HANDBOOK OF INTELLIGENCE

CONSULTING EDITORS

HANDBOOK OF INTELLIGENCE

THEORIES, MEASUREMENTS, AND APPLICATIONS

BENJAMIN B. WOLMAN, Editor

A WILEY-INTERSCIENCE PUBLICATION

JOHN WILEY & SONS

New York   Chichester   Brisbane   Toronto   Singapore

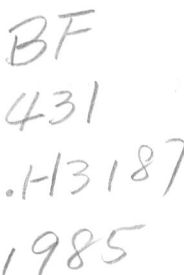
Copyright © 1985 by John Wiley & Sons, Inc.

All rights reserved. Published simultaneously in Canada.

Reproduction or translation of any part of this work
beyond that permitted by Section 107 or 108 of the
1976 United States Copyright Act without the permission
of the copyright owner is unlawful. Requests for
permission or further information should be addressed to
the Permissions Department, John Wiley & Sons, Inc.

This publication is designed to provide accurate and
authoritative information in regard to the subject
matter covered. It is sold with the understanding that
the publisher is not engaged in rendering legal, accounting,
or other professional service. If legal advice or other
expert assistance is required, the services of a competent
professional person should be sought. *From a Declaration
of Principles jointly adopted by a Committee of the
American Bar Association and a Committee of Publishers.*

Library of Congress Cataloging in Publication Data:
Main entry under title:
Handbook of intelligence.

"A Wiley-Interscience publication."
Includes index.
1. Intellect. 2. Intelligence tests. I. Wolman,
Benjamin B.
BF431.H3187   1985   153.9   85-3355
ISBN 0-471-89738-8

Printed in the United States of America

10 9 8 7 6 5 4 3 2 1

In memory of David Wechsler

CONTRIBUTORS

Paul B. Baltes
Max Planck Institute for Human Development and Education
Berlin, German Federal Republic

Ann E. Boehm
Teachers College, Columbia University
New York, New York

Thomas J. Bouchard, Jr.
Psychology Department
University of Minnesota
Minneapolis, Minnesota

Nathan Brody
Psychology Department
Wesleyan University
Middletown, Connecticut

Valerie J. Cook
George Peabody College of Vanderbilt University
Nashville, Tennessee

Roger A. Dixon
Max Planck Institute for Human Development and Education
Berlin, German Federal Republic

Gerald E. Gruen
Psychology Department
Purdue University
West Lafayette, Indiana

J. P. Guilford
Department of Psychology
University of Southern California
Los Angeles, California

David O. Herman
Psychological Corporation
New York, New York

John L. Horn
University of Denver
Denver, Colorado

Lloyd G. Humphreys
Department of Psychology
University of Illinois
Champaign, Illinois

George W. Hynd
College of Education
University of Georgia
Athens, Georgia

Randy W. Kamphaus
California School of Professional Psychology
San Diego, California

Robert M. Kaplan
University of California
School of Medicine
La Jolla, California

Alan S. Kaufman
California School of Professional Psychology
San Diego, California

Nadeen L. Kaufman
California School of Professional Psychology
San Diego, California

Deirdre A. Kramer
Max Planck Institute for Human Development and Education
Berlin, German Federal Republic

Roger T. Lennon
Psychological Corporation
New York, New York

Michael Lewis
Department of Pediatrics
Rutgers Medical School
New Brunswick, New Jersey

Joseph D. Matarazzo
Department of Medical Psychology
Oregon Health Sciences University
Portland, Oregon

Damian McShane
Department of Psychiatry
Oregon Health Sciences University
Portland, Oregon

Mary N. Meeker
S. O. I. Institute
El Sugundo, California

Kazuo Nihira
University of California
Los Angeles, California

Thomas Oakland
Department of Educational Psychology
College of Education
University of Texas
Austin, Texas

Ronald Parmelee
College of Education
University of Texas
Austin, Texas

Cecil R. Reynolds
Department of Educational Psychology
College of Education
Texas A & M University
College Station, Texas

Nancy L. Segal
Department of Psychology
University of Minnesota
Minneapolis, Minnesota

Robert J. Sternberg
Department of Psychology
Yale University
New Haven, Connecticut

Margaret Wolan Sullivan
Department of Pediatrics
Rutgers Medical School
New Brunswick, New Jersey

Steven G. Vandenberg
Institute for Behavioral Genetics
University of Colorado
Boulder, Colorado

George P. Vogler
Institute for Behavioral Genetics
University of Colorado
Boulder, Colorado

W. Grant Willis
Department of Educational Psychology
University of Georgia
Athens, Georgia

Benjamin B. Wolman
International Encyclopedia of Psychiatry, Psychology,
    Psychoanalysis, & Neurology
New York, New York

James M. Woo-Sam
Neuropsychiatric Institute
University of California
Los Angeles, California

Irla Lee Zimmerman
Neuropsychiatric Institute
University of California
Los Angeles, California

PREFACE

David Wechsler was the first American psychologist I met upon my arrival in this country thirty-five years ago. We became instant friends and had frequent scientific and social meetings. Whether in his or my home, our lunches and dinners always turned into scholarly discussions, sort of Platonic feasts, with David being the mentor and myself the enthusiastic disciple.

David Wechsler was an intellectual giant, a one-man encyclopedia, full of universal knowledge. He was always ready to help, explain, and guide. A few years ago, after reading one of my handbooks and perusing my twelve-volume *Encyclopedia of Psychiatry, Psychology, Psychoanalysis and Neurology,* Wechsler came up with the idea of the present handbook. "Why not," he said, "why not put together a high-level, encyclopedia handbook on Intelligence? I will be your consulting editor."

And that is how things began to roll. I contacted Richard Zeldin and Thurman Poston at Wiley. Thurman Poston was assigned as my counterpart, and I never had a more cordial and more efficient editor. I was fortunate to obtain the cooperation of three distinguished psychologists—D. K. Detterman, A. S. Kaufman, and J. Matarazzo—who helped me in the planning of the Handbook and choice of contributors.

The present Handbook was planned and written on the highest scholarly level. It deals with a galaxy of issues and problems and intends to serve as a *vademecum* for researchers and scientists. The authors of the 23 chapters are leading authorities in their respective fields who did not spare time and effort in contributing to this monumental work, worthy of the memory of David Wechsler.

The present Handbook is composed of three parts. The first part deals with theories and conceptual issues related to intelligence. The second part describes the various measurement methods, tests, their rationale and their limitations. The third part is devoted to clinical, educational, and other applications.

As this volume is going to press I feel confident that we have done a good job in honor of David Wechsler, our friend and teacher.

BENJAMIN B. WOLMAN

New York, New York
June 1985

CONTENTS

PART THREE   APPLICATIONS

HANDBOOK OF INTELLIGENCE

PART ONE

THEORIES

ONE

GENETIC DETERMINANTS OF INTELLIGENCE

STEVEN G. VANDENBERG
GEORGE P. VOGLER
Institute for Behavioral Genetics, University of Colorado Boulder, Colorado

The nature-nurture controversy regarding intelligence probably is the best known among the various topics covered by behavioral genetics texts, including those written by Fuller and Thompson (1967, 1978), McClearn and DeFries (1973), Ehrman and Parsons (1976), Dixon and Johnson (1980), Plomin, DeFries, and McClearn (1980), and Fuller and Simmel (1983). In this chapter we will restrict ourselves to that topic. We will present data that have been advanced as evidence for hereditary influence on intelligence, and we will usually interpret the data in this way, without considering objections raised by critics such as Kamin (1974) and Lewontin (1975). Even though individual studies may be faulted for particular reasons, we feel that in their totality they present a convincing story. Furthermore, we are not aware of any detailed theory without a genetic component that can explain the various types of data nearly as well as a genetic hypothesis.

People accepting a role for heredity in human psychological traits are often suspected of being conservative politically, yet it should be remembered that heredity not only makes children similar to their parents, but also at times makes them dissimilar. To see this, we will designate genes for high intelligence by capital letters (A,B,C, and so on) and genes for low intelligence by lowercase letters (a,b,c, and so on). Whenever two parents are heterozygous for any of these genes, say Aa, there will be a probability of ¼ that a child will receive AA, ½ that it will receive Aa, and ¼ that it will receive aa; in other words, only half the children on average will be similar to the parents in this respect. This can be generalized for all gene loci involved with intelligence. These results confirm empirical findings that the majority of very intelligent children come

This work was supported in part by NICHD research grant HD-11681 and by NIMH training grant MH-16880.

3

from the very large pool of parents who are themselves average, rather than from exceptionally intelligent parents. Figure 1 shows the results of one such study (Nuttin, 1965), in which it was found that of the children in the top 10% on each of four ability measures, only between 9.5% and 14.8% came from the highest socioeconomic class, and almost as many came from the lowest class. Of course this intelligence distribution is one of the driving forces behind upward mobility. Countries may differ in how much they facilitate upward mobility— by open educational systems and by inheritance taxes, among other things— but the process occurs everywhere. Hence, heredity is as much a force for change as it is for conservation of the status quo.

THE NATURE OF INTELLIGENCE

Before we review the evidence for genetic determinants, we will have to discuss the various ways in which intelligence has been conceived and measured. In most early studies of the genetics of intelligence a variety of tests were used that claimed to measure general intelligence, most of which were called IQ tests.

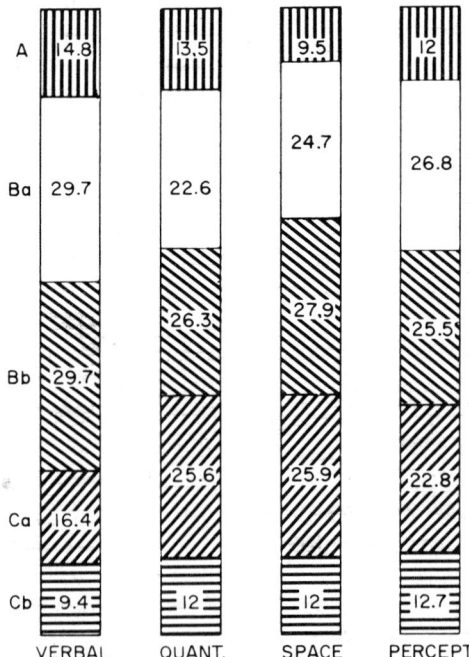

Figure 1. Contribution of five socioeconomic groups to the top ten percent of children for four ability factors. A is the highest group. (*Source:* Reprinted with permission from S. G. Vandenberg. The future of human genetics. In L. Ehrman, G. S. Omenn, & E. Caspari (Eds.), *Genetics, environment, and behavior*. New York: Academic Press, 1972.)

Only in recent years have measures of several different mental abilities been used with increasing frequency. The tests of general intelligence, especially those designed for adults, measure primarily verbal skills such as comprehension, vocabulary, and information rather than the ability to solve problems of a nonverbal nature, such as those involving spatial reasoning or mechanical aptitude, for example. Most of these tests use either the ratio ("intelligence quotient") between the earned score—called mental age—and the chronological age of the child or a deviation IQ, used mainly for adults, in which the performance of the person tested is compared to the distribution of scores for a norm group of the same age as the test-taker. The first method is used with children and is the basis for the Binet-type test. The second method is used in the Wechsler tests and many others. In principle there is not a great difference between the two methods because both use a comparison to the standard for a specific age group. In the Binet-type test such a norm group was used to find items suitable for the given age. Norms are not provided or needed to determine the score, because correct responses to those items show that the child is comparable to the children of the same age on whom the items were standardized. For deviation IQ tests, the published norms are used to determine a person's IQ; the items are presumed to be suitable for the full range of ages for which the test is intended.

There is much to recommend the conception of intelligence as one general entity. First, it conforms to popular usage. It makes it possible to define degrees of mental retardation, which for administrative purposes has obvious advantages over a multidimensional classification. For most retardates, it seems to fit rather well. It is when we approach the average level of ability that one number, the IQ, may not suffice. Most individuals do not perform equally well in various school subjects and show special skills and weaknesses. The strongest argument in favor of the concept of general intelligence is that virtually all measures of different abilities correlate positively. For that reason Spearman (1904) proposed that general intelligence be defined by whatever all those tests have in common, which he thought was induction and abstraction. Spearman's procedure for finding this general factor was a forerunner of factor analysis and multivariate analysis. It tends to favor verbal ability, since all tests require an understanding of the instructions, and many tests contain verbal problems of one type or another. It is only when several similar tests of an entirely different type are included in the analysis that a separate ability factor—spatial ability, for example—can be isolated and measured. Actually one can find several separate ability factors, even among retarded children, provided that one includes measures that allow such abilities to show. Meyers, Dingman et al. (1962, 1964) constructed the Pacific Multifactor Test battery for just that purpose and found four similar factors for retarded and normal children. Kebbon (1965) also reported finding four similar factors in five groups of children of different ages and different overall levels of ability, although these factors differed somewhat from the Pacific test factors.

One argument against the general intelligence concept, especially as measured

Table 1.   Variance and Factors Measured at Various Ages

**A. Percentage of Variance at Four Ages Contributed by Eight Factors
in the Stanford-Binet**

Content	Ages			
	7	9	11	13
Verbal	21.1	15.0	25.2	19.4
Reasoning I	18.3	13.7	—	11.8
Reasoning II	—	—	—	6.4
Memory	9.4	9.6	11.5	8.3
Visualization	—	—	—	7.8
Spatial	—	8.9	12.2	7.0
Residual	—	3.1	2.8	—
Number	8.8	—	—	—

B. Number of Items at Four Ages Measuring Eight Kinds of Factors

Content	Ages			
	7	9	11	13
Verbal	11	15	14	13
Reasoning I	9	14	—	7
Reasoning II	—	—	—	4
Memory	7	7	9	6
Visualization	—	—	—	3
Spatial	—	10	11	4
Number	6	—	—	—

Source.   Reprinted with permission from S. G. Vandenberg. Comparative studies of multiple factor ability measures. In J. Royce (Ed.), *Theoretical Problems in Multivariate Research. Proceedings from the Third Banff Conference on Theoretical Problems in Psychology.* New York: Academic Press, 1973.

by the Stanford-Binet test, is the lack of consistency from year to year in what the test measures. Jones (1949) performed factor analyses of the items at four age levels (7, 9, 11, and 13 years) and found that a total of eight factors were being measured at various ages, each accounting for different amounts of variance at each age. His results are summarized in Table 1. The varying content may account in part for the apparent changes in IQ in some children, reported by several investigators (Bayley, 1956; Hindley & Owen, 1978; Honzik, Macfarlane, & Allen, 1948; McCall, Appelbaum, & Hogarty, 1973; Sontag, Baker, & Nelson, 1958). It may also account for apparent changes in the degree of hereditary control at varying ages.

Against the argument that all ability tests correlate positively and therefore measure the same ability, one can point out that height and weight also correlate, and rather substantially, yet we consider them to be separate characteristics.

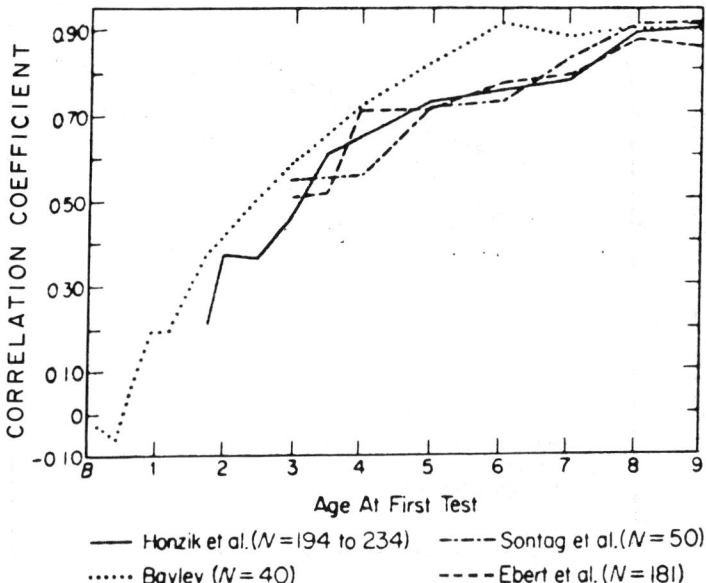

Figure 2. Prediction of IQ at 10 years from scores at earlier ages. (*Source:* Reprinted with permission from S. G. Vandenberg. Hereditary abilities in man. In A. Oliverio (Ed.), *Genetics, environment, and intelligence.* Amsterdam: Elsevier/North-Holland Biomedical Press, 1977.)

However, in the final analysis, it depends on the purpose for which one wants ability measures, as well as one's personal taste. There will always be splitters and lumpers. For that reason we look at some of the evidence for genetic determinants in general intelligence *and* in separate mental abilities. We will start with general intelligence.

Despite individual changes in IQ, the predictability of the IQ score at age 10 improves steadily from age 1 to age 9, as shown in Figure 2. Performance on an individually administered verbal test is the best predictor, followed by a group verbal test. A nonverbal group test is the poorest predictor of later intelligence, as shown in Figure 3.

Intelligence is assumed to be normally distributed—in fact most test norms are constructed to ensure this. However, too many cases appear at the lower end of the distribution, as may be seen in Figure 4. It is thought that this excess is due to a variety of genetically caused disorders, many of which are the result of single gene abnormalities (seen in Tay Sachs disease for example, and phenylketonuria, before the introduction of screening and diet) or due to an incorrect number of chromosomes as seen in Down's or Klinefelter's syndrome.

Single gene abnormalities such as these have been found to occur equally often at all socioeconomic levels. In contrast, milder forms of retardation, shading into low normal intelligence, are more common in lower socioeconomic classes. Whether these mild retardates owe their condition to genetic or environmental causes is still a matter of debate, as is the origin of average and superior

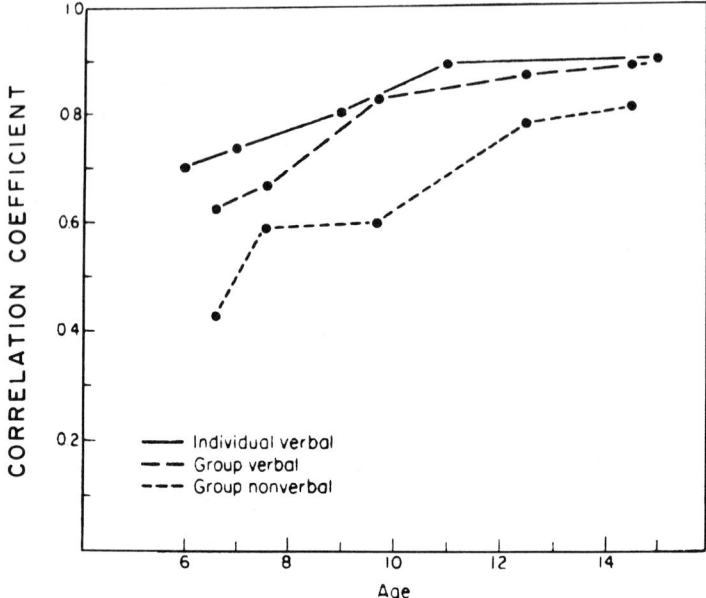

Figure 3. Correlation between IQ scores at varying ages and IQ at age 17 for individual verbal, group verbal, and group nonverbal tests. (*Source:* Reprinted with permission from S. G. Vandenberg. Hereditary abilities in man. In A. Oliverio (Ed.), *Genetics, environment, and intelligence.* Amsterdam: Elsevier/North-Holland Biomedical Press, 1977.)

intelligence. However, in the fifth edition of the catalog of autosomal and X-linked dominant and recessive conditions, McKusick (1978) listed a large number of abnormalities in which mental retardation is part of the syndrome. We will review a few examples of these known genetic defects first.

Phenylketonuria (PKU) is the best known of these, because it represents one of the successes in human genetics research that paved the way for research into

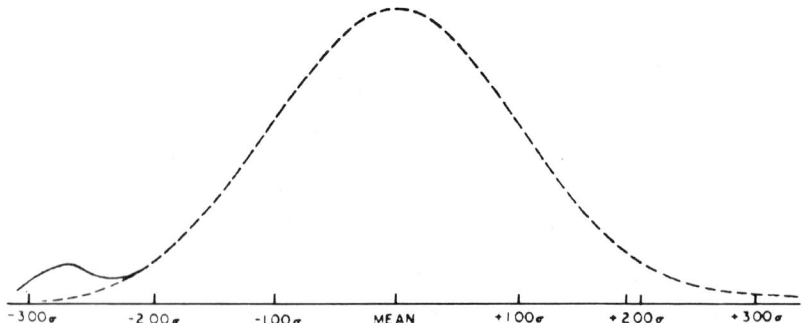

Figure 4. The distribution of IQ compared to a normal distribution. (*Source:* Reprinted with permission from S. G. Vandenberg. What do we know about the inheritance of intelligence and how do we know it? In R. Cancro (Ed.), *Intelligence: Genetic and environmental influences.* New York: Grune and Stratton, 1971.)

other diseases. PKU is an autosomal recessive disorder with an estimated incidence rate of 1 per 10,000 to 40,000 in Caucasian populations, which corresponds to a gene-frequency of 1 in 100 to 200. In other words, .5% to 1% is the estimated incidence of "carriers"—people who have one abnormal gene and who run the risk, when they marry other carriers, that one out of four of their children will be affected. The basic defect in PKU is the absence of the enzyme phenylalanine hydroxylase, which converts phenylalanine to tyrosine. In carriers there seems to be less of the enzyme, and these individuals can be detected by a "loading" test in which a large amount of phenylalanine is ingested. Carriers are unable to metabolize the phenylalanine as completely as normal people and as a result will excrete some phenylpyruvic acid in their urine. This is because they have just one normal allele, which produces sufficient phenylalanine hydroxylase to metabolize normal amounts of phenylalanine, but not enough to metabolize the excessive dose used in the loading test.

PKU led to serious mental retardation in the past. Figure 5 shows the distribution of IQs of untreated children: all but two have IQs below 50, and more than two-thirds have IQs below 25. The treatment consists of instituting, immediately after birth, a diet low in phenylalanine, which if maintained long enough eliminates the expression of retardation. The precise length of time required for maintaining the child on this diet is still being studied, but may be

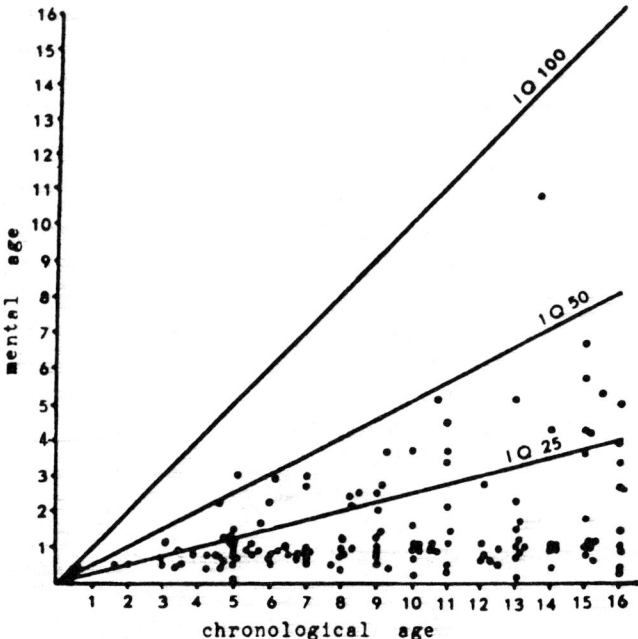

Figure 5. The distribution of IQs in PKY patients. (*Source:* Reprinted with permission from R. S. Paine. The variability in manifestations of untreated patients with phenylketonuria (phenylpyruvic aciduria). *Pediatrics,* 1957, **20,** 290–301.)

as little as six years. This may be related to the fact that untreated PKU retards or prevents the myelinization of neurons in the brain, and this process should be completed by 6 years of age, if not earlier. Treated (and untreated) PKU women may produce babies who are already affected by the phenylpyruvic acid in their mother's blood, so that it may be necessary to place the mothers on the diet during their pregnancy (Hsia, 1970). Most states have instituted screening programs for newborns, and the incidence of retardation has been reduced, resulting in substantial savings in the cost of institutional care for severely retarded individuals. The story of PKU is more complex than this account suggests, however. Some individuals who have hyperphenylalaninemia do not become retarded, and when placed on the PKU diet they may suffer nutritional deficits and become retarded or die (Scriver & Clow, 1980). Other similar types of metabolic errors have been discovered, some of which are also amenable to dietary control.

Another breakthrough occurred when methods were elaborated for photographing human chromosomes, allowing them to be counted and identified. When these chromosomes are arranged by size in order of magnitude, such a photo is called a *karyotype*. The individual identification of each chromosome was a later accomplishment, but the accurate count alone permitted the discovery of a variety of abnormalities. An abnormal number of chromosomes is called *aneuploidy* (*an* = not, *eu* = good or correct, *ploidy* = number of chromosomes). The first such abnormality described was Down's syndrome, formerly called mongolism, which is now called trisomy–21 (trisomy = three chromosomes), although the most recent evidence indicates that the trisomy is for chromosome 22.

Down's syndrome is an example of an *autosomal aneuploidy. Autosomal* means that it is not a sex chromosome. *Monosomy* (or complete absence of the second chromosome of a pair) or *trisomy* (the presence of three chromosomes instead of a pair) are much more common for the sex chromosomes X and Y. In autosomes, monosomy or trisomy usually leads to early spontaneous abortion, which may occur so early that it is not even noted. All kinds of sex chromosome aneuploidies have been reported, with up to six X and Y chromosomes observed in various combinations. The X chromosome is one of the larger chromosomes, while the Y is one of the smallest. A compilation by Moor (1967) suggests that each extra X lowers the IQ substantially, while each extra Y has much less of an effect. Figure 6 summarizes her findings.

The sex chromosome aneuploidies fall into several groups:

Turner's Syndrome.   Turner's syndrome is XO, that is, a single X. Although phenotypically female, such an individual has a number of anomalies: absence of ovaries and breasts, heavy musculature at the back of the neck, and usually poor spatial ability. The latter may be the result of infantilization by the parents, who tend to see such a child as younger than the real age.

Klinefelter's Syndrome.   A normal male has one X chromosome and one Y chromosome. Any male with more than one X is representative of Klinefelter's syndrome: XXY, XXXY, XXYY, XXXYY, and so on. These individuals

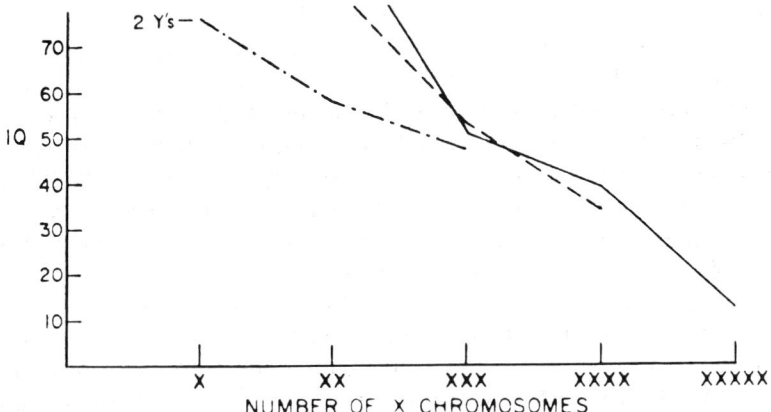

Figure 6. Mean IQ of individuals with various numbers of sex chromosomes. (*Source:* Reprinted with permission from S. G. Vandenberg. What do we know about the inheritance of intelligence and how do we know it? In R. Cancro (Ed.), *Intelligence: Genetic and environmental influences.* New York: Grune & Stratton, 1971. Adapted from Moore, 1967.)

tend to be retarded, and the degree of mental retardation depends on the number of excess X chromosomes.

"Superfemales." "Superfemales" include any female with more than two Xs (XXX, XXXX, and so on). Although morphologically normal, such individuals also have lower IQs depending on the number of excess Xs.

Jacob's Syndrome. Jacob's syndrome, the *XYY type*, was initially discovered in some of the inmates of maximum security prisons, and such individuals were thought to be genetically predisposed toward violent crime because of the extra Y, which was thought to produce more androgen and greater height. Only the latter tends to be true. In representative samples it is found that the mean height is increased, but there is virtually no increase in criminality. What little increase there is consists of petty property crimes, which may be due in part to the small decrease in intelligence that is also present.

X-inactivation. To explain why there are no greater abnormalities in people with an abnormal number of sex chromosomes, the Lyon hypothesis is invoked (Lyon, 1961). This theory states that every X except one is inactivated soon after the first few cell divisions. This hypothesis might also explain why women do not differ much from men, except for sexual characteristics, despite the excess genetic material represented by the second X chromosome (which is one of the larger ones). Which X is inactivated in a cell is presumed to be a matter of chance, but thereafter all of the cell's descendants are thought to have the same X inactivated. There is a large body of evidence in support of this theory (see Lyon, 1961).

Individual Identification of Chromosomes. In 1971, Caspersson and associates described the first method for identifying each of the 22 autosomes and the X and Y by producing a banding pattern that is unique for each chromosome.

There are now a number of procedures that differ with respect to ease versus resolution. Application of such procedures has revealed a wide variety of minor abnormalities, such as deletions or duplications of specific narrow bands within a given region of a chromosome. Some of these abnormalities have been associated with specific abnormalities in morphology or biochemistry. Segments of a chromosome may also be inverted, or even inserted into or added to another chromosome. Sometimes there is an interchange of materials between two nonhomologous chromosomes. This is called a translocation. As long as an individual retains both abnormal chromosomal segments, no obvious abnormalities appear to result, but such an individual can produce two abnormal types of eggs or sperm: one with the abnormal chromosome that has the additional material, and the other with the chromosome that is lacking some of its material. Offspring resulting from such abnormal chromosomes are usually affected, unless the other parent also carries a similar, balanced translocation and the offspring receive the two types of chromosomes that balance each other by having complementary interchanges of material. The best-known case of a translocation, involving chromosomes 22 and 15, produces a milder form of Down's syndrome when the excess material derived from 22 is added to 15, resulting in a partial trisomy.

One of the newest discoveries is the existence of so-called *fragile sites*, which are small segments of a chromosome that do not stain normally. Their precise nature is not yet known. Fragile sites appear in only a small proportion of the cells of an individual that are cultured in the preparation of a karyotype. The best-known of the fragile sites is located on the X chromosome, and it appears to be associated with a sex-linked type of mental retardation (Sutherland & Ashforth, 1979). Females are usually heterozygous for the fragile X, and, depending on which X is inactivated in each cell, they may be mildly retarded or normal (Uchida & Joyce, 1982). The discovery of the fragile X syndrome is too recent to permit estimation of the number of retardates thus affected. Perhaps this type of sex-linked mental retardation can explain the excess number of male retardates.

Inheritance of Normal Intelligence

A very large number of studies have attempted to estimate the contribution of heredity (or nature) to the total variance of intelligence. In earlier studies nature was pitted against nurture, and it was sometimes thought that one could subtract the genetic percentage of variance from the total and thus obtain the environmental contribution. Currently, the importance of both genetic and environmental influences is acknowledged.

In more recent, sophisticated models, gene-environment interaction and correlation are considered, as well as the effects of assortative mating and cultural transmission. A number of methods have been used for this purpose: (1) the comparison of identical (MZ) and fraternal (DZ) twin similarities, (2) correlations between parents and children, (3) correlations between siblings, (4) correlations between various other types of relatives, (5) adoption studies, (6) correlation between MZ twins reared apart from another, and (7) studies combining a number of these relationships. We will discuss each briefly:

Twin Studies

The idea of comparing identical or monozygous (MZ) twins and fraternal or dizygous (DZ) twins goes back to Galton (1876). It is based on the fact that MZ twins have the same genetic makeup because they originate from a single fertilized egg that split into two developing embryos. In some cases this division occurs after only a few cell divisions; in other cases it occurs somewhat later, when a right-left orientation has been formed, so that one twin may be, for example, right-handed and the other left-handed. Because such twins may be implanted some distance apart in the uterus, each twin is enclosed in a separate chorionic membrane. DZ twins result from two fertilized ova, so that genetically they are no more alike than two siblings born at different times. It is assumed that prenatal and postnatal environmental conditions are comparable for the two types of twins. There are indications that some MZ twins differ more in birth weight than do most DZ pairs, due to an unequal supply of blood from the single placenta (Falkner, Banik, & Westland, 1962). On the other hand, MZ twins may be treated more alike than are most DZ twins. There is disagreement on whether such treatment is due to the greater MZ similarity in appearance (which may invoke similar reactions from others, so that it should be regarded as a type of genotype-environment interaction) or as environmental in origin, because the treatment might be relatively independent of the physical appearance of the twins. Vandenberg and Wilson (1979) found no correlation between the degree to which twins were treated alike and similarity on the six subtests of the Primary Mental Abilities test battery. While several authors have reported that MZ twins were treated more alike, no other study has determined whether such treatment had an effect on twin similarity in test scores.

Blood typing can be used to determine whether a twin pair is MZ or DZ. It can rule out MZ status for any pair in which a difference is found in any of the many blood group systems that can be tested, and it provides the probability that a given pair may be DZ even though there is concordance for all blood groups tested. Such probabilities are very small—of the order of 10^{-5} or smaller, depending on the number of blood groups tested. In most studies it is sufficient to use physical similarity and a history of one twin being mistaken for the other—by teachers, friends, or even parents—to separate MZ from DZ pairs, so that blood typing is not necessary. A rare misclassification usually will not seriously affect the results of an analysis of a trait that cannot be measured too precisely anyway.

Bouchard and McGue (1981) have summarized a large number of correlations for intelligence between various paired relatives, including MZ and DZ twins. They report a weighted average MZ correlation, based on 4672 pairs from 34 studies, of .86, and a weighted average for 5546 DZ pairs from 41 studies of .60. If there were nothing but genetic factors, we would expect values of 1.00 and .50. It is clear that this hypothesis is untenable: the MZ correlation is too low, suggesting that environmental influences made the MZ twins less than perfectly similar. On the other hand, the DZ correlation is too high, suggesting that even DZ twins share a more similar environment than do two children born at different times, for which Bouchard and McGue report a correlation of .47, based on 26,473 pairs from 68 reports. This last value comes close to the expected genetic value of .50, but still could be environmental in origin. Since the hypothesis that nothing but genetic factors determine the twin correlations is rejected, what is one to conclude from these correlations? A variety of formulas have been proposed that attempt to express the proportion of the total variance that is due to heredity. This quantity, H, is usually called the broad heritability of the trait.

The symbol h^2 is commonly used to denote narrow-sense heritability, or the proportion of phenotypic variance due to additive genetic variation. Because of a number of technical problems, we will not review the older formulas for heritability. A simple test of the genetic component of variance is the ratio between the two within-pair variances, where $F = \dfrac{\text{Var}_{wDZ}}{\text{Var}_{wMZ}}$. This is a standard F-test with degrees of freedom N_{DZ} and N_{MZ}, where N is the number of pairs. This test does not give the proportion of the total variance that is genetic in origin, however. Falconer (1960) has proposed $2(r_{MZ} - r_{DZ})$ as a reasonable approximation of h^2. This formula, using the MZ and DZ intraclass correlations r_{MZ} and r_{DZ}, essentially entails a comparison of the between-pair components of variance, under the assumption that the total phenotypic variance in the two zygosities is equal, and that the MZ and DZ samples are equally representative of the same population. This method will overestimate heritability if there is dominance variance for the trait being studied or if environmental influences are not equally distributed for the two types of twins. The method favored by the Birmingham school of Mather and Jinks (1971) and others uses both the within- and the between-pair variances to estimate the genetic and environmental variances as follows:

First the mean squares are calculated between and within pairs, separately for the MZ and DZ twins. These provide the observed variances, as shown in Table 2. The second step consists of fitting the theoretically expected components of variances to these observed values, using either the least squares or the maximum likelihood method. One set of theoretical expectations is shown in Table 2, where two types of environmental influences are included—V_{ec}, the common environment of each pair of twins, and V_{ew}, the individual environment of each member of a pair—and additive genetic influences constitute the expected parameter V_{ga}.

The great advantage of this method over previous ones is that it not only specifies environmental influences explicitly, but it also permits a test of the importance of the three expected variance components.

In the full model there are four observations (between- and within-pair variance for both MZ and DZ twins), but only three expected parameters to be estimated (V_{ew}, V_{ec}, and V_{ga}), leaving a single degree of freedom. The least squares

Table 2. Analysis of Variance Model for Twin Data, with Polygenic Variance and Two Sources of Environmental Variance

Sum of Squares	df	Expected Mean Squares	Expected Variance Components
MZ Pairs			
Between	$n_{MZ} - 1$	$\sigma^2_{W_{MZ}} + 2\sigma^2_{B_{MZ}}$	$V_{Ew} + 2V_{Ec} + 2V_{GA}$
Within	n_{MZ}	$\sigma^2_{W_{MZ}}$	V_{Ew}
DZ Pairs			
Between	$n_{DZ} - 1$	$\sigma^2_{W_{DZ}} + 2\sigma^2_{B_{DZ}}$	$V_{Ew} + 2V_{Ec} + 1\frac{1}{2}V_{GA}$
Within	n_{DZ}	$\sigma^2_{W_{DZ}}$	$V_{Ew} + \quad\quad \frac{1}{2}V_{GA}$

Note. n_{MZ} and n_{DZ} are the number of MZ and DZ twin *pairs*, respectively.

or maximum likelihood procedures provide a chi-square test of the goodness-of-fit of the observed data to the model, with the degrees of freedom being the number of observed variances minus the number of expected variance components estimated.

In the full model shown in Table 2, the single degree of freedom provides a test of the equality of the MZ and DZ total variances. If the chi-square is significant, the cause of the variance in one type of twin being greater than that of the other type of twin should be investigated. More important, if the variances are statistically equivalent, more specific hypotheses involving the three expected variance components are possible. For example, the hypothesis of no genetic influence on the trait under consideration can be tested by dropping the parameter V_{ga} (that is, fixing it at zero). The model then becomes a completely environmental model, with only two variance components to be estimated (V_{ew} and V_{ec}), leaving two degrees of freedom for the goodness-of-fit test. From the complete model, we know that one degree of freedom tests for the equality of MZ and DZ variances, and we know the value of the chi-square associated with that test. In the reduced model (with V_{ga} dropped), a larger chi-square with two degrees of freedom is obtained. By subtracting from this chi-square the chi-square value of the equal-variance test, and by subtracting the degrees of freedom, a new chi-square with one degree of freedom is obtained. This provides a direct test of the importance of V_{ga} to the fit of the data to the model; if it is not significant, there are no important additive genetic influences on the phenotypic variation, but if it is significant, it suggests that a genetic hypothesis is necessary to explain the data. The same procedure can be used to assess the importance of the environmental parameters.

If enough data are available, it is possible to expand the model to include, for instance, a sex difference or a special environment for MZ twins.

Parent Offspring Studies

In the absence of assortative mating, the correlation of the midparental value with that of the offspring is a direct estimate of the degree of familiality of the trait, where familiality includes both genetic and shared environmental factors. In the presence of assortative mating, the regression of midoffspring on midparent is a more appropriate statistic to use, since it is not inflated by the influence of assortative mating (DeFries, Kuse, & Vandenberg, 1979). Bouchard and McGue (1981) report a weighted mean correlation of .72 for 410 midparent-midchild pairings in three studies, and .50 for 982 midparental-single offspring pairings in eight studies. Many more correlations are included in the Bouchard and McGue paper, as can be seen in Figure 7, which is reproduced from that report. What is perhaps most important to note in that figure is the overall trend of increasing correlation with an increase in the biological closeness of the individuals who were being compared. A large study that has been published since the summary by Bouchard and McGue was based on 2029 pairs of parents tested when in their teens, with one or more children also tested at that age. The regression of offspring on midparental value was .613 ± .022 (Reed & Rich, 1982). The authors noted a slightly higher correlation between mother and offspring than between father and offspring, and a sibling correlation of .387. (Actually the influence of assortative mating, when separately estimated, turns out to be almost negligible.)

Resemblance Between Siblings

The correlations between brothers, between sisters, and between brother-sister pairs are valuable as additional entries in a table of all possible biological relationships, for they help to demonstrate the consistent trend toward increased correlation with increased biological relatedness. In addition, they permit one test of sex-linkage: brothers would have a 50% chance of receiving the same X chromosomes from their mother (while both share their father's Y), while sisters would receive an X chromosome from each parent, with a probability of .25 that both are the same for the two girls. The consequence of this would be that boys would correlate higher on a sex-linked trait than would girls, and boy-girl pairs should be in between. This strategy has been used only a few times. We will return to this topic a little later when discussing spatial ability.

Bouchard and McGue report a weighted average sibling correlation of .47, based on 26,473 pairs from 68 studies. This is only a little lower than the correlation of DZ twins reared together (.60, according to the same study), suggesting that the twin situation and the fact that the twins are of the same age, and therefore might be treated somewhat more alike, has little effect on observed DZ similarity for intelligence.

Resemblance Between Other Relatives

There are few reports of correlations between more distant relatives, such as uncles or aunts and nephews or nieces; grandparents and grandchildren; cousins,

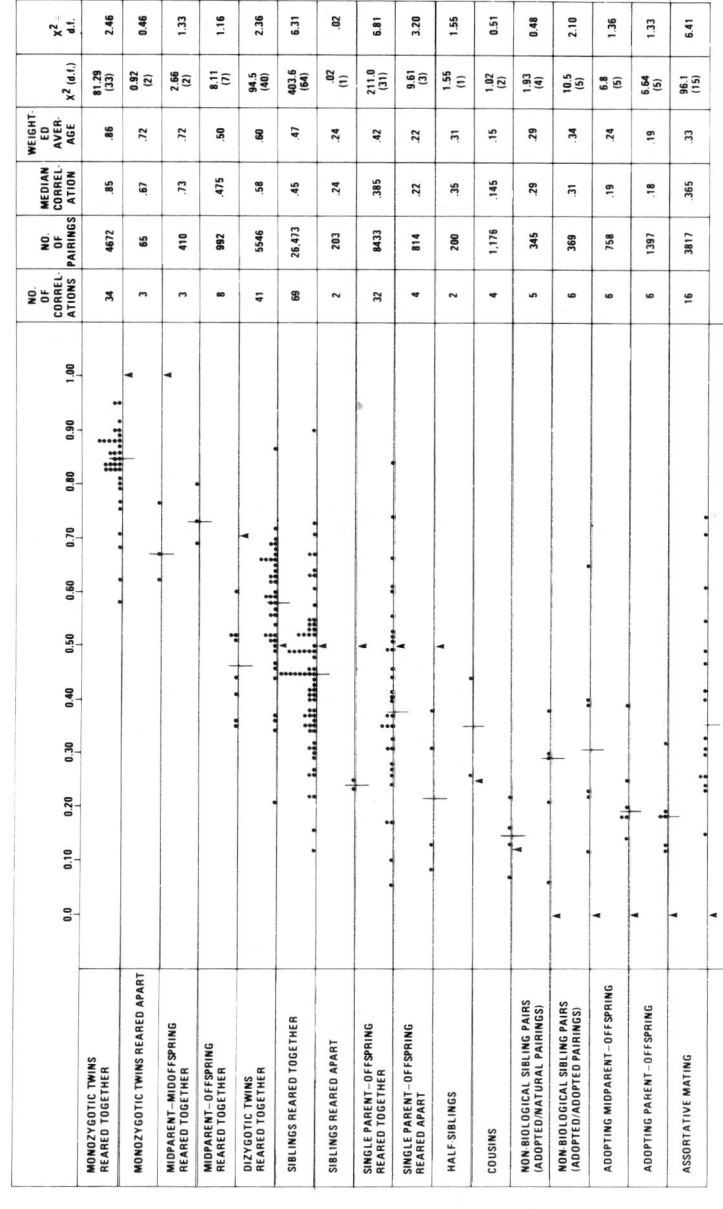

	NO. OF CORREL- ATIONS	NO. OF PAIRINGS	MEDIAN CORREL- ATION	WEIGHT- ED AVER- AGE	χ^2 (d.f.)	χ^2 d.f.
MONOZYGOTIC TWINS REARED TOGETHER	34	4672	.85	.86	81.29 (33)	2.46
MONOZYGOTIC TWINS REARED APART	3	65	.67	.72	0.92 (2)	0.46
MIDPARENT—MIDOFFSPRING REARED TOGETHER	3	410	.73	.72	2.66 (2)	1.33
MIDPARENT—OFFSPRING REARED TOGETHER	8	992	.475	.50	8.11 (7)	1.16
DIZYGOTIC TWINS REARED TOGETHER	41	5546	.58	.60	94.5 (40)	2.36
SIBLINGS REARED TOGETHER	69	26,473	.45	.47	403.6 (64)	6.31
SIBLINGS REARED APART	2	203	.24	.24	.02 (1)	.02
SINGLE PARENT—OFFSPRING REARED TOGETHER	32	8433	.385	.42	211.0 (31)	6.81
SINGLE PARENT—OFFSPRING REARED APART	4	814	.22	.22	9.61 (3)	3.20
HALF SIBLINGS	2	200	.35	.31	1.55 (1)	1.55
COUSINS	4	1,176	.145	.15	1.02 (2)	0.51
NON-BIOLOGICAL SIBLING PAIRS (ADOPTED/NATURAL PAIRINGS)	5	345	.29	.29	1.93 (4)	0.48
NON-BIOLOGICAL SIBLING PAIRS (ADOPTED/ADOPTED PAIRINGS)	6	369	.31	.34	10.5 (5)	2.10
ADOPTING MIDPARENT—OFFSPRING	6	758	.19	.24	6.8 (5)	1.36
ADOPTING PARENT—OFFSPRING	6	1397	.18	.19	6.64 (5)	1.33
ASSORTATIVE MATING	16	3817	.365	.33	96.1 (15)	6.41

Figure 7. Familial correlations for IQ. The vertical bar indicates the median correlation; the arrow indicates the correlation predicted by a simple polygenic model. (*Source:* Reprinted with permission from T. J. Bouchard & M. McGue. Familial studies of intelligence: A review. *Science*, 1981, 212, 1055–1059. Copyright 1981 by the AAAS.)

17

and so on. Bouchard and McGue (1981) report four studies with 1176 pairs of cousins, with a weighted average of .15.

In a study in Hawaii in which many families participated, some of the nuclear families were related, that is, some of the parents were brothers or brother and sister. As a consequence, some of the children from two families were cousins; more interesting, some uncles and aunts were "in-laws" who were not biologically related to their nieces or nephews. It was thus possible to compare the similarity of nieces/nephews to (1) uncles/aunts that were biological relatives and (2) uncles/aunts that were married into the family. Table 3 shows these results for 15 tests, four composites of specific cognitive abilities, and the first principal component that is a measure of general intelligence. It can be seen that when there was no biological relationship all of the measures of resemblance (except one) are not significant and are close to zero. In contrast, for the biological relatives (uncles/aunts and nieces/nephews, as well as cousins), most values were significant.

Adoption Studies

Adoption studies are frequently cited as giving the best estimate of genetic and environmental components of variance. However, for this to be true several essential conditions must be met. First of all, the children should not have contact with their biological mothers for any length of time after birth. Second, there should not be any selective placement, because that practice can produce a correlation between the biological and the adoptive parents that inflates the correlation between the child and both its biological and adoptive parents. In the past, many agencies practiced such selective placement in order to match the child with the expectations of the adoptive parents—expectations that were often focused on school and career achievements. Currently, the principal concerns of most adoption agencies are with the stability of the adoptive home and the ability of the family to provide a loving, accepting atmosphere. Ho, Plomin, and DeFries (1979) reported a very low correlation between the test scores of adoptive and biological parents, suggesting an absence of selective placement for the parents participating in the Colorado Adoption Project. These results are shown in Table 4. (The Colorado study was started too recently to provide relevant data for this chapter. At the time this was written, most of the children were still too young to be tested with Binet or Wechsler tests, but reports should soon be appearing.)

As mentioned above, an adoption study provides independent estimates of genetic and environmental variance components simultaneously. The correlation between the child and the biological parents provides the former, and the correlation between the child and the adoptive parents provides the latter. The famous graphs in Figure 8 from Honzik's (1957) reanalysis of the data collected by Skodak and Skeels (1949) show that the correlation of the child's intelligence with the education (as proxy for intelligence) of the biological parents increased with age to a value of about .35, while the correlation with the adoptive parents

Table 3. Resemblances of Collateral Relatives on Cognitive-Test Scores

Tests and Composites	Biological Uncles/Aunts and Nephews/Nieces[a]	Unrelated Uncles/Aunts and Nephews/Nieces[a]	Cousins[b]
Tests			
Vocabulary	.27**	.06	.31**
Visual memory (immediate)	.11	.09	.08
Things	.11	.09	.26**
Mental rotations	.15*	−.01	.12
Subtraction and multiplication	.20**	.04	.21**
"Lines and dots" (Elithorn mazes)	.05	−.07	.17**
Word beginnings and endings	.14*	−.01	.23**
Card rotations	.18**	−.10	.17**
Visual memory (delayed)	.12	.06	.14*
Pedigrees	.20**	.11	.26**
Hidden patterns	.23**	.06	.19
Paper form board	.26**	.14*	.23**
Number comparisons	.21**	.06	.18**
Social perception	.01	.11	.23**
Progressive matrices	.20**	.12	.22**
Composites			
Verbal	.15*	.11	.24**
Spatial	.14*	−.06	.11
Perceptual speed	.20**	.07	.15*
Visual memory	.14*	.03	.07
First Principal Component	.18**	.04	.29**

[a] Regressions; pairwise deletions for missing data.
[b] Interclass correlations; pairwise deletions for missing data.
*p < .05.
**p < .01.

Table 4. Selective Placement Correlations for Cognitive Measures

Measure	Biological vs. Adoptive Mother	Biological vs. Adoptive Father
General cognitive ability	−0.10	0.15
Verbal ability	0.03	0.20
Spatial ability	−0.03	−0.08
Perceptual speed	−0.10	−0.03
Memory	−0.07	−0.14
N	110	22

Source. Reprinted with permission from J. C. DeFries, R. C. Plomin, S. G. Vandenberg, & A. R. Kuse. Parent-offspring resemblance for cognitive abilities in the Colorado Adoption Project: Biological, adoptive, and control parents and one-year-old children. *Intelligence*, 1981, *5*, 245–277.

did not at any time exceed .10. Yet the children's IQ was raised 20 points over that of their mothers, as shown in Figure 9.

Later studies by Scarr and Weinberg (1976, 1978) and by Horn, Loehlin, and Willerman (1979) obtained similar results, as shown in Table 5. The first study by Scarr and Weinberg is particularly interesting, because it involved adoption of 176 children that were black or racially mixed into white families. The study by Horn et al. involved 469 adopted children and 300 families. The results are remarkably similar for the three studies: the average correlation of the child's IQ with that of the adoptive parents was .16, whereas with the biological parents it was .36. Note, however, that in the study by Horn et al. the correlations with the biological parents are for parents and their own biological children reared at home, so that these include environmental family influences. The corresponding values for two older studies by Burks (1928) and Leahy (1935) were .15 and .48, respectively. In general many older studies of whatever kind tend to arrive at somewhat higher estimates of the genetic component. This may not be due only to biased sampling or accident; perhaps genetic differences were clearer and were not obscured by the more uniform schooling the present generation has received.

MZ Twins Raised Apart

The review of studies of MZ twins reared apart presents a problem. Ideally, only similarity of MZ pairs randomly placed in separate environments at birth would have to be attributed to genetic similarity or prenatal maternal influences. However, some of the pairs in the few studies that have been reported of MZs reared apart were apparently not as separated as is necessary in order to assume no common environment. For example, some pairs were living close together, and in some cases one twin was raised by the biological mother and the other twin by the mother's sister. Farber (1981) calculated the correlations in IQ for the Newman, Freeman, and Holzinger (1937), Juel-Nielsen (1965), and Shields (1962) studies, as well as for some isolated reports, after taking into account the degree of contact there might have been between the twins. This was done

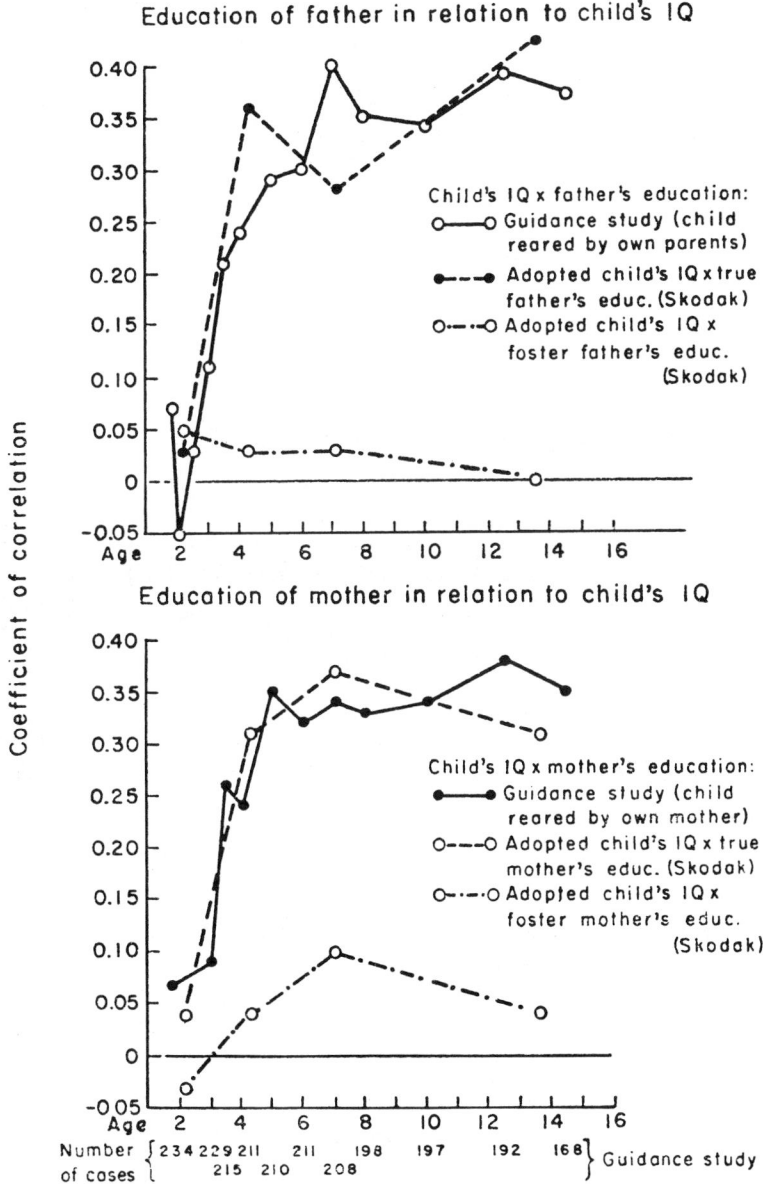

Figure 8. IQ resemblance of adopted children to foster- and biological-parents. (*Source:* Reprinted with permission from S. G. Vandenberg. What do we know about the intelligence and how do we know it? In R. Cancro (Ed.) *Intelligence: Genetic and environmental influences.* New York: Grune & Stratton, 1971.)

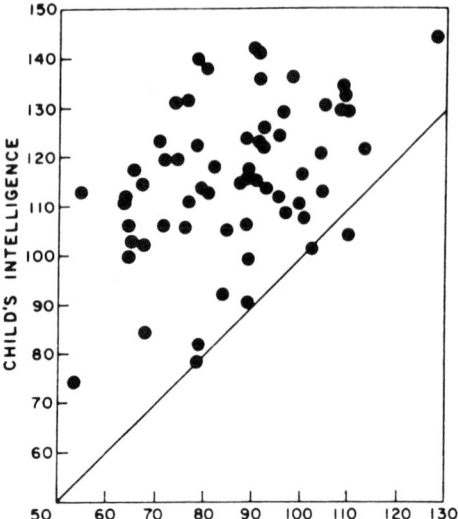

Figure 9. Correlation Between child's IQ and IQ of biological mother for 67 adopted children. (*Source:* Reprinted with permission from S. G. Vandenberg. The future of human behavior genetics. In L. Ehrman, G. S. Omenn, & E. Caspari (Eds.), *Genetics, environment, and behavior.* New York: Academic Press, 1972.)

in two ways: (1) adjusting for the degree of contact in each of several age periods, and (2) considering the total frequency and degree of contact. The results of these two adjustments were .67 and .76, respectively, for the male and female pairs together. These values are lower than the value of .86 for the weighted average correlation of MZ twins reared together (Bouchard & McGue, 1981), but not strikingly so, even though in the latter case the twins are continuously in contact and in the same environment.

Since then a group of investigators at the University of Minnesota, under the direction of Bouchard, has been collecting data on twins reared apart. About half of the present sample of 30 pairs had not met prior to the study. The correlation for 27 pairs was .66 on the Wechsler Adult Intelligence scale and .78 on a combination of the Raven Progressive Matrices and the Mill-Hill vocabulary test—both of which were used in the Shields and Juel-Nielsen studies.

Table 5. Parent-Child IQ Correlations in Three Adoption Studies

Study		Adoptive		Biological	
		r	N	r	N
Scarr & Weinberg (1976)	Fathers	.27	170	.39	142
	Mothers	.23	174	.34	141
Scarr & Weinberg (1978)	Fathers	.15	150	.39	237
	Mothers	.04	150	.39	237
Horn et al. (1979)	Fathers	.17	457	.42	162
	Mothers	.19	455	.23	162

If a value intermediate between the last two correlations is taken, the resulting correlation of .72 is nearly identical to the average of the two correlations corrected by Farber for amount of contact between the twins.

A correlation between twins reared apart of .72 is indeed very high. Most other attempts to estimate the genetic part of the total variance come out substantially lower. It should be kept in mind that MZ twins, whether reared together or not, still had the same prenatal environment and also that they share the same total nonadditive variance—variance due to dominance and epistasis that is less largely shared by other siblings, parents and their children, or more distant relatives. Perhaps those nonadditive components are more important than is usually thought.

Studies Combining a Number of Relationships

In recent years there have been several attempts to integrate many of the findings of different studies by proposing models that specify, for a number of relationships, the expected degree of similarity among relatives due to genotypic similarity, environmental similarity, or assortative mating. These expectations are then equated to the observed values for the various combinations of relatives, in order to solve for the components of variance and covariance. In principle, this is the best way to obtain estimates for the various parameters, but practical problems arise when different observed relationships are derived from different studies. Because different tests have been used in the various studies, it is often not possible to make age-corrections, or the shared environment in one study is not the same as in another study, and so on. Nevertheless, we will summarize the results of a few of these efforts.

There are two types of techniques that are used to analyze multiple familial relationships simultaneously. One is the biometrical approach of the Birmingham school (see, for example, Eaves, Last, Young, & Martin, 1978), which was introduced in the section on twin studies. This approach is basically an extension of the analysis of variance. The second technique is called path analysis, which resembles multiple regression analysis. Although the two methods were developed relatively independently, they will yield identical results if the models employed contain the same assumptions about the contributions of various factors to familial resemblance. This section of the review focuses on studies that have used the latter method.

The statistical technique of path analysis has several advantages over the simpler analyses outlined above. First of all, information about the observed correlation or covariation among *many* classes of relatives is used in the estimation of the contribution of genetic and environmental influences on phenotypic variation, so that it is not necessary to rely solely on the assumptions of a single method, such as the MZ-DZ twin comparison. Second, when a model is developed, the assumptions an investigator is willing to make can be incorporated explicitly and graphically into the model. These assumptions are concerned with causality, genotype-environment correlation, and such controversial issues as the mechanisms of assortative mating and heritable cultural transmission, dominance variation, and the degree of shared environmental influences among MZ twins, DZ twins, and siblings. Third, statistical evaluation of the goodness-of-fit of a model to the observed correlations or covariances can be obtained. In particular, it is possible to explicitly test assumptions, such as those listed above, by statistically comparing alternative models—one in which a given assumption is included and another in which it is not.

Conversely, the complexity of the method results in a number of complications. First, while the simpler analyses can be executed by hand, path analysis usually involves the use of complex iterative optimization routines that require a computer for execution. Second, it is necessary to obtain data either on infrequently occurring familial relationships—such as twin separation or adoption data—or on more common relationships—such as nuclear families—where a good index of strictly environmental influences is available. In the case of rare familial relationships, it is difficult to obtain adequate samples, and even if available, the assumption that the sample represents the same population as the samples of more common relationships is questionable. The use of only nuclear families and environmental indices alleviates this problem, but introduces the further complications of finding true indices of the environment and of incorporating these indices into the model. Third, there are a number of mathematical requirements that must be met for the statistical evaluation of a model to be valid. These include assumptions of linearity and additivity, and distributional properties of the data. Fourth, there is a temptation to overinterpret the results of path analysis (see Cliff, 1983).

The pros and cons of path analysis have been widely debated in the literature (for example, Goldberger, 1978a, 1978b; Karlin, Cameron, & Chakraborty, 1983, with responses by Cloninger, Rao, Rice, Reich, & Morton, 1983, and Wright, 1983; Rao, Morton, & Yee, 1978; Taylor, 1980). Some propose abandonment of the technique altogether (Karlin, Cameron, & Chakraborty, 1983), although this is an extreme view that would preclude future refinements of the method, which might overcome some of the current criticisms. Furthermore, the critics have not proposed alternative methods that are potentially as informative as the path analysis technique.

PATH ANALYSIS TECHNIQUE IN GENETIC STUDIES

Wide application of path analysis to problems in genetics and other fields has occurred only within the past decade, paralleling the general availability of high-speed computers. However, the technique was first proposed by Sewall Wright in 1918 as a means to analyze observed relationships among variables in terms of known or postulated causal systems by setting up a system of linear equations based on a causal model.

A simple causal model of intelligence is shown in Figure 10a. P is the phenotype of intelligence as measured by some IQ test, E represents environmental causal influences on P, and G denotes additive genetic influences on intelligence.

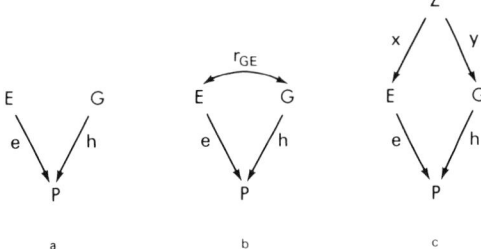

Figure 10. Simple causal models of intelligence. (a) Uncorrelated environmental and genetic influences on the phenotype; (b) Genotype-environment correlation included; (c) Cause of genotype-environment correlation explicitly modeled.

The single-headed arrows denote causality, with the "path coefficients" e and h representing the degree to which the phenotypic standard deviation is a function of variability among the environmental and additive genetic causes. This simple model assumes that P is measured without error and is caused entirely by uncorrelated environmental and genetic factors. If P is standardized to have a mean of zero and unit variance, the path coefficients are standardized partial regression coefficients. The phenotypic variance V_P equals $h^2 + e^2$, or 1. In other words, all phenotypic variance is due to environmental and genetic variation. A double-headed arrow (Figure 10b) represents a correlation between two variables and implies that there are common causal factors of the two correlated variables (Figure 10c, where $xy = r_{GE}$), but that the common cause or causes are not important or not defined in the model. In Figure 10b, $V_P = h^2 + e^2 + 2her_{GE} = 1$.

In the path models of Figure 10, we have only a single observed variable (P), and the variables G and E are unobserved (latent), hypothesized causes of P. The model is thus underdetermined, and it is not possible to estimate any of the path coefficients or correlations. In Figure 11, the phenotype is measured for both a parent and a child. Since a child will share, on the average, 50% of the parent's genes, the path from G_P to G_0 can be fixed at ½, so the expectation for parent-offspring correlation can be derived from Figure 11. To obtain the expectation, the product of the path coefficients and correlations connecting the two phenotypes is taken, and if there is more than one way to connect the phenotypes, the sum of the resulting products yields the expectation for the total correlation between the two phenotypes. To do this, several rules must be observed: a path can be traced back from one variable through a common cause and forward to the second variable, but a path cannot be traced forward and then backward, since two causal variables are not necessarily correlated as a result of both contributing to a common effect; directions can be changed only once in tracing a path; and any given variable can be passed through only once in deriving a product.

By observing these rules, the expectation for the parent-offspring correla-

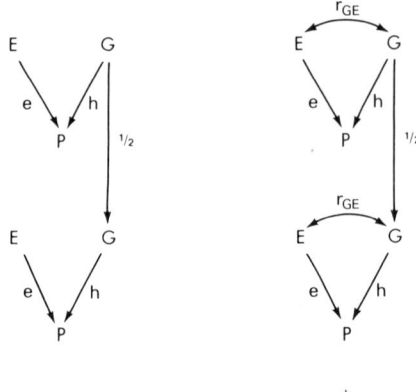

Figure 11. Simple causal models of parent-offspring resemblance (a) Without genotype-environment correlation; (b) with genotype-environment correlation.

tion from Figure 11a is $\frac{1}{2} h^2$, and from Figure 11b it is $\frac{1}{2} h^2 + \frac{1}{2} her_{GE}$, or $\frac{1}{2} h(h + er_{GE})$. The model of Figure 11b is still underdetermined, but by taking the expectation of $\frac{1}{2} h^2$ for the model of Figure 11a, and the additional information that $h^2 + e^2 = 1$, it is possible to solve for the two free parameters, h and e. However, this simple model contains a number of restrictive assumptions: no assortative mating; no cultural or environmental transmission from parent to offspring; no genotype-environment correlation or interaction; equilibrium of h and e across generations; absence of measurement error; only linear and additive genetic and environmental influences, and so on.

The inclusion of additional familial relationships—such as both of the parents, siblings, MZ and DZ twins, relationships resulting from adoption, and other more remote relatives—permits empirical testing of many assumptions. This is because another parameter (involving an additional assumption) can be estimated with each additional independent relationship included in the model. Specific parameters can then be dropped or fixed at hypothesized values. By doing so, the model becomes overdetermined, with more observed correlations than free parameters in the model. A perfect fit is no longer obtained, but the difference between the number of observed correlations and the number of free parameters in the model is the degrees of freedom available for a maximum likelihood or least squares test of the goodness-of-fit of the observed data to the model, given the assumptions made by dropping free parameters from the model.

The Application of Path Analysis to Studies of Intelligence

The first application of path analysis to human data on intelligence was Wright's (1931) analysis of adoption data collected by Burks (1928). Despite some understandable methodological problems, this study represents a landmark in the use of causal modeling in the context of familial resemblance for IQ (see Loehlin, 1979, for a historical overview). In this review, we will concentrate on more recent applications.

Widespread use of path analysis began when Jencks et al. (1972) attempted to estimate heritability from a compilation of previously published studies of familial resemblance for IQ. These included parent-offspring, sibling, twin, and adoption data. Their model incorporated phenotypic assortative mating, cultural transmission such that the parental phenotype for IQ directly influences the environment in the offspring generation, shared environmental influences unique to twins, and genotype-environment correlation. Jencks et al. proceeded in a stepwise fashion, analyzing different relationships separately, so that they obtained a number of estimates of heritability for IQ, but no overall test of the model. They conclude that a guess of overall heritability for IQ is .45, and cultural transmission is approximately .35.

In the mid-1970s, a series of developments in the application of path analysis to studies of familial resemblance were primarily due to the work of a group of investigators in Hawaii and later of a group in St. Louis. In the first of a series of papers by the Hawaii group, Morton (1974) presents a possible model for the sibling correlation, incorporating midparental genotype and common family environment, both of which directly influence the sibling phenotypes, and which are permitted to be correlated. The use of an index of the common environment is an important feature of the model.

In the second paper of this series (Rao, Morton, & Yee, 1974), the use of statistical tests of hypotheses for models of familial resemblance is introduced. The use of path analysis to test null hypotheses, rather than simply to obtain heritability estimates, represented a major methodological advance. The model, influenced in part by the controversy over Jensen's (1969) paper, provides for variables having an influence on the phenotype, which account for among-group variation, so that samples that are not from a homogeneous population can be analyzed together. The authors concentrate primarily on relationships from the offspring generation—siblings, half-sibs, and twins, reared together or by various combinations of foster parents—while parent-offspring resemblance is considered only briefly. Within groups, the phenotype is influenced by midparental genotype and indexed common-family environment. These two influences are permitted to be correlated. Heritable and common-family environmental influence on the phenotype can differ by generation when parent-offspring resemblance is considered.

This model was used in an analysis of published correlations for IQ from the data of Burks (1928) and from a partial set of the studies summarized by Jencks et al. (1972). The samples included siblings, MZ and DZ twins, parents, and adoptees, so that the model combined the family, twin, and adoption study designs simultaneously. Burks's (1928) culture index was used as the index for common-family environment. No allowance was made to permit parental genotypes to be correlated. The estimates of the direct genetic and cultural components of phenotypic variance for IQ from this analysis are 75% for children and 12% for parents resulting from genotypic variation, with 9% and 52% due to cultural variation in children and parents. The goodness-of-fit test indicated that the model could not be rejected ($\chi^2_4 = 2.80$, $p > .50$).

The next developments from the Hawaii group (Rao, Morton, & Yee, 1976,

1978) included a more thorough treatment of the spouse correlation in the parental generation and a refinement of the modeling of cultural transmission. In the 1976 model (Figure 12), the spouse phenotypic correlation is assumed to result from primary correlations among all possible combinations of the parents' childhood family environments and parental genotypes. Cultural transmission can occur by both the childhood family environment of the parents and the parental adult phenotype influencing the environment in the offspring generation. The common environment is indexed for each individual. Generational differences are permitted for the effects of both genotype and family environment on the phenotype, and the genotype and family environment can be correlated.

Rao, Morton, & Yee (1976) reanalyzed the data used in their earlier paper (1974) with the addition of an observed spouse correlation. The model that the authors favored showed no correlation between the two parental genotypes or between parental genotype and environment within individuals, suggesting that the spouse correlation is a result of assortative mating solely for environmental factors. They also found that the influence on the child's environment by either parental childhood environment or adult phenotype (but not both) could be assumed to be zero. The final estimates of genetic and cultural influences on phenotypic variance (from corrigenda by Rao, Morton, & Yee, 1978) are as follows: 71% for children and 32% for adults resulting from genotypic variation, and 8% and 50% due to cultural variation in children and adults, respectively. The fit of the data to the model was satisfactory but not outstanding ($\chi^2_3 = 6.45$, $p > .05$).

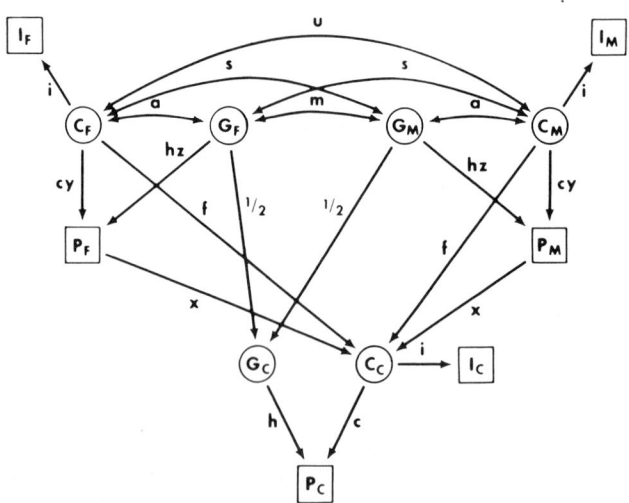

Figure 12. Marital and parent-offspring path diagram. The subscripts F, M, and C, denote father, mother, and child; G is genotype, P is phenotype, and C is common environment with index I. (*Source:* Reprinted with permission from D. C. Rao, N. E. Mortin, & S. Yee, Resolution of cultural and biological inheritance by path analysis. *American Journal of Human Genetics*, 1976 **28**, 228–242. Copyright 1976 University of Chicago.)

The same model was used for an analysis of a more extensive compilation of American studies of intelligence (Rao & Morton, 1978) consisting of 65 correlations involving 16 familial relationships. The authors conclude that the most parsimonious model is the one in which the parental genotypic correlation, parental genotype-environmental correlation, and direct influence of parental phenotype on childhood environment are all zero. This model results in the following estimates of sources of phenotypic variation for IQ: 69% genotypic variation in children and 30% in adults; 16% cultural variation in children and 55% in adults. The overall residual chi-square is 39.83 with eight degrees of freedom, which is highly significant, but Rao and Morton (1978) use an *F*-ratio statistic that adjusts for heterogeneity among the samples as an adjusted goodness-of-fit test. This statistic results in an acceptable fit.

The most recent series of papers from the Hawaii group have dealt extensively with the issue of the mechanism of assortative mating. In the above models, the spouse correlation was viewed as primarily due to assortative mating for social factors, which then induced all possible correlations among parental genotypic and environmental influences on IQ and ultimately between the parental phenotypes. The authors name this model of assortative mating *social homogamy*. Since the results summarized above demonstrate that the spouse genotypic correlation can be fixed at zero, this means that mate selection occurs solely on the basis of cultural or environmental factors, which are related to IQ independently of the genotype. An alternative model, termed *phenotypic homogamy*, represents assortative mating as primarily due to selection on the basis of the IQ phenotype of the spouse, which then induces secondary correlations among the genotypes and environments of the spouses. This mechanism for assortative mating was assumed in models proposed by Jencks et al. (1972), Wright (1978), and Cloninger, Rice, and Reich (1979a). These two approaches were combined in a model developed by Rao, Morton, and Cloninger (1979).

Rao, Morton, Lalouel, and Lew (1982) applied this model to the data set compiled by Rao and Morton (1978), with the addition of four more observed correlations, and with several additional distinctions made among the samples, for a total of 69 correlations on 22 familial relationships. The general model is presented in Figure 13.

Two sets of analyses were performed. The first set, which included the fourteen phenotypic correlations, did not involve environmental indices. The full model fit the data well, with χ_5^2 of 3.60 ($p > .60$). A number of hypotheses were then tested by dropping parameters. Two models were found to be acceptable: phenotypic homogamy with no generational differences (the influence of heritable variation on phenotypic variance was 31%, and cultural variation contributed 42%) and social homogamy with no generational differences for genetic heritability (heritable variation was 44%, and cultural variation was 33% for children and 48% for adults). The second set of analyses included correlations involving indices. The full model showed a marginal fit ($\chi_{10}^2 = 16.99$, $p > .07$). Attempts to drop parameters demonstrated that it was necessary to retain both social and phenotypic homogamy, but generational differences were not significant. Esti-

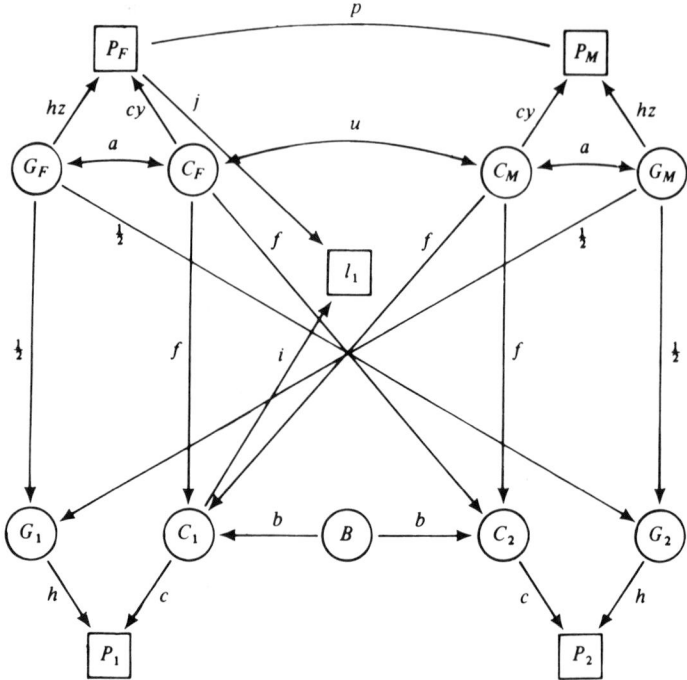

Figure 13. Mixed homogamy model for U.S. IQ. The variables *P, G, C, I,* and *B*, denote phenotype, genotype, transmissible environment, index, and nontransmitted sibling common environment. Subscripts *F, M, 1,* and *2* denote father, mother, and two children. For simplicity, only the index of the first child is shown. (*Source:* Reprinted with permission from D. C. Rao & N. E. Morton. IQ as a paradigm in genetic epidemiology. In N. E. Morton & C. S. Chung (Eds.), *Genetic epidemiology,* New York: Academic Press, 1978.)

mates of the contribution of genetic variation and cultural variation on phenotypic variation are .34 and .26, respectively. Clearly, additional work is required on the issues of the mechanism of assortative mating, environmental indices, and generational differences, since alternative models cannot be clearly rejected but yield inconsistent results.

A related group of models was developed by a group of investigators in St. Louis. In the first paper of a series, Rice, Cloninger, and Reich (1978) describe three models of multifactorial inheritance: the *cultural model* assumes transmission from parent to offspring of only cultural influences; the *polygenic model* describes the case when parent-offspring resemblance is due entirely to genetic transmission; and the *pseudopolygenic model* results when the value of the path coefficient from the parent's cultural factors to those of the offspring is equal to the value of the path from the genotype of parent to offspring (in essence, ½). Genetic heritability and cultural transmission cannot be separated in the pseudopolygenic model. Each of the three models is a special case of a *unitary model* (later termed the *TAU model*). Assortative mating is assumed to be for the parental phenotype.

The second paper of this series (Cloninger, Rice, & Reich, 1979a) describes a model (the *BETA model*) that combines the cultural and polygenic models for simultaneous analysis of both cultural and genetic transmission from parent to child. As in the TAU model, assortative mating is due to phenotypic preference. Cloninger, Rice, & Reich (1979a) are more conservative in their use of indices than is the Hawaii group, preferring to analyze data about phenotypic resemblance separately from data involving indices. Sibling nontransmissible environments can be correlated, with separate estimates for siblings, DZ twins, and MZ twins.

American IQ data (mainly the studies analyzed by Rao & Morton, 1978) are analyzed using this model. The general model fits acceptably ($\chi_2^2 = 3.73$, $p > .25$). The hypothesis that the sibling and DZ twin nontransmissible environmental correlations are equivalent is also acceptable. Both transmissible, additive genetic and cultural effects are necessary in the model for an acceptable fit. The contributions of genotypic and cultural variation to phenotypic variation are 33% and 27%, respectively (the model does not specify generational differences).

The same analysis is reported by Rice, Cloninger, and Reich (1980), using a nearly identical data set (heritability = 30%, cultural transmission = 29%). In addition, they report an analysis of socioeconomic status (SES) as an index of cultural determinants of IQ. They conclude that the relationship between SES and IQ is more complex than the model can allow, but the notion that SES is simply a cultural index is certainly not acceptable.

Loehlin (1979) used path analysis for an analysis of familial resemblance for IQ in an adoption study conducted in Texas (Horn, 1983; Horn, Loehlin, & Willerman, 1979). The study contained 300 families who had adopted at least one child, some of whom also had natural children. IQ scores were also available for the biological mothers of the adopted children. Adult IQs were from the Revised Beta Test; the Wechsler performance scale was used to obtain IQ for the children. The design resulted in correlations for 21 familial relationships for IQ. Loehlin's (1979) model assumes that intelligence is a function of additive genetic factors, dominance deviation, common environment shared by siblings, and a residual term called unique environment. An index of SES for the adoptive home was derived by a combination of both parents' education and the father's occupation. This adds seven additional observed correlations between the index and IQ phenotypes. Additive genetic and common environmental factors are correlated. Environmental transmission occurs by a direct influence of parental phenotype on the shared environment of the children, and also by a variable termed "social and economic advantages of the home" (indexed by the SES composite and correlated with parental genotype and phenotype) to the childhood shared environment. Assortative mating in the general model is assumed to be phenotypic. The possibility of selective placement was incorporated into the model. In general, no generational or sex differences were assumed.

Four tests of the full model were conducted: the first is the general model outlined above; the second assumes that assortative mating between the biological parents of the adopted children is half that of the adopting parents (no direct estimate of assortative mating in the biological parents was available, since biological fathers were not tested); the third assumes that assortative mating is for some variable correlated with IQ, such that the parental genotypic correlation is one-half that expected under direct assortative mating for IQ; and the fourth assumes that parental values for the paths from genotype and cultural factors to IQ are half the values in the offspring generation. The goodness-of-fit test of these models could not distinguish among the four ($\chi^2_{19} = 23.24$ to 23.81, $p >$ .20 for all four tests).

Several exploratory techniques were also employed. Various combinations of parameters were fixed at zero or other hypothesized values, and the change in chi-square from the full model was used as a test of the various hypotheses. In addition, the values of several "observed" correlations were changed to assess the effects of sampling fluctuations on the parameter estimates. Although Loehlin (1979) emphasizes that the results of this study are only illustrative, using a sample of adoptees that may or may not represent the general population and a model that could possibly be formulated in alternative ways, there are several conclusions that can be drawn. The contribution of dominance variation is only weakly estimated, since the model cannot be rejected at any value from zero to one for the dominance parameter. Both genetic and cultural transmission are necessary to account for the data, but alternative models of cultural transmission are not distinguishable with this data set. Tentative estimates of the contribution of genetic and cultural factors on phenotypic variation using this sample and general model are as follows: 38% genotypic, 19% transmissible cultural influences, 12% dominance variation, 10% genotype-common environment covariation, and 21% residual (including unique environment, epistasis, and genotype-environment interaction).

In a subsequent report (Horn, Loehlin, & Willerman, 1982), the data from the Texas Adoption Project are scrutinized in even greater detail. Ten analyses are undertaken on the data, which were randomly modified to include the potential influence of sampling fluctuations among all of the correlations simultaneously. The heritability and common family environmental path coefficient estimates remain stable; the value of the dominance path fluctuates wildly; and estimates for the two paths representing the two types of cultural transmission are variable but complementary (in essence, when one is high, the other is low). This confirms the general conclusions of the original report. Separate analyses by the sex of the offspring reveal no evidence for differential heritability for boys and girls. When the data are divided on the basis of the age of the child (5–7 years old and 8 or older), there is a suggestion of greater genetic heritability in younger children than in older children. Dividing the sample at the mean SES value results in a slightly higher estimate of the influence of heritable genetic and cultural transmission in the lower SES group. When the sample is divided at the mean IQ for the adoptive family midparental Beta IQ or the biological mother's IQ, analyses of the resulting subsamples suggest that the overall results are not identical, but the differences are probably not due to differential heritability or to cultural transmission, and the analyses are confounded by restriction of range for IQ. The use of different reliability adjustments and divisions of the sibling comparisons on the basis of the sexes of the siblings resulted in no substantially different results from those of the general model. Thus the conclusions from the original analyses (Loehlin, 1979) appear to be warranted. The analysis of the Texas Adoption data is exemplary for its rigorous examination of potential sources of bias resulting from invalid modeling assumptions.

The Colorado Adoption Project is currently being conducted at the Institute for Behavioral Genetics, University of Colorado, Boulder (DeFries, Plomin, Vandenberg, & Kuse, 1981; Plomin & DeFries, 1983). This study obtains information on some of the biological fathers in addition to the relationships studied in the Texas Adoption Project, and it includes control families that did not adopt a child. The study is longitudinal, and the children are still young. Fulker and DeFries (1983) present analyses of familial resemblance for intelligence when the children were 1 and 2 years old. Parental cognitive ability was assessed using the first principal component of a battery of sixteen tests of specific cognitive abilities. The measure of infant cognitive ability is the Bayley Mental Index. The model with which the data were analyzed is basically identical to the model used by Jencks et al. (1972), with minor modifications to permit differential phenotypic assortative mating for the biological parents versus the adoptive parents, selective placement parameters of the form of correlations for each biological parent with each adoptive parent, and an index of the home environment caused by the phenotypes of the rearing parents and having a causal influence on the environment of the child. Covariance matrices rather than correlations are analyzed, using a maximum likelihood technique analogous to that of Jöreskog and Sörbom (1981) for analyzing multiple matrices (adoptive and control families, along with incomplete matrices due to missing family members).

Because the children are so young, and given different measures of cognitive ability in parents and children, the two measures are probably not isomorphic. Therefore, the authors caution that the data are mainly illustrative of the model and the results should be interpreted cautiously. Nevertheless, the results show an absence of selective placement in the sample. Genotype-environment correlation can be entirely accounted for by the influence of the paternal phenotype (which is connected to the child's genotype) on the home index, and the influence of the index on the child's environment. The heritability parameter is significant, with a value ranging from .14 to .17, indicating that there are genetic contributions to familial resemblance. Cultural influences on familial resemblance appear to be due primarily to the father's influence on the home index, and the influence of the home index on the childhood environment. Residual influences of the parental phenotype on the childhood environment were small and not significant. Future reports from the Colorado Adoption Project should provide more compelling evidence about the nature of genetic and environmental influences on familial resemblance for cognitive ability as the children approach the age at which the parents were originally tested.

SUMMARY

Table 6 presents a summary of the proportions of phenotypic variance due to genotype, cultural or environmental influences, and the covariance between genotype and culture. The estimates are from the most parsimonious model of each study in the summary. The estimates should not be viewed as replications, since there is a great deal of overlap among the samples analyzed in most of the studies. In fact, most of the fluctuation among the estimates is due primarily to different assumptions in the various reports regarding the modeling of cultural transmission, assortative mating, and other phenomena.

There are several observations worth noting from Table 6. Heritable genetic contributions (h^2) to phenotypic variation occur, with the estimates of h^2 generally falling in the range of .3 to .4. Transmissible cultural or environmental influences are usually of similar magnitude, but the estimates are considerably more variable, reflecting the lack of a consensus concerning the modeling of the mechanisms of these influences. Genotype-environmental covariation contributes little as transmissible influences on phenotypic variation—probably less than 10%. In fact, the summary in Table 6 probably represents overestimates of the effect of genotype-environmental covariation, since in many of the studies the empirical estimate of the correlation between genotype and environment (r_{GE}) did not differ statistically from zero. Some of the earlier studies that estimated h^2 and c^2 separately for the offspring and parental generations showed high heritability and low cultural transmission in the children, with a trend in the opposite direction in adults. Evidence that this is a real effect is not convincing.

Table 6. Proportion of Phenotypic Variance Due to Genetic (h^2) and Cultural (c^2) Influences and Their Covariance ($2hcr_{GC}$)

Children		Adults			
h^2	c^2	h^2	c^2	$2hcr_{GE}$	Source
.50	.07	.30	.36	.12–.13[a]	Wright (1931)
.45	.35	.45	.35	.20	Jencks et al. (1972)
.75	.09	.12	.52	.12	Rao et al. (1974)
.71	.08	.32	.50	.09–.14[a]	Rao et al. (1976, 1978)
.69	.16	.30	.55	.01	Rao & Morton (1978)
.38	.19	.38	.19	.10	Loehlin (1979)
.33	.27	.33	.27	.09	Cloninger et al. (1979)
.30	.29	.30	.29	.09	Rice et al. (1980)
.31	.42	.31	.42	.07	Rao et al. (1982)[b]
.44	.33	.44	.48	0	Rao et al. (1982)[c]
.34	.26	.34	.26	.05	Rao et al. (1982)[d]

[a] Lower value for children; higher value for adults.
[b] Phenotypic homogamy; no indices.
[c] Social homogamy; no indices.
[d] Mixed homogamy; indices included.

Subsequent analyses using alternative models of assortative mating and environmental transmission, along with more prudent use of environmental indices, failed to find intergenerational differences. Furthermore, Loehlin (1978) attempted to resolve the different results obtained with essentially the same data by Jencks et al. (1972) and Rao, Morton, & Yee (1974, 1976), as well as a biometrical genetic analysis by Jinks and Eaves (1974) and Eaves (1975). Loehlin (1978) demonstrated that by incorporating dominance into the model and by assuming that assortative mating is for the phenotype for IQ rather than only for common environmental influences, the intergenerational differences disappear.

From a historical perspective, path analytic studies of familial resemblance have been concerned with obtaining quantitative estimates of h^2. This emphasis is somewhat misplaced. The most important outcome is the demonstration that both transmissible genetic and environmental influences are moderately important with respect to phenotypic variation in measures of intelligence, but the actual estimates are only of secondary importance. The advantage of path analysis is that environmental influences can be identified and the mechanism of environmental transmission can be studied while the influence of genetic transmission is controlled for. The next step is to identify those aspects of environmental variation that influence the phenotype for intelligence. Currently, too little is known about the nature of the environmental influences to justify the assumption by the Hawaii group that true indices of the environment are available and can be directly incorporated into a model as environmental variables. Attention should now be focused on the development of realistic indices. The approach of the St. Louis group to determine the relationship of indices to the phenotype, genotype, and culture and environment after analyzing phenotypic resemblance could be fruitful in this respect.

Another promising approach is the extensive analysis of the families of adult twins. Nance (1976) and Nance and Corey (1976) propose studying MZ twins, their spouses, and their children. The children of MZ twins are genetically half-siblings without the potential bias due to broken homes, death of a parent, and so forth, which is introduced in conventional half-sib samples. Genetically related maternal effects can be studied by comparing the offspring of MZ females to those of MZ males. Cloninger, Rice, and Reich (1979b) adapt their BETA model, which includes cultural transmission, to the analysis of children of MZ twins. Corey and Nance (1978) extend the model to include grandchildren of identical twins. The grandchildren of one twin are 1 ½ cousins of the grandchildren of the other twin. When broken down by the sex of the twins, their offspring, and the grandchildren, there are twenty distinct 1 ½ cousin relationships. These relationships can be used to distinguish among different types of maternal effects—cytoplasmic effects, effects of prenatal environment, and genetically determined maternal effects. Crumpacker et al. (1979) used a model that included both MZ and DZ twins and their offspring in an analysis of human smoking behavior. This model permits the assessment of additive genetic influences and assortative mating, of "cultural" transmission defined as the influence of parental genotype on offspring environment, and of prenatal and postnatal familial environmental effects.

Thus far, data on intelligence have not been presented using the offspring of twins method. Such an analysis, combined with the family, twin, and adoption relationships that have been used before, promises to contribute to the understanding of environmental influences on familial resemblance when genetic factors are statistically controlled. In combination with a concerted effort to identify relevant aspects of the environment by studying the relationship of indices of potential environmental factors to the phenotype, the full story behind phenotypic variation for intelligence may be within reach.

GENETIC FACTORS IN SEPARATE MENTAL ABILITIES

Many twin studies have used tests designed to measure separate mental abilities. Most of these tests had been found in factor analytic studies to represent some factor that characterizes a specific cognitive ability and is largely independent of other specific mental ability factors. However, most of these tests would correlate positively with general intelligence. There have been too many such studies to review each of them. In 1972 Nancy Breland, working with Robert C. Nichols, summarized the results of a number of these studies (the summary was published in Nichols, 1976), shown in Figure 14 and Table 7, which are taken from Osborne (1980). Although there are 211 pairs of intraclass correlations, they do not all come from different studies, but rather from several studies that report results for a variety of tests. These studies were done over a considerable time span, using different tests of varying reliabilities. Nevertheless, the overall trends displayed provide the best summary possible.

The first thing to notice is the high correlation between the degree of MZ and DZ similarity. In general, the higher the MZ concordance, the higher the DZ concordance. One would expect such a pattern for traits that are to a considerable extent influenced by genes. Indeed, if environment played no role at all, one would expect values of 1.00 and .50 for the MZ and DZ concordances. The averages for all tests are .74 and .54. The MZ twin scores are thus less similar than expected on a purely genetic hypothesis, while the DZ twin scores are close to what would be expected. One might conclude that environmental factors make MZ twins less similar, rather than more.

As shown before, Bouchard and McGue (1981) reported weighted averages of .86 and .60 for MZ and DZ concordances for general intelligence. Allowing for the possibility of lower reliabilities for at least some of the tests of special abilities, the results are remarkably similar. Of course the 30 paired correlations for general intelligence in Table 7 are probably also included in the Bouchard and McGue results.

Is it possible to say anything about difference in heritability among the various abilities? Figure 15 shows that the tests of spatial ability and of reasoning have larger MZ–DZ differences in concordance than the other tests, and therefore

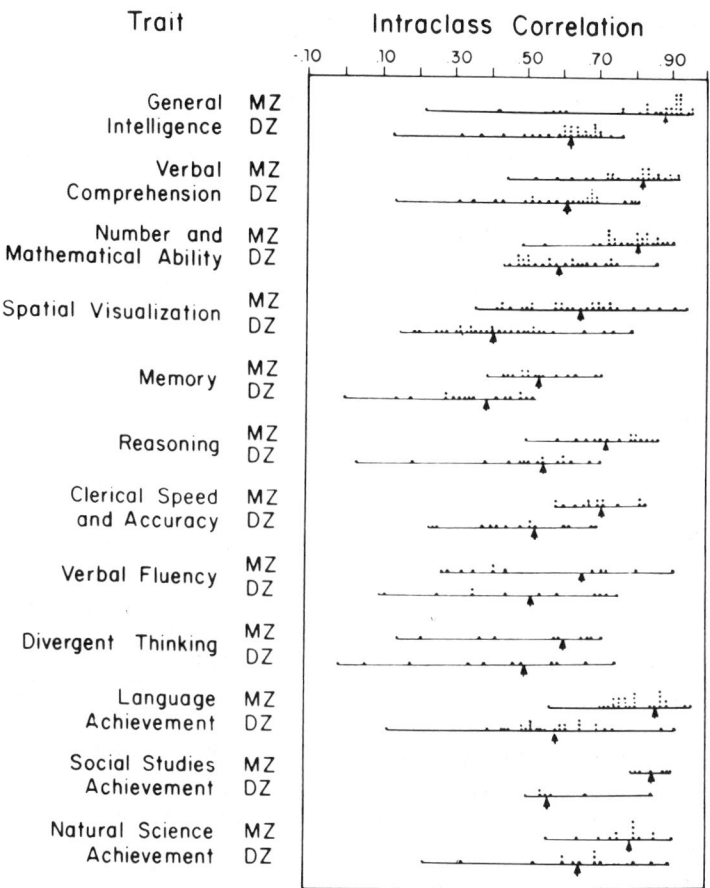

Figure 14. Intraclass correlations from twin studies of various abilities. Each correlation is shown by a dot. The mean weighted value is shown by an arrow. (*Source:* Reprinted with permission from R. T. Osbourne. *Twins, black and white.* Athens, GA: Foundation for Human Understanding, 1980.)

are probably influenced to a greater degree by heredity. The differences are not large, however.

Independent evidence for differential familial influences on specific cognitive abilities was obtained from a study in which a large number of parents and children were tested with a battery of 15 tests of specific abilities. For details of this study the reader is referred to DeFries, Kuse, and Vandenberg (1979). Some of these families were Americans of Japanese ancestry (AJA), because the study was done in Hawaii, but we will discuss only the results for the 830 families that were of European ancestry (AEA), although the results for the other families were similar. The rank order correlation between the values for the AEA and AJA was .77. The regression of midchild on midparent was used as the measure of parent-offspring resemblance, because this eliminates the effect

Table 7.   Weighted Average Intraclass Correlations from Twin Studies
of Various Abilities

Ability	Number of Studies	Average Correlation		$2(r_{MZ} - r_{DZ})$
		r_{MZ}	r_{DZ}	
General intelligence	30	.82	.59	.46
Verbal comprehension	27	.78	.59	.38
Number ability	27	.78	.59	.38
Spatial visualization	31	.65	.41	.48
Memory	16	.52	.36	.32
Reasoning	16	.74	.50	.48
Clerical speed and accuracy	15	.70	.47	.46
Verbal fluency	12	.67	.52	.30
Divergent thinking	10	.61	.50	.22
All abilities	211	.74	.54	.40

Source.   Adapted from Osborne (1980).

of assortative mating and is less influenced by potential truncation of the distribution of either parental or children's scores. Between-family environmental influences do affect the regression, which consequently is interpreted as a measure of "familial" effects rather than heredity. The results of the 15 tests corrected for age effects are shown in Table 8 as well as the results for four factors (spatial, verbal, perceptual speed and accuracy, and visual memory) and for the first principal component of the covariance of the 15 tests. The first principal com-

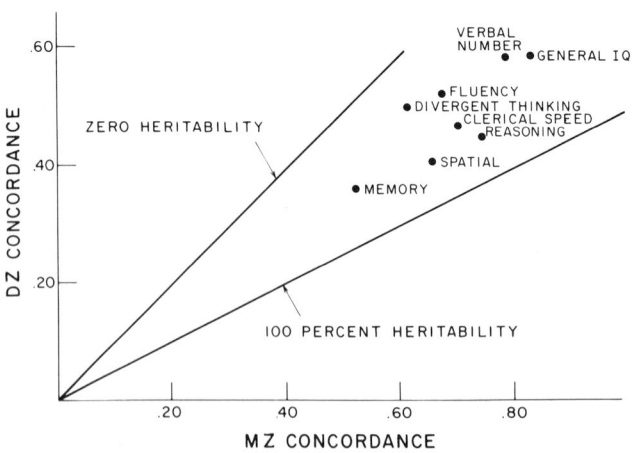

Figure 15.   MZ and DZ correlations for ten abilities and for general IQ plotted against each other. Lines of zero and one-hundred percent heritability are shown for comparison.

Table 8. **Regressions of Midchild on Midparent for Cognitive Test and Principal Component Scores in Total Hawaiian AEA and AJA Samples**

Tests and Composites	Uncorrected		Corrected[a]	
	AEA	AJA	AEA	AJA
Tests				
Vocabulary	0.64	0.55	0.67	0.57
Visual memory (immediate)	0.15	0.12	0.26	0.21
Things	0.41	0.35	0.55	0.47
Mental rotations	0.43	0.40	0.49	0.45
Subtraction and multiplication	0.38	0.34	0.40	0.35
Elithorn mazes ("lines and dots")	0.24	0.23	0.27	0.26
Word beginnings and endings	0.39	0.42	0.55	0.59
Card rotations[b]	0.46	0.30	0.52	0.34
Visual memory (delayed)	0.31	0.18	0.50	0.29
Pedigrees	0.52	0.45	0.72	0.63
Hidden patterns[b]	0.45	0.27	0.49	0.29
Paper form board	0.51	0.46	0.61	0.55
Number comparisons	0.38	0.29	0.46	0.36
Social perception	0.26	0.18	0.38	0.26
Progressive matrices[b]	0.52	0.24	0.60	0.28
Composites				
Spatial[b]	0.60	0.42	0.64	0.45
Verbal	0.54	0.48	0.61	0.55
Perceptual speed and accuracy	0.41	0.34	0.46	0.38
Visual memory	0.31	0.18	0.43	0.25
First Principal Component[b] (Unrotated)	0.60	0.42	0.62	0.43
Number of Families	830	305	830	305

Source. Reprinted with permission from J. C. DeFries, R. C. Johnson, A. R. Kuse, G. E. McClearn, J. Polovina, S. G. Vandenberg, & J. R. Wilson. Familial resemblance for specific cognitive abilities. *Behavior Genetics*, 1979, *9*, 23–43.

Note. AEA and AJA are Americans of European and Japanese ancestry, respectively. Standard errors for AEA and AJA coefficients range from .04 to .05 and from .06 to .08.

[a]Corrected for test reliability.
[b]AEA and AJA regression coefficients significantly ($p \leq .05$) different.

ponent is equivalent to a measure of general intelligence, since Kuse (1977) found a correlation of .73 with the Wechsler IQ in a subsample of 118 families. The spatial and verbal tests, the spatial and verbal composite, and the first principal component show the familial influences.

Because spatial tests seem to be most consistently influenced by heredity, and because they show the most consistent sex difference in favor of males, it has been proposed that spatial ability might be sex-linked—that is, influenced by a gene or genes on the X-chromosome (Stafford, 1961; Bock & Kolakowski, 1973). This hypothesis would lead to the prediction that the correlation between father and son would be lower than that between mother and daughter, which in turn should be lower than the mother and son or father and daughter correlations when considering only genetic influences.

Vandenberg and Kuse (1979) reviewed the evidence for such sex-based differential values of the parent-child correlations for spatial ability. Their summaries are shown in Tables 9 and 10. Only the earliest studies reported values close to the expected pattern, which is shown in the bottom line of Table 9, while the majority of more recent studies do not conform to the sex-linkage expectation. This rules out the idea of X-linkage for spatial ability.

Genetic Analysis of the Wechsler Subtests

There have been three studies in which the Wechsler scales have been used to investigate the importance of genetic influence: Block (1968) administered the WAIS to 120 pairs of twins, 5 male and 5 female at each age from 13 through 18 years of age. To evaluate the importance of heredity, he used the F-test suggested by Dahlberg (1926): the ratio between the within-pair variance for the DZ twins and that for the MZ twins, which was introduced in an earlier section. An increase in the DZ within-pair variance relative to that of the MZ twins can be interpreted as due to the presence of genetic variation between members of a DZ twin pair. The results of Block's study are shown in Table 11. All but two of the subtests showed a significant contribution by heredity. The F-tests for the two subtests that were not significant (Picture Completion and Object Assembly) fell just short of the 5% level of significance.

The second study was by Williams (1975 a, b), who administered the WISC to 55 10-year-old boys and the WAIS to both parents of each boy. His regressions of the sons' scores on the midparental scores (an estimate of the familiality) are also shown in Table 11. Again Picture Completion and Object Assembly fail to reach significance, but so do Digit Span and Picture Arrangement.

The third study was by Kuse (1977), who analyzed the Wechsler scores for 118 families tested as part of the Hawaii study mentioned before. His results are shown in the right-most column in Table 11. These are regressions of the midchild score on the midparental score. In general, the results are remarkably similar to Williams's values, except that Picture Completion reached a significant value.

If one assumes that the total variance for each subtest is the same for the

Table 9. Familial Correlations for Tests of Spatial Visualization

Author	Test	Father/ Son	Mother/ Daughter	Mother/ Son	Father/ Daughter	Father/ Mother
Stafford (1961)	Identical blocks[a]	.02(51)	.18(64)	.39(50)	.36(63)	.04(99)
Hartlage (1970)	DAT space relations	.18(25)	.25(25)	.39(25)	.34(25)	—
Bock & Kolakowski (1973)[b]	Guilford-Zimmerman spatial visualization	.15(99)	.12(97)	.20(115)	.25(84)	.26(121)
DeFries et al. (1976)	Mental rotations	.15(434)	.32(438)	.16(434)	.23(438)	.10[c](555)
Spuhler (1976)	Mental rotations	.25(81)	.04(81)	.10(81)	.32(81)	−.07(104)
Carter-Saltzman (1977)	Mental rotations	.04(94)	.23(119)	.04(94)	.17(119)	.02(93)
McGee (1978)	Mental rotations	.23(185)	.16(196)	.20(204)	.17(172)	.06(144)
Loehlin et al. (1978)	Cube comparisons	.16(183)	.19(201)	.04(183)	.17(201)	.01(192)
Expected values for X-linked variable with recessive gene frequency of .5.		.00	.33	.58	.58	.00

Source. Reprinted with permission from S. G. Vandenberg & A. R. Kuse. Spatial ability: A critical review of the sex-linked major gene hypothesis. In M. C. Wittig & A. C. Peterson (Eds.). *Sex-related differences in cognitive functioning.* New York: Academic Press, 1979.

Note. All scores are age-corrected. The number of pairs entering into each correlation is given in parentheses.

[a]Corrected for reliability.

[b]The exact number of pairs of each correlation was reported by Bock (1970).

[c]The parental correlation was reported in a study of assortative mating by Johnson et al. (1976).

Table 10. Familial Correlations for a Variety of Spatial Tests

Author	Test	Father/Son	Mother/Daughter	Mother/Son	Father/Daughter	Father/Mother
Corah (1965)	Embedded figures tests (EFT AND CEFT)	.18(30)	.02(30)	.31(30)	.28(30)	.14(60)
Bock (1970)	Embedded figures (EFT)	−.05(25)	.36(26)	.18(26)	.49(22)	.18(60)
Williams (1975a,b)	WAIS block design	.28(55)	—	.05(55)	—	.19(55)
Carter-Saltzman (1977)	WAIS block design	.33(95)	.17(119)	.37(97)	.38(117)	.15(96)
Kuse (1977)	WAIS block design	.26(80)	.18(81)	.24(80)	.06(81)	.07(118)
DeFries et al. (1976)	Paper form board	.27(434)	.36(438)	.30(434)	.40(438)	.20[b](555)
	Hidden patterns	.21(434)	.32(438)	.20(434)	.27(438)	.23[b](555)
	Card rotations	.26(434)	.36(438)	.19(434)	.22(438)	.13[b](555)
	Spatial factor[a]	.27(434)	.41(438)	.28(434)	.32(438)	.16[b](555)
Spuhler (1976)	Paper form board	.37(81)	.24(81)	.12(81)	.35(81)	.08(104)
	Hidden patterns	.29(81)	.35(81)	.29(81)	.34(81)	.15(104)
	Card rotations	.25(81)	.03(81)	.16(81)	.15(81)	.02(104)
	Spatial factor[a]	.35(81)	.24(81)	.13(81)	.40(81)	.05(104)
McGee (1978)	Hidden patterns	.09(185)	.20(196)	.22(204)	.11(172)	.28(144)
Loehlin et al. (1978)	Card rotations	.27(183)	.40(201)	.27(183)	.32(201)	.28(192)
	Hidden patterns	.40(183)	.22(201)	.40(183)	.38(201)	.21(192)
	Paper folding	.27(183)	.21(201)	.27(183)	.30(201)	.09(192)
	Spatial composite	.28(183)	.28(201)	.28(183)	.30(201)	.14(192)

Source. Reprinted with permission from S. G. Vandenberg & A. R. Kuse. Spatial ability: A critical review of the sex-linked major gene hypothesis. In M. C. Wittig & A. C. Peterson (Eds.), *Sex-related differences in cognitive functioning*. New York: Academic Press, 1979.

Note. All scores are age-corrected. The number of pairs entering into each correlation is given in parentheses.

[a]These spatial factors had major loadings on mental rotations, paper form board, hidden patterns, card rotations, Elithorn mazes, progressive matrices, and pedigrees tests.

[b]These parental correlations were reported in a separate paper by Johnson et al. (1976).

Table 11. Resemblance among Relatives on Wechsler Subtests

Subtests	Twin Resemblance		Midparent-Offspring Regressions	
	$F = \dfrac{V_{WDZ}}{V_{WMZ}}{}^a$	$1 - 1/F^b$	Williams (1975b)^c	Kuse (1977)^d
Information	3.88***	.74	.25 ± .13*	.34 ± .09***
Comprehension	2.55**	.61	.26 ± .13*	.44 ± .10***
Arithmetic	2.78***	.68	.45 ± .12**	.33 ± .10***
Similarities	1.81*	.45	.36 ± .15*	.27 ± .09***
Digit span	1.53*	.35	.13 ± .15	.19 ± .10
Vocabulary	3.14***	.68	.53 ± .10**	.52 ± .09***
Digit symbol	2.06**	.52	.56 ± .15**	.52 ± .10***
Picture completion	1.50	.34	−.12 ± .20	.25 ± .10**
Block design	2.35**	.58	.34 ± .19*	.31 ± .11***
Picture arrange-ment	1.74*	.43	.07 ± .18	−.01 ± .10
Object assembly	1.36	.27	.02 ± .24	.12 ± .10

^{a}F-ratios of within-pair variances (from Block, 1968); $N = 60$ MZ and 60 DZ pairs.
^{b}When the MZ and DZ total variances are equal, the heritability (h^2) equals $1 - 1/F$.
^{c}$N = 55$ midparent and son pairs.
^{d}$N = 118$ midparent and midchild pairs.
* $p < .05$.
** $p < .01$.
*** $p < .001$.

DZ and MZ twins in Block's (1968) study, it is possible to convert the F-ratio in that study to a value somewhat akin to a heritability estimate by calculating $1 - \dfrac{1}{F}$. These values, shown to the right of the F-values in Table 11, are larger than the measures of familiality in the Williams (1975) and Kuse (1977) studies. This is probably because the comparison of MZ and DZ twins includes variance due to dominance and epistasis, and possibly variance due to the special twin situation of the MZ pairs, which inflates these estimates.

Four PMA Twin Studies

The other test that has been used in several studies is the Primary Mental Abilities test of Thurstone. In contrast with the rather highly correlated Wechsler subtests, the Primary Mental Abilities test measures six relatively independent abilities: verbal ability, spatial ability, number ability, reasoning ability, word fluency, and memory. Blewett (1954) was the first to use this test battery with twins, followed by Thurstone himself in 1955 and by Vandenberg in his 1962 and 1965 studies. The results of these four studies are shown in Table 12. The statistics used is the ratio between the DZ and MZ within-pair variances, as in

Table 12.   F-Ratios of Dizygous and Monozygous Twin Within-Pair Variance

Name of PMA Subtest	Blewett	Thurstone et al.	Vandenberg (Michigan)	Vandenberg (Louisville)
Verbal	3.13**	2.81**	2.65**	1.74*
Space	2.04*	4.19**	1.77*	3.51**
Number	1.07	1.52	2.58**	2.26**
Reasoning	2.78**	1.35	1.40	1.10
Word fluency	2.78**	2.47**	2.57**	2.24**
Memory	Not used	1.62	1.26	Not used
N_{MZ}	26	45	45	76
N_{DZ}	26	53	37	36

Source. Reprinted with permission from S. G. Vandenberg. The nature and nurture of intelligence. In D. C. Glass (Ed.), *Genetics.* New York: The Rockefeller University Press and Russell Sage Foundation, 1968.
*$p < .05$.
**$p < .01$.

Block's (1968) study. There are significant genetic components in the verbal ability, spatial ability, and word fluency scores in all four studies, but in only two studies are the number ability scores significant. In the two studies where the memory subtests were used there was no indication of a genetic component. This seems to have been due in part to the fact that group tests of memory are usually unreliable, because they depend on the motivation of the testees to memorize the materials during the study time provided. The reasoning subtests also failed to show a genetic component in three of the four studies. This may have been due to the fact that problems in these tests can be solved in different ways, so that members of a twin pair may have used different strategies at times.

The fact that different cognitive tests show different degrees of genetic determination raises the question of whether this reflects random error or different reliability, or whether it is indeed due to variation in genetic control. One way to examine this issue is to see how much genetic covariation the tests share. There have been several multivariate analyses of twin data to determine whether the underlying genetic components for the various tests are largely the same or different (Bock & Vandenberg, 1968; Bramble, Bock, & Vandenberg, 1970; Kolakowski, Bock, & Vandenberg, 1968; Loehlin & Vandenberg, 1968; Partanen, Bruun, & Markkanen, 1966; and Vandenberg, 1965a, 1965b). In general, these studies show that the increased within-pair variance of fraternal twins compared to that for identical twins, which is due to hereditary differences within the fraternal twins, is not due solely to a general hereditary superiority of one twin over the other on all tests. Rather, one twin will do better on one test and the other twin on another test, so that performance on different ability tests appears to be due at least partly to different genetic factors.

In addition to the analyses of twin data, there has been one multivariate analysis of parent-offspring data. DeFries, Kuse, and Vandenberg (1979) partitioned the observed cross covariances of test i for midparent and test j for midchild into genetic covariances and environmental covariances, where i and j were each of the 15 cognitive tests in turn of the Hawaii Family Study of Cognition (DeFries et al., 1976). The genetic covariances were then converted into correlations by dividing them by the product of the square roots of the genetic variances associated with each pair of variables. This provided a 15 by 15 matrix of the genetic correlations. The environmental covariances were similarly divided by the product of the square roots of the environmental variances for the two variables concerned. Finally, the genetic and the environmental correlation matrices were factor analyzed.

Table 13 presents three sets of four factors: the phenotypic factors (those in the original correlations), the genetic factors, and the environmental factors. It can be seen that the three factor structures are rather similar. In fact, the similarity between the last two sets of factors is shown in Table 14, in which the diagonal elements, representing the congruence between corresponding factors, are .99, .82, .84, and 1.00! This perhaps somewhat surprising result has been interpreted as evidence that environment—for example, educational influences—can develop only abilities that are potentially there. Note that the environment need not consist only of formal, academic instruction.

We know next to nothing about brain mechanisms responsible for performance on tests, other than that the two hemispheres may play somewhat different roles. In addition, there must be differential involvement of various subsystems, such as visual and auditory processing systems, short- and long-term memory, and so forth.

Since the "cognitive revolution" there has been a return of interest in the possibility of finding basic laboratory measures of information processing that might replace conventional measures of intelligence. As a first step, such explorations have in general used conventional paper-and-pencil ability tests to demonstrate that the new measures indeed relate to intelligence. Another strategy has been to contrast the performance of retarded and normal subjects. The tasks used include multiple choice reaction time (Jensen, 1981), minimum inspection time required to decide which of two lines is longer or whether a letter is in lowercase or capital form, and variations of that technique, including comparisons of tones (Raz & Willerman, 1983); as well as aspects of the EEG and auditory or visual evoked potentials (Eysenck, 1982; Hunt, 1983). Most of this mental chronometry has been concerned with one variable only, plus possibly one or more paper-and-pencil tests used as criterion measures. At an in-between level, Sternberg (1977) analyzes various types of analogical reasoning into (sequential) information processing components. Perhaps much of the history of factor analyzing collections of test scores will have to be repeated, in order to isolate information-processing components.

There has been only one behavior-genetic study of tasks derived from an information-processing viewpoint (Cole et al., 1979). Members of 118 families were administered a version of Sperling's (1970) task in which one row of a 3 by 3 matrix of letters is to be recalled. The matrix is displayed for one-half

Table 13. Varimax Rotated Factor Loadings Obtained from AEA Phenotypic, Genetic, and Environmental Correlation Matrices

Variables	Phenotypic Factors				Genetic Factors				Environmental Factors			
	1	2	3	4	1	2	3	4	1	2	3	4
VOC	.13	<u>.77</u>	.22	.08	.18	<u>.85</u>	.26	.17	−.04	<u>.69</u>	−.36	−.02
VMI	.08	.11	.03	<u>.85</u>	<u>.42</u>	.16	.05	<u>.91</u>	−.10	.12	−.06	<u>.78</u>
TH	.13	<u>.66</u>	.01	−.01	.28	<u>.68</u>	−.06	.03	−.03	<u>.64</u>	.03	−.03
MR	<u>.75</u>	.20	−.07	.09	<u>.88</u>	.37	−.02	.06	<u>.66</u>	−.19	−.20	.15
S&M	.08	.22	<u>.85</u>	.00	.00	.25	<u>.92</u>	−.07	.39	<u>.54</u>	.20	.17
L&D	<u>.56</u>	.01	.20	.02	<u>.78</u>	.37	.29	.21	.06	.08	<u>.85</u>	.02
WB&E	.16	<u>.67</u>	.21	.03	.21	<u>.78</u>	.25	.05	.18	<u>.55</u>	.01	.07
CR	<u>.74</u>	.11	.16	.05	<u>.87</u>	.17	.15	.25	<u>.60</u>	.09	.10	−.11
VMD	.07	.08	.06	<u>.85</u>	.11	.14	.01	<u>.99</u>	.05	.00	.01	<u>.81</u>
PED	.36	<u>.59</u>	.30	.16	.32	<u>.74</u>	.21	.29	<u>.44</u>	<u>.53</u>	.04	.08
HP	<u>.63</u>	.29	.23	.07	<u>.74</u>	.33	.25	.24	<u>.49</u>	.32	.07	−.08
PFB	<u>.67</u>	.30	.01	.04	<u>.75</u>	.41	.05	.14	<u>.55</u>	.11	.04	−.12
NC	.25	.14	<u>.81</u>	.10	.31	.11	<u>.87</u>	.14	<u>.45</u>	<u>.44</u>	.10	.18
SPV	.19	<u>.67</u>	.01	.12	.39	<u>.87</u>	.14	.09	.18	.31	−.36	.18
PM	<u>.54</u>	<u>.50</u>	.08	.07	<u>.59</u>	<u>.68</u>	.06	.11	<u>.53</u>	.14	.14	.10

Source. Reprinted with permission from J. C. DeFries, A. R. Kuse, & S. G. Vandenberg. Genetic correlations, environmental correlations, and behavior. In J. R. Royce & L. P. Mos (Eds.), *Theoretical advances in behavior genetics.* Alphen aan den Rijn, Netherlands: Sijthoff & Noordhoff, 1979.

Note. AEA = Americans of European ancestry. Relatively high loadings (.40 or greater) on each factor are underlined.

Table 14.   Factor Structure Comparisons Between R_A and R_E

| Environmental | Genetic Factors | | | |
Factors	1	2	3	4
1	.99	.17	−.01	.04
2	−.14	.82	.55	−.01
3	.10	−.54	.84	−.01
4	−.05	.01	.02	1.00

Source. Reprinted with permission from J. C. DeFries, A. R. Kuse, & S. G. Vandenberg. Genetic correlations, environmental correlations, and behavior. In J. R. Royce & L. P. Mos (Eds.), *Theoretical advances in behavior genetics.* Alphen aan den Rijn, Netherlands: Sijthoff & Noordhoff, 1979.

second, and after another half-second delay the subject is told which row to report. This is a measure of short-term visual (iconic) memory (VIS3). In other trials, there was no interval before the row was specified (VIS2). Finally, the subjects were asked to report as many of the nine letters as possible (VIS1). There were three similar auditory tasks, except that in AUD3 the interval before reporting one of the three letter groups was filled with serial subtraction (100 minus 3 = 97, 97 minus 3 = 94, and so on).

Regressions of midchild on midparental values were VIS1 .33, VIS3 .43, AUD2 .31, AUD3 .53. (Regressions for VIS2 and AUD1 were not significant.) These values are of the same magnitude as those for some conventional psychometric memory tests that were also administered: Wechsler Digit Span .23; memory for abstract designs, immediate .39, after delay of over an hour .35; memory for pictures of objects, immediate .45, and after one hour delay .20. This study suggests that information-processing tasks may be under genetic control to about the same degree as standard measures of intelligence, but more work is clearly needed before we can be certain of this.

Piaget has developed a theory that presents an alternative to the psychometric approach to intelligence. This raises the question of whether Piaget's stages are influenced by hereditary factors. Piaget himself took no clear position on this issue. There is one study that begins to answer this question.

Piaget (1965) formulated theories concerning the stages in children's conceptions of numbers. Garfinkle developed the Piagetian Mathematical Concepts Battery (PMCB) to assess those stages with quantitative scales (Garfinkle & Vandenberg, 1978, 1979). The PMCB was administered to 137 MZ and 72 same-sexed DZ twin pairs, aged 4 to 8 years, from Caucasian, middle- and upper-middle-class homes. In addition, Raven's Colored Progressive Matrices test (PM), the Peabody Picture Vocabulary Test (PPVT), and a Visual Memory test (VM) were administered. The MZ and DZ intraclass correlations are shown in Table 15. It can be seen that the hereditary component for the PMCB is of the same order of magnitude as those for the psychometric tests. The correlations of the PPVT and PM with the PMCB were .36 and .41, respectively, demonstrating that the Piagetian tasks are tapping something that is largely independent of conventional psychometrically measured intelligence, as reported repeatedly by others.

Table 15. Intraclass Correlations and Estimates of Broad Heritabilities (h^2) for the Cognitive Tests and for Height and Weight, for 137 MZ and 72 DZ Twin Pairs

Measure	Intraclass Correlation		h^2
	MZ	DZ	
PMCB	.73 ± .04	.56 ± .08	.34* ± .18
	(.86)[a]	(.66)	(.40)**
PM	.49 ± .07	.39 ± .10	.20 ± .24
PPVT	.69 ± .04	.52 ± .09	.34* ± .19
	(.90)	(.68)	(.44)**
VM	.17 ± .08	−.08 ± .12	
	(.27)	(−.13)	
Height	.94 ± .01	.54 ± .09	.80** ± .17
Weight	.91 ± .01	.67 ± .06	.48** ± .13

Source. Reprinted with permission from A. S. Garfinkle. Genetic and environmental influences on the development of Piagetian logico-mathematical concepts and other specific cognitive abilities: A twin study. *Acta Genetical Medical et Genellologiae*, 1982, *31*, 10–61.

Note. Broad heritability, $h^2 = 2(r_{MZ} - r_{DZ})$, from Falconer (1960).

[a]Numbers in parentheses are the appropriate values corrected for test reliability.

*$p < .05$.

**$p < .01$.

Inbreeding Depression

In earlier papers Vandenberg considered the reduced intelligence due to consanguinity or inbreeding to be another piece of evidence for genetic factors in intelligence. However, Kamin's 1980 review has persuaded us that only one study (Schull & Neel, 1965) provides support for a lowering of IQ as a result of cousin marriages. Kamin ascribes this depressed IQ partly to socioeconomic differences between inbreds and controls, while we accept the measures used by Schull and Neel (1965) to remove this socioeconomic effect: house size as indicated by the number of tatami mats, and education and occupation of parent. However, in a second study in Japan (Schull & Neel, 1972) the effects of inbreeding on IQ were not significant, weakening the case of the first study.

Is the National Average IQ Declining?

From time to time this question is raised because of several considerations: (1) IQ is genetically influenced; (2) lower socioeconomic classes have lower IQs; and (3) these classes have more children. Let us discuss each of these points.

Regarding the first point, we noted in our introduction that even with perfect hereditary control there would be segregation, that is, children would differ from their parents as often as they would be similar. Furthermore, heritability is far less than 100%, and environmental conditions certainly play a large role. Point 2 is only true as far as averages go, and there is a great deal of overlap in ability between the classes. The best illustration of this is provided by a large study of Belgian recruits (Cliquet, 1963). In this study 3621 recruits were measured on seven abilities, and the mean scores and standard deviations were calculated for men whose fathers were from nine different socioeconomic levels. The results are shown in Figure 16. It can be seen that in general the mean score decreases with a decrease in social status. However, the overlap is such that even the lowest class overlaps substantially the highest class. Note that the range level shown in the figure represents only a single standard deviation above and below the mean. With respect to the third point in the argument, the evidence is mixed. Bajema (1963, 1971), Higgins, Reed, and Reed (1962), Olneck and Wolfe (1980), Spuhler (1962), and Waller (1971) have reported a positive relationship between socioeconomic status (or IQ) and number of children, especially when persons with low IQ who do not reproduce are taken into account. However, Vining (1982) has found a negative correlation and has argued that the earlier studies are based on small, perhaps unrepresentative samples, who had children during the baby boom period. His study used a national probability sample and represents a post–World War II cohort with a falling birth rate. He regards his results as reflecting more nearly the true state of affairs. Even though all three steps in the chain of reasoning may be accurate statements, we expect that the middle class forms such a very large reservoir of genes for high intelligence that it far outweighs the possibility of a small decrease in average IQ, which might be due to the lower reproductive rate of the upper class.

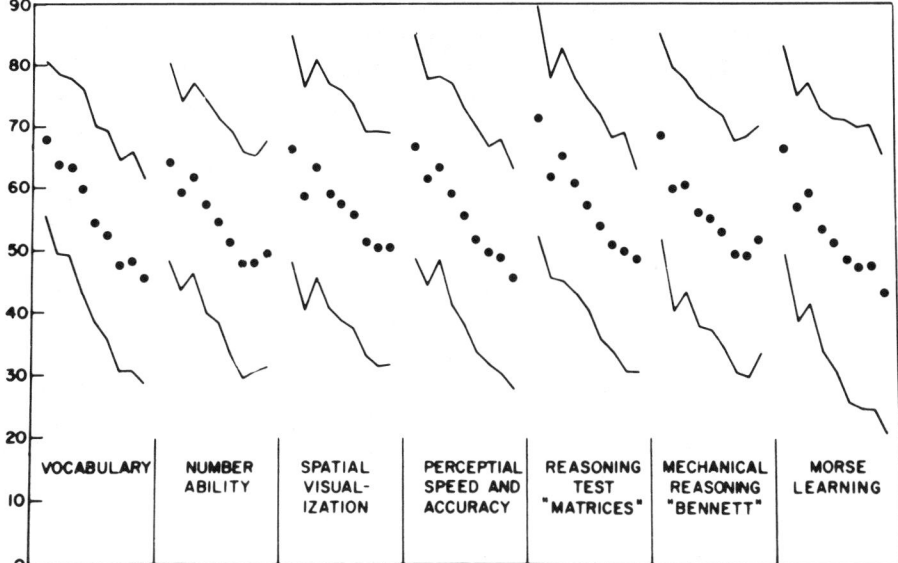

Figure 16.   Mean scores (and range of one standard deviation above and below the mean) for seven abilities in Belgian recruits from nine socioecomonic levels. (*Source:* Reprinted with permission from S. G. Vandenberg. The future of human behavior genetics. In L. Ehrman, G. S. Omenn, & E. Caspari (Eds.), *Genetics, environment, and behavior.* New York: Academic Press, 1972.)

CONCLUSION

In its entirety, the body of literature we summarized justifies the conclusion that hereditary influences on intelligence exist. While individual studies can be criticized for various shortcomings, there are no compelling alternative explanations for the resemblance among relatives. While methodological advances have resulted in a refinement of estimates of the genetic contribution to phenotypic variability from around 80% to a more moderate 30% to 40%, studies have consistently demonstrated familial resemblance for measures of intelligence for more than a century.

There are two questions that should be addressed at this point. First, of what practical use is the demonstration of hereditary influences on intelligence? Presumably we have no ethical means to control such influences. Indeed, there is historical precedent to demonstrate that the misinterpretation of such information by individuals with political motives can lead to disastrous abuses. Furthermore, a heritability of 30% to 40% means that 60% to 70% of the variation in general cognitive ability is due to nongenetic influences over which we may have some degree of control. Nevertheless, genetic influences represent the *single* most important influence that has been identified. Controversy regarding such findings has led to the refinement of analytic techniques, so that it is now possible to control for genetic influences in the search for salient environmental influences, of which we know little. This leads directly to the second question: Where do we go from here?

The next logical step is to use the methodology that now exists to study the 60% to 70% of variation remaining after genetic variation is accounted for. To date, most studies have tried to use some global indices of the environment, such as SES or parental education, which probably also are influenced to some degree by genetic factors—possibly some of the same genetic factors that influence intelligence. Such research has met with only mixed success. What is needed is rigorous study of numerous specific environmental factors, such as nutrition, variability in the educational system, and other more detailed aspects of the individual's home environment and personal experience. It is likely that numerous influences will be found, each with a small effect, rather than one or two major environmental influences. Intervention programs designed to improve environmental influences will have to be comprehensive, rather than focused narrowly on only a few aspects of the environment, in order to be successful. The methodology that has been developed to study genetic influences appears to have the greatest potential for identifying the relevant aspects of the environment.

REFERENCES

Bajema, C. (1963). Estimation of the direction and intensity of natural selection in relation to human intelligence by means of the intrinsic rate of natural increase. *Eugenics Quarterly, 10*, 175–187.

Bajema, C. (1971). The genetic implications of population control. *Bio-Science, 21*, 71–75.

Bayley, N. (1956). Individual patterns of development. *Child Development, 27,* 45–74.

Blewett, D. B. (1954). An experimental study of the inheritance of intelligence. *Journal of Mental Science, 100,* 922–933.

Block, J. B. (1968). Hereditary components in the performance of twins on the WAIS. In S. G. Vandenberg (Ed.), *Progress in human behavior genetics.* Baltimore: Johns Hopkins Press.

Bock, R. D. (1970). *A study of familial effects in certain cognitive and perceptual variables.* Final Report of the Illinois Psychiatric Training and Research Grant No. 17-137 to the University of Chicago.

Bock, R. D., & Kolakowski, D. (1973). Further evidence of sex-linked major-gene influence on human spatial visualizing ability. *American Journal of Human Genetics, 25,* 1–14.

Bock, R. D., & Vandenberg, S. G. (1968). Components of heritable variation in test scores. In S. G. Vandenberg (Ed.), *Progress in human bahavior genetics.* Baltimore: Johns Hopkins Press.

Bouchard, T. J., & McGue, M. (1981). Familial studies of intelligence: A review. *Science, 212,* 1055–1059.

Bramble, W. J., Bock, R. D., & Vandenberg, S. G. (1970). *Components of heritable variation in the Primary Mental Abilities test (PMA).* Research report from the Institute for Behavioral Genetics, University of Colorado, Boulder, Colorado.

Breland, N. S. (1972). *A new approach to estimates of heritability from twin data.* Unpublished research qualifying paper, Department of Educational Psychology, State University of New York at Buffalo.

Burks, B. S. (1928). The relative influence of nature and nurture upon mental development: A comparative study of foster parent–foster child resemblance and true parent–true child resemblance. *Yearbook of the National Society for the Study of Education, 27,* 219–316.

Carter-Saltzman, I. (1977). Patterns of cognitive abilities and lateralization in adoptive and biological families. *Behavior Genetics, 7,* 48. (Abstract)

Caspersson, T., Lomakka, G., & Møller, A. (1971). Computerized chromosome identification by aid of the quinacrine mustard fluorescence technique. *Hereditas, 67,* 103–109.

Cliff, N. (1983). Some cautions concerning the application of causal modeling methods. *Multivariate Behavioral Research, 18,* 115–126.

Cliquet, R. L. (1963). Bijdrage tot de kennis van het verband tussen de sociale status en een aantal antrobiologische kenmerken (Contribution to the knowledge of the relation between social status and a number of anthrobiological characteristics). *Verh. Kon. Vlaam. Acad. Wetensch. Lett. Schone Kunsten Belg. Kl. Wetensch. No. 72,* Brussels.

Cloninger, C. R., Rao, D. C., Rice, J., Reich, T., & Morton, N. E. (1983). A defense of path analysis in genetic epidemiology. *American Journal of Human Genetics, 35,* 733–756.

Cloninger, C. R., Rice, J., & Reich, T. (1979). Multifactorial inheritance with cultural transmission and assortative mating—II: A general model of combined polygenic and cultural inheritance. *American Journal of Human Genetics, 31,* 176–198.

Cloninger, C. R., Rice, J., & Reich, T. (1979). Multifactorial inheritance with cultural transmission and assortative mating—III: Family structure and the analysis of separation experiments. *American Journal of Human Genetics, 31,* 366–388.

Cole, R. E., Johnson, R. C., Ahern, F. M., Kuse, A. R., McClearn, G. E., Vandenberg, S. G., & Wilson, J. R. (1979). A family study of memory processes and their relations to cognitive test scores. *Intelligence, 3,* 127–138.

Corah, N. L. (1965). Differentiation in children and their parents. *Journal of Personality, 33,* 300–308.

Corey, L. A., & Nance, W. E. (1978). The monozygotic half-sib model: A tool for epidemiologic research. In W. E. Nance (Ed.), *Twin research: Part A. Psychology and methodology.* New York: Alan R. Liss.

Crumpacker, D. W., Cederlöf, R., Friberg, L., Kimberling, W. J., Sörensen, S., Vandenberg, S. G.,

Williams, J. S., McClearn, G. E., Grever, B., Iyer, H., Krier, M. J., Pedersen, N. L., Price, R. A., & Roulette, I. (1979). A twin methodology for the study of genetic and environmental control of variation in human smoking behavior. *Acta Geneticae Medicae et Gemellologiae, 28,* 173–195.

Dahlberg, G. (1926). *Twin births and twins from a hereditary point of view.* Stockholm: Tidens Tryckeri.

DeFries, J. C., Ashton, G. C., Johnson, R. C., Kuse, A. R., McClearn, G. E., Mi, M. P., Rashad, M. N., Vandenberg, S. G., & Wilson, J. R. (1976). Parent-offspring resemblance for specific cognitive abilities in two ethnic groups. *Nature, 261,* 131–133.

DeFries, J. C., Johnson, R. C., Kuse, A. R., McClearn, G. E., Polovina, J., Vandenberg, S. G., & Wilson, J. R. (1979). Familial resemblance for specific cognitive abilities. *Bahavior Genetics, 9,* 23–43.

DeFries, J. C., Kuse, A. R., & Vandenberg, S. G. (1979). Genetic correlations, environmental correlations, and behavior. In J. R. Royce & L. P. Mos (Eds.), *Theoretical advances in behavior genetics.* Alphen aan den Rijn, Netherlands: Sijthoff and Noordhoff.

DeFries, J. C., Plomin, R., Vandenberg, S. G., & Kuse, A. R. (1981). Parent-offspring resemblance for cognitive abilities in the Colorado Adoption Project: Biological, adoptive, and control parents and one-year-old children. *Intelligence, 5,* 245–277.

Dixon, L. K., & Johnson, R. C. (1980). *The roots of individuality.* Monterey, CA: Brooks/Cole.

Eaves, L. J. (1975). Testing models for variation in intelligence. *Heredity, 34,* 132–136.

Eaves, L. J., Last, K. A., Young, P. A., & Martin, N. G. (1978). Model-fitting approaches to the analysis of human behavior. *Heredity, 41,* 249–320.

Ehrman, L., & Parsons, P. A. (1976). *The genetics of behavior.* Sunderland, MA: Sinauer Associates.

Eysenck, H. J. (1982). The psychophysiology of intelligence. In C. D. Spielberger & J. N. Butcher (Eds.), *Advances in personality assessment* (Vol. 1). Hillsdale, NJ: Erlbaum.

Falconer, D. S. (1960). *Introduction to quantitative genetics.* London: Oliver and Boyd.

Falconer, D. S. (1981). *Introduction to quantitative genetics* (2nd ed.). London: Longman.

Falkner, F. T., Banik, N. D. D., & Westland, R. (1962). Intra-uterine blood transfer between uniovular twins. *Biology of the Neonate, 4,* 52.

Farber, S. L. (1981). *Identical twins reared apart.* New York: Basic Books.

Fulker, D. W., & DeFries, J. C. (1983). Genetic and environmental transmission in the Colorado Adoption Project: Path analysis. *British Journal of Mathematical and Statistical Psychology, 36,* 175–188.

Fuller, J. L., & Simmel, E. C. (1983). *Behavior genetics: Principles and applications.* Hillsdale, NJ: Erlbaum.

Fuller, J. L., & Thompson, W. R. (1967). *Behavior genetics.* New York: Wiley.

Fuller, J. L., & Thompson, W. R. (1978). *Foundations of behavior genetics.* St. Louis: Mosby.

Galton, F. (1876). The history of twins as a criterion of the relative power of nature and nurture. *Royal Anthropological Institute of Great Britain and Ireland Journal, 6,* 391–406.

Garfinkle, A. S. (1982). Genetic and environmental influences on the development of Piagetian logico-mathematical concepts and other specific cognitive abilities: A twin study. *Acta Geneticae Medicae et Gemellologiae, 31,* 10–61.

Garfinkle, A. S., & Vandenberg, S. G. (1978). Development of Piagetian logico-mathematical concepts: Preliminary results of a twin study. In W. E. Nance (Ed.), *Twin research: Part A. Psychology and methodology.* New York: Alan R. Liss.

Garfinkle, A. S., & Vandenberg, S. G. (1979). Verification of the psychometric value of the Piagetian Mathematical Concepts Battery. In M. K. Poulson & G. I. Lubin (Eds.), *Piagetian theory and the helping professions.* Los Angeles: University of Southern California.

Goldberger, A. S. (1978a). The nonresolution of IQ inheritance by path analysis. *American Journal of Human Genetics, 30,* 442–445.

Goldberger, A. S. (1978b). Pitfalls in the resolution of IQ inheritance. In N. E. Morton & C. S. Chung (Eds.), *Genetic epidemiology.* New York: Academic Press.

Hartlage, L. C. (1970). Sex-linked inheritance of spatial ability. *Perceptual and Motor Skills, 31,* 610.

Herbst, D. S., & Miller, J. R. (1980). Non-specific X-linked mental retardation. II. The frequency in British Columbia. *American Journal of Medical Genetics, 7,* 461–469.

Higgins, J., Reed, E., & Reed, S. (1962). Intelligence and family size: A paradox resolved. *Eugenics Quarterly, 9,* 84–90.

Hindley, C. B., & Owen, C. F. (1978). The extent of individual changes in IQ for ages between six months and seventeen years, in a British longitudinal sample. *Journal of Child Psychology and Psychiatry, 19,* 329–350.

Ho, H., Plomin, R., & DeFries, J. C. (1979). Selective placement in adoption. *Social Biology, 26,* 1–6.

Honzik, M. P. (1957). Developmental studies of parent-child resemblance in intelligence. *Child Development, 28,* 215–228.

Honzik, M. P., Macfarlane, J. W., & Allen, L. (1948). The stability of mental test performance between two and eighteen years. *Journal of Experimental Psychology, 17,* 309–324.

Horn, J. M. (1983). The Texas Adoption Project: Adopted children and their intellectual resemblance to biological and adoptive parents. *Child Development, 54,* 268–275.

Horn, J. M., Loehlin, J. C., & Willerman, L. (1979). Intellectual resemblance among adoptive and biological relatives: The Texas Adoption Project. *Behavior Genetics, 9,* 177–207.

Horn, J. M., Loehlin, J. C., & Willerman, L. (1982). Aspects of the inheritance of intellectual abilities. *Behavior Genetics, 12,* 479–516.

Hsia, D. Y. (1970). Phenylketonuria and its variants. In A. G. Steinberg & A. G. Bearn (Eds.), *Progress in medical genetics* (Vol. 7). New York: Grune and Stratton.

Hunt, E. (1983). On the nature of intelligence. *Science, 219,* 141–146.

Jencks, C., Smith, M., Acland, H., Bane, M. J., Cohen, D., Gintis, H., Heyns, B., & Michelson, S. (1972). *Inequality: A reassessment of the effect of family and schooling in America.* New York: Basic Books.

Jensen, A. R. (1969). How much can we boost IQ and scholastic achievement? *Harvard Educational Review, 39,* 1–123.

Jensen, A. R. (1981). The chronometry of intelligence. In R. J. Sternberg (Ed.), *Advances in research on intelligence* (Vol. 1). Hillsdale, NJ: Erlbaum.

Jinks, J. L., & Eaves, L. J. (1974). IQ and inequality. *Nature, 248,* 287–289.

Johnson, R. C., DeFries, J. C., Wilson, J. R., McClearn, G. E., Vandenberg, S. G., Ashton, G. C., Mi, M. P., & Rashad, M. N. (1976). Assortative marriage for specific cognitive abilities in two ethnic groups. *Human Biology, 48,* 343–352.

Jones, L. V. (1949). A factor analysis of the Stanford-Binet at four age levels. *Psychometrika, 14,* 299–330.

Jöreskog, K. G., & Sörbom, D. (1981). *Lisrel: Analysis of linear structural relationships by the method of maximum likelihood* (Version V). Chicago: International Educational Services.

Juel-Nielsen, N. (1965). Individual and environment: A psychiatric-psychological investigation of MZ twins reared apart. *Acta Psychiatrica Scandinavica (Suppl. 183).* Copenhagen: Munksgaard.

Kamin, L. J. (1974). *The science and politics of IQ.* Potomac, MD: Erlbaum.

Kamin, L. J. (1980). Inbreeding depression and IQ. *Psychological Bulletin, 87,* 469–478.

Karlin, S., Cameron, E. C., & Chakraborty, R. (1983). Path analysis in genetic epidemiology: A critique. *American Journal of Human Genetics, 35,* 695–732.

Kebbon, L. (1965). *The structure of abilities at lower levels of intelligence.* Stockholm: Skandinaviska Test Forlaget AB.

Kolakowski, D., Bock, R. D., & Vandenberg, S. G. (1968). *A study of components of variation in some perceptual and cognitive tests* (Research Report No. 29). Louisville Twin Study, University of Louisville School of Medicine, Louisville, Kentucky.

Kuse, A. R. (1977). *Familial resemblance for cognitive abilities estimated from two test batteries in Hawaii.* Unpublished doctoral dissertation, University of Colorado.

Leahy, A. M. (1935). Nature-nurture and intelligence. *Genetic Psychology Monographs, 17,* 236–308.

Lehrke, R. G. (1974). *X-linked mental retardation and verbal disability.* New York: Intercontinental Medical Book.

Lewontin, R. C. (1975). Genetic aspects of intelligence. *Annual Review of Genetics, 9,* 387–405.

Loehlin, J. C. (1978). Heredity-environment analyses of Jencks's IQ correlations. *Behavior Genetics, 8,* 415–436.

Loehlin, J. C. (1979). Combining data from different groups in human behavior genetics. In J. R. Royce & L. P. Mos (Eds.), *Theoretical advances in behavior genetics.* Alphen aan den Rijn, Netherlands: Sijthoff and Noordhoff.

Loehlin, J., Sharan, S., & Jacoby, R. (1978). In pursuit of the "spatial gene": A family study. *Behavior Genetics, 8,* 27–42.

Loehlin, J. C., & Vandenberg, S. G. (1968). Genetic and environmental components in the covariation of cognitive abilities: An additive model. In S. G. Vandenberg (Ed.), *Progress in human behavior genetics.* Baltimore: Johns Hopkins Press.

Lyon, M. F. (1962). Sex chromatin and gene action in the mammalian X-chromosome. *American Journal of Human Genetics, 14,* 135–148.

Mather, K., & Jinks, J. L. (1971). *Biometrical genetics* (2nd ed.). London: Chapman and Hall.

McCall, R. B., Appelbaum, M. I., & Hogarty, P. S. (1973). Developmental changes in mental performance. *Monographs of the Society for Research in Child Development, 38* (Whole No. 150).

McClearn, G. E., & DeFries, J. C. (1973). *Introduction to behavior genetics.* San Francisco: Freeman.

McGee, M. G. (1978). Interfamilial correlations and heritability estimates for human spatial abilities in a Minnesota sample. *Behavior Genetics, 8,* 77–80.

McKusick, V. A. (1978). Mendelian inheritance in Man; catalogs of autosomal dominant, autosomal recessive, and X-linked phenotypes (5th ed.). Baltimore: Johns Hopkins Press.

Meyers, C. E., Dingman, H. F., Orpet, R. E., Sitkei, E. G., & Watts, C. A. (1964). Four ability factor hypotheses at three preliterate levels in normal and retarded children. *Monographs of the Society for Research in Child Development, 29* (4, Serial No. 96).

Meyers, C. E., Orpet, R. E., Atwell, A. A., & Dingman, H. F. (1962). Primary abilities at mental age six. *Monographs of the Society for Research in Child Development, 27* (1, Serial No. 82).

Moor, L. (1967). Niveau intellectuel et polygonosomie: Confrontation du carotype et du niveau mental de 374 malades dont le carotype comporte un excess de chromosomes x ou y (Intellectual level and polyploidy: A comparison of karyotype and intelligence of 374 patients with extra x or y chromosomes). *Revue de Neuropsychiatrie Infantile et d'Hygiene Mentale de l'Enfance, 15,* 325–348.

Morton, N. E. (1974). Analysis of family resemblance. I. Introduction. *American Journal of Human Genetics, 26,* 318–330.

Nance, W. E. (1976). Genetic studies of the offspring of identical twins. *Acta Geneticae Medicae et Gemellologiae, 25,* 103–113.

Nance, W. E., & Corey, L. A. (1976). Genetic models for the analysis of data from the families of identical twins. *Genetics, 83,* 811–826.

Newman, H. H., Freeman, F. N., & Holzinger, K. J. (1937). *Twins: A study of heredity and environment.* Chicago: University of Chicago Press.

Nichols, R. C. (1976). *Heredity and environment: Major findings from twin studies of ability, personality, and interests*. Invited address presented at the American Psychological Association meeting, Washington, DC.

Nuttin, J. (1965). De verstandelijke begaaftheid van de jeugd in de verschillende sociale klassen en woonplaatsen (The intellectual ability of youth in different socioeconomic classes and urban and rural backgrounds). *Meded. Kon. Vlaam. Acad. Wetensch. Lett. Schone Kunsten Belg. Kl. Wetensch. 27* (7), Brussels.

Olneck, M., & Wolfe, B. (1980). Intelligence and family size: Another look. *Review of Economics and Statistics, 62*, 241–247.

Osborne, R. T. (1980). *Twins, black and white*. Athens, GA: Foundation for Human Understanding.

Paine, R. S. (1957). The variability in manifestations of untreated patients with phenylketonuria (phenylpyruvic aciduria). *Pediatrics, 20*, 290–301.

Partanen, J., Bruun, K., & Markkanen, T. (1966). *Inheritance of drinking behavior*. Helsinki: The Finnish Foundation for Alcohol Studies.

Piaget, J. (1965). *The child's conception of number*. New York: Norton.

Plomin, R., & DeFries, J. C. (1983). The Colorado Adoption Project. *Child Development, 54*, 276–289.

Plomin, R., DeFries, J. C., & McClearn, G. E. (1980). *Behavioral genetics: A primer*. San Francisco: Freeman.

Rao, D. C., & Morton, N. E. (1978). IQ as a paradigm in genetic epidemiology. In N. E. Morton & C. S. Chung (Eds.), *Genetic epidemiology*. New York: Academic Press.

Rao, D. C., Morton, N. E., & Cloninger, C. R. (1979). Path analysis under generalized assortative mating. I. Theory. *Genetical Research, 33*, 175–188.

Rao, D. C., Morton, N. E., Lalouel, J. M., & Lew, R. (1982). Path analysis under generalized assortative mating. II. American IQ. *Genetical Research, 39*, 187–198.

Rao, D. C., Morton, N. E., & Yee, S. (1974). Analysis of familial resemblance. II. A linear model for familial correlation. *American Journal of Human Genetics, 26*, 331–359.

Rao, D. C., Morton, N. E., & Yee, S. (1976). Resolution of cultural and biological inheritance by path analysis. *American Journal of Human Genetics, 28*, 228–242.

Rao, D. C., Morton, N. E., & Yee, S. (1978). Resolution of cultural and biological inheritance by path analysis: Corrigenda and reply to Goldberger. *American Journal of Human Genetics, 30*, 445–448.

Raz, N., & Willerman, L. (1983). Backward masking and intelligence. *Behavior Genetics, 13*, 549. (Abstract)

Reed, S. C., & Rich, S. S. (1982). Parent-offspring correlations and regressions for IQ. *Behavior Genetics, 12*, 535–542.

Rice, J., Cloninger, C. R., & Reich, T. (1978). Multifactorial inheritance with cultural transmission and assortative mating. I. Description and basic properties of the unitary models. *American Journal of Human Genetics, 30*, 618–643.

Rice, J., Cloninger, C. R., & Reich, T. (1980). Analysis of behavioral traits in the presence of cultural transmission and assortative mating: Applications to IQ and SES. *Behavior Genetics, 10*, 73–92.

Scarr, S., & Weinberg, R. A. (1976). IQ test performance of black children adopted by white families. *American Psychologist, 31*, 726–739.

Scarr, S., & Weinberg, R. A. (1978). The influence of "family background" on intellectual attainment. *American Sociological Review, 43*, 674–692.

Schull, W. J., & Neel, J. V. (1965). *The effects of inbreeding on Japanese children*. New York: Harper & Sons.

Schull, W. J., & Neel, J. V. (1972). The effects of parental consanguinity and inbreeding in Hirado, Japan: V. Summary and interpretation. *American Journal of Human Genetics, 24*, 425–453.

Scriver, C. R., & Clow, C. L. (1980). Phenylketonuria and other phenylalanine hydroxylation mutants in man. *Annual Review of Genetics, 14,* 179–202.

Shields, J. (1962). *Monozygotic twins brought up apart and brought up together.* London: Oxford University Press.

Skodak, M., & Skeels, M. H. (1949). A final follow-up study of one hundred adopted children. *Journal of Genetic Psychology, 75,* 85–125.

Sontag, L. W., Baker, C. T., & Nelson, V. L. (1958). Mental growth and personality development: A longitudinal study. *Monographs of the Society for Research in Child Development, 23* (Whole No. 2).

Spearman, C. (1904). General intelligence, objectively determined and measured. *American Journal of Psychology, 15,* 201–293.

Sperling, C. (1970). Short-term memory, long-term memory, and scanning in the process of visual information. In F. A. Young & D. B. Lindsley (Eds.), *Early experience and visual information processing and perceptual and reading disorders.* Washington: National Academy of Sciences.

Spuhler, J. (1962). Empirical studies on quantitative human genetics. In *The use of vital and health statistics for genetic and radiation studies.* New York: United Nations.

Spuhler, K. P. (1976). *Family resemblance for cognitive performance: An assessment of genetic and environmental contributions to variation.* Unpublished doctoral dissertation, Univ. of Colorado.

Stafford, R. C. (1961). Sex differences in spatial visualization as evidence of sex-linked inheritance. *Perceptual and Motor Skills, 13,* 300–308.

Sternberg, R. J. (1977). *Intelligence, information processing, and analogical reasoning: The componential analysis of human abilities.* Hillsdale, NJ: Erlbaum.

Sutherland, C. R., & Ashforth, P. L. C. (1979). X-linked mental retardation with macro-orchidism and the fragile site at Xg 27 or 28. *Human Genetics, 48,* 117–120.

Taylor, H. F. (1980). *The IQ game: A methodological inquiry into the heredity-environment controversy.* New Brunswick, NJ: Rutgers University Press.

Thurstone, T. G., Thurstone, L. L., & Strandskov, H. H. (1955). *A psychological study of twins* (Report No. 4). Chapel Hill, NC: Psychometric Laboratory, University of North Carolina.

Uchida, I. A., Freeman, V. C., Jamro, H., Partington, M. W., & Soltan, H. C. (1983). Additional evidence for fragile X activity in heterozygous carriers. *American Journal of Human Genetics, 35,* 861–868.

Uchida, I. A., & Joyce, E. M. (1982). Activity in the fragile X in heterozygous carriers. *American Journal of Human Genetics, 34,* 286–293.

Vandenberg, S. G. (1962). The hereditary abilities study: Hereditary components in a psychological test battery. *American Journal of Human Genetics, 14,* 220–237.

Vandenberg, S. G. (1965a). Multivariate analysis of twin differences. In S. G. Vandenberg (Ed.), *Methods and goals in human behavior genetics.* New York: Academic Press.

Vandenberg, S. G. (1965b). Innate abilities, one or many? A new method and some results. *Acta Geneticae Medicae et Gemellologiae, 14,* 41–47.

Vandenberg, S. G. (1968). The nature and nurture of intelligence. In D. C. Glass (Ed.), *Genetics.* New York: Rockefeller Press and Russell Sage Foundation.

Vandenberg, S. G. (1971). What do we know about the inheritance of intelligence and how do we know it? In R. Cancro (Ed.), *Intelligence: Genetic and environmental influences.* New York: Grune & Stratton.

Vandenberg, S. G. (1972). The future of human behavior genetics. In L. Ehrman, G. S. Omenn, & E. Caspari (Eds.), *Genetics, environment, and behavior.* New York: Academic Press.

Vandenberg, S. G. (1973). Comparative studies of multiple factor ability measures. In J. Royce (Ed.), *Theoretical problems in multivariate research. Proceedings from the Third Banff Conference on Theoretical Problems in Psychology.* New York: Academic Press.

Vandenberg, S. G. (1977). Hereditary abilities in man. In A. Oliverio (Ed.), *Genetics, environment and intelligence*. Amsterdam: Elsevier-North-Holland Biomedical Press.

Vandenberg, S. G., & Kuse, A. R. (1979). Spatial ability: A critical review of the sex-linked major gene hypothesis. In M. C. Wittig & A. C. Peterson (Eds.), *Sex-related differences in cognitive functioning*. New York: Academic Press.

Vandenberg, S. G., & Wilson, K. (1979). Failure of the twin situation to influence twin differences in cognition. *Behavior Genetics, 9*, 55–60.

Vining, D. R. (1982). On the possibility of the reemergence of a dysgenic trend with respect to intelligence in American fertility differentials. *Intelligence, 6*, 241–264.

Waller, J. (1971). Differential reproduction: Its relation to IQ test score, education, and occupation. *Social Biology, 81*, 122–136.

Williams, T. (1975a). The Wechsler scales: Parents and (male) children. *Journal of Educational Measurement, 12*, 119–128.

Williams, T. (1975b). Family resemblance in abilities: The Wechsler scales. *Behavior Genetics, 5*, 405–409.

Witkin, H. A., Mednick, S. A., Schulsinger, F., Bakkestrom, E., Christiansen, K. O., Goodenough, D. R., Hirschhorn, K., Lundsteen, C., Owen, D. R., Philip, J., Rubin, D. B., & Stocking, M. (1977). Criminality, aggressiveness, and intelligence among XYY and XXY men. In S. A. Mednick & K. O. Christiansen (Eds.), *Biosocial bases of criminal behavior*. New York: Gardner Press.

Wright, S. (1918). On the nature of size factors. *Genetics, 3*, 367–374.

Wright, S. (1931). Statistical methods in biology. *Journal of the American Statistical Association, 26* (Suppl.), 155–163.

Wright, S. (1978). *Evolution and the genetics of populations* (Vol. 4): *Variability within and among natural populations*. Chicago: University of Chicago Press.

Wright, S. (1983). On "Path analysis in genetic epidemiology: A critique." *American Journal of Human Genetics, 35*, 757–768.

TWO

COGNITIVE APPROACHES TO INTELLIGENCE

ROBERT J. STERNBERG
Yale University
New Haven, Connecticut

During most of this century, the dominant approach to theory, research, and practice in the field of human intelligence has been the psychometric approach. Investigators using this approach have sought to understand intelligence by examining patterns of individual differences in scores on various kinds of mental tests, such as vocabulary, number facility, figure analogies, mental rotation of geometric objects, and so forth.

The thesis of this chapter is that psychometric and cognitive (information-processing) approaches to studying intelligence are complementary and mutually beneficial. The role of cognitive theory is not to overthrow psychometric theories, but rather to fill in their details. Cognitive theories elaborate on rather than replace psychometric ones. Both forms of theory are needed for a comprehensive understanding of intelligence. Psychometric theories deal with intelligence primarily in its structural aspects; cognitive theories deal with it primarily in its processing aspects.

THE NATURE OF INFORMATION-PROCESSING COMPONENTS

Whereas the fundamental unit of analysis in most psychometric theories is the factor, the fundamental unit of analysis in most cognitive theories is the information-processing component. A *component* is an elementary information process that operates on internal representations of objects or symbols (Newell & Simon, 1972; Sternberg, 1977). The components may translate a sensory input into a conceptual representation, transform one conceptual representation into another, or translate a conceptual representation into a motor output.

Preparation of this chapter was supported by contract N0001483K0013 from the Office of Naval Research and Army Research Institute.

The component is a unit of process, just as the factor is a unit of structure. It is fruitless to claim that one of these units is more "basic" in some sense. First, it is not clear just what is meant psychologically by "more basic." Second, even if it were clear, no empirical operations exist for discerning which unit is more basic. On the one hand, it is possible to do factor analyses of identified components of human intelligence; on the other hand, it is also possible to do componential analyses of identified factors of human intelligence. In the first case, one seeks to identify the structure interrelating a set of component scores; in the second case, one seeks to identify the processes involved in the behavioral implementation of various factors.

THE ORGANIZATION OF COMPONENTS OF HUMAN INTELLIGENCE

Consider three theories of how the information-processing components of intelligence might be organized: Carroll's, Brown's, and Sternberg's.

Carroll's Theory

According to Carroll (1976, 1981), performance on mental tests can be understood in terms of a relatively small number of basic underlying information-processing components. Carroll has investigated the major tests used in both psychometric and cognitive research. Based on a "logical and partly intuitive analysis of the task" (Carroll, 1981, p. 14), Carroll has identified a tentative list of ten types of cognitive components.

1. **Monitor (MONITR).** This process is a cognitive set or "determining tendency" that drives the operation of other processes during the course of task performance.
2. **Attention (ATFTIM).** This process evolves from an individual's expectations regarding the type and number of stimuli that are to be presented during task performance.
3. **Apprehension (APSTIM).** This process is used in the registering of a stimulus in a sensory buffer.
4. **Perceptual Integration (CLOZR).** This process is used in the perception of the stimulus, or the attainment of perceptual closure of a stimulus, and its matching with any previously formed memory representation.
5. **Encoding (REPFRM).** This process is used in forming a mental representation of the stimulus and in its interpretation in terms of its attributes, associations, or meaning, depending on the requirements of a particular task.
6. **Comparison (TSTFIF).** This process is used to determine whether two stimuli are the same, or at least of the same class.
7. **Co-representation Formation (FOCORT).** This process is used to es-

tablish a new representation in memory in association with a representation that is already there.

8. **Co-representation Retrieval (FICORP).** This process is used in finding in memory a particular representation in association with another representation on the basis of some rule or other basis for the association.

9. **Transformation (TRAREP).** This process is used to transform or change a mental representation on some prespecified basis.

10. **Response Execution (XECUTR).** This process is used to operate on some mental representation to produce either an overt or a covert response.

Carroll (1981) emphasizes that this list is tentative in that it may not exhaustively cover all the processes that might eventually be identified in the analysis of elementary cognitive tasks. He claims, however, that this list does cover all the processes that he has been able to identify in the long list of elementary cognitive tasks that he has considered. Although he is not certain that the processes are all mutually distinct from one another, they seem to be different enough to serve as the basis for an information-processing analysis of intelligent task performance.

In his 1981 article, Carroll analyzes a choice reaction-time task in terms of this set of processes. In the choice reaction-time task, an individual is presented with two or more stimuli: for example, bulbs that can be lit. The subject's task is to make one of several responses as a function of what happens to a given stimulus. Thus, for example, there might be two light bulbs, one on the left and one on the right. The subject's task might be to press a button with his left hand if the bulb on the left lights up, and to press a button with his right hand if the bulb on the right lights up (see also Jensen, 1980). Carroll's task analysis shows that even this simple task requires quite a long and complicated set of information-processing components for its successful execution.

Brown's Theory

Brown (1978; Brown & Campione, 1978; Campione & Brown, 1978) has divided processes of cognition into two kinds: metacognitive processes, which are executive skills used to control one's information processing, and cognitive processes, which are nonexecutive skills used to implement task strategies. An essentially identical distinction has been proposed by a number of other investigators, for example, Butterfield and Belmont (1977), Flavell (1981), Markman (1981), and Reitman (1965). In Brown's particular version of this process dichotomy, five metacognitive processes are of particular importance: (1) *planning* one's next move in executing a strategy, (2) *monitoring* the effectiveness of individual steps in a strategy, (3) *testing* one's strategy as one performs it, (4) *revising* one's strategy as the need arises, and (5) *evaluating* one's strategy in order to determine its effectiveness. Metacognitive processes such as these would be used to decide on the cognitive processes appropriate for task solution. For example, these processes might be used to decide that in a learning task, the cognitive processes involved in rehearsal of material provide an appropriate way of memorizing a list of words.

Sternberg's Theory

Sternberg (1980b, 1985) distinguishes among three different kinds of information-processing components.

Metacomponents are higher-order control processes used for executive planning, monitoring, and evaluation of one's performance in a task. Metacomponents are comparable to what Brown refers to as metacognitive processes. Collectively, these processes are sometimes referred to by psychologists as the "executive" or the "homunculus." The ten metacomponents believed to be most important in intelligent functioning are (1) recognition that a problem of some kind exists, (2) recognition of just what the nature of the problem is, (3) selection of a set of lower-order, nonexecutive components for performance on a task, (4) selection of a strategy for task performance, combining the lower-order components, (5) selection of one or more mental representations for information, (6) decision on how to allocate attentional resources, (7) monitoring or keeping track of one's place in task performance and of what has been done and needs to be done, (8) understanding of internal and external feedback concerning the quality of task performance, (9) knowing how to act on the feedback that is received, and (10) implementation of action as a result of the feedback. Note that this last metacomponent in effect assigns a crucial role to action in the theory of intelligent performance. According to this view, one cannot have an adequate theory of intelligence without considering both thought and the actions that emanate from it.

Performance components are lower-order processes used in the execution of various strategies for task performance. Three examples of such components are (1) *encoding* the nature of a stimulus, (2) *inferring* the relations between two stimulus terms that are similar in some ways and different in others, and (3) *applying* a previously inferred relation to a new situation.

Knowledge-acquisition components are processes involved in learning new information and storing it in memory. The three knowledge-acquisition components believed to be most important in intelligent functioning are (1) *selective encoding*, by which relevant new information is sifted out from irrelevant new information (for the specific purpose for which the learning is taking place), (2) *selective combination*, by which the selectively encoded information is combined in a particular way that maximizes its internal coherence, or connectedness, and (3) *selective comparison*, by which the selectively encoded and combined information is related to information already stored in memory to maximize the connectedness of the newly formed knowledge structure to previously formed knowledge structures.

These three kinds of components are applied in task performance for reaching a solution or other goal. Components can vary widely in the range of tasks to which they apply. Some components, and especially the metacomponents, appear to be broadly applicable over a wide range of tasks. Other components apply to less broad ranges of tasks, and some apply only to a narrow range of tasks. Such components are of little theoretical interest, and generally of little practical interest as well.

Sternberg (1980b) has described four ways in which the various kinds of components can interact with each other: (1) direct activation of one kind of component by another, (2) indirect activation of one kind of component by another via the mediation of a third kind of component, (3) direct feedback from one kind of component to another, (4) indirect feedback from one kind of component to another via a third kind. In the proposed system, only metacomponents can directly activate and receive feedback from each other. Thus all control passes directly from the metacomponents to the system, and all information passes directly from the system to the metacomponents. The other kinds of components can activate each other only indirectly, and receive feedback from each other only indirectly; in every case, mediation must be supplied by the metacomponents. For example, the activation of information affects the retrieval of information and the various kinds of performances that can be done on that information, but only via the link of the two lower-order kinds of components to the higher-order metacomponents. Information from the knowledge-acquisition components is filtered to the performance components through the metacomponents. Metacomponents are also unique among the three kinds of components in that they can directly activate and receive feedback from each other.

Consider a simplified example of how the proposed system might function in the solution of a word puzzle, such as an anagram (where the letters of a word are presented in scrambled fashion). As soon as one decides metacomponentially on a certain tentative strategy for unscrambling the letters of the word, activation of that strategy can pass directly from the metacomponents responsible for deciding on a strategy to the performance components responsible for executing the first step of the strategy; subsequently, activation can pass to the successive performance components needed to execute the strategy. Feedback will return from the performance components, indicating the strategy's level of success. The individual must decide how to act on this feedback, and then must actually perform the required action. As a given strategy is being executed, new information is being acquired about how to solve anagrams in general. This information is also fed back to the metacomponents, which may act on or ignore this information. New information that seems useful is more likely to be transmitted indirectly from the relevant knowledge-acquisition components to the relevant performance components for use in solving new problems, whether anagrams or otherwise.

The metacomponents are able to process only a limited amount of information at a given time. In a difficult task, the amount of information being fed back to the metacomponents may exceed their capacity to act on that information. In this case, the metacomponents become overloaded, and valuable information that cannot be processed may simply be wasted. The total information-handling capacity of the metacomponents of a given system will thus be an important limiting aspect of the system. This capacity can effectively be increased by automatization of componential execution. Automatic processing of information is theorized to require far less in the way of attentional resources than is required by controlled processing.

TAXONOMIES OF SOURCES OF INDIVIDUAL DIFFERENCES IN INFORMATION PROCESSING

To understand information processing and individual differences in information processing, it is not enough simply to examine the processes or kinds of processes individuals use in executing strategies for task solution. One must examine other aspects of processing as well. Consider two theories of what the major aspects of information processing are that need to be examined.

Snow's Theory

Snow (1979) has identified four sources of individual differences in information processing: (1) parameter differences (*p*-variables), (2) sequence differences (*q*-variables), (3) route differences (*r*-variables), and (4) summation or strategic differences (*s*-variables).

> The distinctions between *p*-, *q*-, and *r*-variables can be clarified by imagining two flow charts [box diagrams showing the course of information processing] that characterize the performance of two different individuals on some task; *p*-variables would refer to differences between the individuals on particular steps or components (e.g., capacity of STM, time needed for stimulus encoding, etc.); *q*-variables would be shown by the two flow charts taking the same steps, but in different sequences (e.g., early vs. late work on some subgoal); *r*-variables would be indicated by the inclusion of qualitatively different steps in the two flow charts (e.g., visual image rotation, or double checking, used in one chart and not in the other). [Snow, 1979, p. 110]

Sternberg's Theory

Sternberg (1977) has proposed six primary sources of individual differences in information processing. These sources of differences are as follows:

1. *Components.* Some individuals use more components, fewer components, or different components from those used by other individuals. For example, one individual might solve a problem using components, *a, b,* and *c.* Another individual might solve the same problem using components *b, d,* and *e.*

2. *Combination Rule for Components.* Some individuals combine components according to one rule, whereas others combine them according to a different rule. For example, one individual might combine components additively: $a + b + c$. Another individual might combine them multiplicatively: $a \times b \times c$.

3. *Order of Component Processing.* Some individuals order components in one sequence, others in a different sequence. For example, one individual might order components so that c follows b, which follows a. Another subject might order them in the reverse order, or in some other permutation.

4. *Mode of Component Processing.* Some individuals might process particular components in one mode, others in another mode. For example, one individual might process components a, b, and c in self-terminating mode: he or she will cease execution of a given component process as soon as possible. A second individual might process these same components in exhaustive mode: he or she will execute the processes to completion, even if a solution to the problem presents itself before process execution has been completed. Exhaustive information processing is not necessarily a waste of time, because it is more likely, in many cases, to lead to correct answers than is self-terminating information processing (Sternberg, 1977; Sternberg & Rifkin, 1979).

5. *Component Time or Accuracy.* Some individuals may process particular components more quickly or more accurately than do other individuals. For example, one individual may execute a given component process, a, in considerably less time than is taken by a second individual.

6. *Mental Representation on which Components Act.* Some individuals may use one particular representation for information, whereas others use a different representation. For example, it has been found that in linear syllogistic reasoning (which involves problems such as "John is taller than Pete. Pete is taller than Dick. Who is tallest?"), some individuals represent information about the problems in a primarily linguistic fashion, whereas others represent information in a primarily spatial fashion.

To conclude, investigators studying intelligence from a cognitive viewpoint have proposed several classification schemes for understanding information-processing components, and have proposed several schemes for understanding sources of individual differences in these components and in the ways in which they combine. Next we will consider how cognitive theorists have used information-processing concepts to understand the human abilities that have been identified in psychometric investigations of intelligence.

UNDERSTANDING HUMAN ABILITIES FROM A COGNITIVE VIEWPOINT

In this section, some of the major sources of variation in performance on intelligence tests will be considered with an eye toward understanding the information-processing bases of these abilities. The abilities that will be considered here are verbal abilities, quantitative abilities, learning abilities, inductive and deductive reasoning abilities, and spatial abilities.

Verbal Ability

Verbal ability is sometimes divided into two separate skills: verbal comprehension abilities and verbal fluency abilities (Thurstone, 1938). *Verbal comprehension* refers to a person's ability to understand linguistic material such as newspapers, magazines, textbooks, lectures, and so forth. *Verbal fluency* refers to a person's ability to generate words and strings of words easily and rapidly. Verbal comprehension is typically measured by tests such as reading comprehension and vocabulary. Verbal fluency is typically measured by tests such as word generation, where, for example, an individual might be asked to think of as many words as he or she can think of beginning with the letter *b* in the, say, five minutes allotted for the test. In this section, however, only verbal-comprehension abilities will be considered, because they have received considerably more attention in psychological research.

Verbal-comprehension abilities have been recognized as an integral part of intelligence in both psychometric theories (e.g., Guilford, 1967; Thurstone, 1938; Vernon, 1971) and information-processing theories (e.g., Carroll, 1976; Heim, 1970; Sternberg, 1980b) and have, under a variety of aliases, been a major topic of research in differential and experimental psychology for many years.

Three major information-processing approaches to understanding the nature of verbal comprehension are a knowledge-based approach, a bottom-up approach, and a top-down approach. The knowledge-based approach deals with the role of prior information in the acquisition of new information. The bottom-up approach deals with speed of execution of certain very basic mechanistic cognitive processes. The top-down approach deals with higher-order use of cues in understanding complex verbal material. The three approaches are complementary rather than contradictory.

The Knowledge-Based Approach. The knowledge-based approach assigns a central role to old knowledge in the acquisition of new knowledge. Although "knowledge" is often referred to in the sense of domain-specific knowledge, the knowledge-based approach can also encompass research focusing on general world knowledge, knowledge of structures or classes of text (as in story grammars), and knowledge about strategies for knowledge acquisition and application (see, e.g., Bisanz & Voss, 1981). Proponents of this approach differ in the respective roles that they assign to knowledge and process in the acquisition of new knowledge. A fairly strong version of the approach is taken by Keil (1984), who argues that "structure plays a more important role than process in explanations of many instances of cognitive change" (p. 91).

Proponents of this approach usually cite instances of differences between expert and novice performance—in verbal and other domains—that seem to derive more from knowledge differences than from processing differences. For example, Keil (1984) suggests that development in the use of metaphor and in the use of defining features of words seems to be due more to differential knowledge states than to differential use of processes or speed of process execution. Chi (1978) has shown that whether children's or adults' recall performance is better depends on the knowledge domain in which the recall takes place, and particularly on the relative expertise of the children and the adults in the respective domains. Finally, Chase and Simon (1973) found that differences between expert and novice performance in chess seemed largely due to differential knowledge structures rather than to processes.

I have no argument with the position that the knowledge base is highly important in understanding differences in current performance between experts and novices in both verbal and nonverbal domains. But accounts such as Keil's that essentially slight the role of information processing in the development of expertise seem to beg an important question, namely, that of how the differences in knowledge states came about in the first place. For example, why did some people acquire better vocabularies than others? Or in the well-studied domain of chess, why is it that of two individuals given equally intensive and extensive exposure to the game, one will acquire the knowledge structures needed for expertise and the other will not?

In sum, one can easily accept the importance of old knowledge in the acquisition of new knowledge. But the overemphasis on process that may have characterized some past research should not be replaced by an overemphasis on knowledge in present research. Rather, it should be recognized that knowledge and process work interactively in complex ways. The knowledge-based approach is complementary to the process-oriented approaches, not a replacement for them.

The Bottom-Up Approach.   The bottom-up research has emerged from the tradition of investigation initiated by Earl Hunt (e.g., Hunt, 1978; Hunt, Lunneborg, & Lewis, 1975) and followed up by a number of other investigators (for example, Jackson & McClelland, 1979; Keating & Bobbitt, 1978; see also Perfetti & Lesgold, 1977, for a related approach). According to Hunt (1978), two types of processes underlie verbal-comprehension ability—knowledge-based processes and mechanistic (information-free) processes. Hunt's approach has emphasized the latter kind of process. Hunt, Lunneborg, and Lewis studied three aspects of what they called "current information processing," which they believed to be key determinants of individual differences in developed verbal ability. These were as follows:

(a) Sensitivity of overlearned codes to arousal by incoming stimulus information, (b) the accuracy with which temporal tags can be assigned, and hence order information can be processed, and (c) the speed with which the internal representation in STM and intermediate term memory (ITM, memory for events occurring over minutes) can be created and altered. [Hunt, Lunneborg, & Lewis, 1975, p. 197]

Their basic hypothesis was that individuals varying in verbal ability differ even in these low-level mechanistic skills—skills that are free from any contribution of disparate knowledge or experience. Intelligence tests are hypothesized to measure indirectly these basic information-processing skills by measuring directly the products of these skills, both in terms of their past contribution to the acquisition and storage of knowledge (such as vocabulary) and their present contribution in the current processing of information.

For example, in a typical experiment, subjects are presented with the Posner and Mitchell (1967) letter-matching task. The task comprises two experimental conditions, a physical-match condition and a name-match condition. In the physical-match condition, subjects are presented with pairs of letters that either are or are not physical matches (e.g., *AA* or *bb* versus *Aa* or *Ba*). In the name-match condition, subjects are presented with pairs of letters that either are or are not name matches (e.g., *Aa, BB,* or *bB* versus *Ab, ba,* or *bA*). Subjects must identify the letter pair either as a physical match (or mismatch) or as a name match (or mismatch) as rapidly as possible. The typical finding in these experiments is that the difference between mean name match and physical match times for each of a group of subjects is correlated about $-.30$ with scores on tests of verbal ability. The theoretical interpretation of this finding is that speed of lexical access, as measured by name-match minus physical-match time, is in some sense causal of acquired level of verbal ability.

The finding described above is widely replicable, but its interpretation is a matter of dispute (Carroll, 1981; Hogaboam & Pellegrino, 1978; Sternberg, 1981). As it happens, .30 level correlations are abundant in both the abilities and in the personality literatures (indeed, they are rather low as ability correlations go) and provide a relatively weak basis for causal inference. A further concern is that most of the studies done on the name minus physical-match difference have not used adequate discriminant validation procedures. When such procedures are used, and perceptual speed is considered as well as verbal ability, this difference seems to be much more strongly related to perceptual speed than it is to verbal ability (Lansman, Donaldson, Hunt, & Yantis, 1982; Willis, Cornelius, Blow, & Baltes, 1983), although these findings are subject to alternative interpretations (Hunt, personal communication). Thus the obtained correlation with verbal ability may reflect, at least in part, variance shared with perceptual abilities of the kind that the letter-matching task would seem more, at least on the surface, to measure. But whatever may be the case here, it seems likely that speed of lexical access plays some role in verbal comprehension, and what remains to be clarified is just what this role is (see, for example, Beck, Perfetti, & McKeown, 1982; Curtis, 1981).

The Top-Down Approach. Top-down processing refers to expectation- or inference-driven processing, or to knowledge-based processing, to use Hunt's (1978) terminology. Top-down processing has been an extremely popular focus for research in the past decade, with many researchers attempting to identify and predict the types of inferences a person is likely to draw from a text and how these inferences (or lack thereof) will affect text comprehension (see, for example, Kintsch & van Dijk, 1978; Rieger, 1975; Rumelhart, 1980; Schank & Abelson, 1977; Thorndyke, 1976). Usually, top-down researchers look at how people combine information actually present in the text with their own store of world knowledge to create a new whole representing the meaning of the text (e.g., Bransford, Barclay, & Franks, 1972). To our knowledge, however, the top-down approach, although often used in models of text processing in general, has been only minimally applied to understanding individual differences in verbal ability or to understanding vocabulary acquisition as a special subset of knowledge acquisition in general.

The first of a small handful of investigators who looked at the use of inference in the acquisition of word meanings from context were Werner and Kaplan, who proposed that:

> The child acquires the meaning of words principally in two ways. One is by explicit reference either verbal or objective; he learns to understand verbal symbols through the adult's direct naming of objects or through verbal definition. The second way is through implicit or contextual reference; the meaning of a word is grasped in the course of conversation, i.e., it is inferred from the cues of the verbal context. [Werner and Kaplan, 1952, p. 3]

Werner and Kaplan (1952) were especially interested in the second way of acquiring word meanings (the inference of meaning from context). They devised a task in which subjects were presented with an imaginary word followed by six sentences using that word. The subjects' task was to guess the meaning of the word on the basis of the contextual cues they were given. One example (from the 12 imaginary words they used) is *contavish,* which they intended to mean *hole.* They did not, of course, tell the children in their study the meaning of the word, but rather presented them with six sentences:

1. You can't fill anything with a *contavish.*
2. The more you take out of a *contavish* the larger it gets.
3. Before the house is finished, the walls must have *contavishes.*
4. You can't feel or touch a *contavish.*
5. A bottle has only one *contavish.*
6. John fell into a *contavish* in the road. [Werner and Kaplan, 1952, p. 4]

Children ranging in age from 8 to 13 years were tested in their ability to acquire new words presented in this way. Developmental patterns were analyzed by a number of different means. Werner and Kaplan (1952) found that (1) performance improves gradually with age, although the various processes that underlie performance do not necessarily change gradually; (2) there is an early and abrupt decline in signs of immaturity that relate to inadequate orientation toward the task; (3) the processes of signification for words undergo a rather decisive shift between approximately 10 and 11 years of age; and (4) language behavior shows different organizations at different ages.

Daalen-Kapteijns and Elshout-Mohr (1981) pursued the Werner-Kaplan approach by having subjects think aloud while solving Werner-Kaplan type problems. They proposed an ideal strategy for learning from context with which subjects could form a model (provisional representation) of the meaning of a new word. In this strategy, (1) the sentence is reformulated so that it can be brought to bear directly on the neologism; for example, in sentence 1 above, the strategy might yield the statement that "A *contavish* is not a substance that can be used to fill anything," and (2) the reformulated information is transformed into an aspect of the meaning of the neologism, for example, "A *contavish* may be some kind of absence of substance."

Using ingenious protocol-analysis techniques, the investigators found that (1) word acquisition is guided by models, with an initial model chosen on the basis of the interpretation of the new word's meaning in the first sentence and with subsequent processing guided by this model; (2) the processing of each new word presentation in context can lead to the filling of slots in the model, to adjustment of these slots, or to the formation of a new model altogether; (3) if the model is not sufficiently well articulated to permit active search and evaluation of possibly relevant information, as tends to be the case for low-verbal subjects, model-guided search can be replaced by subsequent use of step 2 of this strategy; and (4) high- and low-verbal subjects learn word meanings differently, with high verbals generally using both steps of the ideal strategy and low verbals generally using only the first step (sentence-based processing).

Whereas Daalen-Kapteijns and Elshout-Mohr (1981) specified strategies for word acquisition in detail but the mental representation (what they referred to as the model) of information about the word in only minimal detail, Keil (1981) has specified representation in considerable detail but strategy in only minimal detail. Keil presented children in kindergarten and grades two and four with simple stories in which an unfamiliar word was described by a single paragraph. An example of such a story is: "*Throstles* are great except when they have to be fixed. And they have to be fixed very often. But it's usually very easy to fix throstles." Subjects were then asked what else they knew about the new word (here, *throstle*) and what types of things the new word described. Keil found that even the youngest children could make sensible inferences about the general categories denoted by the new terms and about the properties the terms might reasonably have. Errors were systematic and in accordance with Keil's (1979, 1981) theory of the structure of ontological knowledge, which provides a powerful basis for inferring a possible structure for storing (at least ontological) information about the meaning of a new word and for inferring the possible predicates of the word.

Jensen (1980) has suggested that vocabulary is a good measure of intelligence "because the acquisition of word meanings is highly dependent on the *eduction* of meaning from the contexts in which the words are encountered" (p. 146). Marshalek (1981) has tested this hypothesis by using a faceted vocabulary test, although he did not directly measure learning from context. The vocabulary test was administered with a battery of standard reasoning and other tests. Marshalek found that (1) subjects sometimes could give correct examples of how a given word is used in sentences, despite their having inferred incorrect defining features of the word; (2) subjects with low reasoning ability had major difficulties in inferring word meanings; and (3) reasoning was related to vocabulary measures at the lower end of the vocabulary difficulty distribution but not at the higher end. Together, these findings suggested that a certain level of reasoning ability may be prerequisite to extracting word meanings. Above this level, the importance of reasoning begins to decrease rapidly.

It has been assumed in the above review that the ability to learn from external context leads to higher vocabulary. It should be pointed out, however, that the relationship between learning from context and level of vocabulary is probably bidirectional (Anderson & Freebody, 1979; Sternberg, 1980b): learning from context can facilitate vocabulary level at the same time that a higher vocabulary level can facilitate learning from context.

Sternberg and Powell (1983) have presented a theory of verbal-comprehension ability based on learning from context. According to this theory, the ability to infer the meanings of unfamiliar words from context deserves a prominent place within a discussion of verbal comprehension, in general, for three reasons. First, a theory describing how people use context to infer the meanings of words could tell us much about vocabulary-building skills. Identifying what types of information people of different ability levels use to construct a tentative definition for a word and how additional information influences a working definition for a word could tell us much about training vocabulary-acquisition skills, thus better enabling people to improve their own vocabularies. Second, a theory of learning from context can help explain why vocabulary is the single best predictor of verbal intelligence overall. A reasonable hypothesis is that learning from context reflects important vocabulary-acquisition skills, the end products of which are measured by the extent of one's vocabulary. Thus vocabulary tests are good predictors of one's overall verbal intelligence because they reflect one's ability to acquire new information. Third, a theory of learning from context is useful in illuminating the relation between the more fluid, inferential aspects of verbal intelligence, usually measured by tests of verbal analogies, and the more crystallized, knowledge-based aspects of verbal intelligence, usually measured by vocabulary tests (see Horn & Cattell, 1966). Learning from context thus provides a way of integrating the two aspects of verbal ability—vocabulary and comprehension—and of placing vocabulary acquisition within the framework of general cognitive theories of language comprehension.

The theory has three parts: context cues, mediating variables, and processes of verbal learning.

Context cues are hints contained in a passage that facilitate (or, in theory and sometimes in practice, impede) deciphering the meaning of an unknown word. An example of the use of some of these cues in textual analysis might help concretize this descriptive framework. Consider the sentence, "At dawn, the *blen* arose on the horizon and shone brightly." This sentence contains several external contextual cues that could facilitate one's inferring that *blen* probably means *sun.* "At dawn" provides a temporal cue, describing when the arising of the *blen* occurred; "arose" provides a functional descriptive cue, describing an action that a *blen* could perform; "on the horizon" provides a spatial cue, describing where the arising of the *blen* took place; "shone" provides another functional descriptive cue, describing a second action a *blen* could do; finally, "brightly" provides a stative descriptive cue, describing a property (brightness) of the shining of the *blen.* With all of these different cues, it is no wonder that most people would find it very easy to figure out that the neologism *blen* is a synonym for the familiar word *sun.*

Whereas the contextual cues describe the types of information that might be used to infer the meaning of a word from a given verbal context, they do not address the problems of recognizing the applicability of a description to a given concept, weaning out irrelevant information, or integrating the information gleaned into a coherent model of the word's meaning. For this reason, a set of mediating variables is also proposed that specifies relations between a previously unknown word and the passage in which it occurs, and that mediates the usefulness of the contextual cues. Thus, whereas the contextual cues specify the particular kinds of information that might be available for an individual to use to figure out the meanings of unfamiliar words, the mediating variables specify those variables that can affect, either positively or negatively, the application of the contextual cues present in a given situation.

Consider, for example, how the variable, "variability of contexts in which multiple occurrences of the unknown word appear," can mediate use of contextual cues. Different types of contexts, such as different kinds of subject matter or different writing styles, and even just different contexts of a given type, such as two different illustrations within a given text of how a word can be used, are likely to supply different types of information about the unknown word. Variability of contexts increases the likelihood that a wide range of cues will be supplied about a given word and thus increases the probability that a reader will get a full picture of the scope of a given word's meaning. In contrast, mere repetition of a given unknown word in essentially the same context in which it previously appeared is unlikely to be as helpful as a variable context repetition because few or no really new cues are provided regarding the word's meaning. Variability can also present a problem in some situations and for some individuals: if the information is presented in a way that makes it difficult to integrate across appearances of the word or if a given individual has difficulties in making such integrations, then the variable repetitions may actually obfuscate rather than clarify the word's meaning. In some situations and for some individuals, variable contexts may cause a stimulus overload to occur, resulting in reduced rather than increased understanding. The other mediating variables for external context can similarly facilitate or inhibit the acquisition of a word's meaning from a given text.

Three components of knowledge acquisition are critical in the acquisition of word meanings and of verbal concepts in general: (1) selective encoding, (2) selective combination, and (3) selective comparison. (See Sternberg & Davidson,

1982, and Sternberg, 1984, for more general discussions of these components as they apply to insightful learning and problem solving.) *Selective encoding* involves sifting out relevant information from irrelevant information. When new information is presented in natural contexts, relevant information for one's given purposes is embedded in the midst of large amounts of purpose-irrelevant information. A critical task facing the individual is that of sifting the wheat from the chaff: recognizing just what information among all the pieces of information presented is relevant for one's purposes. *Selective combination* involves combining selectively encoded information in such a way as to form an integrated, plausible whole. Simply sifting out relevant from irrelevant information is not enough to generate a new knowledge structure; one must know how to combine the pieces of information into an internally connected whole (see Mayer & Greeno, 1972). *Selective comparison* involves relating newly acquired information to information acquired in the past. Deciding what information to encode and how to combine it does not occur in a vacuum. Rather, encoding and combination of new knowledge are guided by retrieval of old information. New information will be all but useless if it cannot somehow be related to old knowledge to form an externally connected whole (Mayer & Greeno, 1972).

The theory of decontextualization was tested by Sternberg and Powell (1983) by asking 123 high school students to read 32 passages of roughly 125 words in length that contained embedded within them from one to four extremely low-frequency words. Thirty-seven of these words (all nouns) were used in the passages; each target word could appear from one to four times, resulting in a total of 71 presentations altogether. Passages were equally divided among four different writing styles: literary, newspaper, scientific, and historical. An additional sample passage was written in the literary style.

The students' task was to define as best they could each low-frequency word within each passage (except for multiple occurrences of a single word within a given passage, which required only a single definition). Students were not permitted to look back to earlier passages and definitions in making their current responses. Experienced personnel rated the quality of the students' definitions. The correlations between predicted and observed goodness ratings were .92 for literary passages, .74 for newspaper passages, .85 for scientific passages, and .77 for historical passages. All these values were statistically significant. In an external-validation procedure, subjects' scores (mean-rated goodness of all written definitions) on the learning-from-context task were correlated with scores on the psychometric tests. Correlations for the various passage types combined were .62 with IQ, .56 with vocabulary, and .65 with reading comprehension. Correlations with the psychometric test scores were quite similar for learning-from-context scores computed for the individual passage types.

Not only were these obtained correlation coefficients statistically significantly greater than zero, but they were also significantly greater than .30, a level of correlation that is fairly typical between measures of cognitive tasks and psychometric verbal tests (see, e.g., Hunt, Lunneborg, & Lewis, 1975). Higher correlations are, of course, to be expected when one increases the complexity of experimental tasks, but what is important here is that the learning-from-context task was very different in form and content from the standardized IQ, vocabulary, and reading comprehension measures used in the study. Yet, high correlations were still obtained. Indications are that the task tapped a basic skill of intermediate complexity between basic information processing and full-scale reading. Identification of basic skills at this intermediate level of complexity provides a fruitful basis for understanding, and eventually for training, verbal comprehension. This intermediate level is high enough to preserve the richness of complex verbal information processing, but low enough to provide explanatory power.

Quantitative Ability

Whereas models of verbal comprehension have been seen as general models of the whole verbal-comprehension domain, models of quantitative ability have generally been regarded as models of more limited subdomains of knowledge and information processing. It is not clear that the models of verbal ability actually are more general; probably the major difference in generality with respect to models of quantitative ability is in the generality of claims rather than in coverage. Because the models of quantitative ability are of specific domains, the coverage of these models will reflect the organization of at least part of the field.

Counting Abilities.   Gelman (1982; Gelman & Gallistel, 1975) has sought to understand counting abilities in terms of five principles that she believes are generated by preschool children: (1) the one-one principle; (2) the stable-order principle; (3) the cardinal principle; (4) the abstraction principle; and (5) the order-irrelevant principle.

The one-one principle involves ticking off items in an array with distinct tags so that just one tag is used for each item in the array. In using this principle, an individual has to coordinate two component processes: partitioning and tagging. Partitioning involves maintaining two categories of items, namely, the to-be-counted and the already counted. Items need to be transferred from the first category to the second. This partitioning process must be coordinated with the tagging process, which involves thinking of distinct tags for the objects, one at a time. These tags are typically numerical ones, but they do not have to be.

The use of the one-one principle is necessary but not sufficient for true counting to occur. At the very least, this principle must be supplemented by the stable-order principle, which requires the use of tags that are arranged in a stable, repeatable order. Use of the principle requires the availability of a stable list of tags that is at least as long as the number of items to be counted.

Whereas the one-one and stable-order principles involve the assignment of tags to each item in a given set, the cardinal principle involves recognition that the final tag in a sequence has a special status. In particular, this tag represents the numerosity of the items in the set. Use of this principle presupposes use of the first two principles.

The fourth of Gelman's principles, the abstraction principle, states that a counting procedure can be applied to any collection of objects, whether real or imagined. This principle develops in children later than the others. It takes some time to realize the full range of kinds of items that can be counted.

Finally, the order-irrelevant principle states that it does not matter in what order tags are assigned to objects when one's goal is simply to count the number of objects in an array. If, for example, one wishes to count the number of books one has on one's bookshelf, it makes no difference in what order the books are counted. The total number of books will be the same, regardless of the order in which the books are counted.

Gelman and Gallistel (1975) describe a wealth of data collected to determine at what ages these various principles of counting are acquired. It appears that the principles are all understood by a majority of five-year-olds, and that understanding the principles is well underway even in three-year-olds. Surprisingly, there is evidence of counting behavior even in infants. In a study by Starkey, Spelke, and Gelman (reported in Gelman, 1982), infants were shown two-item and three-item heterogeneous displays placed side by side. A loudspeaker between these displays emitted either two taps or three taps on each of a set of trials. To the authors' surprise, infants of six to eight months of age showed a significant tendency to look at the two-item display when two taps were sounded and at the three-item display when three taps were sounded. It thus appears that even these young infants have at least rudimentary counting knowledge. Gelman has interpreted these results as suggesting that counting abilities may not only be natural and universal, but that they may also be, at least in part, innate.

Computational Abilities.   Whereas the most salient ability for very young children is probably the ability to count, the most salient ability for children in the primary grades is probably computational ability. At the very least, primary school children need to demonstrate facility in addition and subtraction. The component skills involved in addition and subtraction have been studied by cognitive psychologists.

Groen and Parkman (1972) proposed three alternative models of how children (as well as adults) might add pairs of numbers. These models are predicated on the assumption that addition processes can be understood as a set of discrete, serial operations. A "counter" is set to some initial value. Subsequently, an iterative process is executed whereby the value of the counter is incremented until it reaches the sum of two numbers. Consider how the three proposed models differ from each other. To illustrate these differences, they are applied here to the simple addition problem, $4 + 2 = 6$.

In the first model, Model A, the counter is initially set to zero. Then it is incremented by the value of the first of the two addends. Finally, it is incremented by the value of the second of the two addends. The final value of the counter is the sum of the two numbers. In the example, the counter is initially set to 0; then it is incremented by 4, the value of the first addend; finally, it is incremented by 2, the value of the second addend. The sum is thus found to be equal to 6. Note that in this model, the counter is incremented 6 times. More generally, if M is the first addend and N the second addend, the counter is incremented $M + N$ times. The number of increments made to the counter is important in the prediction of reaction time for the computation of sums. The model predicts that reaction time will vary linearly as a function of $M + N$.

In the second model, Model B, the counter is initiated not at 0, but rather at a value corresponding to the first addend. The counter is then incremented by a number of times corresponding to the value of the second addend. In the example, the counter is initially set at 4. It is then incremented by 2, so that the final value of the sum is 6. Note that in this model, it was necessary to increment the counter only 2, rather than 6, times. In this model, the number of times the counter needs to be incremented is equal to N, where N is the value of the second addend. Note that this model makes quite different predictions about reaction time from those predictions made by the first model. Whereas in the first model, reaction time is a linear function of $M + N$, in this model, reaction time is a linear function simply of N.

In a third model, Model C, the counter is initially set to the value of whichever addend is greater. The incrementing procedure is then applied to the other of the two addends. In the example, the counter would initially be set to 4 and then incremented by 2. Thus for this problem, the predictions of Models B and C are identical. However, for the example, $2 + 4 = 6$, the predictions of the models would be different. In Model B, the counter would initially be set to 2, and then incremented by 4; in Model C, the counter would initially be set to 4, and then incremented by 2. In Model C, therefore, reaction time is a linear function of either M or N, depending on whichever value is smaller.

Groen has conducted many experiments to compare the fits of these three alternative models to reaction-time data for subjects solving addition problems. In one such study (Groen & Parkman, 1972), the models were compared in their ability to account for the reaction times of first graders. Groen and Parkman found that virtually all the first-grade children used Model C, the most sophisticated of the three models. It thus appears that even young children are able to employ a relatively sophisticated strategy in solving simple addition problems. Note, however, that the model does not apply to problems in which both of the addends have the same value, for example, $3 + 3 = 6$ or $4 + 4 = 8$. Such problems are solved more rapidly than would be predicted by the model. This result suggests that the sums of addition problems in which both addends have the same value may be prestored in long-term memory. Some of these sums need not be computed when children are presented with such problems.

Woods, Resnick, and Groen (1975) extended this kind of information-processing modeling to subtraction. In particular, they compared the ability of three information-processing models to account for the subtraction performance of second and fourth graders. Consider as an example the subtraction problem $6 - 4 = 2$.

In the first model, Model *A*, the counter is initially set to the value of the minuend (first term in the subtraction), and then decremented the number of times specified by the subtrahend (second term in the subtraction). In the example, the counter would initially be set to 6, and then decremented by 2. The result would be a difference of 4. Note that this model assumes that reaction time will be a linear function of the value of the subtrahend. In the general case, $M - S = D$, reaction time will be a linear function of *S*.

In the second model, Model *B*, the counter is initially set at the value of the subtrahend. The counter is then incremented until it reaches the value of the minuend. The number of increments required equals the value of the difference. In the example, therefore, the counter is initially set to 2. It is then incremented 4 times to reach the value, 6. The difference is therefore 4. Note that in this model, reaction time is a linear function of the difference in the subtraction. In the general case, it is a function of the value of *D*.

In the third model, Model *C*, individuals are assumed to follow either Model *A* or Model *B*, depending on which is the quickest. Thus, in the example 6 − 2 = 4, the individual would be assumed to use Model *A*, because the number of decrementing operations required (2) specified by Model *A* is less than the number of incrementing operations (4) specified by Model *B*. In the subtraction problem, 6 − 4 = 2, however, the individual would be assumed to prefer Model *B* over Model *A*. In this problem, the number of incrementing operations specified by Model *B* (2) is less than the number of decrementing operations specified by Model *A* (4). This last model was called a "choice model," because the strategy followed in subtraction is assumed to be a choice on the part of the individual performing the subtraction.

The straightforward algorithm suggested by Model *A* is the algorithm that we usually assume is taught in schools, where the individual starts with the value of the minuend, subtracts the value of the subtrahend from the minuend, and thereby computes the difference. One might therefore expect that second graders would display performance along the lines suggested by Model *A*. It might be reasonable to expect, however, that at some point children might discover that in some instances it is more efficient to count upward from *S* to *M*, rather than downward from *M* to *S*. One might therefore expect that, by fourth grade, individuals would show a preference for Model *C*. The data obtained by Woods, Resnick, and Groen (1975) did not quite conform to this expectation. At the second-grade level, 20% of the children showed a pattern of reaction-time data similar to that predicted by Model *A*; the other 80% showed reaction-time data in accord with Model *C*. All the fourth graders seemed to solve the subtraction problem in accordance with Model *C*. Thus it appears that most children learn very early to solve subtraction problems in the most efficacious way. Although most individuals at both grade levels used Model *C*, they did not use it with equal celerity. At the second-grade level, the average time for incrementing or decrementing operations was roughly 400 milliseconds. At the fourth-grade level, the average time for this operation was roughly 250 milliseconds. Thus fourth graders were quite a bit faster than second graders in performing the computations.

The linear-modeling approach that characterizes the above research is not the only approach that has been taken to understanding arithmetic computation. Brown and Burton (1978) and Ginsburg (1977) have sought to understand the sources of error in children's algorithms for computation. Brown and Burton even developed a computer program, BUGGY, that analyzes students' algorithms for three-column subtraction. The program analyzes students' answers to a large number of three-column subtractions, for example, 436 − 281 = 155. If the student answers all items correctly, BUGGY categorizes students as using the correct algorithm for subtraction. If there are errors, however, BUGGY attempts to find the one or more "bugs" that best account for the source of the errors in subtraction. Some examples of bugs are: (1) not knowing how to borrow from zero, (2) not knowing how to subtract a larger digit from a smaller digit, and (3) not knowing how to subtract a digit from zero. It is interesting to note that although the BUGGY program was able to identify hundreds of bugs or combinations of bugs in students' performance, it was by no means totally successful in diagnosing all the sources of students' errors. In fact, the program was able to find algorithms that either totally or partially produced the answers given by only 43% of the students. The remaining errors were either random or were at least partly inconsistent in the kinds of bugs involved. Thus, although the approach used by Brown and Burton enables one to identify quite precisely the kinds of knowledge about computations students lack, it can do so only for some problems and for some people.

To conclude, then, at least two approaches have yielded some success in understanding how people solve arithmetic computation problems. A first approach is based on information-processing modeling of the components individuals use in solving problems such as addition and subtraction. The approach is used to predict *reaction time* in solving computation problems. The second approach is used to predict *errors* in solving computation problems. The idea in this approach is to use a computer program to analyze the kinds of errors students make in order to understand what facts about computation they lack. Clearly, the two approaches are complementary rather than mutually exclusive. It would be useful to use them in combination in order to understand both the speed and accuracy with which people solve arithmetic computation problems.

Problem-Solving Ability. Mathematical problem solving is often broken down into two basic steps (Bobrow, 1968; Hayes, 1981; Mayer, 1983): problem representation and problem solution. In *problem representation,* a problem is converted from a series of words and numbers into an internal mental representation of the terms of the problem. In *problem solution,* operations are performed to deduce a solution to the problem from the internal mental representation. Each stage in problem solving is a source of individual differences in overall problem-solving ability.

A striking example of how difficult problem representation can be, even for college students, was provided by Soloway, Lochhead, and Clement (1982). These investigators asked college students to represent statements such as, "There are six times as many students as professors at this university," in terms of an equation. Roughly 33% of the college students represented problems such as this one incorrectly. In this example, they would have represented it by the incorrect equation, $6S = P$, where S refers to student and P to professor. An interesting sideline to this experiment showed the powerful effect of mental representation on students' ability to represent the problems correctly. Consider the following problem: "At the last company cocktail party, for every six people who drank hard liquor, there were eleven people who drank beer." Some students were asked to translate this statement into a mathematical equation; other students were asked to translate this statement into a little program in the BASIC computer language. The error rate for students translating the problem into an equation was 55%, whereas the error rate for students translating the problem into the computer language was only 31%.

Mayer (1982) has also studied the abilities of college students to represent mathematical problems. Two sets of data analyses are of particular interest in this research. To illustrate these analyses, consider the algebra problem: "A river steamer travels 36 miles downstream in the same time that it travels 24 miles upstream. The steamer's engine drives in still water at a rate of 12 miles per hour more than the rate of the current. Find the rate of the current." The students were asked to recall problems such as these as best they could.

In the first set of data analyses, Mayer looked at which kinds of content students most tended to forget. He divided problem content into three kinds: *assignments,* which assign a value to a variable, for example, "A river steamer travels 36 miles downstream"; *relations,* which express a quantitative relation between two variables, for example, "The steamer's engines drive in still water at a rate of 12 miles per hour more than the rate of the current"; and *questions,* which ask for a solution to the problem, for example, "Find the rate of the current." Mayer found that students made about three times as many errors in recalling relational propositions (error rate: 29%) as in recalling assignment propositions (error rate: 9%). This result is consistent with that of Soloway et al. (1982) and others in suggesting students' greatest difficulty is in representing relational information about mathematical problems.

In the second data analysis, Mayer examined the kinds of errors students make in recalling propositions: *omission errors,* in which the proposition is not recalled; *specification errors,* in which a variable in the original proposition is somehow changed to a different variable in recall (for example, "A river steamer travels 36 miles downstream" is recalled as "A boat travels 36 miles downstream"; and *conversion errors,* in which the form of the proposition is changed from an assignment to a relation, or vice versa (for example, "The steamer's engine drives in still water at 12 miles per hour more than the rate of the current" is translated into "The steamer's engine drives in still water at 12 miles per hour"). By far, the largest proportion of errors was in errors of omission. The smallest number of errors was in errors of conversion. This pattern held true for assignment relations and questions. It is interesting to note that there was a systematic bias in the form taken by conversion errors. Of 21 cases of conversion, 20 involved changing a relation into an assignment, whereas only one involved changing an assignment into a relation. Thus, one can begin to see that students' greatest difficulty appears to be in representing relational information.

Davidson and Sternberg (1983) compared the abilities of gifted and nongifted students to solve quantitative insight problems. An example of such a problem is, "A man has black socks and blue socks in a drawer mixed in a ratio of 4 to 5. It is dark, and the man cannot see the colors of the socks he removes from the drawer. How many socks must the man remove from the drawer to ensure having a pair of socks of the same color?" The correct answer to the problem is 3. Davidson and Sternberg tested the hypothesis that the reduced performance of the nongifted students could be traced in part to their failure to generate spontaneously three kinds of insights: (1) *selective encoding,* in which relevant information for problem solution is distinguished from irrelevant information; (2) *selective combination,* in which relevant information is combined in a meaningful way to allow problem solutions; and (3) *selective comparison,* in which new information in the problem is related to old information that one previously had stored in long-term memory. To test this hypothesis, problems, such as the socks problem, were presented in either of two fashions. In one, the problems were presented in the standard way. The students would see the problem and have to solve it. In the second, students were given one of the three kinds of insights to facilitate their problem solution. For example, selective-encoding insights were provided by underlining in each given problem only information that was relevant for problem solution. In the socks problem, for instance, the ratio information is irrelevant to the solution of the problem; yet many students attempt to use it to solve the problem. Davidson and Sternberg found that providing insights of each of the three kinds significantly facilitated performance only in the nongifted students. The gifted students seemed to generate the insights on their own; providing them with insights did not facilitate their performance.

The steps involved in representing and solving mathematical problems can become quite complicated, and some investigators have sought to do justice to this degree of complication by constructing computer simulations of students' problem-solving processes. For example, Greeno (1978) has written a computer program, PERDIX, that simulates the performance of high school students in solving geometry problems. In fact, Greeno formulated the project on the basis of a fairly extensive study of students' thinking-aloud protocols as provided in the course of their actual solutions of geometry problems. Two important features of this program are its use of a generate-and-test strategy, and its use of subgoals. The generate-and-test strategy is used when one knows what type of information is needed at a given point during problem solution, but does not know which particular items of information in the problem are of this kind. In this strategy, one scans the list of possible items that may provide the needed information and tests each one to see if it fits. Resnick and Ford (1981) provide a good example of the generate-and-test strategy. Suppose one needs to find the list of all prime numbers (that is, numbers whose only factors are themselves and 1) in the range from 1 to 50. Usually, a person will generate the numbers between 1 and 50 one at a time, and test each one to see if it has any factors other than itself and 1. Only those numbers that have no other factors are retained in the list of primes.

The use of subgoals is a reflection of the fact that plane-geometry theorem proving is usually too complicated for the use of just a single goal. To construct a proof, students usually set up a series of subgoals that represent states in the proof that they need to reach along the way toward the final solution of the proof.

In conclusion, mathematical abilities involve a number of information-processing skills, at least some of which are hierarchically related. For example, computational skills presuppose counting skills, and problem-solving skills presuppose at least some computational skills. Information-processing analyses of ability can tend to obscure the "big picture" as far as quantitative abilities are concerned. Although quantitative abilities can be decomposed into a large number of component information processes, the abilities to use these processes are certainly correlated. Thus some people are better quantitatively, overall, than are other people. There seems to be a need for theories that combine the best aspects of psychometric and information-processing analysis. Psychometric analysis gives one a good sense of quantitative ability as comprising one factor or, at most, a small number of factors. It does not, however, specify the processing components involved in this factor. Information-processing analysis can specify processing components, but it is often hard to see how they fit together into an overall ability structure. Thus a theory is needed to specify the information-processing components of quantitative abilities, but also to specify how these components fit together into a higher-order ability that distinguishes more quantitatively able people from less quantitatively able ones.

Learning Ability

The relation between learning ability and intelligence has been a perplexing one. Intuitively, learning ability would seem to be closely related to, and perhaps central in, intelligence. This theory is captured by many definitions of intelligence. For example, in a 1921 symposium Buckingham defined intelligence as the ability to learn; similarly, Dearborn defined intelligence as a capacity to learn and profit by experience. Investigators such as these have not only believed that learning is the central ingredient in intelligence, but have proposed that measures of learning would form the most suitable measures of intelligence. For example, Thorndike (1924) argued that measures of learning could well form a single basis for evaluation of intelligence.

Between the 1920s and 1940s, a considerable amount of research was done on the relation between learning ability and intelligence as measured by standard intelligence tests. To the surprise of many investigators, the results were largely negative: learning performance was not highly related to intelligence. Indeed, most of the studies found no relation at all. (For a review of this literature, see Estes, 1982.) By 1946, Woodrow, as much a learning theorist as Thorndike, claimed that "Intelligence, far from being identical with the amount of improvement shown by practice, has practically nothing to do with the matter" (p. 151). It is no surprise that Woodrow came to this conclusion. His own work had yielded some of the most disappointing findings of all. In one study, Woodrow (1917) found no differences in learning performance between normal and mentally retarded children. In another study (1938), he found no relation between level of intelligence of college students and their learning ability.

Why might the studies of Woodrow and many others have failed to find a link between learning performance and intelligence? There seem to be at least five reasons.

First, the investigators may have been focusing on the wrong aspects of learning, at least to the extent that the purpose was to relate learning to intelligence. Consider some recent work suggesting that differences can be found in the learning performance of normal and retarded subjects if one investigates the right phenomena of learning.

A frequent observation in the memory literature is the serial-position curve, whereby items presented near the beginning and near the end of a list tend to be recalled better than items near the middle of the list. Superior recall of the earlier items (the primacy effect) is usually attributed to the effects of long-term memory, whereas the superior recall of the later items (the recency effect) is usually attributed to the effects of short-term memory (Crowder, 1976). Several investigators have found that manipulating the rate at which items are presented has an effect on recall of earlier items by normal subjects; specifically, faster presentation reduces recall of words near the beginning of the list (Glanzer & Cunitz, 1966). Glanzer and Cunitz suggested that slow presentation permits more rehearsal than does fast presentation and that increased rehearsal of earlier items leads to higher recall of these items.

Retarded subjects do not show a reduction in primacy with faster presentation. This interaction between the performance of the normal and the retarded led Ellis (1970) to conclude that mentally retarded performers simply do not rehearse (or minimally rehearse) items, even under conditions of slow presentation. It seems unlikely that the deficit of the retarded results from their inability to rehearse items. Presumably, almost anyone is capable of repeating presented words subvocally; it seems more likely, however, that retarded performers simply do not choose to rehearse. Belmont and Butterfield (1971) conducted an experiment to test this hypothesis. They concluded that, indeed, the deficiency of retarded performers in recall of early items is due in large part to their failure to rehearse, but that this failure stems from their failure to generate an appropriate strategy for learning the items. When the retarded subjects were told to rehearse, significant gains in primacy recall were obtained. Thus the difficulty of the retarded subject is not in learning processes, but in the executive processes by which a strategy for learning is generated. Early investigators, however, studied learning per se rather than the executive processes that contribute to learning.

Another example of research with a more analytic focus is that of Zeaman and House (1963). These investigators had subjects perform a concept-learning task, in which they had to learn to attend to a relevant dimension in concept learning and to learn to choose the correct value along that dimension. In a typical experiment, subjects would see two objects on each of a series of trials. The objects would differ along a number of dimensions, such as color, shape, size, and number. The subjects' task was to choose the correct object. What made a specific object "correct" was its having a particular value along a particular dimension. For example, the experimenter might define in advance the color red as constituting the basis for a correct answer. In this case, an object would be correct if it were red, and incorrect otherwise. The subjects would thus have to learn to attend to the dimension of color and the value of red in the concept-learning task. Zeaman and House used an elegant mathematical-modeling technique to find the locus of the difference between retarded and normal subjects in performing this concept-learning task. They found that the major source of differences between the two groups was attentional. The normal subjects were more likely to attend to the relevant dimension for concept learning early during the learning trial. Note that in this work, as in the work of Belmont and Butterfield, simply studying learning per se would not have been enough: whereas the Belmont and Butterfield research showed the locus of differences between retarded and normal subjects to be in executive processes, the Zeaman and House work showed the differences between retarded and normal subjects in concept learning to be in attentional processes. In both cases, simply studying learning would not have been enough.

A second reason for the generally poor correlation between scores on simple learning tasks and scores on intelligence tests may be the nature of the tasks that were used. Typical memory tasks involve exercises such as learning and remembering a list of words in the exact order that the words were presented (serial recall), learning pairs of words so that later, when only the first word of the pair is presented, the examinee can recall the second word in the pair (paired-associate recall), and learning a list of words that can later be recalled in any order (free recall). These so-called "episodic" memory tasks are notable for their simplicity and relative impoverishment of meaningful content. For example, the words used in a list are usually either unrelated to each other or related to each other in only the most casual ways.

More recent research has focused on learning of meaningful materials. For example, it was noted earlier that performance on the Sternberg-Powell (1983) learning-from-context task is correlated at a level of approximately .60 with scores on standard IQ tests. The ability to recall final words of successive sentences is correlated at about the same level with tests of verbal intelligence (Daneman & Carpenter, 1980). Brown and Smiley (1977, 1978) studied the ability of students from grade three to grade twelve to identify essential organizing features and crucial elements of meaningful texts. These texts had previously been rated by college students as involving material at four levels of importance for learning the content in the text. Third graders made no reliable distinctions between levels of importance in their attempts to rate such levels. Fifth graders could only distinguish the highest level of importance from the other levels. Seventh graders did not differentiate the two intermediate levels of importance but were able to distinguish the least important and the most important elements in the text. Twelfth graders were able to distinguish reliably all four levels of importance in the text. Brown and Smiley also found that when children were given extra time for studying, their tendency to use active strategies for learning, such as note taking or underlining, increased with age. The youngest students favored a passive strategy involving nothing more than rereading the text, whereas the older children tended to favor the more active strategies. Subsequent recall of material was better for strategy users than for those who failed to use an active strategy.

The third reason why early studies may have failed to find a relation between learning and intelligence is, ironically, the completeness and clarity of the directions for the tasks. A number of investigators, including Resnick and Glaser (1976) and Campione, Brown, and Bryant (1984), have suggested that intelligence may involve largely the ability to learn from incomplete instruction. Rohwer (1973) performed a study that happens to be relevant to testing this hypothesis. He investigated the use of elaborative processes in facilitating paired-associate learning. An example of an elaborative process would be learning a paired associate by mentally creating a sentence linking the two words. So, for example, if the paired associate to be learned was "lion–potato," the subject might form a sentence such as "The lion mashed the potato." Alternatively, the subject might form an interactive visual image showing a possible physical relation between the two items in the paired associates. For example, the subject might imagine a scene in which a lion is chomping on a large potato. Rohwer provided various cues to facilitate subjects' use of elaborative strategies. Some of these cues were more explicit than others. Rohwer found that the younger or less intelligent the subject, the more he or she needed a more explicit cue in order to use an elaborative strategy and to enhance subsequent performance.

A fourth reason why early studies may have found no relation between learning and intelligence was their concentration on the immediate results of learning rather than on the transfer of learning. In much of our lives, the typical real use of learning is in the transfer of what is learned in old situations to new situations. If we are unable to carry over knowledge to new situations, the knowledge remains essentially useless to us. Ferrara (1982) studied the possibility that a major distinguisher of students of average versus above-average mental ability is in their respective levels of transfer of learning. She taught students rules for solving series-completion problems, which require inductive reasoning. A typical series completion of the kind used by Ferrara is $A\ B\ A\ C\ A\ D\ \_\ \_$. The subject's task is to fill in the letters that belong in the blanks.

Ferrara had all subjects learn how to solve these problems to a uniform criterion. She then investigated three kinds of learning via new series-completion items. *Maintenance* items were new examples of the same problem types that the subjects had been taught. *Near-transfer* items involved the same types of relations that the subjects had been taught, but with new combinations of letters. *Far-transfer* items included new relations as well as other potentially new features. Ferrara found that above-average children learned more quickly than did average children, although all children were able to learn the original material to criterion. The more interesting results concerned transfer. On the maintenance items, performance of both the average and above-average subjects was almost perfect; the groups did not differ. Similarly, both groups did quite well on the near-transfer problems. On the far-transfer problems, however, large group differences emerged. The above-average subjects performed at a distinctly higher level than did the average subjects. Thus the above-average subjects showed greater ability to transfer learning, even though their original learning was to the same criterion as for the average subjects.

Fifth, whereas the early studies used impoverished content with minimal semantic relatedness to test the relation between learning and intelligence, it may be precisely the opposite kind of material that most shows the relation. A number of investigators have now shown the strong effect of prior knowledge on new learning, and because more intelligent individuals can be expected, on the average, to have an enriched knowledge base with respect to lower-ability individuals, the more intelligent, higher-knowledge individuals may learn more quickly.

What has become the classic study of the effect of knowledge on learning and recall was performed by Chase and Simon (1973). These investigators had individuals at various levels of expertise in chess learn and later recall patterns of chess pieces on a chessboard. The critical finding was that the better chess players were no better than the worse chess players at recalling the board configurations when the configurations were random (i.e., the pieces were placed on the board in a way that bore no correspondence to the way in which they would appear in a normal chess game). However, when the pieces were placed in sensible configurations, the chess experts' recall of the pieces was quite a bit better than the recall of the lesser players. A developmental twist to this finding was demonstrated by Chi (1978). Chi showed that when child chess experts were pitted against adult chess novices in recall, the adults performed better on a standard task of memory span (serial recall of digits), but the children performed better in recalling configurations of pieces on a chessboard. In other words, the greater level of knowledge of the children for chess enabled them to outperform the adults on the chess-recall task, even though their memories of less meaningful materials were inferior. In a related study, Chi and Koeske (1983) studied children's recall for names of dinosaurs. Chi and Koeske had previously determined that some of the dinosaurs on the list to be learned were more widely and well known than were others. The investigators found that recall of dinosaur names was largely a function of prior knowledge. In other words, the more familiar the dinosaur was before the experiment began, the more likely that the name of the dinosaur would be recalled when it was presented in a list of words. Similar results to those reported in the Chase and Simon study and the Chi studies have been reported in other domains, such as in the learning of baseball information (Chiesi, Spilich, & Voss, 1979).

An intriguing notion about the relation between learning and intelligence has been proposed by Vygotsky (1978) and expanded on by Feuerstein (1979). This notion is the so-called "zone of potential development." The idea is that a person's latent, or unexpressed, ability may be measured by the extent to which the person profits from guided instruction in performing a task. In other words, one would measure a person's zone of potential development by comparing the person's performance on a task without guided instruction to the person's performance with guided and graded instruction. Vygotsky and Feuerstein have claimed that individuals who profit more from such sequenced instruction have latent ability that may not be measured by standard tests of intelligence. Brown and Ferrara (1984) have provided some additional evidence that this may be the case, but at present the zone of potential development remains an intriguing but unverified construct.

To conclude, there definitely appears to be a relation between learning and intelligence, but this relation tended not to be expressed in early correlational studies using simple learning tasks. More recent studies emphasizing the role of fairly complex information processing in learning have tended to demonstrate the relation. It now appears that learning is central to intelligence, rather than peripheral or unrelated to it. But the learning that is related to intelligence is the kind of learning that occurs in our everyday interactions with the environment, rather than the very simple types of learning that have often been studied in the laboratories of experimental psychologists. Psychologists are often implored to make their research "ecologically valid," that is, relevant to performance in the real world. The results of the research on the relations between learning and intelligence show that the quest for ecological validity is not merely well intentioned but inconsequential. On the contrary, ecologically valid research can yield results quite different from results that have less real-world relevance.

Inductive Reasoning Ability

Inductive reasoning problems are characterized by the absence of a single, logically certain response. Although such reasoning problems may have one solution that seems better than alternative solutions, this solution is a consensually agreed on one rather than a logically necessary one. Consider, for example, what might be viewed as a prototypical inductive reasoning problem: the series completion. One might see in an inductive reasoning test the series completion: 1, 2, 3, 4, _. One's task is to complete the series. Most people would not hesitate to complete the series with the number 5, and indeed, if this problem appeared in an intelligence test for children, it is virtually certain that 5 would be viewed as the correct answer. However, 5 is not the only possible answer. On the contrary, an equation can be generated that will yield as a correct answer any rational number at all (Skyrms, 1975). In the typical interpretation of this problem, the generating equation is $K + 1$, where K takes on the value of each successive number in the series. An alternative equation, however, is $(K - 1)$ $(K - 2) (K - 3) (K - 4) + K$. This equation generates 29 as the fifth value in the series. Other equations would generate other completions. One might argue that some completions are simpler, more elegant, or more natural than others. That is precisely the point: in inductive reasoning problems, some completions may seem better than others; but there is no logically defined, uniquely correct response.

Inductive-reasoning performance has long been considered a keystone of intelligence. One of the first theorists of general intelligence, Spearman (1923), used analogies as the prototypes for intelligent performance. Spearman exemplified three basic principles of cognition through the use of the analogy. The ability to perceive second-order relations, or relations between relations, has served as the touchstone marking the transition between concrete and formal operations in Piaget's (1972) theory of intelligence, and analogies, since they require the ability to perceive relations between relations for their solution, can serve as a useful measure for distinguishing concrete-operational from formal-operational children (Sternberg & Rifkin, 1979). Certain forms of series completion and classification problems can also require the ability to perceive second-order relations. Finally, induction problems, and especially analogies, have played a major role in information-processing theories of intelligence. Reitman (1965) and Sternberg (1977) have used analogies as cornerstones for information-processing theories of intelligence, and other investigators have also seen analogies, as well as other kinds of induction problems, as fundamental to information-processing notions of intelligence (e.g., Pellegrino & Glaser, 1980; Whitely, 1977). Thus induction problems have played a central part in the theorizing of differential, Piagetian, and information-processing theorists of intelligence.

Whereas in some areas of the study of intelligence, the disagreements among theorists are more salient than the agreements, in other areas, the agreements are more salient. In the study of inductive reasoning, the agreements among investigators regarding how induction problems are solved are much more striking than the disagreements. Consider three of the more well-known cognitive theories: Sternberg's, Pellegrino and Glaser's, and Embretson's.

Sternberg's Theory. Sternberg (1977, 1979; Sternberg & Gardner, 1983; Sternberg & Nigro, 1980) has proposed a theory of inductive reasoning that he has applied to analogies, series completions, classifications, and metaphorical understanding. (For a complete review of this theory and the research it has generated, see Sternberg, 1985.)

The theory of information processing specifies the processing components alleged to be involved in inductive reasoning. Consider what these components are, with a simple analogy used to facilitate their explanation: LAWYER : CLIENT :: DOCTOR : (a) MEDICINE, (b) SICK PERSON. The seven components are (1) *encoding,* by which the individual recognizes the terms of the problem and accesses attributes of the analogy terms that are stored in semantic memory and that might be relevant for task solutions; (2) *inference*, by which the individual figures out the relation between the first two terms of the analogy (e.g., that a lawyer renders professional consulting services to a client); (3) *mapping*, by which the individual figures out the higher-order relation between the two halves of the analogy (e.g., that both a lawyer and a doctor render professional services); (4) *application*, by which the individual takes the relation inferred between the terms in the first half of the analogy as mapped to the third term in the second half of the analogy and uses this relation to generate an "ideal" completion to the analogy, (e.g., the individual might generate PATIENT as an ideal completion); (5) *comparison*, by which the individual compares each answer option (in multiple-choice analogies) to the ideal, and decides which is better (in the sense of more closely resembling the ideal) (e.g., the individual will compare each of MEDICINE and SICK PERSON to PATIENT); (6) *justification*, in which the individual decides whether the preferred answer option is close enough to the ideal option to warrant its selection, or whether the possibility ought to be entertained and possibly acted on that an error has been made in earlier information processing (e.g., the individual might decide that SICK PERSON, although not an ideal response, is at or above some criterion for a minimally acceptable response); and (7) *response*, by which the individual communicates his or her choice of an answer (for example, the individual might circle an answer or press a button indicating his or her choice of SICK PERSON as the preferred answer).

As noted above, the theory can also be applied to other kinds of induction problems. Consider, for example, the series completion: 2, 5, 8, 11, (a) 14, (b) 15. In this series completion, the individual must *encode* the terms of the problem, *infer* the relation between each successive pair of given digits, *apply* this relation to generate the next digit in the series, *compare* each of the two answer options to the generated option, possibly *justify* the chosen option if it does not correspond exactly to one of the given options, and *respond*. Note that *mapping* is not required in the series completion because the problem did not require any recognition of higher-order relations between relations. The series completion problem thus requires only a subset of the component processes required by the analogy.

This theory was first tested in a set of experiments on Stanford undergraduates (Sternberg, 1977). In these experiments, subjects solved schematic-picture, verbal, and geometric analogies, and were timed while they did so. The reaction-time data provided strong support for the theory. In a later set of experiments, the theory was extended to series completions and classifications presented to adult subjects. Again, there were three contents (schematic pictures, words, and geometric figures) (Sternberg & Gardner, 1983). This research showed that the theory could be successfully extended to the other kinds of induction problems. In both sets of experiments, individuals' scores on each component of inductive reasoning were correlated with scores on standard psychometric tests of inductive-reasoning abilities and perceptual-speed abilities. The idea was to show that the components of reasoning did correlate strongly with inductive reasoning but did not correlate strongly with perceptual speed. The results of the first set of studies were somewhat ambiguous, but the results of the second set of studies, which entailed far more reliable observations than did the first set of studies, were not. The three components of inductive reasoning alleged to be most critical for reasoning—inference, mapping, and application—were strongly correlated with psychometric tests of inductive-reasoning ability but not at all correlated with psychometric tests of perceptual-speed ability. The comparison component also correlated significantly and substantially with psychometrically measured reasoning abilities. The encoding and justification parameters showed mixed patterns of correlation (some statistically significant, but others not). The response parameter did not correlate significantly with reasoning in any of the second set of studies, although it did show significant correlations in the first set of studies.

In a set of further experiments, the theory was tested developmentally (Sternberg & Nigro, 1980; Sternberg & Rifkin, 1979). In the Sternberg-Nigro study, verbal items were used, and the investigators looked at use of word association as well as of reasoning in the solution of the items. For example, in the analogy, TREE : ANIMATE :: PENCIL : (a) INANIMATE, (b) PAPER, PAPER has the greater associative relation to PENCIL, even though the correct answer to the analogy is INANIMATE. Children ranging in educational levels from grade two to college received either one of two kinds of schematic-picture analogies (Sternberg-Rifkin) or verbal analogies (Sternberg-Nigro). In these experiments, the most interesting data proved to be qualitative data illustrating the functioning of metacomponents rather than quantitative data illustrating the functioning of performance components. With regard to the latter, the main result was that the theory of analogical reasoning was supported for both kinds of contents and at all grade levels.

In summary, Sternberg's theory of inductive reasoning contains two parts: a theory of information processing and a theory of response choice. The theory of information processing specifies the processing components used by individuals as they actually solve an induction problem. It includes processing components such as inferring relations, applying relations, and mapping relations. The theory of response choice, based on a theory proposed by Rumelhart and Abrahamson (1973), seeks to predict individuals' response choices in inductive reasoning. It uses a representation of a multidimensional psychological space to make its predictions. Both theories have been tested on a number of empirically collected data sets and have been found to predict both reaction time and response-choice data with high accuracy.

Pellegrino and Glaser's Theory. Pellegrino and Glaser's theory of inductive reasoning (Mulholland, Pellegrino, & Glaser, 1980; Pellegrino & Glaser, 1980, 1982) differs from Sternberg's theory in two major respects: (1) a second inference component is substituted for the application component; (2) mapping (which these investigators call "comparison") occurs near the end of analogy solution rather than in the middle and is slightly different in character from mapping in Sternberg's theory. Consider the sequence of events in the solution of an analogy such as LAWYER : CLIENT :: DOCTOR : (a) MEDICINE, (b) PATIENT.

In Sternberg's theory, (1) the individual encodes LAWYER, (2) then CLIENT, (3) infers the relation between LAWYER and CLIENT, (4) encodes DOCTOR, (5) maps the higher-order relation of the first half of the analogy starting with LAWYER to the second half of the analogy starting with DOC-TOR, (6) encodes MEDICINE and PATIENT, (7) applies the inferred relation as mapped to the second half of the analogy starting with DOCTOR to create an ideal solution, (8) compares each answer option to the ideal solution, (9) justifies the better of the answer options in terms of whether it is good enough, and (10) responds.

Now, consider how solution of the analogy would proceed in Pellegrino and Glaser's theory. The individual would (1) encode LAWYER, (2) encode CLIENT, (3) infer the relation between LAWYER and CLIENT, (4) encode DOCTOR, (5) encode MEDICINE, (6) encode PATIENT, (7) infer the relation between DOCTOR and MEDICINE, (8) infer the relation between DOCTOR and PATIENT, (9) compare the relation between LAWYER and CLIENT to the relation between DOCTOR and MEDICINE, on the one hand, and DOC-TOR and PATIENT, on the other, and (10) respond. Note that in this model the comparison operation essentially takes the place of mapping, comparison, and justification collectively in Sternberg's theory. This theory is similar to and derives from an earlier theory proposed by Evans (1968) in the form of a computer program for solving geometric analogies. Pellegrino and Glaser have tested their theory directly only on analogy problems (Mulholland, Pellegrino, & Glaser, 1980), and have found good support for it. However, they did not quantitatively test the predictions of their theory against the predictions of Sternberg's theory.

Goldman, Pellegrino, Parseghian, and Sallis (1982) studied developmental differences in verbal analogical reasoning. Goldman and her colleagues conducted two experiments with eight- and ten-year-olds. Although this work was loosely motivated by the Pellegrino and Glaser theory, it did not directly test it. Rather, it sought explicitly to study developmental changes in solution processes and strategies for solving verbal analogies. Goldman et al. (1982) found evidence for both quantitative and qualitative changes in children's solutions of the analogies. Older children were more accurate than younger children in inference and ap-plication processes and they also were more likely to recognize the correct response from among a set of alternatives when either their inference or appli-cation had been incorrect. (Note that although Pellegrino and Glaser did not have an application process in their theory, Goldman et al. did make use of such a process, following Sternberg's theory.) In addition, older children were less likely to be distracted by associative choices in the alternative set. These are choices in which one of the options is highly related to the third term in the analogy stem, but is nevertheless an incorrect analogical completion. An example of an analogy in which the answer option that is a high associate to the third term of the stem is nevertheless incorrect is LEMON : SOUR ::

APPLE : (a) FRUIT, (b) SWEET. Although FRUIT is more highly associated with APPLE than is SWEET, SWEET is the correct answer to the analogy.

In both of Goldman et al.'s experiments, children were also asked to state why they had selected the particular answer they preferred. Responses were classified into three major categories: parallel relations, nonparallel relations, and no relation. Statements indicating comprehension that the $A : B$ and $C : D$ relations of an analogy must match were classified in the "parallel relations" category. Statements that violated the property of matching relations were classified in the "nonparallel" category. Statements about the chosen response that did not relate this response to anything else were classified in the "no-relation" category. Goldman and her colleagues found that 10-year-olds had significantly more statements in the parallel relations category (.50) than did eight-year-olds (.34). The investigators interpreted these results as indicating that younger children understand that they are supposed to use parallel relations when they solve analogy problems, but that they do not always, in fact, use these relations when solving the analogies. When they do choose the correct alternative to an analogy problem, they are just as likely as the older children to verbalize the appropriate reason. But they choose inappropriate answers more often than do older children, and when they do so, they come up with rationalizations for their answers that show little cognizance of the relational properties of the four analogy terms (see Pellegrino, 1984). The developmental trends observed by Goldman and her colleagues have also been observed in older students. Heller (1979) studied the performance of vocational high school and college students in verbal analogical reasoning. She found that the college students used analogical solutions 99% of the time. However, the best (upper 25% in verbal ability) of the high school students used analogical solutions 71% of the time, whereas the worst (lower 25% of verbal ability) of the high school students used analogical solutions only 34% of the time.

In collaboration with Holzman (Holzman, Glaser, & Pellegrino, 1976; Holzman, Pellegrino, & Glaser, 1983), Pellegrino and Glaser have examined the processes, strategies, and knowledge involved in the solution of series-completion problems. However, the empirical work has not been based primarily on the Pellegrino and Glaser theory of analogical reasoning. Rather, the Holzman, Glaser, and Pellegrino (1976) work derives from a model of series completions formulated by Simon and Kotovsky (1963), whereas the Holzman, Pellegrino, and Glaser (1983) study emphasizes the role of knowledge in series completions rather than the processes of the Simon and Kotovsky theory.

In the Simon and Kotovsky (1963) theory (also Kotovsky & Simon, 1973), there are three basic components of solution of series completions. The theory applies most clearly for letter series, and it can be applied as well to number series. It does not apply as straightforwardly to other kinds of series problems, such as verbal or geometric series.

The first component is detection of relations. This component requires an individual to scan the terms of a series and to hypothesize how each element of a series is related to another. Thus this component is similar to inference in

Sternberg's theory. For letter-series problems, only three relations must be considered: identity (which is adjacent repetitions of a given letter), next (which is transition from a given letter of the alphabet to the next letter of the alphabet, as in *AB*), and backward next (which is transition from one letter to another in reverse alphabetical order, as in *BA*). In number-series problems, a much greater variety of relations is possible. For example, number series can involve relations of addition, subtraction, multiplication, division, exponentiation, and so on.

The second component of solution is the discovery of periodicity. The period of a series is the number of elements that constitutes one complete cycle of the pattern that makes up the series. For example, in the series problem, 1, 5, 2, 6, 3, 7, 4, . . . , a period consists of just two relations, +4 and −3. A longer period would be possible in a more complex series problem. Individuals can use either of two principal methods for discovering the periodicity of a series (see Pellegrino, 1984). In an "adjacent" approach, periodicity is discovered by noting regularly occurring breaks in relations between adjacent elements. To take a simple example, in the series, 1, 2, 5, 6, 1, 2, 5, 6, 1, 2, . . . , it is easily noted that there is a break that separates the 1, 2 sequence from the 5, 6 sequence. A "nonadjacent" approach involves discovery of period length by the individual's noting regular intervals at which a given relation repeats itself. For example, if an individual notices that the relation +4, −3 repeats itself again and again, the individual would have used a nonadjacent approach to discovering the periodicity of the series.

The third component of series-completion solution is completion of the pattern description using this component, whereby the individual extrapolates the rule that he or she has discovered in order to generate the next term or terms of the series problem. Extrapolation involves identifying the position in the period of the problem in which the answer should occur, discovering that part of the rule of the problem that governs the answer position, and applying that part of the rule to generate the correct solution to the problem. Whereas Simon and Kotovsky (1963) tested this theory by computer simulation in comparing the computer's performance to the performance of human subjects, Kotovsky and Simon (1973) tested the theory primarily by looking at data of human subjects. On series problems, Holzman and his colleagues (1976) tested the theory via a training experiment. All three studies were supportive of the theory.

To conclude, Pellegrino and Glaser, together with their colleagues, have studied inductive reasoning in analogies and series problems. They have been eclectic in the theories they have applied to understanding inductive reasoning in each of these kinds of problems. On the whole, it would probably be fair to say that Sternberg has been more theory-driven in his approach to studying induction, whereas Pellegrino and Glaser have been more data-driven. This is not to say that Sternberg's work is theoretical and Pellegrino and Glaser's work is strictly empirical. Rather, Sternberg has taken a theory and attempted to apply it with as little change as possible to a variety of induction problems. Pellegrino and Glaser have been more willing to change the theory they test as a function of the particular problem type and age of subjects. Each approach has its advantages and disadvantages.

The theory-driven approach has the advantage of a level of theoretical coherence that is absent in more empirically oriented approaches. Instead of specific theories that vary as a function of tasks and subjects, a single theory is applied in multiple instances. The primary disadvantage of a highly theory-driven approach is that it may be blind to the limitations of the theory. All theories have domains in which they apply more strongly and more weakly. As one moves from the stronger domains to the weaker domains, the fit of the theory to data starts to break down. It is therefore necessary to know just how far a given theory can be extended before it breaks down irretrievably in its attempts to account for data.

The advantages and disadvantages of a more data-driven approach are almost opposite. The advantage is that one retains a degree of flexibility in applying a theory that optimally suits a given set of data. One is less likely to be blinded by an attempt to apply a single theory to all types of data. The main disadvantage is the lack of theoretical coherence and the danger of ad hoc theory formulation. One may find oneself fitting a different theory to each data set, such that a fit to any one data set is quite impressive, but at the expense of generality of a given theory across data sets. Neither Sternberg nor Pellegrino and Glaser is at the extremes in their use of theory and data, and the differences in their approaches reflect differences in styles of research rather than differences in substantive beliefs about the processes of induction. In fact, as noted earlier, the similarities between the two theories are more striking than the differences.

Embretson's Theory. Embretson (who has also published under the name Whitely) has proposed that at least three strategies may be involved in the solution of induction problems (Embretson, in press). She has used elegant psychometric techniques (latent-trait analyses) to study individuals' uses of these three strategies (Whitely, 1980a, 1980b, 1981).

The first strategy uses what Embretson refers to as the rule-oriented approach (Whitely, 1981; Whitely & Barnes, 1979). In this approach, the individual infers properties of an ideal solution from relations in the stem of an analogy item, and then evaluates response alternatives according to the properties that were inferred from the item stem. According to Embretson, the rule-oriented strategy involves two basic information-processing components: rule construction and response evaluation. Rule construction involves figuring out the rules that relate the first term of the analogy to the second term, and the third term of the analogy to the correct solution. It thus incorporates the inference, mapping, and application components of Sternberg's theory, and the inference and comparison components of Pellegrino and Glaser's theory. Response evaluation involves selecting the correct alternative from among several alternatives, given the rule underlying the analogy. This component incorporates the comparison and justification components of Sternberg's theory. It does not relate clearly to information-processing components in Pellegrino and Glaser's theory. The second strategy proposed by Embretson to be used by individuals solving analogies is one of association. Embretson suggests use of this strategy on the basis of past research by Gentile, Kessler, and Gentile (1969), who found that many items on conventional analogy tests can be solved and are solved by some individuals by selecting the answer option that is the highest associate to the third term of the analogy. As noted earlier, Goldman and her colleagues found evidence of the use of associative strategies by high school students. Achenbach (1970) has even devised a test that measures children's tendencies to use associative as opposed to reasoning strategies in solving analogies. Achenbach has contended that such a test actually provides an alternative to standard group intelligence tests.

The third strategy noted by Embretson is a response-elimination strategy (see Whitely & Barnes, 1979). In this strategy, processing is influenced by the number and types of answer options that are presented. Options are processed in two stages. The first stage eliminates response alternatives that are not members of a "target domain" for the ideal answer. If more than one response option remains, then a second stage is employed in which a more exact rule of correspondence is applied. Thus in the first stage an approximate rule eliminates most or possibly all of these answer options. If necessary, an exact rule is applied in the second stage to select the one best response (Embretson & Curtright, 1982).

Embretson's data suggest the possibility of at least some use of all these strategies by various individuals. Although the response-elimination model is the most complex one, it does not seem to provide a better fit to data than do either of the others. The first two strategies thus appear by themselves sufficient to provide a good account of how a variety of individuals solve analogies (Embretson, in press). Embretson has also studied these and related strategies in the solution of classification tests, again using latent-trait analysis. For a lucid description of this research and of the latent-trait method used in its implementation, see Whitely (1980a).

In conclusion, a variety of theories have been proposed to account for information processing in inductive reasoning. The general consensus is that the components of information processing are the same, or at least highly overlapping, across a variety of induction tasks (Greeno, 1978; Pellegrino & Glaser, 1980; Simon, 1976; Sternberg & Gardner, 1983; Whitely, 1980a). If this contention is correct, and the data described above suggest that it is, then we may have at least one basis for understanding why it is that tests of general intelligence tend to be highly intercorrelated and to yield a general (g) factor. Tests of general intelligence almost always involve at least some induction items. The Raven Progressive Matrices (Raven, 1938, 1960) and the Cattell Culture-Fair Test of g (Cattell & Cattell, 1963), for example, involve induction items exclusively. The general factor may arise as a function of common information-processing components that are relevant for item solution across the various types of induction items, and other items as well.

The theories and experiments described in this section have concentrated on commonalities in what Sternberg (1980b) has referred to as performance components (that is, encoding, inference, mapping, application, and so on). However, the general factor is likely to arise from commonalities in metacomponents as well (that is, defining the nature of a problem, deciding what performance components are relevant for solving the problem, deciding on a strategy by which to combine the performance components, and so on). Thus it is possible to understand the general factor and other factors as well in terms of the information-processing components that combine to contribute to individual differences in individuals' scores on psychometric tests. Components that tend to co-occur generate the factors that are derived from ability tests. A general factor would arise from components that are common to all of a set of tasks; group factors would arise from factors that are common to subsets of the tasks; and specific factors would arise from components that are unique to single tasks. Although information-processing psychologists would try to understand factors in terms of information-processing components, differential psychologists would more likely attempt to understand information-processing components in terms of factors. Such psychologists might claim, for example, that it is actually a general factor of intelligence that gives rise to individual differences in information-processing components. According to this view, individual differences in processes, such as inference, mapping, and application, are derivative rather than causative of individual differences in the general factor. At present no way exists empirically to distinguish between these two positions. Thus various claims, such as Sternberg's (1980b) that components are more basic and Carroll's (1980) that factors are more basic, appear, at least at present, to be basically articles of faith. For the present, a conclusion that does appear safe to draw is that information-processing components and structural factors are intermappable. Each helps us understand some aspect of human intelligence.

Deductive Reasoning

In deductive reasoning, the information contained in the premises of a problem is logically (although not necessarily psychologically) sufficient to reach a valid conclusion. A number of different kinds of deductive-reasoning problems have been studied. For example, mathematical word problems, propositional reasoning, and syllogistic reasoning all involve primarily deductive inference. Because mathematical word problems were considered in an earlier section, and studies of propositional reasoning do not intersect with the human-abilities domain, the focus of this section will be on the study of syllogistic reasoning.

The three most commonly studied types of syllogisms are categorical syllogisms, conditional syllogisms, and linear syllogisms.

A *categorical syllogism* usually contains three statements: a major premise, a minor premise, and a conclusion. The individual's task may be to decide whether a given conclusion is logically valid, or to decide which of several conclusions is logically valid or best serves as a conclusion for the syllogism. An example of a categorical syllogism is as follows: "All Danians are Eleuseans. Some Richters are Danians. Can one conclude that all Richters are Eleuseans?" Premises of categorical syllogisms can be presented in either affirmative or negative form (that is, "All Etruscans are ancients" versus "No Etruscans are ancients"). Furthermore, the premises can be presented in either universal or particular form (that is, "All Etruscans are ancients" versus "Some Etruscans are ancients"). By combining polarity (affirmative versus negative) with quantification (universal versus particular), it is possible to obtain four basic types of syllogistic statements: universal affirmatives (all X are Y), universal negatives (no X are Y), particular affirmatives (some X are Y), and particular negatives (some X are not Y). Some of the major theories of categorical syllogistic reasoning that have been proposed are the atmosphere theory of Woodworth and Sells (1935), the conversion theory of Chapman and Chapman (1959), the complete- and random-combination theories of Erickson (1974, 1978), the analogical theory of Johnson-Laird and Steedman (1978), and the transitive-chain theory of Guyote and Sternberg (1981).

Conditional syllogisms also involve a major premise, a minor premise, and a conclusion. However, these problems are different in form from categorical syllogisms. An example of a conditional syllogism is as follows: "If Conrad the Clown performs, people laugh. Conrad the Clown performs. Can one conclude that people laugh?" As with categorical syllogisms, premises may be negated (that is, "If Conrad the Clown performs, people do not laugh," or "Conrad the Clown does not perform"). People solve categorical and conditional syllogisms in a similar way, but the commonalities in these two forms of deductive reasoning have received less theoretical and empirical attention than have the commonalities in inductive reasoning (but see Guyote & Sternberg, 1981).

A third type of syllogism is the *linear syllogism*. In this type of syllogism, two relations are presented between each of two pairs of items. One item of each pair overlaps between the two pairs. The individual's task is to figure out the relation between the nonoverlapping terms in the two linear-syllogistic premises. An example of a linear syllogism is as follows: "John is taller than Pete. Pete is taller than Bill. Who is tallest?" In these problems, a logically valid conclusion is implied by the premises only if it is assumed that the relations linking the terms are transitive. For example, the relation *taller than* would satisfy transitivity, whereas the relation *plays better tennis than* might not. Of the three types of syllogisms, linear syllogisms have received the greatest attention in the literature on human intelligence; thus the remainder of this section is devoted to a review of theories and research pertinent to such syllogisms.

The linear syllogism has played an important part in theorizing about intelligence. In Piaget's (1928, 1955) developmental theory of intelligence, the ability to perform transitive inferences, as required by linear syllogisms, differentiates preoperational from concrete-operational children. In a more psychometric vein, Burt (1919) used linear syllogisms for measuring the intelligence of school children, and such problems have been used on subsequent tests as well. In more recent work, performance on linear syllogisms has been found to be highly correlated with performance on verbal, spatial, and abstract-reasoning ability tests (Shaver, Pierson, & Lang, 1974; Sternberg, 1980a; Sternberg & Weil, 1980): Correlations with such tests usually fall in the range from .30 to .60.

Although theorists of intelligence and cognitive processes agree that the ability to do linear syllogistic reasoning is an important ingredient of intelligence, these theorists disagree regarding just how linear syllogisms are solved. The major disagreement centers on how information encoded in the linear syllogism is mentally represented. The three major classes of theories have been spatial theories, linguistic theories, and spatial-linguistic mixture theories. We will review each of these types of theories.

Spatial Theories.   Spatial theorists, such as DeSoto, London, and Handel (1965), Huttenlocher (1968), and Huttenlocher and Higgins (1971), have argued that information from linear syllogisms is represented in the form of a spatial array that functions as an internal analog to a physically realized or realizable array. At least eight types of evidence have been adduced to argue in favor of a spatial mental representation for information encoded during linear syllogistic reasoning. In such a representation, a linear syllogism (such as "John is taller than Bill. Bill is taller than Pete. Who is tallest?") would be represented by a mental spatial array, perhaps with John at the top, Pete in the middle, and Bill at the bottom. Consider each of the eight types of evidence that have been offered in favor of a spatial mental representation.

1.   *Introspective Reports.*   Many subjects in various experiments have reported using spatial imagery to solve transitive inference problems. (An inference is transitive when if *A* is related in a certain way to *B*, and *B* is related in a certain way to *C*, then *A* is related in the same way to *C* that *A* is to *B* and *B* is to *C*.) Transitivity can be extended to more than three terms. Subjects frequently claim to use imagery when solving problems such as the linear syllogism (Clark, 1969a; DeSoto, London, & Handel, 1965; Huttenlocher & Higgins, 1971).

2.   *Need for Spatial Array to Combine Premise Information.*   At some point during the course of problem solution, individuals must comprehend the higher-order relations between the two lower-order relations expressed in the individual premises. Such comprehension is tantamount to making the transitive inference needed to solve the problem. Spatial-imagery theorists have specified at a reasonable level of detail how such comprehensions can take place (see, for example, Huttenlocher, 1968). It is not clear how any nonspatial theory could account for the integration of information from these two premises. Clark (1971), the major exponent of the competing linguistic theory, has admitted as much. He has said that "The linguistic theory is not complete. For one thing, it does not fully specify how information from two premises are [sic] combined" (p. 513).

3.   *Comparability of Data Patterns for Purported Imaginal Arrays to Those of Physical Arrays.*   One of Huttenlocher's main arguments in favor of spatial imagery has been that the difficulty of solving different forms of linear syllogisms

parallels the difficulty of arranging real objects according to comparable instructions (Huttenlocher, Eisenberg, & Strauss, 1970). A series of experiments has shown that the two types of items—linear syllogisms and arrangements of real objects in a spatial array—do indeed show parallel patterns of data (Huttenlocher, Eisenberg, & Strauss, 1970; Huttenlocher & Strauss, 1968).

4. *Symbolic-Distance Effect.* Data reported by Potts (1972, 1974) and by Trabasso and his colleagues (Trabasso & Riley, 1975; Trabasso, Riley, & Wilson, 1975) seem strongly to implicate some kind of spatial process in linear-ordering problems. In a typical experiment, subjects are taught a linear ordering of items that takes the form (A, B, C, D, E, F). Subjects are trained only on adjacent pairs of items. Subjects are able to judge the untrained relation between B and E more rapidly than they are able to judge the trained relation between B and C. The further apart the two items are, the easier the judgment is. This symbolic-distance effect is compatible with the kind of "internal psychophysics" proposed by Moyer (1973) and by Moyer and Bayer (1976), whereby a spatial analog presentation is constructed for the array, and elements of this analog representation are compared to one another.

5. *Serial Position Effects.* In the linear-ordering experiments described above, subjects are trained on all adjacent pairs of items in the linear ordering. Trabasso and his colleagues (Lutkus & Trabasso, 1974; Riley & Trabasso, 1974; Trabasso, Riley, & Wilson, 1975) have found that errors made during training and retraining exhibit a serial-position effect with respect to position of the pairs in the linear ordering: maximum errors occur on middle pairs and fewer errors occur on pairs near the end of the ordering. This serial-position effect is interpreted as prima facie evidence for an underlying spatial array (see Bower, 1971).

6. *Directional Preferences within Linear Orderings.* In many of the adjective pairs used in linear syllogism problems, one adjective of a bipolar pair results in more rapid or more accurate solutions than the other. For example, use of the adjectives *taller* and *better* results in facilitated performance relative to the adjectives *shorter* and *worse* (Handel, DeSoto, & London, 1968). These investigators have proposed that faster solutions for the adjectives *taller* and *better* can be accounted for by the fact that (a) *taller-shorter* is represented along a continuum proceeding from top to bottom, whereas *better-worse* is represented along a continuum proceeding from right to left, and (b) people proceed more readily in a downward direction than in an upward direction, and in a rightward direction than in a leftward direction.

7. *End-Anchoring Effects.* Investigators of transitive inference have repeatedly found end-anchoring effects in their data (see DeSoto, London, & Handel, 1965; Huttenlocher, 1968). These effects are observed when it is easier to solve a transitive-inference problem presented from the end of an array inward than it is to solve the problem presented from the middle of the array outward. Such effects are consistent with a spatial representation of information.

8. *Correlations with Spatial Visualization Tests.* Shaver, Pierson, and Lang (1974) have reported correlations across subjects between errors in the solution of linear syllogisms and scores on tests of spatial visualization. These correlations

varied in magnitude, but an impressive number reached statistical significance. These correlations were interpreted as evidence that spatial imagery is used in the solution of linear syllogisms. Sternberg (1980a) and Sternberg and Weil (1980) have also reported significant correlations between scores on linear syllogisms tasks and tests of spatial ability. It thus seems plausible to believe that spatial imagery plays at least some role in the solution of linear syllogisms.

With eight types of evidence converging on the same conclusion, one is tempted to accept the conclusion without further ado. Yet theorists are still actively arguing for other theoretical positions. The reason that such arguments are possible is that none of the eight types of evidence proves to be conclusive, considered either by itself or in conjunction with the remaining types of evidence.

Consider first introspective reports. These are common and are acknowledged even by the most prominent linguistic theorists (Clark, 1969b). A long-standing question in psychology, however, has been whether such reports can be accepted at face value (see, for example, Nisbett & Wilson, 1977). Although such reports are suggestive, they are certainly not conclusive. Consider next the combination of premise information, symbolic-distance effects, serial-position effects, and end-anchoring effects. Can a linguistic representation account for any or all of these effects? The answer appears to be affirmative: a small modification and extension of a linguistic representation suggested by Holyoak (1976) will predict all these effects. Consider next the comparability of data patterns for imaginal arrays. Huttenlocher's (1968) argument that data patterns for reasoning with purported imaginal arrays are quite similar to those for placement with actual physical arrays presents a reasonable case for the analogy between the two types of arrays. The correspondence does not always hold, however (Clark, 1969b, 1972). Consider now directional preferences. In general, adjectives that encourage top-down or right-left processing are also those that are linguistically unmarked. Thus linguistic theory also predicts facilitated processing for these adjectives. Consider finally correlations with spatial tests. Available correlational evidence from the Shaver, Pierson, and Lang (1974) study provides convergent validation for the spatial hypothesis, but does not provide discriminant validation with respect to one or more alternative hypotheses. In other words, errors on the linear syllogism task might well have correlated with tests of spatial-visualization ability because of a general factor that pervades performance on both spatial and linguistic-ability tests. In order to provide a stronger test of the spatial hypothesis, one would have to show high correlations between linear syllogism performance and spatial test performance coupled with low correlations between linear syllogism performance and linguistic test performance. In the Sternberg (1980a) and Sternberg and Weil (1980) data, correlations were computed between linear syllogism scores and linguistic as well as spatial tests. The correlations with linguistic tests also generally turned out to be statistically significant.

Linguistic Theories. Linguistic theorists argue that information is represented in the form of linguistic, deep-structural propositions of the type originally proposed by Chomsky (1965). For example, the sentence "John is taller than Pete" might be represented by (John is tall +; Pete is tall). Three principal types of evidence have been adduced in favor of a linguistic representation for information in linear syllogistic reasoning.

1. *The Principle of Primacy of Functional Relations.* This principle states that "Functional relations, like those of subject, verb, and direct object, are stored, immediately after comprehension in a more readily available form than other kinds of information, like that of themes" (Clark, 1969b, p. 388). This principle forms the basis for the linguistic representation of information in terms of base strings and underlying deep-structural transformations on these base strings. Clark, the main linguistic theorist, has not offered any direct experimental evidence to support the principle, although he does claim indirect support from several sources (Donaldson, 1963; Piaget, 1928).

2. *The Principle of Lexical Marking.* According to Clark's (1969b) lexical-marking principle, the senses of certain "positive" adjectives, like *good* and *tall,* are stored in memory in a less complex form than the senses of their opposites. The "positive" adjectives are the unmarked ones, and their opposites are the marked ones. If, as Clark claims, marked adjectives are stored in memory in a more linguistically complex form than is needed for unmarked adjectives, then one might well expect the encoding of marked adjectives to be more time consuming than the encoding of unmarked adjectives, and indeed all studies of linear syllogistic reasoning that have investigated both marked and unmarked adjectives have found longer latencies or more errors associated with items containing marked adjectives than with items containing unmarked adjectives. This evidence therefore seems on its face to support the principle of lexical marking.

3. *The Principle of Congruence.* According to Clark (1969b), "information cannot be retrieved from the senses unless it is congruent in its functional relations with the information that is being sought" (p. 392). If the information from the premises is not congruent with the information being sought, then additional time will be needed to establish congruence between the question and response. Suppose, for example, the question were "Who is best?" and the answer were *A.* If *A* were encoded from a premise that shows "*A* is better than *B*," then solution should be relatively rapid, in that *A* was encoded in terms of the comparative, *better,* and the question asks, *Who is best*? Suppose that, instead, a relevant premise were "*B* is worse than *A*," which, according to Clark, can be expanded to "*B* is worse than *A* is bad." This premise does not contain information congruent with the question. The question can be answered only if it is reformulated to read, "Who is least bad?"

Evidence in favor of a linguistic representation of information is certainly no more solid than that in favor of a spatial representation. First, the observational evidence to support the principle of primacy of functional relations is suggestive at best, and certainly no stronger than subjects' direct introspective reports of spatial imagery. At present, the principle seems to stand more as a presupposition for the remaining principles than as a principle that is testable in its own right. Second, the mere existence of a marking effect as predicted by the principle of lexical marking does not in itself argue for a linguistic representation for information. As noted earlier, a number of investigators have noticed that the unmarked form of a bipolar adjective pair is in general the form that would be expected to appear at the top of the spatial array (DeSoto, London, & Handel, 1965; Huttenlocher & Higgins, 1971). If an adjective pair could be found in which the marked form suggested the top of a spatial array and the unmarked form suggested the bottom of a spatial array, then, according to Clark (1969b), it would be possible to disentangle the spatial and linguistic accounts of the marking effect. Such an adjective pair is found in *deep-shallow*, where *deep*, the unmarked adjective in the pair, suggests the lower end of a spatial array. Clark (1969b) has reported that when subjects are presented with linear syllogisms containing the adjective pair, *deep-shallow*, the standard marking effect is obtained. Another adjective pair, *early-late*, however, is reported by Clark (1969b) to show results opposite to those predicted for the principle of lexical marking. Finally, consider again the principle of congruence. Spatial theorists are skeptical that the available data provide adequate support for the principle of congruence. In a series of recent experiments, Potts and Scholz (1975) obtained the congruence effect under some circumstances but not under others. Clark's (1969b) data provide only weak support for the principle of congruence. Sternberg's (1980a) data suggest that the principle of congruence palls when items are presented in standard form, but not when they are presented premise by premise, with subjects pacing the rate of premise presentation. The reason for this difference can be found in the relative quality of encoding in the two types of experimental situations. The principle of congruence applies only for weaker encodings (see Sternberg, 1980a).

Spatial-Linguistic Mixture Theories. Mixture theories are of two basic kinds. One postulates that individuals solve linear syllogisms via different forms of mental representation at different points during practice. Thus Shaver, Pierson, and Lang (1974) proposed that during the course of practice with linear syllogisms, individuals use a linguistic representation for information during initial trials, but then switch to a spatial representation for information. Johnson-Laird (1972) has made the opposite proposal, namely, that individuals use a spatial representation early during practice and then switch to a linguistic representation (see also Wood, Shotter, & Godden, 1974). Thus these two theories postulate that individuals switch formats of mental representation during the course of practice with linear syllogisms. The theories differ in terms of the direction that the switch takes.

Sternberg (1980a) has proposed a different type of mixture model in which individuals are proposed to use both spatial and linguistic representations for information during the course of solution of a single linear syllogism. In other words, the mixture of representations occurs within problems rather than between problems, as in the above two theories. Sternberg (1980a) offered two major classes of evidence to support this claim.

First, he performed *internal validation* of a mixture theory of linear syllogistic reasoning. In a series of experiments with college students, Sternberg quantified alternative information-processing models of task performance and compared their ability to fit reaction-time data. Regardless of experimental manipulations (whether the question came after or before the two premises), adjective pair, or session of practice, the mixture theory provided a better fit to the group reaction-time data than did either of the spatial or linguistic theories. Moreover, there was no evidence of an interaction between quantitative fit and amount of practice. The squared correlation (R^2) between predicted and observed reaction time was usually in the range of .80 to .90 across experiments. Evidence for the mixture theory can also be found in the fact that parameter estimates (mathematically estimated latencies for particular component operations) were highly similar across experiments in which the mixture theory was tested. This fact, combined with the good fit of the mixture theory to the data, suggests that the component processes specified by the mixture theory give a good account of individuals' processing of linear syllogisms.

Although the mixture theory could better account for latency data than could either the spatial theory or the linguistic theory, it should be noted that individuals process these problems differently. When the latency data of individual subjects is mathematically modeled, although most individuals use a strategy for solving the linear syllogisms that is specified by the mixture theory, nontrivial proportions of individuals use either a spatial strategy or a linguistic strategy. In other words, the group model that fits basically reflects what the majority of subjects are doing. However, when data are modeled individually, individual differences can, and in fact do, show up (Sternberg, 1980a; Sternberg & Weil, 1980).

External validation procedures also support the mixture theory over the alternative theories. Sternberg (1980a) found that latencies for solving linear syllogisms are significantly correlated with scores on both verbal and spatial ability tests. Moreover, when individuals' scores on particular components of information processing are correlated with the psychometric tests, information-processing components that are theorized to be linguistic tend to show higher correlations with verbal ability tests and lower correlations with spatial ability tests; conversely, when information-processing components theorized to be spatial are correlated with the psychometric ability tests, these components show high correlations with spatial tests and relatively lower correlations with verbal tests. In other words, the correlations of component latencies with the verbal and spatial ability tests show the pattern of convergent-discriminant validation predicted by the mixture theory. Again, it should be remembered that there are individual differences in strategies. For individuals who use a basically spatial strategy, significant correlations are obtained only with spatial, but not with verbal, tests. Conversely, for subjects who use a basically linguistic strategy, significant correlations are obtained only with verbal, but not with spatial, tests

(Sternberg & Weil, 1980). None of the quantitative fits of theory to data were consistent with the notion of strategy change across time. In other words, the theories of Shaver, Pierson, and Lang (1974) and of Johnson-Laird (1972) received no support from the data.

To conclude, the mixture theory appears to give the best general account of performance in the solution of linear syllogisms. There are, however, individual differences in subject strategies. In general, though, individuals appear to use both spatial and linguistic mental representation in solving linear syllogisms. Other types of syllogisms, such as categorical and conditional syllogisms, rely even more heavily on the use of spatial representations than do linear syllogisms (Guyote & Sternberg, 1981). In all these types of syllogisms, one's working memory capacity plays an important part in one's ability to solve syllogisms. This is especially true in categorical syllogisms, where the working-memory requirements can be simply overwhelming.

The data that have been collected on syllogistic reasoning suggest why Thurstone (1938) and others have not found the same factorial purity for deductive reasoning that they have found for inductive reasoning. First, inductive-reasoning tasks share a common set of information-processing components across almost the full range of tasks. This is not the case for deductive reasoning tasks. Linear syllogisms involve one set of information-processing components, categorical and conditional syllogisms involve another set of information-processing components, and propositional reasoning involves still another set. Second, the solution of deductive-reasoning problems draws heavily on what seem to be more basic abilities. Thus spatial ability, verbal ability, inferential ability, and memory ability are all heavily implicated in deductive reasoning. Deductive reasoning thus appears to require a mix of skills, which would decrease the probability of its appearing as a unitary factor in factor analyses of tests involving deductive reasoning. The factorial impurity of deductive-reasoning tests should not be construed as implying their unsuitability for the measurement of intelligence. On the contrary, the problems provide a good measure of intelligence precisely because they draw on a number of different intellectual abilities. Deductive reasoning is essential to performance in disciplines such as mathematics and the sciences and hence it is essential to measure it in at least some way on a test that assesses individuals' intellectual abilities.

Spatial Ability

Although many tests of intelligence include items measuring spatial ability, the construct of spatial ability remains somewhat ill-defined to the present day. All such items require some type of mental manipulation of objects such that the mental manipulation simulates a manipulation that could occur physically as well.

Lohman (1979) reanalyzed data from several well-known studies of spatial ability in an attempt to identify common factors, or constellations, of individual differences that underlie spatial ability. In other words, his hypothesis was that spatial ability might be several things, rather than just one thing. Lohman's analysis revealed three distinct factors of spatial ability.

One factor, *spatial orientation*, involves the ability to imagine how a given object or set of objects would appear from a spatial perspective different from that in which the object or objects are shown. Usually, spatial-orientation tasks require people to reorient themselves relative to the object or objects in question. In a typical test item measuring the spatial-orientation factor, one might see an airplane or a boat heading for a certain landmass. One's task is to figure out what the plane or boat would look like if viewed from another perspective. For example, one perspective might be the perspective of the pilot or ship captain heading for the landmass. Another perspective might be that of someone on the landmass observing the plane or boat about to approach the landmass. Of course, many other perspectives are possible, and this task will be more difficult depending on how different one perspective is from another.

A second factor identified by Lohman is *spatial relations*. This factor appears to involve the ability rapidly and accurately to engage in mental rotation of one or more visualized objects. For example, one might see a geometric object at the left of the page. Following the geometric object is a set of other objects, each of which is identical to the first object except for (1) orientation of the object in space, and (2) the possible reflection of the object. With respect to (2), it is customary for half of the objects shown in the answer options to be rotated versions of the original object, and the other half of the objects to be rotated versions of mirror images of the original objects. The examinee's task is to indicate whether each object at the right is a rotated version of the original object or a rotated version of a mirror image of that object.

The *spatial-visualization* factor is assessed by tests that require rather complex mental manipulations, such as those involved in mental paper folding or mental rearrangement of pieces of an object to form the whole object. In one type of item, the examinee must consider an unfolded object at the left, and indicate what it would look like if it were physically folded. In a second type of item, the examinee must consider the pieces of a geometric form at the left, and indicate what the pieces would look like if they were rearranged into a unified geometric figure of which each of the pieces is a part. The spatial-visualization factor might be a "difficulty factor" with respect to the spatial-relations factor. A difficulty factor can arise when two tests differ from each other quantitatively in difficulty rather than qualitatively in the mental processes or mental representations used to solve the test items. The difference between spatial relations and spatial visualization is clearly not simply one of two- versus three-dimensional mental manipulations of the figures. It is possible to have three-dimensional mental rotation problems (problems requiring rotation in depth with respect to the picture plane), and, indeed, Shepard and Metzler (1971) found that performance on problems requiring three-dimensional mental rotations was no worse than performance on problems requiring two-dimensional mental rotations. Similarly, spatial-visualization test items can require mental manipulations in either two or three dimensions. Thus it would remain for information-processing analysis to ascertain the processes that define either of these two factors, or the spatial orientation factor.

The classic experiment that essentially initiated information-processing research on spatial ability was done by Shepard and Metzler (1971). In their experiment, Shepard and Metzler asked subjects to determine whether pairs of perspective drawings of three-dimensional geometric forms were either identical to each other in shape or were mirror images. The complexity that they introduced into the task was that the objects could differ from each other in angle of orientation either in the picture plane or about an axis of depth. Thus, for example, a subject might see on the left a picture of a given geometric form, and, on the right, a picture of that same form rotated 45 degrees. In this case, the subject would have to indicate that the two forms are the same. If the 45-degree rotated object had been a mirror image of the original object, the subject would have had to indicate that the two forms are different. The most striking result of the study was that the time subjects required to make the same-different discrimination increased linearly as a function of the difference in the portrayed orientations of the two objects in each (same-shaped) pair. Shepard and Metzler interpreted these results as suggesting that subjects perform the mental-rotation task by imagining one of the two objects mentally rotated into a congruent orientation with the other object. Once the two objects are in the same orientation, the subject then determines whether they match or mismatch in shape. The investigators interpreted the slope of the reaction-time function as indicating the rate at which mental rotation takes place. An interesting subsidiary finding was that rate of rotation did not differ as a function of whether the rotation was in the picture plane or in a third dimension that cut across the picture plane.

In more recent work, Cooper and Shepard (1973) have shown that when familiar visual stimuli, such as letters of the alphabet, are shown individually in nonstandard orientations, the time to determine whether the stimuli are in their normal version or in a reflected version increases approximately linearly as a function of the extent of the form's departure from the standard, upright position. In other words, the hardest position would be a 90-degree departure from the upright position of, say, a letter. Linear reaction-time functions for a mental-rotation task have also been demonstrated for random polygons (Cooper, 1975). Cooper and Podgorny (1976) showed that the rate of mental rotation for such random polygons is unaffected by the complexity of the polygon. The linear reaction-time function found in the mental-rotation task can be found in other spatial tasks as well. For example, Shepard and Feng (1972) found that reaction times for a mental paper-folding task, where subjects have to fold shapes mentally, increase approximately linearly with the number of foldings to be performed.

Although Cooper and Podgorny found no effect of complexity of a figure on mental-rotation time, it would seem that at some point, variations in figures would affect time for mental rotation. Pellegrino, Mumaw, Kail, and Carter (1979) investigated this hypothesis. They had 99 adults engage in mental-rotation tasks either for alphanumeric characters or for two-dimensional geometric forms of the type on the spatial subtest of the Primary Mental Abilities Test. They found that the more familiar figures, the alphanumeric ones, had a significantly higher rate of mental rotation. Moreover, the time to encode the alphanumerics, as measured by the intercept of the reaction-time function, was less than the time to encode the geometric forms.

There now appears to be substantial evidence for the existence of sex differences in scores on psychometric measures of spatial ability. According to Maccoby and Jacklin (1974), reliable sex differences do not appear until early adolescence, but once they appear, they are maintained throughout adulthood. Information-processing studies of spatial ability help isolate the locus of the difference between males and females. Metzler and Shepard (1974) found a nonsignificant trend for women to have steeper slopes (slower rates of mental rotation) than men, and also for them to have greater intercepts (slower rates of figural encoding). Tapley and Bryden (1977) performed some experiments related to those of Metzler and Shepard. In experiments with concrete rather than abstract three-dimensional stimuli, women had nonsignificantly larger intercepts than men. In an experiment with abstract stimuli, women had significantly steeper slopes than men and nonsignificantly greater intercepts. Kail, Carter, and Pellegrino (1979) did a more definitive study than these to test for sex differences. They found that men rotated stimuli significantly faster than did women, both for familiar alphanumeric characters and for unfamiliar geometric characters of the type found on the Primary Mental Abilities Test. These authors argued that the main locus of the difference between men and women in spatial-information processing is in the rate of mental rotation.

The studies described above have all been conducted on adults. However, work has been conducted on children as well. Kail, Pellegrino, and Carter (1980) tested 8-year-olds, 9-year-olds, 11-year-olds, and 19-year-olds on a mental-rotation task, again using both alphanumeric stimuli and geometric characters of a form found on the Primary Mental Abilities Test. Error rates were quite low (under 10%) at each grade level, indicating that even children as young as 8 can perform the mental-rotation task with little difficulty. Moreover, the reaction-time data at each age level were well fit by a linear function, again implicating an analog mental-rotation process. The main developmental findings were as follows: First, rates of mental rotation decreased approximately monotonically with grade level; thus older children were faster in their rate of mental rotation. Second, the unfamiliar geometric stimuli were rotated more quickly than were the familiar alphanumerics by all groups except the 8-year-olds, where interpretation of the results proved to be problematic due to reduced fit of the model to the data. Third, intercepts (encoding and response time) also declined monotonically over age. Children improved in all aspects of performance with increasing age.

The data described above suggest that there are systematic differences in rates of mental rotation both for subjects of different ages and even within subjects of the same age. These differences might be viewed as "quantitative" ones, in that they portray differences in amounts of spatial ability, but not differences in strategies in spatial ability. One might ask whether there are also "qualitative" differences between subjects in the ways they process spatial information. Data collected by Cooper (1980) suggest at least some qualitative differences do exist in strategies for solving spatial problems. In her research, Cooper has shown subjects two randomly constructed geometric forms in various degrees of angular orientation with respect to each other. The subjects' task was to determine whether the two forms are identical to each other or different from each other. Forms that are different may differ in varying amounts. In other words, different forms may either be quite close to each other in appearance, or quite different from each other in appearance. Cooper discovered two types of subjects in her research. For one type of subject, speed of deciding whether the two forms were the same or different was a monotonically decreasing function of the difference between the two stimuli. In other words, the more different the two geometric forms were, the easier it was for these subjects to tell the geometric forms apart. For the other group of subjects, however, there was no effect of degree of difference between the two forms on reaction time. Reaction time exhibited a flat function no matter what the degree of difference between the two forms.

Cooper (1980, 1982) has suggested that individuals may be characterized as either analytic or as holistic spatial-information processors. The analytic information processors compare the two spatial forms feature by feature and, hence, take longer to differentiate stimuli that are more similar to each other. Subjects in her experiments would respond "different" as soon as they found a difference between two stimuli, but it would take longer to find such a difference with more similar stimuli than it would with more different stimuli. For holistic processors, the degree of difference between the two geometric figures would have no effect on reaction time because the two figures would be compared holistically only. If they were not identical, they would be characterized as "different," regardless of the degree of difference between the two figures.

The results described indicate that information-processing analyses of spatial aptitude can be useful in pinpointing the sources of obtained differences on spatial ability tests. However, they do not provide a comprehensive information-processing theory of spatial ability. Such a theory has been provided by Kosslyn (1980, 1981). The theory specifies both the mental structures and the mental processes that comprise spatial abilities. We will describe here only the classes of processes specified by the theory. There are four classes of processes: image generation, image inspection, image transformation, and image utilization.

Image generation occurs when a person forms a visual image on the basis of information stored in long-term memory. *Image inspection* occurs when one surveys a mental image in order to answer a question about it. For example, if one is asked, "Which is larger, a mouse or a beaver?" one might picture a mouse and picture a beaver, and then compare them in size. The process of inspecting the images to determine their size is the critical process here. *Image transformation* occurs when one changes an image from appearing one way to appearing another way. For example, one might be imagining an elephant in one context and then, on hearing the term "white elephant," change the image so that the elephant that appeared gray now appears white. *Image utilization* occurs when an image is used in some other mental operation, such as fact retrieval. For example, suppose someone is asked whether a kangaroo has a tail. If one does not remember spontaneously the answer to this question, one might generate a mental image of a kangaroo and search for a tail. If one's mental image has a tail, then one responds affirmatively to the question; otherwise, one responds negatively.

Kosslyn's (1980, 1981) theory assumes that mental images are represented in an analog fashion. In other words, the mental images have associated with them certain of the spatial properties that actual physical objects demonstrate. Indeed, Kosslyn defines mental processes such as *scan, zoom,* and *rotate* that sound like operations that could be performed as well on physical objects as they could be on mental objects. The other investigators whose work is cited in this section also assume spatial analog representations. It should be noted, however, that not all theorists share this assumption. For example, Pylyshyn (1973, 1979) has disputed whether such analog representations really exist in the head. He has claimed instead that all mental representations can be viewed as fundamentally propositional in quality. Moreover, he has attempted to show how propositional representations of information might generate the empirical results that Kosslyn, Shepard, Cooper, and others have obtained. Anderson and Bower (1973) took a similar position, although Anderson (1978) has concluded that there is probably no conclusive way of distinguishing between propositional and analog representational theories. At the present time, the debate among theorists continues, with some arguing for analog representations of spatial information, some arguing for propositional representation, and still others arguing that the debate is not likely to be a fruitful one. Whatever the underlying representation, however, the work on information processing suggests that it is possible to understand at least some of the sources of individual differences in psychometric test and factor scores in terms of differences in rates and strategies of spatial-information processing.

CONCLUSIONS

In this chapter, I have reviewed a small subset of the research done on the relations between cognition and intelligence. Research along these lines has been actively pursued over the last decade and shows no sign of abatement. Several conclusions follow from the work that has been pursued so far.

First, cognitive approaches to intelligence are basically compatible with psychometric and other approaches. To a large extent, they address different questions about the same basic phenomena. For example, whereas the psychometric approach dwells primarily on questions of mental structures, cognitive approaches dwell primarily on questions of mental processes. Much of the research described in this chapter can be viewed as elucidating earlier psychometric models. Thus, for example, Thurstone (1938) identified primary mental abilities, such as verbal-comprehension ability, mathematical ability, inductive-reasoning ability, spatial ability, and so on. What research of the type described in this chapter does is to specify the information processing involved in these abilities. During the early and mid-1970s, a number of investigators, including myself, viewed research on components of intelligence as potentially superseding research in the psychometric tradition. It now appears more likely that psychometric and cognitive research will go hand in hand and develop in parallel. This parallel development is possible at least in part because of the recent formulation of confirmatory techniques for factor analysis, which strengthen factor analysis as a means for hypothesis testing, as opposed merely to hypothesis formation.

Second, it has become clear that identification of the components of infor-mation processing does not in itself give an adequate account of the nature of intelligent performance. One must also identify the strategies into which the components combine and the mental representations on which both the com-ponents and the strategies act. It has been customary in much psychometric and cognitive research to pursue a *nomothetic* approach to understanding in-dividual differences. In this approach, it is assumed that all individuals have essentially the same abilities, whether these abilities are measured by factors or components. Thus the factors and components of mental abilities would be the same across subjects, with only their values differing in quantitative fashion. It now appears, however, that individuals differ qualitatively as well as quantita-tively and that, as a result, a more *idiographic* approach is needed for the study of human abilities. Several investigators have now found that individuals can differ quite widely in the strategies they use in information-processing tasks measuring intelligence performance. Averaging over these strategies yields a composite that may mean little or nothing in individual cases. Thus it is necessary to understand data at the individual as well as the group level. In practice, cognitive techniques probably lend themselves more readily to this type of analysis than do psychometric techniques, although it is possible, in theory, to perform factor analysis on data of individual subjects obtained over multiple trials.

Third, it is becoming increasingly apparent that in order to understand in-telligent behavior, we need to move beyond the fairly restrictive tasks that have been used both in experimental laboratories and in psychometric tests of intel-ligence. The work on learning, in particular, shows how quite different patterns of results may be obtained as a function of the ecological validity of the learning task. More generally, the abilities one applies to laboratory tasks or intelligence tests may not transfer to one's performance in everyday life, or conversely, the abilities one exercises in everyday life may not express themselves in laboratory tasks or on intelligence tests. Thus there is a pressing need to investigate the components of intelligence as they operate in everyday life as well as in fairly artificial laboratory settings.

Fourth, there is a need to integrate theory and research on various aspects of intellectual performance. At present, research on topics such as verbal com-prehension, learning, inductive reasoning, deductive reasoning, and spatial relations is quite distinct. It is usually a simple matter to classify a given theory or research project as falling into a single domain. But to the extent that mental abilities cross-cut the domains that we so readily assign to them, there is a need to understand how this cross-cutting takes place. The appearance of general and major group factors in intelligence tests argues strongly for the generality of at least some abilities. Clearly, not all abilities are domain-general: in fact, the current *Zeitgeist* (some might prefer the word, *fad*) in cognitive psychology is toward emphasis on domain-specific abilities. It appears, however, that at least some abilities, such as those represented by metacomponents or executive processes, are quite general, and their application in various domains of endeavor needs to be understood better.

Fifth and finally, there is a need to bring developments in cognitive research into the arenas of current technology. The technologies of testing and training of intellectual skills are still largely dominated by psychometric perspectives. Although this in itself is not bad, it appears certain that the cognitive perspective could have a great deal to contribute to technologies of testing (Sternberg, 1981) and training (Sternberg, 1983). A cognitive perspective is not a panacea for efforts in these domains, but it may well prove to be a useful contribution toward the improvement of the outcome of these efforts.

In sum, the cognitive approach to understanding intelligence has provided a new and exciting perspective on the nature and function of intelligence. It has provided much more detail regarding the nature of various mental abilities than have any of the other approaches that have been used to date. No one approach to studying intelligence is apt to be "complete," and thus the cognitive approach, like any other, needs supplementation by other approaches. A continuing challenge for the future will be the integration of results from various paradigms of research so that our understanding of intelligence will be transparadigmatic rather than specific to the research approach that it happens to use. Regardless of the theoretical or methodological approach one happens to prefer, one should not forget that our ultimate goal is understanding of the psychological phenomenon of *intelligence*, and that understanding this mental construct must transcend any one paradigm for its investigation.

REFERENCES

Achenbach, T. M. (1970). The children's associative responding test: A possible alternative to group IQ tests. *Journal of Educational Psychology, 61*, 340–348.

Anderson, J. R. (1978). Arguments concerning representations for mental imagery. *Psychological Review, 85*, 249–277.

Anderson, J. R., & Bower, G. H. (1973). *Human associative memory.* New York: Wiley.

Anderson, R. C., & Freebody, P. (1979). *Vocabulary knowledge* (Tech. Rep. No. 136). Champaign, IL: University of Illinois, Center for the Study of Reading.

Beck, I. L., Perfetti, C. A., & McKeown, M. G. (1982). The effects of long-term vocabulary instruction on lexical access and reading comprehension. *Journal of Educational Psychology, 74,* 506–521.

Belmont, J. M., & Butterfield, E. C. (1971). Learning strategies as determinants of memory performance. *Cognitive Psychology, 2,* 411–420.

Bisanz, G. L., & Voss, J. F. (1981). Sources of knowledge in reading comprehension. In A. Lesgold & C. A. Perfetti (Eds.), *Interactive processes in reading.* Hillsdale, NJ: Erlbaum.

Bobrow, D. G. (1968). Natural language input for a computer problem solving system. In M. Minsky (Ed.), *Semantic information processing.* Cambridge, MA: MIT Press.

Bower, G. H. (1971). Adaptation-level coding of stimuli and serial position effects. In M. H. Appley (Ed.), *Adaptation-level theory.* New York: Academic Press.

Bransford, J. D., Barclay, J. R., & Franks, J. J. (1972). Sentence memory: A constructive versus interpretive approach. *Cognitive Psychology, 3,* 193–209.

Brown, A. L. (1978). Knowing when, where, and how to remember: A problem of metacognition. In R. Glaser (Ed.), *Advances in instructional psychology* (Vol. 1). Hillsdale, NJ: Erlbaum.

Brown, A. L., & Campione, J. C. (1978). Permissible inferences from cognitive training studies in developmental research. In W. S. Hall & M. Cole (Eds.), *Quarterly Newsletter of the Laboratory of Comparative Human Cognition, 2,* 46–53.

Brown, A. L., & DeLoache, J. S. (1978). Skills, plans and self-regulation. In R. Siegler (Ed.), *Children's thinking: What develops?* Hillsdale, NJ: Erlbaum.

Brown, A. L., & Ferrara, R. A. (1984). Diagnosing zones of proximal development. In J. Wertsch (Ed.), *Culture, communication, and cognition: Vygotskian perspectives.* New York: Cambridge University Press.

Brown, A. L., & Smiley, S. S. (1977). Rating the importance of structural units of prose passages: A problem of metacognitive development. *Child Development, 48,* 1–8.

Brown, A. L., & Smiley, S. S. (1978). The development of strategies for studying texts. *Child Development, 49,* 1076–1088.

Brown, J. S., & Burton, R. R. (1978). Diagnostic models for procedural bugs in basic mathematical skills. *Cognitive Science, 2,* 155–192.

Buckingham, B. R. (1921). Intelligence and its measurement: A symposium. *Journal of Educational Psychology, 12,* 271–275.

Burt, C. (1919). The development of reasoning in school children. *Journal of Experimental Pedagogy, 5,* 68–77.

Butterfield, E. C., & Belmont, J. M. (1977). Assessing and improving the executive cognitive functions of mentally retarded people. In I. Bialer & M. Sternlicht (Eds.), *Psychological issues in mental retardation.* New York: Psychological Dimensions.

Campione, J. C., & Brown, A. L. (1978). Toward a theory of intelligence: Contributions from research with retarded children. *Intelligence, 2,* 279–304.

Campione, J. C., Brown, A. L., & Bryant, N. R. (1984). Learning and memory abilities. In R. J. Sternberg (Ed.), *Human abilities: An information-processing approach.* San Francisco: Freeman.

Carroll, J. B. (1976). Psychometric tests as cognitive tasks: A new "structure of intellect." In L. B. Resnick (Ed.), *The nature of intelligence.* Hillsdale, NJ: Erlbaum.

Carroll, J. B. (1978). How shall we study individual differences in cognitive abilities? Methodological and theoretical perspectives. *Intelligence, 2,* 87–115.

Carroll, J. B. (1980). *Individual differences in psychometric and experimental cognitive tasks* (NR 150-406 ONR Final Report). Chapel Hill, NC: L. L. Thurstone Psychometric Laboratory, University of North Carolina.

Carroll, J. B. (1981). Ability and task difficulty in cognitive psychology. *Educational Researcher, 10,* 11–21.

Cattell, R. B., & Cattell, A. K. (1963). *Test of g: Culture fair, scale 3.* Champaign, IL: Institute for Personality and Ability Testing.

Chapman, L. J., & Chapman, J. P. (1959). Atmosphere effect re-examined. *Journal of Experimental Psychology, 58,* 220–226.

Chase, W. G., & Simon, H. A. (1973). The mind's eye in chess. In W. G. Chase (Ed.), *Visual information processing.* New York: Academic Press.

Chi, M. T. H. (1978). Knowledge structure and memory development. In R. S. Siegler (Ed.), *Children's thinking: What develops?* Hillsdale, NJ: Erlbaum.

Chi, M. T. H., & Koeske, R. D. (1983). Network representations of a child's dinosaur knowledge. *Developmental Psychology, 19,* 29–39.

Chiesi, H. L., Spilich, G. J., & Voss, J. F. (1979). Acquisition of domain-related information in relation to high and low domain knowledge. *Journal of Verbal Learning and Verbal Behavior, 18,* 257–274.

Chomsky, N. (1965). *Aspects of the theory of syntax.* Cambridge, MA: MIT Press.

Clark, H. H. (1969a). The influence of language in solving three-term series problems. *Journal of Experimental Psychology, 82,* 205–215.

Clark, H. H. (1969b). Linguistic processes in deductive reasoning. *Psychological Review, 76,* 387–404.

Clark, H. H. (1971). More about "Adjectives, comparatives, and syllogisms": A reply to Huttenlocher and Higgins. *Psychological Review, 78,* 505–514.

Clark, H. H. (1972). Difficulties people have answering the question "Where is it?" *Journal of Verbal Learning and Verbal Behavior, 11,* 265–277.

Cooper, L. A. (1975). Mental rotation of random two-dimensional shapes. *Cognitive Psychology, 7,* 20–43.

Cooper, L. A. (1980). Spatial information processing: Strategies for research. In R. Snow, P. A. Federico, & W. E. Montague (Eds.), *Aptitude, learning, and instruction: Cognitive process analyses of aptitude* (Vol. 1). Hillsdale, NJ: Erlbaum.

Cooper, L. A. (1982). Strategies for visual comparison and representation: Individual differences. In R. J. Sternberg (Ed.), *Advances in the psychology of human intelligence* (Vol. 1). Hillsdale, NJ: Erlbaum.

Cooper, L. A., & Podgorny, P. (1976). Mental transformations and visual comparison processes: Effects of complexity and similarity. *Journal of Experimental Psychology: Human Perception and Performance, 2,* 503–514.

Cooper, L. A., & Shepard, R. N. (1973). Chronometric studies of the rotation of mental images. In W. G. Chase (Ed.), *Visual information processing.* New York: Academic Press.

Crowder, R. G. (1976). *Principles of learning and memory.* Hillsdale, NJ: Erlbaum.

Curtis, M. E. (1981). *Word knowledge and verbal aptitude.* Unpublished manuscript, University of Pittsburgh, Pittsburgh.

Daalen-Kapteijns, M. M. van, & Elshout-Mohr, M. (1981). The acquisition of word meanings as a cognitive learning process. *Journal of Verbal Learning and Verbal Behavior, 20,* 386–399.

Daneman, M., & Carpenter, P. A. (1980). Individual differences in working memory and reading. *Journal of Verbal Learning and Verbal Behavior, 19,* 450–466.

Davidson, J. E., & Sternberg, R. J. (1983). *Insight in the gifted.* Paper presented at the Annual Meeting of the Society for Research in Child Development, April, Detroit, MI.

Dearborn, W. G. (1921). Intelligence and its measurement: A symposium. *Journal of Educational Psychology, 12,* 210–212.

DeSoto, C. B., London, M., & Handel, S. (1965). Social reasoning and spatial paralogic. *Journal of Personality and Social Psychology, 2,* 513–521.

Donaldson, M. (1963). *A study of children's thinking*. London: Tavistock.

Ellis, N. R. (1970). Memory processes in retardates and normals. In N. R. Ellis (Ed.), *International review of research in mental retardation*. New York: Academic Press.

Embretson, S. (in press). Latent trait models for assessing and analyzing individual differences. In R. J. Sternberg (Ed.), *Advances in the psychology of human intelligence* (Vol. 3). Hillsdale, NJ: Erlbaum.

Embretson, S., & Curtright, C. (1982). *Problem structure and response format in solving verbal analogies* (N.I.E. Tech. Rep. No. NIE082-2). Lawrence, KS: University of Kansas.

Erickson, J. R. (1974). A set analysis theory of behavior in formal syllogistic reasoning tasks. In R. L. Solso (Ed.), *Theories of cognitive psychology: The Loyola Symposium*. Hillsdale, NJ: Erlbaum.

Erickson, J. R. (1978). Research on syllogistic reasoning. In R. Revlin & R. E. Mayer (Eds.), *Human reasoning*. New York: Wiley.

Estes, W. K. (1982). Learning, memory, and intelligence. In R. J. Sternberg (Ed.), *Handbook of human intelligence*. New York: Cambridge University Press.

Evans, T. G. (1968). A program for the solution of geometric analogy intelligence test questions. In M. Minsky (Ed.), *Semantic information processing*. Cambridge, MA: MIT Press.

Ferrara, R. A. (1982). *Children's learning and transfer of inductive reasoning rules: A study of proximal development*. Unpublished Master's Thesis, University of Illinois, Champaign, IL.

Feuerstein, R. (1979). *The dynamic assessment of retarded performers: The learning potential assessment device, theory, instruments, and techniques*. Baltimore: University Park Press.

Flavell, J. H. (1981). Cognitive monitoring. In W. P. Dickson (Ed.), *Children's oral communication skills*. New York: Academic Press.

Gelman, R. (1982). Basic numerical abilities. In R. J. Sternberg (Ed.), *Advances in the psychology of human intelligence* (Vol. 1). Hillsdale, NJ: Erlbaum.

Gelman, R., & Gallistel, C. R. (1975). *The child's understanding of number*. Cambridge, MA: Harvard University Press.

Gentile, J. R., Kessler, D. K., & Gentile, P. K. (1969). Process of solving analogy items. *Journal of Educational Psychology, 60*, 494–502.

Ginsburg, H. (1977). *Children's arithmetic*. New York: Van Nostrand.

Glanzer, M., & Cunitz, A. R. (1966). Two storage mechanisms in free recall. *Journal of Verbal Learning and Verbal Behavior, 5*, 351–360.

Goldman, S. R., Pellegrino, J. W., Parseghian, P. E., & Sallis, R. (1982). Developmental and individual differences in verbal analogical reasoning by children. *Child Development, 53*, 550–559.

Greeno, J. G. (1978). A study of problem solving. In R. Glaser (Ed.), *Advances in instructional psychology*. Hillsdale, NJ: Erlbaum.

Groen, G. J., & Parkman, J. M. (1972). A chronometric analysis of simple addition. *Psychological Review, 79*, 329–343.

Guilford, J. P. (1967). *The nature of human intelligence*. New York: McGraw-Hill.

Guilford, J. P. (1982). Cognitive psychology's ambiguities: Some suggested remedies. *Psychological Review, 89*, 48–59.

Guyote, M. J., & Sternberg, R. J. (1981). A transitive-chain theory of syllogistic reasoning. *Cognitive Psychology, 13*, 461–525.

Handel, S., DeSoto, C. B., & London, M. (1968). Reasoning and spatial representations. *Journal of Verbal Learning and Verbal Behavior, 7*, 351–357.

Hayes, J. R. (1981). *The complete problem solver*. Philadelphia: Franklin Institute Press.

Heim, A. (1970). *Intelligence and personality: Their assessment and relationship*. Harmondsworth, England: Penguin.

Heller, J. I. (1979). *Cognitive processing in verbal analogy solution.* Unpublished doctoral dissertation, University of Pittsburgh, Pittsburgh.

Henley, N. M. (1979). A psychological study of the semantics of animal terms. *Journal of Verbal Learning and Verbal Behavior, 8,* 176–184.

Hogaboam, T. W., & Pellegrino, J. W. (1978). Hunting for individual differences: Verbal ability and semantic processing of pictures and words. *Memory and Cognition, 6,* 189–193.

Holyoak, K. J. (1976). *Symbolic processes in mental comparisons.* Unpublished doctoral dissertation, Stanford University, Stanford, CA.

Holzman, T. G., Glaser, R., & Pellegrino, J. W. (1976). Process training derived from a computer simulation theory. *Memory and Cognition, 4,* 349–356.

Holzman, T. G., Pellegrino, J. W., & Glaser, R. (1983). Cognitive variables in series completion. *Journal of Educational Psychology, 75,* 602–617.

Horn, J. L., & Cattell, R. B. (1966). Refinement and test of the theory of fluid and crystallized ability intelligences. *Journal of Educational Psychology, 57,* 253–270.

Hunt, E. B. (1978). Mechanics of verbal ability. *Psychological Review, 85,* 109–130.

Hunt, E. B., Frost, N., & Lunneborg, C. (1973). Individual differences in cognition: A new approach to intelligence. In G. Bower (Ed.), *The psychology of learning and motivation* (Vol. 7). New York: Academic Press.

Hunt, E. B., Lunneborg, C., & Lewis, J. (1975). What does it mean to be high verbal? *Cognitive Psychology, 7,* 194–227.

Huttenlocher, J. (1968). Constructing spatial images: A strategy in reasoning. *Psychological Review, 75,* 550–560.

Huttenlocher, J., Eisenberg, K., & Strauss, S. (1970). Comprehension: Relation between perceived actor and logical subject. *Journal of Verbal Learning and Verbal Behavior, 9,* 334–341.

Huttenlocher, J., & Higgins, E. T. (1971). Adjectives, comparatives, and syllogisms. *Psychological Review, 78,* 487–504.

Huttenlocher, J., & Strauss, S. (1968). Comprehension and a statement's relation to the situation it describes. *Journal of Verbal Learning and Verbal Behavior, 7,* 300–304.

Jackson, M. D., & McClelland, J. L. (1979). Processing determinants of reading speed. *Journal of Experimental Psychology: General, 108,* 151–181.

Jensen, A. R. (1980). *Bias in mental testing.* New York: Free Press.

Johnson-Laird, P. N. (1972). The three-term series problem. *Cognition, 1,* 57–82.

Johnson-Laird, P. N., & Steedman, M. (1978). The psychology of syllogisms. *Cognitive Psychology, 10,* 64–99.

Kail, R. V., Carter, P., & Pellegrino, J. W. (1979). The locus of sex differences in spatial ability. *Perception & Psychophysics, 26,* 182–186.

Kail, R. V., Pellegrino, J. W., & Carter, P. (1980). Developmental changes in mental rotation. *Journal of Experimental Child Psychology, 29,* 102–116.

Kaye, D. B., & Sternberg, R. J. (1982). *Development of lexical decomposition ability.* Unpublished manuscript.

Keating, D. P., & Bobbitt, B. L. (1978). Individual and developmental differences in cognitive-processing components of mental ability. *Child Development, 49,* 155–167.

Keil, F. C. (1979). *Semantic and conceptual development.* Cambridge, MA: Harvard University Press.

Keil, F. C. (1981). Constraints on knowledge and cognitive development. *Psychological Review, 88,* 197–227.

Keil, F. C. (1984). Transition mechanisms in cognitive development and the structure of knowledge. In R. J. Sternberg (Ed.), *Mechanisms of cognitive development.* San Francisco: Freeman.

Kintsch, W., & van Dijk, T. A. (1978). Toward a model of text comprehension and production. *Psychological Review, 85,* 363–394.

Kosslyn, S. M. (1980). *Image and mind.* Cambridge, MA: Harvard University Press.

Kosslyn, S. M. (1981). The medium and the message in mental imagery. *Psychological Review, 88,* 46–66.

Kotovsky, K., & Simon, H. A. (1973). Empirical tests of a theory of human acquisition of concepts for sequential events. *Cognitive Psychology, 4,* 399–424.

Lansman, M., Donaldson, G., Hunt, E., & Yantis, S. (1982). Ability factors and cognitive processes. *Intelligence, 6,* 347–386.

Larkin, J., McDermott, J., Simon, D. P., & Simon, H. A. (1980). Expert and novice performance in solving physics problems. *Science, 208,* 1335–1342.

Lohman, D. F. (1979). *Spatial ability: A review and reanalysis of the correlational literature* (Tech. Rep. No. 8). Stanford, CA: Aptitude Research Project, School of Education, Stanford University.

Lutkus, A. D., & Trabasso, T. (1974). Transitive inferences in preoperational retarded adolescents. *American Journal of Mental Deficiency, 78,* 599–606.

Maccoby, E. E., & Jacklin, C. N. (1974). *The psychology of sex differences.* Stanford, CA: Stanford University Press.

Markman, E. M. (1981). Comprehension monitoring. In W. P. Dickson (Ed.), *Children's oral communication skills.* New York: Academic Press.

Marshalek, B. (1981). *Trait and process aspects of vocabulary knowledge and verbal ability* (NR 154-376 ONR Tech. Rep. No. 15). Stanford, CA: School of Education, Stanford University.

Mayer, R. E. (1982). Memory for algebra story problems. *Journal of Educational Psychology, 74,* 199–216.

Mayer, R. E. (1983). *Thinking, problem solving, and cognition.* San Francisco: Freeman.

Mayer, R. E., & Greeno, J. G. (1972). Structural differences between learning outcomes produced by different instructional methods. *Journal of Educational Psychology, 63,* 165–173.

Metzler, J., & Shepard, R. N. (1974). Transformational studies of internal representations of three-dimensional objects. In R. Solso (Ed.), *Theories in cognitive psychology: The Loyola Symposium.* Hillsdale, NJ: Erlbaum.

Moyer, R. S. (1973). Comparing objects in memory: Evidence suggesting an internal psychophysics. *Perception and Psychophysics, 13,* 180–184.

Moyer, R. S., & Bayer, R. H. (1976). Mental comparison and the symbolic distance effect. *Cognitive Psychology, 8,* 228–246.

Mulholland, T. M., Pellegrino, J. W., & Glaser, R. (1980). Components of geometric analogy solution. *Cognitive Psychology, 12,* 252–284.

Newell, A., & Simon, H. A. (1972). *Human problem solving.* Englewood Cliffs, NJ: Prentice-Hall.

Nisbett, R. E., & Wilson, T. D. (1977). Telling more than we can know: Verbal reports on mental processes. *Psychological Review, 84,* 231–259.

O'Rourke, J. P. (1974). *Toward a science of vocabulary development.* The Hague: Mouton.

Pellegrino, J. W. (1984). Inductive reasoning ability. In R. J. Sternberg (Ed.), *Human abilities: An information-processing approach.* San Francisco: Freeman.

Pellegrino, J. W., & Glaser, R. (1980). Components of inductive reasoning. In R. E. Snow, P. A. Federico, & W. E. Montague (Eds.), *Aptitude, learning, and instruction: Cognitive process analyses of aptitude* (Vol. 1). Hillsdale, NJ: Erlbaum.

Pellegrino, J. W., & Glaser, R. (1982). Analyzing aptitudes for learning: Inductive reasoning. In R. Glaser (Ed.), *Advances in instructional psychology* (Vol. 2). Hillsdale, NJ: Erlbaum.

Pellegrino, J. W., Mumaw, R. J., Kail, R. V., & Carter, P. (1979). *Different slopes for different folks: Analyses of spatial ability.* Paper presented at annual meeting of Psychonomic Society, Phoenix, AZ.

Perfetti, C. A., & Lesgold, A. M. (1977). Discourse comprehension and individual differences. In

P. Carpenter & M. Just (Eds.), *Cognitive processes in comprehension: The 12th annual Carnegie Symposium on cognition.* Hillsdale, NJ: Erlbaum.

Piaget, J. (1928). *Judgment and reasoning in the child.* London: Routledge & Kegan Paul.

Piaget, J. (1955). *The language and thought of the child.* New York: Meridian Books.

Piaget, J. (1972). *The psychology of intelligence.* Totowa, NJ: Littlefield, Adams.

Posner, M. I., & Mitchell, R. F. (1967). Chronometric analysis of classification. *Psychological Review, 74,* 392–409.

Potts, G. R. (1972). Information processing strategies used in the encoding of linear orderings. *Journal of Verbal Learning and Verbal Behavior, 11,* 727–740.

Potts, G. R. (1974). Storing and retrieving information about ordered relationships. *Journal of Experimental Psychology, 103,* 431–439.

Potts, G. R., & Scholz, K. W. (1975). The internal representation of a three-term series problem. *Journal of Verbal Learning and Verbal Behavior, 14,* 439–452.

Pylyshyn, Z. W. (1973). What the mind's eye tells the mind's brain: A critique of mental imagery. *Psychological Bulletin, 80,* 1–24.

Pylyshyn, Z. W. (1979). Validating computational models: A critique of Anderson's indeterminacy of representation claim. *Psychological Review, 86,* 383–394.

Raven, J. C. (1938). *Progressive matrices: A perceptual test of intelligence.* London: Lewis.

Raven, J. C. (1960). *Guide to the standard progressive matrices.* London: Lewis.

Reitman, W. (1965). *Cognition and thought.* New York: Wiley.

Resnick, L. B., & Ford, W. W. (1981). *The psychology of mathematics for instruction.* Hillsdale, NJ: Erlbaum.

Resnick, L. B., & Glaser, L. (1976). Problem solving and intelligence. In L. B. Resnick (Ed.), *The nature of intelligence.* Hillsdale, NJ: Erlbaum.

Rieger, C. (1975). Conceptual memory. In R. C. Schank (Ed.), *Conceptual information processing.* Amsterdam: North-Holland.

Riley, C. A., & Trabasso, T. (1974). Comparatives, logical structures, and encoding in a transitive inference task. *Journal of Experimental Child Psychology, 17,* 187–203.

Rohwer, W. D., Jr. (1973). Elaboration and learning in childhood and adolescence. In H. W. Reese (Ed.), *Advances in child development and behavior* (Vol 8). New York: Academic Press.

Rumelhart, D. E. (1980). Schemata: The building blocks of cognition. In R. J. Spiro, B. C. Bruce, & W. F. Brewer (Eds.), *Theoretical issues in reading comprehension: Perspectives from cognitive psychology, linguistics, artificial intelligence and education.* Hillsdale, NJ: Erlbaum.

Rumelhart, D. E., & Abrahamson, A. A. (1973). A model for analogical reasoning. *Cognitive Psychology, 5,* 1–28.

Schank, R. C., & Abelson, R. P. (1977). *Scripts, plans, goals, and understanding.* Hillsdale, NJ: Erlbaum.

Shaver, P., Pierson, L., & Lang, S. (1974). Converging evidence for the functional significance of imagery in problem solving. *Cognition, 3,* 359–375.

Shepard, R. N., & Feng, C. (1972). A chronometric study of mental paper folding. *Cognitive Psychology, 3,* 228–243.

Shepard, R. N., & Metzler, J. (1971). Mental rotation of three-dimensional objects. *Science, 171,* 701–705.

Simon, H. A. (1976). Identifying basic abilities underlying intelligent performance of complex tasks. In L. B. Resnick (Ed.), *The nature of intelligence.* Hillsdale, NJ: Erlbaum.

Simon, H. A. (1978). Information processing theories of human problem solving. In W. K. Estes (Ed.), *Handbook of learning and cognitive processes* (Vol. 5). Hillsdale, NJ: Erlbaum.

Simon, H. A., & Kotovsky, K. (1963). Human acquisition of concepts for sequential patterns. *Psychological Review, 70,* 534–546.

Skyrms, B. (1975). *Choice and chance* (2nd ed.). Encino, CA: Dickenson.

Snow, R. E. (1979). Theory and method for research on aptitude processes. In R. J. Sternberg & D. K. Detterman (Eds.), *Human intelligence: Perspectives on its theory and measurement.* Norwood, NJ: Ablex.

Soloway, E., Lochhead, J., & Clement, J. (1982). Does computer programming enhance problem solving ability? Some positive evidence on algebra word problems. In R. J. Seidel, R. E. Anderson, & B. Hunter (Eds.), *Computer literacy.* New York: Academic Press.

Spearman, C. (1923). *The nature of "intelligence" and the principles of cognition.* London: Macmillan.

Spearman, C. (1927). *The abilities of man.* New York: Macmillan.

Sternberg, R. J. (1977). *Intelligence, information processing, and analogical reasoning: The componential analysis of human abilities.* Hillsdale, NJ: Erlbaum.

Sternberg, R. J. (1979). The nature of mental abilities. *American Psychologist, 34,* 214–230.

Sternberg, R. J. (1980a). Representation and process in linear syllogistic reasoning. *Journal of Experimental Psychology: General, 109,* 119–159.

Sternberg, R. J. (1980b). Sketch of a componential subtheory of human intelligence. *Behavioral and Brain Sciences, 3,* 573–614.

Sternberg, R. J. (1981). Testing and cognitive psychology. *American Psychologist, 36,* 1187–1189.

Sternberg, R. J. (1983). Criteria for intellectual skills training. *Educational Researcher, 12,* 6–12, 26.

Sternberg, R. J. (1985). *Beyond IQ: A triarchic theory of human intelligence.* New York: Cambridge University Press.

Sternberg, R. J., & Davidson, J. E. (1982, June). The mind of the puzzler. *Psychology Today,* pp. 37–44.

Sternberg, R. J., & Gardner, M. K. (1983). Unities in inductive reasoning. *Journal of Experimental Psychology: General, 112,* 80–116.

Sternberg, R. J., & Nigro, G. (1980). Developmental patterns in the solution of verbal analogies. *Child Development, 51,* 27–38.

Sternberg, R. J., & Powell, J. S. (1983). Comprehending verbal comprehension. *American Psychologist, 38,* 878–893.

Sternberg, R. J., Powell, J. S., & Kaye, D. B. (1983). Teaching vocabulary-building skills: A contextual approach. In A. C. Wilkinson (Ed.), *Classroom computers and cognitive science.* New York: Academic Press.

Sternberg, R. J., & Rifkin, B. (1979). The development of analogical reasoning processes. *Journal of Experimental Child Psychology, 27,* 195–232.

Sternberg, R. J., & Weil, E. M. (1980). An aptitude-strategy interaction in linear syllogistic reasoning. *Journal of Educational Psychology, 72,* 226–234.

Tapley, S. M., & Bryden, M. P. (1977). An investigation of sex differences in spatial ability: Mental rotation of three-dimensional objects. *Canadian Journal of Psychology, 31,* 122–130.

Thorndike, E. L. (1924). The measurement of intelligence: Present status. *Psychological Review, 31,* 219–252.

Thorndyke, P. W. (1976). The role of inferences in discourse comprehension. *Journal of Verbal Learning and Verbal Behavior, 15,* 437–446.

Thurstone, L. L. (1938). *Primary mental abilities.* Chicago: University of Chicago Press.

Thurstone, L. L. (1947). *Multiple factor analysis.* Chicago: University of Chicago Press.

Trabasso, T., & Riley, C. A. (1975). On the construction and use of representations involving linear order. In R. J. Solso (Ed.), *Information processing and cognition: The Loyola Symposium.* Hillsdale, NJ: Erlbaum.

Trabasso, T., Riley, C. A., & Wilson E. G. (1975). The representation of linear order and spatial strategies in reasoning: A developmental study. In R. Falmagne (Ed.), *Reasoning: Representation and process.* Hillsdale, NJ: Erlbaum.

Vernon, P. E. (1971). *Structure of human abilities.* London: Methuen.

Vygotsky, L. S. (1978). *Mind in society: The development of higher psychological processes.* Cambridge, MA: Harvard University Press.

Werner, H., & Kaplan, E. (1952). The acquisition of word meanings: A developmental study. *Monographs of the Society for Research in Child Development* (No. 51).

Whitely, S. E. (1977). Information-processing on intelligence test items: Some response components. *Applied Psychological Measurement, 1,* 465–476.

Whitely, S. E. (1980a). Latent trait models in the study of intelligence. *Intelligence, 4,* 97–132.

Whitely, S. E. (1980b). Multicomponent latent trait models for ability tests. *Psychometrika, 45,* 479–494.

Whitely, S. E. (1981). Measuring aptitude processes with multicomponent latent trait models. *Journal of Educational Measurement, 18,* 67–84.

Whitely, S. E., & Barnes, G. M. (1979). The implications of processing event sequences for theories of analogical reasoning. *Memory & Cognition, 7* (4), 323–331.

Willis, S. L., Cornelius, S. W., Blow, F. C., & Baltes, P. B. (1983). Training research in aging: Attentional processes. *Journal of Educational Psychology, 75,* 257–270.

Wood, D., Shotter, J., & Godden, D. (1974). An investigation of the relationships between problem solving strategies, representation, and memory. *Quarterly Journal of Experimental Psychology, 26,* 252–257.

Woodrow, H. A. (1917). Practice and transference in normal and feeble-minded children. 1. Practice. *Journal of Educational Psychology, 8,* 85–96.

Woodrow, H. A. (1938). The effect of practice on groups of different initial ability. *Journal of Educational Psychology, 29,* 268–278.

Woodrow, H. A. (1946). The ability to learn. *Psychological Review, 53,* 147–158.

Woods, S. S., Resnick, L. B., & Groen, G. J. (1975). An experimental test of five process models for subtraction. *Journal of Educational Psychology, 67,* 17–21.

Woodworth, R. S., & Sells, S. B. (1935). An atmosphere effect in formal syllogistic reasoning. *Journal of Experimental Psychology, 18,* 451–460.

Zeaman, P., & House, B. J. (1963). The role of attention in retardate discrimination learning. In N. R. Ellis (Ed.), *Handbook of mental deficiency.* New York: McGraw-Hill.

THREE

NEUROLOGICAL FOUNDATIONS OF INTELLIGENCE

GEORGE W. HYND and W. GRANT WILLIS
University of Georgia
Athens, Georgia

Attempts to understand the mind or soul of man have unquestionably been a preoccupation of the earliest philosophers. Certainly, differences in Plato's and Aristotle's conceptualization of the mind or intellect formed one of the most basic of all differences between these two Greek philosophers. Plato, a student of Socrates, believed in the immortality and preexistence of the mind or soul. Aristotle believed that, like the body, the mind ceased to exist with death.

Other philosophers continued to refine their ideas of how the seat of human intellect might indeed be housed in the brain. Hippocrates of Croton in the fifth century B.C. proposed this notion about the brain. He also speculated that the heart housed the senses. Perhaps of all the earliest philosophers, Galen in the second century B.C. advanced the most accurate conceptualization of how the brain and intellect were related when he proposed that the intellect was not housed in the ventricular system as proposed by Herophilus, but rather that cognitive processes were the result of interacting processes in the cortical and subcortical matter. It remained for Vesalius some 1800 years later to confirm Galen's early ideas through his brilliant anatomical research (Heilman & Valenstein, 1979).

Since the work of Vesalius, truly enormous leaps in our understanding of how the brain contributes to intelligent behavior have occurred. Unfortunately, the march of progress in search of scientific truth has advanced more rapidly in comprehending basic neurophysiological structures and processes than in the realm of clearly articulated notions of brain-intellect relationships. In this respect, leaps in logic and premature applications of theory have resulted in some rather absurd ideas. Three examples may illustrate this point.

Gall (1825), for instance, correctly theorized that cognitive processes were the result of the interacting relationship of the two cerebral hemispheres. He also contributed to our understanding of the structure and function of the brain by suggesting that the subcortical structures were responsible for life-sustaining functions. These ideas have been validated repeatedly during the past 150 years. Gall's contributions to neurology have largely been eclipsed, however, by his elaboration of his ideas of the relationship between structure and function. Gall (1825), of course, made the observation that his brightest students had protruding eyes. He incorrectly decided that this was because of enhanced development of the frontal lobes (Pirozzolo, 1978). To Gall, the conclusion was obvious—the frontal lobes were indeed the seat of intellect! Through further elaboration on this theme, he is perhaps now better known for the ideas that served as the foundation for phrenology than for his largely correct theories regarding cortical and subcortical processes. Luria (1980) notes that Gall's ideas on phrenology were so "fantastic" even at the time he published his findings that he was never taken seriously by the scientific community. His ideas, however, were widely circulated in the popular literature and pseudoscientific circles and had a greater impact on the developing discipline of psychology than on neurology and medicine in general.

In retrospect, other conclusions regarding brain-behavior relationships published years ago seem equally absurd today. For instance, it has long been observed on a case-to-case basis that mixed or incomplete dominance, usually hand or eye dominance, may be correlated with neurologic dysfunction. Years of research relating left handedness or "mixed cerebral dominance" to deficient intelligence led the now infamous Cyril Burt (1937) to conclude that left-handed people " . . . Squint, they stammer, they shuffle and shamble, they flounder about like seals out of water. Awkward in the house, and clumsy in their games, they are fumblers and bunglers at whatever they do" (quoted by Corballis, 1980, p. 287).

Although some subtle cognitive differences may exist between right handers and some subgroups of left handers, it now seems more prudent to conclude that differences in intelligence probably do not exist but, if differences do exist, they relate to the manner in which information is processed (Hardyck, Petrinovitch, & Goldman, 1976; Hynd, Obrzut, & Obrzut, 1981; Kaufman, Zalma, & Kaufman, 1978; Ullman, 1977).

Finally, early neuroanatomists who were interested in the cytoarchitectonic structure of the corpus callosum (thick bundle of neurons that "interconnect" the two cerebral hemispheres) proposed that the total number of fibers reflected intellectual level. Considering that the range of estimated fibers varies from approximately one million to 250 million fibers (Blinkov & Glezer, 1968), considerable variability in intelligence could indeed be accounted for. Those who studied the corpus callosum in African blacks in the 1930s (Schepers, 1938) and in eminent scientists (for example, Spitzka, 1905) proposed indexes to quantify the relationship between the number of neurons and intelligence. More recent indexes have also appeared including Kapper's "callosal index" (cited by Selnes, 1974) and Bremer's (1966) "calloso-bulbar index."

It is certainly inviting to speculate about the relationships that must exist between neural structures and intelligence. In considering these three examples it is easy to understand how simple minded our earlier conceptualizations of brain-behavior relationships appeared. One must appreciate, however, that such speculation is indeed important, if not critical, to our developing knowledge of how the brain does indeed receive, process, store, and make use of sensory stimulation in an "intelligent" fashion. Although the ideas of Gall (1825), Burt (1937), and the neuroanatomists may seem simple today, the examination of their ideas and theories have led to more well-documented "truths" regarding the neurological correlates of intelligence.

Consider, for example, Gall's notions regarding asymmetrical variations of the skull as reflecting underlying cognitive processes and their neural foundation. We now know that brain asymmetries do exist. The brain is not symmetrical. The left temporal speech region (planum temporale) is enlarged in 65% of cases (Galaburda, Sanides, & Geschwind, 1978; Geschwind & Levitsky, 1968; Falzi, Perrone, & Vignolo, 1982). Evidence exists that this asymmetry is unique to humans, existed in Neanderthals, and may relate to the neurolinguistic abilities associated with this region of the cortex (Galaburda, LeMay, Kemper, & Geschwind, 1978). Other structural asymmetries exist as well. Further research may similarly show these asymmetries favoring the right frontal cortex, left occipital region (Weinberger, Luchins, Morihisa, & Wyatt, 1982) and the lateral posterior nucleus of the thalamus (Eidelberg & Galaburda, 1983) to be related to cognitive functions.

The study of handedness and lateralized processes using techniques vastly superior to those employed by Burt (1937) and others has led us to speculate on cognitive processes that are related to the right and left cerebral hemispheres. It is now believed by some that simultaneous and successive processes may be lateralized to different hemispheres (Kaufman, 1979) and it is this notion, of course, that has stimulated further refinements of the nature of basic human intellectual abilities (Kaufman & Kaufman, 1983). These recent advances are largely due to efforts conducted decades ago in attempting to understand how handedness and lateralized processes were related to language dominance.

The research that attempted to correlate the estimated number of fibers in the corpus callosum to intelligence has also led to new findings about possible sexual dimorphism in the human corpus callosum. A recent study by de Lacoste-Utamsing and Holloway (1982) provides evidence that females may have a larger splenium (posterior portion of the corpus callosum) than do males. If one is to believe that an anatomically larger neural structure reflects more neural fibers, then these results may shed light on why males are more lateralized for visuo-spatial functions than are females. It may simply be that females are more interconnected insofar as the projection of interhemispheric occipital-parietal fibers are concerned.

Based on this brief introduction, it would appear that any attempt the authors may make in relating their understanding of functional neurology to the neuropsychological research on intelligence will, in all likelihood, result in three possible outcomes. First, due to the considerable progress made recently in relating aspects of intelligence to their neurological foundations, a chapter will result that adequately reflects our current state of knowledge. Second, viewed several decades hence, some of our conclusions may well seem naive and erroneous. On a positive side, however, a third eventual outcome is that the conclusions drawn here will encourage further research into the intriguing relationship between intelligence and its neurological correlates. It is in this respect that we commit our efforts.

The remainder of this chapter will be devoted to providing a perspective on how the psychological research on intelligence can be correlated to neurological conceptualizations of brain-behavior relationships. The following section will provide a basic foundation on functional neurology. It will conclude by discussing Luria's notion of the functional system. From this perspective, the psychological research on intelligence will then be integrated within a neurological conceptualization.

PERSPECTIVES ON FUNCTIONAL NEUROLOGY

Early Contributions

Gall's (1825) notions regarding functional localization did make an impact on Jean Baptiste Bouillaud, the Dean of the Medical Faculty in Paris. Bouillaud's contributions were many but, most important, his advocacy of localizationist thought influenced his son-in-law, Ernest Auburtin. It was Auburtin who first presented an address to the Paris Society of Anthropology in which he argued that several case studies demonstrated that the anterior region of the brain was important to speech. Pierre Paul Broca (1861) heard Auburtin's presentation; because a patient of his who had an expressive speech deficit and a right-sided paralysis exemplified what Auburtin had spoken about; thus, after the patient died, Broca performed an autopsy. A lesion existed in the region of the left first temporal gyrus, the insular cortex, corpus striatum, and in aspects of the inferior transverse convolution. A number of similar patients were eventually seen by Broca and he termed their loss of expressive speech *aphemia*. The term *aphasia*, was later introduced by Trusseau. Broca and Auburtin are vitally important from a historical perspective, since it was they who first clearly articulated the brain-behavior mechanisms involved in expressive speech.

Although we now recognize these contributions as significant, the evidence presented by Broca and Auburtin was not accepted at that time as without containing flaws. Pierre Marie (1906) proposed that the lesion sites described by Broca were not so neatly defined as he had indicated. Others questioned whether his patients even had the basic intellect required for speech. The antilocalizationists continued to hold sway in their arguments but evidence continued to mount that suggested discrete localization of some cognitive functions. Bastian (1869), for example, showed that some aphasic patients not only lost the ability to speak but could not identify common objects in their environment. He also proposed cortical centers for visual, auditory, and some specific motor (in essence, tongue) functions.

It remained, however, for a 26-year-old doctoral student named Wernicke (1874) to demonstrate that damage to the posterior aspects of the left temporal lobe resulted in linguistic-comprehension deficits. It was his notion that what is now known as Wernicke's region was responsible for auditory-linguistic images while Broca's region was important to motor-speech images. Also, Wernicke correctly believed that these two regions in the left cerebral cortex were connected by intrahemispheric fibers. Thus by the end of the nineteenth century a simple but nonetheless correct cortical network had been conceptualized for receptive and expressive language functions.

The right cerebral cortex had also been the focus of some investigation during this time. Jackson (1874) believed not in functional localization but that the brain was organized in a hierarchical manner and that brain disease disrupted higher cognitive functions first and eventually allowed more basic or primitive neurological systems to operate (Filskov, Grimm, & Lewis, 1981). It was Jackson's notion that "the left (hemisphere) is the side for automatic revival of images, and the right the side for their voluntary revival for recognition." He believed that the left hemisphere functioned automatically, while the right hemisphere "led" cognition. Jackson (1876) also demonstrated that patients with right-sided lesions often experienced difficulty in dressing themselves.

Equipotential versus Localizationist Theory

The idea that brain function was localizable held sway through World War I, which provided an outstanding opportunity to examine the psychological effects of penetrating head injuries. Those who provided evidence of the localization of brain function (for example, Charcot, 1889; Dejerine, 1914; Henschen, 1922; Lichtheim, 1885) were challenged by those who held that the brain acted as a whole (for example, Head, 1926; Wilson, 1926). Perhaps most important in this respect, however, was the work of Lashley (1938), which demonstrated that it was not so much the site of brain damage that determined functional loss but rather the mass of cortical tissue compromised. Lashley's research was very influential and supported the work of others who argued the notion of equipotentiality (for example, Conrad, 1948; Goldstein, 1948; Weisenburg & McBride, 1964).

It has been suggested that the reemergence of interest in localizationist theory can be traced to several factors (Heilman & Valenstein, 1979). First, clinical and experimental neurologists continue to publish replicable clinical findings. Second, medical technology has provided researchers with sophisticated new instruments to examine brain-behavior relationships. Third, work continues to articulate the exact nature of neuroanatomical structures important to behavior and cognition. Finally, work has progressed dramatically in comprehending the specific interaction between neurological structures and behavioral-chemical relationships.

Concurrent to these factors, psychologists have been actively involved in developing practical clinical procedures for diagnosing brain-behavior deficiencies (e.g., Halstead, 1947; Reitan, 1955, 1956, 1974). In addition, theorists have also contributed greatly in developing working models of neuroanatomical-behavioral interactions (Geschwind, 1965, 1974; Luria, 1970; Penfield, 1959). In fact, as will be seen, it was Luria (1970) who provided a conceptual model that is generally accepted today in which he proposed that, "It is now widely accepted that each kind of mental activity has a distinct psychological structure and is effected through the joint activity of discrete cortical zones."

Luria's (1970, 1980) conceptualization is important because it allows in some modified fashion for an integrated view of brain-behavior relationships. Indeed, some basic motor and sensory processes are more localized than are higher-order cognitive processes, which in turn involve many interactive subcortical and cortical structures. With this current perspective it is appropriate to examine in some detail both neurological development and subcortical and cortical organization.

FUNCTIONAL NEUROLOGY

Development and Organization of the Brain

It has been estimated that the human brain is comprised of between 5 to 25 billion nerve cells, or neurons. The differentiation of these neurons in development begins at about the end of the second week of gestation. Two defined areas can be seen by the twentieth day of development. At one end of the neural tube is a tubule, which becomes the basis for the spinal column. A larger area at the other end eventually becomes the brain. At approximately ten weeks of gestation the telencephalon is differentiated from those structures destined to become the brain stem and midbrain, and it begins its development leading to the formation of the frontal cortex. By five months of age the fetal brain resembles its adult counterpart as the central and Sylvian fissure are prominent and most sulci and gyri are visible (Jacobson, 1972).

The human brain takes considerably longer than that of other primates to develop because at birth the human brain is only 40% of its eventual 1500 grams. In contrast the brain of a newborn ape is approximately 70% of its eventual adult size (Geschwind, 1974). Not surprisingly, perhaps, some have proposed that the relative weight of the brain correlates to intellectual capacity (Jerison, 1961; Witherspoon, 1960). Since the focus of this chapter is on interaction between neural organization and intellectual behavior, a more in-depth discussion of Luria's (1980) conceptualization of brain organization is in order.

Basically Luria (1980) proposed that the brain could be conceptually organized into three units. The first unit, the arousal unit, includes the brain stem and midbrain structures. This includes the medulla, reticular activating system (RAS), pons, thalamus, and hypothalamus. The second unit, the sensory-input unit, includes the temporal, parietal, and occipital lobes. Last, the third unit of the brain, the frontal-cortex or organizational-planning unit, incorporates all cortical structures anterior to the central fissure or sulcus (see Figure 1).

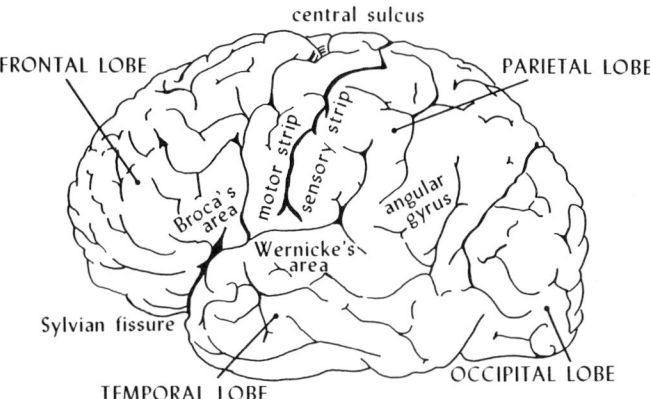

Figure 1. Cerebral cortex and associated landmarks and lobes.

Subcortical Organization

The hindbrain includes the medulla, RAS, and pons. These structures are generally considered to be the oldest and most simply organized in the brain. Respiration, regulation of heart rate, and maintenance of blood pressure are the responsibility of the medulla. The crossover of neural tracts from one side of the body to the other (neural decussation) occurs at this level of the brain. Death may result from damage to this structure.

The RAS in reality is a series of neural structures that run throughout the brain stem. Inattention, drowsiness, stupor, or hyperactivity may result from disorders associated with the RAS. It was Luria's (1980) notion that the RAS partly regulates cortical tone or arousal and that this function is especially important in early development. Several theorists (for example, Dykman, Wallis, Suzuki, Ackerman, & Peters, 1970; Dykman, Wallis, Suzuki, Ackerman, & Peters, 1971) have advanced the notion that the hyperactive and distractible tendencies noted in some developmental learning disorders may well result from delayed or deficient maturation to the RAS. Golden (1981) has even proposed that the "disappearance" of hyperactive behaviors in some children at puberty reflects the regulatory control of the deficient RAS by the developing frontal cortex.

The pons works in conjunction with the cerebellum in the coordination of posture, kinesthetic abilities, and refined motor movements. Neural pathways pass through the pons from the cerebellum to the cortex.

The thalamus and hypothalamus are conceptually part of the diencephalon. Thalamic lesions can result in sensory loss, intellectual deficits, and even the "withering" of speech (Gardner, 1975). The hypothalamus is important in regulating functions such as thirst, sexual arousal, and appetite. Changes in drive state or "libido" have also been associated with lesions in the diencephalon.

Thus to any knowledgeable neurologist or clinician, the drive, motivation, and arousal necessary to behave "intelligently" is most certainly related to the participation of important subcortical structures. Those who would discuss popularized "right-" or "left-brained" behaviors in isolation of references to the notion of interactive subcortical or cortical functional systems are portraying a simple-minded conceptualization of brain-behavior relationships (for example, Fadely & Hosler, 1983). Any model of intelligence must take into account the participation of regulatory drive and motivational mechanisms related to these subcortical structures.

Cortical Organization

The outer convoluted layer of the brain is called the cerebral cortex. It has been estimated that at completed development almost 70% of the cortex is hidden from view deep within the fissures and sulci (Jacobson, 1972). Each of the two roughly equivalent cerebral hemispheres is divided into four lobes: the temporal, parietal, occipital, and frontal lobes. The Sylvian or lateral fissure separates the temporal lobe from the parietal and frontal lobes, while the central fissure separates the frontal lobes from the parietal cortex.

It can be stated in general that in approximately 91% to 95% of the population, the left cerebral hemisphere is dominant for linguistic-semantic function (Sperry, 1974). Other abilities associated with the left cerebral hemisphere include complex motor functions, vigilance, paired-associate learning (Dimond & Beaumont, 1974), ideation, temporal analysis (Eccles, 1977), calculation, finger naming, right-left orientation (Gerstmann, 1924), and sequential processing (Bogen, 1975).

Cortical functions often associated with the right cerebral hemisphere include spatial orientation, simple language comprehension, nonverbal ideation (Sperry, 1974), picture and pattern sense (Eccles, 1977), facial recognition, environmental sound recognition (Milner, 1967), gestalt perception, and simultaneous processing (Bogen, 1969, 1975).

Two points need to be made in the context of the current discussion. First, the experimental methodologies used to arrive at these generalizations will be discussed in a later section. Second, the dichotomizing of brain-behavior relationships along a right-left dimension can result in an incomplete view and can mislead one into not examining the specific parameters used to define a lateralized function. For instance, most would agree that expressive language results from participation of Broca's region and semantic-linguistic comprehension from cortical structures in Wernicke's region. Speech and language are not so simply organized. Evidence indicates that prosody or the affective nature of language (intonations, expression, pitch) may well result from input received from the right cerebral cortex (Butler & Norrsell, 1968). Furthermore, good evidence indicates that fluent bilinguals may demonstrate deviant cortical patterns of organization (Galloway, 1982).

With this caution in mind, it is now appropriate to examine in more detail those abilities assumed to be associated with cortical regions in Luria's (1980) second and third units of the brain. The following discussion serves as a backdrop for the integrative discussion of brain-intelligence theory found in the second half of this chapter.

The Sensory-Input Cortex: The Occipital, Temporal, and Parietal Lobes

Broadly defined, each of the three lobes, discussed as the second unit of the brain according to Luria's (1980) formulation, is conceptually divided into three cortical regions. The primary cortex simply receives and sorts incoming sensation. Little or no processing is thought to occur. The secondary cortex immediately adjacent to the primary cortex is where intramodal associations and processing are thought to occur. Cross-modal integration occurs with the participation of the third cortical region in each lobe, the tertiary zone. This tertiary cortex borders on the secondary cortex for each lobe and the tertiary cortex of the other two lobes. The region of the angular gyrus comprises the zone of overlap, or tertiary cortex for the parietal, temporal, and occipital lobes (see Figure 1).

The occipital lobe is considered to be the visual cortex with most visual sensation registering in the medial aspects of the visual cortex. It has been well established that the left side of each retina is connected to the left occipital cortex, while the right side of each retina is connected to the right occipital cortex (Marcus, 1972). Fibers do cross over but, most important, it seems that stimuli appearing in the right visual field are projected to the left hemiretinas and, hence, to the left visual cortex. Consequently, any damage to the primary visual cortex will typically result in a contralateral visual-field blind spot.

Damage to the secondary visual-association cortex will result in *agnosia*—an inability to match visual stimuli with a visual association. Some controversy surrounds the concept of agnosia, and it is important when one speaks of intelligence (Rubens, 1979). First, it should be noted that an agnosia can occur in any sensory modality. Bay (1953) and others (for example, Bender & Feldman, 1972) have proposed that the symptoms of agnosia are due to a mental deficit that is correlated to a primary sensory loss. Luria (1959), however, has argued that agnostic symptoms are not related to a mental deficit but to incomplete perceptual exploration. An alternate hypothesis proposed by Geschwind (1965) questions the very notion of agnosia and proposes that the symptoms are con-fabulations resulting from disconnected cortical regions. Relative to our present discussion, it does seem important to realize that poor intrasensory association on any task, including tasks appearing on intelligence tests, may well result from neurodevelopmental deficits in either the primary or secondary sensory cortex.

The primary sensory cortex in the parietal lobe is located adjacent to the central fissure with a proportionate representation of cortical space devoted to various tactile-sensory abilities. According to Penfield and Rasmussen (1955), approximately 40% of the sensory cortex is devoted to the face and another 40% to the hand. The tactile-sensory abilities pertaining to the rest of the body account for the remaining 20% of cortical space. It is now believed that the actual perception of sensation occurs in the thalamus but the postcentral cortex locates sensation and evaluates its intensity (Gardner, 1975).

Based on the work of Benton (1959), Critchley (1953), Luria (1973), and others, it is widely recognized that the postcentral cortex, including the primary and sensory parietal cortex, is involved contralaterally for positional sense, tactile localization, two-point discrimination, stereognosis, haptic recognition, and graphesthesia. Dysfunction to the left parietal cortex often manifests itself in the Gerstmann (1957) syndrome, which includes a constellation of four symptoms: dysgraphia, dyscalcalia, left-right disorientation, and finger agnosia. Despite the common appearance of the Gerstmann syndrome in children with developmental learning problems like dyslexia (Hynd & Cohen, 1983), some disagree about the clinical significance of these symptoms (for example, Benton, 1961, 1977). Ideomotor and ideational apraxia are also commonly found in left parietal lobe lesions. Disorders in body sense, perception of space, and constructional apraxia are often found in nondominant or right parietal-lobe lesions (Marcus, 1972).

The left temporal lobe in humans is typically somewhat enlarged over the right temporal region. This is especially true in the region of the planum temporale (Geschwind, 1979; Geschwind & Levitsky, 1968; Witelson & Pallie, 1973). Damage to Heschl's gyrus in the superior aspect of the left temporal cortex can result in cortical deafness, since this is the region of the primary auditory cortex. Congenital or neurodevelopmental/neuroanatomical anomalies (Galaburda & Kemper, 1979) in the primary or secondary auditory cortex may result in deficient auditory discrimination, association, and linguistic-semantic processes (Mahl, Rothenberg, Delgado, & Hamlin, 1964; Meyer & Yates, 1955; Penfield & Roberts, 1959). It is important to realize that the optic radiations traverse the inferior temporal cortex such that dysfunction in this region can result in visual-field or visual-associative deficits (Fuster & Jervey, 1981; Marcus, 1972).

Right temporal-lobe dysfunction may result in nonverbal-pattern or sound-discrimination deficits. Primitive musical ability and abilities associated with picture completion may also be associated with right-sided lesions (Milner, 1958).

In addition to the optic radiations that underlie much of the temporal cortex are important subcortical structures, the function of which can be disrupted due to temporal-lobe lesions. The amygdala, hippocampus, and uncus are involved in emotional expression and for this reason it is not unusual to see in temporal-lobe epileptics alterations in perception, fear, hallucinations, confusion, memory deficits, and occasionally automatisms.

So far, our discussion has focused on the primary and secondary sensory cortexes. Since it is so central to our conceptualization of the integrative and cross-modal aspects of intelligence, the tertiary cortex has not yet been discussed. The region of the angular gyrus in the left cerebral hemisphere "may well be termed 'the association cortex' of the association cortexes" (Geschwind, 1974, p. 99). This is the zone of overlap where the tertiary cortex of the parietal, occipital, and temporal lobes provides the interactive cortical structures necessary for cross-modal integration. As Gaddes (1980) has observed, lesions in this region of the cortex do not produce discrete circumscribed deficits but disrupt the sharing of information perceived in one sensory modality from its correlated association in another sensory modality.

It has long been proposed that neurodevelopmental deficits, such as those found in dyslexia, are attributable to neuroanatomical anomalies in the region of the angular gyrus (Hynd & Cohen, 1983). Until recently, conclusive proof of this notion was lacking. However, case studies published by Drake (1968), Galaburda and Kemper (1979), and Galaburda, Sherman, and Geschwind (1984) document abnormal convolutional patterns, dysplasia, and ectopic cortex in this region of the brain as well as in areas in the temporal and occipital cortex known to be important to the cognitive processes involved in reading. Recognizing that the left hemisphere generally lags behind the right in neural development, Rosen and Galaburda (1984) have even proposed a genetic-autoimmune etiology for some neurodevelopmental learning disorders. Clearly the continued articulation of the hierarchical interplay between neurological development, congenital factors, autoimmune processes, and cognitive development in children will play a vital role in the formulation of meaningful neurological models of intelligence.

Speculation regarding the interaction of congenital and autoimmune factors as they relate to the development of intellectual processes is, although tempting, probably inappropriate. It can be stated, though, that it is in Luria's (1980) second unit or block of the brain where most associative learning takes place. The use of functional cortical systems in the parietal, temporal, and occipital lobes is most central to those cognitive processes incorporated in models of intelligence.

The Third Unit of the Brain: The Frontal Cortex

The advanced development of the frontal lobes is truly what distinguishes humans from other animals. In general, it can be said that the frontal lobes comprise about 40% of the total area of the brain in humans. Since the time of Gall, the frontal cortex has been thought to be the seat of intelligence. Today, however, we have a different view of the frontal cortex.

Directly anterior to the central sulcus is the motor strip that is involved in initiating contralateral movement. Short intrahemispheric association fibers connect the motor strip with the cortical region directly anterior to the motor strip. It was formerly believed that this second region served as a cortical structure that inhibited motor activity (McCulloch, 1944). It is now thought that this premotor area acts as a motor-association cortex similar to the organizational pattern found in the temporal, parietal, and occipital cortex (Filskov, Grimm, & Lewis, 1981).

Luria (1969, 1980) believed that the most anterior aspects of the frontal cortex were involved in the planning, organization, and sequencing of behavior and took command in the direction of behavior at a later developmental time than did the first or second unit of the brain. Golden (1981) suggested that the disappearance of hyperactive behaviors in adolescents and the appearance of adult-onset schizophrenia argue for an even more delayed onset of frontal-lobe development than that proposed by Luria. The most recent evidence indicates that behaviors normally attributed to frontal-lobe control mature in a slow but steady developmental sequence with some reaching full maturity by 6 or 8 years of age and others not yet developed until 10 or 12 years (Passler, Isaac, & Hynd, 1984).

Frontal-lobe lesions seem to produce deficits in complex motivational systems most likely due to the many neural connections between the frontal lobes and subcortical structures (Milner, 1970). Although intellectual impairment does not seem to be a typical result of frontal-lobe lesions (Hebb & Penfield, 1940), dysfunctions in attention, volution, emotion, perception, and the control of motor behavior may result (Gross & Weiskrantz, 1964). Neurological signs often associated with frontal-lobe pathology include more primitive behaviors including abnormal grasp, sucking and snout reflexes, bradykinesia, abnormal gait or posture, occular control deficits, and changes in emotional or orienting responses (Damasio, 1979).

With this discussion as a foundation for understanding some of the neurological underpinnings associated with behavior, it is now appropriate to consider some ideas advanced by Luria on how the brain functions as it pertains to cognitive/intellectual abilities.

LURIA'S NEUROPSYCHOLOGICAL THEORY

Luria has provided us with the most comprehensive view of how the brain functions. Central to his notions is the idea of a functional system. Luria (1980) suggested:

> If the higher mental functions are complex, organized functional systems that are social in origin, any attempt to localize them in special circumscribed areas ("centrex") of the cerebral cortex is even less justifiable than the attempt to seek narrow circumscribed "centers" for biological functional systems. The modern view regarding the possible lateralization of the higher mental functions is that they have a wide, dynamic representation throughout the cerebral cortex based on constellations of territorially scattered groups of "synchronously working ganglion cells, mutually exciting one another" (Ukhtomskii, 1945). . . . We therefore suggest that *the material basis of the higher nervous processes is the brain as a whole but that the brain is a highly differentiated system whose parts are responsible for different* aspects of the unified whole. [Italics original, pp. 32–33]

Thus for Luria (1980) the very notion of a cognitive/intellectual process implies that discrete cortical regions act in concert to produce a given result. Further, he makes the point that structural variation may occur depending not only on the demands of the task but also because of development. In elaborating on this notion he states:

> The structural variation of the higher mental functions at different stages of ontogenetic (and, in some cases, functional) development means that their cortical organization likewise does not remain unchanged and that at different stages of development they are carried out by different constellations of cortical zones. [Thus], . . . *the character of the cortical intercentral relationship does not remain*

the same at different stages of development of a function and that the effects of a lesion of a particular part of the brain will differ at different stages of functional development. [Luria, 1980, pp. 34–35, italics original]

It is well known that different regions of the cortex mature at different rates (Whitaker, 1976). In general, the motor cortex reaches maturity first with the temporal and frontal cortexes maturing last. Our current intelligence tests reflect this maturational sequence in that at the younger ages we rely more on motor and simple auditory and visual-perceptual measures for our estimates of development. In adults, of course, we differentiate individuals based on linguistic-semantic processing skills and on organizational, decision-making abilities, all reflective of later maturing regions of the cortex.

Based on Luria's ideas it can be suggested that a functional system probably exists for nearly all motor and cognitive/intellectual processes. In fact, Roeltgen and Heilman (1984) make the excellent point that for even quite similar processes, such as writing, spelling, and reading, the functional systems involved may well be parallel, duplicated, or even dissociable from each other.

Consequently, considering the variability of human behavior, any number of uniquely different or correlated functional systems may indeed exist. If this is the case, it might help explain the incredibly inconsistent body of literature produced by those who study intelligence and related cognitive processes. Any variability whatsoever in experimental procedures probably results in the involvement of different functional systems and, hence, yields different results. (This notion will be expanded on in a following section.)

It may be helpful to consider one possible functional system. Based on a neurolinguistic model derived from studies with patients with deep, surface, and phonological dyslexia (Coltheart, 1980; Marshall & Newcombe, 1973), a "model" functional system can be hypothesized that is consistent with our knowledge of functional neurology (see Figure 2).

In this hypothesized functional system for reading it can be seen that many cortical areas are involved. A breakdown or deficit due to damage or developmental anomaly could easily disrupt the functional system and, hence, reading. In addition, with regard to anomalies in cortical maturation (for example, dysplasia, ectopic cortex, polymicrogyria) that have been associated with developmental learning disorders (Drake, 1968; Galaburda & Kemper, 1979), if one assumes a random distribution of these anomalies it can be seen that the potential variations of pathological subtypes is nearly limitless. If one accepts this perspective, many of the inconsistencies and variability between subjects seen clinically with regard to learning and cognitive abilities can be better understood. These notions have been further elaborated on by Hynd and Cohen (1983) and Hynd and Hynd (1984).

Clearly the ideas associated with functional systems, cortical maturation and neurodevelopment, and cognitive processes have significant implications for interpreting much of the research on the parameters of intelligence and its measurement. The following sections will integrate these neurological principles with intelligence.

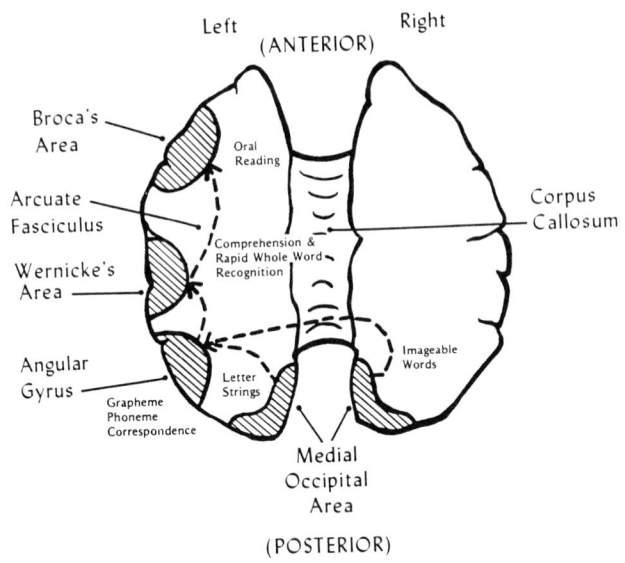

Left (ANTERIOR) Right

Broca's Area

Oral Reading

Arcuate Fasciculus

Corpus Callosum

Comprehension & Rapid Whole Word Recognition

Wernicke's Area

Angular Gyrus

Imageable Words

Letter Strings

Grapheme Phoneme Correspondence

Medial Occipital Area

(POSTERIOR)

Figure 2. The brain as viewed in horizontal section, including the major pathways and cortical regions thought to be involved in reading. Neurolinguistic processes important in reading are also noted.

THE NATURE OF INTELLIGENCE

The nature of intelligence is a highly complex issue, and the definition of this construct is a particularly important, yet theoretically differentiated, task. To synthesize current neurological thought adequately with theories of how humans process information, it is necessary to specify clearly the meaning of intellectual behavior. Given the working assumption that all behavior is physiologically (and therefore neurologically) based, how can intellectual or cognitive behavior be differentiated from other classes of behavior? One important distinction is that intellectual behavior is a covariate of learned behavior. Thus intellectual behavior comprises those unique variables that contribute to within-group variances or individual differences. As Jensen (1979) noted, such variables represent a nearly infinite number of highly diverse tasks. Furthermore, those tasks are delimited only by the necessity for their reliable gradation in terms of behavioral measurement and their orthogonal relationships with variance due to sensory acuity or muscular strength. Intellectual behavior, therefore, represents that general class of behavior that accounts for the correlations between other diversified classes of behavior in a wide variety of situations (see, for example, Jensen, 1979).

To assert that the construct of intelligence accounts for the shared variance among any number of classes of behavior does not, of course, provide an unambiguous orientation on its nature. Moreover, it still does not account for the presumed neurological basis of intelligence. It does, however, contribute to our understanding of the concept by suggesting that a meaningful approach to the study of intellectual behavior involves the thorough investigation of those relatively discrete tasks comprised by that class of behavior.

How can those tasks be identified? In essence, it is important to invoke our knowledge of the anatomy of the human central nervous system and principles of specialization of function within the brain. Our orientation is to approach this task with healthy skepticism, especially considering the abundance of many popular-press conceptualizations of the "left brain" and the "right brain" (for example, Fadely & Hosler, 1983) and the highly divergent abilities ascribed to the cerebral hemispheres. The vast literature available on cerebral hemispheric organization, for example, has prompted numerous dichotomous labels for the cerebral hemispheres (Segalowitz, 1983). One of these dichotomies is verbal versus nonverbal/visuo-spatial for the left and right cerebral hemispheres, respectively. Another dichotomy has resulted from an attempt to classify the cognitive or processing styles of the cerebral hemispheres. This distinction has been made in terms of analytic (or serial) versus holistic (or parallel) styles for the left and right cerebral hemispheres, respectively. As Segalowitz (1983) emphasized, although these dichotomies provide useful theoretical orientations on functional cerebral organization, there are potential associated dangers. For example, once a cerebral hemisphere is labeled, there is a tendency to infer logical extrapolations from that label. Thus the verbal versus visuo-spatial and analytic versus holistic contrasts have given rise to popular-press notions that the left cerebral hemisphere, due to its verbal and logical nature, is unimaginative and stodgy and the right cerebral hemisphere is imaginative, irrational, creative, fun, and often repressed (Segalowitz, 1983). Such traits, of course, clearly are not supported by data; instead, they are extrapolations based on dichotomous labels.

Aside from the speculative nature of these arguments, our primary objection to attempts to label the cerebral hemispheres is the accompanying implicit assumption that the cerebral hemispheres function independently as separate systems. As Valsiner (1983) suggested, given such a simple approach, the presence of an absolute psychological mechanism in a given cerebral hemisphere can be too easily inferred from the relative efficiency of that hemisphere in the processing of a particular behavior. Moreover, this kind of approach is maximally inconsistent with the concepts of pluripotentiality and functional systems originally proposed by Luria (1980).

Our approach to the integration of neurology with intelligence then is to begin with neuroanatomical substrata and to suggest functional aspects or classes of behavior mediated by those substrata. Alternatively, in the absence of empirical support for brain-behavior relationships, methodologies for their investigation are proposed. This approach is in contradistinction to other approaches in which classes of behavior have assumed the primary focus with neurological substrata subsequently inferred. In this respect, an important initial step in the integration of neurology with intelligence is a brief historical perspective on theories of intelligence in order to derive a more refined concept of that general class of behavior that accounts for individual differences in human performance across a wide variety of situations.

Historical Perspective

Speculation about the neurological underpinnings of intelligence, of course, is not a recent endeavor. Such speculation extends as early as the fifth century B.C., when Alcaeon of Croton considered the relationship between the brain and mind and suggested that the brain was the origin of intellectual activity (Matarazzo, 1976). In this century, Thorndike, Bregman, Cobb, and Woodyard (1927) postulated that intelligence comprises a number of orthogonal, specific abilities and, moreover, that each of those abilities involves a particular neuronal substrate. Guilford (1968) proposed three basic facets of intellectual behavior that include the following: (1) contents, (2) operations, and (3) productions. The different abilities comprised by this three-dimensional matrix, currently estimated at 150, have generated theories concerning their relationships to neuroanatomical and neurophysiological substrata (for example, Guilford & Hoepfner, 1971). In a similar vein, Cattell's (1963) explanation of fluid intelligence relies heavily on neurology and suggests that this aspect of intelligence is distinct from crystallized intelligence primarily with respect to the integrity of an individual's neuronal interconnectedness. Finally, Halstead (1951) distinguished four basic components of biological intelligence (integrative field factor, C; abstraction factor, A; power factor, P; and directional factor, D), and he suggested that their maximal representation occurs in the cortex of the frontal lobes.

Significantly, for all these examples the theories of intelligence were established largely on a priori bases. Tasks designed to measure intellectual behaviors were then developed and administered, and results were subsequently factor analyzed. The resulting factor-analytic structures were next interpreted in fashions consistent with the original hypotheses and, finally, possible, neurological substrata were inferred. Moreover, with the possible exception of Halstead's (1951), this final step has occupied only a peripheral focus for each theory of intelligence.

Thus the history of the nature of intelligence, which is inextricably tied to definitional issues, has largely given only secondary emphasis to its neurological basis. Our primary criticism of these theories is addressed to the general orientations from which they were developed. We believe that a more fundamental approach to the definition of intelligence and its eventual and necessary integration with neurology is to begin with the neurological or functional systems hypothesized to be involved in intellectual behavior and to investigate functions associated with the individual components of those systems. In this instance, the neurological basis of intellectual behavior assumes a primary as opposed to secondary (or even perfunctory) focus. This kind of integration of neurological principles with intellectual behavior has the potential to provide a more complete explanation for human individual differences. Clearly, as Matarazzo (1976) identified, the history of the nature of intelligence has been largely determined by the following: (1) the specific samples of individuals who have been studied; (2) the specific tasks and measures applied; and (3) the specific methods used to analyze the data. Thus we have accumulated many hypotheses on the nature and definition of intelligence, including Binet's atheoretical approach, Spearman's

(1927) two-factor theory, Thurstone's (1938) multiple-factor theory, Guilford's (1968) tri-dimensional theory, and Cattell's theory of fluid and crystallized intelligence (Horn, 1968), among others. Although some attempts have been made to relate these differential theories of intelligence to neurology, most were developed independently of neurological principles.

Toward a Definition of Intelligence

By necessity, we must consider intelligence as a general class of behavior. Furthermore, the unifying element for the individual behaviors composing that class is g. Although there may be some disagreement among primary theorists regarding the exact nature of g, the presence of this factor is at least implicitly understood in nearly all theories of intelligence. The intercorrelations of a wide variety of tasks attest to the presence of g. In addition, such intercorrelations are a prerequisite to including differential tasks or tests in a single battery with the resultant arithmetic combination of response variables. To deny the presence of g is to assert that such combination is inappropriate. Thus even Binet with his pragmatic approach to the nature of intelligence implicitly acknowledged the presence of g through his willingness to obtain a psychometric sum of the number of tests passed on his scale of intelligence. That intercorrelations among tasks are not perfect, however, while some groups of tasks intercorrelate more highly than do others, provide evidence that secondary or specific factors are also involved in that general class of intellectual behavior. As Matarazzo (1976) articulated, intelligence is a component of all behavior and consequently should be considered as an attribute of behavior rather than an attribute of a person. We would agree with this conceptualization but would exclude those behaviors limited to sensory acuity or muscular strength.

Given a similar orientation, Wechsler defined intelligence as

The aggregate or global capacity of the individual to act purposefully, to think rationally, and to deal effectively with his [sic] *environment.* It is aggregate or global because it is composed of elements or abilities (features) which, although not entirely independent, are qualitatively differentiable. [Matarazzo, 1976, p. 79, emphasis original]

We propose that the elements of these global abilities are subserved by differential functional systems and, further, that the specific tasks comprised by those elements may be neurologically represented as individual components of those functional systems.

To invoke the concept of functional systems in developing a definition of intelligence is to acknowledge the contribution of Luria (1980) to our present understanding of the integration of neurology and behavior. In this respect, Luria conceptualized intelligence as a "particularly complex form of mental activity, taking place only when the problem demands preliminary analysis and synthesis of the situation and special auxiliary operations by means of which it can be solved" (1980, p. 562). In emphasizing the complexity of the intellectual processes, Luria warned that their particular disturbances in patients with brain lesions often cannot be used directly to infer localization. Implicit within Luria's conceptualization of intelligence and related to his assumption of the highly complex nature of these processes are a number of relatively less complex processes subserved by differential functional systems. Thus, unlike the activity of reading for which a single, albeit individualized, functional system was proposed, intellectual processes may involve several functional systems, each comprising any number of individual components that may, perhaps, operate in isolation or concurrently. For example, the preliminary analysis of a situation necessarily includes the creation of a general plan or scheme by which a complex action can be initiated in order to solve the task, putatively involving tertiary cortical regions or the output/planning unit of the brain. Moreover, within that scheme, an individual must be able to focus attention on relevant information with concomitant inhibition of attention to irrelevant stimuli. These abilities are necessarily highly dependent on a particular level of cortical tone involving the arousal unit of the brain with corresponding subcortical structures included. Finally, for appropriate synthesis, results obtained at each stage of the intellectual process must be compared with the initial conditions or demands of the task in order to eliminate inappropriate solutions (Luria, 1980). This latter stage putatively involves the sensory input unit of the brain. Thus the active participation of all three main units are accounted for in the process of execution of an intellectual behavior.

Crucial to Luria's (1980) method of neuropsychological investigation is the concept of *syndrome analysis*. A well-known neurological principle is that a lesion of a circumscribed area of the cerebral cortex is frequently associated with a group of dysfunctions as opposed to an isolated deficit. The reason for this is that different functional systems have common components. Consequently, a lesion in a circumscribed cortical area inevitably leads to disturbances in a group of functional systems, giving rise to a syndrome of seemingly independent, yet actually neuronally interconnected, symptoms. The neuropsychological examination attempts to analyze the entire syndrome by investigating various functional systems and elucidating the common component or components associated with the dysfunction. Thus Luria (1980) likened the process of syndrome analysis to the statistical technique of factor analysis. In this instance, particular functional systems comprise common components and, to the extent that they overlap, show various degrees of correlations among themselves. The neuropsychological examination, then, is concerned with the cerebroanatomical pathology associated with higher mental functions (such as intellectual behavior) and the primary difference between this technique and factor analysis, in a conceptual sense, is that the former is directed toward the elucidation of cortical functioning in a single individual.

Our approach to a definition of intelligence and its integration with neurology relies heavily on Luria's (1980) fundamental concepts of functional systems and syndrome analysis. Equally important, our approach is also heavily influenced by more psychometric orientations and the belief that any discussion on the nature of intelligence should be well grounded in principles of behavioral measurement. Finally, our approach is primarily neurological in origin and, as such, the neuroanatomical substrata of behavior assume a major focus. Intelligence is a class of behavior that, similar to a statistical covariate, accounts for individual variability in human performance across a wide variety of situations. This class of behavior is believed to be orthogonal to sensory acuity and muscular strength. Furthermore, intelligence (or intellectual behavior) can be neurologically represented by a number of individualized functional systems and through proper analysis the individual components of those functional systems, which correspond to relatively discrete cortical zones, can potentially be identified. To illustrate these concepts a brief discussion of functional cerebral organization follows.

FUNCTIONAL CEREBRAL ORGANIZATION

The vast majority of research conducted in the area of functional cerebral organization has focused on asymmetries between the general cortical regions known as the cerebral hemispheres. These so-called asymmetries have been observed in both functional and morphological terms (Gazzaniga, 1970; Kinsbourne, 1978; Segalowitz, 1983; Springer & Deutsch, 1981) and are here defined to indicate the relative specialization of one cerebral hemisphere in a particular intellectual/cognitive behavior or process. To review the literature in this area is, of course, beyond the scope of this chapter. However, an overview of several primary methods of research in this area is presented, and several behaviors that have been most extensively studied are identified. Although the contributions of many important methodologies are recognized, those selected for presentation here include commissurotomies, Wada procedures, morphological investigations, and various behavioral techniques. Two additional research methods—time-sharing paradigms and regional cerebral blood flow—are also discussed in somewhat greater detail, considering their recent discovery and potential for the noninvasive investigation of functional cerebral organization in groups of normal individuals as well as clinical populations.

Research with Commissurotomy Patients

Patients for whom the cerebral hemispheres have been surgically disconnected have been extensively studied by Sperry (1968) with reference to cerebral hemispheric specialization. This procedure, which entails resection of commissural (or intercerebral) fibers, is sometimes selected as a treatment for intractable epilepsy. At the present time, the procedure usually involves sparing the most posterior aspect of the corpus callosum (that is, the splenium); thus total hemispheric disconnection is rare. The series of investigations reported by Sperry (1968), however, was conducted with patients with radical surgical disconnection. Results of these and similar investigations have indicated that the disconnected cerebral hemispheres can function independently. Moreover, in this disconnected state, they may be specialized for the processing of different classes of behavior (Sperry, 1968). As previously noted, because the visual fields are contralaterally represented in the cerebral hemispheres, a stimulus projected to one visual half-field can be recognized again by these patients only if it reappears in that same visual half-field. Furthermore, whereas visual stimuli projected to the right visual half-field (that is, the left cerebral hemisphere) can be accurately described verbally and in writing, stimuli projected to the left visual half-field (that is, the right cerebral hemisphere) can be identified only by pointing (or through some other nonverbal response mode) on the left side. Similar results have been obtained when the modality of stimulus input has been tactual. This line of research has shown that the disconnected left cerebral hemisphere is relatively specialized for verbal communication, including comprehension, speech, writing, and organization of language, in addition to execution of motor behavior on the right side of the body. In contrast, the disconnected right cerebral hemisphere does not appear to be involved in verbal communication, although comprehension of rudimentary verbal stimuli and of visual and tactual stimuli perceived contralaterally can be demonstrated through nonverbal responses. In addition, the disconnected right cerebral hemisphere appears relatively specialized for execution of responses on the left side of the body.

Other research with commissurotomy patients has demonstrated relative right-cerebral hemispheric superiority for the processing of a variety of visuo-spatial tasks, including drawing a cube (Gazzaniga & Le Doux, 1978), arranging blocks into a pattern (Springer & Deutsch, 1981), and solving a spatial apprehension and reasoning assignment (Zaidel & Sperry, 1973). In addition, some of this work has focused on information-processing styles as opposed to verbal/nonverbal task differences. In this respect, an analytic style for processing information has been attributed to the disconnected left cerebral hemisphere and a holistic style to the right (Levy & Trevarthen, 1976).

There are three major criticisms of this approach to studying functional cerebral organization. First, because of the history of intractable epilepsy in these patients, cerebral functions may be atypically organized. Second, the functioning of the cerebral hemispheres in isolation may differ radically from the normal interactive state. Third, the number of subjects used in this type of research is, of course, usually quite low. Nevertheless, this approach has led to a variety of hypotheses regarding functional cerebral organization and has provided an impetus for research with normal individuals (Rosenzweig & Leiman, 1982).

Research Using the Wada Procedure

A common clinical neurological procedure for assessing cerebral hemispheric specialization for speech was introduced by Wada in 1949 (Wada & Rasmussen, 1960). This procedure entails the injection of an amylobarbital sodium solution (that is, a short-acting anesthetic) in sequential trials into one common carotid artery. The circulation from each common carotid artery is primarily restricted to the ipsilateral cerebral hemisphere, and the injection produces an immediate and temporary loss of function of the cortical structures within that hemisphere (Brodal, 1981). Results of this procedure have shown that, in about 95% of normal adults, the left cerebral hemisphere is specialized for speech (Milner, Branch, & Rasmussen, 1964). This procedure has also been used to study functional cerebral specializations for various other tasks and processes as well. In one study, for example, when the right cerebral hemisphere was anesthetized, although rhythmic elements of singing were maintained, melodies were reduced to monotones (Bogen & Gordon, 1971). This suggests that the right cerebral hemisphere is specialized for melodic aspects of music.

Morphological Research

Asymmetries between the cerebral hemispheres have also been studied with respect to their morphological differences with the corresponding implicit assumption that structure precedes function. Witelson (1983), for example, reported data demonstrating associations between anatomical and functional factors. Such associations suggest neurological precursors of functional cerebral organization. As noted in the first section of this chapter, these morphological differences have included right-left cerebral hemispheric asymmetries in the (1) planum temporale (Geschwind & Levitsky, 1968; Wada, Clarke, & Hamm, 1975; Witelson & Pallie, 1973); (2) pyramidal tract (Benson & Geschwind, 1968); and (3) angle of the Sylvian fissure (Geschwind, 1979). Nevertheless, a number of investigators (for example, Weinstein, 1978; Witelson, 1983) have expressed criticism of the morphological approach to studying functional cerebral organization. Weinstein, for example, emphasized that many of the results of these studies have demonstrated conflicting anatomical asymmetries, and Witelson noted the discrepancy between proportions of subjects identified as left-cerebral hemispheric lateralized for speech and those with a larger left, rather than right, planum temporale.

Behavioral Research with Normal Subjects

In contrast to these invasive procedures, behavioral techniques often have been used to study functional cerebral organization in normal individuals. Three common techniques include the following: (1) dichotic listening; (2) tachistoscopic presentations to the visual half-fields; and (3) dichhaptic tasks. The purpose of all three techniques is to direct stimulus presentations to a particular cerebral hemisphere. The techniques are based on the finding that the auditory, visual, and tactual sensory receptors are more strongly neuronally connected to the contralateral than to the ipsilateral cerebral hemisphere (although, particularly within the auditory system, ipsilateral connections are not absent).

Dichotic Listening.   For dichotic-listening tasks, different auditory stimuli are presented simultaneously to each ear. Results of this type of research have demonstrated that verbal stimuli (such as, words or syllables) presented to the right ear, which has more neuronal connections to the left than right cerebral hemisphere, are perceived more accurately than those presented to the left ear (Kimura, 1973a). This phenomenon has been termed the *right-ear effect* (Kimura, 1961). In contrast, nonverbal auditory stimuli (such as musical and environmental sounds) presented to the left ear, which has more neuronal connections to the right than left cerebral hemisphere, are perceived more accurately than those presented to the right ear (King & Kimura, 1972).

Tachistoscopic Presentations.   In the visual modality, stimuli are presented to the visual half-fields with a tachistoscope. This instrument is used to limit the exposure time of the stimulus so that subjects are unable to shift the direction of their eyes, thus allowing only unilateral cerebral hemispheric perception. Results of research using this technique have shown that verbal stimuli (such as words) projected to the right visual half-field, with left cerebral hemispheric representation, are perceived more accurately than are stimuli presented to the left visual half-field, with right cerebral hemispheric representation (Heron, 1957; Mishkin & Forgays, 1952). Nonverbal stimuli (such as faces and configurations of dots), however, are perceived either equally well in both visual half-fields or more accurately in the left visual half-field (Kimura, 1966; Ley & Bryden, 1979).

Dichhaptic Tasks.   For dichhaptic tasks, an object is presented to either the right or left hand for tactual identification. Controlling for handedness, Witelson (1974) found that abstract shapes were generally perceived more accurately with the left hand, with right cerebral hemispheric neuronal connections, than with the right hand, whereas letter shapes were perceived more accurately with the right hand, with left cerebral hemispheric neuronal connections, than with the left hand.

Results of all three behavioral techniques suggest that a variety of verbal behaviors are relatively more lateralized to the left than to the right cerebral hemisphere and that nonverbal behaviors may be either relatively more lateralized to the right than to the left cerebral hemisphere or bilaterally represented.

Time-Sharing Paradigms

A somewhat more recent approach to the investigation of functional cerebral organization is through time-sharing (or dual-task) paradigms. Since it is noninvasive procedures, such as time sharing and the investigation of cerebral blood flow patterns, that hold much promise theoretically, more in-depth discussion is warranted. The theoretical rationale of time-sharing paradigms is based on the principle of functional cerebral distance, and some of these basic concepts are discussed next.

The Principle of Functional Cerebral Distance.   The principle of functional cerebral distance was proposed by Kinsbourne and Hicks (1978) as an alternative to single- and multiple-channel, limited-capacity models for human information processing (Kinsbourne, 1981). The principle of functional cerebral distance involves an integration of research conducted in cognitive psychology in the areas of information processing and divided attention (Friedman & Polsan, 1981; Kantowitz & Knight, 1976; Navon & Gopher, 1979, 1980; Norman & Bobrow, 1975, 1976) with neuropsychological principles of localization of functional systems within the brain.

A primary assumption of this principle is that the brain comprises networks of neurons and that these networks are specialized for different functions. Due to the interconnected nature of these networks and to the spread of neuronal activation throughout them, the performance of any particular behavior involves a larger portion of the total cerebral space than do the cerebral locus where the processing for that behavior is initiated (Kinsbourne & Hiscock, 1983). Given a dual-task paradigm, then, the degree of interference of one behavior on another, orthogonal behavior should be inversely related to the functional distance between the cerebral foci for the processing of the two behaviors (Hiscock, 1982).

Two orthogonal behaviors, for example, comparable in terms of components of their functional systems, would be expected to generate more mutual interference because of their functionally closer foci than would behaviors processed through less related functional systems involving functionally distant foci. Hence, the principle of functional cerebral distance predicts that the greater the degree of overlap between functional systems involved in the processing of concurrent but orthogonal behaviors, the greater the interference between the behaviors and consequent poorer performance on them. Similarly, concurrent, orthogonal behaviors processed through more distinct (or less overlapping) functional systems would be expected to exert relatively less mutual interference resulting in comparably better performances (Kinsbourne & Hicks, 1978).

Functional asymmetries between the cerebral hemispheres are often considered in terms of the principle of functional cerebral distance. In this respect, a behavior processed primarily in one cerebral hemisphere is predicted to exert relatively minimal interference on an orthogonal, concurrent behavior processed primarily in the opposite hemisphere (Kinsbourne, 1981). This prediction is based on the distribution of association (or intracerebral) fibers that interconnect various regions within one hemisphere. With the exception of "mirror-image" foci in opposite hemispheres that are closely connected via commissural (or intercerebral) fibers, the neuronal connectivity within a cerebral hemisphere is expected in general to be greater than that between cerebral hemispheres (Kinsbourne & Hiscock, 1983). Consequently, with the exception of mirror-image foci, a given functional system primarily within one cerebral hemisphere should be more highly interconnected with other functional systems primarily within that same hemisphere than with those primarily within the opposite hemisphere.

Because interfering effects of one behavior on another can be reliably measured via comparisons of single- versus dual-task performance (Hiscock, 1982), the degree of overlap between functional systems involved in their processing can be inferred. In typical dual-task experimental paradigms, for example, a particular behavior is performed concurrently with left- or right-handed motor performance.

Because the cerebral control of the motor activity is represented primarily along the precentral gyrus (that is, the posterior frontal lobe) of the contralateral cerebral hemisphere, right-handed motor performance is associated with a relatively higher concentration of neuronal activation in the left cerebral hemisphere than in the right. If performance of the behavior requires neuronal activation of a functional system primarily within the left cerebral hemisphere, the degree of interference on right-handed motor performance will be impaired relatively more than will left-handed motor performance in comparison with such performance in the absence of the performance of that behavior.*

Empirical support for the principle of functional cerebral distance has derived from a number of investigations designed specifically to test its hypotheses in addition to reinterpretations of data when viewed retrospectively (Kinsbourne & Hicks, 1978). These investigations, as reviewed by Kinsbourne and Hicks (1978), have focused on simultaneous imitative effects between contralateral limbs (Cernacek, 1961; Cohen, 1970) and between speech and manual-motor behaviors (Kimura, 1973b, 1973c; Kinsbourne & Sewitch, 1975), sequential transfer effects involving reaction times for response shifts (Bertelson, 1963, 1965; Rabbitt, 1965), transfer of training from one limb to another (Ammons & Ammons, 1970; Cook, 1933a, 1933b, 1934), and, more recently, simultaneous interference effects between limbs (Briggs & Kinsbourne, 1978) and between speech or other verbal tasks and manual-motor behaviors (Bowers, Heilman, Satz, & Altman, 1975; Briggs, 1975; Hicks, 1975; Hicks, Bradshaw, Kinsbourne, & Feigin, 1978; Hicks, Provenzano, & Rybstein, 1975; Kinsbourne & Cook, 1971). Results of all these investigations have been compatible with predictions based on the principle of functional cerebral distance. In this respect, relative amounts of motor overflow, transfer, or interference have been explained in terms of degrees of overlap between functional systems involved in the processing of those behaviors.

There are, however, some important criticisms of the principle of functional cerebral distance, especially when considered in terms of functional cerebral hemispheric asymmetries. As Valsiner (1983) suggested, the introduction of a concurrent behavior, which is expected to interfere with an orthogonal, primary behavior, may modify the activity of the entire brain in some fashion, influencing the information processing rather than selectively interfering with a localizable functional system responsible for the processing of the primary behavior. Thus relative asymmetries in the performance of a primary behavior, demonstrated through differential lateralized interference by an orthogonal, concurrent behavior, may be the result of an interaction between the two hemispheres rather

---

*Here it is important to note that these behavioral measures of functional cerebral distance, often used to derive *laterality indexes,* must be viewed in relative rather than in absolute terms. There are two primary reasons for this. First, the concept of localization, even as applied to motor (output) behavior, is probably most accurately viewed in terms of relative concentrations of activated neurons rather than of highly distinct cortical regions. Second, not only do association fibers spread activation homolaterally, but commissural fibers, passing through the corpus callosum, spread activation to mirror-image foci in the contralateral hemisphere, which is subsequently spread homolaterally.

than a demonstration of the lateralized processing of the primary behavior. Valsiner's primary objection to empirical attempts to discover the lateralization for the processing of particular behaviors, therefore, derives from an objection to the assumption that the cerebral hemispheres function independently as separate systems.

Such an assumption, however, is unnecessary and, in fact, contrary to the principle of functional cerebral distance. As Kinsbourne and Hicks (1978) indicated, the specializations of the cerebral hemispheres are complementary rather than in conflict. In this respect, the hemispheres are viewed as typically concurrent in action with functional cerebral space organized to facilitate efficient concurrent functioning of different types of neuronal activity or modes of information processing. Thus, although it is important to consider localization of function in relative rather than in absolute terms, the criticism that dual-task paradigms lead to the oversimplified view of independent cerebral hemispheric functioning may be unfounded.

Results of Research.   Kinsbourne and Hiscock (1983) have provided a comprehensive review of the recent time-sharing research as it applies to functional cerebral organization and that information will not be reiterated here. Research investigations, however, may be classified into two groups: one associated with the time sharing for two output (or motor) behaviors and one with time sharing for an output with a cognitive behavior. This latter classification, especially, shows promise for the integration of intellectual behavior with neurology because it represents an empirical attempt to determine the general cerebroanatomical specializations for the functional systems involved in those tasks comprised by the class of intellectual behavior. In this respect, the cerebral hemispheric specializations for systems involved in the processing of such diverse cognitive tasks as finding hidden figures, solving geometric problems, performing arithmetic calculations, listening to stories, reading passages, scanning photographs of faces and shapes, and various memory tasks have been investigated (Kinsbourne & Hiscock, 1983).

Regional Cerebral Blood Flow

A final methodological technique for the investigation of functional cerebral organization is regional cerebral blood flow. This technique is differentiated from the other methods discussed in terms of its potential for the investigation of more discrete cortical regions than is the general cerebral hemispheres.

Since the corpus of the brain has no store of directly accessible reservoir of energy for processing, it is assumed that the blood circulating in the brain reflects energy demands directly. Within this context, one assumption is paramount; that is, the distribution of cerebral blood flow is directly coupled with metabolic demands that are regulated, in part, by activated cognitive processes. The genesis of the regional cerebral blood flow (RCBF) technique can be traced back more than 30 years (Kety & Schmidt, 1944), and the validation supporting this non-invasive technique is impressive (Prohovnik, 1980).

Essentially, the subject inhales [133]Xenon through a mouthpiece for one minute, and the washout of the [133]Xenon is monitored during a ten-minute desaturation period by 32 sodium iodide crystal detectors placed anteriorly to posteriorly over the right and left cerebral cortex (actually these detectors simply rest on the scalp). Each detector records the [133]Xenon washout for the primary cortex, the underlying white matter, and the overlying extracranial tissues. By charting the washout of [133]Xenon one can develop rate constants for each detector compartment at rest and during the demands of activation (typically some cognitive task). In this fashion, regional and specific compartment comparisons can be made, and shifts in metabolic demands due to specific cognitive activation charted and studied.

To date, investigators have documented differentiated patterns of RCBF in normals for speech and sensory-motor functions (Ingvar & Schwartz, 1974; Oleson, 1971), visual-spatial functions (Risberg, Halsey, Wills, & Wilson, 1975; Risberg, Maximilian, & Prohovnik, 1977), and memory and learning (Hagberg, 1978). Differentiated patterns consistent with our theoretical conceptualization of brain-behavior relationships have also been documented in clinical populations, including chronic schizophrenia (Ariel & Golden, 1981), brain damage (Maximilian, 1980), and in various dementias (MacInnes, 1981; Risberg, 1980).

The fact that these investigations have provided evidence supporting our previous notions regarding the relationships between the functional geography of the brain and cognition attests to the potential impact such a procedure could make in investigating the functional cortical zones activated during performance on tests designed to assess intelligence. Coupled with the time-sharing paradigm, noninvasive procedures, such as the RCBF technique, will probably add substantially to future validation of the interrelationships between brain function and intelligence.

SUCCESSIVE AND SIMULTANEOUS PROCESSING

Any theoretical discussion on intelligence, especially with reference to its neurological basis, would be incomplete without the description of information-processing styles. Successive and simultaneous styles of human information processing have generated considerable speculation regarding the neural basis of these intellectual processes. The concepts of successive and simultaneous processing have a long history, and, in fact, date back to the writings of Sechenov in 1878 (Das, Kirby, & Jarman, 1979). The study of these two theoretically orthogonal constructs has continued to progress and, recently, Kaufman and Kaufman (1983) developed a standardized battery of tests, namely, the Kaufman Assessment Battery for Children (K-ABC), to measure these separate styles of human information processing. Extensive reviews of successive and simultaneous processing have been reported by Das, Kirby, and Jarman (1975, 1979) who, in their conceptual analyses, were heavily influenced by the theoretical orientation of Luria (1980).

Labels and Definitions

As Kaufman and Kaufman (1983) identified, in addition to the terms, successive and simultaneous, other dichotomous labels for these fundamental styles of human information processing have included the following: time ordered versus time independent (Gordon & Bogen, 1974); sequential versus parallel; serial versus multiple (Neisser, 1967); and controlled versus automatic (Schneider & Sheffrin, 1977). A common concept that can be abstracted from all of these terms is derived from the structure of the task involved, that is, the style of information processing.

Das, Kirby, and Jarman (1975) provided conceptual definitions of successive and simultaneous processing. These definitions are interpreted in this instance to indicate that information processed in a successive fashion is considered in terms of serial order. Hence, for successive processing, a system of relationships is surveyed consecutively (rather than unitarily), and the individual components of that system are activated by cues. For some types of tasks, accurate perception is dependent on the analysis of a series of sequential relationships.

In contrast, information processed in a simultaneous fashion involves the synthesis of separate elements into a group, thus permitting integration and the construction of a gestalt perception. For simultaneous processing, a system of relationships is surveyed unitarily, and the order in which an individual component of that system is surveyed is orthogonal to the perception of the whole. Thus, for other types of tasks, simultaneous representation of individual components is necessary so that relationships can be appropriately synthesized.

Other investigators have defined these styles of information processing more operationally. Cohen (1973), for example, presented a variable number of stimuli to individuals. Successive processing was assumed if response time increased with respect to the number of stimuli presented. Conversely, simultaneous processing was assumed if response time remained invariant with respect to the number of stimuli presented.

Research Approaches

From these two approaches to definition—that is, one conceptual and one operational—two primary types of research programs have emerged. Given the conceptual orientation of Das, Kirby, and Jarman (1975, 1979), these researchers have chosen factor-analytic techniques to investigate task-structure variables. Other researchers (for example, Beller, 1970; Cohen, 1972, 1973) have relied on analyses of response reaction times when investigating successive and simultaneous processing.

Theoretically, both successive and simultaneous information-processing styles are available to individuals, and the choice of processing style depends not only on task structure but also on sociocultural and genetic factors (Das, Kirby, & Jarman, 1975). Hence, at one level of analysis, individual differences essentially are regarded as error variance and, at another level, individual differences are of primary interest. The former conceptualization has been reported more extensively in the research literature, although some effort has been directed to the assessment of individual differences in information-processing styles (for example, Kaufman & Kaufman, 1983).

As Kaufman and Kaufman (1983) summarized, although many different tasks and techniques of data analysis have been used, these two styles of human information processing have emerged for a variety of groups, including samples from differing developmental, IQ, and achievement levels, as well as from differing socioeconomic backgrounds, cultures, and clinical subgroups (Das, Kirby, & Jarman, 1975, 1979; McCallum & Merritt, 1983). Thus these constructs appear fairly robust to variations in samples, tasks, and analytic techniques, and evidence for convergent validity is increasing (Beller, 1970; Cohen, 1972, 1973; Klatzky & Atkinson, 1971; Patterson & Bradshaw, 1975; Schneider & Sheffrin, 1977; Sheffrin & Schneider, 1977).

Neuropsychological Issues

There is some controversy among neuropsychologically oriented researchers and practitioners regarding the functional cerebral organization for successive and simultaneous processing. In describing the construction of their battery, Kaufman and Kaufman (1983) suggested that linking these two types of processing to particular anatomical areas in the brain should not affect interpretations of their tests and, in this sense, suggested that the concept of cerebral organization for successive and simultaneous processing may be unimportant, at least in terms of individual assessment. Conversely, many neuropsychologists have shown interest in this topic, and Luria (1980), in particular, considered successive processing to be primarily a function of fronto-temporal (or anterior) regions of the brain, but simultaneous processing to be primarily a function of occipito-parietal (or posterior) regions. Thus, although it may be inaccurate to impose a strict localizationist orientation on this issue, relative cerebral specializatons for the processing of certain types of tasks are not unimportant. Although writing from a perspective of relative degrees of specialization of the cerebral hemispheres, Kinsbourne and Hiscock (1983) articulated the importance of this issue by emphasizing the value of research efforts directed at an empirically based understanding of brain organization. Similarly, Luria (1980) emphasized the importance of specific contributions of components of functional systems to the performance of various cognitive processes.

In contrast to Luria's conceptualization of the cerebral specializations for successive and simultaneous processing, other researchers have suggested anatomical divisions in terms of the cerebral hemispheres. As noted previously, results of a number of investigations (for example, Gazzaniga, 1970; Levy & Trevarthen, 1976; Nebes, 1974) have suggested that successive (or analytic) processing is primarily a function of the left cerebral hemisphere and simultaneous (or holistic) processing is primarily a function of the right cerebral hemisphere.

Processing-Style and Presentation/Response-Modality Confound.

Much of the research in this area has been difficult to interpret appropriately because of a confound inherent within many cognitive behaviors. This confound involves two variables: style of processing and modality of presentation/response. The distinction between these variables is important particularly in consideration of the relatively robust verbal/nonverbal distinctions of the left and right cerebral hemispheres (for example, Gazzaniga, 1970; Kinsbourne, 1978; Segalowitz, 1983; Springer & Deutsch, 1981), which were previously discussed. Successively processed tasks are more often presented and responded to verbally, and simultaneously processed tasks are more often presented and responded to nonverbally. Hence, unless predictor variables are precisely identified and clearly separated, results of research and efforts to assess the effectiveness of strategies employing these variables cannot be appropriately evaluated.

This confound, although relatively neglected in this literature, has not been completely ignored. Torgesen, Bowen, and Ivey (1978), for example, studied both variables in samples of good and poor readers. Results suggested that task structure was a more powerful predictor of individual differences on a test related to reading difficulty than to presentation/response modality. Although these results should be replicated with other tasks and samples in order to ensure their generalizability, they emphasize the dangers associated with ignoring this confound. Such results, for example, may account for the common finding that teaching to preferred modalities does not result in better academic performances for children. The assumption that children learn best when taught via a method that capitalizes on their strongest sensory modality is intuitively appealing, particularly to educators, but comprehensive reviews of research (for example, Kampwirth, 1979) have shown that data simply do not support this assumption.

THE INTEGRATION OF INTELLIGENCE AND NEUROLOGY: DIRECTIONS FOR FUTURE RESEARCH

The integration of known neurological principles with definitions of intelligence is a speculative endeavor at the present time. As discussed, much is currently known about neuroanatomy, and the theoretical framework imposed on this field by Luria (1980) has provided a useful organizational scheme for its continued study. The three functional units of the brain—namely the arousal, the sensory input, and the organization and planning (output) units—are particularly important in understanding the neurological basis for intellectual behavior. Past research efforts have provided some significant insights, as well, regarding functional (as opposed to anatomical) cerebral organization. These research efforts have suggested possible cortical and subcortical regions specialized for the processing of particular intellectual/cognitive behaviors. However, much research continues to be necessary to refine our understanding of the integration of intelligence and neurology—concepts that are essential for all human performance.

One major issue remaining to be resolved concerns the relative cerebro-anatomical specializations for two fundamental styles of information processing—successive and simultaneous. The robust statistical independence of these factors strongly suggests that differential neurological substrata are involved. Although some research has suggested a cerebral hemispheric division (for example, Levy & Trevarthen, 1976), Luria (1980), on the basis of extensive clinical investigation, postulated an anterior/posterior division for successive and simultaneous processing, respectively. Possibly because of greater availability for study, higher level of saliency, or lack of appropriate methodology, most American researchers in functional cerebral organization have chosen to study the cortical functions of the cerebral hemispheres. Currently, the study of functional cerebral organization would benefit from additional interest to include other orientations to cortical division. For example, to date, functional cerebral distance has been studied primarily in the context of cerebral hemispheric divisions of the brain. The logic of the principle, however, could be extended to include anterior/posterior divisions as well. Here, a behavior processed through a given functional system involving components primarily associated with fronto-temporal regions of the brain would be predicted to exert relatively minimal interference (within limits imposed by association fibers) on an orthogonal, concurrent behavior processed through a functional system involving components primarily associated with occipito-parietal regions of the brain. If this is a reasonable generalization from the principle of functional cerebral distance, then time-sharing (or dual-task) paradigms could be used to demonstrate this extrapolation. Thus, although right- and left-handed motor performances are generally contralaterally represented, the concentrations of cortical neuronal activation are relatively more anterior than posterior. Based on the principle of functional cerebral distance, manual-motor performance (regardless of the hand used) would therefore be predicted to interfere to a greater extent with behaviors processed in fronto-temporal than in occipito-parietal cortical regions of the brain.

Particularly important in future investigations of successive and simultaneous processing is the clear separation of potential processing style and presentation/response modality confounds. Within the four cells of the two-by-two matrix delimited by these variables, two cells—that is, successive-nonverbal and simultaneous-verbal—have been relatively neglected in the research literature. Given the importance of both variables to our understanding of intellectual behavior and brain functioning, their clear separation will permit more meaningful interpretations of data on functional cerebral organization. Initial research might seek to establish empirically tasks comprised by these two relatively neglected cells. In this instance, continued factor-analytic investigations may prove useful. Is it meaningful, for example, to consider simultaneous-verbal tasks, and, if so, what relationships do they have with the general class of intellectual behavior or g?

Although requiring perhaps a higher degree of technical sophistication, techniques to assess regional cerebral blood flow present substantial opportunities to improve on our current level of knowledge concerning the integration of intelligence with neurology (or cortical functioning). Such techniques provide more direct, as opposed to inferential, evidence for functional cerebral organization and the elucidation of the functional systems involved in a variety of intellectual behaviors.

Researchers investigating functional cerebral organization should also be aware of the highly differentiated and complex neural connections involved in even the most seemingly discrete behaviors and avoid the too common exclusive focus on cortical structures. As noted previously, our understanding of the importance of subcortical structures to intellectual behavior has improved substantially in recent years. Even so, much is still to be learned about the anatomical organization of the central nervous system, and serious students of the field of intelligence should at least be aware of the ongoing research in this area. As Brodal (1981) articulated,

> *The investigation of the nervous system in all its detail is a prerequisite for progress in studies of its function.* Every function is carried out by a structure, and conclusions about functions without reference to the structures involved will remain incomplete and easily may lead us astray. [p. 851, emphasis original]

It is in this spirit that we have approached the task of describing the neurological basis of intelligence. We believe that any understanding of the nature of intellectual behavior is incomplete in the absence of consideration, albeit speculative at this point, of the neurological substrata involved. The basic structural (morphologic) organization of the brain as presented here has provided a working, fundamental orientation for subsequent discussion of possible functional aspects of the general systems involved in the processing of intellectual behavior. We have presented an empirical view of functional cerebral organization, but we have emphasized more the methodological aspects of this research and less the results of data. Through such emphasis we recognize the evolving nature of research in, and our potential for the eventual understanding of, the neurological basis of intelligence.

REFERENCES

Ammons, R. B., & Ammons, C. H. (1970). Decremental and related processes in skilled performance. In L. E. Smith (Ed.), *Psychology of motor learning.* Chicago: Athletic Institute.

Ariel, R. N., & Golden, C. J. (1981, October). *Regional cerebral blood flow in schizophrenics with the ¹³³Xenon Inhalation method.* Paper presented at the annual convention of the National Academy of Neuropsychologists, Orlando.

Bastian, H. C. (1869). On the various forms of loss of speech in cerebral disease. *British and Foreign Medico-Surgical Review, 43,* 470–492.

Bay, E. (1953). Disturbances of visual perception and their examination. *Brain, 76,* 515–550.

Beller, H. K. (1970). Parallel and serial stages in matching. *Journal of Experimental Psychology, 84,* 213–219.

Bender, M. B., & Feldman, M. (1972). The so-called 'visual agnosias.' *Brain, 9,* 173–186.

Benson, D. F., & Geschwind, N. (1968). Cerebral dominance and its disturbances. *Pediatric Clinics of North America, 15,* 759–769.

Benton, A. L. (1959). *Right-left discrimination and finger localization: Development and pathology.* New York: Hoeber.

Benton, A. L. (1961). The fiction of the Gerstmann syndrome. *Journal of Neurology, Neurosurgery, and Psychiatry, 24,* 176–181.

Benton, A. L. (1977). Reflections on the Gerstmann syndrome. *Brain and Language, 4,* 45–62.

Bertelson, P. (1963). S-R relationships and reaction times to new versus repeated signals in a serial task. *Journal of Experimental Psychology, 65,* 478–484.

Bertelson, P. (1965). Serial choice reaction-time as a function of response versus signal-and-response repetition. *Nature, 206,* 217–218.

Blinkov, S. M., & Glezer, I. I. (1968). *The human brain in figures and tables.* New York: Plenum.

Bogen, J. (1969). The other side of the brain. II. An appositional mind. *Bulletin of the Los Angeles Neurological Society, 34,* 135–162.

Bogen, J. E. (1975). Some educational aspects of hemispheric specialization. *U.C.L.A. Educator, 17,* 24–32.

Bogen, J. E., & Gordon, H. W. (1971). Musical tests for functional lateralization with intracarotid amobarbital. *Nature, 230,* 524–525.

Bowers, D., Heilman, K. M., Satz, P., & Altman, A. (1975). *Intrahemispheric competition. Simultaneous performance on motor, verbal, and nonverbal tasks by right-handed adults.* Paper presented at the meeting of the International Neuropsychological Society, Toronto.

Bremer, F. (1966). Le corps calleux dans la dynamique cérébrale. *Experientia, 22,* 1–8.

Briggs, G. G. (1975). A comparison of attentional and control shift models of the performance of concurrent tasks. *Acta Psychologica, 39,* 183–191.

Briggs, G. G., & Kinsbourne, M. (1978). *Cerebral organization revealed by multilimb tracking performance.* Manuscript submitted for publication.

Broca, P. (1861). Nouvelle observation d'aphemie produite par une lesion de la moite posterieure des deuxieme et troisieme circonvolutions frontales. *Bulletin de la Society Anatomique de Paris, 36,* 398–407.

Brodal, A. (1981). *Neurological anatomy in relation to clinical medicine* (3rd ed.). New York: Oxford University Press.

Burt, C. (1937). *The backward child.* New York: Appleton-Century-Crofts.

Butler, S. R., & Norrsell, U. (1968). Vocalization possibly initiated by the minor hemisphere. *Nature, 220,* 793–794.

Cattell, R. B. (1963). Theory of fluid and crystallized intelligence: A critical experiment. *Journal of Educational Psychology, 54,* 1–22.

Cernacek, J. (1961). Contralateral motor irradiation-cerebral dominance: Its changes in hemisparesis. *Archives of Neurology, 4,* 165–172.

Charcot, J. M. (1889). On a case of sudden and isolated suppression of the mental vision of signs and objects (forms and colours). *Clinical Lectures of Diseases of the Nervous System* (Vol. III). London: The New Sydenham Society.

Cohen, G. (1972). Hemispheric differences in a letter classification task. *Perception & Psychophysics, 11,* 139–142.

Cohen, G. (1973). Hemispheric differences in serial versus parallel processing. *Journal of Experimental Psychology, 97,* 349–356.

Cohen, L. (1970). Interaction between limbs during bimanual activity. *Brain, 93,* 259–272.

Coltheart, M. (1980). Deep dyslexia: A review of the syndrome. In M. Coltheart, K. Patterson, & J. C. Marshall (Eds.), *Deep dyslexia.* Boston: Routledge & Kegan Paul.

Conrad, K. (1948). Beitrag zum problem der parietalen alexia. *Archives Psychologie, 181,* 398–420.

Cook, T. W. (1933a). Studies in cross education. I. Mirror tracing the star-shaped maze. *Journal of Experimental Psychology, 16,* 144–160.

Cook, T. W. (1933b). Studies in cross education. II. Further experiments in mirror tracing the star-shaped maze. *Journal of Experimental Psychology, 16,* 679–700.

Cook, T. W. (1934). Studies in cross education. III. Kinesthetic learning of an irregular pattern. *Journal of Experimental Psychology, 17,* 749–762.

Corballis, M. C. (1980). Laterality and myth. *American Psychologist, 35,* 284–295.

Critchley, M. (1953). *The parietal lobes.* London: Edward Arnold.

Damasio, A. (1979). The frontal lobes. In K. M. Heilman & E. Valenstein (Eds.), *Clinical neuropsychology.* New York: Oxford University Press.

Das, J. P., Kirby, J. R., & Jarman, R. F. (1975). Simultaneous and successive synthesis: An alternative model for cognitive abilities. *Psychological Bulletin, 82,* 87–103.

Das, J. P., Kirby, J. R., & Jarman, R. F. (1979). *Simultaneous and successive cognitive processes.* New York: Academic Press.

Dejerine, J. (1914). *Semiologie des affections du systeme nerveaux.* Paris: Masson.

de Lacoste-Utamsing, C., & Holloway, R. L. (1982). Sexual dimorphism in the human corpus callosum. *Science, 216,* 1431–1432.

Dimond, S. J., & Beaumont, J. G. (1974). Experimental studies of hemisphere function in the human brain. In S. J. Dimond & J. G. Beaumont (Eds.), *Hemisphere function in the human brain.* New York: Wiley.

Drake, W. E. (1968). Clinical and pathological findings in a child with a developmental learning disability. *Journal of Learning Disabilities, 1,* 486–502.

Dykman, R. A., Wallis, R. C., Suzuki, T., Ackerman, P. T., & Peters, J. E. (1970). Children with learning disabilities: Conditioning differentiation and the effect of distraction. *American Journal of Orthopsychiatry, 40,* 766–782.

Dykman, R. A., Wallis, R. C., Suzuki, T., Ackerman, P. T., & Peters, J. E. (1971). Children with learning disabilities: An attentional deficit syndrome. In H. R. Myklebust (Ed.), *Progress in learning disabilities* (Vol. III). New York: Grune & Stratton.

Eccles, J. C. (1977). Evolution of the brain in relation to the development of the self-conscious mind. In S. J. Dimond & D. A. Blizard (Eds.), Evolution and lateralization of the brain. *Annals of the New York Academy of Science, 299,* 161–279.

Eidelberg, D., & Galaburda, A. M. (1983). Symmetry and asymmetry in the human posterior thalamus: I. Cytoarchitectonic analysis in normal persons. *Archives of Neurology, 39,* 325–332.

Fadely, J. L., & Hosler, V. N. (1983). *Case studies in left and right hemisphere functioning.* Springfield, IL: Thomas.

Falzi, G., Perrone, P., & Vignolo, L. A. (1982). Right-left asymmetry in anterior speech region. *Archives of Neurology, 39,* 239–240.

Filskov, S. B., Grimm, B. H., & Lewis, J. A. (1981). Brain-behavior relationships. In S. B. Filskov & T. J. Boll (Eds.), *Handbook of clinical neuropsychology.* New York: Wiley.

Friedman, A., & Polsan, M. C. (1981). Hemispheres as independent resource systems: Limited-capacity processing and cerebral specialization. *Journal of Experimental Psychology: Human Perception and Performance, 7,* 1031–1058.

Fuster, J. M., & Jervey, J. P. (1981). Inferotemporal neurons distinguish and retain behaviorally relevant features of visual stimuli. *Science, 212,* 952–955.

Gaddes, W. H. (1980). *Learning disabilities and brain function: A neuropsychological approach.* New York: Springer-Verlag.

Galaburda, A. M., & Kemper, T. L. (1979). Cytoarchitectonic abnormalities in developmental dyslexia: A case study. *Annals of Neurology, 6,* 94–100.

Galaburda, A. M., LeMay, M., Kemper, T. L., & Geschwind, N. (1978). Right-left asymmetries in the brain. *Science, 199,* 852–856.

Galaburda, A. M., Sanides, F., & Geschwind, N. (1978). Human brain: Cytoarchitectonic left-right asymmetries in temporal speech region. *Archives of Neurology, 35,* 812.

Galaburda, A. M., Sherman, G. F., & Geschwind, N. (1984). Developmental dyslexia: Third consecutive case with cortical abnormalities. *Science.*

Gall, F. J. (1825). *Sur les fonctions du cerveau et sur cells de ses parties* (six volumes). Paris: Bailliere.

Galloway, L. M. (1982). Bilingualism: Neuropsychological considerations. *Journal of Research and Development in Education, 15,* 12–28.

Gardner, E. (1975). *Fundamentals of neurology.* Philadelphia: Saunders.

Gazzaniga, M. S. (1970). *The bisected brain.* New York: Appleton-Century-Crofts.

Gazzaniga, M. S., & Le Doux, J. E. (1978). *The integrated mind.* New York: Plenum.

Gerstmann, J. (1924). Fingeragnosie: eine unschriebene störung der orientierung am eigerst körper. *Wein Klin. Wchnschr., 37,* 1010–1012.

Gerstmann, J. (1957). Some notes on the Gerstmann Syndrome. *Neurology, 7,* 866–869.

Geschwind, N. (1965). Disconnection syndromes in animals and man. *Brain, 88,* 237–294.

Geschwind, N. (1974). Anatomical foundations of language and dominance. In C. L. Ludlow & M. E. Doran-Quine (Eds.), *The neurological bases of language disorders in children: Methods and directions for research.* Bethesda: U.S. Department of Health, Education and Welfare (NIH Publication No. 79-440).

Geschwind, N. (1979). Anatomical foundations of language and dominance. In C. L. Ludlow & M. E. Doran-Quine (Eds.), *The neurological bases of language disorders in children: Methods and directions for research* (NIH Publication No. 79-440). Bethesda: U.S. Department of Health, Education and Welfare.

Geschwind, N., & Levitsky, W. (1968). Human brain: Left-right asymmetries in temporal speech region. *Science, 161,* 186–187.

Golden, C. J. (1981). The Luria-Nebraska Children's Battery: Theory and initial formulation. In G. W. Hynd & J. E. Obrzut (Eds.), *Neuropyschologicial assessment and the school-age child: Issues and procedures.* New York: Grune & Stratton.

Goldstein, K. (1948). *Language and language disturbances.* New York: Grune & Stratton.

Gordon, H. W., & Bogen, J. E. (1974). Hemispheric lateralization of singing after intracarotid sodium amylobarbitone. *Journal of Neurology, Neurosurgery, and Psychiatry, 37,* 727–738.

Gross, C. G., & Weiskrantz, L. (1964). Some changes in behavior produced by lateral frontal lesions in the macaque. In J. M. Warren & K. Akert (Eds.), *The frontal granular cortex and behavior.* New York: McGraw-Hill.

Guilford, J. P. (1968). Intelligence has three facets. *Science, 160,* 615–620.

Guilford, J. P., & Hoepfner, R. (1971). *The analysis of intelligence.* New York: McGraw-Hill.

Hagberg, B. (1978). Defects of immediate memory related to the cerebral blood flow distribution. *Brain and Language, 5,* 366–377.

Halstead, W. C. (1947). *Brain and intelligence: A quantitative study of the frontal lobes.* Chicago: University of Chicago Press.

Halstead, W. C. (1951). Biological intelligence. *Journal of Personality, 20,* 118–130.

Hardyck, C., Petrinovitch, L. F., & Goldman, R. (1976). Left handedness and cognitive deficit. *Cortex, 12,* 266–278.

Head, H. (1926). *Aphasia and kindred disorders of speech.* Cambridge: Cambridge University Press.

Hebb, D. O., & Penfield, W. (1940). Human behavior after extensive bilateral removals from the frontal lobes. *Archives of Neurology and Psychiatry, 44,* 421–438.

Heilman, K. M., & Valenstein, E. (Eds.) (1979). *Clinical neuropsychology.* New York: Oxford University Press.

Henschen, S. E. (1922). *Klinische und anatomische bertrage zur pathologie der gehirns.* Stockholm: Almquist und Wiksell.

Heron, W. (1957). Perception as a function of retinal locus and attention. *American Journal of Psychology, 70,* 38–48.

Hicks, R. E. (1975). Intrahemispheric response competition between vocal and unimanual performance in normal adult human males. *Journal of Comparative and Physiological Psychology, 89,* 50–60.

Hicks, R. E., Bradshaw, G. J., Kinsbourne, M., & Feigin, D. S. (1978). Vocal-manual trade-offs in hemispheric sharing of performance control. *Journal of Motor Behavior, 10,* 1–6.

Hicks, R. E., Provenzano, F. J., & Rybstein, E. D. (1975). Generalized and lateralized effects of concurrent verbal rehearsal upon performance of sequential movements of the fingers by the left and right hands. *Acta Psychologica, 39,* 119–130.

Hiscock, M. (1982). Verbal-manual time sharing in children as a function of task priority. *Brain and Cognition, 1,* 119–131.

Horn, J. L. (1968). Organization of abilities and the development of intelligence. *Psychological Review, 75,* 242–259.

Hynd, G. W., & Cohen, M. (1983). *Dyslexia: Neuropsychological theory, research and clinical differentiation.* New York: Grune & Stratton.

Hynd, G. W., & Hynd, C. R. (1984). Dyslexia: Neuroanatomical/neurolinguistic perspectives. *Reading Research Quarterly, 19,* 482–498.

Hynd, G. W., Obrzut, J. E., & Obrzut, A. (1981). Are lateral and perceptual asymmetries related to WISC-R and achievement test performance in normal and learning disabled children? *Journal of Consulting and Clinical Psychology, 49,* 977–979.

Ingvar, D. H., & Schwartz, M. (1974). Blood flow patterns induced in the dominant hemisphere by speech and reading. *Brain, 97,* 274–288.

Jackson, J. H. (1874). On the nature of the duality of the brain. *Medical Press Circulator, 1,* 19, 41, 46.

Jackson, J. H. (1876). Case of large cerebral tumor without optic neuritis and with left hemiplegia and imperception. *Review Ophthalmology Hospital Report, 8,* 434.

Jacobson, S. (1972). Neuroembryology. In B. A. Curtis, S. Jacobson, & E. M. Marcus (Eds.), *An introduction to the neurosciences.* Philadelphia: Saunders.

Jensen, A. R. (1979). The nature of intelligence and its relation to learning. *Journal of Research and Development in Education, 12,* 79–95.

Jerison, H. J. (1961). Quantitative analysis of evolution of the brain in mammals. *Science, 133,* 1012–1014.

Kampwirth, T. J. (1979). Teaching to preferred modalities: Is it worth it? *Claremont Reading Conference,* 163–176.

Kantowitz, B. H., & Knight, J. L., Jr. (1976). An experimenter-limited processes. *Psychological Review, 83,* 502–507.

Kaufman, A. S. (1979). Cerebral specialization and intelligence testing. *Journal of Research and Development in Education, 12,* 96–107.

Kaufman, A. S., & Kaufman, N. L. (1983). *Kaufman Assessment Battery for Children: Interpretive manual.* Circle Pines, MN: American Guidance Service.

Kaufman, A. S., Zalma, R., & Kaufman, N. L. (1978). The relationship of hand dominance to the motor coordination, mental ability, and right-left awareness of young normal children: *Child Development, 49,* 885–888.

Kety, S. S., & Schmidt, C. F. (1945). The determination of cerebral blood flow in man by use of nitrous oxide in low concentrations. *American Journal of Physiology, 143,* 53–66.

Kimura, D. (1961). Cerebral dominance and the perception of verbal stimuli. *Canadian Journal of Psychology, 15,* 166–171.

Kimura, D. (1966). Dual functional asymmetry of the brain in visual perception. *Neuropsychologia, 4*, 275–285.

Kimura, D. (1973a). The asymmetry of the human brain. *Scientific American, 288*, 360–368.

Kimura, D. (1973b). Manual activity during speaking—I. Right-handers. *Neuropsychologia, 11*, 45–50.

Kimura, D. (1973c). Manual activity during speaking—II. Left-handers. *Neuropsychologia, 11*, 51–55.

King, F. L., & Kimura, D. (1972). Left-ear superiority in dichotic perception of vocal nonverbal sounds. *Canadian Journal of Psychology, 26*, 111–116.

Kinsbourne, M. (Ed.) (1978). *Asymmetrical function of the brain.* New York: Cambridge University Press.

Kinsbourne, M. (1981). Single-channel theory. In D. Holding (Ed.), *Human skills.* New York: Wiley.

Kinsbourne, M., & Cook, J. (1971). Generalized and lateralized effects of concurrent verbalization on a unimanual skill. *Quarterly Journal of Experimental Psychology, 23*, 341–345.

Kinsbourne, M., & Hicks, R. E. (1978). Functional cerebral space: A model for overflow, transfer and interference effects in human performance: A tutorial review. In J. Requin (Ed.), *Attention and performance VII.* Hillsdale, NJ: Erlbaum.

Kinsbourne, M., & Hiscock, M. (1983). Asymmetires of dual-task performance. In J. B. Hellige (Ed.), *Cerebral hemisphere asymmetry.* New York: Praeger.

Kinsbourne, M., & Sewitch, D. (1975). *Gaze and gesture during mental activity.* Paper presented at the meeting of the International Neuropsychology Society, Tampa, Florida.

Klatzky, R., & Atkinson, R. (1971). Specialization of the cerebral hemispheres in scanning for information in short-term memory. *Perception & Psychophysics, 10*, 335–338.

Lashley, K. S. (1938). Factors limiting recovery after central nervous lesion. *Journal of Nervous and Mental Diseases, 88*, 733–755.

Levy, J., & Trevarthen, C. (1976). Metacontrol of hemispheric function in human split-brain patients. *Journal of Experimental Psychology: Human Perception and Performance, 2*, 299–312.

Ley, R. G., & Bryden, M. P. (1979). Hemispheric differences in recognizing faces and emotions. *Brain and Language, 7*, 127–138.

Lichtheim, L. (1885). On aphasia. *Brain, 7*, 433–484.

Luria, A. R. (1959). Disorders of simultaneous perception in a case of bilateral occipito-parietal brain injury. *Brain, 82*, 437–449.

Luria, A. R. (1969). Frontal lobe syndromes. In P. J. Vicken & G. W. Bruyn (Eds.), *Handbook of clinical neurology* (Vol. II). Amsterdam: North Holland Publishing Company.

Luria, A. R. (1970). *Traumatic aphasia: Its syndromes, psychology and treatment.* The Hague: Mouton.

Luria, A. R. (1973). *The working brain.* New York: Basic Books.

Luria, A. R. (1980). *Higher cortical functions in man.* New York: Basic Books.

MacInnes, W. D. (1981, October). *Aging and its relationship to neuropsychological and neurological measures.* Paper presented at the annual convention of the National Academy of Neuropsychologists, Orlando.

Mahl, G. F., Rothenberg, A., Delgado, J. M., & Hamlin, H. (1964). Psychological responses in the human to intracerebral electrical stimulation. *Psychosomatic Medicine, 26*, 337–368.

Marcus, E. M. (1972). Cerebral cortex. In B. A. Curtis, S. Jacobson, & E. M. Marcus (Eds.), *An introduction to the neurosciences.* Philadelphia: Saunders.

Marie, P. (1906, May). Revision de la question de l'aphasie: Le 3ᵉ circonvolution frontale gauche ne jove aucum role speciale dans la fonction du language. *Semaine Medicale,* pp. 241–247.

Marshall, J. C., & Newcombe, F. (1973). Patterns of paralexia: A psycholinguistic approach. *Journal of Psycholinguistic Research, 2*, 175–199.

Matarazzo, J. D. (1976). *Wechsler's measurement and appraisal of adult intelligence.* Baltimore: Williams & Wilkins.

Maximilian, V. A. (1980). *Functional changes in the cortex during mental activation.* Sweden: CWK Gleerup.

McCallum, R. S., & Merritt, F. M. (1983). Simultaneous-successive processing among college students. *Journal of Psychoeducational Assessment, 1,* 85–93.

McCulloch, M. S. (1944). Functional organization of the cerebral cortex. *Psychological Review, 23,* 390–407.

Meyer, V., & Yates, A. J. (1955). Intellectual changes following temporal lobectomy for psychomotor epilepsy. *Journal of Neurology, Neurosurgery and Psychiatry, 18,* 44–52.

Milner, B. (1958). Psychological deficits produced by temporal lobe excision. *Research Publications of the Association for Research on Nervous and Mental Disease, 36,* 244–257.

Milner, B. (1967). Brain mechanisms suggested by studies of the temporal lobes. In C. H. Millikan & F. L. Darley (Eds.), *Brain mechanisms underlying speech and language.* New York: Grune & Stratton.

Milner, B., Branch, C., & Rasmussen, T. (1964). Observations on cerebral dominance. In A. V. S. deKeuck & M. O'Connor (Eds.), *Ciba foundation symposium on disorders of language.* London: Churchill.

Milner, P. M. (1970). *Physiological psychology.* New York: Holt, Rinehart and Winston.

Mishkin, M., & Forgays, D. G. (1952). Word recognition as a function of retinal locus. *Journal of Experimental Psychology, 43,* 43–48.

Navon, D., & Gopher, D. (1979). On the economy of the human-processing system. *Psychological Review, 86,* 214–225.

Navon, D., & Gopher, D. (1980). Task difficulty, resources and dual task performance. In R. S. Nickerson (Ed.), *Attention and performance VIII.* Hillsdale, NJ: Erlbaum.

Nebes, R. D. (1974). Hemispheric specialization in commissurotomized man. *Psychological Bulletin, 81,* 1–14.

Neisser, U. (1967). *Cognitive psychology.* New York: Appleton-Century-Crofts.

Norman, D. A., & Bobrow, D. G. (1975). On data-limited and resource-limited processes. *Cognitive Psychology, 7,* 44–64.

Norman, D. A., & Bobrow, D. G. (1976). On the analysis of performance operating characteristics. *Psychological Review, 83,* 508–510.

Olesen, J. (1971). Contralateral focal increase of cerebral blood flow in man during arm work. *Brain, 94,* 635–646.

Passler, M., Isaac, W., & Hynd, G. W. (1984). *Development of frontal lobe behaviors in children.* Manuscript submitted for publication.

Patterson, K., & Bradshaw, J. L. (1975). Differential hemispheric mediation of nonverbal visual stimuli. *Journal of Experimental Psychology: Human Perception and Performance, 1,* 246–252.

Penfield, W. (1959). The interpretive cortex. *Science, 129,* 1719–1725.

Penfield, W., & Rasmussen, T. (1955). *The cerebral cortex of man.* New York: Macmillan.

Penfield, W., & Roberts, L. (1959). *Speech and brain mechanisms.* Princeton: Princeton University Press.

Pirozzolo, F. J. (1978). Cerebral asymmetries and reading acquisition. *Academic Therapy, 13,* 261–266.

Prohovnik, I. (1980). *Mapping brainwork.* Gotab, Sweden: Gleerup.

Rabbitt, P. (1965). Response facilitation on repetition of a limb movement. *British Journal of Psychology, 56,* 303–304.

Reitan, R. M. (1955). Certain differential effects of left and right cerebral lesions in human adults. *Journal of Comparative Physiological Psychology, 48,* 474.

Reitan, R. M. (1956). Investigation of relationships between "psychometric" and "biological" intelligence. *Journal of Nervous and Mental Disease, 123,* 536–541.

Reitan, R. M. (1974). Psychological effects of cerebral lesions in children of early school-age. In R. M. Reitan & L. A. Davison (Eds.), *Clinical neuropsychology: Current status and applications.* Washington, DC: Winston.

Risberg, J. (1980). Regional cerebral blood flow measurements by [133]XE inhalation: Methodology and application in neuropsychology and psychiatry. *Brain and Language, 9,* 9–34.

Risberg, J., Halsey, J. H., Wills, E. L., & Wilson, E. M. (1975). Hemispheric specialization in normal man studied by bilateral measurement of the regional cerebral blood flow. *Brain, 98,* 511–524.

Risberg, J., Maximilian, V. A., & Prohovnik, I. (1977). Changes of cortical activity patterns during habituation to a reasoning task. A study with the [133]XE inhalation technique for measurement of regional cerebral blood flow. *Neuropsychologia, 15,* 793–798.

Roeltgen, D. P., & Heilman, K. M. (1984). *A neuropsychological and anatomic model of writing.* Manuscript submitted for publication.

Rosen, G. D., & Galaburda, A. M. (1984). Development of language: A question of asymmetry and deviation. In J. Mehler & R. Fox (Eds.), *Neonate cognition: Beyond the blooming buzzing confusion.* Hillsdale, NJ: Erlbaum.

Rosenzweig, M. R., & Leiman, A. L. (1982). *Physiological psychology.* Lexington, MA: Heath.

Rubens, A. B. (1979). Agnosia. In K. M. Heilman & E. Valenstein (Eds.), *Clinical neuropsychology.* New York: Oxford University Press.

Schepers, G. W. H. (1938). The corpus callosum and related structures in the South African negro brain. *American Journal of Physical Anthropology, 24,* 161–184.

Schneider, W., & Sheffrin, R. M. (1977). Controlled and automatic human information processing: I. Detection, search, and attention. *Psychological Review, 84,* 1–66.

Segalowitz, S. J. (1983). *Two sides of the brain.* Englewood Cliffs, NJ: Prentice-Hall.

Selnes, O. A. (1974). The corpus callosum: Some anatomical and functional considerations with special reference to language. *Brain and Language, 1,* 111–140.

Sheffrin, R. M., & Schneider, W. (1977). Controlled and automatic human information processing: II. Perceptual learning, automatic attending, and a general theory. *Psychological Review, 84,* 127–190.

Spearman, C. (1927). *The abilities of man: Their nature and measurement.* New York: Macmillan.

Sperry, R. W. (1964). The great cerebral commissure. *Scientific American, 210,* 240–250.

Sperry, R. W. (1968). Hemispheric deconnection and unity in conscious awareness. *American Psychologist, 23,* 723–733.

Sperry, R. W. (1974). Lateral specialization in the surgically separated hemispheres. In F. O. Schmitt & F. G. Worden (Eds.), *The neurosciences third study program.* Cambridge: MIT Press.

Spitzka, E. A. (1905). Report of a study of the brains of six eminent scientists and scholars belonging to the American Anthropometric Society; Together with a brief description of the skull of one of them. *American Journal of Anatomy, 4,* 3.

Springer, S. P., & Deutsch, G. (1981). *Left brain, right brain.* San Francisco: Freeman.

Thorndike, E. L., Bregman, E. O., Cobb, M. V., & Woodyard, E. (1927). *The measurement of intelligence.* New York: Teachers College.

Thurstone, L. L. (1938). Primary mental abilities. *Psychometric Monographs* (No. 1). Chicago: University of Chicago Press.

Torgesen, J. K., Bowen, C., & Ivey, C. (1978). Task structure versus modality of presentation: A study of the construct validity of the Visual-Aural Digit Span Test. *Journal of Educational Psychology, 70,* 451–456.

Ukhtomskii, A.A., (1945). *Essays on the physiology of the nervous system,* collected works (Vol. 4). Leningrad.

Ullman, D. G. (1977). Children's lateral preference patterns: Frequency and relationships with achievement and intelligence. *Journal of School Psychology, 15,* 36–43.

Valsiner, J. (1983). Hemispheric specialization and integration in child development. In S. J. Segalowitz (Ed.), *Language functions and brain organization.* New York: Academic Press.

Wada, J. A., Clarke, R., & Hamm, A. (1975). Cerebral hemispheric asymmetry in humans. *Archives of Neurology, 32,* 239–246.

Wada, J. A., & Rasmussen, T. (1960). Intracarotid injection of sodium amytal for the lateralization of cerebral speech dominance: Experimental and clinical observations. *Journal of Neurosurgery, 17,* 266–282.

Weinberger, D. R., Luchins, D. J., Morihisa, J., & Wyatt, R. J. (1982). Asymmetrical volumes of the right and left frontal and occipital regions of the human brain. *Neurology, 11,* 97–100.

Weinstein, S. (1978). Functional cerebral hemispheric asymmetry. In M. Kinsbourne (Ed.), *Asymmetrical function of the brain.* New York: Cambridge University Press.

Weisenburg, T. S., & McBride, K. C. (1964). *Aphasia.* New York: Hafner.

Wernicke, C. (1874). *Der aphasiche symptemkomplex.* Breslaw: Cohn and Weigert.

Whitaker, H. A. (1976). Neurobiology of language. In E. R. Carterette & M. P. Friedman (Eds.), *Handbook of perception* (Vol. VII). New York: Academic Press.

Wilson, S. A. K. (1926). *Aphasia.* London: Kegan Paul.

Witelson, S. F. (1974). Hemispheric specialization for linguistic and nonlinguistic tactual perception using a dichotomous stimulation technique. *Cortex, 10,* 3–17.

Witelson, S. F. (1983). Bumps on the brain: Right-left anatomic asymmetry as a key to functional lateralization. In S. J. Segalowitz (Ed.), *Language functions and brain organization.* New York: Academic Press.

Witelson, S. F., & Pallie, W. (1973). Left hemisphere specialization for language in the newborn: Neuroanatomical evidence of asymmetry. *Brain, 96,* 641–646.

Witherspoon, Y. T. (1960). Brain weight and behavior. *Human Biology, 32,* 366–369.

Zaidel, D., & Sperry, R. W. (1973). Performance on the Raven's Coloured Progressive Matrices Test by subjects with cerebral commissurotomy. *Cortex, 9,* 34–39.

FOUR

GENETIC EPISTEMOLOGY AND THE DEVELOPMENT OF INTELLIGENCE

GERALD E. GRUEN
Purdue University
West Lafayette, Indiana

OVERVIEW

Jean Piaget was a remarkable person who spent the major portion of his life trying to integrate two diverse areas of intellectual endeavor: biology and epistemology. He became interested in problems of a biological nature in his youth and published his first article, a description of an albino sparrow, in a natural history magazine when he was only 11 years old. His interest in living things deepened throughout his adolescent years. Between 15 and 18 years of age (cf. Piaget, 1952a, for his autobiography), he published a series of articles reporting studies of sea molluscs.

While still an adolescent, Piaget was introduced by his godfather, a Swiss scholar named Samuel Cornut, to that branch of philosophy known as epistemology. Epistemology is the philosophical study of the origin, nature, and limits of knowledge. Piaget became especially curious about the basic questions of epistemology: what knowledge is, how it is acquired, and whether one can have an objective understanding of external reality apart from a subjective projection or externalization of one's own thought. In other words, is there an absolute reality or only a constructed reality?

The differences between the two separate disciplines of biology and epistemology intrigued Piaget. He began to wonder whether it was possible to study the fascinating problems of knowledge within the scientific framework of biology. He was critical of what he considered to be the overly speculative approach of philosophy as well as the sometimes too strictly empirical approach employed in biology. What was needed, he felt, was a linkage or integration of the two.

The conceptually rich theory of intellectual development that Piaget created grew out of these early puzzlements. The intensive pursuit of answers to these basic questions led him to establish the discipline of *genetic epistemology* (Piaget, 1970b). The essential problem of natural genetic epistemology has been to discover the basic psychological structures that underlie the formation of concepts fundamental to philosophy and science.

Piaget believed that he could clarify the theoretical problems of epistemology if he could study these psychological structures as they developed in children. In a very real sense, his insistence on experimentally studying the growth of thought processes in children was a protest against the armchair-speculation approach employed by philosophers. In contrast to speculation about the origins of knowledge, for example, Piaget observed firsthand the actual development of children's concepts about the world. He reasoned that the philosophers' speculations, if they had any validity, should be demonstrable in the way children develop and continually modify their notions of reality.

The idea of studying the development of philosophical and scientific concepts in children was crucial in determining the direction of Piaget's work. An important experience was his association in 1920 with Theophile Simon during Piaget's brief tenure in the Binet Laboratory in Paris. Dr. Binet had earlier constructed the first successful intelligence test. Attempts were being made in his laboratory to develop additional reasoning tests. In the process of trying to develop a standardized French version of certain English reasoning tests, Piaget discovered that the *errors* children made on these tests were much more intriguing than their correct responses. The errors made by young children were not random and unsystematic, but appeared to have peculiar features that could be identified. Older children were not only quantitatively more intelligent than younger children but their thought was qualitatively different. This was one of the findings that led Piaget to reject quantitative approaches to the measurement of intelligence and to focus on the qualitatively different ways of thinking used by children of various ages. This became *the* problem of intelligence for Piaget; studying it became his task for many years.

THE MULTI-DISCIPLINARY FOUNDATIONS OF PIAGET'S THEORY

Piaget's theory has both a history and a future. He created a new system, which is still evolving and which has a multi-disciplinary flavor in that it draws on concepts from biology, philosophy, logic, and psychology. Piaget's most enduring contribution may be his integration of concepts from disciplines as diverse as these into a coherent system. It is interesting to note that Piaget did not passively accept the previously established views in these disciplines, but, consistent with his notion of assimilation, he actively and creatively modified concepts and fitted them together in a unique manner.

Biological Considerations

Piaget's theory has often been misinterpreted as primarily a theory of the development of logic. The importance of his biological model, and the relationship in his theory between cognitive processes and their biological roots, has been less well understood. Gallagher and Reid (1981) point out that the most likely reason for this is that the important concepts of Piaget's biological model were available only in untranslated works until recently. In 1977, the English translation of Piaget's book *L'Equilibration des Structures Cognitives* was made available and entitled *The Development of Thought: Equilibrium of Cognitive Structures*. In addition, Gallagher (1977) and Gallagher and Reid (1981) have provided a clear exposition of the biological model proposed by Piaget.

Gallagher and Reid (1981) have described in some detail how Piaget's studies of snails (*Limnea stagnalis*) and herbs (*Crassucelae*) led him to formulate a new viewpoint on evolution. According to them, Piaget's view stands midway between Lamarck's emphasis on the role of environmental influences and Darwin's emphasis on the role of chance mutations of the gene pool in explaining an organism's adaptation and consequent structural changes. The views of both Lamarck and Darwin imply a passive organism that is shaped by either external or internal forces. In contrast, Piaget's notion of the genotype, or genome, was that of a controlling system:

> Another way of expressing the controlling system of the interacting genes is to use the term *reaction norm,* or range of reaction to environmental influences. An organism's range of reaction becomes expressed through the phenotype—that is, through the physical makeup of an organism that results from the interaction between the genotype and the environment. Therefore, the phenotype as an interacting concept places the emphasis on the organism's selecting into the environment rather than being controlled by that environment. [Gallagher & Reid, 1981, p. 18]

Thus the organism is not only dependent on its environment but actively chooses its environment.

Piaget (1978) repeatedly stressed internal and directive factors that are not passively received from the environment nor built in by hereditary givens in explaining adaptation and development. He used the term *regulations* to refer to this process. Regulations are systematic reorganizations that lead to new ways of functioning. But the important point is that these modifications and reorganizations are *self-regulated*—they are neither genetically given nor imposed from the outside. This applies to the regulation of both biological and cognitive processes.

The internal directiveness of cognitive development can be seen most clearly in examples in which children make inferences that require going beyond the information that is given. Again, Gallagher and Reid provide a clear example:

> We begin with a little story that Piaget (1970a) himself is fond of telling. One of his friends, then 5 years old, was playing with some pebbles on the beach. After arranging the pebbles in a row, he proceeded to count them from left to right: ten. Next he counted them from right to left: again ten. What would happen if he put them in a circle? First, he marked his starting place and counted clockwise: ten! Next, he counted counterclockwise: still ten! Piaget's friend, now a noted mathematician, still remembers the joy and enthusiasm of that moment. He had discovered that the sum is independent of order—what is called *commutativity.* [1981, p. 2]

From such illustrations Gallagher and Reid conclude, with Piaget, that learning—at least, learning in the broad sense—is fundamentally an internal process of construction. Growth in knowledge and cognitive structures, like change in physical structures, results from self-regulated, internally directed organizations. These reorganizations occur in response to both internal and external events, but they are primarily the result of continued interactions between the organism and his or her environment. The child's *activities* with the pebbles resulted in a new understanding—neither the objects themselves nor maturation alone could account for this change.

A further instance of Piaget's application of a biological model can be seen in his general conception of intelligence. Not surprisingly, he views intelligence as "a particular instance of biological adaptation" and as an extension of it. Every act, whether directed toward the outside world or internalized as thought, takes the form of an adaptation—or, even better, a readaptation. Individuals act as though they experience a need if the *equilibrium* between their cognitive structures and their perceived environment is momentarily upset, as for example happens when an expectation one has is not confirmed. This disequilibrium implies an imbalance between the person's mental activities (the cognitive structures) and perceived environment. Piaget viewed living organisms as active, rather than passive, observers and was interested in what individuals do in order to reestablish the equilibrium between themselves and their environment once it is upset. When a state of disequilibrium exists, the individual acts to reestablish the equilibrium, or to readapt. Thus Piaget stated that "Intelligence constitutes the state of equilibrium towards which tend all successive adaptations of a sensori-motor and cognitive nature" (Piaget, 1952b, p. 11).

Piaget's view is that both the *functional* and *structural* characteristics of intelligence must be analyzed and adequately observed. We will consider the functional characteristics first because they are a natural part of our discussion of adaptation and equilibrium. They grow most clearly out of Piaget's biological concern and lay the foundations for the growth of the cognitive structures that define Piaget's stages of intellectual development.

There are two invariant functional properties of all organic life inherited by all living organisms: *organization* and *adaptation.* The first does not refer to a specific structure but to the general tendency to organize both physical and psychological processes into coherent systems. Ginsburg and Opper explain the first of these systematizing tendencies as it exists in all organisms:

> Let us first consider organization. This term refers to the tendency for all species to systematize or organize their processes into coherent systems which may be either physical or psychological. In the former case, fish possess a number of structures which allow functioning in water—for example gills, a particular circulatory system, and temperature mechanisms. All these structures interact and are coordinated into an efficient system. This coordination is the result of the organization tendency. It should be emphasized that organization refers not to gills or the circulatory structure in particular, but to the tendency observed in all life to integrate their structures into a composite system (or higher-order structure).

At a psychological level, too, the tendency to organize is present. In his interaction with the world, the individual tends to integrate his psychological structures into coherent systems. For example, the very young infant has available the separate behavioral structures of either looking at objects or of grasping them. He does not initially combine the two. After a period of development, he organizes these two separate structures into a higher-order structure which enables him to grasp something at the same time he looks at it. Organization, then, is the tendency common to all forms of life to integrate structures, which may be physical or psychological, into higher-order systems or structures. [1969, pp. 17–18]

The second of these inherited properties, adaptation, has been touched on in our discussion of intelligence. All living organisms must adapt to their environment. For Piaget, adaptation can be described in terms of two complementary processes: *assimilation* and *accommodation*. These two processes are simultaneously present in every act.

An example may clarify these processes. The male infant who is born with the sucking reflex at first attempts to apply that reflex indiscriminately. That is, he will not only suck the nipple of the breast or bottle to obtain food, but he will also suck on his hand, his rattle, or his mother's finger. As he brings various objects to his mouth, he has to modify his sucking reflex to fit the object. He has to open his mouth a little wider to suck on his rattle than he does on the nipple, he may suck with varying degress of intensity on different objects, and he gradually learns that sucking leads to obtaining food with some objects but not others. In short, as he develops he moves from indiscriminately making the same sucking response to any object to modifying his sucking response as he adapts to objects with different qualities.

In this example, both assimilation and accommodation have occurred. The sucking reflex was already a well-formed structure with which the infant could act on his environment at birth. Various objects in his environment were made to fit into this structure; they were *assimilated* to this structure. At the same time, the structure itself was modified as a result of environmental demands; the structure (sucking reflex) *accommodated* to the consequence of action on environmental events.

In a similar way, psychological structures continually go through the processes of assimilation and accommodation. For example, the young female child who learns to call a large four-legged animal a *horse* has obtained a concept, a psychological structure, into which she attempts to fit certain animals. At first, she may overgeneralize and call virtually any large, four-legged animal (such as a cow) *horse*. She is actively fitting (assimilating) various animals, more or less well, into the most relevant structure she has available. When she makes mistakes, she is corrected and narrows her concept of *horse* to apply only to a particular kind of four-legged animal and learns other terms for other animals. From the time she first acquires the concept *horse* she has continuously attempted to assimilate various objects in her environment to this structure and, at the same time, must continually revise, or accommodate, the structure to environmental demands.

What Piaget is essentially describing through these processes of assimilation and accommodation is the way in which individuals interact with their perceived environment. Clearly assimilation and accommodation are complementary processes, two sides of the same coin, that continue throughout development. At the lower levels of development, assimilation usually refers to the way in which young children attempt to deal with new objects by incorporating them into habitual patterns of behavior. At higher levels of development, this process continues but is extended to include children's attempts to fit both new objects and ideas into already existing habits and concepts. In effect, the assimilating child continually attempts to deal with new objects and ideas by relating them to familiar objects and ideas. Accommodation, on the other hand, refers to the way in which behavioral and psychological structures are constantly being modified in response to environmental events.

Thus two general biological principles of functioning affect intelligence, organization, and adaptation. Adaptation includes the processes of assimilation and accommodation. As human beings, we possess these tendencies, along with all other living organisms, as a result of our biological heritage. However, the particular ways in which we adapt and organize our behavioral and intellectual processes is dependent on our experience. The effect of a given environmental event for the child is always dependent on his or her current habits and patterns of conceptualizing events.

Philosophical Considerations

Piaget's emphasis on self-regulation in the development of both physical and cognitive structures is consistent with his philosophical viewpoint. He has adopted the *constructivist's* view of knowledge acquisition, a position that differs radically from the *naive realism* that underlies much of modern-day empiricism. From this viewpoint, whether or not an objective reality external to ourselves actually exists can never be directly known. Individuals do not respond passively to events occurring in their external environment, but actively construct their reality. Thus the traditional distinction between self and environment does not exist in Piaget's system: the environment is itself internally organized and can never be directly known. Events in the environment are filtered through and shaped by the child's own constructions. Thus children do not grow in knowledge by a simple registering of experience, but by actively constructing their own understandings. In the example of the child counting pebbles, the child's recognition of gaps in his understanding led to activities that resulted in a reorganization of his thought processes. Neither biologically given maturational tendencies nor environmental pressures *by themselves* can explain such phenomena. It is in the interaction between the child and objects in the environment that knowledge originates. To quote Inhelder, Sinclair, and Bovet (1974, p. 8): "No human knowledge is preformed in the structures of either the subject or the object." This is basic to the constructivist and biological position adopted by Piaget.

Piaget's constructivist position is reminiscent of some of the revelations emerging from relativity theory in physics with respect to concepts of space, time, and causality. One fundamental parallel is that these concepts are interdependent and always relative to (that is, vary according to) the observer's frame of reference. As we stated in an earlier paper,

> Piaget's view is that we interact with our environment through our cognitive structures (our "organs of knowing") and that our cognitive structures transform the basic sensory data we receive from the environment through the process of assimilation. That is, when we come into contact with reality, we always bend and shape it according to the network of concepts that we bring to the situation. At the same time, this network is constantly being reorganized in order to accommodate to the reality which is being assimilated. It is the continual reorganization of cognitive structures which constitutes cognitive development. [Gruen & Doherty, 1977, p. 301]

Logico-Mathematical Considerations

The term *structure* is a prominent one in Piaget's theory and is a concept he borrowed from mathematics. It refers to a system with a set of laws that applies to the system as a whole. Because he believed thought processes were systematically organized at certain stages of intellectual development, he attempted to draw parallels between the properties of certain logico-mathematical systems and the systems of thought that characterize the stages of intellectual development. Using the formal language of logic and mathematics had the added advantage of communicating his descriptions of each stage in a precise manner.

For example, Piaget (1937, 1950) employed a logico-mathematical model called a *group* (or *groupment*) to describe the organization of the thought structures of the concrete-operational child (roughly, the elementary-school child). In mathematics, a group refers to a particular set of elements (such as classes, relations, numbers) on which certain operations can be performed (such as addition/subtraction or multiplication/division). The elements in a group exist as a part of a hierarchical system. Laws of combination—reversibility, identity, composition (closure), and associativity—govern the whole system. (See the section, "The Concrete-Operational Period.")

How does such a mathematical group relate to the way a young child thinks? Piaget thought that the more or less systematic way in which concrete-operational children approached certain problems suggested that their thought processes had properties analogous to those of a group, that is, reversibility, identity, composition, and associativity. An example from Piaget's well-known conservation task (a task he considered very important for studying children's thinking) may help to illustrate this (see Piaget, 1977). If a young boy given the conservation problem consistently believes that the amount of water in a tall, thin beaker is greater than that in a short, wide beaker (even though he observed the same water being poured from one to the other), his thought lacks certain logical properties. He does not understand that the water could be poured back into its original beaker and returned to its original level (reversibility), or that the amount of water in either beaker has to be the same because nothing has been added or taken away (identity), or that the taller beaker is thinner, as well as taller, than the shorter beaker and thus the greater height and lesser width must be considered simultaneously (associativity). The child who conserves, on the other hand, is immediately aware of the logic underlying these facts and regularly reports that the beakers have the same amount of water. On the basis of these kinds of observations, Piaget concluded that the nonconserving child exhibits behavior that indicates that his or her thought processes lack reversibility and other logical properties, while the conserving child's thought can be said to have these properties.

The conserving child, of course, is not aware that his or her thought processes have such logical properties. An observer infers that the child's thought processes conform or do not conform to a logical model from the way the child responds to conservation problems. Piaget used the term *structure* to refer to these inferred organizational properties of thought, the regularities that underlie the child's systematic behavior or thought. The stages of intellectual development that he describes detail the qualitative changes that occur in these psychological structures as the child develops.

At more advanced levels of intellectual development, Piaget employed somewhat more complex logico-mathematical models to describe formal-operational thought. These will be discussed later. At this point, it is important to recognize that the mathematical groups are nothing more nor less than *models* of the organization of children's or adolescents' thought processes. Piaget (1949) did not believe that children are aware of these formal properties of thought. Rather, children classify, seriate, or conserve objects in such a way that their actions allow one to infer that their thoughts possess (or do not possess) these logical properties. Neither did Piaget believe that children's or even adults' thinking can always be described as "logical." The use of the formal language of logic and mathematics simply was his way of communicating as precisely as possible the way children think at each stage of development.

The Determinants of Development

What is the mechanism by which the child goes from one level of development to another? For Piaget it is not simply *learning* in the narrow sense of acquiring new responses, or new information. When major developments take place, as when the child, for example, goes from preoperational to concrete-operational thinking, a fundamental change in the way the child perceives, understands, and operates on the environment has occurred.

Piaget (1970b) has discussed four factors affecting development and the transition from one stage to another: (1) *maturation*, (2) *experience* (derived from physical objects and from one's own actions on physical objects), (3) *social transmission* (including social interactions, culture, education, and language), and (4) *equilibration.*

Piaget believed that all children progress through the stages of intellectual development in the same order—from sensori-motor to preoperational intelligence, then to concrete operational intelligence, and finally to formal-operational intelligence. This insistence on an invariant sequence of development for all children in itself indicates that he views maturation as a very important part of development. Inhelder (1968) has shown also that mentally retarded children progress through the same stages as nonretarded children, but at a slower rate. This again suggests that maturation plays a crucial role in development. However, maturation clearly does not account for everything. Children in different cultures and socioeconomic groups may progress through the stages at different rates.

Experience that involves contact with the physical environment is a second factor that affects development. Some experiences may not lead to new knowledge, such as exercising already acquired skills by repeated practice. For example, practicing throwing a ball or repeatedly ordering the same series of different sized sticks may improve one's skill at these activities, but nothing new is necessarily learned. Other experiences with the physical environment do lead to new knowledge and these are of two types: (1) physical experience—object manipulation in which the child discovers directly the properties inherent in the object (such as it is cold, round, hard, and smooth); and (2) logico-mathematical experience—knowledge that is gained indirectly from the child's manipulation of objects and his or her subsequent reflection on such activities (Piaget, 1977b). The first kind of knowledge comes directly through sensory experience of the objects, but the latter results from reflexively thinking about the results of one's own activities on objects. The example given earlier of the boy arranging and rearranging the pebbles and observing that their sum did not change despite spatial transformations is an example of logico-mathematical experience.

Social experience, of course, involves interaction with people. Ordinary social relationships, culture, education, and language are included here. Social interactions force children to become aware of other peoples' points of view, to be more flexible in their reasoning, and to be more observant of attributes of objects with which others concern themselves.

Neither physical experience, social transmission, nor maturation can account for both the sequential nature of development and the variations in children's rates of development. There is a fourth factor, equilibration, which involves aspects of all three of the other factors affecting development. Piaget viewed equilibration as the most important factor affecting development; through equilibration the child organizes the other three factors into a coherent whole. In a general sense it involves the process of going from a state of relative disequilibrium to a state of greater equilibrium. Equilibrium refers to the relative balance that exists between the individual's psychological structures and perceived events in the environment—the balance between assimilation and accommodation processes, or that between different domains of knowledge (for example, some children conserve number but not length at one point in development), and between the parts and the whole (see Gallagher & Reid, 1981, pp. 47–59, for an excellent discussion of this concept). Piaget assumes that developing structures continually move toward more and more stable kinds of relative equilibrium;

they also reach plateaus where relatively little disequilibrium exists. However, it is a moderate level of disequilibrium, rather than equilibrium, that leads to readaptation and reorganization of existing psychological structures. Disequilibrium, therefore, plays an important role in energizing structural change.

Let us take an example from the physical world, the ordinary thermostat, to illustrate this process. If you set your home thermostat for 68° and the temperature in the room falls below that level, a signal is sent to the furnace that triggers its operation. The thermostat is constructed to detect incoming information (room temperature) that is discrepant from the standard (68°) at which it is set. When a discrepancy exists, that message starts the furnace into operation until the gap is closed—until room temperature reaches a level of 68° or higher. The thermostat again reads that information, signals the furnace that the gap is closed, and the furnace ceases its operation.

In a similar way, whenever children are made aware of gaps in their knowledge, or come across an intriguing problem, the solution of which is not immediately obvious, or have an expectancy (hypothesis) disconfirmed, their cognitive processes begin to operate. During this time, they are in a state of relative disequilibrium. If they are successful in resolving the problem, they will return to a state of relative equilibrium. In the process of achieving this equilibrium, however, their cognitive processes will have become reorganized in a slightly different way than before—in essence, they will have obtained a new concept or modified their expectancies.

It should be emphasized here that the metaphor of the thermostat regulating the temperature in the room is actually too static a model to capture what Piaget intends with his notion of equilibration. Cognitive equilibrium never leads back to the original state in the same way that the thermostat brings the temperature in the room back to the originally set temperature. Once a child has resolved a conflict between predictions and reality, new understanding permits the appreciation of problems that were not even recognizable prior to this progress.

Children continually reach plateaus where relatively little disequilibrium exists, have this equilibrium upset by discrepant incoming information, and then actively reduce the disequilibrium by reorganizing their thought processes. In other words, they pass through *stages* of relative equilibrium. Levels of equilibrium are not static; they are continually being upset. Gradually, children develop more stable, more balanced, and more integrated psychological structures that permit the maintenance of increasingly higher levels of equilibrium. Thus they can deal with an increasingly wider variety of problems without running into logical inconsistencies or contradictions.

In Piaget's stages, for example, children at the preoperational stage who lack conservation are not, at first, particularly troubled by their inability to conserve quantity. The logical fact that water poured from a short, wide beaker into a tall, thin beaker could not become greater in amount unless some water was added or taken away never occurs to them. They center, or focus, their attention on one salient dimension, such as the height of the beaker, and conclude that the tall, thin beaker has more water. If the other dimension, width, is made more salient by using wider and wider beakers, they may center on that dimension and judge the wider beaker to have more water. In either case, they are in a state of relative equilibrium. They are not troubled by the inconsistency in their thinking. As they become older and become capable of considering two dimensions at once, they—often suddenly—realize that the taller beaker is thinner as well as taller and they may vacillate in their conclusions as to which beaker has more water. Once this correlation is noticed, children are able to focus on transformations rather than static states. At this point, they are able to recognize the discrepancy between their earlier notion that the taller beaker always has more, regardless of its width, and the possibility that a short, but very wide, beaker may actually contain more water than a tall, but very thin one. In short, they are in a state of relative disequilibrium at this time. When they arrive at the point where they realize that the amount of water is conserved (does not change) despite spatial rearrangements (being poured into beakers of different size and/or shape) they come to a new, higher level of equilibrium.

Gallagher and Reid (1981) point out that late in his career Piaget (1977) slightly revised his concept of equilibration. In his earlier writings, as the previous example illustrates, equilibration was seen as a process based on increasing sequential probabilities. In his later writings, Piaget suggested that children first focus on *affirmations*—the most salient, positive, observable characteristics of objects. For example, they notice that one beaker is taller than the other. Next, they take into account *negations*—those things that are less salient and that must be constructed. For progress to be made in knowledge development, children must link several features of observations they make into a system of inferences—for example, that the taller beaker is also thinner, while the shorter beaker is wider. It is not the observable features themselves that lead to a change in thought processes, but an internal regulation. As in Piaget's earlier explanations of equilibration, noticing the correlation between height and width is still necessary and the new model is still one of increasing sequential probabilities to some extent. However, progress now is explained as the progressive substitution of endogenous (the negations) for exogenous (the affirmations) knowledge. Again, the child's activities and inferences control and direct development—not environmental events. And, again, disequilibrium motivates the search for a solution.

Thus psychological structures are modified and reorganized as the child progresses from lower levels of relative equilibrium, through states of disequilibrium, to higher levels of equilibrium—in essence, to more mobile, more stable, and more widely applicable thought structures.

THE STAGES

Piaget has divided intellectual development into four major periods (see Tanner & Inhelder, 1956): the sensori-motor period (birth to 1½ or 2 years), the preoperational period (2 to 7 years), the concrete-operational period (7 to 11 years), and the formal-operational period (11 or 12 years and above). It is important to keep in mind that the ages at which these stages typically emerge is not fixed and is not as important as their sequential nature. As implied earlier, this invariant sequence does not implicate maturation as the primary determiner of development. The interactive and self-regulatory processes involved in equili-bration are the primary mechanisms responsible for movement through the sequence. The stages are meant to be descriptive, not predictive. Thus they describe the characteristics of children's thinking within broad periods in de-velopment. They do suggest that these stage-specific characteristics can be applied to all events and all reasoning during a given period.

The Sensori-Motor Period

Piaget's observations and investigations of his own infants (Laurent, Lucienne, and Jacqueline) led him to describe in his book, *The Origins of Intelligence*, six stages within the sensori-motor period. Readers of his book have been impressed by the intricate detail with which Piaget describes the infant's behavior and by his carefulness in arriving at appropriate explanations of the behavior.

The First Stage. The first of Piaget's six stages of the sensori-motor period includes the first month of life. The newborn infant is not a *tabula rasa*, but makes his or her appearance into the world with a number of primarily heredity-determined functional capabilities and structures. For example, the reflexive schemes of sucking, looking, listening, phonation, and grasping are all present at birth. From the beginning the infant responds reflexively to external stimuli and actively incorporates (assimilates) various external stimuli into ready-made reflexive schemes. These reflexes are provided by the physical structure of the infant and furnish the basis for future intellectual development. From the be-ginning, however, experience plays an important role in modifying these schemes.

Accommodation of these reflexes to environmental events begins early. For example, in the case of the sucking reflex, progress during this first stage is made in the continuity of searching for the nipple, in distinguishing between sucking-and-swallowing and sucking-without-swallowing, and in fitting the mouth to the nipple.

Similar progress is made with the looking scheme, in that the infant acquires the ability to follow an object with his or her eyes through an arc for a short duration. Progress is also made with the hearing scheme, in that the infant begins to stop activity when a sound such as the approaching footsteps of the mother are heard.

Assimilation and accommodation are going on from the beginning. The in-fant's interaction with his or her immediate environment results in the modifi-cation of the ready-made reflexive schemes present at birth. The effect of external stimuli impinging on the infant is then determined by the physical structures as modified by previous experience as well as by the nature of the stimuli themselves.

The Second Stage. This stage occurs approximately between one and four to five months. The major development during this time is that of the *primary circular reaction*, which refers to the repetitive way in which the infant of this age performs an act involving the coordination of two or more independent schemes. For example, Piaget conceives sucking the thumb to be a coordination of arm movements and the sucking schema. He describes how, as his son's thumb and fingers came into contact with his face, Laurent grasped them with his mouth. With repetition, this coordination became skillful. Once such coordinations of reflexes have become established they may be repeated often and become habits.

Consider the following example at one month, three days of age:

> At 0;1(3) . . . Laurent, after nursing remained wide awake and continued trying to suck, interspersing his attempts with vigorous cries. I then grasped his right arm and held it until his mouth began to suck his hand. As soon as the lips were in contact with the hand, the arms stopped resisting and remained still for several moments . . . the arm remained immobile for a moment, although the back of the hand only was in contact with the lips; the latter obviously tried to explore the whole hand. After a moment, the hand lost the contact but rediscovered it. It is no longer the mouth that seeks the hand, but the hand which reaches the mouth. Thirteen times in succession I have been able to observe the hand go back into the mouth. There is no longer any doubt that coordination exists. [Piaget, 1952b, p. 52]

Examples of such primitive coordinations of schemes in infants are numerous: things heard become things to look at, things seen become things to grasp, and things grasped soon become things to suck. *Handwatching*, the infant's bringing his hand to a position over his eyes and observing it for a duration, is often reported with infants of this age, too, and is another example of a primary circular reaction (see Hunt, 1961).

A general principle in Piaget's theory is illustrated by these simple coordinations of schemes: the behaviors characteristic of a given stage do not disappear when the infant reaches the next higher stage; rather the "old" behaviors are simply *organized* in a different way so that they have a new relationship to each other. Thus behavior patterns characteristic of stage 1 (sucking, looking, grasping schemata) are *integrated* into superordinate structures that are defined by the way in which these schemata are coordinated at stage 2. This kind of coordinating, reorganizing, and integrating of lower-level schemata into higher-level (supraordinate) structures goes on throughout the developmental period.

The Third Stage. The major development at this stage, which occurs roughly between four and one-half to nine months of age, is that of *secondary circular reactions*. The primary circular reactions of stage 2 always involved coordinations centered around the child's own body (such as bringing the thumb to the mouth). The secondary circular reactions of stage 3, on the other hand, are called "secondary" because they involve events or objects in the external environment.

Piaget (1952) states that after applying circular reactions to his own body, the infant will use them sooner or later in order to adapt himself or herself to unforeseen phenomena of the external world, hence the behavior patterns of exploration, experimentation, and so on. As a result, the infant's behavior becomes centered on the results produced by his or her actions. Piaget infers that the infant thereby begins making the distinction between *means* and *ends* (intentionality). That is, behavior patterns that were initially discovered by chance to reproduce interesting events are performed in *anticipation* of their consequences.

Let us consider the following example:

> Finally two other procedures were employed by Jacqueline, Lucienne, and Laurent in order to shake their bassinet or the objects hanging from the hood. At 0;7(20) Lucienne looks at the hood and the hanging ribbons; her arms are outstretched and slightly straightened, at an equal distance from her face. She gently opens and closes her hands, then more and more rapidly with involuntary arm movements which thus gently shake the hood. Lucienne then repeats these movements with increasing speed. Same reaction at 0;7(27) etc. I again observe the phenomenon at 0;10(27): she moves her bassinet while waving her hands.
>
> At 0;8(5), Lucienne shakes her head from side to side in order to shake her bassinet, the hood, ribbons, fringes, etc. [Piaget, 1952b, p. 165]

Thus infants of this stage become interested in contact with the external environment and their behavior becomes more extensive, away from their body. The increasing number and range of schemes result in children becoming more capable than previously of imitating the behavior of a model. However, infants at this stage are quite limited in their ability to imitate—they can imitate only those actions that are already in their repertoire and thus are familiar. They cannot yet reproduce novel acts.

Another development at this stage concerns the formation of the object concept. Whereas at stage 2 the infant makes no attempt to search for a vanished object, the stage 3 infant will attempt a visual or tactual search for an object *if the infant has caused its disappearance.* If the infant has made certain movements of the hand in order to grasp an object, and then loses it, he or she will search for the object by continuing the movements. Thus the object exists only in relation to the action the infant was performing when it vanished, or eluded his or her grasp, which indicates only a subjective permanence of the object. No new movements to retrieve the lost object are initiated, but the infant merely repeats past movements directed toward the object.

This is also the first stage at which infants can recognize an object when they are able to see only certain parts of it. The stage 3 infant makes no attempt to search for a toy completely covered by a cloth, but if certain parts remain visible (such as either end of a milk bottle), the infant will try to lift the cloth to discover the rest of the toy. This trend toward a greater degree of permanence attributed to objects by infants continues to progress through the later stages.

The Fourth Stage. This stage includes approximately months nine through twelve and the primary developments occurring here are the increasing coordination of the secondary schemes developed in stage 3 and an increasing differentiation of means and ends. The following observation illustrates these developments:

> Likewise at 0;9(17), Laurent lifts a cushion in order to look for a cigar case. When the object is entirely hidden, the child lifts the screen with hesitation, but when one end of the case appears, Laurent removes the cushion with one hand and with the other tries to extricate the objective. The act of lifting the screen is therefore entirely separate from that of grasping the desired object and constitutes an autonomous "means" no doubt derived from earlier analogous acts (removing the obstacle, displacing and pushing away objects which are a barrier, etc.). [Piaget, 1952b, p. 222]

At stage 3, it will be recalled, the infant pursued a goal after having *accidentally* discovered it. At stage 4, on the other hand, the infant has the goal in mind from the beginning and employs one scheme for obtaining the goal and another scheme for dealing with it. The infant's behavior here is truly purposive, or intentional. When an obstacle prevents direct attainment of a goal, the infant uses a scheme that is different from the one employed previously with the goal object. There is thus a novel coordination between two schemes not previously associated.

Infants' abilities to perform the above kinds of coordinated behavior patterns teach them something about the relationships between objects. For example, they gain a concrete understanding of the relations *in front of* and *before* when they recognize that the obstacle is in front of the goal and must be removed before they can attain the goal.

Imitation becomes more genuine at this stage as the infant begins to imitate novel actions, some of which he or she cannot see himself or herself perform. For example, when Piaget (1952) put out his tongue to Jacqueline at this stage, she bit her lips, indicating that she had at least assimilated her father's action to the proper organ.

There is also progress in infant concepts of the permanence of objects at this stage. Infants engage in a variety of behaviors to search for vanished objects. For example, if a toy is completely covered with a cloth while they are looking, they will remove the cloth to obtain the toy. However, if the place of the object is changed through several displacements, they will return to the place where they first found it. Clearly infants attribute a degree of permanence to objects and conceive of them as independent of their own subjective state. Thus increased objectification has occurred.

The Fifth Stage. This stage occurs at approximately 1 year to 18 months of age. The major development here is that of *tertiary circular reactions,* the discovery of new means through active experimentation. The infant at this stage becomes interested in the properties of objects for their own sake, and, especially, the effect of his or her own actions on objects. Many of the infant's actions appear to be "experiments in order to see." The infant's response to new objects consists first of applying familiar schemes and then varying the schemes. For example, consider the observation reported below:

> One recalls . . . how at 0;10(2) Laurent discovered in "exploring" a case of soap, the possibility of throwing this object and letting it fall. Now, what interested him at first was not the objective phenomenon of the fall—that is to say, the object's trajectory—but the very act of letting go. He therefore limited himself, at the beginning, merely to reproducing the result observed fortuitously, which still constitutes a "secondary" reaction, "derived," it is true, but of typical structure.

> On the other hand, at 0;10(10) the reaction changes and becomes "tertiary." That day Laurent manipulates a small piece of bread (without any alimentary interest: he had never eaten any and has not thought of tasting it) and lets it go continually. He even breaks off fragments which he lets drop. Now, in contradistinction to what has happened on the preceding days, he pays no attention to the act of letting go whereas he watches with great interest the body in motion; in particular, he looks at it for a long time when it has fallen, and picks it up when he can.

> At 0;10(11) Laurent is lying on his back but nevertheless resumes his experiments of the day before. He grasps in succession a celluloid swan, a box, etc., stretches out his arm and lets them fall. He distinctly varies the positions of the fall. Sometimes he stretches out his arm vertically, sometimes he holds it obliquely, in front of or behind his eyes, etc. When the object falls in a new position (for example on his pillow), he lets it fall two or three times more on the same place, as though to study the spatial relation. [Piaget, 1952b, pp. 268–269]

New developments also occur at this stage with regard to imitation and the development of object concepts. The infant is now capable of imitating new actions of models such as producing sounds uttered before. He or she is also able to follow an object through a series of visible displacements and search for it in its proper place. But if the object disappears successively in a number of places, the infant will search for it where it was last seen. Thus the infant's belief in the permanence of the object depends partly on the opportunity to follow it visually at this stage.

The Sixth Stage.   This stage covers from about 18 months to 2 years and forms the transition from sensori-motor to symbolic thought. Although the infant at stage 5 was capable of exploring objects, and even inventing new means for dealing with objects, he or she was still tied to the concrete here and now. His or her strategies for dealing with objects were still mainly trial and error, showing no evidence of being able to combine symbols mentally to reach solutions to simple problems. The exciting development that distinguishes the stage 6 from the stage 5 child is the ability to use symbols and words to refer to absent objects and to "think" about possible ways of solving a problem before acting. Consider the following example:

At 1;4(0) . . . I play at hiding the chain in the same box . . . I begin by opening the box as wide as possible and putting the chain into its cover (where Lucienne herself put it, but deeper). Lucienne, who has already practiced filling and emptying her pail and various receptacles, then grasps the box and turns it over without hesitation. No invention is involved of course (it is the simple application of a schema, acquired through groping) but knowledge of this behavior pattern of Lucienne is useful for understanding what follows.

Then I put the chain inside an empty matchbox (where the matches belong), then close the box leaving an opening of 10 mm. Lucienne begins by turning the whole thing over, then tries to grasp the chain through the opening. Not succeeding, she simply puts her index finger into the slit and so succeeds in getting out a small fragment of the chain; she then pulls it until she has completely solved the problems.

Here begins the experiment which we want to emphasize. I put the chain back into the box and reduce the opening to 3 mm. It is understood that Lucienne is not aware of the functioning of the opening and closing of the matchbox and has not seen me prepare the experiment. She only possesses the two preceding schemata: turning the box over in order to empty it of its contents, and sliding her finger into the slit to make the chain come out. It is of course this last procedure that she tries out first: she puts her finger inside and gropes to reach the chain, but fails completely. A pause follows during which Lucienne manifests a very curious reaction bearing witness not only to the fact that she tries to think out the situation and to represent to herself through mental combination the operations to be performed, but also to the role played by imitation in the genesis of representations. Lucienne mimics the widening of the slit.

She looks at the slit with great attention; then, several times in succession, she opens and shuts her mouth, at first slightly, then wider and wider! Apparently Lucienne understands the existence of a cavity subjacent to the slit and wishes to enlarge that cavity. The attempt at representation which she thus furnishes is expressed plastically, that is to say, due to inability to think out the situation in words or clear visual images she uses a simple motor indication as "signifier" or symbol.

Soon after this phase of plastic reflection, Lucienne unhesitatingly puts her finger in the slit and, instead of trying as before to reach the chain, she pulls so as to enlarge the opening. She succeeds and grasps the chain. [Piaget, 1952b, pp. 377–378]

Whereas the stage 5 child would have tried out various new means for dealing with the problems of getting the chain out of the matchbox until he or she stumbled onto the correct solution, Lucienne is beginning to internalize this procedure. Lucienne is not yet capable of representing the problem to herself completely in mental terms, as evidenced by the movements of her mouth. But now she is developing a shortcut to the strictly trial and error procedure. She can symbolically combine various actions "in her head," or think, and is on the threshold of true mental activity.

The ability of stage 6 infants to represent objects or models symbolically enables them to imitate a model that is absent. They are able to observe a model's actions at one point in time, form a mental representation of it, and then reproduce the actions of the model at a later time. Similarly, their newfound ability to represent objects symbolically enables them to make further progress in the area of object concepts. When Piaget hides a desired object in his hand and then successively makes his hand disappear under three separate scarves, Jacqueline goes directly to the last scarf to get the object. She apparently believes the object continues to exist within Piaget's hand throughout the whole sequence of invisible displacements. Piaget believes that is because she can form a mental image of the object and can maintain it representationally.

Summary of the Sensori-Motor Period. Piaget documents how the infant develops from the newborn, who was heavily dependent on heredity-determined reflexes for interaction with the environment, to the stage 6 child, who is now engaging in mental combinations and capable of representing objects and events symbolically. Throughout these developments, infants are seen as *actively* seeking out contact with their environment rather than passively responding to it; they are seen as interpreting (assimilating) environmental events according to the schemes they have for dealing with them; and they are seen as both modifying, and being modified by, their environment. Though the age norms reported are only approximate, the order in which these stages develop is considered invariant as each stage is a preparation for the next one to follow. Development is a continual process in which older schemes are coordinated together into supraordinate structures. At higher stage levels the older schemes are integrated together to form new, more complex, systems of actions.

The Preoperational Period

In this section we will discuss the two phases of what Piaget calls the preoperational period: the *preconceptual* phase (2–4 years) and the *intuitive* phase (4–7 years). The fact that these phases are still *pre*operational emphasizes that the child at this level is still a long way from mature logical thought. However, some very significant developments occur at this time that prepare the way for such thought, including the development of the symbolic function, language, and the preconcepts.

The Preconceptual Phase. The best source of Piaget's description of the child from 2–4 years is his book *Play, Dreams and Imitation* (Piaget, 1962). The phase begins where we left the child at the end of the sensori-motor period— just at the threshold of being able to use symbols to represent objects and events in his or her environment. This is a major development because it permits children to function on a new level. They are no longer limited to manipulating and reasoning with concrete objects that are present in their immediate environment. Now they are capable of using symbols to represent objects and events with which they had experience in the past but are no longer present. This provides them with an increased scope and speed of thought that permits them to go beyond what is immediate and local in time and space. This phase involves, in general, a transition from sensori-motor to reflective intelligence.

One of the most important issues concerning the child's development during this phase is the nature of the symbols used. Are the first symbols mental pictures, or templates, of perceived objects and events? Or are they words that permit the encoding of such phenomena? Or, finally, are they action patterns, schemes, that have been internalized in some way?

The Nature of Mental Symbols.   Piaget (1962) does not believe that the first mental symbols involve language. By the end of the sensori-motor period, children are able to engage in symbolic actions involving mental combinations without the use of words. For example, they can stand in their playpen and use a stick to rake toward them a desired toy outside their normal reach. They are capable of "deferred imitation," that is, they can imitate objects or events they observed in the past. And they are capable of reconstructing a series of invisible displacements of an object and to search for the object after its displacement. All these things they can do *prior* to the development of language. In addition, Piaget points out that apes are capable of many of these kinds of activities without the benefit of language. For all these reasons, he rejects the idea that thought depends on language and that the first mental symbols are words.

Neither does Piaget believe that the first mental symbols are limited to visual, or other kinds, of perceptual images. Some symbols certainly involve visual images but Piaget does not believe that symbolic activity can be equated with visual imagery.

What, then, is the nature of the child's first mental symbols? Piaget's answer is that mental symbols derive from imitation. The young child's symbols are an interiorization of actions either made by the child or observed by him or her in other people or objects. You will recall the example where overt imitation played the role that symbols later play in directing behavior. You may remember that when Piaget hid a chain in a matchbox, Lucienne first opened and shut her mouth just slightly, and then wider and wider. Following this motor action, apparently used in much the same way as a mental symbol might be, she opened the box to get the chain. This motor "thinking out loud" becomes more internalized as the child develops so that such patterns of action are not so readily observable.

However, symbols still remain, basically, interiorized actions. A couple of examples may help to clarify this point. The child who observes a grasshopper jump and then imitates the grasshopper's actions may be employing either visual images or patterns of motor movements, or both, to represent the grasshopper's actions. But Piaget views visual perception itself as an *activity.* Even when a child observes a stationary object such as a chair, his or her eyes are actively scanning its outline, noting its texture, and observing its location—in short, actively searching and taking in information about the chair. The child's perception of the chair derives as much from his or her own activity as it does from the stimulus characteristics of the chair. The child's visual image of the chair, when it is absent, will involve an abbreviated, internal imitation of the perceptual activity engaged in when the chair was present. Thus Piaget defines imitation very broadly to include not only the reproduction of overt activity, such as jumping like a grasshopper, but also the reproduction of more subtle activity, such as scanning an object visually. Visual imagining is itself a perceptual activity: "Now it is this perception activity, and not perception as such, which produces the image, which is a kind of scheme or summary of the perceived object" (Piaget, 1962, p. 77).

Internal imitation, of course, primarily involves accommodation because imitation involves modifying one's own schemes, or behavior, to fit those of another person or object. This is the process that first provides the child with mental symbols. The child then assimilates these symbols into mental schemes and endows them with meaning by relating them to that with which he or she is already familiar.

The mental symbol is a *signifier* that represents something (the signified) to the individual, but its nature may be highly idiosyncratic. The grasshopper may be symbolized by one child by its jumping movements, while a visual image of a stationary grasshopper may be the symbol employed by another child. Such symbols are, therefore, not very useful for transmitting information from one individual to another. Words, on the other hand, are social and not as idiosyncratic to the individual. They are more arbitrary than the mental symbol in that they do not resemble the object to which they refer, but they eventually obtain an agreed on meaning by a linguistic community.

The Role of Language.   Even though the first mental symbols do not involve language, one major evidence of symbolic function in the young child is the development of language. However, the first words are not used in a symbolic way. They are, rather, mere expressions, or accompaniments, of actions. For example, Piaget observed the following example in Laurent:

> At 1;2(22) he cried "Mummy!" when his mother, who had been with him for more than an hour, began to swing to and fro. This was therefore an exclamatory appreciation of unsuspected powers on the part of his mother. At 1;2(23) he said "daddy" to Jacqueline who held out her arms to him like his father. . . . At 1;4(4) . . . he said "mummy" as he pointed to what he wanted, even when he was referring to his father or to some other person. [Piaget, 1962, p. 217]

Piaget refers to these first words as semi-verbal signs that lie between sensorimotor and conceptual intelligence. That such words are not symbolic is indicated by the fact that they are used in connection with immediately present objects, are used mainly to express immediate desires, and are very unstable.

At about 2 years of age the child begins to use words in a symbolic way. One evidence of this is the child's ability to describe action, to talk *about* it, rather than just to associate a word with it. For example:

At 1;7(28) Jacqueline told her mother about a grasshopper she had just seen in the garden: "Hopper, hopper jump boy," meaning that the grasshopper jumped as a boy had made her jump. A boy cousin had in fact made her jump two days earlier.

At 1;11(28), a few minutes after it had happened Lucienne said: "Auntie Madame in car, gone in car." Then, an hour later, when she was alone in the garden, she said to herself: "Mummy gone, Jacqueline gone with mummy." [Piaget, 1962, p. 222]

Thus language ceases to be merely an accompaniment of action in progress and is used in a representational way. This descriptive aspect of language gives it a new degree of objectification.

The transition to a representational use of language is also marked by the appearance of the question, "What is it?" For example, at about 2 years of age Jacqueline was observed asking herself and others the names for parts of her doll (nose, mouth, and so on) and for a stone (Piaget, 1962). Learning the names of objects involves learning the concept or class to which they belong—not just their labels. Piaget believes that the important process going on here, then, is the child's acquisition of general classes of objects and their relationships to one another.

However, the fact that preconceptual children use language in a symbolic way does not indicate that they use words in the same way, or with the same meaning, as an adult might use them. Children still use subjective generalizations (all animals are "dogs") but the answers to their "what is it?" questions continually serve to correct these subjective generalizations and move them toward the collectively agreed-on relationships between words and their referents. We will return to several more examples of this phenomenon when we discuss preconceptual reasoning.

Symbolic Play. A third example of the use of the symbolic function (in addition to imitation and language) is seen in the preconceptual child's play, which Piaget views as primarily an assimilative process. Toward the end of the sensori-motor period, playful make-believe is observed:

At 1;3(17) . . . [Jacqueline] . . . saw a cloth whose fringed edges vaguely recalled those of her pillow; she seized it, held a fold of it in her right hand, sucked the thumb of the same hand and lay down on her side, laughing hard. She kept her eyes open, but blinked from time to time as if she were alluding to closed eyes. Finally, laughing more and more she cried "Néné" (No no). . . . At 1;3(13) she treated the collar of her mother's coat in the same way. At 1;3(30) it was the tail of her donkey which represented the pillow! [Piaget, 1962, p. 96]

In this example, Jacqueline is not yet employing mental symbols but she is using the cloth (collar, donkey's tail) as a concrete symbol—it was used as a signifier and its referent was a pillow. She assimilated several different materials into this action pattern, or scheme.

At a little later stage of development the child becomes capable of holding in memory and imitating that which he or she has seen others do in a playful manner. For example:

> At 1;3(20), a quarter of an hour after I blew a hunting horn in his presence, [Laurent] picked up a doll's chair a couple of inches high, put it to his mouth and pretended to sound it. "Tantara." [Piaget, 1962, p. 122]

This was the first example of symbolic play observed in Laurent.

A further development in symbolic play activity occurs when the child identifies with another person and playfully pretends to be that person for a moment. Jacqueline was about 2 years old when she pretended to be ironing like a washerwoman and a moment later become the washerwoman: "It's Mrs. Sechaud ironing" (Piaget, 1962, p. 125). At other times she pretended to be her mother, or her little sister, or her cousin. In each case she imitated some activity of each person.

A still further development occurs when the child becomes capable of re-evaluating or reconstructing combinations of scenes and activities rather than isolated imitations or assimilations of one object to another.

Preconceptual Reasoning.   The child of this age displays many confusions in language and concepts that are not only amusing to adults but also provide evidence of the nature of the reasoning process. One outstanding feature of preconcepts is the absence of general classes in categorizing objects. Piaget (1962) provides many examples of this from observations: the child seeing first one red slug and, at a later time, another red slug, believes them both to be the same slug reappearing; all gardens are uncle Alfred's gardens; all streams are the same stream, and so on. In each instance, the slugs (gardens, streams) are not ascribed individual identities because the child lacks the ability to include individual representatives of a class into a superordinate class of which they are members.

Another salient feature of preconceptual reasoning is the lack of either hypothetical-deductive reasoning (reasoning from the general to the particular) or inductive reasoning (reasoning from the particular to the general). Instead the child reasons from particular to particular, a kind of reasoning Piaget calls *transductive.* For example:

> At 2;1(13), Jacqueline wanted to see a little hunchbacked neighbor whom she used to meet on her walks. A few days earlier she had asked why he had a hump, and after I had explained she said: "Poor boy, he's ill, he has a hump." The day before, Jacqueline had also wanted to go and see him, but he had influenza, which Jacqueline called being "ill in bed." We started out for our walk and on the way Jacqueline said, "Is he still in bed?" "No. I saw him this morning, he isn't in bed now." "He hasn't a big hump now!" [Piaget, 1962, p. 231]

Children at this age center on one outstanding feature of an event and draw conclusions from it that are not logically compelling. This is because they are reasoning without real concepts—they cannot classify objects or events into conceptual categories. This reasoning seems to be that if A is like B in one respect, then A is like B in all respects. As a result, the child's transductive reasoning often results in his seeing a relationship between two or more particular events when there is none.

The Intuitive Phase. The second phase of the preoperational period is the intuitive phase, which includes children from approximately 4–7 years of age. A number of characteristics of intuitive thought describe preoperational thinking in general. These include egocentrism, centration, static immobility, and irreversibility.

Egocentrism refers primarily to the child's inability to take the view of another person. One of the most dramatic illustrations of egocentricity in the thought of the young child occurs when he or she is presented with a visual display such as Piaget's "mountain scene" (Piaget, 1948, p. 211). The scene is looked at from one point, A, and the child is then asked to represent what the display would look like from another point, B (from the side, or from behind it). Typically, the egocentric child believes the display would look the same from other perspectives as it does from his or her own perspective.

A related characteristic of the preoperational child's thought is *centration*. Flavell (1963, p. 157) defines centration as "The tendency to *center*, as Piaget says, attention on a single striking feature of the object of its reasoning to the neglect of other important aspects, and by so doing, to distort the reasoning." When asked if a tall, thin beaker (B) has the same amount of water as a short, wide beaker (A), immediately after having observed the water being poured from A into B, the child may center only on the height (or only on the width) of the beakers and say that B has more "because it is tall" (or A has more "because it is wide"). The child is unable to *decenter*, to consider both the width and height of the beakers simultaneously in making the judgment.

In the last illustration the child seems able to focus on the initial state of the water (while in beaker A) and on the terminal state of the water (while in beaker B), but has difficulty focusing on the successive states of the water as it is transformed from one state to another. In this sense, the thought of the preoperational child is *static*.

Irreversibility is another and probably the most emphasized characteristic of preoperational thought for Piaget. It refers to the inability of the child at this stage to reverse the direction of his or her thought processes. A cognitive organization is reversible

> If it is able to travel along a cognitive route (pursue a series of reasonings, follow a series of transformations in a display, etc.) and then reverse direction in thought to find an unchanged point of departure (the beginning premise, the original state of the display, etc). [Flavell, 1963, p. 159]

The preoperational child does not realize, in the water-conservation problem described above, that pouring water from beaker B to A would reverse or negate the action of pouring from A to B. The child cannot reverse the pouring in his or her mind. Neither can the child cancel out the differences between the two beakers by an action of reciprocity—seeing that the greater height of one beaker is balanced by the greater width of the other beaker.

Other Characteristics of the Intuitive Phase.   The intuitive-phase child can best be thought of as in transition from preoperational to concrete-operational thinking. In many respects, the child at this stage is described by Piaget mainly in terms of what he or she *cannot* do that concrete-operational children *can* do. Children from 4–11 years of age are presented with specified tasks. The concrete-operational child (7–11 years) consistently solves them while the intuitive-phase child fails them. The thinking of the intuitive-phase child lacks certain logical properties, which is illustrated by his or her failure to solve these tasks; intuitive thinking, therefore, is largely defined in terms of the absence of these logical properties. For that reason, we will discuss some of the characteristics of intuitive and concrete-operational thinking in more detail in the next section.

The Concrete-Operational Period

One major transition in cognitive development is that from preoperational to concrete-operational thought. The static, centered, and irreversible thought of the preoperational child gives way to more mobile, flexible, and reversible thought. Though the transition is gradual, the regulations of the intuitive phase seem to reach their limits almost suddenly. The child is no longer limited to approaching new problems through a succession of actual and mental experiments. When asked to classify objects according to different dimensions, or to order them in a series along a single dimension, the concrete-operational child acts immediately in a systematic, organized manner. His or her actions indicate a qualitative change in thought processes and the existence of more complex cognitive structures than had existed heretofore.

What is the *nature* of these cognitive structures that develop in most children by 7 or 8 years of age; and *how* does the child get from preoperational to concrete-operational thought? Piaget (1937, 1949) has developed logico-mathematical models, called *groupings,* that help to communicate, more precisely than would otherwise be possible, the manner in which the child's thought processes are organized (that is, their structure).

Before we discuss *groupings,* however, it might be helpful to discuss the reasons this period of development is called *concrete-operational.* First, it is necessary to ask what is an *operation.* You will recall that when Piaget discussed the development of symbols in the young child he indicated that they were first and foremost internalized actions. It should come as no surprise, then, that operations, which depend on symbolic thinking, are also internalized actions. They are actions, since they are carried out on objects before being performed on symbols. They are internalizable, since they can also be carried out in thought without losing their original character of actions.

A unique characteristic of operations is that they can never occur in isolation. They are coordinated and integrated with other actions to form systems characterized by laws that apply to the system as a whole. One cannot place objects into a class, for example, without considering the relationship of that class to other classes. That is, all classes derive from some sort of supraordinate classification system. Thus when school-aged children classify objects, they demonstrate that they are capable of implementing a whole classification *system* and not just a single class. Similarly, when they order sticks along a single dimension (for example, by length, from the longest to the shortest), their actions demonstrate the presence of an implicit strategy that is itself an internalized, organized system of actions.

Second, why are the concrete operations called *concrete*? They are concrete because they are operations limited to being performed on concrete, manipulable objects. The concrete-operational child is only able to organize and order objects, numbers, and events that are real and that exist in the immediate here and now. Later, in the formal-operational period, the adolescent will be able to think of possibilities that do not exist in reality and to see that reality is just a special case of what is possible (Flavell, 1963). However, at this stage the child is concrete-operational and can deal only with the possible.

Groupings. We stated earlier that Piaget employs a logico-mathematical model to describe the organization of the thought structures underlying the activities of the concrete-operational child. He calls this formal descriptive model a *grouping* (Piaget, 1937). From a strictly logico-mathematical view, a grouping refers to a set of elements (such as classes or relations) on which (1) certain operations can be performed (such as addition, subtraction, multiplication, division, and so on) and that (2) exist as a part of a hierarchical system in which (3) the elements follow a law (or laws) of combination so that the whole system has the properties of reversibility, identity, composition (closure), and associativity (Piaget, 1950).

Rather than attempting to explain fully the logico-mathematical meaning of the term *grouping* in the abstract, it may be more meaningful to illustrate groupings and their properties with concrete examples. Piaget provides many such examples, which illustrate the way in which he attempts to relate the child's activities and his underlying thought structures to groupings.

It is important to recognize at this point that groupings are nothing more or less than *models* of the organization of the thought processes of the concrete-operational child. Piaget believes that the properties of groupings (reversibility, identity, combinativity, and associativity) closely resemble the properties of concrete-operational thought structures. But he does not believe that children are aware of the structure of their concrete operations or its formal properties. Rather, children classify, seriate, conserve, and so on, in such a way that their actions allow one to *infer* that their thought structures possess the properties of reversibility, identity, and so on. It is in this way that the logico-mathematical structures, the groupings, are useful—simply as a formal description of concrete-operational thought.

Nine groupings characterize concrete-operational thought. However, we will discuss only the first because these groupings have been adequately described earlier by a number of authors (see, for example, Flavell, 1963). In addition, the groupings all possess the same properties (composition, associativity, identity, and reversibility), which are used by Piaget to describe concrete-operational thought. These properties, rather than the groupings, will be emphasized.

To study the way in which they develop and operate logically with "classes," Piaget often presented children of different ages with flat, plastic geometric designs such as squares, circles, triangles, and so on, of various colors. These were then mixed and the child was told to put together the things that were alike. Piaget was interested in finding out whether the child could form true classes, that is, classes that were (1) mutually exclusive (no objects being included in two classes at once) and (2) defined by a certain property (squareness, circleness, and so on) that determined the members of each class.

He found that toward the end of the preoperational period, children of about 5 to 7 years of age became capable of forming true classes. If presented with a collection containing red and yellow squares and triangles, for example, the intuitive-phase child can arrange them into four classes as shown in Table 1. These are true classes because they are mutally exclusive and are defined by specific properties. But the late preoperational child goes even beyond that—he or she can arrange the designs in hierarchical fashion, so that the general class of squares is subdivided into red squares and yellow squares and the general class of triangles is divided into red triangles and yellow triangles.

However, the preoperational child still lacks a very important understanding of the hierarchies he or she is able to arrange: the child does not understand the relation between subclasses and their supraordinate class. This is illustrated by the fact that the child is unable to solve the problem that Piaget calls *class-inclusion*. One example is an experiment by Piaget (1952) in which he presented children with 20 wooden beads, *B*, 17 of them brown, *A*, and 3 of them white, *A'*. Although preoperational children could readily determine that they "could make a longer necklace" with the brown beads than the white beads, they could

Table 1. Classification by Color and Shape

		Shape	
		Squares	Triangles
Color	Red	Red Squares	Red Triangles
	Yellow	Yellow Squares	Yellow Triangles

not correctly answer the question of whether the *wooden* beads or the *brown* beads would make a longer necklace. Typically, children from 5 to 7 years of age responded that the brown beads would make a longer necklace. Piaget interprets this kind of behavior to mean that the child cannot yet keep in mind the supraordinate class B and the subordinate classes A and A' simultaneously. When the preoperational child's attention is centered on the larger subordinate class A, "brownness" is salient but "woodenness" seems to fade from awareness. Thus only the white beads remain for comparison.

In contrast, the concrete-operational child immediately understands that there are more wooden beads than either brown or white beads ($B > A$ or A'), that both the brown and white beads are wooden, that removing the brown wooden beads leaves only the white wooden beads ($B - A = A'$), and that removing the white wooden beads leaves only the brown wooden beads ($B - A' = A$). In other words, the concrete-operational child grasps the relation of the parts to the whole and to each other. The concrete-operational child can think *simultaneously* in terms of the whole and its parts. Thus the child at this stage has decentered to the point where he or she is not limited to being exclusively preoccupied with either the part or the whole.

Although concrete-operational children are able to construct a hierarchical arrangement and understand the relation of the parts to the whole when dealing with concrete objects, they still may not be able to solve class-inclusion problems in which concrete objects are not present. For example, it may be difficult for them to grasp fully the notion that Lafayette is a city within the state of Indiana. When the child at this stage leaves Lafayette, he or she may think Indiana has been left, too; or when he or she returns to Indiana from out of state, the child may be confused by the fact that he or she is not necessarily in Lafayette as well. But concrete-operational children have made considerable progress from preoperational thought in that they can deal with the part–whole problem logically as long as they interact with concrete objects.

The Addition of Classes: Grouping I. Earlier we said that the logico-mathematical groupings had certain properties that are very similar to the properties of concrete-operational thought. We are now to the point where we can understand the relationship of the grouping to the kind of concrete-operational thought demonstrated by the class-inclusion problem (see Piaget, 1950).

The first grouping is a system with a set of implicit rules that regulate class operations such as those we saw in the wooden-beads problem. Five properties define the structure of the grouping and, by analogy, the concrete-operational child's thought structure.

The first property is *composition,* or *combinativity,* which mandates that the combination of any two elements (classes) of the system will result in another element within the system. For example, if we combine brown and white beads in the class-inclusion problem, we obtain the general class of wooden beads; or if we combine red and yellow triangles, we obtain the general class of triangles. In general, we find that $A + A' = B$. This property can, of course, be extended to hierarchies having greater numbers of subelements than two, such as $A + A' + A'' = A^n = B$.

The second property is *associativity*, which mandates that the sum of a series of elements is independent of the way they are grouped. Suppose, in the class-inclusion problem, we have three colors of wooden beads: brown, A, white, A', and yellow, A''. It makes no difference in our final result if we first group $(A + A')$ together and add that sum to A''; or, if we first group $(A' + A'')$ together and add that sum to A—in either case, we arrive at the sum B: $(A + A') + A'' = A + (A' + A'') = B$.

The third property is *identity*, which requires that there be one element in the system, which, when combined with any other element, produces no change. The obvious identity element with classes is the null class. If we do not add any other class to the brown beads, A, we will still have only brown beads, A.

The fourth property is *reversibility*, which states that for every element in the system, there is one element (the *inverse*), which when combined with the first, produces the identity element. Every logical operation is reversible in the sense that an inverse operation cancels, or *negates*, it. For example, the inverse operation of adding white beads, A', to brown beads, A, to get the class of all wooden beads, B, is to subtract the white beads from the wooden beads. This produces the class of brown beads again, that is, $A + A' = B$ but $B - A' = A$, which brings us back to the starting point. Thus the inverse operation of adding a class is subtracting the same class—a negation that cancels out the first operation.

The fifth property has to do with the *special identities* and has two versions: tautology and resorption. Piaget uses the word *tautology* to refer to what happens if we combine a class with itself: namely, the class is unchanged—brown beads plus brown beads yields brown beads $(A + A = A)$. Thus every class functions as its own identity element. Another aspect of this is *resorption*: if we combine brown beads and wooden beads, we get wooden beads $(A + B = B)$. Adding A to B is like adding nothing to B so that A functions like an identity element.

These five properties, then, provide a formal description of grouping I, the addition of classes. By analogy, they also describe the processes underlying the child's performance on class-inclusion problems.

The same properties hold in providing a formal description of the manner in which the concrete-operational child can find the intersect, or the logical product, of two classes of objects. For example, given two objects in a sequence—a three-inch, dark-green square and a two-inch medium-green square—the child can complete the sequence with a one-inch light-green square (Piaget calls this the *multiplication* of classes). This requires the consideration of the attributes of two classes simultaneously, to form and operate on double matrices.

Similarly, the concrete-operational child can perform logical operations on the *relations* that exist between two or more objects. For example, he or she can order a set of ten sticks from large to small and even establish a one-to-one correspondence between two ordered series of objects (Piaget & Szeminska, 1952). The child can make transitive inferences as demonstrated by his or her ability to understand that stick number five, for instance, is both longer than stick number six and shorter than stick number four—at the *same time*. The child can go beyond the information given in a task based on transitive relations, that is, he or she can logically deduce that stick *A* is longer than stick *C* even though no direct comparison of those two sticks was made *if* the relationship *A* > *B* and *B* > *C* was previously made known.

Finally, the properties of combinativity, associativity, reversibility, and identity provide a formal description of how the concrete-operational child operates on numbers. This is not surpising since number is essentially a synthesis of two components, classes (for example, a group of six days and a group of six flowers have in common their "sixness") and asymmetrical relations (the ordinal relationship between numbers, such as three is greater than two but less than four).

Summary of Concrete-Operational Structures. The most outstanding feature of concrete-operational thought structure is that it is *reversible*. This is evident in the way children at this stage can *negate*, or cancel out, an action on classes by an inverse action; it is evident in the way they can grasp the *reciprocity* inherent in an ordered series of relations; and it is evident in their ability to *conserve* number. Concrete-operational children can *coordinate* two dimensions at once, whether they are constructing a double-entry matrix of classes or relations or recognizing that the change in length of a row of objects is balanced by a compensating, and inverse, change in its density in a number-conservation task. In these and other ways, their thought structures exhibit the grouping properties of composition, associativity, reversibility, general identity, and the special identities.

In short, concrete-operational children's thought is *operational* in that it is characterized by representational, or internalized, actions that are part of an organized network of related acts. But it is still *concrete*. Their thought is only operational as long as they are dealing with concrete, manipulable objects or real events. Further development must occur before the child will be able to think in terms of abstract logical propositions, to separate the form of a logical argument from its specific content.

The Formal-Operational Period

Concrete-operational children's thought achieves some major advances over that of the preoperational child. One important advance is the beginnings of going beyond the information immediately before them. However, they always begin with what is real; extrapolations only occur to them as they interact with the concrete objects before them.

The major transformation in thought that takes place around 11 or 12 years of age is the ability to see reality as only one special case among the possible. In contrast to younger children, adolescents begin their consideration of the data before them by thinking of all the possible relations that could hold true and *then* test out which possibilities exist in reality. In other words, they use the *hypothetico-deductive* method. The formal-operational adolescent reverses the concrete-operational child's approach of going from the actual to the potential—

the adolescent starts with a number of logical possibilities and determines which are realized or realizable.

The thought structures of concrete-operational children are not yet integrated into a single system. The operations deriving from the separate groupings are still uncoordinated to some degree. For example, they are capable of two kinds of reversibility—*negation* for operating on classes and *reciprocity* for operating on relations. But they are not yet capable of coordinating these two kinds of reversibility. We shall see in a moment that such coordination is necessary for dealing with many problems of a more abstract nature.

The formal-operational adolescent, on the other hand, can make such coordinations because he or she is capable of thinking in terms of propositions, or formal statements. Formal-operational thought is not limited to "first-order" operations with classes and relations, as is the thought of the concrete-operational child:

> He takes the *results* of these concrete operations, casts them in the form of propositions, and then proceeds to operate further upon them, i.e., make various kinds of logical connections between them. . . . Formal operations, then, are really operations performed upon the results of prior (concrete) operations. [Flavell, 1963, p. 205]

Piaget refers to formal operations, then, as *operations of the second power,* or "second-order" operations (Piaget, 1950, p. 148). This ability to operate on operations, to think propositionally, permits a more integrated reversibility of thought than was possible at the concrete-operational level. For example, the adolescent operating with propositions such as "*q* implies *p*" can employ two kinds of reversible operations with respect to that statement, that is, "*q* does *not* imply *p*," a *negation* of the original statement, or "*p* implies *q*," the *reciprocal* of the original statement. This increased reversibility of the thought structures underlies the adolescent's ability to go beyond the real to the possible and to use the hypothetico-deductive method.

Formal operations, then, enable the adolescent to follow the *form* of an argument rather than its concrete content. The concrete-operational child's thought is not sufficiently detached or dissociated from the raw data with which he or she is operating to permit this kind of content-free, "formal" thinking. Propositional thinking frees the adolescent from the immediate here and now and results in a more flexible, integrated system of thought that possesses a very high degree of equilibrium.

Just as he did at the concrete-operational level, Piaget employs logico-mathematical models to describe formal-operational thought. These models are complex but basically involve two logical models, the *combinatorial system* and the *INRC group.* We will consider only limited portions of these models. We will consider first the 16 binary operations as a special case of the combinatorial system.

The Combinatorial System: Sixteen Binary Operations.   The adolescent, like the mature adult, is capable of combining propositions or hypotheses in a

way that is best described by modern symbolic or algorithmic logic. We will consider two examples of adolescent thinking that demonstrate this in a moment. First, we need to illustrate some of the propositional symbols used in a symbolic logic in a hypothetical example.

Piaget and Inhelder (1969) provided an example in which p is a proposition (an animal is a swan), $\bar{p}$ is its negative (an animal is not a swan), q is another proposition (an animal is white), and $\bar{q}$ is its negative (an animal is not white). These propositions can be combined in a "conjunctive" or "disjunctive" manner. We will use the sign "·" for conjunctions and "V" for disjunctions. For example, the expression $p \cdot q$ reads that both p and q are true at the same time, that is, an animal is both a swan and white. The expression p V q, the disjunction, reads that *either* only p is true, *or* only q is true, *or* that *both* are true. The only possibility that disjunction leaves out is that neither p nor q is true. Thus, p V q could also be stated as $(p \cdot \bar{q})$ V $(\bar{p} \cdot q)$ V $(p \cdot q)$, that is, either the animal is a swan and not white, or the animal is white and not a swan, or the animal is both a swan *and* white.

The concrete-operational child, given the task of classifying animals as either swans or not swans and, at the same time, classifying them as either white or not white, is capable of filling in a matrix like that in Table 2. That is, the child of seven or eight can form a simple multiplicative grouping.

However, the formal-operational child can not only complete this kind of matrix but can take the four multiplicative associations (the propositions) that result and derive sixteen combinations. He or she does that by taking them one at a time, two at a time, three at a time, or four at a time.

1. 0
2. $p \cdot q$
3. $p \cdot \bar{q}$
4. $\bar{p} \cdot q$
5. $\bar{p} \cdot \bar{q}$
6. $(p \cdot q)$ V $(p \cdot \bar{q})$
7. $(p \cdot q)$ V $(\bar{p} \cdot q)$
8. $(p \cdot q)$ V $(\bar{p} \cdot \bar{q})$
9. $(p \cdot \bar{q})$ V $(\bar{p} \cdot q)$
10. $(p \cdot \bar{q})$ V $(\bar{p} \cdot \bar{q})$
11. $(\bar{p} \cdot q)$ V $(\bar{p} \cdot \bar{q})$
12. $(p \cdot q)$ V $(p \cdot \bar{q})$ V $(\bar{p} \cdot q)$
13. $(p \cdot q)$ V $(\bar{p} \cdot \bar{q})$ V $(\bar{p} \cdot \bar{q})$
14. $(p \cdot q)$ V $(\bar{p} \cdot q)$ V $(\bar{p} \cdot q)$
15. $(p \cdot \bar{q})$ V $(\bar{p} \cdot q)$ V $(\bar{p} \cdot q)$
16. $(p \cdot q)$ V $(p \cdot \bar{q})$ V $(\bar{p} \cdot q)$ V $(\bar{p} \cdot \bar{q})$

Each of these 16 statements can be thought of as a hypothesis about the possible attributes of an animal. For example, statement 6 is the hypothesis that the animal is either a white swan $(p \cdot q)$ or just a swan, but not white $(p \cdot \bar{q})$; statement 13 is the fairly loose hypothesis that either the animal is a white swan $(p \cdot q)$, or it is a swan, but not white $(p \cdot \bar{q})$, or the animal is neither a swan nor white $(\bar{p} \cdot \bar{q})$.

Piaget and Inhelder state:

These sixteen combinations (or 256 combinations in the case of three propositions, etc.) constitute new and altogether distinct operations which may be called "propositional," since they consist in combining propositions from the point of view only of their being true or false. For example, if the four associations indicated [in

Table 2] are true, then there is no relation necessarily between swans and whiteness. Before the discovery of the black swans of Australia, however, we would have said that the association $p \cdot \bar{q}$ was false. That would have left "$p \cdot q$ or $\bar{p} \cdot q$ or $\bar{p} \cdot \bar{q}$;" that is, an implication: swan implies whiteness because if it is a swan it is white; but an object may be white without being a swan ($\bar{p} \cdot q$) or be neither white nor a swan ($\bar{p} \cdot \bar{q}$). [1969, p. 135n]

Inhelder and Piaget (1958) have demonstrated these differences between concrete and formal-operational thought in the process of investigating the manner in which children of different ages deal with problems of physics and chemistry. For example, in one experiment subjects were given the opportunity to discover Archimedes' law of floating bodies. They were presented with several buckets of water and a variety of objects and asked to classify the objects according to whether or not they float on water. They were then asked to summarize their observations and to look for a law.

In the early phases of the concrete-operational period, children typically classify objects in one of three ways: (1) objects that float, (2) objects that sink, and (3) objects that float or sink depending on conditions. They are still somewhat confused by the fact that some heavy objects (such as a large piece of wood) float while some light objects (such as a needle) sink, and they attempt to resolve this contradiction. Eventually, they arrive at a double-entry classification: small light objects, small heavy objects, large light objects, and large heavy objects.

Formal-operational children, on the other hand, approach the problem in quite a different way even though they may start out by considering the same kind of double-entry classification as concrete-operational children do. Formal-operational children typically form hypotheses without recourse to observation and then reject their own hypotheses. For example, they might eliminate absolute weight as a factor by noting that wood can be heavy and it floats or that some light objects sink. Inhelder and Piaget (1958) say that adolescents view the problem in terms of all possible combinations and proceed in terms of the "implications or nonimplications" of the possible hypotheses they derive.

Formal-operational adolescents also feel the need to prove, or verify, their assertions. Their proofs take into account the totality of possible combinations and consist of a logical demonstration of the truth or falseness of a general

Table 2. Classification of Animals by Two Attributes

		White	
		Yes (q)	No ($\bar{q}$)
Swan	Yes (p)	$p \cdot q$	$p \cdot \bar{q}$
	No ($\bar{p}$)	$\bar{p} \cdot q$	$\bar{p} \cdot \bar{q}$

assertion. However, it is usually not until 13 or 15 years of age that they discover "the rule of one variable." That is, they attempt to hold everything else constant but the one variable they manipulate. Typically, it is easier for them on this particular problem to vary weight and leave volume constant than to operate the other way around. For example, one 14-year-old subject said: "I take a wooden cube and a plastic cube which I fill with water. (The cubes are the same size.) I weigh them, and the difference can be seen on the scale according to whether an object is heavier or lighter than water" (Inhelder & Piaget, 1958, p. 44). Obviously, this subject has discovered, and proved, that the weight of the object must be considered *in proportion to* the weight of the water it displaces.

Thus the combinatorial system, and, in particular, the 16 binary operations, provides a model that describes the adolescent's ability to generate hypotheses. It is the systematic, orderly, and exhaustive manner of the adolescent in approaching problem-solving tasks that Piaget attempts to emphasize by this model. Piaget is not, of course, implying that the adolescent is familiar with logical symbols, or the 16 binary operations. But, his or her activities in solving problems suggest that his or her thought structures resemble, and have many of the same properties as, the combinatorial system. This is one of the logical models Piaget uses, then, to describe adolescent thought.

The INRC Group. A second model that Piaget uses to describe adolescent thought is the system of operations known to logicians as the INRC group (Inhelder & Piaget, 1958, pp. 150–181). The four transformations that the letters *I, N, R,* and *C* refer to are:

1. *Identity (I).* This is the "null" transformation which, when performed on any proposition, leaves it unchanged. Thus, the identity transformation for the proposition $p \cdot q$ is $p \cdot q$; similarly, $I(p \vee q) = p \vee q; I(\bar{p} \cdot q) = \bar{p} \cdot q$, and so on.

2. *Negation (N).* This transformation changes everything in the proposition to which it is applied: assertions become negations, negations become assertions, conjunctions become disjunctions, and disjunctions become conjunctions. Thus $N(p \cdot q) = \bar{p} \vee \bar{q}; N(\bar{p} \vee q) = p \cdot \bar{q}$, and so on.

3. *Reciprocal (R).* This transformation changes assertions and negations but leaves conjunctions and disjunctions unchanged. Thus $R(p \cdot q) = \bar{p} \cdot \bar{q}; R(\bar{p} \vee \bar{q}) = p \vee q; R(\bar{p} \cdot q) = p \cdot \bar{q}$, and so on.

4. *Correlative (C).* This transformation changes conjunctions and disjunctions but does not change assertions and negations. Thus, $C(p \cdot q) = p \vee q; C(\bar{p} \cdot q) = \bar{p} \vee q$, and so on.

These four elements form a group that has the same properties as the groupings of the concrete-operational period (composition, associativity, reversibility, and identity) when they are combined (cf. Inhelder & Piaget, 1958).

What activities do adolescents perform that indicate that their underlying thought processes correspond to the INRC group? That is, how do they show that they can operate with these transformations on propositions? Inhelder and Piaget (1958) have attempted to demonstrate this by presenting children of various ages with problems from physics and chemistry and observing how they approach them.

An example of one such problem involves a balance-type weighing instrument that is used in studying the child's discovery of the law of equilibrium. In this problem the child is required to discover the relationships between weight, distance, and height in a weighing instrument similar to that in Figure 1. The task is to make the crossbar balance and to discover the factors that control this balance.

In the early phases of the concrete-operational period, children discover that equal weights located at equal distances from the fulcrum will balance, that is, come into equilibrium through symmetry. They also recognize that equal weights at unequal distances do not balance and they can substitute a number of lighter weights for a heavier weight. In the process of trying out various relationships between the weights and distances on the balance, they discover that there is some kind of relationship between a smaller weight at a greater distance from the fulcrum and a greater weight at a smaller distance. For example, they may discover that a 5-gram weight at a distance of 10 holes from the fulcrum balances a 10-gram weight at the distance of 5 holes, a weight $\times$ distance multiplicative relationship. But they have difficulty generalizing from this relationship. For example, they cannot immediately invert this kind of relationship on opposite sides of the fulcrum. Another period of trial and error is required. In the later phase of concrete operations they develop the general notion that things "weigh more" when they are farther from the fulcrum. If they have a heavier weight on one side of the balance, they know that a lighter weight on the opposite side will have to be a greater distance from the fulcrum to achieve balance. In other words, they begin to coordinate unequal weights and distances.

In the early phases of the formal-operational period, the adolescent begins to use what Piaget calls "the proportionality scheme." For example, if he or she is given two weights to balance, one weighing exactly twice as much as the other,

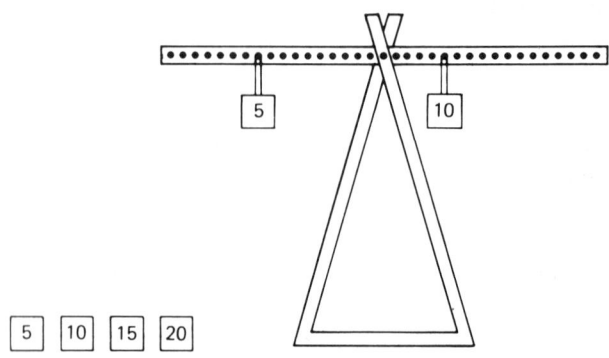

Figure 1. Balance Weighing Instrument.

he or she knows, and usually can state, that the heavier weight will have to be placed half the distance from the fulcrum than the lighter weight. Later, he or she can clearly recognize the proportional relationship between weight, W, and distance, D, such that $W1/W2 = D1/D2$. For example, one 13-year-old demonstrated the physics concept of work when he said, "You need more force to raise weights placed at the extremes than when it's closer to the center . . . because it has to cover a greater distance." This same boy also demonstrated the proportionality scheme: "If one weight on the balance is three times the other, you put it a third of the way because the distance (upward) it goes is three times less" (Inhelder and Piaget, 1958, pp. 174–175).

How does this kind of performance by the adolescent correspond to the INRC group? Inhelder and Piaget (1958) cast the problem into propositional language: let p stand for a fixed increase in weight, and $\bar{p}$ a corresponding decrease in weight; q represents a fixed increase in distance and $\bar{q}$ a corresponding decrease of distance on the same arm of the balance. Similarly, p' and q' correspond to p and q on the opposite arm and $\bar{p}'$ and $\bar{q}'$ correspond to $\bar{p}$ and $\bar{q}$.

Thus, the statement $p \cdot q$ can be used to indicate that the weight and the distance have been increased simultaneously on one of the arms. The identity transformation of that statement, $I(p \cdot q)$, will, of course, leave it unchanged. If such an operation were carried out by the adolescent on the left side, for example, the effect would be to lower the arm on that side of the fulcrum.

The negation transformation would have the opposite effect, that is, cause the left side to move upward. This could be accomplished by reducing the distance of the weight from the fulcrum, by diminishing the weight on the left side of the balance, or by doing both. These three operations correspond to the logical statement of the negation transformation discussed earlier: $N(p \cdot q) = (\bar{p} \lor \bar{q}) = (p \cdot \bar{q}) \lor (\bar{p} \cdot q) \lor (\bar{p} \cdot \bar{q})$.

The reciprocal transformation would have the same effect on the crossbar as the negation transformation, that is, cause the left side to move upward. In this case, the reciprocal operation of increasing the weight and distance on the left side would be to increase the weight and distance on the right side. This can be written as $R(p \cdot q) = (p' \cdot q')$, which is equivalent to compensating increasing weight and distance on the left side by decreasing both on that side. In other words, $R(p \cdot q) = (p' \cdot q') = \bar{p} \cdot \bar{q}$.

Finally, the correlative transformation has the same effect on the crossbar as the identity transformation, that is, it causes the left side to lower. This could be accomplished by decreasing the weight and distance of the weight from the fulcrum on the right side $(\bar{p}' \cdot \bar{q}')$, by increasing the weight on the left side, by increasing the distance of the weight from the fulcrum on the left side, or by doing both. Recall that the latter three operations correspond to the logical statement of the correlative transformation discussed earlier: $C(p \cdot q) = (p \lor q) = (p \cdot \bar{q}) \lor (\bar{p} \cdot q) \lor (p \cdot q)$.

What formal-operational adolescents understand is that there is more than one way to lower the left arm of the crossbar of a balance in equilibrium: in addition to increasing the weight and distance simultaneously on the left side (the identity operation), they can, on the left side, increase the weight alone or increase the distance alone; on the right side, they can decrease the weight and/or distance (the correlative operations). They also understand that they can cancel out the effect of increasing weight and distance on the left side by decreasing the weight, or decreasing the distance, or doing both simultaneously (the negation transformation); or, they can accomplish the same thing by increasing the weight and distance on the right side of the crossbar (the reciprocal transformation). Further, this is equivalent to the proportional statement

$$\frac{I\,(p\cdot q)}{R\,(p\cdot q)} = \frac{C\,(p\cdot q)}{N\,(p\cdot q)},$$

that is, the increase of weight and distance on one arm of the balance (the left) is to the increase of weight and distance on the other side of the balance (the symmetrical operation) as decreasing the weight and distance on the second arm of the balance (the right) is to decreasing the weight or distance on the first arm (the left).

Adolescents demonstrate an implicit understanding of this kind of proportionality schema by their reasoning with the balance problem. They do a very similar thing when they prove that they are capable of solving such verbal analogies as "Indianapolis is to Indiana as Boston is to Massachusetts" or "Boys are to men as girls are to women." This kind of reasoning has long been thought to be one of the hallmarks of intelligence (Spearman, 1923).

Summary of the Formal Operations.   Piaget advances the combinatorial system (16 binary operations) and the INRC group as logical models that are intended to provide a formal description of the adolescent's thought structure. They describe the structure underlying the adolescent's activities, but they do not exactly reproduce every detail of his or her performance. Neither do these models imply that the adolescent understands symbolic logic in any explicit way. They are integrated systems that have properties analogous to those of the adolescent's system of thought. These models are intended to describe the adolescents' basic capacities, or competencies, and not their actual performance in any given situation. But, it is at the same time, adolescents' activities in various problem-solving tasks from which Piaget infers that their thought structures resemble these models.

In general, formal-operational adolescents are capable of using the hypothetico-deductive method of reasoning. They think in terms of the possible rather than the real and are able to test out possibilities in a systematic and orderly fashion to determine which exist in reality. They can "operate on operations," or propositions, to exhaust all the possibilities in a problem situation. Adolescents can conduct controlled experiments, holding all variables constant but one, to determine the effects of that variable. In short, they are capable of acting like scientists.

The thought structures of the adolescent have reached a very high degree of equilibrium. Thought is now reversible in two distinct, but integrated, ways. An action in one direction can be reversed in several different ways, resulting in a return to the starting point. The adolescent reaches this high degree of equilibrium as he or she attempts to resolve the contradictions and failures experienced during the concrete-operational period. An internal reorganization of thought structures occurs as a result of the subjective uncertainty that is thereby felt in many problem situations. But the reorganization occurs very gradually as the adolescent continually develops a more flexible, more integrated, and better equilibrated system of thought operations.

Piaget believes that it is the acquisition of formal operations that often causes adolescents to be idealistic (even social reformers), as well as being able to solve physical problems. Because the attention of adolescents is no longer confined to reality, they can think of various alternative ways that the world might be run besides the particular present way. They take delight in thinking of these alternatives and comparing their views with others. In many ways, they have acquired the intellectual apparatus that enables them to function as mature adults, adapting to, and modifying, their physical and social surroundings.

PIAGET'S IMPACT ON CURRENT MODELS OF INTELLECTUAL DEVELOPMENT

In this final section, the growing interest in the relationship (or potential relationship) between Piaget's theory and information-processing approaches to studying cognitive development will be briefly explored. Both approaches have had a significant impact on current research and models of development, but they have usually been considered antagonistic to each other. We are now beginning to see that they also have many common features. As the metaphor of the digital computer is used more and more frequently to characterize the representation of human thought, many of Piaget's core concepts are finding renewed application. This is despite some important differences between the "organismic" approach of Piaget and the more "mechanistic" approach that computer metaphors provide.

Hunt (1961) was one of the first to see the analogy between the active and constructive strategies for information processing of computer models and Piaget's model of intelligence. In both approaches, mental processes are viewed as internalized activities that transform or manipulate information. Also, stored information is viewed in both models as hierarchically arranged and accessed. However, it is true that information-processing approaches tend to emphasize, more than Piaget did, how such conceptually related items are linked associatively.

Another point of some similarity between these two approaches is the mechanism by which the child's knowledge base is modified. In a particularly lucid account of the information-processing approach to cognitive development, Kail and Bisanz have drawn a parallel between what they call "inconsistency detectors" in informational systems and Piaget's notions of equilibration:

> Consider problem solving as an example. The outcome of a particular solution process may be disconfirmed by information from the environment (e.g., Kendler, 1979), or the results of two different processes may be inconsistent with each other (e.g., Inhelder, Sinclair, & Bovet, 1974). When an inconsistency is detected, . . . functions are activated until the inconsistency is reduced or eliminated. This notion of inconsistency detectors parallels Piaget's ideas about "disequilibrium" and "equilibration" and is related to the widely used concept of "match" between cognitive structures and environmental events (e.g., Hunt, 1961). [1982, p. 66]

Kail and Bisanz point out that the computer metaphor includes characteristics of both the machine and the programs associated with the machine. Thus information-processing systems cannot be assumed to be passive. The "program" component is very flexible and allows for the inclusion of *active* strategies for processing information. As they state, "The metaphoric and representational use of the computer extends to its operations and organization but does not include its physical characteristics" (Kail & Bisanz, 1982, p. 70).

Other investigators with an information-processing orientation have applied their approach to problem-solving tasks devised by Piaget. For example, Siegler (1976, 1981, 1983) identified a set of four rules to describe the developmental changes in children's judgments on a balance-scale problem from the ages of five to seventeen. These rules became increasingly comprehensive and more powerful with development. Although his approach to studying children's judgments on the balance-scale task was different from Piaget's and more consistent with an information-processing approach, his findings were highly consistent with those of Piaget.

Interestingly, many findings of investigators whose work derives from an information-processing view, and who see their work as contradicting Piaget's theory, could actually be construed as supporting his theory. Because this is an important point, the controversy surrounding children's making of transitive inferences will be presented next in some detail. This controversy illustrates how the two approaches are often unnecessarily presented as contradictory when a careful analysis reveals that they are actually complementary. Much of what follows was taken from a previously unpublished paper by the author (Gruen & Paris, 1979).

The Controversy over Transitive Inferences in Children

Piaget's Original Work.   Logical transitivity among a set of elements exists when a set of paired relations $A : B$ and $B : C$ necessarily determines the relation between $A : C$. The number of elements and type of relation can vary considerably as long as the logical relationship is preserved. For example, one can instantiate transitive relations based on *identity* $(A = B, B = C, A = C)$, *hierarchical classification* $(A > B, B > C, A > C)$, and *comparative relations* $(A > B, B >$

C, $A > C$). Transitive relations may include symmetrical or asymmetrical relations and seriated or nonseriated arrays. In any case, Piaget (Piaget & Szeminska, 1952) has argued that the critical steps in logical or psychological analysis are: (1) the recognition that the middle term linking successive pairs is the *same* element, (2) the recognition of the middle term's *reversible* role to different elements (that is, B is smaller than A and bigger than C), and (3) the *coordination* of discrete elements by deduction of the role of the middle term. Since the concepts of identity, reversibility, and coordination are not attained until the concrete-operational period, transitivity should not be observed until approximately seven–eleven years according to Piaget's theory.

Trabasso's Work. Bryant and Trabasso (1971) conducted an initial study on young children's ability to make transitive inferences. They tested four- to seven-year-olds with an array of five sticks. A five-element array was used rather than Piaget's three-element array to avoid always labeling the first term "tall" and the last element "short." A three-element array confounds absolute responses with transitive judgments while a five-term array includes middle terms (B and D) that are labeled tall and short equally often. Bryant and Trabasso (1971) hypothesized that young children's failure to make transitive inferences was due to memory failure for the premises. Therefore, they included extensive training phases. In the first phase, children were presented each pair of colored sticks in a box of different depth holes (so all sticks protruded equally) and asked which stick was longer or shorter. During learning of the pairs, children were given either verbal or visual feedback regarding the correct choice. In the second phase of training, children were presented all pairs of adjacent sticks until they correctly responded to each pair on six consecutive choices. This procedure ensured memory for the original pairs by overlearning. The test phase involved presentation of all possible pairs (adjacent and inferred) and children were asked either which is shorter or which is longer.

In subsequent studies (cf. Trabasso, 1975), Trabasso and his colleagues provided children with training with both comparatives (longer and shorter), permitting subjects to construct contrastive and ordinal relations rather than nominal labels of long and short. With striking consistency, Trabasso and his colleagues have found that four- to seven-year-olds can judge actual and implied pair relations nearly perfectly. Transitive judgments are made readily by children when they remember the original premises. In fact, conditionalizing transitive judgments on the premises reveals that the observed values are very close to the predicted values.

According to Trabasso, children solve transitive-order problems in a manner similar to adults. The first stage of processing involves construction of a linear array of all elements. This array may be spatial or linguistic in nature. The child first isolates the end points of the array and begins to construct paired relations in an ends-inward fashion. The error data during training show more errors and more trials to reach criterion for middle pairs in support of this interpretation. The use of both comparative terms during training (or presentation of premises) is critical here because it promotes the child's construction of an ordinal array and not simply a nominal division of the dimension (that is, tall and short sticks). In a sense, the child is learning the *identity* of middle terms, the *reversible* role of terms, and the *coordination* of elements by placing them in a linear array. Once the array has been constructed (and memory for original pairs ensured by overlearning to a stringent criterion), children access the array easily to make all paired comparisons. The serial positions for errors and reaction times parallel those observed for adults, older children, and retarded children.

Children perform more poorly than adults on this task (1) when only verbal feedback is used and (2) when memory for premises is not ensured. Trabasso concludes that these difficulties are linguistic and mnemonic but not logical deficiencies of children and therefore Piaget's interpretation is incorrect.

Resolution of the Controversy.   Trabasso's research evidence is impressive and his findings are highly consistent. Undoubtedly children and adults *can* solve transitive problems based on comparative relations by accessing a constructed linear array. The processes are influenced similarly for all ages by memory, linguistics, training, and distance parameters. There is also little doubt that Piaget's analysis is not complete since four- and five-year-olds *can learn* to reason accurately about transitive relations.

However, several points need to be made here. Although young children can be trained to reason transitively, they usually fail to do so *spontaneously*. That is, they may not *remember* the premises or *construct* the array ($A > B > C > D > E$) as subgoals that are necessary for later access to implied pairs (such as BD). The often cited failure by four- to seven-year-olds to reason transitively may indicate their *failure to produce* such constructive skills rather than their inability to *comprehend* them.

Second, Trabasso's data indicate training itself shows important developmental differences in learning rates. Children with lower chronological ages and mental ages generally take longer to learn the original pairs *and* longer to construct the linear order. These differences are critical since they reflect poor understanding of the relations among elements and the seriated organization of the ordinal array (as well as poorer linguistic and mnemonic skills). Trabasso's procedure of extensive training eliminates the primary source of developmental differences and so reasoning from a known array appears very similar across ages.

Third, it may be that there are *many* possible strategies children could use to solve transitive reasoning tasks. The demonstration that four- to seven-year-olds *can* learn linear-order strategies or that they do not spontaneously apply logical analyses does not necessarily indicate the developmental progression of what children actually do (that is, their evolving interpretations and solutions of the task).

The Piaget versus Trabasso conflict may actually be artificial since the processes proposed by both may be isomorphic. Training in Trabasso's procedure involves the learning of a seriated, ordinal, linear array and *presupposes* that children know about the *identity, reversibility,* and *coordination* of elements. The array cannot be constructed without this knowledge. Since training and construction of the array yield the largest developmental differences, it seems reasonable to hypothesize that young children have difficulty learning these conceptual relationships.

CONCLUSION

Piaget produced a very rich, logically consistent theory of intellectual development. He chose to represent human thought in terms of formal logic and to use biological metaphors to emphasize the adaptive nature of intelligence. Although his theory doubtlessly will have to be revised and refined as empirical research accumulates, his incredibly detailed descriptions of children's thought processes will continue to be a source of hypotheses regarding intellectual development. His hypothetico-deductive approach to theory building has provided principles that have helped us understand some of the more important parameters of cognitive-structural development. The more inductive approaches of many contemporary investigators of cognitive development, such as information processing, will undoubtedly lead to many worthwhile refinements of these principles and even to the modification of some. But the heuristic value of Piaget's theory is made evident in these efforts, as well as in those that verify his system. Our scientifically based knowledge of intellectual development has been advanced enormously by his contribution.

REFERENCES

Bryant, P. E., & Trabasso, T. (1971). Transitive inference and memory in young children. *Nature, 232,* 456–58.

Flavell, J. H. (1963). *The developmental psychology of Jean Piaget.* Princeton, NJ: Van Nostrand.

Gallagher, J. M. (1977). Piaget's equilibration theory: Biological, cybernetic, and logical roots. In M. H. Appel & L. S. Goldberg (Eds.), *Topics in cognitive development*, Vol. 1, *Equilibration: Theory, research, and application.* New York: Plenum.

Gallagher, J. M., & Reid, D. K. (1981). *The learning theory of Piaget and Inhelder.* Monterey, CA: Brook/Cole.

Ginsburg, H., & Opper, S. (1969). *Piaget's theory of intellectual development: An introduction.* Englewood Cliffs, NJ: Prentice-Hall.

Gruen, G. E., & Doherty, J. A. (1977). Constructivist view of a major developmental shift in early childhood. In I. C. Uzgiris & F. Weizmann (Eds.), *The structuring of experience.* New York: Plenum.

Gruen, G. E., & Paris, S. G. (1979). *Transitive inferencing in children.* Unpublished manuscript.

Hunt, J. McV. (1961). *Intelligence and experience.* New York: Ronald Press.

Inhelder, B. (1968). *The diagnosis of reasoning in the mentally retarded.* New York: Day.

Inhelder, B., & Piaget, J. (1958). *The growth of logical thinking from childhood to adolescence.* New York: Basic Books.

Inhelder, B., Sinclair, H., & Bovet, M. (1974). *Learning and the development of cognition.* Cambridge, MA: Harvard University Press.

Kail, R., & Bisanz, J. (1982). Information processing and cognitive development. *Advances in child development and behavior, 17*, 45–81.

Kendler, T. S. (1979). The development of discrimination learning: A levels of functioning explanation. In H. W. Reese & L. P. Lipsitt (Eds.), *Advances in child development and behavior* (Vol. 13). New York: Academic Press.

Piaget, J. (1937). La réversibilité des operations el l'importance de la notion de "group" pour la psychologie de la pensée. *Proceedings of the 11th International Congress of Psychology,* pp. 433–434.

Piaget, J. (1948). *La représentation de l'espace chez l'enfant.* Paris: Prenes Universitaires de France.

Piaget, J. (1949). *Traité de logique.* Paris: Colin.

Piaget, J. (1950). *The psychology of intelligence.* New York: Harcourt, Brace.

Piaget, J. (1952a). Autobiography. In E. G. Boring, N. S. Langfeld, H. Werner, & R. M. Yerkes (Eds.), *History of psychology in autobiography* (Vol. 4). Worcester, MA: Clark University Press.

Piaget, J. (1952b). *The origins of intelligence in children.* New York: International Universities Press.

Piaget, J. (1962). *Play, dreams and imitation in childhood.* New York: Norton.

Piaget, J. (1970a). *Genetic epistemology.* New York: Columbia University Press.

Piaget, J. (1970b). Piaget's theory. In P. H. Mussen (Ed.), *Carmichael's manual of child psychology* (Vol. 1). New York: Wiley.

Piaget, J. (1971). *Biology and knowledge.* Chicago: University of Chicago Press.

Piaget, J. (1977a). *The development of thought: Equilibrium of cognitive structures.* New York: Viking Press.

Piaget, J. (1977b). The role of action in the development of thinking. In W. Overton & J. M. Gallagher (Eds.), *Knowledge and development,* Vol. 1, *Advances in research and theory.* New York: Plenum.

Piaget, J. (1978). *Behavior and evolution.* New York: Pantheon Books.

Piaget, J., & Inhelder, B. (1956). *The child's conception of space.* London: Routledge & Kegan Paul.

Piaget, J., & Inhelder, B. (1969). *The psychology of the child.* New York: Basic Books.

Piaget, J., & Szeminska, A. (1952). *The child's conception of number.* London: Routledge & Kegan Paul.

Siegler, R. S. (1976). Three aspects of cognitive development. *Cognitive Psychology, 8,* 481–520.

Siegler, R. S. (1981). Developmental sequences within and between concepts. *Monographs of the Society for Research in Child Development, 46* (2, Serial No. 189).

Siegler, R. S. (1983). Information-processing approaches to development. In P. H. Mussen (Ed.), *Carmichael's manual of child psychology.* (Vol. 1) New York: Wiley.

Spearman, C. E. (1923). *The nature of intelligence and the principles of cognition.* New York: MacMillan.

Tanner, J. M., & Inhelder, B. (Eds.) (1956). *Discussions on child development* (Vol. 1). London: Tavistock Publications, Ltd.

Trabasso, T. (1975). Representation, memory, and reasoning: How do we make transitive inferences? In A. D. Pick (Ed.), *Minnesota Symposium on Child Psychology* (Vol. 9). MN: University of Minnesota Press.

FIVE

GENERAL INTELLIGENCE

AN INTEGRATION OF FACTOR, TEST, AND SIMPLEX THEORY

LLOYD G. HUMPHREYS
University of Illinois
Champaign, Illinois

This chapter opens with a short discussion of different approaches to the definition of intelligence and follows with an extended development of the writer's position. After reaching a satisfactory quantitative definition, a modification of current test theory is presented. This approach is congruent with the construction of tests as broad as those for general intelligence. A theory of intelligence requires an appropriate measurement theory. This theory differs from the prevailing doctrine in that it rejects the goals of high item homogeneity and a rigid definition of unidimensionality. The final section presents a description of the construct of general intelligence and integrates this concept with the important information concerning the stability during the course of human development of scores on intelligence tests.

DEFINITIONS OF INTELLIGENCE

The Traditional

Most accounts in the psychological literature assume that intelligence is an innate capacity or learning potential. This is especially characteristic of those who use and interpret clients' scores on intelligence tests. It was also true of most of the pioneers who developed and popularized the first intelligence tests. This is quite clear in the writings of Terman (1916), Wechsler (1939), and Goddard (1913), for example, although Binet's (1916) position was more ambiguous. The latter can be quoted on both sides of this issue. In part test users take their cue from these pioneers, but intelligence as an innate capacity is endemic in Western culture.

People who have been active in test development do tend to narrow the scope of the supposed capacity. They use descriptive phrases, such as manipulation of symbols, dealing with abstractions, mental adaptability, adjustment of thinking to new requirements, and so on. These statements about intelligence are, in effect, content analyses of the items that appear in the tests. For the layman, in contrast, the capacity can refer to almost any human activity and becomes adaptability to one's environment. Intelligence may, in these terms, include physical and personality traits.

Although subjective, the content analysis of items is desirable because it represents the first step in tying the construct of intelligence to the nature of the measuring instrument. It is the teaming of content descriptions with capacity or potential that creates a serious, even insurmountable, problem. Capacity and potential are neither congruent with the measurement operations nor with the correlates of scores on intelligence tests. They are not even congruent with any conceivable measurement operations that depend on behavioral acts. A construct that can be neither measured directly nor inferred from measurements has no place in science. The ubiquity of inferences about capacity from test scores does not make these inferences acceptable.

Cognitive Processes

In recent years interest has risen in defining intelligence in terms of fundamental cognitive operations or processes. This research is closely tied to measurements of the hypothetical processes that are obtained under controlled conditions. This line of research has much to recommend it. The data have suggested intriguing insights into the operations involved in various types of problem-solving, attentive behaviors, and so on.

Individual differences in these laboratory tasks have been correlated with scores on intelligence tests, but it is not possible to make highly definitive generalizations about the size of these relationships. It is fair to conclude that this approach to the definition of intelligence is still in the exploratory phase. Samples are usually small and confidence intervals large; samples are frequently categorized into extreme groups based on the measure of intelligence; the populations sampled are frequently highly restricted in range of talent; the laboratory paradigms have been standardized to a limited extent only. For the applied needs of the clinician, the educational psychologist, or the industrial psychologist, it is also fair to conclude that this approach is promising but any application is still a matter of the distant future.

Factor Analytic

A third approach is the factor analytic, based on the intercorrelations of various measures of individual differences. It is noteworthy that Spearman's (1904) factor-analytic construct of general intelligence antedated the first actual intelligence test of Binet and Simon (1905). Spearman's measures were academic grades. Based on the discrepancy between the reliabilities of his measures and the size of their correlations with other measures, he also required specific factors in addition to the general factor in his theory.

In a sense the last 75–80 years of factor-analytic research have been concerned with the conversion of Spearman's specifics to common factors. This has been done in a readily understandable fashion: namely, by inventing more and more tests, or other measures, that were more and more similar to existing tests. Thurstone (1938) extracted 13 factors from more than 50 tests, interpreted nine, and was sufficiently confident about their definitions to publish tests for seven. In contrast Guilford has had available many more tests and, in his structure-of-intellect model (1967), has hypothesized 150 factors. Humphreys (1981) has suggested that the logic of converting larger and larger proportions of true score variance to common factors actually provides for far more than 150 factors in the domain of intelligence.

The English psychometricians after Spearman, such as Burt (1949) and Vernon (1960), were also describing more factors than Spearman had envisioned, but they retained Spearman's construct of general intelligence as well. They viewed the "structure of intellect" as a hierarchy of progressively broader factors. Thus Vernon placed general intelligence at the top of his hierarchy, followed by major group factors, and then by minor group factors. During this period the English psychometricians did not have available an objective methodology for extracting the factors in the full hierarchical model that could be applied to large correlation matrices.

THEORY OF GENERAL INTELLIGENCE

Thurstone's Error

In retrospect it was a serious error psychologically for Thurstone to call first-order factors, the only ones most investigators report and describe, primary mental abilities. Factor analysis capitalizes on differences in the size of correlations. Any determinants that produce slightly higher correlations among a subset of tests than their correlations with other subsets also produce factors. Tests are invented; therefore factors are invented. Some differences among the determinants of responses to the items in psychological tests produce larger differences in the rank order of individuals than do other differences. Consequently some factors are more easily defined in small samples than others, but ease of definition is not a sufficient basis for a *primary* mental ability. First-order factors are frequently based on differences in the size of correlations that reflect trivial differences in behavior outside the testing room.

The interpretation of first-order factors starts with a content analysis of the test items that define the factors, but it does not typically stop with description. Factors become entities, such as primary mental abilities, and are likened to the chemical elements. This is the error of reification of measurement operations. General intelligence at the level of first-order factoring often becomes a collection of innate capacities.

Higher-Order Factors

It is necessary for those in the tradition initiated by Thurstone to look for broader factors that appear in higher-order factoring if they are concerned with factors of broad psychological meaning. Thurstone (1947) abandoned orthogonal for oblique rotations early in his research and recognized that the rather substantial intercorrelations of his measures of the seven primary mental abilities reflected Spearman's general intelligence. However, many investigators avoided higher-order factors because such factors were seemingly too far removed from the original measures. What is the meaning of a factor defined by factors? Such factors were considered to be highly esoteric and fundamentally different from primary mental abilities.

These problems were solved by Schmid and Leiman (1957) when they showed how simple transformations of oblique factors in two or more orders could produce an orthogonal matrix of hierarchical factors, each defined by a linear combination of the original tests. A higher-order factor is nothing more than a factor defined by more variables than the factors subordinate to it in the hierarchy. Higher-order factors are merely broader factors. Schmid and Leiman provided a bridge between English and American theorists, but it is a bridge that many users of the factor methodology have not yet traversed.

The broad factors arrived at by means of higher-order factoring and the Schmid-Leiman transformations have several important properties. In data in which the model fits well, the communalities of the variables are invariant from the first order to the complete hierarchy. Higher-order factoring does not increase the communalities of the individual variables. Group factors, when considered in the first order only, are not conceptually equivalent to the group factors in the full hierarchy although both are defined by the same variables. The first-order factors that now appear low in the hierarchy "explain" less variance. They represent the traditional verbal, numerical, spatial, and other factors after the variance associated with general intelligence has been removed.

Problems with Hierarchical Solutions

Factors high in the hierarchy have an undesirable attribute from the mathematical point of view. The broader factors are linearly dependent on the narrower factors that are extracted earlier in the process. One can solve this problem rather easily, however, by discarding the residual information furnished by the narrower factors and by using only that portion of their variance that enters the broader factors. For most applied purposes, information relevant to behavior outside the testing room is rarely lost by doing this.

There are also difficulties in finding acceptable hierarchical solutions in many investigations. Small samples cause problems in the factor analysis of variables that, in the population, are fit well by the hierarchical model. In many factor-analytic investigations, however, the population correlations are not fit well. So many different facets may have been used in constructing the tests that overlapping hierarchies may result. Furthermore, there is no current consensus concerning choice of an oblique rotational program. These problems lead to errors in the determination of the number of factors and to uncertainties in the placement of oblique axes.

The interpretation of higher-order factors is, if anything, more subject to reification than first-order factors, but reification is not intrinsic to factor analysis or to a conceptualization of general intelligence. Factors of all degrees of breadth are, in the first instance, merely convenient mathematical dimensions. It is useful theoretically to develop measures of these dimensions, and it is useful practically to develop measures of some of them. The dimensions acquire additional meaning as research proceeds. One can also conclude that the dimension is "real" when it is replicable under carefully defined and acceptable methodological procedures and when it enters into a theoretical framework. More than this is required, however, for a factor to become the equivalent of a chemical element or an entity within the organism. Factors can be described on the basis of the defining tests without assuming an *underlying* trait. Entities lead to misuse and misinterpretation of test scores. All tests sample phenotypic behavioral acts, and phenotypes have many determinants.

An Alternative to Factor Analysis

The empirical basis for the construct of general intelligence does not depend on one's ability to obtain a clean hierarchical solution by factor-analytic methods. The basis for the most general factor lies in the ubiquity in a wide range of talent of positive correlations among measures of cognitive functioning (Humphreys, 1979). One has to look long and hard to find, in a suitable range of talent, a cognitive variable having a confidence interval about a sample correlation that does not include positive values of the population correlation. Sheer number of attempts of very simple items on highly speeded tests may have negative population correlations with the number right on highly cognitive tests of word meaning, arithmetic reasoning, spatial visualization, and so on, but a score that penalizes errors brings this activity back into the intellectual domain.

It is instructive to relate hierarchical factors to the correlations among the tests. The general factor depends on the lowest correlations in the R matrix. A correlation of .09 is seemingly trivial, but if the general factor is all that the two tests have in common, then that correlation is congruent with two factor loadings that can vary from .30 and .30 to .09 and 1.00. If one of the two tests is a measure of abstract reasoning, it can still be a highly valid indicator of the general factor. In contrast, the very highest correlations in the R matrix define not only the narrowest factors, but also help to define a series of broader factors in the hierarchy. The highest correlations determine the first-order factors. The narrowest possible group factor is defined by a correlation between two tests that is slightly but dependably lower than the square root of the product of their respective reliabilities. This situation also defines two small but dependable specific factors.

TEST THEORY MODIFIED

The hierarchical view of the cognitive domain does not presently have a test theory that is congruent with that view. As Jensen (1980) correctly points out, to construct an intelligence test requires compromises with prevailing theory. Tests are supposed to be factor pure. Items must be highly homogeneous. The test must be unidimensional. Test theorists are beguiled by the association of first-order factors and so-called primary mental abilities. Yet the intelligence tests that do not conform to present theory furnish some of the most important information a test user can gather about an individual, a group, or a population. To conclude that one must compromise with theoretical principles in order to construct a valid test of general intelligence puts the cart before the horse. Perhaps test theory should be revised.

Bases for an Alternative Theory

In a series of papers extending over many years, the present writer has questioned and criticized components of standard test theory (Humphreys, 1952, 1956, 1962, 1970, 1981; Hulin & Humphreys, 1980). A summary of the positions reached in these papers will serve as a useful starting point for the discussion of an alternative test theory.

1. Tests of seemingly high homogeneity can frequently be "splintered" into several different tests each more homogeneous than the original and with intercorrelations of estimated true scores less than unity.

2. There are many more facets in ability tests than Guilford's three dimensions. With two or more elements per facet thousands of different tests can be defined in the cognitive domain. These thousands of tests will each approach unidimensionality quite closely.

3. Two homogeneous tests differing in only one element of one facet will have a correlation between estimated true scores of less than unity. In other words there are literally thousands of factors as well as thousands of homogeneous tests.

4. The information furnished by these thousands of tests is highly redundant. The intercorrelations of tests in the ability domain in a wide range of talent are overwhelmingly positive in sign and substantial in size.

5. The test for each combination of facets in the Cartesian product of all facets is psychologically complex although statistically homogeneous. Each such test is an inextricable combination of content, operation, product, and so on. Factor purity is not equivalent to psychological purity.

6. If one establishes factor-pure tests of high homogeneity as the goal of test construction, one is faced with the dilemma of dealing with the thousands of tests and factors that are the result. The common solution

in practice is not to carry a good thing too far, but this is not satisfactory theoretically. How much homogeneity is enough but not too much? There is no way that a psychologist can deal with the myriad tests and factors that conventional theory, based on high homogeneity and unidimensionality, produces. Selection of a much smaller number of tests and factors from the thousands possible omits information. It will be seen that the alternative approach focuses on construct validity, but it also emphasizes the importance of content, defined by facet analysis, in achieving valid measurement of the hypothetical construct. It also produces higher validities for the prediction of socially important criteria.

Item Theory

The approach starts with a discussion of the determinants of responses to items and assumes that examinees are well motivated. There is no reason to administer an ability test to an examinee who is not trying to obtain right answers. When examinees are well motivated, there is no *random* guessing. Choices, whether the test is multiple choice or free response, are determined. The host of determinants can be described more in the manner of Godfrey Thomson (1919) and Edward Thorndike (1926) than in the tradition of Spearman (1914) and Thurstone (1938). Psychologists have been slow to realize that many different subsets of items can be treated as if they measure an underlying dimension or latent trait even though there are multiple determinants. Overlapping multiple determinants can produce correlations and, hence, factors. There is nothing gained, and typically a good deal lost scientifically, by the ubiquitous reification of factors.

Determinants of only one item on a particular occasion constitute measurement error. Most determinants affect more than one item, many on more than one occasion. Situational determinants arise, for example, from instructions concerning guessing and speed of response. Whether the item is presented visually or orally also contributes differentially to its variance. There are major contributions to item variance of determinants considered under the dimensions of content, product, and operation.

A perfect Guttman scale (1944) is a valid model for measuring traits as readily observable and isolatable as the physical traits of height and weight. Tests of height and weight can readily be devised. Each test is of course composed of multiple pass-fail items. The sum of all of the items passed is the measure of the physical attribute. With careful standardization of measurement operations, the items in these tests will scale as long as there is moderate separation of item difficulties. Scalability is the one trustworthy criterion of unidimensionality in a set of items, but this is an unattainable ideal for important psychological (that is, behavioral), attributes. There are simply too many determinants of the response to an item that are unrelated to the attribute one wishes to measure. The item variance associated with the psychological attribute is typically minor compared to the unique variance of the item. Critics of psychological tests who point to specific items in a test and ask rhetorically, "How can anyone believe that this item really measures intelligence?" document their ignorance of psychometric properties.

Modest approximations to a perfect scale for psychological traits are rare and, when they do occur as in attitude measurement, they are based on restricting the number of items to a very small number that are widely spaced in attractiveness by the appropriate choice of modifiers inserted into an essentially common item. Such a test has very limited use.

The mean level of item product-moment correlations in the most homogeneous of ability tests is relatively low, and the range of these mean correlations from quite heterogeneous tests, such as the Stanford-Binet, to a test of information concerning automotive mechanical information is relatively small. This is revealed by the application of the Spearman-Brown formula in reverse, that is, to the estimation of the correlation between any pair of items from the Kuder-Richardson coefficients for the total scores on the tests. Mean item correlations as large as one-third or as small as one-twentieth are rare.

Use of multiple items in a psychological test has three separate functions. The first is obvious. Multiple items convert a series of dichotomies based on the separate items into a quasi-continuous total score. A second function is the one on which uninformed critics stub their toes. The linear combination of a properly selected set of items maximizes the contribution to the variance of the total score of the attribute being measured. Every item is highly fallible as a measure of the attribute. Note that if behavioral traits were like height and weight, this property would not be needed.

Even though the attribute makes only a tiny, nonzero contribution to the variance of the separate items, as long as different items do not share large chunks of nonattribute variance, a large enough number of items will build up the attribute variance in the total score to an extent that makes that score interesting and useful psychologically for theory or application. In building up the variance of the attribute in the total score, a third function of multiple items is observed. Reliability of the total score is increased as items are added, but if the attribute variance is large enough to be psychologically interesting, the number of items is large enough for the reliability needed.

Interrelationships among Test Parameters

Homogeneity is not a parameter of measurement in classical theory. It is this property that sets psychological tests apart from physical measures. The larger the number of determinants the items in a test have in common, the higher the homogeneity of the items. It is measured by the mean product-moment correlation among the items even though these correlations are in part a function of the distribution of item difficulties. Product-moment correlations also have the advantage of being acceptable for algebraic manipulation. Characteristics of the total score can be analyzed in terms of the characteristics of the items.

The Kuder-Richardson coefficient and coefficient alpha are not suitable as measures of homogeneity of the items in a test because these coefficients are confounded with the number of items or components in the composite. Allowing the number of items to vary, these statistics are useful in determining whether the amount of attribute variance in the total score has reached a preestablished, desirable level.

Reliability of a test is defined in classical measurement theory as the correlation between parallel, independent measurement operations. It is estimated from the correlation between a first and a second administration of the same test or, if memory determinants destroy the independence required on the two occasions, it is estimated from the correlation between two parallel forms. Because the total score on the test is a linear combination of the items, the reliability of the test can be expressed in terms of the n parallel item covariances and $n(n - 1)$ interitem covariances in the numerator and n item variances and $n(n - 1)$ covariances in the denominator. Because there are only n parallel item covariances in comparison to $n(n - 1)$ interitem covariances, the reliability of the total score on the test is confounded with item homogeneity. It is essential to maintain the separation of the two concepts even though under certain restricted circumstances a Kuder-Richardson estimate of the homogeneity of the total score can be substituted for a parallel-forms reliability estimate with little error.

The confounding of test reliability and item homogeneity requires, if one doubts the goal of maximum homogeneity, rejection also of the goal of maximum reliability for a given number of items. Striving for maximum reliability can distort the attribute being measured by the test. If item homogeneity is low, the test constructer should compensate by increasing the number of items, not by narrowing the focus of the test. Items should be constructed, however, to be individually as reliable as possible. Even when one expects fairly low item intercorrelations as a function of item heterogeneity, the correlations should not be reduced further by item unreliability. Maximum item reliability is a dependable goal; maximum test reliability for a fixed number of items is not.

Holding homogeneity constant, the relationship between reliability and predictive validity of a test follows the expectation from classical measurement theory. When homogeneity varies, however, the interrelationships become complex. The predictive validity of a test, as its reliability, can be written in terms of item variances and covariances. There are n covariances of the items with the criterion measure in the numerator of the correlation between test and criterion. This numerator is divided by the square root of n^2 variances and covariances of the items with each other. If a highly homogeneous test is compared with a heterogeneous one having the same number of items with the same level of correlations with the criterion, the homogeneous one will have the lower predictive validity and higher reliability. Thus homogeneity, validity, and reliability are confounded.

An Alternative Formulation

An alternative formulation starts with the outright rejection of the goal of high homogeneity or unidimensionality. The attribute one wishes to measure can be as broad or as narrow as needed for either theory or application. Positive correlations among any subset of items indicate some degree of overlap among determinants. Obtaining a measure of the effects of those determinants is an interesting and potentially useful endeavor for theory or practice. When positively correlated items are placed in a linear composite, no matter how low those correlations are, the total score will reflect the common determinants more directly than will any one item. The first principle of this approach, therefore, is: items can be added together to form a total score as long as they are positively correlated with each other. The level of item homogeneity is independent of whether one can or should add items together in the attempt to measure a hypothetical attribute. Low correlations are the basis for broad attributes, higher correlations for narrower attributes.

To have the total score reflect most validly the attribute desired and to minimize confounding with other attributes, it is necessary to follow a closely related second principle: select items as heterogeneous as possible within the limits of the attribute that has been defined. This requires analyzing in one's items all the facets that are independent of the attribute and writing items that share the attribute but differ as widely as possible on other facets. One can tolerate small subsets of items more highly intercorrelated than the mean item correlation when their number is small and the number of subsets is large. No matter how narrow the attribute in which one is interested, there is always unwanted variance in psychological items arising from the huge number of determinants of responses. Thus this is a very general principle, but it is especially important for broad attributes. One cannot measure general intelligence, for example, with items lacking content, operations, or products. No one source of unwanted variance should be allowed to predominate. The unwanted variance in the total score is minimized by maximizing the heterogeneity of the determinants of responses to the items over and beyond the common core of determinants associated with the attribute of general intelligence.

Although an attribute can be as broad or as narrow as necessary for the measurement of the hypothetical attribute, there are limitations to the degree of narrowness that are imposed by good professional practice. The third principle is: a test should be as broad as possible without loss of information for the purposes the test is to serve. Stated in another way, tests should be no narrower than the differential inferences about behavior outside the testing room one can legitimately draw from the scores. Here differential is used in the older sense—not in the majority-minority groups sense—of two or more tests having differential validity for two or more research hypotheses or practical criteria. By legitimate is meant that the inferences are based on research, not on free associations to the name of the test or to the description of the factor supposedly measured by the test. The reference to behavior outside the testing room implies that differences among tests per se are not very interesting or important psychologically. Something more than a reliable difference score for two tests is needed. Differences should indeed make a difference in important behaviors.

For many purposes a broad test of general intelligence may furnish all the information needed. An intelligence test is the single most important test that can be administered for vocational guidance purposes. For students at the level of high school graduation, approximately age 18, who have experienced the typical high school curricula, however, the predictor tests can measure somewhat narrower attributes than general intelligence. Scores on two major group factors from Philip Vernon's hierarchical model of intelligence (1961) do furnish differential information for guidance into two broad job families: clerical and mechanical. It is doubtful whether narrower group factors, whether they are the Thurstone (1938) primaries or the Guilford (1967) structure-of-intellect components, than the academic-intellectual and spatial-mechanical furnish dependable differential information for entry into the world of work.

The fourth principle is briefly stated: psychometric analyses are used to check one's assumptions, procedures, and so on, but should not be used to determine the decisions made in constructing a test. To measure certain hypothetical attributes, it may be necessary to use items whose intercorrelations are little more than zero, or a given item may belong in a test even though its correlation with the total score may be low relative to the majority of items in the item pool. It may be difficult at times to distinguish between an unreliable item and one that merely has low homogeneity, but this can be done.

When these principles are followed, the parameter of test homogeneity is seen in a new light. Homogeneity has not been discarded as an important parameter. Only the goal of high homogeneity, or unidimensionality, or of factorial purity has been rejected. This suggests a fifth summary principle: within the limitations of behavioral measurement a test should be as homogeneous as possible with respect to the attribute being measured. Because the most interesting and most useful attributes are broad ones, however, the degree of homogeneity obtainable may be quite modest. In addition to attribute variance in the total score, one must tolerate small amounts of unwanted, systematic, nonerror variance in that score. This is a necessity that goes along with behavioral measurement. This unwanted variance can be minimized by selecting items as heterogeneous as possible within the limits set by the definition of the attribute. It can also be minimized by using a sufficient number of items to build up the total score's homogeneity to an acceptable level. It appears paradoxical, but the larger the number of different types of unwanted sources of variance in the test, the smaller is their total contribution to test score variance. This summary principle can also be stated as follows: the requirements for construct validity of the score are met if the items measure one dominant dimension or factor and if secondary factors are both equalized and minimized in their contributions to the variance of the total score. One dominant dimension should be substituted for unidimensionality as the appropriate goal of test construction.

A Concrete Example

This approach to test theory can be illustrated with an analysis of sources of variance in a Piagetian task. A single conservation of volume task has the following components of variance as a minimum: general intelligence, generalized Piagetian reasoning, generalized conservation, conservation of volume, specifics associated with the wording of the instructions, the equipment used, the manner of presentation, and so on, and measurement error. The combination of specifics and error in a single task may produce a score named conservation of volume that is not highly valid for that attribute. One should plan on measuring conservation of volume in several different ways. Vary systematically the equipment, the instructions, and any other facets of the situation that might make a difference in the rank order of persons on the task. Standardization of measurement operations does not require uniformity of nonattribute sources of variance among the elements.

The more valid conservation-of-volume composite has less specific and error variance, but it also includes variance associated with broader attributes whose contributions to variance have increased along with the narrower volume conservation variance. There is no way to avoid this development, but one can develop more valid measures of the broader attributes. Generalized conservation can be measured more validly by including all types of conservation in the test, with each type being measured in a fashion to minimize specifics and error. The larger the number of types of conservation that can be included in the broader measure, the smaller will be the contribution to variance of any one type, such as volume, or the sum of all of the types.

Simultaneously with the building up of the variance of general conservation has been an increase in the variance of generalized Piagetian reasoning and of general intelligence. Present data indicate that a composite Piagetian measure is as highly correlated with Wechsler verbal and performance scales as the latter two are with each other. The Piagetian composite, furthermore, is correlated with the performance IQ only a little more highly than with the verbal. (See Humphreys & Parsons, 1979a; Humphreys, 1980.) The inclusion of Piagetian tasks in a standard test of intelligence adds to the construct validity of the measure. The contributions of the Piagetian tasks to variance of factors other than general intelligence are minimized by the many different, but similarly subordinate, factors in the current Wechsler test. All such factors make a virtually zero contribution to the variance of the total score (Humphreys, Rich, & Davey, in press) in a wide range of talent.

This step-wise, hierarchical definition of attributes varying in breadth points up an important problem in a great many experimental and post hoc correlational analyses. If interesting and important relationships are obtained with an independent variable for a particular test serving as a dependent variable, how does one know which component of variance is primarily involved in the observed relationship? The answer appears to be that psychology of necessity is a multivariate discipline. Several carefully selected dependent variables are required in many experiments as well as in post hoc correlational investigations if the relationships obtained are to be interpreted unequivocally.

Implications of the Theory

Several implications of this approach to test theory can be briefly summarized. It is more difficult to obtain high reliability of broad tests than of narrow tests, and high construct validity of broad tests requires large numbers of items. On the other hand, predictive validities of tests having maximum heterogeneity of the items within the limits set by the attribute will usually be higher than of tests constructed in accordance with the goal of unidimensionality.

Is information likely to be lost in broad tests? Why not separate a broad test into as many homogeneous tests as needed? One argument against proceeding in this fashion is based on feasibility. How much time would be required to obtain reliable scores on the 150 possible tests in Guilford's structure-of-intellect model? Can the potential information in 150 tests that are substantially intercorrelated be obtained in dependable form using the samples typical of psychological research? A second argument is the one of greater importance. Given the nature of the psychological test, there is no reason to assume that first-order factors are in any sense primary psychologically. Because of the host of possible determinants there are literally thousands of different abilities, or of latent traits, if the sole criterion is differences in the rank order of scores on these tests. Some groupings of determinants may be more fundamental psychologically than will others. The primary mental ability may indeed be the attribute called general intelligence.

The construct validity of a measure of human ability does not depend on unidimensionality of the items. It does require one major or dominant dimension, and standard tests of intelligence do have one dominant dimension. Even though the same raw score can be attained by somewhat different routes by different examinees, in a well-constructed test the two scores on the general factor can still be equivalent. Although more research needs to be done, it seems probable that item response theory (IRT) methodology in its current form can be applied to tests that are maximally heterogeneous within the limits set by the definition of the attribute and meaningful solutions obtained. Drasgow and Parsons (1983) provided a rather severe test of this possibility. An assumption of one dominant dimension can be substituted for unidimensionality.

On the other hand, it is useful to consider the consequences if the IRT methodology cannot be used with some of the broadest tests developed in accordance with the present model. This would not invalidate the model. The characteristics of psychological data, and the needs of psychologists for mathematical models, are not determined by the current availability of models. If the IRT model does not fit, or if present programs do not provide reasonable solutions, it is not necessarily the test that is at fault. Perhaps the model or the program should be changed to fit the needs of psychologists and the nature of the data with which they have to work.

THEORY OF INTELLIGENCE

General intelligence is represented by the broadest factor in a fully developed hierarchical solution based on the principal factors in a large set of cognitive tests. It is also represented by the smallest positive, nonzero correlations among those tests. These are statistical definitions. A test theory suitable for a hierarchical view of human abilities has also been presented. This theory has a statistical basis in the intercorrelations of items. It is always suitable to add items together whose intercorrelations are generally at a similar positive, nonzero level. Once the level of the attribute in the hierarchy has been decided, item selection is as heterogeneous as possible within the limits of the attribute. One does not have to compromise with a suitable test theory to construct a test of general intelligence. The theory does reject the need for a test to be strictly unidimensional. It does accept the need for theoretical purposes for a test to measure one dominant dimension, but that dominant dimension can represent a very broad hypothetical attribute.

Intelligence as Phenotype

It is now appropriate to turn to a more descriptive account of the construct of general intelligence. First, intelligence is a phenotypic, behavioral construct. Each item in a test evokes a behavioral response. These responses were acquired during the course of development and have both a genetic and an environmental substrate. Height is also a phenotypic characteristic that is acquired during development and has both a genetic and an environmental substrate. Height differs from intelligence in that it is not behavioral. It also differs in being more readily observable and easier to specify for measurement purposes. Nevertheless, intelligence is observable. It is not a capacity.

Height measures taken during the period of physical development are not interpreted as a fixed capacity for growing in stature. The phenotype for height changes during development whether measured on the absolute ratio scale for length or on a relative scale that controls for chronological age. Either score can be used to predict height at a later age with equivalent accuracy, but the degree of accuracy is a function of the ages when the measurements occur and the amount of time that elapses between the two measurements. These are the expected characteristics of a phenotypic trait that changes during development. Measures of intelligence have similar characteristics. The intelligence test score is an estimate of the phenotypic trait at a particular point in time.

Intelligence is also a "public" trait. Observers can evaluate levels of intelligence on rating scales with considerable accuracy. Intelligence differs from height, however, because reasonably accurate judgments of the former require more opportunities to judge. There is also more agreement among judges when the behaviors for which they are looking are defined in advance. As noted earlier, some observers would include character traits in their definitions. Nevertheless, the similarities with height outweigh differences. Judgments of height can be confounded with extraneous variables, such as body shape. If judgments include observations of sitting height, there is further confounding. For both traits objective measurement is preferred to subjective judgment.

Height and intelligence as phenotypic traits also have in common the possibility of estimating the correlation between phenotype and genotype. For continuous measures of fingerprint characteristics, the phenotype/genotype correlation can be estimated with confidence from several different comparisons of family-resemblance correlations in uncontrolled data. The confidence arises from one's difficulty in imagining nontrivial environmental influences on these characteristics. For both height and intelligence, on the other hand, it is easier to imagine nontrivial environmental effects. Most family-resemblance data involve confounding between genetic and environmental influences. Adoption studies with random assignment to foster families in infancy control for postnatal confounding. Only in recent months has it become technically possible—but hardly feasible—to control for prenatal confounding.

In the absence of experimental controls, it seems best not to estimate a person's genotypic intelligence. Those who do place confidence in estimates of the heritability of intelligence, however, must recognize that the estimation of genotype is not the equivalent of the estimation of capacity. This is not an argument about the accuracy of the estimate. The capacity so much desired by so many test users is a construct critically different from genotype. An individual of any age performs, functions, and achieves with his or her phenotypic traits. The extent to which a phenotype can be influenced by environmental manipulations at any given point during the life span does not covary inversely with the size of the heritability coefficient. A person who might have been taller if there had been no experience of early malnutrition plays basketball at his or her phenotypic height.

The Behavioral Repertoire

One can also characterize intelligence by means of a content analysis of items on standard tests of intelligence, such as the Wechsler and the Stanford-Binet. Items require the examinee to deal with abstractions and to manipulate symbols. Examinees are faced with novel problems. Mental adjustments are required. As a matter of fact, there has been surprisingly little change in item content from the first decade of this century to the Wechsler and Stanford-Binet tests in use today.

There are, of course, differences among standard tests. Rather than identifying intelligence with the operations required to administer and score a particular test, it is advisable to define intelligence in terms of a repertoire of skills and knowledge that is sampled by standard tests. The intellectual repertoire does not include all knowledge and skills, but is limited by the consensus existing among psychologists who are experts in the area. As noted earlier, there has historically been a rather remarkable consensus. The statistical definition of general intelligence, as a matter of fact, indicates that the consensus may have been too restrictive. Based on the evidence from correlations, many types of information not usually included in intelligence tests belong in the intellectual repertoire. Piagetian reasoning tasks clearly belong also.

The behavioral repertoire is not completely homogeneous with respect to which the different elements measure the construct of general intelligence. Some elements are closer to the centroid of the space spanned by the domain than others. One can construct a good test with relatively few items if selection is made from the most central items. On the other hand, a test can still be a good measure of general intelligence if items are sampled entirely from the periphery. In the latter case one must exercise more care in the construction and selection of the items, and one must have more items, but the one dominant dimension can still be that of general intelligence. For example, it is highly probable that an excellent measure of general intelligence as revealed by correlations with a Wechsler or Stanford-Binet scale could be constructed from a broad enough pool of rote-memory items. This would require seeking maximum heterogeneity of every facet on which such measures differ from each other.

A person's behavioral repertoire changes during development, and the rate of change is itself a function of period during development. Until late in life change is largely characterized by growth. People of all ages forget, but there is little forgetting of the well-learned and practiced skills and knowledge in the repertoire sampled by standard tests of intelligence, particularly during the school years. This emphasizes the importance of intelligence being defined as status at a given point in time.

The repertoire is the phenotypic trait, not the intelligence quotient. This emphasizes the importance of interpreting intelligence test scores in terms of absolute level as well as relative to age. The latter score standing alone provides no information about the size of the repertoire. For many theoretical and applied purposes, the level of intelligence is more important than the IQ. It is unfortunate that mental-age scores were largely abandoned with the advent of deviation IQs. Once the need for MA in the formula for IQ disappeared, there was no compelling argument against the assignment of MAs to adults. The MA designation for a level score could also have been abandoned without loss if another score indicating level of performance had been substituted. The obtained test score equivalent to the 50th centile in a given norm group is an appropriate-level score for a person from any other norm group who has obtained that score on the test. Absolute and relative scores are useful for both height and intelligence.

Stability of Intelligence

It is of utmost importance that not only does intelligence change or grow when measured by mental-age units or their equivalent but intelligence also changes with learning and growth when measured by a deviation IQ or its equivalent. The rank order of individuals changes continuously during development. A large number of longitudinal studies in the literature describe this type of change. These are cited and described in sufficient detail by Anastasi (1982) that further review is unnecessary.

The conventional interpretation of the data in such studies is that early preschool tests do not measure intelligence but appropriate tests do measure intelligence by the age of entrance into elementary school. There may be some unevenness in development for a few years thereafter, but intelligence soon stabilizes. The rationale for the British Eleven-Plus Examination was that intelligence stabilized by age 11. The observed correlations from year to year during adolescence are high and conventional wisdom has assumed that departures from unity were due to measurement error. Many of the reported correlations are also based on relatively small samples so that confidence intervals are large.

The assumption (hope?) that intelligence tests really assessed capacity is congruent with the conventional wisdom described above. It may even be responsible for the conventional wisdom, but there were "voices crying in the wilderness" quite early. Anderson (1939, 1940) pointed out that the stability of IQs from year to year could be explained by a model in which gains in intelligence from the base year to the next occasion of measurement were uncorrelated with the base. The model, based on the nature of part/whole correlations, explained year-to-year high stability and increasing instability as the number of years increased between test and retest. The model also suggested that year-to-year stability should increase as the age at the first test increases. Roff (1941) published several additional series of correlations between gains and the initial base, confirming that these correlations in several samples were essentially zero. The Anderson model and Roff's support for it are hardly compatible with intelligence as capacity.

Humphreys (1960) followed up on the Anderson and Roff research some 20 years later by applying Guttman's simplex model of intercorrelations to longitudinal data such as those for intelligence. The simplex matrix characterizes the intercorrelations of items in a perfect Guttman scale (1944). Such items all measure the same factor or dimension, but differ in difficulty level. Guttman later (1955) applied this model to the intercorrelations of tests measuring the same content but differing in complexity of cognitive processing. This was, of course, another application to a single occasion of measurement. Humphreys, in contrast, discussed the relationship between uncorrelated gains during learning and maturation, the phenomenon of Anderson and Roff, to the simplex.

The Simplex Matrix

In these applications, when all the measures are placed in their ordinal positions, the form of the observed correlations is highly distinctive. The highest correlation in a given row or column is the one adjacent to the principal diagonal. The lowest correlation in the matrix is the one between the two most extreme ordinal positions.

A quantitative definition of the simplex assumes that the correlations are population values among true scores. These characteristics of the model represent a double whammy for the theorist interested in studying its goodness of fit. When these two conditions are met, if i, j, and k refer to any three items of increasing difficulty, to any three tests of increasing complexity, or to any three occasions of measurement varying from early to late during learning or maturation, all $r_{ik.j}$ in a simplex matrix are zero. It also follows, for the matrix as a whole, that the only nonzero regression weights in estimating any given item, test, or occasion selected as the criterion are for the items, tests, or occasions adjacent to the criterion. Thus the measures at the beginning and end of a given series have only one predictor with a nonzero weight while all others have two. There is no information in i not in j when k is the criterion, but there is information in the adjacent variable beyond k not in j. If true score gains are independent of the true score base, these conditions are met.

The simplex model was not particularly useful until recent years because it was not possible to do more than guess about its fit to observed correlations in most sets of data. It was the true score assumption that created the principal problem. There is rarely an alternate form for an item, and alternate forms of learning trials cannot be constructed. Now, following the methodological contributions of Joreskog and his coworkers (see Joreskog & Surbom, 1978), it is possible to obtain unique estimates of reliabilities of all variables except the first and last in the continua of item difficulty, test complexity, and learning/maturation from the matrix of intercorrelations. With estimates of reliabilities, correlations can be corrected for attenuation and the hypothesis of zero partial correlations tested.

Fitting the Simplex

Humphreys, Parsons, and Park (1979) in the Growth Study data of the Educational Testing Service (Hilton, Beaton, & Bower, 1971) found numerous cognitive variables for which data at two-year intervals from the fifth through the eleventh grade showed acceptable-to-excellent fits for the simplex model. This was true for white and black males and females. The fit to the simplex of a composite of 16 separate tests weighted by canonical weights in Humphreys and Parsons (1979b) for the white sample of the combined sexes was spectacularly good. This composite can be considered an excellent measure of general intelligence. With reliabilities for only the seventh and ninth grades, however, only one stability was uniquely determined. They reported a value in excess of .96. Because the canonical weights capitalized on chance, this stability has recently been computed for the unit-weighted composite of the same 16 tests. For white boys and girls separately the new stabilities are just above .95.

Humphreys, Davey, and Park (1984) have recently submitted a manuscript in which the data of the Harvard Growth Study were reanalyzed. Dearborn, Rothney, and Shuttleworth (1938) had published raw scores on intelligence tests, along with several anatomical variables, for relatively large groups of boys and girls from age 7 through age 18. In these data it is possible to obtain unique estimates of reliabilities from ages 8 through 17, but with less confidence than in the earlier model fitting. In contrast to the ETS data many more different tests were used during the period of development studied, and the tests were not by any means parallel forms. All tests were group tests, even for the youngest ages. Futhermore, it was not possible, without sacrifice of large amounts of information to obtain a sample of constant size. In contrast, the ETS tests were constructed to be as similar as possible, and a large constant N could be obtained for all correlations.

Considering these characteristics of the Harvard data it is not surprising that a chi square test of goodness of fit conclusively rejects the simplex model. On the other hand, samples were relatively large for most correlations. At maximum there were about 600 boys and 700 girls. The residuals also appeared in the matrix in seemingly random locations. There is also seemingly random variability in the size of the estimated stabilities from one age to another, but there is a hint of some systematic variation as well. Humphreys and Davey (1984a) suggest that there may be increased instability for girls at 15 after most had had their first menstruation. Boys may show similar instability a year or two later. Even when this relatively late instability is included, the mean year-to-year correlation from ages 9 through 17 is slightly larger than .96. During a two-year interval a representative value is .93. This compares with the .95 in the more nearly ideal ETS data. Estimated stabilities between ages 8 and 9, and 8 and 10, are .89 and .87, respectively. These reduced stabilities presumably reflect problems associated with measuring intelligence with group tests at this age.

With year-to-year stabilities estimated for the ages 8 through 17, it is possible to estimate the stabilities for all longer intervals by the product of the appropriate r_{ij} and r_{jk}. In the Harvard data a quick and fairly accurate estimate of a given stability for any interval between ages 9 and 17 is to raise .96 to the power of the number of years in the interval. Thus the stability of intelligence in these data between ages 9 and 17 is approximately $(.96)^8$.

A third test of the simplex model (Humphreys & Davey, 1984b) has been made with data published by Wilson (1983) for a large sample of twins. All tests were individually administered. One subsample was tested from 3 months to 9 years, first at 3-month, later at 6-month, and still later at 12-month intervals. A second and overlapping subsample was tested from 18 months to 9 years and then retested at 15. An acceptable fit of the simplex is obtained in the second subsample, thus providing estimates of stabilities from 24 months through 9 years. In the first subsample an acceptable fit is obtained from 9 months through 9 years. Data from the infant tests administered at 3 and 6 months produce many large residuals for the first two occasions, indicating that these tests are not measuring the dimension of general intelligence. The stability from 9 to 12 months is indeterminate, but the first subsample does provide two unique stability estimates missing from the second: from 12 to 18 and from 18 to 24 months. In these data, as in the Harvard data, sample sizes vary from one correlation to another, but test selection and administration were superior.

Interpretation of the Stabilities

One-year stabilities, starting at 12 months and ending for 4 and 5 years, are .64, .77, .89, .91, and .94. From 5 to 6 years the estimate reaches .96 and, although there is some variability thereafter, this value is representative of the remaining years to age 9. The reliability at 15 is indeterminate, but a reasonable guess of reliability at 15 provides a stability from ages 9 to 15 of .84. This is consistent with year-to-year stabilities of .97.

The ETS, Harvard, and the twin data have overlapping age measurements.

Between grades seven and nine, typically ages 13 and 15, the stability estimate was .95. The square root of this correlation, about .975, is the estimate for a single year. A representative figure for the Harvard data was .96. In the twin data the .96 level is reached between 5 and 6. This is only a little lower than the value expected from a best guess for the same sample concerning stabilities from ages 11 to 13. The only stability in the three sets of data in which there is overlap in age that is not reasonably congruent with the value from another set is the stability from ages 8 to 9 in the Harvard group test data.

By integrating data from the three sets it is possible to estimate the stabilities for all age separations between 12 months and 17 years. For the two extreme ordinal positions the estimate is in the low twenties. The lowest correlation in a simplex cannot be zero, and an investigator is not able to reject the simplex hypothesis by finding zero or small negative correlations in a small sample of preschool children. The progressive increase in the size of year-to-year stabilities apparently ends fairly early. These values are more or less constant during the public school years. The belief that intelligence stabilized may have been influenced partly by increases in the size of observed score stabilities to values close to the reliabilities of the scores. Correcting for the effects of measurement error is essential. It is also essential to estimate stabilities for a series of occasions.

It is also possible to study these results from the viewpoint of the reasonableness of the estimates of reliabilities and stabilities. The former are not bizarre and are in line with expectations based on knowledge of the tests and of the populations of examinees. The stabilities become close to unity, but estimates of unity or in excess of unity occur rarely and in the least adequate data. It becomes easy to understand the belief in a fixed intelligence when one looks only at the small difference in true score stability from year to year between an estimated .97 and the 1.00 required by a fixed intelligence during the preteen and teen years. An estimate of $(.97)^8$ or $(.76)$ between ages 9 and 17, however, allows for substantial instability of individual differences.

It is the implication of these analyses that infant tests of intelligence, despite much lower correlations during comparable time periods, are measuring the same dimension as the tests in late adolescence. This hypothesis is in direct contradiction to the prevailing wisdom. Individual differences in intelligence as defined heretofore in this paper are expected to change rapidly in the early years when the intellectual repertoire is small. Correlations less than unity after correcting for attenuation are insufficient evidence for the rejection of a common dimension when the examinees are learning and maturing. Even a correlation in the low twenties between intelligence at 12 months and at 17 years is congruent with the model, and one can with high confidence reject the hypothesis that the intelligence test at any age is a measure of capacity or potential.

Alternative Explanation for the Simplex

As noted earlier, if true score gains are independent of the true score base, the zero partial correlations that define the simplex are intuitively obvious and, of course, can readily be derived. The simplex model does fit the data reasonably well, and the better the data, the better the fit. Is one forced to accept Markov processes in intellectual development? The observed correlations of Anderson and Roff have been for observed bases and observed gains. A bias, arising from measurement error, in these correlations would mask small positive correlations between true score gains and true score bases. It is also possible to relax the assumption of independent gains, but to do so requires a very complex model. This is seen in the equations for the numerators of three successive partial correlations. The symbols are defined as follows:

$$x_0 = \text{Initial base}$$
$$x_1 = x_0 + d_1$$
$$x_2 = x_0 + d_1 + d_2$$

x_3 to x_n are defined similarly:

$$r_{x_0 x_2 \cdot x_1}: \{C_{x_1 d_2}(S^2_{x_1} - S^2_{x_0}) - S^2_{x_0} C_{d_1 d_2}\}/S_{x_0} S^2_{x_1} S_{x_2}$$
$$r_{x_1 x_3 \cdot x_2}: \{(C_{x_1 d_3} + C_{d_1 d_3})(S^2_{x_2} - S^2_{x_1}) - S^2_{x_1} C_{d_2 d_3}\}/S_{x_1} S^2_{x_2} S_{x_3}$$
$$r_{x_2 x_4 \cdot x_3}: \{(C_{x_1 d_4} + C_{d_1 d_4} + C_{d_2 d_4})(S^2_{x_3} - S^2_{x_2}) - S^2_{x_2} C_{d_3 d_4}\}/S_{x_2} S^2_{x_3} S_{x_4}$$

Although at first glance the numerators of the partials all seem to be trivial in size, the residual standard deviations in the missing denominators are also small. These equations allow one to reject correlations of a constant size between gains across all ages. It may be that no reasonable model of growth will provide a precise fit to these equations, but it is also possible that the correlations between true score gains and true score bases are so small that the simplex model for which independent gains are the simplest explanation cannot be rejected unequivocally in samples of reasonable size.

It does seem that independence of gains is too strong an assumption on both genetic and environmental grounds. The surprising thing is that the correlations are so close to zero. The intellectual repertoire is acquired by a biological organism learning and maturing in an environment that contains many systematic elements. There may be many determinants of growth, but the integrity of the organism alone should be sufficient to produce nonzero correlations.

It is known that identical twins show correlated gains over any one time period (see, for example, Wilson, 1983). This is difficult to reconcile with a Markov process for each individual. It is also known (Humphreys & Parsons, 1979b) that individual differences in one measure of cognitive development, "Listening" from the Sequential Tests of Educational Progress, anticipate by two to four years individual differences in a cognitive composite formed from the School and College Aptitude Test, the five other tests of STEP, and the eight scores from the Test of General Information. Both Listening and the cognitive composite have intercorrelations over occasions considered independently that are fit by the simplex model, that is, gains are relatively independent of bases, but the cross-correlations follow a different pattern. The anticipation of gains is also difficult to reconcile with a Markov process.

Although one can accept the possibility of small correlations among gains, it is still necessary to question the conventional wisdom concerning family-resemblance correlations that one sees in the literature. These questions can be answered only by investigations based on large samples and careful selection of the testing instruments. Do the correlations between identical twins, fraternal twins, and siblings stabilize at some early period in development? Does the correlation between parent and child in intelligence or the correlation between child's intelligence and parents' socioeconomic status stabilize early in development? Is it reasonable to assume constant values for these various correlations when the true score correlation in intelligence for the child between ages 6 and 17 appears to be somewhere between .96 and .97 to the *11th* power?

SUMMARY

The approach to the construct of general intelligence described in the preceding pages has several key attributes. Most basic is the ubiquitous finding of positive intercorrelations among cognitive items in a wide range of human talent. These intercorrelations can be modeled by a hierarchy of factors extending from the highly general to specifics. These factors are convenient mathematical dimensions that are accurately described as abstractions rather than things.

Items can be assembled in a test and a total score accumulated linearly on the basis of a systematic theory of test construction that is of general applicability. The objective in test construction is to build a test of the breadth required for the purposes for which it will be used rather than the breadth (narrowness) required to obtain maximum homogeneity of the items. The theory allows the construction of a test at any level of the hierarchy.

The intelligence measured by the test is the repertoire of cognitive skills and knowledge available to the examinee at a given point in time. The test samples this repertoire. Human judgment can also assess the repertoire. Both test scores and judgments are based on observations of behavior that has been acquired during the course of development. Neither the test nor the judge can observe a capacity or a potential.

There appears to be continuity in the development of intelligence from 12 months to 17 years. This development is along a single dimension on which children change both absolutely and relatively to each other during this time frame. This hypothesis accounts for the intercorrelations of test scores during the many occasions for which data are available. There is no break in the simplex pattern. Change proceeds smoothly and, apparently, inexorably. One must use different content to measure intelligence at 12 months and at 17 years, but it is not necessary to invoke the difference in content to explain the low correlation between intelligence test scores during this interval of time. The rate of relative change is most rapid early in development, but has become relatively level by the time of school entrance. The rate stabilizes, but change continues.

The construct of general intelligence that emerges *requires* one to infer a multiplicity of causes of individual differences. One subset of these causes is certainly the many genes involved. There is widespread agreement that the inheritance of intelligence is polygenic. Although these genes are largely fixed at the time of conception, there is no reason to consider their resultant an entity. To the extent that there are genetic determinants of instability, individual genes in the complex may be "coming on line" at different times during development. It is also clear that there are environmental determinants of the intellectual repertoire, and there are both genetic and environmental determinants of the many structures within the central nervous system. Both sets of determinants affect how those structures are used in the acquisition of the behaviors sampled by standard intelligence tests.

REFERENCES

Anastasi, A. (1982). *Psychological testing* (5th ed.). New York: Macmillan.

Anderson, J. E. (1939). The limitations of infant and preschool tests in the measurement of intelligence. *Journal of Psychology, 8*, 351–379.

Anderson, J. E. (1940). The prediction of terminal intelligence from infant and preschool tests. *Thirty-ninth Yearbook, National Society for the Study of Education*, Part I, pp. 385–403.

Binet, A., & Simon, T. (1905). Methodes nouvelles pour le diagnostic du niveau intellectuel des anormaux. *L'Année Psychologique, 11*, 191–244.

Binet, A., & Simon, T. (1916). The development of intelligence in children (translated from articles in *L'Année Psychologique* from 1905, 1908, and 1911 by Elizabeth S. Kite). Baltimore: Williams and Wilkins.

Burt, C. (1949). *The factors of the mind: An introduction to factor-analysis in psychology.* New York: Macmillan.

Dearborn, W. F., Rothney, J. W. M., & Shuttleworth, F. K. (1938). Data on the growth of public school children. *Monographs of the Society for Research on Child Development, 3*, (1).

Drasgow, F., & Parsons, C. K. (1983). Application of unidimensional item response theory models to multidimensional data. *Applied Psychological Measurement, 7*, 189–200.

Goddard, H. H. (1913). *Feeblemindedness: Its causes and consequences.* New York: Macmillan.

Guilford, J. P. (1967). *The nature of human intelligence.* New York: McGraw-Hill.

Guttman, L. (1944). A basis for scaling qualitative data. *American Sociological Review, 9*, 139–150.

Guttman, L. (1955). A generalized simplex for factor analysis. *Psychometrika, 20*, 173–192.

Hilton, T., Beaton, A., & Bower, C. (1971). *Stability and instability in academic growth—A compilation of longitudinal data.* Final Report, Washington, DC: United States Office of Education. (Research No. 0-0140)

Hulin, C. L., & Humphreys, L. G. (1980). Foundations of test theory. In *Construct validity in psychological measurement*. Proceedings of a Colloquium on theory and application in education and employment. U.S. Office of Personnel Management and Educational Testing Service, Princeton, NJ.

Humphreys, L. G. (1952). Individual differences. In C. P. Stone & D. Taylor (Eds.), *Annual Review of Psychology* (Vol. III), pp. 131–147.

Humphreys, L. G. (1956). The normal curve and the attenuation paradox in test theory. *Psychological Bulletin, 53*, 472–476.

Humphreys, L. G. (1960). Investigations of the simplex. *Psychometrika, 25*, 475–483.

Humphreys, L. G. (1962). The organization of human abilities. *American Psychologist, 17*, 475–483.

Humphreys, L. G. (1970). A skeptical look at the factor pure test. In C. E. Lunneborg (Ed.), *Current problems and techniques in multivariate psychology.* Proceedings of a conference honoring Professor Paul Horst (pp. 23–32). Seattle, WA: The University of Washington.

Humphreys, L. G. (1979). The construct of general intelligence. *Intelligence, 3*, 105–120.

Humphreys, L. G. (1980). Methinks they do protest too much. *Intelligence, 4*, 179–183.

Humphreys, L. G. (1981). The primary mental ability. In M. P. Friedman, J. P. Das, and N. O'Connor (Eds.), *Intelligence and Learning.* New York: Plenum Press.

Humphreys, L. G., & Davey, T. C. (1984a). *Instability in intelligence from infancy to age 17.* Unpublished manuscript.

Humphreys, L. G., & Davey, T. C. (1984b). *Critique of correlated growth spurts in brain and in intelligence.* Unpublished manuscript.

Humphreys, L. G., Davey, T. C., & Park, R. K. (1984). *Longitudinal correlational analysis of standing height and intelligence.* Unpublished manuscript.

Humphreys, L. G., & Parsons, C. K. (1979a). Piagetian tasks measure intelligence and intelligence tests assess cognitive development. *Intelligence, 3*, 369–382.

Humphreys, L. G., & Parsons, C. K. (1979b). A simplex process model for describing differences between cross-lagged correlations. *Psychological Bulletin, 86*, 325–334.

Humphreys, L. G., Parsons, C. K., & Park, R. K. (1979). Application of a simplex process model to six years of cognitive development in four demographic groups. *Applied Psychological Measurement, 3*, 51–64.

Humphreys, L. G., Rich, S. A., & Davey, T. C. (in press). A Piagetian test of general intelligence, *Psychological Bulletin.*

Jensen, A. R. (1980). *Bias in mental testing.* New York: Free Press.

Joreskog, K., & Sorbom, D. (1978). *LISREL IV, a general computer program for the estimation of linear structural equation systems by maximum likelihood methods.* University of Uppsala, Department of Statistics, Uppsala, Sweden.

Roff, M. (1941). A statistical study of the development of intelligence performance. *Journal of Psychology, 11*, 371–386.

Schmid, J., & Leiman, J. M. (1957). The development of hierarchical factor solutions. *Psychometrika, 22*, 53–61.

Spearman, C. (1904). General intelligence, objectively determined and measured. *American Journal of Psychology, 15*, 201–293.

Spearman, C. (1914). The theory of two factors. *Psychological Review, 21*, 101–115.

Terman, L. M. (1916). *The measurement of intelligence.* Boston: Houghton Mifflin.

Thomson, G. H. (1919). On the cause of hierarchical order among correlation coefficients. *Proceedings of Royal Society,* A, 95.

Thorndike, E. L. (1926). *The measurement of intelligence.* New York: Bureau of Publications, Teachers College, Columbia University.

Thurstone, L. L. (1938). Primary mental abilities. *Psychometric Monograph,* 1.

Thurstone, L. L. (1947). *Multiple factor analysis.* Chicago: University of Chicago Press.

Vernon, P. (1960). *The structure of human abilities.* London: Methuen.

Wechsler, D. (1939). *The measurement of adult intelligence.* Baltimore: Williams and Wilkins.

Wilson, R. S. (1983). The Louisville twin study: Developmental synchronies in behavior. *Child Development, 54*, 298–316.

SIX

THE STRUCTURE-OF-INTELLECT MODEL

J. P. GUILFORD
Emeritus Professor of Psychology
University of Southern California

From the time when Alfred Binet offered the world the first acceptable scale for the assessment of a person's intelligence, those who were concerned about the nature of intelligence faced the important issue of whether that human commodity is a single, all-inclusive entity or a collection of many different abilities. That issue is the main concern of this chapter.

Being a good experimental psychologist with investigations of thinking to his credit, Binet was well aware of the complexities of mental functioning. Asked to develop a means of distinguishing potentially slow learners in the Paris schools, he wisely extended the sampling of children's capabilities in different kinds of tasks. Binet actually believed that individuals are not uniformly capable in all kinds of mental functions. In fact, he thought that there are several kinds of memory abilities, and later experiences have proved him to be right. The structure-of-intellect (SOI) model, which this chapter is about, has places for 30 different memory abilities, of which about two-thirds have been investigated and demonstrated (Guilford, 1971, 1977a).

Binet's use of a single score was for pragmatic reasons. His aim was to make easy a single administrative decision on the placement of each child in one of two groups. A single score was sufficient and it was simple. He had also demonstrated that for every test item a common mental-age value could be determined, which may have implied for some that every item was measuring the same thing. The common scale, however, was no indication that every item measures the same quality.

Intelligence-test developers following Binet, Lewis M. Terman being the most prominent, were mostly unconcerned about the nature of what they were measuring. Their chief aim was to find something that worked, thus proceeding with a pragmatic rather than a scientific motivation. A few psychologists *were* concerned, however. A number of writers sought to define intelligence, but they did so in terms that themselves needed definition and there was little consensus. One writer, E. G. Boring (1923), made the unique suggestion that intelligence is whatever intelligence tests measure. This could have been taken as a facetious remark, but it turned out to be a profound suggestion. He implied that recognized tests of intelligence should be studied scientifically to determine what it is that they require individuals to do in order to pass items and to make good scores.

In this chapter we will try to accomplish several purposes. We will first look at how the study of tests in the domain of human intelligence has been conducted, by means of correlations between pairs of tests, and how factor analyses have provided answers such as Boring called for. We will consider briefly the historical models that were derived from factor analysis, culminating in the structure-of-intellect model, with a full account of the nature of that model and some of its consequences.

Among those consequences are some important implications for psychological theory, for intelligence testing, and for applications in the areas of education and personnel matters. Bearings of the features of the model on brain functioning, on hereditary and environmental determination of intelligence, and on development and decline will be treated. Discussion of these implications should serve to provide deeper understanding of the model and of its significance.

SOME BACKGROUND ON CORRELATION AND FACTOR ANALYSIS

On first thought it may seem curious that in learning about the nature of human intelligence, which is what all of us have in common, we have had to resort to studies of how we are all different. The phenomenon of individual differences is of course obvious to any observing person. It can be noted that person A excels in mathematics, person B in making puns, and person C in understanding and controlling other individuals. One who is well aware of this situation may feel the need for investigating different talents, their causes and their consequences.

Karl Pearson laid the foundation for a scientific method for studying such human variations when he devised the correlation method and its coefficient of correlation. A zero correlation between two tests of different skills, of course, indicates that they measure nothing whatever in common. A positive correlation indicates something in common, and the higher the coefficient the more in common. This is the basis for deriving information as to what tests do measure. The further steps needed are factor analysis and an interpretation of the factors in terms of psychological variables.

Spearman and His Universal *g* Factor

A one-time student of Pearson, Charles Spearman was the father of factor analysis. Contrary to Binet, Spearman concluded after his early research that there is only one underlying ability common to all tests of an intellectual nature because he found positive correlations among all tests. Degrees of correlations differed, but he could attribute that to uneven involvements with *g* in different tests. He called his universal factor *g*, for *general.*

The proposal of only one common-factor ability undoubtedly lent comfort to those who were proceeding under the simple and attractive idea of a single "general intelligence." Spearman's view also probably forestalled efforts to investigate the possible multivariate nature of intelligence. To make Spearman's view complete, it should be said that he thought that each test measures in addition to g its own "specific" factor, which is independent of all other specific factors.

Later in his research Spearman discovered something that was contrary to his earlier view, which proved to be of considerable significance. He found that in a certain set of tests each test correlated higher with other tests within the set but lower with tests in other such sets. One set included verbal tests only and other sets featured visual items, number items, and items calling for awareness of the mental states of observed persons. Spearman therefore had to recognize what he called "group factors," which were of moderate degrees of generality, in addition to g. As reported later in this chapter, the structure-of-intellect model has places for *several* abilities involving each of the four kinds of information featured by Spearman's group factors.

Early Models of Intelligence

Factor analyses in Britain subsequent to Spearman's led to the belief in other group factors of different degrees of generality. With the growing number of factors in view, some efforts were made to see whether they could be logically related. The first kind of model suggested was of a hierarchical nature, as proposed by Burt (1949) and by Vernon (1950). These models were alike in placing Spearman's g at the apex. They differed otherwise. In Vernon's model, immediately below g were two broad abilities—v:ed (verbal-educational) and k:m (spatial and practical). Under v:ed were verbal and numerical abilities and under k:m came spatial and mechanical abilities.

Thurstone and His Multiple-Group Factors

During the 1930s L. L. Thurstone, at the University of Chicago, gave birth to a quite different direction in factor analysis. His general theory viewed intelligence as a multidimensional phenomenon, each dimension in space representing a unique mental ability. He thought that his centroid method of factor analysis would discover abilities like Spearman's group factors, but he apparently expected the basic factors to be of narrower scope. At any rate that is how things turned out.

An important novel feature of Thurstone's method of factor analysis was that he based it on matrix algebra. He regarded a table of intercorrelations among n tests as being an n-by-n matrix, with its n columns and n rows. The end result of a factor analysis, mathematically, was in the form of a factor matrix, a table of r columns, one for each factor, and n rows, one for each test, r being much smaller than n. Each numerical value in this table is known as a "factor loading" or "factor coefficient." Each one indicates the degree of correlation between a test and a factor.*

Psychological Interpretation of Factors.   The factors found by factor analysis are actually mathematical constructs. In gaining psychological information from them something more must be done. The psychological nature of each factor is decided from the features that the tests substantially loaded on it (usually from .30 to .70) have in common, as distinct from those with lower loadings on it.

Thurstone's Primary Mental Abilities (PMA).   Thurstone's first historical analysis of intellectual abilities (Thurstone, 1938), using some 50 tests with a large number of college students, yielded several factors, seven of which he felt confident. They were identified as verbal comprehension, numerical facility, spatial ability, perceptual speed, rote memory, induction, and deduction. He called them *primary mental abilities* (PMA). Later analyses by Thurstone and his students added a few more factorial abilities to the list.

The Army Air Force Analyses

During World War II I happened to be Director of an Aviation Psychology Research Unit that had the responsibility for developing tests in the general area of intelligence, for use in the classification of Aviation Cadets for training in the specializations of pilots, navigators, bombardiers, and flight engineers. Tests were developed for measuring hypothesized abilities in the areas of perception, reasoning, judgment, planning, foresight, and problem solving. Thurstone's multivariate factor theory was adopted and his methods of factor analysis were applied. The supply of experimental subjects was abundant, and the population was homogeneous as to age and sex.

Most of Thurstone's PMAs were well verified, one exception being that instead of his spatial-ability factor, we found two factors dealing with visual space. One involves the awareness of *arrangements* of objects in space and the other is concerned with visualizing *changes* in visual objects. The reason for this distinction became clear in view of the SOI model.

Altogether the number of demonstrated intellectual factors came to about 25. All the AAF analyses and the resulting factors were reviewed in a governmental volume (Guilford & Lacey, 1947). These factors and those from other sources were reviewed by French (1951). No attempt was made to organize the known intellectual abilities in a logical system in either publication.

Thurstone did tolerate the idea of an eventual hierarchical model such as Burt and Vernon had proposed, although he regarded the factorial abilities such as he found as being rather narrow and basic. He thought that there are broader, higher-order factors, which can be demonstrated by intercorrelating the basic

*An introduction to theory and operations of factor analysis may be found in Comrey (1971) and Gorsuch (1974).

factors and performing factor analyses of them. Having found the second-order factors, one could also intercorrelate them and analyze them, and so on, perhaps eventually arriving at Spearman's *g*.

Analyses by the Aptitudes Research Project (ARP)

After World War II, I had the good fortune of financial support, continuing over 20 years, through contracts with the Office of Naval Research. Additional grants were made by the National Science Foundation and by the Office of Education of the Department of Health, Education, and Welfare. With the aid of capable and devoted graduate students some 40 large factor analyses were performed, each with large numbers of subjects, in homogeneous groups, from grade six to young maturity. These analyses were in the same areas as mentioned for the Air Force research with the added area of creative thinking.

The category of creative thinking was added because it had long seemed to me that a person who exhibits this kind of talent is especially intelligent. Tests or items of this type were conspicuously missing from standard intelligence scales. Terman (1905) had tried out some items calling for ingenuity in his early study of potential intelligence-scale items. He tried out his experimental items by comparing the results from the seven brightest and the seven dullest boys in a group of 500, as rated by teachers. None of the ingenuity items appeared to be valid. It is now realized that teachers are often slow to recognize ingenuity as a sign of intelligence (Getzels & Jackson, 1961). Teachers typically want children to give "right" answers, not clever ones.

Origin of the Structure-of-Intellect Model

After five years of operation the ARP had verified almost all the factors reported from the Thurstone and the AAF analyses and had added a few more to the list, bringing the number to about 40. By that time, certain similarities and differences among the abilities were standing out, as were some parallels; thus an attempt was made to organize them.

The abilities could be grouped according to the kinds of mental processes involved—comprehension, memory, and fluency of ideas, for example. But the very same abilities could also be classified according to the kinds of information featured—visual, symbolic, and semantic (meaningful), for example. A third way of classification dawned more slowly, but it became realized that sets of abilities were also similar in the form that the items of information took—classes, relations, and systems, for example. The grouping of the abilities in three different ways called for a cross-classification in three dimensions. Visually conceived this became a cubical figure (see Figure 1). Such an arrangement is sometimes called a morphological model. Mathematically, it probably qualifies as a "product of sets."

Actually, at that stage we had found abilities with only three kinds of content, the three just mentioned. A fourth category of content was added on the basis of pure speculation. Aware that Spearman had found evidence for a "psycho-

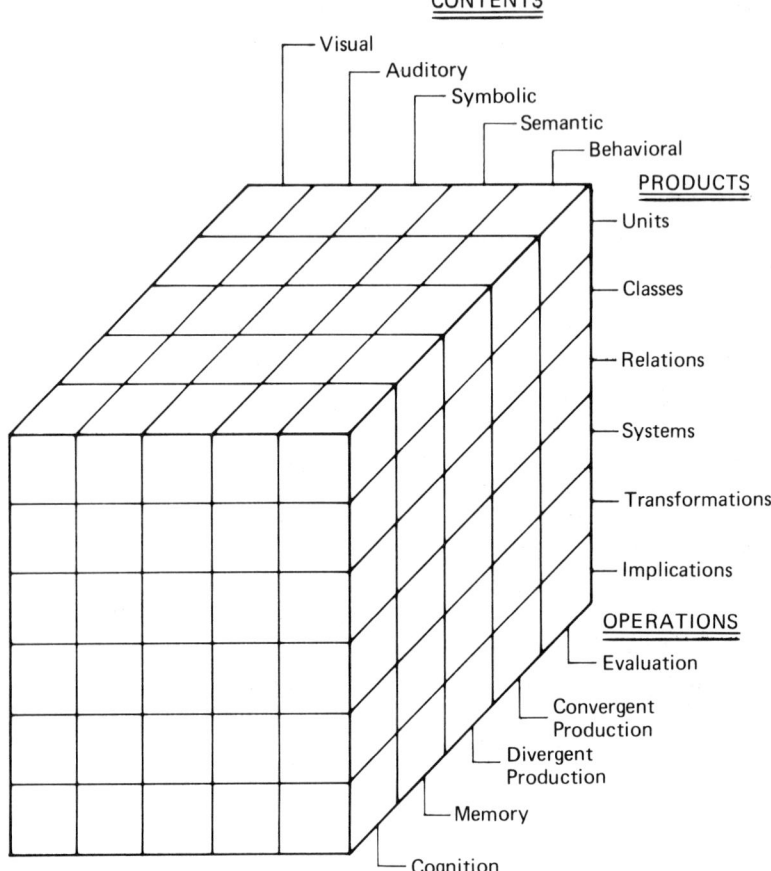

Figure 1. The visual form of the structure-of-intellect model.

logical" content category of information and that E. L. Thorndike (1920) had argued vigorously for a "social intelligence" that would involve the awareness of the mental states of others, it was hypothesized that this area would possess the same kinds of abilities as had already appeared in the other categories of information. Later analyses have provided strong evidence that this is the case (Hendricks, Guilford, & Hoepfner, 1969; O'Sullivan & Guilford, 1975). The earliest form of the structure-of-intellect model presented in print in 1959 (Guilford, 1959) was with the behavioral-content category included.

On the other hand a content category was not included that might well have been. This would have been for auditory abilities. A very few such abilities had been reported, such as two factors found by Fleishman, Roberts, and Friedman (1958). They were listed under the label of auditory-figural along with visual-figural in an early account (Guilford, 1967a). This column was divided in a later account (Guilford, 1977a), as seen in Figure 1. Feldman (1969) had found further evidence for three auditory factors and Horn (1973) presented evidence for five such factors, all of which fitted into the model.

Description of the SOI Model

The nature of the SOI model has suggested that intelligence should be defined as *a systematic collection of abilities or functions for processing information of different kinds in various forms.* The term "ability" is used in the context of individual differences and "functions" in the behaving individual. Thus in such a manner, the two major psychologies, bivariate experimental and multivariate experimental, are brought together. More will be said about this later in discussing relations of SOI to general psychological theory.

As the definition implies, each basic ability is identified by its conjunction of three variables or *facets.* Each ability has a unique kind of mental activity or *operation,* informational *content,* and informational *product.* The term "product" is well chosen because the brain has to produce it, in its own kind of structure.

Each column in Figure 1 represents a kind of operation. The rows going one way represent kinds of contents and rows going the other way stand for the kinds of products. The three-faceted nature of the model has probably been a major source of difficulty in factor analysis, for reasons that will become clearer later.

One example of an SOI ability is denoted by the three-letter symbol *CVR* (cognition of visual relations), as commonly found in multiple-choice figural-analogies tests. Another would be *MSS* (memory for symbolic systems), as seen in common memory-span tests. Still another would be *EMC* (evaluation of semantic classes), found in a test that calls on the examinee to accept or reject a set of word meanings as belonging to the same class. Each three-letter symbol includes the three initial letters of the three categories represented, except, to avoid duplications, convergent production is symbolized by N (C is for cognition) and M is for semantic (S is for symbolic). The order of the three letters is always (1) operation, (2) then content, (3) then product.

SOI Categories Defined

Since it is claimed that the SOI categories are unambiguous and operationally defined (Guilford, 1982), it is incumbent on me to state those definitions very explicitly.

Kinds of Operations or Mental Processes

Cognition. Discovering, knowing, or comprehending items of information, such as seeing that the red patch of color is in the form of a cow, or knowing the meaning of the word *love.* More technically, cognition is a process of structuring items of information by the brain.

Memory.   Committing cognized items of information to storage in the brain with persistence at least beyond the moments of activation by direct stimulation, such as memorizing the license number of an automobile or a recipe for cooking. This operation does *not* include retrieving items of information from storage. The latter activity involves one or the other of two different SOI operations to be mentioned next.

Divergent Production.   Producing a number of alternative items of information from memory storage, either verbatim or in modified form, to satisfy a given need, such as naming objects that are both hard and edible, or suggesting a number of different titles for a given short story. Thus it is a matter of retrieving from memory storage members of a specified class. It is optimally revealed by individual differences in test scores when *two* class specifications are given (Christensen & Guilford, 1963).

Convergent Production.   Retrieving from memory storage a particular, fully specified item of information, such as thinking of a special word to fit a given place in a crossword puzzle or drawing the correct conclusion from given facts, à la Sherlock Holmes. It may seem strange that events of retrieving items of information from memory storage should involve two different psychological functions, but factor analysis consistently shows this to be the case. One function involves a broad search, as in reviving members of a class while the other entails a focused search for a particular class member.

Evaluation.   Deciding whether or not, or how well, a certain item of information satisfies certain logical requirements, such as deciding whether an incomplete circle will pass through a given point if it is completed, or deciding which of four given objects is both round and hard. This operation does not apply to aesthetic judgments or choices (Hoffman, Guilford, Hoepfner, & Doherty, 1968). It is not known whether it applies to moral judgments, but it should theoretically apply to judgments of the actuality of behavioral events and to legal decisions.

Kinds of Informational Substances—Content Categories

Visual.   Information arising directly from stimulation of the retina or indirectly in the form of images of the same character.

Auditory.   Information arising from the direct stimulation of the receptors in the cochlea of the inner ear or indirectly in the form of images of the same character.

Symbolic.   Items of information that ordinarily stand for other kinds of items, such as digits or letters and their combinations; a basis for mathematics and languages.

Semantic.   Meanings, usually but not always attached to word symbols.

Behavioral.   Items of information about the mental states and about the behavior of individuals, as transmitted by their expressive actions—their "body language." Abilities involving behavioral information provide a "social intelligence."

Kinds of Informational Forms—Product Categories

In this section illustrations of products will be given from all the content categories just discussed. Products differ in the kinds of structures that the brain produces.

Unit. An entity like an object, having its own unique combination of properties or attributes, such as a blue triangular patch, the sound of a musical chord, a printed word, the meaning of *crime*, or a person's intention to hit someone.

Class. A conception behind a set of similar units (or other kinds of products, even classes of classes), as given by a set of rectangles, or high-pitched tones, or words ending in *-ing*, or set of occupations, or of doubting Thomases.

Relation. An observed connection between two items, as one boy taller than another, two tones an octave apart, two names in alphabetical order, Alice married to Jim, or Maggie angry with Henry.

System. Three or more items interrelated in a recognizable whole, as the arrangement of objects seen on your desk, a melody or a rhythm, a telephone number, a plan for a sequence of actions, or three persons interacting in a cartoon.

Transformation. Any change in an item of information, including substitutions, as in a visually perceived movement of an object, a variation in a melody, a correction of a misspelling, a pun, or a revised impression of a person's mood.

Implication. An item of information suggested by a given item of information, as adding a line to a doodle, thunder expected following lightning, seeing 4×5 and thinking 20, hearing the word *light* and thinking of *heavy*, or thinking what your frowning friend is likely to say or do next.

The product of implication has been recommended as a replacement for that time-honored concept of *association*, which has served psychology so well in its theories (Guilford, 1966b). This suggestion includes the conditioned response, in line with those who have regarded it as an instance of expectation (Tolman, 1932). An interesting advantage is that an association thus acquires a logical status, for it satisfies the logical proposition "If *A*, then *B*."

A Psychologic and a Psychoepistemology

Concluding that a psychological implication has a genuine logical status has suggested that other kinds of products might also share that honor. The best candidates for this recognition are classes and relations. And if these three products qualify, how about units, systems, and transformations?

The thought then occurs that all six kinds of products are found in mathematics (Guilford, 1980b), suggesting that the brain operates according to a "psychologic" (Guilford, 1966b). Although mathematics features symbolic and visual information, it shares with all other kinds of intellectual functioning the same set of informational products. An important difference is that in mathematics all items of information are precisely defined whereas in other content areas the brain does the best it can with less precise information. Psychologic is broader than mathematics, however, having many more kinds of relations and systems, and so on.

Considering only the kinds of SOI contents and products, we have a matrix of five columns for kinds of content and six rows for kinds of products, yielding 30 unique kinds of items of information. I have suggested that such a set be recognized as a "psychoepistemology" (Guilford, 1966b). This is the kind of thing that philosophers at one time were looking for.

HIGHER-ORDER SOI ABILITIES

Some Rotational Problems

The rectangular nature of the SOI model has for some reason sometimes given the impression that the basic SOI abilities are orthogonal or mutually independent. Adding to this implication is the fact that I have always employed orthogonal rotation of factor axes in the second major step in factor analysis. I have done so without assuming that the factors are independent. The several reasons for this will be mentioned shortly. At this point it will be said that the methods used yielded well-replicated, meaningful factors. That was our main goal. We need to be reasonably sure of the meaningful factors before we inquire about their intercorrelations and higher-order factors.

Another feature of our rotational procedures apparently needs some defense. Before computerized procedures of rotation became available, we used the Thurstone graphic method. Results from such rotations had had a history of ready replication of psychological factors, from one analysis to another and from one investigator to another. This was shown by Thurstone's work and that of the AAF analyses. As computerized methods became available, we tried them out. We found that they provided poor replications of factors from one analysis to another and interpretability of factors was very poor. Evidently too much depended on what sets of tests were analyzed together. The nature of factors should not depend on such circumstances.

Rotations to Hypothesized Targets.   Later in ARP activities the Cliff (1966) computerized method of rotating orthogonally all axes simultaneously toward logically hypothesized factor loadings became available. We tried it and found that psychological factors could be very satisfactorily interpreted and replicated, so we used the method thereafter. We also rotated the axes in all the previous ARP analyses and found that, with minor improvements in places, the earlier results were well verified. As in the graphic method, one rotates to hypotheses and after the rotation one checks the goodness of fit of obtained results to hypotheses and also notes whether there are any unacceptable negative factor loadings for a positive manifold. If necessary, a new set of hypotheses can be set up and new rotations executed, which we commonly did.

Our use of Cliff's method of rotation came under attack because of the involvement of the subjective element in setting up hypotheses of factor loadings (Horn & Knapp, 1973). These authors illustrated their case by applying some chance-generated factor loading as targets in rotation. For their illustrative rotation they selected one of the earlier ARP analyses, applying their rotation operation to the unrotated factor matrix for that ARP analysis. They claimed that their resulting solution came nearly as close to their hypothesized set of loadings as had the ARP results to ARP hypotheses.

Elshout, Van Hemert, and Van Hemert (1975) came to our rescue. They objected that Horn and Knapp applied only *one* chance-generated set of hypotheses, which might have been by chance a lucky one for those authors. Generating by computer a fairly large number of alternative sets of chance hypotheses for the same problem, and using a more rigorous index of goodness of fit, they found that the index of fit in the case of our logically generated hypotheses was way outside the total distribution of the chance-generated indices. Thus our use of Cliff's method seems to have been vindicated.

Estimating the Correlations among the Basic Factors

The orthodox method for estimating the correlations between basic or first-order factors has been to rotate the axes obliquely and to use the cosines of the angles between pairs of axes as the estimates of their correlations. My orthogonal rotations precluded the use of this procedure. My alternative method was to start with the obtained loadings of tests on the orthogonal factors. Having selected the factors that were to be analyzed together, a set of from two to five tests were selected to represent each factor. The loadings for all the tests of a set on every factor to be analyzed were averaged. This gave the coordinates of the *centroid* of the set of tests on each of the factors. These steps gave a factor matrix of the loadings of the factor centroids on all the factors involved in the analysis. These loadings were used in the equation for estimating a coefficient of correlation between two variables from their common-factor loadings. The result was a correlation matrix for the basic-factor centroids. These procedures are more fully explained elsewhere (Guilford, 1981).

Analysis of the Basic Factors

Possible Kinds of Higher-Order Factors.   The analyses of basic factors that I have performed have employed data available from some of the ARP analyses. Most of those analyses had fortunately been planned to provide useful sets of factors, as will be seen from a few examples.

Consider first the kinds of higher-order factors that could be expected in view of the nature of the SOI model. Pairs of basic factors can differ in the number of facet categories that they have in common, from none to two. The more in common, the higher the correlation is expected between them.

Second-order factors would have two categories in common. For example, the common factor for *CMU* and *CMI* would be *CM*; the common factor for *CVC* and *NVC* would be *VC*; and that for *ESR* and *EMR* would be *ER*. These three second-order factors would be described as a semantic-cognition ability, a visual-classes ability, and an evaluation-of-relations ability.

Third-order factors would have only one SOI category in common—a divergent-production ability (*D*), a semantic ability (*M*), or a transformation ability (*T*), for example. We should expect to find 16 third-order factors, one for each of the SOI categories, and 85 second-order factors, one for each pair of categories, the members of each pair coming from different facets of the model.

An Analysis of Memory and Divergent-Production Factors

One strategy that I followed was to analyze together two parallel sets of basic factors, such as the six semantic-memory factors and the six semantic-divergent-production factors. In the ARP basic analysis there had been an interest in determining whether memory and divergent production are after all two different operations, since both depend on tests that call for retrieval of items of information from memory storage (Brown, Guilford, & Hoepfner, 1968). The basic analysis did show a separation of the two sets of factors, but a second-order analysis could show something about the degree of separation of the two kinds of abilities.

The results of the second-order analysis are shown in Figure 2, where the basic memory and divergent-production abilities are seen to be completely separated on either side of the first centroid axis. The oblique axes are each placed through the centroid of the two most extreme vectors in a search for bounding hyperplanes. The positive correlation between the factors *DM* and *MM* indicates a third-order factor in common to the two. This suggests a very general third-order factor, *M*, an ability to process semantic information. From these results alone, however, we cannot be sure about how general this factor is. It does apparently apply to all six kinds of products but possibly not to operations other than *D* and *M*, to which this analysis was limited.

Incidentally, I would equate a general *M* (semantic) factor to the Horn-Cattell ability they call "crystallized intelligence" (Guilford, 1980a; Horn & Cattell, 1966). Their "fluid intelligence" factor would appear to be a confounding of two other third-order factors, *V* (visual) and *S* (symbolic).

A Brief Summary of Results on Higher-Order Factors.   A few highlights can be mentioned here with respect to the higher-order SOI factors revealed thus far. Within the scope of the usable data, more than half of the 85 second-order abilities have been demonstrated, many more than once. The angles of separation have ranged widely, from about 30 to 80 degrees. Generally the

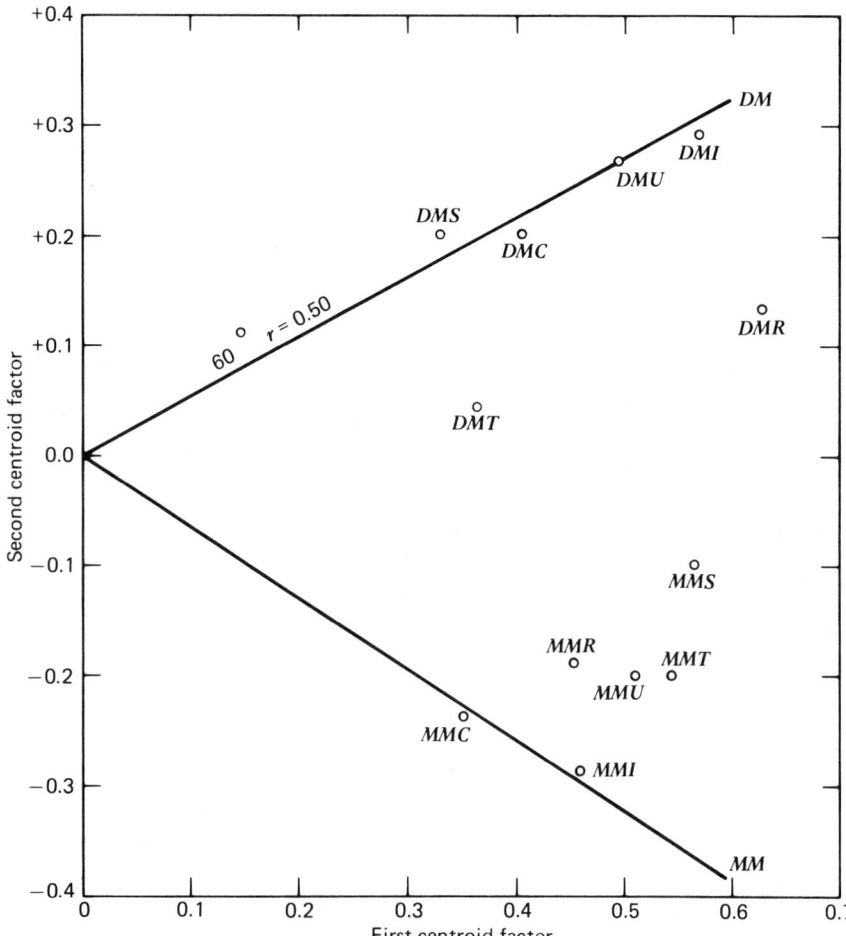

Figure 2. A plot of the points representing the centroid vectors for the six basic semantic-memory factors and the six basic semantic-divergent-production factors, showing an oblique rotation to locate roughly the two second-order factors DM and MM.

separations of pairs of operation factors have been widest and those for pairs of product factors have been narrowest.

An important exception was that evaluation factors could not be satisfactorily separated from cognition and from convergent-production factors. This appeared to be due to inadequate controls built into the tests. For all three operations, the common format for tests was the multiple-choice type. If the alternative answers given in this kind of test call for fine distinctions, more than one of them being acceptable, some evaluation is needed in order to make a good score. It could also happen that in evaluation tests either the stem or the alternative answers are not familiar to many examinees, thus bringing in some cognition variance.

Of all the operation categories, divergent production was most easily distinguished from all others and memory came next. Those two areas had the most distinctive test formats, which may have helped. The surprising distinction between divergent and convergent production was mentioned earlier. The distinction of both from the memory operation led to defining the latter as merely a process of recording items of information.

Hierarchical Model for SOI Abilities?   The oblique nature of the SOI model has also been demonstrated with another approach by Kelderman, Mellenbergh, and Elshout (1981). The finding of abilities at three levels of generality within the model naturally suggests the hierarchical type of model as of Burt and Vernon. Such models could be constructed, as I have shown for the divergent-production abilities (Guilford, 1984). But getting all such operation models combined in one overall pattern would seem to be precluded, owing to the many linkages of factors in different directions of the facets.

Furthermore, there is no good evidence for anything more general than the third-order factors. From results from ARP research there is certainly evidence against the idea of an all-embracing g factor. Of some 48,000 correlations between pairs of tests, about 18% were below .10, many of them being below zero (Guilford, 1964; Guilford & Hoepfner, 1971). In such analyses the typical standard error for a correlation of zero was about .07 or less, so that more than 20% of the r's failed to reach the .05 level of significance. Spearman had not carried his research far enough.

IMPLICATIONS FOR PSYCHOLOGICAL THEORY

From time to time in the history of psychology there have been some attempts, or at least expressions of desire, to bring intelligence under the tent of general psychological theory. Accomplishing this would bring about a kind of marriage between bivariate experimental and multivariate experimental psychologies. Such a connection is possible through the use of the SOI model.

Current thinking in cognitive psychology has often emphasized information processing as the appropriate approach to understanding mental events, with the implication that the brain is "that computer between our ears." Some experts on the nature of computers have been attempting to arrive at psychological understanding by investigating what they call "artificial intelligence" (Norman, 1981). In this connection, however, is the danger of trying to picture human information processing too much in the image of computer performance. The fact that the computer and the brain achieve similar results is not proof that they do so in the same manner. It is evident that the brain does have some crucial features that the best computers still do not possess. Any light that these investigators can throw on psychological events will of course be welcome.

Much can still be learned about these matters by attending directly to human information-processing activities. The SOI model has much to offer as a general map of this field. Recall the definition given earlier, that intelligence is a systematic collection of abilities *or functions* for processing information of different kinds in various forms. This definition indicates that attention should be paid to all three facets of that phenomenon; all category concepts need to be used to cover the field and perhaps more of similar kinds.

Elsewhere I have proposed that the SOI model can serve as a frame of reference for cognitive psychology (Guilford, 1974, 1979a). In doing so it offers a systematic array of unambiguous and operationally defined concepts—a psychological taxonomy. The operational definitions are in the form of references to kinds of tests or tasks that represent the factors and their categories. Some of the areas of cognitive psychology will be discussed briefly from the SOI point of view.

An SOI View of Perception

To some readers it may seem somewhat surprising to find perception brought within the sphere of intelligence, since the latter has been traditionally tied to thinking. For example, Terman defined intelligence as an ability to do abstract thinking. The extension of intelligence to include perception was forecast by Spearman, with his visual group factor; by Thurstone, with his two visual-PMA abilities; and by Wechsler, who included visual tests in his intelligence scale.

The SOI model has places for 30 visual abilities and 30 auditory abilities. The best justification for including them is that the abilities that have been found in these two categories are completely parallel with those in other content categories. It is even quite possible that when investigations have been made from the SOI point of view that columns in the model may have to be added for kinesthetic and possibly cutaneous abilities. Information in these areas is probably sufficiently structured to justify their additions. Kinesthetic information and its abilities should be very relevant in athletics, acrobatics, the dance, and also in all other motor skills, which have intellectual management. Cutaneous information should be of special value in the reading of Braille.

Some SOI Views of Learning

One very early view of intelligence as an overall ability was that it is the ability to learn. This idea came from the prescientific naturalists, who pointed out that while lower animals cope with their environments by virtue of inborn instincts, man does his coping largely through learning, which also meant through intelligence. Apart from the implication of a single ability, Binet shared this view when he developed his intelligence scale to distinguish between slow and normal learners.

Correlations with Rates of Learning. As psychologists developed methods for measuring the effects of learning in the laboratory, at different stages of practice, a rate-of-learning index could be obtained. It was hypothesized that such an index should correlate substantially with measures of intelligence. Such correlations proved to be disappointingly small. But it was noted that the sizes of the correlation coefficients varied with the kind of learning task and the kind of test. This should have led to the implication that learning in different kinds of tasks depends on different kinds of abilities.

Correlations at Different Stages of Practice.

After factorial abilities had become known efforts were made to find out how tests of different abilities correlated with learning scores at different stages of practice. This effort hypothesized that different abilities were of different degrees of importance at different stages of practice. From the nature of the learning task one could hypothesize what abilities might be relevant and thus choose the tests to use. Fleishman and Hempel (1954, 1955) were leaders in this kind of experiment, considering first the learning in psychomotor tasks, such as keeping a pointer on a moving target. They found that learning in different tasks did depend on different abilities, as found previously, but also that the same ability can change in importance as learning progresses. A general finding was that in psychomotor tasks intellectual abilities were relatively more important early in learning and psychomotor abilities more important later.

The same kind of experiment was later performed on the learning of concepts (Dunham, Guilford, & Hoepfner, 1967, 1969). Each concept was a class idea. The study covered class concepts in three areas of content—visual, symbolic, and semantic. In each case, four concepts were to be learned, denoted as *A*, *B*, *C*, and *D*. On one page of a teaching booklet an exemplar of one of the four concepts was shown, with the subject to guess to which class it belonged. The next page gave the answer that should have been chosen, in immediate feedback information, and presented a new exemplar for his decision.

In general the involvement of SOI abilities increased in importance as learning progressed, but not always in linear fashion. Quite generally the SOI content category of the relevant abilities coincided with that of the concept. An interesting exception was that semantic abilities seemed to play some roles also when the concepts were visual and symbolic. This might suggest that learners were tending to translate the information into semantic form, taking advantage of the fact that semantic information is more readily learned and remembered.

Of the operations involved, memory abilities seemed most pertinent, probably because of the need to remember earlier exposures and answers. Convergent production came into play relatively late in the learning exercise, probably because only after concepts were sufficiently learned could such events occur. Divergent production showed little or no relevance at any stage of learning. Evaluative abilities were not presented in the experiment. Curiously, ability *CMU*, which dominates IQ scales, showed little involvement even in the semantic task.

The Essential Nature of the Learning Process.

From the immediately preceding discussion it would appear that a total learning episode can be a very complicated affair, involving a number of the SOI operations and perhaps more than one content category. As a concept, can "learning" be better focused? Only in this way can we avoid ambiguity. What is the *sine qua non* of learning, if there is one?

Historically it has been the almost universal view that learning is a matter of forming new associative connections between elements. In SOI terms that is a matter of constructing new implications. A structuring act is the SOI operation of cognition. Is the cognition of implications the *only* process in learning? A little thought should lead to the question about the items of information that become connected in learning. Those items have had to be structured also. This step has been generally overlooked in learning theory. *All* items of information must be structured, as must *all* kinds of products. Thus it is argued that the essence of learning is the operation of cognition. This conception is essentially the same as that of Gestalt psychology. During the learning episode the other SOI operations are merely contributory to the main event. Problem solving in the total learning event involves all the operations, as will be described soon.

The Role of Repetition in Learning. The Gestalt view has been that repetitions of actions in learning serve the purpose of sharpening the newly structured products, thus increasing clarity and differentiation from other items of information. We may add that there is also improvement in item relations, class memberships, and roles in systems, all of which improves the ease of retrieval and the utility of the information on later occasions.

Transfer of Learning. The phenomenon of transfers from acquired skills to others receives some illumination from SOI concepts. The key to transfer is similarity; similarity generally means class membership. The SOI model provides three bases for similarity, in terms of operations, contents, or products and their combinations. Heinonen (1962) hypothesized that maximum transfer will occur between two tasks if both feature the same underlying ability, which means three reasons for similarity, and he provided evidence to support the idea. Earlier Ferguson (1954) had proposed that factorial intellectual abilities themselves develop by virtue of transfers due to similarities of tasks. What Ferguson proposed would seem to apply more to the higher-order abilities, which probably develop by transfers across facet lines.

One can speculate as to which kinds of similarity are most effective and what the consequences are. Similarity of operations should contribute in terms of strategies and tactics in mental functioning. Kinds of products in common should provide formal similarities. Similarity in content might be of some help, but it is probably easier to find instances of transfer across content boundaries, as in the experiment cited on the learning of concepts. Such transfers are translations between psychological languages.

Transformations in Learning. Almost entirely overlooked in theory of learning is the fact that transformations of items of information play an important role. One ARP study was focused on abilities involving transformations, in connection with all kinds of operations and two kinds of content—symbolic and semantic (Hoepfner, Guilford, & Bradley, 1970a). Added to the study was a test designed to indicate how much of short reading selections some high school students could understand and remember in taking a multiple-choice reading-comprehension test. Since reading to gain information is the almost overwhelming academic approach to learning, such a study could be illuminating. It was.

Very briefly, a stepwise multiple-regression approach was used, with scores for the various factors included in the study as predictors of the score for reading comprehension. Although the leading contributor to prediction was the commonly expected *CMU*, or verbal-comprehension factor, two transformation abilities were not far behind—*MMT* (memory for semantic transformations) and *CMT* (cognition of the same). Other significant contributors were *DMC* (divergent production of semantic classes) and *NMT* (convergent production of semantic transformations). Two *symbolic* abilities were surprisingly relevant; surprising until it was remembered that two of the three reading selections contained some numerical data. These abilities were *DST* (divergent production of symbolic transformations) and *EST* (evaluation of symbolic transformations). This might imply that the examinees indulged in some trial-and-error thinking as they answered the reading-test items. The most significant suggestion from all the results is that a learner's corrections of his own errors involves cognition of, memory of, and evaluation of transformations of items of information. It is probably not surprising to find that much learning is actually relearning, but it is not generally realized that abilities other than *CMU* can be so prominently involved.

Reinforcement in Learning.   Acquired mental structures are accepted, and thus likely to be committed to memory storage, or they are rejected, leading to new attempts and corrections of errors. Many different explanations have been offered to explain the nature of reinforcement. The SOI view offers the suggestion that the operation of *evaluation* is the key process. The opening statement of this paragraph essentially describes evaluation. A living organism is a confirmed pragmatist. It keeps what works and rejects what does not. Deciding what works and what does not are acts of evaluation. Reinforcement thus receives an information-processing interpretation. Feedback information plays an important role, cybernetic-wise. Incidentally, all previously suggested interpretations of reinforcement can also be envisaged in terms of evaluation and thus in terms of information processing (Guilford, 1966a).

SOI Views of Memory

Historically the textbook concept of memory included the steps of memorizing (learning), retention, recall, and recognition. The SOI view presents a quite different picture. As previously stated, learning is a matter of cognition, so learning and memorizing are different SOI functions. SOI memory is the fixation of cognized items of information in storage. It was defined to include some degree of retention, for, as far as events went, retention could be regarded as merely a persisting brain condition rather than an operation.

As reported earlier, recall is not a single kind of operation, for retrieval of information from storage involves the two different operations of divergent and convergent production, which are always clearly distinguished in factor analyses. Recognition is partly just what the term says, a re-cognition, but it is obviously more than that. A feeling of deja vu is often mentioned in this connection, a kind of awareness that it is a rerun. There is possible revival of background information. It can be positively reported that recognition tests do just as well as recall tests in detecting individual differences in the memory operation. Both kinds of tests possibly merely provide evidence that storage has taken place.

There is, after all, some evidence for retention abilities or functions. This evidence is in the form of factor-analytic information indicating a distinction between short-term and long-term retention, a distinction long known in bivariate psychology. Kamstra (1971) performed analyses of memory tests, some with immediate-recall testing and some with long-term-recall testing, both based on hypothesized SOI kinds of memory factors. He found two parallel sets of memory factors. Parallel factors were positively correlated, as one might expect. A deduction is that a column may need to be added to the SOI model for an operation of retention.

SOI Functions in Problem Solving

Although "problem solving" is one term, which may mean for some a single psychological function, just as the term "intelligence" has for so many, it actually refers to a varied set of intellectual functions. Incidentally, both instances seemed to have a psychological fallacy that one word refers to one thing. In the case of problem solving, also, a very large number of functions play roles, varying from one occasion to another.

It is well known that some psychologists, such as John Dewey, have suggested a number of typical steps in a problem-solving episode. The steps are now much clearer. First there must be an awareness that a problem exists. There follows a structuring of the nature of the problem, including an awareness of what is missing or lacking. This information calls for producing solutions. The solution or solutions are judged as to suitability and are rejected or accepted.

These steps have been put in SOI terms and displayed in a model (Guilford, 1966b), also in a slightly revised model (Guilford, 1977a). A view of the revised model is shown in Figure 3.

Seeing that a problem exists appears to be a matter of cognition of implications. In the ARP research a special ability was hypothesized for "sensitivity to problems." In an Apparatus Test, for example, we asked "What needs to be done to improve an ordinary telephone?" In another test one item asked "What is wrong with the institution of divorce?" Such tests did give rise to a factor that

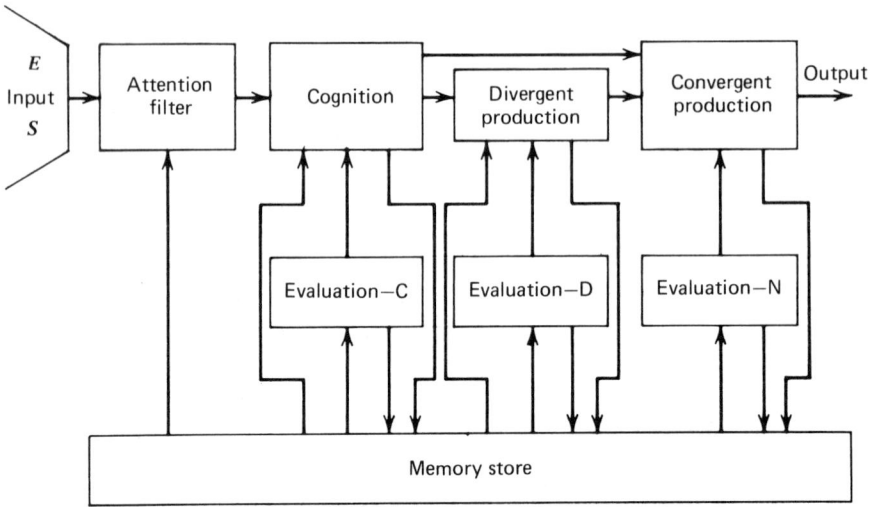

Figure 3. The structure-of-intellect problem-solving model, showing the interrelationships of the SOI operations in a time series.

was later identified as *CMI* (cognition of semantic implications). A parallel factor was found for *CSI*, involving symbolic information. Tests for this factor also called for finding problems. A sample item was "What can be done with the following material: $X - 0 - 0 X - X$?"

Structuring a problem is also largely a matter of cognition. If the problem is at all complex it is a matter of systems, as has often been found in arithmetical-reasoning test items. The dominant factor is *CMS*. But the system has a missing element. In dealing with strictly mathematical problems, equations are symbolic systems, the content being usually symbolic but sometimes visual. With verbally stated arithmetical problems, the solver must translate from one psychological language to another.

The step of finding solution or solutions to a problem involves convergent production in the first instance and divergent production in the second. Frequently both occur. The roles of memory and evaluation appear all along the way. Every step may be evaluated. In sensing a problem one may ask "Is there a problem or not?" Failure at a later step may call for a reevaluation of the structuring of the problem. Suggested solutions may run the gauntlet of inspection. Memory in problem solving consists of recording steps taken for possible uses in renewed efforts.

Decision Making

The key, the *sine qua non,* of decision making is SOI evaluation. It may be a simple case of choosing which implement to use with a certain new dish at the dining table. Or it may be a decision as to which stock to buy from a broker, using a windfall of dollars (Guilford, 1968b).

Creative Thinking

Some years ago in facing logically the general problem of creative thinking, I suggested that one of the common functions involved is fluency in the production of ideas—a readiness to think of alternatives to meet a need (Guilford, 1950). Already Thurstone and his students had turned up three such factors (Carroll, 1941; Taylor, 1947; Thurstone, 1938).

In the ARP research other kinds of fluency abilities were hypothesized and a number of factor analyses were concentrated in this area (Christensen & Guilford, 1963; Gershon, Guilford, & Merrifield, 1963; Hendricks, Guilford, & Hoepfner, 1969; Hoepfner & Guilford, 1966; Wilson, Guilford, Christensen, & Lewis, 1954).

In constructing the SOI model, fluency factors were placed in the operation category of divergent production. Of the 30 basic abilities in this category 24 have been investigated and demonstrated. The six auditory abilities in this category have not been investigated. Such auditory abilities seem quite possible when one thinks of the many alternative melodies and rhythms a composer may try out before reaching the final product.

Another hypothesis (Guilford, 1950) was that creative thinking is flexible thinking, calling for readiness to change items of perception or thought. Such factors were found and were identified with the layer of transformation abilities in the model. Two major analyses supplied most of the desired information (Frick, Guilford, Christensen, & Merrifield, 1959; Hoepfner, Guilford, & Bradley, 1970a). All told, 17 basic transformation abilities were accounted for out of a possible 25. No ARP analyses were made in the auditory area, but Horn (1973) has reported a factor that qualifies for the spot for NAT (convergent production of auditory transformations).

An incidental hypothesis that developed along the way was that a highly creative person is an elaborative thinker. A test developed for this hypothesis presented outlines of different plans, asking the examinee to round out the plans with needed details. The focal ability proved to be DMI (divergent production of semantic implications). Parallel abilities were found in other content areas. For ability DVI we presented outline drawings of items of furniture or costume, asking for added decorative elements in repeated test items.

It may be of interest to report that two 1950 hypotheses did not pan out as expected. I suggested that there should be an ability to analyze and an ability to synthesize. Incidentally, Bloom (1956) later proposed such abilities for a taxonomy of mental functions important in education. Tests of the two kinds were developed and were analyzed (Wilson, Guilford, Christensen, & Lewis, 1954). Tests of each set failed completely to determine a factor, going instead in the direction of other factors with other interpretations. This does not mean that a person does not analyze and synthesize, but, as in the case of problem solving, those popular activities can be accounted for unambiguously in terms of other functions.

Divergent Production and Transformations in Creative Performance.

In addition to many studies that have indicated the validity of divergent-production and transformation tests for predicting creative performance in daily life (see, for example, Elliott, 1964 or Jones, 1960) there have been other indications. Before divergent-production and transformation abilities had become known, Alex Osborn, an advertising executive who was concerned about making advertising writers more creative, had been using a method that he called "brainstorming." In this procedure, individuals sitting around a table are given a specific problem and are asked to suggest as many alternative solutions as they can, just as in a test of divergent production. Another exercise asks the group to suggest changes in familiar objects, having had previous instruction as to the kinds of changes commonly made. Thus, transformations were to be seen or produced.

Another source of support came from an ARP study (Allen, Guilford, & Merrifield, 1960; Guilford, 1963), in which Allen interviewed a fairly large number of highly productive scientists and others. As a part of his contact with these people, he described for them some of the SOI abilities that had become known at that time, giving examples of test items. Each subject was asked to rank the abilities as to importance to him or her. The scientists tended to rate divergent-production abilities high, but transformation abilities came out highest. Other highly creative persons gave similar judgments.*

Speech and Language

Speaking, listening, writing, and reading present numerous problems that can receive enlightenment from the use of SOI concepts. A very large number of SOI abilities can be found involved at some points. Symbolically, words can be in either visual or auditory form.† The meaning conveyed is of course semantic. Behavioral information may be conveyed by tone of voice as well as by what the speaker says.

A special problem involving speech was investigated by Feldman (1969) in his study of the relevance of certain SOI abilities in learning to read in the first grade. He found that relatively more important than *CMU* (cognition of semantic units), which is of leading importance later in reading, were six other abilities. They were concerned with the cognition memory, and evaluation of visual and auditory information—abilities *CVU, CAU, MVU, MAU, EVU,* and *EAU.* Further investigations would probably show other abilities to be relevant (transformations, for example, since much of a child's time and effort are taken up with correcting mistakes, which means transformations).

*For general theoretical discussions of creativity see Guilford (1967a, b).

†The question is open as to whether there are two distinct symbolic categories—visual and auditory. Investigations of symbolic abilities have thus far been confined to visual symbols.

The semantic aspects of speech and language are of course numerous. Since much of human communication is in symbolic form, with some in visual form, there are translation problems (translation from one content language to another). The greatest difficulty is that whereas symbolic and visual items are very precisely structured, those in semantic form are imprecise and varying from person to person and from time to time in the same person. This fact has apparently caused no end of trouble for those who deal with artificial intelligence (Norman, 1981). Much meaning that a speaker tries to communicate also depends on the contexts of speaker and listener. It is no wonder that much effort in communication misfires and that disorders of speech are so numerous and varied. Wiig and Semel (1976) have found many semantic abilities especially relevant in illuminating certain speech disorders.

Cognitive Styles

In the past three decades investigators have discovered by factor analysis quite a number of personality traits that have to do with selecting or controlling intellectual functioning of different kinds. A survey of these traits (Guilford, 1979a, 1980c) has led to the conclusion that the cognitive styles can be aligned with the categories of the SOI model. It would appear that the brain has some recognition of the SOI categories and the direction that intellectual functioning takes is somewhat determined by this information.

Some cognitive styles are concerned with the initiation and the control of intellectual processes at the moment. I have interpreted these styles as "intellectual executive functions." Styles that are concerned with preferences for the use of certain SOI categories may be regarded as "intellectual interests."

The most noteworthy style of the first kind is Witkin's field independence versus field dependence (Witkin, Dyk, Faterson, Goodenough, & Karp, 1962). Originally found in tests involving correct visual perception of the vertical position of a line under distorting influences, the trait can also be found in connection with tests of seeing hidden figures. The latter kind of test is also known as a measure of SOI ability *NVT* (convergent production of visual transformations). This fact provided a clue for interpretation of the Witkin variable. Field independence may be regarded as a person's being all set to *transform* visual items of information. In the hidden-figures test it is a matter of transforming lines belonging to the perceived larger figure into lines of the smaller hidden figure. In Witkin's rod-and-frame test it is a matter of transforming an illusory view into a realistic one. Studies have shown that the Witkin trait applies to information other than visual (Messick, 1976). It would seem to be a rather general preparedness for seeing or producing transformations.

Examples of intellectual-interest traits bearing logical relations to SOI categories are also easy to find. There are habitual preferences for using visual versus symbolic versus semantic information, and it would not be surprising to find special interests for auditory and behavioral categories of information. There are demonstrated traits of interest in divergent thinking and in convergent thinking

(Guilford, Christensen, Frick, & Merrifield, 1961). From the contrasting nature of these two kinds of actions, one might expect to find a strong negative correlation between them, perhaps even a bipolar trait. One estimate of the correlation between these interests I found to be only $-.30$, however. Another example of an interest style is a perference for broad classes versus narrow classes. Others pertaining to SOI categories have been mentioned (Guilford, 1980c).

SOI Concepts and Motor Functions

A little further speculation suggests that the SOI concepts can apply to motor activities. In fact, it was an aptitude-factor investigation that led to the concept of a "motor executive function." It was in an investigation of divergent production in connection with behavioral information that this concept came about. The printed tests that were developed for this analysis (Hendricks, Guilford, & Hoepfner, 1969) called for the usual written answers. Then it occurred to us that we might call for alternative responses in the form of expressional behavior— facial and vocal responses—in different tests. These responses were photographed and tape recorded, respectively. In the factor analysis it would have been possible for these tests to go along with the conventional ones, but they did not. Instead, they determined two new unique factors, for facial and vocal expression. The results later gave rise to the concept of motor executive functions (Guilford, 1972).

This concept led to further thinking about motor activities and functions. Movements, of an intentional nature at least, are shaped by the brain under the influence of intellectual functioning. Do they not, therefore, partake of some of the same properties as intellectual functioning? And does this go so far as a modeling of motor functions in a way similar to that for intellectual functions? Are motor functions distinguishable in terms of operations, contents, and products?

The product categories would seem to have the most promise for such discriminations. There are indeed simple movements (units) and there are organized motor coordinations (systems). There are sets of similar movements (classes), certain movements naturally following one another (implications), and pairs of movements are often called for (relations). Transformations would be found as learners of skills modify or correct movements.

As to operations, there can be no question that motor *memory* is a real phenomenon. *Evaluation* undoubtedly occurs as a learner accepts or rejects a completed movement or a movement in progress, with feedback information playing a role. There might seem to be no clear coordinate for *convergent production,* yet there are recognized "right" movements. *Divergent production* would appear in trial-and-error motor learning along with evaluation, and transformations as a learner corrects his errors. And how about *cognition?* Earlier, cognition was identified with learning. The structuring of movements could fulfill that category.

And how about kinds of content in connection with motor activity? At first thought there seems to be no possibility. It was mentioned earlier that there may be a need for a kinesthetic-content category in the SOI model, but that would be in the intellectual domain. It would, of course, be intimately linked with motor activity. This decision leaves motor functioning without a content facet. But it can be suggested that, as in a model for psychomotor abilities that I have suggested (Guilford, 1958), the part of the body involved supplies a possible motor-content facet. On the intellectual side the content facet also depends on bodily (brain) locations. At any rate, such thinking brings motor activity into an information-processing psychology. This move would call for a broadening of the label of "cognitive psychology" to an "informational psychology," which I have previously suggested (Guilford, 1971, 1982).

Physical Correlates

As to anatomical and physiological correlates of SOI categories, only those for contents seem clear. The cortical localizations for visual and auditory functioning have long been known. Split-brain investigations have associated semantic content with the left hemisphere (in right-handed individuals). Presumably because of the intimate operating connection between semantic and symbolic content, the latter would share that localization. Behavioral information, possibly because of the phenomenon of empathy, would involve some subcortical elements. Since all kinds of operations and all kinds of products occur in all content areas, some features other than localization for these categories will have to be found.

The physiological correlates of learning have long attracted the attention of theorists. The telephone-line analogy of brain functioning in learning has been giving way to electronic-computer parallels. As stated earlier, the SOI view is that learning is the process of structuring items of information. What could underlie the formation of items of information in all its forms? Each form is a different kind of construct, as noted in the definitions of kinds of products. A pathway neural structure cannot be ruled out as a contender for this purpose. But there are other reasonable possibilities, such as patterns of firing neurones, digit-wise. There could also be molecular patterns within cells, like genes. Gestalt psychologists favored the idea of generation of electrical fields. Such fields could be spatially expansive, thus accounting for transmission activities.

DEVELOPMENT AND DECLINE OF INTELLIGENCE

The description of neither growth nor decline of intelligence is adequately instructive unless it is viewed in terms of the components of that composite phenomenon. Investigations of these problems have usually been aimed at possible interventions that may promote growth or delay decline. With as many as 150 distinguishable features of intelligence, each possibly responding differently to treatments, it is important to have more detailed information regarding the general problem.

Effects of Heredity and Environment

This is not the place to go into the perennial issue of how heredity and environment influence the development of intelligence in individuals. In this and other sections I have had to limit discussions to some selected examples to show how SOI abilities or functions are relevant.

As to heredity there is as yet very limited information from the component approach, but a few appropriate items can be mentioned. A study by Stafford (1961) found evidence for the heredibility of ability to visualize, evidently the SOI ability *CVT* (cognition of visual transformations). Furthermore, he found that this trait is sex linked in inheritance. Two studies have shown heredibility of some divergent-production abilities (Barron, 1970; Thurstone & Strandskov, 1953). Thus at least one important aspect of creativeness has some hereditary foundation.

The environmental influences that affect intellectual development are much more numerous. A most pertinent study for our purposes here was performed by Broyler, Thorndike, and Woolyard (1927). It is relevant here because it considered effects of different kinds of educational instruction on different kinds of abilities. Some 13,000 high school students were given a variety of tests at the beginning of the school year and again at the end. The most interesting result was that, in general, students taking courses emphasizing visual versus symbolic versus semantic information improved most in the corresponding kinds of abilities distinguished as to the SOI kinds of content.

An Enlightened Formal Discipline.   At one time educators believed that they could strengthen intelligence in their students by teaching them languages and mathematics. When tests were eventually given to determine the effects of such teaching, the results were disappointing, and faith in that educational regimen lost support. We can now see that there should have been some benefits, but the wrong kinds of tests were given to detect them. Exercise was in symbolic form but perhaps tests were for semantic abilities.

If one is concerned with educational efforts for the promotion of intellectual development, the SOI model tells precisely what functions need to be exercised to achieve the desired results. Today, in Japan, and also in some areas of the United States, there is a growing enlightened formal discipline, in the form of applying exercises frankly designed to strengthen each SOI ability (Chiba, 1977). These efforts have been somewhat concentrated at the kindergarten level, but they can be applied at any level, including preschool years (as in Headstart programs). In Japan some mothers are being enlisted and trained to apply the exercises to their preschool youngsters.

There is information on such a program at the college level. At the State University College in Buffalo a two-year course has been designed for improving the creative thinking of students. A major experiment compared a large trained group with a matched control group on selected SOI tests before and after a two-year interval (Reese, Parnes, Treffinger, & Kaltsounis, 1976). They found significant differences in development in measures of both divergent production and transformation abilities. There were indications of superior performances by the trained students in connection with their other courses.

Rate of Growth of Intelligence

There has been general interest in the question of how rapidly intelligence develops in individuals at different age levels and the age at which maturity is reached. This is true for both global changes, as indicated by IQ tests, and for special abilities of the SOI type.

For the global picture the best indication was given by Thurstone and Ackerson (1929). They used an absolute-scale measure, that is, one with equal units and an absolute zero point. With the zero point coming slightly before birth, the curve relating their mental-age index to chronological age was S-shaped, with an inflection point near the age of 10 and a maturity level approached during the late teens.

When Thurstone (1955) developed similar growth curves for his PMA abilities, the function was also S-shaped, but the curves differed considerably from one ability to another, in inflection points and in age levels of maturity. The perceptual-speed score, for SOI ability EVU (evaluation of visual units), approached maturity earliest and the word-fluency test, for SOI ability DSU (divergent production of symbolic units), showed maturity was reached during the twenties. Trembly (1964) similarly found that as a group the divergent-production abilities gave maximum scores in the range of 20 to 25 years of age.

Other indications also show that divergent-production functions in general mature later than others. Indirect evidence comes from studies of the ages at which recognized creative people have exhibited output, in terms of both quality and quantity. Rossman (1931) reported results concerning inventors and Lehman (1953) reported findings with regard to creative people in other fields. There is agreement that *quality* of output is generally maximum between the ages of 25 and 30, but this varies depending on the field, with philosophers peaking near age 40. *Quantity* rose along with excellence but tends to remain higher longer.

An interesting incidental finding has been reported by Torrance (1975). Using divergent-production tests with children he found that at about the fourth grade boys tend to show slight losses, from which they tend to recover later. He found this to be true in different races and different cultures. He has attributed this event to the fact that boys at that age are becoming aware of sex roles and may regard such activities as being feminine. In agreement with this finding is the fact that females tend to excel in tests of divergent production, and it is possible that creative males tend to have a bit of feminine streak in them.

Early Development of SOI Abilities.   With the early success of IQ tests, which were typically made for children no lower than mental age three, efforts were made to extend testing to younger children, even to infants. A general finding was that IQs obtained at such early ages correlated low with IQs obtained for the same children in later years with standard IQ tests. This should have alerted testers to the fact that different abilities were being measured with the infant and younger-children tests.

After PMAs and other SOI abilities became known it was naturally asked whether the abilities found in later years also existed as such in the early years. For information on this question we are indebted to Stott and Ball (1963) and to Meyers, Dingman, Orpet, Sitkei, and Watt (1964). This information and that from other sources have been summarized (Guilford, 1977b). Stott and Ball analyzed the Merrill-Palmer and other standard tests for early childhood, with resulting factors that were interpreted as SOI abilities. Meyers, Dingman, Orpet, Sitkei, and Watt designed for use with young children some new tests, modeled after tests for certain abilities at later ages. The investigators administered those tests to both normal and mentally retarded children whose mental ages were two, four, and six. The results of the analyses yielded factors like those for older persons.

An examination of the many descriptions of what infants and young children can do, as reported by Piaget and his followers, when examined in the light of SOI functions, shows that a large number of the SOI functions are exhibited down to the earliest years (Guilford, 1977b).

Garrett (1946) proposed the principle that the first intelligence to appear in the infant is a single, general ability like Spearman's *g*, and that through life experiences this ability becomes divided and subdivided evenutally into abilities of the PMA type. My own view is essentially the opposite. The infant's and the young child's encounters with the world give his brain restricted inputs along the lines of the SOI contents and products, or his brain sorts them out that way. There develops accordingly some very limited skills like the SOI functions. Later, through transfers, as mentioned earlier, the broader abilities of higher order develop. Increasing, not decreasing, correlation among the basic abilities occurs. But these transfers never become complete, to achieve one universal ability.

Declines in Intelligence

The phenomenon of the waning of intelligence in individuals with advancing age is of increasing interest as the population lives longer. Here, again, we do not find that changes are equally evident in all respects.

When Wechsler (1958) related his general index of intelligence to age he found the curve comes to a maximum between ages 20 and 25, declines rather gradually to the age of 50, continuing at an accelerated rate to age 75, as far as his curve went. When he considered the rates of decline for his different component tests he found some marked differences. The lowest rate of decline came for his Information Test, which probably measures mostly CMU (cognition of semantic units) or verbal comprehension.

This finding is consistent with others and is interesting because Cattell regards a score from such a test as being a measure of his proposed "crystallized intelligence." He chose this metaphorical name because development in vocabulary is obviously dependent on accumulated learning. He also proposed that numerical-operation tests measure the same broad ability for the same reason. But such number tests have had a long history of correlating near zero with vocabulary tests (Guilford, 1980a). I think it is much safer to interpret this Cattell factor as a third-order *semantic* ability.

Wechsler found the most rapid declines occurred in his digit-symbol test. In SOI terms, this test probably measures two basic abilities—*MSI* (memory for symbolic implications) and *NSI* (convergent production of symbolic implications). Examinees can obtain good scores by quickly committing to memory storage the given pairings of digits and symbols (cognition is no problem, since the connections are presented to the examinee), or by making the stored implications functional in convergent production.

From the two cases just mentioned and from other information there is evidence that semantic abilities hold up better than symbolic ones in old age. There is not much information regarding declines with other kinds of content, although Cattell's "fluid intelligence" is said to decline more rapidly. I suggested earlier that this factor seems to be a combination of both symbolic and visual third-order abilities.

There is not much information regarding declines with respect to different kinds of products with aging. It does appear that information involving systems presents earlier difficulties in old age. This is shown by the elderly who have difficulty in comprehending complicated instructions and in solving complicated problems.

With respect to kinds of operations, common observations note failing recalls of information in the elderly. The loss is mainly in convergent production. The fact that divergent production holds up well has been mentioned. There is a noteworthy loss in flexibility, which probably means in connection with transformations. The last two items are consistent with the greater loss in quality of creative productions in old age than in quantity. The elderly also show difficulties with evaluation in sometimes being too sure of themselves (Guilford, 1968a).

IMPLICATIONS FOR PSYCHOLOGICAL MEASUREMENT

The detailed information provided by the SOI model has naturally numerous implications in various spheres of living. The most direct effects should be found in the assessment of individuals with respect to intellectual status. There are also applications in many areas of education, in vocational guidance, and in personnel selection and placement in business and industry.

Implications in Intelligence Testing

An examination of the component items of the Stanford Binet Scale as Meeker (1969) has done shows just how much of the whole of intelligence as displayed by the SOI model is missing and how unbalanced the representation is at different age levels of the scale. On the whole, the Stanford Binet emphasizes the operations of cognition and memory, to a relative neglect of productive thinking and evaluation. It is heavily weighted with semantic content with some attention to symbolic information, with behavioral information missing. Among the products, units and systems are featured with nothing of any consequence on classes. The SOI model has places for 25 abilities involving classes, 17 of which have been investigated and demonstrated (Dunham, Guilford, & Hoepfner, 1969).

There have been a number of factor analyses of the components of the Wechsler scales. For the adult scale probably the best analysis has been that of Davis (1956), since he included other tests that proved to be helpful in interpreting obtained factors. From this source and from logical considerations of the Wechsler component tests, the leading abilities are probably as follows:

Tests	SOI Abilities
Information test	*CMU* (cognition of semantic units)
Comprehension	*CMU*
Arithmetical reasoning	*CMS* (cognition of semantic systems)
Memory span digits	*MSS* (memory for symbolic systems)
Similarities	*CMC* and *CMR* (cognition of semantic classes and relations)
Picture arrangement	*NMS* (convergent production of semantic systems)
Picture completion	*CVU* and *CVT* (cognition of visual units and transformations)
Block design	*CVT*
Object assembly	*CVU* and *EVU* (cognition and evaluation of visual units)
Vocabulary	*CMU*
Digit symbol	*MSI* and *NIS* (memory and convergent production of symbolic implications)

This account gives some idea of the coverage and the sort of balance offered by the adult Wechsler scale as of the 1950s. It does show how his extension to visual content succeeded. Like other IQ scales it misses behavioral and auditory abilities.

Intelligence Profiles. Although the Wechsler scale went in the right direction it did not go far enough or diversify enough. In view of the testing time it uses there is much redundancy. What is needed is a profile of scores for well-distinguished and well-defined abilities. Such an approach has been taken by the SOI Institute of El Segundo, California, with its battery of SOI tests. From such a battery one can obtain a picture of a person's strengths and weaknesses. It is especially useful for vocational guidance, for diagnosing particular deficiencies in children with learning problems, and for suggesting remedial instruction. For any learner it can be determined how individualized instruction can be planned.

Weighted Composite Scores. Another kind of use for factorial-ability scores has been found most effective. Predictions of the goodness of performance in a particular task can be best achieved by means of a selected combination of such scores, optimally weighted in a regression equation. Such predictions are most effective when the intercorrelations among the component scores are minimal, thus with the least redundancy. Factorial-ability scores provide that condition. For example, the AAF group during World War II, using that approach, could claim much of the credit for cutting the failure rate in Primary pilot training from about 30% at the beginning of the war down to about 10% near the end (Guilford, 1948a, b). Another indication of effectiveness of assignment in terms of the pilot "stanine" or composite pilot-aptitude score, was that students assigned to pilot training against the psychologists' recommendations were twice as likely to fail. Also a large group was sent to pilot training without psychological judgment. The correlation between the pilot stanine and the pass-fail criterion was about .60.

IMPLICATIONS FOR EDUCATION

I have discussed at length this general subject (Guilford, 1968a, 1978a, 1978b, 1979b). Only a few highlights will be mentioned here, regarding curriculum, the selection of students, teaching, and examinations.

Curriculum and Intellectual Development

For those who are concerned with the development of the intellectual resources of the children or students who are under their care, the SOI model provides a clearly designed map of the field to be covered. It could serve as the "periodic table" of the educator and teacher as well as the psychologist. Its first application could be in making a survey of the present balances and imbalances in education. Many other considerations, of course, should help determine choices in curriculum.

Some Educational Imbalances. An examination of the distribution of efforts in education will show the same kinds of imbalances as occur in standard intelligence scales. This is rather natural because of the latter's traditional uses. Aschner (1963) made a study of what goes on in typical classrooms, in terms of exercising different SOI functions. The results showed an overwhelming emphasis on cognition and memory to the relative neglect of productive thinking and evaluative functioning as in IQ scales.

As for informational content, the kinds of coverage are well known and some of it has been touched on earlier. A possible suggestion might be that exercise of visual abilities might be given more attention, in view of the economy provided by visual thinking and its use in problem solving and creative thinking. As the Chinese adage says, a picture is worth a thousand words. Exercise in translations between visual and semantic content would also be useful.

Among the products a possible neglect is in the use of transformations. Teaching emphasizes finding right answers and thus does not encourage explorations into other conditions and views, and thus development in creativity. As noted earlier, transformations also play an important role in correcting errors.

Selection of Students

The selection of students is of course generally limited to the college level. General college-entrance examinations seem to have functioned rather well, having been given a good start by Thurstone. But there is always room for improvements. There has been a realization that for selection of students in special curricula, such as law, medicine, or engineering, some special testing is needed, but this has been without the benefit of full knowledge of special abilities. And it is one thing to select students who will pass their courses and graduate but something else to predict professional success, as in diagnosing ailments and prescribing treatments in medicine or in winning cases in law.

Within the general undergraduate program more detailed information as to aptitudes could probably be useful in guiding students into courses and majors. Many studies have been made validating SOI tests for the prediction of achievement in different subjects. Some of them will be reviewed briefly next.

Aptitude for Mathematics. Three studies have provided detailed information regarding aptitudes for mathematics. One was concerned with general mathematics and algebra at the 9th-grade level, one with geometry at the 10th-grade level, and one with advanced courses in mathematics at undergraduate and graduate levels in college.

In the 9th-grade study (Guilford, Hoepfner, & Peterson, 1965) the criteria were in the form of comprehensive examinations at the end of the school year. Standard aptitude tests had been given, including the CTMM (California Test of Mental Maturity), with its language and nonlanguage scores, and four parts of the DAT (Differential Aptitudes Test). These scores appear to cover six SOI abilities, two on a univocal basis.

One aspect of this study that is most relevant here was designed to see whether tests selected for 13 SOI abilities would contribute something novel to prediction of achievement. Table 1 summarizes some of these results. Information is given concerning how well optimally weighted part scores of the standard tests predicted the criteria and also multiple correlations when the equations were extended to include the SOI test scores.

The general result was that for the two general-mathematics courses there were gains in prediction but none was statistically significant. For regular algebra there was one significant gain out of two. For accelerated (college-preparatory) algebra there were two significant gains from the addition of SOI tests. The latter emphasized symbolic abilities, which probably accounts for the differences in gains.

The study in connection with geometry was made by Caldwell, Schroder, and Michael (1970). Applying the stepwise addition of predictors in a multiple-

Table 1. Multiple Correlations for Different Standard-Test Composites and for
These Composites Plus Thirteen SOI Tests in Predicting Achievement in General
Mathematics and Algebra

Test Combination	Mathematics Course		Algebra Courses	
	General Basic	Noncollege Algebra	Regular	Accelerated
CTMM	.35	.41	.21	.38
CTMM + SOI tests	.59	.59	.54[a]	.80[b]
DAT	.58	.55	.29	.72
DAT + SOI tests	.64	.59	.55	.85[b]
Thirteen SOI tests	.46	.45	.39	.75
N	77	95	101	73

[a]Significant gain at .05 level.
[b]Significant gain at .01 level.

regression analysis, they found that the multiple R was .60 in both of two
different schools, with five relevant SOI tests in the one case and four in the
other. The criterion was a standard geometry test. With a score in 9th-grade
algebra achievement as a sole predictor the validity coefficients were .45 and
.58. Including this variable with the SOI tests gave R's of .65 and .70. Thus the
small SOI composites did better than the algebra score alone but each made
unique contributions.

The college-level study was performed by Hills (1957). Students in physics
and engineering as well as in mathematics specializations were subjects. They
were administered nine selected SOI tests in 23 groups. The criteria in most
cases were grades in mathematics, most of them in calculus courses, with ratings
of general achievement in mathematics in graduate groups.

Some of Hills' results are summarized in Table 2, giving the number of
instances of correlations that were statistically significant at the .05 level or
better. Ranges of the values of the significant coefficients are given for the tests.
In general, the semantic abilities, two of which are usually dominant in standard

Table 2. Validity Coefficients in Predicting Achievement in Higher Mathematics

SOI Ability	Number of Significant Correlations	Range of These Coefficients
CVS	4	.33 to .68
CVT	3	.31 to .34
CMU	0	———
CMS	1	.31
MSI + NSI	4	.29 to .44
DMU	0	———
DVT	3	.35 to .68
EMI	4	.38 to .72

college-entrance examinations (*CMU* and *CMS*), showed little or no validity. Tests for visual abilities were among the best (*CVU, CVT,* and *DVT*), indicating that visual thinking is an important asset in advanced mathematics, including calculus. Only one symbolic test was in Hills' battery and it performed well. Curiously, this was the common numerical-operations test, which, in SOI terms, represents abilities *MSI* and *NSI* about equally well (Thurstone's "numerical facility" factor proved to be a confounding of these two SOI abilities). Other symbolic abilities not covered in Hills' battery would probably add to predictions of mathematical achievement. One semantic test did do well, the one for *EMI* (evaluation of semantic implications), or Thurstone's deduction ability. Some of the correlations with single tests were so high that one could expect multiple correlations to be very high in multiple predictions of mathematical achievement.

Achievement in Physics.   Ignatz (1982) compared the validity for a set of SOI tests in the prediction of achievement in high school physics with that of a standard Florida Statewide Twelfth-Grade Test. His selected SOI tests took two hours to administer, while the Florida test required two days. In two high schools, and with a standard test in physics as the criterion, the multiple *R*'s for the SOI tests came to .48 and .54. For the Florida test the correlations were .43 and .54. For the two predictors together the coefficients were .58 and .74. Thus the two-hour testing was as valid as the two-day testing, and both could have been improved as predictors of physics achievement.

Teaching for SOI Development

Of considerable importance would be the teacher's awareness of the SOI concepts, in making assignments, in preparing lesson plans, and in classroom performance. In this connection, some teachers have told me that knowledge of the products is of greatest use. These are the forms in which learning occurs, so knowledge of them can serve as a teacher's goals. The teaching of different products involves different problems and calls for different tactics, which I have discussed elsewhere (Guilford, 1967a). I have also recommended that as soon as they are ready for it, learners be taught SOI concepts so that they can apply this information in the management of their own learning.

Examinations

Students naturally learn subject matter of a course in ways that they have found successful in taking examinations in the course. The nature of the examination then has much to do with the kind of intellectual development that occurs. True-false and multiple-choice examinations generally call for limited exercises of intellectual functions. This is not a new observation, but the kind of shortcoming is now clearer. It is no wonder that employers sometimes complain that although college graduates seem to know the information that they have been taught, they sometimes fall short in using the information in solving problems or in creative production (Guilford, 1950).

PERSONNEL SELECTION AND PLACEMENT

The kind of success described in the selection and classification of aircraft pilots mentioned earlier offers much promise for similar outcomes with other personnel, but it takes some research. This activity can be very much facilitated when applying the SOI model as a map. It would guide one clearly to hypotheses as to what kinds of measures of talent are probably needed to fit a particular situation. In other words, the model can serve in a systematic job analysis.

Job Analysis with the SOI Model

In the approach suggested, after examining the more critical tasks to be performed in an assignment, only three decisions need be made in zeroing in on each intellectual ability that is probably needed: which kind of operation, kind of content, and kind of product are relevant? These are the specifications to be satisfied.

Suppose the position is that of a probation officer. There is little doubt that the critical kind of informational content is behavioral. Probation officers must be prepared through their own observations to understand their ward: the latters' motivations, attitudes, and any quirks of personality. In addition to their understanding, officers will sometimes need to think of kinds of treatment to apply, which falls in the area of divergent production. They must perpetually evaluate their perceptions and their considered treatments. As to products of information, their clients' relations to other individuals and their possible roles in groups need to be considered, thus the involvement of behavioral relations and systems. Among the abilities thus suggested would be *CBR* and *CBS,* as well as *DBU* and *DBS.* One probation officer who made a minor psychological study of the matter told me that he found tests for *CBC* (cognition of behavioral classes) relevant, perhaps because the officer needs to diagnose behavior in terms of classes in order to prescribe treatment.

Some Occupational Roles and Informational Content

One who is concerned with personnel problems in a more general way can look for more common links between jobs and SOI abilities. Making a general survey of both fields, decisions can be reached about common matchings, considering the three facets of the model. The following suggestions are made along that line. There is some scattered information to support some of the suggestions (for example, Guilford & Hoepfner, 1971).

The clearest connections can be seen in the case of the kinds of informational content. With content categories considered in turn, here are a few suggestions:

Visual. Artist, architect, engineer, surgeon, mathematician, plumber, auto or truck driver, aircraft pilot, inventor, acrobat.

Auditory. Musical performer or teacher, composer or arranger, speech teacher or therapist, poet.

Symbolic. Mathematician, code maker or breaker, linguist, accountant, clerk, computer programmer.

Semantic. Scientist, writer, speaker, teacher, lawyer, legislator, journalist, crossword-puzzle writer.

Behavioral. Foreman, lawyer, judge, juror, salesman, politician, statesman, probation officer, welfare worker, policeman, security guard, football player, coach, teacher, speaker, physician, parent, detective, novelist.

In view of the length of this last list it should be surprising that there have been so few calls for the assessment of behavioral abilities. It has apparently been assumed that a measure of "general intelligence" would suffice for these purposes. It won't.

Occupations and SOI Operations

Occupations are not nearly so easily classified in terms of the kinds of operations that are relevant. Cognition and memory are of very general use, so most decisions need to be made on the basis of some other facet. A few suggestions can be made, however. Because of their dominant roles in learning, both students and teachers come to mind. Because of cognition's role in discovery, it should be of importance for scientists, investigators, and detectives.

Everyone profits from having good facilities for recording and retaining information, although the spreading use of personal computers may make this less true. Not everyone will carry a vest-pocket computer with him or her. Some for whom this SOI operation is of special utility include the actor and actress who must memorize their lines; performing musicians; bridge players and gamblers who need to remember the moves of their opponents and of themselves; lawyers who must remember lists of cases; and coaches who must remember the player who has the special kind of skill to meet the present crisis.

Divergent production is the operational resource of the fertile problem solver and the creative thinker. It is needed by scientists, who must think of alternative hypotheses and of alternate ways for testing each hypothesis. Planners need this kind of skill, including high-level managers of organizations (Berger, Guilford, & Christensen, 1957).

Convergent production is the area commonly known as deductive reasoning (Guilford, 1961). The mathematician comes naturally to mind, as well as the logician and philosophers in general. Others are legal experts and theorists in science.

Being the area of judgment and decision making, evaluation is needed by anyone who wants to see problem solving through to correct or wisest conclusions. Some specialists for whom evaluation is an important asset include editors, who must decide on the acceptance or rejection of manuscripts, and those who must eliminate errors from printers' proof. Judges of the various courts of law, of course, derive their titles from the main psychological process involved.

Places for Some Products of Information

As in the case of operations, products of information have use in many places. A few cases of unusual needs can be mentioned, however. Semantic units, or vocabulary, or ability *CMU*, have dominated IQ tests from the beginning, with very good reasons. But, for one thing, it must be remembered that there are also "vocabularies" in all other content categories as well. No particular occupations will be mentioned in connection with units, for so much more depends on the content area involved.

Special groups can be mentioned for their unusual dependence on classes. At lower levels of industrial activity are sorters and pairers of socks, and of nuts and bolts, and so on. At the higher levels of such activity are the scientists who are concerned with taxonomic problems as in chemistry, biology, pathology, and psychology. The SOI model is itself a taxonomy.

A few persons who are especially concerned with relations are novelists, who relate their characters; scientists, who are looking for functional relationships; politicians, who look at the issues in relation to getting votes; and historians, who find critical relations in historical events, thus making history more plausible and intelligible.

Many types of people are concerned with systems. When life becomes complex, of course, all of us are concerned with systems, for we live in frames of reference in time and in space, in families, in organizations and political affairs. Especially concerned are planners, high-level managers, who must encompass many conditions and events, and on a more detailed level a computer programmer. And then there are builders of houses and other edifices, and there are directors of motion pictures and television programs.

It was mentioned earlier that scientists themselves confess to the need for using transformations in their work. Humorists, and others involved with producing humor use transformations, for so much depends on them (punsters, for example). Government officials and political campaigners need to be ready to meet changing conditions with transformations in their thinking and in their views. Governmental rigidity can cause much distress.

People who need to be ready with predictions and with conclusions must be prepared to see and to produce implications. Among them are lawyers, judges, mathematicians, planners, and decision makers in government and industry, who need to foresee consequences of actions and decisions.

SOME GENERAL CONCLUDING REMARKS

The search for the nature of human intelligence has required the exploration of a very large range of cognitive functioning, thus contributing to a broad and detailed view of psychological theory in an informational psychology. The exploring has had to capitalize on studies of individual differences, which are variations that nature has provided for us, by correlational and factor-analytic procedures, used in a hypothesis-testing regime.

There is still much to be done to round out the general picture. Of the 150 distinct abilities or functions in the SOI model, only a few over 100 have been investigated and demonstrated. Many have been demonstrated a number of times. The remaining intellectual-aptitude variables are already clearly hypothesized and can be fully expected to achieve demonstrated status with appropriate test development and factor analysis. The model has abundantly demonstrated its heuristic value, not only in pointing to undemonstrated abilities but also to the kinds of tests it would take to reveal them. The greatest need is for investigation in the auditory-content area. In the behavioral-content area there is need to analyze for abilities involving the operations of memory, convergent production, and evaluation. As mentioned, there may be whole sets of discoverable functions in the areas of kinesthetic and cutaneous information.

For the first time, intelligence and intelligence testing have a detailed and systematic, scientific foundation. On the side of psychological theory a wide range of phenomena receive new, coherent interpretations. It was also suggested that SOI concepts can be extended to cover motor functioning. It was suggested how both motor and motivational functioning can be envisaged in terms of information processing.

From the standpoint of applications a detailed map or taxonomy has been provided for promoting the development of intelligence in individuals by educational procedures. The map also shows that assessment of individual status in intelligence is most revealingly achieved in terms of profiles of scores rather than a single conglomerate of unrecognized composition.

Detailed pictures of development and of decline of intellectual functioning are now attainable. Predictions of achievement, in school learning or in the world of work, can be best achieved with the use of optimally weighted composite scores tailored for the purpose. In all these connections one can proceed with broad and deep understanding of what results or findings mean.

REFERENCES

Allen, M. S., Guilford, J. P., & Merrifield, P. R. (1960). The evaluation of selected intellectual factors by creative research scientists. *Reports from the Psychological Laboratory, University of Southern California* (No. 25).

Aschner, M. J. (1963). The analysis of verbal interaction in the classroom. In A. Bellack (Ed.), *Theory and research in teaching.* New York: Teachers College.

Barron, F. (1970). Heritability of factors of creative thinking and aesthetic judgment. *Acta Geneticae Medicae et Gemelogie, 19,* 204–208.

Berger, R. M., Guilford, J. P., & Christensen, P. R. (1957). A factor-analytic study of planning abilities, *Psychological Monographs, 71* (Whole No. 436).

Bloom, B. S. (Ed.) (1956). *Taxonomy of educational objectives. Handbook I, Cognitive domain.* New York: Longmans.

Boring, E. G. (1929). Intelligence as the tests test it. *New Republic, 34,* 33–37.

Brown, S. W., Guilford, J. P., & Hoepfner, R. (1968). Six semantic-memory abilities, *Educational and Psychological Measurement, 28,* 691–717.

Broyler, C. R., Thorndike, E. L., & Woolyard, E. (1927). A second study of mental discipline in high school students. *Journal of Educational Psychology, 18,* 377–404.

Burt, C. (1949). The structure of the mind: A review of the results of factor analysis. *British Journal of Educational Psychology, 19,* 100–111, 176–199.

Caldwell, J. R., Schroder, J. P., & Michael, W. B. (1970). SOI measures and other tests as predictors of success in 10th grade modern geometry. *Educational and Psychological Measurement, 30,* 437–441.

Carroll, J. B. (1941). A factor analysis of verbal abilities. *Psychometrika, 6,* 379–397.

Chiba, A. (1977). *The Learned Society of Intelligence Education: Outline of the history and activities.* Tokyo: Information Center.

Christensen, P. R., & Guilford, J. P. (1963). An experimental study of fluency factors. *British Journal of Statistical Psychology, 16,* 1–26.

Cliff, N. (1966). Orthogonal rotation to congruence. *Psychometrika, 31,* 33–42.

Comrey, A. L. (1971). *A first course in factor analysis.* New York: Academic Press.

Davis, P. C. (1956). A factor analysis of the Wechsler Bellevue Scale. *Educational and Psychological Measurements, 16,* 127–146.

Dunham, J. L., Guilford, J. P., & Hoepfner, R. (1967). Multivariate approaches to the discovering of the intellectual components of concept learning. *Psychological Review, 75,* 206–221.

Dunham, J. L., Guilford, J. P., & Hoepfner, R. (1969). Cognition, production, and memory of class concepts. *Educational and Psychological Measurements, 29,* 515–538.

El Abt, H. A. (1971). The intellect of East African students. *Multivariate Behavioral Research, 5,* 423–435.

Elliott, J. M. (1964). Measuring creative abilities in public relations and advertising work. In C. W. Taylor (Ed.), *Widening horizons in creativity.* New York: Wiley.

Elshout, J. J., Van Hemert, N. A. D., & Van Hemert, M. (1975). Comment on Horn and Knapp on the subjective character of the empirical base of Guilford's structure-of-intellect model. *Onderswijdresearch, 1,* 15–25.

Feldman, B. (1969). *Prediction of first grade reading achievement from selected structure of intellect tests.* Unpublished doctoral dissertation, University of Southern California.

Ferguson, G. A. (1956). On transfer and the abilities of man. *Canadian Journal of Psychology, 10,* 121–131.

Fleishman, E. A., & Hempel, W. E. Jr. (1954). Changes in factor structure of a complex psychomotor test as a function of practice. *Psychometrika, 19,* 239–252.

Fleishman, E. A., & Hempel, W. E. Jr. (1955). The relation between abilities and improvement with practice in a visual-discrimination reaction-time test. *Journal of Experimental Psychology, 49,* 301–312.

Fleishman, E. A., Roberts, M. M., & Friedman, M. P. (1958). A factor analysis of aptitude and proficiency measures in radiotelegraphy. *Journal of Applied Psychology, 42,* 129–137.

French, J. W. (1951). The description of aptitude and achievement tests in terms of factors. *Psychometric Monographs* (No. 5).

Frick, J. W., Guilford, J. P., Christensen, P. R., & Merrifield, P. R. (1959). A factor-analytic study of flexibility or thinking. *Educational and Psychological Measurement, 19,* 469–480.

Garrett, H. E. (1946). A developmental theory of intelligence. *American Psychologist, 1,* 372–378.

Gershon, A., Guilford, J. P., & Merrifield, P. R. (1963). Figural and Symbolic divergent production abilities in adolescent and adult populations. *Reports from the Psychological Laboratory, University of Southern California* (No. 20).

Getzels, J. W., & Jackson, P. W. (1961). *Creativity and intelligence.* New York: Wiley.

Gorsuch, R. L. (1974). *Factor analysis.* Philadelphia: Saunders.

Guilford, J. P. (1948a). Some lessons from aviation psychology. *American Psychologist, 3,* 3–11.

Guilford, J. P. (1948b). Factor analysis in a test development program. *Psychological Review, 55,* 79–94.

Guilford, J. P. (1950). Creativity. *American Psychologist, 4,* 444–454.

Guilford, J. P. (1958). A system of psychomotor abilities. *American Journal of Psychology, 71,* 164–174.

Guilford, J. P. (1959). Three faces of intellect. *American Psychologist, 14,* 459–479.

Guilford, J. P. (1961). Basic conceptual problems in the psychology of thinking. In E. Harms (Ed.), *Proceedings of the New York Academy of Sciences, 91,* 6–21.

Guilford, J. P. (1963). Intellectual resources and their values as seen by scientists. In C. W. Taylor & F. Barron (Eds.), *Scientific creativity: Its recognition and development.* New York: Wiley.

Guilford, J. P. (1964). Zero intercorrelations among tests of intellectual abilities. *Psychological Bulletin, 61,* 401–404.

Guilford, J. P. (1966a). Motivation in an informational psychology. In D. Levine (Ed.), *Nebraska symposium on motivation 1965.* Lincoln, NB: University of Nebraska Press.

Guilford, J. P. (1966b). Intelligence: 1965 model. *American Psychologist, 21,* 20–26.

Guilford, J. P. (1967a). *The nature of human intelligence.* New York: McGraw-Hill.

Guilford, J. P. (1967b). Some theoretical views of creativity. In H. Helson & W. Bevan (Eds.), *Contemporary approaches to psychology.* Princeton, NJ: Van Nostrand.

Guilford, J. P. (1968a). *Intelligence, creativity, and their educational implications.* San Diego, CA: EdITS.

Guilford, J. P. (1968b). Intellectual aspects of decision making. In A. F. Wolford & J. E. Birren (Eds.), *Interdisciplinary topics in gerentology* (Vol. 4). Basel: Karger.

Guilford, J. P. (1971). Varieties of memory abilities. *Journal of General Psychology, 86,* 207–228.

Guilford, J. P. (1972). Executive functions and a model of behavior. *Journal of General Psychology, 86,* 279–287.

Guilford, J. P. (1974). A psychology with act, content, and form. *Journal of General Psychology, 90,* 90–100.

Guilford, J. P. (1977a). *Way beyond the IQ guide to improving intelligence and creativity.* Buffalo, NY: Creative Education Foundation.

Guilford, J. P. (1977b). Development of intelligence: A multivariate view. In C. Uzgiris & E. Weizman (Eds.), *The structuring of experience.* New York: Plenum.

Guilford, J. P. (1978a). Education with an informational psychology. *Education, 98,* 3–16.

Guilford, J. P. (1978b). Intelligence education is intelligent education. In A. Chiba (Ed.), *Intelligence education is intelligent education.* Tokyo: International Society for Intelligence Education.

Guilford, J. P. (1979a). *Cognitive Psychology with a Frame of Reference.* San Diego, CA: EdITS.

Guilford, J. P. (1979b). Intelligence isn't what it used to be: What to do about it. *Journal of Research and Development in Education, 12,* 34–46.

Guilford, J. P. (1980a). Fluid and crystallized intelligence: Two fanciful concepts. *Psychological Bulletin, 88,* 406–412.

Guilford, J. P. (1980b). La Intelligencia desde el punto de vista processimiento de la informacion. *Intersciencia, 5,* 285–292.

Guilford, J. P. (1980c). Cognitive styles: What are they? *Educational and Psychological measurement, 40,* 715–735.

Guilford, J. P. (1981). Higher-order structure-of-intellect abilities, *Multivariate Behavioral Research, 16,* 411–435.

Guilford, J. P. (1982). Cognitive psychology's ambiguities: Some suggested remedies. *Psychological Review, 89,* 48–59.

Guilford, J. P. (1984). Varieties of divergent production. *Journal of Creative Behavior, 18,* 1–10.

Guilford, J. P., Christensen, P. R., Frick, J. W., & Merrifield, P. R. (1961). Factors of interest in thinking. *Journal of General Psychology, 65,* 39–52.

Guilford, J. P., & Hoepfner, R. (1971). *The analysis of intelligence.* New York: McGraw-Hill.

Guilford, J. P., Hoepfner, R., & Peterson, H. (1965). Predicting achievement in mathematics from measures of intellectual-aptitude factors. *Educational and Psychological Measurements, 15,* 659–682.

Guilford, J. P., & Lacey, J. I. (Eds.). (1947). *Printed classification tests: Army Air Forces Aviation Psychology Research Program (Report No. 5).* Washington DC: Government Printing Office.

Guthrie, G. M. (1963). Structure of abilities in a non-western culture. *Journal of Educational Psychology, 54,* 94–103.

Heinonen, V. A. (1962). Factor analysis study of transfer of learning. *Scandinavian Journal of Psychology, 8,* 177–188.

Hendricks, M., Guilford, J. P., & Hoepfner, R. (1969). Measuring creative social intelligence. *Reports from the Psychological Laboratory, University of Southern California* (No. 42).

Hills, J. R. (1957). Factorized abilities and success in college mathematics. *Educational and Psychological Measurement, 17,* 615–622.

Hoepfner, R., & Guilford, J. P. (1966). Sixteen divergent-production abilities at the ninth-grade level. *Multivariate Behavioral Research, 1,* 43–66.

Hoepfner, R., Guilford, J. P., & Bradley, P.A. (1970a). Information-transformation abilities. *Educational and psychological Measurement, 30,* 385–402.

Hoepfner, R., Guilford, J. P., & Bradley, P. A. (1970b). Transformation of information in learning. *Journal of Educational Psychology, 61,* 316–323.

Hoffman, K. I., Guilford, J. P., Hoepfner, R., & Doherty, W. J. (1968). A factor analysis of the figural-cognition and figural-evaluation abilities. *Reports from the Psychological Laboratory, University of Southern California* (No. 40).

Horn, J. L. (1973). Theory and functions represented among auditory and visual test performances. In J. R. Royce (Ed.), *Multivariate analysis and psychological theory.* New York: Academic Press.

Horn, J. L., & Cattell, R. B. (1966). Refinement and test of fluid and crystallized intelligence. *Journal of Educational Psychology, 57,* 253–270.

Horn, J. L. & Knapp, J. R. (1973). On the subjective character of the empirical base of Guilford's structure-of-intellect model, *Psychological Buttetin, 80,* 33–43.

Ignatz, M. (1982). A comparison of S-O-I factors with the Florida State Wide Twelfth Grade Test in predicting physics achievement. *Educational and Psychological Measurement, 42,* 935–939.

Jones, C. A. (1960). *Some relationships between creative writing and creative drawing of sixth-grade children.* Unpublished Doctoral Dissertation, Pennsylvania State University.

Kamstra, O. W. M. (1971). *De dimensionaliteit van het geheugen: Ein faktoranalytisch onderzook.* Amsterdam: Drukherin van Soest.

Kelderman, H., Mellenbergh, G. J., & Elshout, J. J. (1981). Guilford's facet theory of intelligence: An empirical comparison of models. *Multivariate Behavioral Research, 16,* 37–61.

Lehman, H. C. (1953). *Age and achievement.* Princeton, NJ: Princeton Press.

Meeker, M. N. (1969). *The structure of intellect: Its interpretation and uses.* Columbus, OH: Merrill.

Messick, S. (Ed.). (1976). *Individuality in learning.* San Francisco: Jossey-Bass.

Meyers, C. E., Dingman, H. F., Orpet, R. F., Sitkei, E. G., & Watt, C. A. (1964). Four ability hypotheses at three preliterate levels in normal and retarded children. *Monographs for the Society for Research in Child Development, 29* (5).

Norman, D. A. (Ed.). (1981). *Perspectives on cognitive science.* Norwood, NJ: Ablex.

Nsereko-Gyagenda, T. (1970). *An investigation of eleven metal abilities in Uganda children.* Thesis, Makerare University.

Osborn, A. (1963). *Applied Imagination.* New York: Scribners.

O'Sullivan, M., & Guilford, J. P. (1975). Six factors of behavioral cognition: Understanding people. *Educational Measurement, 12,* 255–271.

Reese, H. W., Parnes, S. J., Treffinger, D. J., & Kaltsounis, G. (1976). Effects of a creative studies program on structure-of-intellect factors. *Journal of Educational Psychology, 68,* 401–410.

Rossman, J. (1931). *The psychology of the inventor.* Washington DC: The Inventor Press.

Stafford, R. E. (1961). Sex differences in visualization as evidence of sex-linked inheritance. *Perceptual and Motor Skills, 12,* 428.

Stott, L. H., & Ball, R. S. (1963). *Evaluation of infant and preschool tests.* Detroit, MI: Merrill Palmer.

Taylor, C. W. (1947). A factorial study of fluency in writing. *Psychometrika, 12,* 239–262.

Terman, L. M. (1905). Genius and stupidity: A study of some of the intellectual processes of seven "bright" and seven "stupid" boys. *Pedagogical Seminary, 13,* 307–373.

Thorndike, E. L. (1920). Intelligence and its uses. *Harpers Magazine, 140,* 227–235.

Thurstone, L. L. (1935). *Vectors of mind.* Chicago: University of Chicago Press.

Thurstone, L. L. (1938). Primary mental abilities. *Psychometric monographs,* No. 1.

Thurstone, L. L. (1955). *The differential growth of mental abilities.* Chapel Hill, NC: Psychometric Laboratory.

Thurstone, L. L., & Ackerson, L. (1929). The mental growth curve for the Binet tests. *Journal of Educational Psychology, 20,* 569–583.

Thurstone, T. G., & Strandskov, H. H. (1953). *A psychological study of twins: Differences for identical and fraternal twins (No. 4).* Chapel Hill, NC: Psychometric Laboratory.

Tolman, E. C. (1932). *Purposive behavior in animals and man.* New York: Appleton-Century-Crofts.

Torrance, E. P. (1975). Creativity research in education: Still alive. In I. A. Taylor & J. W. Getzels (Eds.), *Perspectives in creativity.* Chicago: Aldine.

Trembly, D. (1964). Age and differences in creative thinking. *American Psychologist,* p. 516 (Abstract).

Vernon, P. E. (1950). *The structure of human intelligence.* New York: Wiley.

Wechsler, D. (1958). *The measurement and appraisal of adult intelligence.* Baltimore: Williams and Wilkins.

Wiig, E. H., & Semel, E. M. (1976). *Language disabilities in children and adolescents.* Columbus, OH: Merrill.

Wilson, R. C., Guilford, J. P., Christensen, P. R., & Lewis, D. J. (1954). factoranalytic study of creative-thinking abilities. *Psychometrika, 19,* 247–311.

Witkin, H. A., Dyk, R. B., Faterson, H. F., Goodenough, E. R., & Karp, C. A. (1962). *Psychological differentiation.* New York: Wiley.

SEVEN

REMODELING OLD MODELS OF INTELLIGENCE

JOHN L. HORN
University of Denver
Denver, Colorado

PROBLEMS WITH OLD MODELS

Beliefs are very curious phenomena. They can enter our cultures on the basis of only the very slimmest of evidence, but once they have become embedded in a culture—once they have been passed from one generation to the next—they can become strangely resistant to change, very difficult to eliminate. They can persist and persist despite the mounting of huge amounts of evidence that they are wrong. The inertia of tradition keeps them alive.

This occurs despite education designed to prevent it. In our early school years we are taught that people believed that the earth was flat and the center of the universe, and that people like Columbus and Galileo had great difficulties in dislodging these beliefs despite the accumulation of evidence. We are taught the story of Lysenko. We are taught to be "on guard" because incorrect beliefs can be so emotionally based that it is very difficult to accept the evidence that threatens them. Yet this teaching can have very little influence. We can look back at the examples from our history and say, "My, how absurd," but not let that lesson do much to alter incorrect beliefs in our own time.

The example of such a belief that I wish to bring to your attention in this chapter is the belief in a concept of general intelligence. I will not proclaim that there is absolutely *no* version of this belief that can be correct, but I will remind you that a large mound of evidence persistently indicates that all inclusive *unifactor* concepts of intelligence are almost certainly incorrect and not very useful. Most of the evidence we have before us in 1984—from biology, from genetics, from sociology, from education, and from common sense—suggests that it is

I am grateful to Hill Goldsmith, Jack McArdle, Pat Ellison and Ann Hogan for the many constructive criticisms they gave me as I struggled to put this chapter together. Production of the chapter was supported by grants ROI-HD17552 from the National Institute of Child Health and Human Development and ROI-AG02695 from the National Institute of Aging.

extremely unlikely that all of the many human performances that are classified as intellectual represent a unitary attribute, determined by a unitary set of influences such as might be specified in a polygenetic theory. Instead, a great mound and variety of evidence indicates that what is called intelligence is a mixture of quite different things—different attributes having different genetical and environmental determinants and different developmental courses over the life span.

In contrast to intelligence, skin color can be regarded as a unitary polygenetic trait. The alleles of perhaps nine genes add up to determine dark color; inheriting none of these genetic determiners would make one very pale indeed; inheriting all nine alleles would make one a very black individual. The colors of most people are between these extremes, distributed in accordance with a symmetrical binomial distribution—that is, an approximation to a normal distribution.

A polygenetic theory like this one for skin color should be considered, of course, when we try to make scientific sense out of the phenomena of human intellectual abilities. Indeed, such a theory has been considered. It has been proclaimed to be the most plausible account of the major source of variance in intellectual performances. But it is not plausible. When we look at the variety of intellectual abilities that humans evince, when we consider that these abilities are behavioral characteristics, and when we relate these observations to what we know about brain functions and experiential influences, we must conclude, I think, that it is very unlikely that a singular polygenetic theory will provide a valid explanatory basis for what is classified as intellectual behavior.

Let me suggest a couple of analogies that may help illustrate this main point. The analogies I have in mind are for the structure of brains and for the concept of facial beauty. Brains are very much like faces. At first glance—as to an "outsider"—one brain looks very much like another. But as you examine brains carefully you discover that they have tremendous variability. Indeed, when you think about human brains, think about the variety you know in the faces you meet (as you prepare a face to meet the faces you meet). Behind these very different faces are very different brains. And when you think about the possibility that intelligence is a unitary polygenetic characteristic, think also about the possibility that facial beauty, and the brains behind the faces, are unitary characteristics. When one considers the idea of general intelligence in the context of such analogies, one can see rather clearly that the idea represents a motley of different things.

Consider facial beauty for a moment longer. If we analyze features of what we mean by facial beauty—nose length, nose breadth, eye size, eye shape, and so on—we can find a substantial first principal component, just as we find such a component among different abilities. Moreover, we can obtain reasonable agreement in our society about who has, and who does not have, facial beauty, just as we can obtain reasonable agreement among ratings for general intelligence. But when we examine what comprises these principal components and ratings—as viewed through physiology, biology, genetics, sociology, anthropology, and psychology—we conclude that it is extremely unlikely that what we see in facial beauty is a unitary trait. At the level of measurement we find beautiful faces that have long, thin noses—Meryl Streep's, for example—and we find beautiful faces that have short, wide noses—Sally Fields comes to mind. At the level of genetics we now know that several distinct features of noses, ears, eyebrows, upper and lower jaw, hair color, hair form, and skin color are all inherited independently. These distinct features yield distinctly different physiognomies that we identify with the single label "beautiful face." If we consider beauty from an anthropological or sociological perspective, we realize that what is highly regarded as beautiful in one society is not so highly regarded in another society.

That which we label intelligence is more analogous to facial beauty than it is to skin color. Just as distinct features form a face, so distinct capacities make up distinctly different mixtures of abilities that we identify with the single label "intelligence." Research in behavioral genetics indicates that there are distinct genetic influences operating to produce the separate capacities that are grouped under the heading of intelligence. When we look away from genetic determiners toward environmental determiners it becomes apparent again that distinct abilities are outgrowths of distinct pathways of learning that diverge more and more as development proceeds.

Analogies do not tell the whole story, of course; my point is that the evidence supports the analogies. I will present some—just a small part—of this evidence. Before doing that, however, let me again raise the question: "Why in scientific research and clinical practice do we persist in using, under the name of intelligence, various hodgepodges of distinct abilities?"

I have noted that when beliefs become imbedded in a culture, they can become very resistant to change. Such inertia represents one of the reasons why we persist in using hodgepodge concepts of general intelligence. This cultural inertia is imbedded in federal and state laws that require children to be classified in accordance with hodgepodge measures—for example, for the purpose of determining eligibility for special-education programs. Such laws virtually force clinical psychologists to give obeisance to a false belief.

Also, of course, a hodgepodge concept can be useful in everyday discourse. We need not give up the idea of "beautiful face" simply because we know that the idea represents quite different things. Similarly, I do not propose that the everyday use of the word "intelligence" be abandoned simply because it does not represent a genetical, functional, or developmental unity. What I do suggest, however, is that vernacular language should not dictate scientific theory and clinical practice. The man on the street can continue to use the word intelligence to represent all manner of different combinations of basic abilities, and we (psychologists) can do this when we act in the role of a man or woman on the street. But when we are trying to clear up mysteries about human functioning, and when we aim to provide good therapy—good remedial programs—then, I think, we should not talk about general intelligence, but instead do our work with what we know about separate and distinct human capacities.

One reason the concept of IQ and general intelligence continues to be so widely used is that many psychologists sponsor a mistaken belief that a positive manifold among the intercorrelations for various abilities, and a finding of a large first principal component among such correlations, provide convincing evidence in support of a theory of general intelligence. Jensen (1984), for example, sponsors this mistaken belief. He says that the positive intercorrelations among ability measures and the large first principal component for such data are convincing evidences in support of Spearman's theory of *g*. This is not true. In a recent review of Jensen's (1980) book on bias, Hill Goldsmith and I (Horn & Goldsmith, 1981) pointed to some of the reasons why this is not true. In particular, two important features of Spearman's theory are not at all supported by the evidence Jensen cites.

First, Spearman's model for *g* is a one, and *only one*, common factor theory. It specifies that each ability in a set of abilities represents a separate component of a gestalt that is defined by all of the set of abilities. These separate components are, as discussed by Spearman, necessary parts of the whole. This is a very demanding substantive theory and mathematical model. It is not arbitrary. It is an elegant specification of necessary conditions. One cannot easily design studies that truly test hypotheses of this theory. Jensen has not designed such studies. In a moment I will mention results from studies that have been designed to test Spearman's theory. Jensen's studies are not among these. In his work Jensen has simply calculated the first principal component in various collections of abilities, announced that this component is large and, for that reason, well represents Spearman's *g*. But the size of the first principal component is not relevant to a test of *g*. Spearman's model does not require that this component be large. Indeed, it is well known that the size of the first principal component is mainly a function of how many similar variables are included in a battery. The first principal component among ability measures is no more than a good weighted linear combination of the abilities of a battery, whatever these abilities might be. Calculating this component does not provide a test of a model specifying that these abilities represent necessary components of a single attribute. Calculating the first principal component is not a test of Spearman's model.

A second important thing we should remember about Spearman's work is that although he used the term "general" factor to distinguish one common factor from many specific factors, he did not try to account for *all* the common variance among *all* of what is called intellectual performance with the general factor. Instead, he was very careful to specify the particular features, the particular components, of the one-and-only-one common factor of his theory, and he insisted that any well-designed study to test his theory must be based on very careful selection of such components. The variables must represent necessary features of *g*, but not share common factors other than *g*.

It is *not* in accordance with these design strictures to throw together just any collection of ability measures and assert, or assume, that one such collection measures the same thing as any other collection. Different collections of tests— different collections of primary abilities—measure different principal components. A principal component is not a stable indicator of any particular common factor. It represents arbitrary collections. To calculate the first principal component for a collection of abilities is not to produce an operational definition of Spearman's g or any other common factor. Jensen speaks of a singular g, but the so-called g that he picks up on one occasion is a different mixture than the so-called g he picks up on other occasions.

Different IQ tests measure different first principal components. Not one is based on a representative sample of the known primary mental abilities. Not one is based on any rationale of sampling from a universe of abilities to obtain those abilities that are necessary, not to mention sufficient, to represent a unitary concept of general intelligence. The tests measure only arbitrary collections of abilities. It is as if one of them measures beauty when the breadth of eyes and length of nose is counted, while another measures beauty in terms of fullness of lips and arch of eyebrows. No IQ test has been constructed on the basis of research designed to demonstrate a gestalt of general intelligence—the ability equivalent of a beautiful face.

Studies that have been adequately designed to test Spearman's theory have demonstrated time and time again that the theory does not describe human intellectual capacities. It is a good theory because it is clear enough to have a test, but it is not a correct theory because it does not account for the phenomena. I have reviewed this evidence in, for example, a chapter in the Cattell-Dreger handbook (Horn, 1977). There I point out that Rimoldi (1948) made a good attempt to show support for Spearman's theory, but the evidence he obtained forced him to conclude that more than one common factor was required to properly account for the data. The same conclusion was reached in the studies of Alexander (1935), El Koussy (1935), Botzum (1951), Corter (1952), Martin and Adkins (1954), Cohen (1959), and others. Researchers who followed closely in Spearman's footsteps and performed well-conceived and well-executed studies to test hypotheses of Spearman's theory in each case concluded that the results simply cannot be described in accordance with a one-common-factor model. Instead, the results indicate that several factors are required to adequately represent data that are carefully chosen to identify the one common factor of Spearman's theory.

A few years ago (Horn, 1968) my reviews of this research led me to the conclusion that no fewer than four broad dimensions are needed to account for the processes Spearman identified as essential in his substantive theory of g. Two of these four dimensions seemed to represent what Cattell (1941, 1957) had talked about as fluid and crystallized intelligence and what Hebb (1941, 1949) had discussed as intelligence A and intelligence B. Largely because Cattell's concepts more surely pointed toward operational definition in measurement, I preferred to build on his ideas rather than on Hebb's. In either case, however, I found that two concepts—two dimensions—are not enough to represent what Spearman had identified as human intellectual functioning. Moreover, two factors are not enough to describe what others have referred to as intelligence. The evidence I will review in this chapter indicates that although at least two concepts should replace the concept of general intelligence, probably we should be thinking in terms of upward from four distinctly different concepts of intellect.

Those who speak of general intelligence sometimes cite my work as supporting their views. They may do this for two reasons: first, because I emphasize that adequate theory must take account of the ubiquitous and persistent finding of positive intercorrelations among performances that represent human intellectual capacities (although I note, too, those instances where ability intercorrelations are near zero and negative, Guilford, 1964; Horn, 1968); second, because I sometimes calculate a high-order factor, as in a Schmid-Leiman transformation, to represent the positive intercorrelations among a given set of ability measures. When my work (or other such work) is cited in these ways one should recognize two things.

First, the calculation of a high-order factor, like the calculation of a first principal component, is *not* a test of a hypothesis of a one-factor theory of intelligence. One can calculate a general factor for any conglomerate of abilities. That does not mean that the conglomerate represents anything *unitary*. Conglomerates are not compounds.

Second, many nonintellectual performances are positively correlated with intellectual abilities. For example, contrary to what some believe, good measures of athletic performance are, in broad samples of normal people, positively correlated with intellectual abilities, and the same can be said about ethical beliefs, absence of neurotic symptoms, assertiveness, and a host of other things. Positive correlations do not indicate the boundaries for a domain of human intellect. Positive intercorrelations among human behaviors may require a concept of general organization of behavior, as in Hebb's (1949) theory, but that is quite a different matter than a theory of general intelligence.

Psychologists who sponsor mistaken beliefs about general intelligence often cite the evidence indicating that there are heritable components in the mixtures they refer to as *g* (see Loehlin, Lindzey, & Spuhler, 1975, for a balanced review). One need not discount this evidence to see that it is irrelevant to arguments that *g* is unitary. Recall the analogy of facial beauty. No one who recognizes that facial beauty is not a unitary genetical trait need deny that the shape of noses, the color of eyes, and so on, are inherited traits and that conglomerate measures of these attributes in ratings of beauty can have high heritabilities. If the distinct components that go into mixture-measures of general intelligence are separately inherited, then the heritabilities calculated for these different measures can be high and numerically similar—even when the components are differently weighted. This is what the evidence on the heritability of general intelligence indicates, not that there is support for a hypothesis that intelligence is a unitary attribute.

Similarly, evidence suggesting that there is some cross-cultural communality in measures of general intelligence can be accepted for what it is worth and still be recognized as quite irrelevant to claims that "*g* exists." People of different races and cultures have some similar ideas about facial beauty, but that does not prevent us from seeing that beauty in one race and culture is not the same as beauty in other races and cultures.

In sum, then, I suggest that despite the prevalence of belief in general intelligence, despite the emotional intensity with which this belief is held, and despite the fact that this belief is proclaimed as true by some of the high priests of our science, the belief should be cast out—or at least put far away from research and clinical practice. Existing evidence about the nature of human capacities provides little basis for the belief. This evidence indicates that several distinct functions are involved in performances that are classified under the heading of intelligence. These distinct functions probably have distinct genetic bases, distinct courses of development in infancy, childhood, and adulthood, and distinct implications for understanding human retardation, human accomplishments, human creativity, and human happiness. This position has clear ties to viewpoints developed earlier by Thomson (1948) and Humphreys (1979).

PARTS FOR NEW MODELS

When we throw the concept of general intelligence out the window in rooms where scientific investigation can progress, a question that naturally arises is "What theory about human abilities should replace current ideas about general intelligence?" There are several alternatives. I sponsor a *Gf-Gc* theory. This is not necessarily the best of available theories. More detailed concepts might be better—concepts such as are found in the work of Butterfield, Nielsen, Tangen, and Richardson (1984), the Pellegrino-Glaser-Holzman group (Holzman, Pellegrino, & Glaser, 1982; Pellegrino & Glaser, 1979), Buzz Hunt's group (Hunt, 1978; Hunt, Frost, & Lunneborg, 1973), Robert Sternberg and his coworkers (Sternberg, 1977), Jack Carroll (1976), the Detterman (1984) group, or Susan Embretson and her coworkers (Embretson, 1984; Whitely, 1980; Whitely & Schneider, 1981). *Gf-Gc* theory has the virtue of pertaining to a broader array of human abilities than is referenced in these other works, but for some purposes that is a defect. *Gf-Gc* theory is only a few small steps away from ideas about general intelligence. For this reason it may have a chance to overcome the cultural inertia that perpetrates use of the idea of general intelligence. It has the virtue of being responsive to evidence that is largely ignored in statements about general intelligence.

I will summarize results that indicate the nature of *Gf-Gc* theory. You will see that the current theory is notably different from the theory of a similar name that was put forth some 40 years ago by Raymond Cattell. The current theory is built on Cattell's theory much in the same way as current theory in physics is built on Newtonian physics, but research results have accumulated to indicate that early formulations must be reformulated. Also, several new features, particularly in respect to development, have been added to Cattell's early statement of the theory.

The studies I will review can be usefully classified under the following three main headings:

1. **Structural.** Under this heading I will refer to studies indicating distinct intellectual abilities, analogous to distinct features of faces.

2. **Developmental.** The evidence summarized under this heading shows that different dimensions of intellect have different developmental courses over the life span. In particular, the averages for some abilities increase with age in adulthood while the averages for other abilities decrease over this same age span. I will point to some of the elementary processes that seem to be involved in the abilities that decline in adulthood.

3. **Genetic.** Under this heading I will report briefly on studies indicating separate-but-equal lines of genetic determination of major dimensions of intellect.

Structural Evidence

I will begin with a glimpse at some correlational and factor-analytic results. These findings indicate that although the intercorrelations for measures of different abilities are usually positive, reliably different sources of variance—different factors—are found again and again and again. We will always have questions about the precise nature of these different forms of what is called intelligence, but the available evidence leaves virtually no doubt about a conclusion that there are several distinct factors among performances, all of which are said to indicate intelligence. The results I will present to illustrate this evidence are only a very small part of the whole.

In the study represented by Table 1, Lazar Stankov and I developed several tests to measure intellectual abilities with auditory rather than visual problems. In studies preceding the one I summarize in the table, we demonstrated (Stankov & Horn, 1980) that a number of different factors are needed to account for the variability measured with our auditory tests. We likened those factors to primary mental abilities—the set of ability factors first demonstrated by Thurstone (1936) and very much expanded by the work of many investigators since Thurstone's time (as summarized in, for example, Ekstrom, French, & Harman, 1979). The factors I show in Table 1 are found among auditory primary abilities, as so defined, and a sample of visual primary abilities established on the basis of much previous work.

These results indicate some five distinct forms of what is called intelligence. The fluid and crystallized dimensions involve both visual and auditory abilities. In addition to these two factors are factors that indicate intellectual abilities in solving spatial-visual problems, auditory problems, and problems in which there is a premium for working quickly. This evidence thus suggests that there is something we might call auditory intelligence, such as might be evinced in the extreme by great musicians, and something we might call visual intelligence, the extremes of which might be seen in great painters, sculptors, and photographers. These intelligences, as well as a speediness function, are independent in measurement from the analytic-thinking form of intelligence indicated by Gf and the acculturation-absorption form of intelligence indicated by Gc.

Table 1. Second-Order Oblique Dimensions Determined on Auditory and Visual Primary Factors

Primary Factors	Symbol	Second-Order Factors				
		Ga	aSD	Gc	Gf	Gv
Auditory						
Discrimination among sound patterns	DASP	50			21	
Maintaining and judging rhythms	MaJR	35				29
Temporal tracking of sounds	Tc	29			26	20
Auditory cognition of relations	ACoR	23			24	
Auditory immediate memory	Msa	22			55	
Speech perception under distraction/distortion	SPUD		61			
Auditory acuity	Ac		39			
Listening verbal comprehension	Va		30	43		
Visual						
Verbal comprehension	V			50		
Semantic systems	EMS			51		
Semantic relations	CMR			47		
Induction	I			28	26	
Figural relations	CFR				57	
Visualization	Vz				46	24
Figural classes	CFC				20	40
Speed of closure	Cs		22			20
Flexibility of closure	Cf					50
Spatial orientation	S					47

Source. After Horn & Stankov (1982).

Note. Loadings less than .20 and decimal points omitted. $N = 241$ males.

Column abbreviations.   *Ga:* Auditory General Ability. *aSD:* Auditory Sensory Detection. *Gc:* Crystallized Intellect. *Gf:* Fluid Intellect. *Gv:* Visual General Ability.

Table 2 tells a similar story, this time in terms of results from two studies (Horn, 1977b, 1978) based on a variety of measures of mainstream cognitive psychology. The findings of these studies indicate that in addition to the *Gf, Gc,* and visual forms of intelligence (*Gv*), there are two kinds of intelligence in which memory is emphasized. The *SAR* dimension represents a broad variety of performances in which there is emphasis on abilities in storing and retrieving information over short periods of time—a few seconds or perhaps a minute or two at most. The *TSR* dimension, on the other hand, indicates abilities of storing and retrieving information over long periods of time (many minutes, hours, and days). The results indicate that these two memory capacities are not only in-

Table 2. Extract from Second-Order Results Indicating Memory Organizations Distinct from *Gf*, *Gc*, and *Gv*

	Symbol	SAR	TSR	Gc	Gf	Gv
Short-Time Retention						
Recency (primary memory)		30			23	
Murdock intercept (primary memory?)		58		26		
Primacy (secondary memory)		46		23		
Murdock slope (secondary memory)		56				
Memory span (forward, serial recall)	Ms	57				
Recall after Mandler sorting		26	38	25	35	
Incidental recall			36	27	34	
Long-Term Retrieval						
Associations for a word	Fa		28	58		
Things fitting a definition	Fe		28	33		
Uses for objects	DMC			56	20	
Encoding Behavior						
Classes in Mandler sorting			31			
Knowledge Retrieval						
Vocabulary	V			75		
Remote associations	DMT			44	38	
Reasoning						
Esoteric word analogies	CMR			72		
Common word analogies	CMR			45	50	
Letter series	I			32	53	
Matrices	CFR			21	56	
Visualizing						
Paper folding	Vz				44	47
Gestalt closure	Cs				44	38
Reassembling cutouts (Hooper)			28		38	38
Matching figures	P					30

Note. Loadings less than .20 and decimal points omitted. Loadings are averages of factor coefficients obtained in two studies of progress reports for National Science Foundation and Army Research Institute grants. The *N*'s on which the analyses were based were 122 and 147.

Column abbreviations. *SAR:* Short-term Apprehension and Retrieval. *TSR:* Long-term Storage and Retrieval. *Gc:* Crystallized Intellect. *Gf:* Fluid Intellect. *Gv:* Visual General Ability.

dependent one from the other, but also independent of the capacities represented by *Gf, Gc,* and *Gv.*

In a third set of studies (Horn, 1978, 1981) we focused on the very old and widely believed idea that the speed with which people solve problems is indicative of the difficulty of the problems they can solve. It is often assumed that speed of intellectual processing is almost equivalent to quality of intellectual thought. Teachers at all levels of education give speeded tests to measure learning outcomes. This practice seems to be based on an assumption that speed in dealing with problems is highly indicative of quality of thinking about the problems.

A limitation of many studies of the relation between intellectual speed and power is that speed and power have not been defined in an operationally independent manner. Investigators have used time-limit tests in which speediness scores are derived from the same items on which power scores are based. Also, in most studies subjects have been encouraged to—in effect, forced to—provide an answer choice even when they are not confident that they have a correct answer to a problem. These conditions force artifactual correlations between measures of power and speed. In the studies summarized in Table 3 (Horn, 1978, 1981) we avoided the problem of artifactual correlation by using quite different sets of comparable items to derive speed and power scores, by measuring power in terms of level of difficulty of problems actually attempted and solved, by measuring speed as quickness in actually solving problems, and by teaching subjects to give no answer to a problem if they have not satisfied themselves that they have a correct answer.

Under these conditions of measurement in samples of adults we found that speediness in obtaining correct answers to intellectual problems of nontrivial difficulty is correlated *positively* with speediness in obtaining *incorrect* answers, and these two measures of speediness correlate at only a low level with power scores based on the same kinds of items. A correlation of .20 indicates the typical relation we found between speediness in obtaining correct answers and level of difficulty of problems solved.

Thus contrary to a widely held belief, speed of thinking and power of thinking are not highly correlated. Moreover, the results of Table 3 suggest that speed of arriving at correct solutions to problems—the factor labeled *CDS*—is a separate capacity of what we call intelligence. Some people are much quicker than others in solving problems, but this quickness of thinking is independent of the qualities of thinking represented by *Gf* and *Gc.*

The results of this table also indicate that the quickness of thinking factor, *CDS,* is separate from a scanning speediness factor, symbolized as *Gs.* This latter is demonstrated in performances in which one must quickly glance through visual symbols to find elements that satisfy a given criterion—as if, for example, you were asked to underline all the *a*'s on a page of print. Contrary to what we had expected when we began our studies of speediness, such speed-of-scanning performances are only very lowly correlated with speed of obtaining correct answers to problems of nontrivial difficulty. Even more surprising, we found in our samples of adults that speed of scanning correlates more highly with power measures of fluid ability than does speed in obtaining correct answers. I think

Table 3.   Extract from Second-Order Results Suggesting How Speediness Organizations Are Distinct from *Gf*, *Gc*, and *Gv*

	Gs	CDS	WDS	Gc	Gf
Clerical Speed					
Matching figures	77				
Finding *a*'s and numbers	49				
Comparing lists of names	79				
Speed in Providing Correct Answers					
Analogies		*63*	*22*		
Remote associations	35	55		20	
Letter series		*46*	*40*		
Paper folding		*47*	*33*		
Speed in Providing Incorrect Answers					
Matrices		20	*54*		
Gestalt closure			64		
Remote associations			41		
Vocabulary		52	*28*	*26*	
Number Correct					
Vocabulary				80	30
Esoteric analogies				71	23
Remote associations				51	47
Matrices					60
Letter series				37	59
Paper folding					49
Gestalt closure					58

Note.   Loadings less than .20 and decimal points omitted. Italicized loadings are averages over the two studies. Loadings that are not italicized were obtained in one but not the other study because the variable was not included in both studies.

Column abbreviations.   Gs: Scanning General Ability. *CDS:* Correct Decision Speed. *WDS:* Wrong Decision Speed. *Gc:* Crystallized Intellect. *Gf:* Fluid Intellect.

this *Gs* factor is closely related to the kind of reaction-time speediness that Jensen (1982), has been studying. I will have more to say about this when we look at some of the developmental evidence.

Before looking at developmental results, let me show you one more item of structural evidence derived from our recent studies of the Wechsler Adult Intelligence Scales (WAIS), the set of tests on which this volume might be said to rest. Pioneering in their day, the Wechsler tests are today known to provide measures of only a very limited range of the abilities people refer to when they talk about intelligence. Nevertheless our studies indicate that several different intelligences are measured by these tests.

McArdle and I (McArdle & Horn, 1983) have modeled the WAIS in over 100 different samples of subjects. The latent dimensions are not the same in detail in each of our samples, but in every sample there is need to recognize that no fewer than four dimensions are needed in a proper model. In other words, although only a very limited set of abilities is sampled by the subscales of the WAIS, even in this limited set of data we need to recognize four distinctly different concepts of intelligence.

The results shown in Figure 1 indicate the futility of trying to fit a single-factor model to Wechsler scale performances. If a model for one general intelligence was indeed a reasonable model for these data, the chi-square would be approximately equal to the degrees of freedom. But the chi-square is almost 3,000—20 times as large as the 152 degrees of freedom of the model. Such results provide no support for a hypothesis stipulating that the Wechsler scales represent a concept of general intelligence.

Incidentally, many multiple factor models do not fit these data either. For example, Kaufman's (1979) specification of right-brain and left-brain functions measured by the Wechsler scales does not approximate a good model for these abilities (see Figure 2). No two-factor model provides a good fit to the Wechsler data, but several two-factor models provide a better fit than the Kaufman model. Moreover, if the Kaufman laterality hypotheses are imbedded in a four-factor model, the fit of this model is inferior to other four-factor models, some of which do approximate a reasonable fit to the Wechsler data.

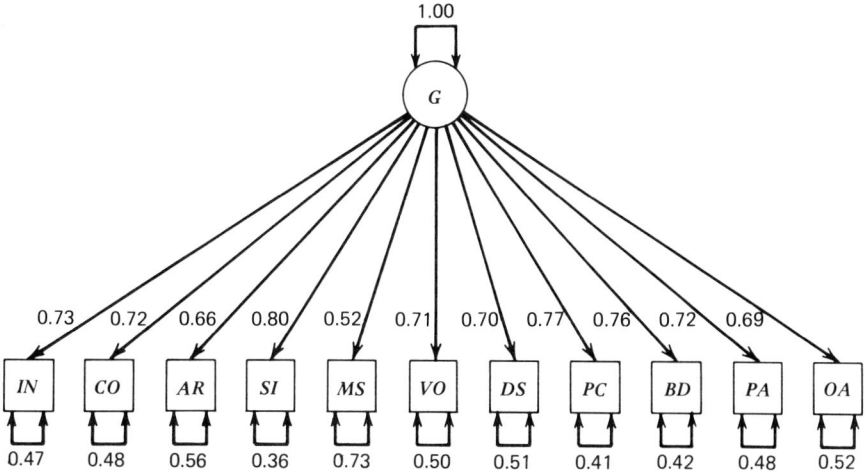

Figure 1. Spearman's (1904) Single Common Factor Model of the WAIS. (Chi-square= 2982; df= 152; Z= 60; D= .73) Abbreviations: *IN:* Information. *CO:* Comprehension. *AR:* Arithmetic. *SI:* Similarities. *MS:* Memory Span. *VO:* Vocabulary. *DS:* Digit Symbols. *PC:* Picture Completion. *BD:* Block Design. *PA:* Picture Arrangement. *OA:* Object Assembly.

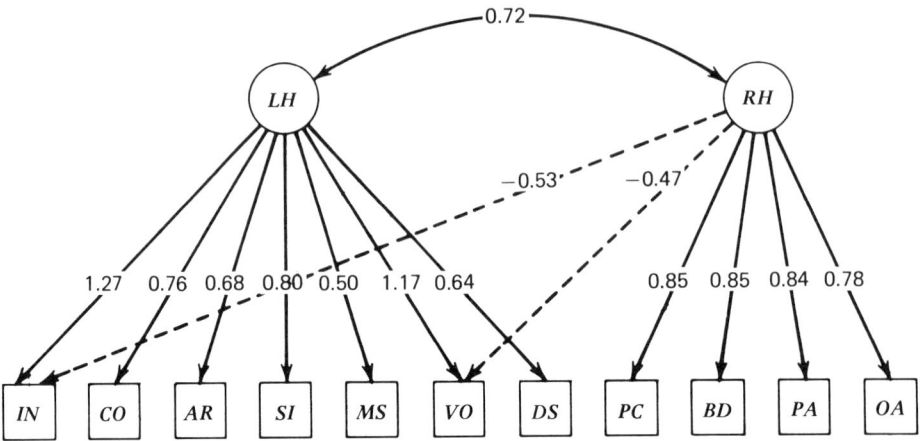

Figure 2. Kaufman's (1974) Left-Right Hemisphere Model of the WAIS. (Chi-square = 1034; df = 142, Z = 21) Abbreviations: *IN:* Information. *CO:* Comprehension. *AR:* Arithmetic. *SI:* Similarities. *MS:* Memory Span. *VO:* Vocabulary. *DS:* Digit Symbols. *PC:* Picture Completion. *BD:* Block Design. *PA:* Picture Arrangement. *OA:* Object Assembly.

The results shown in Figure 3 indicate the kind of model that we have found to provide a reasonable fit to Wechsler data obtained in quite different samples of subjects.

Developmental Evidence

Recall results such as those shown in Figure 4. In these results we see that if we put together a motley of abilities and call the result "general intelligence," we are in danger of throwing away an interesting developmental distinction between abilities. From young adulthood to old age there is regular year-to-year decline in the averages for some of the abilities of intelligence—namely, the *Gf*, *Gv*, and *Gs* abilities; in the same samples of subjects there is also regular year-to-year increase in the averages for other abilities that are said to indicate intelligence—namely, the *Gc* and *TSR* abilities. If *Gf* and *Gc* are combined in a mixture that might be labeled *g*, or general intelligence, then the distinction between intellectual abilities that decline with age and intellectual abilities that improve with age can very well be lost; or, depending on the relative proportion of *Gf* and *Gc* in the *g* mixtures of different studies, we can have all manner of different results suggesting that *g* declines with age, that *g* improves with age, and that *g* neither declines nor improves with age. Thus we can have lots of argument in the literature, as we have had in the past, but argument that is largely a waste of time because it stems from poor definition of concepts.

The particular results referred to in this figure happen to be based on cross-sectional data—that is, data in which age is equivalent to year of birth. In my judgment, based on several analyses (Horn, 1970, 1976, 1980, 1982a; Horn & Donaldson, 1976, 1980), the cross-sectional data tell the same story at a general

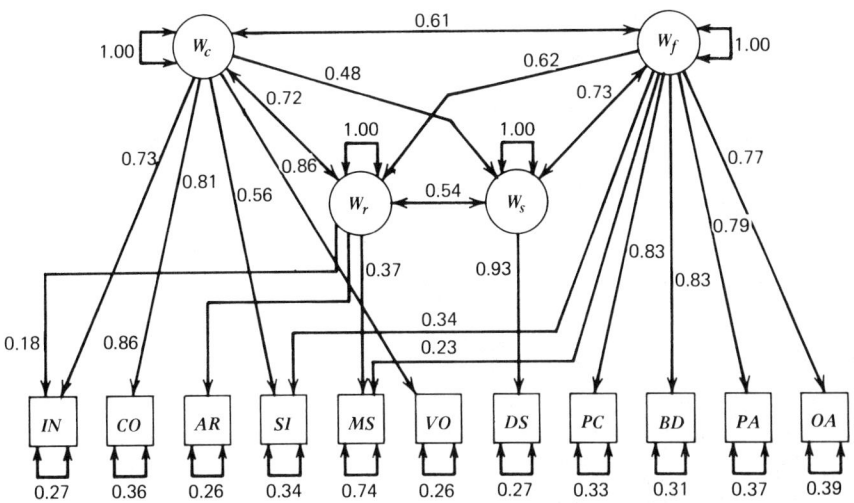

Figure 3. Horn & McArdle (1980) Revised *Gf-Gc* Model of the WAIS. (Chi-square= 436, df= 127, Z= 9.5) Abbreviations: *IN:* Information. *CO:* Comprehension. *AR:* Arithmetic. *SI:* Similarities. *MS:* Memory Span. *VO:* Vocabulary. *DS:* Digit Symbols. *PC:* Picture Completion. *BD:* Block Design. *PA:* Picture Arrangement. *OA:* Object Assembly.

level as do results based on longitudinal data. But whether or not one accepts my judgment on this matter, the cross-sectional findings alone, which have been documented in several studies, indicate why we should not regard mixture-measures of general intelligence as representing a unitary concept. Different intellectual abilities follow different paths of development. What is shown in this figure for adulthood development applies also to childhood development (see Lewis, 1976; Lewis & McGurk, 1972). Different abilities that are said to indicate intelligence reach peaks in development at quite different ages in child-hood and young adulthood, when viewed both within individuals and in comparisons between individuals.

Let me quickly show you some results that indicate separate processes involved in the decline of *Gf* abilities—analogous to processes of wrinkling and double-chin formation in the decline of facial beauty.

In Figure 5 we see aging decline in sensory-detector (*vSD*) capacities—simple abilities in discriminating stimuli and determining whether or not a stimulus is present. It is reasonable to suppose that aging loss of such capacities would distort perception of the problems one must solve to demonstrate *Gf* abilities, and thereby be an underlying cause of the observed decline in *Gf*.

The results summarized in Figure 6 provide no support for this hypothesis, however. When we control for the aging decline of sensory detectors we do not reduce the aging decline of *Gf*.

In contrast when we control for abilities of organizing information at the time of encoding (abbreviated *EOG*), as measured with a paradigm developed by George Mandler (1968), we find that such control produces a notable and

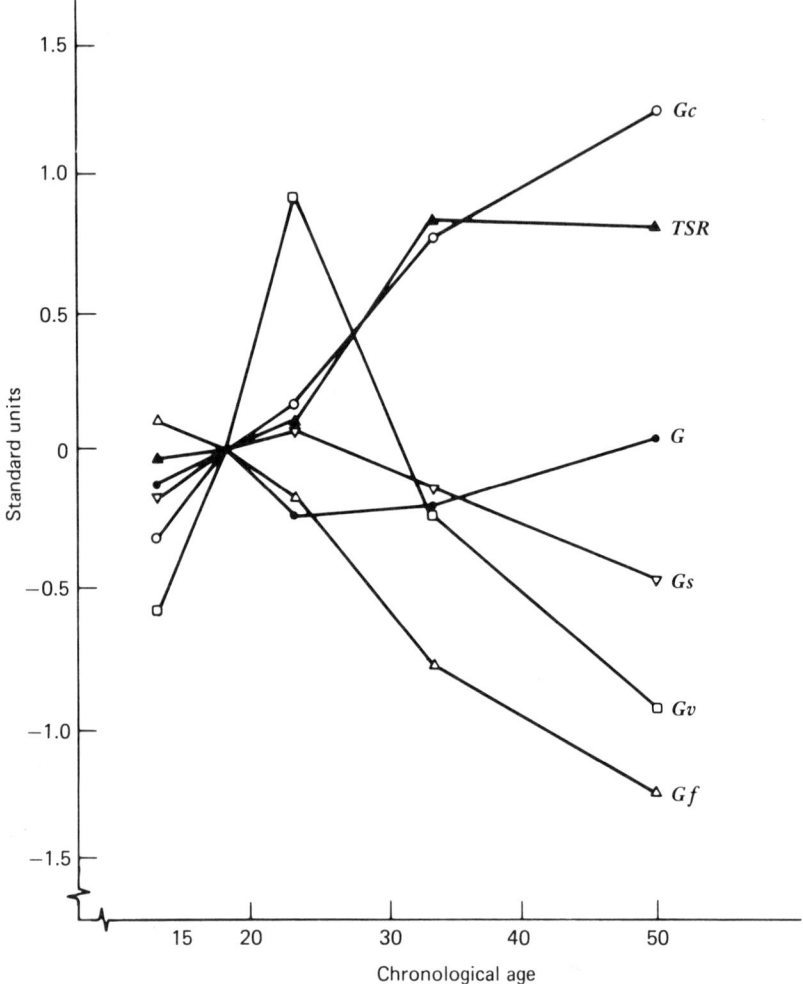

Figure 4. Adulthood Age Differences in Dimensions of Human Intellect. (Based on Horn & Cattell, 1967). Abbreviations: *Gc:* Crystallized Intellect. *TSR:* Long-term Storage and Retrieval. *G:* General Factor. *GS:* Scanning General Ability. *GV:* Visual General Ability. *Gf:* Fluid Intellects.

significant alteration in the decline curve for *Gf*; thus there is support for a hypothesis stipulating that decline in an encoding-organization ability is a part of the decline of *Gf*. This *EOG* variable accounts for the decline of short-term memory (abbreviated *SAR*) in adulthood, and the extent to which this is implicated in the decline of *Gf*.

In Figure 7, I summarize results that analytically demonstrate what happens to *Gf* decline when measures of speed of performance and carefulness are controlled. As I mentioned before, one interesting finding of our studies is that speed of obtaining correct answers to problems of nontrivial difficulty—abbre-

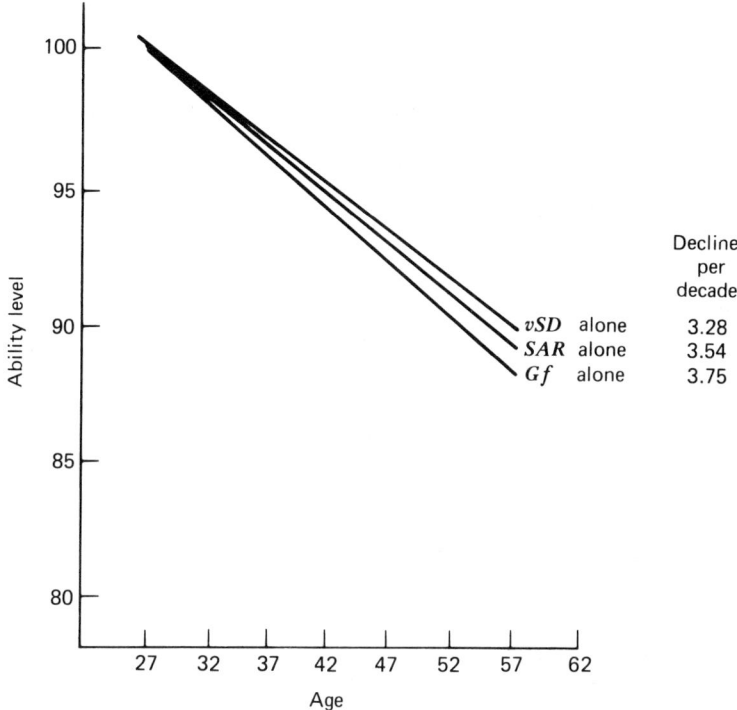

Figure 5. Aging Decline of Visual Sensory Detectors (*vSD*), Short-term Acquisition-Retrieval (*SAR*), and Fluid Ability (*Gf*). Abbreviations: *vSD:* Visual Sensory Detection. *SAR:* Short-term Apprehension and Retrieval. *Gf:* Fluid Intellect.

viated *CDS* in this figure—has very little correlation with power measures of *Gf*; in the figure we see that such intellectual speediness is not implicated in the aging decline of *Gf*. In contrast, when we control for *Gs*—what I believe is similar to the complex reaction time of Jensen's studies—we remove some of the *Gf* decline. We also show in these results that this *Gs* (scanning) speediness, and the aging decline of such speediness, are linked to abilities in maintaining close concentration (abbreviated *COS*) and attention (abbreviated *ATD*). Indeed, it seems that declines in capacities for maintaining attention and close concentration are mainly responsible for both the aging decline of speed of performance and the aging decline of *Gf*-ability in solving complex reasoning problems.

   Also shown in Figure 7 is evidence indicating that although older adults tend to be more careful and more persistent than younger adults when working on intellectual problems, this carefulness and persistence is not responsible for *Gf* decline. Older adults give fewer incorrect answers than younger adults when there is opportunity to abandon a problem if one is not sure about an answer. This is the *CAR* variable in the figure. Older adults also work longer before abandoning difficult problems than do younger adults. This is the variable abbreviated as *PRS* in the figure. It can be seen in the results that when carefulness

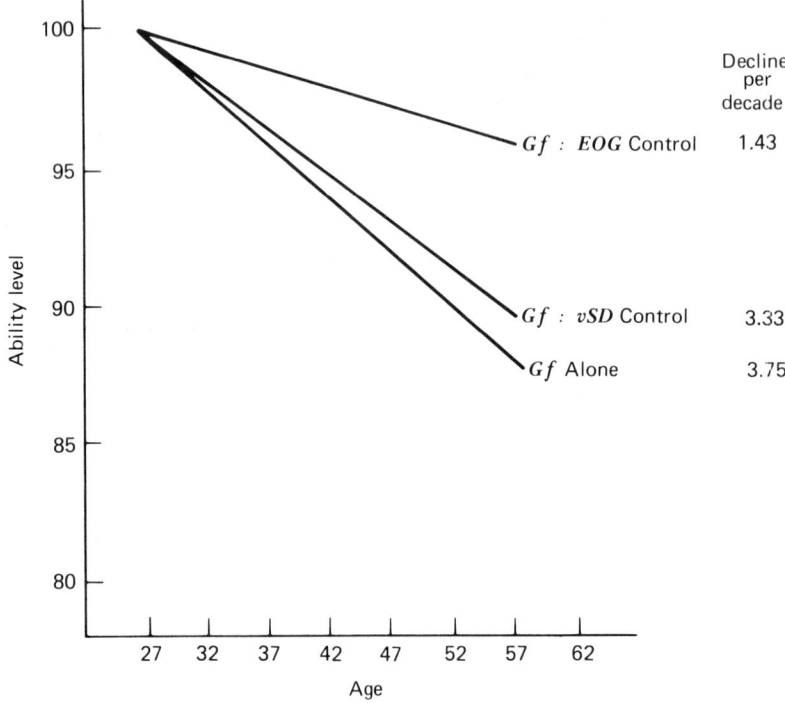

Figure 6. Aging Decline of *Gf* Under Linear Control of Visual Sensory Detectors (*vSD*) and Encoding Organization (*EOG*). Abbreviations: *EOG:* Encoding. *vSD:* Visual Sensory Detection *Gf:* Fluid Intellect.

and persistence are controlled, not only is there no decrease in the aging decline of *Gf,* there is increase in this decline. Such results indicate that carefulness and persistence are advantages that accrue to older adults, on the average, more than to younger adults. These advantages enable older adults to do relatively better in solving *Gf* problems than they would do if opportunities to exercise carefulness and persistence were removed. When the advantages associated with carefulness and persistence are partialed out, there is significant increase in the aging decline for *Gf.*

These figures are a part of other results I will not discuss here, but summarize in Figure 8. The studies in which these results were obtained are reported rather fully elsewhere (Horn, Donaldson, & Engstrom, 1981).

My reason for pointing to such results in the present context is to suggest that even if one were to regard a particular factor—*Gf,* say—as representing "the" concept of general intelligence (which would imply that *Gc* is something different from general intelligence), our theory and our clinical practice should take account of findings, such as I have just illustrated, showing that separate processes, very possibly having separate genetical and environmental determinants, are involved in that which we would have chosen to call intelligence.

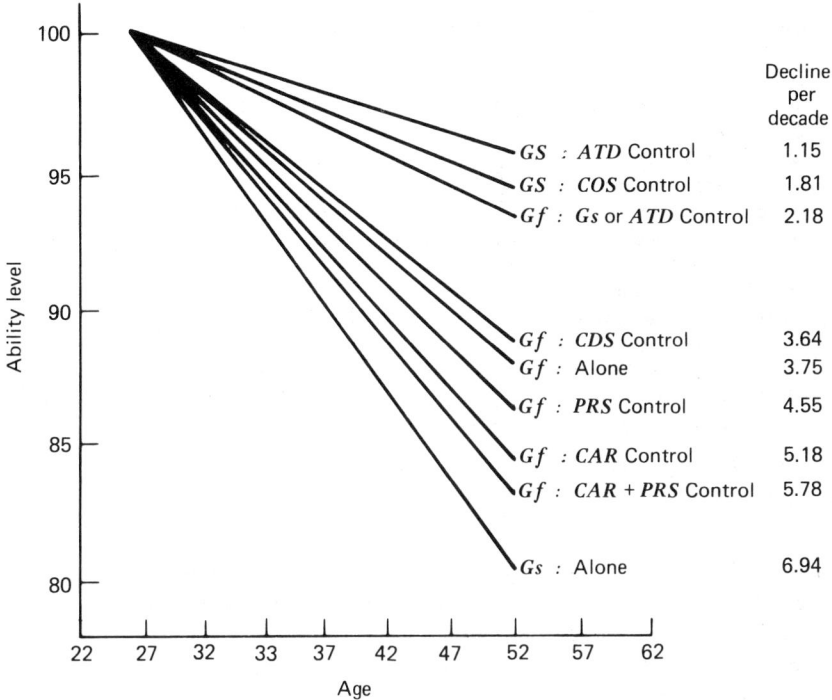

Figure 7. Aging Decline of *Gf* and Clerical Perceptual Speed (*Gs*) under Linear Control of Correct Decision Speed (*CDS*), Concentration on Slowness (*COS*), Attention Division (*ATD*), Persistence (*PRS*), and Carefulness (*CAR*).

Of course, given the results showing that *Gf* declines with age in adulthood, and given that research psychologists are themselves aging, it is very possible that many researchers will not choose to define *Gf* as general intelligence: *Gc* might be a better candidate for that title. But of course my main point is that neither *Gf* nor *Gc* is general intelligence, because there is no such thing—except in parlor conversation.

Genetic Evidence

My main point in regard to genetic evidence does not stem from any argument one might have about the scientific value of a concept of heritability. I will assume that we all know that heritability is a high-level abstraction, that estimates of heritability depend very much on the variability of measures and the variability of environmental opportunities within a society where the estimates are obtained. As with almost all the evidence we have on important issues in psychology, the evidence we can derive from studies of heritability is cankered with equivocality. Nevertheless, I think we can learn from this kind of evidence if we guard against social-political posturing and interpret results skillfully and cautiously.

Choose your favorite three (for any three will do the job of all under cross-validation).

PROCESS	SYMBOL
1. *Concentration*: Maintaining close attention, as in doing a task very slowly.	COS
2. *Encoding Organization*: Classifying incoming information in ways that facilitate subsequent recall.	EOG
3. *Incidental Memory*: Remembering small things for minutes-hours—in essence, things that would seem to be insignificant.	ICM
4. *Eschewing Attentional Irrelevancies*: Not attending to what has proved to be irrelevant.	EIR
5. *Dividing Attention*: Attending to other things while remembering a given thing.	ATD
6. *Working Memory*: Holding several distinct ideas in mind at once.	MSB
7. *Speediness*: Speed in "seeing" and "marking" and "comparing."	SPD
8. *Hypothesizing*: Forming ideas about what is likely.	HYP

Figure 8. Summary of Processes Involved in the Decline of Fluid Abilities During the "Vital Years" of Adulthood. (Source: Horn, Donaldson, and Engstrom, Research on Aging, 1981.)

Evidence such as I have reviewed thus far—on the organization and development of intellectual abilities—provide the raison d'être for *Gf-Gc* theory. It follows from these two sets of findings that different abilities are likely to be determined by different sets of genetic and environmental determinants. There has been considerable speculation about this matter. The position that is most frequently cited as representing *Gf-Gc* theory was put forth in Cattell's early statements. According to this view, *Gf* represents only, or primarily, genetic influences, while *Gc* represents environmental influences that have modified the genetically determined *Gf*. Thus, *Gc* is thought to develop out of *Gf* as individual differences in environmental influences accumulate.

If this view is correct, then we might expect to find that the heritability of *Gf* is larger than the heritability of *Gc*. We might expect also that in the earliest years of life there is virtually no distinction between *Gf* and *Gc*. This would follow if individual differences in environmental influences are not very large in the first years of life, and thus could not have done much to change genetically determined *Gf*.

Of course, it is possible that there are large individual differences in environmental influences even prior to birth and in infancy. If this were true, or if *Gf* and *Gc* had distinct genetic determinants, we might expect to find a distinction between *Gf* and *Gc* at an early age in childhood.

It does not follow necessarily, only colorably, that an early separation of *Gf* and *Gc* indicates genetic determination, while absence of the distinction threatens this case. It need not be true that genetic influences become manifest early in childhood: many developmental geneticists hold open the possibility that some genes are not expressed until, say, puberty. Nevertheless, if a distinction between *Gf* and *Gc* is found among very young children, then one logical interpretation of these findings is that the two intelligences stem from different genetic determiners.

Indeed, the distinction between *Gf* and *Gc* does show up at an early age. Pat Ellison, David Prasse, and I (Horn & Ellison, 1983; Horn, Ellison, & Prasse, 1985) found the distinction in samples of four-year-old and seven-year-old children who, for a variety of reasons, had been hospitalized in neonatal intensive care units (NICU) at the time of birth. Early results from our studies (now in progress) are summarized in Table 4.

These results might be interpreted as supporting a hypothesis that *Gf* and *Gc* have separate genetic determinants, but the results can indicate also that *Gf* and *Gc* rest on the same set of genetic determinants, but powerful individual differences in environmental influences operate in the earliest periods of life. In our samples of NICU children, quite different medical conditions necessitated intensive care in the first place, and the children received quite different treatments during their stay in the hospital. We are currently studying quite a number of infancy and early-childhood correlates of four-year-old and seven-year-old outcomes such as are illustrated in the table. Such study may shed light on the question of whether or not the *Gf-Gc* distinction is determined largely by early environmental influences, but I do not yet have results from this work that might dependably indicate the answer to this question.

Table 4. Equimax Rotated Factors of the McCarthy Scales

	Symbol[a]	*Gc*	*Gf*	*SAR?*	*TSR?*	*CORD*
Number Questions	*N*	27	06	11	08	03
Word Knowledge	*V*	53	25	32	30	27
Opposite Analogies	*CMR*	66	23	29	23	15
Conceptual Grouping	*CMC*	61	40	10	20	25
Counting and Sorting	*CSS*	48	34	18	27	28
Tapping Sequences	*TC*	22	56	10	36	16
Puzzle Solving	*RG*	26	53	27	05	00
Block Building	*CFR*	25	45	23	14	33
Draw-a-Child	*DBU*	13	52	22	24	30
Draw-a-Design	*DFU*	19	48	01	29	28
Verbal Fluency	*Fe*	33	29	45	27	23
Picture Memory	*MV*	14	11	36	06	39
Verbal Memory II	*MSU*	14	13	73	05	06
Verbal Memory I	*MMU*	23	01	61	44	14
Numerical Memory I	*MSR*	20	16	14	71	17
Numerical Memory II	*MSC*	10	13	08	37	03
Leg Coordination	*LC*	08	08	25	40	43
Arm Coordination	*AC*	02	18	15	03	59
Imitative Action	*IA*	28	05	−05	20	55

[a]Derived from identifications with the primary factors indicated in the Ekstrom, French, and Harman (1979), Guilford (1967), Guilford and Hoepfner (1971), Horn (1982b), and Stankov and Horn (1980) reviews and studies.

Column abbreviations. Gc: Crystallized Intellect. *Gf:* Fluid Intellect. *SAR:* Short-term Apprehension and Recall. *TSR:* Long-term Storage and Retrieval. *CORD:* Coordination.

Another line of research, however, suggests that the *Gf-Gc* distinction is determined in heredity by the independent operation of separate sets of genetic factors. This evidence suggests, also, that the heritability of *Gf* is *not* larger than the heritability of *Gc*, that genteic influences are about equally important in determining individual differences in each kind of intelligence.

Nichols (1978), collating over almost all (if not all) the available studies of twins, obtained the results I have summarized in Table 5. In such studies, twice the difference between the intraclass correlations for monozygotic and dizygotic twins provides Falconer's (1960) estimate of broad-sense heritability. We need

Table 5.   Averages of Intraclass Correlations for Primary Abilities Measurements of Fraternal and Identical Twins

		MZ	*DZ*	Dif.	2 Dif.[a]
Crystallized Markers					
V:	Verbal comprehension	.82	.61	.21	.42
	Vocabulary	.84	.60	.24	.48
N:	Number facility	.80	.60	.20	.40
Fw:	Word fluency	.65	.51	.14	.28
Fe:	Expressional fluency	.60	.49	.11	.22
	Social studies	.83	.57	.26	.52
	Natural sciences	.80	.64	.16	.32
	Averages	.76	.58	.18	.37
Fluid Markers					
I:	Inductive reasoning	.70	.55	.15	.30
S:	Spatial reasoning	.64	.40	.24	.48
P:	Perceptual speed	.70	.53	.17	.34
N:	Number facility	.80	.60	.20	.40
Ma:	Associative memory	.53	.39	.14	.28
	Averages	.67	.49	.18	.36

Source.   After Nichols (1978).

[a]Falconer's estimate of broad-sense heritability, h^2.

Column abbreviations.   *MZ:* Monozygotic.   *DZ:* Dizygotic.   *Dif.:* Difference.

not get into questions about whether or not Falconer's is a best estimate of heritability. It is a commonly accepted index and is calculated in the same way for *Gf* as for *Gc*; here we are interested in a comparison of the two indices, not with the magnitude of heritability, as such.

Nichols' results indicate that heritability is virtually the same for *Gc* abilities as for *Gf* abilities. Similar groupings of the results reviewed by Plomin, DeFries, and McClearn (1980) and by DeFries, Kuse, and Vandenberg (1979) lead to the same conclusion. Such results suggest that, if anything, *Gc* has greater heritability than *Gf*. The average of the heritability estimates for markers of *Gf* is less than the corresponding average for *Gc* markers.

It seems, then, that heritability is *not* larger for *Gf* than for *Gc*. There are good reasons for such a result. In particular, there are good reasons to believe that *Gf* is learned as much as *Gc*, and that *Gc* is inherited as much as *Gf*.

Contrary to suggestions that *Gf* represents unlearned capacities, if one looks carefully at the tests that define *Gf*, it becomes apparent that much learning must precede good performance on such tests. Consider in Figure 9 an item from the letter series test, items of the kind that Butterfield, Nielsen, Tangen, and Richardson (1984) now generate with a rational computer program. Letter series is one of the better markers for *Gf*. But to get an item of this test correct, one must have learned that people who make up tests assume that the letters of the alphabet are ordered in the way we conventionally teach children to say the alphabet; one must have learned also that makers of tests assume that when one comes to the end of the conventional order of listing the letters of the alphabet, one goes back and starts at the beginning; and one must have learned how to count and think in terms of serial order. Given all these things, one must have learned how to reason with the idea of progressions—in the examples, a simple linear progression.

Incidentally, several years ago Banish Hoffman (1962), a mathematician, showed that most of the progressions we ask people to solve in such tests as letter series are not determinable, so, mathematically speaking, such problems do not have solutions. Thus to do well on a letter series test one must have learned to give wrong answers!

It is clear, then, that performance on letter series tests depends heavily on learning. Every one of the tests that define *Gf* requires learning. This is not to say that, necessarily, individual differences in *Gf* reflect individual differences in opportunities for learning. A complex ability can be an outcome of learning and still be mainly determined by genetic factors if that learning is mainly determined by genetic factors. But the difference between *Gc* and *Gf* is not that one is learned and the other is not; both depend heavily on learning. The distinction between the two reflects differences in the kind of learning on which performances are based.

Gc is based on, and reflects, individual differences in acculturation learning; *Gf* is based on, and reflects, individual differences in what I refer to as casual learning—learning that is not heavily shaped by acculturation. In our society much emphasis in education is placed on what might be called fact-learning or knowledge absorption, and relatively little emphasis is placed on learning to

Inductive Reasoning: What number or letter comes next in the following?

4 5 6 3 4 5 6 2 3 4 5 6 $\dfrac{?}{?}$

B D A C Z B Y A

Figural Reasoning: Choose a figure from the right to fit the empty box in the left figure.

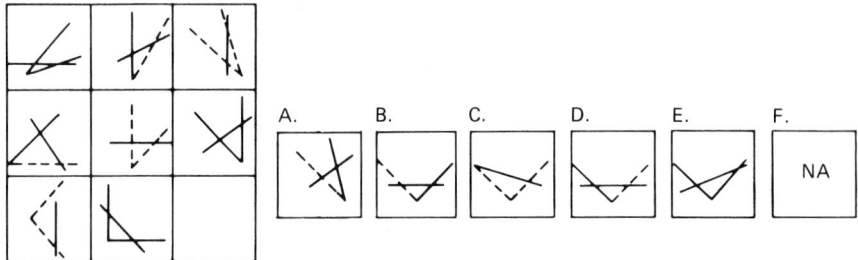

Common Word Analogies: SOON is to NEVER as NEAR is to ?
NOT FAR, SELDOM, NOWHERE, WIDELY

Koh's Blocks: (from the WAIS — i.e., Wechsler)
Put together blocks on the left to make pattern on the right.

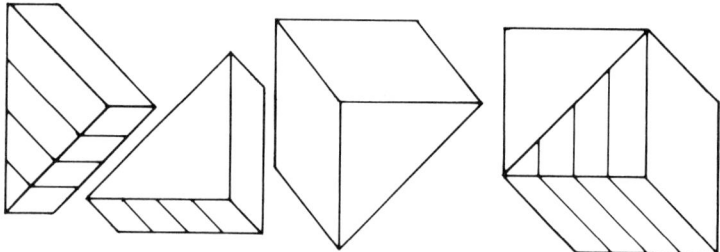

Figure 9. Some Examples of Fluid Abilities Tasks.

assume what is given and reason from that. In our society much learning is based on promotion and ability-placement procedures that systematically include some and exclude others from that learning. These procedures reward conformance to a considerable extent, rather than independent thinking. This is part of what I refer to as cohesive acculturation. *Gc* is a principal outgrowth of acculturation. *Gf*, on the other hand, is based on independent thinking brought on in part by avoidance of, or exclusion from, acculturation.

Evidence also indicates that some of the determinants of *Gc* are linked to heredity. *Gc* is heavily based on verbal skills and language development. It is well established that girls learn language earlier and more readily than do boys.

An essential determinant of the differences between girls and boys is genetic. Very likely some of the same kinds of genetic differences that exist between boys and girls exist within gender. Certainly some boys learn language earlier than other boys, and some girls learn language later than some boys. And what can be seen in language development occurs also for other conditions leading to early development of *Gc*.

Thus it seems that differences in *Gc* stem in part from genetic differences. These factors may become manifest in assimilation as Piagetians identify this concept. In consequence of hereditary predispositions that appear early in life, some individuals may more readily assimilate acculturational learning than do others. This would lead to the highly learned individual differences we see in crystallized abilities. Other genetic factors may produce the individual differences in accommodation that Piagetians have described. These early-appearing differences could put some individuals more than others on a path leading to more development of *Gf* than of *Gc*.

Results from one of our recent studies (McArdle, Horn, & Goldsmith, 1984) provide some support for this line of reasoning. In this work we fitted a *Gf-Gc* model using data from the Thurstone, Thurstone, and Standskov (1955) study of twins. Four sets of variance-covariance coefficients, as shown in Figure 10, can be obtained from these data to indicate the relative strength of genetic and environmental influences. These sets of coefficients can be described as follows.

First, there is a matrix of between-family variances and covariances for monozygotic twins—the matrix symbolized as *MZB* in Figure 10. For example, if the vocabulary scores of the two twins of a family are summed, so for each family there is one score, then the variability from one family to another of these summed scores is the between-family variance for vocabulary. If the vocabulary sum score is covaried with the same kind of sum score for a fluency test, then a between-family covariance is obtained.

A matrix of within-family variances and covariances—abbreviated *MZW*—can be obtained by making the basic unit the *difference* between the vocabulary scores of the two twins of a family. The variance of these differences indicates the within-family variability, and the covariability of the differences in vocabulary with the differences in fluency test scores provides the within-family covariance.

The same kinds of matrices can be calculated for a sample of dizygotic twins. A *DZB* matrix of between-family variances and covariances is defined by using the sum of two twins' scores as the basic measure for analysis. The matrix of within-family variances and covariances, *DZW*, is defined by analyzing the differences between the scores for each pair of fraternal twins.

As can be seen in the figure, logic and theory in genetics suggest the *MZB*, *MZW*, *DZB*, and *DZW* represent different proportions of genetic and environmental influences. What is known in genetics now suggests, for example, that monozygotic twins have the same genetic structure, which implies that none of the within variance of *MZW*—none of the variability within pairs of twins—is due to genetic factors. Since the within-twin and between-twin genetic variance must add up to the total variance in the sample of monozygotic twins, and because within-twin variance is zero, the total genetic variance (set conveniently

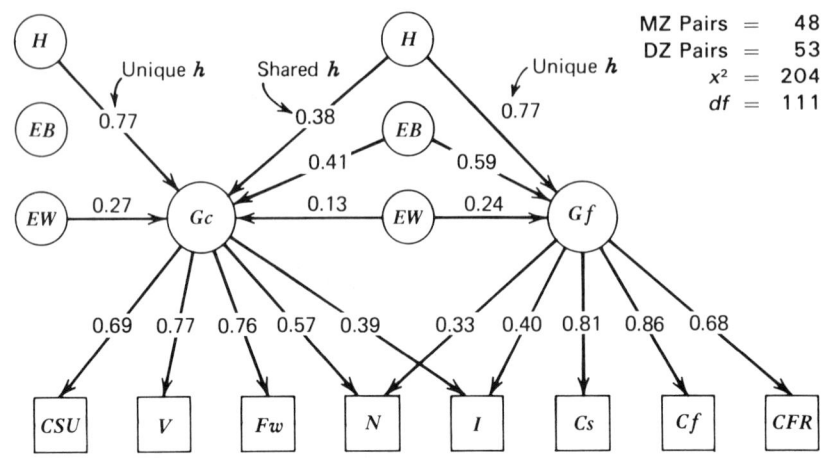

Fit the following four
 Variance-Covariance Matrices: Genetical theory
                                       Relative Involvements*

		H	EB	EW
Monozygot Between Families:	MZB	1	1	1
Monozygot Within Families:	MZW	0	0	1
Dizygot Between Families:	DZB	3/4	1	1
Dizygot With Families:	DZW	1/4	0	1

Abbreviations CSU: Cognition of System Units. V: Vocabulary. Fw: Word Fluency. N:
Number Ability. I: Induction. Cs: Speed of Closure. Cf: Flexibility of Closure. CFR:
Cognition of Figural Relations.
*After Eaves & Eysenck (1977).

Figure 10. A Genetical Model of *Gf* and *Gc*. (Source: After Eaves & Eysenck, 1977.) Abbreviations
not defined in previous Figures or tables: *R:* Reasoning. *I:* Induction. *S:* Spatial. *P:* Perceptual Speed.
Ma: Associative Memory. *MS:* Span Memory. *Mm:* Meaningful Memory. *SMT:* Sperling Matrices.
VLA: Visual Locations. *SPD:* Sensory Pattern Detection. *Ac:* Auditory Acuity. *Va:* Voice Acuity.
SM: Semantic Memory. *Fe:* Expressive Fluency. *Fa:* Associational Fluency. *Fi:* Idiational Fluency.

at 1.00) must be associated with the *MZB* matrix alone. In the dizygotic twins,
on the other hand, only 50% of the genes are common to both twins. The
contribution to within-family variance of this shared set of genes is thus the
square of the shared component, or 25%. Since again the within-twin and between-twin genetic variances must add to unity, it follows that the between-twin
genetic variance in the sample of dizygotic twins must be 75% when the comparable within-twin variance is 25%. Through the same kinds of analyses the
proportionate contributions to within-family (*EW*) and between-family (*EB*)
environmental influences are derived from theory in genetics, as represented in
Jinks and Fulker (1970; Eaves & Eysenck, 1977). By definition, there can be no
between-family environmental variance within families; so *EB* must be zero for
both the *MZW* and *DZW* matrices. All this variance and covariance must
therefore be associated with the *MZB* and *DZB* matrices.

Now, then, given that genetic and environmental influences are distributed in these different ways in the four variance-covariance matrices, the question we asked of these data is the following: "Does a *Gf-Gc* structural model fit these data in accordance with the partitioning I have just outlined for genetic and environmental determinants, and if so, does *Gf* have significantly larger heritability than *Gc*?" The answers to these questions are suggested by the results I summarize in the figure. The model we specified provides a reasonable fit to the data, and the heritability is not larger for *Gf* than for *Gc*. This outcome is quite consistent with the results of other studies (as summarized earlier).

In our modeling analyses the variances of all variables, both latent and manifest, have been set at unity over the total sample of subjects. This means that the sum of the squares is unity for the coefficients on the directed arrows leading to any particular variable in the figure. Specifically, for example, the sum of the squares is unity for the three directed arrows leading into Gf—$(.77)^2 + (.59)^2 + (.24)^2 = 1.00$. The unique broad-sense heritability of *Gf* can thus be seen to be $(.77)^2 = .59$. In mind of the embroglio generated by some of Cyril Burt's results, I am reluctant to point out that this is also precisely the unique broad-sense heritability for *Gc*! These unique heritability estimates suggest that *Gf* and *Gc* are based on separate sets of genetic determinants.

There is also some correlation between the genetic influences for *Gf* and *Gc*. This is represented by the directed arrow to *Gc* from *H*, representing the genetic influence of *Gf*. This means that in addition to its unique heritability, *Gc* involves heritability that stems from *Gf*. It is as if Cattell's hypothesis that *Gc* is an outgrowth of *Gf* is partly correct, that some (but not all) of the genetic determination of *Gc* is an outgrowth of genetic determinants of *Gf*. In concrete terms this means that the overall heritability of *Gc* is larger than the heritability of *Gf*. For the heritability of *Gc* is the unique heritability, $(.77)^2$, plus the heritability stemming from *Gf*, $(.38)^2$; this sum is .74. This total heritability is similar to broad-sense heritabilities reported for conglomerate measures of general intelligence.

These results thus indicate that there are independent components of heritability for *Gf* and *Gc*, and the heritability for *Gf* is not larger than the heritability for *Gc*; indeed, it is probably smaller.

A REMODELED MODEL

Let me now summarize major points and lay out some features of a recently remodeled model with which I have been working. First, however, I need to acknowledge that I know very little about human abilities. All I can do is write articles about them, talk about them, and specify models for them. The more I talk and write and model, the more I realize how little I really know about this complex realm of human functioning. But what little I think I do know brings me to a clear awareness that in scientific work and applied work that purports to derive from scientific understanding we simply must get rid of current concepts of general intelligence; they do more to cloud than to clarify major issues. My remodeling should be regarded as nothing more than a step along the way to a truly adequate theory, but it is a positive step because it is concordant with major features of what is presently known about human abilities (as outlined in previous sections).

We need to consider a broad organization of several main intellectual functions, perhaps ten major capacities, as illustrated in Figures 11 and 12. Any one of the ten factors of these figures might, in someone's theory, be chosen to indicate the basic capacities of general intelligence. For example, Jensen (1982)

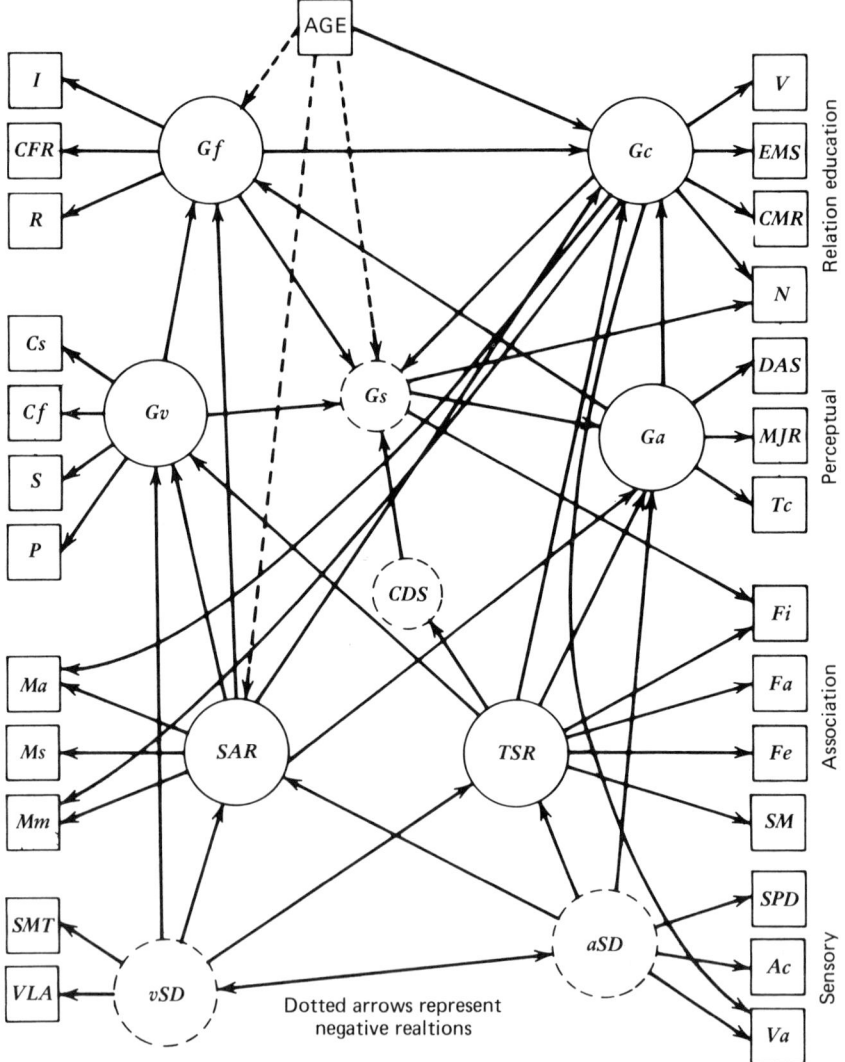

Figure 11. Function Organization of Intellect. Abbreviations: *CSU:* Cognition of System Unit. *V:* Vocabulary. *Fw:* Word Fluency. *N:* Number Ability. *Cs:* Speed of Closure. *Cf:* Flexibility of Closure. *CFR:* Cognition of Figural Relations.

seems to have chosen complex reaction time for the core of what he thinks of as general intelligence. Maybe so, but such an idea has a long way to go before it can be said to be a convincing theory about any one of the different "intelligences" I summarize in Figure 11. It is extremely unlikely that any feature of complex reaction time is the (singular) determinant of all the intelligent behavior adumbrated in the figure. It is unlikely that this variability can be derived from

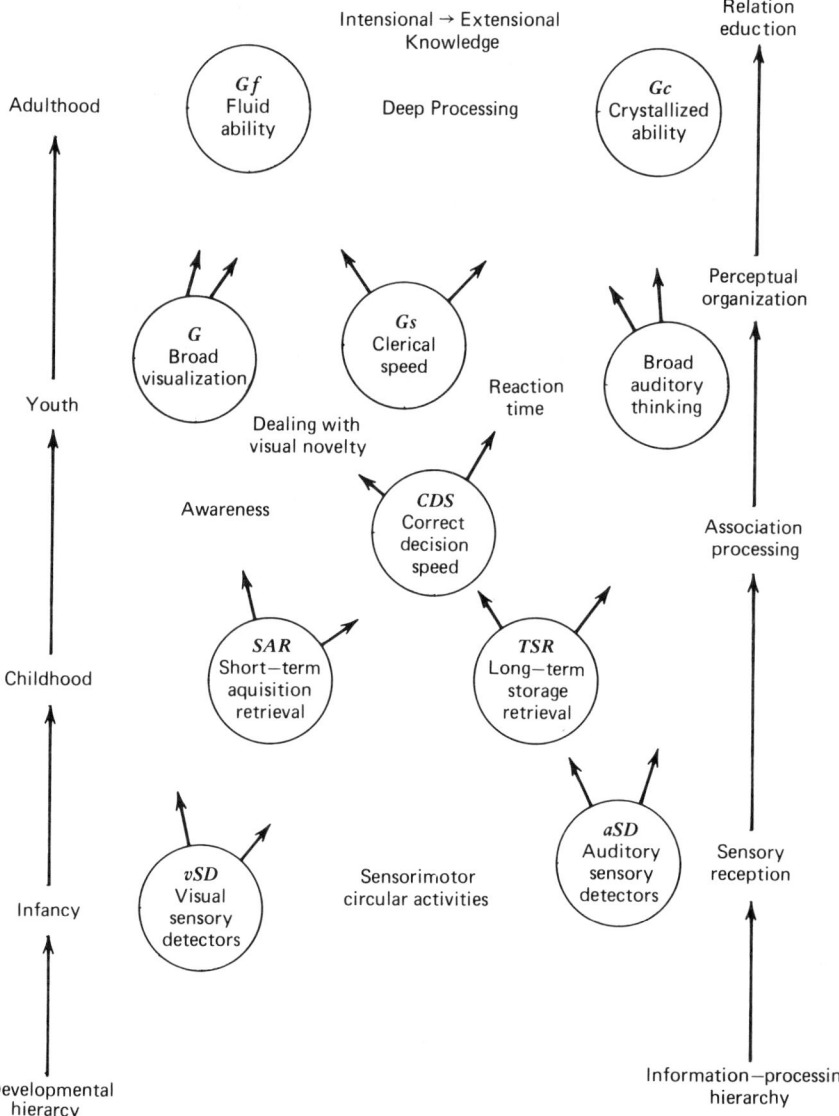

Figure 12. Ability Organizations within Developmental and Information-Processing Hierarchies.

any single source. It is more reasonable to suppose that each of the separate capacities of the figure cannot be derived one from the other—that these factors, and the even more elementary factors of which these are combinations, derive from quite different sets of environmental and genetic determinants. The capacities are probably interrelated, both in function and in development, but as Godfrey Thomson (1948) argued many years ago, this need not imply a general factor of intelligence.

In the model there is a hierarchy of functions: the *Gf* and *Gc* capacities for eduction of relations depend on perceptual organizations (auditory, visual, and so on), which in turn depend on associational processing, which is based on sensory detection. This hierarchy of functions runs parallel to a developmental hierarchy extending from infancy to old age. In each hierarchy, the distance from top to bottom is inversely proportional to the magnitude of correlation between abilities. The abilities near the bottom of the figure have low correlations with the abilities near the top of the figure.

The processes represented by the abilities of the figure no doubt interact in complex ways, and an organization among such interactions might be specified in a theory of general intelligence. I know of no such theory. Similarly, one might someday specify a theory of general intelligence that describes how each of the capacities of the figure become organized along a developmental pathway, but no theory currently on the market—including Piaget's theory, of course—

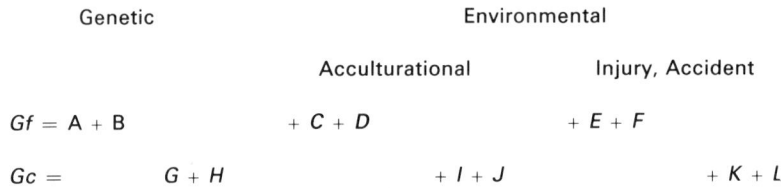

	Genetic		Environmental	
		Acculturational		Injury, Accident
$Gf = A + B$		$+ C + D$		$+ E + F$
$Gc =$	$G + H$		$+ I + J$	$+ K + L$

Symbols Used to Represent Determinants

A, B = Different genetical determinants of *Gf*
G, H = Different genetical determinants of *Gc*
C, D = Casual learning influences of *Gf*
I, J = Acculturation influences on *Gc*
E, F = Direct injuries and indirect physiological influences on *Gf*
K, L = Injury and indirect physiological influences on *Gc*

Gc and *Gf* (*Gs, Gv,* and so on) are functions of:

Different genetical factors (for example, assimilation, accommodation).
Different life-course patterns of learning (for example, acculturation, casual).
Different factors that act on physiological process directly (for example, neurotransmitters, hippocampus).

We understand some aspects of some of these things.

Figure 13.   Determinants of *Gf* and *Gc*.

comes at all close to even asking the questions I have raised, much less formulating an integration.

In Figure 13 I illustrate several main features of the *Gf-Gc* remodeling. The basic idea is that any two of the 10 intellectual functions I mentioned in Figures 11 and 12—for example, *Gf* and *Gc*—are based on separate genetic and environmental influences. For *Gf* and *Gc*, the genetic determinants might produce differences in such basic processes as assimilation and accommodation, as discussed by Piaget. Separate classes of environmental determinants interact with the genetic factors throughout development. In *Gc* development, genetic determiners of assimilation interact favorably with the environmental determiners classified as acculturational. In *Gf* development, genetic determinants of accommodation interact favorably with development deriving from casual learning experiences. The outcomes we see in *Gf* and *Gc* reflect the fact that some genetic factors predispose one to be more receptive to some kinds of environmental influences than to others. Highly developed assimilation capacities predispose one to acculturational influences that underlie development of *Gc*.

Also important are a number of nutritional and physical injury factors. Neurological injuries occurring late in development affect the reasoning capacities of *Gf* more than they influence the abilities of *Gc*. Several sets of this kind of evidence have been considered elsewhere (Horn, 1982a, 1982b).

There is much we must learn before we become enamored with a model of the kind I have outlined. The model incorporates a considerable range of evidence, but much relevant evidence has not been built into the model. Much of the evidence needed to evaluate the model does not exist. The remodeling is an improvement over the old model, but do not take it too seriously. We do not want the new model to become one of those embedded beliefs of which I spoke at the beginning of this chapter.

REFERENCES

Alexander, W. P. (1935). Intelligence, concrete and abstract. *British Journal of Psychology* (Monograph Supplement).

Botzum, W. A. (1951). A factorial study of reasoning and closure factors. *Psychometrika, 16,* 361–386.

Boyd, B. D., & Ellis, N. R. (1984). *Levels of processing and memory in retarded and nonretarded persons.* Gatlinburg, Tennessee: Conference on Theory and Research.

Butterfield, E. G., Nielsen, D., Tangen, K. L., & Richardson, M. B. (1984). Theoretically based psychometric measures of inductive reasoning. In S. Embretson (Ed.), *Test design: Contributions from psychology, education, and psychometrics.* New York: Academic Press.

Carroll, J. (1976). Psychometric tests as cognitive tasks: A new structure of intellect. In L. Resnick (Ed.), *The nature of intelligence.* Hillsdale, NJ: Erlbaum.

Caruso, D. R. (1984). *Role of encoding in the short-term memory processes of mentally retarded and nonretarded persons.* Gatlinburg, Tennessee: Conference on Theory and Research.

Cattell, R. B. (1941). Some theoretical issues in adult intelligence testing. *Psychological Bulletin, 38,* 592 (Abstract).

Cattell, R. B. (1957). *Personality and motivation structure and measurement.* Yonkers-on-Hudson, NY: World Book.

Cohen, J. (1959). A factor analytically based rationale of the Wechsler Adult Intelligence Scale. *Journal of Consulting Psychology, 21,* 451–457.

Corter, H. M. (1952). Factor analysis of some reasoning tests. *Psychological Monographs.*

DeFries, J. C., Kuse, A. R., & Vandenberg, S. G. (1979). Genetic correlations, environmental correlations and behavior. In J. R. Royce (Ed.), *Theoretical advances in behavior genetics.* Alphen aan den Rijn, Netherlands: Sigthoff Noordhoff.

Detterman, D. K. (1984). *Assessing cognitive deficits in the mentally retarded: Conclusions.* Gatlinburg, Tennessee: Conference on Theory and Research.

Eaves, L. J., & Eysenck, H. J. (1977). A genotype-environmental model for psychoticism. *Advances in Behavioral Research Theory, 1,* 5–26.

Ekstrom, R. B., French, J. W., & Harman, M. H. (1979). Cognitive factors: Their identification and replication. *Multivariate Behavior Research Monographs* (No. 79), 2.

El Koussy, A. A. H. (1935). The visual perception of space. *British Journal of Psychology* (Monograph Supplement).

Embretson, S. (1984). *Test design: Contributions from psychology, education and psychometrics.* New York: Academic Press.

Fagan, J. F. (1984). *Infants' attention to visual novelty as a measure of intelligence: Overview and implications.* Gatlinburg, Tennessee: Conference on Theory and Research.

Falconer, D. S. (1960). *Introduction to quantitative genetics.* New York: Ronald Press.

Greenfield, D. B., Scott, M. S., & Sterental, E. (1984). *Intensional superordinate category knowledge as a predictor of school failure.* Gatlinburg, Tennessee: Conference on Theory and Research.

Guilford, J. P. (1964). Zero intercorrelations among tests of intellectual abilities. *Psychological Bulletin, 61,* 401–404.

Guilford, J. P. (1967). *The nature of human intelligence.* New York: McGraw-Hill.

Guilford, J. P., & Hoepfner, R. (1971). *The analysis of intelligence.* New York: McGraw-Hill.

Hebb, D. O. (1941). Clinical evidence concerning the nature of normal adult test performance. *Psychological Bulletin, 38,* 593 (Abstract).

Hebb, D. O. (1949). *The Organization of behavior.* New York: Wiley.

Hoffman, B. (1962). *The tyranny of testing.* New York: Collier.

Holzman, T. G., Pellegrino, J. W., & Glaser, R. (1982). Cognitive dimensions of numerical rule induction. *Journal of Educational Psychology, 74,* 360–373.

Horn, J. L. (1968). Organization of abilities and the development of intelligence. *Psychological Review, 75,* 242–259.

Horn, J. L. (1970). Organization of data on life-span development of human abilities. In L. R. Goulet & P. B. Baltes (Eds.), *Life-span development in psychology.* New York: Academic Press.

Horn, J. L. (1974). Educability and group differences by A. R. Jensen. *American Journal of Psychology, 87,* 546–551.

Horn, J. L. (1976). Human abilities: A review of research and theory in the early 1970s. *Annual Review of Psychology, 27,* 437–485.

Horn, J. L. (1977a). Personality and ability theory. In R. B. Cattell & R. M. Dreger (Eds.), *Handbook of modern personality theory.* London: Hemisphere.

Horn, J. L. (1977b). *Intellectual development through the vital years: Final report.* Washington, DC: Army Research Institute.

Horn, J. L. (1978). *Individual differences in cognitive development: Final Report.* Bethesda, Maryland: National Science Foundation.

Horn, J. L. (1980). Concepts of intellect in relation to learning and adult development. *Intelligence, 4,* 285–317.

Horn, J. L. (1981). *Age differences in human abilities: Final report.* Bethesda, Maryland: National Institute on Aging.

Horn, J. L. (1982a). The aging of human abilities. In B. B. Wolman (Ed.), *Handbook of developmental psychology.* New York: Prentice-Hall.

Horn, J. L. (1982b). The theory of fluid and crystallized intelligence in relation to concepts of cognitive psychology and aging in adulthood. In F. I. M. Craik & S. E. Trehub (Eds.), *Aging and cognitive processes.* Boston: Plenum.

Horn, J. L., & Cattell, R. B. (1967). Age differences in fluid and crystallized intelligence. *Acta Psychologica, 26,* 107–129.

Horn, J. L., & Donaldson, G. (1976). On the myth of intellectual decline in adulthood. *American Psychologist, 31,* 701–719.

Horn, J. L., & Donaldson, G. (1980). Cognitive development in adulthood. In O. G. Brim & J. Kagan (Eds.), *Constancy and change in human development.* Cambridge: Harvard University Press.

Horn, J. L., Donaldson, G., & Engstrom, R. (1981). Apprehension, memory and fluid intelligence decline in adulthood. *Research on Aging, 3,* 33–84.

Horn, J. L., & Ellison, P. H. (1983). *A proposal to study developmental paths of children treated in intensive care units.* Grant Application, National Institute of Child Health and Human Development.

Horn, J. L., Ellison, P. H., & Prasse, D. (1985). A structural equation model of the McCarthy scales of early childhood abilities. In preparation.

Horn, J. L., & Goldsmith H. (1981). Reader be cautious: Bias in mental testing by Arthur R. Jensen. *American Journal of Education, 89,* 305–329.

Horn, J. L., & Stankov, L. (1982). Auditory and visual factors of intelligence. *Intelligence, 6,* 165–185.

Humphreys, L. G. (1979). The construct of general intelligence. *Intelligence, 3,* 105–120.

Hunt, E. (1978). Mechanics of verbal ability. *Psychological Review, 85,* 109–130.

Hunt, E., Frost, N., & Lunneborg, C. (1973). Individual differences in cognition: A new approach to intelligence. In G. Bower (Ed.), *The psychology of learning and motivation* (Vol. 7). New York: Academic Press.

Jensen, A. R. (1980). *Bias in mental testing.* New York: Free Press.

Jensen, A. R. (1982). Reaction time and psychometric *g.* In H. J. Eysenck (Ed.), *A model for intelligence.* New York: Springer-Verlag.

Jensen, A. R. (1984). *Alternative models of "g."* Invited address, Gatlinburg, Tennessee: Conference on Theory and Research.

Jinks, J. L., & Fulker, D. V. (1970). Comparisons of the biometrical and genetical, MAVA and classical approaches to the analysis of human behavior. *Psychological Bulletin, 73,* 311–349.

Johnson-Martin, N. M., & Goldman, R. D. (1984). *Capturing cognitive competence: Alternative assessments for handicapped infants.* Gatlinburg, Tennessee: Conference on Theory and Research.

Kahn, J. V. (1984). *Sensorimotor prediction of adaptive behavior in severely and profoundly mentally retarded children.* Gatlinburg, Tennessee: Conference on Theory and Research.

Kaufman, A. S. (1979). *Cerebral specialization and intelligence testing.* New York: Wiley.

Lewis, M. (Ed.). (1976). *Of intelligence: Infancy and early childhood.* London: Plenum.

Lewis, M., & McGurk, H. (1972). Evaluation of infant intelligence: Infant intelligence scores—true or false. *Science, 178,* 1174–1177.

Loehlin, J. C., Lindzey, G., & Spuhler, J. N. (1975). *Race differences in intelligence.* San Francisco: Freeman.

Mandler, G. (1968). Organized recall: Individual functions. *Psychonomic Science, 13,* 230–236.

Martin, L., & Adkins, D. C. (1954). A second-order analysis of reasoning abilities. *Psychometrika, 19,* 71–78.

McArdle, J. J., & Horn, J. L. (1983). *Validation by systems modeling of WAIS abilities.* National Institute of Aging.

McArdle, J. J., Horn, J. L., & Goldsmith, H. H. (1984). *A structural equation model of the genetical components of Gf and Gc.* In preparation.

McDonough, S. C. (1984). *Comparison of cerebral palsied infants: Cognitive performance and visual information-processing tasks and the Bayley scales.* Gatlinburg, Tennessee: Conference on Theory and Research.

Nichols, R. C. (1978). Twin studies of ability, personality and interests. *Homo, 29,* 158–173.

Pellegrino, J. W., & Glaser, R. (1979). Cognitive correlates and components of inductive reasoning. In Rabbitt (P. M. A.), How old and young subjects monitor and control responses for accuracy and speed. *British Journal of Psychology, 49,* 305–311.

Plomin, R., DeFries, J. C., & McClearn, G. E. (1980). *Behavioral genetics.* San Francisco: Freeman.

Rimoldi, H. J. (1948). Study of some factors related to intelligence. *Psychometrika, 13,* 27–46.

Stankov, L., & Horn, J. L. (1980). Human abilities revealed through auditory tests. *Journal of Educational Psychology, 72,* 21–44.

Sternberg, R. J. (1977). *Intelligence, information processing and analogical reasoning: The componential analysis of human abilities.* Hillsdale, NJ: Erlbaum.

Sternberg, R., & Defferman, D. K. (Eds.) (1979). *Human intelligence: Perspectives on its theory and measurement.* New York: Ablex.

Thomson, G. A. (1948). The factorial analysis of human ability (3rd ed.). Boston: Houghton Mifflin.

Thurstone, L. L. (1936). The factorial isolation of primary abilities. *Psychometrika, 1,* 175–182.

Thurstone, T. G., Thurstone, L. L., & Standskov, H. H. (1955). *Psychological study of twins. Scores of one hundred and twenty-five pairs of twins on fifty-nine tests.* Chapel Hill, NC: The Psychometric Laboratory, University of North Carolina.

Whitely, S. E. (1980). Multicomponent latent trait models for ability tests. *Psychometrika, 45,* 479–494.

Whitely, S. E., & Schneider, L. M. (1981). Information structure for geometric analogies: A tests theory approach. *Applied Psychological Measurement, 5,* 383–397.

EIGHT

INTELLIGENCE: A LIFE-SPAN DEVELOPMENTAL PERSPECTIVE

ROGER A. DIXON, DEIRDRE A. KRAMER,
PAUL B. BALTES
Max Planck Institute for Human Development and Education
Berlin, West Germany

The study of mature intelligence, of intellectual development in adulthood, has a long and venerable past. When allied with the study of infant, child, adolescent, and early adult intelligence (e.g., Bayley, 1970; Flavell, 1977; McCall, 1979; Wohlwill, 1980), the history of psychological research is voluminous and often impressive. Whereas the *developmental* stories told for these earlier age groups are often quite similar—that is, stories primarily optimistic in their accounts of progression, aggrandizement, and actuated potential—the stories told for the adult and aging years are often fundamentally different. Whereas the course of normal child and adolescent intellectual development is portrayed as growthlike, with interindividual differences in level and rate but not in directionality, there is a lack of consensus concerning whether the course of adult intelligence is typified by progression, decrement, or both; after more than half a century of systematic research, this is still an unresolved issue. It is apparent, however, that interindividual variation rather than universality is a central theme of research in adulthood.

Contrasting Trends in Life-span Development

From a life-span developmental perspective, the evidence pertaining to intellectual development during the first third of life can be summarized in a few relatively stable findings. This orderly pattern of findings applies especially to Western cultures, partly because it is here that most systematic investigation has occurred and partly because of the high degree of methodical organization of education, occupation, health care, and other macro-social and biological conditions.

The authors appreciate the helpful comments of Freya Dittmann-Kohli, Reinhold Kliegl, John Nesselroade, and Jacqui Smith on an earlier version of this chapter.

First, until early adulthood, intellectual development is characterized primarily in terms of growth or progression in cognitive operations and knowledge. Second, the structure of mental abilities and associated interindividual differences reach a fairly high level of stabilization by early adolescence. The level of stabilization is not perfect—there is room for further change—but present genetic and social conditions appear to be prevalent. Third, by early adulthood, most individuals can exercise sufficient cognitive skills to engage in further knowledge acquisition, providing that social and ecological conditions (for example, occupation) permit, since the capacity for continued learning and for maintaining and expanding on both general knowledge systems and specific knowledge domains is a prototypical feature of adulthood. Fourth, deviations from this general pattern of intellectual development are often the result of environmental insult, serious disease, or substantial social deprivation. Many reviews (see Bayley, 1970; Bertram, 1981; Jencks, 1972; Jensen, 1973; McCall, 1979; Scarr & Carter-Saltzman, 1982; Wohlwill, 1980) address the relevant evidence in considerably more detail and with varying degrees of emphasis and preference (for example, regarding the contributing role of social versus genetic factors).

With regard to adulthood and old age, this general pattern of universal growth and stabilization of interindividual differences in structure and function is not (or is not yet) the dominant position in research and theory. If applied to the adult portion of the life span, most such summary statements regarding childhood intelligence would represent issues of controversy. Although it is possible to argue that because life-span research on intelligence is still in its infancy the general patterns have not yet been determined, it is also possible that the conditions of life-long change in intelligence simply do not display the level of biological and cultural stabilization that is apparent for the first part of life. The widespread aging of the population is a fairly recent phenomenon. Thus it may be understandable that the course of intellectual development during adulthood and old age is less structured, less stable, and less predictable than it is during childhood.

Organization of This Chapter

In the present review we assume that our task is to narrate and interpret the story of research on intellectual development in adulthood and old age, and we speculate about future directions. We have chosen to focus our attention on this portion of the life span for several reasons. First, earlier portions of the life span are adequately reviewed in other chapters in this volume. Second, the life-span movement originated partly from a concern for disparate, seemingly contradictory, results in the initial studies of adult intelligence. Third, much research in the tradition of life-span developmental psychology coincides with research in adult development and aging.

Several general reviews of intellectual development in adulthood have appeared in recent years (Baltes & Labouvie, 1973; Botwinick, 1977; Denney, 1982; Horn, 1982; Horn & Donaldson, 1980; Labouvie-Vief, in press; Salthouse, 1982;

Schaie, 1979, 1983a; Willis & Baltes, 1980). Moreover, several recent reviews, adopting a more interpretive approach, have summarized the state of the art from a particular viewpoint and have proffered models for further investigation (see, for example, Baltes, 1984; Baltes, Dittmann-Kohli, & Dixon, 1984; Berg & Sternberg, 1983; Labouvie-Vief, 1977, 1982, inpress). The present review begins with a selective historical review, focusing on the era when the study of the life-span development of intelligence began in earnest. We shall focus on the development of knowledge about adult intelligence and, in particular, we shall argue that if there is ambiguity in this research domain, it may well represent the variegated nature of normal adult intellectual development in the present social and cultural conditions. Furthermore, we shall suggest that many of the recent conceptual advances in this domain have been anticipated in various ways and from various sources during the last century; to this extent, the story of intellectual development in adulthood is supported by social- and method-related robustness.

INTELLIGENCE: FROM CONCEPT TO CONSTRUCT

Recently, four concepts have been abstracted from the literature pertaining to life-span intellectual development (Baltes & Willis, 1979; Willis & Baltes, 1980). Together, these abstractions have been advanced as a coherent and useful characterization of the development of intelligence in adulthood and old age. In brief, these four concepts are as follows: (1) *multidimensionality,* or the notion that intelligence is composed of multiple mental abilities, each with potentially distinct structural, functional, and developmental properties; (2) *multidirectionality,* which signifies that there are multiple distinct change patterns associated with these abilities; (3) *interindividual variability,* a concept reflecting the large differences in the life-course change patterns of individuals; and (4) *intraindividual plasticity,* which indicates that, in general, throughout the life-course individual behavioral patterns are modifiable. These abstractions reflect a particular interpretation of predominantly recent research on the process of intelligence. This interpretation presupposes both an active organism as well as pragmatic and functional tenets (Baltes et al., 1984). As we shall see in this section, however, this view, in rudimentary form, was actually advanced long before intelligence was addressed in explicit life-span developmental terms, even before the concept of intelligence became an empirically accessible, developmental construct.

Therefore, it will become clear that much of the substance of these ideas has been a part of the landscape of developmental work in intelligence for many decades. Indeed, even prior to the initial systematic empirical work of the post-1920 era, some instances, however isolated, of these ideas may be located. Although our task is certainly not one of reviewing exhaustively the concept of intelligence per se, nor the evolution of this concept (see Woodruff, 1982), we shall note several historical precursors to contemporary portrayals of life-span intelligence, and, examine concepts of intelligence that, even if entirely disjunctive with later developments or completely unknown to later researchers, demonstrate that the recently refined methods of developmental research have not so much allowed us to propagate new interpretations as they have entitled us to begin deciding among alternative explications of the data.

Selected Nineteenth Century Conceptions

Several recent articles on intelligence (see, for example, Beilin, 1983; Dörner, 1982; Sternberg, 1982, 1984), and especially on adult intelligence (Dittmann-Kohli, 1984; Dittmann-Kohli & Baltes, in press; Edelstein & Noam, 1982; Labouvie-Vief, 1982, in press; Mergler & Goldstein, 1983), have emphasized active, functional, pragmatic, or contextual properties of intellectual behavior and development. In this subsection we identify several historical precursors to this recent set of emphases.

Histories of intelligence and mental testing (Freeman, 1939; Goodenough, 1949; Goslin, 1963; Jenkins & Paterson, 1961; Peterson, 1925) often identify the Frenchman Esquirol (1838), who conducted work on mental disorders, as having initiated the era of mental testing. The term *mental test* apparently first appeared in the literature in an article by James McKeen Cattell (1890) in which ten physical and mental measurements are proposed (see also Sharp, 1899; Wissler, 1901). The nineteenth century work on human inheritance by Darwin (1859, 1872) and Galton (1869), as well as Quetelet's (1835, 1838, 1842) applications of probability theory to measurement and review of empirically based observations on life-span indicators of intelligence and other domains, have also been noted in these histories. Quetelet, for example, used the term "intelligence" and emphasized its varying expression in terms of distinct subabilities and historical relativity. Furthermore, British associationism and the individual differences perspective of Darwinism influenced some early testing work (for example, Cattell and Galton). Still, beginning to measure intelligence is not necessarily tantamount to defining it, and many of the more persuasive nineteenth-century works on intelligence derived from other sources and often under distinctive rubrics.

In addition to Quetelet (1838), another pre-Darwinian writer, Abercrombie (1839), foreshadowed more recent portrayals of the active, adaptive functions of "intellectual power" or reason. In describing features of the "well regulated mind," Abercrombie (1839, p. 267) asserted that it is not only contemplative, properly directed and attentive, and carefully regulated, but that it is also selective, active, and inquiring. Furthermore, reason, described in a problem-solving way as consisting of the comparison of facts with each other and mental impressions with external things, was viewed as "that power by which we combine means for accomplishing our end . . . even though this may be regarded rather as the practical application of the knowledge to which reason leads us, than as a primary part of the province of reason itself" (Abercrombie, 1839, p. 137).

The emphasis on an active, functional conceptualization of intelligence in this period was derived in part from the intellectual climate provided by evolutionary biology (Dixon & Lerner, 1984). Among intelligence theorists influenced by evolutionary thinking, salient (and controversial) topics included the following: the nature of the relationship between internal and external relations, the function of this relationship in the development of knowledge, and the adequacy of correspondence between consciousness and environmental uniformities (James, 1890, 1909/1975; Spencer, 1855). In a chapter entitled "The Human Intellect: Its Function, Development, and Faculties," Porter (1891) argued that to know is a preeminently active operation of the intellect, that in "knowing, we are not so much recipients as actors" (p. 61). Still, Porter continued, this intellective activity is delimited, as are all other agents in nature, by the conditions under which it exercises its action:

> While, on the one hand, the intellect, in knowing, must act or operate upon, and in some sense create, its products, it cannot produce results at its will but must be governed by the objects which are furnished, as to what it knows and as to how it shall know them. [p. 62]

Not only did Porter present the act of knowledge as a process, but he also offered a synopsis of intellectual development in which the easier and more natural processes are matured prior to the more difficult and artificial, with not all adults attaining the highest levels of performance. In general, Porter's scheme represented the easiest and most natural processes as "the powers of sense and outward observation," which are followed by memory and imagination, and finally reflection, thought, and reason. This progression was viewed as being influenced by other "faculties," such as "feeling" and "will," and each of the individual intellectual "powers" were thought to be sensitive to activity or progress in the others.

Intelligence, it was argued, "functioned" so as to adapt a complex organism to complex environments; it acts as a "selecting agency," an efficacious instrument of survival (James, 1890). From this perspective, attention came to be focused on the *modus operandi* of the phenomenon (Angell, 1907), on the *process* of intelligence, called cognition or intellection (Stout & Baldwin, 1901), especially under conditions of practical significance or actual experience (Dixon & Hertzog, in press). More consideration was given to the practical operations of intelligence than to the analysis and comparison of its contents. Thus practical judgment and practical reasoning, both of which denote the involvement of purpose or valuing, was differentiated from logical reasoning (Baldwin & Stout, 1902; Peirce, 1902) much as it is today. Furthermore, this conceptualization of intelligence as an active form of "consciousness" was combined with a "genetic" (or developmental) approach (Angell, 1907; Baldwin, 1895, 1902) to psychological ontogenesis. According to James (1909/1975), the purpose of knowing is to bring oneself into fruitful relations with reality. Intelligence is directed at problems of living, whether those problems be of a mundane everyday sort, a veritable matter of survival, or of a self-selected, purely intellectual variety. Dewey's (1916, 1938) theory of intelligence was, similarly, equally applicable at all levels of active thinking, in all realms of active interchange between the organism and the environment.* In all instances requiring intelligent thinking, the presentation or identification of a problem—defined as the blockage of action—is pivotal (Dewey, 1938). The function of intelligence, then, is to solve problems (or to alter the environment).

As mentioned above, numerous recent writers have reasserted the significance of an active, functional, pragmatic depiction of mature intelligence (Baltes et al., 1984; Beilin, 1983; Berg & Sternberg, 1983; Dittmann-Kohli & Baltes, in press; Dixon & Baltes, in press; Dixon & Hertzog, in press; Sternberg, 1984) and argued that adequate consideration will alter extant research approaches and interpretations. In the following sections we shall see that these depictions did not lie entirely dormant during the intervening half century. Instead, they may have suffered a fate similar to that of the functional psychology movement from which they were in part derived. That is, after these conceptions achieved a certain common-sense appeal (James, 1890), they were distributed in a nonparadigmatic fashion across several traditions of psychological research. In addition, the emerging emphasis on methods of operationalization may have been associated with a decline in the scientific prestige of these depictions of mental activity (Matarazzo, 1972). In the following subsection we review selectively this tension between common-sense conceptualization and the exigencies of operationalization, especially as it applies to the past, present, and future study of mature intelligence.

The Proliferation of Testing

The functional concepts of intelligence, however contemporary they may seem, did not immediately spawn widely circulated methods of mental measurement. Indeed, the most notable advances in the early twentieth century were made in the design and production of practical methods of assessment. It is well known that Binet, after an unsatisfying flirtation with craniometry, was commissioned (in 1904) to develop a practical means of identifying children academically at risk. His early tasks, although tapping such processes as reasoning and comprehension, were representative of everyday problems (Binet, 1909). Binet was quite clear about his rejection of both an atomistic approach to measuring the complexities of intelligence and a unitary portrayal of the nature of intelligence (Binet & Henri, 1895; Binet & Simon, 1911; Gould, 1981; Peterson, 1925). Although he had devised a rudimentary form of scaling, it was Stern (1912) who proposed the enduring mental quotient as an indication of overall mental caliber. Binet, however, continued to emphasize the aspect of mental orthopedics, indicating that intelligence scores could be improved by training, an emphasis that is maintained in recent life-span research (Baltes & Willis, 1982; Denney, 1982). Underlying this accentuation of mental orthopedics was Binet's postulate of voluntary attention—even goal-seeking activity—a concept construed in terms

*Angell (1922) pointed out that intelligent actions are not, at base, unique to the human species, although there are, of course, significant differences in the intelligent behavior of humans and animals (see, for example, Baldwin, 1895; Spencer, 1895; Thorndike, 1911).

of adaptability. Indeed, adaptation—along with direction, autocriticism, and comprehension—became the cornerstone of his emerging emphasis on thinking and problem solving (Binet, 1909; Peterson, 1925).

Thus Binet's work was congruent with much of the conceptual work of this period and, moreover, is consistent with much of contemporary life-span thinking. His more immediate legacy, however, was in his methods, which contributed to the growth of psychometric formulations and procedures, such as those of Spearman.* According to Guilford (1967) these ensuing psychometric procedures were less informative about fundamental issues in, and concepts of, intelligence than were those of Binet. They did, however, properly emphasize "the need for a multiple-aptitude view of intelligence" (Guilford, 1967, p. 23), which is itself a precursor to one of the four contemporary life-span concepts of intelligence (multidimensionality).

An operational definition of a construct such as intelligence is often limited in its generalizability. The assessment of group (for example, age) differences with group-specific tests is problematic. Nevertheless, intelligence tests, designed to identify individuals similar to a given standard (often the test maker; see Neisser, 1976) and proffered as diagnostic or orthopedic devices, were applied to the investigation of developmental, racial, and other group differences.† The observer could not help but be impressed by the sheer range of human mental abilities, at least as indicated by the many mental tests and the multiple groups to which they were applied.

Theories and definitions of intelligence reflected this range both substantively (that is, incorporating the notion of intellectual variability) and illustratively (that is, exemplifying the range of concepts in the very diversity of definitions). As several observers have pointed out (for example, Bayley, 1970), some definitions and subsequent explanations reflected a decidedly hereditary or maturational orientation (for example, Boynton, 1933; Burt, Jones, Miller, & Moodie, 1934; Galton, 1869), whereas others reflected a strongly environmental or learning viewpoint (for example, Hayes, 1962; Hunt, 1961), and still others defined intelligence in terms of the activities to which effective operations could be brought to bear (for example, Reinert, 1970; Stoddard, 1941, 1943). The fact of interindividual variability in developmental trajectories influenced the con-

---

*It should be noted that Binet influenced Spearman in a somewhat paradoxical manner. Spearman (1927) argued against the proliferation of heterogenous scales (such as Binet's) and yet claimed that his g was the theoretical justification of such intelligence testing (Herrnstein, 1971; Spearman, 1904, 1914a, 1914b, 1927).

†For example, age-related differences among infants and children were heavily investigated (see Bayley, 1955, 1956, 1970; Gesell, 1925; Goodenough, 1954; Griffiths, 1954; Jones, 1954; Piaget, 1952, for reviews). Similarly, group differences pertaining to blacks and whites and to immigrants and nonimmigrants were popular topics of study (for example, Blackwood, 1927; Boody, 1926; Brigham, 1930; Kirkpatrick, 1926; Loehlin, Lindzey, & Spuhler, 1975; Peterson, 1929; Witty & Jenkins, 1936). For recent reviews of the controversy surrounding the investigation of group differences in intelligence see Gould (1981), Hirsch (1981), Kamin (1974), and Lerner (1985, Chapter 4).

ceptualization of Garrett (1946). In his formulation of the "differentiation hypothesis," Garrett addressed the issue of multidimensionality (to wit, with age, intelligence is transformed from a general ability to a loosely organized group of abilities), as well as the issue of interindividual variability (to wit, because of this transformation, methods of measurement may require age-related modification or have demonstrable sensitivity to differences in developmental status or age).

Wechsler (1952), however, placed the concern for the range of human mental abilities in a slightly different perspective, suggesting that the range was wide, but:

> When compared to that of other phenomena in nature . . . [it is] extremely limited, and that the differences which separate human beings from one another with respect to whatsoever trait or ability we may wish to compare, are far smaller than is ordinarily supposed. [pp. 7–8]

As we shall see in the following section this observation, when applied to adult age-related performance variability, resonates with some contemporary perspectives (for example, Baltes et al., 1984). If, as Neisser (1976) suggested, intelligence testing was in part conducted in order to distinguish between those who resembled the tester and those who did not, and if this may be applied judiciously to the case of life-span intelligence testing, then one may speculate that work on intellectual development in adulthood has been in part conducted in the interest of finding older adults who resemble younger adults ("pure research") and, when they do not, training them to do so ("training research"). In turn, these younger adults, who together comprise the "model" of intellectual performance, were selected because they resemble the creators of the test(s). In the following sections we shall have more to say concerning this youth-oriented strategy and about the alternatives that have been proposed.

INTELLECTUAL DEVELOPMENT IN ADULTHOOD: THE FIRST REPORTS

Several of the early works on "child study" devoted some attention to the comparison along selected facets of children and adults (for example, Drummond, 1912; Kirkpatrick, 1903). In a chapter entitled "Development of Intellect," Kirkpatrick (1903) compared children and adults on several dimensions of intelligence, arguing that in the development of "conscious intelligence" experience contributed greatly to the observed age-related differences (p. 247). Presaging several contemporary motifs, Kirkpatrick (1) considered both reasoning and practical reasoning, (2) asserted that interest and familiarity are important elements in adult learning, (3) alluded to the issue of brain plasticity in maturity (claiming it decreased after puberty), and (4) discussed the transfer of training issue (whether training on specific tasks could generalize to overall mental powers). Conscious intelligence, according to Kirkpatrick (1903), was active, because, as it developed, it selected "from the various possibilities presented to it by the results of previous action, those objects and acts that are most pleasing" (p. 247). Thus, for Kirkpatrick, conscious intelligence was modifiable; it may be changed either gradually and unconsciously or suddenly and consciously.

Other early commentators foreshadowed other aspects of the modern approach. For example, although Sanford (1902) associates mental decay with the inevitable physical decline that occurs in the later years of life he does emphasize that with care, effort, and continued activity some stability in intellectual functioning is possible. Considering the Period of the Elderly (ages 55–70), Sanford writes that:

> Intellectual vigor may survive (and as sometimes happens, much more than compensate the failure on the physical side), but a man must take care of himself; he must retire from positions demanding physical strength and must have a care that his body be able to support the demands of his mind. In intellectual matters, even, he may find that he must fight his indolence. [p. 447]

In his discussion of the subsequent Period of Old Age Sanford notes that the apparent diminished intellectual plasticity is "partly enforced by the exclusion of the aged from active participation in current affairs" (p. 448). Furthermore, Sanford argues that the fact of diminished intellectual powers should not preclude the distinctive contentment of later life, a contentment that derives from viewing this period as a special opportunity to participate and serve others in a unique age-related manner.

Hollingworth (1927) virtually premised his work in developmental psychology (which to him was the study of both mental growth and decline) on the fact of human diversity. Hollingworth's (1927) perspective on the centrality of the developmental perspective in the science of psychology was lucid and unequivocal. His perspective on multidimensionality and multidirectionality of life-span developmental change was similarly vivid:

> If we try to represent the course of human life by a curve of growth or a curve of development, we find at once that no single curve is adequate to portray the actual complexity of the individual's history. Different features begin to appear at different times; mature at different rates; begin to decline, if decline they do, at different times and proceed here also at different rates. [Hollingworth, 1927, p. 324]

Hollingworth defined intelligence as a uniquely mental activity, the fundamental feature of which was the operation of symbols. When considered as a mental ability, intelligence was defined by Hollingworth (1927) as the "capacity for dealing with symbols, under the influence of a symbolic context" (p. 273). He developed a simplistic normal curve of intellectual capacity in adulthood in which the "average man" (the middle 50%) was associated with occupations appropriate to his or her abilities, as were the next ±20% and the extreme ±5%. More germane, perhaps, was his report concerning his own adult intelligence study ($n = 534$, with ages ranging from less than 20 to 45). Hollingworth reported the results of five tests, four of which (*completion, naming opposites, word building,* and *digit span*) revealed no age-related decline. On the other hand, the fifth test, *substitution,* which was said to require the establishment and exercise of new associations, did show evidence of age-related decline. Hollingworth also cited the master's essay of a former student who tested older adults (from ages 65 to 83) and compared these results to those obtained from testing much younger "army men." A similar mixed pattern of equivalent performance on some tests and age-related decline on others was obtained (Werner, 1924, as cited in Hollingworth, 1927). Still, Hollingworth found sufficient grounds for optimism, calling for more studies but asserting that "even if these tentative results point to the actual limitations to the establishment of new associations in age, *they do not yet prove that learning capacity ever completely ceases in the average case*" (Hollingworth, 1927, p. 312; italics added).*

Although other researchers of this era may not have been as theoretically prescient as Hollingworth, many of them conducted rather more memorable empirical investigations. Compared to Hollingworth, many of his contemporaries emphasized the empirical side of the study of life-span intelligence, and it is to these contributions that we now turn. From a perspective prepossessed by contemporary standards, it would be possible to critique these studies with respect to several methodological considerations (for example, experimental design, sampling). Nevertheless, we shall hold such critiques in abeyance and direct the interested reader to other reviews that address these issues more specifically (Baltes & Labouvie, 1973; Botwinick, 1977; Guilford, 1967; Jones, 1959; Schaie, 1979; Wechsler, 1958). In this section, our review is organized in roughly chronological fashion, an approach that corresponds to the use of cross-sectional and longitudinal designs, respectively.

Initial Empirical Investigations

Almost as soon as evidence pertaining to intellectual development throughout adulthood began to accumulate, commentators recognized theoretical, methodological, and interpretive problems that are of critical concern today. After reviewing a portion of the literature, Weisenburg, Roe, and McBride (1936) observed the following: (1) there was a notable inter-test variability in developmental trajectories, including wide variation in the ages at which various test performances reached their peak; (2) when there was decline, it occurred more slowly than did the corresponding growth curve; and (3) interindividual variations were large. Other reviewers of early work in this area reached similar conclusions, arguing, for example, for the consideration of life circumstances, real-life problem situations, and for the broadening of the concept of intelligence to incorporate the total matrix of psychological functioning, including personality

---

*Nevertheless, despite his own mixed pattern of results and the optimism apparent in this quotation, Hollingworth quoted with approval the words of Paton that "generally speaking, the acquisition of new facts and intellectual expansion in the individual do not continue after the fiftieth year" (Paton, as quoted by Hollingworth, 1927, p. 311).

and morality (Guilford, 1967; Jones, 1959; Pressey & Kuhlen, 1957; Wechsler, 1958).

Among the earliest pieces of evidence on which these initial judgments were made was a set of studies by Pressey (1917, 1919), which found positive adult age differences for a vocabulary test and negative age differences for a rote recall test (Pressey & Kuhlen, 1957). Other early age-comparative studies (for example, Beeson, 1920; Foster & Taylor, 1920) also found some stability in vocabulary measures, but considerable negative age differences for other abilities. Foster and Taylor (1920) accounted for the decrements by referring to such age-related performance factors as diminished familiarity, practice, and interest. Yerkes (1921, 1923) examined Army Alpha intelligence data for officers in World War I and found a gradual, apparently universal, age-related decline in performance across the adult life span. Nevertheless, Yerkes argued, older officers are selected because of their experience and command of specific knowledge domains.

The core of this period of research is formed, however, by an ensemble of three studies—Jones and Conrad (1933), Miles and Miles (1932), and Willoughby (1927). Willoughby's contribution, originally designed to be an analysis of family resemblance, was conducted with an academically highly selected sample and suffered from a high (almost 50%) refusal rate. Multiple intelligence tests were administered to 13-year-old school children and their families, and peak performances ranged from the ages of 17 to 27. Although the tests revealed variable growth and decline curves, there was less apparent age-related decrement—that is, the decline curves were not as sharp—for such tests of accumulated experience as vocabulary, science-nature information, and arithmetic reasoning. Those tests associated with the most rapid decline curves were number-series completion and analogies. Willoughby reasoned that performance on those tests associated with relatively slow growth and slow decline curves may result from life conditions disposing for continuous practice and effort.

Jones and Conrad (1933) administered the Army Alpha to inhabitants, ranging in age from 10 to 60, of small New England communities ($n = 1191$). Although a very gradual decline became evident in their early 20s, the authors reported that there was a similar, wide range of performance at all ages across the adult life span. In examining the diverse age trends in subtest performance, the authors reported that no age-related decline was found for tests of vocabulary or for general information, whereas evidence for the most severe decline was found for tests of analogies, common sense, and numerical completions. The overall performance decline rate was accelerated for those subjects who, failing to participate in the initial voluntary phase of testing, were contacted and tested in their own homes. This observation suggested to the authors that education and social status were important considerations in such sample selections. Moreover, Jones and Conrad concluded that, as Thorndike (1928) had already remarked, the most adverse effect of advancing age in adulthood is on "native capacity," "sheer modifiability," or, in more modern parlance, reserve capacity and plasticity. Finally, in addition to sampling problems, the authors discussed certain limitations of their conclusions and more general factors potentially influencing the interpretation of aging research. Prominent among these were age-related deficits in motivation, familiarity, sensory-motor functioning (eyesight, hearing), ability to work rapidly, and recency of educational experience.

Results similar to those of Jones and Conrad (1933) were obtained by Miles and Miles (1932). They, however, used a different test (Otis Self-Administering Test of Intelligence) and sampled a quite different population (urban California). They reported that peak performance occurred at around age 20 and thereafter a gradual decline was observed through the remainder of the life span (age range from 7–94; $n = 823$). This conclusion was supported in a later study in which there were approximately 250 adults over age 70 (Miles, 1934). Again, items rated as difficult—defined as those requiring speed or organization—were associated with steeper decline curves than were other items, such as those requiring verbal associations, generalizations, and interpretations. A note of optimism was sounded for those older adults who, declining slowly in overall functioning, were able to draw on their experience and continued to lead active and intellectually effective lives (Miles & Miles, 1932).

With only minor variations, other cross-sectional studies of this period reported similar results. Weisenberg et al. (1936) found only slight decrements for "language tests" and virtually no decline (to age 60) in vocabulary performance. Lorge (1936) also found negative age differences but, because of his design, was able to interpret them as primarily due to age-related deficits on speeded (rather than power) tests. In a learning study, Ruch (1934) found evidence for a decline in the ability to modify one's behavior (plasticity), and, although older subjects performed at lower levels than did younger adults on all tests, they did better, in comparison to younger subjects, on tasks with familiar content or which were related to long-established habits (see also Miles, 1933). In line with this familiar finding, Marsh (1933) reported that there was only a slight indication that aging was associated with a decline in adaptability.

An early version of what was to become the Wechsler Adult Intelligence Scale (WAIS) was used in a cross-sectional study of a stratified sample of New York adults (see Wechsler, 1939, 1955, 1958). For the first and the subsequent standardization studies, average scores rose rapidly until about age 20 and then gradually declined throughout the adult years. Considering the norms established by Doppelt and Wallace (1955), most cross-sectional studies using the WAIS have found less evidence for age-related decline for the verbal subtests (for example, information, vocabulary, comprehension, similarities) than for the nonverbal or performance subtests (for example, block design, picture arrangement, digit symbol substitution) (Berkowitz, 1953; Botwinick & Storandt, 1974; Wechsler, 1958).* This pattern, substantially replicated in West Germany (Riegel,

*It is worth noting that, in addition to the considerable empirical resources accruing to the WAIS, Wechsler's legacy to the study of adult intelligence includes contributions to at least two of the recent themes described at the beginning of the second section and noted repeatedly throughout the second and third sections. His definition of intelligence, however nonoperational, explicitly incorporates the notions of purposeful action and adaptiveness to the context. The sophistication of the WAIS, and of its component abilities, has lent an unmistakable measure of support to two of the general observations of life-span work in intelligence: that is, intelligence is composed of multiple mental abilities, each with its distinct life-course change patterns.

1958), is analogous to that obtained by many other researchers using different but parallel intelligence tests (see Botwinick, 1977; Salthouse, 1982).

The life-span cross-sectional investigations of intelligence conducted in subsequent decades (for example, Corsini & Fassett, 1953; Eisdorfer, Busse, & Cohen, 1959; Foulds & Raven, 1948; Raven, 1948; Schaie, 1958; Welford, 1958) testified further to a gradual decline picture of intelligence in adulthood. It should be evident, however, that even the early investigators did not promulgate blindly the decline model. Although precise methodological critiques of the cross-sectional design were not yet available, there were ample criticisms of other potential methodological flaws, as well as empirical evidence of stability, to at least extend the imagination of several observers (Bayley, 1955; Doppelt & Wallace, 1955; Jones, 1959; Jones & Conrad, 1933; Kuhlen, 1940; Weisenberg et al., 1936). These observers pointed to factors that, when viewed through the lens of what is presently known about research methodology, are at least consistent with arguments associated with cohort effects—that is, aging effects may be generated because of historically related differences among generations in educational and social experience. It was known, for example, that the results of cross-sectional studies could be vitiated by historical factors modifying not only the ability of successive cohorts, but also by performance factors such as motivation (Jones, 1959; Kuhlen, 1963).*

Thus, as the first longitudinal studies of adult intelligence began to be published in the 1950s, cross-sectional work, some results of which indeed challenged simple interpretations of aging decline, continued to appear. Demming and Pressey (1957), for example, informally surveyed everyday adult activities and then constructed tests, cast in colloquial language, designed to assess such matters of practical intelligence as knowledge of legal terms, occupations, how to use a telephone directory, and social manners and tact (see also Pressey & Kuhlen, 1957). On these tests, which Demming and Pressey referred to as indigenous to adult life, middle-aged and older adults performed better than younger adults. Pressey and Kuhlen (1957) go even further in arguing that an empirical approach sympathetic to the life experiences and distinctive abilities of middle-aged and older adults—abilities such as capacity for effective living, social perception and knowledge, foresight, carefulness, and broad understanding—might often reveal "growth" in the mature years.

Much of the controversy concerning the interpretation of cross-sectional investigations revolves around the issue of the nature of the test used. As Botwinick (1977) observed, the heart of the no-decline argument was that "appropriate" tests revealed little evidence of decline, even in cross-sectional studies. How tests come to be defined as "appropriate" seems to depend on more than simply theoretical or empirical information. Whereas some authors argued that power tests are more representative of adult intelligence (Corsini & Fassett, 1953; Green, 1969; Lorge, 1936), others argued that speeded performance tests are equally

---

*Recent evidence indicates that there has been indeed substantial malleability in American intelligence test scores since the early 1930s (Flynn, 1984). Whether it is real change or an artifact, mean intelligence test scores improved dramatically between 1932 and 1978.

important indicators (Birren, 1952; Botwinick & Storandt, 1973). The stakes in the controversy were not small; whereas the former were usually associated with patterns of intellectual stability, the latter were associated with patterns of decline (see Botwinick, 1977).

The Advent of Longitudinal Studies

Several longitudinal investigations of psychological development in adulthood began as either unpremeditated second-wave extensions of earlier cross-sectional studies or as long-term extensions of child studies. Because such unplanned follow-up studies are necessarily restricted by the characteristics of the original design, it is often difficult to improve them significantly by incorporating intervening methodological and theoretical advances. Of course, such complications also occur in planned long-term longitudinal investigations. In principle, the advantage of observing intraindividual change accrues to longitudinal studies in general, whether they are planned initially or not.

In any event, because of their own inherent biases, longitudinal designs may have contributed to the frequent observation of positive age-change functions (see, for example, Baltes, Reese, & Nesselroade, 1977; Nesselroade & Baltes, 1979; Schaie, 1983b). In aging research such sampling biases as the twin concerns of selective sampling and selective dropout are prominent (Baltes, Schaie, & Nardi, 1971; Jarvik & Falek, 1963; Riegel & Riegel, 1972). In brief, subjects volunteering to participate in longitudinal studies and continuing participation are those who perform at relatively higher levels. Obviously, such factors may influence results and conclusions in a deleterious manner. In addition to issues of sampling and dropout, single-cohort longitudinal designs are subject to other threats to both internal validity and external validity. Internal validity is threatened by retest effects (practice, reactivity). Retest effects in intelligence research with adults can be sizable (for example, Hofland, Willis, & Baltes, 1981; Willis, Blieszner, & Baltes, 1981). With respect to external validity, the major issue is one of cohort generalizability (Salthouse, 1982; Schaie, 1983b). Again, because reviews of these issues are plentiful, we shall attend to substantive results of selected early longitudinal studies, with methodological comments noted *passim*, rather than focusing specific attention on them.

It should be noted, then, that early longitudinal studies documented the existence of some stability patterns, and even the recurring appearance of continued growthlike curves, throughout the adult years. As we have seen, cross-sectional investigations presented an overall picture of gradual intellectual decline, but this research was not without evidence for stability and, indeed, progression. Although interpretations of the matter have varied (Bayley, 1955; Botwinick, 1967, 1977; Jones, 1959), this early longitudinal research did not conflict completely with many of the conclusions emerging from the cross-sectional literature. The difference is more one of weight—due to the presumed superiority of longitudinal designs—than one of basic discrepancy. Longitudinal evidence accumulated that improvement on intelligence tests could be found through early adulthood (Bayley, 1955, with notable interindividual differences; see also Bradway, Thompson, & Cravens, 1958), as well as throughout middle and old age (Bayley & Oden, 1955, with gifted adults; Nisbet, 1957; Owens, 1953; Rudinger & Lantermann, 1980).

Bayley and Oden (1955) retested subjects of the Terman Study of Gifted Children, a sample ranging in age from approximately 20 to 50. Using a revision of the Concept Mastery Test, a difficult verbal measure, the scores of all five-year age groups increased at the second wave, 12 years after the first. Like the Bayley and Oden study, which targeted gifted adults, Nisbet (1957) administered a verbal skills test (Simplex Group Test) to talented individuals (graduate students) on two occasions, one during graduate school and one 24 years later when all subjects were in their late 40s. Again, positive age changes were found. Both of these studies used well-educated or gifted adults, most of whom were intellectually active between the measurements. In addition to the common problem of a highly selective sample, both studies employed verbal skill measures, performance on which, even in cross-sectional studies, rarely declines significantly until very late in the life span. Finally, both studies were limited because the age range covered was only from young to middle adulthood. None of these criticisms, of course, is necessarily a serious flaw. Some similar results have been found in average or below-average adults (Charles, 1953; Thompson, 1951), but it is not always replicated (Tuddenham, Blumenkranz, & Wilkin, 1968).

Thirty-one years after the first wave of data collection, Owens (1953) readministered the Army Alpha intelligence test to 127 of the 363 original male subjects (see also Cunningham & Owens, 1983; McHugh & Owens, 1954). The original sample was drawn from the freshman class of Iowa State College in 1919. When they were retested, at an average age of 50, their overall scores were found to have improved (by .55 standard deviations). It should be noted that, with the same test, a similar difference, but in the opposite direction, was found in the cross-sectional study of Jones and Conrad (1933), a difference Jones (1959) attributes in part to differences in initial ability levels of the two samples. Specifically, Owens found that overall stability or gain was a function of seven of the eight subtests, but especially attributable to four verbal (information, vocabulary, practical judgment, disarranged sentences) subtests. Although the 31-year interval makes it impossible to identify whether the improvement occurred gradually or during (for example) the college years (length of college attendance was positively related to amount of improvement), it is not exposed to the typical threat of practice effects. All second-wave participants were volunteers. Most of the remaining original participants could not be located or were deceased and the resultant sampling bias has been discussed (Jones, 1959).

Owens (1966; see also Cunningham & Owens, 1983) retested about 75% of the second sample in 1961, approximately 11 years after the first retesting, as the subjects were entering their 60s. Compared to the second occasion, only one of the verbal subtests (vocabulary) continued to gain. Of the three factors abstracted from them one mean (numerical) declined significantly, one (verbal) declined slightly (although it remained at a level higher than that on the first occasion), and one (relations) continued to gain. In an additional analysis, Owens compared the scores of a new student sample in 1961 to those of the original 1919 sample. He found that the more recent sample scored better than the original sample, a result he attributed to the impact of historical and cultural change (Cunningham & Birren, 1976; Cunningham & Owens, 1983; Flynn, 1984).

Certainly not all of the early longitudinal studies reported unambiguous positive age changes, or even stability, in late adulthood. Jarvik, Kallmann, and Falek (1962) tested older (age > 60) pairs of twins on three occasions at intervals of about one and seven years. Overall, the means of the scores improved at the first retesting, a gain the authors attributed to practice effects. At the second retesting the verbal subtests revealed stable performance curves, whereas the speeded tests showed evidence of decline. At a later 12-year follow-up, the performance of the subjects (who were now over 80) declined in all subtests except for vocabulary (Blum, Jarvik, & Clark, 1970). General maintenance of nonspeeded intellectual performance through the 70s was observed, with performance on speeded tasks falling off rather earlier. It is impossible to overlook the similarity of this pattern of results to that suggested by many cross-sectional and even longitudinal studies; this bifurcation for normal subjects is what Botwinick (1977) termed the *classic intellectual aging pattern.*

The extension of this pattern—and indeed the very possibility of stability or progression—is problematic when the very late years of life are considered (Blum, Fosshage, & Jarvik, 1972; Jarvik & Bank, 1983) or when nonnormal adults are tested (Berkowitz & Green, 1963). In both cases firm evidence for decrements have been found, evidence emanating from both verbal and performance test results. As the human organism approaches the limits of life and the limits of survival, as the organism must cope with progressively more serious biological deterioration (for example, in oxygen supply and detrimental chemical changes), and environmental insults, performance on psychometric intelligence tests becomes increasingly difficult (and perhaps irrelevant) to sustain. For whatever reason, it is possible that under extreme conditions intellectual performance may decline ineluctably. In the following section we shall examine several recent programs of research bearing upon this and other issues in the life-span development of intelligence.

THE TALE RETOLD: PROGRAMS AND ISSUES

It should be clear by now that several investigators throughout the history of research in life-span intellectual development would agree with Guilford's (1967) comment that the study of intelligence throughout adulthood presents many unusual difficulties "owing to the multitude of variations in life circumstances that interfere with experimental control" (p. 461). Many would indeed go further and argue that these variable life circumstances affect not just experimental control, but the very process of intelligence itself. Indeed, although they are

variable both across- and within-cohorts in their occurrence, timing, norma-
tiveness, and salience, such circumstances and events are an integral part of any
portrayal of overall intellectual development. Nevertheless, as we shall see in
the present section, this not-so-recently promulgated posture is, like the nature
of the evidence itself, subject to some debate in the contemporary literature.

The primary purposes of the present section are threefold. We first review
two of the major programs of research in intellectual development in adulthood.
Here the intent is to summarize the most prominent results and emerging interpretations. Second, we shift our focus from this descriptive work to intervention
research: why it has been conducted, and what it may contribute to our understanding of intellectual aging. Third, we identify selected continuing (unresolved or controversial) issues in the investigation of adult intelligence. We shall
concentrate less on criticizing the present state of affairs and more on (1) how
current thinking is not entirely disjunctive with past conceptions, and (2) what
current thinking suggests for the future understanding of mental development
in adulthood.

Schaie's Seattle Longitudinal Study

In 1956, K.W. Schaie began a carefully designed and exhaustive longitudinal
and cohort-sequential study of intelligence in adulthood (Schaie, 1979; Schaie,
1983a). Schaie administered Thurstone's test of five Primary Mental Abilities
(PMA—1948 version; Thurstone & Thurstone, 1949) and additional intelligence-
related measures to an initial sample of some 500 community-dwelling adult
subjects (carefully stratified and ranging in age from 20 to 70). This first cross-
sectional study, following a pilot age-comparison study indicating age-related
decrements in all five PMA tests beginning by age 60 (Schaie, Rosenthal, &
Perlman, 1953), found relatively late peaks for three of the tests (verbal, word
fluency, and, especially, number, which did not peak until 46–50) and peaks in
the 20s for the reasoning and space tests (Schaie, 1958). Beginning at about age
60, negative age-differences in performance were observed across all five tests
(Schaie, 1958), a pattern that remained unchanged even when the effects of
covariates, such as income and education, were considered (Schaie, 1959).

A second wave of data was collected in 1963, seven years after the original
cross-sectional investigation. While 60.6% of the original sample were retested,
a new random sample covering the original age range (20–70), as well as a new
random sample comparable in age to the oldest members of the original sample,
were also tested. The addition of these two new samples—a scheme similar to
that of Owens (1966) which was done in 1961, and attributed by Schaie (1979)
to Kuhlen's (1940, 1963) work on disentangling ontogenetic and sociocultural
changes—provided Schaie with an empirically rich and theoretically provocative
data set. This eventually led to the generation of strategies specifically designed
to regulate and measure the differential effects of age and cohort (Baltes, 1968;
Riley, Johnson, & Foner, 1972; Ryder, 1965; Schaie, 1965; Schaie & Baltes,
1975).

The cross-sectional findings in 1963 were quite similar to those reported in 1956, except that the level of performance in all but the word fluency test was noticeably higher at the later testing. At the same time, the longitudinal results suggested general stability in performance (on all but the word fluency test) until the 60s (Schaie & Strother, 1968a, 1968b). In accordance with Schaie (1965), the cross-sequential method, which at that time was thought to provide a means of contrasting the effects of age changes (as indicated in repeated measures designs) and age differences (as cohort differences, such as those obtained in cross-sectional designs), was applied. These results suggested that, at least until about age 50, a substantial portion of the age differences often found in cross-sectional studies was actually due to cohort effects (Nesselroade, Schaie, & Baltes, 1972; Schaie & Strother, 1968a, 1968b). That is, the decline in intellectual functioning suggested by many cross-sectional studies is not as universal as is often presumed. These data indicate that such observed age differences may be in part a function of cultural and historical differences (as represented in cohort differences), and not entirely due to universal ontogenetic functions.

A third wave of data was collected in 1970, 14 years after the original testing (32.4% of the 1956 panel, and 42.0% of the 1963 panel were retested). Again, new random samples were drawn from what was presumed to be the same parent population. Extending the results from the second wave, it was found that there were successively higher mean test scores for the independent cross-sectional samples as the time of measurement became more recent, again pointing to the effects of sociocultural change (Schaie, Labouvie, & Buech, 1973). The results of the 14-year longitudinal study (Schaie & Labouvie-Vief, 1974) and of the cohort-sequential study—in which two independent seven-year longitudinal change studies are compared (longitudinal sequences), which is more appropriate than the cross-sequential design for separating age and cohort (see Schaie & Baltes, 1975; Schaie & Parham, 1977)—generally replicated the earlier results.

These results substantiated the position that cohort differences exert profound effects in observed patterns of intellectual development in adulthood. The source of these cohort effects remains undetermined. Substantively, the 14-year longitudinal analysis found reliable decrements before age 60 only for word fluency, and indeed a reliable increment in verbal meaning to age 39. Finally, certain aspects of life circumstances (noted at the outset of this section as important features of intellectual development) and their influence on intellectual development were examined. Some evidence was found for an indirect causal effect of cardiovascular disease (Hertzog, Schaie, & Gribbin, 1978) and certain elements (for example, social deprivation) of the family environment (Gribbin, Schaie, & Parham, 1975).

The discord surrounding these results has been notable (Baltes & Schaie, 1976; Botwinick, 1977; Horn & Donaldson, 1976; Schaie & Baltes, 1977). The controversy stems primarily from (1) Schaie's interpretation of stability in most functions through middle age, (2) the relative emphasis placed on cohort effects in the interpretation of the age/cohort relationship, and (3) the interpretation of the apparent ameliorative effects of intervention. Especially pertinent is the use of the cross-sequential design, which is ill-suited for assessing age changes. Specifically, reanalyses of Schaie's data seemed to uncover rather more evidence of age-related decline (as well as earlier onset) in intellectual functioning than had been indicated in the original research reports (for example, Horn & Donaldson, 1976). Botwinick (1977; see also Schaie, 1979) argued that Schaie's data supported his own claim that, in general, there are no major differences in the results of such cross-sectional and longitudinal studies. The questions pertaining to the empirical evidence may be settled in part through the development of additional data sets supplementing the (1956, 1963, 1970) cohort-sequential arrangement in the form of extended longitudinal sequences (Schaie, 1983a).

In 1977, 21 years after the start of the study, a fourth wave of data was collected. Schaie and Hertzog (1983) have reported the first results from this wave in the form of 14-year cohort sequential analyses. Thus two independent longitudinal samples were considered (longitudinal sequences), the first comprised of those subjects tested in 1956, 1963, and 1970, and the second comprised of those subjects tested in 1963, 1970, and 1977. Unlike the earlier studies, these results indicated the existence of reliable decrements on some PMA tests beginning in the decade prior to age 60, and decidedly clear evidence for decline on all PMA tests after age 60.

The authors remark, however, that the decrements observed should be seen in the context of their other findings. The decrements in the 50s are small enough to be of little practical importance, whereas the decrements observed in old age (60–80) are of considerably more salience, partly because performance declines on a similar order of magnitude across all PMA tests (including verbal meaning) (see also Schaie, 1983a). Furthermore, the authors emphasize that there are not only sex differences present in the data, but also large interindividual performance differences across the 14-year longitudinal sequences. Indeed, up to age 70 there are still some subjects who do not decline at all (Schaie, 1983a). Finally, it is important to consider that cohort differences for same-age older adults (for example, age 70) are of a magnitude comparable to that of the observed age-related decrements. Such a finding lends some support to the interpretation that what is seen in descriptive aging research as decline may be, at least in part, a reflection of age differences in social and environmental opportunities (Baltes, 1984), a position echoing the remarks of some of the earliest commentators (for example, Sanford, 1902).

Horn and Cattell: Fluid and Crystallized Intelligence

Horn and Cattell (1966) (see also Horn, 1980, 1982; Horn & Donaldson, 1976) have offered an alternative view of the "classic aging pattern" described by Botwinick (1977). The classic aging pattern is based on a series of cross-sectional results (including those of Horn & Cattell, 1967), which indicate higher (and more stable) performance in late adulthood in verbal than in nonverbal intelligence tests. Compared to Schaie's cohort-sequential arrangement and investment in systematic longitudinal data collection, the empirical contribution to the model of Horn and Cattell is less complete. The model itself, however, is conceptually attractive and ambitious.

Arguing that it is premature to identify a set of primary mental abilities, Horn and Cattell (1966) generated a set of second-order factors most prominently represented by the abilities termed *fluid* and *crystallized intelligence* (see also Cattell, 1943, 1963, 1971; Horn, 1978). *Fluid intelligence* reflects the level of intellectual competence associated with casual (formerly termed incidental) learning processes and assessed by performance on novel, usually nonverbal tests. *Crystallized intelligence*, on the other hand, reflects intellectual competence associated with intentional learning processes and is assessed by measures of acculturated knowledge and skills, such as most verbal tests.

Horn's alternative version of the "classic aging pattern" takes the following shape. Crystallized intelligence, because it is indexed by the life-long accumulation of cultural knowledge, usually increases over the adult years. Fluid intelligence is more dependent on physiological functioning and especially on the support of a relatively determinate neurological base. If this neurological base, which is continually subject to change, is impaired, the ability to perform the associated intellectual skills is undermined. Furthermore, the growth of the cognitive competence associated with crystallized intelligence may also contribute to the eventual age-related decline in fluid performance levels. Thus the functional prediction is that, from a peak in late adolescence, fluid intelligence will decline throughout the adult years, whereas crystallized intelligence will evince progressive increases in performance levels throughout adulthood (Horn, 1970, 1978; Horn & Cattell, 1966, 1967).

Although the data base for the support of this theory is clearly not as rich as, for example, Schaie's cohort-sequential longitudinal study, it has unquestionably moved the conceptualization of adult intellectual development forward. It appears to some observers to provide a certain rationale for the verbal-nonverbal distinction (of the classic aging pattern), but the distinction between these two representations of the cross-sectional data base should not be lost. In principle, it is possible to conceptualize a critical experiment, but, to date, pertinent data are lacking. Also lacking are details concerning the mechanics of the relationship between, for example, the neurological base and fluid intelligence on the one hand, and experience and crystallized intelligence on the other. In the absence of such hypothesized mechanisms suitable empirical work may not be immediately forthcoming.

In the final section of this chapter, in which we discuss several alternative conceptions of adult intelligence, we describe one way of conceptually unpacking crystallized intelligence. Viewing the phenomenon circumscribed by crystallized intelligence through the lens of recent process-oriented work on knowledge systems may prove to be more theoretically fertile. That is, it is important to consider not only the amount of accumulated knowledge as indicated by traditional psychometric instruments, but also the amount of knowledge in specific domains and the ability to mobilize that knowledge in relevant problem-solving situations. Such a perspective may hold promise also for further advances in understanding the verbal component of the classic aging pattern.

Intervention Research

Although this review has concentrated thus far on primarily descriptive work, an important aspect of the intellectual aging research scene, especially since the early 1970s, has been intervention (Baltes, 1973; Denney, 1979; Sterns & Sanders, 1980; Willis, in press; Woodruff, 1982). It is possible that much of the extant variation in the interpretation of the descriptive work can be assigned to contrasting accounts of both the evidence for age-related decline (or stability) and the purported demonstrations of intraindividual plasticity as a result of both naturally occurring experiential differences and concerted efforts at intervention. As we have seen, there is considerable descriptive evidence against a universal and irreversible decline model of intellectual aging. If experiential differences (for example, those associated with cohort) are in part responsible for observed interindividual and inter-task performance differences, then the programmatic manipulation of specific experiences may have the effect of enhancing specific performances. Such manipulations may take the form of practice, modeling, education, training, or other techniques of ecological intervention.

The effect of further educational experience on the intellectual performance of adults has been of interest since the dawn of the empirical era of life-span intelligence (Snow, 1982; Sorenson, 1933; Thorndike, 1928; Willis, in press). From the beginning it was suggested that continued intellectual activity—for example, continued involvement in professional training, as well as continued efforts to develop or maintain widely applicable heuristics—might mitigate some of the otherwise "naturally occurring" effects of age-related intellectual decline. An experimental model—an interest in manipulation, contrasted with pure observation or description—was implicated and, given some limitations of the extant scientific context, pursued.* The history of programmatic educational intervention in late adulthood is spotted at best, and that which is available reaches but a small, positively biased proportion of older adults (Willis, in press). To the extent that such programmatic efforts are successful in facilitating long-term adaptation to the cognitive demands of aging, arguments for the plasticity of intellectual aging are enhanced. To date, the evidence for such long-term, generalized effects is meager.

Nevertheless, suggestive results of more specific research on short-term intraindividual variability in life-span intellectual performance have appeared. This

*Whether—as was alluded to in an earlier section of this chapter—this effort was a function of the investigators' desire to make older adults behave/perform more like younger adults or whether the motivation stemmed from other (for example, academic, altruistic) sources cannot be answered (then, as now) with certainty. In this subsection we are concerned with the second of these motivational streams, that is, the use of experimental intervention to understand better the processes involved in intellectual aging (Baltes & Goulet, 1971).

training research has examined the modifiability, flexibility, and plasticity of intelligence in late adulthood as a function of a given experimental treatment. One such treatment, associated with the experiential deficits argument previously cited, is that of test practice: that is, perhaps some of the observed age-related performance differences may be accounted for by the fact that older adults are less knowledgeable of, familiar with, and practiced at taking psychometric tests. In general, older adults who have practiced taking standard psychometric and cognitive tests are differentiated from those who have not (Baltes & Willis, 1982; Denney, 1979, 1982; Jones, 1959; Kamin, 1957; Rabbitt, 1982; Taub, 1973). Intraindividually, continued increments in performance across multiple occasions as a function of practice have been found, even in such fluid intelligence measures as induction and figural relations (Hofland, Willis, & Baltes, 1981; Plemons, Willis, & Baltes, 1978).

Indeed, fluid intelligence, which is thought to be associated with inevitable age-related decline, has been the target of a series of studies investigating the potential intraindividual psychometric performance variability of older adults (see Baltes & Willis, 1982; Willis, in press). In these studies older adults (average age approximately 70) displayed and maintained improvement in performance levels due to training in ability-specific reasoning over multiple occasions (across several months). As the authors of these studies had predicted, differential transfer of training effects were observed; that is, they found near transfer within the target dimension, and not far transfer, for example, to indices of crystallized intelligence (Baltes, Dittmann-Kohli, & Kliegl, 1985; Baltes & Willis, 1982; Blieszner, Willis, & Baltes, 1981; Willis, Blieszner, & Baltes, 1981). Despite the fact that such a restricted range of transfer effects were predicted by the investigators, the absence of far transfer may also be of theoretical interest (Birren, Cunningham, & Yamamoto, 1982). Parenthetically, it may be noted that the contrast between these two positions on transfer of training effects reiterates a long-standing debate in educational psychology (for example, Thorndike & Woodworth, 1901). As is the case with descriptive work, training studies using traditional psychometric tests that fail to demonstrate either transfer to, or a predictive relationship with, other domains of intelligent behavior (for example, to nonexperimental, everyday, practical performance situations) are often called on to show theoretical relevance or power in other ways. Equally important (and as yet unexamined) is the question of whether such improved posttest performance is a better predictor of intelligent behavior in nonexperimental situations than is pretest performance.

The theoretical contribution of such research, however, is more evident. Overall, the magnitude of observed improvement due to practice and training in ability-specific reasoning is approximately one standard deviation. As shown in Figure 1, this amount of improvement is roughly equivalent to the amount of the 21-year longitudinal decrement in older adults (as observed by Schaie & Hertzog, 1983). Although it is impossible to compare precisely these two sets of results, it is conceivable that observed age-related decline in psychometric test performance—even in performance on dimensions predicted to decline ine-

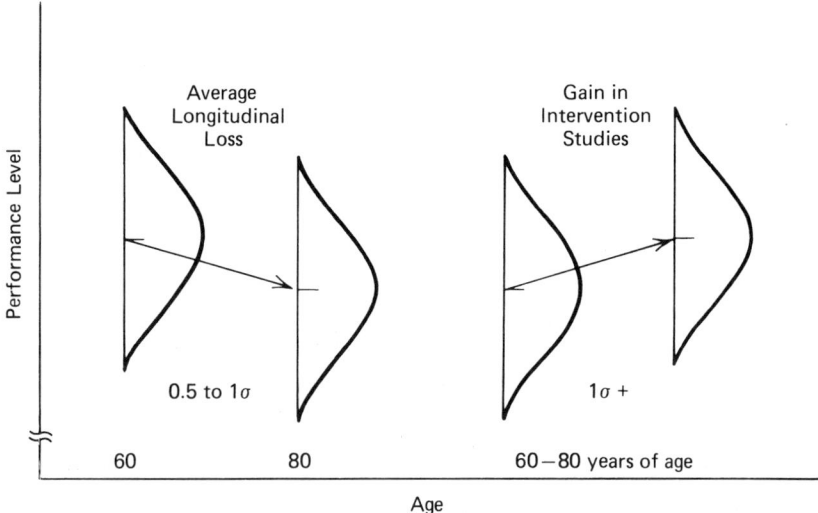

Figure 1. Fluid intelligence: average aging loss (descriptive) and magnitude of gain following training. (Source: Baltes et al., 1984.)

luctably—is potentially modifiable. More specifically, in late adulthood age and cohort effects may be mitigated as a function of (1) specific training and (2) the individuals' reserve capacity. Two important questions in cognitive training research have not yet been resolved. First, it is not known whether younger adults would display similar gain patterns. Second, it is open to question whether the gains observed in older adults reflect reactivation of previously existing levels of performance or whether they involve learning of new cognitive skills as well (Baltes et al., 1985).

Moderate levels of success in cognitive training in adulthood have been found also in the problem-solving and neo-Piagetian literatures (Denney, 1979; Hornblum & Overton, 1976; Labouvie-Vief, 1976; Willis, in press). Similar to the psychometric research, specific training on specific abilities often results in short-term specific improvements for older adults. Overall, psychometric and cognitive training work has both methodological implications and theoretical overtones. Methodologically, if age changes can be manipulated or simulated then it renders the yeoman efforts involved in conducting long-term longitudinal studies, such as Schaie's (1983), important but not absolutely critical. Theoretically, if reliable intraindividual variability in late adulthood can be demonstrated on a variety of both "pure" and ecologically relevant tasks, then the generalizability of the decrement model of intellectual aging is further called into question.

The effect of supplemental experience in ameliorating intellectual performance (and, especially, adaptiveness) in older adults is an enduring issue in the study of life-span intelligence. Furthermore, it represents a pivotal aspect of the contrasting accounts of intellectual development in adulthood (Wolman, 1982).

Continuing Issues

Botwinick (1977) has argued that the depictions of intellectual development generated from cross-sectional data are only quantitatively (and not qualitatively) different from those derived from longitudinal data (see also Salthouse, 1982). Aside from the added perspective of intervention research, our argument is similar, but extends somewhat deeper: we suggest that, despite apparently refined designs and methods of analysis, the data base is interpreted in similar ways partly because of continuity in other fundamental dimensions. We have mentioned these dimensions at several junctures throughout the present chapter; indeed, we have employed one contemporary view (but we could have chosen others) as the vortex of our discussion. This view described the contemporary literature in the form of four generalizations or abstractions: namely, multidimensionality, multidirectionality, interindividual variability, and intraindividual plasticity (Baltes & Willis, 1979; Willis & Baltes, 1980). In this chapter we have focused some attention on the precursors to the literature from which these abstractions were derived. In so doing, we have found, at the very least, isolated instances of similar notions appearing in several historical and intellectual contexts.

The inescapable conclusion is that, whether based on no formal data or cross-sectional data or longitudinal data, these (or similar) abstractions regarding the nature of mature intelligence have been derived from either casual observation or from a similar definitional and conceptual system. Indeed, we have seen how, from a variety of sources (not all of which were primarily psychometric), many definitions of intelligence have converged on one or more of such themes as multidimensionality, multidirectionality, interindividual variability, and functional activity. That such themes reappear in contemporary settings (for example, Baltes et al., 1984; Belmont, 1983; Berg & Sternberg, 1983; Dittmann-Kohli & Baltes, in press; Hunt, 1982, 1983; Labouvie-Vief, in press; Sternberg, 1980; Wechsler, 1975) is not to discredit contemporary writers any more than it is to credit their predecessors. One interpretation—that the study of the life-span development of intelligence, and its parent field, the psychology of intelligence, has not moved very far—is arguable, but not as important, perhaps, as the question of what comes next. In this realm there appears to have been some movement, and perhaps this movement is in the forward direction. In the remainder of the present subsection, we shall identify some of the recurring issues in this area of study that, because they are recurring and seem to reach deeply into the heart of the matter, have led to the formulation of some of the alternative approaches described in the following section.

Age- and Cohort-Appropriate Tests. The discussion of this issue, as the discussions of most issues in this chapter, should begin with a brief glance backward. As we have already commented, the appropriateness issue pertains both to arguments within the psychometric tradition (regarding the relative suitability of power or speeded tests in the study of aging) and to debates concerning the legitimacy of applying psychometric tests designed for adolescents or young adults to aging samples. Considering the latter topic first, Pressey and Kuhlen (1957) called for a testing approach that is sympathetic to the distinctive life demands and abilities of older adults, in the same manner that cross-cultural cognitive and intellectual testing must be conducted (see also Baltes & Willis, 1979; Jones, 1959). In support of this argument they cite an exploratory study (Demming & Pressey, 1957) in which older adults performed better than younger adults on tests of activities indigenous to adulthood (practical intelligence). Indeed, Hilgard (1948) had already suggested that in learning studies some attention be devoted to ecologically relevant problem situations.

Nevertheless, attempts to develop such real-world problem solving and intelligence tests, and to apply them to older adults, have not been entirely successful. Furthermore, contrary to the results obtained by Demming and Pressey (1957; see also Gardner & Monge, 1977), few have demonstrated unquestionable indications of stability or growth in performance in late adulthood (for example, Burton & Joel, 1945; Jones & Conrad, 1933). More recently, efforts to distinguish practical and academic intelligence have focused on (1) differences in the ecological or adaptive relevance of the problems, (2) relatively low correlations between academic intelligence and indicators of real-world success, and (3) differences in the range of psychological resources (for example, motivation, interest, coping strategies, cognitive process involvement) brought to bear on the problem (Berg & Sternberg, 1983; Charlesworth, 1976; Cornelius & Kenney, 1982; Neisser, 1976; Wagner & Sternberg, 1984). It is apparent that the content of traditional psychometric tests is generally unfamiliar to older adults (especially fluid intelligence tasks) (Cornelius, 1984). One reason for this unfamiliarity is that these tests are designed to assess intellectual functioning as defined by school-related criteria.

Schaie (1978) and colleagues (Popkin, Schaie, & Krauss, 1983), adopting an approach from within the psychometric tradition, have identified several features of standard instruments that may present test-taking difficulties for older adults; for example, small type size, and complexity of directions, demands, and answer sheets. In an initial effort to construct an "age-fair" psychometric instrument, Popkin et al. (1983) adapted the PMA for use with older adults by enlarging the type size and decreasing the complexity of presentation. Some evidence was obtained that performance factors (unrelated to the cognitive operations underlying intelligent behavior) were minimized with this test. Such an approach is, of course, addressed to minimizing age-related performance factors associated with traditional psychometric tests, rather than to postulating age-fair alternative formulations of intelligent behavior and generating complementary measurement instruments.

Within the psychometric tradition the issue of whether power tests are better indicators of adult intelligence than are speeded tests has been raised (Birren, 1952; Botwinick, 1977; Botwinick & Storandt, 1973; Corsini & Fassett, 1953; Green, 1969; Lorge, 1936). The question, in other words, is whether it is more or less appropriate in aging research to produce individual differences that are a function of the difficulty of the test (power) or the ability to solve problems quickly (speed). It is abundantly clear, for example, that the version of the PMA used by Schaie in his 21-year longitudinal study is weighted on the side of high speed (and low power). Appropriate data to address the question of the validity of the Schaie results (for example, a comparable design using a low speed and high power test) are simply not available. Schaie (1978, 1979) acknowledges this potential limitation and, as have others (for example, Baltes & Willis, 1979), called for more studies of the efficiency of instruments to assess the construct of intelligence throughout adulthood. As Schaie (1979) argues, there is a "need for a new series of investigations which will link both the present and ecologically more defensible tasks to multiple situational criteria of relevance in the last third of life" (p. 107).

The Role of Cognitive Skills. If mental testing had developed differently after Binet, the relationship between psychometric performance and the underlying cognitive skills might not be one of the leading continuing issues in intelligence research in general, and in life-span work in particular (Resnick, 1976; Tyler, 1976). Binet's early emphasis on processes underlying intelligent behavior and his less quantitative view of mental test performance, however, did not continue to inform the emerging field of psychometric mental testing.* Nor did the early cognitive psychologists attend to issues of measurement in a way acceptable to psychometricians. It is well known that bridging the subsequent division between experimental psychology (which concentrates on variance among treatments) and correlational or psychometric psychology (which concentrates on variance among organisms) is as important to initiate as it is difficult to consummate (Anastasi, 1983; Cronbach, 1957, 1975; Resnick, 1976).

In life-span intelligence research it is imperative not only to describe interindividual or intraindividual differences in performance, but also to examine the processes presumably underlying those differences. The emphasis in our discussion has been on the descriptive facts regarding inter- and intraindividual differences in intellectual performance. Such facts do not address, nor allow for inferences regarding, the relative status of the cognitive processes involved in that performance. Consequently, the processes that either support or fail to support intellectual stability throughout the adult years have not been identified.

Research on plasticity (described previously) represents one effort to move in the direction of identifying relevant factors or variables involved in regulation of performance. Such an approach, however, is often insufficiently grounded in cognitive theory. Another approach is to focus directly on the cognitive processes involved in intellectual functioning. Holding special promise, perhaps, is the cognitive components approach (Berg & Sternberg, 1983; Kliegl & Baltes, 1984; Pellegrino & Glaser, 1979; Sternberg, 1980, 1981, 1983), which attempts to decompose the tasks of intelligence tests into their component processes, and investigate these processes via methods normally identified with experimental

---

*This occurred, as Matarazzo (1972) pointed out, partly because of pressing social contingencies, such as the need to evaluate and classify large numbers of World War I recruits.

psychology (but see also Neisser, 1983). As applied to life-span research, one goal would be to recover the information-processing components of intelligence test performance and to identify those components associated with age-related change. Such a componential analysis may contribute to the understanding of the classic aging pattern described above; that is, it may shed light on why some dimensions of intelligence appear to decline with advancing age and why others appear to remain stable, and, furthermore, why there are substantial interindividual differences in change profiles. In any event, whether one pursues a cognitive components approach, applies another programmatic cognitive approach (such as that associated with Hunt, 1978, 1982, 1983; or that of Carroll & Maxwell, 1979) to the study of aging, or follows up one of the occasional nonprogrammatic efforts (for example, Cornelius, Willis, Nesselroade, & Baltes, 1983; Hultsch, Hertzog, & Dixon, 1984), the role of information-processing skills involved in intelligence test performance is a topic of considerable importance. In the long run, cross-domain information on the relationship between cognitive processes and psychometric constructs, especially with regard to their potentially changing relationship across the life span, is a necessary precursor to the understanding of intelligent behavior as both product and process.

Additional Issues.   Several additional continuing issues should be mentioned in passing. Most have been at least identified in the previous sections. For example, the methodological question of *research design* (cross-sectional, longitudinal, sequential) was previously addressed (see also Baltes & Labouvie, 1973; Baltes et al., 1977), as well as the accompanying issue of the age-cohort relationship. Similarly, we have alluded to the issue of such potentially confounding *performance factors* as motivational level, fatigue, and practice (see also Furry & Baltes, 1973; Hoyer, Labouvie, & Baltes, 1973; Kamin, 1957; Salthouse, 1982), as well as such ancillary individual differences as health status and life style (Gribbin et al., 1975; Hertzog et al., 1978). Another important (and continuing) issue is the *prediction of later by earlier ability levels* (for example, Botwinick, 1977; McCall, 1979; Owens, 1959; Riegel & Riegel, 1972). In adulthood there is virtually no evidence to support the contention that the initially higher ability adults continue to gain as compared to their lower ability counterparts. Indeed, some evidence of extreme group regression to the mean has been found (Baltes, Nesselroade, Schaie, & Labouvie, 1972; Nesselroade, Stigler, & Baltes, 1980).

Together, these six issues—training, age-appropriate tests, the role of cognitive skills, research design, performance factors, and prediction of later by earlier levels—represent both the past and the future of life-span intelligence research. Although not all of them are relevant to any given research effort, it is difficult to imagine a study (past or present) that safely avoids them all. Some of them— perhaps the three we have chosen to highlight (namely, training, age-appropriate tests, and the role of cognitive skills)—may provide fertile sources for future research. Certainly, it is in part because of some of these recurring issues, or at least as a function of addressing them, that the alternative approaches described in the following section were articulated. It is to a selective overview of three of these alternative approaches to life-span intelligence research that we now turn.

ALTERNATIVE CONCEPTIONS OF INTELLECTUAL DEVELOPMENT

In this section we present three alternative conceptions of intellectual development in adulthood: (1) an interdisciplinary framework from which a dual-process model is generated, (2) a generalized effort to focus on some forms of intellectual phenomena that may be resistant to decline or may be selected for in the adaptive context of the mature years (e.g., expertise and wisdom), and (3) a programmatic effort to extend cognitive structuralism from childhood and adolescence into adulthood.

An Interdisciplinary Framework

Throughout this chapter we have referred to four abstractions derived from the literature on the life-span development of intelligence. These abstractions—multidimensionality, multidirectionality, interindividual variability, and intraindividual plasticity—are thought to represent both the extant data base and to have considerable historical precedent. Recently, we have proceeded to formulate propositions that focus directly on the dynamic interplay between growth, decline, and stability, and, at the same time, promote further understanding of intelligence during adulthood and old age. This effort has led to the generation of eight propositions that are based on a review of a wider range of information (Baltes et al., 1984). These propositions are designed to integrate the data base at a somewhat lower level of analysis than were the four abstractions, and at the same time provide a more thorough foundation for the delineation of one alternative approach to intellectual development in adulthood.

By distinguishing between capacity and performance (Baltes et al., 1984; Fries & Crapo, 1981), the first three propositions maintain as follows: (1) there is stability in capacity for "average" intellectual functioning until the 60s; (2) nevertheless, there are some dimensions of intellectual ability that may show decided decrements, particularly in very difficult performance situations; and (3) there is at the same time some suggestive (but not conclusive) evidence for intellectual progression continuing in some individuals through even late adulthood. In each of the instances described by the first three propositions, there is marked interindividual variability in onset, rate, and patterning. The fourth and fifth propositions were derived from the more general field of the psychology of adult development and aging. From this perspective, it is important for the researcher in life-span intellectual development to recognize that (4) with aging there is often a change in the structure of life goals such that the acquisition and maintenance of school-related cognitive skills becomes deemphasized and replaced by an accentuation of pragmatic and more immediate realms of functioning (such as problem solving in social, family, personal, and professional activities). Furthermore, there is, with aging, (5) increasing individualization and interindividual differentiation, such that maintenance, growth, and decline in select domains of intellectual functioning is regulated by both external resources and internal performance conditions (for example, interest, motivation, familiarity).

This latter notion is supported by sociological evidence pertaining to the sixth proposition, namely, (6) that aging-related changes in the social and environmental conditions of (and expectations for) performance seem to structure this increasing individualization, a process which results in both growthlike change (in the area of specialization) and decline (in most remaining and often unattended realms). The seventh and eighth propositions derive from research on age-related biological functioning: (7) as with psychological functioning, there is, with aging, increased vulnerability and a concomitant reduction in maximum levels of performance. A psychological implication of this is that there may be a growing awareness on the part of aging individuals that they are both psychologically and biologically at risk. Given, however, the final proposition, that (8) because some important features of the biological status of aging individuals are, in principle, modifiable, efforts to compensate for specific debilitations or vulnerabilities may result in selective optimization of functioning. Of course, whether it is psychological or biological, this optimization would operate within proscriptions imposed by, among other things, these very systems (Baltes et al., 1984).

Selective Optimization with Compensation.

There are several ways in which this set of propositions could provide a foundation for theory building. The approach of interest to us has been called selective optimization with compensation (Baltes et al., 1984; Baltes & Willis, 1982). This inchoate approach proceeds, of course, from the assumption that intellectual aging displays features of growth, stability, and decline. It suggests that the process of "successful aging" may be typified by the individual's own aptitude in "selecting" life goals and trajectories for which internal and external conditions are supported. As long as this support is garnered, intellectual skills and domains of expertise may be maintained and, more important, may compensate for those realms that are not supported (or supportable).

A first application of this approach to intellectual aging distributes the province of mental functioning into two interrelated domains, and, as such, has been called a dual-process conception. The first domain, described as the "mechanics of intelligence," includes the content-free architecture of information processing and problem solving. It represents those tasks and abilities on which (like fluid intelligence or speeded nonverbal tests) one might expect aging-related decline. The second domain is termed the "pragmatics of intelligence." It includes both pragmatic and specialized features of intelligence, as well as accumulated systems of knowledge and skills of application. This second domain may be the reservoir from which compensatory efforts are marshalled and adaptive intellectual functioning is derived. In this way, the second domain may (like crystallized and verbal intelligence) be associated with patterns of stability and even select progression in intellectual functioning throughout adulthood.

Adaptive Forms of Intelligence in Adulthood

An emerging emphasis in research on intellectual development in adulthood is typified less by its ambition to theoretical coherence than by its assiduous attention to special forms of intellectual phenomena. This emphasis is influenced more by current trends in cognitive psychology (Hoyer, 1984) than by either the psychometric model of intelligence (Hunt, 1983) or by the extension of cognitive structuralism (Labouvie-Vief, in press). The strategy employed is to identify domains of knowledge and problem solving that are characteristic of aging adults and the varying conditions of their life courses. The effort to identify tasks that are indigenous to adulthood is reminiscent of the Demming and Pressey (1957) study discussed above. The recent efforts, however, are more concentrated in their attention to the mechanics of intelligence and its associated processes of problem solving. Explicit concern with both the contents of knowledge and the component processes of intelligence leads to the specification of adaptive forms of functioning. In this subsection we describe this strategy of research as it applies to two such forms of intellectual functioning especially relevant to adulthood—namely, expertise and wisdom.

Knowledge, Expertise, and Specialization.   Recent cognitive science research on knowledge systems, expertise, and specialization has informed one set of alternative strategies to the study of life-span intelligence (for example, Baltes et al., 1984; Hoyer, 1984; Kuhn, Pennington, & Leadbeater, 1983). Other current reformulations of intellectual or cognitive functioning stress similar modalities of practical or everyday mental activity (Beilin, 1983; Charlesworth, 1983; Cornelius & Kenney, 1982, Dörner, 1982; 1983; Sternberg, 1982, 1984).

One assumption of these approaches is that much of intellectual development beyond adolescence is not related to further evolution of basic cognitive processes. Possible adult trajectories, it is argued, involve the elaboration, maintenance, and transformation of knowledge rather than basic cognitive skills (Edelstein & Noam, 1982; Labouvie-Vief, 1980, 1982). Thus the primary form of intellectual development during the second part of human life is not represented by further changes of the basic processing capacities and associated cognitive structures, but by the procedural and factual knowledge systems (Anderson, 1982; Brown, 1982; Chi, Glaser, & Rees, 1983) associated with education, occupational life, and other pragmatic aspects of adult development and aging (Goodnow, Knight, & Cashmore, in press). A related assumption of such a view is that further acquisition, maintenance, and transformation of intelligence can be best studied by understanding it in terms of indices of cumulative evolution of effectiveness and high levels of performance. Among the key concepts are those of expertise and specialization.

As alluded to earlier, such a cognitive psychology approach may be an alternative treatment of the notion of crystallized intelligence, which has been described as the centerpiece of intellectual growth during the second part of the life span (Horn, 1970, 1982). This linkage of cognitive psychology work to research on psychometric intelligence is plausible. In this instance, work on knowledge systems and expertise would make explicit how insufficient current psychometric measures of crystallized intelligence are (they consist primarily of measures of vocabulary and social intelligence) and how further refinement and expansion of crystallized intelligence could proceed. However, cognitive science work on knowledge and expertise represents an approach that in itself deserves more attention by life-span researchers on intelligence; that is, it is not simply an elaboration of the concept of crystallized intelligence. Two examples of some of the applications of this approach are given.

Example: Study of Wisdom.   As Kekes (1983) has observed, wisdom is a kind of interpretive knowledge, combining breadth and depth, an understanding of the significance of what is commonly known. Issuing from wisdom is good judgment regarding the factors of life and the tasks of the life course, a deep and yet practical understanding of the limitations and possibilities that accrue as a function of the species, the individual, and the individual's stage of life (Kekes, 1983). With time, wisdom can be acquired but whether it can be learned or taught is questionable (Hall, 1922; Kekes, 1983). Because of this temporal dependency, wisdom is often associated with late adulthood, and the emergence of noetic or meditative urges, philosophic calm, impartiality, and the desire to draw moral lessons (Hall, 1922). Recently, some authors have begun to examine the concept of wisdom as a progressive feature of aging and to explore its amenability to operational and empirical investigation. Its association with such indistinct concepts as self-direction, action-guidance, and good judgment—as well as its frequent confusion with simple accumulated knowledge —make such a task particularly formidable.

Following earlier suggestions on this topic (Clayton, 1975, 1982; Clayton & Birren, 1980; Hall, 1922; Meacham, 1982), Dittmann-Kohli and Baltes in press define wisdom as a mental skill indexing "good judgment about important but uncertain matters of life." Using cognitive science perspectives, they began the task of specifying heuristic criteria by which to identify and assess wisdom. The following aspects appear to be salient: (1) an expertise (including descriptive and procedural knowledge) in the pragmatics of life, (2) interpretive and evaluative knowledge about the significance of this content domain, (3) contextual richness (breadth) of problem definition and solution, (4) uncertainty (especially complexity and difficulty) of problem definition, and (5) good (relativisitic, practical, action-guiding) judgment (Dittmann-Kohli & Baltes, in press; Dixon & Baltes, 1985). Classifying wisdom as an expertise in the pragmatics of life connotes that it is an ability associated with a highly developed form of factual and procedural knowledge and, furthermore, that its acquisition and development is enhanced by the existence of a long-term series of experiences with the human condition and its varying processes and outcomes. Living longer and into old age, in this instance, may be advantageous.

Identifying and defining wisdom in this manner facilitate the tasks of specifying and expanding on the psychometric concept of verbal or crystallized intelligence. At the same time, however, as conceptualized in the framework of cognitive psychology, the study of wisdom can focus on mechanisms and process rather than product, as would be true for the bulk of the psychometric orientation. Note in this context that a concern with wisdom does not imply that wisdom-related phenomena do not exist at earlier stages of life nor that it is the only highlight of adult intellectual development. The study of wisdom is given as an example of how some forms of mental activity in adulthood may be progressive and adaptive and how ontogenetically earlier facets of intelligence (for example, social intelligence) may be refined and transformed as adulthood progresses.

Example: Professional Specialization and Productivity.   Additional examples of forms of intelligence that may evince further growth in adulthood are seen in the study of professional knowledge and productivity (Bertram, 1981; Birren, 1969; Cole, 1979; Featherman, 1980; Kohn & Schooler, 1978, 1982; Miller, Slomczynski, & Kohn, 1984). Occupational careers belong to the experiences of adult life that may involve maintenance and further transformation of factual and procedural knowledge. Intellectual performances of scientists as studied in the field of scientific productivity will be used here as a sample case. From its inception, research on knowledge systems and expertise (Chi et al., 1983) has addressed such occupational and professional knowledge domains as chess, physics, and mathematics. Such work has demonstrated, not unlike cognitive training research in aging (Baltes & Willis, 1982; Denney, 1979), that older adults in good health and in supportive environments have the capacity to maintain or increase high levels of functioning in select areas. Longitudinal research on the relationship between characteristics of work environments and cognitive functioning (Kohn & Schooler, 1978, 1982) have substantiated this view in natural settings. Level and rate of intellectual development during adulthood vary as a function of cognitive complexity and demands of work environments. Such research exemplifies the notion that interindividual differences in adult cognition and the nature of intellectual aging reflect in part the socio-professional structure of society and everyday life (Bertram, 1981).

The study of age and scientific productivity, which has undergone a trend similar to research on intellectual aging, is a concrete example. Early cross-sectional studies revealed a general pattern of age-related decline in scientific productivity (Lehman, 1953). Later work, however, based on cohort and citation analysis, failed to corroborate the incidences of such widespread decrement (Cole, 1979; Dennis, 1966). Cole (1979), for example, found that for scientists who remain active, the dominant finding is one of stability in scientific performance up to ages 60–65, and not one of decline. This finding of age invariance applies to all fields studied by Cole, including physics and mathematics.

Recent work has suggested that age-related changes in the socio-professional context may serve to maintain or promote scholarly productivity among successful scientists. The scientific productivity of aging individuals is influenced by such features of the context as normative, age-graded professional tasks (for example, assumption of administrative duties in later life) (Roe, 1972), psychosocial tasks and their influence on the meaning of productivity for different aged individuals (Jaques, 1970), and the scientific reward system, including the relative availability of research resources to different aged individuals (Cole, 1979; Dennis, 1966). Cultural dimensions may also be a feature in the consideration of differential creative productivity for different aged individuals (for example, Maduro, 1974). Although the potential for continued productivity exists, the functional adaptiveness and meaning of such productivity must be considered in the context of the aging individual's life goals and life structure.

In our view, research on professional knowledge and specialization, particularly if connected with a cognitive science approach, is an important vehicle for better conceptualization of dimensions of efficacy in the domain of verbal intelligence during adulthood and old age. On the one hand, such research represents the structure and function of intelligence as a system of factual and procedural knowledge. On the other hand, it makes explicit two related major features of adult development and aging: (1) increased specialization, and (2) a dynamic interplay between aspects of selective growth and decline. We described this interplay earlier as a process of selective optimization with compensation. Finally, this research highlights the importance of representing aging in terms of adaptations to changing social and professional contexts, rather than simply comparing the performance and products of aging adults to those of young adults.

Applications of Cognitive Structuralism

We have concentrated thus far on portrayals of adult intellectual development derived from the psychometric tradition. When we have referred to the relationship between intelligence test performance and cognitive processing, we have adopted (or addressed) the information-processing view of cognition. In this subsection we describe a perspective on intelligence with rather different historical and theoretical roots. In particular, we focus on the application of this perspective, Piagetian theory, to the study of the development of intelligence in adulthood. This view encourages a focus on mechanisms and process rather than on product.

Like the functional approach described above, the Piagetian conception of intelligence contains a crucial adaptive feature (Piaget, 1960, 1972). By design, the Piagetian approach focuses on similarities in ontogeny, rather than on interindividual differences, which are treated primarily as questions of décalage or unattained optimal functioning. The consequent emphasis on universal and invariant sequences of developmental progression, of qualitative structural transformations, is a well-known feature of the Piagetian approach to intellectual development (Flavell, 1970). According to Piagetian theory, the final qualitative stage of cognitive development—formal operations—is usually attained (if it is attained at all) by early adolescence (Inhelder & Piaget, 1958; Sigel & Hooper, 1968). Beyond this mature stage of abstract reasoning, no structural change was posited by Piaget (1972): that is, within the original theory, further changes are more quantitative than qualitative (Flavell, 1970).

At first, the original cognitive structuralism of Piaget was applied as a framework for understanding intellectual aging (Hooper, Fitzgerald, & Papalia, 1971). Initial efforts to apply this approach to changes in intellectual functioning in adulthood involved the administration of concrete and formal operational tasks designed for use with children to adult samples. This research has resulted in primarily descriptive accounts of age-related performance differences. Although these differences have been related to the graded difficulty of the problem (that is, the more difficult the problem, the less likely older adults will be able to solve it), the understanding of what makes some problems difficult and others easy has not been achieved (Rabbitt, 1977; Reese & Rodeheaver, in press): that is, a structural-qualitative explanation for these observed changes has not been forthcoming. In addition, explanations in terms of reverse developmental sequences (for example, involution—see Papalia & Bielby, 1974) or further developmental stages (for example, Arlin, 1975; Riegel, 1973) have yet to receive rich empirical support. Attempts to address empirically progressive structural change have generally suffered from methodological problems pertaining to sampling, measurement, and scoring. This situation has resulted in the appearance of occasionally ambiguous findings (for example, Arlin, 1975; Basseches, 1980; Blanchard-Fields, 1983; Commons, Richards, & Kuhn, 1982; Hartley, 1980; King, Kitchener, Davison, Parker, & Wood, 1983; Kramer & Woodruff, in press; Kuhn et al., 1983; Perry, 1970; Powell, 1980; Sinnott, 1983).

As is the case with the psychometric approach, the component processes of observed performance differences have been incompletely addressed. Indeed, observed differences are often accounted for in methodological terms, for example, as an artifact of (cross-sectional) research design or (changing) measurement validity (Papalia & Bielby, 1974), or the competence-performance distinction (Overton & Newman, 1982). As Reese and Rodeheaver (in press) noted, there are multiple performance factors that may influence observed age-related differences, a situation that also applies to research in the psychometric tradition. Finally, those age differences in concrete and formal operational tasks that have been observed are by no means universal. Several recent studies have failed to corroborate earlier findings of performance deficits among the elderly (for example, Chance, Overcast, & Dollinger, 1978; Papalia-Finlay, Blackburn, Davis, Dellmann, & Roberts, 1981; Protinsky & Hughston, 1978; Schaier & Cicirelli, 1976). Attempts to extend Piagetian structuralism beyond adolescence may be more fruitfully directed at the exploration of the unique competencies and skills of adults than in the single assessment of their performance on traditional Piagetian tasks.

Insofar as adult intellectual development is reversible, nonuniversal, and relatively independent of maturation, then the identification of progressive structural transformations is problematic (Flavell, 1970; Labouvie-Vief, 1977). In general, however, although the Piagetian approach still requires an adequate performance theory (Broughton, 1981; Chapman, 1985; Overton & Newman, 1982), a structural view of cognitive development is not necessarily incompatible with such conceptions as multidimensionality, multidirectionality, plasticity, and interindividual variability. The frequent criticism that developmental perform-ance on Piagetian tasks lacks sufficient synchrony to indicate structural change has, on the basis of Piaget's own writing, been challenged (Broughton, 1981; Chapman, 1985). In addition, the degree of synchrony necessary in developmental transitions may be in part a function of other epistemological considerations (Overton & Newman, 1982). The view that mental development in childhood is structural in nature, as well as biologically and socially constrained, whereas mental development in adulthood is nonstructural, as well as experientially based, may have been prematurely advanced.

The continued search for progressive transformations is one alternative to a decrement model of life-span intellectual development. Reformulations and ex-pansions have been proffered (Arlin, 1975; Basseches, 1980; Broughton, 1978; Commons, 1983; Edelstein & Noam, 1982; Kitchener & King, 1981; Kramer, 1983; Labouvie-Vief, 1980, 1982; Pascual-Leone, 1983; Riegel, 1973; Sinnott, 1983). According to Kramer (1983), for example, common features of such models suggest that adult thought is "relativistic and dialectical" in nature. Such processes are believed to represent adaptations that occur due to the limitations of formal operations in adjusting to the increased complexity of the adult en-vironment. From a neo-Piagetian perspective, Labouvie-Vief (1980, 1981, 1982) argued that progressive structural change in adulthood may be not only adaptive, but also responsive to the unique pragmatic concerns of adult life and the continuing evolution of the system of self. Labouvie-Vief (1982) proposed three adult stages of logic that are designed to integrate such related domains of psychological functioning and self-regulation as cognitive, affective, and social development, and result in the inclusion of the self as a reference point in the construction of knowledge (see also Pascual-Leone, 1983, and Sinnott, 1983, for similar sequences). Movement through these stages (or regulatory schemes) was viewed both as progressive and as involving structural transformations. The fact that individual differences in the mechanisms and rates of movement were ex-pected (and expected to be pervasive) did not, according to Labouvie-Vief (1982), necessarily invalidate the principles on which this stage model was based. Never-theless, the identification and specification of the mechanisms by which structural transformations in adulthood are accomplished remain important problems for future research.

CONCLUSIONS

In this chapter, we have reviewed research and theory on intellectual development from a life-span developmental perspective. This perspective focuses on the study of intellectual functioning from birth to death. Life-span scholars portray human development as consisting of both continuous and discontinuous (newly emerging) processes of constancy and change. Furthermore, they emphasize the embeddedness of ontogeny within historical, biocultural change. In addition, the life-span perspective concentrates on the study of the conditions of interindividual differences and intraindividual plasticity. The search is not only for universals of development, but also for conditions that produce differential development and regulate individual uniqueness.

In the first part of the chapter it was shown that there exists considerable historical continuity to current issues and themes of life-span research on intelligence. This is accomplished by using four central concepts of current life-span work on intelligence (multidimensionality, multidirectionality, intraindividual plasticity, and interindividual differentiation) and by examining the writing of early life-span scholars on these topics. A much higher degree of historical continuity is observed than might have been expected.

Although we have not addressed this issue in the present chapter, perspectives similar to the ones mentioned as typical for adult intelligence are also part of the literature on intellectual development during the first part of life. In our view, however, the pattern of perspectives and their relative weighting are different. In research on intelligence in childhood and adolescence, the central focus is on unidirectional growth trends with interindividual differences and predictability being embedded within a general view of progression and stability. Furthermore, the relative magnitude of, and concern with, intraindividual plasticity, while extant in early life work, is not a core feature of theorizing. In adulthood research, on the contrary, multidimensionality and multidirectionality (for example, verbal versus nonverbal intelligence), interindividual differences (for example, large interindividual variation in occurrence of further growth or decline), and substantial intraindividual plasticity (for example, results of cognitive intervention work in older adults) are paramount. Advances are sought in ways to make such phenomena a direct integral concern of theory development. In life-span work, such phenomena attain a core thematic status; they are not treated as inconsequential conditions or as noise in the system.

Why is there such a difference in outcome pattern and weighting of features when comparing research on intellectual development at different points of the life span? Our central position is that the structure and function of intelligence in the first third of life evinces a high degree of biocultural stabilization. For the first part of life, the macro-cultural and macro-biological conditions affecting the course of intellectual development have become fairly stabilized (at least in developed countries). In adulthood and old age the situation is markedly different. Processes of adult development and aging, in part due to their fairly recent occurrence as widespread phenomena, are part of a less stable and, conversely, more labile set of societal and biological conditions. Consequently, the system of conditions affecting adult intellectual development is less predetermined and perhaps more individualized than is true for earlier parts of the life course. Nevertheless, as we have seen, work continues in the direction of articulating possible forms of qualitative and structural transformation in adult cognition. It is unclear whether the apparent higher degree of biological and societal indeterminacy is intrinsic to the adult and aging years per se, or whether it reflects a transitory state that will be transformed into a higher level of constraint in the future, for example, in conjunction with further biocultural evolution.

Finally, within a framework of multidimensionality, multidirectionality, interindividual differentiation, and plasticity, we discuss the types of continuities and discontinuities in intellectual functioning that are proffered as characteristic of adulthood and old-age intelligence. We address explicitly several conceptions that may aid in further refinement. One conception useful in organizing available evidence is a dual-process model of life-span intelligence; this model distinguishes between the mechanics and the pragmatic aspects of intelligence. We argue that interactive and compensatory relationships involving growth and decline in these two processes constitute much of intellectual aging. Furthermore, we describe intellectual development during adulthood and old age as a process of selective optimization with compensation. Finally, we present conceptions that are aimed at delineating forms of intelligence that may be particularly adaptive or otherwise prone to occur and develop during adulthood and old age. Practical intelligence, knowledge systems, wisdom, and further cognitive (post-formal) operations are examples. We consider these forms of intelligence to be adaptive and pragmatic, considerably influenced by the situations and demands characteristic of adult life. Under specific life-long conditions, their structure and level of efficacy may become more pronounced in adulthood than is typical for earlier periods.

One may expect that the psychometric work will continue: the advances associated with Schaie's longitudinal study, the theory of crystallized and fluid intelligence, as well as psychometric perspectives on recurring issues, such as training and age-appropriate tests, have provided a foundation for future endeavors. Nevertheless, broadening the concept of intelligence in adulthood to include both alternative conceptions (for example, dual-process model) and alternative forms (for example, practical intelligence), and to promote further investigation of the sources of individual differences (for example, component cognitive skills) and the possibility of structural change, will result in a more thorough understanding of the nature of life-span intellectual development.

REFERENCES

Abercrombie, J. (1839). *Inquiries concerning the intellectual powers and their investigation of truth.* Boston: Otis, Broaders.

Anastasi, A. (1983). Evolving trait concepts. *American Psychologist, 38,* 175–184.

Anderson, J. R. (1982). Acquisition of cognitive skill. *Psychological Review, 89,* 369–406.

Angell, J. R. (1907). The province of functional psychology. *Psychological Review, 14,* 61–91.

Angell, J. R. (1922). The evolution of intelligence. In G. E. Baitsell (Ed.), *The evolution of man.* New Haven: Yale University Press.

Arlin, P. K. (1975). Cognitive development in adulthood: A fifth stage? *Developmental Psychology, 11,* 602–606.

Baldwin, J. M. (1895). *Mental development in the child and the race.* New York: Macmillan.

Baldwin, J. M. (1902). Pragmatic and pragmatism. In J. M. Baldwin (Ed.), *Dictionary of philosophy and psychology* (Vol. 2). New York: Peter Smith.

Baldwin, J. M., & Stout, G. F. (1902). Practical judgment. In J. M. Baldwin (Ed.), *Dictionary of philosophy and psychology* (Vol. 2). New York: Peter Smith.

Baltes, P. B. (1968). Longitudinal and cross-sectional sequences in the study of age and generation effects. *Human Development, 11,* 145–171.

Baltes, P. B. (Ed.). (1973). Strategies for psychological intervention in old age: A symposium. *The Gerontologist, 13,* 4–38.

Baltes, P. B. (1984, May). Intelligenz im Alter. *Spektrum der Wissenschaft,* pp. 46–60.

Baltes, P. B., Dittmann-Kohli, F., & Dixon, R. A. (1984). New perspectives on the development of intelligence in adulthood: Toward a dual-process conception and a model of selective optimization with compensation. In P. B. Baltes & O. G. Brim, Jr. (Eds.), *Life-span development and behavior* (Vol. 6). New York: Academic Press.

Baltes, P. B., Dittmann-Kohli, F., & Kliegl, R. (1985). *Reserve capacity of the elderly in aging-sensitive tests of fluid intelligence.* Unpublished manuscript. Max Planck Institute for Human Development and Education, Berlin, West Germany.

Baltes, P. B., & Goulet, L. R. (1971). Exploration of developmental variables by simulation and manipulation of age differences in behavior. *Human Development, 14,* 149–170.

Baltes, P. B., & Labouvie, G. V. (1973). Adult development of intellectual performance: Description, explanation, and modification. In C. Eisdorfer & M. P. Lawton (Eds.), *The psychology of adult development and aging.* Washington: American Psychological Association.

Baltes, P. B., Nesselroade, J. R., Schaie, K. W., & Labouvie, E. W. (1972). On the dilemma of regression effects in examining ability level-related differentials in ontogenetic patterns of adult intelligence. *Developmental Psychology, 6,* 78–84.

Baltes, P. B., Reese, H. W., & Lipsitt, L. P. (1980). Life-span developmental psychology. *Annual Review of Psychology, 31,* 65–110.

Baltes, P. B., Reese, H. W., & Nesselroade, J. R. (1977). *Life-span developmental psychology: Introduction to research methods.* Monterey, CA: Brooks/Cole.

Baltes, P. B., & Schaie, K. W. (1976). On the plasticity of intelligence in adulthood and old age: Where Horn and Donaldson fail. *American Psychologist, 31,* 720–725.

Baltes, P. B., Schaie, K. W., & Nardi, A. H. (1971). Age and experimental mortality in a seven-year longitudinal study of cognitive behavior. *Developmental Psychology, 5,* 18–26.

Baltes, P. B., & Willis, S. L. (1979). The critical importance of appropriate methodology in the study of aging: The sample case of psychometric intelligence. In F. Hoffmeister & C. Müller (Eds.), *Brain function in old age.* Heidelberg: Springer.

Baltes, P. B., & Willis, S. L. (1982). Plasticity and enhancement of intellectual functioning in old age: Penn State's Adult Development and Enrichment Project (ADEPT). In F. I. M. Craik & S. E. Trehub (Eds.), *Aging and cognitive processes.* New York: Plenum Press.

Basseches, M. (1980). Dialectical schemata: A framework for the empirical study of the development of dialectical thinking. *Human Development, 23,* 400–421.

Bayley, N. (1955). On the growth of intelligence. *American Psychologist, 10,* 805–818.

Bayley, N. (1956). Individual patterns of development. *Child Development, 27,* 45–74.

Bayley, N. (1970). Development of mental abilities. In P. H. Mussen (Ed.), *Carmichael's Manual of Child Psychology* (Vol. 1, 3rd ed.). New York: Wiley.

Bayley, N., & Oden, M. H. (1955). The maintenance of intellectual ability in gifted adults. *Journal of Gerontology, 10,* 91–107.

Beeson, M. F. (1920). Intelligence at senescence. *Journal of Applied Psychology, 4,* 219–234.

Beilin, H. (1983). The new functionalism and Piaget's program. In E. K. Scholnick (Ed.), *New trends in conceptual representation.* Hillsdale, NJ: Erlbaum.

Belmont, J. M. (1983). Concerning Hunt's new ways of assessing intelligence. *Intelligence, 7,* 1–7.

Berg, C. A., & Sternberg, R. J. (1983). Toward a triarchic theory of intellectual development during adulthood. Unpublished manuscript, Department of Psychology, Yale University, New Haven.

Berkowitz, B. (1953). The Wechsler-Bellevue performance of white males past age 50. *Journal of Gerontology, 8,* 76–80.

Berkowitz, B., & Green, R. F. (1963). Changes in intellect with age. I. Longitudinal study of Wechsler-Bellevue scores. *Journal of Genetic Psychology, 103,* 3–21.

Bertram, H. (1981). *Sozialstruktur und Sozialisation: Zur mikrosoziologischen Analyse von Chancenungleichheit.* Darmstadt: Luchterhand.

Binet, A. (1909). *Les idées modernes sur les enfants.* Paris: Flammarion.

Binet, A., & Henri, V. (1895). La psychologie individuelle. *L'Année Psychologique, 2,* 411–465.

Binet, A., & Simon, T. (1911). *A method of measuring the development of the intelligence of young children.* Lincoln, IL: Courier.

Birren, J. E. (1952). A factorial analysis of the Wechsler-Bellevue Scale given to an elderly population. *Journal of Consulting Psychology, 16,* 399–405.

Birren, J. E. (1969). Age and decision strategies. In A. T. Welford & J. E. Birren (Eds.), *Decision making and age: Interdisciplinary topics in gerontology* (Vol. 4). Basel, Switzerland: S. Karger.

Birren, J. E., Cunningham, W. R., & Yamamoto, K. (1982). Psychology of adult development and aging. *Annual Review of Psychology, 34,* 543–575.

Blackwood, B. (1927, December). A study of mental testing in relation to anthropology. *Mental Measurement Monographs* (Serial No. 4).

Blanchard-Fields, F. (1983). *The socio-emotional integration of logical reasoning in adolescent and adult development.* Unpublished doctoral dissertation, Wayne State University, Detroit, MI.

Blieszner, R., Willis, S. L., & Baltes, P. B. (1981). Training research in aging on the fluid ability of inductive reasoning. *Journal of Applied Developmental Psychology, 2,* 247–265.

Blum, J. E., Fosshage, J. L., & Jarvik, L. F. (1972). Intellectual changes and sex differences in octogenarians: A twenty-year longitudinal study of aging. *Developmental Psychology, 7,* 178–187.

Blum, J. E., Jarvik, L. F., & Clark, E. T. (1970). Rate of change on selective tests of intelligence: A twenty-year longitudinal study of aging. *Journal of Gerontology, 25,* 171–176.

Boody, B. M. (1926, February). A psychological study of immigrant children at Ellis Island. *Mental Measurement Monographs* (Serial No. 3).

Botwinick, J. (1967). *Cognitive processes in maturity and old age.* New York: Springer.

Botwinick, J. (1977). Intellectual abilities. In J. E. Birren & K. W. Schaie (Eds.), *Handbook of the psychology of aging.* New York: Van Nostrand Reinhold.

Botwinick, J., & Storandt, M. (1973). Speed functions, vocabulary ability, and age. *Perceptual and Motor Skills, 36,* 1123–1128.

Botwinick, J., & Storandt, M. (1974). Vocabulary ability in later life. *Journal of Genetic Psychology, 125,* 303–308.

Boynton, P. (1933). *Intelligence: Its manifestations and measurement.* New York: Appleton-Century-Crofts.

Bradway, K. P., Thompson, C. W., & Cravens, R. B. (1958). Preschool IQs after twenty-five years. *Journal of Educational Psychology, 49,* 278–281.

Brigham, C. C. (1930). Intelligence tests of immigrant groups. *Psychological Review, 37,* 158–165.

Broughton, J. (1978). Development of concepts of self, mind, reality, and knowledge. *New Directions for Child Development, 1,* 75–100.

Broughton, J. M. (1981). Piaget's structural developmental psychology: II. Logic and psychology. *Human Development, 24,* 195–224.

Brown, A. L. (1982). Learning and development: The problem of compatibility, access, and induction. *Human Development, 25,* 89–115.

Burt, C., Jones, E., Miller, E., & Moodie, W. (1934). *How the mind works.* New York: Appleton-Century-Crofts.

Burton, A., & Joel, W. (1945). Adult norms for the Watson-Glaser Tests of Critical Thinking. *Journal of Psychology, 19,* 43–48.

Carroll, J. B., & Maxwell, S. E. (1979). Individual differences in cognitive abilities. *Annual Review of Psychology, 30,* 603–640.

Cattell, J. McK. (1890). Mental tests and measurement. *Mind, 15,* 373–380.

Cattell, R. B. (1943). The measurement of adult intelligence. *Psychological Bulletin, 40,* 153–193.

Cattell, R. B. (1963). Theory of fluid and crystallized intelligence: A critical experiment. *Journal of Educational Psychology, 54,* 1–22.

Cattell, R. B. (1971). *Abilities: Their structure, growth, and action.* Boston: Houghton-Mifflin.

Chance, J., Overcast, T., & Dollinger, S. J. (1978). Aging and cognitive regression: Contrary findings. *Journal of Psychology, 98,* 177–183.

Chapman, M. (1985). *Piaget, and structures of the whole: A reinterpretation.* Unpublished manuscript, for Max Planck Institute for Human Development and Education, Berlin, West Germany.

Charles, D. C. (1953). Ability and accomplishment of persons earlier judged to be mentally defective. *Genetic Psychology Monographs, 47,* 3–71.

Charlesworth, W. R. (1976). Intelligence as adaptation: An ethological approach. In L. B. Resnick (Ed.), *The nature of intelligence.* Hillsdale, NJ: Erlbaum.

Charlesworth, W. R. (1983). An ethological approach to cognitive development. In C. J. Brainerd (Ed.), *Recent advances in cognitive-developmental theory: Progress in cognitive development research.* New York: Springer.

Chi, M. T. H., Glaser, R., & Rees, E. (1983). Expertise in problem solving. In R. J. Sternberg (Ed.), *Advances in the psychology of human intelligence* (Vol. 1). Hillsdale, NJ: Erlbaum.

Clayton, V. P. (1975). Erikson's theory of human development as it applies to the aged: Wisdom as contradictory cognition. *Human Development, 18,* 119–128.

Clayton, V. P. (1982). Wisdom and intelligence: The nature and function of knowledge in the later years. *International Journal of Aging and Human Development, 15,* 315–323.

Clayton, V. P., & Birren, J. E. (1980). The development of wisdom across the life span: A reexamination of an ancient topic. In P. B. Baltes & O. G. Brim, Jr. (Eds.), *Life-span development and behavior* (Vol. 3). New York: Academic Press.

Cole, S. (1979). Age and scientific performance. *American Journal of Sociology, 84,* 958–977.

Commons, M. (Ed.). (1983). *Post-formal operations.* New York: Praeger Press.

Commons, M. L., Richards, F., & Kuhn, D. (1982). Metasystematic reasoning: A case for a level of systematic reasoning beyond Piaget's stage of formal operations. *Child Development, 53,* 1058–1069.

Cornelius, S. W. (1984). Classic pattern of intellectual aging: Test familiarity, difficulty, and performance. *Journal of Gerontology, 39,* 201–206.

Cornelius, S. W., & Kenney, S. R. (1982). *Academic and everyday intelligence in adulthood and old age.* Unpublished manuscript, Department of Human Development and Family Studies, Cornell University, Ithaca, NY.

Cornelius, S. W., Willis, S. L., Nesselroade, J. R., & Baltes, P. B. (1983). Convergence between attention variables and factors of psychometric intelligence in older adults. *Intelligence, 7,* 253–270.

Corsini, R. J., & Fassett, K. K. (1953). Intelligence and aging. *Journal of Genetic Psychology, 83,* 249–264.

Cronbach, L. J. (1957). The two disciplines of scientific psychology. *American Psychologist, 12,* 671–684.

Cronbach, L. J. (1975). Beyond the two disciplines of scientific psychology. *American Psychologist, 30*, 116–127.

Cunningham, W. R., & Birren, J. E. (1976). Age changes in human abilities: A 28-year longitudinal study. *Developmental Psychology, 12*, 81–82.

Cunningham, W. R., & Owens, Jr., W. A. (1983). The Iowa State study of the adult development of intellectual abilities. In K. W. Schaie (Ed.), *Longitudinal studies of adult psychological development*. New York: Guilford.

Darwin, C. (1859). *On the origin of species*. London: John Murray.

Darwin, C. (1872). *The expression of emotions in man and animals*. London: John Murray.

Demming, J. A., & Pressey, S. L. (1957). Tests indigenous to the adult and older years. *Journal of Counseling Psychology, 4*, 144–148.

Denney, N. W. (1979). Problem solving in later adulthood: Intervention research. In P. B. Baltes & O. G. Brim, Jr. (Eds.), *Life-span development and behavior* (Vol. 2). New York: Academic Press.

Denney, N. W. (1982). Aging and cognitive changes. In B. B. Wolman (Ed.), *Handbook of developmental psychology*. Englewood Cliffs, NJ: Prentice-Hall.

Dennis, W. (1966). Creative productivity between the ages of 20 and 80 years. *Journal of Gerontology, 21*, 1–18.

Dewey, J. (1916). *Democracy and education*. New York: Macmillan.

Dewey, J. (1938). *Experience and education*. New York: Macmillan.

Dittmann-Kohli, F. (1984). Weisheit als mögliches Ergebnis der Intelligenzentwicklung im Erwachsenenalter. *Sprache und Kognition, 2*, 112–132.

Dittmann-Kohli, F. (1984). Weisheit als mögliches Ergebnis der Intelligenzentwicklung im Erwachsenenalter. *Sprache und Kognition, 2*, 112–132.

Dittmann-Kohli, F., & Baltes, P. B. (in press). Toward a neofunctionalist conception of adult intellectual development: Wisdom as a prototypical case of intellectual growth. In C. Alexander & E. Langer (Eds.), *Beyond formal operations: Alternative endpoints to human development*. New York: Oxford University Press.

Dixon, R. A., & Baltes, P. B. (in press). Toward life-span research on the functions and pragmatics of intelligence. In R. J. Sternberg & R. K. Wagner (Eds.), *Practical intelligence: Origins of competence in the everyday world*. Cambridge: Cambridge University Press.

Dixon, R. A., & Hertzog, C. (in press). A functional approach to memory and metamemory development in adulthood. In F. E. Weinert & M. Perlmutter (Eds.), *Memory development across the life span*.

Dixon, R. A., & Lerner, R. M. (1984). A history of systems in developmental psychology. In M. H. Bornstein & M. E. Lamb (Eds.), *Developmental psychology: An advanced textbook*. Hillsdale, NJ: Erlbaum.

Doppelt, J. E., & Wallace, W. L. (1955). Standardization of the Wechsler Adult Intelligence Scale for older persons. *Journal of Abnormal and Social Psychology, 51*, 312–330.

Dörner, D. (1982). The ecological conditions of thinking. In D. R. Griffin (Ed.), *Animal mind—Human mind (Dahlem Konferenzen)*. New York: Springer.

Dörner, D. (1983). Heuristic and cognition in complex systems. In R. Groner, M. Groner, & W. F. Bischof (Eds.), *Methods of heuristics*. Hillsdale, NJ: Erlbaum.

Drummond, W. B. (1912). *An introduction to child-study*. New York: Longmans, Green.

Edelstein, W., & Noam, G. (1982). Regulatory structures of the self and "postformal" stages in adulthood. *Human Development, 6*, 407–422.

Eisdorfer, C., Busse, E. W., & Cohen, L. D. (1959). The WAIS performance of an aged sample: The relationship between verbal and performance IQs. *Journal of Gerontology, 14*, 197–201.

Esquirol, J. -E. D. (1838). *Des maladies mentales considérées sous les rapports médical, hygiénique, et médico-légal* (3 vols.). Paris: Bailliere.

Featherman, D. L. (1980). Schooling and occupational careers: Constancy and change in worldly success. In O. G. Brim, Jr. & J. Kagan (Eds.), *Constancy and change in human development*. Cambridge, MA: Harvard University Press.

Flavell, J. H. (1970). Cognitive change in adulthood. In L. R. Goulet & P. B. Baltes (Eds.), *Life-span developmental psychology: Research and theory*. New York: Academic Press.

Flavell, J. H. (1977). *Cognitive development*. Englewood Cliffs, NJ: Prentice-Hall.

Flynn, J. R. (1984). The mean IQ of Americans: Massive gains 1932 to 1978. *Psychological Bulletin, 95*, 29–51.

Foster, J. C., & Taylor, G. A. (1920). The applicability of mental tests to persons over fifty years of age. *Journal of Applied Psychology, 4*, 39–58.

Foulds, G. A., & Raven, J. C. (1948). Normal changes in mental abilities of adults as age advances. *Journal of Mental Science, 94*, 133–142.

Freeman, F. N. (1939). *Mental tests: Their history, principles and applications*. Boston: Houghton-Mifflin.

Fries, J. F., & Crapo, L. M. (1981). *Vitality and aging*. San Francisco: Freeman.

Furry, C. A., & Baltes, P. B. (1973). The effect of age differences in ability-extraneous performance variables on the assessment of intelligence in children, adults, and the elderly. *Journal of Gerontology, 28*, 73–80.

Galton, F. (1869). *Hereditary genius*. London: Macmillan.

Gardner, E. F., & Monge, R. H. (1977). Adult age differences in cognitive abilities and educational background. *Experimental Aging Research, 3*, 337–383.

Garrett, H. E. (1946). A developmental theory of intelligence. *American Psychologist, 1*, 372–378.

Gesell, A. (1925). *The mental growth of the preschool child*. New York: Macmillan.

Goodenough, F. L. (1949). *Mental testing*. New York: Holt, Rinehart, and Winston.

Goodenough, F. L. (1954). The measurement of mental growth in childhood. In L. Carmichael (Ed.), *Manual of child psychology* (2nd ed.). New York: Wiley.

Goodnow, J. J., Knight, R., & Cashmore, J. (in press). Adult social cognition: Implications of parents' ideas for approaches to development. In M. Perlmutter (Ed.), *Minnesota Symposium on Child Development*. Minneapolis: University of Minnesota Press.

Goslin, D. A. (1963). *The search for ability: Standardized testing in social perspective*. New York: Russell Sage Foundation.

Gould, S. J. (1981). *The mismeasure of man*. New York: Norton.

Green, R. F. (1969). Age-intelligence relationship between ages sixteen and sixty-four: A rising trend. *Developmental Psychology, 1*, 618–627.

Gribbin, K., Schaie, K. W., & Parham, I. A. (1975). *Cognitive complexity and maintenance of intellectual abilities*. Paper presented at the 10th International Congress of Gerontology, Jerusalem, Israel.

Griffiths, R. (1954). *The abilities of babies: A study in mental measurement*. New York: McGraw-Hill.

Guilford, J. P. (1967). *The nature of human intelligence*. New York: McGraw-Hill.

Hall, G. S. (1922). *Senescence: The last half of life*. New York: Appleton.

Hartley, D. G. (1980). *Adult cognitive development: Problem finding and problem solving*. Paper presented at the Southeast Conference on Human Development, Alexandria, VA.

Hayes, K. J. (1962). Genes, drive, and intellect. *Psychological Reports, 10*, 299–342.

Herrnstein, R. J. (1971). IQ. *Atlantic, 22*, 43–64.

Hertzog, C., Schaie, K. W., & Gribbin, K. (1978). Cardiovascular disease and changes in intellectual functioning from middle to old age. *Journal of Gerontology, 33*, 872–883.

Hilgard, E. R. (1948). *Theories of learning*. New York: Appleton-Century-Crofts.

Hirsch, J. (1981). To "unfrock the charlatans." *Sage Race Relations Abstracts, 6*(2), 1–67.

Hofland, B. F., Willis, S. L., & Baltes, P. B. (1981). Fluid intelligence performance in the elderly: Intraindividual variability and conditions of assessment. *Journal of Educational Psychology, 73*, 573–586.

Hollingworth, H. L. (1927). *Mental growth and decline: A survey of developmental psychology.* New York: Appleton.

Hooper, F., Fitzgerald, J., & Papalia, D. (1971). Piagetian theory and the aging process: Extensions and speculations. *International Journal of Aging and Human Development, 2*, 3–20.

Horn, J. L. (1970). Organization of data on life-span development of human abilities. In L. R. Goulet & P. B. Baltes (Eds.), *Life-span developmental psychology: Research and theory.* New York: Academic Press.

Horn, J. L. (1978). Human ability systems. In P. B. Baltes (Ed.), *Life-span development and behavior* (Vol. 1). New York: Academic Press.

Horn, J. L. (1980). Concepts of intellect in relation to learning and adult development. *Intelligence, 4*, 285–317.

Horn, J. L. (1982). The theory of fluid and crystallized intelligence in relation to concepts of cognitive psychology and aging in adulthood. In F. I. M. Craik & S. Trehub (Eds.), *Aging and cognitive processes.* New York: Plenum Press.

Horn, J. L., & Cattell, R. B. (1966). Refinement and test of the theory of fluid and crystallized intelligence. *Journal of Educational Psychology, 57*, 253–270.

Horn, J. L., & Cattell, R. B. (1967). Age differences in fluid and crystallized intelligence. *Acta Psychologica, 26*, 107–129.

Horn, J. L., & Donaldson, G. (1976). On the myth of intellectual decline in adulthood. *American Psychologist, 31*, 701–719.

Horn, J. L., & Donaldson, G. (1980). Cognitive development in adulthood. In O. G. Brim, Jr. & J. Kagan (Eds.), *Constancy and change in human development.* Cambridge: Harvard University Press.

Hornblum, J. N., & Overton, W. F. (1976). Area and volume conservation among the elderly: Assessment and training. *Developmental Psychology, 12*, 68–74.

Hoyer, W. J. (1984). Aging and the development of expert cognition. In T. M. Schlechter & M. P. Toglia (Eds.), *New directions in cognitive science.* Norwood, NJ: Ablex.

Hoyer, W. J., Labouvie, G. V., & Baltes, P. B. (1973). Modification of response speed deficits and intellectual performance in the elderly. *Human Development, 16*, 233–242.

Hultsch, D. F., Hertzog, C., & Dixon, R. A. (1984). Text recall in adulthood: The role of intellectual abilities. *Developmental Psychology, 20*, 1193–1209.

Hunt, E. B. (1978). Mechanics of verbal ability. *Psychological Review, 85*, 109–130.

Hunt, E. (1982). Towards new ways of assessing intelligence. *Intelligence, 6*, 231–240.

Hunt, E. (1983). On the nature of intelligences. *Science, 219*, 141–146.

Hunt, J. McV. (1961). *Intelligence and experience.* New York: Ronald Press.

Inhelder, B., & Piaget, J. (1958). *The growth of logical thinking from childhood to adolescence.* New York: Basic Books.

James, W. (1890). *The principles of psychology* (2 vols.). New York: Dover.

James, W. (1975). *The meaning of truth.* Cambridge: Harvard University Press. (Original work published 1909)

Jaques, E. (1970). *Work, creativity, and social justice.* London: Heinemann.

Jarvik, L. F., & Bank, L. (1983). Aging twins: Longitudinal psychometric data. In K. W. Schaie (Ed.), *Longitudinal studies of adult psychological development.* New York: Guilford.

Jarvik, L. F., & Falek, A. (1963). Intellectual stability and survival in the aged. *Journal of Gerontology, 18*, 173–176.

Jarvik, L. F., Kallmann, F. J., & Falek, A. (1962). Intellectual changes in aged twins. *Journal of Gerontology, 17*, 289–294.

Jencks, C. (1972). *Inequality: A reassessment of the effect of family and schooling in America.* New York: Harper & Row.

Jenkins, J. J., & Paterson, D. G. (Eds.). (1961). *Studies in individual differences: The search for intelligence.* New York: Appleton-Century-Crofts.

Jensen, A. R. (1973). *Genetics and education.* New York: Harper & Row.

Jones, H. E. (1954). The environment and mental development. In L. Carmichael (Ed.), *Manual of child psychology* (2nd ed.). New York: Wiley.

Jones, H. E. (1959). Intelligence and problem solving. In J. E. Birren (Ed.), *Handbook of aging and the individual: Psychological and biological aspects.* Chicago: University of Chicago Press.

Jones, H. E., & Conrad, H. S. (1933). The growth and decline of intelligence: A study of a homogeneous group between the ages of ten and sixty. *Genetic Psychology Monographs, 13,* 223–298.

Kamin, L. J. (1957). Differential changes in mental abilities in old age. *Journal of Gerontology, 12,* 66–70.

Kamin, L. J. (1974). *The science and politics of IQ.* Potomac, MD: Erlbaum.

Kekes, J. (1983). Wisdom. *American Philosophical Quarterly, 20,* 277–286.

King, P. M., Kitchener, K. S., Davison, M. L., Parker, M. L., & Wood, P. K. (1983). The justification of beliefs in young adults: A longitudinal study. *Human Development, 26,* 106–116.

Kirkpatrick, C. (1926, January). Intelligence and immigration. *Mental Measurement Monographs* (Serial No. 2).

Kirkpatrick, E. A. (1903). *Fundamentals of child study: A discussion of instincts and other factors in human development with practical applications.* New York: Macmillan.

Kitchener, K. S., & King, P. M. (1981). Reflective judgment: Concepts of justification and their relationship to age and education. *Journal of Applied Developmental Psychology, 2,* 89–116.

Kliegl, R., & Baltes, P. B. (1984). *Cognitive reserve capacity, expertise, and aging.* Unpublished manuscript, Max Planck Institute for Human Development and Education, Berlin, West Germany.

Kohn, M. L., & Schooler, C. (1978). The reciprocal effects of the substantive complexity of work and intellectual flexibility: A longitudinal assessment. *American Journal of Sociology, 84,* 24–52.

Kohn, M. L., & Schooler, C. (1982). Job conditions and personality: A longitudinal assessment of their reciprocal effects. *American Journal of Sociology, 87,* 1257–1286.

Kramer, D. A. (1983). Post-formal operations? A need for further conceptualization. *Human Development, 26,* 91–105.

Kramer, D. A., & Woodruff, D. S. (in press). Relativistic and dialectical thought in three adult age groups. *Human Development.*

Kuhlen, R. G. (1940). Social change: A neglected factor in psychological studies of the life span. *School and Society, 52,* 14–16.

Kuhlen, R. G. (1963). Age and intelligence: The significance of cultural change in longitudinal vs. cross-sectional findings. *Vita Humana, 6,* 113–124.

Kuhn, D., Pennington, N., & Leadbeater, B. (1983). Adult thinking in developmental perspective. In P. B. Baltes & O. G. Brim, Jr. (Eds.), *Life-span development and behavior* (Vol. 5). New York: Academic Press.

Labouvie-Vief, G. (1976). Toward optimizing cognitive competence in later life. *Educational Gerontology, 1,* 75–92.

Labouvie-Vief, G. (1977). Adult cognitive development: In search of alternative interpretations. *Merrill-Palmer Quarterly, 23,* 227–263.

Labouvie-Vief, G. (1980). Beyond formal operations: Uses and limits of pure logic in life-span development. *Human Development, 23,* 141–161.

Labouvie-Vief, G. (1981). Pro-active and re-active aspects of constructivism: Growth and aging in life-span perspective. In R. M. Lerner & N. A. Busch-Rossnagel (Eds.), *Individuals as producers of their development: A life span perspective.* New York: Academic Press.

Labouvie-Vief, G. (1982). Dynamic development and mature autonomy: A theoretical prologue. *Human Development, 25,* 161–191.

Labouvie-Vief, G. (in press). Intelligence and cognition. In J. E. Birren & K. W. Schaie (Eds.), *Handbook of the psychology of aging* (rev. ed.). New York: Van Nostrand Reinhold.

Lehman, H. C. (1953). *Age and achievement.* Princeton, NJ: Princeton University Press.

Lerner, R. M. (1985). *Concepts and theories of human development* (2nd ed.). Reading, MA: Addison-Wesley.

Loehlin, J. C., Lindzey, G., & Spuhler, J. N. (1975). *Race differences in intelligence.* San Francisco: Freeman.

Lorge, I. (1936). The influence of the test upon the nature of mental decline as a function of age. *Journal of Educational Psychology, 27,* 100–110.

Maduro, R. (1974). Artistic creativity and aging in India. *International Journal of Aging and Human Development, 5,* 303–327.

Marsh, C. J. (1933). Human adaptability as related to age. *Psychological Bulletin, 30,* 589.

Matarazzo, J. D. (1972). *Wechsler's measurement and appraisal of adult intelligence.* Baltimore: Williams & Wilkins.

McCall, R. B. (1979). The development of intellectual functioning in infancy and the prediction of later IQ. In J. D. Osofsky (Ed.), *Handbook of infant development.* New York: Wiley.

McHugh, R. B., & Owens, W. A. (1954). Age changes in mental organization—A longitudinal study. *Journal of Gerontology, 9,* 296–302.

Meacham, J. A. (1982). Wisdom and the context of knowledge: Knowing that one doesn't know. In D. Kuhn & J. A. Meacham (Eds.), *On the development of developmental psychology.* Basel: Karger.

Mergler, N. L., & Goldstein, M. D. (1983). Why are there old people: Senescence as biological and cultural preparedness for the transmission of information. *Human Development, 26,* 72–90.

Miles, C. C. (1934). Influence of speed and age on intelligence scores of adults. *Journal of Genetic Psychology, 10,* 208–210.

Miles, C. C., & Miles, W. R. (1932). The correlation of intelligence scores and chronological age from early to late maturity. *American Journal of Psychology, 44,* 44–78.

Miles, W. R. (1933). Age and human ability. *Psychological Review, 40,* 387–414.

Miller, J., Slomczynski, K. M., & Kohn, M. L. (1984). *The impact of job on intellective process in the United States and Poland: Continuity of learning-generalization throughout adult life.* Unpublished paper, National Institute of Health, Bethesda, MD.

Neisser, U. (1976). General, academic, and artificial intelligence. In L. B. Resnick (Ed.), *The nature of intelligence.* Hillsdale, NJ: Erlbaum.

Neisser, U. (1983). Components of intelligence or steps in routine procedures? *Cognition, 15,* 189–197.

Nesselroade, J. R., & Baltes, P. B. (Eds.). (1979). *Longitudinal research in the study of behavior and development.* New York: Academic Press.

Nesselroade, J. R., Schaie, K. W., & Baltes, P. B. (1972). Ontogenetic and generational components of structural and quantitative change in adult behavior. *Journal of Gerontology, 27,* 222–228.

Nesselroade, J. R., Stigler, S. M., & Baltes, P. B. (1980). Regression towards the mean and the study of change. *Psychological Bulletin, 88,* 622–637.

Nisbet, J. D. (1957). IV.—Intelligence and age: Retesting with twenty-four years interval. *British Journal of Educational Psychology, 27,* 190–198.

Overton, W. F., & Newman, J. L. (1982). Cognitive development: A competence-activation/utilization approach. In T. Field, A. Houston, H. Quay, L. Troll, & G. Finley (Eds.), *Review of human development.* New York: Wiley.

Owens, W. A., Jr. (1953). Age and mental abilities: A longitudinal study. *Genetic Psychology Monographs, 48,* 3–54.

Owens, W. A., Jr. (1959). Is age kinder to the initially more able? *Journal of Gerontology, 14,* 334–337.

Owens, W. A., Jr. (1966). Age and mental abilities: A second adult follow-up. *Journal of Educational Psychology, 51,* 311–325.

Papalia, D. E., & Bielby, D. D. V. (1974). Cognitive functioning in middle and old age adults: A review of research based on Piaget's theory. *Human Development, 17,* 424–443.

Papalia-Finlay, D., Blackburn, J., Davis, E., Dellmann, M., & Roberts, P. (1981). Training cognitive functioning in the elderly—Inability to replicate previous findings. *International Journal of Aging and Human Development, 12,* 111–117.

Pascual-Leone, J. (1983). Growing into human maturity: Towards a metasubjective theory of adulthood stages. In P. B. Baltes & O. G. Brim, Jr. (Eds.), *Life-span development and behavior* (Vol. 5). New York: Academic Press.

Peirce, C. S. (1902). Reasoning. In J. M. Baldwin (Ed.), *Dictionary of philosophy and psychology* (Vol. 2). New York: Peter Smith.

Pellegrino, J. W., & Glaser, R. (1979). Cognitive correlates and components in the analysis of individual differences. In R. J. Sternberg & D. K. Detterman (Eds.), *Human intelligence: Perspectives on its theory and measurement.* Norwood, NJ: Ablex.

Perry, W. G. (1970). *Forms of intellectual and ethical development in the college years: A scheme.* New York: Holt, Rinehart & Winston.

Peterson, J. (1925). *Early conceptions and tests of intelligence.* New York: Harcourt, Brace & World.

Peterson, J. (1929, February). Studies in the comparative abilities of whites and negroes. *Mental Measurement Monographs* (Serial No. 5).

Piaget, J. (1952). *Origins of intelligence in children.* New York: International Universities Press.

Piaget, J. (1960). *The psychology of intelligence.* Paterson, NJ: Littlefield, Adams.

Piaget, J. (1972). Intellectual evolution from adolescence to adulthood. *Human Development, 15,* 1–12.

Plemons, J. K., Willis, S. L., & Baltes, P. B. (1978). Modifiability of fluid intelligence in aging: A short-term longitudinal training approach. *Journal of Gerontology, 33,* 224–231.

Popkin, S. J., Schaie, K. W., & Krauss, I. K. (1983). Age-fair assessment of psychometric intelligence. *Educational Gerontology, 9,* 47–55.

Porter, N. (1891). *The human intellect with an introduction upon psychology and the soul* (4th ed.). New York: Charles Scribner's Sons.

Powell, P. M. (1980). Advanced social role-taking and cognitive development in gifted adults. *International Journal of Aging and Human Development, 11,* 177–192.

Pressey, S. L. (1917). Distinctive features in psychological test measurements made upon dementia praecox and chronic alcoholic patients. *Journal of Abnormal Psychology, 12,* 130–139.

Pressey, S. L. (1919). Are the present psychological scales reliable for adults? *Journal of Abnormal Psychology, 14,* 314–324.

Pressey, S. L., & Kuhlen, R. G. (1957). *Psychological development through the life span.* New York: Harper.

Protinsky, H., & Hughston, G. (1978). Conservation in elderly males. *Developmental Psychology, 14,* 114.

Quetelet, A. (1835). *Sur l'homme et le développement de ses facultés.* Paris: Bachelier.

Quetelet, A. (1838). *Über den Menschen und die Entwicklung seiner Fähigkeiten.* Stuttgart: Schweizerbarts.

Quetelet, A. (1842). *A treatise on man and the development of his faculties.* Edinburgh: William & Robert Chambers.

Rabbitt, P. M. A. (1977). Changes in problem solving ability in old age. In J. E. Birren & K. W. Schaie (Eds.), *Handbook of the psychology of aging.* New York: Van Nostrand Reinhold.

Rabbitt, P. M. A. (1982). How do old people know what to do next? In F. I. M. Craik & S. Trehub (Eds.), *Aging and cognitive processes.* New York: Plenum Press.

Raven, J. C. (1948). The comparative assessment of intellectual ability. *British Journal of Psychology, 39,* 12–19.

Reese, H. W., & Rodeheaver, D. (in press). Problem solving and complex decision making. In J. E. Birren & K. W. Schaie (Eds.), *Handbook of the psychology of aging* (rev. ed.). New York: Van Nostrand Reinhold.

Reinert, G. (1970). Comparative factor analytic studies of intelligence throughout the human life span. In L. R. Goulet & P. B. Baltes (Eds.), *Life-span developmental psychology: Research and theory.* New York: Academic Press.

Resnick, L. B. (1976). Introduction: Changing conceptions of intelligence. In L. B. Resnick (Ed.), *The nature of intelligence.* Hillsdale, NJ: Erlbaum.

Riegel, K. F. (1958). Ergebnisse und Probleme der psychologischen Altersforschung. *Vita Humana, 1,* 52–64.

Riegel, K. F. (1973). Dialectic operations: The final period of cognitive development. *Human Development, 16,* 371–381.

Riegel, K. F., & Riegel, R. M. (1972). Development, drop, and death. *Developmental Psychology, 6,* 306–319.

Riley, M. W., Johnson, M., & Foner, A. (Eds.). (1972). *Aging and society: A sociology of age stratification.* New York: Russell Sage Foundation.

Roe, A. (1972). Maintenance of creative output through the years. In C. W. Taylor (Ed.), *Climate for creativity.* New York: Pergamon Press.

Ruch, F. L. (1934). The differentiative effects of age upon human learning. *Journal of General Psychology, 11,* 261–286.

Rudinger, G., & Lantermann, E. D. (1980). Soziale Bedingungen der Intelligenz im Alter. *Zeitschrift für Gerontologie, 13,* 433–441.

Ryder, N. B. (1965). The cohort as a concept in the study of social change. *American Sociological Review, 30,* 843–861.

Salthouse, T. A. (1982). *Adult cognition: An experimental psychology of human aging.* New York: Springer.

Sanford, E. C. (1902). Mental growth and decay. *American Journal of Psychology, 13,* 426–449.

Scarr, S., & Carter-Saltzman, L. (1982). Genetics and intelligence. In R. J. Sternberg (Ed.), *Handbook of human intelligence.* Cambridge: Cambridge University Press.

Schaie, K. W. (1958). Rigidity-flexibility and intelligence: A cross-sectional study of the adult life span from 20 to 70. *Psychological Monographs, 72,* No. 462 (Whole No. 9).

Schaie, K. W. (1959). Cross-sectional methods in the study of psychological aspects of aging. *Journal of Gerontology, 14,* 208–215.

Schaie, K. W. (1965). A general model for the study of developmental problems. *Psychological Bulletin, 64,* 92–107.

Schaie, K. W. (1978). External validity in the assessment of intellectual development in adulthood. *Journal of Gerontology, 33,* 695–701.

Schaie, K. W. (1979). The Primary Mental Abilities in adulthood: An exploration in the development of psychometric intelligence. In P. B. Baltes & O. G. Brim, Jr. (Eds.), *Life-span development and behavior* (Vol. 2). New York: Academic Press.

Schaie, K. W. (1983a). The Seattle Longitudinal Study: A 21-year exploration of psychometric intelligence in adulthood. In K. W. Schaie (Ed.), *Longitudinal studies of adult psychological development.* New York: Guilford.

Schaie, K. W. (1983b). What can we learn from the longitudinal study of adult psychological development? In K. W. Schaie (Ed.), *Longitudinal studies of adult psychological development.* New York: Guilford.

Schaie, K. W., & Baltes, P. B. (1975). On sequential strategies in developmental research and the Schaie-Baltes controversy: Description or explanation? *Human Development, 18,* 384–390.

Schaie, K. W., & Baltes, P. B. (1977). Some faith helps to see the forest: A final comment on the Horn and Donaldson myth of the Baltes-Schaie position on adult intelligence. *American Psychologist, 32,* 1118–1120.

Schaie, K. W., & Hertzog, C. (1983). Fourteen-year cohort-sequential analyses of adult intellectual development. *Developmental Psychology, 19,* 531–543.

Schaie, K. W., & Labouvie-Vief, G. (1974). Generational vs. ontogenetic components of change in adult cognitive behavior: A fourteen-year cross-sequential study. *Developmental Psychology, 10,* 305–320.

Schaie, K. W., Labouvie, G. V., & Buech, B. U. (1973). Generational and cohort-specific differences in adult cognitive functioning: A fourteen-year study of independent samples. *Developmental Psychology, 9,* 151–166.

Schaie, K. W., & Parham, I. A. (1977). Cohort-sequential analyses of adult intellectual development. *Developmental Psychology, 13,* 649–653.

Schaie, K. W., Rosenthal, F., & Perlman, R. M. (1953). Differential deterioration of factorially "pure" mental abilities. *Journal of Gerontology, 8,* 191–196.

Schaie, K. W., & Strother, C. R. (1968a). The cross-sequential study of age changes in cognitive behavior. *Psychological Bulletin, 70,* 671–680.

Schaie, K. W., & Strother, C. R. (1968b). The effects of time and cohort differences on the interpretation of age changes in cognitive behavior. *Multivariate Behavioral Research, 3,* 259–293.

Schaier, A. H., & Cicirelli, V. G. (1976). Age differences in humor comprehension and appreciation in old age. *Journal of Gerontology, 31,* 577–582.

Sharp, S. E. (1899). Individual psychology: A study in psychological method. *American Journal of Psychology, 10,* 329–391.

Sigel, I. E., & Hooper, F. H. (Eds.). (1968). *Logical thinking in children: Research based on Piaget's theory.* New York: Holt, Rinehart & Winston.

Sinnott, J. D. (1983). Post-formal reasoning: The relativistic stage. In M. Commons (Ed.), *Post-formal operations.* New York: Praeger.

Snow, R. E. (1982). The training of intellectual aptitude. In D. K. Detterman & R. J. Sternberg (Eds.), *How and how much can intelligence be increased.* Norwood, NJ: Ablex.

Sorenson, H. (1933). Mental ability over a wide range of adult ages. *Journal of Applied Psychology, 17,* 729–741.

Spearman, C. (1904). "General intelligence" objectively determined and measured. *American Journal of Psychology, 15,* 201–293.

Spearman, C. (1914a). The heredity of abilities. *Eugenics Review, 6,* 219–237.

Spearman, C. (1914b). The measurement of intelligence. *Eugenics Review, 6,* 312–313.

Spearman, C. (1927). *The abilities of man.* New York: Macmillan.

Spencer, H. (1855). *The principles of psychology* (2 vols.). New York: Appleton.

Spencer, H. (1895). *The principles of biology* (3rd ed.). New York: Macmillan.

Stern, W. (1912). *Die psychologischen Methoden der Intelligenzprüfung.* Leipzig: Barth.

Sternberg, R. J. (1980). Sketch of a componential subtheory of human intelligence. *Behavioral and Brain Sciences, 3,* 573–614.

Sternberg, R. J. (1981). Testing and cognitive psychology. *American Psychologist, 36,* 1181–1189.

Sternberg, R. J. (Ed.). (1982). *Handbook of human intelligence.* Cambridge: Cambridge University Press.

Sternberg, R. J. (1983). Components of human intelligence. *Cognition, 15,* 1–48.

Sternberg, R. J. (1984). Toward a triarchic theory of human intelligence. *Behavioral and Brain Sciences, 7,* 269–315.

Sterns, H. L., & Sanders, R. E. (1980). Training and education of the elderly. In R. R. Turner & H. W. Reese (Eds.), *Life-span developmental psychology: Intervention.* New York: Academic Press.

Stoddard, G. D. (1941). On the meaning of intelligence. *Psychological Review, 48,* 250–260.

Stoddard, G. D. (1943). *The meaning of intelligence.* New York: Macmillan.

Stout, G. F., & Baldwin, J. M. (1901). Intellect (or intelligence). In J. M. Baldwin (Ed.), *Dictionary of philosophy and psychology* (Vol. 1). New York: Macmillan.

Taub, H. A. (1973). Memory span, practice and aging. *Journal of Gerontology, 28,* 335–358.

Thompson, C. W. (1951). Decline in limit of performance among adult morons. *American Journal of Psychology, 64,* 203–215.

Thorndike, E. L. (1911). *Animal intelligence: Experimental studies.* New York: Macmillan.

Thorndike, E. L. (1928). *Adult learning.* New York: Macmillan.

Thorndike, E. L., & Woodworth, R. S. (1901). The influence of improvement in one mental function upon the efficiency of other functions. *Psychological Review, 8,* 247–256.

Thurstone, L. L., & Thurstone, T. G. (1949). *Examiner manual for the SRA Primary Mental Abilities Test.* Chicago: Science Research Associates.

Tuddenham, R. D., Blumenkranz, J., & Wilkin, W. R. (1968). Age changes on AGCT: A longitudinal study of average adults. *Journal of Consulting and Clinical Psychology, 32,* 659–663.

Tyler, L. E. (1976). The intelligence we test—An evolving concept. In L. B. Resnick (Ed.), *The nature of intelligence.* Hillsdale, NJ: Erlbaum.

Vernon, P. A. (1983). Speed of information processing and general intelligence. *Intelligence, 7,* 53–70.

Wagner, R. K., & Sternberg, R. J. (1984). *Practical intelligence in real-world pursuits: The role of tacit knowledge.* Unpublished manuscript, Department of Psychology, Yale University, New Haven.

Wechsler, D. (1939). *The measurement of adult intelligence.* Baltimore: Williams & Wilkins.

Wechsler, D. (1952). *The range of human capacities.* Baltimore: Williams & Wilkins.

Wechsler, D. (1955). *Wechsler Adult Intelligence Scale, manual.* New York: Psychological Corporation.

Wechsler, D. (1958). *The measurement and appraisal of adult intelligence* (4th ed.). Baltimore: Williams & Wilkins.

Wechsler, D. (1975). Intelligence defined and undefined: A relativistic appraisal. *American Psychologist, 30,* 135–139.

Weisenburg, T., Roe, A., & McBride, K. E. (1936). *Adult intelligence: A psychological study of test performance.* London: Commonwealth Fund.

Welford, A. T. (1958). *Aging and human skill.* London: Oxford University Press.

Willis, S. L. (in press). Towards an educational psychology of the adult learner. In J. E. Birren & K. W. Schaie (Eds.), *Handbook of the psychology of aging* (rev. ed.). New York: Van Nostrand Reinhold.

Willis, S. L., & Baltes, P. B. (1980). Intelligence in adulthood and aging: Contemporary issues. In L. W. Poon (Ed.), *Aging in the 1980s: Psychological issues.* Washington, DC: American Psychological Association.

Willis, S. L., Blieszner, R., & Baltes, P. B. (1981). Intellectual training research in aging: Modification of performance on the fluid ability of figural relations. *Journal of Educational Psychology, 73,* 41–50.

Willoughby, R. R. (1927). Family similarities in mental-test abilities. *Genetic Psychology Monographs, 2,* 239–277.

Wissler, C. (1901). The correlation of mental and physical tests. *The Psychological Review Monograph Supplements 3,* No. 6 (Whole No. 16), 4, 27, 29, 34–36.

Witty, P. A., & Jenkins, M. D. (1936). Intra-race testing and Negro intelligence. *The Journal of Psychology, 1,* 179–192.

Wohlwill, J. F. (1980). Cognitive development in childhood. In O. G. Brim, Jr., & J. Kagan (Eds.), *Constancy and change in human development.* Cambridge: Harvard University Press.

Wolman, B. B. (Ed.). (1982). *Handbook of developmental psychology.* Englewood Cliffs, NJ: Prentice-Hall.

Woodruff, D. S. (1982). *Age and intelligence: The history of an idea.* Unpublished manuscript, Department of Psychology, Temple University, Philadelphia.

Woodruff, D. S. (1983). A review of aging and cognitive processes. *Research on Aging, 5,* 139–153.

Yerkes, R. M. (1921). *Psychological examining in the United States Army.* Washington, DC: Government Printing Office.

Yerkes, R. M. (1923). Testing and the human mind. *Atlantic Monthly, 131,* 358–370.

PART TWO

MEASUREMENTS

NINE

THE VALIDITY OF TESTS OF INTELLIGENCE

NATHAN BRODY
Wesleyan University
Middletown, Connecticut

Do intelligence tests measure intelligence? To ask this question is to recognize implicitly the distinction between the construct, intelligence, and the instruments that are alleged to be measures of the construct. Further, the question implies that the meaning of the construct must be independent of the measurement instruments. That meaning, for the purposes of this chapter, is found in the common-sense or ordinary-language definition of the term intelligence, and in the slightly more refined rendition offered by Spearman in his famous article of 1904. It is not, however, a meaning totally devoid of the accumulated results of over a century of research and empirical relationships that provide a nomological network of meanings that triangulate the construct in logical space. Thus the full answer to the question posed would require one, in effect, to reproduce the contents of all the chapters in this handbook. The review of research in this chapter will of necessity be diffuse. Its coherence shall derive from the attempt to ascertain if more recent and refined empirical efforts require modification in the common-sense views of intelligence and in the views stated in 1904 by Spearman.

Many of the meanings that are relevant for technical discourse about intelligence are implicit in the ordinary understanding of the term (see Sternberg, Conway, Ketron, & Bernstein, 1981, for a related assertion). Or, perhaps, one might argue that the ordinary understanding of the term has shaped technical discourse and research on intelligence. The ordinary connotations of the term appear to include the following.

1. The term is singular rather than plural. Hence, whatever intelligence is, it must be one thing rather than many things.

2. The singular entity called intelligence may be construed as a measure of the ability to acquire knowledge as a result of exposure to culturally relevant information.

3.   To define intelligence in terms of ability is to imply that whatever intelligence is, it must partly be construed as something independent of and different from achievement and what is actually learned. Ability to learn is logically prior to what is learned. One can speak of an ability that has not yet had an opportunity to manifest itself. This notion implies that ability, even as an unmeasurable or unactualized potential, must exist in a historically prior sense. Ability notions do not, strictly speaking, require one to assume that the ability is influenced by genotypes or is constitutionally present. However, the historically prior status of the construct is at least compatible with, if not conducive to, the view that intelligence is a genetically influenced and constitutionally present characteristic of the person. Further, abilities stand in a causal relationship to achievements. They are necessary but not sufficient determinants of what is achieved. It is logically inconsistent to assert that someone has learned or achieved knowledge without the ability to do so. It is not, however, logically inconsistent to assert that someone has the ability to acquire knowledge but has failed to do so. Indeed, it is part and parcel of our ordinary knowledge of the world that there are many reasons why abilities may not be actualized. An individual may be deprived of the opportunities to learn and acquire knowledge, or an individual may be provided with the opportunity to acquire knowledge but may choose not to do so for a variety of temperamental or motivational reasons. Thus intelligence stands in a causal but not in a unicausal relationship to the acquisition of knowledge.

4.   It is certainly the case that one's ability to learn ought not to be independent of what one has learned. Thus intelligence should not be a fixed or invariant characteristic of a person. Rather, it should be modified as a result of experience. However, if the ability to learn is causally related to what has been learned, modifications in intelligence should not be independent of the initial level of intelligence. And, given relatively invariant opportunities, and assuming no changes in the nonintellective abilities that may influence what is learned, the position of an individual relative to others who differ in ability should remain relatively invariant. Changes in ability may occur through the life span, and certainly over the initial part of the life span, without necessarily influencing a person's ability relative to others. Differences in opportunities to learn ought to result in differences in ability to learn. Thus the ordinary conception of intelligence does not imply that it is a fixed characteristic, and it allows for a relative degree of invariance. But we tend to think of abilities as being resistant to change. Thus we ought to expect that the underlying construct intelligence is relatively nonmalleable.

5.   If intelligence is logically distinct from achievement, we should expect that the indices that are appropriate to the measure of intelligence are initially distinct and independent from those that assess actual knowledge. At the same time we should recognize that achievement and intelligence ought to become, over time, relatively intertwined, and it ought to be difficult to distinguish between such measures if individuals are given considerable opportunity to actualize their ability to learn.

6.   Since intelligence changes over the life span (although an individual's ability relative to others may remain relatively invariant), then it follows that the indices used to infer ability necessarily must change. Moreover, if individuals have had different opportunities to actualize their ability, it is, in principle, possible that the relationship between indices of intelligence (that is, intelligence test scores) and the underlying construct of which such indices are considered manifestations may be variable.

Spearman (1904) may be viewed as providing three technical refinements and emendations on the ordinary meaning of intelligence sketched above. First, Spearman made explicit in his two-factor theory that intelligence is really a singular entity, and he established the algebraic consequences of that view. He noted that the correlation between any two measures of intelligence ought to be determined by the extent to which they are measures of the single construct called g. This assumption permits one to derive the law of tetrad differences and to define the relationships that exist among all the correlations in a matrix of correlations of ability measures. The matrix should be subject to a hierarchical arrangement in which tests can be arrayed across both columns and rows in order of their g loading. In such a matrix the magnitude of the positive correlations should decrease in a predictable fashion as one reads down the horizontal columns or across the rows. Second, returning to the earlier methods of Galton (1869, 1883), Spearman proposed to test intelligence not in terms of the clinical methods of Binet and Simon (1905) but rather in terms of the allegedly more rigorous methods of the experimental psychology laboratory. Third, by proposing the correction for attenuation Spearman, in effect, distinguished between the construct intelligence and the test of intelligence and indicated that the latter index may be subject to any of a host of random fluctuations or perturbations that result in an inaccurate measure. In effect, Spearman provided a formal method both for the correction of the measure and provided the basis for distinguishing between the error-prone index of the construct and the true construct. Thus for Spearman, intelligence was a theoretical entity apart from and distinct from any of its empirical constituents and manifestations.

To what extent does contemporary research on intelligence support this naive view of intelligence including the emendations of Spearman?

THE ONE-MANY PROBLEM

Let us begin with the question of whether intelligence is one or many things. One must postulate the existence of more than one factor to account for all the patterns of correlations in the matrix—a fact that Spearman was aware of as early as 1906 (see Spearman, 1927). Also a single general factor accounts for a substantial portion of the variance in any matrix of correlations among diverse ability tests given to a group of individuals who do not represent a sharply restricted range of talent for intelligence (Brody & Brody, 1976; McNemar,

1964). Moreover, the existence of a general factor is relatively independent of the factor-analytic procedures that are used to extract the factor. Jensen (1981, 1983a) notes that the general factor that is empirically derived from factor analysis is not dependent on the method of analysis. Whether g is extracted as the first principle component of an initially unrotated factor or is derived as a second-order factor does not appreciably influence the existence of a general factor that accounts for a substantial portion of the relationship among the diverse tests. Further, such general factors derived in different ways from the same matrix are highly correlated and empirically nondistinguishable. The existence of a general factor is simply a more abstract way of noting that virtually all general matrices of correlations among diverse measures of intellectual ability given to a sample of individuals not restricted in range of talent will exhibit a positive manifold. That is, the correlations will tend to be all positive. In this sense, the empirical literature supports Spearman's concept of the indifference of the indicator. Virtually any measure that seems to reflect some type of intellectual ability will correlate positively with virtually any other measure and in this sense the composition of many different heterogeneous batteries of ability measures will empirically result in roughly comparable measures (see Spearman, 1927). And it is for this reason that all omnibus measures of intelligence are substantially positively correlated (see Matarazzo, 1972).

Gould (1981; see also Schonemann, 1983) has noted that factor-analytic solutions of matrices are indeterminate and that one can, using oblique or orthogonal rotations, resolve the indeterminacy of the matrices in any of several ways without necessarily positing the existence of a general factor of ability. Although it is certainly the case that one can factor analyze a matrix of ability using oblique factor-analytic methods and find a factor solution that does not include a general factor, it should be noted that the obliquely defined factors will themselves be correlated and that tests that load highly on the primary factors will also have substantial loading on the g factor.

Several modern theories are extant that in various ways would argue that it is a mistake to construe intelligence as a single entity. Guilford (1964, 1967; Guilford & Hoepfner, 1971), more than any other contemporary theorist, has proposed a model of intelligence that has no provision for g and in fact postulates the existence of 120 orthogonal independent dimensions of intellect that are alleged to be discoverable in factor-analytic investigations. The mere postulation of such a radical alternative to g may be wrongly construed to imply that the factor-analytic investigation of intelligence is either at best indeterminate with respect to the existence of a general factor of intelligence or, if Guilford is correct, then the factor-analytic evidence directly contradicts the existence of g. I have argued that the factor-analytic evidence does not support Guilford (Brody & Brody, 1976; see also Cronbach & Snow, 1977; Eysenck, 1979). Guilford's factor structures are often nonreplicable. In one analysis of a matrix of correlations for memory factors where Guilford postulated the existence of 18 orthogonal factors, an analysis of the correlations indicated that a single standard measure of verbal ability correlated positively and significantly with every other measure with correlations ranging between .16 and .70 and had a median correlation value of .39 (see Brody & Brody, 1976).

Guilford's factor-analytic procedures through the use of targeted or Procrutean methods submerge the general factor and replace it with a host of allegedly independent orthogonal but poorly defined factors. However, this is a forced solution. Also Guilford's theoretical factors have very little predictive validity. Any theory of the structure of intellect that proposes to replace g with a more differentiated concept ought to have predictive validity that exceeds that obtained from a general factor. Guilford's system has failed that requirement. Predictions of intellectual performance by using several intellectual indices derived from Guilford's model do not in general exceed the predictive validity coefficients obtained from a single general index (see Brody & Brody, 1976). Similarly, Jensen (1981) has argued that the diverse relationships between measures of intellectual ability and performance in a variety of occupational settings are better accounted for by the g factor than by specialized intellectual abilities.

To a considerable degree the pervasiveness of g as a component of measures of ability has posed difficulties for a variety of factor-analytically derived models that have attempted to decompose g. Consider as an example of a widely accepted factor-analytically based theory of intelligence, Cattell's fluid and crystallized ability distinction (Cattell, 1971). His theoretical distinction largely duplicates the ability achievement distinction within the domain of ability itself. Cattell argues that g may be divided into two components: g_f or fluid ability, represents a biologically based measure of general ability that stands in a causal relationship to ability that is acquired as a result of acculturation, g_c or crystallized ability. Cattell finds that measures of fluid and crystallized ability are separable using oblique rotations. They are, however, substantially correlated (approximately .50). Cattell prefers to derive these measures as second-order factors using oblique rotations. In some of his studies Cattell has factor analyzed second-order factors including g_c and g_f. He derives two third-order factors that are presumed to represent more general factors and considers one of them to be a historically prior measure of fluid ability. He assumes that the second factor (the educational effectiveness factor) represents the impact of educational experiences. At this still more abstract hierarchical level a number of Cattell's analyses indicate that the historical fluid ability factor that is most reminiscent of Spearman's g seems to account for more variance than the educational effectiveness factor. Thus at its most abstract level, Cattell's factor-analytic research reduces to postulation of a single general factor (see Cattell, 1971; Brody & Brody, 1976). In this respect Cattell's factor-analytic system is only marginally different from the factor solutions favored by such British theorists as Vernon (1961) who extract g as a general factor before attempting to account for additional variance in the matrix.

It is not only the case that Cattell's psychometric analyses have not invariably been successful in distinguishing between components of g; a number of conceptual distinctions that are essential to the argument that the different components of g do measure different aspects of intelligence have not always been unequivocally supported in the research literature. For example, Cattell asserts that fluid ability is more likely to be influenced by biological variables than crystallized ability. A number of implications of this general position have been the subject of empirical investigations. Cattell has argued that the heritability of fluid intelligence should be higher than the heritability of crystallized intelligence. Cattell (1982) has provided a comprehensive review of research dealing with this issue, indicating that the hypothesis has received only partial support in the literature. In his first study of this problem (see Cattell, Stice, & Kristy, 1957; Cattell, Blewett, & Beloff, 1955), Cattell found that the heritability of fluid and crystallized intelligence measures was essentially equal, although he notes (Cattell, 1982) that the heritability estimates based on twin data are discrepant with respect to the influence of genotypes on measures of fluid and crystallized ability from the estimates provided by analyses of between-family relationships. The latter analyses suggested that between-family heritability for fluid ability is higher than the between-family heritability for crystallized ability. More recent studies using somewhat more comprehensive analytic procedures appear partly to confirm these results. Averaged across all forms of analysis, Cattell finds heritability of fluid ability to be .59 and the heritability of crystallized ability to be .33. The discrepancy in heritability is attributable to a large difference in between-family heritability. Fluid and crystallized ability do not differ at all in the heritability estimates based on within-family variances derived from twin data. It should be noted that there are a number of somewhat arbitrary statistical assumptions involved in calculating these heritability estimates and that the data sets that provide the basis for the heritability estimates are incomplete (not all the possible correlations that might be used to estimate parameters in the model for the determination of the several components of variance that are included in the full specification of the equations for estimating heritability are represented in the data set). This brief excursion into research on the differential heritability of fluid and crystallized ability is presented as an illustration that is suggestive of several more general conclusions. Because of the relatedness of separate components of g, it is somewhat difficult to obtain unambiguous empirical demonstrations indicating that different components of g have different theoretical properties. It may require somewhat extensive arbitrary statistical manipulations to obtain distinctions between highly related components of general intelligence.

Another theoretical distinction between crystallized and fluid ability is the assumption of differential decline over the age span. Fluid ability is assumed to exhibit larger declines with age since it is more reflective of the underlying integrity of the nervous system. Cattell (1971) argues that there is an inexorable decline in the efficiency of neural processing with age. Crystallized intelligence, since it is less directly tied to the nervous system, and since it reflects the results of a lifetime of acquisition of knowledge, is not assumed to decline with age. It is now known that the picture of inevitable decline of intelligence with age is partly an artifact of using cross-sectional data that does not take account of cohort differences (Schaie & Strother, 1968). There is, however, some debate in the literature about the existence of differential decline in crystallized and fluid ability over the age span. Cattell (1971) cites an unpublished reanalysis by Wackwitz of Schaie and Strother's combined cross-sectional and longitudinal data and other data collected by Horn and Cattell (1967) that indicates there is very little difference in age-related declines between fluid and crystallized ability measures (see Horn & Donaldson, 1976; Baltes & Schaie, 1976). Horn and Donaldson argue that the data cited by Baltes and Schaie indicating a lack of inevitable decline in intelligence with age is based on measures that are not unambiguous markers for fluid ability factors. It should be noted that the evidence for differential decline in ability over time is substantially derived from cross-sectional rather than longitudinal data that confounds cohort effects and longitudinal changes attributable to the effects of age. The debate between Horn and Donaldson and Baltes and Schaie exemplifies the difficulty of developing unambiguous distinctions between indices of g that are themselves substantially correlated.

INTELLIGENCE AND THE ABILITY TO ACQUIRE KNOWLEDGE

Binet (Binet & Simon, 1905) wanted to develop measures of ability that would predict success in school and Spearman (1904) assumed that the demonstration of a high correlation between laboratory measures and judgments of intelligence based on school performance demonstrated that his intellectual ability measures were in fact valid. There is no doubt that intelligence test scores are correlated with academic success (see Lavin, 1965, for a comprehensive review). The usual correlations reported are about .50. Usually the correlations are somewhat higher for the elementary grades and decrease at the college level due to restrictions in range of talent. Intelligence test scores are also related to the number of years of education that an individual attains; the correlation is approximately .70 (Miner, 1957; Wechsler, 1958). Intelligence test scores also have a predictive relationship to academic achievement. Tests given early in school can predict the number of years of education that a person will obtain. For example, Benson (1942) reported a correlation of .57 between intelligence test scores in the sixth grade and the number of years of education subsequently completed. The fact that intelligence test scores and academic success are correlated is supportive of the view that intelligence tests are measures of ability. However, the correlations do not clearly establish that tests stand in the required causal relationship implied by the assertion that intelligence tests are measures of ability to learn what is taught in schools. Crano, Kenny, and Campbell (1972) have attempted to use cross-lagged panel analysis to establish that tests of intelligence in general, and those tests that are presumed to be more reflective of fluid rather than crystallized ability in particular, are more predictive of subsequent achievement test scores than achievement test scores are predictive of subsequent scores on intelligence tests. They found some support for this hypothesis (see Rogosa, 1980, for a critique of the logic of cross-lagged panel analysis). There is other evidence for the notion that intelligence tests are independent of achievement tests. Intelligence tests may be given to children prior to school entry and such measures will be at least weakly predictive of academic achievement. Items on tests that appear only tangentially related to the standard curriculum of the schools will predict academic performance. Thus omnibus measures of intelligence are not merely a surrogate of academic achievement and appear to measure something that is independent of academic achievement but is nevertheless substantially predictive of achievement. Of course, over time, one would expect on theoretical grounds that measures of academic achievement and intelligence test scores would tend to coalesce.

The relationship between general intelligence and the ability to acquire knowledge appears to be ubiquitous. It is rather difficult to circumvent by variations in the context of learning. Many arguments that have been developed to suggest that general intelligence does not pervasively relate to the ability to acquire knowledge may well be spurious. For example, in a well-known analysis of the relationship between intelligence test scores and performance in a variety of laboratory tasks of learning, Woodrow (1940; see also Munn, 1954) argued that intelligence test scores are not substantially related to performance in laboratory measures of learning. Zeaman and House (1967) reanalyzed these data and indicated that many of the low correlations were attributable to restrictions in the range of talent and to unreliability of measurement of performance in laboratory tasks. They argued that tests of intelligence correlate moderately with a variety of verbal learning measures.

Cronbach and Snow (1977) reviewed the literature on what they called "aptitude X treatment" interactions. They were particularly interested in the possibility that certain types of instructional methods would benefit individuals who are low in intellectual ability while other methods of instruction would benefit individuals who are high in intellectual ability. They also investigated the possibility that different instructional methods interact differentially with different components of intelligence. Two rather striking conclusions are suggested by their comprehensive review of the literature. First, most of the interactions of instructional methods with measures of ability are between general ability measures rather than between specialized abilities and instructional methods. Thus with occasional exceptions a more differentiated view of intellectual abilities has not been found to be the most useful basis for individuating the curriculum. Second, there are very few disordinal interactions with ability such that certain instructional treatment lead to poorer performance for individuals of higher ability than for individuals of lower ability. Snow and Yalow (1982) have summarized the more recent literature on this issue. They found that some treatments benefit individuals with high intellectual ability and lead to poorer performance of individuals with low intellectual ability. Most of these treatments may be characterized as providing more opportunities for students to develop their own ideas and to deal with more complex materials. A number of instructional procedures appear to benefit individuals of low ability without harming individuals of high ability. Many of these may be described as providing students with structured information that relieves them of the burden of organizing materials for themselves. There are few, if any, replicated findings suggesting that there are instructional conditions permitting individuals of low intellectual ability to exceed the learning performance of individuals of high ability. Essentially similar conclusions may be derived from Bloom's analysis of mastery learning procedures (Bloom, 1974). Bloom notes that one reason for the ubiquitous correlation of measures of general intellectual ability and school achievement is that individuals of high ability are able to master concepts more rapidly than individuals of low ability. Schools typically do not provide enough time for individuals of low ability to acquire the concepts that are necessry to master new materials; hence slower students tend to develop cumulative deficits. Under mastery learning procedures students are given sufficient time to master a concept before being introduced to a new concept. Under such procedures Bloom asserts that the correlation between intelligence test scores and the acquisition of knowledge in school settings is reduced. However, Bloom does not claim that mastery learning procedures eliminate individual differences in general ability. He asserts only that the acquisition of conceptual knowledge may be made less dependent on individual differences in general intelligence. It may be the case that educational changes in instructional formats may help students with lower ability to develop greater mastery of the educational program of the schools. However, no known instructional formats will eliminate individual differences in general ability as an index of the ability to acquire more complex intellectual skills. The matter has been well put by Cronbach and Snow who conclude their review of the relationship between general ability and treatment interactions for instructions as follows:

> We once hoped that instructional methods might be found whose outcomes correlate very little with general ability. This does not appear to be a viable hope. Outcomes from extended instruction almost always correlate with pretested ability unless a ceiling is artificially imposed.
>
> The pervasive correlations of general ability with learning rate or outcomes in education limits the power of ATI findings to reduce individual differences. [Cronbach & Snow, 1977, p. 500]

The number of years of education attained is the single most important determinant of occupational status in United States society. Therefore, it is not surprising to find that intelligence test scores relate to occupational status. There have been a number of attempts to study the relationship between intelligence test scores and occupational status within the framework of path-analytic models that attempt to relate parental social status, intelligence test scores obtained during the school-age years, and educational attainment as determinants of occupational status (see Blau & Duncan, 1967; Fulker & Eysenck, 1979; and Jencks, 1972). The general picture that has emerged from these analyses is that parental social and educational status influences intelligence test scores and has relatively little influence on educational attainment that is independent of its influence on intelligence test scores. Intelligence test scores have a large influence on educational attainment and relatively little indirect influence on occupational status that is independent of their relationship to education. Taubman (1976) has studied occupational attainment in a large sample of monozygotic and dizygotic twins. His analysis permits one to construct somewhat more complex models that take into account the influence of separate genetic and environmental components of general intelligence that are related to occupational status. Taubman's refined study adds textured detail and precision to our understanding of the influence of intelligence on academic success and subsequent occupational success. It is, however, possible to argue that the relatively central role of intelligence and its predictive relationship to occupational attainment were prefigured by the results of Terman's classic longitudinal study that demonstrated that school children selected solely on the basis of high intelligence test scores tend to become intellectually eminent in adulthood and tend to have high occupational status (Terman, 1925; Terman & Oden, 1959).

Occupational status and intelligence may also be studied concurrently (see Harrell & Harrell, 1945). The median intelligence test scores of individuals in different occupations is positively related to ratings of the prestige of the occupation. The range and variability of intelligence test scores is inversely related to the social prestige of the occupation. Intelligence test score acts as a threshold variable for occupational success. Individuals with low scores have a low probability of being found in prestige occupations. However, individuals of all intellectual levels are found in low prestige occupations. This "threshold" relationship is substantially mediated by the relationship between intelligence test scores and academic success. High-prestige occupations require extensive years of education as a condition of entry and individuals with low intelligence test scores tend to have difficulty completing higher education (see Hartson & Sprow, 1941).

Literature also relates intelligence test performance to success within an occupation, although this is not a simple matter. Since intelligence test scores act as a threshold variable for entry into many occupations, there is often a restricted range of talent of intelligence within an occupation, reducing the magnitude of the correlation. Also, for many occupations it is difficult to obtain relatively unbiased indices of occupational success. Also, the relationship between success within an occupation and intelligence may be variable across occupations for a variety of reasons. Success in some occupations may be determined substantially by nonintellective factors. For example, some admittedly dated evidence suggests that success as a salesman is unrelated to intelligence test scores (Kenagy & Yockum, 1925). Also, we should expect on theoretical grounds that the correlation between occupational success and intelligence should be dependent on the intellectual demands of the occupation. Jensen (1981) has reported the results of an extensive analysis of the data provided by the U.S. Department of Labor manual for the USES General Aptitude Test Battery. The manual reports correlations between special measures of intellectual ability and some specialized aptitudes such as manual dexterity and measures of success at a variety of different occupations. Jensen's analysis indicates that the median validity for the multifactor battery using an optimally weighted composite of nine aptitudes including general intelligence and such specializing ability measures as verbal, numerical, and spatial ability and success in 446 different occupations is .36. The median validity for a general intelligence score alone is .27. It should be noted that the validity coefficient for the optimally weighted multifactorial prediction is inflated by sampling error. The relatively small difference in these validity coefficients suggests that a substantial portion of the predictive validity for occupational success within an occupation is attributable to general ability. Of course, specialized aptitudes may add useful incremental validity in certain specialized situations, but to a remarkable extent what appears to determine occupational success in a great variety of occupations is general intellectual ability rather than more specialized components of intellect. Jensen also cites an unpublished analysis of these data by Hunter that indicates that the predictive validity of general intelligence increases as the intellectual demands of the occupation increase (see Jensen, 1980).

IS INTELLIGENCE MALLEABLE?

It is a mistake to argue that our concept of ability requires that intelligence is fixed or invariant. However, we assume that abilities are somewhat resistant to change and that intelligence should be a relatively invariant characteristic of a person. In this section I will review studies dealing with stability and change in intelligence test scores. Intelligence test scores are among the most stable indices of individual differences over the life span. The position of an individual with respect to his or her age cohorts in intellectual ability remains relatively invariant over the life span. Conley (1984) has summarized the results of longitudinal studies of intelligence over the adult years. With the exception of one value using a test of intelligence with undefined reliability, his review of the literature indicates that the uncorrected test-retest correlations found in 10 studies ranged from .62 to .94 for intervals ranging between 7 and 40 years. Data from the Berkeley Growth Study (see Jones & Bayley, 1941; Pinneau, 1961), in which a group of individuals were repeatedly given intelligence tests, indicate that scores obtained at ages 10, 11, and 12 when averaged predict the average of test scores obtained at ages 17 and 18 with a correlation of .96. Thus the average of intelligence test scores prior to the start of secondary school predict performance at the end of secondary school. Although these findings support the view that intelligence test scores are remarkably stable characteristics of individuals they should not necessarily be entirely surprising, since our knowledge of the determinants of intelligence test scores suggests that the major determinants of test performance have already had a substantial impact on individuals by the time they are aged 10. Among the influences on test scores are genetic influences, the impact of the family, and the school environment. One would expect that, in large measure, the impact of these variables has helped to determine intelligence test scores during the early school-age years. It is unlikely that the typical child experiences a dramatic change in the influence of the several determinants of intelligence during the high school years. That is, one's genes, the impact of the family environment, and the quality of schooling one experiences are not likely to change during this period. And the small likelihood of large changes may help to create stability in performance over time.

Although there is considerable evidence for the stability of general intelligence test scores, several different kinds of evidence have been cited by individuals who tend to argue that intelligence is not fixed. Hunt (1961) argued that the relatively low correlations usually found betwen measures of ability obtained in infancy from such tests as the Bayley Scales of Infant Development and subsequent intelligence test scores was evidence for the malleability of intelligence. There is little doubt that scores on infant intelligence tests given during the first year of life have relatively low and often near-zero correlations with later measures of intelligence (see McCall, 1979, for a review of this literature). However, many of the items on such tests as the Bayley seem only tangentially related to intellectual ability. The lack of strong predictive relationships between early measures of intelligence is interpretable in two rather different ways. It may be that it is wrong to construe general intelligence as a constitutionally present characteristic of a person. There may be several different components of intelligence that develop at different rates, some of which may be preconditions for the subsequent development of later emerging abilities. In such a particularistic developmental view one would not expect to find strong relationships between early measures of ability and subsequent measures of ability. A different interpretation of the low correlation between infant intelligence test scores and later intellectual development is that maybe intelligence is constitutionally present but the tests available in infancy do not permit one to assess this potential until it has more clearly emerged at a later age. Some findings support this latter view. Cameron, Livson, and Bayley (1967) reported a correlation between an index of the age at which a girl first acquired several developmental markers for early language development as noted in 6-, 9-, and 12-month examinations and verbal intelligence test score at age 26 of .74 (see also Moore, 1967). This result suggests that some indices of early intellectual development may be substantially predictive of later intellectual ability (although in this case the results hold for females and not for males). There is at least other suggestive evidence that early measures of ability may be predictive of later intelligence. Fagan and McGrath (1981) have reported correlations of .37 and .57 between measures of infant memory recognition obtained at 4 and 7 months of age and measures of intelligence obtained at 4 and 7 years of age, respectively. Lewis and Brooks-Gunn (1981) have reported correlations for measures of the magnitude of recovery of visual fixation time for changed stimuli obtained at 3 months of age and Bayley scores of intellectual ability obtained at 2 years of age in two different samples of .52 and .40. Also, in their data, the magnitude of the correlations exceeded those obtained from omnibus measures of infant intelligence. McCall (1981) has written a thoughtful critique of the Fagan and McGrath and Lewis and Brooks-Gunn studies. He noted that their procedures for obtaining measures of infant memory recognition and response recovery were not ideal and concluded that the results, although not definitive, are at least promising. The failure to find predictive relationships between measures of intelligence obtained in the first year of life and later measures of ability may be attributable to technological problems and to the tendency to develop omnibus measures of intellectual ability in infancy that rely on the Binet tradition of using items that can be administered without elaborate equipment and facilities that are useful in clinical settings. It may very well be the case that more refined measures are needed to assess intellectual ability for preverbal children relying on the techniques of the experimental laboratory. The preliminary results reported by Lewis and Brooks-Gunn with what may be less than optimal methods for the assessment of visual response recovery are sufficiently promising as to leave open the possibility that there may be more continuity in intellectual functioning over the life span than was previously believed to be the case. Just as our earlier beliefs in the decline in intelligence with age now seem to be, in part, an artifact of cohort effects, so, too, the failure to relate early indices of intelligence to later measures of ability may partly be the result of the use of an inadequate methodology for the assessment of infant intelligence.

Evidence for the relative invariance of measures of intellectual ability over the life span provide only indirect evidence for the view that intelligence test scores are invariant. They do not deal with the responsiveness of such test scores to specific manipulations designed to create changes in intelligence. There have been attempts to increase intelligence test scores of both preschool children and older individuals. There have been several attempts to increase intelligence test scores by the provision of special enrichment experiences to preschool children who come from economically deprived backgrounds. Several studies reported gains of 10 to 15 points in intelligence test scores as a result of a two- or three-year preschool intervention (see Weikart, 1967, for a typical study of this type). Although these studies suggest that the provision of adequate early intellectual enrichment can lead to relatively substantial increments in intellectual ability, we now have reasons to interpret these results with more caution. Many of these results may be attributable to rather superficial test-taking skills that are relatively more important determinants of test performance among young children than they are of older children or adults. Also some of these results may be attributable to motivational changes (see Zigler, Abelson, & Seitz, 1973). The possibility that 10 to 15 point increments in test performance for preschool children growing up in poverty may not be of great importance is suggested by the results of a study by Jacobsen, Berger, Bergman, Milham, and Greeson (1971). They found that preschool children exposed to 20 hours of training in solving two choice discrimination problems of increasing complexity had a 13.3 point increase in intelligence test score as assessed by the Stanford-Binet. The largest increments in intelligence test scores were obtained by the children who initially had the lowest scores. We are not inclined to assume that 20 hours of instruction in two choice discrimination problems has dramatically altered intellectual ability. A more sensible interpretation of these results would require us to question the meaning of low scores on intelligence tests for preschool age children with impoverished backgrounds. The potential ease of manipulation of test scores for very young children leads us to interpret the findings of 10 to 15 point increments in intelligence test scores obtained for intellectual interventions of two years' duration cautiously. There is an additional reason to be skeptical of these findings. The typical result for these studies is that the intellectual gains fade over time (see Bronfenbrenner, 1975; Zigler and Seitz, 1982; Zigler and Valentine, 1979). The decline in intelligence test scores to the point where the experimental group is no longer substantially different from the control group may occur because of the failure of the public schools to provide adequate intellectual enrichment for children who have been intellectually enriched in the preschool period. However, one finds the fadings of intelligence test gains as a result of enrichment even where children exhibit some gains in intellectual achievement in the schools (see Zigler & Valentine's 1979 assessment of the benefits of Headstart programs). These results suggest that the fading of intelligence test scores are not so much attributable to inadequate intellectual stimulation provided by the schools but rather to the possibility that the score increases obtained during the preschool years did not reflect true gains in ability.

More dramatic gains in ability were reported by Heber and Garber (1970) in a study in which a group of black children whose mothers had intelligence test scores below 70 were exposed to an intensive intellectual enrichment program starting shortly after birth. The preliminary reports of the outcomes of this project indicated gains in intelligence test scores relative to the control group at age 4 of over 30 points. These children had a mean test score of 120. Clarke and Clarke (1976) reported on the basis of a personal communication that the intelligence test scores of the experimental group of children had faded to 106 shortly after school entry. The results of the Heber and Garber research, although widely cited as demonstrating the possibility of dramatic gains for children from deprived backgrounds who are provided intensive intellectual interventions starting shortly after birth, have never been presented in referred journals. All the information about the study has been gleaned from personal presentations at meetings and from a variety of technical reports. Moreover, the principal investigators have not responded to requests for technical details of their research (Beller, 1979; Page, 1975). And more recently there have been suggestions that the results may be fraudulent (see Sommer & Sommer, 1983).

Ramey and Haskins (1981a) have reported the results of an early intervention program starting at 3 months of age. They reported a 14 point increment in Binet test scores for their experimental children compared to their control-group children at 36 months of age. However, by age 5 the differences between the experimental and the control group had faded to 7 points and were only marginally significant (Ramey & Haskins, 1981b). The results of the Ramey and Haskins study require longer follow-up for full evaluation. However, the preliminary data suggest that the changes in intelligence test scores as a result of intensive interventions were marginal. To my knowledge no one has reported gains in intelligence test scores as a result of preschool interventions that are of enduring significance or that even persist as far as the third grade. This assertion should not be construed as a negative statement about the value of such preschool interventions. There is at least preliminary evidence that some of these programs have had a positive impact on the school performance of children (see Zigler & Valentine, 1979). But these benefits occur independent of changes in intelligence test scores. The only intervention in the preschool period that has been found to produce increments in intelligence test scores is adoption. Scarr and Weinburg (1976) have reported that a group of black children adopted by white middle-class parents had intelligence test scores of 106 at age 7. Similarly Schiff, Duyme, Dumaret, Stewart, Tomkiewicz, and Feingold (1978) reported that 26 children whose biological mothers had working-class backgrounds who were adopted by middle-class parents before 6 months of age had intelligence test scores of 111.5, over 16 points higher than the intelligence test scores of their sibling controls who were raised with their biological mothers. Of course, adoption is a dramatic intervention that can have a substantial impact on the kind of environment to which a child is exposed. The adoption studies suggest that the provision of optimal intellectual environments will result in changes in intelligence test scores over and above those that would be obtained if the adopted children experienced a less stimulating environment. Of course, adoption is not a socially viable program for the production of intellectual improvements for children whose parents are poor and uneducated. The research reviewed here supports the vague common-sense view that abilities are not subject to a "quick fix" but that they are modifiable slowly over time as the result of the provision of optimal environments.

In addition to the attempts to increase intelligence as a result of interventions in the preschool period, there are several attempts to study changes in general intelligence as result of experiences during the school years. Harnquist (1968a, 1968b) has studied the effects of tracking in the Swedish school system at the secondary level. His analysis, based on a complex set of statistical manipulations, suggests that pupils who select more rigorous educational experience at the secondary school level may gain as much as two-thirds of a standard deviation in intelligence test score in comparison to pupils who select vocational educational experiences designed to be terminal. Jensen (1974, 1977) has reported two studies of the cumulative-deficit hypothesis according to which children experiencing inadequate educational experiences will demonstrate declines in intellectual ability. Although the hypothesis is obviously correct for environments that are extremely deficient, it is not obvious that a typical secondary school in an urban neighborhood whose pupils come from economically deprived families does, in fact, provide an environment sufficiently impoverished to create progressive intellectual declines in a substantial number of its pupils. Jensen (1974) reviewed a number of studies of the cumulative-deficit hypothesis and concluded that the majority of them were methodologically flawed. He proposed the use of a sibling control study. Cumulative deficits would be found if older siblings had lower intelligence test scores than their younger siblings. In his first study using California school children aged 5 to 12 years Jensen found very little evidence for the cumulative-deficit hypothesis. He did find some small declines in verbal scores for his black sample, but there were no corresponding declines in scores for the same sample on a nonverbal measure of intelligence. Jensen (1977) conducted a comparable study using a sample of black children attending a rural school in Georgia. He also obtained data for the white children attending these schools. The white sample had a mean intelligence test score that exceeded the mean of the black sample by over 30 points, more than twice the usual black-white difference in intelligence test score, suggesting that the black sample was extremely disadvantaged. Jensen found evidence for a significant age-related decline in both verbal and nonverbal intelligence test scores for the black sample but not for the white sample. He estimates that among the black children intelligence test scores decline at the rate of approximately 1.42 points per year producing a one standard deviation decline over the school-age years. Jensen's data do not provide us with any indications of the kinds of intellectual deprivations that lead to such substantial declines in intelligence. Also, his study is not longitudinal and some of these effects may be attributed to cohort effects. However, his results, combined with those of Harnquist, do suggest that over a period of time large variations in the kinds of intellectual stimulation that individuals are exposed to will have an impact on intelligence test scores. These results are also buttressed by the results of differences in intelligence test performance of individuals born at the turn of the century and prior to World War II, which suggest that there were substantial increases in intelligence test performance probably associated with changes in the duration of formal schooling over this period.

The studies we have reviewed on the changes in intelligence test scores deal with the effects of exposure to naturally occurring environments. There have also been studies of attempts to provide individuals with intensive, but relatively brief, learning experiences in an attempt to increase their performance on tests of intellectual ability. Some of these studies are little more than clinical reports (for example, Whimbey, 1975). Others are more systematic. There have been several attempts to increase the scores of individuals on Scholastic Aptitude Tests. Messick and Jungeblut (1981) have published a comprehensive review of this literature. Their analysis indicates that the average increment in S.A.T. score as a function of coaching is a nonlinear function of the duration of training. Small increments are achieved rather quickly, but the rate of gain in test score then slows and longer and longer periods of instruction are necessary to produce equal increments in score. Although a gain of approximately one-tenth of a standard deviation in score would require approximately 12 hours of instruction, a gain of one-third of a standard deviation would require approximately 260 hours of instruction. These results are based on fitting regression lines to a variety of studies that are often, in various ways, flawed. They do suggest, however, that S.A.T. scores, which are highly related to measures of general ability, are not easily changed by exposure to intensive intellectual training.

Perhaps the most systematic challenge to the view that intelligence test scores are malleable is contained in Feuerstein's research leading to the development of the Learning Potential Assessment Device (see Feuerstein, 1979). Feuerstein's clinical experience with standard tests of intelligence administered to children in Israel with non-Western backgrounds led him to become dissatisfied with the value of such tests. Israeli children with non-Western backgrounds frequently scored low on such tests. Differences between Oriental Jews and Jews with European backgrounds on the order of two standard deviations were not uncommon. The children with Oriental backgrounds frequently responded impulsively to the tests, were not able to reason in a planned manner, and in general exhibited a variety of cognitive deficits in their test performance. Although Feuerstein is a critic of the use of standard tests for the assessment of individuals, he does not challenge the view that such tests are measures of the current cognitive functioning of individuals. Where Feuerstein differs from the conventional view of intelligence tests is that he does not conceive of the results of such tests as a fundamental index of ability to learn. That is, he asserts that such tests do not measure the extent to which intellectual ability is modifiable as a result of new experience. Feuerstein believes that many individuals whose scores are low on the test may respond to cognitive interventions that are designed to increase intellectual skills.

Feuerstein has developed a quasi-clinical procedure called the Learning Potential Assessment Device that is designed to provide more adequate assessments of the ability of an individual who has had an intellectually deprived background to respond to intensive instruction designed to increase intelligence. Feuerstein's procedures change the relationship between the examiner and the examinee. The examiner, rather than acting as an impersonal judge of the responses of the examinee, attempts to create a supportive atmosphere in which he or she assists the examinee. Moreover, the examiner actually demonstrates and models algorithms for correct solutions in order to see if the examinee is able to benefit from the tutoring provided by the examiner. Feuerstein's approach to the assessment of intelligence is reminiscent of the methods used to measure hypnotic susceptibility. In order to predict an individual's response to hypnotic inductions one exposes the individual to hypnotic inductions and then assesses the actual degree of responsiveness of the individual. So, too, if one wants to have a measure of responsiveness of an individual to attempts to train intelligence, one could expose the individual to actual attempts to train the individual to improve intellectual performance. In summary, Feuerstein views intelligence tests as measures of current rather than potential ability. He believes that the tests have limited predictive validity as measures of the ability to learn. And, most critically, he views abilities as highly malleable.

Feuerstein provides several different kinds of evidence in support of his assertions and presents many clinical examples. He reports the results of a variety of empirical studies that demonstrate that groups of individuals who score low on tests of intelligence can, as a result of specialized tutoring, show large increases in their performance on tests. Do these demonstrations constitute convincing evidence of the proposition that intelligence tests are not measures of the ability to learn? Several comments are in order. A good deal of Feuerstein's work is with individuals who have non-Western cultural backgrounds. There is little doubt that the assessment of intellectual functioning in a group of individuals who have not had extensive exposure to the appropriate cultural background surrounding tests is fraught with difficulty. And certainly it is the case that one would want to be particularly cautious when making clinically relevant decisions about children such as placement in special classes on the basis of tests obtained from children who had experienced a culturally different background. One should be cautious, however, in translating his experiences to variations in performance among children with different socioeconomic status in the United States. It is not at all clear that cultural variations associated with differences in social-class background are sufficient to render intelligence tests invalid in quite as dramatic a way as Feuerstein implies. In any case the attempt to see if a child can benefit from attempts to increase his or her performance by using Feuerstein's assessment procedures would appear to be sound clinical practice in any context in which important decisions about a child will be made. Although I have a generally positive view of the clinical relevance of Feuerstein's work, I am somewhat less persuaded by the more radical aspects of his critique of the validity of intelligence tests for the great majority of the population in Western countries. I suspect that the magnitude of cultural differences encountered by Feuerstein in Israeli society are less commonly present in the United States. There are few, if any, defined social groups whose intelligence test scores fall two standard deviations below the mean in the United States. Feuerstein has refused to quantify his procedures and has resisted the development of an index of modifiability. However, it should be possible to derive a measure of the clinical judgment of modifiability as a result of an outcome of his assessment procedures. It would be very interesting to compare the predictions of future academic and intellectual attainments for representative samples of the population for clinical judgments derived from Feuerstein's assessment procedures with predictions derived from standard omnibus measures of intelligence. In the absence of such data it is very difficult to assess the validity of Feuerstein's critique of intelligence tests.

In most of the research reported by Feuerstein the effects of his interventions on standard omnibus measures of intelligence are not reported. One exception to this assertion is reported in what he calls the Hodayot study—a study involving heterogeneous grouping of pupils attending a residential vocational school in Israel. The study dealt with the effects of heterogeneous grouping of ninth- and tenth-grade pupils who had previously been kept apart. The low-scoring pupils were described as culturally deprived, functionally illiterate, and of borderline mental ability. Feuerstein notes a number of improvements in the functioning of the low-scoring groups following their placement for over a year in heterogeneously grouped classes. Feuerstein reports the differences between the low- and high-scoring groups on Thurstone's Primary Mental Abilities Test prior to the start of the educational intervention and after one year of heterogeneous grouping. The ninth-grade pupils in the superior group had scores of .68 standard deviations higher at the start of the study on the Primary Mental Abilities battery than the low-scoring group. After one year they exceeded the low-scoring group by .71 standard deviation units. Thus the intervention had no influence on the magnitude of the difference in intelligence for the ninth-grade pupils. The tenth-grade pupils in the low group started the experiment 1.07 standard deviation units lower than the high-scoring group on the PMA test and, after one year, were .26 standard deviation units lower on the test. Thus the intervention did decrease the difference in test scores for the tenth-grade pupils. The sample size for the high- and low-scoring pupils in the tenth grade were 32 and 16 respectively. Given the small samples it is perhaps appropriate to average the results for both grades. This leaves us with an initial difference of .88 standard deviation units that is reduced to a difference of .48 standard deviation units. The .40 reduction is not large in magnitude. When looked at in this fashion the study does not provide dramatic evidence for increments in intelligence test scores as a result of the educational interventions. Feuerstein's research demonstrates that changes in test performance can occur for specific tests that are the focal point of the intervention but does not indicate that these changes generalize to scores on omnibus measures of intelligence. Thus little convincing data supports the claim that scores on intelligence tests are modifiable as the result of his training procedures.

It is possible to summarize this section by a series of assertions that extend beyond the available empirical literature but are not contraindicated by the available data.

Intelligence tends to remain relatively invariant over the life span. It may be capable of being assessed in infancy, and it is certainly assessable during the preschool period. There is very little evidence for the decline in intelligence over the life span. Intelligence defined as position with respect to age cohorts as well as in absolute terms is unlikely to change dramatically over the adult life span. Although intelligence is modifiable by means of the cumulative impacts of schooling, highly deprived backgrounds, and variations in environments provided by upper-middle-class rearing as opposed to rearing by parents who are not well educated, there is little evidence that short-term interventions will lead to enduring changes in intelligence. The available data on the malleability of intelligence and its responsiveness to environmental interventions is congruent with our ordinary intuitions about the meaning of the construct intelligence. In this sense the data on the malleability of intelligence tests suggest that intelligence tests are valid measures of the construct intelligence.

COMPONENTS AND REDUCTION: THE REFINEMENT OF *g*

Spearman attempted to develop a more refined conception of *g*. Although he thought that Binet's tests were an adequate measure of general intelligence, he preferred to use procedures based on the laboratory psychology of his day. Subsequently, he speculated that general intelligence was related to "mental energy" and to intellectual processes that he called the education of correlates and relations (see Spearman, 1927). In this section I shall examine several attempts to relate intelligence to performance in laboratory settings with respect to their implications for understanding the validity of intelligence tests.

Hendrickson (1982a, 1982b) has reported the results of a series of studies relating evoked potential measures derived from the EEG response to auditory stimuli to measures of general intelligence. The most dramatic evidence reported by Hendrickson is contained in a study of the evoked potential responses of 219 English secondary school students. Hendrickson derives measures of the variability and complexity of the pattern of EEG responses. He reports that a measure of the variance of the response pattern correlates with the WAIS .83. Further, he reports that this relationship was replicated in a smaller sample of adults. In another study Blinkhorn and Hendrickson (1982) report that the correlation between the EEG measure and the Ravens test in a sample of students attending a Polytechnic was .47.

The magnitude of the correlations reported by Hendrickson exceeds those typically found between biologically based measures and psychometric indices. Moreover, there has been some difficulty in replicating some of the earlier claims of a relationship between EEG measures and intelligence (see Ertl & Schafer, 1969; Rust, 1975). Therefore, these results should be accepted cautiously until there are replications. Nevertheless, given the large sample and the absence of any obvious defects in the studies reported by Hendrickson, it is entirely possible that there is a substantial relationship between particular EEG measures and psychometric measures of intelligence. Eysenck (1982) has argued that Hendrickson's measures are more fundamental and more accurate indices of general intelligence than standard psychometric tests. He indicates that the Hendrickson EEG measure correlates more highly with the first principal component of a factor analysis of WAIS subscales than any of the WAIS subscales. Thus the EEG measure is said to be the best marker for the general intelligence factor. Eysenck also reported that the difference between high and low socioeconomic groups on intelligence in his sample was 1.67 standard deviation units and the differences between the same groups on the EEG measure was 1.18 standard deviation units. Eysenck argued that the EEG measure is a better measure of general intelligence than the usual psychometric measures in at least two senses— it has a higher *g* loading and it is more reflective of basic biological ability and is less responsive to differences in social background that may interfere with the true assessment of underlying intellectual potential. Again these claims should be taken cautiously pending replication. Eysenck tends to view the development of a biological marker for intelligence as providing a theoretically refined measure of the underlying construct of general intelligence. He accords privileged status to biologically based rather than psychologically based measures. It is possible that such unwanted sources of variance as attitude toward the test and motivation may also influence biologically based measures. Hendrickson has noted that a number of conditions must be fulfilled in order to maximize the correlation between EEG based measures and psychometric intelligence. For example measurements based on the first 256 milliseconds are assumed to be better indices based on 512 milliseconds following stimulus presentation. This is explained by reference to Osborne's finding that the heritability of EEG measures based on 256 millisecond episodes is higher than the heritability of EEG measures derived

from 512 millisecond epochs (Osborne, 1970). Also the same methods of measurement that provided good indices of individual differences among individuals
within the normal range of intelligence did not discriminate between retarded
and normal individuals. The EEG records of retarded individuals were so different from those of the normals that the particular derived measures used by
Hendrickson were not meaningful. It is possible that the relationship between
the EEG indices and the construct of which they are alleged to be a manifestation
may be variable among different classes of individuals. I am somewhat skeptical
of the argument that the EEG measures, even if they prove to be consistently
correlated with psychometric indices of intelligence, are privileged and are to be
construced as pure measures of *g* that are more fundamental and unbiased than
mere psychometric indices.

There have been several attempts to assess the relationship between general
intelligence and performance on experimental tasks. This research may be viewed
as the continuation of Spearman's research reported in 1904 that was in turn
based on the efforts of Galton in the 1860s. A considerable body of evidence
indicates that various measures of reaction time in simple laboratory tasks are
inversely related to general intelligence. Several different kinds of measures may
be used to discriminate between retarded and normal individuals and, in addition,
may be used to discriminate among individuals within the normal range of
intelligence. (See, for a general discussion of these data, Jensen, 1980, 1982;
Vernon, 1983.) Jensen has explored the relationship between a number of measures of reaction time derived from choice reaction time paradigms and measures
of general intelligence. It is well known that the reaction time increases as the
number of alternative choices among which one must choose increases. Hick's
law (Hick, 1952) states that reaction time increases linearly with increases in
the uncertainty of the stimulus alternatives defined in the familiar information
theory metric of log to the base 2. A linear function defining an increase in
reaction time with increases in stimulus uncertainty may be obtained for an
individual. One can then define the slope and the intercept of the function for
a person. In addition, one can obtain measures of the intrasubject variability of
reaction times for an individual at each level of stimulus uncertainty. Jensen
(1982) has summarized a considerable body of research relating these parameters
to psychometric indices of intelligence in diverse samples. Most of the research
has used samples that are restricted in range of talent with respect to intelligence.
Several studies have used samples that are grossly discrepant in intelligence and
demonstrated that there are mean differences in various parameters of reaction
time among such grossly discrepant groups. Since a variety of methods of
measurement and samples have been used in this research it is difficult to specify
the simple correlation or multiple correlation value that may be used as a best
estimate of the relationship between these parameters and intelligence. However,
several generalizations seem warranted. All the parameters have been consistently
found to be negatively correlated with intelligence. That is, individuals of high
intelligence have been found to have low slopes and intercepts of the function
defining increases in reaction time with increases in stimulus uncertainty and

lower intrasubject variability of reaction times. The usual correlations reported for each parameter is approximately −.35. However, in several respects correlations of this magnitude should definitely not be thought of as the upper limit of predictability that can be attained. Correlations of this magnitude should be construed as lower bound estimates. Many of these variables may not be consistently related to intelligence over the entire range of intelligence. Measures of simple reaction time may be more discriminating between retarded and normal individuals than they are among normal individuals. Some of these parameters may have low test-retest coefficients of stability and as a result the relationship between such measures and scores on intelligence tests may be subject to significant attenuations. For example, Jensen (1982) has reported that among college students the intrasubject variability of reaction times was the parameter that most consistently correlated with measures of general intelligence. This parameter had a test-retest correlation in a sample of 100 college students of −.42. If one corrects a correlation of −.35 for attenuation, the correlation becomes −.55. Of course, this correlation should also be corrected for restrictions in range of talent, but the precise magnitude of the correction may be difficult to determine since there is no guarantee that the correlation is uniform over the population. The discriminability of this parameter may, in fact, be lower among individuals with lower intelligence test scores. Correlations between reaction time parameters and intelligence are usually larger in samples with larger ranges of talent. For example, Lally and Nettlebeck (1977) studied the relationship between choice reaction time and intelligence test scores in a sample of 48 individuals with Wechsler intelligence test scores between 57 and 130. They found that the magnitude of the correlation between reaction times and intelligence test scores increased in a linear fashion as the uncertainty in bits of the number of stimulus alternatives increased. The correlation ranged from .50 to .70. The several parameters derived from reaction time studies are themselves less than perfectly correlated. It should be possible to define a multiple correlation between measures of reaction time and intelligence that exceeds the simple correlation. If the above reasoning is correct it should be possible, using a large and heterogeneous sample of individuals who are not restricted with respect to range of talent to derive a multiple correlation including the possibility of using nonlinear functions of reaction time parameters to predict scores on intelligence tests with some degree of accuracy. Given the available data, shrunken multiple correlations of the order of magnitude of .60 to .70 do not appear to represent an unreasonable possibility.

Several other reaction time measures have been related to general intelligence. Hunt, Lunneborg, and Lewis (1975) were the first to relate individual differences in a task originally devised by Posner and coworkers to individual difference in intelligence (see Posner & Mitchell, 1967; and Posner, Boies, Eichelman, & Taylor, 1969). In this task individuals are presented with pairs of letters that are identical in both name and typecase (*AA*) and pairs of letters that are identical in name but not in typecase (*Aa*). The subjects must decide if such pairs and others are either the same or different. Subjects have been found to take longer to respond to stimulus pairs that are the same in name only. The increase in reaction time is taken to be a measure of the time taken to access relatively overlearned semantic codes in long-term memory. The difference in reaction times between these two tasks is negatively related to differences in verbal ability among college students. This measure has also been found to discriminate between normal and retarded individuals (Hunt, 1978). Keating and Bobbitt (1978) found that the difference in reaction times in these two tasks correlated more substantially with individual differences in intelligence as children grew older. They found correlations in excess of .50 among their oldest children.

The fact that several different measures of reaction time derived from experimental tasks may correlate with intelligence test scores suggests the possibility that one could combine several such measures into a predictive index of intelligence. Vernon (1983) has reported the results of such a study. Vernon administered the Ravens and WAIS tests to 100 college students. He then obtained several reaction time measures including a measure of the threshold for judgments of the lengths of two lines presented tachistoscopically that are masked and a scanning task in which subjects were presented with strings of digits from 1 to 7 in length followed by a single probe digit. Subjects were required to state whether or not the probe digit appeared in the string. The reaction times for judgments were obtained, a variation in the Posner type task in which subjects were required to make same-different judgments about pairs of words, and measures of choice reaction time. Vernon derived a number of different measures from these mental measures. He was able to show that there were both pervasive general speed of processing factors present in matrices of correlations of derived measures as well as more refined factors that were somewhat independent. Vernon found a shrunken multiple correlation between measures of reaction time on his various tasks and intelligence of .46 that, when corrected for attenuation and restrictions in range of talent in this sample, implies a multiple correlation of .668. Measures of intraindividual variability derived from these tasks had a comparable multiple correlation. Measures derived from the choice reaction time task had the best single predictive relationship to intelligence and measures derived from the inspection time task had the lowest correlations, although they had been found useful in discriminating between retarded and normal subjects in previous research (see Lally & Nettlebeck, 1977).

These results buttress our earlier conclusion that relatively simple measures of basic information processing may correlate with general intelligence in a representative sample with correlations close to .70. Vernon suggested that differences in speed of information processing may determine the ability to acquire the more complex knowledge and skills that are assessed by omnibus measures of intelligence. He implies that such measures stand in a causal relationship to other components of intelligence. However, given the absence of appropriate longitudinal research, such a causal account of these relationships remains conjectural. His research does support the notion that speed and efficiency of information processing are components of intelligence. Vernon's paper may be viewed as a culmination of the program of research started by Galton and endorsed by Spearman.

The attempt to relate performance on intelligence test scores to tasks that have been of interest to the experimental psychologist has not been restricted to the analysis of very fundamental levels of information processing. There have been many attempts to understand the fundamental nature of general intelligence by relating scores on omnibus tests of intelligence to more cognitively complex tasks. Sternberg and Powell (1983) have advocated the use of tasks of intermediate degrees of complexity for this purpose. They report the results of a study designed to explore the processes that lead to the acquisition of new vocabulary. They note that individual differences in vocabulary have been consistently found to be highly related to individual differences in general intelligence and may indeed be one of the best single indices of overall mental ability. They suggest that the ability to increase one's vocabulary is highly related to the ability to acquire new meanings from experimental contexts that are not well specified and to infer the meaning of new words from incompletely specified contextual cues. In order to test this theory they provided high school students with passages containing extremely low-frequency nouns. The students were not familiar with the meaning of the words prior to encountering them one or more times in the context of different types of prose passages. The students were asked to write definitions of the words. They found that ratings of the quality of the definitions of the words correlated .62 with scores on intelligence tests.

The search for defining attributes to intelligence has also included a number of other characteristics. Some theorists have sought to emphasize individuals' differences in knowledge as one of the most defining attributes of individual differences in general intelligence. Such an approach does not deal with the question of how such differences come about. The acquisition of knowledge is probably related to individual differences in intelligence. Differences in the extensity of the knowledge base relevant to a domain may, in turn, influence the ways in which individuals solve relevant problems and reason. For example, Chi, Glaser, and Rees (1982) have studied individual differences in the ways in which individuals with different expertise in physics solve physical problems. They note that expert learners are more able than novice learners to use inferences and abstractions derived from past experience as aids in the representations of a problem. In addition, expert learners are skilled in the manipulations of their knowledge structures and this skill assists them in problem solution.

Individuals who differ in intelligence may also differ with respect to what has been called metacognitive abilities. Metacognitive skills may include capacity to monitor cognitive processes, detect inconsistencies in reasoning, and to allocate time and intellectual resources to various components of a solution to a particular problem (see Sternberg, 1980).

It is obvious from this brief review that any of a large number of cognitive skills and parameters of cognitive processing may be found to be related to differences in intelligence. There is the temptation to view some of these as being more fundamental or more defining than others, or to construct causal models such that the more elementary cognitive processes such as the kinds of processes assessed in reaction time experiments or in measures of the evoked response to tones are seen as being logically prior or causally related to the more complex processes. However, we have very little evidence that permits us to ascertain such causal or reductive sequences. Moreover, we can at least plausibly infer quite different models of causality. The relationship between the complexity of the evoked potential response and individual differences in intelligence may be mediated partly by motivational and temperamental characteristics that influence both the development of intelligence and the ability to attend to auditory stimuli. Or, perhaps, individuals who develop complex intellectual skills may learn to focus attention in ways that influence the form of the evoked potential response. In a related context, Sternberg and Powell (1983) have argued that it is important to analyze the interactive relations among top-down and bottom-up conceptions of the acquisition of verbal skills. Focusing on a particular cognitive skill as the fundamental aspect of ability tends to give a partial and incomplete overview of the interactive relations among the multiple components of skill that combine to determine individual differences in ability. Such reductive analyses are reminiscent of the parable of the blind men and the elephant, each focusing on a different part of the elephant, each convinced that he has determined the nature of the whole.

The recent emphases on the analysis of individual differences in parameters of experimental tasks that may relate to individual differences in general intelligence has contributed to the understanding of the nature of general intelligence by indicating just what aspect of performance on a task might relate to general ability. Also, such analyses contribute greatly to the understanding of the cognitive processes that are engaged when individuals solve particular kinds of intellectual tasks. However, the impressive progress in understanding the components of intellectual skills that has been attained in recent years does not imply that Spearman's conception of intelligence as a single entity is substantially false. Much of the current cognitive research has had as its focus intratask analysis while Spearman's conception of general intelligence is based on intertask relationships. Insofar as performance on a particular task or some parameter of performance on a task relates to general intelligence one would suspect that in a representative group of individuals that it would relate to performance on any other component of task performance that is substantially related to general intelligence. Often long periods of time and extensive involvement with subjects are required to obtain measures of performance on tasks that are used in the psychological laboratory. Such an intensive investment in obtaining measures on single tasks tends to preclude the possibility of obtaining performance measures on a large number of tasks from a representative sample of individuals. However, insofar as measurable components of task performance are highly correlated with general intelligence we would expect that a correlation matrix of such measures would have a general factor. In other words one could argue that componential approaches to intelligence permit the rediscovery and redefinition of Spearman's general factor albeit with greater precision of understanding of some of the components of general intelligence.

It should also be noted that in several respects contemporary experimental analyses of individual differences in performance on cognitive tasks have provided us with a more particularistic and differentiated view of the nature of intelligence.

A frequently encountered theme in these research efforts is that different individuals may use different processes of solution for a particular task. Therefore, a model that may accurately describe the performance of the typical individual may not at all be descriptive of the performance of particular individuals. Different models may be necessary to explain the behavior of different individuals on the same tasks. Some of these individual differences in the processes of solution of a task may relate to individual differences in ability—others may be independent of individual differences in ability. Sternberg and Weil (1980) have presented a particularly clear demonstration of a task in which different processes of solution are used by different individuals. They studied the performance of individuals in syllogistic reasoning tasks. They were able to distinguish between two groups of individuals—one group relied on a linguistic model and one group apparently relied on a spatial reasoning model for solution. Individuals whose reponses were best fitted by a model assuming linguistic processing tended to have solution latencies that had substantial inverse correlations with measures of verbal ability ($r = -.76$ for a sample of college students) and relatively low correlations with measures of spatial ability ($r = -.28$). Individuals whose performance on the task was best modeled by a spatial model had correlations between solution latencies and performance on a measure of verbal ability of $-.08$. The comparable correlation for a measure of spatial ability was $-.60$. These results provide impressive external validation for the assertion that different individuals rely on different approaches to the same task. Moreover, the pattern of correlations between a task and other measures will vary as a function of the particular strategy used by an individual to solve a particular problem.

Differences in the processes of solution that are used to solve a task have been noted on tasks that appear to assess very simple and fundamental abilities. For example, Cooper (1982) has studied performance on a task in which Ss are required to make same-different judgments for visually presented polygons. She was able to identify two different strategies and approaches to the task that are used by different subjects. One type of subject is described as using a holistic strategy in which comparisons are made not in terms of searching for differentiating features but rather in terms of an overall match between the standard and comparison stimuli. Other subjects are described as using an analytic strategy in which there is a specific comparison of the features of the standard and comparison stimuli in an attempt to ascertain if there are differentiating or distinguishing features.

If there are important individual differences in the way in which individuals solve the same problem, does this suggest that intelligence should not be conceived as a single entity? Not necessarily. One could interpret individual differences in general intelligence in a way that is analogous to the interpretation provided by Thomson (1939) rather than Spearman. Thomson asserted that the mind consisted of a large number of bonds that were nonrandomly involved in the solution of different tasks. (For a brief discussion of the affinity between Thomson's views of intelligence and process-oriented conceptions that are compatible with the existence of a general factor see Carroll, 1976, and Humphreys,

1976.) This analysis suggests that individuals who differ in general ability may differ in various specific intellectual skills and in capacities and knowledge. These differences, in turn, may lead them to exhibit differences in performance on various tasks and to use different methods of solution for the same task. Thus a nomothetic theory of intelligence that stresses the importance of a single general dimension to account for individual differences in intelligence is not logically incompatible with an idiographic theory of intelligence that emphasizes special abilities and the unique configuration of skills and acquisitions of knowledge structures and algorithms that may characterize the ability structure of each person. What justifies us in the retention of the construction is not the belief that individuals who differ in g will invariably have the same set of competencies and skills and will solve problems in the same way but rather the belief that the likelihood that an individual will be capable of finding successful solutions to diverse intellectual tasks increases as a function of general ability. If we wish to individualize the curriculum or to provide algorithms that will be useful to individuals in solving a particular intellectual task, the particularistic analysis of individual differences in the processes of solution may provide an optimal knowledge base for improving performance on that task. However, we should recognize that there are individual differences in average ability to profit from various types of instructions and to acquire knowledge under conditions in which instructional procedures are less than optimal. And it is this general ability that defines general intelligence. Thus intelligence is both many different things, indeed, even idiographically present within an individual, and is also, in a coherent and meaningful sense, one thing.

MOTIVATIONAL AND TEMPERAMENTAL PERTURBATIONS

Although common sense suggests that individual differences in personality, temperament, and motivation may influence the relationship between intelligence and achievement, there is relatively little systematic research on this topic. There are, however, several different kinds of studies that provide relevant information. Matheny, Dolan, and Wilson (1976) have reported a twin study in which they asked school authorities to nominate children from a large cohort of twins who were experiencing academic difficulty, who then formed an index group. They formed a control group from the same cohort. The children who were nominated were described as having reading test scores that were 1.9 grade equivalents lower than the children in the control group at a median age of 10.

They found that twins in the index group had Wechsler intelligence test scores at age 6 that were 8 points lower than the twins in the control group. These results suggest that the differences in academic performance between the index and the control children are not likely to be attributable to differences in their intelligence. The standard deviation of grade equivalent scores at an average age of 10 is not given in their report. However, it is unlikely to be very much larger than 1. Differences in reading score and the general school difficulty exhibited by the index twins relative to the control-group twins cannot be accounted for by the relatively small difference they exhibited in intelligence test scores. Matheny, Dolan, and Wilson report that the index twins were significantly different from the control twins on measures of temperament derived from the preschool period. They were reported as being overly active (87% vs. 26% for the control group), distractible (89% vs. 22% for the control group), and they were more likely to be described as experiencing feeding and sleeping problems. They also found that the variables that differentiated between the index twin cases and the control cases were heritable. That is, the concordance rates for monozygotic twin pairs for these variables were higher than the concordance rates for same-sex dizygotic pairs for these variables. These results suggest that temperamental variables that are genetically influenced moderate the relationship between intelligence and academic achievement.

The results of the Matheny, Dolan, and Wilson study dovetail with the findings of Taubman (1976) who used a sample of twins in his study of occupational achievement. He found that there was a large component of variance in occupational and academic success that was independent of intelligence but was nevertheless heritable. Although he did not include measures of personality and temperament in his analysis, it is possible that preschool measures of the sort found to discriminate between index and control children in the Matheny, Dolan, and Wilson study would account for some of the heritable variance in occupational and educational outcomes that is independent of intelligence.

Further evidence for the possible influence of heritable personality characteristics on individual differences in the use of intelligence is contained in a twin study reported by Lykken (1982). Lykken used a computer-administered version of the Ravens test in his study. The use of computer-administered formats permits subjects to perform tasks at their own rate of speed. It also adds a component of persistence to the quality of performance on the task. Thus the test may be transformed to a measure that combines both intelligence and aspects of personality and motivation. Lykken found intraclass correlations on the Ravens for MZ twins reared apart of .71 and .78 for MZ twins reared together. The correlation for DZ twins reared together was .19. This latter value is clearly deviant. The usual DZ correlation for tests of intelligence is close to .6. The correlation of .19 is far more characteristic of correlations usually reported for DZ twins for personality measures. An admittedly speculative account of these findings that extends beyond the available data is as follows: genetic and environmental influences act quite differently on the traits of personality and intelligence (see Henderson, 1982). Genetic influences on personality traits are more likely to be epistatic and nonadditive than genetic influences on intelligence, which are likely to have higher narrow heritability (see Price, Vandenberg, Iyer, & Williams, 1982). Also, the environmental influences on intelligence are likely to consist of both within- and between-family influences while the environmental influences on personality are apparently exclusively within-family environmental influences (see Loehlin & Nichols, 1976). If these assertions are correct, we should expect that DZ twins should tend to have relatively low degrees of resemblance for measures of personality. The low intraclass correlation for the Ravens reported by Lykken for DZ twin pairs is exactly the result we would expect given this theoretical analysis, if his method of administration has converted the Ravens from a measure of intelligence to a measure that combines the measurement of intellectual capacity with the measurement of personality and temperamental characteristics.

Temperamental and motivational influences may influence scores on intelligence tests as well as the relationship between intelligence and achievement. A particularly clear demonstration of such an influence is contained in a series of studies performed by Revelle, Humphreys, Simon, and Gilliland (1980). They were interested in variables that were assumed to influence arousal level. They compared the performance of individuals who scored either high or low on the impulsivity dimension of the personality trait "extraversion." Their subjects were tested in the morning or afternoon following the ingestion of caffeine or a placebo on measures of cognitive ability. Subjects who scored high on impulsivity scored higher on tests of cognitive ability in the morning if they were assigned to a caffeine ingestion group rather than to a placebo group. Individuals who scored low on impulsivity had the opposite pattern of performance in the morning. That is, their performance was poorer if they ingested caffeine rather than a placebo. In the afternoon the results were reversed. Subjects who scored high on a test of impulsivity had poorer performance if they ingested caffeine rather than a placebo. Subjects who scored low on impulsivity improved their performance in the afternoon if they ingested caffeine. The triple interaction between impulsivity, time of day, and caffeine ingestion was replicated in several different experiments. Also, the magnitude of the interaction effects was relatively large— occasionally in excess of one half a standard deviation. Although the interpretation of the finding is in dispute (see Eysenck & Folkard, 1980), the results provide a clear demonstration of the importance of a number of transitory, complex, and perhaps poorly understood variables that influence performance on tests of cognitive ability. Empirically, such influences can be minimized by averaging over several administrations of a test in order to provide a more accurate indication of an individual's ability. With respect to the issue of the validity of intelligence tests it certainly can be argued that it is part and parcel of our ordinary understanding of the meaning of test scores that they may fluctuate and be subject to perturbations and influences that are independent of cognitive ability. While on a somewhat more orthodox view of validity, such perturbations might be assumed to be an indication of low validity or that the test contains sources of variance that are noncognitive and contribute to the error. Once the distinction between the construct and the measure of the construct is recognized we expect and even require that tests should have such nonintellective influences. Of course, this argument should not be carried to its reductio ad absurdum. Obviously we require that a major portion of the variance in test score be cognitive rather than noncognitive if the test is to have construct validity.

DIFFERENTIAL VALIDITY

The relationship between measures of intelligence and the construct intelligence may be variable for individuals who have had different opportunities to develop their intellectual capacity. And intelligence tests may not be equally valid measures for individuals who have had different cultural experiences. It is indisputable that individuals may have potentially high levels of ability and not be able to actualize their abilities due to cultural deprivations. What is more problematic is the nature of the deprivations that must occur to render intelligence tests invalid. This issue is particularly germane to discussions of the differences in intelligence test scores among members of different social groups and has received the most attention with respect to the black-white difference in intelligence test scores (see Loehlin, Lindzey, & Spuhler, 1975). Scarr and Weinberg (1976) found that black children adopted into advantaged white families have intelligence test scores above the white mean. This supports the hypothesis that the black-white difference in intelligence is substantially attributable to the environmental conditions surrounding the experience of being reared within the black subculture of the United States. This interpretation is buttressed by the results of Eyferth's (1961) study of children whose mothers were native Germans and whose fathers were black American soldiers. Eyferth found that such children had intelligence test scores that were comparable to a control group of children with German mothers whose fathers were white American soldiers. Whatever the reason for the differences in intelligence test scores between black and white Americans it is well established that such differences exist and that they are of the order of magnitude of one standard deviation. It is clear that levels of deprivation exist that prohibit individuals from developing their potential ability. If one understands by the term intelligence, native ability, and one can establish that the differences between black and white Americans is in part attributable to differences in subcultural experiences—a result strongly implied by the adoption studies—then the scores of a black person are less likely to reflect the construct of native ability. Moreover, the results reported by Jensen (1977) for his rural black sample are also evidence that tests are not as likely to reflect true ability among individuals who experience cumulative deficits.

   Several other issues are germane to the possible existence of differential intelligence test validity among individuals in different racial groups in the United States. It is quite clear that black-white differences in intelligence are not a function of type of item or tests. As far as is known, it is pervasive and exists on virtually all measures that are generally assumed to be measures of general intelligence. Jensen (1983b) has reported that black-white differences in performance on tests of cognitive ability extend to the reaction time measures used by Vernon (1983). Jensen has suggested that the magnitude of the black-white difference in intelligence is a function of the extent to which the tests are measures of g. He calls this the Spearman hypothesis. He reports that the magnitude of the black-white difference on a particular test correlates with its average loading on a g factor, .59. Tests that show the largest black-white difference with whites exceeding the black mean also turn out to have the largest g loading. I find Jensen's analysis of argument on this issue somewhat unconvincing. Many of the studies he cites use the Wechsler scales, and it is likely that there are subscales on the Wechsler that probably are not very good measures of general intelligence. I have not seen any convincing data that indicates support for the Spearman hypothesis among a large battery of tests that are clearly good measures of general ability. Jensen (1971) finds in one of his own studies with large samples that the magnitude of black and white differences for the Ravens—presumably a good measure of g was less than the comparable difference on the Peabody— presumably a poor test of general ability. The white mean minus the black mean for the Ravens was 1.12 standard deviation units and 1.24 standard deviation units on the Peabody test. Whatever the status of the "Spearman" hypothesis there is no doubt that the differences between blacks and whites in the United States on tests of intelligence are quite pervasive and exist on any and all measures that are generally construed as measures of general intelligence.

Not only are racial differences in test scores quite pervasive, the predictive validity of test scores is, at least in certain contexts, similar for both racial groups. For example, Cleary, Humphreys, Kendrick, and Wesman (1975) have summarized research on the predictive validity of tests of ability for grade point average in college. Their analysis indicates that, in large measure, a common regression line will result in accurate predictions for both racial groups. There is very little evidence that the predictive validity of test scores is influenced by the racial designation of the individual from whom the score is obtained.

However, predictive validity is not equivalent to construct validity. We have already argued that the adoption data supports the view that the intelligence test scores are not likely to provide equally good measures of the native ability of black and white Americans. If this analysis is correct, we should expect that the heritability of test scores might be different in black and white samples (see Scarr & Carter-Saltzman, 1982). There have been few large-scale convincing studies on this issue (see Scarr-Salapatek, 1971). One study that provides information about the possibility of differential heritability of intelligence test scores among individuals of social class backgrounds is contained in a twin study reported by Fischbein (1980). Fischbein separated twin pairs into three different groups based on the social class backgrounds of their families. He found that the heritability of intelligence test scores increased with increases in the social status of the twin pairs. Among the twins in the lowest social group he calculated intraclass correlations of .66 and .51 for his samples of MZ and DZ twins on a measure of verbal ability. Among the twins in the highest socioeconomic group the correlation of the MZ twins on the verbal battery measure was .76 and the comparable correlation of the DZ twins was .37. These data suggest the possible existence of differential heritability among individuals in different social groups. They raise the possibility that tests given to individuals with different social backgrounds, notwithstanding their possible similarities in many contexts with respect to predictive validity, may nevertheless not be equally valid indices of the construct intelligence.

Additional evidence for the proposition that tests of intelligence may not have equivalent construct validities for individuals with different social backgrounds is contained in the findings of the cross-lagged panel study of Crano, Kenny, and Campbell (1972). They found evidence that tests of intelligence stood in the theoretically required causal relationship to tests of achievement. However, these findings were restricted to a sample of suburban, predominantly white children. For a predominantly black sample of children attending urban schools they found no evidence of a causal relationship between intelligence and achievement. These results suggest that the black-white differences in test scores may reflect not only a difference in intelligence level but also a difference in the nature of the relationship between the test and the underlying construct measured by the test.

CONCLUDING COMMENTS

In this chapter I have briefly touched on various issues that appear to me to be germane to the issue of the validity of tests of intelligence. I have argued that in large measure the evidence supports a conception of intelligence that is congruent with our ordinary conceptions of the meaning of the term. Considerable progress has been made in recent years in understanding the processes of reasoning involved in solution of cognitive tasks and these developments have carried contemporary research on intelligence far beyond our ordinary understanding of the implicit meaning of the term. Despite these impressive developments it is still possible to argue in a general way that our ordinary conceptions of intelligence are supported by contemporary research. It is still valid to assert that intelligence is unitary, incompletely malleable, relatively invariant over the life span, substantially related to socially relevant intellectual achievements, related to the capacity to acquire knowledge in diverse settings, subject to the influences of motivational and temperamental processes that influence both scores on tests and the tendency to actualize one's intellectual ability, and subject to cultural influences that change the relationship between the test and the construct. In all these respects the available literature is congruent with a conception of intelligence that is implicit in our everyday understanding of the terms. In this sense intelligence tests are valid.

REFERENCES

Baltes, P. B., & Schaie, K. W. (1976). On the plasticity of intelligence in adulthood and old age: Where Horn and Donaldson fail. *American Psychologist, 31,* 720–725.

Beller, E. K. (1979). Early intervention program. In J. D. Osofsky (Ed.), *Handbook of infant development.* New York: Wiley.

Benson, V. E. (1942). The intelligence and later scholastic success of sixth grade pupils. *School and Society, 55,* 163–167.

Binet, A., & Simon, T. (1905). Methodes nouvelle pour le diagnostic du niveau intellectuel des anormaux. *Année Psychologie, 11,* 191–244.

Blau, P., & Duncan, O. D. (1967). *The American occupational structure.* New York: Wiley.

Blinkhorn, S. F., & Hendrickson, D. E. (1982). Averaged evoked responses in psychometric intelligence. *Nature, 295,* 596–597.

Bloom, B. S. (1974). Time and learning. *American Psychologist, 29,* 682–688.

Brody, E. B., & Brody, N. (1976). *Nature, determinants, and consequences.* New York: Academic Press.

Bronfenbrenner, U. (1975). Is early intervention effective? Some studies of early education in familial and extrafamilial settings. In A. Montagu (Ed.), *Race and IQ.* New York: Oxford University Press.

Cameron, J., Livson, N., & Bayley, N. (1967). Infant socializations and their relationship to mature intelligence. *Science, 157,* 331–333.

Carroll, J. B. (1976). Supplementing comment: Carroll's response to Cooley. In L. B. Resnick (Ed.), *The nature of intelligence.* Hillsdale, NJ: Erlbaum.

Cattell, R. B. (1971). *Abilities: Their structure, growth, and action.* Boston: Houghton Mifflin.

Cattell, R. B. (1982). *The inheritance of personality and ability.* New York: Academic Press.

Cattell, R. B., Blewett, D. B., & Beloff, J. R. (1955). The inheritance of personality: A multiple-variance analysis determination of approximate nature-nurture ratios for primary personality factors in Q data. *American Journal of Human Genetics, 7,* 123–146.

Cattell, R. B., Stice, G. F., & Kristy, N. T. (1957). A first approximation of nature-nurture ratios for eleven primary personality factors in objective tests. *Journal of Abnormal and Social Psychology, 54,* 143–159.

Chi, M. T. H., Glaser, R., & Rees, E. (1982). Expertise in problem solving. In R. J. Sternberg (Ed.), *Advances in the psychology of human intelligence.* Hillsdale, NJ: Erlbaum.

Clarke, A. M., & Clarke, A. D. B. (1976). *Early experience: Myth and evidence.* New York: Free Press.

Cleary, T. A., Humphreys, L. G., Kendrick, S. A., & Wesman, A. (1975). Educational uses of tests with disadvantaged students. *American Psychologist, 30,* 15–41.

Conley, J. J. (1984). The hierarchy of consistency: A review and model of longitudinal findings on adult individual differences in intelligence, personality and self opinion. *Personality and Individual Differences, 5,* 11–26.

Cooper, L. A. (1982). Strategies for visual comparison and representation: Individual differences. In R. J. Sternberg (Ed.), *Advances in the psychology of human intelligence.* Hillsdale, NJ: Erlbaum.

Crano, W. D., Kenny, J., & Campbell, D. T. (1972). Does intelligence cause achievement? A cross-lagged panel analysis. *Journal of Educational Psychology, 63,* 258–275.

Cronbach, L. J., & Snow, R. E. (1977). *Aptitudes and instructional methods.* New York: Irvington.

Ertl, J., & Schafer, E. W. P. (1969). Brain response correlates of psychometric intelligence. *Nature, 223,* 421–422.

Eyferth, K. (1961). Lerstungen verschiedener Gruppen von Besatzunfskindern in Hamburg-Wechsler Intelligenztest fur Kinder (HAWK). *Archiv fur die Gesante Psychologie, 113,* 222–241.

Eysenck, H. J. (1979). *The structure and measurement of intelligence.* Berlin: Springer-Verlag.

Eysenck, H. J. (1982). Is intelligence? An epilogue. In H. J. Eysenck (Ed.), *A model for intelligence.* Berlin: Springer-Verlag.

Eysenck, M. W., & Folkard, S. (1980). Personality, time of day, and caffeine: Some theoretical and conceptual problems in Revelle et al. *Journal of Experimental Psychology: General, 109,* 32–41.

Fagan, J. F., III, & McGrath, S. K. (1981). Infant recognition memory and later intelligence. *Intelligence, 5,* 121–130.

Feuerstein, R. (1979). *The dynamic assessment of retarded performers: The learning potential assessment device, theory, instruments, and techniques.* Baltimore, MD: Baltimore University Park Press.

Fischbein, S. (1980). IQ and social class. *Intelligence, 4,* 51–63.

Fulker, O. W., & Eysenck, H. J. (1979). Nature, nurture and socio-economic status. In H. J. Eysenck, *The structure and measurement of intelligence.* Berlin: Springer-Verlag.

Galton, F. (1869). *Heredity genius.* London: MacMillan.

Galton, F. (1883). *Inquiries into human faculty and its development.* London: MacMillan.

Gould, S. J. (1981). *The mismeasure of man.* New York: Norton.

Guilford, J. P. (1964). Zero intercorrelations among tests of intellectual abilities. *Psychological Bulletin, 61,* 401–404.

Guilford, J. P. (1967). *The nature of human intelligence.* New York: McGraw-Hill.

Guilford, J. P., & Hoepfner, R. (1971). *The analysis of intelligence.* New York: McGraw-Hill.

Harnquist, K. (1968a). Relative changes in intelligence from 13–18. I. Background and methodology. *Scandinavian Journal of Psychology, 9,* 50–64.

Harnquist, K. (1968b). Relative changes in intelligence from 13–18. II. Results. *Scandinavian Journal of Psychology, 9,* 65–82.

Harrell, T. W., & Harrell, M. S. (1945). Army General Classification Test scores for civilian occupations. *Educational and Psychological Measurement, 5,* 229–239.

Hartson, L. D., & Sprow, A. J. (1941). Value of intelligence quotients obtained in secondary school for predicting college scholarship. *Educational and Psychological Measurement, 1,* 387–398.

Heber, R., & Garber, H. (1970). *An experiment in the prevention of cultural-familial mental retardation.* Paper presented at the Second Congress of the International Association for the Scientific Study of Mental Deficiency, Warsaw, Poland.

Henderson, N. D. (1982). Human behavior genetics. *Annual Review of Psychology, 33,* 403–440.

Hendrickson, A. E. (1982a). The biological basis of intelligence. Part I. Theory. In H. J. Eysenck (Ed.), *A model of intelligence.* Berlin: Springer-Verlag.

Hendrickson, A. (1982b). The biological basis of intelligence. Part II. Measurement. In H. J. Eysenck (Ed.), *A model for intelligence.* Berlin: Springer-Verlag.

Hick, W. (1952). On the rate of gain of information. *Quarterly Journal of Experimental Psychology, 4,* 11–26.

Horn, J. L., & Cattell, R. B. (1967). Age differences in fluid and crystallized intelligence. *Acta Psychologia, 26,* 107–129.

Horn, J. L., & Donaldson, G. (1976). On the myth of intellectual decline in adulthood. *American Psychologist, 31,* 701–719.

Humphreys, L. G. (1976). A factor model for research on intelligence and problem solving. In L. B. Resnick (Ed.), *The nature of intelligence.* Hillsdale, NJ: Erlbaum.

Hunt, E. (1978). Mechanics of verbal ability. *Psychological Review, 85,* 109–130.

Hunt, E., Lunneborg, C., & Lewis, J. (1975). What does it mean to be high verbal? *Cognitive Psychology, 7,* 194–227.

Hunt, J. McV. (1961). *Intelligence and experience.* New York: Ronald.

Jacobsen, L. L., Berger, S. M., Bergman, R. L., Millham, J., & Greeson, L. E. (1971). Effects of age, sex, systematic conceptual learning sets and programmed social interaction on the intellectual and conceptual development of pre-school children from poverty backgrounds. *Child Development, 42,* 1399–1415.

Jencks, C. (1972). *Inequality: A reassessment of the effect of family and schooling in America.* New York: Basic Books.

Jensen, A. R. (1971). The race $\times$ sex $\times$ ability interaction. In R. Canero (Ed.), *Contributions to intelligence.* New York: Grune & Stratton.

Jensen, A. R. (1974). Cumulative deficit: A testable hypothesis. *Developmental Psychology, 10,* 996–1019.

Jensen, A. R. (1977). Cumulative deficit in IQ of blacks in the rural south. *Developmental Psychology, 13,* 184–191.

Jensen, A. R. (1980). *Bias in mental testing.* New York: Free Press.

Jensen, A. R. (1981). *Test validity g versus the specificity doctrine.* Invited address at the annual convention of the American Psychological Association, Los Angeles, California.

Jensen, A. R. (1982). The chronometry of intelligence. In R. J. Sternberg (Ed.), *Recent advances in research on intelligence.* Hillsdale, NJ: Erlbaum.

Jensen, A. R. (1983a). The definition of intelligence and factor score indeterminacy. *The Behavioral and Brain Sciences, 6,* 313–315.

Jensen, A. R. (1983b). *The nature of the white-black difference on various psychometric tests.* Invited address at the annual convention of the American Psychological Association, Anaheim, California.

Jones, H. E., & Bayley, N. (1941). The Berkeley growth study. *Child Development, 12,* 167–173.

Keating, D. P., & Bobbitt, B. L. (1978). Individual and developmental differences in cognitive processing components of mental ability. *Child Development, 49,* 155–167.

Kenagy, H. G., & Yockum, C. E. (1925). *The selection and training of salesmen.* New York: McGraw-Hill.

Lally, M., & Nettlebeck, T. (1977). Intelligence, reaction time, and inspection time. *American Journal of Mental Deficiency, 82,* 273–281.

Lavin, D. E. (1965). *The prediction of academic performance: A theoretical analysis and review of research.* New York: Russell Sage Foundation.

Lewis, M., & Brooks-Gunn, J. (1981). Visual attention at three months as a predictor of cognitive functioning at two years of age. *Intelligence, 5,* 131–140.

Loehlin, J. C., & Lindzey, G., & Spuhler, J. N. (1975). *Race differences in intelligence.* San Francisco: Freeman.

Loehlin, J. C., & Nichols, R. C. (1976). *Heredity and environment and personality: A study of 850 sets of twins.* Austin: University of Texas Press.

Lykken, D. T. (1982). Research with twins: The concept of emergenesis. *Psychophysiology, 19,* 361–373.

Matarazzo, J. D. (1972). *Wechsler's measurement and appraisal of adult intelligence* (5th ed.). Baltimore: Williams & Wilkins.

Matheny, A. P., Jr., Dolan, A. B., & Wilson, R. S. (1976). Twins with academic learning problems. *American Journal of Orthopsychiatry, 46,* 464–469.

McCall, R. B. (1979). The development of intellectual functioning in infancy and the prediction of later IQ. In J. D. Osofsky (Ed.), *Handbook of Development.* New York: Wiley.

McCall, R. B. (1981). Early predictors of later IQ: The search continues. *Intelligence, 5,* 141–147.

McNemar, Q. (1964). Lost: Our intelligence? Why? *American Psychologist, 19,* 871–882.

Messick, S., & Jungeblut, A. (1981). Time and method in coaching for the SAT. *Psychological Bulletin, 89,* 191–216.

Miner, J. B. (1957). *Intelligence in the United States.* New York: Springer.

Moore, T. (1967). Language and intelligence: A longitudinal study of the first eight years. *Human Development, 10,* 88–106.

Munn, N. L. (1954). Learning in children. In L. Carmichael (Ed.), *Manual of Child Psychology* (2nd ed.). New York: Wiley.

Osborne, R. T. (1970). Heritability estimates for the visual evoked potential. *Life Science, 9,* 481–490.

Page, E. G. (1975). Miracle in Milwaukee: Raising the IQ. In B. Z. Friedlander, G. M. Sterritt, & G. E. Kirk (Eds.), *The exceptional infant.* New York: Brunner/Mazel.

Pinneau, S. R. (1961). *Changes in intelligence quotient: Infancy to maturity.* Boston: Houghton Mifflin.

Posner, M., Boies, S., Eichelman, W., & Taylor, R. (1969). Retention of visual and name codes of single letters. *Journal of Experimental Psychology Monograph, 79* (I, Pt. 2).

Posner, M., & Mitchell, R. (1967). Chronometric analysis of classification. *Psychological Review, 74,* 392–409.

Price, R. A., Vandenberg, S. G., Iyer, H., & Williams, J. S. (1982). Components of variation in normal personality. *Journal of Personality and Social Psychology, 43,* 328–340.

Ramey, C. T., & Haskins, R. (1981a). The modification of intelligence through early experience. *Intelligence, 5,* 5–19.

Ramey, C. T., & Haskins, R. (1981b). Early education, intellectual development, and school performance: A reply to Arthur Jensen and J. McVicker Hunt. *Intelligence, 5,* 41–48.

Revelle, W., Humphreys, M. S., Simon, L., & Gilliland, K. (1980). The interactive effect of personality, time of day, and caffeine: A test of the arousal model. *Journal of Experimental Psychology: General, 109,* 1–31.

Rogosa, D. (1980). A critique of cross-lagged correlation. *Psychological Bulletin, 88,* 245–258.

Rust, J. (1975). Cortical evoked potential, personality, and intelligence. *Journal of Comparative and Physiological Psychology, 89,* 1220–1226.

Scarr, S., & Carter-Saltzman, L. (1982). Genetics and intelligence. In R. J. Sternberg (Ed.), *Handbook of human intelligence.* Cambridge: Cambridge University Press.

Scarr, S., & Weinberg, R. A. (1976). IQ test performance of black children adopted by white families. *American Psychologist, 31,* 726–739.

Scarr-Salapatek, S. (1971). Race, social class, and IQ. *Science, 174,* 1285–1295.

Schaie, K. W., & Strother, C. R. (1968). A cross-sequential study of age changes in cognitive behavior. *Psychological Bulletin, 70,* 671–680.

Schiff, M., Duyme, M., Dumaret, A., Stewart, J., Tomkiewicz, S., & Feingold, J. (1978). Intellectual status of working-class children adopted early into upper-middle class families. *Science, 200,* 1503–1504.

Schonemann, P. H. (1983). Do IQ tests really measure intelligence? *The Behavioral and Brain Sciences, 6,* 311–313.

Snow, R. E., & Yalow, E. (1982). Education and intelligence. In R. Sternberg (Ed.), *Handbook of human intelligence.* Cambridge: Cambridge University Press.

Sommer, R., & Sommer, B. A. (1983). Mystery in Milwaukee: Early intervention, IQ, and psychology textbooks. *American Psychologist, 38,* 982–985.

Spearman, C. (1904). General intelligence, objectively determined and measured. *American Journal of Psychology, 15,* 201–293.

Spearman, C. (1927). *The abilities of man.* New York: Macmillan.

Sternberg, R. J. (1980). Sketch of a componential subtheory of human intelligence. *Behavioral and Brain Sciences, 3,* 573–614.

Sternberg, R. J., Conway, B. E., Ketron, J. L., & Bernstein, M. (1981). People's conceptions of intelligence. *Journal of Personality and Social Psychology, 41,* 37–55.

Sternberg, R. J., & Powell, J. S. (1983). Comprehending verbal comprehension. *American Psychologist, 38,* 878–893.

Sternberg, R. J., & Weil, E. M. (1980). An aptitude-strategy interaction in linear syllogistic reasoning. *Journal of Educational Psychology, 72,* 226-234.

Taubman, P. (1976). The determinants of earnings: Genetics, family and other environments: A study of white male twins. *American Economic Review, 66,* 858–870.

Terman, L. M. (Ed.) (1925). *Genetic studies of genius,* Vol. I, *Mental and physical traits of a thousand gifted children.* Stanford, California: Stanford University Press.

Terman, L. M., & Oden, M. H. (1959). *The gifted group at mid-life.* Stanford, California: Stanford University Press.

Thomson, G. H. (1939). *The factorial analysis of human ability.* Boston: Houghton Mifflin.

Vernon, P. E. (1961). *The structure of human abilities* (2nd ed.). London: Methuen.

Vernon, P. (1983). Speed of information processing and general intelligence. *Intelligence, 7,* 53–70.

Wechsler, D. (1958). *The measurement and appraisal of adult intelligence.* Baltimore: Williams & Wilkins.

Weikart, D. P. (1967). *Preschool intervention: A preliminary report of the Perry preschool project.* Ann Arbor, Michigan: Campus Publishers.

Whimbey, A. (1975). *Intelligence can be taught.* New York: Dutton.

Woodrow, H. (1940). Interrelations of measures of learning. *Journal of Psychology, 10,* 49–73.

Zeaman, D., & House, B. J. (1967). The relation of IQ and learning. In R. M. Gagne (Ed.), *Learning and individual differences.* Columbus, OH: Merrill, 1967.

Zigler, E., Abelson, W. D., & Seitz, V. (1973). Motivational factors in the performance of economically disadvantaged children on the Peabody Picture Vocabulary Test. *Child Development, 44,* 295–303.

Zigler, E., & Seitz, C. (1982). Social policy and intelligence. In R. J. Sternberg (Ed.), *Handbook of human intelligence.* Cambridge: Cambridge University Press.

Zigler, E., & Valentine, J. (Eds.) (1979). *Project Head Start: A legacy of the war on poverty.* New York: Free Press.

TEN

ENVIRONMENT AND IQ

THOMAS J. BOUCHARD, JR.
NANCY L. SEGAL
University of Minnesota
Minneapolis, Minnesota

INTRODUCTION

The literature dealing with the influence of environmental factors on IQ is quite large. Entire books have been written to summarize studies dealing with the effects of preschool intervention (Royce, Darlington, & Murray, 1983; Zigler & Valentine, 1979), famine (Stein, Susser, Saenger, & Marolla, 1975), malnutrition (Lloyd-Still, 1976), prenatal and early developmental factors (Broman, Nichols, & Kennedy, 1975), early experience (Clarke & Clarke, 1976), and social class and education (Jencks, Smith, Acland, Bane, Cohen, Gintis, Heyns, & Michelson, 1972; Herrnstein, 1973). White (1982), for example, found more than 200 studies that reported on the relationship between socioeconomic status and achievement. In addition, a large number of books have focused on the heredity-environment controversy (Jencks et al., 1972; Jensen, 1972, 1973; Kamin, 1974; Loehlin, Lindzey, & Spuhler, 1975; Scarr, 1981; Taylor, 1980; Vernon, 1979). Consequently, we will be selective in our choice of topics and breadth of coverage. The focus will be on a number of enduring issues that have continued to stimulate research for many years and around which large bodies of data have been built. In all instances, the selection of studies is illustrative rather than exhaustive. It is no longer possible to review properly a domain of content without either carrying out a series of meta-analyses or drawing on such a series (Glass, McGaw, & Smith, 1981; Hunter, Schmidt, & Jackson, 1982). Unfortunately the literature on environment and IQ contains few such meta-analyses.

The majority of studies we will summarize in this chapter report correlations between particular environmental variables, such as social class, parental education, nutritional status, conditions of birth, birth weight, and so forth, and

We wish to acknowledge the Pioneer Fund and Koch Foundation for providing financial support during the preparation of this chapter.

IQ measures. Some of these reports imply that these measures "explain" individual and group differences in IQ in some causal sense. There are a number of fallacies in this line of thinking. In almost every instance, a number of interpretations of a particular correlation are possible. We will first discuss the major possibilities, however, so that it will not be necessary to caution the reader repeatedly when we cover the empirical findings in each section of this chapter.

Confounding Genetic and Environmental Influences

The vast majority of the studies to be examined have been carried out within biologically related families (within-families). Biological parents pass on genes to their children, in addition to providing social and physical environments. The physical and social environments provided by these parents are, in turn, correlated with characteristics of the parents, such as their IQs. Consequently, correlations between environmental measures and IQs obtained in such settings are confounded with genetic variance. Adoption designs are mandatory for disentangling specific environmental and genetic factors (DeFries & Plomin, 1978).

Multiple Regression and Partial Correlation

In general, trait-relevant features of the environment are positively correlated. As a result, the enumeration of a large number of possible environmental correlates of IQ reveals very little. It is necessary to show, through using either multiple regression techniques or a specific theoretical model that incorporates nonadditive effects, that each environmental factor makes an independent contribution to the explanation of the IQ variance, after removing whatever IQ variance it has in common with factors already included. The value of the beta weights or regression coefficients for particular variables in such equations should be interpreted with caution. Such weights will fluctuate as a function of the intercorrelations among the predictor variables, and in some instances the equations are difficult, if not impossible, to interpret (see Vandenberg & Kuse, 1981).

Aggregation Fallacies

Occasionally an investigator will use aggregated data (for example, average IQ of a classroom, average SES of a classroom, average birth order of a cohort, and so forth) instead of individual data. Correlations based on such measures, called ecological correlations, are usually inflated relative to individual correlations, and they may be entirely misleading (see Robinson, 1950; and our subsequent discussion of the work by White, 1976, 1982). Hypotheses about individual level phenomena should be tested using individual level data.

Direction of Causation

It is easy to assume that a variable, such as level of education, is a cause of enhanced IQ. It is more difficult to remember that individuals with low IQs may, because of frustration, repeated failure, problems of self-esteem, and so on, drop out of school sooner than do individuals with higher IQs, and thereby reverse the direction of causation. It has become widely recognized in the domain of child development that the direction of effects of socialization is an empirical problem, not one to be assumed away (Bell, 1968).

Genotype × Environment Interaction

It is common for theorists of the heredity × environment controversy to confuse the statistical concept of interaction with a viewpoint called interactionism. The problem arises because each concept applies at a different level of analysis. A statistical interaction supposedly exists when variance not accounted for by the main effects can be accounted for by some interactive function (for example, multiplicative) of the main effects. The concept of statistical interaction, therefore, applies at the population level of analysis. The interactionist viewpoint asserts that an "organism is a product of its genes and its past environment" (Anastasi, 1958, p. 197). This is true at the level of development for the individual. It says nothing, however, about the existence or nonexistence of interaction variance at the population level. Bouchard (1976) has suggested that, in order to avoid confusion when we discuss individual development, we should refer to trans-actions with the environment.

Interactions, in principle, can take a variety of forms (Haldane, 1946; Vale, 1980). The most plausible form of an interaction for IQ is an ordinal interaction of the type popularized by Gottesman (1963, 1968) in his well-known reaction range curves. In this scheme, genotypes for higher intelligence respond more rapidly (steeper slope) to increasing favorableness of the environment than do genotypes for lower intelligence. There is very little convincing evidence for any genotype × environment interaction (Bouchard, 1976; Jinks & Fulker, 1970), but this is due in part to the lack of adequate data to test for it (Plomin, DeFries, & Loehlin, 1977).

Genotype × Environment Correlation

Genotype × environment correlations refer to the differential exposure of specific genotypes to specific environments. Plomin, DeFries, and Loehlin (1977) discuss three types of genotype × environment correlation. The first type of correlation is *passive*. If intelligent parents provide a favorable trait-relevant environment for the development of intelligence in their children, and less intelligent parents provide a less favorable trait-relevant environment, children in natural biological families will experience a passive genotype × environment correlation. We specifically refer to the concept of "trait-relevant environment" because, as we will show, our knowledge of the "trait-relevant environment" for intelligence is so meager that it is not safe to assume that natural families experience a significant passive genotype × environment correlation. The second type of correlation is *reactive*. In this case, other individuals (including family and nonfamily members) react to the child on the basis of his or her genotype (often referred to as natural ability). In actual fact, the response, is always to a developed phenotype. A child who draws with whatever he or she gets into his or her hands is more likely to receive crayons, pencils, and drawing instruments on his or her birthday. The third type of correlation is *active*. In this instance, the child seeks out an environment consistent with his or her genotype propensities. Bright children may, for example, seek reading material earlier and in greater quantities than do less bright children. Although the concept of genotype × environment correlation is beginning to be taken seriously by theoreticians and investigators in the domain of intelligence (Scarr & Grajek, 1982), very little empirical data have been gathered. Many of the findings generated with the various home environment instruments discussed later in this chapter should, however, be scrutinized with this model in mind. Again, Plomin, DeFries, and Loehlin (1977) have outlined a number of research strategies for assessing genotype × environment correlation, but they remain unimplemented.

Means and Correlations

Researchers interested in human behavior genetics almost always use correlational approaches to any question being investigated. In contrast, investigators interested in environmental effects, particularly those carrying out intervention studies, usually compare means between groups. Behavior geneticists tend to ignore mean differences, or use them in very limited ways, because they realize that means are far more susceptible to a variety of artifacts than are correlations and covariances. Examples of such artifacts are inadequate sampling of participants, poorly normed tests, and cohort effects.

Correlational methods take advantage of the natural variability that exists in a population. By contrasting correlations and covariances, obtained from appropriate groups, it is possible to draw inferences about the relative effects of heredity and environment (Jinks & Fulker, 1970; Li, 1975; Plomin, DeFries, & McClearn, 1980). These methods would not, however, enable us to detect the power of a new intervention to change the IQ of the population. A high heritability for IQ does not necessarily mean that IQ is unchangeable. It may simply mean that there is limited variation in the kinds of environmental factors that influence IQ.

A useful contrast is that of stature. Familial correlations for stature fit the polygenic model quite well and support the interpretation of strong genetic determination. Nevertheless, there has been a strong secular trend for an increase in stature in developed countries. The increase is still occurring even in the privileged classes, and it is linked with numerous factors that characterize a good physical environment. Thus the trait is being influenced by trends in the environment that affect almost everyone.

A similar phenomenon may be occurring for IQ. Flynn (1984) has recently argued that the mean IQ of Americans has shown a gain of 13.8 IQ points during the period from 1932 to 1978. This increase has resulted, and it has been hidden, because each new standardization sample for the Stanford-Binet and Wechsler tests has established norms of a higher standard. (Flynn's arguments may or may not be correct, and we will discuss them briefly later in this chapter.) Regardless of whether Flynn is correct in interpreting these gains as real changes in intelligence, they still have important implications. As he notes, "IQ gains produce obsolete norms and obsolete norms have acted as unrecognized confounding variables in literally hundreds of studies, misleading researchers about the nature and significance of their results" (p. 39). These gains can, to some extent, be understood within the same framework as the secular increase in stature.

PRENATAL AND EARLY DEVELOPMENTAL INFLUENCES

Complications of Labor and Delivery

Obstetrical complications have been reported to occur more frequently in low socioeconomic groups (see, for example, Birch & Gussow, 1970), implying that this may be associated with their lower IQ relative to higher SES groups. The collaborative study (Broman, Nichols, & Kennedy, 1975) found 31 obstetrical variables, measured at age 4 years, in both white and black samples to be almost totally unrelated to IQ. Similar negative results have been reported by Drillien (1968).

Birth Weight

Birth weight is often implicated as a variable causally related to IQ, due in part to its association with social class. Birth-weight differences, particularly large ones, may be associated with IQ differences between twins. Scarr (1969) reported a sizable IQ difference (13 points) within monozygotic (MZ) pairs in which one co-twin weighed above 2,500 grams and the other weighed below 2,500 grams at birth. When both twins were above or below this weight, the IQ differences were 5 and 6 points, respectively. Caputo and Mandell (1970) conclude that only children with very low birth weights (between 1,000–1,500 grams) have impaired IQs. They cite correlations in the range of .14 to .20 between IQ and birth weight. The collaborative project (Broman, Nichols, & Kennedy, 1975) reports correlations of .07 (whites) and .11 (blacks), uncorrected for SES.

Melnick, Myrianthopoulos, and Christian (1978) found significantly greater within-pair variation for members of white (but not black) MZ dichorionic pairs, relative to MZ monochorionic pairs, reflecting greater IQ-discordance within the former. In this study, IQ testing was performed when the twins were 7 years of age. A plausible interpretation offered by the investigators, based on research by Corey, Kang, Christian, Norton, and Harris (1976), is that the developmental asynchrony between embryos sharing a common uterus may be offset by single placentation and circulatory anastomoses in the case of monochorionic MZ twins, but not in dichorionic MZ twins.

A more recent study by Wilson (1979) is additionally informative. Ten pairs of MZ twins, whose birth weights differed by at least 750 grams (mean = 1064 grams), did *not* show significant within-pair differences in IQ measured at 6 years of age. We concur with Wilson's explanation that there may be a "high degree of buffering for intelligence against the effects of nutritional deficit in the prenatal period" (1979, p. 205), yet appreciate the vast complexity of factors that may underlie IQ-discordance between MZ co-twins. Future investigators may be advised to examine also the percent difference in birth weight and difference in IQ. The reader interested in attempting to interpret the IQ advantage of the heavier twin and the effect of the twin transfusion syndrome should read the paper by James (1982) and references therein.

Finally, only small correlations between birth order and IQ have been detected in studies of twins (Babson, Kangas, Young, & Bramhall, 1964; Loehlin & Nichols, 1976; Scarr 1969), despite some reports that the second-born twin may be somewhat "handicapped," relative to the first-born twin (Derom & Thiery, 1974; Pollin & Stabenau, 1968). Record, McKeown, and Edwards (1969), using sibs, have shown that, if birth order is held constant, there is no difference in verbal reasoning ability between light and heavy sibs of either sex. Sibs are excellent controls for SES, mother's genotype for weight, and so forth, as are dizygotic (DZ) twins. We agree, therefore, with Record et al. (1969) that the correlation between IQ and birth weight found in the general population is due primarily to between-family differences, such as SES, and not to birth weight.

It has been well documented that twins score 5-10 points below the singleton population on standard tests of intelligence (Drillien, 1961; Myrianthopoulos, Nichols, Broman, & Anderson, 1972). Explanations for this finding include both adverse prenatal and perinatal influences and/or restricted social experiences at the postnatal level due to the "twin situation," or close relationship shared by MZ twins. In an attempt to address this issue, Record, McKeown, and Edwards (1970) identified a sample of 148 twins whose co-twins were still-born or died within four weeks after birth. Their mean score on a test of verbal reasoning was 98.8, which is just slightly lower than the mean score (99.5) typically reported for singletons. The investigators concluded that the commonly observed "twin deficit" could be explained with reference to postnatal, rather than to biological factors. While the unique twin relationship might be responsible, or partially responsible, for reduced intellectual performance in some cases (see Luria & Yudovitch, 1959; Lytton, 1980), it is hardly a complete explanation. First, the mean score of the surviving twins was still somewhat below that of the singletons. Second, parents of these survivors may have provided additional efforts toward the care and education of these children to compensate for the possibility that they were also influenced by adverse prenatal effects. Third, the zygosity of these pairs was unknown. DZ pairs are not subject to the same intrauterine influences (for example, mutual circulation) as are MZ pairs. It is also the case that they do not appear to show the same degree of deficit as do MZ twins. DZ twins do not show the same close social relationship as do MZ twins. To the extent that Record et al. (1970) included a disproportionate number of DZ survivors in their sample, their conclusions could be biased (see, for example, James, 1982). A study by Myrianthopoulos, Broman, Nichols, and Anderson (1972) also addressed this issue. They compared mental test performance at age 4 years and 7 years for twins raised as singletons and for twins raised together. They found no differences at either age level. The results were also consistent for both the black and white portions of their sample. The average IQ, at age 7 years, for the white twins raised as singletons was 97.0. The average IQ, at the same age, of the white twin sample as a whole was 96.9. The white singleton sample obtained a mean IQ of 101.9.

We emphasize here that the functions relating birth weight, birth order, and maternal age are quite complex (Selvin & Janerich, 1971). Social mobility occurs as a function of height (a correlate of weight) (Scott, Illsley, & Thomson, 1956; Tanner, 1966; Thomson, 1958) and ability (discussed next), an event that may explain the modest birth weight $\times$ IQ correlation usually found. Weight, head circumference, and height do not, however, correlate very highly with IQ after infancy. Data from a representative sample of the north-central part of the United States ($N = 2,023$, 94% Caucasian) are shown in Table 1.

Weight at birth correlates only .08 with 7-year Binet IQ, but 1-year, 4-year, and 7-year weights correlate .11, .14, and .13, respectively, with this score. Broman, Nichols, and Kennedy (1975) report correlations of .08 and .10 between head circumference at birth and 4-year IQ for blacks and whites, respectively. Table 1 shows correlations of .17, .22, and .23 between head circumference measured at ages 1 year, 4 years, and 7 years, and 7-year Binet IQ.

Myrianthopoulos et al. (1971) have shown that there is no difference in birth weight for identical twins discordant for mental retardation. Thus birth weight does not seem to be a deciding factor in mental retardation either.

Anoxia

The collaborative project found that children judged to have a moderate degree of respiratory distress at birth had mean 4-year IQs of 4 points (blacks) and 7 points (whites) below children who did not experience such difficulties (correlations were $-.05$ and $-.06$, for the white and black samples, respectively). These correlations are small because only a tiny portion of the population was affected. (Interestingly, the incidence of respiratory distress at birth does not vary by class or by race.) These very modest correlations are consistent with

Table 1. Correlations Between Physical Growth Measures Taken at Ages 1 Year, 4 Years, and 7 Years and 7-Year IQ

	7-Year IQ									Correlation Coefficient With 7-Yr IQ
	Superior (≥120)			Average (80–119)			Low (≤79)			
	N	Mean	SD	N	Mean	SD	N	Mean	SD	
Birth weight, gm	258	3,333.2	472.9	1,667	3,312.3	535.5	96	3,279.4	635.5	.08
1 Year Old										
Weight, kg	234	10.1	1.2	1,518	10.1	1.3	86	9.6	1.4	.11
Height, cm	233	75.8	3.4	1,512	75.5	3.6	85	74.1*	3.0	.14
Head circumference, cm	238	46.5*	1.5	1,514	46.0	1.6	87	45.7	2.1	.17
4 Years Old										
Weight, kg	174	16.9	1.9	1,269	16.5	2.0	75	15.9	2.4	.14
Height, cm	174	103.1*	4.0	1,268	101.7	4.2	75	99.2	4.3	.23
Head circumference, cm	174	51.0*	1.5	1,262	50.3	1.6	75	49.8	1.9	.22
7 Years Old										
Weight, kg	258	24.2	4.2	1,665	23.5	3.6	96	22.3*	4.8	.13
Height, cm	258	123.0	5.2	1,659	121.9	5.3	96	118.5	5.4	.21
Head circumference, cm	258	52.6*	1.4	1,656	52.0	2.2	96	51.4	2.0	.23

Source. From Fisch, Bilek, Horrobin, and Chang, 1976.

*Significant mean differences at $p < .05$ level from average IQ group.

Gottfried's (1973) finding of a 4.6 IQ point deficit, due to anoxia, based on a summary of the literature. Gottfried felt that, although these studies were methodologically problematic, the anoxic infants as a group did not appear to become retarded. Reviews by Sameroff and Chandler (1975) and Sameroff (1975) lead to the same conclusion. Of particular note is the fact that when the effects of anoxia were documented in terms of impairment of biological functioning in the first few days of life (Graham, Matarazzo, & Caldwell, 1956; Graham, Pennoyer, Caldwell, Greenman, & Hartman, 1957) and related to impaired IQ at age 3 years (Graham, Ernhart, Thurston, & Craft, 1962), the difference between anoxic children and controls had disappeared by age 7 (Corah, Anthony, Painter, Stern, & Thurston, 1965).

Children experiencing primary apnea (failure to develop spontaneous respiration in the first two minutes after birth) had mean IQs of 3 points (blacks) and 8 points (whites) below those not afflicted ($r = -.04$ and $-.02$, respectively). Blacks are afflicted at a higher rate than are whites (.85% vs. 1.59%), but rates do not vary by class within race. Detailed reviews of the effects of other perinatal factors (for example, prematurity, maternal history of smoking, use of forceps or medications at delivery, and so forth), is beyond the scope of this chapter. The results from such studies suggest that perinatal stress may be associated with suboptimal intellectual functioning in only a small portion of these children.

Childhood Illnesses

Investigation of the relationship of childhood illnesses to later IQ are fraught with difficulties. It is necessary to correct for maternal age, birth order, social class, and so forth. An extensive study of the verbal scores on the 11+ examination of 43,820 Birmingham (England) children (McKeown & Record, 1976) suggests that there is no relationship between these test scores and the following diseases: measles, pertussis, rubella, mumps, and scarlet fever. These results are consistent in general with the previous literature reviewed by those authors. They also report that the data on the relationship between these diseases and mental subnormality (defined as IQ < 75) are inconclusive.

Lead Poisoning

Lead poisoning poses a serious problem in some central cities (Oberle, 1969), due to the widespread use of leaded paints prior to 1940. Children have been known to eat peeling paint chips and putty sticks (Aronow, 1969), a phenomenon termed pica. In addition, lead fallout from smelters is known to accumulate in children who live nearby and can lead to subtle neurological dysfunctions and minor psychomotor abnormalities (Roberts, Hutchinson, Paciga, Chattapadhyay, Jervis, Nan Loon, & Parkinson, 1974). Some studies have found that the blood levels of children living near lead sources are elevated, but that they were unrelated to IQ (Landsdown, Clayton, Graham, Shephard, Delves, & Turner, 1974). There were methodological problems with this study, however (see, for

example, Hebel, Kinch, & Armstrong, 1976). Hebel et al. (1976) were unable
to show any effect of lead pollution on the 11+ scores of Birmingham children
who lived in lead-polluted areas. The authors do admit that the design of this
study allowed for the detection of only very large effects. A widely cited study
by Needleman, Gunnoe, Leviton, Reed, Peresie, Maher, and Barrett (1979),
which unequivocally implicated low levels of lead as a cause of lower IQs, has
recently been criticized by the Environmental Protection Agency (Marshall,
1983). Bellinger and Needleman (1983) have reported an additional analysis of
the original report, which has also been criticized (Colliver, Kolm, & Verhulst,
1983). Other American results have been inconsistent (see Perino & Ernhart,
1974; and the follow-up study by Ernhart, Landa, & Schell, 1981). Other useful
references in this area are Chisolm and O'Hara (1982) and Rutter and Jones
(1983). The influence of low-level lead exposure (documented by low levels of
lead in the blood and by analysis of teeth shed by children) on children's IQs
remains unresolved. See, however, a reanalysis of relationships between lead and
IQ scores by Needleman et al. (1985), in which the neurotoxicity of low dose
exposure is demonstrated.

Summary

Both the collaborative study and a large-scale longitudinal study in Hawaii
(Werner, Bierman, & French, 1971) strongly suggest that the effects of perinatal
stress on intellectual functioning, broadly defined (for example, IQ), are small.
Joffe's (1969) review of the previous literature reaches a similar negative conclusion. These results can be placed within a broader research and theoretical
perspective that will make the results more meaningful. In the 1950s, the concept
of a broad continuum of reproductive causality was advanced. On the basis of
a number of studies (Lilienfeld & Parkhurst, 1951; Lilienfeld & Pasamanick,
1955, 1956; see also Joffe, 1969, for a careful review), it has been argued that
the severity and number of insults experienced during the prenatal period (for
example, nutritional deficiency, toxemia, low birth weight, anoxia, complications
of pregnancy, and so on) resulted in a hierarchy of injuries ranging from prenatal
death (a period in which the death rate is four times greater than at other ages)
to severe disorders of the brain (for example, cerebral palsy, epilepsy, mental
retardation) and milder disorders (for example, reading problems, as well as
speech and behavior disorders). Explicit in some formulations and implicit in
others is the critical period hypothesis, which states that some organ systems
are more vulnerable at the period of maximum growth than at other times. The
alternative hypothesis, favored previously, was that the developing fetus was
extremely well buffered from many types of insult during pregnancy. An extreme
form of this hypothesis is that the response of the fetus to insult is closer to an
all-or-none effect. If the insult is powerful, it causes death; otherwise, the organism has the capacity to recover. The results of the largest and best studies
(Broman, Nichols, & Kennedy, 1975; Werner, Bierman, & French, 1971) do not
support the hypothesis of a continuum of reproductive causality (see also Brody

& Brody, 1976, Chapter 5; Sameroff, 1975). Indeed they can, in our opinion, be said to support a weak version of the all-or-none hypothesis (allowing for compensation in response to insult). As indicated by Stein, Susser, Saenger, and Marolla (1975) (with reference to the famine study to be discussed), perhaps early biological insult *does* affect subsequent intellectual functioning, but our tools are not sufficiently sensitive to detect this. Observable and measurable differences, however (for example, SES differences and preliminary results from poorly controlled studies), lead to the continuum or reproductive casualty hypothesis. It is clear, therefore, that at least on one level this hypothesis is refuted.

MALNUTRITION AND FAMINE

Although some investigators contend that there is "compelling evidence that early malnutrition is a contributing factor in the incidence of mental deficiency" (Kaplan, 1972), others feel that "it remains a rather open question whether, to what extent, in what way, and by what means malnutrition lastingly influences psychological development" (Warren, 1973). Progress has been made in this area, although most of the important questions are unresolved.

Research on Malnutrition

Assessing the effects of malnutrition on IQ poses some extremely difficult problems because malnutrition occurs in association with poverty, crowding, large family size, inadequate medical care, short birth intervals between children, premature birth, poor sanitation and health practices, and so forth (Christiansen, Mora, & Herrera, 1975; Lloyd-Still, 1976). Although several studies have compared malnourished children with various control groups and have found differences in IQ in favor of the controls (Birch & Gussow, 1970; Hoorweg, 1976; Lloyd-Still, 1976; Stein & Kassab, 1970), the authors are unwilling to attribute the difference exclusively to malnutrition. The more recent the study, the more carefully the conclusions are stated.

Typically, an index sample of malnourished children is hospitalized for severe clinical malnutrition. One or more control samples are then created. For the control to be convincing, the children in the control group must be similar to the index cases in all relevant respects (age, sex, size of family, birth order, SES, education of parents, and so on), except for being malnourished. While no one would expect perfect controls, most studies conducted before the 1970s used extremely poor controls. They often failed to match on such basic factors as SES. Few conclusions can, therefore, be reliably based upon these analyses (Warren, 1973). Some early studies (Cravioto, DeLicardie, & Birch, 1966) compared tall and short children in communities in which malnutrition was endemic. The short children were assumed to have been at a greater nutritional risk. Aside from not demonstrating that malnutrition had even occurred, such a design confounds possible correlations between SES and height, as well as a possible biological correlation between height and IQ.

A widely used and generally powerful control is a sibling comparison group. The IQs of nearest-age siblings are compared to the IQs of the malnourished children (Hertzig, Birch, Richardson, & Tizzard, 1972). This design controls for many background factors but, even here, there are biases. For example, one must ask: Why did a particular child experience malnutrition and not the other? Did the mother overtly, or covertly, show preference for one child over the other? If so, why? Did the preferred child show greater potential or greater need? Some additional problems with sibling controls are outlined by Lloyd-Still (1976). Common paternity may be questionable, particularly among lower SES groups. The effects of hospitalization of the probands may bias sib comparisons, since this identifies families with children at risk. In addition, hospitalizations may have adverse effects. Finally, sibs may be subclinically malnourished and have suffered complications from secondary deprivation. This may, in fact, partly explain failure to demonstrate group differences on intelligence tests, in some cases. Jay (1972) has shown that if malnourished children are divided into two groups—(1) those who showed signs of psychomotor retardation or evidence of adverse event(s) that may have inflicted brain damage and (2) children with normal developmental antecedents—the children with normal antecedents have higher IQs. These data suggest that malnutrition is more likely to strike children with initially lower IQs.

Studies of the long-term consequences of severe malnutrition during the first two years of life (Hertzig et al., 1972; Richardson, Birch, & Hertzig, 1973) illustrate the methodological constraints, interpretive difficulties, and general findings of malnutrition studies of children. One such study was conducted in Jamaica. The index children had been hospitalized for severe clinical malnutrition, prior to the age of two years. Two comparison groups were formed: (1) a group of nearest-age sibs and (2) a group of unrelated classmates or neighbors closest in age to the index child. The authors note that, "The comparison children should, however, in no way be regarded as 'controls,' [because] there may be systematic differences between the index and comparisons in their social and biological histories which contribute to the differences in cognitive functioning other than the presence or absence of severe malnutrition" (Richardson et al., 1973, p. 632). At the time of testing with the WISC (Wechsler Intelligence Scale for Children), the children were between 5 years, 11 months, and 10 years of age. The IQ data are shown in Table 2.

The sibs do not differ significantly from the comparison group except on Performance IQ. They do, however, score lower than the comparison group on all other measures. The index group scores lower than the comparison group on all three measures and lower than the sibs on Full Scale and Verbal IQ. The most reliable effect would be the 4.12 point difference in Full Scale IQ. Given that the WISC has not been normed on a Jamaican sample, however, the absolute values in Table 2 may not be valid. The authors show that these effects are not due to artifacts of age differences or to ordinal position. Additional behavioral effects of malnutrition are reported in Richardson, Birch, and Ragbeer (1975).

Table 2. Means and Standard Deviations of WISC Scores for Three
Comparison Groups

| | Contrast Groups | | |
Scale	Sibs $N = 38$	Malnourished $N = 71$	Comparison $N = 71$
Full Scale IQ	61.84 $\pm$ 10.82	57.72 $\pm$ 10.75	65.99 $\pm$ 13.59
Verbal IQ	71.03 $\pm$ 12.87	64.92 $\pm$ 11.80	73.70 $\pm$ 14.55
Performance IQ	58.03 $\pm$ 10.47	56.30 $\pm$ 11.85	63.69 $\pm$ 13.30

Source. From Hertzig, Birch, Richardson, and Tizard, 1972.
Note. Means connected by lines are significantly different at $p < .02$.

Several studies (Winick, 1969; Winick, 1973; Winick, Brasel, & Rosso, 1972) show that severe malnutrition results in microscopic and biochemical changes in the brain (for example, cell number is reduced, myelination is decreased, DNA measures are lowered, and so on). Indeed, the evidence from animal studies and human autopsies convinces us that suboptimal diets sufficient to keep the organism alive will affect the central nervous system (Dobbing, 1973). It has been postulated that the period of most active growth of a target organ is the time of maximum vulnerability (Dobbing, 1968). In the case of cell division in the human brain, this period runs from the third trimester of pregnancy through the early postnatal months. The growth of dendrites and neuronal interconnections, however, continues to 24 months, and myelination is not well established until age 4 (Dobbing, 1973). Several authors have postulated that interferences with growth at this time tend to be irreversible. Severe malnutrition in adulthood, however, has not been associated with any impairment in cognitive ability (Keys, Brožek, Henschel, Mickelson, & Taylor, 1950).

The Effects of Famine

If, because of brain vulnerability, malnutrition during the early postnatal months is more serious than later malnutrition, one would expect a correlation between age of hospitalization and degree of impairment. Tests of this relationship have not been confirmatory (Hertzig et al., 1972; Jay, 1972). In addition, a large epidemiological study by Stein, Susser, Saenger, and Marolla (1972) casts further doubt on this hypothesis. The authors examined the mental performance (Raven Progressive Matrices) of approximately 98% of all males, living in cities, whose dates of birth bracketed the famine period imposed by the Nazis in western Holland during 1944–1945. Their performance was also compared with a control group drawn from the southern, eastern, and northern parts of that country. The tests were administered at age 19 when the subjects appeared for military induction, making this a very long-term study. The military in Holland also obtains files on all institutionalized individuals (handicapped or mentally retarded) in order to certify rejection. One limitation of the study is that only males were included. This should *increase* the sensitivity of this study to the famine effect, because of the phenomenon of general male vulnerability (Hutt, 1972). The three dependent variables studies were as follows: (1) severe mental retardation, (2) mild mental retardation, and (3) IQ (Raven Progressive Matrices score). Children subjected to famine during the third trimester of pregnancy, which is the period of high velocity brain growth, are of particular interest. Under the hypothesis that "developing organ systems are most vulnerable at the period of maximum growth," children subject to famine at this time should show more loss in IQ than would any other group.

Figures 1 and 2 depict the fluctuations in the dependent variables across the birth dates on the various cohorts. The mild mental retardation rates and Raven Progressive Matrices scores are presented by social class of the father. The period bracketed by the dotted lines shows conceptions during the famine. (Figure 2 will be discussed later.)

The rate of severe mental retardation increases during the period of famine, but it is accompanied by an equal rise in the control group; thus impairment appears to be associated with factors other than famine. The rates of mild mental retardation differ for the two social classes just as would be expected from a polygenic theory of inheritance. There is no effect due to famine. Most of the fluctuation within classes is a response to famine.

There is no association between famine and Raven Progressive Matrices scores. Again, however, large social class differences are observed. Bradley (1973) has pointed out the possibility of an ecological fallacy in this study, namely that pregnant mothers received larger rations than the population as a whole, because of differential sharing within the family. In fact, pregnant mothers *did* receive larger rations, but they were still exceedingly low (Smith, 1947). In any event, there is no doubt that the mothers did undergo severe malnutrition. Figure 2

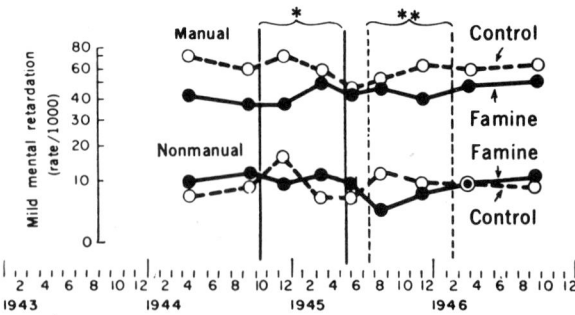

Figure 1. Rates of mild mental retardation in Netherlands men examined at age 19, for manual and nonmanual classes according to father's occupation, by cohort of birth in famine and control cities. Solid vertical lines bracket period of famine, and broken vertical lines show the period of births conceived during famine. (*Source:* From Stein, Susser, Saenger, and Marolla, 1972; Copyright© 1972 by the AAAS.)

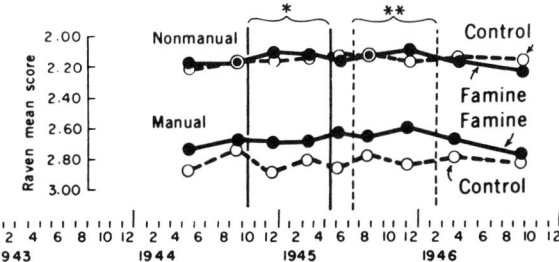

Figure 2. Mean grouped scores on Raven progressive matrices test of Netherlands men examined at age 19, for manual and nonmanual classes according to father's occupation, by cohort of birth in famine cities and control cities. Solid vertical lines bracket period of famine, and broken vertical lines show the period of births conceived during famine. (*Source:* From Stein, Susser, Saenger, and Marolla, 1972; Copyright© 1972 by the AAAS.)

shows that for children born in hospitals in which birth records were available, there was a dramatic loss in weight during the famine period. Bradley (1973) also suggests that there may be a threshold below which one must go in order to influence mental performance. According to Stein and Susser (1976), there was a threshold for fetal growth that was not met because of the retarded growth of the children. There was excess infant mortality, and maternal weight was severely depressed immediately after birth, but, "No threshold below which mental performance is affected could be detected in our data, however. If there is such a threshold, it must be very close to that below which reproduction cannot be maintained" (Susser, 1976, p. 134).

It is striking that the growth variable least affected by famine was head size. Why didn't starvation during pregnancy (confirmed partially by birth weight reduction in a selected hospital sample of the famine group) influence mental performance 19 years later? There are a number of possibilities. First, it must be understood that this was a study of episodic malnutrition, not chronic malnutrition, and that the mothers had previously been well nourished; as such, their bodies may have helped supply essential nutrients. This is in contrast with conditions of chronic undernutrition in many developing countries and among very poor people in other countries. A second possibility, favored by Stein (personal communication, 1973), is that at least among infants exposed to famine in the third trimester (for which there is evidence of reduction in head size), there was organic impairment, but that the cerebral reserve was large enough to prevent the impairment from becoming sufficiently manifest in any form to be measurable. This is a plausible hypothesis, but real advances in the measurement of both mental ability and human biochemistry are required to test it adequately. Another possibility is that impairment was later offset by compensatory learning. A weak test of this hypothesis would require an interaction between exposure or nonexposure to famine and social class. No such interaction was found. A very reasonable hypothesis is that the brain of a developing child is exceedingly well buffered from the effects of malnutrition, and that death is likely to occur only when mechanisms influencing mental functioning are impacted. If, due to evolutionary pressure (for example, many periods of starvation

selectively decimating populations), most animals are built "hierarchically"—
that is, in such a way that the least essential organs are influenced first, and the
least "important" part of essential organs are influenced next—we would have
a sound explanation for the great difficulty researchers have had in showing a
large intellectual deficit due to malnutrition. This hypothesis is rendered more
plausible by the fact that "the known, *major*, qualitative evolutionary trends in
animal nutrition were established long before the origin of the human species
some 300,000 years ago" (Loehlin, Lindzey, & Spuhler, 1975, p. 197).

Regardless of the accuracy of the above hypothesis, buffering of the brain
under malnutrition is dramatic, as can be seen in data collected by Naeye,
Diener, Dellinger, and Blane (1969). These investigators examined 445 consecutive cases in which children were stillborn or died within 48 hours after birth.
They excluded 193 cases in which it was clear that some type of disorder had
affected growth. The remaining cases were divided into "poor" and "nonpoor"
groups on the basis of income and family size. Organ and body weights of the
two groups were compared. The results are shown in Table 3. The data are
scaled in terms of percent of "normal" published values.

Table 3. **Mean Organ and Body Weights ($\pm$1 SD) in Newborn Infants
of Poor and Nonpoor Families in Percent of "Normal" Published
Values, and Additional Contrasts**

Item	Poor	Nonpoor	Difference
Organ Weight			
Placenta	84 $\pm$ 35	88 $\pm$ 29	4
Brain	101 $\pm$ 19	107 $\pm$ 25	6*
Kidney	91 $\pm$ 34	101 $\pm$ 37	10*
Heart	90 $\pm$ 27	105 $\pm$ 28	15**
Liver	83 $\pm$ 22	104 $\pm$ 31	21**
Spleen	81 $\pm$ 45	104 $\pm$ 49	23**
Adrenal	77 $\pm$ 38	102 $\pm$ 46	25**
Thymus	66 $\pm$ 31	104 $\pm$ 49	38**
Body	92 $\pm$ 18	107 $\pm$ 23	15*
Miscellaneous			
N	49	203	
Percent stillborn	37%	27%	
Mean no. of gestations	3.9	2.8	
Percent previous preg- nancies with surviv- ing children	85%	76%	
Gestational age (weeks)	29	29	

Source. Naeye, Diener, Dellinger, and Blane, 1969; Copyright© 1972 by the AAAS.
*$p < .05$.
**$p < .005$.

Among the children's organs studied, the brain was the *least* affected. This same particular ranking of organs has also been shown in animals subjected to undernutrition. The authors conclude that, "Undernutrition appears responsible for prenatal growth retardation in infants from poor families," but they caution that, "other environmental or genetic factors have not been excluded" (Naeye et al., 1969, p. 1026).

Summary

While the magnitude of the effects of malnutrition on intellectual and physical development is apparently much less than one would expect on first consideration, even difficult to establish conclusively, the relationships appear to be real. Given these facts, are the effects reversible? While the necessary microscopic and biochemical studies have not been conducted, radiological case histories of rehabilitated malnourished children have revealed dramatic increases in brain size following proper nutrition, with once closed cranial sutures reopening, due to brain expansion (De Levie & Nogrady, 1970). An adoption study of Korean children (all females), who apparently underwent severe nutritional deprivation during the first two to three years of life and were adopted into American middle-class homes before age 3, showed remarkable gains in height and weight six years later. In addition, their scores on IQ and achievement tests were outstanding (Winick, Meyer, & Harris, 1975). A large nutritional and educational supplementation study of deprived children from Colombian families additionally indicated impressive gains in cognitive performance (McKay, Sinisterra, McKay, Gomez, & Lloreda, 1978). These studies strongly suggest that the prospects for rehabilitation of severely malnourished infants and children are not necessarily hopeless.

Given these findings, we nevertheless do not believe that malnutrition, at least at the level experienced in developed economies, has substantial impact on mental retardation or on the general distribution of IQ. The question, however, deserves considerably more study (see, for example, Loehlin et al., 1975; they have drawn a similar conclusion). A small effect on the population does *not*, however, mean a small effect on individuals. Individual children are not only mentally and physically stunted by malnutrition, but they also die from it (Chase & Martin, 1970).

FAMILY BACKGROUND AND IQ

Data from Biological Families

Parental socioeconomic status is widely believed to be an important determinant of childhood IQ and success in school. Consequently, it is often recommended that SES be controlled in educational studies prior to an assessment of school factors. St. John (1970), for example, concluded:

So powerful is the apparent effect of social class, that the influence of other background and school factors can be detected only if socioeconomic status (SES) is first neutralized through matching or statistical control. Accurate measurement of SES, therefore, is crucial to any social research in schools. [p. 255]

Recommendations to control for SES are sometimes based on the assumption that the influence of SES on IQ is environmental in origin. That assumption, unfortunately, is not correct. In open societies with high degrees of occupational mobility, individuals with higher IQs migrate, relative to their parents, to occupations of higher SES, and individuals with lower IQs migrate to occupations of lower SES. There is excellent evidence for this phenomenon in both England and the United States (Bouchard, 1976; Gibson, 1970; Waller, 1971). Since IQ has a high heritability—that is, there is a high correlation between the genotype and phenotype—it must follow that SES differences between individuals are, in part, genetic (Bouchard, 1976; Eckland, 1967; Herrnstein, 1973). If this is true, then statistical controls for SES partial out genetic, as well as environmental, variance, and they are fallacious if used in a context in which the relative roles of heredity versus environment are at issue (see Meehl, 1970).

The terms "family background," "social class," "economic status," and "SES" are used almost interchangeably by many social scientists. In fact, most measures of SES intercorrelate so highly that for many purposes they can be used interchangeably. For our purposes, however, a more careful articulation of the components is necessary. Fortunately, this literature has been recently subjected to a meta-analysis by White (1982). The results are in many respects surprising. (Table 4 is constructed from data presented by White in Table 1 and Table 5 of his paper.)

Under the section titled "unit of analysis," we can see that when correlations are computed on aggregate data, using school districts, schools, and classrooms as the units of analysis, the correlations are seriously inflated, relative to the correlations based on students as the unit of analysis. The student correlation is the proper descriptive statistic for our purposes. Surprisingly, the correlation for SES and achievement (which includes IQ) is lower than that found for SES and IQ. One would expect that the various achievement measures used in the literature would, on the average, be more culture-loaded than are IQ scores. One might suspect that achievement measures tend, on the average, to be less reliable than are IQ measures, but in an extended treatment of the topic White (1976) demonstrates that most achievement measures are highly reliable.

There is also a large difference in the magnitude of the SES achievement correlation as a function of type of publication. Books overstate the magnitude of the relationship, while unpublished sources, such as doctoral dissertations, tend toward understatement. When classified by degree of internal validity of the study, the relatively less valid studies report a higher correlation for achievement than do more valid studies. The opposite is true, however, for IQ.

The most meaningful correlation in the table, for our purposes, uses the student as the unit of analysis. This correlation (.333) is lower than popular

Table 4.   Magnitude of the Mean Correlation Between SES and
Achievement and IQ as a Function of Different Study Characteristics

Category	Achievement		IQ	
	Mean	*N*	Mean	*N*
Unit of Analysis				
Aggregated	.680	93	.731	18
Confounded	.338	39	.337	10
Student	.245	489	.333	74
Type of Publication				
Books	.508	88	.592	19
Journals	.343	219	.387	63
Unpublished	.292	313	.273	20
Validity				
Valid	.296	489	.419	81
Fairly valid	.357	107	.306	17
Invalid	.486	28	**	**

Source. Compiled from White, 1982, Tables 1 and 5.
**$N < 10$.

discussion of the topic would lead one to believe, but it is far from insignificant. Figure 3 shows the frequency distribution of SES × achievement correlation coefficients for studies using the student as the unit of analysis.

The enormous variance is readily apparent. There are even some negative correlations. A single study, for whatever reason, may yield a wide range of results. Clearly, reliance on the results of a single study could be very misleading. Much of the variation arises from the diversity of measures of SES used, as shown in Table 5.

Income is the highest single correlate of achievement, followed by occupation and education. Various composites work better, and the variable home atmosphere works best of all. (We will discuss home atmosphere in the next section of this chapter.) The high correlation of income with achievement shown in Table 5 was discrepant with our own expectations. A summary of the results of four large-scale studies (not included in the White tabulations) are shown in Table 6. They suggest that IQ relates to parental education, income, and oc-

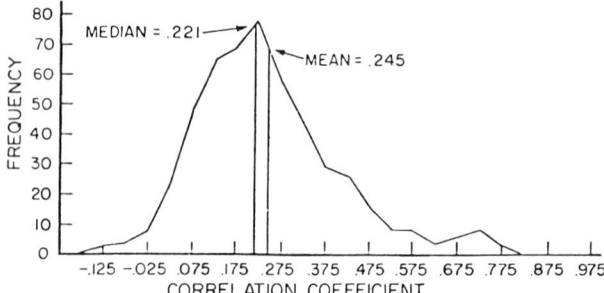

Figure 3. Frequency distribution of SES/achievement correlation coefficients for studies using the student as the unit of analysis ($N = 489$). (*Source:* From White, 1982. Copyright© 1972 by the American Psychological Association. Reprinted by permission of the publisher and author.)

cupation somewhat differently than does achievement. The Educational Testing Service, however, reports a correlation of .23 ($N = 650,000$) between the Scholastic Aptitude Test (SAT) and income (Educational Testing Service, 1980). When computed on a more recent group, using income reported on a finer scale, the correlation was .29. Thus, income may correlate as highly with children's IQs as does parental education.

The Bahr and Leigh (1978) study used the National Longitudinal Surveys of Labor Market Experience. IQ was obtained from the high school records of each participant. The Mercy and Steelman (1982) data derive from Cycle II of the National Health Examination Survey. The IQ measure is composed of the Vocabulary and Block Design subtests of the Wechsler Adult Intelligence Scale. We averaged the correlations with each of these subtests. The Firkowska, Ostrowska, Sokolowska, Stein, Susser, and Wald (1978) data were gathered in 1974 on 13,695 children (96% of the children born in 1963) in Warsaw, Poland. The Project Talent Data are reported by White (1976) in his doctoral dissertation. They were included in order to compare the results of the meta-analysis with a single large-scale study.

These results suggest that the educational histories of both parents are equally related to IQ, and yield a correlation of about .30. This is in contrast to the figure of .185 for SES reported by White in Table 5. The correlation for occupation is .28 and is, therefore, quite close to that for parental education. The correlation for income (.22) is much lower than that for either education or occupation and much lower than the figure of .315 for SES reported by White, but, as we mentioned previously, the very large ETS sample gives a higher figure. A meta-analysis of the parental income × children's IQ correlation is clearly warranted. We should also note that the correlation between parental education and child's IQ (.52) in the large twin study conducted by Wilson (1983) deviates considerably from the mean correlation given in Table 5.

Jencks et al. (1972), based on an analysis of the relevant literature, concluded the following:

Table 5. Magnitude of the Mean Correlation Between SES and Achievement for Different Kinds of SES Measures

SES Measure	Mean	N
Income only	.315	19
Education only	.185	116
Occupation only	.201	65
Home atmosphere only	.577	21
Income and education	.230	36
Income and occupation	.332	15
Education and occupation	.325	20
Income, education, and occupation	.318	27
Income, education, and occupation plus something else major	.365	22

Source. From White, 1982, Table 6.

Taking all the evidence together, however, we estimate that a family's economic status probably correlates about 0.35 with the children's test scores. . . . If we merely equalize everyone's economic status, test score inequality would fall by 6% or less. [pp. 80–109]

If economic inequality were to be measured only by income, then our results suggest that Jencks et al. may have overstated the possible reduction in cognitive inequality if income inequality is eliminated.

As we will explain in the next section, it may well be that parental education is a reasonable proxy for intelligence, and the intrinsic factors in this study are to a large extent genetic, rather than environmental.

Table 6. Correlations Between Parental Socioeconomic Status Measures and Child's IQ in Large Scale Studies of Biological Families

Status Variable	Study and Sample Size					
	1 (2,700)	2 (2,700)	3 (7,119)	4 (13,695)	5 (8,500)	Mean
Fathers' Education	.32	.34	.36	.29	.26	.314
Mothers' Education	.29	.34	.36	.27	.23	.298
Fathers' Occupation	.26	.30	—	.28	.27	.278
Income	.22	.20	.28	—	.19	.223

Note. 1 = Bahr & Leigh, 1978 (Males); 2 = Bahr & Leigh, 1978 (Females); 3 = Mercy & Steelman, 1982; 4 = Firkowska, 1978; 5 = Flanagan et al., 1972, as analyzed and reported by White, 1976.

Data from Nonbiological Families

Orphanage Studies.   The influence of SES variables can be usefully assessed via studies of institutionalized children. We can, for example, examine the IQs of institutionalized children when they are ordered by the SES of their biological parents. Two studies of this type—one by Lawrence (1931) and one by Jones and Carr-Saunders (1927)—are available. Lawrence (1931) studied illegitimate children who had never lived with their father and whose average age of placement in the institution was six months. The children were tested at about age 12.6 years (SD = 18 months) with the Stanford-Binet and the Simplex. A control group of children (in what the author describes as a typically large, London elementary school) was also tested with the Simplex. SES was determined on the basis of occupation of the father. The results are displayed in Table 7.

Dropping the two males in class E, the range becomes 7.8 IQ points for boys and 8.3 IQ points for girls. Notice that the standard deviation of the IQ for these children has been reduced. This reduction is due to the dearth of cases at both extremes. It may, in part, be associated with the restriction of environmental variation in the institution.

Jones and Carr-Saunders (1927) studied children from a number of different orphanages. These children were placed much later than those in the Lawrence study; therefore, the data are broken down by years of residence. SES was again determined by occupation of the father. The test used was the Simplex. The children were all between 9.5 and 14.0 years of age when tested. These data are presented in Table 8.

Age of placement does not appear to affect the results. The range of IQs in the early placement group spans 14.1 IQ points. While these studies are far from perfect (see Eysenck & Kamin, 1982), the most parsimonious explanation of the results is that part of the variation in IQ across the different social classes is genetically determined.

At this point, we cannot fail to mention briefly a widely cited study by Skeels (1966). This study purported to raise significantly the IQs of orphanage children by placing them in an institution for the mentally retarded that resulted in close personal care at the hands of older inmates. The critique of this study by Longstreth (1981) is sufficiently trenchant that we do not feel the study requires discussion.

Adoption Studies.   Burks (1928) carried out one of the first adoption studies designed to assess the influence of family background variables on IQ. She examined two matched groups, a group of foster (legally adopted) children ($N = 124$) and their parents, and a control group of children reared by their biological parents ($N = 105$). The two groups were quite well matched on a variety of family background characteristics. Those few factors on which matching was not accomplished are discussed in detail and convincingly shown not to be crucial to an interpretation of the results. The SES (Barr ratings) of the parents showed a distribution similar to that of the general American population.

Table 7. **Means,** *N*'s, **Standard Deviations, and Correlation Ratios of Simplex and Stanford-Binet IQ for London Elementary School Children and Institutionalized Children by Social Class of Father**

Social Class of Father	London Elementary School Children				Institutionalized Children			
	Boys		Girls		Boys		Girls	
	Mean	N	Mean	N	Mean	N	Mean	N
Simplex Test								
A	111.3	6	109.9	8	97.9	16	100.8	12
B	108.8	28	104.8	38	104.4	27	98.5	19
C	100.2	136	100.8	137	97.5	44	93.2	34
D	94.9	37	96.6	39	93.8	14	93.6	17
E	97.8	4	94.8	6	98.0	2	—	—
Total	100.7	211	100.9	228	98.9	103	95.6	82
SD	15.8		14.1		13.7		12.3	
Correlation ratio	.27±.04		.22±.04		.26±.06		.25±.07	
Stanford-Binet								
A					102.0	20	100.1	15
B		Not applicable			106.0	43	102.8	24
C					99.9	72	95.3	50
D					98.2	23	94.5	20
E					92.0	2	—	—
Total					101.5	160	97.5	109
SD					12.6		12.5	
Correlation ratio					.22±.05		.26±.06	

Source. Lawrence, 1931.

Table 8. Mean IQs of Institutionalized Children According to Years of Residence and Occupational Class of Biological Father

Class	0 to 3 Years of Residence		3 to N Years of Residence	
	N	Mean IQ	N	Mean IQ
1	92	107.3	117	106.0
2	46	104.4	46	105.6
3	98	96.3	65	95.5
4	91	95.5	74	96.0
5	149	93.2	102	93.7
Weighted Mean		98.1		99.3

Source. From Jones and Carr-Saunders, 1927.

A great deal of evidence was generated to demonstrate that selective placement had not occurred. For example, the correlation between true fathers' and foster fathers' Barr ratings was −.02. This same careful checking of placement effects revealed that the Barr ratings of the true fathers (91 cases on whom the information could be obtained) correlated only .07 with the adopted away child's IQ. The home environments of all the children were carefully and extensively analyzed. The results are shown in Table 9.

Concerning ourselves first with the correlations shown above the dotted line in Table 9, we see that the parents' mental ages and vocabulary scores correlated highly with the IQ scores of the control (biological) children. Both the Whittier Index and the Culture Index correlated with the children's IQs, as well as with the parental status measures. Parental education (last grade completed) and income correlated much less strongly (.27 and .24, respectively) and at the same level as reported in more recent studies (see Table 6). These results are, then, remarkably consistent with modern data on biological families.

The correlations for the foster children–foster parent pairs are approximately half as large as those of the control pairs. Burks corrected most of the correlations above the dotted line for attenuation. This considerably increased the difference between the two groups. While theoretically correct, this practice always raises objections, and we have not reported those correlations here. The foster children correlations are, as we explained previously, estimates of environmental effects unconfounded by heredity.

Burks (1928) calculated the multiple correlation between four of these measures and child's IQ in each group. The four variables were selected from the nine in such a way as to minimize computational difficulties, since computers were not available at that time. For the foster group the multiple *r* was .35 (.42 using *r*'s corrected for attenuation) and for the control group it was .53 (.61 using *r*'s corrected for attenuation). While the corrected figures are most often cited in the literature, we will use the uncorrected figures here, both because

Table 9. Child's IQ Correlated with Environmental and Hereditary Factors

Factor	Type of r	Foster			Control		
		r	P.E.	N	r	P.E.	N
Father's M. A.	P.M.	.07	.05	178	.45	.05	100
Mother's M. A.	P.M.	.19	.05	204	.46	.05	105
Mid-parent M. A.	P.M.	.20	.05	174	.52	.05	100
Father's vocabulary	P.M.	.13	.05	181	.47	.05	101
Mother's vocabulary	P.M.	.23	.04	202	.43	.05	104
Whittier index	P.M.	.21	.04	206	.42	.05	104
Whittier index (using 5-yr.-olds only)	P.M.	.29	.08	63	—	—	—
Culture index	P.M.	.25	.05	186	.44	.05	101
Culture index (using 5-yr.-olds only)	P.M.	.23	.08	60	—	—	—
Grade reached by father	P.M.	.01	.05	173	.27	.06	102
Grade reached by mother	P.M.	.17	.05	194	.27	.06	103
Parental supervision rating 3 or 4 *vs.* 5 or 6	B.	.12	.05	206	.40	.09	104
Income	P.M.,K.	.23	.05	181	.24	.06	99
No. of books in home library	P.M.,K.	.16	.05	194	.34	.06	100
Owning or renting home	B.	.25	.07	149	.32	.10	100
No. of books in child's library	P.M.,K.	.32	.04	191	.32	.06	101
Private tutoring (in music, dancing, etc.)	B.						
Boys		.06	.10	77	.43	.11	46
Girls		.31	.08	108	.52	.09	56
Five-year girls only		.50	.12	31	—	—	—

Table 9. (*Continued*)

Factor	Type of *r*	Foster			Control		
		r	P.E.	*N*	*r*	P.E.	*N*
Home instruction by members of							
household (hrs. weekly)	P.M.						
Ages 2 and 3		.34	.04	181	−.05	.07	101
Ages 4 and 5 (children over 5)		.15	.06	129	−.03	.08	71
Ages 6 and 7 (children over 7)		.03	.07	88	.24	.09	46
Ages 2 and 3 (5-yr.-olds only)		.18	.09	51	—	—	—
Ages 4 and 5 (5-yr.-olds only)		.13	.09	52	—	—	—
Father's rating of child's							
intelligence	P.M.	.49	.04	164	.32	.06	98
Mother's rating of child's							
intelligence	P.M.	.39	.04	181	.52	.05	101

Source. From Burks, 1928.

Note. The following abbreviations are used in this table: M.A. for mental age; P.M. for product-moment correlation; B. for biserial correlation; K. for Professor Kelley's auxiliary score method.

See also the tables of correlation arrays for child's IQ with Father's M.A. and Mother's M.A., from which the corresponding *r*'s in this table were computed (Appendix II).

The significance of the division of the table by the dotted line is explained in the text, p. 536.

current investigators tend to avoid using corrected figures and because the figures based on correction for attenuation probably should be corrected for shrinkage. Squaring the multiple *r*'s gives us the amount of variance accounted for by the environmental factors. Thus, in the foster situation in which the multiple correlation represents only environmental influence, the amount of explained variance in children's IQ is 12%. In the control condition it is 28%, which is more than twice as much.

We now turn to the data below the dotted line in Table 9. Burks regarded these figures as more ambiguous than those above the line because of the problem of reciprocal effects. Addressing the variable, "number of books in the child's library," as opposed to "number of books in home library," she asked, "Do the books in a child's library stimulate the growth of his IQ or does the child of high intelligence tend to collect more books around him? Does reading the Burgess bedtime stories to a two-year-old enhance his mental potentiality, or does the child with high mental potentiality clamor loudest for the bedtime stories?" This is the problem of genotype × environment correlation discussed earlier. In this instance we have an active genotype × environment correlation. For "number of books in child's library," the correlation is .32 for both groups. It is very unfortunate that Burks did not report the intercorrelations between all of her variables. If this information were available, we could carry out additional analyses and compare her results more directly with modern studies.

Freeman, Holzinger, and Mitchell (1928) published a study of foster children in the same issue of the *National Society for the Study of Education Yearbook* in which the Burks study appeared. This study has been heavily criticized by Munsinger (1975) and defended by Kamin (1978). For our purposes the interesting findings are shown in Tables 10 and 11.

Table 10 shows the mean IQs of the foster children as a function of the occupational class of their foster parents. The correlation is .37. We have computed the weighted average IQ, excluding cases in the unskilled labor class because their scores were not reported. The mean IQ is 97.56. This is very close to the mean of 97.5 reported for the entire 401 cases. These data suggest a strong influence of occupational status on IQ variance (14% of the variance). It is of interest, however, to compare the IQs of the foster children with those of biological children of the same parents. A subgroup of 36 biological children showed an average IQ of 112.4 (SD = 13.9), while 34 foster children raised in the *same homes* showed an average IQ of 95.1 (SD = 14.8). The difference (17.3) is greater than one full standard deviation and equal to the average difference one finds between any two unrelated individuals paired at random (see Plomin & DeFries, 1980). Nevertheless, the correlation between the IQs of the 40 pairs of unrelated siblings in this group was .34. This correlation is a direct estimate of common family environmental effects (unless there is placement bias). It is a variance estimator and should not be squared (Jensen, 1971).

Table 11 gives the correlations between child's IQ and foster home rating. The rating is comprised from ratings of material environment, evidences of culture, occupational standing, education, and social activity. Freeman, Holzinger, and Mitchell (1928) emphasize the correlation of .48 for the Binet IQ.

Table 10. Intelligence of Children According to the Occupational Status of Their Foster Fathers

Occupational Class	Mean Intelligence Quotient of Foster Children	N
Professional	106.8	61
Semi-professional & Business	101.1	160
Skilled labor	91.6	149
Semi-skilled to slightly skilled labor	84.9	19
Unskilled labor	*	5
	(Mean 97.56)**	394

Source. From Freeman, Holzinger, and Mitchell, 1928, Table 37, p. 178.
*Not reported by the authors.
**Weighted mean computed by us.

Table 11. Correlations Between Children's IQ and Foster Home Rating

	Stanford-Binet IQ		International Test Score	
Group	N	r	N	r
Home Group	401	.48	298	.24
Entered Before 2 Years	156	.52	80	.28
Entered Before 9 Months	111	.46	58	.30

Source. Compiled from Freeman, Holzinger, and Mitchell, 1928, Table 34.

Unfortunately, there is a significant degree of placement bias in this study, and it is readily acknowledged by the original authors. They note that for an important subgroup the correlation between home rating and IQ of the child was .34 *at the time of placement.* They argue, and we agree, that for the group as a whole the degree of placement bias is probably less. The problem is: How much less? They downplay placement bias by noting that after four years in the home the correlation rises to .52. This value (.52) is the same as for the children from the entire group (Home Group) who entered their foster home before 2 years of age. These data are shown in Table 11. In the same table we show the results for the International Test. The International Test is a nonverbal measure of intelligence. According to the investigators, "The fact that no norms were available for the test did not limit its value, in as much as only the point scores were used and these only in comparisons and correlations within a given group" (Freeman et al., 1928, p. 109). While the entire sample did not take this test, we see immediately that the authors' arguments do not constructively replicate the results. First, the overall correlation for the home group is .24. This is much less than the placement bias discussed above and may be only slightly above the level of placement bias for the entire group. Second, the correlation for the early placement group is also very modest (.28). We do note that the sample sizes for the International Test are smaller than for the Binet IQ and there may be sampling differences. Nevertheless, the constructive replication is in the range of possible placement bias. Finally, if we look at the very early placement group, the correlation is actually slightly less than that for the entire group. Regarding the International Test, the authors show, in an earlier section of their very long paper, that the International Test is less correlated with age than is the Binet test, and that the "International Test may depend somewhat less on training and be a closer measure of native capacity" (Freeman et al., 1928, p. 110). Interestingly enough, these same authors used the International Test in their study of monozygotic twins reared apart (MZA) reported nine years later (Newman, Freeman, & Holzinger, 1937). In that study the International Test shows an MZA correlation of .82 versus .68 for the Binet. In the MZA study the correlation between the two tests was .62, and in the adoption study it was .70 (with age held constant). These correlations are typical of the correlations reported between the Stanford-Binet and other IQ tests (Jensen, 1980, p. 314).

In adoption studies, parental IQ is an environmental indicator unconfounded by genetics (but probably confounded by placement). The parent-offspring IQ correlation for fathers was .37 ($N = 180$) and for mothers it was .28 ($N = 255$). The correlation for parental education $\times$ child's IQ was .42. These correlations are, of course, consistent with the adopted child-foster parent correlation of .34 reported above. These figures all index the influence of common family environment. They can be compared to the correlation of .41 for biological parents and offspring reared together, the latter figure reflecting the joint effects of common heredity and common family environment (Bouchard & McGue, 1981). (We will return to these correlations after we review several additional studies.)

Leahy (1935) has also reported environmental correlations gathered on an adoptive sample. Like Burks (1928), Leahy compared two matched groups, a set of foster children and their parents, and a control group of children reared by their biological parents. Considerable effort was devoted to finding children who had been placed very early in order to avoid placement bias. Nevertheless, there is evidence for placement bias based on mothers' education. This bias will work to enhance environmental estimates, relative to genetic ones. The children were at least 5 years old and not more than 14 years old at the time of testing. No families from rural-agricultural settings were included and all children had been legally adopted. The correlational data are shown in Table 12.

The correlations between parental and home characteristics and child's IQ are somewhat higher for the control sample than for those reported by Burks (mean of .51 versus .41 for the eight variables in common). They are also higher than what we find in more recent samples. The adoptive correlations are very similar to those of Burks (mean of .19 versus .16). Leahy did not carry out a multiple correlation analysis, but it appears that the results for the adopted children would be very close to those obtained by Burks. The means, standard deviations, and sample sizes for the two groups by SES categories are shown in Table 13.

The range of IQs for the adopted children is 4.8 IQ points, while the range for control children is 17.5 IQ points. If we omit classes VI and VII from each group, because they are poorly matched on environmental status (74.5 versus 40.1) and the sample sizes are small, we see that, despite having a much higher mean environmental status score and just as much variation on this score, the adopted children have the same mean IQ as the control children.

Scarr and Weinberg (1978) have reported an adoption study that examines a variety of directly measured environmental influences in 120 biological and 104 adoptive families. The adoptive families were recruited through the Minnesota Department of Welfare. Families who had adopted children between 1953 and 1959 were contacted and asked to participate. The biological families were recruited through newspaper articles, personal referrals, and the adoptive fam-

Table 12.   Child's IQ Correlated with Other Factors

Correlated Factor	Adopted Children		Control Children	
	r	N	r	N
Father's Otis score	.15	178	.51	175
Mother's Otis score	.20	186	.51	191
Mid-parent Otis score	.18	177	.60	173
Father's S.B. vocabulary	.22	177	.47	168
Mother's S.B. vocabulary	.20	185	.49	190
Mid-parent S.B. vocabulary	.24	174	.56	164
Environmental status score	.19	194	.53	194
Cultural index of home	.21	194	.51	194
Child training index of home	.18	194	.52	194
Economic index of home	.12	194	.37	194
Sociality index of home	.11	194	.42	194
Father's education	.16	193	.48	193
Mother's education	.21	192	.50	194
Mid-parent education	.20	193	.54	194
Father's occupational status	.12	194	.45	194

Source.   From Leahy, 1935.

ilies. The two groups are clearly upper-middle-class volunteer samples. The mean age of placement of the adoptive children was, however, very young—2.6 months. IQs were based on four subtests from the WAIS (Vocabulary, Arithmetic, Block Design, and Picture Arrangement). The principal results of this study are shown in Table 14.

The top part of Table 14 summarizes the result of a multiple regression analysis. The first four variables (fathers' education, mothers' education, fathers' occupation, and income) yield a multiple correlation of .33 ($R^2 = .107$) for biological families and .14 ($R^2 = .019$) for adoptive families. The addition of

Table 13. Comparative Analysis of Intelligence of Adopted and Control Children and Environmental Status of Homes Classified According to Occupation of Father

	Adopted Children					Control Children				
		Intelligence Quotient		Environmental Status			Intelligence Quotient		Environmental Status	
Occupation of Father	N	M	SD	M	SD	N	M	SD	M	SD
I Professional	43	112.6	11.8	194.6	27.2	40	118.6	12.6	180.4	29.1
II Business manager	38	111.6	10.9	171.3	40.2	42	117.6	15.6	160.7	31.1
III Skilled trades	44	110.6	14.2	133.2	35.2	43	106.9	14.3	106.3	43.4
IV Farmers	—	—	—	—	—	—	—	—	—	—
V Semi-skilled	45	109.4	11.8	94.0	30.3	46	101.1	12.5	77.6	37.4
VI Slightly skilled and VII Day labor	24	107.8	13.6	74.7	28.7	23	102.1	11.0	40.1	26.7

Source. From Leahy, 1935.

Table 14. Multiple Regressions (R) and Simple Correlations Between Children's IQ and Family Background Characteristics in Biological and Adoptive Families

Family Type	Family Background Characteristics										
	Rearing Family								Natural Mother		
	Fathers' Ed.	Mothers' Ed.	Fathers' Occup.	Income	Birth Rank	Number Child.	Fathers' IQ	Mothers' IQ	Age	Ed.	Occup.
Multiple Regressions (variables added stepwise from the left to right)											
Biological	→			.33		.38 →	→	.56			
Adoptive	→			.14		.24 →	→	.27		.37 →	.40
Simple Correlations											
Biological	.26	.24	.10	.22	−.19	−.21	.39	.39	−.10	.21	
Adoptive	.10	.10	.12	.06	−.19	−.05	.15	.04			.12

Source. Compiled from Scarr and Weinberg, 1978

Note. N for biological families is 257 children. N for adoptive families is 150 children.

birth rank and number of children raises the correlations to .38 and .24, respectively, which represents a modest increase. The addition of rearing parent IQ, however, causes a sizable increase in the multiple correlation for the biological families (an increase of 16% of the variance explained), but very little increase for the adoptive families (an increase of 1.6% of the explained variance). Even more striking is the increase in variance accounted for in the IQs of the adoptive children when the biological mother's age, education, and occupation are added (an increase of 8.2% of the variance explained). The latter effects must be entirely genetic in origin. For the adoptive sample, the largest single correlation with children's IQ is the natural mothers' education (.21). This correlation is not as high as that found in the biological families (see Table 6), but it is substantial. There is every reason to believe that the biological mothers' actual IQs would generate a higher correlation. A comparison of the Scarr and Weinberg correlations in the lower part of Table 14 with those in Table 6 suggest that the pattern of correlations between family background characteristics and children's IQ, for their biological sample, is quite representative (except for fathers' occupation). The authors conclude, and we agree, that the regression of family variables on children's IQs, when using biologically related individuals, largely reflects genetic variance.

The final adoption research to be discussed in this section is that of Schiff, Duyme, Dumaret, Stewart, Tomkiewicz, and Feingold (1978) and Schiff, Duyme, Dumaret, and Tomkiewicz (1982). Both reports deal with the same data. By a variety of stratagems, these authors were able to locate (through adoption files) and test (surreptitiously at an average age of 10.3 years) 32 adoptees, whose biological parents were unskilled laborers, and who were abandoned at birth and adopted at about 4 months of age into families spanning the top 13% of the socioprofessional scale. In addition, they were able to find an internal control group of 20 biological half-sibs of the index cases, who were reared in their "natural" environment (raised by their mothers). The average IQ of the index cases, based on two IQ tests, was 108.7. The average IQ of the controls was 94.6. The difference of 14.1 IQ points reflects the effect of environment mediated by social class, since the design supposedly holds heredity constant. The IQ of biological offspring reared in the top 13% of the socio-professional scale is estimated to be 110.0. The authors conclude that these results furnish the answer to Jensen's (1969) famous question, "How much can we boost IQ and scholastic achievement?" The authors further suggest that virtually none of the IQ difference between upper- and lower-class French men and women is genetic in origin. The results of this study, then, stand in sharp contrast to all others we have discussed, including that of Freeman, Holzinger, and Mitchell (1928). Recall that in the Freeman et al. study, the biological offspring of the rearing parents had IQs of 112.4, almost the same as the children in the top 13% of the socio-professional group in the Schiff et al. study. The adopted cases in the Freeman et al. study who were reared in the same families had an IQ of only 97.5. Since they are unlikely to have been selected from biological parents with a less favorable background than those in the Schiff et al. cases, this lack of agreement with the Schiff et al. results is quite striking. The Schiff et al. results also contrast with some findings we have not discussed (Fisch, Bilek, Deinard, & Chang, 1976; Horn, Loehlin, & Willerman, 1982; Teasdale, 1979; Willerman, 1979). The interested reader should consult Loehlin (1980) for a discussion of recent adoption studies from the viewpoint of assessing heritability; see Munsinger (1975) for a more detailed analysis of all adoption studies; and see Kamin (1974, 1977) for extensive critiques of these studies and for various analyses presented in the literature. We do, however, regard Kamin's approach to interpreting much of this evidence to be occasionally misleading (see Bouchard, 1982). Finally, because of its very small sample size, we refrain from placing too much emphasis on the Schiff et al. study.

The correlations between various parental SES measures and children's IQ from the adoption studies are summarized in Table 15. The most striking feature of Table 15 is the deviance of the Freeman et al. (1928) correlations: they are all outliers. Without the Freeman et al. data, the means for the first three variables would be .164, .168, and .10. We do not believe that the Freeman et al. study is methodologically superior to the other five studies summarized in the table. The most plausible explanation for the results is that placement bias was a much more serious problem in that study than its authors realized.

Summary

The evidence from biological families, reviewed in this chapter, suggests that family background characteristics are significantly correlated with children's IQs. The absolute magnitude of these correlations is, however, smaller than most social scientists might have expected.

Studies of adoptive children demonstrate that family background characteristics do influence adoptive children's IQs, but only to a modest extent. These

Table 15. Correlations Between Rearing Parent Socioeconomic Status Measures and Children's IQ in Six Adoption Studies

Status Variable	Study and Sample Size						
	1 (178)	2 (178)	3 (401)	4 (455)	5 (150)	6 (130)	Mean
Fathers' Education	.01	.16	(.42)*	.21	.10	.34	.207
Mothers' Education	.17	.21	(.42)*	.14	.10	.22	.210
Fathers' Occupation	—	.12	.37	.17	.12	−.01	.154
Income	.23	—	—	.06	.06	−.00	.088

Note. 1 = Burks, 1928; 2 = Leahy, 1935; 3 = Freeman, Holzinger, & Newman, 1928; 4 = Horn, Loehlin, & Willerman, 1979; 5 = Scarr & Weinberg, 1978; 6 = Scarr & Weinberg, 1976.
*Freeman, et al. only report the correlation for parents' education.

studies clearly show that the regression of family variables on children's IQs, when using biological families, largely reflects genetic variance. These studies also converge on the related conclusion that a significant portion of the IQ difference between social classes is genetic in origin. Scarr and Weinberg (1978) suggest that genetic differences among the SES groups account for about two-thirds to three-fourths of the average IQ difference among children in the various social classes. This finding should be interpreted in light of the fact that the IQ variance within families, not to mention social classes, is very large. The Schiff et al. (1982) study, which examined the IQs of children born to lower SES parents and reared by upper SES families, suggests no genetic differences in IQ between the various social classes. Because of its small sample size and the fact that the findings of this study are inconsistent with those of many other studies, we refrain from placing too much emphasis on its findings.

THE INFLUENCE OF SPECIFIC HOME ENVIRONMENTAL FACTORS ON IQ

The Home Interview Method

In the previous section we reviewed the influence of rather global environmental factors. Parents' education and fathers' occupation do not differ very much from child to child within a single family. Consequently, these effects are often called "common family environmental factors" or, more concisely, "common environment." We know from behavior-genetic studies that common environment accounts for only about half of the environmental variance (Rowe & Plomin, 1981; Willerman, 1979). The other half is unique. Consequently, these unique environmental factors, which make biologically related people who are reared together different from one another, are just as important as the common environmental factors. We now turn to attempts to assess home environments that focus, in part, on unique psychosocial factors that impinge upon individual children.

Twenty years ago Bloom (1964) asserted that:

> Our catalog of tests of individual differences is enormous, whereas our instruments for measuring environmental differences consists of a few techniques for measuring social class status and socioeconomic status. . . . just as a general index of intelligence or IQ has obscured many of the very important differences among individuals, so the general index of social or economic status has obscured many very important differences among environments. . . . It is likely that factorial research which has proven so powerful in the identification of the major dimensions on which individuals differ may prove to be equally powerful in defining the dimensions on which environments differ. [pp. 185–186]

As we will show, just as the issue of whether a global factor of intelligence, or *g*, should be superseded by a multivariate model of intelligence has not been resolved (Detterman, 1982; Humphreys, 1979; Jensen, 1980), the issue of the dimensionality of the environment also remains unsettled. Through the work of his students, Bloom did, however, launch an attack on this problem.

Wolf (reported in Bloom, 1964; and later in Wolf, 1965) reviewed the literature on the effects of environments on intelligence. On the basis of this review he hypothesized 13 different variables that might influence the development of intelligence. Using an interview form with sixty questions, he interviewed sixty mothers of fifth-grade students and generated measures on the 13 variables listed below:

A. Press for Achievement Motivation

   1. Nature of intellectual expectations of child.

   2. Nature of intellectual aspirations for child.

   3. Amount of information about child's intellectual development.

   4. Nature of rewards for intellectual development.

B. Press for Language Development

   5. Emphasis on use of language in a variety of situations.

   6. Opportunities provided for enlarging vocabulary.

   7. Emphasis on correctness of usage.

   8. Quality of language models available.

C. Provisions for General Learning

   9. Opportunities for learning in the home.

   10. Opportunities provided for learning outside the home (excluding school).

   11. Availability of learning supplies.

   12. Availability of books (including reference works), periodicals, and library facilities.

   13. Nature and amount of assistance provided to facilitate learning in a variety of situations.

Wolf recognized that some of these variables were interactive, or what we prefer to call transactive: that is, the response of the parent depends on the behavior of the child. Variables 1, 2, 3, 4, 9, 10, and 13 were seen as responses of the parent to the specific behavior of the child. Some of these variables would index what we earlier called a reactive genotype × environment correlation, and others would correspond to what we have called an active genotype × environment correlation. The other variables (5, 6, 7, 8, 11, 12) were seen as being more stable characteristics of the parents and home, but independent of the child's characteristics. Wolf obtained a multiple correlation of +.76 between his rating variables and the children's IQs. It is significant to note that both sets of variables correlated equally with child's IQ (+.70).

Marjoribanks (1972), building on Wolf's work, prepared a semi-structured interview schedule to measure "eight environmental forces." Interviews, lasting approximately two hours, were conducted with the parents of 90 middle-class and 95 lower-class 11-year-old boys to obtain these measures. This selection procedure could possibly exaggerate the correlations reported. In addition, six social status variables were assessed. The boys were also administered the Primary Mental Abilities Verbal, Number, Spatial, and Reasoning subtests. Part of the results are shown in Tables 16 and 17.

Table 16 shows the individual correlations between each of the environmental measures and total scores on the PMA. The highest correlation between the environmental measures and subtests are also reported. In every instance, except one (number of children in the family), the highest correlation is with the verbal subtests. In the exceptional instance the difference is .33 versus .32. In every instance, except two (both of which are quite close), Number is the subtest showing the second-highest correlation. Notice, also, that the correlation with the total score is never significantly higher than that with the Verbal subtest.

Table 17 shows that in a multiple correlation the *environmental* forces correlate more highly with mental ability than do the *status* variables. In addition, the status variables do not add anything to predictability over and above what is already accounted for in the environmental force variables (except for the Spatial subtest). Again, the Verbal and Number subtests are equally predictable and at about the same magnitude as the total score. The composite multiple regression with total score is $+.75$, almost identical to the $+.76$ reported by Wolf.

There is some controversy concerning the interpretation of these data. Harris and McArthur (1974) have shown that if we ask the question, "How many latent (underlying) variables are required to 'account for' or reproduce the correlations between environmental measures (press and status) and mental ability scores?" (p. 457), the answer is one. These authors conclude that Marjoribanks has designed a set of "press" variables that are factorially similar to the "status" variables, but are better predictors of mental test scores. Walberg and Marjoribanks (1973), using a different method, have shown that at least two factors are at work and that "verbal and number abilities and to a lesser extent reasoning ability, are more closely associated with the environmental force scores than is spatial ability" (pp. 365–366). The crucial issue is: Do environmental forces shape abilities differently? Keeping in mind the confounded meaning of the term "environmental" in the context of these studies (in essence, it could mean reactive covariance), we believe they do. There is a great deal of evidence that spatial skill is a distinct ability, over and above g, and that scores on spatial tests have lower correlations with all environmental measures than do any other mental abilities (McGee, 1979).

Several developmental studies with very young children, using procedures similar to those used by Marjoribanks and Wolf, have reported similar results (Bradley & Caldwell, 1976; Elardo, Bradley, & Caldwell, 1975; Hanson, 1975). In the Elardo et al. (1975) study, the multiple correlation between 24-month

Table 16. Correlations Between Total Mental Ability Score, Special Ability Score, Special Ability with the Highest Correlation, and Environmental Force and Status Factors

Variable	Correlation	
	Total Score	Highest Ability
Environmental Forces		
Press for achievement	.60**	.66 (V,N)
Press for activeness	.47**	.52 (V)
Press for intellectuality	.59**	.61 (V)
Press for independence	.38**	.42 (V)
Press for English	.40**	.50 (V)
Press for ethlanguage	.28**	.35 (V)
Father dominance	.15	.16 (V)
Mother dominance	.16*	.21 (V)
Status Factors		
Education of father	.31**	.29 (V)
Education of mother	.36**	.39 (V)
Occupation of father	.43**	.43 (V)
Number of children in family	−.31**	−.33 (N)
Crowding ratio	−.33**	−.34 (V,N)
Ordinal position in family	−.24**	−.26 (V)

Source. Compiled from Marjoribanks, 1972.
 *$p < .05$.
 **$p < .10$.

measures of home environmental variables (6 measures) and 3-year Stanford-Binet scores ($N = 77$ black and white children) was .718 ($p < .01$). The results of this study are shown in Table 18.

A later study (Bradley, Caldwell, & Elardo, 1977), using a larger sample ($N = 105$; this sample appears to incorporate the sample in the study cited above), contrasted the multiple correlation between the 3-year Stanford-Binet

Table 17.   Corrected Multiple Correlations of Each of the Mental Ability Scores
with the Eight Environmental Forces, the Six Status Variables, and the
Environmental and Status Variables Taken Together

Ability	Eight Environmental Forces	Six Status Variables	Environmental Plus Status Variables
Verbal	.71**	.51***	.71***
Number	.71**	.40***	.71***
Spatial	.26	.28*	.36*
Reasoning	.40**	.25	.42**
Total	.72**	.53***	.75***

Source. Compiled from Marjoribanks, 1972.
  $*p < .05.$
 $**p < .01.$
$***p < .001.$

scores, six home environment variables, and four status variables (mother's education, father's education, occupation of head of household, and father's absence). The status variables yielded a multiple correlation of .56, and the environmental variables yielded a multiple correlation of .77. As in the Marjoribanks (1972) study, the status measures did not add to the home factors. Notice that the variable, "provisions of appropriate play material" alone accounts for a large portion of the predictable variance.

As indicated above, one use of the results of a correlational study is to pinpoint variables that might be manipulated in an experimental context. There is one well-designed preschool compensatory education study that has manipulated "provisions of appropriate play materials." That study (Busse, Ree, Gutride, Alexander, & Powell, 1972) also used the Stanford-Binet as one criterion instrument. In addition, the children in the study were close in age to those in the Elardo et al. study. These similarities make this study a good test of the hypothesis that provision of appropriate play materials is a powerful environmental variable. The subjects were black Headstart students about 4 years of age. At the beginning of the school year, sixty-two children were randomly assigned to enriched classrooms and sixty-one children were assigned to control classrooms. The enriched condition consisted of adding a large number of specially selected items to the classrooms. According to the authors, "The effect of adding to the classrooms was to take meagerly equipped classrooms and turn them into dream classrooms." At the end of the school year the enriched subjects had *not* improved, relative to the controls, on the Stanford-Binet and tests of auditory reception and auditory sequential memory. In fact, they fell significantly

**Table 18. Correlations Between 24-Month Inventory of Home Stimulation Scores
and Mental Test Scores at 36 Months**

Home Environment Variables	Mental Test Scores, 36-Month Binet
1. Emotional and verbal responsivity of mother	.495*
2. Avoidance of restriction and punishment	.406*
3. Organization of physical and temporal environment	.413*
4. Provision of appropriate play materials	.635*
5. Maternal involvement with child	.545*
6. Opportunities for variety in daily stimulation	.499*
Total score	.695*
Multiple correlation[a]	.718*

Source. From Elardo, Bradley, and Caldwell, 1975.
[a]This represents the correlation of all subscales with mental test scores.
*$p < .01$.

behind the controls on the Wechsler Preschool and Primary Scale of Intelligence
(WPPSI) Performance IQ and on a test of visual perception. They were, however,
superior to the control group on a test of visual sequential memory. Overall,
the study must be considered a failure to confirm the hypothesis. The failure of
complex compensatory education studies such as this one, as well as those
discussed next can, however, be due to many factors other than the ineffectiveness
of the particular treatment. Nevertheless, in this case, the results are compatible
with the conclusions of other investigators. Bereiter and Engelmann (1966) have
argued that "an object-rich environment is ineffective in compensating for the
child's toy deficit and in stimulating learning" (p. 72). Clearly, it is dangerous
to generalize in a simple way from a correlational study of home environment
to the results of classroom manipulation. There still remains the question: What
would happen if the treatment were applied in the child's home, beginning at
an early age and extending over a long period of time? Such a study would be
far more similar to the context in which the original correlational data were
collected and would be a far more effective test of the hypothesis.

Recent studies by Wilson (1983) and Wilson and Matheny (1983) have also
addressed the question: How many home environmental factors influence mental
development? Like Marjoribanks, they were also interested in the comparative
predictive power of home variables versus status variables. Information on parental education and occupation (status variables) were initially obtained through
maternal interviews for 116 families with twins under age 8 years. A subsequent
detailed home assessment composed of 200 items (interview questions and direct
observation by a trained social worker) were also conducted. These items were
selected from the following sources: Harvard Preschool Interview (White, Kaban,
& Attanucci, 1979); HOME: Caldwell's Inventory of Home Stimulation (Caldwell, 1978); Family Environment Scales (Moos, 1974); as well as from the series
of interviews that are administered by the Louisville Twin Study (Matheny,

Thoben, & Wilson, 1982; Wilson & Matheny, 1983, p. 201). Four factor scores were identified: (1) "adequacy of the home environment" (judgments of quality of interpersonal and physical environment for encouraging intellectual and social development, play space, qualitative features of the home); (2) "maternal temperament" (ratings of mother's emotional reactivity); (3) "maternal cognitive" (ratings of mother's intellectual and verbal facility); and (4) "maternal social affect" (ratings of mother's sociability, talkativeness, and interpersonal warmth).

A multiple regression analysis was conducted using mental development scores obtained at three ages: 6 months, 24 months, and 6 years. The results are shown in Table 19.

At age 6 months, of the seven variables, only father's education correlated significantly with child's mental development scores. At 2 years of age, adequacy of home environment and maternal temperament were added to father's education, and they increase the correlation to .56. At 6 years of age, the same three variables yield a correlation of .64, and maternal cognitive and maternal

Table 19. Multiple Regression Analysis of Home-Visit Variables and Mental Development Scores

Age, Step, and Variable	Multiple R	Partial R	Initial r with Criterion
6 months:			
Step 1—Father's education (no other variable significant)	.28	—	.28
24 months:			
Step 1—Adequacy of home environment	.45	—	.45
Step 2—Father's education	.54	.23	.38
Step 3—Maternal temperament (−)	.56	−.13	.01
6 years:			
Step 1—Adequacy of home environment	.55	—	.55
Step 2—Father's education	.62	.33	.53
Step 3—Maternal temperament (−)	.64	−.23	−.08
Step 4—Maternal cognitive	.65	.15	.52
Step 5—Maternal social affect	.66	.13	.25
6 years (minimum set of predictors):			
Step 1—Father's education	.53	—	.53
Step 2—Mother's education	.58	.23	.50
Step 3—Socioeconomic status	.59	.17	.51

Source. From Wilson, 1983.

social affect raise it to .66. Wilson also asked the question: If a home assessment is not feasible, what minimum set of predictors would relate to mental development? The answer, shown at the bottom of Table 19, is parental education and SES. These three variables yield a multiple correlation of .59, which is only slightly below the .66 generated by the full set of variables. Socioeconomic status correlates only slightly less with mental development scores at every age than does adequacy of the home environment. The two variables correlate .62. The detailed home ratings, therefore, make only a modest, but meaningful, addition to the prediction of mental development scores. Wilson interprets these findings in light of his own twin results (reported in the same paper), as well as adoption studies. He asserts that it is reasonable to view parental education as a broad approximation or surrogate for parental IQ and that the joint contribution of both variables is consistent with genetic transmission. Longstreth, Davis, Carter, Flint, Owen, Rickert, and Taylor (1981), using a procedure very similar to that of Wolf (they administered a variation of his questionnaire), have made a very similar argument.

The Observation Method

Hanson (1975) has studied a different set of environmental correlates of IQ. His analysis included 50 males and 50 females who were part of the Fels Institute Longitudinal Study (Kagan & Moss, 1962). Using data in the Fels files, he constructed ten environmental variables. The measures were similar to those of Wolf (1965) and Marjoribanks (1972), but also included several additional indices to test specific hypotheses. The variables and their correlations with Stanford-Binet IQ obtained at 9.5 years are given in Table 20.

Surprisingly, there were no mean differences between the sexes on any of the ten variables. Nevertheless, there are striking correlational differences between the two sexes: In every instance, except one, the female correlation is larger in magnitude. Particularly striking are the correlations between variables 1 and 2 and IQ for females. They are in the same range as the multiple correlations reported by Marjoribanks (1972) and Bradley et al. (1976). Females, on the average, are known to be superior to males on tests of verbal fluency (Hutt, 1972; Levy, 1980). Since there are no mean differences on these environmental variables, the correlational differences may reflect basic differences between the sexes, perhaps in cerebral organization (Springer & Deutsch, 1981). Hanson did not report the multiple correlation between his variables and IQ. He did, however, report a factor analysis of the first seven variables; this analysis is summarized in Table 21. A varimax rotation yielded two factors. The first factor, defined by all variables, except numbers five (emphasis on performing independently) and four (emphasis on achievement), accounted for 40% of the common variance. The second factor, defined by variables four and five, accounted for only 7% of the common variance. These results suggest that the corrected multiple correlation would not exceed .70–.75 and support the hypothesis of a single large

Table 20.   Concurrent Correlations Between Environmental Variables and 9½-Year
Binet Male and Female IQs

	Variable	Males (N=60)	Females (N=60)	Sex Difference
1.	Freedom to engage in verbal expression	.26*	.73**	**
2.	Direct teaching of language behavior	.30*	.69**	*
3.	Parental involvement with the child	.42*	.31*	
4.	Emphasis on school achievement	.22	.44**	
5.	Emphasis on performing independently	.26*	.39*	
6.	Models of intellectual interests	.34*	.61**	*
7.	Models of language development	.25	.64*	**
8.	Emphasis on female sex role development	−.05	−.21	
9.	Freedom to explore the environment	.09	.14	
10.	Models of task orientation	−.05	.20	
	Mean correlation	.23	.45**	

Source.   Compiled from Hanson, 1975.
*$p < .05$.
**$p < .01$.

environmental factor similar to that found by Harris and McArthur (1974) in the Marjoribanks (1972) data.

Three environmental variables were included in the Hanson study to test specific predictions. First, Maccoby (1966) has suggested that societal emphasis on female sex role development would be positively correlated with verbal measures. The correlations are negative, thereby refuting this hypothesis. Furthermore, direct measures of language emphasis (variables 1 and 2) correlated strongly with IQ, thus eliminating the competing hypothesis that the criterion is inadequate. Second, Bing (1962) has suggested that freedom to explore the

Table 21. Factor Analyses of Environmental Variables

	Variable Name	Period 1 (0–3 Years)		Period 2 (4–6 Years)		Period 3 (7–10 Years)	
		Factor 1	Factor 2	Factor 1	Factor 2	Factor 1	Factor 2
1.	Emphasis on independence	.03	.67	−.01	.54	.07	.50
2.	Freedom of verbal expression	.73	.25	.75	.05	.69	.06
3.	Teaching of language	.75	.31	.76	.06	.58	.38
4.	Involvement with child	.80	.06	.80	−.21	.65	.16
5.	Emphasis on achievement	.31	.64	.68	.28	.28	.72
6.	Models of intellectual behavior	.29	.67	.62	.39	.61	.43
7.	Models of language behavior	.49	.45	.73	.08	.68	.21
	Eigenvalue	3.04	0.79	3.19	0.54	2.77	0.54
	Variance (%)	43	12	46	7	40	7

Source. From Hanson, 1975.

Note. This table gives the results of the three factor analyses (one for each time period) carried out on the environmental variables.

environment should be negatively related to the development of verbal abilities. This hypothesis was clearly refuted. Finally, Douglas (1964) and others have suggested that parental models of task orientation could be positively related to cognitive behavior in general. This hypothesis was also refuted.

Notice that, while this study could not distinguish between environmental and genetic causes of correlations, it was able to refute decisively specific environmental hypotheses.

Hanson (1975) also reported an interesting instance of an active genotype by environment correlation. With respect to "obtaining the frequency with which parents or other adults read aloud to the child," he found a wide range of responsiveness:

> At the extremes, some children would beg and plead to be read to, while others would resist such efforts by refusing to sit still, making noise, or being generally inattentive. Various degrees of acceptance or rejection were presented between these extremes. The end result was that the measures of the environment, that is, frequency of times adults read aloud to the child, was very definitely influenced by the child's reaction to it. [Hanson, 1975, pp. 478–479]

The Twin Difference Method

An infrequently used design for studying specific environmental effects is the twin difference design. Since identical twins are genetically alike, any differences between them must be environmental in origin. The environmental effects may, of course, be physicochemical as well as psychosocial. It is important to recognize that environmental difference $\times$ twin difference correlations have a narrow meaning. It means that the environmental factor, which generates the correlation, accounts for a proportion of the variance not already accounted for by heredity. Thus it is a useful technique for searching for difference-producing influences. Obviously the twin difference method is more likely to reveal environmental effects in the adopted-away design than in the within-family design.

Loehlin and Nichols (1976) have reported correlations between identical twins' absolute difference scores on the various National Merit Scholarship Qualifying Test (NMSQT) subtests and a variety of experience measures. The correlations were all remarkably small. The only significant replicable correlations were with reports of "better in grade school." In this instance, the correlations were about .11. These correlations demonstrate that the method has some sensitivity. They are better interpreted as outcome correlations than as causal correlations. None of the causal variables, such as serious illness in infancy, illness in childhood, mother's attention, birth order, heavier at birth, and so on, showed a significant and replicable correlation. These results suggest that the differences in early treatment of identical twins within families play only a minor role in explaining the differences between them when measured at adolescence.

Newman, Freeman, and Holzinger (1937) have reported the correlation between five ability measures (Binet IQ, Otis IQ, International Test, American Council Test, and Stanford Educational Age) and ratings of educational differences, social differences, and physical health differences. They demonstrated interjudge reliabilities of .90 and above for the ratings. The correlations between the educational difference ratings and ability measures were .791, .547, .462, .570, and .908, respectively. The correlations between the social difference ratings and ability differences were .507, .533, .534, .321, and .349, respectively. The physical and health ratings yielded inconsistent results. The educational and social ratings in this case clearly reflect sizable between-family factors or some factor of potential importance in determining IQ variance.

A number of investigators have suggested that the reared-apart twin data seriously overestimate the influence of heredity on IQ because of a variety of artifacts and placement biases. Farber (1981) has argued that the amount of contact between the co-twins is a powerful explanatory variable. Bouchard (1982) and Loehlin (1981) have shown that this analysis is faulty. The direction of effects would, for example, have to work in opposite directions for males and females. There is no plausible theory, nor empirical evidence, to suggest that an important environmental factor works in this manner. Taylor (1980) has argued that similarity of rearing environments of the MZA cases in the literature is a major cause of their similarity. Bouchard (1983) has shown that these results cannot be constructively replicated when the same analysis is applied to the alternate IQ measures used in two of the three studies. Farber's and Taylor's conclusions are simply wrong. They are based on an approach to data analysis that Bouchard (1982a, 1982b) has called "pseudoanalysis." The data are subgrouped using a variety of criteria, some plausible, some not plausible, in search of the smallest genetic estimates possible. Other anomalies created in the data are not considered, and the enormous sampling errors that accompany correlations based on small sample sizes are ignored.

Excellent discussions of the possible uses of twin studies for exploring environmental influences can be found in Eaves (1982) and Rowe and Plomin (1981).

Summary

Measures of specific home environmental factors have yielded multiple correlations with children's IQs that are, in some studies, much higher than are family background characteristics. Whether the environmental factors assessed by these measures are different from those measured by family background or status measures is still an open question. In assessing the specific home measures, it is important to recognize that they are confounded with genetic variance, serving, in part, as surrogate measures of parental IQ and education. They also reflect reciprocal effects. Parental "press for achievement," for example, may correlate highly with children's IQ because high IQ children elicit more of this press variable from their parents than do low IQ children.

FAMILY CONFIGURATION AND IQ

The Confluence Theory

Since Galton's (1874) report that first-born individuals were overrepresented among fellows of the British Royal Society, there has been a great deal of research on birth order and its behavioral correlates (Altus, 1966; Breland, 1974; Clarke, 1916; Ellis, 1926; Schacter, 1959). The statistical pitfalls (Ernst & Angst, 1983; Poole, 1974) and small sample sizes used, however, have made it extremely difficult to detect reliable, systematic effects. Schooler (1972), in a review of this area, concluded that when statistical precautions were taken, there was little reliable scientific evidence of birth order effects on psychological traits. This conclusion echoed that of epidemiologists, who have examined birth order across many years and generations (Ernst & Angst, 1983; see also Chapter 1). In 1973, Belmont and Marolla (1973) published data collected for the Dutch Famine study (to be discussed later in this chapter), arranged by birth order and family size. The seemingly impressive regularities apparent in these data are displayed in modified form in Figure 4.

These data have generated some very interesting theorizing by Zajonc and

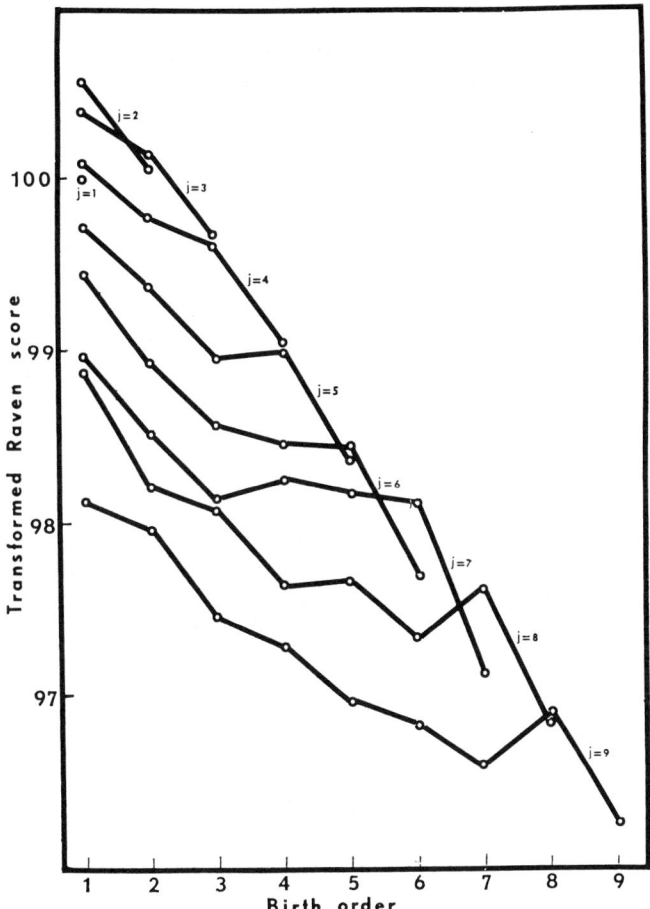

Figure 4. Average transformed Raven scores as a function of birth order (i) and family size (*j*), recalculated from Belmont and Marolla (1973). (The Raven scores were reported by Belmont and Marolla in terms of six categories from 1, high, to 6, low. For the purposes of the present analysis a linear transformation, $X_{tr} = 113.45 - 5.0047X$, was performed on these scores, inverting the scale so that increasing values now indicate increasing intelligence and setting the score of the only child at 100.) (*Source:* From Zajonc and Markus, 1975; Copyright© 1975 by the American Psychological Association.)

his colleagues (Berbaum, Markus, & Zajonc, 1982; Zajonc & Markus, 1975; Zajonc, Markus, & Markus, 1979). Their theory, called the *confluence model,* is the first good example of a quantitative environmental model proposed to explain individual differences in IQ.

Before discussing the model in detail, several points deserve emphasis. First, notice the narrow range of scores within which we are working. The average family size in this sample is about 4.1, plus or minus 2.1. The vast bulk of the variation is, therefore, between 98.5 and 100.5. This means that only a very small portion of the full variation in IQ, which ranges from 55–145, or 100 plus or minus 3 SDs, is related to birth order and family size. As we will point out, the confluence model has most often been fit to data at the aggregate level and not to individual subject scores. The small amount of total variance potentially explainable by this theory, relative to genetic effects, for example, is seldom discussed by its authors. Sometimes, however, the data force the issue. In their discussion of the failure of the confluence model to explain the drop in SAT scores during the years 1965 to 1977, a prediction made by Zajonc in 1976, they admit that the theory would predict a decline of 5.6 points out of a total decline of 34.5 points (Zajonc & Bargh, 1980a). In a recent defense of the theory, Zajonc (1983) admits that "the size of the differences associated with differences in family size, birth order, or birth interval are, to be sure, quite small" (p. 478).

In the Dutch sample, the Raven scores correlate −.10 with birth order, −.19 with family size, and +.24 with social class (Stein et al., 1975, p. 214).

What aspects of these data require explanation? The data in Figure 4 have five salient features:

1. IQ declines with increases in family size.
2. Within each family size, IQ declines with increasing birth order.
3. Excluding last-borns, the data assume the form of a quadratic function. This means that, until the last-born child, there is a progressive reduction in IQ decrement, and an eventual upswing for families of eight and nine children.
4. Within each family size, last-borns show a greater decline than do children of any other birth rank.
5. Only children score at about the same level as second-borns in two-child families, or first-borns in four-child families.

The confluence model is offered by Zajonc and Markus (1975) to explain these results. In its initial form, it was simple and elegant in its reasoning. The principal assumptions were as follows:

1. The trait-relevant environment is the average of the absolute intellectual levels of the number of individuals in a family, and it includes the value of the child being considered. Keep in mind that there is a large body of data showing that the intellectual level of the family members is, in part, genetic in origin. This point is never mentioned by Zajonc et al. Using arbitrary values, the confluence model can be illustrated quite simply: If two parents have levels of 100, the absolute value of the environment is 100, but when a newborn child enters, the value drops to 66.6 ([100 + 100 + 0]/3 = 66.6). Assuming a child reached half of his or her absolute intellectual value by the time a second sib is born, the absolute value of the environment becomes 62.5 ([100 + 100 + 50 + 0]/4 = 62.5). The quality of the environment for the second sib is

lower than for the first sib and, therefore, his or her IQ will be lower, on the average. Notice that if the second sib is delayed until after the first sib has reached more than two-thirds of his or her absolute mental growth (say 70%), the second sib would come into a richer environment than did the first sib ($[100 + 100 + 70 + 0]/4 = 67.5$). This model, therefore, predicts either a positive or a negative effect of birth order, depending on the interval between births. On the assumption that the interval between births in the Dutch data is shorter than the time needed for a child to reach two-thirds of his or her absolute level of mental ability, the form of the data in Figure 4 (including the quadratic component, but *not* the only-born and last-born effect) is predicted by the model. Another excellent check on the model would compare the absolute growth function of IQ needed to fit birth order and family size data, with the same absolute growth function established by other means (see Thurstone, 1928).

2. The only child and the last child are deprived of an opportunity to serve as intellectual resources ("teachers") to their siblings. This lack of stimulation results in a failure to develop their IQs as thoroughly as their siblings.

The confluence model has undergone considerable elaboration and revision (see Berbaum, Markus, & Zajonc, 1982). Consequently, refutations of earlier versions are not always relevant to the current model. This is a normal process in model development in any science.

Tests of the Model

Until growth functions on individuals become available, the most important tests of this model involve data on age spacing. Zajonc (1976) has purported to explain a large number of phenomena with the so-called age spacing effect. Although it has not yet been made explicitly clear, it is the case that decreases in IQ with increases in family size must occur in every social class. Otherwise, some features of the data in Figure 4 might be a function of social class differences. Indeed, social class differences in the shape of the function relating family size and birth order make the Zajonc and Markus model a much less plausible explanation of the effects of birth order and family size on IQ than it first appears. Marjoribanks and Walberg (1975) have shown that the Dutch data are characterized by some strong, statistically significant interactions: that is, family size and birth order do not relate in the same way within each social group. (Their data are shown in Figure 5.)

These authors excluded only children from their data. Their reasoning suggests an alternative explanation to that of Zajonc and Markus (1975) concerning the position of these children in Figure 5. They argue that "a number of the single-borns may have been mentally deficient at birth, which influenced the parents

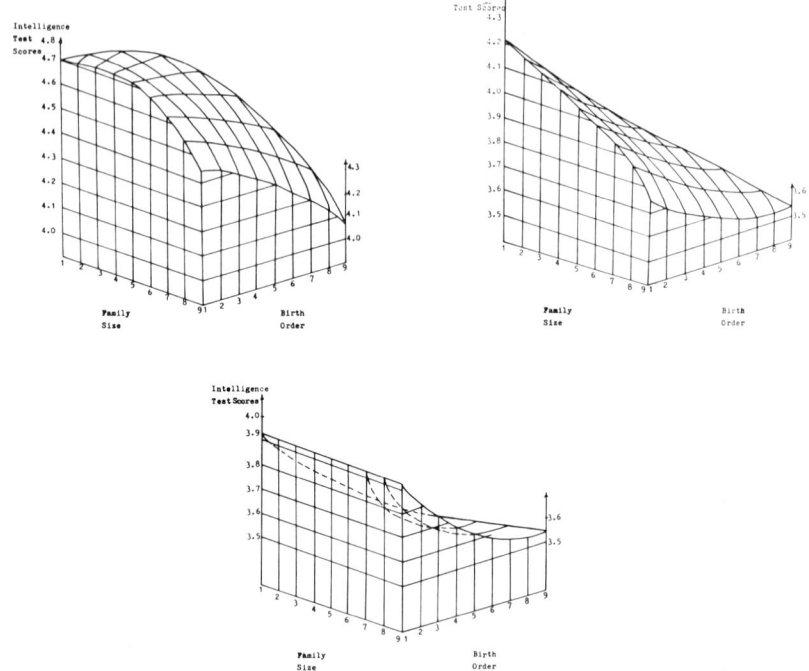

Figure 5. Fitted intelligence test scores in relation to family size and birth order in three social class groups. (*Source:* Compiled from Marjoribanks & Walberg, 1975.)

not to have further children" (Markus, 1975, p. 263). The so-called teacher effect for last-born children is not, however, a systematic feature of the data. As the figures show, there is no reduction in the IQs of last-born children in the highest SES group until family size six is reached, whereas in the other two classes, the decrease for last-borns occurs for small and intermediate family sizes. Indeed, for the lowest SES group, there is a trend toward an increase in IQ for large family sizes. The last-born effect and the particular shape of the curves in Figure 4 appear to be statistical artifacts, due to the mixing of quite different curves from the three social classes. These differences between social classes seriously challenge the simple theory of age spacing as an explanation of family size and birth order effects. For example, in the highest SES group, there is an average increase in IQ with family size until size three, and the average IQ does not drop until we reach family size six. In contrast, in the lowest SES group, there is no statistically significant effect due to family size, but there is a birth order effect. Zajonc (1983) has recently addressed the problem of SES differences. He does not, however, control for this important factor before fitting models to the data.

It is very important to recognize that the explanatory mechanism in the model, age spacing effects on IQ, is a within-family effect. The evidence from which the theory was derived (see, for example, Figure 4) and on which it is still often tested by the authors (Zajonc, Markus, & Markus, 1979) is, however, based on data that confounds between-family and within-family effects. The theory explains why large families have low IQs on the basis of age spacing (a within-family effect). It may be, however, that children from large families have lower IQs partly because their parents have lower IQs (a between-family effect). Useful, but not crucial, information could come from a contrast between the IQs of large and small families when the IQs of the parents are the same. Another way to circumvent the problem of confounded data is to look only at within-family evidence. If we contrast children within the same families, between-family effects are excluded. As evidence in support of the age-gap hypothesis, Zajonc cites the lower than average IQs of twins, triplets, and other multiples. These individuals have no age gap at all, and the theory predicts large decrements in their IQ, relative to normally spaced children. Such differences do exist, but, as we noted in the section on prenatal effects, the causes are multiple and complex.

A second approach is to examine differences between siblings. Record, McKeown, and Edwards (1969) have reported data using this technique. The sample consisted of all children born in the five-year interval 1950–1954, who completed the English 11 + examination. These data are conveniently organized in two ways and displayed in Table 22.

The between-family comparison shows large differences for all adjacent birth ranks. The within-family comparison shows a difference only half as large for the first versus second comparison (1.5 versus 2.9), with differences continually reduced by half for each subsequent birth rank comparison. It is clear that between-family comparisons seriously confound within-family and between-family effects. The within-family differences in Table 22 order themselves in much the same way as that shown in Figure 4. The difference decreases as birth order increases. The Record et al. (1969) data, unfortunately, do not allow a breakdown by family size or an examination of only-borns or last-borns. They do, however, allow a social class contrast that confirms the Marjoribanks and Walberg (1975) analysis. Using a three-class grouping system, the difference for the upper class, between earlier- and later-born sibs was 0.7 (109.0 versus 108.3, $N = 222$ pairs), the difference for the middle class was 0.9 (98.0 versus 97.1, $N = 2,209$ pairs), while the difference for the lower class was 2.0 (99.2 versus 98.4, $N = 473$ pairs). Again, social class moderates the effect of birth order. Record et al. (1969) conclude that "the striking association of measured intelligence with maternal age and birth order in a general population of children is determined mainly by differences between rather than within families" (p. 68). Berbaum, Markus, and Zajonc (1982) reluctantly agree with this conclusion, adding that "among the between-family factors to consider are differences in the spacing and number of children" (p. 178).

Grotevant, Scarr, and Weinberg (1977) were able to measure the important components of the Zajonc and Markus model for a population of transracial adoptive families (Scarr & Weinberg, 1976). Using a regression model they were

Table 22. Relation of Verbal Reasoning Score to Birth Rank Obtained by Two Different Methods

Between-Family Birth Rank Comparisons

N	Contrast	Verbal Reasoning Score			Difference
11,724	1st w/2nd	104.8	vs.	101.9	2.9
10,353	2nd w/3rd	101.9	vs.	98.2	3.7
6,220	3rd w/4th	98.2	vs.	95.4	2.8
3,425	4th w/5th	95.4	vs.	92.8	2.6
1,794	5th w/6th plus[a]	92.8	vs.	89.4	3.4

Within-Family Birth Rank Comparisons

No. Pairs	Contrast	Verbal Reasoning Score			Difference
2,193	1st w/2nd	101.8	vs.	100.3	1.5
1,279	2nd w/3rd	98.8	vs.	97.9	0.9
1,111	3rd w/4th	95.4	vs.	94.9	0.5
	4th w/5th				
	5th w/6th				
472	6th w/7th	91.8	vs.	91.9	−0.1
	7th w/8th				
	8th w/9th				

Source. Compiled from Record, McKeown, & Edwards, 1969.

Note. The data are standardized for maternal age. This increases all differences.

[a]N for 6th and later = 2,347.

able to account for, at most, 4.5% of the individual IQ variance. Child spacing did not generate a statistically significant effect. The regression method of testing the confluence model has been severely criticized by Howell and Malone (1979), Zajonc et al. (1979), Berbaum et al. (1982), and Zajonc (1983). These authors argue that an additive regression model is not a good representation of the nonlinear, nonadditive confluence model. This is technically correct, but it is important to realize that the dramatic failure of the additive models places a tremendous demand on the nonlinear and interactive aspects of the confluence model. Nonadditive components of any model are very difficult to replicate. Furthermore, the specific components of the model should be shown to have some effect before the complex configuration of the model (which capitalizes on chance when fit uniquely to each data set) is taken too seriously. It has been difficult to demonstrate such effects.

Belmont, Stein, and Zybert (1978), for example, were able to obtain birth interval and Raven test scores from a series of 535 pairs of brothers and a population series of first-borns and second-borns ($N = 1111$ individuals). The subjects were from the same data set used to construct Figure 4, and from which Zajonc and Markus (1975) derived their theory. The confluence theory predicts that for brothers, the difference score (first-born score minus second-born score) should be negatively related to spacing. The group was divided into two social classes, based on father's occupation (manual and nonmanual). The correlations were .07 and −.01 (both not significantly different from zero). In both the population series and the brother series, the confluence theory predicts a *positive* relationship between spacing interval and ability level of both first- and second-borns. All correlations were *negative* and not significantly different from zero. Zajonc (1983) argues that spacing effects are age-specific and that these data fit the theoretical expectation.

Brackbill and Nichols (1982) also directly tested four hypotheses previously derived from the confluence model and a fifth one not previously formulated. The predictions were as follows: (1) children in two-parent homes should have higher ability levels than children in father-absent homes; (2) twins from intact pairs should have lower ability levels than surviving twins (cases in which one twin is lost at birth or shortly thereafter); (3) as the birth interval increases, the effect of family size on ability should decrease; (4) first-borns should score higher than only children because the latter have fewer opportunities to teach; and (5) children raised in homes with an extra adult should score higher than children reared in homes in which the father and mother are the only adults. The sample used in this study consisted of the well-known National Collaborative Perinatal Project (Broman, Nichols, & Kennedy, 1975) and includes both blacks and whites. The two groups were analyzed separately. Ability was assessed using an IQ test (Stanford-Binet Intelligence Scale) administered at 4 years and at 7 years, and an achievement test (Wide Range Achievement Test) administered at 7 years. The data are, of course, individual, not aggregate. There was a significant negative effect due to father absence for all three measures in both racial groups. When socioeconomic status was partialled out, the effect on IQ reversed itself, and three of the four correlations were statistically significant. The effects on achievement were still statistically significant and positive, but very small. It is important to realize that this study used a very large sample so that even very tiny effects are statistically significant. An examination of the father-absent effect within very narrow SES intervals also showed no significant effects. Thus we have a clear failure to confirm the theory and an additional demonstration of the important confounding effects of social class. The second hypothesis was also clearly refuted. Single twins did not score higher than twins from intact pairs. The third hypothesis was tested using a multiple regression approach. In only one out of six analyses was there evidence that birth interval mediated the effects of family size, after controlling for social class. The fourth hypothesis was tested by predicting the ability and achievement scores of first-born children in families with two to five children. These equations were then used to predict the only children's scores given family size of one and their SES score. No significant effects were found for any of the six groups. The fifth hypothesis was tested in two ways, and none of the twelve tests supported the hypothesis.

Thus several direct tests of components of the confluence theory fail to support it. In addition, careful control of between-family effects reduces birth order effects on ability to near insignificance. There is also some suggestive evidence that prenatal factors differentially influence children of different birth orders (reviewed previously), making the postnatal explanation of the confluence theory even more tenuous. Galbraith (1982b) has recently applied the confluence theory to a large set of data collected on Mormon families. As in the above studies, specific components of the model did not work as expected, and the overall model did not explain very much of the individual difference variance in IQ (see, however, the rebuttal by Berbaum et al., 1982; the reply by Galbraith, 1982a; and the discussion by Zajonc, 1983). Berbaum et al. (1982) have argued that the use of Mormon families, who are characterized by distinctive child-rearing and family-living practices, may be an important reason for the lack of fit of the model. This may be so, but the argument seems ad hoc in light of attempts by Zajonc and Bargh (1980b) to fit the confluence model to data from other societies without regard to such differences in child-rearing practices.

Galbraith (1982b, 1982c) has also criticized the confluence model on a number of quantitative and logical grounds. His criticisms are detailed and extensive, and the rebuttals are weak and unconvincing (Berbaum et al., 1982). (In light of the problems that we have discussed, little would be gained by repeating Galbraith's criticisms here, and we refer the interested reader to the original articles.)

Perhaps the strongest formal criticism of the confluence model is that of Price, Walsh, and Vilberg (1984). As they point out, strong empirical support for the model has come from studies that use mental age (MA) as the dependent variable and chronological age (CA) as a parameter of the model. Price et al. have shown that "the confluence model's ability to predict MA is no accident; it is an artifact" (p. 195). Without the use of any empirical data these authors show that a model based on only one of the confluence model's parameters (CA) does at least as well as the confluence model. It is important to recognize that the Price et al. criticism applies not to the model itself, but to one approach to testing the model. Unfortunately, that approach to testing the model is the one that has provided the greatest support.

Summary

If we look at all the data as a whole (primarily aggregate level data), the confluence model has not been refuted. It has, however, been placed under considerable strain. Analyses at the individual level are much less impressive and raise a number of questions about the adequacy of the model. The formal criticism raised by Price et al. (1984), cited above, further undermines the model. Current defenses of the theory (Zajonc, 1983), while not *ad hoc*, do appear to involve some special pleading. The model, at best, explains a very small amount of the total variance in IQ, and it should not be overinterpreted as it was in early presentations (Zajonc, 1976).

The confluence theorists, like many others, assume that birth order effects are not genetic or biological. As Record, McKeown, and Edwards (1969) argue, "the fact that there are small differences related to birth order between children in the same families, whose environment is relatively uniform and for whom no question of genetic variation arises, suggests that the much larger differences which exist between families also reflect, in part, experience in the postnatal environment" (p. 68).

Although it is theoretically the case that, because of random segregation, sibs should not differ genetically and, therefore, the birth order effects should not be genetic, perhaps we should not close the door too quickly. ABO blood group frequencies have been shown to be birth order dependent in a Japanese sample: in essence, the frequency of type AB children increases among second- and later-borns, relative to first-borns (Hiraizumi, Spradlin, Ito, & Anderson, 1973). The mechanism(s) underlying this effect are unknown. In addition, other biological factors have simply not been explored.

Finally, in an extensive review of more than 15,000 scientific studies concerning relationships between birth order and behavior, Ernst and Angst (1983) find little that is of merit. They claim that associations previously thought to be meaningful can most often be explained by sampling biases. For example, larger families tend to come from the lower socioeconomic classes. As such, first-born children may represent a valid cross-section of society, whereas fifth-born and later-borns come from disproportionately less-advantaged homes.

SCHOOLING AND IQ

Inequality of Schooling and IQ

Inequality of schooling is a popular explanation of individual, class, and race differences in IQ. While the quality of primary and secondary education is an important concern (see our discussion of mean effects versus causes of individual differences), there is no firm evidence that it is a major source of individual differences in IQ. It is important to recognize that *most* of the differences in IQ under discussion here exist before children attend school. Table 23, for example, shows the mean IQ for children classified by father's occupation, at four different ages (cross-sectional data).

The correlation between IQ measured at age 5 and at maturity is quite high. Interpolation of a summary graph of relevant data presented by Bloom (1964) suggests a correlation of about .70. Wilson (1983) reports a correlation of .67 between IQ measures at 5 years and IQ measured at 15 years ($N = 343$). Consequently, the numbers shown in Table 23 for ages 6 through 9 can be considered stable.

The Coleman Report (Coleman et al., 1966) was a large scale study commissioned by the federal government to determine the extent to which inequalities

Table 23. Mean IQs of Children According to Fathers' Occupations

Fathers' Occupational Classification	Chronological Ages			
	2–5½	6–9	10–14	15–18
I Professional	114.8	114.9	117.5	116.4
II Semi-professional and Managerial	112.4	107.3	112.2	116.7
III Clerical, Skilled Trades, and Retail Business	108.0	104.9	107.4	109.6
IV Rural Owners	97.8	94.6	92.4	94.3
V Semi-skilled, Minor Clerical and Business	104.3	104.6	103.4	106.7
VI Slightly Skilled	97.2	100.0	100.6	96.2
VII Day Labor, Urban and Rural	93.8	96.0	97.2	97.6

Source. From McNemar, 1942. The data cited pertain to the 1937 revision of the Stanford-Binet Scale by Quinn McNemar; Copyright© 1942. Reproduced by permission of the Riverside Publishing Company.

in educational performance were due to inequalities in school facilities. The report concluded:

> Taking all these results together, one implication stands out above all: That schools bring little influence to bear on a child's achievement that is independent of his background and general social context; and that this very lack of an independent effect means that the inequalities imposed on children by their home, neighborhood, and peer environment are carried along to become the inequalities with which they confront life at the end of school. For equality of educational opportunity through the schools must imply a strong effect of schools that is independent of the child's immediate social environment, and that strong independent effect is not present in American schools. [Coleman et al., 1966, p. 325]

The estimated variance accounted for by school quality ranged between 2% and 10%. These (Jencks et al., 1972; Mosteller & Moynihan, 1972) and other data (Sewell, Hauser, & Featherman, 1976) have been repeatedly analyzed, yielding similar conclusions. Jencks et al. (1972), for example, conclude as follows:

> Equalizing the quality of elementary school would reduce cognitive inequality by 3 percent, or less. . . . Equalizing the quality of high schools would reduce cognitive equality by 1 percent, or less. [p. 109]

The Warsaw Study

There are dissenters from this view (Bowles & Gintis, 1976; *Harvard Educational Review*, 1973). Their arguments remain selective, *ad hoc,* and untested (Jencks, 1973; Kamin, 1977), but constitute a fertile source of new hypotheses. One of the main sources of uneasiness regarding the conclusions about schooling is their total dependence on statistical analyses. The results do not depend on the purposive manipulation of the variable. The results of one large social experiment dealing with schooling have now been published, and they support the previous conclusions (Firkowska, Ostrowska, Sokolowska, Stein, Susser, & Wald, 1978).

During World War II, the city of Warsaw was almost totally destroyed (70%). The city was rebuilt in a planned manner, under a socialist egalitarian system. Individuals and families representing all levels of education and occupation were almost randomly allocated to dwellings, schools, and health facilities. Two classes of ecological factors (called extrinsic factors)—quality of the district and quality of the schools—and one within-family factor (called intrinsic factors) were assessed. The district measures were as follows: (1) city center—a measure of access to well-developed cultural and consumer facilities; and (2) social marginality— a measure of degree of social dependency of the district. High-scoring districts have many old people and few young people, higher crime rates, more people collecting welfare, and so on. The school measures were as follows: (1) average number of pupils per class; (2) percentage of teachers with university degrees; and (3) percentage of children repeating grades. The subjects of the study were not a sample, but were *all* children born in 1963 (14,238) and living in Warsaw at the time of the survey (March, 1974–June, 1974). The Raven Progressive Matrices test was administered to 96.2% of the enumerated population. The correlations between the variables and the children's Raven scores were as follows: education of father and mother (.29, .27); occupation of father and mother (.28, .29); city center (.11); marginality ($-.02$); class size (.06); graduate teachers (.07); and repeaters ($-.08$). The educational and occupational correlates of the Raven are essentially the same as those in the Western samples and in the Dutch data discussed previously.

The data were analyzed by regressing the children's Raven scores on the three factors (district, school, and family) in the three possible orders. These results are shown in Table 24.

The three factors account for 10.6% of the variance. No matter how the data are analyzed, family variables make the major contribution and extrinsic variables make a minor contribution. Model 1 shows that the district and school variables taken together can account for only 2.1% of the total variance, while the family adds 8.5%. The 2.1% figure is a maximum because under the other two models, family accounts for 9.2% and 10.3% of the total variance. In terms of the proportion of explained variance in the Raven scores, family variance can account for no less than 80%, and as much as 97%.

On the assumption that children with less well-educated parents would benefit more from schooling than would those with better-educated parents (in essence, they would receive intellectual and social stimulation at school that they would not receive at home), this analysis was repeated for children of parents who did not complete a primary school education. Schooling could not be shown to contribute proportionally more variance to their mental performance. Notice that the 2.1% of the variance accounted for is very close to Jencks's estimate of 3% or less.

Regardless of which model is chosen, extrinsic factors explain only a minor part of the variance. It may well be that social policy has so well equalized

Table 24. **Multiple Correlation and Proportion of Variance in Raven Scores**
Accounted for by District, Family, and School Variables in Three Causal Models

Step	Variable Entered	Multiple Correlation (R)	Variance Accounted for (R^2)	R^2 Change
		Model 1		
1	District	.126	.01586	.01586
2	School	.147	.12161	.00575
3	Family	.326	.10618	.08458
		Model 2		
1	School	.115	.01315	.01315
2	Family	.324	.10482	.09168
3	District	.326	.10618	.00136
		Model 3		
1	Family	.320	.10271	.10271
2	District	.324	.10514	.00244
3	School	.326	.10618	.00104

Source. From Firkowska et al., 1978; Copyright© 1978 by the AAAS.

extrinsic factors that they have been removed from consideration. Their removal, however, has had virtually no influence on the relation of intrinsic factors to IQ. It is also readily apparent that the Firkowska et al. (1978) data are entirely consistent with the three other surveys reported in Table 24. The authors conclude as follows:

> It is plain, nevertheless, that societal changes over a generation have failed to override forces that determine the social class distribution of mental performance among children. For further elucidation of the determinants of cognitive abilities, we need to turn our attention to intrinsic factors. [p. 1362]

Amount of Schooling and IQ

The correlation between adult IQ and amount of schooling completed is quite high. Matarazzo (1972, p. 373) reports the full-scale correlations for three age groups in the WAIS standardization sample as .69 (ages 18–19), .66 (ages 25–34), and .72 (ages 45–54, $N = 300$). These are typical figures. This correlation may develop because bright individuals continue in school (selection) and/or because schooling increases IQ. Surprisingly few studies have attempted to distinguish between these two possibilities. Lorge (1945), in a study of 131 New York City boys, showed that IQ measures at age 14 correlated .64 with IQ measures taken at age 34. This large increase (from .64 to .79) suggests that schooling enhances IQ. Unfortunately, only 17% of the original subjects remained in the follow-up sample. Although the follow-up sample did not differ from the original sample in terms of mean score on a variety of tests, it appears that they did differ in terms of the correlations among significant variables. The correlation between IQ at 14 years and eventual education in the follow-up sample was only .36. This is much lower than the figure of about .54 (Duncan, 1968) usually found in this age range, and it raises the possibility of an unrepresentative sample. The design used by Lorge is also subject to regression artifacts. Thus these data must be interpreted cautiously. Bradway, Thompson, & Cravens (1958), in a follow-up study of children in the 1937 Binet standardization sample, found no effect due to additional schooling. Both Husen (1951) and Harnqvist (1968), using more adequate procedures and larger samples than Lorge's, were able to demonstrate an effect due to additional years of education.

No ex-post facto (after the fact) design that allows subjects to self-select can conclusively settle this question. Without randomized assignment, one can always argue that preexisting differences between the group that attends school and the group that does not attend school underlie group differences in IQ. We know, however, from studies of monozygotic (MZA) twins reared apart that differences in amount of education correlate with differences in IQ. Newman, Freeman, and Holzinger (1937) report correlations of .79 and .55 between MZA twin IQ differences on the Stanford-Binet and Otis IQ tests, respectively, and educational difference ratings. Since studies of separated MZ twins are subject to somewhat different sources of error, our confidence that education makes a difference is enhanced by similar findings in both contexts. Even using this design, however, it is possible to reason that prenatal biological differences influencing IQ have a subsequent effect on level of education completed.

Based upon the accumulation of evidence from studies of schooling and IQ, Jencks (1972) has estimated "that each extra year of education boosts an individual's adult IQ score about 1 point above the expected level" (p. 88). This is a reasonable estimate.

Preschool Enrichment Programs

In 1969, Arthur Jensen began his now famous article, "How much can we boost IQ and scholastic achievement?" with the following statement:

> Compensatory education has failed. . . . The chief goal of compensatory education— to remedy the educational lag of disadvantaged children and thereby narrow the achievement gap between "minority" pupils—has been utterly unrealized in any of the large compensatory education programs that have been evaluated so far. [Jensen, 1969, pp. 2–3]

Jensen's evaluation received wide publicity, and a storm of protest followed. (See Jensen, 1972, for a bibliography of articles on this controversy.) Jensen specifically targeted Headstart-type programs in his critique. He also specifically allowed that these programs probably provided other benefits even if they did not raise IQ or academic achievement. Are Jensen's conclusions still valid 15 years later? The answer is yes, more or less.

In 1975, the Consortium for Longitudinal Studies was founded. This group was comprised of pjarticipants in many of the important preschool projects of the time. One of their goals was to assess the effects of preschool intervention programs on a large data base provided by a series of individual projects. They pooled the data from eleven such projects, undertaken between 1961 and 1969. They also collected follow-up data (Royce, Darlington, & Murray, 1983). The available data were collected in four "waves."

Wave I. Participants ranged in age from 3 months to 5 years, $N = 3,656$; IQ tests included the Stanford-Binet and PPVT (Peabody Picture Vocabulary Test); 60 family background variables were assessed.

Wave II. Participants ranged in age from 5 to 10 years, $N = 2,107$; IQ tests included the Stanford-Binet and PPVT administered annually. These data were collected prior to 1976.

Wave III. This was the 1976 consortium follow-up sample. Participants ranged in age from 10 to 19 years, $N = 2,008$ (these individuals received at least one follow-up measure); test instruments included the School Record Form, 1976 Youth Interviews, 1976 Parental Interview, and Wechsler Intelligence Scale for Children (WISC and WISC-R).

Wave IV. Participants ranged in age from 14 to 21 years, $N = 1,104$. (This sample constituted the 1980 consortium follow-up [1979–1981].) Test instruments included the 1980 School Data Form and 1980 Youth Interview. Comparison of outcomes between program group and control group children from the different projects was done by converting the significance level to a standard score (z-score); standard scores from the different projects were then pooled. Program group-control group differences, based on the median unstandardized coefficients across projects (for example, IQ points, percentage difference) are presented. The authors report a large number of outcome measures, many of them significant and important. We, however, will focus primarily on the IQ data.

Group differences at immediate post-testing (7.42 IQ points) were significant ($p < .001$) and robust. Program children scored significantly higher on the Stanford-Binet at 1 year (4.32 IQ points, $p < .001$) and 2 years (4.62 IQ points, $p < .001$) after termination of the program. Both of these results were robust. Program children also demonstrated an initial advantage at the time of entry into the first grade (age 6 years), relative to the nonprogram children (5.80 IQ points, $p < .001$). At 3 or 4 years after program participation, a group difference was maintained (3.04 IQ points, $p < .002$), but was no longer robust. In greater contrast, by 1976, when the children were 10–19 years old, program group-control group differences on the WISC were not observed on most consortium projects. Some superiority in achievement test scores was maintained by the program children, especially in mathematics, in grades three through six. Some other benefits were in the areas of achievement orientation, school competence, educational attainment, and career accomplishments. For example, at age 15 years, program participants cited a school-related activity when asked to name something that makes them proud (achievement orientation). Parents of these children voiced high aspirations for these children. Furthermore, only 13% of the program children, compared with 31% of the nonprogram children, were eventually enrolled in special education classes.

A recent critical review of this research effort (Glass & Ellwein, 1984) outlines two possible interpretations of the findings. The first position (adopted by members of the consortium) recognizes that some important first steps toward improving IQ and the quality of children's lives have been taken. A second view holds that school officials' knowledge of the elevated scores among program participants, as well as their experience in the program, might function to prevent their placement in remedial education classes (they already have had their share), in contrast with nonprogram pupils. The nonprogram controls, who may be no less talented, enter these special classes. As a result, their parents, their teachers, and they themselves come to expect less of themselves, and thus the twig is bent. But:

> Once the child is out of the institution, the distinctions and differences disappear . . . . the true lasting effects of a child's preschool experiences may be detected only in the attitudes of the professionals and in the records of the institutions that will husband his or her life after preschool. [Glass & Ellwein, 1984, p. 274]

We will not discuss the controversial findings of Heber and the Milwaukee Project (Herrnstein, 1982; Sommer & Sommer, 1983). Nevertheless, because we have found so many colleagues who were not aware of the controversy surrounding this project, we will alert the reader to some of the key references (Clarke, 1981; Herrnstein, 1982; Sommer & Sommer, 1983). To our knowledge this study has never been reported in an edited scientific journal. Finally, we recommend an examination of Flynn's (1984) analysis of the Heber data from the viewpoint of outdated norms.

Summary

As we have found with most other environmental variables, quality of schooling, amount of schooling, and preschool enrichment do have an influence on IQ. The magnitude of the influence is, however, much more modest than someone unfamiliar with this literature would expect. The Warsaw study strengthens conclusions previously based on correlational findings alone. It does not, of course, prove the case for a lack of influence. Preschool enrichment programs, of the type designed during the "War on Poverty," have had, at best, a transitory impact on children's IQs; this is not to deny, however, that such programs have not had other types of positive influence.

CHAPTER SUMMARY

The principal finding in this review of environmental effects on IQ is that no single environmental factor appears to have a large influence on IQ. Variables widely believed to be important are usually weak. Some social scientists have been discouraged by this finding, and they have argued that we simply do not know very much about how the environment works. We would like to argue differently: Even though many studies fail to find strong environmental effects, and some misinterpret genetic for environmental variance, most of the factors studied *do* influence IQ in the direction predicted by the investigator. What does not exist is a small subset of variables, which, when manipulated simultaneously, leads to substantial improvement in IQ. The message here is straightforward and does not originate with us. It is simply that environmental effects are multifactorial and largely unrelated to each other.

Rowe and Plomin (1981) have argued persuasively, but not completely convincingly, that most environmental influences are within-families as opposed to between-families. This translates into E1, as opposed to E2, in the Birmingham biometric notation:

> Although a number of E1 variables have been proposed, the effects of these variables are generally limited either because only a small number of people encounter the variable or because its effects are weak. We suggest that behavioral scientists may have to settle for a large number of environmental explanations of behavior each with fairly circumscribed applicability. [Rowe and Plomin, 1981, p. 523]

Their list of specific sources of possible E1 influences is shown in Table 25. Several of these sources, which have been discussed in this chapter, seem to have, at best, small effects. Other sources have simply not been studied in such a way as to estimate their influence on IQ. Rowe and Plomin do, however, suggest a number of useful designs.

Jensen (1981) has also addressed the issue of what we call multifactorial effects. After a discussion of how little we know about environmental influences on IQ, he asserts as follows:

> My hunch is that the nongenetic variance in IQ is the result of such a myriad of microenvironmental events as to make it extremely difficult, if not impossible, to bring more than a small fraction of these influences under experimental control. The results of all such attempts to date would seem to be consistent with this interpretation. [Jensen, 1981, p. 33]

Willerman (1979), in a concise review of family effects on intellectual development, has concluded as follows:

> The picture is beginning to emerge that here are many psychological and biological environmental factors, each contributing a small fraction to the variance in IQ scores. Many of the detrimental environmental factors may be uncorrelated with

Table 25. Specific Sources of E1 Influences

Measurement	Sources				
	Accidental Factors	Sibling Interaction	Family Structure	Parental Treatment	Extra-familial Networks
Error of measurement	Tetratogenic agents Physical illness Prenatal and post-natal trauma Separation	Differential treatment Deidentification	Birth order Sibling spacing	Differential treatment of children Interactions of parent and child characteristics	Peer group members not shared by siblings Relatives Teachers Television

Source. From Rowe and Plomin, 1981; Copyright© 1981 by the American Psychological Association.

each other or with social class (particularly for those not severely deprived) and for that reason will be especially hard to eliminate. [p. 927]

A second, and not mutually exclusive, possibility is that genotype-environmental correlations are more important than previously believed. This question is divided into two parts in Table 25: Differential treatment, under the heading "Sibling Interaction"; and Differential treatment of children, under the heading, "Parental Treatment." Both questions have been dealt with by Rowe and Plomin (1981). They conclude that there is limited evidence in support of either factor as an important source of IQ variance, but that the methods for studying these questions have hardly been sufficiently exploited. Scarr and Grajek (1982) have taken a much more optimistic stance toward the possibility that genotype-environment correlations explain a significant part of the environmental variance in IQ. Their treatment of the topic is primarily qualitative and heuristic, and their very interesting speculations remain to be rigorously tested. In summary, there is little question that unraveling the complexity of environmental influences on IQ will pose a continuing challenge to behavioral science researchers in future years.

REFERENCES

Altus, W. D. (1966). Birth order and its sequelae. *Science, 151,* 44–48.

Anastasi, A. (1958). Heredity, environment, and the question "how?" *Psychological Review, 65,* 197–208.

Aronow, A. M. (1969). Lead poison in putty. *Science, 166,* 552.

Babson, S. G., Kangas, J., Young, N., & Bramhall, J. L. (1964). Growth and development of twins of dissimilar size at birth. *Pediatrics, 33,* 327–333.

Bahr, S. J., & Leigh, G. K. (1978). Family size, intelligence, and expected education. *Journal of Marriage and the Family, 40,* 331–335.

Bell, R. Q. (1968). A reinterpretation of the direction of the effects in studies of socialization. *Psychological Review, 75,* 81–95.

Bellinger, D. C., & Needleman, H. L. (1983). Lead and the relationship between maternal and child intelligence. *Journal of Pediatrics, 102,* 523–527.

Belmont, L., & Marolla, F. A. (1973). Birth order, family size, and intelligence. *Science, 182,* 1096–1101.

Belmont, L., Stein, Z., & Zybert, P. (1978). Child spacing and birth order: Effect on intellectual ability in two child families. *Science, 202,* 995–996.

Berbaum, M. L., Markus, G. B., & Zajonc, R. B. (1982). A closer look at Galbraith's "closer look." *Developmental Psychology, 18,* 174–180.

Bereiter, C., & Engelmann, S. (1966). *Teaching disadvantaged children in preschool.* Englewood Cliffs, NJ: Prentice-Hall.

Bing, E. (1962). The effects of child-rearing practices on development of differential cognitive abilities. In E. E. Maccoby & L. Raus (Eds.), *Differential cognitive abilities.* Stanford, CA: Stanford University Press.

Birch, H. G., & Gussow, J. D. (1970). *Disadvantaged children: Health, nutrition and school failure.* New York: Grune & Stratton.

Bloom, B. S. (1964). *Stability and change in human characteristics.* New York: Wiley.

Bouchard, T. J., Jr. (1976). Genetic factors in intelligence. In A. R. Kaplan (Ed.), *Human behavior genetics.* Springfield, MA: Thomas.

Bouchard, T. J., Jr. (1982a). Review of identical twins reared apart: A reanalysis. *Contemporary Psychology, 27,* 190–191.

Bouchard, T. J., Jr. (1982b). Review of the intelligence controversy. *American Journal of Psychology, 95,* 346–349.

Bouchard, T. J., Jr. (1983). Do environmental similarities explain the similarity in intelligence of identical twins reared apart? *Intelligence, 7,* 175–184.

Bouchard, T. J., Jr., & McGue, M. (1981). Familial studies of intelligence: A review. *Science, 212,* 1055–1059.

Bowles, S., & Gintis, H. (1976). *Schooling in capitalist America: Educational reform and the contradictions of economic life.* New York: Basic Books.

Brackbill, Y., & Nichols, P. L. (1982). A test of the confluence model of intellectual development. *Development Psychology, 18,* 192–198.

Bradley, M. N. (1973). Pregnancy and famine. *Science, 180,* 133–134.

Bradley, R. H., & Caldwell, B. M. (1976). Early home environment and changes in mental test performance in children from 6 to 36 months. *Developmental Psychology, 12,* 93–97.

Bradley, R. H., & Caldwell, B. M. (1976). The relation of infants' home environment to mental test performance at fifty-four months: A follow-up study. *Child Development, 47,* 1172–1175.

Bradley, R. H., Caldwell, B. M., & Elardo, R. (1977). Home environment, social status, and mental test performance. *Journal of Educational Psychology, 69,* 697–701.

Bradway, K. P., Thompson, C. W., & Cravens, R. B. (1958). Preschool IQs after twenty-five years. *Journal of Educational Psychology, 49,* 278–281.

Breland, H. M. (1974). Birth order, family configuration, and verbal achievement. *Child Development, 45,* 1011–1019.

Brody, E. B., & Brody, N. (1976). *Intelligence: Nature, determinants, and consequences.* New York: Academic Press.

Broman, S., Nichols, P. L., & Kennedy, W. A. (1975). *Preschool IQ: Prenatal and early developmental correlates.* Hillsdale, NJ: Erlbaum.

Burks, B. S. (1928). The relative influence of nature and nurture upon mental development: A comparative study of foster parent-foster child resemblance and true parent-true child resemblance. *Twenty-seventh Yearbook of the National Society for the Study of Education, 27,* 219–316.

Busse, T. V., Ree, M., Gutride, M., Alexander, T., & Powell, L. S. (1972). Environmentally enriched classrooms and the cognitive perceptual development of Negro preschool children. *Journal of Educational Psychology, 63,* 15–21.

Caldwell, B. M. (1978). Home observation for measurement of the environment. Little Rock: University of Arkansas.

Caputo, D. V., & Mandell, W. (1970). Consequences of low birth weight. *Developmental Psychology, 3,* 363–383.

Chase, H. P., & Martin, H. P. (1970). Undernutrition and child development. *The New England Journal of Medicine, 282,* 933–939.

Chisolm J. J., Jr., & O'Hara, D. M. (1982). *Lead absorption in children.* Baltimore: Urban & Schwarzenberg.

Christiansen, N., Mora, J. O., & Herrera, M. G. (1975). Family social characteristics related to physical growth of young children. *British Journal of Preventive Social Medicine, 29,* 121–130.

Clarke, A. (1981). Sir Cyril Burt and Rick Heber. *Bulletin of the British Psychological Society, 34,* 324.

Clarke, A. M., & Clarke, A. D. B. (1976). *Early experience: Myth and evidence*. New York: Free Press.

Clarke, E. L. (1916). *American men of letters, their nature and nurture*. New York: Columbia University Press.

Coleman, J. S., Campbell, E. O., Hobson, C. J., McPartland, J., Moody, A. M., Weinfeld, F. D., & York, R. L. (1966). Equality of educational opportunity. Washington, DC: U.S. Government Printing Office.

Colliver, J. A., Kolm, P., & Verhulst, S. J. (1983). Dentine lead and IQ: Interpretation of results of residuals analysis. *Journal of Pediatrics, 102*, 573–574.

Corah, N. L., Anthony, E. J., Painter, P., Stern, J. A., & Thurston, D. L. (1965). Effects of perinatal anoxia after seven years. *Psychological Monographs, 79* (Whole No. 596).

Corey, L. A., Kang, K. W., Christian, J. C., Norton, J. A., & Harris, R. E. (1976). Effects of chorion type on variation in cord blood cholesterol of monozygotic twins. *American Journal of Human Genetics, 28*, 433–441.

Cravioto, J., DeLicardie, M. S., & Birch, H. G. (1966). Nutrition, growth and neurointegrative development: An experimental and ecological study. *Pediatrics, 38*, 319–372.

DeFries, J. C., & Plomin, R. (1978). Behavior genetics. *Annual Review of Psychology, 29*, 473–515.

De Levie, M., & Nogrady, M. B. (1970). Rapid brain growth upon restoration of adequate nutrition causing false radiologic evidence of increased intracranial pressure. *Journal of Pediatrics, 76*, 523–528.

Derom, R., & Thiery, M. (1974). Intrauterine hypoxia—A phenomenon proper to the second twin. *Acta Geneticae Medicae et Gemellologiae, 23*, 54.

Detterman, D. K. (1982). Does "g" exist? *Intelligence, 6*, 99–108.

Dobbing, J. (1968). Vulnerable periods in developing brains. In A. N. Davison & J. Dobbing (Eds.), *Applied neurochemistry*. London and Oxford: Blackwell.

Dobbing, J. (1973). The later development of the central nervous system and its vulnerability. In J. A. Davis & J. Dobbing (Eds.), *Scientific foundations of pediatrics*. London: William Heinemann Medical Books.

Douglas, J. W. B. (1964). *The home and the school*. London: MacGibbon.

Drillien, C. M. (1961). The incidence of mental and physical handicaps in school age children of very low birth weight. *Pediatrics, 27*, 452–464.

Drillien, C. M. (1968). Studies in mental handicap. *Archives of Disease in Childhood, 43*, 283.

Drillien, C. M. (1969). School disposal and performance of children of different birth weight born 1953–1960. *Archives of Disease in Childhood, 44*, 562–570.

Duncan, O. D. (1968). Ability and achievement. *Eugenics Quarterly, 15*, 1–11.

Eaves, L. J. (1982). The utility of twins. In V. E. Anderson, W. A. Hauser, J. K. Penry, & C. F. Sing (Eds.), *Genetic basis of the epilepsies*. New York: Raven.

Eckland, B. K. (1967). Genetics and sociology: A reconsideration. *American Sociological Review, 32*, 173–194.

Educational Testing Service (1980). *Test scores and family income: A response to charges in the Nader/Narin report on ETS*. Princeton: Educational Testing Service.

Elardo, R., Bradley, R., & Caldwell, B. M. (1975). The relation of infants' home environments to mental test performance from six to thirty-six months: A longitudinal analysis. *Child Development, 46*, 71–76.

Ellis, H. (1926). *A study of British genius*. Boston: Houghton Mifflin.

Ernhart, C. B., Landa, B., & Schell, N. B. (1981). Subclinical levels of lead and developmental deficit—A mutivariate follow-up reassessment. *Pediatrics, 67*, 911–919.

Ernst, C., & Angst, J. (1983). *Birth order: Its influence on personality*. New York: Springer-Verlag.

Eysenck, H. J., & Kamin, L. J. (1982). *The intelligence controversy*. New York: Wiley.

Fairweather, D. V. I., & Illsley, R. (1969). Obstetric and social origins of mentally handicapped children. *British Journal of Preventive and Social Medicine, 14,* 149–159.

Farber, S. L. (1981). Identical twins reared apart: A reanalysis. New York: Basic Books.

Firkowska, A., Ostrowska, A., Sokolowska, M., Stein, A., Susser, M., & Wald, I. (1978). Cognitive development and social policy: The contribution of parental occupation and education to mental performance in 11-year-olds in Warsaw. *Science, 200,* 1357–1362.

Fisch, R. O., Bilek, M. K., Deinard, A. S., & Chang, P.-N. (1976). Growth, behavioral, and psychologic measurements of adopted children: The influences of genetic and socioeconomic factors in a prospective study. *Journal of Pediatrics, 89,* 494–500.

Fisch, R. O., Bilek, M. K., Horrobin, J. M., & Chang, P.-N. (1976). Children with superior intelligence at 7 years of age. *Archives of American Journal of Diseases of Children, 130,* 481–487.

Flynn, J. R. (1984). The mean IQ of Americans: Massive gains 1932 to 1978. *Psychological Bulletin, 95,* 29–51.

Freeman, F. N., Holzinger, K. H., & Mitchell, B. C. (1928). The influence of environment on the intelligence, school achievement, and conduct of foster children. *Yearbook of the National Society for the Study of Education, 27,* 103–217.

Galbraith, R. C. (1982a). Just one look was all it took: Reply to Berman, Markus and Zajonc. *Developmental Psychology, 18,* 181–191.

Galbraith, R. C. (1982b). Sibling spacing and intellectual development: A closer look at the confluence models. *Developmental Psychology, 18,* 151–173.

Galbraith, R. C. (1982c). The confluence model and six divergent data sets: Comments on Zajonc and Bargh. *Intelligence, 6,* 305–310.

Galton, F. (1874). *English men of science, their nature and their nurture.* London: Macmillan.

Gibson, J. B. (1970). Biological aspects of a high socio-economic group: I. IQ, education and social mobility. *Journal of Biosocial Science, 2,* 1–16.

Glass, G. V., & Ellwein, M. C. (1984). Early education. [Review of *As the twig is bent . . . Lasting effects of preschool programs.*] *Science, 223,* 273–274.

Glass, G. V., McGaw, B., & Smith, M. L. (1981). Meta-analysis in social research. Beverly Hills: Sage.

Gottesman, I. I. (1963). Genetic aspects of intelligent behavior. In N. Ellis (Ed.), *Handbook of mental deficiency: Psychological theory and research.* New York: McGraw-Hill.

Gottesman, I. I. (1968). Biogenetics of race and class. In M. Deutsch, I. Katz, & A. R. Jensen (Eds.), *Social class, race, and psychological development.* New York: Holt, Rinehart and Winston.

Gottfried, A. W. (1973). Intellectual consequences of perinatal anoxia. *Psychological Bulletin, 80,* 231–242.

Graham, F. K., Ernhart, C. B., Thurston, D., & Craft, M. (1962). Development three years after perinatal anoxia and other potentially damaging newborn experiences. *Psychological Monographs: General and Applied, 76* (3, Whole No. 522).

Graham, F. K., Matarazzo, R. G., & Caldwell, B. M. (1956). Behavioral differences between normal and traumatized newborns: II. Standardization, reliability, and validity. *Psychological Monographs, 70* (21, Whole No. 428).

Graham, F. K., Pennoyer, M. M., Caldwell, B. M., Greenman, M., & Hartman, A. F. (1957). Relationship between clinical status and behavior test performance in a newborn group with histories suggesting anoxia. *Journal of Pediatrics, 50,* 177–189.

Grotevant, H. D., Scarr, S., & Weinberg, R. A. (1977). Intellectual development in family constellations with adopted children and natural children: A test of the Zajonc & Markus model. *Child Development, 48,* 1699–1703.

Haldane, J. B. S. (1946). The interaction of nature and nurture. *Annals of Eugenics, 13,* 197–205.

Hanson, R. A. (1975). Consistency and stability of home environmental measures related to IQ. *Child Development, 46,* 470–480.

Harnqvist, K. (1968). Relative changes in intelligence from 13 to 18. *Scandinavian Journal of Psychology, 9,* 50–64.

Harper, L. V. (1975). The scope of offspring effects: From caregiver to culture. *Psychological Bulletin, 82,* 784–801.

Harris, C. W., & McArthur, D. L. (1974). Another view of the relation of environment to mental abilities. *Journal of Educational Psychology, 66,* 457–459.

Harvard Educational Review (1973). Perspectives on inequality: A reassessment of the effects of family and schooling in America. *Harvard Educational Review, 43,* 37–164.

Hebel, J. R., Kinch, D., & Armstrong, E. (1976). Mental capability of children exposed to lead pollution. *British Journal of Preventive and Social Medicine, 30,* 170–175.

Herrnstein, R. J. (1973). *IQ in the meritocracy.* Boston: Little, Brown.

Herrnstein, R. J. (1982, August). IQ testing and the media. *The Atlantic Monthly,* 68–74.

Hertzig, M. E., Birch, H. G., Richardson, S. A., & Tizard, J. (1972). Intellectual levels of school children severely malnourished during the first two years of life. *Pediatrics, 49,* 814–824.

Hiraizumi, Y., Spradlin, C. T., Ito, R., & Anderson, S. A. (1973). Birth-order dependent segregation frequency in the ABO blood groups of man. *American Journal of Human Genetics, 25,* 277–286.

Hoorweg, J. C. (1976). *Protein-energy malnutrition and intellectual abilities: A study of teenage Ugandan children.* The Hague: Mouton.

Horn, J., Loehlin, J. C., & Willerman, L. (1982). Aspects of the inheritance of intellectual abilities. *Behavior Genetics, 12,* 479–516.

Howell, F. H., & Malone, L. C. (1979). Comment on Kunz and Peterson: Family size, birth order and academic achievement. *Social Biology, 26,* 80–85.

Humphreys, L. G. (1979). The construct of general intelligence. *Intelligence, 3,* 105–120.

Hunter, J. E., Schmidt, F. L., & Jackson, G. B. (1982). *Meta-analysis: Cumulative research findings across studies.* Beverly Hills: Sage Publications.

Husen, T. (1951). The influence of schooling upon IQ. *Theoria, 17,* 61–68.

Hutt, C. (1972). *Males and females.* Baltimore: Penguin Books.

James, W. H. (1982). The IQ advantage of the heavier twin. *British Journal of Psychology, 73,* 513–517.

Jay, M. (1972). Le developpement intellectuel apres les carences protidiques. *Revue de Neuropsychiatrie Infantile, 20,* 267–295.

Jay, M., Collin, P., Andre, J., & Tracadas (1965). Les performances des enfants d'age scolaire aux tests de niveau mental dans le departement de la reunion. *Revue de Neuropsychiatrie Infantile, 13,* 659–680.

Jencks, C. (1973). Inequality in retrospect. *Harvard Educational Review, 43,* 138–164.

Jencks, C., Smith, M., Acland, H., Bane, M. J., Cohen, B., Gintis, H., Heyns, B., & Michelson, S. (1972). *Inequality: A reassessment of the effects of family and schooling in America.* New York: Basic Books.

Jensen, A. R. (1969). How much can we boost IQ and scholastic achievement? *Harvard Educational Review, 39,* 1–123.

Jensen, A. R. (1971). A note on why genetic correlations are not squared. *Psychological Bulletin, 75,* 223–224.

Jensen, A. R. (1972). *Genetics and education.* New York: Harper & Row.

Jensen, A. R. (1973). *Educability and group differences.* New York: Harper & Row.

Jensen, A. R. (1980). *Bias in mental testing.* New York: Free Press.

Jensen, A. R. (1981). Raising the IQ: The Ramey and Haskins Study. *Intelligence, 5,* 29–40.

Jinks, J. L., & Fulker, D. W. (1970). A comparison of the biometrical, genetical, MAVA, and classical approaches to the analysis of human behavior. *Psychological Bulletin, 73,* 311–349.

Joffe, J. M. (1969). *Prenatal determinants of behavior.* Oxford: Pergamon Press.

Jones, D. C., & Carr-Saunders, A. M. (1927). The relation between intelligence and social status among orphan children. *British Journal of Psychology, 17,* 343–364.

Kagan, J., & Moss, H. A. (1962). *Birth to maturity.* New York: Wiley.

Kamin, L. J. (1974). *The science and politics of IQ.* Potomac, MD: Erlbaum.

Kamin, L. J. (1977). Comment on Munsinger's adoption study. *Behavior Genetics, 7,* 403–406.

Kamin, L. J. (1978). Comment on Munsinger's review of adoption studies. *Psychological Bulletin, 85,* 194–210.

Kaplan, B. J. (1972). Malnutrition and mental deficiency. *Psychological Bulletin, 78,* 321–334.

Keys, A. B., Brožek, J., Henschel, A., Mickelson, O., & Taylor, H. L. (1950). *Biology of human starvation.* Minneapolis: University of Minnesota Press.

Lansdown, R. G., Clayton, B. E., Graham, P. J., Shephard, J., Delves, H. T., & Turner, W. C. (1974). Blood-lead levels, behavior and intelligence: A population study. *Lancet, 1,* 538.

Lawrence, E. M. (1931). An investigation into the relation between intelligence and inheritance. *British Journal of Psychology* (Monograph Supplement), No. 16, 1–80.

Leahy, A. (1935). Nature-nurture and intelligence. *Genetic Psychology Monographs, 17,* 236–308.

Levy, J. (1980). Cerebral asymmetry and the psychology of man. In M. Wittrock (Ed.), *The brain and psychology.* New York: Academic Press.

Li, C. C. (1975). *Path analysis—A primer.* Pacific Grove, CA: Boxwood Press.

Lilienfeld, A. M., & Parkhurst, E. (1951). A study of the association of factors of pregnancy and parturition with the development of cerebral palsy: A preliminary report. *American Journal of Hygiene, 53,* 262–282.

Lilienfeld, A. M., & Pasamanick, B. (1955). A study of variations in the frequency of twin births by race and socio-economic status. *American Journal of Human Genetics, 7,* 204–217.

Lilienfeld, A. M., & Pasamanick, B. (1956). The association of maternal and fetal factors with the development of mental deficiency. Relationships to maternal age, birth order, previous reproductive loss, and degree of mental deficiency. *American Journal of Mental Deficiency, 60,* 557–569.

Lilienfeld, A. M., Pasamanick, B., & Rogers, M. (1955). Relationship between pregnancy experience and the development of certain neuropsychiatric disorders in childhood. *American Journal of Public Health, 45,* 637–643.

Lloyd-Still, J. D. (1976). Clinical studies on the effects of malnutrition during infancy and subsequent physical and intellectual development. In J. D. Lloyd-Still (Ed.), *Malnutrition and intellectual development.* Littleton, MA: Publishing Sciences Group.

Loehlin, J. C. (1980). Recent adoption studies of IQ. *Human Genetics, 55,* 297–302.

Loehlin, J. C. (1981). Review of *Identical twins reared apart: A reanalysis. Acta Geneticae Medicae et Gemellologiae, 30,* 297–298.

Loehlin, J. C., Lindzey, G., & Spuhler, J. C. (1975). *Race differences in intelligence.* San Francisco: Freeman.

Loehlin, J. C., & Nichols, R. C. (1976). *Heredity, environment and personality: A study of 850 twins.* Austin: University of Texas Press.

Longstreth, L. E. (1981). Revisiting Skeels' final study: A critique. *Developmental Psychology, 17,* 620–625.

Longstreth, L. E., Davis, B., Carter, L., Flint, D., Owen, J., Rickert, M., & Taylor, E. (1981). Separation of home intellectual environment and maternal IQ as determinants of child's IQ. *Developmental Psychology, 17,* 532–541.

Lorge, I. (1945). Schooling makes a difference. *Teachers College Record, 46,* 483–492.

Luria, A. R., & Yudovitch, F. I. (1959). In J. Simon (Ed.), *Speech and the development of mental processes in the child.* London: Staples.

Lytton, H. (1980). *Parent-child interaction.* New York: Plenum Press.

Maccoby, E. E. (1966). Sex differences in intellectual functioning. In E. E. Maccoby (Ed.), *The development of sex differences.* Stanford: Stanford University Press.

Marjoribanks, K. (1972). Ethnic and environmental influences on mental abilities. *American Journal of Sociology, 78,* 323–337.

Marjoribanks, K. (1974). Another view of the relation of environment to mental abilities: A reply. *Journal of Educational Psychology, 66,* 460–463.

Marjoribanks, K., & Walberg, H. J. (1975). Birth order, family size, social class, and intelligence. *Social Biology, 22,* 261–268.

Marshall, E. (1983). EPA faults classic lead poisoning study. *Science, 222,* 906–907.

Matarazzo, J. D. (1972). *Wechsler's measurement and appraisal of adult intelligence.* Baltimore: Williams & Wilkins Co.

Matheny, A. P., Jr., Thoben, A. S., & Wilson, R. S. (1982). Appraisals of basic opportunities for developmental experiences (ABODE): Manual for home assessments of twin children. *JSAS Catalog of Selected Documents in Psychology, 12,* 31.

McCall, R. B., Hogarty, P. S., & Hurlburt, N. (1972). Transitions in infant sensorimotor development and the predictions of childhood IQ. *American Psychologist, 27,* 728–748.

McGee, M. (1979). Human spatial abilities: Psychometric studies and environmental, genetic, hormonal, and neurological influences. *Psychological Bulletin, 86,* 889–918.

McKay, H., Sinisterra, L., McKay, A., Gomez, H., & Lloreda, P. (1978). Improving cognitive ability in chronically deprived children. *Science, 200,* 270–278.

McKeown T., & Record, R. G. (1976). Relationship between childhood infections and measured intelligence. *British Journal of Preventive & Social Medicine, 30,* 101–106.

McNemar, Q. (1942). *The revision of the Stanford-Binet scale.* Boston: Houghton Mifflin.

Meehl, P. E. (1970). Nuisance variables and the ex-post facto design. In M. Radner & S. Winokur (Eds.), *Minnesota studies in the philosophy of science* (Vol. 4). Minneapolis: University of Minnesota Press.

Melnick, M., Myrianthopoulos, N. C., & Christian, J. C. (1978). The effects of chorion type on variation in IQ in the NCPP twin population. *American Journal of Human Genetics, 30,* 425–433.

Mercy, J. A., & Steelman, L. C. (1982). Familial influence on the intellectual attainment of children. *American Sociological Review, 47,* 532–542.

Moos, R. H. (1974). Family environment scale. Palo Alto: Social Ecology Laboratory, Stanford University. Moss (1962).

Mosteller, F., & Moynihan, D. P. (Eds.) (1972). *On equality of educational opportunity.* New York: Random House.

Munsinger, H. (1975). The adopted child's IQ: A critical review. *Psychological Bulletin, 82,* 623–659.

Munsinger, H. (1978). Reply to Kamin. *Psychological Bulletin, 85,* 202–206.

Myrianthopoulos, N. C., Nichols, P. L., Broman, S. H., & Anderson, V. E. (1972). Intellectual development of a prospectively studied population of twins and comparison with singletons. In J. de Grouchy, F. J. G. Ebling, & I. W. Henderson (Eds.), *Human genetics: Proceedings of the Fourth International Congress of Human Genetics,* 243–257.

Naeye, R. L., Diener, M. M., Dellinger, W. S., & Blanc, W. A. (1969). Urban poverty: Effect on prenatal nutrition. *Science, 166,* 1026.

Needleman, H. L., Geiger, S. K., & Frank, R. (1985). Lead and IQ scores: a reanalysis. *Science, 227,* 701–703.

Needleman, H. L., Gunnoe, C., Leviton, A., Reed, R., Peresie, H., Maher, C., & Barrett, P. (1979). Deficits in psychologic and classroom performance of children with elevated dentine lead levels. *The New England Journal of Medicine, 300,* 689–695.

Newman, H. H., Freeman, F. N., & Holzinger, K. H. (1937). *Twins: A study of heredity and environment.* Chicago: University of Chicago Press.

Oberle, M. W. (1969). Lead poisoning: A preventable childhood disease of the slums. *Science, 165,* 991–992.

Pasamanick, B., & Knobloch, H., & Lilienfeld, A. M. (1956). Socio-economic status and some precursors of neuropsychiatric disorders. *American Journal of Orthopsychiatry, 26,* 594–601.

Perino, J., & Ernhurst, C. B. (1974). The relation of subclinical lead level to cognitive and sensorimotor impairment in Black preschoolers. *Journal of Learning Disabilities, 7,* 616–620.

Plomin, R., & DeFries, J. C. (1980). Genetics and intelligence: Recent data. *Intelligence, 4,* 15–24.

Plomin, R., DeFries, J. C., & Loehlin, J. C. (1977). Genotype-environment interaction and correlation in the analysis of human behavior. *Psychological Bulletin, 84,* 309–322.

Plomin, R., DeFries, J. C., & McClearn, G. E. (1980). *Behavior genetics: A primer.* San Francisco: Freeman.

Pollin, W., & Stabenau, J. R. (1968). Biological, psychological and historical differences in a series of monozygotic twins discordant for schizophrenia. In D. Rosenthal & S. S. Kety (Eds.), *The transmission of schizophrenia.* London: Pergamon Press.

Poole, A. (1974). Bytheway's statistical trap. *Journal of Biosocial Science, 6,* 73.

Price, G. G., Walsh, D. J., & Vilberg, W. R. (1984). The confluence model's good predictions of mental age beg the question. *Psychological Bulletin, 96,* 195–200.

Record, R. G., McKeown, T., & Edwards, J. H. (1969). The relation of measured intelligence to birth order and maternal age. *Annals of Human Genetics, 33,* 61–69.

Record, R. G., McKeown, T., & Edwards, J. H. (1970). An investigation of the differences in measured intelligence between twins and single births. *Annals of Human Genetics, 34,* 11–20.

Richardson, S. A., Birch, H. G., & Hertzig, M. E. (1973). School performance of children who were severely malnourished in infancy. *American Journal of Mental Deficiency, 77,* 633–644.

Richardson, S. A., Birch, H. G., & Ragbeer, C. (1975). The behaviour of children at home who were severely malnourished in the first 2 years of life. *Journal of Biosocial Science, 7,* 255–267.

Roberts, T. M., Hutchinson, T. C., Paciga, J., Chattopadhyay, Jervis, R. E., Van Loon, J., & Parkinson, D. K. (1974). Lead contamination around secondary smelters: Estimation of dispersal and accumulation by humans. *Science, 186,* 1120–1123.

Robinson, W. S. (1950). Ecological correlations and the behavior of individuals. *American Sociological Review, 15,* 351–357.

Rowe, D. C., & Plomin, R. (1981). The importance of nonshared (E1) environmental influences in behavioral development. *Developmental Psychology, 17,* 517–531.

Royce, J. M., Darlington, R. B., & Murray, H. W. (1983). Pooled analyses: Findings across studies. In *As the twig is bent . . . Lasting effects of preschool programs* (Consortium for Longitudinal Studies). Hillsdale, NJ: Erlbaum.

Rutter, M., & Jones, R. R. (Eds.) (1983). *Lead versus health.* New York: Wiley.

St. John, N. (1970). The validity of children's reports of their parents' educational level: A methodological note. *Sociology of Education, 43,* 255–269.

Sameroff, A. J. (1975). Early influences in development: Fact or fantasy? *Merrill-Palmer Quarterly, 21,* 267–294.

Sameroff, A. J., & Chandler, M. J. (1975). Reproductive risk and the continuum of caretaking causality. In F. D. Horowitz, M. Hetherington, S. Scarr-Salapatek, & G. Siegel (Eds.), *Review of Child Development Research* (Vol. 4). Chicago: University of Chicago Press.

Santrock, J. W. (1972). Relation of type and onset of father absence to cognitive development. *Child Development, 43,* 455–469.

Scarr, S. (1969). Effects of birth weight on later intelligence. *Social Biology, 16,* 249–256.

Scarr, S. (1981). *Race, social class, and individual differences in IQ.* Hillsdale, NJ: Erlbaum.

Scarr, S., & Grajek, S. (1982). Similarities and differences among siblings. In M. E. Lamb & B. Sutton-Smith (Eds.), *Sibling relationships.* Hillsdale, NJ: Erlbaum.

Scarr, S., & Weinberg, R. A. (1976). IQ test performance of Black children adopted by White families. *American Psychologist, 10,* 726–739.

Scarr, S., & Weinberg, R. A. (1978). The influence of "family background" on intellectual attainment. *American Sociological Review, 43,* 674–692.

Schacter, S. (1959). *The psychology of affiliation.* Palo Alto: Stanford University Press.

Schiff, M., Duyme, M., Dumaret, A., Stewart, J., Tomkiewicz, S., & Feingold, J. (1978). Intellectual status of working-class children adopted early into upper-middle-class families. *Science, 200,* 1503–1504.

Schiff, M., Duyme, M., Dumaret, A., & Tomkiewicz, S. (1982). How much could we boost scholastic achievement and IQ scores? A direct answer from a French adoption study. *Cognition, 12,* 165–196.

Schooler, C. (1972). Birth order effects: Not here, not now! *Psychological Bulletin, 78,* 161–175.

Scott, E. M., Illsley, R., & Thomson, A. M. (1956). A psychological investigation of primigravidae. II. Maternal social class, age, physique and intelligence. *Journal of Obstetrics and Gynaecology, 63,* 338–343.

Selvin, S., & Janerich, D. T. (1971). Four factors influencing birth weight. *British Journal of Preventive and Social Medicine, 25,* 12–16.

Sewell, W. H., Hauser, R. M., & Featherman, D. L. (Eds.) (1976). *Schooling and achievement in American society.* New York: Academic Press.

Skeels, H. M. (1966). Adult status of children with contrasting early life experiences. *Child Development Monographs, 31* (No. 3).

Smith, C. A. (1947). Effects of wartime starvation in Holland on pregnancy and its products. *American Journal of Obstetrics and Gynecology, 53,* 599–608.

Sommer, R., & Sommer, B. A. (1983). Mystery in Milwaukee: Early intervention, IQ and psychology. *American Psychologist, 34,* 923–929.

Springer, S. P., & Deutsch, G. (1981). *Left brain, right brain.* San Francisco: Freeman.

Stein, Z. A., & Kassab, H. (1970). Nutrition. In J. Wortis (Ed.), *Mental retardation.* New York: Grune & Stratton.

Stein, Z. A., & Susser, M. W. (1976). Prenatal nutrition and mental competence. In J. D. Lloyd-Still (Ed.), *Malnutrition and intellectual development.* Littleton, MA: Publishing Sciences Group.

Stein, Z. A., Susser, M., Saenger, G., & Marolla, F. (1972). Nutrition and mental performance. *Science, 178,* 708–713.

Stein, Z. A., Susser, M., Saenger, G., & Marolla, F. (1975). *Famine and human development: The Dutch hunger winter of 1944/45.* New York: Oxford University Press.

Susser, M. W. (1973). *Causal thinking in the health sciences: Concepts and strategies in epidemiology.* New York: Oxford University Press.

Svanum, S., & Bringle, R. G. (1980). Evaluation of confluence model variables on IQ and achievement test scores in a sample of 6- to 11-year-old children. *Journal of Educational Psychology, 72,* 427–436.

Tanner, J. M. (1966). Galtonian eugenics and the study of growth: The relation of body size, intelligence test scores, and social circumstances in children and adults. *Eugenics Review, 58,* 122–135.

Taylor, H. F. (1980). *The IQ game: A methodological inquiry into the heredity-environment controversy.* New Brunswick, NJ: Rutgers University Press.

Teasdale, T. W. (1979). Social class correlations among adoptees and their biological adoptive parents. *Behavior Genetics, 9,* 103–114.

Terman, L. M. (1916). *The measurement of intelligence.* Boston: Houghton Mifflin.

Thomson, A. M. (1958). Diet in pregnancy. I. Dietary survey technique and the nutritive value of diets taken by primigravidae. *British Journal of Nutrition, 12,* 446–461.

Thurstone, L. L. (1928). The absolute zero in intelligence measurement. *Psychological Review, 35,* 175–197.

Vale, J. R. (1980). *Genes, environment, and behavior.* New York: Harper & Row.

Vandenberg, S. G., & Kuse, A. R. (1981). In search of the missing environmental variance in cognitive ability. In L. Gedda, P. Parisi, & W. E. Nance (Eds.), *Twin Research 3: Intelligence, personality, and development.* New York: Alan R. Liss.

Vernon, P. E. (1979). *Intelligence: Heredity and environment.* San Francisco: Freeman.

Walberg, H. J., & Marjoribanks, K. (1973). Differential mental abilities and home environment: A canonical analysis. *Developmental Psychology, 9,* 363–368.

Waller, J. H. (1971). Achievement and social mobility: Relationships among IQ score, education, and occupation in two generations. *Social Biology, 18,* 252–259.

Warren, N. (1973). Malnutrition and mental development. *Psychological Bulletin, 80,* 324–328.

Werner, E. E., Bierman, J. M., & French, F. E. (1971). *The children of Kauai.* Honolulu: University of Hawaii Press.

White, B. L., Kaban, B. T., & Atanucci, J. S. (1979). *The origins of human competence.* Lexington: Heath.

White, K. R. (1976). *The relationship between socioeconomic status and academic achievement.* Unpublished doctoral dissertation, University of Colorado School of Education.

White, K. R. (1982). The relation between socioeconomic status and academic achievement. *Psychological Bulletin, 91,* 461–481.

White, B. L., Kaban, B. T., & Atanucci, J. S. (1979). *The origins of human competence.* Lexington: Heath.

Willerman, L. (1979). Effects of families on intellectual development. *American Psychologist, 34,* 923–929.

Wilson, R. S. (1979). Twin growth: Initial deficit, recovery, and trends in concordance from birth to nine years. *Annals of Human Biology, 6,* 205–220.

Wilson, R. S. (1983). The Louisville Twin Study: Developmental synchronies in behavior. *Child Development, 54,* 298–316.

Wilson, R. S., & Matheny, A. P. (1983). Mental development: Family environment and genetic influences. *Intelligence, 7,* 195–215.

Winick, M. (1969). Malnutrition and brain development. *Journal of Pediatrics, 74,* 667–679.

Winick, M. (1973). Fetal malnutrition and future development. *Pediatric Annals, 2,* 10–15.

Winick, M., Brasel, J. P., & Rosso, P. (1972). Nutrition and cell growth. In Winick, M. (Ed.), *Current Concepts in Nutrition. I. Nutrition and development.* New York: Wiley.

Winick, M., Meyer, K., & Harris, R. C. (1975). Malnutrition and environmental enrichment by early adoption. *Science, 190,* 1173–1175.

Wolf, R. M. (1965). The measurement of environments. In C. W. Harris (Ed.), *Proceedings of the 1964 Invited Conference on Testing Problems.* Princeton: Educational Testing Service.

Zajonc, R. B. (1976). Family configuration and intelligence. *Science, 192,* 227–236.

Zajonc, R. B. (1983). Validating the confluence model. *Psychological Bulletin, 93,* 457–480.

Zajonc, R. B., & Bargh, J. (1980a). Birth order, family size, and decline of SAT scores. *American Psychologist, 35,* 662–668.

Zajonc, R. B., & Bargh, J. (1980b). The confluence model: Parameter estimation for six divergent data sets on family factors and intelligence. *Intelligence, 4,* 349–361.

Zajonc, R. B., & Markus, G. B. (1975). Birth order and intellectual development. *Psychological Review, 82,* 74–88.

Zajonc, R. B., Markus, H., & Markus, G. B. (1979). The birth order puzzle. *Journal of Personality and Social Psychology, 37,* 1325–1341.

Zigler, E. (1967). Familial mental retardation: A continuing dilemma. *Science, 155,* 292–298.

Zigler, E., & Valentine, J. (1979). *Project Head Start: A legacy of the war on poverty.* New York: Free Press.

ELEVEN

THE CONTROVERSY RELATED TO THE USE OF PSYCHOLOGICAL TESTS

ROBERT M. KAPLAN

San Diego State University, and University of California, San Diego
La Jolla, California

Emotional public debates about the meaning of psychological tests have become common occurrences in classrooms, courtrooms, and professional conversations. This chapter reviews the issue of test bias, which is at the heart of the controversy. The issue of test bias is so controversial that it has inspired legislation controlling the use of tests to evaluate minority group members. Other legislation and judicial decisions have forced major changes in the testing industry.

Although test bias is the unmistakable issue of the day, we should not give the impression that it is the first controversy about mental testing. Controversy has surrounded mental testing since test reports began in 1905, and the issues have been debated on and off since the 1920s (Cronbach, 1975; Haney, 1981).

WHY IS THE ISSUE CONTROVERSIAL?

A basic tenet of U.S. society is that all people are created equal. This cornerstone of political and social thought is clearly defended in the Constitution. Yet all individuals are not treated equally, and the history of social action is replete with attempts to remedy this situation. Psychological tests are among the many practices that counteract the idea that all people are the same. Tests are designed to measure differences between people, and often the differences tests measure are in desirable personal characteristics such as intelligence and aptitude. Test scores that demonstrate differences between people may suggest to some that people are not created with the same basic abilities.

The most aggravating problem is that certain ethnic groups, on the average, score differently on some psychological tests. The most controversial case concerns intelligence tests. On the average, black Americans score 15 points or one standard deviation lower than do white Americans on standardized IQ tests. Nobody disagrees that the two distributions greatly overlap and that there are some Blacks who score as high as the highest whites. There are also some whites who score as low as the lowest blacks. Yet only about 15% to 20% of the White population score below the average black score (Jensen, 1980).

The dispute has not concerned whether these differences exist, but rather has focused on where the responsibility for the differences lies. Many have argued that the differences are due to environmental factors (Kamin, 1974; Rosenthal & Jacobson, 1968), while others have suggested that the differences are biological (Jensen, 1969, 1972; Munsinger, 1975). The environmental versus the biological debate continues to flourish and is the topic of many publications (Loehlin, Lindzey & Spuhler, 1975). This chapter will not consider the nature-nuture question. Instead, the focus will be on tests and their use.

The review in this chapter is not limited to IQ tests. The principles discussed here are also applicable to achievement and aptitude tests. As Anastasi (1980) has suggested, it is often difficult to distinguish between the constructs of aptitude, achievement, and intelligence.

PSYCHOMETRIC STUDIES OF BIAS

This section considers the following question: Are standardized tests as valid for blacks and other minority groups as they are for whites? All the types of validity must be evaluated when the issue of test bias is considered (Cole, 1981). Some psychologists argue that the tests are differentially valid for black and white people. Because the issue of differential validity is so controversial and so emotionally arousing, it has forced a careful rethinking of many issues in test validation. Differences between ethnic groups on test performance do not necessarily indicate that the test is biased. The question is whether the test has different meanings for different groups. In psychometrics, validity defines the meaning of a test.

Item Content

Many researchers also argue that intelligence or aptitude tests are affected by language skills that are inculcated as part of a white, middle-class upbringing but are foreign to inner-city children (Kagan, Moss, & Siegel, 1963; Lesser, Fifer, & Clark, 1965; Mercer, 1971; Pettigrew, 1964; Scarr-Salapatek, 1971; Woodring, 1966). As a result of being unfamiliar with the language, some children have no chance of doing well on standardized IQ tests. For example, an American child is not likely to know what a schilling is, but a British child probably does. Similarly, the American child would not be expected to know where one puts the petrol. We assume that only a British child would understand this term. Some psychologists argue that asking an inner-city child about opera is just as unfair as asking an American child about petrol. In both cases, the term is not familiar to the child (Hardy, Welcher, Mellits, & Kagan, 1976).

Flaugher (1978) considered the accusations about the bias in psychological tests and concluded that many of them are based on misunderstandings. Many people feel that a fair test is one that asks questions they can answer. By contrast, a biased test is one that does not reveal all the test taker's strengths. Flaugher argued that the purpose of aptitude and achievement tests is to determine whether a person knows certain bits of information that are drawn from large potential pools of items. The test developers are indifferent to the opportunities people have to learn the information on the tests. The meaning they eventually assign to the tests derives from correlations of the test scores with other variables.

It has been argued that the linguistic bias in standardized tests does not cause the observed differences (Clarizio, 1979a). For example, Quay (1971) administered the Stanford-Binet to 100 children in an inner-city Head Start program. Half of the children in this sample were given a version of the test that used a black dialect, while the others were given the standard version. The results demonstrated that the advantage produced by having the test in a black dialect translates into less than a one-point increase in test scores. This finding is consistent with other research findings demonstrating that black children can comprehend standard English about as well as they can comprehend nonstandard black dialect (Clarizio, 1979a; Copple & Succi, 1974). This finding does not hold for white children, who seem to be functional only in standard dialect.

Systematic studies have failed to demonstrate that biased items in well-known standardized tests are responsible for the differences between ethnic groups (Flaugher, 1978). One approach has been to allow expert judges to eliminate particular unfair items. Unexpectedly, the many attempts to purify tests using this approach have not yielded positive results. In one study 16% of the items in an elementary reading test were eliminated after experts reviewed them and labeled them as potentially biased toward the majority group. However, when the new version of the test, which had the bad items "purged", was used, the differences between the majority and the minority school populations were no smaller than they had been when the original form of the test was used (Biachini, 1976).

Another approach to the same problem is to find classes of items that are most likely to be missed by members of a particular minority group. If a test is biased against that group, there should be significant differences between the minority and nonminority groups on certain categories of items. These studies are particularly important because if they identify certain types of items that discriminate between groups, these types of items can be avoided on future tests. Again, the results have not been encouraging; studies have not been able to identify clearly categories of items that discriminate between groups (Flaugher, 1974). The studies do show that groups differ on certain items, but it has not been clear whether these are real or chance differences. When groups are compared on a large number of items, some differences will occur for chance reasons.

A different strategy is to find items that systematically show differences between ethnic groups. Then these items are eliminated, and the test is rescored. In one study, 27 items from the SAT were eliminated because they were the specific items on which ethnic groups differed. Then the test was rescored for everyone. Although it seems as though this procedure should have eliminated the differences between groups, it actually had only slight effects because the items that differentiated the two groups tended to be the easiest items in the set. When these items were eliminated, the test was harder for everyone (Flaugher & Schrader, 1978).

There is at least some evidence that test items do not accurately portray the distribution of sexes and races in the population. Zores and Williams (1980) reviewed the WAIS, WISC-R, Stanford-Binet, and Slosson Intelligence test items for race and sex characterization and found white males shown with disproportionate frequency. Nevertheless, it has not yet been established that bias in the frequencies with which different groups are pictured in items is relevant to the issue of test bias. Various studies have failed to demonstrate that there is serious bias in item content. Most critics argue that the verbal content of test items is most objectionable because it is unfamiliar to minority groups. However, Scheuneman (1981) reviewed the problem and concluded that the verbal material in tests is usually closer to the life experiences of blacks than is the nonverbal material.

Other statistical models have been employed to evaluate item fairness. Across these different studies, with different populations and different methods of analysis, little evidence has been produced for bias in test items (Gotkin & Reynolds, 1981). However, different models may identify different items as biased. In one comparison Ironson and Sebkovial (1979) applied four different methods to analyze item bias in the National Longitudinal Study test battery. Three methods (chi-square for group differences, transformed item difficulty, and item characteristic curves) identified many of the same items as biased in evaluating 1,691 black high school seniors contrasted to 1,794 white twelfth graders. However, there was little agreement between these item evaluations and the bias items selected using a method proposed by Green and Draper (1972).

Recently, there has been debate about the effects of biased test items upon the differential validity of a test. In one theoretical example, 25% of the items on a test were presumed to be so biased that minority test takers would be expected to perform at chance level. Despite random performance, according to this simulation, there would be only slight and perhaps undetectable differences in validity coefficients for minority and majority group members (Drasgow, 1982). One year after the publication of this paper, Dobko and Kehoe (1983) reported that the result was artificial and dependent on an unusual usage of the term "test bias." Using a more general definition of test bias and biased items, they suggested that failure to find differences in validity coefficients is consistent with the belief that the tests are equally valid for members of different ethnic and racial groups.

In summary, studies have tended not to support the popular belief that items have different meanings for different groups. However, we must continue to evaluate the fairness of test items. On some occasions careful reviews of tests have identified questionable items. Many tests are carelessly constructed, and every effort should be taken to purge items that have the potential for being biased.

Criterion Validity

College administrators who use standardized test scores to forecast first-year performance are faced with difficult problems. On the average, minority applicants have lower test scores than do nonminority applicants. At the same time most universities and colleges are attempting to increase their minority enrollments. Because minority applicants are considered as a separate category, it is appropriate to ask whether the tests have differential predictive power for the two groups of applicants.

Criterion validity of a test is typically evaluated using the coefficient of correlation between the test and some criterion and by examining regression plots and scatter diagrams. If college grades are the criterion (the variable we are trying to forecast), the validity of a test such as the SAT would be represented by the correlation between the SAT and first-year college grades.

To understand criterion validity, it is often valuable to study regression lines separately for different groups. Figure 1 shows a regression line that represents each of two groups equally well. Group A appears to be performing less well than Group B on both the test (predictor) and the criterion scores. For example, the regression for Group A and for Group B have the same slope and intercept. There is little evidence for test bias in Figure 1; Group B has high scores on the test and exhibits better performance on the criterion.

Figure 2 represents a different situation. In this instance, there is a separate regression line for each group. The slopes of the two lines are the same, and that is why the two are parallel. However, the intercepts, or points at which the lines cross the vertical axis, differ. A particular test score gives one expected criterion score for regression line A and another expected criterion score for regression line B. For a test score of 8, the expected criterion score from regression line A is 6, while the expected criterion score from regression line B is 10. The

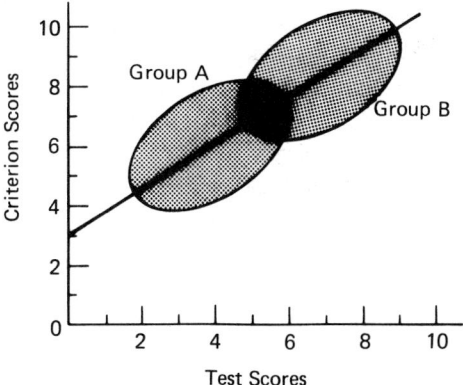

Figure 1. A single regression slope can predict performance equally well for two groups. However, the means for the two groups differ. (*Source:* From *Psychological Testing: Principles, Applications and Issues,* by R. Kaplan and D. Sacuzzo. Copyright (©) 1982 by Wadsworth, Inc. Reprinted by permission of Brooks/Cole Publishing Company, Monterey, California.)

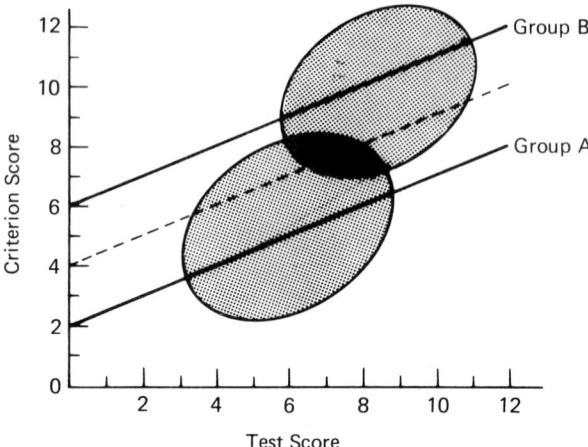

Figure 2. Regression lines with equal slopes but different intercepts. (*Source:* From *Psychological Testing: Principles, Applications and Issues*, by R. Kaplan and D. Sacuzzo. Copyright (©) 1982 by Wadsworth, Inc. Reprinted by permission of Brooks/Cole Publishing Company, Monterey, California.)

dotted line in Figure 2 is based on a combination of regression lines A and B. A test score of 8 from this combined (dotted) regression line gives an expected criterion score of 8. Thus the combined regression line actually overpredicts performance on the criterion for Group A and underpredicts performance for Group B. According to this example, the use of a single regression line produces discrimination in favor of Group A and against Group B.

Some evidence suggests that this situation is descriptive of the relationship between the SAT and college grade point average (Cleary, 1968, Kallingal, 1971; Pfeifer & Sedlacek, 1971; Temp, 1971). Each of the studies cited above showed that the relationship between college performance and SAT scores was best described by two separate regression equations. Using a combined regression equation, which is commonly the case in practice, overpredicts how well minority students will do in college and tends to underpredict the performance of majority-group students. In other words, it appears that the SAT used with a single regression line yields biased predictions, and the bias is in favor of minority groups and against majority group students.

Since the lines in Figure 2 are parallel, the slope of the lines is about the same for each group. The equal slopes suggest equal predictive validity. Most standardized intelligence, aptitude, and achievement tests do confirm the relationships shown in the figure (Reynolds, 1980; Reynolds & Nigl, 1981; Reschly & Sabers, 1979). Thus there is little evidence that tests such as the SAT predict college performance differently for different groups or that IQ tests have different correlations with achievement tests for black, white, or Hispanic children. This finding has been reported for the SAT (Temp, 1971), preschool tests (Reynolds, 1980), and IQ tests such as the WISC-R (Reschly & Sabers, 1979). Whether separate or combined regression lines are used depends on different definitions of bias. (We return to this issue later in the chapter. The interpretation of tests for assessing different groups can be strongly influenced by personal and moral convictions.) It is worth noting that the situation shown in Figure 2 is independent of differences in mean scores. The differences in mean scores in the figure are equal to the differences between the two regression lines.

A third situation outlined by Cleary and her colleagues (Cleary, Humphreys, Kendrick, & Wesman, 1975) is shown in Figure 3. In this figure, there are two regression lines, but the lines are no longer parallel. In this situation, the coefficient for one group is different from the coefficient for the other group. In the situation presented in Figure 2, we found that each group was best represented by its own regression line. In this case, using a common regression line causes error in predicting scores for each group. However, the situation depicted in Figure 2 is not hopeless, and indeed some practitioners feel that this situation is useful because it may help increase the accuracy of predictions (Cleary, 1968). However, Figure 3 demonstrates a more hopeless situation. In this case the test is differentially valid for the two groups, meaning that the test will have an entirely different meaning for each group. Although empirical studies have rarely turned up such a case, there are some known examples of differential slopes (Mercer, 1979). An extensive discussion of differential validity is presented by Bartlett and O'Leary (1969).

ALTERNATIVE TESTS

To many American psychologists the defense of psychological tests has not been totally satisfactory. Those who do not think that the tests are fair suggest one

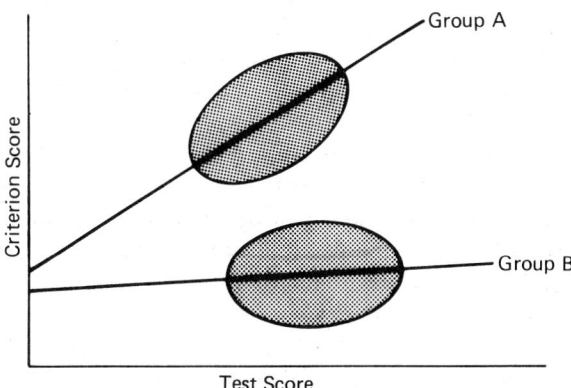

Figure 3. Regression lines with different slopes suggest that a test has different meanings for different groups. This is the most clear-cut example of test bias. (*Source:* From *Psychological Testing: Principles, Applications and Issues,* by R. Kaplan and D. Sacuzzo. Copyright (©) 1982 by Wadsworth, Inc. Reprinted by permission by Brooks/Cole Publishing Company, Monterey, California.)

of two alternatives: restrict the use of psychological tests for minority students (Williams, 1974), or develop psychological assessment strategies that suit minority children. Advocates of the first alternative have launched a legal battle to establish restrictions on the use of tests. This group emphasizes that we must try to find selection procedures that will end all discriminatory practices and protect the interests of minority-group members.

In this section various approaches to the second alternative are reviewed. In particular, five different assessment approaches are examined: the Chitling Test, the Black Intelligence Test of Cultural Homogeneity, the System of Multicultural Pluralistic Assessment, the Kaufman Assessment Battery for Children, and a Reaction time measure. Each of these approaches is different, yet they are all based on one common assumption: minority children have not had the opportunity to learn how to answer items on tests that reflect traditional, white, middle-class values.

Ignorance versus Stupidity

In a California trial about the use of testing in public schools, *Larry P. v. Wilson Riles*, the judge made an abrasive but insightful comment. Both sides in the case agreed that minority children perform more poorly on the standardized tests. The major issue debated by the witnesses was the meaning of the scores. One side argued that the scores reflect the underlying trait of intelligence. In other words, they allegedly measure how smart a child is. Witnesses for the other side suggested that the tests measure only whether the child has learned the appropriate responses needed to perform well on the test. This position claims that the tests do not measure how smart the child is, but only whether the child has been exposed to the information on the test. After hearing the testimony for the different points of view, the judge concluded that the issue was really one of ignorance versus stupidity. Although this comment appears abrasive and racist, it is quite insightful. There are two potential explanations for why some children do more poorly on standardized tests than do other children. One explanation is that they are less intelligent. In the words of the judge, this would be the stupidity explanation. The other explanation is that some children performed more poorly because they are ignorant. In other words, they simply have not learned the right responses for a particular test. If ignorance is the explanation, differences in IQ scores are less to be concerned about because they can be changed. The stupidity explanation is more damaging because it implies that the lower test scores obtained by black students are a product of some deficit that cannot be easily changed.

The term ignorance implies that differences can easily be abolished. Just as some minority children are ignorant about how to answer items that might predict success in the white, middle-class culture, some white, middle-class children could be labeled ignorant about how to succeed in the world of a ghetto child. This proposition is illustrated by the Chitling Test.

The Chitling Test

Many years ago animal psychologists talked about higher and lower animals. The higher animals were considered to be intelligent because they could do some of the same things humans can do, and the lower animals were considered to be unintelligent because they could not perform like humans. However, in 1969, a famous article by Hodos and Campbell changed the thinking of many students of animal behavior. Hodos and Campbell argued that all animals are equally intelligent for the environments in which they live. We cannot compare the intelligence of a rat with that of a cat because a rat is adapted to a rat's environment and a cat is adapted to a cat's environment. Both animals are best suited to survive in the environment they occupy.

The same insight seems not to have permeated the world of human affairs. Because of poverty and discrimination, minority and nonminority children grow up in different environments. To be successful in each of these environments requires different skills and knowledge. A psychological test may consider survival in only one of these environments, and this is usually the white, middle-class environment. Using one of these tests for impoverished children is analogous, therefore, to testing a cat on a task designed to determine how well a rat is adapted to a rat's environment.

The Chitling Test was developed by black sociologist Adrian Dove to demonstrate that there is a body of information about which the white middle class is ignorant. Dove named his effort the Dove Counterbalance General Intelligence Test, but it has become known as just the Chitling Test ("Taking the Chitling Test," 1968). A major aim in developing the Chitling Test was to show that blacks and whites have different approaches to communication.

Items on the Chitling Test ask about the definitions of a "handkerchief head," a "gas head," a "blood," "Dixie Hummingbirds," and several other items. In 1968, those who had grown up in a ghetto outperformed white, middle-class students.

However, no more than face validity has been established for the Chitling Test. No body of evidence demonstrates that the test successfully predicts performance on any important criterion. In fact, standardized tests predict performance for both minority and nonminority students, and the Chitling Test predicts performance for neither group. The Chitling Test may turn out to be a valid test of how streetwise someone is. Yet any generalizations must await validity evidence. Dove described his efforts to develop an intelligence test as "half-serious." But we have seen that the test does identify an area of content on which the races differ and blacks outperform whites.

The Black Intelligence Test of Cultural Homogeneity

To many observers, the use of intelligence tests is seen as a subtle and dangerous form of racism. Since the tests are supported by validity studies, they are given the endorsement of scientific objectivity (Garcia, 1981). Robert Williams, a well-known black psychologist, has labeled this phenomenon scientific racism (1974). Williams views IQ and standardized achievement tests as "nothing but updated versions of the old signs down South that read 'for Whites only' (1974, p. 34).

Of particular interest to Williams and his colleagues is the assessment of survival potential with a Survival Quotient (SQ). This quotient is more important than is assessment of IQ, which only indicates the likelihood of succeeding in the white community. As a beginning, Williams developed the Black Intelligence Test of Cultural Homogeneity (BITCH), which asks respondents to define 100 vocabulary words relevant to Afro-American culture. The words came from the Afro-American Slang Dictionary and from William's personal experience interacting with black Americans. Black people obtain higher scores than did their white counterparts on the BITCH. When Williams administered the BITCH to 100 16- to 18-year-olds from each group, the average score for black subjects was 87.07 (out of 100). The mean score for the whites was significantly lower (51.07). Williams argues that traditional IQ and achievement tests are nothing more than culture-specific tests that assess how much white children know about white culture. The BITCH is also a culture-specific test, but one on which the black subjects outperform the whites.

Although the BITCH does tell us a lot about the cultural loading in intelligence and achievement tests, it has received mixed reviews. The reliability data reported by Williams show that the BITCH is quite reliable for black test takers (standard error less than 3 points on the 100-point scale) and acceptably reliable for white test takers (standard error about 6). (Conventional tests have similar reliabilities for both groups; Oakland & Feigenbaum, 1979.) However, little convincing data on the BITCH are available. Although the test manual does report some studies, the samples are small and not representative of any clearly defined population (Cronbach, 1978). Low correlations between the BITCH and California Achievement Test are reported in the manual (Williams, 1972). The difficulty is that we cannot determine whether the BITCH does predict how well a person will survive on the streets, how well he or she will do in school, in life, or in anything else. The test does assess word association, but it seems to give no information on reasoning abilities.

Further studies are needed to determine whether the BITCH does what it is supposed to do. One of the rationales for the test is that it will identify children who have been unfairly assigned to classes for the Educable Mentally Retarded (EMR) on the basis of IQ scores. In one study, Long and Anthony (1974) attempted to determine how many Black EMR children would be reclassified if they were retested with the BITCH. Among a small and limited sample of 30 Black EMR high school students from Gainesville, Florida, all the students who performed poorly on the WISC also performed below the first percentile on the BITCH. Using the BITCH served to reclassify none of the students. In another study, middle-class black seventh graders obtained higher BITCH scores than did their white middle-class counterparts. However, there were no differences between lower-class blacks and whites (Andre, 1976). These data do not strongly support the value of the BITCH. In its present state, the BITCH can be a valuable tool for measuring white familiarity with the black community. When white teachers or administrators are sent to schools that have predominantly black enrollments, the BITCH may be used to determine how much they know about the culture. Furthermore, the BITCH may be used to assess the extent to which a black person is in touch with his or her own community and may be useful in building black pride (Milgram, 1974). As Cronbach (1978) notes, people with good abstract reasoning skills may function poorly if they are unfamiliar with the community in which they live. Similarly, people with poor reasoning skills may get along just fine if they are familiar with the community.

The System of Multicultural Pluralistic Assessment

The system of Multicultural Pluralistic Assessment (SOMPA) (Mercer, 1979), developed by sociologist Jane Mercer, offers a strong challenge to traditional views of testing. Before reviewing the SOMPA and the evaluations of it, it is instructive to review Mercer's beliefs about the social and political implications of testing.

Mercer argues that beliefs about fairness are related to the social structure. She agrees with sociologist K. Mannheim (1936) that members of the politically dominant group provide the interpretation of events within a society and they do so from their own perspective. The traditional psychometric literature on IQ tests provides a scientific rationale for the dominant group to restrict minority-group members by demonstrating that the minority-group members do not have the language and knowledge skills to perform well in a white cultural setting. The feedback given to the minority groups is not that they are ignorant about the rules of success in another culture (just as the dominant group would be in a minority culture), but that they are stupid and unlikely to succeed. Mercer emphasizes that we must take into consideration that some individuals are working from a different knowledge base.

It is not possible to give a complete description of the SOMPA here. The system is complex, and many technical issues have been raised about its validity and its applicability (Brown, 1979a, 1979b; Clarizio, 1979a, 1979b; Goodman, 1977, 1979; Mercer, 1979; Oakland, 1979).

One important philosophical assumption underlies the development of the SOMPA. This assumption is that all cultural groups have the same average potential. Any differences between cultural groups are assumed to be caused by differences in access to cultural experiences. Those who do not perform well on the tests are not well informed about the criteria for success that are usually set forth by the dominant group. However, within groups that have had the same cultural experiences, not all individuals are expected to be the same; and assessments of these differences is a better measure of ability than is assessment of differences between cultural groups.

Mercer has been concerned about the consequences of labeling a child as mentally retarded (Mercer, 1972). She has convincingly argued that many children are incorrectly identified as retarded and that they suffer severely as a result of this inaccurate branding. In particular, she is distressed that classes for EMR students contain a disproportionate number of minority children. Mercer maintains that some minority students score low on the traditional tests because they are merely ignorant about the ways of the dominant culture, but they are not mentally retarded. Students may also be misclassified due to medical problems. Thus a fair system of evaluation must include medical assessment. It must also include the assessment of children relative to other children who have had similar life experiences. The basic point of divergence between the SOMPA and earlier approaches to assessment is the SOMPA attempts to integrate three different approaches to assessment: medical, social, and pluralistic.

SOMPA System.   One of the most consistent findings in the field of public health is that members of low-income groups have more health problems than do those who are economically better off. The medical component of the SOMPA system asks: "Is the child an intact organism?" (Mercer, 1979, p. 92). The rationale for this portion is that medical problems can interfere with a child's performance on mental measures and in school.

The social system component attempts to determine whether a child is functioning at a level that would be expected by social norms. For example, does the child do what is expected by family members, peer groups, or the community? Mercer feels that test users and developers typically adopt only a social-system orientation. For example, if a test predicts who will do well in school, it is forecasting behavior that is expected by the dominant social system. However, Mercer emphasizes that the social-system approach is a narrow one because only the dominant group in society defines the criteria for success (Reschly, 1981).

The pluralistic component of the SOMPA recognizes that different subcultures are associated with different life experiences. Only within these subgroups do individuals have common experiences. Thus tests should assess individuals against others in the same subculture. It is important to recognize the distinction between the criteria for defining deviance in the pluralistic model and in the social-system mode. The social-system model used the norms of society as the criteria, while the pluralistic model uses the norms within a particular group.

The SOMPA attempts to assess children relative to each of these models. The medical portion of the SOMPA package includes physical measures such as visual tests, tests of hearing, and tests of motor functioning. The social-system portion is similar to most assessment procedures. The entire WISC-R is given and evaluated according to the regular criteria. Finally, the pluralistic portion also uses WISC-R scores but evaluates them against those for groups that have similar social and cultural backgrounds. In other words, the WISC-R scores are adjusted for socioeconomic background. These adjusted scores are known as estimated learning potentials (ELP).

The major dispute between Mercer and her many critics concerns the validity of the SOMPA. Mercer (1979) points out that a test itself is not valid or invalid but the inferences that are made on the basis of the test scores are. She insists that the ELPs cannot be validated in the same way as are other test scores. (Validating a test by predicting who will do well in school is appropriate only for the social-system model.) Mercer argues that the criteria for evaluating the ELP must be different. She states that the appropriate validity criteria for ELPs should be the percentage of variance in WISC-R scores that is accounted for by sociocultural variables. Many SOMPA critics (Brown, 1979a; Clarizio, 1979b; Goodman, 1979; Oakland, 1979), however, feel that a test should always be validated by demonstrating that it predicts performance. The correlation between ELPs and school achievement is around .40, while the correlation between the WISC-R and school achievement is around .60 (Oakland, 1979). Thus ELPs are a poorer predictor than WISC-R scores of school success. Mercer refutes these critics by arguing that the test is not designed to identify which children will do well in school. Its purpose is to determine which children are mentally retarded. Yet it gives minority students additional IQ points to compensate for their impoverished backgrounds. In one example, Sattler (1982) showed that the system can boost a child with a full-scale WISC-R score in the 2nd percentile all the way up to the 70th percentile. This can be done only by comparing children with others who have had the same life experiences.

Accepting Mercer's argument may produce a quota system for EMR classes. Using ELPs should make the proportions of ethnic groups in EMR classes more representative than they now are. Because several states have adopted the SOMPA, we may soon be able to determine the ultimate effect of the system. There is no question that it will identify fewer minority children as EMR students. This may produce cost reductions because the costs of educating EMR students are higher than average. Only time will tell whether children no longer considered EMR students will benefit. Mercer's (1972) research suggests that a big part of the battle is just getting more children labeled as normal. Her critics retaliate by suggesting that the effects of labeling are weak and inconsequential (Thorndike, 1968). They argue that no matter what these children are called they will need some special help in school.

The Kaufman Assessment Battery for Children (KABC)

In 1983, Kaufman and Kaufman introduced a new approach to the assessment of intellectual abilities in children. Their tests, known as the Kaufman Assessment Battery for Children (K-ABC), separates two fundamental components of human information processing: simultaneous processing and sequential processing. Similar distinctions have been made by several cognitive psychologists with only slight variations in the label. For instance, the Kaufman's Sequential-Simultaneous distinction is quite similar to the Successive-Simultaneous distinction (Das, Kirby and Járman, 1975, 1979; Luria, 1966), the Analytic-Holistic Distinction (Ornstein, 1972) or the Serial-Parallel/Sequential-Multiple Distinction (Neisser, 1967). As Kaufman (1983) argues, there has been a strong concensus that there is a basic dichotomy in types of human information processing. However, there has been less concensus about the neuroanatomical site responsible for this distinction. Some attributed it to a temporal/occipital-parietal distinction while others describe it as left brain/right brain difference (Kaufman and Kaufman, 1983).

The K-ABC is an individually administered intelligence test that was standardized on a nationwide (American) sample of normal and exceptional children ranging in age from 2½ to 12½ years. In each age range, the test measures sequential and simultaneous information processing. In addition, it has a separate section for achievement. One of the features of the K-ABC is that it proportedly does not have the same racial bias that characterizes most other IQ tests. Data for the WISC-R Standardization program show the mean score of white children (ages 6 through 16) to be 102.3, while the mean for black children in the same age range is 86.4 (Kaufman and Doppelt, 1976). A separate study on WISC-R data showed the mean for a sample of Hispanic children to be 91.9 (Mercer, 1979).

Mean scores for the K-ABC are considerably closer together for black and white students. For white students, K-ABC scores are nearly equivalent to the WISC-R scores (Mean = 102.0). For the 807 black students in the standardization sample, the mean was 95.0, while it was 98.9 for the 106 Hispanic students in the standardization program (Kaufman and Kaufman, 1983). For the sequential processing portion of the K-ABC, black, white, and Hispanics in the 2½- through 12½-age range performed at near equivalent levels. In addition, Hispanic students performed at near equivalent levels to the white standardization sample.

Although predictive validity data are not presented separately for race or ethnic groups, some evidence suggests that the concurrent validity of the K-ABC is comparable for different groups. For example, the correlation between the K-ABC mental processing composite score and the Woodcock Reading Mastery Test was .60 for the white sample in one validation study. For the black and Mexican-American subsamples, these correlations were .56 and .70, respectively. In another study, the K-ABC correlated slightly more highly with the KeyMath Diagnostic Arithmetic Test for black and Hispanic samples than it did for a white sample (Kaufman and Kaufman, 1983). Although a majority of the 43 validity studies reported in the manual had at least some minority subjects, these are the only studies that reported validity data separately for different ethnic or racial groups. In summary, the K-ABC appears to be a promising approach. Mean differences between racial groups are smaller than they are for other intelligence tests. Yet the K-ABC appears to have firm roots in empirical psychology and to have a substantial record of reliability and validity. Further validity data will be required to confirm or disconfirm these encouraging observations.

Factor Theory and IQ Differences

In 1927, Charles Spearman presented a discussion of racial differences in intelligence. He argued that the amount by which groups differed was not consistent across different mental tasks. However, he suggested that there was a g factor or general intelligence factor that was common to many mental tasks. The g factor is widely discussed in the psychological literature and the concept has endured for more than a half century. The g factor can be obtained from a factor analysis of mental tasks. It is the primary factor representing tests of verbal, numerical, spatial, and other general mental abilities.

The degree to which black and white subjects differ in mental test scores differs across studies. Jensen (1983) argued that these different results can be explained by the tasks used in the different studies. He suggested that tasks that loaded highly on the g factor are more likely to show the differences than will tasks with low g loading. Furthermore, he suggested that scores on a reaction time task are highly correlated with the g factor. Black and white subjects differ in their mean performance on these reaction time tests. Nevertheless, the tasks do not require language and should be no more familiar to one group than to the other.

In Jensen's most recent work, he has been careful not to offer a causal mechanism for these differences. Yet many of his critics assume that Jensen's view of intelligence regards abilities as fixed and unchangable over the course of time. Robert Sternberg (cited in Cordes, 1983) disagrees that intelligence tests measure a fixed trait. Instead, he suggests that they measure cognitive processes that may be altered through experience. Jones (1983) and others have demonstrated that Black-White differences in standardized achievement scores narrowed between 1971 and 1980. They noted that math scores tended to diverge during the course of time. Yet multiple regression analysis demonstrated that math scores are well predicted from the number of algebra and geometry courses a student has completed. Black children took fewer of these courses and thus did more poorly on the math tests. It was argued that the difference in test scores could be irradicated by providing more mathematics training for black youth.

In summary, it was suggested that cognitive abilities measured by IQ and achievement tests can be modified by educational experiences. It is these complex abilities that load highly on the g factor. We expect research to shed more light on this debate in the years to come.

Ethical Concerns and the Definition of Test Bias

It is difficult to define the term *test bias* since different authors have different views (Cole, 1981; Darlington, 1978; Flaugher, 1978; Hunter & Schmidt, 1976). These different definitions represent commitments to underlying ethical viewpoints about the way various groups ought to be treated. Hunter and Schmidt (1976) identify three ethical positions that set the tone for much of the debate: unqualified individualism, the use of quotas, and qualified individualism. All these positions are concerned with the use of tests to select people either for jobs or for training programs (including college).

Supporters of unqualified individualism would use tests to select the most qualified individuals they could find. In this case, users of tests would be indifferent to the race or sex of applicants. The goal would be to predict those who would be expected to perform best on the job or in school. According to this viewpoint, a test is fair if it finds the best candidates for the job or for admission to school. If race or sex were a valid predictor of performance beyond the information in the test, the unqualified individualist would see nothing wrong with considering this information in the selection process.

A quite different ethical approach to selection is to use quotas. Quota systems explicitly recognize race and sex differences. If the population of a state is 20% black, then supporters of a quota system might argue that 20% of the new medical students in the state-supported medical school should also be black. Selection procedures are regarded as biased if the actual percentage of applicants admitted is different from the percentage in the population; each group should have a fair share of the representation (Gordon & Terrell, 1981). This fair-share selection process gives less emphasis than the testing process to how well people in the different groups are expected to do once they are selected (Darlington, 1971; Hunter & Schmidt, 1976; S. Thorndike, 1971).

The final moral position considered by Hunter and Schmidt might be viewed as a compromise between unqualified individualism and a quota system. Qualified individualism, like unqualified individualism, embraces the notion that the best-qualified persons should be the ones selected. But unqualified individualists also take information about race, sex, and religion into consideration if it helps predict performance on the criterion. Not to do so results in underprediction of performance for one group and overprediction of performance for another group. Qualified individualists, however, recognize that, although failing to include group characteristics (race, sex, and religion) may lead to differential accuracy in prediction, this differential prediction may counteract known effects of discrimination. It may, for example, lead to underprediction of the performance of the majority group and overprediction of the performance of the minority group. The qualified individualist may choose not to include information about personal characteristics in selection because ignoring this information may serve the interest of minority-group members.

Each of these ethical positions can be related to a particular statistical definition of test bias, and we now turn to these definitions. Table 1 shows several different models of test bias based on different definitions of fairness. All these models are based on different definitions of fairness. All these models are based on regression lines as we discussed above. The models discussed in Table 1 are relevant to tests that are used for selection purposes, including job-placement tests and tests used to select students for college or for advanced-degree programs.

The straight regression approach described in Table 1 (see also Cleary, 1968) represents the unqualified individualism position. The result of this approach is that a large number of majority-group members may be selected. In other words, this approach maintains that an employer or a school should be absolutely color and gender blind. The reason for considering ethnicity or sex is to improve prediction of future performance. This approach has been favored by business

Table 1. Different Models of Test Fairness

Model	Reference	Use of Regression	Rationale	Effect on Minority Selection	Effect on Average Criterion Performance
Regression	Cleary (1968)	Separate regression lines are used for different groups. Those with the highest predicted criterion scores are selected.	This is fair because those with the highest estimated level of success are selected.	Few minority-group members selected.	High.
Constant Ratio	R. L. Thorndike (1971)	Points equal to about half of the average difference between the groups are added to the test scores of the group with the lower score. Then a single regression line is used, and those with the highest predicted scores are selected.	This is fair because it better reflects the potential of the lower-scoring group.	Some increase in the numbr of minority-group members selected.	Somewhat lower.
Cole/Darlington	Cole (1973); Darlington (1971, 1978)	Separate regression equations are used for each group, and	This is fair because it selects more potentially successful	Larger increase in the number of minority-group mem-	Lower.

Table 1. (*Continued*)

Model	Reference	Use of Regression	Rationale	Effect on Minority Selection	Effect on Average Criterion Performance
Cole/Darlington		points are added to scores of those from the lower group to assure that those with the same criterion score have the same predictor score.	persons from the lower group.	bers selected.	
Quota	Dunnette and Borman (1979)	The proportion of persons to be selected from each group is predetermined. Separate regression equations are used to select those persons from each group who are expected to perform highest on the criterion.	This is fair because members of different subgroups are selected based on their proportions in the community.	Best representation of minority groups.	About the same as for the Cole/Darlington model.

Source. Kaplan and Saccuzzo (1982, p. 456).
Note. Based on Dunnette and Borman (1979).

because it ensures the highest rate of productivity among the employees who are selected by the procedure.

At the other extreme is the quota system. To achieve fair-share representation, separate selection procedures are developed. One procedure, for example, is used to select the best available black applicants, and another procedure is used to select the best available nonblack applicants. If a community has 42% black residents, the first procedure would be used to select 42% of the employees and the other procedure would be used to select the other 58%.

The difficulty with the quota system is that it may lead to greater rates of failure among some groups. Suppose, for example, that a test had been devised to select telephone operators and that the test did indeed predict who would succeed on the job. However, the test selected 70% women and only 30% men. The quota system would encourage the use of separate cutoff scores so that the proportion of men selected would approach 50%. But, because the women scored higher on the average, they would perform better on the job, resulting in a higher rate of failure among men. Thus, although quota systems often aid in increasing the selection of underrepresented groups, they also make it likely that the underrepresented groups will experience failure.

Table 1 shows two other models (Cole, 1973; Darlington, 1971; Thorndike, 1971). These models represent compromises between the quota and the un-qualified-individualism points of view. In each of these cases, there is an attempt to select the most qualified people, yet there is some adjustment for being from a minority group. When people from two different groups have the same test score, these procedures give a slight edge to the person from the lower group and places the person from the higher group to a slight disadvantage. Although these approaches have been attacked for being based on faulty logic (Hunter & Schmidt, 1976, 1978), plausible defenses have been offered. The effect of these procedures is to increase the number of people selected from underrepresented groups. However, these procedures also result in lower expected performance scores on the criterion.

Which of these approaches is right and which is wrong? That is a value decision that embraces different philosophical beliefs about fairness.

LEGAL CONTROVERSIES

The U.S. government has attempted to establish clear standards for the use of psychological tests. Regulation of tests comes in many forms, including executive orders, laws created by legislative bodies, and actions by the courts. The most important legal development was the passage of the 1964 Civil Rights Act. Title VII of this act created the Equal Employment Opportunity Commission (EEOC). The EEOC in 1970 published guidelines for employee-selection procedures. In 1978, it released a new document entitled, "Uniform Guidelines on Employee Selection Procedure." These are the major guidelines for the use of psychological tests in education and in industry.

The 1978 guidelines are stricter, more condensed, and less ambiguous about the allowable use of psychological test scores than were the 1970 guidelines. The original act clearly prohibited discrimination in employment on the basis of race, color, religion, sex, or national origin. However, the 1978 guidelines made clear that any screening procedure, including the use of psychological tests, may be viewed as having adverse impact if it systematically rejects substantially higher proportions of minority than nonminority applicants. When any selection procedure does so, the employer must demonstrate that the procedure has documented validity. However, the guidelines are specific about the acceptable criteria for the use of a test. The guidelines have been adopted by a variety of federal agencies including the Civil Service Commission, the Department of Justice, the Department of Labor, and the Department of the Treasury. The Office of Federal Contract Compliance has the direct power to cancel government contracts held by employers who do not comply with these guidelines. In the next few years it is almost certain that these guidelines will provide the basis for law suits filed by both minority and nonminority job applicants who feel they have been mistreated in their employment pursuits.

It is worth noting that the guidelines are used only for cases in which adverse impact is suspected. When adverse impact is not suspected, organizations are under little pressure to use valid selection procedures (McCormick & Ilgen, 1980). As Guion (1976) observes, "organizations have the right to even be fairly stupid in their employment practices as long as they are stupid fairly" (p. 811).

Specific Laws

Other regulatory schemes attempt to control the use of tests. Recently, Truth in Testing Laws have been passed in two states (New York and California) and similar bills have been introduced in several other states and at the federal level.

The New York Truth in Testing Law is one of the most controversial measures ever to hit the testing field. The New York law was motivated by an extensive investigation of the Educational Testing Service (ETS) by the New York Public Interest Research Group (NYPIRG). Other testing companies are affected by the law, but the New York law was written with ETS specifically in mind.

ETS was created by the College Entrance Examination Board, the American Council on Education, and the Carnegie Foundation in 1948. Its original and best-known mission was to create and administer aptitude tests such as the SAT. By 1979, ETS was responsible for more than 300 testing programs, including the Graduate Management Admission Test (GMAT), the Graduate Record Examination (GRE), the Multi-State Bar Exam, and the Law School Admission Test (LSAT). The assets of the company exceeded $25 million, and its gross yearly income exceeded $80 million.

NYPIRG seemed upset by the wealth and success of ETS, yet what bothered NYPIRG more was the power ETS has. Each year several million people take tests designed and administered by ETS, and the results of these tests have pronounced effects on their lives (Brill, 1973; Kiersh, 1979; Levy, 1979). Many educational programs take the scores seriously. Students scoring poorly on the LSAT, for example, may be denied entrance to law school, and this rejection may eventually affect many important aspects of their lives. Higher scores may have resulted in a higher income, more occupational status, and greater self-esteem for them.

On investigation, NYPIRG became dissatisfied with the available information on test validity, the calculation of test scores, and the financial accounting of ETS. The Truth in Testing Law responds to these objections by requiring testing companies to (1) disclose all studies on the validity of a test, (2) provide a complete disclosure to students about what scores mean and how they were calculated, and (3) on request by a student, provide a copy of the test questions, the correct answers, and the student's answers.

The first two portions are essentially noncontroversial. The test developers argue that they do disclose all pertinent information on validity, and they do release many public documents highlighting the strengths and weaknesses of their tests. Furthermore, ETS strongly encourages institutions using their tests to perform local validity studies. Any of these studies can be published in scholarly journals with no interference from ETS. However, NYPIRG provided some evidence that ETS and other testing companies have files of secret data that they do not make public because these data may reflect poorly on the product. The second aspect of the law was included because ETS sometimes reports index scores without telling students how the index was calculated and the exact index value being reported.

The controversial third portion of the law may turn out to seriously decrease the value of testing programs. Requiring that the test questions be returned to students means that the same questions cannot be used in future versions of the test. Several problems are expected to result from this policy. First, it decreases the validity of the test. With the items constantly changing, the test essentially becomes a new test each time the items change. As a result, it is impossible to accumulate a record of construct validity.

Second, it is difficult to equate scores across years. For example, a graduate school must often consider students who took the GRE in different years. If the test itself is different each year, it is difficult to compare the score of students who took the test at different times. Although the bill eventually adopted in New York did allow testing companies to keep some of the items secret for equating purposes, this practice falls short of being a satisfactory solution. Equating can be accomplished, but it may be difficult without increasing the chances of error.

Third, the most debated problem associated with the disclosure of test items is that it will greatly increase the costs to ETS and other testing companies. It has been estimated that test construction costs range from $50,000 to $165,000 (APA, Committee on Psychological Tests and Assessment, 1983). ETS will probably not absorb these inflated costs but will pass them on to the consumer. Just how high the cost of taking a test will go is a matter of conjecture. Experts within the testing industry warn that the costs could be more than twice what they were before the law was passed. NYPIRG doubts that the cost of writing new items will have any substantial impact on the cost of taking the test. Only 5% of the students' fees for taking a test go to question development, while 22% to 27% go to company profit. Backers of the law feel there should be only minimal increases in fees and that ETS, as a nonprofit and tax-exempt institution, should take the cost of writing new items out of its substantial profits.

One immediate impact of the New York Truth in Testing Law was that it stimulated other similar proposals. A similar law was passed in California and bills were introduced in several other states. The Educational Testing Act of 1979 was offered to the U.S. House of Representatives in July 1979. The Educational Testing Act, which was proposed by Representatives Ted Weiss, Shirley Chisholm, and George Miller, was essentially the same as the New York Truth in Testing Law; the major provisions of the bills were almost identical. In effect, the Educational Testing Act of 1979 attempted to make the New York law a federal law. However, the federal bill was not enacted into law.

There is no question that the truth-in-testing bills were introduced by sincere and well-intentioned legislators. However, the laws are disturbing for two reasons. First, they politicize a process that has in the past been primarily academic. The issues in the debate were not presented in a scholarly fashion. Instead, they were presented (on both sides) in an adversarial manner. The debate thus got out of the hands of psychologists who have the training to interpret some of the complex technical issues. For example, in his testimony before a subcommittee of the House of Education and Labor Committee, Representative Weiss made many references to the bias in the tests. His major argument was that there are mean differences between different ethnic groups in test scores, yet mean difference is not usually considered evidence for test bias.

ETS does make booklets available to the public that present information on the scoring system, the validity, the reliability, and the standard error of measurement for each of their tests. People with no background in testing probably will not comprehend all this information, and the authors of the bills fail to recognize that the proper use of tests and test results is a technical problem that requires technical training in advanced courses such as psychological testing. For instance, we do not expect people to be able to practice medicine without the technical training given in medical school.

Second, we must consider the ultimate impact of the truth-in-testing legislation. One side argues that the new laws will make for a fairer and more honest testing industry. The other argues that students will now have to pay a higher price for a poorer product. If the requirement of test-item disclosure results in lower validity of the tests (which it most likely will), there will be greater error in selecting students than now exists. In other words, selection for admissions may become more random.

By summer of 1983, the Committee on Psychological Tests and Assessment of the American Psychological Association issued a formal statement on test-item disclosure legislation. The statement suggested that proposals for truth-in-testing legislation be postponed until the impact of the bills passed in California

Table 2.   Summary of American Psychological Association Statement on Testing Legislation

1. We recommend a "wait and see" period prior to enacting further legislation. The legislation enacted in New York and California has created a situation that can be viewed as a naturally occurring field experiment. A few years of studying this "experiment" is warranted before other legislation is passed or rejected.

2. We strongly support provisions encouraging the dissemination of information about test content, test purpose, validity, reliability, and interpretation of test scores. Test takers should have access to their individual results and interpretative information, especially where such test results are used for educational or employment decisions.

3. We oppose total disclosure of items from low volume tests or tests where item domains are finite (for instance measuring specific content areas).

4. We oppose disclosure of tests where interpretation is dependent upon a long history of research (for example, extensive norming); disclosure would result in loss of valid interpretation. This is particularly true of interest and personality measures.

5. In disclosure cases involving large volume tests testing a broad domain, we recommend at a minimum that only items used to determine test performance be disclosed. Pretesting and equating items should be protected from disclosure.

6. Where disclosure is deemed desirable, we encourage examination of alternative methods of conveying this information to test takers, such as partial disclosure (disclosure of one test after several administrations) or making sample tests available for perusal at a secure location.

7. We urge that any personnel selection or licensing procedure in use should be subject to the same scrutiny as tests, provided that sample size is sufficient for meaningful statistical analyses.

Source.   American Psychological Association Statement on Test Item Disclosure Legislation (August, 1983).

and New York could be evaluated. The committee's conclusions and recommendations are shown in Table 2.

Some Major Lawsuits

There have already been many lawsuits concerning the use of psychological tests, and the number can be expected to increase dramatically in the years to come. Some of the most important of these lawsuits are discussed in this chapter. It is important to realize that each of these cases was complex and involved considerably more evidence than can be reviewed here.

Early Desegregation Cases.   The fourteenth Amendment requires that all citizens be granted the equal protection of the laws. At the end of the nineteenth century, it was being argued that segregated schools did not offer such protection. In the famous 1896 case of *Plessy v. Ferguson,** the Supreme Court ruled that

*163 U.S. 537 (1896).

schools could remain segregated, but that the quality of the schools must be equal. This was the much acclaimed separate but equal ruling.

Perhaps the most influential ruling in the history of American public school education came in the case of *Brown v. Board of Education** in 1954. In the Brown case, the Supreme Court overturned the *Plessy v. Ferguson* decision and ruled that the schools must provide nonsegregated facilities for black and white students. In its opinion the court raised several issues that would eventually affect the use of psychological tests.

The most important pronouncement of Brown was that segregation was a denial of equal protection. In coming to its decision, the court made extensive use of testimony by psychologists. This testimony suggested that black children could be made to feel inferior if the school system kept the two races separate.

The story of the Brown case is well known, but what is less often discussed is the ugly history that followed. Many school districts did not want to desegregate, and the battle over busing and other mechanisms for desegregation continues today in many areas. Many of the current arguments against desegregation are based on fear of children leaving their own neighborhoods or on the stress on children who must endure long bus rides. The early resistance to the Brown decision was more clearly linked to the racist belief of Black inferiority.

Stell v. Savannah-Chatham County Board of Education.†

The most significant racist court case occurred when legal action was taken to desegregate the school system of Savannah, Georgia, on behalf of a group of black children. The conflict began when attorneys for two white children intervened. They argued that they were not opposed to desegregating on the basis of race but that black children did not have the ability to be in the same classrooms as Whites. Testimony from psychologists indicated that the median IQ score for black children was 81 while that for white children was 101. Because there was such a large difference in this trait (which was assumed to be genetic), the attorneys argued that it could be to the mutual disadvantage of both groups to congregate them in the same schools. Doing so might create even greater feelings of inferiority among black children and might create frustration that would eventually result in antisocial behavior.

The court essentially agreed with this testimony and ruled that the district should not desegregate. The judge's opinion reflected his view of what was in the best interest of all of the children. Later, this decision was reversed by Judge Griffin Bell of the U.S. Court of Appeal for the Fifth Circuit. In doing so, the court used the precedent set forth by Brown as the reason for requiring the Savannah district to desegregate. It is important to note that the validity of the

---

*347 U.S. 483 (1954), 349 U.S. (1955).
†220 F. Supp. 667, 668(S.D. Ga. 1963, rev'd 333 F.2d 55(5th Cir. 1964 cert. denied, 379 U.S. 933 (1964).

test scores, which were the primary evidence, was never discussed (Bersoff, 1979, 1981).

Hobson v. Hansen.[*] Stell was just one of many cases that attempted to resist the order set forth in the famous Brown desegregation case. Like Stell, many of these cases introduced test scores as evidence that black children were genetically incapable of learning or being educated in the same classrooms as white children. The courts routinely accepted this evidence. Given the current controversy regarding the use of psychological tests, it is remarkable that several years passed before the validity of the test scores became an issue.

The first major case to examine the validity of psychological tests was *Hobson v. Hansen.* The Hobson case is relevant to many of the current lawsuits. Unlike the early desegregation cases, it did not deal with sending black and white children to different schools. Instead, it concerned the placement of children once they arrived at a school. Although the courts had been consistent in requiring schools to desegregate, they tend to take a hands off approach with regard to placement of students in tracks once they arrived at their desegregated schools.

The Hobson case contested the use of group standardized ability tests to place students in different learning tracks. Julius W. Hobson was the father of two black children placed in a basic track by the District of Columbia School District. Carl F. Hansen was the superintendent for the district. Within the district, children were placed in honors, regular, general, and basic tracks on the basis of group ability tests. The honors track was designed to prepare children for college, while the basic track focused on skills and preparation for blue-collar jobs. Placement in the basic track makes it essentially impossible to prepare for a high income/high prestige profession.

The rub in Hobson was that racial groups were not equally represented among those assigned to the basic track. In effect, the tracking system served to racially segregate groups by placing black children in the basic track and white children in the other tracks. Psychological tests were the primary mechanism used to justify this separation. The Hobson case was decided in 1967 by Judge Skelly Wright of the federal district court of Washington, D.C. Just two years before the decision, the Supreme Court had ruled that a group is not denied equal protection by "mere classification" (Bersoff, 1979). Nevertheless, Judge Wright ruled against the use of the tracking system when based on group ability tests. After extensive expert testimony on the validity of the tests for minority children, the judge concluded that the tests discriminated against them. An interesting aspect of the opinion was that it claimed that grouping would be permissible if it were based on innate ability. The judge asserted that ability test scores were influenced by cultural experiences, and the dominant cultural group had an

[*]269 F. Supp. 401 (D.D.C. 1967).

unfair advantage on the tests and thereby gained admission to the tracks that provided the best preparation for high income/high prestige jobs.

Diana v. State Board of Education.* The decision in *Hobson v. Hansen* opened the door for a thorough examination of the use of standardized tests for the placement of students in EMR tracks. The case of Diana has particular implications for the use of standardized tests for bilingual children. Diana was one of nine Mexican-American elementary school children who had been placed in EMR classes on the basis of the WISC or Stanford-Binet. These nine children represented a class of bilingual children. They brought a class action suit against the California State Board of Education, contending that the use of standardized IQ tests for placement in EMR classes denied equal protection because the tests were standardized only for whites and had been administered by a non-Spanish-speaking psychometrist. Although only 18% of the children in Diana's school district had Spanish surnames, this group made up nearly one-third of the enrollment in EMR classes.

When originally tested in English, Diana achieved an IQ score of only 30. However, when retested in Spanish and English, her IQ was 79, which was high enough to keep her out of the EMR classes in her school district. Seven of the other eight plaintiffs also achieved scores high enough on retesting in Spanish to be taken out of the EMR classes.

When faced with this evidence, the California State Board of Education decided not to take the case to court. Instead, they adopted special provisions for the testing of Mexican-American and Chinese-American children. These provisions included the following:

1. If English was not the primary language, the children would be tested in their primary language.
2. Questions based on certain vocabulary and information that the children could not be expected to know would be eliminated.
3. The Mexican-American and Chinese-American children who had been assigned to EMR classes would be reevaluated with tests that used their primary language and nonverbal items.
4. New tests would be developed by the state that reflected Mexican-American culture and that were normed for Mexican-American children (Bersoff, 1979).

Later studies confirmed that bilingual children do score higher when tested in their primary language (Bergan & Parra, 1979).

The combination of the judgment in Hobson and the change in policy brought about by Diana forced many to question seriously the use of IQ tests for the assignment of children to EMR classes. However, these decisions were quite

*401 U.S. 424(a)(1971).

specific to the circumstances in the particular cases. Hobson dealt with group tests but did not discuss individual tests. However, individual tests are used more often than group tests to make final decisions for EMR placement. The ruling in Diana was limited strictly to bilingual children. These two cases were thus not relevant to black children placed in EMR classes on the basis of individual IQ tests. This specific area was left for the most important court battle of them all—*Larry P. v. Wilson Riles.*

Larry P. v. Wilson Riles*. In October 1979, Judge Robert Peckman of the Federal District Court for the Northern District of California handed down an opinion that declared that "The use of IQ tests which had a disproportionate effect on Black children violated the Rehabilitation Act, the Education for All Handicapped Children Act, Title VI, and the 14th Amendment when used to place children in EMR classes." Attorneys for Larry P., one of six black elementary school students who were assigned to EMR classes on the basis of IQ test results, had argued that the use of standardized IQ tests to place black children in EMR classes violated both the California constitution and the equal protection clause of the fourteenth Amendment (Opton, 1979), as well as those laws mentioned above.

The court first ruled in the case of Larry P. in 1972. It found that the school district incorrectly labeled Larry as EMR and violated his right to equal educational opportunity. As a result, a preliminary injunction was issued that prohibited that particular school district from using IQ tests for EMR placement decisions. Later, the California Department of Education called for a temporary moratorium on IQ testing until another court opinion on the validity of the tests could be obtained (Opton, 1979). The Larry P. case came before the same court that had issued the preliminary injunction in order to obtain a ruling on test validity for black children.

During the trial, both sides geared up for a particularly intense battle. Wilson Riles was the black superintendent of public instruction in California; he had instituted many significant reforms that benefited minority children. Thus it was particularly awkward to have a nationally recognized spokesperson for progressive programs named as the defendant in an allegedly racist scheme.

In defense of the use of tests, Riles and the state called many nationally recognized experts on IQ tests, including Lloyd Humphreys, Jerome Sattler, Robert Thorndike, Nadine Lambert, and Robert Gordon. These witnesses presented rather extensive evidence that IQ tests, particularly the Stanford-Binet and the WISC (which were used to test Larry and others), were not biased against blacks. Although the tests had not originally been normed for black populations, studies had demonstrated that they were equally valid for use with black and white children. (Many of the arguments supporting the use of tests for all races were summarized earlier.) If the tests were not biased, then why

---

*442 U.S. 405 (1975).

did Larry and the others receive higher scores when they were retested by black psychologists? The defense argued that the black psychologists did not follow standard testing procedures and that IQ test scores are not changed when standardized procedures are followed.

Statements from special-education teachers were also presented. The teachers argued that the children involved in the case could not cope with the standard curriculum and that they required the special tutoring available in the EMR classes. The children had not been learning in regular classes, and the schools investigated cases in which there was doubt about the placement. For all these children, the assignment to EMR classes was deemed appropriate (Sattler, 1979).

The Larry P. side of the case also had its share of distinguished experts, including George Albee, Leon Kamin, and Jane Mercer. The arguments for Larry were varied. His lawyers argued that all humans are born with equal capacity and that any test that assigns disproportionate numbers of children from one race to an EMR category is racist and discriminatory. The witnesses testified that dominant social groups had historically used devices such as IQ tests to discriminate against less powerful social groups and that the school district had intentionally discriminated against black children by using unvalidated IQ tests. Specifically, the tests were used to keep blacks in dead-end classes for the mentally retarded, in which they would not get the training they needed to move up in the social strata. Furthermore, the plaintiffs suggested that labeling someone as EMR has devastating social consequences. Children who are labeled as EMR lose confidence and self-esteem (Mercer, 1973), and eventually the label becomes a self-fulfilling prophecy (Rosenthal & Jacobson, 1968). In other words, labeling a child as mentally retarded may cause the child to behave as though mentally retarded.

The judge was clearly persuaded more by the plaintiffs than by the defense. He declared that the tests "are racially and culturally biased, have a discriminatory impact on black children, and have not been validated for the purpose of (consigning) black children into educationally dead-end, isolated, and stigmatizing classes." Furthermore, the judge stated that the Department of Education had "desired to perpetuate the segregation of minorities in inferior, dead-end, and stigmatizing classes for the retarded."

The effect of the ruling, was a discontinuance of IQ testing to place black children in EMR classes. The decision immediately affected all black California school children who had been labeled as EMR. More than 6000 of these children must be reassessed in some other manner.

There are strong differences of opinion about the meaning of the Larry P. decision. Harold Dent, one of the black psychologists who had retested Larry P. and the other children, hailed the decision as a victory for black children:

> For more than 60 years psychologists have used tests primarily to justify the majorities desire to "track" minorities into inferior education and dead-end jobs. The message of Larry P. is that psychologists must involve themselves in the task mandated in the last sentence of the court's opinion: "this will clear the way for more constructive educational reform" (quoted in Opton, 1979).

Others did not share the belief that the Larry P. decision was a social victory. Nadine Lambert, who was an expert witness for the state, felt it was a terrible decision. On learning of it, she remarked, "I think the people who will be most hurt by it are the Black children" (quoted in Opton, 1979, p. 1). Banning the use of IQ tests opens the door to completely subjective judgments, which may be even more racist than the test results. Opponents of the Larry P. decision cite many instances in which gifted black children were assumed to be average by their teachers but were recognized as highly intelligent because of IQ test scores.

The Larry P. decision has been frequently cited in subsequent cases. Some of these are actually remote from the issues in Larry P. For example, in the matter of Ana Maria R.*, parental rights were terminated on the grounds that the mother was mentally retarded. However, the mother was Spanish speaking and Larry P. was cited as precedent that tests and classification of mental retardation are discriminatory against blacks and Hispanics. In contrast to the case of Ana Maria R., the factual situation in an Illinois case was quite similar to Larry P. That case is described in the following section.

Parents in Action on Special Education v. Hannon.[†]

Just as the case of Larry P. was making headlines in California, a similar case came to trial in Illinois. The case was a class-action lawsuit filed on behalf of two black children (representing the class of all similar children) who had been placed in special classes for the educable mentally handicapped (EMH) on the basis of IQ test scores. Attorneys for the two student plaintiffs argued that the children were inappropriately placed in EMH classes because of racial bias in the IQ tests. They suggested that the use of IQ tests for black children violates the equal protection clause of the Constitution and many federal statutes.

In their presentation to the court, the plaintiffs relied heavily on the recent Larry P. decision, which held that the WISC, the WISC-R, and the Stanford-Binet IQ tests are biased and inappropriate for the testing of minority children. However, Judge John Grady of the U.S. District Court came to exactly the opposite conclusion of Judge Peckham, who had presided over the Larry P. case. Judge Grady found evidence for racial bias in the three major IQ tests to be unconvincing. In his opinion, he noted that the items objected to were only a fraction of the items on the entire test. For example, witnesses for the plaintiffs never mentioned whole subtests on the WISC and WISC-R, such as arithmetic, digit span, block design, mazes, coding, and object assembly. The judge noted that these subtests were not biased in favor of either black or white children because most youngsters of both groups would have never confronted problems of this type before. The items for which there were legitimate objections were too few to have an impact on test scores.

Thus, less than one year after the historic Larry P. case, another court concluded, "Evidence of racial bias in standardized IQ tests is not sufficient to

*96 U.S. 2040(c)(1976).
[†]C.A. No. C-70 37 RFP (N.D. Cal., filed Feb 3, 1970).

render their use as part of classifications procedures to place black children in 'educable mentally handicapped' classes violative of statutes prohibiting discrimination in federally funded programs." In early 1984 the ninth district court of appeals considered an appeal citing both Larry P. and Parents in action. The court upheld Larry P. by a 2–1 vote (*Los Angeles Times,* January 24, 1984).

Debra P. V. Turlington.* Some people feel that a test is biased if it contains questions that particular test takers cannot answer. One 1979 lawsuit in Florida involved ten black students who had failed their first attempt to pass Florida's minimum competence test, the State Student Assessment Test. Debra P. was one of the students, and the case took her name. In Hillsborough County, where the suit was filed, about 19% of the students in the public school system were black. However, black students constituted 64% of those who had failed the test.

Minimum competence tests similar to the one used in Florida have been adopted by more than 30 states, and 19 states require the exam for graduation. If they meet other requirements, students who do not pass the exam are given a certificate of completion that acknowledges that they attended high school but does not carry the same status as a high school diploma. The Florida suit charged that the test should not be used for minority students when most of their education occurred before the schools were desegregated. Thus the dispute concerned whether the same test should be used for students who may have had unequal opportunities to learn in school. Attorneys for the students argued that their clients had been in inferior schools and had been the subjects of continued discrimination. Thus they should not be held to the standards for majority students, who had better opportunities.

Ralph D. Turlington was the commissioner of education and one of the defendants in the case. He argued that basic minimum standards must be applied in order to certify that students have enough information to survive in situations that require high school level sophistication. These standards, it was argued, must be absolute. Either students know the basic information or they do not. According to the commissioner, "To demand that a 12th-grade student with a 3rd-grade reading level be given a diploma is silly."

The Florida case illustrates the kind of lawsuits we might expect in the future. It pits two sides with reasonable arguments against each other. One side argues that minority children have worked hard in school under great disadvantage and cannot be expected to have learned the things majority children know. In recognition of their work they deserve a diploma. The other side argues that there should be an absolute standard for basic information (Seligmann, Coppola, Howard, & Lee, 1979).

The court essentially sided with the commissioner. The judge did not challenge the validity of the test. However, he did suspend the use of the test for four years, after which all the students who had any part of their education in

*347 F Supp. 1306 (N.D. Cal 1972). aff'd 502 F.2d 963 (9th Cir. 1979).

segregated schools would have graduated. Then, according to the opinion, the test could be used.

In a 1981 paper, Lerner argued that minimum competency exams, such as the SSAT II used in the State of Florida, benefit both students and society. As an attorney, she found little legal justification for court involvement. However, the court reopened the Debra P. case the same year as Lerner's paper was published. This new consideration came after those students who had begun their education under a segregated system had graduated and differences in performance could not be attributed to segregation. In the new evaluation, the U.S. district court of appeal considered the validity of the test. It stated that the test would violate the Equal Protection Clause if, "the test by dividing students into two categories, passers and failers, did so without a rational relation to the purpose for which it was designed, then the Court would be compelled to find the test unconstitutional" (474 F. Supp at 260). However, in this case, the Court concluded that the test did have adequate construct validity and that it could be used to evaluate functional literacy. In the same opinion, the Court stressed that the test must reflect what is taught in school and that continual surveillance of test fairness is warranted.

Regents of the University of California v. Bakke. Alan Bakke was an engineer in his thirties who decided to apply to the University of California, Davis, medical school in the early 1970s. Although Bakke had a high grade point average and good MCAT scores, he was denied admission. Bakke decided to investigate the matter. He discovered that his test scores were higher than those of minority students who had gained admission to the medical school under a special affirmative action program. Bakke eventually sued the university on grounds that he had been discriminated against because he was not a minority-group member. The suit ended in the Supreme Court and is considered to be one of the most important cases of the century.

Although many arguments were presented in the Bakke case, one of the major ones concerned the use of test scores. Under the affirmative action program, the cutoff value for MCAT scores was higher for nonminority than for minority students. In defense of the special admissions program it was argued that the tests were not meaningful (valid) for minority students. However, evidence was also presented that the tests were equally meaningful for both groups.

The Supreme Court ruling was not specific with regard to the use of tests. The court ruled that the university had to admit Bakke and that it had denied him due process in the original consideration of the case. It also implied that the use of different cutoff scores was not appropriate. However, the court did acknowledge that race could be taken into consideration in selection decisions. This acknowledgment was interpreted by the EEOC as meaning that affirmative action programs based on numerical quotas could continue (Norton, 1978).

After the Bakke decision, the high court seemed unwilling to hear further reverse-discrimination cases. For example, a week after Bakke, the court refused to hear a challenge to a strong affirmative action plan that created reverse discrimination (EEOC v. A.T. & T.).

Personnel Cases in Law. Most of the cases we have discussed involved educational tests. Several other important lawsuits have dealt with the use of tests in employment setting. Through a series of Supreme Court decisions, specific restrictions have been placed on the use of tests for the selection of employees. The most important of these cases are *Griggs v. Duke Power Company,** *Albemarle Paper Company v. Moody,* †and *Washington v. Davis.* ‡The effect of these decisions has been to force employers to define the relationship between test scores and job performance and to define the measure of job performance. However, none of the decisions denies that tests are valuable tools in the personnel field and that the use of tests can continue.

The courts have also been asked to decide on issues of test administration. For example, an employee of the Detroit Edison Company was not promoted because of a low test score. In his defense, his union suggested that the low score might have been an error and requested a copy of the test to check the scoring. Detroit Edison did not want to release the test because it feared that the union would distribute the items to other employees. By a vote of five to four, the Supreme Court ruled on the side of Detroit Edison (*Detroit Edison Co. v. NLRB*). It is interesting that in a major decision, such as this, a single vote can make a difference in policy (Cronbach, 1980).

A Critical Look at Lawsuits

The problems that psychologists are unable to resolve themselves will eventually be turned over to someone else for a binding opinion. This procedure may not be in the best interest of the field of psychology or of the people whom we serve.

It is difficult to be an uncritical admirer of the courts. As Lerner (1979) notes, inconsistencies in court decisions are commonplace. Even worse, judges who make important decisions about the use of tests often have little background in psychology or testing. Often judges obtain their entire education about testing during the course of a trial.

In the near future we must grapple with many tough issues. For example, many current social problems seem related to the differential distribution of resources among the races in American society. Changing the income distribution seems to be one of the only ways in which effective social change can occur. To accomplish this redistribution, we must get minority children in appropriate educational tracks, into professional schools, and into high-income positions. The courts have ruled that psychological tests are blocking this progress.

Psychologists themselves are not of one mind regarding the use of psychological tests. However, current research tends not to confirm the widely held belief that the tests are systematically biased. The field of psychometrics, after long and careful consideration of the problems, has come to a conclusion opposite

---

*414 NYS 2d. 982 (1979).
†74 C C3586, USDC (N.D. Ill, 7/7/80).
‡474 F. Supp. 244(M.D. Fla 1979) 644 F.2d 397 (1981).

to that of the courts, which have given the issue a briefer evaluation. In the end, however, the courts have the power, and their judgment is the law.

CONTROVERSIES SURROUNDING THE SOCIAL AND POLITICAL IMPLICATIONS OF TESTING

Psychological testing may lead to undesirable social and political trends. Some groups believe that psychological testing has produced social injustices that are indefensible in a free society. In this final section, two of these controversies will be discussed. The first is the review of the impact of psychological testing by Ralph Nader and his consumer organizations. The second stems from the accusation that psychological testing evidence was used as the basis for a racist immigration policy passed by the Congress in 1924.

Nader's Raid on the Educational Testing Service

Ralph Nader and his associates have established a sound reputation as consumer advocates. In 1980, Nader and junior associate Alan Nairn (1980) issued a report that criticized the testing industry. The prime target of the report was the Educational Testing Service (ETS). In a much publicized report, Nairn characterized ETS as an evil bureaucracy operating under a guise of secrecy. It was suggested that ETS conspired to maintain the status quo by intentionally discriminating against students from low-income families. It is suggested that invalid and biased tests ensure that only those from wealthy families are admitted to prestigious colleges and universities.

There are two major arguments in Nairn's report. First, the report suggests that the Scholastic Aptitude Test (SAT), which was developed by ETS, is not a valid predictor of college success. The second argument is that the only real correlate of the SAT is family income. Thus those selected for college admission through SAT testing programs may be wealthy but not necessarily more likely to succeed in college.

When carefully examined, many of the arguments in the Nairn report were found to be faulty. The report suggested that the SAT is no better than chance in predicting college performance. However, Nairn confused percentage of variance accounted for by the test with percentage of cases perfectly predicted. Reanalysis of the data revealed that the SAT predicts performance better than chance in nearly all cases. In combination with high school grades, the SAT is a relatively good predictor of college success for students from different social classes and with different ethnic group backgrounds. Although SAT scores are correlated with social class, there is no evidence for differential validity at different income levels (Kaplan, 1982).

The Nader report was very influential in the passage of some truth-in-testing legislation. As noted earlier, this legislation requires testing companies to make their items public. One consequence of this legislation is that test items may be included in common instruments without having established a record of validity. The impact of the Nader proposal may serve to decrease the validity of the tests. In other words, the quality of the product may suffer. At the same time as the quality would decrease, costs are expected to increase due to the expense of continually creating and testing new items. Students might expect to pay a higher fee to take a less valid test. In other words, the Nader-Nairn report that was written in advocacy of the consumer may result in higher fees for a less valid product.

The Immigration Act of 1924

In 1924, the United States Congress passed a racially biased immigration law. This Immigration Act of 1924 set quotas for immigration based on the percentages of immigrants from each country who had arrived prior to the 1890 census. Most immigrants from Eastern and Southern Europe had arrived after 1890. As a result, the Immigration Act of 1924 had a strong bias in favor of immigrants from Northern and Western Europe and a bias against those from Southern and Eastern Europe.

Critics of intelligence tests have argued that testing advocates using data from biased intelligence tests played a central role in the passage of this act. This position was forcefully argued by Leon Kamin in a widely cited book entitled, *The Science and Politics of IQ* (Kamin, 1974, p. 16). Kamin deplored the "involvement of the mental testing movement in the passage of an overtly racist immigration act in 1924" (1982, p.16). A popular book by Paleobiologist Steven Gould (1981) entitled, *The Mismeasure of Man*, also attributes the passage of the Immigration Act of 1924 to testing advocates. Gould's book is widely quoted in both scientific and popular literature and has received overwhelmingly positive critical acclaim.

Recently, Snyderman and Herrnstein (1983) reexamined the role of intelligence test data in the passage of the 1924 Act. Evidence frequently cited by Kamin and his many followers include the report by H. H. Goddard (1917) characterizing as feebleminded the great majority of immigrants of Jewish, Hungarian, Italian, and Russian heritage. This attitude presumably led to the increased restrictions against immigration by Eastern and Southern Europeans. Kamin and Gould also cited C. Brigham's analysis of Army Alpha and Beta Intelligence Tests. Brigham (1923) concluded that the average test scores of immigrants from Northern Europe were better than those obtained from immigrants from Southern or Eastern Europe. In addition, an analysis of scores from draftees suggested that average intelligence scores had been declining for about a twenty-year period (in essence, from about the turn of the century). This decline could be accounted for by the increasing proportion of immigrants from Southern and Eastern Europe. Thus he recommended immigration policies that would favor Northern Europeans and restrict immigration from Southern and Eastern Europeans.

Brigham's position is clearly racist and difficult to defend. In addition, it appears that the Immigration Act of 1924 closely coincides with Brigham's recommendations. Nevertheless, Snyderman and Herrnstein's (1983) careful evaluation suggests that Brigham's statements had relatively little influence in the deliberations of the Congress. Critics of intelligence tests, including Kamin and Gould, imply that Brigham's analysis went essentially unchallenged. Yet there is substantial evidence that psychologists of the day were highly critical of Brigham's work and of his position on immigration. In fact, Brigham himself changed his position a few years later (Brigham, 1930).

In a similar vein, it appears that Goddard's (1917) views were largely misrepresented. Goddard had intentionally preselected his sample to include only those of borderline intelligence. In his study of 178 immigrants, there was no intention to make statements about the prevalence of feeble-mindedness among immigrants in any particular group. The purpose was to demonstrate that a test could make fine discriminations in borderline cases. Yet it was well known at the time that the test exaggerated the rate of feeble-mindedness in all adult populations. There is also evidence, contrary to statements by Kamin (1974) and Gould (1981), that Goddard did not attribute poor intelligence test performance to either inheritance or ethnic background. In fact, Goddard attributed poor performance among some immigrants to poor environment (Snyderman and Herrnstein, 1983). The views of both Goddard and Brigham were widely criticized by the time the immigration policies of 1924 were formulated. Gould's book (1981) stated that intelligence test data and the consensus among psychologists were the focal point of Congressional deliberation. As Gould (1981) noted, "Congressional debates leading to the passage of the Immigration Restriction Act of 1924 continually invokes the Army data (p. 232). Upon review of Congressional Record, Snyderman and Herrnstein were unable to substantiate these claims. In fact, the 32 sections of the act make no reference to intelligence tests, intelligence, or feeblemindedness. Kamin (1974) suggested that testimony and written documents had influenced the members of the Congressional committees prior to the floor debates. For example, Kamin quoted a statement from Madison Grant (1916), an anthropologist who praised the value of the Army Intelligence tests. Yet Snyderman and Herrnstein were unable to locate Grant's statement in the Harvard University archives and could find no record that the Senate Immigration Committee had even met on the day Grant proportedly made his statement. In fact, there was no evidence that Grant had ever made a statement to the Committee.

The major advocates of psychological tests, including Goddard, Termin, Yerkes, and Thorndike were never even called to testify. The records show that those few witnesses who mention native differences in intellect were typically criticized by the members of Congress when they presented their testimony. In summary of their review, Schnyderman and Herrnstein (1983) stated, "Summarizing our examination of the Congressional Record and Committee hearings: there is no mention of intelligence testing in the act; tests results of the immigrants appear only briefly in the committee hearings and are largely ignored or criticized, and they are brought up only once in the over 600 pages of the Congressional floor debate where they are subjected to further criticism without rejoinder" (p.

994). Thus there is little evidence supporting the commonly held belief that the unified group of psychologists used intelligence test data to influence the regrettable Immigration Act of 1924.

SUMMARY

This chapter has reviewed several controversies in testing. Most of these controversies are related to differential performance between ethnic and racial groups on standardized tests. At present there is little convincing evidence that content bias in major tests is the major cause of observed differences. Studies of criterion validity are more difficult to evaluate. Interpretation of the results depends on a specific philosophical orientation. Thus disagreements may be a reflection of different moral positions.

Several alternative approaches have been proposed. At present each is still under evaluation. While these issues are debated in academic circles, a greater number of cases has reached the courts. Future court battles can be anticipated, since there has been considerable inconsistency in judgments. Social and political debates about testing have often been emotional and have gained considerable public attention. However, some of the claims have not been well substantiated and many of the anti-testing public statements appear to have been in error.

REFERENCES

Anastasi, A. (1980). Abilities and the measurement of achievement. *New Directions for Testing and Measurement, 5,* 1–10.

Andre, J. (1976). Bi-Cultural Socialization and the Measurement of Intelligence. *Dissertation Abstracts International,* 3676B–3676B.

APA (1983). American psychological association statement on test item disclosure legislation (mimeograph).

Bartlett, C. J., & O'Leary, B. S. (1969). A differential prediction model to moderate the effects of heterogeneous groups in personnel selection and classification. *Personnel Psychology, 22,* 1–17.

Bergan, J. R., & Parra, E. B. (1979). Variations in IQ testing and instruction and the letter learning and achievement of Anglo and bilingual Mexican-American children. *Journal of Educational Psychology, 71,* 819–826.

Bersoff, D. N. (1979). Regarding psychologists testily: Legal regulation of psychological assessment in the public schools. In B. Sales & M. Novick (Eds.), *Perspectives in law and psychology. III: Testing and evaluation.* New York: Plenum.

Bersoff, D. N. (1981). Testing and the law. *American Psychologist, 36,* 1047–1057.

Bianchini, J. C. (1976, May). *Achievement tests and differentiated norms.* Paper presented at the U.S. Office of Education invitational conference on achievement testing of disadvantaged and minority students for educational program evaluation, Reston, Va.

Brigham, C. C. (1923). *A study of American intelligence.* Princeton, NJ: Princeton University Press.

Brigham, C. C. (1930). Intelligence tests of immigrant groups. *Psychological Review, 37,* 158–165.

Brill, S. (1973). The secrecy behind the college boards. *New York Magazine.* (Reprinted by the NYC Corporation.)

Brown, F. G. (1979a). The algebra works—But what does it mean? *School Psychology Digest, 8*(2), 213–218.

Brown, F. G. (1979b). The SOMPA: A system of measuring potential abilities? *School Psychology Digest, 8*(1), 37–46.

Clarizio, H. F. (1979a). In defense of the IQ test. *School Psychology Digest, 8*(1), 79–88.

Clarizio, H. F. (1979b). SOMPA—A symposium continued: Commentaries. *School Psychology Digest, 8*(2), 207–209.

Cleary, T. A. (1968). Test bias: Prediction of grades of Negro and White students in integrated colleges. *Journal of Educational Measurement, 5,* 115–124.

Cleary, T. A. (1975). Humphreys, L. G., Kendrick, S. A., & Wesman, A. Educational uses of tests with disadvantaged populations. *American Psychologist, 30,* 15–41.

Cole, N. S. (1973). Bias in selection. Journal of *Educational Measurement, 10,* 237–255.

Cole, N. S. Bias in testing. (1981). *American Psychologist, 36,* 1067–1077.

Copple, C. E., & Succi, G. J. (1974). The comparative ease of processing standard English and Black nonstandard English by lower-class Black children. *Child Development, 45,* 1048–1053.

Cordes, C. (1983). Jensen Refines Theory Linking G-Factor to Processing Speed. *APA Monitor, 14*(10), 3,20.

Cronbach, L. J. (1975). Five decades of public controversy over mental testing. *American Psychologist, 30,* 1–14.

Cronbach, L. J. (1978). Black Intelligence Test of Cultural Homogeneity: A review. In O. K. Buros (Ed.), *The eighth mental measurements yearbook* (vol. 1). Highland Park, NJ: Gryphon Press, 1978.

Cronbach, L. J. (1980). Validity of parole: How can we go straight? *New Directions for Testing and Measurement, 5,* 99–108.

Darlington, R. B. (1971). Another look at "cultural fairness." *Journal of Educational Measurement, 8,* 71–82.

Darlington, R. B. (1978). Cultural test bias: Comment on Hunter and Schmidt. *Psychological Bulletin, 85,* 673–674.

Das, J. P., Kirby, J., & Jarman, R. F. (1975). Simultaneous and successive syntheses An alternative model for cognitive abilities. *Psychological Bulletin, 82,* 87–103.

Das, J. P., Kirby, J., & Jarman, R. F. (1979). *Simultaneous and successive cognitive processes.* New York: Academic Press, 1979.

Dobko, P., Kehoe, J. F. (1983). On the Fair Use of Bias: A Comment of Drasgow. *Psychological Bulletin, 93,* 604–408.

Drasgow, F. Biased Test Items and Differential Validity. (1982). *Psychological Bulletin, 92,* 526–531.

EEOC (1970). Equal Employment Opportunity Commission guidelines on employee selection procedures. *Federal Register, 35* (19), 12333–12336.

EEOC (1978). *Employment Guidelines,* Washington, D.C.: U.S. Government Printing Office.

Flaugher, R. L. (1974). *Bias in testing: A review and discussion* (TM Rep. 36). Princeton, NJ: ERIC Clearinghouse on Tests, Measurements, and Evaluation.

Flaugher, R. L. (1978). The many definitions of test bias. *American Psychologist, 33,* 671–679.

Flaugher, R. L., & Schrader, W. B. (1978). *Eliminating differentially difficult items as an approach to test bias* (RB-78-4). Princeton, NJ: Educational Testing Service.

Garcia, J. (1981). The logic and limits of mental aptitude testing. *American Psychologist, 36,* 1172–1180.

Goddard, H. H. (1917). Mental tests and the immigrant. *Journal of Delinquency, 2,* 243–277.

Goodman, J. (1977). The diagnostic fallacy: A critique of Jane Mercer's concept of mental retardation. *Journal of School Psychology, 15,* 197–206.

Goodman, J. (1979). "Ignorance" versus "stupidity"—the basic disagreement. *School Psychology Digest,* 1979, 8(2), 218–223.

Gordon, E. W., & Terrell, M. D. (1981). The changed social context of testing. *American Psychologist, 36,* 1167–1171.

Gould, S. J. (1981). *The Mismeasure of Man,* New York: Norton.

Grant, M. (1916). *The passing of the great race.* New York: Scribner's, 1916.

Green, D. R., & Draper, J. F. (1972, September). *Exploratory studies of bias and achievement Association,* Honolulu, Hawaii.

Guion, R. M. (1976). Recruiting, selection and job placement. In M. D. Dunnette (Ed.), *Handbook of industrial and organizational psychology.* Chicago: Rand McNally.

Gutkin, T. D., & Reynolds, C. R. (1981). Factorial similarity of the WISK-R for white and black children from the standardization sample. *Journal of Educational Psychology, 73,* 227–231.

Haney, W. (1981). Validity, vaudeville, and values: A short history of social concerns over standardized testing. *American Psychologist, 36,* 1021–1034.

Hardy, J. B., Welcher, D. W., Mellitis, E. D., & Kagan, J. (1976). Pitfalls in the measurement of intelligent: Are standarized intelligence tests valid for measuring the intellectual potential of urban children? *Journal of Psychology, 94,* 43–51.

Hodos, W., & Campbell, B. C. G. (1969). Scala naturae: Why there is no theory in comparative psychology. *Psychological Review, 76,* 337–350.

Hunter, J. E., & Schmidt, F. L. (1976). Critical analysis of statistical and ethical implications of various definitions of test bias. *Psychological Bulletin, 83,* 1053–1071.

Hunter, J. E., & Schmidt, F. L. (1978). Bias in defining test bias: Reply to Darlington. *Psychological Bulletin, 85,* 675–676.

Ironson, G. H., & Sebkovial, N. J. (1979). A Comparison of Several Methods for Assessing Item Bias. *Journal of Educational Measurement, 16,* 209–225.

Jensen, A. R. (1969). How much can we boost IQ and scholastic achievement? *Harvard Educational Review, 39,* 1–23.

Jensen, A. R. (1972). *Genetics and education.* New York: Harper & Row.

Jenson, A. R. (1980). *Bias in mental testing.* New York: Free Press.

Jensen, A. R. (1983, August). *The nature of black–white difference on various psychometric tests.* Presented at the Meeting of the American Psychological Association Anaheim, California.

Jones, L. V. (1983). White–black achievement differences: The narrowing gap. Invited Address, American Psychological Association, Anaheim, CA, August.

Kagan, J., Moss, H. A., & Siegel, I. E. (1963). Psychological significance of styles of conceptualization. *Monographs of the Society for Research in Child Development, 28*(2, Serial No. 86), 73–124.

Kallingal, A. (1971). The prediction of grades for black and white students at Michigan State University. *Journal of Educational Measurement, 8,* 263–265.

Kamin, L. J. (1974). *The science and politics of IQ.* Hillsdale, NJ: Erlbaum.

Kamin, L. J. (1976). Heredity, intelligence, politics and psychology: II. In N. J. Block & G. Dworkin (Eds.), *The I.Q. controversy.* New York: Pantheon Books.

Kamin, L. J. (1982). Mental testing and immigration. *American Psychologist, 37,* 97–98.

Kaplan, R. M. (1982). Nader's Raid on the testing industry: Is it in the best interest of the consumer? *American Psychologist, 37,* 15–23.

Kaplan, R. M. & Saccuzzo, D. P. (1982). *Psychological testing: Principles, Applications and Issues.* Monterey: Brooks/Cole.

Kaufman, A. S., & Kaufman, N. L. (1983). *K-ABC Kaufman Assessment Battery for Children.* Circle Pines, Minnesota: American Guidance Service.

Kaufman, A. S., & Doppelt, J. D. (1976). Analysis of WISC-R standardization data in terms of the stratification variables. *Child Development, 47*, 165–171.

Kiersh, E. (1979, January 15). Testing is the name, power is the game. *The Village Voice.*

Lerner, B. (1979). Tests and standards today: Attacks, counterattacks, and responses. *New Directions in Testing and Measurement, 1*(3), 15–31.

Lerner, B. (1981). The minimum competence testing movement: Social, scientific, and legal implications. *American Psychologist, 36*, 1057–1066.

Lesser, G. S., Fifer, G., & Clark, D. H. (1965). Mental abilities of children from different social-class and cultural groups. *Monographs of the Society for Research in Child Development, 30*(4, Serial No. 102).

Levy, S. (1979). E.T.S. and the "coaching" cover-up. *New Jersey Monthly, 3*(5), 4–7.

Loehlin, J. C., Lindzey, G., & Spuhler, J. N. (1975). *Race Differences and Intelligence.* San Francisco: Freeman.

Long, P. A., & Anthony, J. J. (1974). The measurement of retardation by a culture-specific test. *Psychology in the Schools, 11*, 310–312.

Luria, A. R. (1966). *Human brain and psychological processes.* New York: Harper & Row.

Luria, A. R. (1966). *Higher Cordical Functions in Man.* New York: Basic Books.

Mannheim, K. (1936). *Ideology and utopia.* London: Kegan, Paul, Trench, Trubner.

McCormick, E. J., & Ilgen, D. (1980). *Industrial psychology* (7th ed.). Englewood Cliffs, NJ: Prentice-Hall.

Mercer, J. R. (1971). Sociocultural factors in labeling mental retardates. *Peabody Journal of Education, 48*, 188–203.

Mercer, J. R. (1973). *Labeling the mentally retarded: Clinical and social system perspective on mental retardation.* Berkeley: University of California Press.

Mercer, J. R. (1972). Anticipated achievement: Computerizing the self-fulfilling prophecy. Presented at the meeting of American Psychological Association, Honolulu.

Mercer, J. R. (1979). In defense of racially and culturally non-discriminatory assessment. *School Psychology Digest, 8*(1), 89–115.

Mercer, J. R., & Lewis, J. F. (1979). *System of multi-cultural pluralistic assessment: Conceptual and technical manual.* New York: Psychological Corporation.

Milgram, M. A. (1974). Danger: Chauvinism, scapegoatism, and euphenism. In G. J. Williams & S. Gordon (Eds) *Clinical Child Psychology: Current Practices and Future Perspectives,* New York: Behavioral Publications.

Munsinger, H. (1975). The adopted child's IQ: A critical review. *Psychological Bulletin, 82*, 623–659.

Nairn, A., & Associates. (1980). *The reign of ETS: The corporation that makes up minds.* Washington, DC: Nader.

Neisser, U. (1967). *Cognitive psychology.* New York: Appleton-Century-Crofts.

Norton, E. H. (1978, July). *The Bakke decision and the future of affirmative action.* Statement of the Chair, U.S. Equal Employment Opportunity Commission, at the National Association for the Advancement of Colored People convention.

Oakland, T. (1979). Research on the ABIC and ELP: A revisit to an old topic. *School Psychology Digest, 8*, 209–213.

Oakland, T., & Feigenbaum, D. (1979). Multiple sources of test bias on the WISC-R and the Bender-Gestalt test. *Journal of Consulting and Clinical Psychology, 47*, 968–974.

Opton, E. A. (1977). A psychologist takes a closer look at the recent landmark Larry P. opinion. *APA Monitor,* December, 1–4.

Opton, E. (1979, December). A psychologist takes a closer look at the recent landmark Larry P. opinion. *APA Monitor,* pp. 1,4.

Ornstein, R. (1972). *The psychology of consciousness.* San Francisco: Freeman.

Pettigrew, T. F. (1964). *A profile of the American Negro.* New York: Van Nostrand Reinhold.

Pfeifer, C., & Sedlacek, W. (1971). The validity of academic predictor for black and white students at a predominantly white university. *Journal of Educational Measurement, 8*, 253–261.

Piersel, W. C., Blake, B. S., Reynolds, C. R., and Harding, R. (1982). Bias and content validity of the Boehm Test of basic concepts for white and Mexican-American children. *Contemporary Educational Psychology, 7*, 181–189.

Quay, L. C. (1971). Language dialect, reinforcement, and the intelligence-test performance of Negro children. *Child Development, 42*, 5–15.

Reschly, D. J., & Sabers, D. L. (1979). Analysis of test bias in four groups with a regression definition. *Journal of Educational Measurement, 16*, 1–9.

Reschly, D. J. (1981). Psychological testing in educational classification and placement. *American Psychologist, 36*, 1094–1102.

Reynolds, C. R. (1980). An examination of bias in the pre-school test battery across race and sex. *Journal of Educational Measurement, 17*, 137–146.

Reynolds, C. R., & Nigl, A. J. (1981). A regression analysis of differential validity: An intellectual assessment for black and white inner-city children. *Journal of Clinical and Child Psychology, 10*, 176–179.

Rosenthal, R., & Jacobson, L. (1968). *Pygmalion in the classroom.* New York: Hold, Rinehart & Winston.

Sattler, J. M. (1979, April). *Intelligence tests on trial; Larry P. et al. vs. Wilson Riles et al.* Paper presented at the meeting of the Western Psychological Association, San Diego.

Sattler, J. M. (1982). *Assessment of children's intelligence and special abilities.* Boston: Allyn & Bacon.

Scarr-Salapatek, S. (1971). Race, social class and IQ. *Science, 174*, 1285–1295.

Scheuneman, J. D. (1981). A new look at Bar S and aptitude tests. *New Directions in Testing and Measurement*, No. 12, 5–25.

Seligmann, J., (1979, May 28). Coppola, V., Howard, L., & Lee, E. D. (1979, May 28). A really final exam. *Newsweek*, pp. 97–98.

Shiffrin, R. M., & Schneider, W. (1977). Controlled and automatic human information processing: II. Perceptual learning, automatic attending, and a general theory. *Psychological Review, 84*, 127–190.

Snyderman, M., & Herrnstein, R. J. (1983). Intelligence tests and the Immigration Act of 1924. *American Psychologist, 38*, 986–995.

Spearman, C. E. (1927). *The abilities of man.* New York: Macmillan.

Taking the Chitling Test. (1968, July 15). *Newsweek*, pp. 51–52, 72.

Temp, G. (1971). Test bias: Validity of the SAT for blacks and whites in thirteen integrated institutions. *Journal of Educational Measurement, 8*, 245–251.

Thorndike, R. L. (1968). Review of *Pygmalion in the Classroom* by R. Rosenthal and L. Jacobson. *American Educational Research Journal, 5*, 708–711.

Thorndike, R. L. (1971). Concepts of culture-fairness. *Journal of Educational Measurement, 8*, 63–70.

Williams, R. L. (1972, September). *The BITCH-100: A culture-specific test.* Paper presented at the Meeting of the American Psychological Association, Honolulu, Hawaii.

Williams, R. L. (1974). Scientific racism and IQ: The silent mugging of the black community. *Psychology Today, 7*, 32–41.

Woodring, P. (1966). Are intelligence tests unfair? *Saturday Review, 49*, 79–80.

Zores, L. S., & Williams, P. B. (1980). A look at content bias in IQ tests. *Journal of Educational Measurement, 17*, 313–322.

TWELVE

INFANT INTELLIGENCE AND ITS ASSESSMENT

MICHAEL LEWIS AND MARGARET WOLAN SULLIVAN

UMDN3–Rutgers Medical School
New Brunswick, New Jersey

If in any field there can be said to exist an intermeshing of scientific method and world view, it is in the study of human intelligence. In this chapter, we will survey the field of infant assessment and its theory. It is our recurring theme, however, that the preconceived assumptions, beliefs, and prejudices held about intelligence have subtly shaped both the nature of the phenomenon and the methods used in its study. Although this theme is not entirely novel (Gould, 1981; Kamin, 1974; Lewis, 1976), it is particularly important to consider this thesis with respect to infant intelligence, be it the history of the field or the theoretical models of developing intelligence.

1. THE HISTORY OF INFANT ASSESSMENT*

Writing in 1954, Florence Goodenough stressed the practical impetus for assessment: "The development of mental testing, like many other scientific procedures of modern times, was by no means the result of the abstract curiosity of the 'pure' scientist. First and primarily, mental tests as we know them today are practical instruments devised to meet some specific need" (p. 463). While

---

* The chapter by Brooks-Gunn & Weinraub (1983) was a valuable resource in preparing this section.

We wish to thank Aileen Wehren for the background research on predictive validity of infant tests in handicapped infants, the Laurie Neurodevelopmental Institute of UMDNJ for loaning us the Griffiths Scales, which are not readily obtainable in the U.S., and the Test Collection Archives of Educational Testing Service for access to many historical tests and references. The preparation of this manuscript was supported by funds from W. T. Grant Foundation and the R. W. Johnson Foundation.

practical need for infant assessment cannot be denied (Yang, 1979), the factors (both the scientific and the practical) to which Goodenough alludes have influenced the state of the art in infant assessment. In our historical outline we will attempt to show how tests originally designed for the clinician or educator have been repeatedly revamped and new assessment tools developed in response to scientific evaluation and critique of the prevailing assumptions about early mental development. In fact, the notion of intelligence that is central to all assessment— an attribute of the mind that is fixed, stable, and quantifiable—had its origins in the nineteenth century scientific and educational communities. It was this notion, among others, which was tacitly adopted by the first developers of tests for young children.

Pre-1900

Infant testing and the assessment of intelligence in children have common origins. Both can be conveniently fixed at the beginning of the twentieth century with the work of Binet. However, the development of early intelligence tests derived from and continued to be influenced by the social, educational, and scientific milieu in western Europe and in the United States prior to 1900 (Brooks-Gunn & Weinraub, 1983). Factors fostering the assessment of intellectual functioning in infants and children included the following: (1) scientific study of psychological processes of perception, sensation, reaction time, and memory originating in German laboratories; (2) British scientific interest in the hereditary aspects of intelligence, particularly giftedness (Lewis & Michalson, 1985); (3) American interest in individual differences and the prediction of scholastic achievement; (4) interest in early human behavioral development; (5) medical and educational progress in the diagnosis and training of the mentally deficient in France and in the United States; and (6) the need for standardized testing and placement criteria demanded by the establishment of compulsory public school in France and America.

The German Contribution.   The nineteenth century laboratories of Kraepelin, Ebbinghaus, and Wundt have been recognized as the indirect impetus for mental testing (Goodenough, 1954). Though individual differences in perception were regarded as errors of measurement and therefore unworthy of study in and of themselves, the early empiricists succeeded in demonstrating the existence of individual differences in performance despite rigorous experimental methods. The stress of the empiricists on uniform, replicable procedures for testing was recognized by test developers. These reliable differences in sensory and perceptual functioning were presumed by many to reflect differences in intellectual capacity and some of these early experimental tasks were deliberately borrowed from and incorporated into general tests of intelligence (Kelley & Surbeck, 1983).

Although the notion that perceptual processes or even anthropometric indices, such as skull size, are related to intellectual capacity seems simplistic today, such measures represent science's first crude attempts to tap some aspects of central processes through behavior and physiology. Motor and sensory processes were, in effect, the first and most obvious way. This "sensory bias," a pitfall of early tests for many years, can still be raised in objection to some of the current infant test items. In fact, research has changed—but thinking about what to measure has not altered as radically. Infant test items have changed little over the years. Moreover, virtually all infant tests have either borrowed or adapted test items from those first introduced by Gesell. According to Honzik (1983),

> All subsequent authors of infant tests raided the Gesell Schedules for test items, with appropriate acknowledgement of indebtedness. The test materials from the Gesell Schedules found most frequently in other tests are the red ring and string, the 1″ red cubes, the sugar pellets and the dinner bell with handle. [p. 71]

In fact, borrowing from and adaptation of items in infant assessment were present from the first. The earliest infant test developers relied on or attempted to scale down existing items for older children, especially nonverbal ones. The earliest performance tests that were incorporated into infant scales included Wittmer form boards (Ide, 1918), Séguin form board, Wallin pegs, and the Manikin Puzzle Test (Hamley, 1935). Fillmore (1936), for example, used the Wallin Pegboard (1918), the Knox Cube Series, and the Skeels Form Boards (1932). These or similar items have continued to appear in some form on other infant tests. The Knox Cubes appear to be an instance of adaptation of materials. Fillmore found that even the earliest items of the series, a performance test used by early clinicians as a nonverbal test to supplement the Stanford-Binet (Grove, 1953), was too difficult for children under 3 years. However, the cubes themselves were useful as stimuli for the very young infants and have become a staple of infant tests. Even the term *cube*, as opposed to block, has persisted in infant test manual language.

This borrowing of items on infant tests is not unlike that which occurred in the early stages of the development of adult assessment instruments. Good items should not be discarded. The net result has been, however, that all infant tests have shared a highly similar pool of items as can be seen in Table 1. The table lists test items for infants and young children through age 36 months as they have appeared on a number of different infant tests. Similar test items are grouped under major conceptual headings. An X in the column indicates the item's presence on that particular test. Tests whose age span begins with toddlers, rather than infants, have infant items left blank.

The table is not exhaustive (for brevit 's sake, for example, only the most commonly assessed motor items are listed) nor is it meant to identify the orig-inator of particular items. It does show, however, that few new items have appeared on any test and that similar behaviors are assessed across tests, with the possible exception of the Uzgiris-Hunt scales. Though test items have become more specific and better standardized, and the reliability of scoring has improved, the skills that the tests attempt to measure have altered little since the 1920s and 1930s. Because, until quite recently (circa 1960), the young infant appeared

Table 1. Infant Test Items (through 36 months) on Selected Infant Scales

Item Category	Kuhlman-Binet, 1922	Stutsman, 1926	Fillmore, 1936	Goodenough et al., 1932	Kuhlman, 1939	Gesell, 1939	Cattell, 1940	Griffiths, 1954/1970	Bayley, 1969	Uzgiris-Hunt, 1976	Frankenberg et al., 1976 (PDQ)	Comments on Stimuli and Item Criteria KEY: Kuhlman-Binet (KB), Stutsman (ST), Fillmore (F), Goodenough (Good), Kuhlman (K), Gesell (G), Cattell (C), Griffiths (Grif), Bayley (B), Uzgiris-Hunt (UH), Frankenberg (FK)
1. Early Auditory Responses												
a. Reacts to sudden sound	X		X+		X+	X		X	X			Distances and stimuli vary with test: bell, rattle, and/or switch click; telephone snapper; quiets or inhibits activity credited by B; Grif includes startle to loud sound.
b. Soft sounds: whisper from								X			X	

508

Item								Comments
behind; tick of clock; music								
c. Quiets to music			X					
2. Auditory Localization								
a. Locates single sound source	X	X	X	X	X		X	Various stimuli used, including snapper, bell, rattle.
b. Searches with eyes for sound (2 different sounds alternated)		X	X					Supine position; bell and rattle.
3. Early Reflexes								
a. Grasps finger or other object			X				X	Grif; 2 different objects as well as resistance to withdrawal.
b. Reacts to paper on face			X					Grif; several levels of response.
c. Blinks at object which threatens eyes						X+		X	B; shadow of hand passing over eyes used as stimulus.
4. Vision								
a. Turns head and eyes to light source							X	B; light source displaced 30° from midline.

Table 1. (*Continued*)

Item Category	Kuhlman-Binet, 1922	Stutsman, 1926	Fillmore, 1936	Goodenough et al., 1932	Kuhlman, 1939	Gesell, 1939	Cattell, 1940	Griffiths, 1954/1970	Bayley, 1969	Uzgiris-Hunt, 1976	Frankenberg et al., 1976 (PDQ)	Comments on Stimuli and Item Criteria — KEY: Kuhlman-Binet (KB), Stutsman (ST), Fillmore (F), Goodenough (Good), Kuhlman (K), Gesell (G), Cattell (C), Griffiths (Grif), Bayley (B), Uzgiris-Hunt (UH), Frankenberg (FK)
b. Momentary regard of object in line of vision	X					X	X	X	X			
c. Locates object in margin					X+	X			X		X	B; red ring displaced 30° from midline.
5. Active Attending												
a. Prolonged regard of objects						X	X		X	X	X	Various stimuli used depending on test and age: red ring, cube, pellet, spoon. UH; examines object.
b. Shifts attention between two								X		X		

510

										Comments
visually presented objects										
c. Inspects surroundings				X	X	X	X			
d. Coordinated visual tracking										Both supine and seated positions on later tests.
1. Eyes follow object in vision	X*			X	X	X				B; 3 different stimuli including light. Grif; 2 different.
2. Horizontal tracking		X+		X	X	X	X			
3. Vertical tracking		X+		X	X	X	X			UH; multicolored ring.
4. 180° arc (seated)							X			
5. Circular tracking					X	X	X	X		
e. Follows rapidly moving object horizontally						X	X	X		B; ball on table top. Grif; object pulled by string.
f. Regards pellet or other small object				X			X		X	
6. Early Awareness										
a. Responses to being picked up				X	X	X	X			
b. Anticipatory responses				X	X	X	X			B & Grif; to lifting, 2 levels. G & C; to food.

Table 1. *(Continued)*

Item Category	Kuhlman-Binet, 1922	Stutsman, 1926	Fillmore, 1936	Goodenough et al., 1932	Kuhlman, 1939	Gesell, 1939	Cattell, 1940	Griffiths, 1954/1970	Bayley, 1969	Uzgiris-Hunt, 1976	Frankenberg et al., 1976 (PDQ)	Comments on Stimuli and Item Criteria KEY: Kuhlman-Binet (KB), Stutsman (ST), Fillmore (F), Goodenough (Good), Kuhlman (K), Gesell (G), Cattell (C), Griffiths (Grif), Bayley (B), Uzgiris-Hunt (UH), Frankenberg (FK)
						Infant Scale						
c. Aware of strange situation						X		X	X			
d. Pulls at dress or clothing						X						
e. Manipulates table edge						X		X	X			
f. Hands inspected						X	X	X	X			
g. Hands and/or feet played with						X	X		X			B; 2 levels.
7. Early Social Responses												
a. Regards person momentarily						X			X			
b. Regards person,										X	X	

512

		Comments
	activity diminishes	
c.	Eyes follow moving person	FK; 2 levels—side to side, 180 arc. Grif; several items.
d.	Responds to voice	
e.	Social smile	
f.	Vocal response to social smile	
g.	Reacts to disappearance of face	
h.	Recognizes mother visually	
i.	Discriminates strangers	
j.	Enjoys bath	
k.	Gives affection	
8.	**Early Vocalizations**	
a.	Occurrence	Once or twice— noncry sounds.
b.	Frequency	B; at least four times.
c.	Quality	
	1. Different sound types	B & Grif; 2 different/ 4 different.
	2. Expresses attitudes	G; 2 different, G; laughs, mmm, grunt. Grif; displeasure at removal of toy.

513

Table 1. (*Continued*)

| Item Category | Infant Scale | | | | | | | | | | | Comments on Stimuli and Item Criteria KEY: Kuhlman-Binet (KB), Stutsman (ST), Fillmore (F), Goodenough (Good), Kuhlman (K), Gesell (G), Cattell (C), Griffiths (Grif), Bayley (B), Uzgiris-Hunt (UH), Frankenberg (FK) |
	Kuhlman-Binet, 1922	Stutsman, 1926	Fillmore, 1936	Goodenough et al., 1932	Kuhlman, 1939	Gesell, 1939	Cattell, 1940	Griffiths, 1954/1970	Bayley, 1969	Uzgiris-Hunt, 1976	Frankenberg et al., 1976 (PDQ)	
3. "Talks" to persons						X		X				FK; laughs.
d. Specific social-vocal responses												
1. Attends familiar speech sounds, sound patterns, words						X		X	X	X		UH; items on Vocal imitation scale—baby must vocalize in response though not necessarily match.
2. Vocalizes to unfamiliar sound patterns										X		

514

	1	2	3	4	5	6	7	8	Notes
9. Exploration of Objects									
a. Glances at rattle in hand	X					X			
b. Object in hand:									
1. Prolonged holding									Grif; resists removal.
2. Examines		X+	X			X			G, B, and C; sustained inspection of ring in hand.
3. Carries to mouth	X		X		X	X			
c. Transfers small object from hand to hand			X	X	X	X		X	
d. Manipulates bell—interest in detail				X	X	X	X		
e. Pokes pellet	X					X			
10. Reaching Objects									Several levels and qualitatively different types of grasp assessed. B; motor scale item designated (M). Tests vary with respect to the nature of stimulus object.

Table 1. (*Continued*)

Item Category	Infant Scale											Comments on Stimuli and Item Criteria — KEY: Kuhlman-Binet (KB), Stutsman (ST), Fillmore (F), Goodenough (Good), Kuhlman (K), Gesell (G), Cattell (C), Griffiths (Grif), Bayley (B), Uzgiris-Hunt (UH), Frankenberg (FK)
	Kuhlman-Binet, 1922	Stutsman, 1926	Fillmore, 1936	Goodenough et al., 1932	Kuhlman, 1939	Gesell, 1939	Cattell, 1940	Griffiths, 1954/1970	Bayley, 1969	Uzgiris-Hunt, 1976	Frankenberg et al., 1976 (PDQ)	
a. Makes effort to reach	X	X	X									
b. Uses thumb in grasping		X	X		X+	X	X	X	XM		X	
c. Hands open		X				X	X					
d. Voluntary closing of fist, moves thumb and fingers independently											X	
e. Attempts to reach for dangling object			X+		X	X	X		X			F; string or yarn used. Others; dangling object is typically a red ring.
f. Attempts to reach for rattle from shoulder							X					

Item	1	2	3	4	5	6	7	8	Notes
g. Recovers rattle in crib			X		X				
h. Eye-hand coordination in reaching		X	X	X		X			
i. Picks up objects in reach deftly and directly	X		X			X			
j. Pursuit of dropped object		X				X			
k. Reaches persistently for objects out of reach	X		X	X	X	X			
l. Uses locomotion to attain objects out of reach		X							
m. Attains dangling object	X		X	X	X	X	X	X+	
n. Retains dangling object			X						
o. Lifts cup			X	X					B; regular and inverted cup placement. Grif; inverted only.
p. Enjoys holding little toys				X					
11. Mirror Responses									
a. Looks attentively in					X			X+	
b. Manipulates/approaches									Touches/leans toward, etc.

Table 1. (Continued)

Item Category	Infant Scale											Comments on Stimuli and Item Criteria. KEY: Kuhlman-Binet (KB), Stutsman (ST), Fillmore (F), Goodenough (Good), Kuhlman (K), Gesell (G), Cattell (C), Griffiths (Grif), Bayley (B), Uzgiris-Hunt (UH), Frankenberg (FK)
	Kuhlman-Binet, 1922	Stutsman, 1926	Fillmore, 1936	Goodenough et al., 1932	Kuhlman, 1939	Gesell, 1939	Cattell, 1940	Griffiths, 1954/1970	Bayley, 1969	Uzgiris-Hunt, 1976	Frankenberg et al., 1976 (PDQ)	
c. Reacts to image in						X	X	X	X			
d. Playful response to						X	X	X	X			Responses scored include pats, bangs, laughs, mouths, reaches to.
e. Smiles at mirror image						X		X	X			
f. Reaches object to mirror/or matches object to mirror						X						
12. Social Games and Play												
a. Plays peek-a-boo or cooperates in other games					X	X		X	X			K; considered as imitative play.

518

Item	1	2	3	4	5	6	7	8	9	10	Notes
b. Likes frolic play							X	X	X		UH; responds consistently (e.g., vocally or other) so as to keep game going.
c. Repeats performance laughed at								X			
d. Responds to bye-bye, or other gesture							X				
e. Behavior to a spectacle produced, etc.					X	X			X		UH; responds consistently (e.g., vocally or other) so as to keep game going.
f. Behavior to recreate an event (agent acting on object)									X		UH; picks up and hands toy to person to operate again (e.g., music box, etc.).
g. Plays ball with throw or cast to another	X	X			X		X			X	
h. Parallel social play					X		X				
i. Cooperative social play					X		X				
j. Tries to sing							X				
k. Disputes/negativism						X					
13. Play with Objects											
a. Simple play with rattle					X			X	X		

Table 1. (Continued)

Item Category	Kuhlman-Binet, 1922	Stutsman, 1926	Fillmore, 1936	Goodenough et al., 1932	Kuhlman, 1939	Gesell, 1939	Cattell, 1940	Griffiths, 1954/1970	Bayley, 1969	Uzgiris-Hunt, 1976	Frankenberg et al., 1976 (PDQ)	Comments on Stimuli and Item Criteria
Infant Scale												KEY: Kuhlman-Binet (KB), Stutsman (ST), Fillmore (F), Goodenough (Good), Kuhlman (K), Gesell (G), Cattell (C), Griffiths (Grif), Bayley (B), Uzgiris-Hunt (UH), Frankenberg (FK)
b. Interest in sound production			X					X	X		X	UH; any simple scheme with object with or without sound; hits, shakes, waves, etc., any two objects.
c. Bangs in play						X	X	X	X			
d. Rings bell purposefully						X		X	X	X		
e. Repetition of actions to activate toy or mechanical toy										X	X	UH; Toy—any which produces audio or visual stimulus change; must consistently swipe at, self-activate or utilize a "procedure"

Item		Notes
f. Pulls toy, walking		to have agent.
14. Complex Motor Schemes with Objects (slides, crumples, tears, stretches, rubs, pats, etc.)	XM*	UH; any of several objects. C, B, Grif; paper only.
15. Acts on Objects with Social Meaning		UH; several different objects available: doll, animal, cup, car, etc.
a. Toys played with in socially appropriate ways		G; hugs doll, and carries, domestic.
b. Uses cup and spoon in play		B and G; pushes car. Grif; 2 levels.
16. Objects in Combination		UH; any objects combined w/ simple motor schemes.
a. Cubes, picks up 1		Others; combines cubes or cube and cup in some way. Test situations vary across test. Maximum number varies as do criteria.
b. Cubes, picks up 2		

521

Table 1. *(Continued)*

Item Category	Infant Scale											Comments on Stimuli and Item Criteria
	Kuhlman-Binet, 1922	Stutsman, 1926	Fillmore, 1936	Goodenough et al., 1932	Kuhlman, 1939	Gesell, 1939	Cattell, 1940	Griffiths, 1954/1970	Bayley, 1969	Uzgiris-Hunt, 1976	Frankenberg et al., 1976 (PDQ)	KEY: Kuhlman-Binet (KB), Stutsman (ST), Fillmore (F), Goodenough (Good), Kuhlman (K), Gesell (G), Cattell (C), Griffiths (Grif), Bayley (B), Uzgiris-Hunt (UH), Frankenberg (FK)
c. Holds first, regards second			X			X						
d. Takes or attempts 3 cubes						X	X	X				
e. Regards third			X			X						
f. Drops 1 or 2 to take third					X			X		X		
g. Retains 2 of 3 offered								X	X			
h. 4 cubes held simultaneously			X			X	X	X				
i. Cubes in cup or box, 1 without demonstration			X			X		X				
j. 2–3 in								X				
k. 3 or more in								X	X			
l. In and out play								X		X		

									Notes
m. 8–9 in			X			X			
n. 10–11 in	X			X		X			
o. 12+ in	X			X		X			
p. 15+ in						X			
q. Removes or attempts to remove both cubes from box							X		
r. Manipulates box, lid, and cubes					X		X		
17. Constructions (S-B)*									
a. Piles some blocks or attempts	X		X		X	X	X	X	Using blocks, cubes, or bricks. Criteria vary with test.
b. Tower of 2		X	X	X	X	X		X	
c. Tower of 3; 4+		X	X		X	X			Good; 3 and 6 cube pyramids rather than tower.
d. Tower of 6 or 7			X		X	X	X		
e. Tower of 8			X		X	X	X		
f. Consecutive play with boxes or other objects						X	X		
g. Constructs bridge	X			X	X	X			
18. Object Permanence									
a. Object search: disappearing objects									UH and FK; light soundless object dropped to floor.

Table 1. (*Continued*)

Item Category	Kuhlman-Binet, 1922	Stutsman, 1926	Fillmore, 1936	Goodenough et al., 1932	Kuhlman, 1939	Gesell, 1939	Cattell, 1940	Griffiths, 1954/1970	Bayley, 1969	Uzgiris-Hunt, 1976	Frankenberg et al., 1976 (PDQ)	Comments on Stimuli and Item Criteria — KEY: Kuhlman-Binet (KB), Stutsman (ST), Fillmore (F), Goodenough (Good), Kuhlman (K), Gesell (G), Cattell (C), Griffiths (Grif), Bayley (B), Uzgiris-Hunt (UH), Frankenberg (FK)
1. Looks after fallen object			X		X+		X	X	X	X	X	B; spoon, age placement at 2 levels depending on response.
2. Notices disappearance of slowly moving object									X	X		
b. Object search: uncover, unwrap												
1. Takes cup off hidden toy			X				X	X	X			UH; object moves both horizontally and vertically. B; spoon, moved behind subject.

2. Hunts for partly covered toy										X		
3. Hunts for cloth covered toy			X		X		X			X		
4. Unwraps object in paper	X*				X		X	X	X			KB; used actual candy. Others; cube or toy.
c. Complex object search												
1. Finds covered object in 2 places; 3 places										X		
2. Finds object in 2 places alternately										X		
3. Finds object after successive visible displacements										X		
4. Finds under superimposed covers										X		
5. Finds after invisible displacements										X		
6. Finds after invisible displacements w/multiple screens										X		

Table 1. (*Continued*)

Item Category	Infant Scale											Comments on Stimuli and Item Criteria
	Kuhlman-Binet, 1922	Stutsman, 1926	Fillmore, 1936	Goodenough et al., 1932	Kuhlman, 1939	Gesell, 1939	Cattell, 1940	Griffiths, 1954/1970	Bayley, 1969	Uzgiris-Hunt, 1976	Frankenberg et al., 1976 (PDQ)	KEY: Kuhlman-Binet (KB), Stutsman (ST), Fillmore (F), Goodenough (Good), Kuhlman (K), Gesell (G), Cattell (C), Griffiths (Grif), Bayley (B), Uzgiris-Hunt (UH), Frankenberg (FK)
7. Finds after series of invisible displacements w/multiple screens										X		
8. Finds in reverse order of hiding							X		X	X		
19. Memory												
a. Finds two different objects hidden simultaneously												
b. Selects correct of												

526

								Comments
3 boxes with toys after 10 count								X	Good; take-away game varies with test/number of trials.
c. Names pictures from memory			X			X			
d. Repeats sentence of 6 syllables			X		X				
e. Repeats digits (S-B)			X					X*	Grif; 1 digit. Others; 2 digits must be repeated.
f. Gives family or full name			X	X					
20. Interest in Gravity									
a. Explores fall of objects by dropping in play	X		X	X	X				G; toys over crib rail. UH; intentional, repeated throwing of objects.
b. Experiments w/ gravity, toy on string, incline		X							
c. Dangles ring	X		X	X		X			
21. Container Problems									
a. Boxes and covers			X				X+		
1. Interest in box			X						
2. Unscrews top			X						

Table 1. *(Continued)*

Item Category	Kuhlman-Binet, 1922	Stutsman, 1926	Fillmore, 1936	Goodenough et al., 1932	Kuhlman, 1939	Gesell, 1939	Cattell, 1940	Griffiths, 1954/1970	Bayley, 1969	Uzgiris-Hunt, 1976	Frankenberg et al., 1976 (PDQ)	Comments on Stimuli and Item Criteria KEY: Kuhlman-Binet (KB), Stutsman (ST), Fillmore (F), Goodenough (Good), Kuhlman (K), Gesell (G), Cattell (C), Griffiths (Grif), Bayley (B), Uzgiris-Hunt (UH), Frankenberg (FK)
3. Uncovers box							X	X	X			
4. Looks for contents of								X	X			
5. Covers box			X				X	X	X			F; assembles 3 matching covers. C and B; closes round; oblong. Grif; lid on boxes w/cube.
b. Getting things in (small, difficult)												
1. Interest in small object in container					X	X						
2. Removes from container							X	X	X		X	UH; see objects in combination. Grif; credits 2 levels, attempts, succeeds.

											Comments
3. Inserts successfully			X		X		X		X	X	F; cork in bottle; penny in bank (2 levels), beads in box, pellet in bottle, sand in bottle used as stimuli.
c. Tall container and necklace problem									X		
d. Nested containers										X	F; 2, 3, all or all nested—4 maximum.
22. Miscellaneous Problems with Objects											
a. Ring and string problem											
1. String play			X		X		X			X	Typically the red ring. UH; any toy.
2. Secures object by string	X		X		X	X	X				UH; both horizontal and vertical pulling assessed.
3. Adaptively pulls			X		X		X				
b. Uses/understands support can be used to attain toy	X						X				
c. Toy-stick problem	X		X		X		X				Attempts to (C, B) or attains (UH) toy

Table 1. (Continued)

Item Category	Kuhlman-Binet, 1922	Stutsman, 1926	Fillmore, 1936	Goodenough et al., 1932	Kuhlman, 1939	Gesell, 1939	Cattell, 1940	Griffiths, 1954/1970	Bayley, 1969	Uzgiris-Hunt, 1976	Frankenberg et al., 1976 (PDQ)	Comments on Stimuli and Item Criteria — KEY: Kuhlman-Binet (KB), Stutsman (ST), Fillmore (F), Goodenough (Good), Kuhlman (K), Gesell (G), Cattell (C), Griffiths (Grif), Bayley (B), Uzgiris-Hunt (UH), Frankenberg (FK)
						Infant Scale						
d. Barrier problem						X				X		after demonstration.
e. Stacking problems												
1. 5 graded bricks		X								X		
2. Solid ring						X						UH; does not try to stack solid ring.
f. Twist to open problems			X			X		X				F; key in padlock, attempts only. Grif and G; doorknob.
g. Take objects apart/puts together						X						
h. Fixes broken doll									X			B; several levels scored.
23. Imitation of Actions												K; includes use of

530

										Notes
a. Arm and hand movements	X+									bell and rattle, dropping of objects in play.
1. Stick in tube				X					X	
2. Examiner's use of block		X			X	X	X	X		ST; makes block walk. G; clicks together.
3. Stirs with spoon in cup						X				C; also bangs with spoon in cup.
4. Pats whistle doll in imitation						X		X	X	UH; listed as a familiar scheme.
5. Pellet in bottle in/out in imitation						X		X		
6. Adds chimney to train					X					
b. Complex actions composed of familiar schemes									X	UH; e.g., places object in container and shakes, etc.
1. Paper folding		X	X		X	X		X		ST and G; at least twice. B; once, attempt counts.
2. Domestic mimicry					X				X	
c. Drawing imitated										
1. Examiner's scribble					X			X		

Table 1. *(Continued)*

Item Category	Infant Scale											Comments on Stimuli and Item Criteria KEY: Kuhlman-Binet (KB), Stutsman (ST), Fillmore (F), Goodenough (Good), Kuhlman (K), Gesell (G), Cattell (C), Griffiths (Grif), Bayley (B), Uzgiris-Hunt (UH), Frankenberg (FK)
	Kuhlman-Binet, 1922	Stutsman, 1926	Fillmore, 1936	Goodenough et al., 1932	Kuhlman, 1939	Gesell, 1939	Cattell, 1940	Griffiths, 1954/1970	Bayley, 1969	Uzgiris-Hunt, 1976	Frankenberg et al., 1976 (PDQ)	
2. Examiner's horizontal or vertical strokes				X	X	X		X	X		X	FK; assesses vertical only.
3. Examiner's "V" or circular stroke						X						
d. Novel but visible gestures										X		
e. Novel but not observable gestures of the body										X		For example, touches top of head, facial expressions.
24. Imitation of Sounds												
a. Nonspeech sounds						X	X					For example, cough, click, raspberry.

		Notes
b.	Vocalizations shift to match	
c.	Novel sound patterns	Criteria vary with test.
d.	Familiar words	ST; 2 of 4 or 4 of 4 imitated.
e.	Novel words	
25.	**Drawing**	
a.	Attends scribbling	
b.	Holds implement adaptively	
c.	Successfully marks or spontaneous scribble	Grif; several levels assessed.
d.	Differentiates stroke from scribble	
e.	Copies circle (SB)	Good; several different figures thru preschool age commencing with circle. FK; not until after 36 mo. K; attempt accepted.
f.	Copies cross	G; 2 or more strokes for cross. Grif; figure must be recognizable.

Table 1. *(Continued)*

Item Category	Kuhlman-Binet, 1922	Stutsman, 1926	Fillmore, 1936	Goodenough et al., 1932	Kuhlman, 1939	Gesell, 1939	Cattell, 1940	Griffiths, 1954/1970	Bayley, 1969	Uzgiris-Hunt, 1976	Frankenberg et al., 1976 (PDQ)	Comments on Stimuli and Item Criteria — KEY: Kuhlman-Binet (KB), Stutsman (ST), Fillmore (F), Goodenough (Good), Kuhlman (K), Gesell (G), Cattell (C), Griffiths (Grif), Bayley (B), Uzgiris-Hunt (UH), Frankenberg (FK)
Infant Scale												
26. Motor Development[a]												
a. Head control			X		X+	X	X	X	XM		X	C, G, Grif, FK; several levels. Bayley Motor Scale item.
b. Sitting			X		X	X		X	XM		X	Typically assessed with and without support.
c. Rolls over			X			X		X	XM		X	
d. Creeps, crawls	X		X									
e. Stands			X		X	X		X	XM		X	Typically assessed with or without support.
f. Walks					X	X		X	XM		X	B, F, Grif; assess reflex and or early weight-bearing attempts.

Item				XM			Notes
g. Stands on one foot			X			X	
h. Cuts with scissor			X			X	Grif; attempts counted.
27. Feeding Behavior							
a. Single night feeding					X		
b. Pats or holds own bottle					X		
c. Uses glass or cup or feeds self	X		X		X	X	G and Grif; several levels assessed.
d. Uses fork or spoon	X		X		X		Grif, uses spoon, uses both.
e. Spits out solids					X		
f. Takes solids			X		X		
28. Self-Help and Personal Skills							
a. Cooperates in dressing	X		X		X		
b. Puts on or removes simple garments	X		X		X	X	G; includes zippering, buttoning. ST; buttons 1, 2 buttons (timed).
c. Puts things away when requested	X				X		
d. Can carry breakable objects or pour without spilling					X		

535

Table 1. (*Continued*)

Item Category	Infant Scale											Comments on Stimuli and Item Criteria
	Kuhlman-Binet, 1922	Stutsman, 1926	Fillmore, 1936	Goodenough et al., 1932	Kuhlman, 1939	Gesell, 1939	Cattell, 1940	Griffiths, 1954/1970	Bayley, 1969	Uzgiris-Hunt, 1976	Frankenberg et al., 1976 (PDQ)	KEY: Kuhlman-Binet (KB), Stutsman (ST), Fillmore (F), Goodenough (Good), Kuhlman (K), Gesell (G), Cattell (C), Griffiths (Grif), Bayley (B), Uzgiris-Hunt (UH), Frankenberg (FK)
e. Toileting						X			X			Several levels assessed.
29. Quantitative Ability												
a. Concept of 1												
b. Counts 1, 2		X	X+						X			
30. Body Parts (S-B, 4+ known)												
a. Points out eyes, nose, mouth on self or doll	X*		X	X	X	X	X	X	X		X	Minimum and maximum number vary with test.
31. Follows Directions (S-B)												

536

Item	Col1	Col2	Col3	Col4	Col5	Col6	Col7	Notes
a. Responds to simple requests (misc.)	X		X		X	X		C; same items as used on S-B, 2 levels.
b. Follows directions with doll			X	X	X	X		A small baby doll which can be fed, made to sit, etc.
c. Give me the/show me/bring me	X			X	X	X		
d. Follows two commands with ball				X				
e. Inhibits on command				X	X			
32. Early Speech								
a. Polysyllabic sounds (babble)								
1. Uses 2–3 syllables in combination (mama, dada, baba, etc.), at least one	X	X	X	X	X	X	X	Grif; several levels by string length.
2. Jargon/jabbers expressively		X	X	X	X	X	X	Grif; 2 levels, credits mama or dada and credits having both.
3. Babbles sentences with embedded word			X		X			

537

Table 1. *(Continued)*

Item Category	Kuhlman-Binet, 1922	Stutsman, 1926	Fillmore, 1936	Goodenough et al., 1932	Kuhlman, 1939	Gesell, 1939	Cattell, 1940	Griffiths, 1954/1970	Bayley, 1969	Uzgiris-Hunt, 1976	Frankenberg et al., 1976 (PDQ)	Comments on Stimuli and Item Criteria — KEY: Kuhlman-Binet (KB), Stutsman (ST), Fillmore (F), Goodenough (Good), Kuhlman (K), Gesell (G), Cattell (C), Griffiths (Grif), Bayley (B), Uzgiris-Hunt (UH), Frankenberg (FK)
b. Uses words												
1. Single word						X	X				X	Other than mama/dada, specified.
2. 2 words						X	X	X	X		X	
3. 3–4 word vocabulary						X		X				
4. 5–7 word vocabulary						X		X				
5. 9–12 word vocabulary								X				
6. Indicates absence of familiar person						X	X		X	X		
7. Uses words to make wants known												

Infant Scale

538

Item						Notes
a. Asks for toilet			X			
b. Asks for another			X			
8. 2-word sentences		X	X			
9. 3-word sentences			X			Grif; length in number of syllables.
10. Incidental speech scored	X			X		
11. 20+ word vocabulary			X		X	
12. 2 descriptive words				X		
13. Tries to tell experiences				X		

33. Picture Book

Item						Notes
a. Looks at pictures			X	X		Grif; several levels scored.
b. Pats pictures/active interest			X	X	X	
c. Turns pages			X		X	
d. Points and names					X	

34. Picture Cards (S-B)

Item						Notes
a. Interest in card only		X				

Table 1. *(Continued)*

Item Category	Kuhlman-Binet, 1922	Stutsman, 1926	Fillmore, 1936	Goodenough et al., 1932	Kuhlman, 1939	Gesell, 1939	Cattell, 1940	Griffiths, 1954/1970	Bayley, 1969	Uzgiris-Hunt, 1976	Frankenberg et al., 1976 (PDQ)	Comments on Stimuli and Item Criteria
												KEY: Kuhlman-Binet (KB), Stutsman (ST), Fillmore (F), Goodenough (Good), Kuhlman (K), Gesell (G), Cattell (C), Griffiths (Grif), Bayley (B), Uzgiris-Hunt (UH), Frankenberg (FK)
b. Recognizes object in picture	X		X	X								Spontaneous response: gaze, voc, or point.
c. Spontaneously names	X+	X	X		X							
d. Points out object in picture	X		X	X	X	X	X	X	X			Several levels, depending on number named; criteria vary with test.
e. Names objects in picture					X	X		X	X			
35. Comprehension and Pragmatics												
a. Uses gesture to make wants known						X		X			X	Grif; specifies, points with index finger.

								Comments
b. Responds to own name				X	X			
c. Pulls to show or shows spontaneously				X	X	X		
d. Likes rhymes/jingles						X		
e. Listens to stories						X		
f. Knows big, little/big, bigger						X		
g. Understands prepositions								
1. On, under, behind, in, to, in front		X		X	X	X		X	Typically at least two assessed, usually on and one other. Second preposition varies with test.
2. Follows complex command with preposition embedded	X		X					
36. Discrimination and Naming of Actual Objects (S-B)								
a. Names objects shown	X		X	X	X	X	X		ST; 1 of 10 or 6 of 10 named. UH; spontaneously names any object.
1. Knows penny, money				X	X				

Grif; 2 different levels scored.

541

Table 1. (*Continued*)

Item Category	Kuhlman-Binet, 1922	Stutsman, 1926	Fillmore, 1936	Goodenough et al., 1932	Kuhlman, 1939	Gesell, 1939	Cattell, 1940	Griffiths, 1954/1970	Bayley, 1969	Uzgiris-Hunt, 1976	Frankenberg et al., 1976 (PDQ)	Comments on Stimuli and Item Criteria
						Infant Scale						KEY: Kuhlman-Binet (KB), Stutsman (ST), Fillmore (F), Goodenough (Good), Kuhlman (K), Gesell (G), Cattell (C), Griffiths (Grif), Bayley (B), Uzgiris-Hunt (UH), Frankenberg (FK)
b. Discriminates 2 or 3 objects of series						X	X	X	X			C; uses S-B objects. Criteria (number named) varies with test.
c. Points to 4 objects						X	X	X				C; 2–3 objects used. B; cup, plate, box.
d. Gives use of test objects												Grif; minimum criteria: 2 or more objects.
e. Matches colored blocks		X										ST; 6 of 20 matches.

						Notes
37. Recognition of Incomplete Pictures						
a. Identifies incomplete watch	X			X		
b. Incomplete picture series						
38. Self-Concept						
a. Identifies self/refers to self by name	X	X	X			ST; in mirror. G; includes first person pronoun. Full name: required; ST.
b. Interest in possessions		X				
39. Form Board Problems						
a. Pegboard	X	X		X	X	Several levels from fingering hole, insert one, to completion, ST and C; Two types of pegboards: round, square. B; scores 4 different completion times.
b. Three-hole form	X	X	X	X	X	Several levels typi-

Table 1. (Continued)

Item Category	Infant Scale											Comments on Stimuli and Item Criteria
	Kuhlman-Binet, 1922	Stutsman, 1926	Fillmore, 1936	Goodenough et al., 1932	Kuhlman, 1939	Gesell, 1939	Cattell, 1940	Griffiths, 1954/1970	Bayley, 1969	Uzgiris-Hunt, 1976	Frankenberg et al., 1976 (PDQ)	KEY: Kuhlman-Binet (KB), Stutsman (ST), Fillmore (F), Goodenough (Good), Kuhlman (K), Gesell (G), Cattell (C), Griffiths (Grif), Bayley (B), Uzgiris-Hunt (UH), Frankenberg (FK)
board (circle, triangle, square) (SD-B)												cally assessed: placing one, two, all, doing board after it has been rotated. Note: UH does not use form board but has items dealing with appreciating reversal of objects.

| c. Other types of form board or form box problems | X | | | X | | X | X | B; times to completion and number of objects placed: circles and squares. Grif; one circle board, 2 circle board, circle/square board, 4 square board, 6 hole board, times to completion on latter two. ST; Séguin form board. |

Note. * = Original Binet-Simon item; S-B = Stanford-Binet item; + = discarded item; M = Bayley Motor Scale item. Only those which are most commonly assessed appear. Bayley items are from MOTOR, not the mental scale.

[a]Motor items are not listed exhaustively.

to be incapable of any sophisticated behavior, sensory and motor performance were the only behaviors that could presumably provide clues concerning emerging intelligence. The choice of such items now appears to be inappropriate but, as we shall describe in Section 4, the basic belief that competence can be assessed by quantifying some aspect of behavior or physiology remains. In many ways much of the history of infant intelligence tests can be regarded as a long search for the "right" measure. The search for new measurement methods continues in the 1980s.

The British Contribution.
Darwin's theory of evolution (1859) fostered the widespread belief that intelligence was fixed by heredity, and thereby essentially unmodifiable. This view, which would remain the predominant theory of human intelligence until the late 1920s and early 1930s (Kelley & Surbeck, 1983), was promoted by Darwin's cousin, Francis Galton (1884). Though Galton's own sensory and anthropometric tests proved no better at prediction than those subsequently developed in America and elsewhere, he has been identified as the "father of mental testing" (Goodenough, 1954). His methodological and theoretical contributions to the field include the following: the study of the role of heredity in intelligence through twin studies, as well as interest in individual differences in general (Brooks-Gunn & Weinraub, 1983), but particularly with respect to giftedness (Lewis & Michalson, 1985); the introduction of large and systematic data collection; the adoption of quantitative methods of data analysis; the development of the concept of variability; and collaborative efforts on correlation coefficient (Kelley & Surbeck, 1983).

The American Contribution.
Cattell, a student of Wundt and the German empirical tradition, initiated the study of individual differences in mental functioning in America and is credited with the introduction of the term "mental test" (Goodenough, 1954). American interest in testing was such that in 1895 a special committee of the American Psychological Association instigated the construction of tests that might predict the scholastic success of college entrants. Cattell was a member of this commission and produced such a test (Goodenough, 1954). At least one test of school-age children was also developed during this period (Gilbert, 1894). The issue of the construct and predictive validity of these early tests, biased as they were toward the sensory and memory processes, was raised as early as 1900 (Brooks-Gunn & Weinraub, 1983). Basic methodological issues, such as the need for standardized testing conditions, adequate sampling, and test reliability, also received attention as a result of this early work. Thus, while the tests themselves may have been inadequate, the research they generated raised important questions concerning assessment, questions which would surface repeatedly in the infant assessment movement.

The Influence of Baby Biographies.
The theory of evolution (Darwin, 1859, 1872) and the publication of Darwin's biography of his own infant son (1877) fostered interest in early human development. Infant diaries dating from

the sixteenth and seventeenth centuries are known; however, infancy study can be said to have become an appropriate area of scientific inquiry with the appearance of Darwin's baby biography. Approximately thirty such biographies appeared in print from 1877 to 1907 (Papalia & Olds, 1975), and they have continued to appear periodically (for example, Church, 1966). Some of the frequently cited biographies, in addition to Darwin's, are Preyer (1882), Shinn (1900), and Stern (1924). Dennis (1936) provides a complete bibliography of the early baby biographies.

Though the appearance of these first observational studies of human development did not impact directly on the construction of the first intelligence test, their influence on the development of infant assessment was quite important. First, they treated human development as a scientific topic and extended inquiry to the youngest ages. Second, they demonstrated an orderly sequence of human behavioral maturation and documented individual variation in the rate of development (Goodenough, 1954). Third, they provided inspiration for later theorists and a source for test situations for the infant scale developers. For example, responses to mirrors, standard infant test fare, were originally described by both Darwin (1877) and Preyer (1882). Furthermore, perhaps the most significant rethinking of infant intellectual development was prompted by Piaget's diary studies of his own children (Piaget, 1952). The maturational perspective (in essence, a belief in the importance of studying differences in patterns of development within normal children rather than intelligence *per se*) was a major school of thought in the early years of infant assessment and was a systematic extension of this first spark of interest. Finally, the baby diaries and their popularity were a visible expression of the historically recent, but already entrenched, concern of parents that their children develop successfully, however that might be defined: "From that point on [that is, the 1800s] interest in raising healthy, virtuous and successful children was to be a primary concern of parents and a topic that would through the years cover enough pages to blanket the earth" (Papalia & Olds, 1975, p. 5). A current rash of popular news articles, as well as telecasts on "how smart is baby," is the most recent evidence of the popular concern with infant intelligence.* The desire of parents to have intelligent and therefore presumably successful children, who develop on or ahead of schedule (although this presumption can be questioned too, according to Lewis & Michalson, 1983), appears to have originated in this preassessment era.

The French Influence. Between 1800 and 1900, a number of French physicians were interested in mental retardation (for example, Esquirol, Itard, Séguin). Their work resulted in the differential diagnosis of mental retardation

---

* See, for example, the following: Babies: What do they know? When do they know it? *Time,* August 15, 1983, pp. 52–59. "Bringing up superbaby," *Newsweek,* March 28, 1983, pp. 62–68. McCall, R. Can you raise a superbaby? *Parents,* November, 1983, p. 120. CBS-TV, New York City local evening newscast, March 22, 1984: Health Wire: Infant communication. ABC-TV Eyewitness News, New York City, local evening newscast, week of November 14, 1983: "How babies learn." (A five-part mini-series hosted by S. Field.)

and insanity, a distinction not made before their time (Brooks-Gunn & Weinraub, 1983). Primarily through the efforts of Séguin, both in France and in his later homeland, the United States, education of the retarded began to be undertaken (Kelley & Surbeck, 1983). Suddenly, there was a need in the educational community for a practical, empirically based identification and classification system for mental deficiency. At the same time, the emergence of public school education for children required an accurate, but efficient, assessment tool so that those who could not benefit from formal schooling could be identified.

In 1904, a commission was created in Paris to address these problems and delineate criteria for school placement. A member of this commission, Alfred Binet, a respected experimental psychologist and a contemporary authority on mental functioning in children had been lead by some 10 years of study to reject the then prevalent notion that intelligence could be assessed by tests of sensory functioning and anthropometrics (Pollack & Brenner, 1969). Although he himself had begun with such measures as head circumference and skin sensitivity, he subsequently rejected these (Hamley, 1935). Instead, he argued that higher mental functions, such as good judgment, reasoning ability, and comprehension, were essential dimensions of intellectual ability (Binet & Simon, 1905). Armed with this unorthodox view, he developed a scale that was based on his own gresearch with children. This scale was subsequently adopted by the commission to identify, classify, and refer for special instruction those public school children who were not of normal intellectual ability. Binet's approach to intelligence was pragmatic and closely tied to intervention (Gould, 1981). Because the focus of the test was the classification of the mentally deficient, it included items thought to be appropriate for infants through age 2 years, but which the lowest functioning retarded could also pass (Binet & Simon, 1905). Thus this test, the 1905 Binet scale, was not only the grandfather of all subsequent IQ tests, but also marked the first widely known test that included items appropriate for children under 2. An earlier test for children up to age 3 predated Binet by some eight years, but remained unknown probably because of its publication in an obscure, local American medical journal (Goodenough, 1954). Because of its historical and conceptual importance, we will consider the Binet-Simon and its American adoption in some detail.

1905–1919: Early IQ Testing

The Binet-Simon Scales (1905, 1908, 1911).   The Binet scale was unique and innovative. It assessed complex mental functioning and problem solving, rather than simple sensory and motor capacity. Items were arranged in increasing difficulty and were passed or failed. The items were simple to administer, score, and had standardized administration procedures. Most important, they discriminated retarded from normal children. The 1908 test, which was standardized on a small sample of Parisian children (both normal and institutionalized), had item difficulty gauged according to the age at which they were typically passed. Thus the concept of mental age was introduced. Of the six items on the original

1905 scale, which presumably tapped the competences of children 2 years of age and/or idiots, at least two have become classic and survive in some form on modern infant tests. Following a lighted match with the eyes and head has a parallel in the several items requiring elaborate visual tracking of a light found on several modern infant tests. Following simple directions and imitating gestures also have modern counterparts. Unfortunately, the infant items were among those that were ultimately dropped from the final scale (1911) because they were not appropriate to the tests' function of assessing the general intelligence of school-age children (Goodenough, 1954).

The Americanization of Binet-Simon.   The Binet-Simon scale was adopted rapidly in America by both the scientific and educational communities. Goddard (1908, 1910) produced an English translation of the original scales and actively promoted their use among the educational community. The scale was adopted by the Vineland Training School for the retarded where Goddard, its director, and his associates offered test administration seminars for teachers (Kelley & Surbeck, 1983). Moreover, Goddard wrote about his use of the test in a series of books and papers from 1910 to 1915 (Goodenough, 1954), which promoted the notion of intelligence as determined by heredity. However, interest in the Binet-Simon scales was not confined to educators of the retarded. Kelley & Surbeck (1983) list no fewer than five additional translations of the scales that appeared between 1910 and 1914. Goodenough (1954) comments: "The extraordinary rapidity with which Binet testing was taken up in America can be traced to a number of conditions. Most important is that the test appeared at the opportune moment" (p. 461). The needs of the educational community with respect to identification and classification of the retarded has already been mentioned. Other factors leading to the rapid adoption of the Binet scales included the following:

1. The need to identify and deal with children of limited ability forcibly retained in the primary grades because of compulsory school attendance laws (Goodenough, 1954).

2. The need for diagnostic and screening tools by organized social welfare agencies (Goodenough, 1954), including child adoption agencies (Brooks-Gunn & Weinraub, 1983).

3. The development of the mental hygiene movement that emphasized well baby/child clinics for children (Goodenough, 1954).

Another, albeit critical, view is that the Binet was adopted because it satisfied the American penchant for identification and selection as opposed to intervention: "The attraction of the Binet approach for American psychologists lay less in its potential for identifying educational problems and thus guiding interventions, and more in the possibility of generating a scale to arrange the population hierarchically in terms of a fixed (and typically inborn) characteristic termed 'intelligence.' The theoretical guide was Galton rather than Binet" (Keating, 1983, p. 4).

Still an additional factor that ensured American interest in the Binet test was a strong child-study movement. Since the turn of the century, psychological clinics devoted to the study of child development had been in existence at major universities throughout the United States (Sears, 1975). Under G. Stanley Hall, Clark University was a major center in the early child-study movement. Several psychologists who would figure prominantly in the early testing movement— Kuhlman, Goddard, Terman, and Gesell—studied at Clark University under Hall (Senn, 1975). Thus, in America at least, there were those who saw an important social and scientific need for examining the psychological development of young children. The Binet-Simon was therefore subjected to scientific study, underwent two American revisions, and eventually became the Stanford-Binet (Terman, 1917; Terman & Merrill, 1937). The 1937 edition, which remained in effect until 1960 (Terman & Merrill, 1960), began at 2 years of age.

Infants, Preschoolers, and the Early IQ Tests.   As we have seen, test items appropriate for infants were included in the original Binet scale only because they were thought to identify severely retarded individuals. The later Binet scales (1908, 1911) contained only 4 or 5 items for each age between 3 and 5 years. The emphasis of the early testing with the revised Binet continued to be as follows: (1) focused on school-age children, rather than on preschoolers and infants, and (2) concerned with a global index of intelligence. Kuhlman (1912) published a version of the Binet scale that included items for children under age 2. However, it was not widely used, and not until 1937 was the Stanford-Binet appropriate for assessing children below school age. Even then, the norms for children 2–6 years of age were not considered adequate until the 1960 revision (Bayley, 1970). It was not until the next decade that tests specifically for preschool children and infants were constructed.

1920–1939

Both theory and practical need continued to push the age of assessment below preschool age. During this period a number of tests for preschoolers and several infant assessment tools appeared. Two of the latter would continue to dominate infant assessment for many years.

The Tests.   The 1920s saw the development of the first tests for preschool children (Burt, 1921; Yerkes & Foster, 1923), as well as the first infant tests (Kuhlman, 1914/1922, 1939; Linfert & Hierholtzer, 1928; Traube & Stockbridge, 1922). According to Brooks-Gunn and Weinraub (1983), Kuhlman (1914/1922) and Linfert and Hierholtzer (1928) represent the first professionally produced infant tests, although neither was widely used in this country. In Britain, Kuhlman's test seemed to enjoy wider usage and was considered an "especially refined instrument" (Hamley, 1935, p. 38). Though these tests have been criticized because standardization was poor and the reliability and validity of the tests were unreported (see Brooks-Gunn & Weinraub, 1983, for a review), these early infant tests indicate the developing interest in providing for assessment at the youngest ages.

Several other tests developed for the very young during this and the following decade should be mentioned, though they typically targeted the preschool child rather than the young infant. Hamley (1935) provides an appendix of the numerous tests of this period for children under age 6; only the better-known or historically interesting will be mentioned here. Stutsman's (1926) Merrill-Palmer Scale, for example, provided assessment from 18 months through preschool age. In addition to testing children under 2 years of age, it used items that influenced later infant tests (Fillmore, 1936, for example). The materials for this test, though known to test researchers, were not widely available until later (Goodenough, 1928; Stutsman, 1931). A similar scale, the Minnesota Pre-School Scale, was also developed by Goodenough, Foster, and Wagenen (1932). Other tests that can be mentioned are Van Alstyne's Picture Vocabulary Test (1929) and Atkins' Object Fitting Test (1931). The former, described by Hamley (1935), may have been a forerunner of today's Peabody Picture Vocabulary Test (Dunn & Dunn, 1959/1981). Designed for children 2 to 5, it had 45 cards with 4 pictures each. The child was required to point to the picture depicting the test word. Atkins' test was a nonverbal test requiring the fitting of various objects into matching recesses. It was standardized with children as young as 2 years and was thought to be appropriate for deaf or non-English speakers.

In the decade between 1930 and 1940, five additional infant scales appeared: Gesell's Developmental Schedules (Gesell & Thompson, 1938); Buhler's Viennese Test Series (1930; Buhler & Hertzer, 1935); Shirley's Minnesota Infant Study (1933); Bayley's California First Year Mental Scale (1933a); and Fillmore's Iowa Tests for Young Children (1936). Table 2 provides a brief history and description of each of the infant tests mentioned above. Of these tests, the work of Gesell and Bayley became widely used and influential in infant assessment. Both currently exist in revised forms (Bayley, 1969; Knobloch, Stevens, & Malone, 1980). We will discuss them in detail as they represent two distinct theoretical approaches to infant assessment.

Gesell's Normative Research

Gesell is acknowledged as a pioneer in infant assessment and an outstanding advocate of infancy study in general (Brooks-Gunn & Weinraub, 1983; Honzik, 1983; Yang, 1979). Gesell and his colleagues developed a scale for the assessment of behavioral development from infancy through 6 years of age during the period from 1925 to 1947 (Gesell, 1925; Gesell & Armatruda, 1947; Gesell & Thompson, 1938). Gesell's Developmental Schedules probably represent the most extensive description of the behavior of infants and young children. Even descriptions of neonatal behavior were included in early work, although the normative data actually published for the scales began at 3 months of age (Yang, 1979). In later scales, normative data was extended downward to 1 month of age.

Unlike his normative work, Gesell's Developmental Schedules have been

Table 2

Test	Age Range	Behaviors Assessed	Scoring and Other Comments
Gesell Developmental Schedules	Birth to 4 months, 6, 9, 12, 18 months, 2, 3, 4, and 5 years (later editions 1 month to 6 years)	Motor development, language development, adaptive behavior, personal-social behaviors.	Age placement, diagnostic purposes, based on normative observations.
Buhler Viennese Series	Birth to 5 years, monthly tests to 8 months, bimonthly to 18 months, yearly 2 to 5 years	Sensory receptivity, bodily movement, social behavior and language, learning and imitation, manipulation, mental productivity.	Developmental age, diagnostic purpose, seeks typical *not* optimal performance, continuous 24-hour observation.
Fillmore's Iowa Tests for Young Children	4.5 to 23.5 months	Areas of concentration vary with age of child.	Assesses mental development intended for research purposes, attempts to use only items predictive of IQ in final test items.
Shirley's Minnesota Infant Study Test Series	Birth to 2 years, weekly exams to 1 year, biweekly 1 to 2 years	Areas of concentration vary with age of child, age motor skills tapped throughout, timed exams of 30 minutes, daily observations of neonates.	Based on normative longitudinal observations.
Bayley Scales of Infant Motor and Mental Development	Birth to 18 months (later edition to 30 months)	Separately scored motor scale, mental scale has numerous items which tap adaptive behavior, visual maturity, response to auditory stimuli, language comprehension, and production and social responses.	Age placement at 0.1 month, separate developmental "quotient" for mental and motor scales, age equivalent scoring also possible.

faulted in reviews of infant assessment for lack of statistical reliability, inadequate standardization, and highly variable if not poor predictability of subsequent IQ scores. In evaluating Gesell's contribution, it is important to consider Gesell's theoretical position and the purpose for which the schedules were designed. Each of the reviewers of Gesell's contribution (Ames, 1967; Brooks-Gunn & Weinraub, 1983; Honzik, 1983; Yang, 1979) notes that Gesell never intended the Schedules to be used as a measure of intellectual functioning. Despite a strong biological orientation, Gesell represented the pragmatic philosophy in infant testing (Yang, 1979). The scales were intended to be diagnostic tools for the modern infant and child hygiene movement. The test situations themselves were practical in that they capitalized on naturally occurring situations in the home or clinic and used objects or tasks that had natural appeal for infants. It is for this reason that they have been repeatedly borrowed.

Gesell's interest in individual differences evolved from a strong biological orientation and his concern was with the maturational unfolding of an individual's biologically determined potential in all areas of functioning. Thus he emphasized the sequence and process of growth rather than predictability. Honzik (1983) likens the orientation to that of "a pediatric neurologist" despite his behavioral training. Yang (1979) also traces Gesell's approach directly to the methods of embryology. Gesell's early emphasis on biological stages and the sequencing of growth is still evident albeit somewhat softened in this excerpt from his forward to *Child Behavior* (Ilg & Ames, 1956), a popular rendition of this work that appeared some 25 years later:

> The opening page . . . sets the theme—namely the theme of **growth** [emphasis in original]. To understand a child, we try to understand his ways of growth, for growth is the prime essence of life, especially child life. The child grows as a unit in mind, body, and personality. He is born into a culture, subject to the powerful influences of home, school, community. But he is also subject to the deep seated growth forces which shape his individuality. Each and every part of the child's nature has to grow—his sense of self, his fears, affections and curiosities, his feelings toward mother and father, brothers, sisters and playmates, his attitudes toward sex, his judgments of good and bad, of ugly, of beautiful. [p. 7]

Note that despite the passing acknowledgment of environmental influences, the major focus is on the innate, biologically determined patterns of maturation, patterns that are evident in all behavioral domains, not just the intellectual. Given this theoretical perspective, Ames (1967) and others have argued that the low to moderately positive correlations that have been obtained between the Gesell Schedules and various measures of intellectual functioning are reasonable and "theoretically appropriate" (Yang, 1979, p. 170).

The Gesell Schedules have been widely used for many years, particularly in pediatric settings, and have spawned at least one other major pediatric screening instrument (Frankenberg & Dodds, 1967; Frankenberg, Dodds, Fandal, Kazuk, & Cohrs, 1975). Yang (1979) provides a thorough history of the scales' further refinements and a summary of research with this instrument.

The Bayley Scales of Infant Mental and Motor Development

The Bayley Mental Scale appeared originally in 1933 as the California First Year Mental Scale, with the motor scale following shortly thereafter (Bayley, 1936). Originally standardized on the longitudinal sample from the Berkeley Growth Study, the scales were the first infant tests specifically designed to predict future competence. Bayley's concern was not with normative data *per se*, but with those specific infant behaviors that were predictive of later competence and the extent to which performance was stable during the first months of life. Although she borrowed from the Gesell Schedules, Bayley developed her scales around those behaviors that she believed represented "significant criteria of development" (Bayley, 1933a). Bayley also departed from her predecessors in her scrupulous concern with the psychometric properties of her tests. She provided validity data and split half reliabilities—a practice that she continued in her 1969 revision of the test. Unfortunately, the early mental scale (1933a) failed to have high predictive validity, a result which Bayley concluded was indicative of the nature of early intellect: "Not until the age of 2 years do these composites exhibit a significant degree of overlapping with aggregations of traits constituting intelligence" (1933b, p. 82). Bayley's scales, though not widely used for many years, were and continue to be the most thoroughly researched infant assessment instrument (Brooks-Gunn & Weinraub, 1983). The most recent version (Bayley, 1969) provides a history of the test and details of the more recent standardization on a representative U.S. sample. The 1969 revision makes Bayley scales the best standardized of the American infant scales. British norms are also available (Francis-Williams & Yule, 1967). Moreover, the split half reliabilities of the tests are not only improved but are more consistent across all ages ($r = .81$ to $.93$), compared to what they were in 1933.

Theoretical Formulations.   During this period, the assessment research on young children focused on very basic issues. Kelley & Surbeck (1983) delineate several major research questions that were addressed in America:

1.   What are the characteristics of normal young children?
2.   What is the role of environment in intelligence?
3.   What can be done to improve the assessment of the very young child?

As we have seen, Gesell's work was directed at the first of these, namely, identifying the developmental characteristics of normal young children, while Bayley's work was concerned with actually improving assessment. Her work inadvertently led to a questioning of a hitherto untested assumption. Until the publication of her results, Bayley herself and most other theorists had assumed intelligence was developmentally stable (Yang, 1979). Subsequent research would continue to explore this now controversial issue.

   This period also saw the initial questioning of the second major assumption made about intelligence: its immutability. The first research with preschoolers appeared and suggested that intelligence was modifiable and was affected by the quality of early environment (Kelley & Surbeck, 1983). With the suggestion that multiple test scores, combined with parent's educational status, improved prediction of later intelligence (Anderson, 1939), the possibility of environmental impact on nonstable emergent intelligence began to be considered. The great debate between heredity and environment with respect to IQ, dubbed the Wellman-Goodenough Controversy after its principal proponents (Kelley & Surbeck, 1983), continues to the present day. However, the current argument centers not on whether environment has any effect, but the extent to which change is possible, the appropriate timing of intervention, and the degree to which the effects of intervention are enduring.

1940–1959

Infant testing during the 1930s has been characterized as a period of "consolidation" as the research on the reliability and predictive validity of the early tests was examined (Brooks-Gunn & Weinraub, 1983). Thereafter followed a period of "growing disillusionment" with infant tests because of the poor predictive validity (see, for example, Irwin, 1942). Of the early validity studies reviewed by Brooks-Gunn & Weinraub (1983), none of the correlations exceeded .50, although some particular test items were more predictive of later Stanford-Binet performance. At least one attempt at factor analysis of Gesell (Richards & Nelson, 1939) was made. This method would be extensively employed in the 1960s in an attempt to improve the predictive validity of infant tests.

Despite such disillusionment, several major efforts were made to improve existing infant tests or develop new instruments (Brunet-Lézine, 1951; Cattell, 1940; Griffiths, 1954; Shotwell & Gilliland, 1943). The attitude of many researchers to the poor prediction offered by infant tests appears to have been that predictability could be improved either by the inclusion of concurrent clinical information or by revamping the tests. Others, most notably Gesell and Griffiths, felt that prediction of subsequent IQ was an inappropriate goal and that the true role of infant assessment was early diagnosis (Honzik, 1983; Yang, 1979).

Each of the new efforts in infant assessment depended in some way on the work of Gesell. The Northwestern Intelligence Scale (Shotwell & Gilliland, 1943) in particular relied heavily on the Gesell Schedules for test items (Brooks-Gunn & Weinraub, 1983). Both the Griffiths Mental Development Scale (1954) and the Brunet-Lézine Test (1951) are close European cousins of the Gesell Schedules. Like the Gesell, their primary purpose is diagnosis rather than prediction of individual intelligence scores (Honzik, 1983). The Griffiths (for ages 2 weeks to 2 years) was standardized on a British sample and resembles the Gesell Schedules in some respects. However, speech and language related items in the first year of life, such as auditory responses, babbling, and so on, are given greater emphasis than on the earlier tests. This innovation may be quite important, however there has been to date very little research on predictive validity with this instrument. According to Honzik (1983), Brunet-Lézine is essentially a French version of the Gesell Schedules that is used extensively in Europe. The test was used in a major Swedish longitudinal study. The Cattell Infant Intelligence Test has the distinction of being the second major American infant scale specifically designed to tap intellectual performance and has often been referred to as the downward extension of the Stanford-Binet. Such was its intention, although in practice, the Cattell has fared little better than the Bayley in predicting subsequent Stanford-Binet scores (Honzik, 1983). Like the Bayley, the Cattell was developed for use in a longitudinal study and has standardized administration and scoring. Internal reliabilities by odd-even method are adequate, being in excess of .71 with the exception of the 3 month test, which is not as reliable (Brooks-Gunn & Weinraub, 1983). The Cattell has a smaller number of items and is therefore quicker to administer and less taxing than are other tests, but its brevity may be a questionable advantage (Honzik, 1983).

In general, the later infant tests were more carefully designed, standardized, and objectively administered than the earlier tests. Predictive validity remained the unresolved and thorny issue as other studies—most notably Cattell (1940), Honzik, McFarlane, and Allen (1948), Hindley (1960), and Wittenborn et al. (1956)—repeatedly confirmed that scores on infant tests correlated minimally with scores earned on IQ tests after school age. Nevertheless, the use of infant tests as assessment/diagnostic tools apparently became more widespread during this time. Stott & Ball's (1965) survey of infant and preschool test use in the early 1960s indicated that of 217 respondents involved with the assessment of children below school age, 81% had used currently available tests for diagnostic purposes. Brooks-Gunn and Weinraub (1983) note that for adoption agencies, who were particularly in need of screening young infants, the tests were the only available diagnostic tools.

1960–1979

The evidence for poor predictive validity, at least within normal populations, continued to mount (Bayley, 1970; Lewis & McGurk, 1972; McCall, Hogarty, & Hurlburt, 1972; Stott & Ball, 1965). This period can be characterized by a gradual rejection of the notion of intelligence as a stable, unitary factor and by an emerging consensus that even improvements in existing tests would not result in better prediction within the population of normal children (Brooks-Gunn & Weinraub, 1983). Increasingly, there was acceptance of the notion that the skills that could be tapped during infancy were qualitatively different from those tapped on later tests and that their relationship to that construct known as intelligence was complex. Acceptability of this premise was no doubt aided by the introduction into American psychology of Piaget's theory (1952) on the origins of intelligence. Despite this newly emerging consensus or perhaps because of it, there was unabated, perhaps even intensified, interest in early assessment (Yang, 1979). In the 1960s preschool education and assessment exploded with the availability of federal monies for preschool and special education (Kelley & Surbeck, 1983). This development had indirect impact on infant testing because it intensified the need to identify deficits or their precursors during or before the preschool years. In the late 1970s and into the present decade there has been increasing concern with the early identification and remediation of learning disabilities (Lewis & Taft, 1982, for example). Once again the preschool child and infant were targeted for assessment, but this time the need to examine the development of specific skills, such as language, became the focus. In infant assessment, where the trend away from general to specific skills and away from strictly normative to process orientated assessment was already apparent, the preschool explosion and concern with various aspects of "readiness" reinforced this development.

Finally, medical and psychological knowledge concerning human infants also expanded greatly during this decade. The phrase "the competent infant" (Stone, Smith, & Murphy, 1973) became the catchword of infant behavioral research, replacing older notions of a passive, ineffective, disorganized creature. The remarkable abilities of even very young infants to attend selectively, process, and act upon the "blooming, buzzing confusion" (James, 1890) were a newly identified set of skills that traditional assessment instruments examined cursorily. Recognition of this fact would foster a number of new approaches to assessment. In the medical domain new technologies and improved care for very young and small infants produced a new population of neonates—those who formerly would not have been viable. There was now a critical need to perform neonatal screening, assessment, and follow-up of these high-risk infants. Once again the type of tests that emerged were a reflection of both shifting practical need and theoretical views about infants and the development of intelligence.

Tests of Specific Skills in Infancy.   For many professionals, the most important aspect of infant tests is their prescriptive rather than their predictive value. Tests have prescriptive value if they provide professionals with a profile of strengths and weaknesses that can be used in designing individually tailored programs for intervention. From this viewpoint infant tests, which for the most part were designed as measures of general ability, fail. They provide only single scores and reveal little about specific aspects of functioning. Equivalent developmental quotients on the Bayley Mental Scale, for example, do not indicate that any two children in question have similar deficits. One child may attain a low score because of motoric disability, another because of perceptual impairment, still a third may fail language items. To circumvent this problem, a number of tests were developed to examine specific sensorimotor, social, and language skills. We will briefly review the major tests in each of these areas.

Sensorimotor Intelligence.   Assessment of various sensorimotor competencies was a major theme in test construction during this period. These tests tap the development of skills achieved by the infant within the first 2 years of life, such as object permanence, imitation, means-ends behavior, tool use, and categorization skills. Brooks-Gunn and Weinraub (1983) mention five such scales of sensory-motor ability (Bell, 1970; Decarie, 1965; Escalona & Corman, 1969;

Ricciuti, 1965; Uzgiris & Hunt, 1975). Johnson (1976) reviews a number of others including Casati-Lézine (Casati & Lézine, 1968, a French scale), the Infant Cognitive Developmental Scale (Mehrabian & Williams, 1971), and a scale of gestural imitation developed by Winkelstein (1974) based on one of the Uzgiris-Hunt subscales. Uzgiris (1983) also mentions some additional research instruments. Of these scales, the most widely known, researched, and widely used has been the Uzgiris-Hunt Ordinal Scales of Development (1975). The test consists of six separate scales, each consisting of test situations arranged in stepwise progressions such that they focus on the sequential milestones attained within the particular sensorimotor skill being assessed. The scales are as follows: (1) visual pursuit and object permanence; (2) means-ends; (3) vocal and gestural imitation; (4) operational causality; (5) construction of objects in space; and (6) the development of schemes relating to objects. Uzgiris (1983) reviews the most recent research with respect to this instrument and provides some comparative information about her scales and several other sensorimotor scales.

The importance of the Uzgiris-Hunt scales lies in a number of significant differences between this instrument and the more traditional infant scales. First, the scales independently assess multiple skills rather than general competence. Second, the scales are focused more directly on problem solving and conceptual understanding than do many of the early infant items on other tests. Moreover, the infant receives developmental credit for the quality of his or her action on the test problem rather than just a simple pass/fail assessment. Third, the test proceeds from the theoretical tenet that intellectual functioning in infancy is a distinct entity and "needs to be understood in its own right" (Uzgiris, 1983) and not solely as it relates to later test scores. As such, any pretense of prediction is eschewed. From such a perspective, the low to modest correlations obtained between the Uzgiris-Hunt and other infant tests in addition to the 30- to 36-month Stanford-Binet are not only reasonable but theoretically consistent. However, it should be noted that the correlations obtained between these scales and the Stanford-Binet are similar to those obtained for other infant tests (Honzik, 1983).

Other Infant Skills

A number of other scales and instruments have been developed to tap skills that first emerge during infancy. For example, the Fantz-Nevis Visual Preference Test (1967) assesses attention for infants under 6 months; the assessment of attention will be discussed in some detail later. The Ring and Cube Test (Kohn-Raz, 1966), which assesses bilateral grasp between 5 and 18 months, was designed to provide more comprehensive information about grasping than is obtainable from the Bayley Motor Scale. However, the two skill domains for which instruments have especially proliferated are social/emotional and language development.

Social/Emotional Assessment. Numerous scales for the assessment of social competencies and behavior problems among preschoolers and handicapped children were developed during this period (see Day Care and Child Developmental Council of America, 1973; New York State Office for Education of Children with Handicap, 1982). The Vineland Social Maturity Scale (Doll, 1953) and the Ring and Peg Tests of Behavioral Development for handicapped children (Banham, 1964) are two such scales. By the late 1970s, measures of specific social skills, such as cooperation, frustration, peer interaction skills, conformity, and interpersonal aggression, were available for the assessment of the very young child (see Johnson, 1976). The proliferation of such tools reflects a growing recognition of the importance of social behaviors in overall competence as well as the growing dissatisfaction with the notion that differences in intellectual capacity alone explain or predict child outcomes. Furthermore, individual differences, as well as the individual's well-being throughout the life cycle, are not due solely to differences in intellectual capacity (Lewis & Michalson, 1983); in fact, the infant literature reveals that social interaction in the earliest months has an impact on both concurrent and subsequent intellectual competence. Lewis and Coates, for example, reported that the occurrence of contingent maternal responsivity is associated with the development of cognitive competencies both concurrently at 3 months of age (Lewis & Coates, 1980), and at 6 years (Coates & Lewis, 1984). Ramey, Farran, & Campbell (1979) have also reported that the prediction of 36-month Stanford-Binet IQ was possible using maternal behavior and attitude measures obtained at the 3-month laboratory visit. Ruddy and Bornstein (1982) reported that both infant attention and type of maternal stimulation at 4 months predicted differences in cognitive skills at 12 months. Babies who exhibited faster habituation and greater response decrements at 4 months had higher Bayley MDIs and a larger speaking vocabulary at 12 months of age. Bayley scores at 4 months did not predict vocabulary size at 12 months. Manipulation of objects at 4 months was predictive of 12-month Bayley MDI, but frequency of maternal encouragement of infant attention to objects at 4 months was correlated with 12-month speaking vocabulary.

There is now a large body of research on infant social development and a number of scales and observational systems for infant social and emotional behavior; for example, the Infant Adaptation Scale (Fowler & Sutherland, 1976), which assesses responsivity of 9- to 30-month-olds to novel physical environments and persons, or APPROACH (Caldwell & Honzig, 1971), a system for coding human interactions in naturalistic situations. The most recent comprehensive scale for infants, called the Scales of Social Emotional Development (Lewis & Michalson, 1983), assesses a number of different emotional responses in infants and young children between 3 and 30 months of age as they occur in common situations. The scale is unique in that its emphasis is primarily on the emotional behaviors exhibited by the child in specific contexts. Moreover, the behaviors are broadly sampled and include facial, vocal, postural, and locomotive behaviors. The scales yield scores with respect to specific emotions, such as fear and sadness, as well as profiles of emotional responsiveness across situations. The scales offer a promising approach to the study of early social-emotional development and perhaps the means to examine the interrelationship between individual variability in the emotional and intellectual domains.

Language.   Language assessment for very young children has been by far the most rapidly expanding area of test development and child research. Language has assumed this importance not only because verbal skills constitute a significant component of IQ, but also because of the recognition that it is language skills that are essential for school success and that the early language learning years are critical for the development of these skills (Cazden, 1983). In both Britain and the United States, scales to quantify language and communicative development have been developed. The pitfall of most of the language assessments is that adequate standardization and norms are lacking. In addition, the psychometric properties, including reliability and validity, are unreported from some of the tests (see Darley, 1979; Kilburg, 1981). McCauley and Swisher (1984) reported that fewer than 6 language assessment instruments (20% of those surveyed) met 5 out of 10 standard psychometric criteria for a well-constructed and validated test. No test met them all, and only one test met 8 of the 10 criteria. The authors concluded that, on the whole, there is little evidence currently available regarding the reliability and validity of these instruments. Table 3 lists a number of frequently referenced language assessment instruments and notes where they are reviewed.

Screening

The goal of screening is neither to provide a measure of intelligence, nor to examine specific skills; instead, the goal is to identify those children who have a high likelihood of having delayed or abnormal development. Diagnosis has always been an important facet of infant assessment, and the increased emphasis on screening has been an important development. Numerous screening instruments designed to uncover neurological problems, developmental delay, or retardation were developed for use by day care and preschool personnel as well as by the pediatric community. The latter are becoming increasingly aware of the new morbidity—problems such as learning disabilities and sleep disturbances. Johnson (1976) lists 10 screening instruments for children under 6. Cross and Johnston (1977) provide an additional compendium. Of these instruments, we will discuss the Denver Developmental Screening Test (DDST—Frankenberg, Dodds, Fandal, Kazuk, & Cohrs, 1975; Frankenberg, Fandal, Sciarillo, & Burgess, 1981) and the related Prescreening Development Questionnaire (PDQ—Frankenberg, van Doornick, Liddell, & Dick, 1976), because these are probably the most widely known and researched pediatric/clinical assessment tools in the United States. The DDST has been standardized on a British (Bryant, Richards, & Voorhees, 1973) and on a Japanese (Ueda, 1978) sample as well. In addition, Frankenberg and colleagues, in their effort to promote routine screening of all infants, have continuously revised and developed their screening tools to meet the needs of pediatric practice. Their goal has been to develop a screening program that has a high likelihood of use given the constraints of pediatric and clinical care.

    The DDST is a battery of 105 items arranged in developmental sequence, which, like the Gesell schedules, taps four major behavioral domains: personal social, fine motor-adaptive, language, and gross motor. Results on 23 to 30 items at any age yield a score that can be categorized as normal, abnormal, suspect, or untestable. Repeated screening is required at 3–6, 9–12, and 18–24 months of age, and yearly thereafter through 5 years of age. The DDST is simple and straightforward to administer and interpret and can be administered by a trained paraprofessional. The original 15–20 minute DDST was felt to be of reasonable length. However, the research on DDST usage indicated that its length was the principal constraint on its routine usage. In response, Frankenberg and colleagues developed two new screening tools and a two-stage screening process. In the new screening protocol, either an abbreviated DDST or the PDQ is used as the first stage of screening. The PDQ is a parent questionnaire that can be administered during office waiting time to parents with at least a high school education. The shortened DDST is recommended for those for whom ability to read or to understand the PDQ items is doubtful. Any child tagged as suspect on either of these prescreening procedures would then be administered the full DDST in the second stage of the screening program. The objective is to reduce the amount of time spent with children who are of low risk, but to screen all children at some level. The attempt to use the observations of parents systematically in screening is an interesting and potentially fruitful approach to the screening problem.

Frankenberg et al. (1975) report in their 6-year follow-up study that the DDST program accurately identifies 85–100% of infant and preschoolers who are developmentally delayed. In that follow-up study at least 89% of children with abnormal DDSTs were failing in school. According to Frankenberg et al. (1975), the DDST is a reliable, economic screening protocol for detecting those children at greatest risk of developmental impairment as well as a valuable tool for screening asymptomatic children. Regarding reliability and validity, the DDST compares favorably to that of other screening instruments. Werner (1972), however, states that the DDST under refers during the first two years of life and over refers thereafter. Hopefully, the latest revision of the DDST (Frankenberg et al., 1981) will assuage these concerns.

Neonatal Assessment

Assessment of the newborn infant (birth through 28 days of age) saw considerable growth during the last two decades. The development of these tests followed the trend in infant assessment away from the prediction of intelligence toward screening, diagnosis, and measurement of specific competencies in the very young. Self and Horowitz (1979) provide a succinct overview of the efforts in neonatal assessment between 1960 and 1979:

> Neonatal assessment is done for a variety of reasons. When motivated by clinical needs, such assessments are largely used to guide practitioners in assessing the *immediate* [emphasis added] status of the infant and in making some decision concerning treatment or special care . . . in the context of a research program . . . the measured status of the neonate is a source of data. [p. 158]

Table 3. Communication and Language Assessments Available for Very Young Children

Test	Authors	Age Range	Reviewers
Communication Evaluation Chart (CEC)	Anderson, Miles, and Catheny, 1963	0–5 years	Kilburg, 1981; Muller, Monro, and Code, 1981
Developmental Sentence Analysis	Lee, 1974	2–4 years	Johnson, 1976; Darley, 1979
Early Language Assessment Scale	Honzig and Caldwell, 1966	Older infants	Kilburg, 1981
Environmental Pre-Language Assessment Scale	McDonald and Horstmeier, 1978	Children with 1-word through 4-word sentences	Kilburg, 1981; Carley, 1979
Fairview Language Evaluation Scale	Boroskin, 1971	0–6 years	Johnson, 1981
Full Range Vocabulary Test	Ammons and Ammons, 1948	2–17 months	Darley, 1979
Houston Test for Language Development	Crabtree, 1958	6–36 months	Kilburg, 1981; Darley, 1979
Manual for Testing Language Abilities of 1- to 3-year-old Children	Maimour and Constable 1971, Revised edition—Stockey and Hare, 1975	1–3 years	Kilburg, 1981
Peabody Picture Vocabulary Test	Dunn, 1965	2–13 months	Darley, 1979
Prelinguistic Infant Vocabulary Analysis	Ringwall, 1965	Prior to 1-word utterances	Muller, Munro, and Code, 1981

Preschool Language Scale	Zimmerman, Steiner, and Pond, 1979	18 months to 7 years	Johnson, 1976; Kilburg, 1981; Darley, 1979
Receptive/Expression Emergent Language Scale (REEL)	Bzoch and League, 1971	0–6 years	Johnson, 1976; Kilburg, 1981; Muller, Munro, and Code, 1981; Darley, 1979
Reynell Developmental Language Scale (Revised)	Reynell, 1977	1–6 years	Kilburg, 1981; Johnson, 1981; Muller, Munro, and Code, 1981
Scales of Early Communication Skill of Hearing Impaired	Moog and Geers, 1979	2 months to 2 years, handicapped	Darley, 1979
Sequenced Inventory of Communication Development (SICD)	Hedrich, Prather, and Tobin, 1975	4 months to 4 years	Kilburg, 1981; Darley, 1979
Shield Speech and Language Scale	Shield Institute for Retarded Children, 1968	Handicapped	Darley, 1979
Speech Rating Scale for Children with Severe Speech Lags	Shapiro and Fish, 1969; 1974	1½–8 years, handicapped	Johnson, 1976
Utah Test of Language Development (Revised)	Mecham, Jex, and Jones, 1967	1½–14½ years	Kilburg, 1981; Darley, 1979
Vane Evaluation of Language (Vane L)	Vane, 1975	2½–6 years	Darley, 1979
Verbal Language Development Scale (Revised)	Mecham, 1971	0–14 years	Kilburg, 1981; Muller, Munro, and Code, 1981; Darley, 1979

Although Self and Horowitz (1979) predict increasing application of neonatal assessment, particularly in research with special populations, they also comment:

> With the current range of neonatal assessment procedures available, there is increasingly less need to develop still additional instruments and the majority of current research efforts using neonatal assessment techniques are designed to answer substantive questions. . . . Almost nobody views the earliest assessment of the infant as being related to any later measurement of IQ. In this consensus is reflected progress in infant assessment. [p. 158]

Prechtl (1982), Sameroff (1978), and Self and Horowitz (1979) review and critically discuss neonatal screening techniques, such as the Apgar (1953), a number of obstetrical complications scales and neurological exams developed by Dubowitz et al. (1970), Prechtl and Bentima (1964), and Parmelee (1975), as well as behavioral assessments for the newborn, such as the Graham-Rosenblith Behavioral Test for Neonates (Rosenblith, 1974, 1979) and the Brazelton Neonatal Behavioral Assessment Scale (1973). Self and Horowitz (1979) also present an informative chart on the various motor and reflexive behaviors, physiological characteristics, and neurological signs that constitute the various neonatal and infant scales, while revealing those items that are common across instruments. We will provide a brief description of only two neonatal behavioral tests.

It should also be noted that Korner and Thoman (1970) have also developed an interesting visual alertness scale for newborns that was used in determining infant behavioral receptivity to soothing stimulation. These two behaviors—visual alertness (cognitive) and soothability (temperament)—were found to be related to the type of stimulation and to exhibit individual differences. Despite excellent reliability (Johnson, 1976), this has remained an infrequently used research tool.

Graham-Rosenblith Behavior Test.   This test is a revision of an original scale developed by Graham, Matarazzo, & Caldwell (1956) and Graham, Ernhart, Thurston, & Craft (1962), which sought to differentiate traumatized and possibly brain-injured infants from normal infants. The test scores reflect average, as opposed to optimal, performance in contrast to the Brazelton. This test predated standardized neurological assessments and thus Graham can be regarded as a pioneer in neonatal assessment. In fact, current neonatal assessment developers are as beholding to her as infant test developers are to Gesell (Prechtl, 1982). Rosenblith's aim in modifying the original test was to enhance its usefulness in identifying infants who, though not medically suspect, might be "at risk." Rosenblith (1979) unequivocally states that she did not assume individual predictions would result from her test. In fact, the measures apparently differentiate at risk infants within the normal population and are predictive of functioning at 8 months and at 4 years on some indices (for instance, gross and fine motor, IQ classification, and aspects of emotional behavior). In general, at age 4, there was a greater relationship between risk-scores and functioning for females than for males (Rosenblith, 1979). In addition, Rosenblith (1979) reported that it was the tactile-adaptive subscale, which assesses the defensive responses of the newborn (in essence, those responses that remove or ward off stimuli occluding the nose and/or mouth), that was the most highly predictive at 4 years. Rosenblith's results indicate that the greatest proportion of suspect and abnormal scores originate from those infants with tactile-adaptive scores in the lowest quartile. The next greatest proportion came from the other extreme—the highest quartile. Thus *either* poor or highly exaggerated defensive responses were related to subsequent problems (suggesting either failure to develop adequate defensive reflexes or rigidity/stereotypy in the central nervous system).

Brazelton Neonatal Behavioral Assessment Scale (NBAS).   These scales include a wide range of behaviors that are believed to reflect the integrity of neonatal CNS. A special strength of the test is that it includes items that are more sophisticated in terms of the infant's capacity than those used in standard neurological examinations. The typical pediatric exam, for example, would assess visual functioning by eliciting the pupillary reflex and examining nystagmoid movements on rotation. But infant research of the last decade indicates that infants are capable of more complex visual behavior. Neonates, for example, can habituate their initial blink and startle responses to a bright light. Complex responses to moving objects, such as widening of the pupils and eyelids, facial softening, inhibition of generalized movements, and coordinated tracking movements with the eyes, are all within the newborn's behavioral repertoire. Furthermore, neonates can attend to and track for lengthy periods particular visual stimuli, such as a human face. They will search for light and exhibit stimulus preferences that can be indexed by the duration of attention. Some of these behaviors are incorporated into the NBAS. The validity of the scale is still being researched but several reviews on the NBAS have appeared (Als, Tronick, Lester, & Brazelton, 1979; Prechtl, 1982; Sameroff, 1978). It should be noted that the very positive endorsement of the Brazelton scale by psychologists and clinicians has not been universal, and a number of important issues have been raised with respect to the test (see Prechtl, 1982; Sameroff, 1978). The Sameroff monograph (1978) concludes that the Brazelton is most useful for assessing concurrent functioning of the neonate rather than stable individual differences. Among the criticisms voiced by Prechtl (1982) are the need for greater precision and specificity of item descriptions and terminology, problems in interpretation, scoring and administration of the neurological items included on the scale, problems with the scale's conceptualization of state, and the lack of items representative of common neonatal situations (for example, feeding). Despite these and various other criticisms, however, the NBAS remains the most comprehensive behavioral assessment tool for the newborn. In addition, norms for healthy preterm infants are emerging (Leijoni & Finnström, 1982a) as is the relationship between neurological and behavioral functioning on the Brazelton in normal and preterm infants (Leijoni & Finnström, 1982b; Palmer, Dubowitz, Verghote, & Dubowitz, 1982).

The NBAS is an attractive scale for those interested in the interactive capacities of the neonate and how neonatal status on such variables may be related to early and subsequent interaction. It has been reported, for example, that aspects of the NBAS are related to concurrent behavior exhibited by healthy term infants during feeding interactions (Osofsky & Danzger, 1974) and to the amount of cuddling received by the infant and its irritability (Horowitz, Sullivan, & Linn, 1978). Moreover, NBAS performance has been related to aspects of temperament and cognitive development at 10 weeks (Sostek & Andus, 1977) and to responsivity during feeding and play contexts at 6 months (Vaughn, Taraldson, Crichton, & Egeland, 1980). Among preterm infants, those suffering from respiratory distress exhibit poor interactive and motor process scores on the NBAS, lower developmental scores on the Bayley at 8 and 12 months, as well as poorer face-to-face interactions (Field, 1977). More recently, Greene, Fox, and Lewis (1983) reported that both term and preterm infants who were ill exhibited lower NBAS orientation and that NBAS orientation was associated with maternal and infant behaviors at 3 months. Thus the preliminary evidence indicates that the Brazelton neonatal competencies may have import for the type of social interactions in which the infant will be engaged. It is the quality of such interaction that ultimately may have predictability for future development (Lewis & Coates, 1980; Coates & Lewis, 1984). Additional research with the NBAS may further theoretical conceptualizations regarding the course of individual differences in early social/cognitive development.

Summary

The verdict regarding the validity and utility of the tests of the last decade or so is still undetermined. It is apparent, however, that the new tests no longer emphasize a single IQ score. Rather, they are increasingly concerned with a specific skill domain or attempt a multifaceted picture of infant abilities (for example, Uzgiris-Hunt scales). This focus has been long in emerging and seems to be linked to a gradual change in theories about both the infant and the nature of intelligence. Before examining existing theories about the nature of IQ in infants, we will briefly summarize the data on long-term predictability of current infant assessment tools.

2. PREDICTING INTELLIGENCE FROM INFANT TEST SCORES: A SUMMARY

In this section we will summarize the major conclusions to be drawn from the numerous studies that have attempted to predict IQ from infant test scores. We begin with a summary of the data on prediction within neurologically intact populations and conclude with an overview of predictability within atypical populations—in essence, those children with known genetic or other organic insult, or those known to be at significant risk for such conditions.

Prediction in Normal Populations

In the history of infant assessment we have repeatedly alluded to the poor predictability of traditional infant assessment tools. After decades of presenting blocks, rattles, and all the wonderful paraphernalia to be found in infant test kits to large groups of babies, the conclusion is inescapable that the ability to grasp and manipulate toys, to follow the red ring, to use a bell or crayon purposefully, and so forth does not result in an index of overall competence that is related to subsequent intellectual functioning (Bayley, 1970; Honzik, 1983; Lewis & McGurk, 1972; McCall, 1979; Stott & Ball, 1965). In fact, there is little evidence that infant test performance, when considered as a single score, is related to other concurrent measures of infant intellectual activity (King & Seegmiller, 1973; Lewis & McGurk, 1972). Even test-retest prediction over short ranges is only moderate. Honzik (1983) states:

> The correlations over developmentally long time periods are negligible, adjacent ages yield moderately high rs. The findings . . . indicate what has become a truism in longitudinal studies of infants and children: The interage correlations are highly related to the age at testing and inversely related to the interval between tests. The negligible and even negative prediction from test scores obtained during the first months of life does not appear to be a chance phenomenon but rather a developmental fact. [p. 76]

McCall (1983) provides several useful tables that corroborate Honzik's conclusions. His summary of median cross-age correlations between infant test scores during the first 24 months of life indicates that the best correlations, which are only moderate, occur for the closest age spans (p. 118). Predictive correlations between infant tests (1 to 30 months) and childhood IQ scores (ages 3 to 8 years) from studies conducted between 1930–1969, with various sized samples and from different geographical regions in the U.S., exhibit median correlations ranging from .06 to .59. Correlations are the greatest for infant scores at 19–30 months and childhood IQ at 3–4 years (McCall, 1983, p. 119). The data indicate that the shortest interval for which prediction was attempted provides the most reliable data, but only over a one- to two-year period. Beyond this time, there is only modest predictive value (.39 to .59, or 16% to 36% of variance). Data from European sources cited by Honzik (1983) are consistent with this analysis as is one other more recent American study (Ramey & Haskins, 1981). Siegal (1981) reported high inter-age correlations on Bayley scores for a group of preterm and full-term infants; however, Honzik (1983) has argued that these correlations may be inflated and that spuriously improved prediction is likely to result given the heterogeneity of the population. Honzik (1983) also adds:

> The results indicating greater stability in the test scores of low-scoring babies are of importance to neurologists, pediatricians, psychologists, and others who depend on infant tests in the diagnosis of mental impairment and subnormality. However, test scores of infants and young children should always be adjusted for prematurity

before correlations suggesting stability, and thus prediction, are computed (Hunt, 1977). This caveat applies equally to test scores of individual children. [pp. 84–85]

Infant tests may offer useful information to clinicians (Honzik, 1983), although this is by no means proven (Lewis, 1983). Even so, most tests are too lengthy to be widely used, hence the move to screening instruments that are less time consuming and more cost efficient, and that can be widely applied, thus reducing the volume of children who should be referred for more detailed assessment.

Predictive Validity of Infant Intelligence Tests for Handicapped Children

Although it is commonly acknowledged that infant intelligence tests have no long-term predictive validity for normal children, it is nevertheless recognized that such tests do have some prognostic value for low-scoring infants (Drillien, 1961; Erickson, 1968; Hallowell, 1941; Holden, 1972; Honzik, 1983; Illingworth, 1961, 1972; Ireton, Thwing, & Gravem, 1970; Knobloch & Pasamanick, 1967; Vanderveer & Schweid, 1974; Werner, Honzik, & Smith, 1968). Some of the highest correlations between infant Developmental Quotient (DQ) and subsequent IQ have been reported by Knobloch and Pasamanick (1967) and Siegel (1981). Knobloch and Pasamanick (1967) followed a heterogeneous sample of 123 infants, some of whom exhibited suspected developmental problems. These infants were assessed with the Gesell in the first year of life and subsequently retested with the Stanford-Binet between the ages of 6 and 10 years. The correlation between infant DQ and childhood IQ for low-scoring infants (DQ < 80) was greater ($r = .68$) than that found for infants with average or better DQs ($r = .48$). In addition, inclusion of information about SES (in essence, parental occupation) and the occurrence of seizures in a multiple regression analysis with infant DQ improved predictability for both low-scoring infants (multiple $r = .87–.90$) and for normal infants (multiple $r = .75$). Similarly, Werner et al. (1968) conducted a longitudinal study of 639 children born on the island of Kauai, Hawaii in 1955. They reported a correlation of .71 between Cattell DQ at 20 months and IQ at 10 years for low-scoring infants (DQ < 80), although the correlation for the whole group was only .49. The general conclusion that low-scoring groups exhibit better predictive correlations has been reported by others as well (Goodman & Cameron, 1978; Honzik, 1983; Vanderveer & Schweid, 1970).

Clearly, infant developmental tests can be useful for identifying children at risk for developmental problems. However, low-scoring infants represent a heterogeneous group of children with a variety of potentially handicapping conditions; some of these handicaps are obvious; others are not. Important developmental functions may be obscured if data from infants with different problems are pooled. Therefore, we will describe the results of investigations of infant tests separately for different diagnostic categories.

Down's Syndrome. Investigators have been concerned with both the predictive validity of infant tests for Down's Syndrome children (Fishler, Graliker, & Koch, 1965; Koch, Share, Webb, & Graliker, 1963; Share, Koch, Webb, & Graliker, 1964) and the form of the intelligence growth curve in such children (Carr, 1975; Dicks-Mireaux, 1972; Koch, Graliker, Fishler, Gottfried, & Ragsdale, 1973; Lewis & Brooks-Gunn, 1984). Moderate correlations between tests administered in the first year of life and tests administered in early childhood (4 to 6 years) have been reported by Fishler et al. (1965; $r = .50$, $n = 28$) and by Share et al. (1964; $r = .57$, $n = 24$). In both of these studies, stronger correlations were found between DQs obtained in the second year of life and IQ in early childhood ($rs = .82$ and $.79$, respectively). The predictive validity of infant tests for these children is much higher than it is for normal children.

Early reports of apparent progressive retardation in Down's Syndrome children (Masland, Sarason, & Gladwin, 1958) have since been recognized as an artifact of the way DQ and IQ are calculated (Carr, 1975; Dicks-Mireaux, 1972; Koch et al., 1963). For most Down's Syndrome infants the ratio of mental age to chronological age, used in the calculation of IQ, decreases. Therefore, although the mental age of these children does increase during development, their IQ apparently decreases. Rather than representing a regression in intelligence, however, this decline in IQ reflects a decrease in the *rate* of mental development relative to normal children. Although this deceleration in mental growth was previously attributed to the transition from sensorimotor to linguistic skills testing at about 2 years of age, recent evidence indicates that deceleration in mental growth can be observed in the first year of life prior to the development of language (Carr, 1975; Dicks-Mireaux, 1972; Lewis & Brooks-Gunn, 1984). Lewis and Brooks-Gunn (in press) found, for example, that Down's infants and two other handicapped groups (physically impaired and developmentally delayed) all exhibited significant deviations from normal rate of cognitive development as assessed on the Bayley Scale of Infant Mental Development. In the Down's infants, however, delays in cognitive functioning were apparent from approximately 5 months of age, with increasingly greater deviation from the norm through 28–36 months. At this later age, there is an apparent leveling off in mental age. At present there is no clear explanation regarding what factors are responsible for the declining rate of mental development in these infants (see Kopp & Parmelee, 1979). Lewis and Brooks-Gunn (1984) report, however, that visual information-processing ability, as indexed by a poorer habituation to redundant visual information, is at least one aspect of deficits seen in Down's infants.

In summary, the predictive validity of infant tests is better for Down's Syndrome children than for normal children. However, the rate of mental development in these children declines with age. Thus, although a Down's Syndrome infant is likely to maintain his ranking with respect to other Down's Syndrome children, his IQ may decline during the first few years of life.

Congenital Central Nervous System Malformations. Congenital malformations of the CNS (spina bifida) subsumes a number of conditions that result from lesions or separation of vertebrae. Infants born with such malformations may show a variety of disabilities, including retardation, neurological impairment, paralysis, sphincter-control difficulties, and sensory deficits. The few researchers who have studied IQ stability during the first few years of life in such children (Fishler, Graliker, & Koch, 1965; Fishman & Palkes, 1974; Nielsen, 1980; Tew & Laurence, 1974) typically report that correlations between DQ in early infancy and IQ in early childhood are low or moderate. The predictive validity of infant tests administered in late infancy is quite good, however. Nielsen (1980) followed a small sample ($n = 14$) of spina bifida children in Denmark and reported that scores on the Cattell at 6 months of age correlated modestly (.56) with performance on the Minnesota Preschool Scale at 3 years. The relationship between performance on the Cattell at 18 months and WISC performance at 6 years was much stronger ($r = .84$, $n = 24$). Nielsen (1971) also noted an overall increase in mean DQ/IQ scores from 80.6 at 6 months to 97.6 at 6 years. Similarly, Fishman and Palkes (1974) found a weak correlation ($r = .24$, $n = 15$) between Cattell scores at 6 months and Stanford-Binet performance at 5 years and a strong one ($r = .82$, $n = 2$) between the 18-month Cattell and the Stanford-Binet. The greatest variation in IQ change from 18 months to 5 years occurred for those infants who had relatively high scores in infancy. Such infants showed increases in IQ with age. Thus early tests appear to *underestimate* the abilities of many of these children. This has been attributed to the depressive effects of repeated hospitalizations for corrective surgery that many of these children undergo in the first year of life (Nielsen, 1980) and to differences in the types of skills earlier and later tests assess (Fishman & Palkes, 1974). It seems reasonable that a child whose handicap is primarily motoric might perform poorly on infant tests that emphasize the manipulation of objects and other sensorimotor dependent skills.

Cerebral Palsy and Multiple Handicaps.   Little evidence concerning the predictive validity of infant tests for cerebral palsied and multiply handicapped children is available. Two studies of cerebral palsied children offer contradictory estimates of the predictive validity of very early tests (Fishler et al., 1965; Nielsen, 1971). Fishler et al. (1965), who followed 15 cerebral palsied children during the first 5 or 6 years of life, reported that the correlation between infant tests in the first year and IQ at 5 or 6 years of age was $-.11$. However, 50% of the sample were considered untestable at this early age. Nevertheless, predictability improved as the children matured. Infant tests administered at 2 and 3 years of age correlated .59 ($n = 10$) and .64 ($n = 9$), respectively, with 5-year IQ.

On the other hand, in a study of 150 cerebral palsied children in Denmark, Nielsen (1971) reported moderate correlations between infant tests administered prior to 2 years of age and tests in early childhood ($r = .46$). Correlation between tests administered from 2 through 7 years of age ranged from .68 to .89. Differences between the results of Fishler et al. (1965) and Nielsen (1971) may reflect differences in the severity of handicaps in the populations studied. Nielsen reported, for example, that only 17% of her sample was untestable, in contrast to the 50% figure obtained by Fishler et al.

Dubose (1977) investigated the predictive value of infant tests for an older, multiply handicapped sample ($n = 28$) who were retested after a 5-year period. For children whose mean age at first testing was 51 months (4.3 years), the correlation between the two tests was .69. For those whose mean age at first testing was 101 months (8.42 years), it was .83 after the 5-year period. Dubose concluded that infant tests were useful in predicting intellectual development in multiply handicapped children of at least preschool age.

As categorical groups, cerebral palsied and multiply handicapped children are often heterogeneous with both a wide range of handicapping conditions and great variation in handicap severity. Given this variability, it is not surprising that the few studies of IQ predictability in such infants should produce divergent results. Lewis & Brooks-Gunn (in press) find that children with physical impairment in fact show two distinct patterns of early mental development—one that closely parallels those of normal children, and a second that exhibits extreme delays in development. These patterns may well reflect the degree of handicap; those children who parallel normal mental growth will be the most likely to catch up or be only moderately impaired.

At-risk Infants. At-risk infants are also a heterogeneous group. These infants are characterized by various factors, such as low birth weight or prematurity, or have been subjected to stressful pre- and perinatal experiences, such as anoxia or prolonged labor. Such infants are considered to be at-risk because retrospective studies have indicated that these factors are more frequent in samples of children who exhibit developmental problems than in normal children (see review by Sameroff & Chandler, 1975). Nevertheless, many long-term prospective studies that have included at-risk infants have not been successful in predicting dysfunction on the basis of either early risk indicators or test results (see reviews by Gottfried, 1973; Hunt, 1983; Kopp & Parmelee, 1979; Sameroff & Chandler, 1975). Others have reported some success (for example, Bee et al., 1982; Rosenblith, 1979).

Special Issues and Problems with Respect to the Handicapped Child

Infant tests can be evaluated with respect to their functions as screening or diagnostic tools and as prescriptive devices. Overall, infant tests do appear to have some predictive value for low-scoring infants, although it varies for different groups of handicapped infants. Predictive validity is comparatively high for children with Down's Syndrome and CNS malformations. This issue has not been settled conclusively and many types of risk assessment schemes are currently being explored (see Field et al., 1982; Littman & Parmelee, 1978; Siegel et al., 1982). Hunt (1983) provides a recent review of this area.

Test information for such infants is most likely to be useful when used in conjunction with other information. A number of researchers have found that in general the inclusion of other predictor variables, such as SES, maternal education, and indices of neurological status, improve the prediction of later functioning (for example, Broman, Nichols, & Kennedy, 1975; Knobloch & Pasamanick, 1967; Werner et al., 1968; Willerman, Broman, & Fiedler, 1970). Nevertheless, there are a number of issues regarding infant tests that need to be addressed. These questions concern the sensitivity, reliability, and prescriptive value of the tests.

To be truly worthwhile, infant tests should be more accurate than the clinical judgments of experienced child-care experts. If an infant's handicap is self-evident, there may be little value in having a specially trained examiner administer a lengthy test. One of the few studies in which the question was considered is the Kauai Pregnancy Study (Werner et al., 1968). In addition to being evaluated by a psychologist, these infants were examined by pediatricians who recorded their impressions of the child's intellectual status at 20 months on a four-point scale. The correlation between the pediatricians' assessments and Cattell IQ at 20 months were moderate ($r = .32$). Pediatric judgments of infant intelligence at 20 months had lower (though still significant) correlations with 10-year IQ ($r = .30$) than did the 20-month Cattell score ($r = .49$). Thus the infant test does appear to provide a better estimate of a child's future status than do pediatric evaluations. However, questions of time and cost-effectiveness may rule out their actual application as screening devices. As we have seen, even the Denver, which was designed to be quick, easy, and cost effective, was not used by pediatricians because of time considerations (Frankenberg et al., 1975).

Another issue, raised by McCall, Hogarty, and Hurlburt (1972) is the sensitivity of infant tests. They noted that correlations in the range of .70–.80 for clinical populations are cited to justify the use of infant tests as screening devices in normal populations. They noted that the false-positive rate in such a situation makes the test impractical as a screening device because it would result in a large number of normal infants being misclassified as abnormal. This objection has been raised about the Denver for preschool-aged populations (Werner et al., 1968).

A third problem concerns the reliability of infant tests when they are administered to handicapped infants. Reliability between examiners in studies of handicapped children is seldom reported. This issue is of particular concern since examiners may often adapt the test items to circumvent some of the limitations imposed by the infant's handicaps and/or use mothers' reports and social histories to supplement their observations (for example, Drillien, 1961; Illingworth, 1972; Nielsen, 1971). Drillien (1961) considered it "diplomatic" to avoid tests where absolute failure was evident to the mother (p. 2). Such modifications may lower the reliability of the test. Moreover, given that SES is a better predictor of later intelligence than are infant tests (see summary by McCall, Hogarty, & Hurlburt, 1972), spuriously high correlations between infant tests and later performance may result if the examiner is influenced by knowledge of the infant's home environment or by a subjective impression of maternal competence.

Perhaps the most frustrating aspect of infant tests with respect to clinicians and educators has been that because they yield only a single score summarizing the infant's general level of functioning, information regarding specific skills and deficits is obscured. As we have seen in the history of infant testing, the field has now begun to move in the direction of skill-based assessments. This trend leads us to the central theoretical questions in the field of infant assessment: What is actually being measured on infant tests? What is the nature of the early development of intelligence?

3. THEORIES OF INTELLIGENCE: A DEVELOPMENTAL PERSPECTIVE

The notion of an easily identifiable attribute of the mind (often called intelligence) is an extremely popular and historically entrenched theoretical conceptualization. But what is intelligence and what does it imply? Two major views of intelligence have competed for supremacy: a single trait or attribute versus a set of skills.

In common with many others, Galton (1884), Goddard (1912), Spearman (1904), and Terman (1906) considered intelligence to be a single, easily measurable factor. It was Burt, Jones, Miller, and Moodie (1934) who articulated the concept of *g*. It is from their theory that the basic features of a single-factor theory of intelligence can be extracted. Their theory included five basic assumptions:

1. *g*, a single real factor within individuals, subsumes all mental activity.
2. *g* predicts all mental performance to a significant degree.
3. *g* can be easily measured by assessing a relatively limited subset of behaviors.
4. *g* is innate and therefore genetically determined to a significant degree.
5. *g* is not subject to qualitative changes or to environmental influence.

A corollary of this last point is that *g* does increase with age up to some innately determined maximum as the child develops, hence the necessity of expressing intelligence as a ratio of mental ability over chronological age. However, while the absolute amount of *g* may increase, the ratio (MA/CA) should remain stable within the bounds of measurement error.

The single factor notion of *g* described is compelling, because of its apparent, though questionable, face validity (Kamin, 1974; Keating, 1983; Lewis, 1976; and others). It is also remarkably convenient because it provides a single two- or three-digit index for the classification of individuals that is supposedly stable and should permit generalizations about performance across a wide variety of tasks and life situations. As soon as one introduces the possibility of having multiple factors of intelligence, even so few as three, the situation becomes more cumbersome. One is forced to deal with the notion of profile. Individuals are no longer easily categorized since one individual may be high on one factor but low on another. Furthermore, there is now a problem of determining which score ultimately predicts to which situations and abilities. The notion of profile, while of interest to educators and clinicians, also makes the theoretical study of intelligence more laborious and convoluted.

In fact, however, there is also a long history of intelligence theory that proposes just such an alternative concept of intelligence. Thurstone (1938), Cattell (1952, 1953), and Guilford (1956) argued for a multiple but finite set of mental abilities as being more representative of the structure of intelligence. The seven factors identified by Thurstone and the complex multidimensional classification of abilities developed by Guilford had impact on test theory and construction. For example, the Wechsler scales (WPPSI, WISC, WAIS), which were developed more recently than the Stanford-Binet, were constructed with verbal and performance subscales (Wechsler, 1949, 1955, 1967). The movement toward skills assessment in infancy appears to be a natural consequence of this theoretical viewpoint as well.

While a single factor model of intelligence can be applied to human intelligence at any age, the discussion here is confined to the opening years of life since our subject is infant intelligence. To focus our discussion we will consider whether there is any support for such a model in infancy. We will consider in particular three central features of single factor theory: its factoral structure, its constancy, and finally its predictability.

Intelligence in Infancy: Is There a Single Factor?

First, in order to understand the multifaceted nature of this question, it is necessary to consider how tests of intelligence are constructed. One central feature in test construction is the production of items and subtests that are related to one another and to the score on the test as a whole. Items are constructed and eliminated so that this must be the case. Thus, if there are 10 test items, nine of which are highly related to one another and to the total test score, the tenth item will be eliminated. It is no wonder that these tests have high inter-item agreement as well as high split-half reliability (consistency); they are designed that way. Thus test construction perpetuates the notion of a single factor by the manipulation of items designed to produce just such an outcome. Infant tests, such as the Bayley and the Cattell are no different in this respect.

Another source of support for single-factor has been the results of factor analysis. As Gould (1981), Lewis (1976), and Sternberg (1977) have pointed out, factor-analytic techniques will yield either single or multiple factors depending on the particular method chosen. For example, principal component analysis yields by design a single factor. By projecting a single axis (others being fixed at right angles), the first component extracted mathematically is a general factor that represents an average of information contained in the different items. Most of the variability loads on the first or other principal components and the remaining factors are usually bipolar, with positive loadings for half of the variables and negative loadings for the remainder. Such bipolar factors are difficult to interpret. Thus this method accounts for the major contributor to variance in terms of a generalized factor, while ignoring or rendering obscure other item contributions. On the other hand, more complex factor analytic techniques using oblique axes that can be rotated for maximal solution allow for the possibility of multiple factors (abilities). Spearman and Burt invented and used principal component analysis because of their theoretical bias; Thurstone invented more complex solutions since he favored a multidimensional view of intelligence and sought a technique that could extract evidence in support of this premise. In fact, it is equally possible to examine the same data with these differing factor analytic techniques and reach opposing conclusions regarding the nature of intelligence. This exercise proves nothing about intelligence but does illustrate that there is a relationship between the analytical technique and the belief system of the scientist. Clearly, the nature of theoretical assumptions about intelligence, the measurement system, and the choice of analytical technique are not independent. The choice of technique, while it appears to be arbitrary, at least in the study of intelligence, is strongly influenced by the prior belief of the investigator (Gould, 1981; Kamin, 1974). Thus it seems that the identification of a single factor is related to the choice of the analytical tool. Consequently, the use of factor analysis results as direct evidence supporting the single-factor view of infant IQ does not appear warranted. A review of them should be undertaken if only to point out the empirical failure to demonstrate a single g factor. McCall, Hogarty, and Hurlburt (1972) painstakingly sought individual or factor-item stability across tests and age; nevertheless, they were forced to conclude that even with this type of analysis and the use of a variety of other multivariate techniques, the correlation between different ages "remains modest and of minimal practical utility." In conclusion, they rejected the simple conceptualization of a g factor in infancy:

> The search for correlational stability across vastly different ages implies a faith in a developmentally constant, general conception of intelligence that presumably governs an enormous variety of mental activities. Under that assumption, the nature of the behavioral manifestations of g would change from age to age, but g itself is presumed constant, and this mental precocity at one age should predict mental precocity at another. Confronted with the evidence reviewed above, this g model of mental development must be questioned. [p. 736]

Lewis and McGurk (1972) obtained and correlated three different types of infant intelligence scores. Infants were seen longitudinally from 3 to 24 months, at which time they received the Bayley Scales of Infant Development (1969) and the object permanence scale from the Corman and Escalona Sensorimotor Scales (1969). In addition, at 24 months children received a modified Peabody Picture Vocabulary Test (Dunn & Dunn, 1959/1981) in which both comprehension and production scores were obtained. Inter-age correlations between the Bayley scales and object permanence proved to be relatively weak. Correlations were also obtained between the Bayley and object permanence at each age and language scores at 24 months. In general, the results failed to provide any consistent pattern across tests that might be likened to a g factor. Likewise, when nontraditional scales of sensorimotor development as measured on Uzgiris and Hunt (1975) are considered, there is no evidence for a single factor (Uzgiris, 1973).

In summary, there is little consistency across different measures of infant functioning (for example, Bayley and sensorimotor performance) and little consistency within sensorimotor scales (Uzgiris-Hunt, 1975) or across different factors, such as those described by McCall et al. (1972) for the Gesell scales. The data, therefore, offer little support for a single factor in infant intelligence.

The Constancy of Intelligence in Infancy

A second central feature of intelligence and one related to the issue of long-term predictability is the notion that intelligence remains relatively stable over time. The principal component studies designed to demonstrate a single factor in infant test scores have actually weakened the constant, single factor model. In much of McCall's work (McCall et al., 1972; McCall, Eichorn, & Hogarty, 1977), a component factor analysis is used as the primary analytic device. McCall's work indicates that the nature of the principal component is both unstable (that is, an individual's score in comparison to the group does not remain constant) and changeable over age (first appearing as an attention factor, then by an active exploration of objects, and finally a verbal factor). Thus McCall's data would appear to support the view that infant intelligence is primarily a single *but changing* structure. This result is at odds with a single factor theory of intelligence, but is more consistent with a Piagetian view of intelligence which posits qualitative transformations in intelligence with development. McCall's work suggests, however, that even within the relatively short period of infant sensorimotor development, there are several major transformations in the factoral structure of intelligence and little consistency in IQ performance within the period of infancy.

Predictive Validity in Infancy

In this chapter we have repeatedly noted that there is little evidence of predictive validity over age within infancy and from infancy to older ages. In terms of concurrent infant behavior, the relationship between IQ performance and other aspects of behavior has received almost no attention. In one study, Lewis and Lee-Painter (1974) related the Bayley intelligence performance scores of 100 12-week-old infants from a wide variety of socioeconomic backgrounds to their behavior in interaction with their mothers in a naturalistic home situation. The results showed that there were no significant relationships between performances on the Bayley intelligence scales and the infant behaviors as measured by the infant-mother interactions. Studies relating infant behavior to other social, cognitive, and affective behaviors also fail to find any correlation with IQ scores. Moreover, although infant IQ performance has been related to infant trauma (Hunt, 1983), there is no evidence that infant IQ test performance is related to other infant intellectual activities. Finally, the findings indicating a lack of relationship between performance on a variety of different infant tests, all reporting to measure intellectual activity, have already been discussed.

Why Is There No Support for a *g* in Infant Tests?

We have now shown that several major aspects of a single factor theory of intelligence are questionable. Why is there little evidence for a single generalized factor in infant intelligence?

Several interpretations are possible. The first is that *g* is an inappropriate model of intelligence. Rather, the multidimensional or skills notion may more accurately reflect intelligence in infancy and perhaps in other ages as well. A second possibility is that regardless of the nature of intelligence, infant test *items* are inappropriate. We have already mentioned that the item pool in infant tests is restricted and highly redundant across most tests. Moreover, infant items tend to emphasize sensori-perceptual and motor skills. The latter may be completely unrelated or only minimally related to intelligence as it is assessed on later tests. For example, these early motor items may have little relationship to later verbal items. Infant tests may also miss completely those functions that are concurrently or subsequently related to infant intellectual functioning. Two such measures are attention to the environment and social-cognitive factors. Both are assessed minimally on tests such as the Bayley, yet it has been shown that the nature of the child's attention to the environment reflects information-processing capabilities (Lewis, 1982) and that aspects of social interaction in infancy may well bear an important relationship to future competence (Lewis & Fox, in press; Ramey et al., 1979; Ruddy & Bornstein, 1982). We will discuss such alternative measures more fully in Section 4.

Finally, even if a skills view of infant intelligence is appropriate, it may be that a simple skills model does not capture either the complexity of intellectual functions or the qualitative changes that may occur during development. That is, skills may develop at various ages and may simply be unrelated to one another, or their relationships may change with time.

If we reject the notion of either a single factor intelligence, which is constant over age or which changes over age, then we are forced to consider a skill model. In any consideration of a skills approach to intelligence, it is necessary to consider that a set of skills can have different developmental patterns. Thus, like a single factor, we can consider a set of skills to remain constant over age only increasing in amount, and/or a set of skills can undergo a variety of qualitative transformations. We consider the "and/or" statement as essential, since with a set of skills it is possible that some skills increase in quantity while others change qualitatively. An example of a developmental skill model is one recently elaborated by Fischer (1980). Fischer's model integrates aspects of both Piagetian and contemporary behavioral theory in a transactional (organism × environment) model of skill development. The theory describes both the structure of skills as they emerge during a lifetime of cognitive development and a limited set of transformational rules that relate skills to one another both within and across levels of development. There are five such transformational rules that describe how skills are combined (intercoordination, or reciprocal coordination of skills, and compounding) and undergo qualitative change (focusing, substitution, and differentiation). The theory posits that unevenness is characteristic of skills development. Furthermore, the nature of skill development is gradual although the theory allows for spurts or periods of acceleration in the rate of transformation. At such times, development may appear discontinuous. Thus the debate between a set of skills versus a single factor (g) conceptualization of intelligence in fact gives rise to four different models of intellectual development.

Models of Intellectual Development in Infancy

Model 1: g—A Single Factor.   This model reflects the traditional model of general intelligence that many, though not all, have rejected (Wilson, Brown, & Mathew, 1971). g is held to be stable over the life span and grows quantitatively rather than qualitatively. Good to excellent prediction across age is theoretically possible (see Figure 1).

Model 2: Qualitative Stages in the Emergence of g.   There is a general factor in intelligence according to this model, but it is subject to qualitative changes with development: that is, intelligence is discontinuous (see Figure 2). Only modest correlations should be found across relatively large age spans.

This model approximates a Piagetian position. For example, skills in infancy are primarily sensorimotor in nature and these skills form the basis of later skills. Later skills, however, are different and essentially independent of the

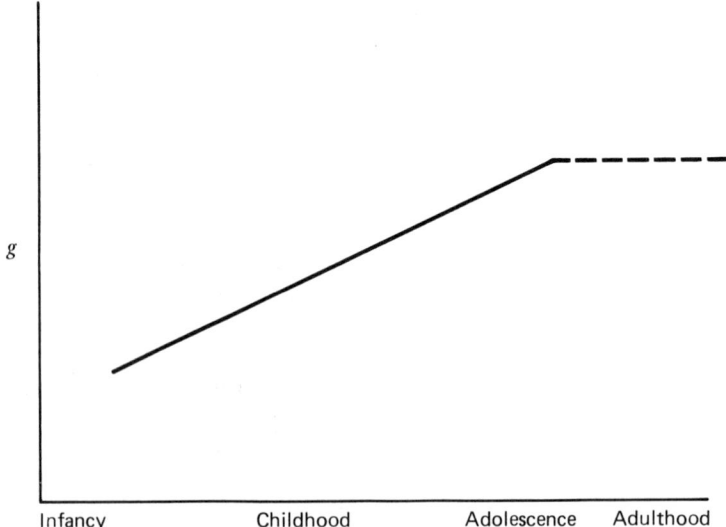

Figure 1.   An illustration of a single-factor model of intelligence.

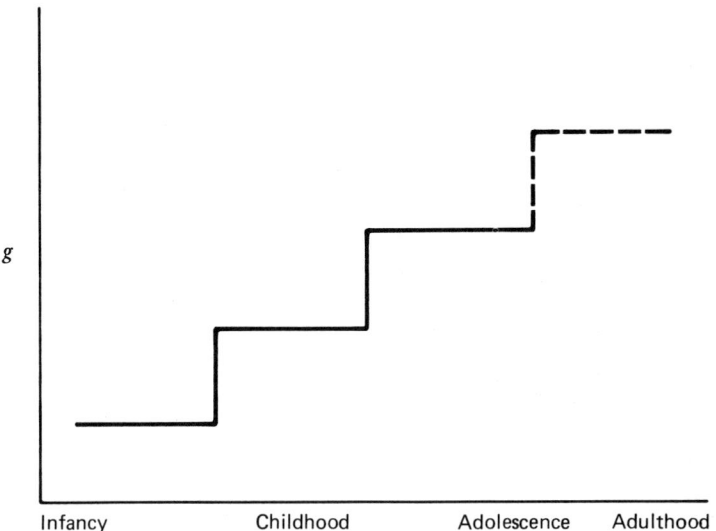

Figure 2. An illustration of a transformational single-factor model of intelligence.

earlier skills. Infants must master sensorimotor competencies, but then they move on to new stages in the development of their intellectual competence. This position is consistent with the modest predictability thus far reported for Piagetian scales, such as the Uzgiris-Hunt and later IQ (Uzgiris, 1983). McCall's factor analytic work (McCall et al., 1972; McCall et al., 1977) can also be interpreted in this light. McCall's work indicates that g, if it does exist, is unstable, first appearing as an attention factor (0–2 months), then as exploratory manipulation of objects (3–7 months), and finally as a verbal factor. It is only after this last verbal factor has emerged that there is any appreciable correlation with subsequent IQ. Thus g can be regarded as a single structure that changes with age, even within the relatively short span of infancy. McCall's work thus integrates an epigenetic view of cognitive development with more traditional psychometric patterns.

Model 3: A Set of Skills. The third model rejects the notion of g entirely and posits that intelligence consists of a disparate but loosely related set of skills. The skills themselves do not change with time but develop incrementally in parallel fashion (see Figure 3). One might expect therefore that motor skills on infant tests would predict to test of such skills later on. Other skills that coexist with motor ability should continue to coexist and will predict subsequent development in their particular skill domains as well. Thus infant attention will predict to subsequent attention abilities, and some aspect of babbling and prelinguistic skills should be related to later language development. This position is probably most closely related to a simple maturational approach. This model, appealing as it is, does not allow for any diversity across skill development nor does it account for transformations of skill structure. In addition, essentially

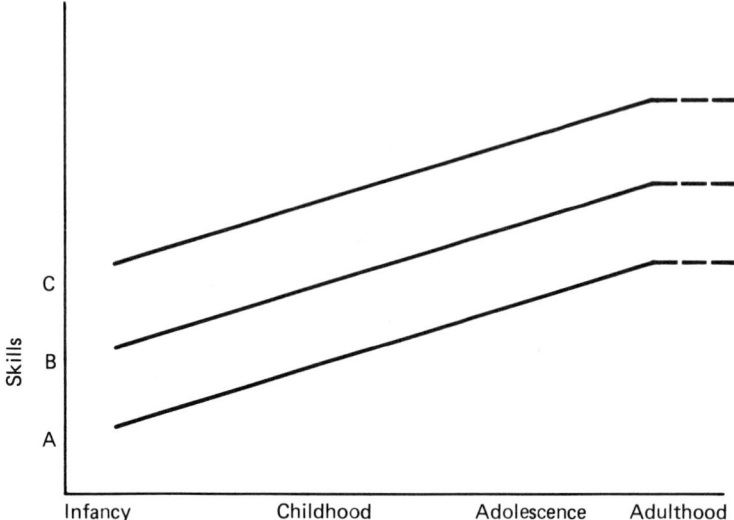

Figure 3. An illustration of a simple skills model of intelligence.

normative observations of quantitative changes in various skills that are implied in this model have little, if any, use for a theory of intellectual development. A fourth and more complex model is also possible.

Model 4: Multiplex Skills in Intelligence. This model is based on a conceptualization of intelligence that is based on a variety of skills or competencies, but it also acknowledges that a variety of transformations may occur with development of these skills:

1. Skills may appear at various points in time independently of one another. Some will be linked, but others will not;
2. Skills may have different patterns of development. Some may increment linearly with age; some may be restricted to a particular phase of development only to disappear; some may be subject to qualitative transformation; still others may drop out or regress only to reappear subsequently.

Theorists (for example, Thurstone, 1938) who view intelligence as multidimensional have used factor rotation methods to isolate item clusters and to identify such discrete mental skills. Lewis and Enright (in press) recently employed an oblique rotation solution to a longitudinal set of Bayley scores. Their results indicate that for each of the three ages studied (3, 12, and 24 months) as set of infant skills can be generated. The relationship of skill over this age range is complex as can be seen in Figure 4. The factors obtained agree for the most part with past research using factor analysis techniques that are amenable to the generation of multiple factors (Bayley, 1970; Richards & Nelson, 1939; Stott & Ball, 1965).

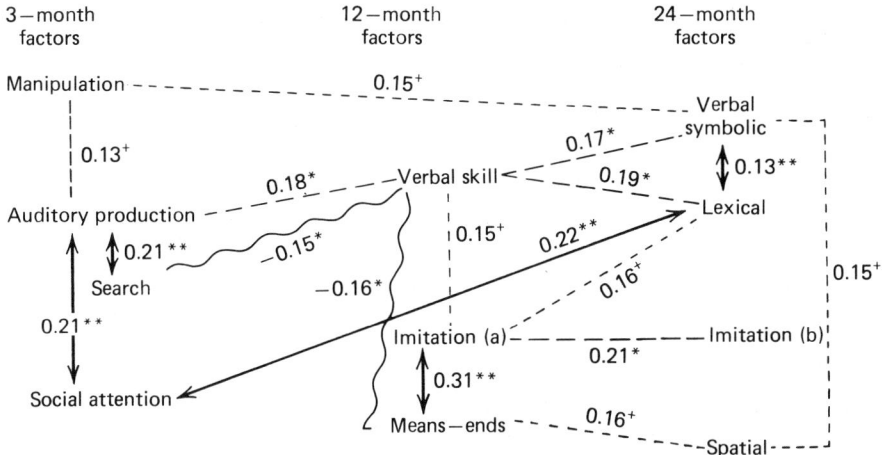

Figure 4. Intercorrelations between Bayley factors in infancy. Significant within-age and between age correlations ($p < .01$**, $p < .05$*, $p < .10$ +) are illustrated, indicating relationships characteristic of the sample of infants as a whole.

Figure 4 indicates that there are at least four major abilities at 3 months, which include the following: a *search factor* composed of orientation and attention items; an *auditory factor* that centers on vocalization and noisemaking; a *social factor,* including smiling at mirror image and frolic play; and finally a *manipulation factor* containing items relating to holding or reaching for objects. These skills are loosely related, with search and social attention being correlated with auditory production, which is in turn correlated with manipulation skills.

By 12 months, three major abilities can be identified, including a *verbal,* an *imitation,* and a *means-end* factor. Imitation and means-ends are essentially independent of 3-month factors, while verbal skills are correlated slightly with auditory production but negatively correlated with search.

Finally, by 24 months another set of abilities appears, including a verbal symbolic, a lexical, an imitation, and a spatial factor. Verbal symbolic skills are related to one another and correlate with earlier developmental skills to a slight degree (for example, 3-month manipulation, 6-month verbal skills, 3-month social attention). Imitation and spatial skills are independent of the two verbal components and of each other. Each is correlated with an earlier 6-month factor (in essence, 6-month imitation or 6-month means-end).

Figure 5 shows the relationship of each of these factors to 36-month Stanford-Binet scores. The figure shows that verbal symbolic, lexical, imitation at 24 months, and verbal skill at 12 months are the factors modestly correlated with 36-month performance with remaining factors at 12 and 24 months contributing significantly but to a small degree. Of the 3-month factors, only social attention has a significant but slight direct association with 36-month performance. Other 3-month factors have no direct association with 36-month IQ. These results

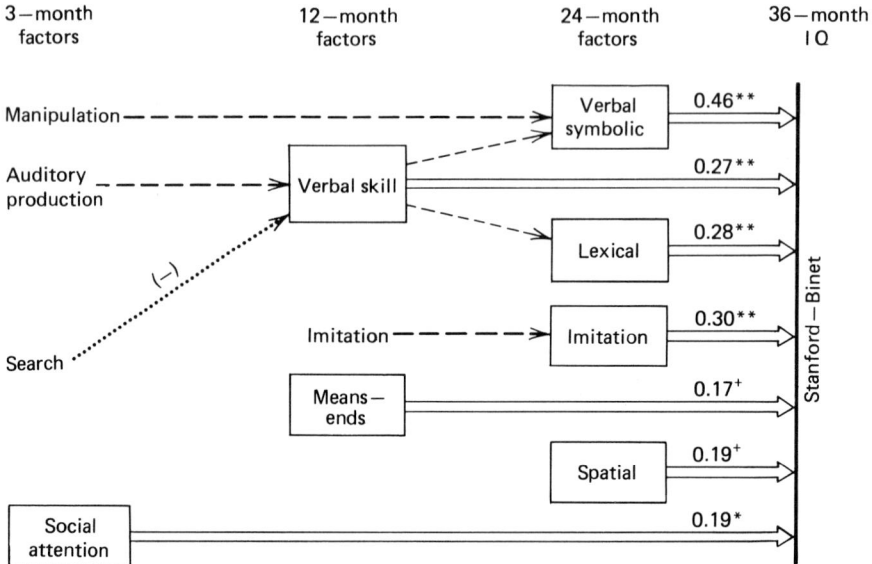

Figure 5. Bayley factors and their relationship to 36-month IQ. Significant cross-age correlations ($p < .01$**, $p < .05$*, and $p < .10$ +) are shown, indicating paths of development characteristic of the same of infants as a whole.

confirm reports from other sources we have reviewed, which indicate the following:

1. The best prediction to subsequent IQ is performance at 24 months;
2. Verbal skills provide the best predictor of subsequent IQ;
3. Attention and social factors (social attention, imitation) are the most significant early factors known to be related to subsequent IQ.

Thus the data indicate three distinct developmental paths: (1) a verbal, (2) a social, and (3) an imitation and means-ends.

Such a multiple abilities analysis indicates that (1) some abilities appear early and then disappear or are only minimally related to IQ (manipulation), (2) some appear and are transformed (auditory), (3) some appear later (spatial), and (4) some appear and remain the same (imitation). Without specific analyses designed to elicit multiple abilities, such observations might not be noted. However, even in this analysis, there is an inherent limitation since a highly specific set of items is used. The items used determine which skills emerge and how they predict subsequent behavior. At present, there is no good theory to indicate which infant items to select.

After having conducted such an analysis, the next step in investigating the development of skills might be to conduct longitudinal investigations in which new measures are employed to tap the specific skill processes identified. The relationship of these new measures to Bayley factor scores and to subsequent functioning can then be explored. Such an approach is potentially fruitful and exciting since it dovetails more closely with the process-approach to competence that characterizes contemporary infant research. Let us turn briefly to a catalog of the likely candidates for a process approach to assessment in infancy.

4. NEW DIRECTIONS IN INFANT ASSESSMENT AND A RECAPITULATION

In the 1970s a number of behavioral and physiological measures were used to assess infant cognitive integrity. Such assessments presumably tap or can be used to localize specific dysfunctions with the CNS. During the decade ahead these measures may contribute significantly to our understanding of individual differences in ability and their relationship or lack of it to subsequent competence. Lewis and Fox (in press) have described a number of such measures in detail. We will review the major themes here.

The New Measures

Attention as a Measure of Cognitive Integrity.   Visual attention has been described as a measure of cognitive integrity as it reflects one of the infant's earliest and most important means of experiencing and processing of information about the external environment (Lewis, Goldberg, & Campbell, 1969). Newborns and young infants are capable of intellectual activity. It is the assessment of attentional processes in the young infant that enables one to obtain measures of information processing, a mental activity that is relatively independent of the infant's limited motoric capability. By observing attentional behavior, one can perhaps examine some of the infant's cognitive abilities, such as memory for example (Werner & Perlmutter, 1979). Several procedures are available for measuring infant attention, and these are described in detail elsewhere (Lewis & Baldini, 1979). In general, such techniques are outstanding for their nonobtrusiveness and the lack of sophisticated equipment required, features which they share with more traditional assessment tools. Given these features, there exists a strong possibility that attention techniques can become an integral part of pediatric primary care assessment. The studies to date have shown that attention distribution is sensitive to mental age differences (Lewis & Brooks-Gunn, 1984), to chronological age (Lewis, 1975), to CNS dysfunction (Lewis, Bartels, Campbell, & Goldberg, 1967; Yoshida, Lewis, Schimpler, Ackerman, Driscoll, & Koenisberger, 1974), and that differences in attention distribution are predictive of subsequent intellectual ability (Fagan & McGrath, 1981; Lewis & Baldini, 1979; Lewis & Brooks-Gunn, 1981). In short, the attention procedure is a sophisticated yet easily administrable measure, which can and should move from exclusively research use to clinical settings.

Electrophysiological Assessment of Infants.   A number of major electrophysiological techniques are currently being used to assess CNS integrity in infants and, in some cases, to discriminate differences in information-processing abilities between learning disabled and normal children. These techniques include somatosensory, visual and brainstem auditory evoked potentials, electroencephalograph (EEG), neurometrics, brain electrical mapping (BEM), and computerized axial tomography (CAT) scan. The population that has been studied with each method varies; the CAT scan in particular has been used to assess neuroanatomical abnormalities in the high-risk infant population. In general, it is true that only a few studies have used these measures to predict subsequent outcomes. Thus there is primarily evidence of concurrent but not predictive validity. Among the primary reasons for the paucity in the predictive research is the relative recency of some of the measures, as well as the more vexing issue of response change; that is, the type and form of a response may change or disappear with CNS maturation. Thus what can be measured at an earlier age may with normal development not exist later. One, in effect, loses the ability to measure longitudinally. Still, these measures offer some promise (see Lewis & Fox, in press). Sonograms are tools that have been used to evaluate the severity of intraventricular hemorrhage (IVH) in very low birth-weight infants who are known to be at significant risk for CNS damage and developmental handicap. Several still ongoing follow-up studies reveal significant correlations between severity of IVH bleed as measured by CAT scan and subsequent mental outcomes at 2 years of age.

Motor Asymmetries.   The use of motor asymmetries as an assessment device is a recent innovation. Consequently, a statement about their ultimate use in identifying dysfunction is not possible at this time. However, such measures hold some promise since they are apparently related to CNS functioning, in particular, language. The tendency for an infant to lie with its head oriented toward the right was first noted by Gesell (1938) and has been studied more systematically in recent years (Turkewitz & Creighton, 1974; Turkewitz, Gordon, & Birch, 1965; Turkewitz, Moreau, & Birch, 1968; Turkewitz, Moreau, Birch, & Crystal, 1967; Turkewitz, Moreau, Davis, & Birch, 1969). There are two distinct types of motor asymmetry: postural asymmetry, the tendency for an infant to lie with its head to the right; and lateral head turning, the tendency for an infant to resume an asymmetrical head placement after its head has been positioned in midline. Prematurity apparently affects the lateral head turning response (see Gardner et al., 1977), and both types of asymmetries are important in the development of handedness according to Michel (1983). Indeed, according to Self & Horowitz (1979), most neonatal behavioral and neurological screening measures include these behaviors as items. Fox and Lewis (1982) recently showed that postural asymmetry can be detected in preterm infants as early as 34–35 weeks of conception and was not disrupted by perinatal illness. In contrast, lateral head turning, which also appeared early (approximately 36 weeks conceptual age), was affected by perinatal distress. Those preterm infants who had suffered from respiratory distress were more likely to maintain a midline head position (in essence, fail to exhibit normal asymmetry) than healthy preterm or term infants of similar chronological age at the time of testing. At least one other study has reported similar findings. These data indicate that motor asymmetries may provide a useful index of the degree of lateralization in the neonatal CNS and/or the potential for deviant lateralization resulting from early perinatal insult that may ultimately result in impaired performance.

Dichotic Attention.   During the 1980s evidence increasingly accumulated in support of anatomical differences in the brains of both the adult and the young infant. In particular, areas in the left hemisphere that have a primary responsibility for speech (for example, the planum temporal) are larger than homologous areas in the right hemisphere (Geschwind & Levitsky, 1968; Wada, Clark, & Hann, 1975; Witelson, 1977; Witelson & Pallie, 1973).

Recent studies have attempted to correlate these neuroanatomical asymmetries with behavioral function. Specifically, using behavioral and electrophysiological measures, researchers have attempted to demonstrate functional hemispheric asymmetry in infants in response to speech or linguistic stimuli. Dichotic attention techniques are used to assess whether information is processed by the contralateral hemisphere during simultaneous stimulation of each ear with differing sounds. After a period of time, during which the subject habituates to the initial dichotic stimuli, the stimulus is changed in either the right or left ear. Greater accuracy in detecting a change in the right ear (or right-ear advantage) is consistent with left-hemisphere specialization for speech sound processing. Behavioral studies include a report by Entus (1977), which reported localization of language function in the left hemisphere and music perception in the right hemisphere. Entus used contingent sucking with habituation of high amplitude sucking as her response measure. Glanville, Best, and Levenson (1975), using heart-rate change as the dependent measure, also found that 3-month-old infants exhibited a right-ear advantage for speech stimuli and a left-ear advantage for music. Although these results are provocative, they have not been readily repeated (Chen, 1982).

Fox and Lewis (1982) attempted to replicate and extend these findings to preterm infants. Two groups of prematures, one of whom underwent perinatal medical complications, were seen at 3 months of age in a dichotic paradigm. While the preterm infants who had been ill did not display a normal pattern of heart rate change or habituation to the stimuli, none of the infants, term or preterm, healthy or sick, exhibited a right-ear advantage for the speech stimuli; again indicating a failure to replicate the earlier findings.

Electrophysiological evidence for the presence of functional asymmetry for language has been more consistent. Molfese (Molfese, Freeman, & Palermo, 1975; Molfese, Nunez, Serbert, & Ramanaia, 1976) has demonstrated that infants in the first year of life display larger left-hemisphere evoked responses to speech stimuli than right-hemisphere evoked responses. Recently, Shucard, Shucard, Cummins, & Campos (1981), using evoked potentials as the response measure, found significant sex differences in hemispheric processing for both language and music stimuli but no evidence of specific left-hemisphere lateralization for speech. Their data suggest that female infants process both speech and music more readily in the left rather than right hemisphere.

At this juncture, the data for lateralization of function in the infant remains unclear. While there are a number of behavioral studies demonstrating functional specialization of the left hemisphere for language, attempts to replicate these experiments have met with mixed success. Even in the area of electrophysiological response, the data remain controversial. While Molfese (1977) has demonstrated asymmetries for certain acoustic features, there are no firm data revealing a relationship between language and EEG activation asymmetries. Such relationships and more information relating the degree of asymmetry or lack of it to language ability will be necessary before dichotic attention becomes a viable assessment tool.

Each of the new techniques described implies many of the assumptions of the traditional tests. There is still the notion of a single skill or test that is related to the construct of some more general ability; it is still assumed that predictability from early functioning to later competence is possible and that measures of the individual independent of the environment in which the child is developing is a valid procedure for understanding individual differences in intellectual growth.

Nevertheless, there is some reason to believe that these techniques may be tapping important specific functions, rather than a more general ability, and that individual differences in these specific functions may well affect later outcome. For example, one of the deficits known to occur in preschool children who were high-risk infants is in the area of reading and language difficulties (Davies & Tizard, 1975). Information regarding infant hemispheric lateralization is thus important to early assessment and diagnosis of speech dysfunctions.

Recapitulation: Intelligence as a Sociopolitical Function

Recall that at the outset, we outlined several features that needed to be reviewed when the concept of intelligence as *g* is being considered. The discussion has revealed that none of them appears free from considerations that are other than scientific. This is not surprising, for it would be naive to believe that science in general and certainly psychology in particular is devoid of human values. Science, although it may try, is not valueless, but value-laden. Holden (cited in Gardner, 1983) states this elegantly: "Themata [beliefs about lawfulness of phenomena and how these principles are best revealed] sometimes held with obstinate loyalty help one to explain the character of the discussion between antagonists far better than do scientific content and social surroundings alone" (p. 150, brackets added). The task of the scientist is to explore these values so that their consequences will be apparent. When science fails to recognize the values associated with the particular scientific effort, scientists fall prey to bias. This point should be clear from Gould's (1981) and Kamin's (1974) analyses of the values of many of the scientists responsible for the current views and data on IQ. If it is true that all the features inherent in the concept of IQ have sociopolitical aspects, it may not be too strong to suggest that the IQ score up until now has been more of a sociopolitical than a scientific construct.

The Use and Function of Infant IQ Scores. A review of the empirical research on infant intelligence tests supports the notion that there is no consistency across or within age in a wide variety of tests purported to measure infant mental functioning. Therefore, the concept of a developmentally constant, general, unitary concept of intelligence is not tenable. Such a model of unitary human capacity must clearly be dealt a severe blow by a review of the infancy literature. Nonetheless, such a conception of people remains, and tests continue to be sold and taken. While infant intelligence scales have been acknowledged to have limited function, they are still widely used in clinical settings in the belief that, although lacking in predictive validity, they provide a valuable aid in assessing the overall health and developmental status of babies at the particular time of testing. This procedure is justified only if the scores are regarded solely as measures of present performance, not as indicators of future potential. What this "present performance" may mean is questionable since superior performance may be followed by poor performance. Just as infant scales are invalid as measures of future potential, it is also unlikely that they alone properly assess a child's current performance compared to that of other children, except when extreme samples of dysfunction are used. Even then, the individual child may possess hidden competencies that are glossed over by traditional infant assessments.

Concurrently, intelligence test scores are widely used as criterion measures in the evaluation of infant intervention or enrichment programs. The experimental subjects are compared with the control subjects in terms of their performance on intelligence tests. If the scores of the experimental group are higher than those of the control group, the program is evaluated positively; if not, it is evaluated negatively. Implicitly assumed is the belief that infant intelligence is a general, unitary capacity, and that mental development can be enhanced as a result of an enrichment experience in a few specific areas. Zigler and Trickett (1978) suggest that the use of IQ as a measure in childhood intervention programs became popular because standard IQ tests are well-developed instruments that are easily administered. Similarly, it was assumed that infant scales are adequate to reflect an improvement that occurs in competence as a consequence of a specific enrichment experience. However, as our previous discussion has made clear, infant intelligence—or intelligence at any age, for that matter—considered as a general unitary capacity is highly questionable. Moreover, that infant skills are adequate to reflect improvement from specific enrichment experiences must also be questioned, since a variety of infant skills tested shows relatively little interscale or intrascale consistency. In part, the need for different measures has been recognized for some time. IQ scores must give way to other measures, such as social competence (Anderson & Messick, 1974; Zigler & Trickett, 1978) or intellectual competence (Scarr, 1981).

The data on infant intelligence tests also cast doubt on whether the scores can be generalized beyond the particular set of abilities or factors sampled at the time of testing. An infant who showed dramatic gains in testing that involved sensorimotor function would not necessarily manifest such gains in tests involving verbal skills. The implication of these conclusions for a wide variety of evaluation policies concerning infant intervention must be considered. For example, infant intelligence scales are quite unsuitable instruments for assessing the effects of specific intervention procedures, primarily because infant intelligence is not a general unitary trait but is rather a composite of skills and abilities that do not necessarily covary. Such a view of intelligence is by no means new (see, for example, Guilford, 1959; Thurstone, 1938), but it is one that must be repeatedly stated in order to counteract the tendency to use simple and single measures of infant intelligence. An example can be used to clarify this issue.

Consider an intervention procedure that is designed primarily to influence sensorimotor intelligence—for example, the development of object permanence. An appropriate curriculum must involve training infants in a variety of peekaboo and hide-and-seek tasks. According to the data presented, a standard infant intelligence scale would be the wrong instrument to use in assessing the efficiency of such a program and is likely to lead to erroneous conclusions concerning the program's efficacy. Even more serious is the possibility that by using the wrong instrument of evaluation over a large number of programs, one would erroneously conclude that intervention in general is ineffective in improving intellectual ability, thus supporting the genetic bias that environment is ineffective in modifying intelligence. There are few who would suggest that schoolchildren be administered a standard intelligence test after a course in geography. Yet such a procedure would be analogous to using an intelligence test to measure the success of teaching the object permanence concept to the infant. The success of a geography course is best assessed by a test of geographical knowledge; by the same token, the success of a program stressing sensorimotor skills is best assessed by specific tests of sensorimotor ability. In both cases there may in some instances be improvement in intelligence test scores; but such improvement must be regarded as fortuitous.

The general view that intelligence is a unitary construct and easily measured cannot be supported by the data. Why, then, should this view of intelligence hold such a dominant position in the thinking of contemporary scientists and public alike? The answer to such a question may be found in a consideration of the functional use of the IQ score in a complex and technological society. The analysis of Gould (1981) on the misuse of the measurement of intelligence suggests that one of the more important functions of the IQ score remains its use in stratifying society into a hierarchy having those with high IQ considered better in all ways than those with low IQ scores. Moreover, the selection of items and procedures for such tests is to benefit those already at the top of that hierarchy. The test then serves to justify the existing order. Moreover, by arguing for the innate quality of the measured difference, the society or those members at the top of the hierarchy can both justify their position and resist any reordering. Such a belief system, supported by the set of a priori beliefs (which are always confirmed "scientifically"), has been labeled "social Darwinism." The purpose of these self-confirming beliefs is in the preservation of the social hierarchy. In complex societies, it serves to maintain a caste system and to create a division of labor within the culture—that is, to determine who will go to school in the first place, who will get into academic programs that lead to college, and so forth. These divisions, in turn, determine the nature of labor the children will perform as adults and, in turn again, will determine the children's socioeconomic status and social, economic, and political position in the society. This division of labor, and, as a consequence, the division of goods and services available to those who succeed, are a necessity in a complex society. This stratification is then justified by scores on a test designed to produce just such a stratification. If we cannot make the claim that IQ differences are genetically determined, then we must base them on differences in cultural learning. But these differences in cultural learning, for the sake of the division of labor, are exactly what the IQ tests are intended to produce. The hierarchy produces the test differences and the test differences are used to maintain the hierarchy. Thus IQ scores have come to replace, in part, the class systems or feudal systems that previously had the function of stratifying society and distributing the goods and wealth of that society. Whereas these earlier systems were supported by the invoking of constructs having to do with the Almighty, the present system invokes Mother Nature instead. In any social system in which stratification is necessary in order to distribute the wealth of that society in a disproportionate fashion, some type of stratifying device is necessary. The twentieth century technological society's stratification device has become the intelligence test. As such, the intelligence test rests more on its function for distribution of wealth than on its predictability and scientific merit.

REFERENCES

Als, H., Tronick, E., Lester, B. M., & Brazelton, T. B. (1979). Specific neonatal measures: The Brazelton neonatal behavioral assessment scale. In J. D. Osofsky (Ed.), *Handbook of infant development.* New York: Wiley.

Ames, L. B. (1967). Predictive value of infant behavior examinations. In J. Hellmuth (Ed.), *Exceptional infant* (Vol. 1). New York: Brunner/Mazel.

Anderson, J. E. (1939). The limitations of infant and preschool tests in the measurement of intelligence. *Journal of Psychology, 8,* 351–379.

Anderson, S., & Messick, S. (1974). Social competency in young children. *Developmental Psychology, 10,* 282–293.

Apgar, V. A. (1953). A proposal for a new method of evaluation of the newborn infant. *Current Research in Anesthesia and Analgesia, 32,* 260–267.

Atkins, R. E. (1931). *The measurement of intelligence by young children by an object fitting test.* Minneapolis: University of Minnesota Press.

Banham, K. M. (1973). Social and emotional adjustment of retarded cerebral palsied infants. *Exceptional Children, 40,* 107.

Banham, K. M. (1964). *Ring and peg tests of behavior development.* Muncie, IN: Psychometric Associates.

Bayley, N. (1933a). *The California first year mental scale.* Berkeley: University of California Press.

Bayley, N. (1933b). Mental growth during the first three years. *Genetic Psychology Monographs, 14,* 1–92.

Bayley, N. (1936). *The California infant scale of motor development.* Berkeley: University of California Press.

Bayley, N. (1969). *Bayley scales of infant development.* New York: The Psychological Corporation.

Bayley, N. (1970). The development of mental abilities. In P. Mussen (Ed.), *Carmichael's manual of child psychology*. New York: Wiley.

Bee, H. L., Barnard, K. E., Eyres, S. J., Gray, C. A., Hammond, M. A., Spietz, A. L., Snyder, C., & Clark, B. (1982). Prediction of IQ and language skill from perinatal status, child performance, family characteristics and mother-infant interaction. *Child Development, 53,* 1134–1156.

Bell, S. B. (1970). The development of the concept of the object as related to infant–mother attachment. *Child Development, 41,* 191–211.

Binet, A., & Simon, T. (1905). Méthodes nouvelles pour le diagnostic du niveau intellectuel des anormaux. *L'Année Psychologique, 11,* 191–244.

Binet, A., & Simon, T. (1908). Le développement de l'intelligence chez les enfants. *L'Année Psychologique, 14,* 1–94.

Binet, A., & Simon, T. (1911). Nouvelle réchèrches sur la mesure du niveau intellectuel chez les enfants d'école. *L'Année Psychologique, 17,* 145–210.

Brazelton, T. B. (1973). Neonatal behavioral assessment scale. *Clinics in Developmental Medicine, 50.*

Broman, S., Nichols, P., & Kennedy, W. A. (1975). Preschool IQ: Prenatal and early developmental correlates. Hillsdale, NJ: Erlbaum.

Brooks-Gunn, J., & Weinraub, M. (1983). A history of infant intelligence tests. In M. Lewis (Ed.), *Origins of intelligence* (2nd ed.). New York: Plenum.

Brunet, O., & Lézine, P. (1951). *Le développement psychologique de la première enfance.* Issy-les-Moulineaux: Éditions Scientifiques et Psychotecniques.

Bryant, G. M., Davies, K. J., Richards, F. M., & Voorhees, S. (1973). A preliminary study of the use of the Denver Developmental Screening Test in a British health department. *Developmental Medicine and Child Neurology, 15,* 33–40.

Buhler, C. (1930). *The first year of life.* New York: John Day.

Buhler, C., & Hertzer, H. (1935). *Testing children from birth to school age.* New York: Farrar & Rhinehart.

Burt, C. (1921). *Mental and scholastic tests.* London: King.

Burt, C., Jones, C., Miller, E., & Moodie, W. (1934). *How the mind works.* New York: Appleton-Century-Crofts.

Caldwell, B., & Honzig, A. S. (1971). APPROACH—A procedure for patterning responses of adults and children. Abstracted in *Catalog of Selected Documents in Psychology, 1,* 1–2. Washington, DC: American Psychological Association Supplemental Abstract Service.

Carr, J. (1975). *Young children with Down's Syndrome: Their development, upbringing and effect on their families.* London: Butterworth.

Casati, I., & Lézine, I. (1968). *Les étages de l'intelligence sensori-motrice.* Paris: Les Éditions du Centre de Psychologie Appliquée. [As cited by I. Uzgiris in M. Lewis (Ed.), *Origins of intelligence* (2nd ed.)]

Cattell, P. (1940). *The measurement of intelligence of infants and young children.* New York: Psychological Corporation.

Cattell, R. B. (1952). *Factor analysis: An introduction and manual for psychologist and social scientist.* New York: Harper.

Cattell, R. B. (1953). Research designs in psychological genetics with special reference to multiple variance. *American Journal of Human Genetics, 5,* 76–91.

Cazden, C. B. (1983). Peekaboo as an instructional discourse model: Discourse development at home and at school. In B. Bain (Ed.), *The sociogenesis of language and human conduct.* New York: Plenum.

Chen, C. (1982). Hemispheric asymmetries to speech sounds in infants. Unpublished manuscript.

Church, J. (1966). *Three babies.* New York: Random House.

Coates, D., & Lewis, M. (1984). Early mother-infant interaction and cognitive status as predictors of school performance and cognitive behavior in 6-year-olds. *Child Development, 55,* 1219–1230.

Corman, H. H., & Escalona, S. K. (1969). Stages of sensorimotor development: A replication study. *Merrill-Palmer Quarterly, 15,* 351.

Cross, L., & Johnston, S. (1977). A bibliography of assessment instruments. In L. Cross (Ed.), *Identifying handicapped children: A guide to case-finding, screening, diagnosis, assessment and evaluation.* New York: Walker.

Darley, F. L. (Ed.) (1979). *Evaluation of appraisal techniques in speech and language pathology.* Reading, MA: Addison-Wesley.

Darwin, C. (1859). *The origin of species.* London: John Murray.

Darwin, C. (1877). A biological sketch of an infant. *Mind, 2,* 285–294.

Darwin, C. (1973). *The expression of emotions in man and animals.* New York: Appleton. (Originally published: London: John Murray, 1872.)

Davies, P. A., & Tizard, J. (1975). Very low birth weight and subsequent neurological defect. *Developmental Medicine and Child Neurology, 17,* 3–17.

Day Care and Child Development Council of America. *Evaluating children's progress: A rating scale for children in day care.* Washington, DC.

DeCarie, T. (1965). *Intelligence and affectivity in early childhood.* New York: International Universities Press.

Dennis, W. (1936). A bibliography of baby biographies. *Child Development, 7,* 71–73.

Dicks-Mireaux, M. J. (1972). Mental development of infants with Down's Syndrome. *American Journal of Mental Deficiency, 77,* 26–32.

Doll, E. A. (1953). *Measurement of social competence.* Educational Test Bureau. (Currently available from American Guidance Service, Circle Pines, MN.)

Drillien, C. M. (1961). The incidence of mental and physical handicaps in school age children of very low birthweight. *Pediatrics, 27,* 452–464.

Dubose, R. F. (1977). Predictive value of infant intelligence scales with multiply handicapped children. *American Journal of Mental Deficiency, 81,* 388–391.

Dubowitz, L. M. S., Dubowitz, V., & Goldberg, C. (1970). Clinical assessment of gestational age in the newborn infant. *Journal of Pediatrics, 77,* 1.

Dunn, R. M., & Dunn, L. (1981). *Peabody picture vocabulary test* (2nd ed.). Circle Pines, MN: American Guidance Service. (First edition, 1959.)

Entus, A. (1977). Hemispheric asymmetry in processing of dichotically presented speech and non-speech stimuli by infants. In S. J. Segalowitz & F. A. Gruber (Eds.), *Language development and neurological theory.* New York: Academic Press.

Erickson, M. T. (1968). The predictive validity of the Cattell Infant Intelligence Scale for very young mentally retarded children. *American Journal of Mental Deficiency, 72,* 728–733.

Escalona, S. K., & Corman, H. (1969). *Albert Einstein scales of sensorimotor development.* New York: Albert Einstein College of Medicine, Yeshiva University.

Fagan, J. F., & McGrath, S. (1981). Infant recognition memory and later intelligence. *Intelligence, 5,* 121–130.

Fantz, R. L., & Nevis, S. (1967). *Fantz-Nevis visual preference test.* Cleveland, OH: Case Western Reserve.

Field, T. (1977). Effects of early separation, interactive deficits and experimental manipulations on infant-mother face-to-face interaction. *Child Development, 48,* 763–771.

Field, T., Widmayer, S., Greenberg, R., & Stoller, S. (1982). Effects of parent training on teenage mothers and their infants. *Pediatrics, 69,* 703–707.

Fillmore, E. A. (1936). Iowa tests for young children. *University of Iowa Studies in Child Welfare, 11,* 4 (New Series No. 315).

Fischer, K. W. (1980). A theory of cognitive development: The control and construction of hierarchies of skills. *Psychological Review, 87*, 477–531.

Fishler, K., Graliker, B. V., & Koch, R. (1965). The predictability of intelligence with the Gesell Developmental Scales in mentally retarded infants and young children. *American Journal of Mental Deficiency, 69*, 515–525.

Fishler, K., Share, J., & Koch, R. (1964). Adaptation of Gesell Developmental Scales for evaluation of development in children with Down's Syndrome. *American Journal of Mental Deficiency, 68*, 642–646.

Fishman, M., & Palkes, N. (1974). The validity of psychometric testing in children with congenital malformations of the central nervous system. *Developmental Medicine and Child Neurology, 16*, 180–185.

Fowler, W., & Sutherland, J. (1976). Infant adaptation scales. In O. Johnson (Ed.), *Tests and measurements in child development: Handbook II*. San Francisco: Jossey-Bass.

Fox, N., & Lewis, M. (1982). Motor asymmetries in preterm infants: Effects of prematurity and illness. *Developmental Psychobiology, 15*, 19–23.

Fox, N., & Lewis, M. (1983). Cardiac response to speech sounds in preterm infants. *Psychophysiology, 20*, 248–480.

Fox, N., & Lewis, M. (in press). Prematurity, illness and experience as factors in development. *Journal of the Division of Early Childhood Development*.

Francis-Williams, J., & Yule, W. (1967). The Bayley Scales of Mental of Motor Development: An exploratory study with an English sample. *Developmental Medicine and Child Neurology, 9*, 391–401.

Frankenberg, W. K., & Dodds, J. B. (1967). The Denver developmental screening tests. *Journal of Pediatrics, 71*, 181–191.

Frankenberg, W. K., Dodds, J. B., Fandal, A. W., Kazuk, E., & Cohrs, M. (1975). *Denver developmental screening test: Reference manual*. Denver: University of Colorado Medical Center.

Frankenberg, W. K., Fandal, A. W., Sciarillo, W., & Burgess, D. (1981). The newly abbreviated and revised Denver Developmental Screening Test. *Journal of Pediatrics, 99*, 995–999.

Frankenberg, W. K., van Doornick, W. D., Liddell, T. N., & Dick, N. P. (1976). The Denver prescreening developmental questionnaire. *Pediatrics, 57*, 744.

Galton, F. (1884). *Hereditary genius*. London: Appleton.

Gardener, H. (1983). *Frames of the mind: The theory of multiple intelligences*. New York: Basic Books.

Gardner, J. D., Lewkowicz, D., & Turkewitz, G. (1977). Development of postural asymmetry in premature human infants. *Developmental Psychobiology, 10*, 471–480.

Greschwind, N., & Levitsky, W. (1968). Human brain: left–right infant asymmetry in temporal speech regions. *Science, 161*, 186–187.

Gesell, A. (1925). *The mental growth of the preschool child*. New York: Macmillan.

Gesell, A. (1938). The tonic neck reflex in the human infant. *Journal of Pediatrics, 13*, 445–464.

Gesell, A., & Armatruda, C. S. (1947). *Developmental diagnosis* (2nd ed.). New York: Harper. (1st edition, Hoeber, 1941.)

Gesell, A., & Thompson, H. (1938). *The psychology of early growth*. New York: Macmillan.

Gilbert, J. A. (1894). Researches on the mental and physical development of school children. *Studies of the Yale Psychology Lab., 2*, 40–100.

Glanville, B. B., Best, C. T., & Levenson, R. (1977). A cardiac measure of cerebral asymmetries in infant auditory perception. *Developmental Psychology, 13*, 54–59.

Goddard, H. H. (1908). The Binet-Simon tests of intellectual capacity. *The Training School, 5*, 3–9.

Goddard, H. H. (1910). A measuring scale for intelligence. *The Training School, 6*, 146–155.

Goddard, H. H. (1912). *The Kallikak family: A study in the heredity of feeblemindedness.* New York: Macmillan.

Goodenough, F. L. (1928). The Kuhlman-Binet tests for children of preschool age: A critical study and evaluation. *Institute of Child Welfare Monograph Series,* (No. 11). Minneapolis: University of Minnesota Press.

Goodenough, F. L. (1954). The measurement of mental growth in childhood. In L. Carmichael (Ed.), *Manual of child psychology.* New York: Wiley.

Goodenough, F. L., Foster, J. C., & Wagenen, M. J. (1932). *The Minnesota preschool scale.* Minneapolis: Educational Test Bureau.

Goodman, J. F., & Cameron, J. (1978). The meaning of IQ constancy in the young retarded child. *Journal of Genetic Psychology, 132,* 109–119.

Gottfried, A. W. (1973). Intellectual consequences of perinatal anoxia. *Psychological Bulletin, 80,* 231–242.

Gould, S. J. (1981). *The mismeasurement of man.* New York: Norton.

Graham, F. K., Ernhart, C., Thurston, D., & Craft, M. (1962). Development three years after perinatal anoxia and other potentially damaging newborn experiences. *Psychological Monographs, 76,* No. 3.

Graham, F. K., Matarazzo, R. G., & Caldwell, B. M. (1956). Behavioral differences between normal and traumatized newborns: I. Test procedures; II. Standardization, reliability and validity. *Psychological Monographs, 70,* 2(Whole Nos. 427–428).

Greene, J., Fox, N., & Lewis, M. (1983). The relationship between neonatal characteristics and three-month mother-infant interaction in high-risk infants. *Child Development, 54,* 1286–1296.

Griffiths, R. (1954). *The abilities of babies.* London: University of London Press.

Griffiths, R. (1970). *The abilities of young children: A comprehensive measurement system for the first eight years of life.* London: Child Development Research Center.

Grove, W. G. (1953). Review of the Arthur Point Performance Tests. In O. Buros (Ed.), *The fourth mental measurement yearbook.* Highland Park, NJ: Gryphon.

Guilford, J. P. (1956). The structure of intellect. *Psychological Bulletin, 53,* 267–293.

Guilford, J. P. (1959). Three faces of intellect. *American Psychologist, 14,* 469–479.

Hallowell, D. K. (1941). Validity of mental tests for young children. *Journal of Genetic Psychology, 58,* 265–288.

Hamley, H. R. (Ed.) (1935). *The testing of intelligence.* London: University of London Press.

Hindley, C. B. (1960). The Griffiths Scale of Infant Development: Scores and predictions from 3 to 18 months. *Journal of Child Psychology and Psychiatry, 1,* 99–112.

Holden, R. (1972). Prediction of mental retardation in infancy. *Mental Retardation, 10,* 28–30.

Honzik, M. P. (1983). Measuring mental abilities in infancy: The value and limitations. In M. Lewis (Ed.), *Origins of intelligence* (2nd ed.). New York: Plenum.

Honzik, M. P., McFarlane, J. W., & Allen, L. (1948). Stability of mental test performance between 2 and 18 years. *Journal of Experimental Education, 17,* 309–324.

Horowitz, F. D., Sullivan, J. W., & Linn, P. (1978). "Stability and instability in the newborn infant: The quest for elusive threads." In A. Sameroff (Ed.), Organization and stability of newborn behavior: A commentary on the Brazelton Behavioral Assessment Scale. *Monographs of the Society for Research in Child Development, 43,* 5–6 (Serial No. 177).

Hunt, J. McV. (1977). Mental development of preterm infants during the first year. *Child Development, 48,* 204–210.

Hunt, J. V. (1983). Environmental risks in fetal and neonatal life as biological determinants of infant intelligence. In M. Lewis (Ed.), *Origins of intelligence* (2nd ed.). New York: Plenum.

Ide, G. G. (1918). Witmer Form Board and Cylinders as tests for children 2 to 6 years of age. *Psychological Clinics, 12,* 65–88.

Ilg, F. L., & Ames, L. B. (1956). *Child behavior.* New York: Dell.

Illingworth, R. S. (1961). The predictive value of developmental tests in the first year with special reference to the diagnosis of mental subnormality. *Journal of Child Psychology and Psychiatry, 2,* 210–215.

Illingworth, R. S. (1972). *The development of the infant and young child, normal and abnormal.* Baltimore, MD: Williams & Wilkins.

Ireton, H., Thwing, E., & Gravem, H. (1970). Infant mental development and neurologic status, and intelligence at age four. *Child Development, 41,* 937–946.

Irwin, O. C. (1942). Can infants have IQ? *Psychological Review, 49,* 69.

James, W. (1890). *The principles of psychology.* New York: Henry Holt.

Johnson, O. (1976). *Tests and measurements in child development: Handbooks I & II.* San Francisco: Jossey-Bass.

Kamin, L. J. (1974). *The science and politics of IQ.* Potomac, MD: Erlbaum.

Keating, D. P. (1983). The emperor's new clothes: The "new look" in intelligence research. In R. J. Sternberg (Ed.), *Advances in the psychology of human intelligence* (Vol. 2). Hillsdale, NJ: Lawrence Erlbaum.

Kelley, M. F., & Surbeck, E. (1983). The history of preschool assessment. In K. D. Paget and B. A. Bracken (Eds.), *The psychoeducational assessment of preschool children.* New York: Grune & Stratton.

Kilburg, G. D. (1981, November). *Assessing emerging communication.* Paper presented at the American Speech and Hearing Association convention, Los Angeles, CA.

King, W., & Seegmiller, B. (1973). Performance of 14- to 22-month-old black, first-born infants on two tests of cognitive development: The Bayley scales and the infant psychological development scale. *Developmental Psychology, 8,* 317–326.

Knobloch, H., & Pasamanick, B. (1967). Prediction from the assessment of neuromotor and intellectual status in infancy. In J. Zubin & G. A. Jervis (Eds.), *Psychopathology of mental development.* New York: Grune & Stratton.

Knobloch, H., & Pasamanick, B. (1974). *Gesell and Armatruda's developmental diagnosis: The evaluation and management of normal and abnormal neuropsychologic development in infancy and childhood* (3rd ed.). New York: Harper & Row.

Knobloch, H., Stevens, F., & Malone, A. (1980). *A manual for developmental diagnosis.* New York: Harper & Row.

Koch, R., Graliker, B., Fishler, K., Gottfried, F., & Ragsdale, N. (1963). Longitudinal study of mentally retarded infants. *Arizona Medicine, 20,* 177–182.

Koch, R., Share, J., Webb, A., & Graliker, B. V. (1963). The predictability of Gesell developmental scales in mongolism. *Journal of Pediatrics, 62,* 93–97.

Kohn-Raz, R. (1966). The ring-cube test: A brief time sampling method for assessing development of coordinated bilateral grasp responses in infancy. *Perceptual and Motor Skills, 23,* 676–688.

Kopp, C. B., & Parmelee, A. M. (1979). Prenatal and perinatal influences on infant behavior. In J. Osofsky (Ed.), *Handbook of infant development.* New York: Wiley.

Korner, A., & Thoman, E. B. (1970). Visual alertness in neonates as evoked by maternal care. *Journal of Experimental Child Psychology, 10,* 67–78.

Kuhlman, F. (1912). A revision of the Binet-Simon system for measuring the intelligence of children. *Journal of Psycho-Asthenics, Monograph Supplement, 1,* 1–41.

Kuhlman, F. (1922). A handbook of mental tests (2nd ed.). Baltimore: Warwick & York. (1st ed., 1914.)

Kuhlman, F. (1939). *Tests of mental development: A complete scale for individual examination.* Minneapolis, MN: Educational Test Bureau.

Leijon, I., & Finnström, O. (1982a). Correlation between the neurologic examination and behavioral assessment of the newborn infant. *Early Human Development, 7,* 119–130.

Leijon, I., & Finnström, O. (1982b). Assessment of behavior on the Brazelton Scale in healthy preterm infants from 32 conceptual weeks until full-term age. *Early Human Development, 7,* 109–118.

Lewis, M. (1975). The development of attention and perception in the young child. In W. M. Cruikshank & D. P. Hallahan (Eds.), *Perceptual and learning disabilities in children* (Vol. 2). Syracuse: Syracuse University Press.

Lewis, M. (1976). What do we mean when we say "Infant intelligence scores"? In M. Lewis (Ed.), *Origins of intelligence.* New York: Plenum.

Lewis, M. (1982). Attention as measure of cognitive integrity. In M. Lewis & L. Taft (Eds.), *Developmental disabilities: Theory, assessment and intervention.* New York: SP Medical and Scientific Books.

Lewis, M. (1983). On the nature of intelligence: Science or bias? In M. Lewis (Ed.), *Origins of intelligence* (2nd ed.). New York: Plenum.

Lewis, M. (1984). Developmental principles and their implications for handicapped infants and children. In M. Hanson (Ed.), *Atypical infant development.* Baltimore: University Park Press.

Lewis, M., & Baldini, N. (1979). Attentional processes and individual differences. In G. A. Hale & M. Lewis (Eds.), *Attention and cognitive development.* New York: Plenum.

Lewis, M., Bartels, B., Campbell, H., & Goldberg, S. (1967). Individual differences in attention: Relationship between infant's condition at birth and attention distribution within the first year. *American Journal of Diseases of Childhood, 113,* 461–465.

Lewis, M., & Brooks-Gunn, J. (1979). *Social cognition and the acquisition of self.* New York: Plenum.

Lewis, M., & Brooks-Gunn, J. (1981). Visual attention at three months as a predictor of cognitive functioning at two years of age. *Intelligence, 5,* 131–140.

Lewis, M., & Brooks-Gunn, J. (1984). Age and handicapped group differences in infants' visual attention. *Child Development, 55,* 858–868.

Lewis, M., & Brooks-Gunn, J. (in press). *The handicapped child: New directions in research and intervention.* New York: McGraw-Hill.

Lewis, M., & Coates, D. (1980). Mother-infant interactions and cognitive development in 12-week-old infants. *Infant Behavior and Development, 3,* 95–105.

Lewis, M., & Enright, M. (in press). The development of mental abilities: A multidimensional model of intelligence in infancy (in press).

Lewis, M., & Fox, N. (in press). Infant assessment: Challenges for the future. In M. Lewis (Ed.), *Prenatal and perinatal factors relevant to learning disabilities: Johnson & Johnson Baby Products Co. Pediatric Roundtable No. 9.* Urbana-Champaign, IL: University of Illinois Press.

Lewis, M., Goldberg, S., & Campbell, H. (1969). Developmental study of information processing within the first 3 years of life. *Monographs of the Society for Research in Child Development, 34* (9, Serial No. 133).

Lewis, M., & Lee-Painter, S. (1974). *Mother-infant interaction and cognitive development.* Paper presented at the meeting of the Eastern Psychological Association, Philadelphia, PA.

Lewis, M., & McGurk, H. (1972). Evaluation of infant intelligence. *Science, 178,* 1174–1177.

Lewis, M., & Michalson, L. (1983). *Children's emotions and moods: Developmental theory and assessment.* New York: Plenum.

Lewis, M., & Michalson, L. (1985). The gifted infant. In J. Freeman (Ed.), *The psychology of gifted children.* New York: Wiley.

Lewis, M., & Taft, L. (Eds.) (1982). *Developmental disabilities: Theory, assessment, and intervention.* New York: SP Medical & Scientific Books.

Linfert, H., & Hierholtzer, H. (1928). A scale for measuring the mental development of babies in the first years of life. *Studies Psychological & Psychiatric,* Catholic University of America, *1,* No. 4.

Littman, B., & Parmelee, A. M. (1978). Medical correlates of infant development. *Pediatrics, 61,* 470–474.

Masland, R. L., Sarason, S. B., & Gladwin, T. (1958). *Mental subnormality.* New York: Basic Books.

McCall, R. B. (1979). The development of intellectual functioning in infancy and the prediction of later IQ. In J. D. Osofsky (Ed.), *Handbook of infant development.* New York: Wiley.

McCall, R. B. (1983). A conceptual approach to early mental development. In M. Lewis (Ed.), *Origins of intelligence* (2nd ed.). New York: Plenum.

McCall, R. B., Eichorn, D. H., & Hogarty, P. S. (1977). Transitions in early mental development. *Monographs of the Society for Research in Child Development, 42* (3, Serial No. 171).

McCall, R. B., Hogarty, P. S., Hurlburt, N. (1972). Transitions in sensorimotor development and the prediction of childhood IQ. *American Psychologist, 27,* 728–748.

McCauley, R. J., & Swisher, L. (1984). Psychometric review of language and articulation tests for preschool children. *Journal of Speech and Hearing Disorders, 49,* 34–42.

Mehrabian, A., & Williams, M. (1971). Piagetian measures of cognitive development for children up to age two. *Journal of Psycholinguistic Research, 1,* 113–116.

Michel, G. F. (1983). *Development of hand use preference in infancy.* Unpublished manuscript.

Molfese, D. L. (1977). Infant cerebral asymmetry. In S. J. Segalowitz & F. A. Gruber (Eds.), *Language and neurological theory.* New York: Academic Press.

Molfese, D. L., Freeman, R. B., & Palermo, D. S. (1975). The ontogeny of brain lateralization for speech and nonspeech stimuli. *Brain and Language, 2,* 356–368.

Molfese, D. L., & Molfese, V. J. (1979). Hemispheric and stimulus differences as reflected in cortical responses of newborn infants to speech stimuli. *Developmental Psychology, 15,* 505–511.

Molfese, D. L., Nunez, V., Serbert, S. M., & Ramanaia, N. V. (1976). Cerebral asymmetry: Changes in factors affecting its development. *Annals of the N.Y. Academy of Sciences, 280,* 821–833.

Muller, D. J., Munro, S. M., & Code, C. (1981). *Language assessment for remediation.* London: Crom Helm.

New York State Office for Education of Children with Handicap (1982). *Identification and referral of young handicapped children: The physician's role.* Albany, New York: State University of New York and the State Department of Education.

Nielsen, H. (1971). Psychological appraisal of children with cerebral palsy: A survey of 128 reassessed cases. *Developmental Medicine and Child Neurology, 13,* 707–720.

Nielsen, H. (1980). A longitudinal study of the psychological aspects of myelomeningiocele. *Scandinavian Journal of Psychology, 21,* 45–54.

Osofsky, J. D., & Danzger, B. (1974). Relationship between neonatal characteristics and mother-infant interaction. *Developmental Psychology, 10,* 124–130.

Palmer, P. G., Dubowitz, L. M. S., Verghote, M., & Dubowitz, V. (1982). Neurological and neurobehavioral differences between preterm infants at term and full term newborn infants. *Neuropediatrics, 13,* 183–189.

Papalia, D. E., & Olds, S. W. (1975). *A child's world: Infancy through adolescence.* New York: McGraw-Hill.

Parmellee, A. H. (1975). Neurophysiological and behavioral examination of premature infants in the first months of life. *Biological Psychiatry, 10,* 501–502.

Piaget, J. (1952). *The origins of intelligence in children.* New York: International Universities Press.

Pollack, R. H., & Brenner, M. W. (1969). *The experimental psychology of Alfred Binet.* New York: Springer.

Prechtl, H. F. (1982). Assessment methods for the newborn infant: A critical evaluation. In P. Stratton (Ed.), *Psychophysiology of the human newborn.* New York: Wiley.

Prechtl, H. F., & Bentima, D. (1964). The neurological examination of the full-term newborn infant. *Little Clinics in Developmental Medicine* (No. 12). London: Spastics Society.

Preyer, W. (1888). *The mind of the child.* New York: Appleton. (Originally published 1882.)

Ramey, C. T., Farran, D. C., & Campbell, F. A. (1979). Predicting IQ from mother-infant interactions. *Child Development, 50,* 804–814.

Ramey, C. T., & Haskins, R. (1981). The modification of intelligence through early experience. *Intelligence, 5,* 21–27.

Ricciuti, H. N. (1965). Object grouping and selective ordering behavior in infants 12 to 24 months old. *Merrill Palmer Quarterly, 11,* 129–148.

Richards, T. W., & Nelson, V. L. (1939). Abilities of infants during the first eighteen months. *Journal of Genetic Psychology, 55,* 299–318.

Rosenblith, J. F. (1974). Relations between neonatal behaviors and those at eight months. *Developmental Psychology, 10,* 779–792.

Rosenblith, J. F. (1979). The Graham/Rosenblith behavioral examination for newborns: Prognostic value and procedural issues. In J. D. Osofsky (Ed.), *Handbook of infant development.* New York: Wiley.

Ruddy, M. G., & Bornstein, M. H. (1982). Cognitive correlates of infant attention and maternal stimulation over the first year of life. *Child Development, 53,* 183–188.

Sameroff, A. J. (Ed.) (1978). Organization and stability of newborn behavior: A commentary on the Brazelton Neonatal Behavioral Assessment Scale. *Monographs of the Society for Research in Child Development, 43* (Serial No. 177, No. 5–6).

Sameroff, A. J., & Chandler, M. J. (1975). Reproductive risk and the continuum of caretaking casuality. In F. Horowitz (Ed.), *Review of child development research* (Vol. 4). Chicago: University of Chicago Press.

Scarr, S. (1981). Testing for children. *American Psychologist, 36,* 1159–1166.

Sears, R. R. (1975). Your ancients revisited: A history of child development. In E. M. Hetherington (Ed.), *Review of child development research* (Vol. 15). Chicago: University of Chicago Press.

Self, P. A., & Horowitz, F. D. (1979). The behavioral assessment of the neonate: An overview. In J. D. Osofsky (Ed.), *Handbook of infant development.* New York: Wiley.

Senn, M. J. E. (1975). Insights on the child development movement in the United States. *Monographs of the Society for Research in Child Development, 40* (Serial No. 3–4, Whole No. 161).

Share, J., Koch, R., Webb, A., & Graliker, B. (1964). The longitudinal development of infants and young children with Down's Syndrome. *American Journal of Mental Deficiency, 68,* 685–692.

Shinn, M. (1900). *The biography of a baby.* Boston: Houghton-Mifflin.

Shirley, M. (1933). *The first three years.* Minneapolis: University of Minnesota Press.

Shotwell, A. M., & Gilliland, A. R. (1943). A preliminary scale for the measurement of the mentality of infants. *Child Development, 74,* 167–177.

Shucard, J. L., Shucard, D. W., Cummins, K. R., & Campos, J. J. (1981). Auditory evoked potentials and sex related differences in brain development. *Brain and Language, 13,* 91–102.

Siegel, L. (1981). Infant tests as predictors of cognitive and language development at two years. *Child Development, 52,* 545–557.

Siegel, L., Saigel, S., Rosenbaum, P., Morton, R. A., Young, A., Berebaum, S., & Stoskof, B. (1982). Predictors of development in preterm and full-term infants: A model for detecting the at-risk child. *Journal of Pediatric Psychology, 7,* 135–147.

Skeels, H. M. (1932). A study of some factors in influencing form-board accomplishment of two- and three-year-old children. *Journal of Genetic Psychology, 40,* 375–395.

Sostek, A. M., & Andus, T. F. (1977). Relationships among the Brazelton neonatal scale, Bayley infant scales and early temperament. *Child Development, 48,* 320–323.

Spearman, C. (1904). General intelligence objectively determined and measured. *American Journal of Psychology, 15,* 201–293.

Stern, W. (1924). *Psychology of early childhood up to the sixth year of age.* New York: Henry Hill.

Sternberg, R. (1977). *Intelligence, information processing and analytical reasoning: The componential analysis of human ability.* Hillsdale, NJ: Erlbaum.

Stone, L. J., Smith, H. T., & Murphy, L. B. (Eds.) (1973). *The competent infant.* New York: Basic Books.

Stott, L. H., & Ball, R. S. (1965). Infant and preschool mental tests: Review and evaluation. *Monographs of the Society for Research in Child Development, 30* (Serial No. 101).

Stutsman, R. (1926). Performance tests for children of preschool age. *Genetic Psychology Monographs, 1,* No. 1.

Stutsman, R. (1931). *Mental measurement of preschool children.* New York: World Book.

Terman, L. M. (1906). Genius and stupidity. A study of some of the intellectual processes of seven "bright" and seven "stupid" boys. *Pedagogical Seminary, 13,* 307–373.

Terman, L. M. (1916). *The measurement of intelligence.* Boston: Houghton-Mifflin.

Terman, L. M. (1917). *The Stanford revision and extension of the Binet-Simon scales for measuring intelligence.* Baltimore: Warwick.

Terman, L. M., & Merrill, M. A. (1937). *Measuring intelligence.* Boston: Houghton-Mifflin.

Terman, L. M., & Merrill, M. A. (1960). *The Stanford-Binet intelligence scale: Form L-M.* Boston: Houghton-Mifflin.

Terman, L. M., & Merrill, M. A. (1973). *Stanford-Binet intelligence scale: Manual for the third revision: (Form L-M).* Boston: Houghton-Mifflin.

Tew, B., Laurence, K. M., & Samuel, P. (1974). Parental estimates of the intelligence of their physically handicapped child. *Developmental Medicine and Child Neurology, 16,* 494–500.

Thurstone, L. L. (1938). *Primary mental abilities.* Chicago: University of Chicago Press.

Traube, M. R., & Stockbridge, F. P. (1922). *Measure your mind.* New York: Doubleday.

Turkewitz, G. M., & Creighton, S. (1974). Changes in lateral differentiation of head posture in the human neonate. *Developmental Psychobiology, 8,* 85–89.

Turkewitz, G. M., Gordon, E. W., & Birch, H. G. (1965). Head turning in the human neonate: Spontaneous patterns. *Journal of Psychology, 107,* 143–158.

Turkewitz, G. M., Moreau, T., & Birch, H. G. (1968). Relation between birth condition and neurobehavioral organization in the neonate. *Pediatric Research, 2,* 243–249.

Turkewitz, G. M., Moreau, T., Birch, H. G., & Crystal, D. (1967). Relationship between prior head position and lateral differences in somesthetic stimulation in the human neonate. *Journal of Experimental Child Psychology, 5,* 548–561.

Turkewitz, G. M., Moreau, T., Davis, L. A., & Birch, H. G. (1969). Factors affecting lateral differences in human newborn. *Journal of Experimental Child Psychology, 8,* 483–493.

Ueda, R. (1978). Child development in Okinawa compared with Tokyo and Denver and the implications for developmental screening. *Developmental Medicine and Child Neurology, 20,* 657–663.

Uzgiris, I. C. (1973). Patterns of cognitive development in infancy. *Merrill-Palmer Quarterly, 19,* 181.

Uzgiris, I. C. (1983). Organization of sensorimotor intelligence. In M. Lewis (Ed.), *Origins of intelligence* (2nd ed.). New York: Plenum.

Uzgiris, I. C., & Hunt, J. McV. (1975). *Assessment in infancy: Ordinal scales of psychological development.* Urbana, IL: University of Illinois Press.

Van Alstyne, D. (1929). The environment of three-year-old children: Factors related to intelligence and vocabulary tests. *Teachers College Contributions to Education,* No. 366, p. 108.

Vanderveer, B., & Schweid, E. (1974). Infant assessment: Stability of mental functioning in young retarded children. *American Journal of Mental Deficiency, 79,* 1–14.

Vaughn, B. E., Taraldson, B., Crichton, L., & Egeland, B. (1980). Relationships between neonatal behavioral organization and infant behavior during the first year of life. *Infant Behavior and Development, 30,* 47–66.

Wada, J., Clark, R., & Hamm, A. (1975). Cerebral hemispheric asymmetries in humans. *Archives of Neurology, 35,* 239–246.

Wallin, J. E. W. (1918). Pegform boards. *Psychological Clinics, 12,* 40–53.

Wechsler, D. (1949). *Wechsler intelligence scale for children. Manual.* New York: Psychological Corporation.

Wechsler, D. (1955). *Wechsler adult intelligence scale. Manual.* New York: Psychological Corporation.

Wechsler, D. (1967). *Wechsler preschool and primary scale of intelligence.* New York: Psychological Corporation.

Werner, E. E. (1972). The Denver Developmental Screening Test. In O. K. Buros (Ed.), *The seventh mental measurement yearbook* (Vol. 1). Highland Park, NJ: Gryphon Press.

Werner, E. E., Honzik, M. P., & Smith, P. S. (1968). Prediction of intelligence and achievement at 10 years from 20-month-old pediatric and psychologic examinations. *Child Development, 39,* 1063–1075.

Werner, J. S., & Perlmutter, M. (1979). The development of memory in infants. *Advances in Child Development and Behavior, 14,* 2–53.

Willerman, L., Broman, S. H., & Fiedler, M. (1970). Infant development, preschool IQ and social class. *Child Development, 41,* 69–77.

Wilson, R. S. (1973). Testing infant intelligence. *Science, 182,* 734–737.

Wilson, R. S., Brown, A. M., & Mathew, A. P. (1971). Emergence and persistence of behavioral differences in twins. *Child Development, 42,* 1381–1398.

Winkelstein, E. (1974). The development of a systematic method by which day care staff can select gestural imitation curriculum procedures for individual infants. *Child Study Journal, 4,* 169–178.

Witelson, E. (1977). Developmental dyslexia: Two right hemispheres and none left. *Science, 195,* 309–311.

Witelson, S. F., & Paille, W. (1973). Left hemisphere specialization of language in newborns. *Brain, 96,* 641–646.

Wittenborn, J. R., Astrachan, M. A., De Gougar, M. W., Grant, W. W., Janoff, I. E., Kugel, R. B., Myers, B. J., Reiss, A., & Russell, E. C. (1956). A study of adoptive children: II. The predictive validity of the Yale developmental examination of infant behavior. *Psychological Monographs, 70* (No. 2).

Yang, R. K. (1979). Early infant assessment: An overview. In J. D. Osofsky (Ed.), *Handbook of infant development.* New York: Wiley.

Yerkes, R. M., & Foster, J. C. (1923). "A new point scale for infants." *Point scales for measuring mental abilities.* Baltimore: Warwick & York.

Yoshida, R. K., Lewis, M., Shimpler, S., Ackerman, J. Z., Driscoll, J., & Koenigsberger, M. R. (1974). The distribution of attention within a group of infants "at risk" (Research Bulletin 74-41). Princeton, NJ: Educational Testing Service.

Zigler, E., & Trickett, P. K. (1978). IQ, social competence, and evaluation of early childhood intervention programs. *American Psychologist, 33,* 789–798.

THIRTEEN

CLINICAL ASSESSMENT OF CHILDREN'S INTELLIGENCE WITH THE WECHSLER SCALES

CECIL R. REYNOLDS
Texas A&M University
College Station, Texas

ALAN S. KAUFMAN

California School of Professional Psychology,
and
University of Alabama
Tuscaloosa, Alabama

The evaluation of intellectual integrity and the level of intellectual functioning of the individual has been the metier, and in many cases the raison d'être of employment, of the psychologist in applied settings since the earliest attempts to apply the special methods of psychology to the human condition. Though the role of the psychologist has expanded considerably since World War II, assessment of intelligence remains an integral component of the psychologist's function whether in private practice or the public sector. The uses of intelligence tests are many and quite varied, ranging from predicting future academic levels, to distinguishing organic from psychiatric syndromes, to evaluating personality. Intelligence tests are among the most frequently administered of all tests by clinical psychologists (Korchin, 1976); school psychologists, who spend more than 60% of their time engaged in testing activities (Hughes, 1979), administer

This chapter is an adaptation and revision of three previous works by the authors: Kaufman, A. S., & Reynolds, C. R., Clinical evaluation of intellectual function, in I. Weiner (Ed.), *Clinical Methods in Psychology*, 2nd Ed., N.Y.: Wiley Interscience, 1983; Kaufman, A. S., The impact of WISC-R research for school psychologists, in C. R. Reynolds & T. B. Gutkin (Eds.), *The Handbook of School Psychology*, N.Y.: Wiley, 1982; and, Kaufman, A. S., & Reynolds, C. R., Assessing intelligence and academic achievement, in T. Ollendick & M. Hersen (Eds.), *Child Behavioral Assessment: Principles and Procedures*, N.Y.: Pergamon, 1984.

intelligence batteries more frequently than any other category of tests (Goh, Teslow, & Fuller, 1981). Despite the controversy over their use, the commercial development and publication of intelligence tests have significantly increased in recent years (Reynolds & Elliott, 1982). Even though psychologists are increasingly engaging in roles that are far removed from assessing intelligence, it seems clear that the clinical evaluation of mental functioning will remain an important aspect of school and clinical psychology for some time.

The present chapter begins with a brief history of intelligence testing followed by the development of a philosophy of intelligent testing. Screening techniques for the brief appraisal of general intellectual level are next addressed before turning to methods of intelligence test interpretation. Applications of the Wechsler scales to diagnosis and evaluation of learning disabilities is then discussed, followed by a treatment of issues and methods in the estimation of premorbid levels of intellectual functioning.

A BRIEF HISTORY OF INDIVIDUAL INTELLIGENCE TESTING

The study of intelligence and its measurement traces its roots to physicians, educators, and psychologists who were deeply involved with populations at the extremes of the intellectual continuum. Esquirol (1838) and Seguin (1907) were committed to the study of mentally retarded individuals, and Galton (1869) was fascinated by the mental abilities of geniuses. The separate contributions of these pioneers have been profoundly felt in the field of intelligence testing; however, it was the innovative research investigations of Binet (1903), who focused on the mental abilities of typical or average children at each age, that have had the longest lasting and most direct effect on individual intelligence testing as we know it today.

Esquirol made several important contributions, most notably by distinguishing "between the idiot, whose intelligence does not develop beyond a very low level, and the demented person" (Peterson, 1925, p. 163). This distinction between mental retardation and emotional disturbance reflected a vital breakthrough for assessment and indicates the primitive state of the art in the early nineteenth century. Esquirol also described a hierarchy of retardation (or feeblemindedness, as it was known in earlier times) with "idiots" occupying the bottom rung, followed by "imbeciles," and peaking with "morons" (Peterson, 1925). He was well ahead of his time in concluding that the use of language was the most dependable criterion for inferring a retarded individual's intelligence level (Anastasi, 1976), and Esquirol (1828) is also credited with developing a precursor of the mental-age concept by pointing out that "an idiot is incapable of acquiring the knowledge common to other persons of his own age" (Peterson, 1925, p. 183).

Seguin was heavily influenced in his work with mentally retarded individuals by Itard, of *Wild Boy of Aveyron* fame. Like Esquirol, Seguin (1907) tried to establish criteria for distinguishing between different levels of retardation, although he focused on sensory discrimination and motor control. Optimism regarding treatment of retarded individuals characterized Seguin's approach, and he instituted a comprehensive program of sense-training and muscle-training techniques, much of which live on in present-day institutions for the mentally retarded (Anastasi, 1976). Tests developed by Seguin such as the Seguin Form Board — which requires the rapid placement of various wooden geometric shapes into their proper holes — are still included in present-day nonverbal performance tests, such as the Arthur Point Scale (Arthur, 1947).

Esquirol and Seguin not only were pioneers in individual intellectual assessment, but their efforts helped bring the world out of the dark ages, instilling more humane treatment of retarded and insane people. Prior to the nineteenth century, "Neglect, ridicule, and even torture had been the common lot of these unfortunates" (Anastasi, 1976, p. 5). However, one conceivably negative consequence of their focus on the differentiation of levels of retardation is the prevalent practice of labelling individuals in various special-education categories. The Esquirol tradition has produced euphemisms for terms like "imbecile," as evidenced by the American Association on Mental Deficiency's (AAMD) classification scheme, which features mild, moderate, severe, and profound levels of retardation. To this day, occasional case reports in folders of retarded individuals will include offensive and archaic labels such as "low-grade moron." Whether a person is considered to suffer from "idiocy" or "profound retardation," the use of unpleasant, pigeon-holing labels remains an unfortunate by-product of the otherwise great contributions of the pioneers in the field of retardation.

The Galton-Cattell Approach to Testing

Francis Galton transformed his enthusiasm for gifted men of genius and the study of the genetics of intelligence into the development of what is apparently the first comprehensive individual intelligence test. Galton's tests, administered for a small fee in his Anthropometric Laboratory, required sensory discrimination and sensory-motor coordination. Based on Galton's (1883) belief that intelligence must be intimately related to sensory abilities because environmental knowledge comes to us via the senses, he developed a series of tests such as weight discrimination, reaction time, visual discrimination, steadiness of hand, keenness of sight, and strength of squeeze. His empirical justification for this test battery came from comparisons between gifted and retarded individuals that, not surprisingly, showed obvious superiority in favor of the gifted (Peterson, 1925). Galton's influence spread far beyond his laboratory as Galton-type tests were developed throughout Europe and the United States. James McKeen Cattell, an assistant at Galton's Anthropometric Laboratory, set up a laboratory in 1890 at the University of Pennsylvania and moved it to Columbia University the following year. Cattell coined the term "mental tests"; Galton's influence was clearly evident in Cattell's 40–60 minute individual examination, as the tests included keenness of hearing, reaction time, after-images, color vision, sensitivity to pain, and the like (Peterson, 1925). However, Cattell's (1890) work was not merely an imitation of Galton's. Cattell elaborated on and improved his mentor's methodology by emphasizing the vital notion that administration procedures must be standardized to obtain results that are strictly comparable from person to person and time to time.

In the meantime, a challenge was being issued to the Galton view of sensory and motor intelligence from Alfred Binet of France. In collaboration with Simon and Henri, Binet conducted numerous investigations of complex mental tasks, rejecting the Galton notion that performance on simple, elementary sensory-discrimination and motor-coordination tasks equates to intelligent behavior. Although Binet and his coworkers developed numerous tests of higher mental processes not long after the time that Galton's laboratory was founded, these tasks of memory, imagination, comprehension, moral sentiments, and so forth did not have an immediate impact on the field of intellectual measurement. In fact, Cattell considered carefully the arguments for "tests of a strictly psycho-logical nature" put forth by Binet and others, but rejected these arguments in favor of "more definite and simple tests" since "measurements of the body and of the senses come as completely within our scope as the higher mental processes" (Cattell & Farrand, 1896; Peterson, 1925, p. 79).

The downfall of the Galton-Cattell approach, and the concomitant upswing of the Binet methodology, came oddly enough as the result of two very flawed investigations. Stella Sharp (1898–99) directly compared sensory-discrimination tests with tests of complex mental functions and concluded that the simplest mental processes yield comparatively unimportant information, whereas the tests of Binet and Henri showed much value in assessing "individual psychical differences." However, these well-respected conclusions of Sharp were based on a sample of only seven advanced college students in psychology along with a "control group" of less advanced undergraduates in an experimental psychology course. Apart from the small and homogeneous nature of the sample, the methodology was weak and quantified only partially.

The second study that spelled doom for the Galton approach was Wissler's (1901) correlational analysis at Barnard College based on data for 250 freshmen and 35 seniors. The tests and anthropometric measures obtained at Cattell's laboratory "showed little more than a mere chance relation" when correlated with each other or when correlated with academic marks (Wissler, 1901). However, the highly selected groups evaluated were extremely restricted in range, which would have depressed coefficients for any tests, including highly complex ones. It is ironical that studies with serious methodological shortcomings would help mark the downfall of the Galton movement. A further irony is that Galton developed a statistical method that was the forerunner of the coefficient of correlation, perfected by his friend Karl Pearson; as indicated, low Pearsonian correlations obtained by Wissler were instrumental in a swing toward the Binet tests.

Even though initial reaction to the two studies was predominantly *antitesting*, causing a lack of enthusiasm for the Galton-Cattell as well as the Binet-Henry approach in the United States, the methodology of Binet eventually triumphed, first throughout Europe and finally in America (Peterson, 1925). Thus support was finally given to what we now know axiomatically to be true, namely the claims repeatedly made by Binet and his collaborators in his own journal (*L'Année Psychologique*), founded in 1895: that efficiency in simple sensory-motor tests bears only a small relationship to other criteria of intellect (Binet used teachers' estimates of ability), and that the tests of higher mental processes, though they give more variable and unstable results than simple tests, are more significant and therefore distinguish between the everyday activities of different individuals (Binet & Henri, 1896; Binet & Simon, 1905). Indeed, the willingness of Binet to accept *error* in measurement as a necessity for proper intellectual assessment constitutes one of his most dynamic contributions to the field (Kaufman, 1983).

Interestingly, recent research by Jensen (1979) and his students (such as Vernon, 1981) has revitalized the early work of Galton to some extent. Although they confirm that simple reaction time measures contribute little to variation in intellectual function, these researchers have found substantial relationships between intelligence and complex reaction time, especially coupled with intraindividual variability in complex reaction time over repeated trials of the same task. Thus adaptations of Galton's work might yet be found to impact on objective intellectual assessment in the future.

Alfred Binet's Legacy in the United States

In addition to recognizing the inevitability of some variability in test performance, Binet "discarded the specific test for the specific ability and took a group of tests which seemed to cover in general the chief psychological characteristics that go to make up intelligence. And, furthermore, as the norm or standard of intelligence he took what the average child at each age could do" (Pintner & Paterson, 1925, p. 7). The age-level approach characterizes the Stanford-Binet Intelligence Scale (Terman & Merrill, 1973) to this day, and the nature of the tasks developed by Binet and his colleagues is extremely similar to the specific tasks constituting every major intelligence test in current use (Kaufman, 1983).

The Binet-Simon scales, including the 1911 revision, which extended through adulthood, were welcomed in Europe and the United States, and their translation and adaptation were begun almost immediately. Town directly translated the Binet-Simon scale into English by 1913; early revisions and adaptations were developed by Bobertag in Germany, Johnston and also Winch in England, and by several investigators in the United States: Goddard, Kuhlman, Wallin, Terman, and Yerkes (Pintner & Paterson, 1925).

Terman's (1916) Stanford Revision and Extension of the Binet-Simon Intelligence Scale, later shortened to Stanford-Binet, emerged victorious despite the earlier appearance of pretenders to the throne such as the Goddard-Binet (Goddard, 1911) and Kuhlman-Binet (Kuhlman, 1912). Terman's success was not due to luck or coincidence. After publishing a revision of the Binet Scale that he termed "tentative" (Terman & Childs, 1912), he spent four years painstakingly and thoroughly standardizing the scale. He was specifically trying to meet the needs of the growing number of practitioners in the field whose demand "for more and more accurate diagnoses . . . raised the whole question of the accurate placing of tests in the scale and the accurate evaluation of the responses made by the child" (Pintner & Paterson, 1925, p. 11). Terman also introduced the term IQ in his 1916 scale, borrowing Stern's (1914) concept, and making his revised Binet even more attractive to individual mental examiners.

Despite the many advantages of Terman's scale over its competitors, there was still much room for improvement: adult intelligence was not adequately measured, standardization was not representative enough, directions for administering and scoring some tasks were unclear, and too many of the tasks were verbal (Sattler, 1982). The 1937 revision of the Binet (Terman & Merrill, 1937) produced two forms (L and M) and corrected many of the problems with the earlier version, for example, more nonverbal tests were added at the preschool levels, the standardization was much improved, and additional levels were added at the lower and upper ends of the scale.

The two most recent Binet revisions have been gross disappointments. In 1960, Forms L and M were combined into its present Form $L-M$, and the deviation IQ (a standard score with a mean of 100 and standard deviation of 16) replaced the ratio IQ (Terman & Merrill, 1937). Astonishingly, there was no restandardization of the 1960 Stanford-Binet. Instead, data from a nonrepresentative sample of 4,498 children, tested in the early 1950s, were used to determine changes in item difficulties obtained in the 1930s. This technique was less than satisfactory as a substitution for a new standardization (Berger, 1970).

The 1972 Stanford-Binet represented a restandardization of the instrument, but no modifications of existing items (except for a couple of trivial substitutions) or switching of tasks from one level to another. Consequently, tests that are placed at year level V, for example, are now solved by the average 4½ year old for reasons such as the impact of mass media on the mental functioning of preschool children. The result is the misplacement of numerous tasks and the total loss of meaning of the mental age (MA) concept. For example, a child of 4 who earns an MA of 4 obtains an IQ of 88 instead of the expected 100! It is ironical that Terman's rigor in determining accurate placements for tasks in his 1916 Scale was instrumental in the triumph of his Binet revision over the versions developed by his competitors; the lack of rigor in this same important endeavor, conducted more than a half-century after Terman's initial work, and about 15 years after his death, has been instrumental in the diminished use of the once-venerated Stanford-Binet. To be sure, the Binet is still used by practitioners throughout the country (Goh, Teslow, & Fuller, 1981), but this one-score, unrevised battery has clearly been superseded in everyday practice by Wechsler's scales, notably the Wechsler Intelligence Scale for Children—Revised (WISC-R; Wechsler, 1974) for school-aged youngsters.

Although Terman and Merrill's battery will continue to be of major historical importance and central to understanding the heritage of intelligence testing, for the practicing psychologist the Stanford-Binet is best eschewed in favor of more contemporary methods. Indeed, the 1972 Stanford-Binet is not a clinical scale to be discussed in latter parts of this chapter because of its many antiquated characteristics; perhaps it is best to accept Friedes' (1972) kind offering of *Requiescat in pace* (Reynolds & Clark, 1982). The impact of the Binet tradition will not be forgotten, however. It is felt whenever an intelligence test is administered; as new scales and procedures have been developed, the prototypical tasks of Binet and of Terman repeatedly appear.

David Wechsler's Contributions to Intellectual Evaluation

The biggest challenge to the Stanford-Binet monopoly came from David Wechsler (to whom this *Handbook* has been dedicated) in 1939 when he published the Wechsler-Bellevue Scale (Wechsler, 1939). Present-day instruments, which trace their heritage to Form I and Form II of the Wechsler-Bellevue, are the WISC-R, Wechsler Preschool and Primary Scale of Intelligence (WPPSI; Wechsler, 1967), and Wechsler Adult Intelligence Scale—Revised (WAIS-R; Wechsler, 1981). All Wechsler scales include 10–12 separate subtests with about half included on a Verbal Scale and half on a Performance Scale; three IQs are yielded, a Verbal IQ, a Performance IQ, and a Full Scale IQ. The yielding of a global IQ, despite the separate subtests and scales, is consistent with Wechsler's (1958) notion about the existence of the construct of global intelligence. He stated:

> The grouping of subtests into Verbal . . . and Performance . . ., while intending to emphasize a dichotomy, as regards possible types of ability called for by the individual tests, does not imply that these are the only abilities involved in the tests. Nor does it presume that there are different kinds of intelligence, e.g., verbal, manipulative, etc. It merely implies that these are different ways in which intelligence may manifest itself. The subtests are different measures of intelligence, not measures of different kinds of intelligence, and the dichotomy into Verbal and Performance areas is only one of several ways in which the tests could be grouped. [Wechsler, 1958, p. 64]

Wechsler was thus basically accepting of the Terman/Binet *definition* of intelligence as a global entity, but he used a different type of *methodology* to measure it. Rather than employ a plethora of brief tasks organized by age level, so that any individual would get an arbitrary sampling of these tasks based on his or her age and ability level, Wechsler limited his scale to a smaller number of reliable tasks, predetermining that all people are administered all tasks. He selected nonverbal tests, conspicuously absent at most age levels of the Stanford-Binet, to constitute fully half of his intelligence scale.

Wechsler followed four procedures before selecting 11 subtests for his original 1939 Wechsler-Bellevue scale: (1) careful analysis of all existing standardized tests regarding functions measured and reliability, (2) empirical assessment of each test's validity claims, (3) subjective judgment of each test's clinical values, and (4) tryout data collected over a two-year period on individuals with "known" levels of intelligence (Wechsler, 1958, p. 63). By limiting his tests to those already in existence, Wechsler selected the best measurement tools available in the mid-1930s; in actuality all his tasks were developed not later than the early 1920s.

Many Wechsler tasks were taken directly from the work of Binet and the Americans who adapted the Binet scales from 1900–1915. These include several direct analogs, namely Comprehension, Similarities, Vocabulary, Digit Span, and Picture Completion, and some that are closely similar to Binet tasks: for example, Arithmetic (Making Change) and Object Assembly (Patience Pictures). Besides Binet's work, other sources of Wechsler subtests were the Army examinations developed during World War I. Extremely similar versions of Wechsler's Information, Arithmetic, and Comprehension subtests appeared in Army Group Examination Alpha; close analogs of Mazes, Digit Symbol (Coding), and Picture Completion appeared on Army Group Examination Beta; and the direct ancestors of Object Assembly, Digit Symbol (Coding), Mazes, Picture Arrangement, and Picture Completion constituted half of the Army Individual Performance Scale Examination (Yoakum & Yerkes, 1920). Whereas a cousin of Wechsler's Block Design subtest appeared on the Army Individual Test (Cube Construction), Wechsler's task follows directly from the test originated by Kohs (1923).

Thus all the subtests in the WISC-R and WAIS-R were developed and used at least 60 years ago. They were constructed without benefit of a theoretical model at a time when diverse and comprehensive theories of learning, cognition, and intelligence had not yet been germinated. Since the 1920s, impressive theories and research investigations have emerged from separate disciplines such as cognition, learning, child development, and neuropsychology, much of which relates directly to the measurement of intelligence. The work of Piaget, Cattell-Horn, Guilford, Gagné, Luria, Bruner, Sperry, Hebb, and many others has been blatantly ignored by the publishers of individual tests of intelligence. The tradition, as well as the tasks, of Alfred Binet and World War I psychologists are alive and well in all popular present-day individual-assessment tools for measuring the intelligence of adults and also of preschool, elementary school, and high school students.

These assertions are not intended to diminish the genius of Alfred Binet and David Wechsler. Binet was a man of vision and a true innovator and pioneer. Wechsler, whose death in May, 1981, was a deep loss to psychology, had the clinical insight to provide verbal and nonverbal scales and the empirical sophistication to select and standardize tasks with exceptional psychometric properties. Many others had developed primarily verbal scales (the Binet adaptions) or performance scales (Cornell & Coxe, 1934; Pintner & Paterson, 1925), but Wechsler was the one who realized just how clinically valuable a verbal/nonverbal comparison would be for all individuals if derived from well-standardized scales.

Binet and Wechsler were both courageous. Binet had the courage to speak out strongly against the sensory-motor view of intelligence that had attained almost worldwide acceptance. Wechsler was bold enough to challenge the Stanford-Binet monopoly in the United States; to many psychologists a Binet age scale was synonymous with intelligence test. Both men ultimately triumphed.

Binet's victory, with an assist from Terman, led to supremacy in the U.S. for about a half-century. Wechsler settled for second place for many years. However, when the Stanford-Binet failed to respond to a changing environment, Wechsler did, indeed, try harder. The two forms of the Wechsler-Bellevue were replaced by improved models known as the WISC and WAIS. As these scales became outmoded, they were replaced by the WPPSI, WISC-R, and WAIS-R, test batteries with better and more representative norms, updated content, and greatly improved psychometric properties.

With the increasing stress on the psychoeducational assessment of learning disabilities in the 1960s, and on neuropsychological evaluation in the 1970s, the V-P IQ discrepancies and subtest profiles yielded by Wechsler's scales were waiting and ready to overtake the one-score Binet. The WISC and WISC-R have been used widely with exceptional populations, and their value has been documented in hundreds of research investigations.

A PHILOSOPHY OF INTELLIGENT TESTING

Conventional intelligence tests and even the entire concept of intelligence testing are currently the focus of considerable controversy. Always the subject of scrutiny, the past decade has witnessed intelligence tests placed on trial in the federal courts (*Larry P.,* 1979; *PASE,* 1980), state legislatures (New York's "truth-in-testing" legislation), the lay press, and open scholarly forums (Reynolds & Brown, 1984; Sattler, Hilliard, Lambert, Albee, & Jensen, 1981). At one extreme of the issues are those such as Albee, Hilliard (1984), and Williams who contend that IQ tests are inherently unacceptable measurement devices with no real utility, while at the other extreme are such well-known figures as Herrnstein (1973) and Jensen who believe the immense value of intelligence tests is by now clearly self-evident. While critics of testing demand a moratorium on their use with children, psychologists are often forced to adhere to rigid administrative rules that require the use of *precise* obtained IQs when making placement or diagnostic decisions with no consideration for measurement error, the influence of behavioral variables on performance, or appropriate sensitivity to the child's cultural or linguistic heritage.

A middle ground is sorely needed. Tests need to be preserved, along with their rich clinical heritage and their prominent place in the neurological, psychological, and educational literature. At the same time the proponents of tests need to be less defensive and more open to rational criticisms of the current popular instruments. Knowledge of the weaknesses as well as the strengths of individually administered intelligence tests can serve the dual functions of improving examiners' ability to interpret profiles of any given instrument, and enabling them to select pertinent supplementary tests and subtests to secure a thorough assessment of the intellectual abilities of any child, adolescent, or adult referred for evaluation. The quality of individual mental assessment is no longer simply a question answered in terms of an instrument's empirical or psychometric characteristics. High reliability and validity coefficients, a meaningful factor structure, and normative data obtained by stratified random-sampling techniques do not ensure that an intelligence test is valuable for all or even most assessment purposes. The skills and training of the psychologist engaged in using intelligence tests will certainly interact with the utility of intelligence testing beyond the level of simple actuarial prediction of academic performance.

Indeed, with low IQ children, the primary role of the intelligent tester is to use the test results to develop a means of intervention that will "beat" the prediction made by global IQs. A plethora of research during this century has amply demonstrated that very low IQ children show concomitantly low levels of academic attainment. The purpose of administering an intelligence test to a low IQ child then is at least twofold: (1) to determine that the child is indeed at high risk for academic failure, and (2) to articulate a set of learning circumstances that defeat the prediction. For individuals with average or high IQs, the specific tasks of the intelligent tester may change, but the philosophy remains the same. When evaluating a learning-disabled child, for example, the task is primarily one of fulfilling the prediction made by the global IQs. Most LD children exhibit average or better general intelligence but have a history of academic performance significantly below what would be predicted from their intelligence test performance. The intelligent tester then takes on the responsibility of preventing the child from becoming an outlier in the prediction, that is, he or she must design a set of environmental conditions that will cause the child to achieve and learn at the level predicted by the intelligence test.

When engaged in intelligent testing, the child or adult becomes the primary focus of the evaluation and the tests fade into the background as only a vehicle to understanding. The test setting becomes completely examinee oriented. Interpretation and communication of test results in the context of the individual's particular background, referral behaviors, and approach to performance on diverse tasks constitute the crux of competent evaluation. Global test scores are deemphasized; flexibility, a broad base of knowledge in psychology, and insight on the part of the psychologist are demanded; and the intelligence test becomes a dynamic helping agent, not an instrument for labeling, placement in dead-end programs, or disillusionment of eager, caring teachers and parents. Intelligent testing through individualization becomes the key to accomplishment and is antithetical to the development of computerized or depersonalized form reporting for individually administered cognitive tests such as espoused by Alcorn and Nicholson (1975) and Vitelli and Goldblatt (1979). (See reviews by Reynolds, 1980a, 1980b.) For the intelligent tester, it is imperative to be sensitive and socially aware, and to be clearly aware that intelligence and cognition do not comprise the total human being.

Intelligent testing urges the use of contemporary measures of intelligence as necessary to achieve a true understanding of the individual's intellectual functioning. The approach to test interpretation adopted under this philosophy has been likened to that of a psychological "detective" (Kaufman, 1979a) and requires a melding of clinical skill, mastery of psychometrics and measurement, and extensive knowledge of differential psychology, especially those aspects related to theories of cognitive development and intelligence. A far more extensive treatment of this approach to test interpretations appears in the book *Intelligent Testing with the WISC-R* (Kaufman, 1979a). Discussion of applications of this philosophy to preschool children may be found in Kaufman and Kaufman (1977) and Reynolds and Clark (1982).

Clinical skills with children are obviously important to the intelligent tester in building rapport and maintaining the proper ambience during the actual testing setting. Although adhering to standardized procedure and obtaining valid scores are quite important, the child must remain the lodestar of the evaluation. Critical to the dynamic understanding of the child's performance is close, insightful observation and recording of behavior during the testing period. Fully half the important information gathered during the administration of an intelligence test comes from observing behavior under a set of standard conditions. Behavior at various points in the course of the assessment will often dictate the proper interpretation of test scores. Many individuals earn IQs of 100, but each in a different manner, with infinite nuances of behavior interacting directly with a person's test performance.

Knowledge and skill in psychometrics and measurement are requisite to intelligent testing. The clinical evaluation of test performance must be directed by careful analyses of the statistical properties of the test scores, the internal psychometric characteristics of the test, and the data regarding its relationship to external factors. As one example, difference scores have long had inherent interest for psychologists, especially between subparts of an intelligence scale. Difference scores are unreliable, and small discrepancies between levels of performance may be best attributed to measurement error. If large enough, however, difference scores can provide valuable information regarding the choice of an appropriate remedial or therapeutic program. The psychometric characteristics of the tests in question dictate the size of the differences needed for statistical confidence in their reflecting real rather than chance fluctuations. Interpretation of subscale differences often requires integrating clinical observations of the child's behaviors with data on the relationship of the test scores to other factors, and with theories of intelligence *but only after first establishing that they are real and not based on error.*

One major limitation of most contemporary intelligence tests is their lack of foundation in theories of intelligence, whether these theories be based on research in neuropsychology, cognitive information processing, factor analysis, learning theory, or other domains. Nevertheless, many profiles obtained by children and adults on intelligence tests are interpretable from diverse theoretical perspectives, and can frequently be shown to display a close fit to one or another theoretical approach to intelligence. Theories then become useful in developing a full understanding of the individual. Competing theories of intelligence literally abound (for example, see Reynolds, 1981b; Vernon, 1979; and White, 1979). Well-grounded, empirically evaluated models of intellectual functioning enable one to reach a broader understanding of the examinee and to make specific predictions regarding behavior outside of the testing situation itself. One will not always be correct; however, the intelligent tester has an excellent chance of making sense out of the predictable individual variations in behavior, cognitive skills, and academic performance by invoking the nomothetic framework provided by theory. The alternative often is to be stymied or forced to rely on trial-and-error or anecdotal, illusionary relationships when each new set of profile fluctuations is encountered. Theories, even speculative ones, are more efficient guides to developing hypotheses for understanding and treating problems than are purely clinical impressions or armchair speculations.

Through the elements of clinical skill, psychometric sophistication, and a broad base of knowledge of theories of individual differences emerges intelligent testing. None is sufficient, yet, when properly implemented, these elements engage in a synergistic interaction to produce the greatest possible understanding. Obviously, all these factors cannot be presented here and occur only as the product of extensive training. The remaining portions of this chapter will focus on providing the psychometric groundwork for intelligent testing. Though the focus will be on the Wechsler scales, the conceptual nature of the methods described is applicable to most standardized tests, including intellectual, neuropsychological (Reynolds, in press), and perhaps even personality scales.

RELIABILITY AND VALIDITY OF INDIVIDUAL INTELLIGENCE MEASURES

Since their first presentation around the turn of the century, the psychometric characteristics of intelligence tests have been improving constantly. Nevertheless, in the early days of testing, and even as late as the 1949 WISC, it was not unusual for standardization samples of individually administered tests to be all white and for reliability and validity data to be reported only for white children. Though the changes have been gradual, such is no longer the case for the premier intelligence scales now available for use with children: Kaufman Assessment Battery for Children (K-ABC; Kaufman & Kaufman, 1983), MSCA (McCarthy, 1972), WPPSI (Wechsler, 1967), and WISC-R (Wechsler, 1974). Other intelligence tests are continuing to be developed and published that do not meet the high standards of the above scales and their use is not encouraged.

Today, the major intelligence scales are developed from large nationally stratified random samples of children. Samples are typically stratified on the basis of age, sex, race, socioeconomic status (usually determined by parental occupation), geographic region of residence (North, South, Central, West), and whether the child resides in an urban or rural setting. Such careful sampling is required to ensure the stability and the generalizability of scores on the battery. Less careful standardization and norming should not be considered acceptable for tests that will impact strongly decisions about children's lives.

The reliability of the major intelligence scales has also reached an impressive level, though it has always been good. Reliability is the benchmark of the accuracy of test scores and is prerequisite to validity. From the ages of 2½ to nearly 17 years, the scales mentioned above report general IQs or summary scores with reliability estimates routinely above .90 and frequently as high as .95 and .96—most impressive statistics, given that the limit of reliability is 1.00 and is itself unattainable. The high level of reliability available from the major scales argues strongly for their use as opposed to other more limited scales. The reliability of these measures has been shown also to be consistent across a host of demographic variables such as race, sex, and socioeconomic status (see Reynolds, 1982, for a review).

The literature regarding the validity of the major intelligence scales as well as the construct of intelligence itself is quite massive in its accumulation over the years. Sattler (1982) has provided a most thorough review of this plethora of evidence. Though one can debate the nature of the construct intelligence and defend many different viewpoints, the data regarding intelligence tests do demonstrate their utility in a number of areas. Intelligence tests are, outside of achievement tests, the best available predictors of academic achievement. Measures of general intelligence also are very good predictors of success in most job-training and vocational-training programs, though prediction of actual job performance is more difficult. Intelligence test scores predict a variety of other criteria as well. General intellectual level consistently has been shown to be one of the best predictors of success in psychotherapy and premorbid IQ is the best available predictor of rehabilitative success of patients with acute brain trauma and a number of neurological diseases (Reynolds, 1981b). The diagnostic use of IQ tests is also quite formidable in such categories as mental retardation and intellectual giftedness (though we do not recommend making any diagnostic statements about any individual on the basis of any single psychological test). Validity has, for the most part, been demonstrated across a host of demographic variables as well (for example, see Jensen, 1980, and Reynolds, 1982).

Though intelligence is omnipresent in our daily activities and influences much of what we do and are able to accomplish, intelligence is not omnipotent. Forgetting this rather simple distinction—omnipresent, not omnipotent—has resulted in many abuses of intelligence tests, abuses that can be avoided if we have an adequate understanding of validity and of the limitations of intelligence as a construct.

WHEN TO TEST INTELLIGENCE

From the ages of 5 years to about 18 years, the vast majority of their nonadult lives, children go to school. Socialization and individuation are doubtless major developmental tasks of this period, and many others could be named, but schooling and the acquisition of an education that allows one to become an independent, contributing member of the larger society take precedence over most other tasks of these years. Academic success, the acquisition of the knowledge base for life in a complex society, and the lack of it are major foci of school administrators, teachers, and parents (the individuals who fill most of the child's waking hours), and are a cause of great consternation and potential distress for the children themselves. It follows then that any evaluation of a child that ignores intellectual and academic development is going to be inadequate for developing a good understanding of children and their reciprocal interactions with the environment. Our response to the question of when to assess intelligence in the context of a psychological evaluation, is—virtually always.

The intellectual level of a child will impact the interpretation given to other assessment outcomes and observations of behavior. Many behaviors could be cited that are developmentally sequenced such that they are considered normal, progressive acts at one age but pathological if persisting beyond a particular age level. Such behaviors and acts are, in most instances, better evaluated relative to the child's mental age and not the chronological age. Pathognomic indicators on certain projective tests such as the kinetic family drawing (KFD) and the human figure drawing (HFD) are age related with regard to their personality interpretation; failure to integrate intellectual level into such interpretations can cause considerable distortion in the final evaluation. Particularly for children, intellectual level can impact a choice of therapeutic programs. A 12 year old with an IQ of 60 is a poor prospect for cognitive-behavior therapy, particularly something along the lines of rational emotive therapy (RET), whereas the 12 year old with an IQ of 120 may be very responsive to such an approach.

An in-depth, comprehensive evaluation of intelligence and achievement (assessment of achievement being equally important for children), although always required when the primary referral questions are problems such as mental retardation or learning disabilities, is not always necessary. The reality of practice and the circumstances of the referral may indicate that only brief or screening measures of IQ and achievement are necessary. Such decisions to defer to a screening measure should not be made lightly, however.

SCREENING FOR INTELLECTUAL DISORDERS

Comprehensive evaluation of intellectual functioning, though highly desirable and recommended when questions of cognitive function arise, realistically is time consuming, expensive, and not always necessary. Hence a variety of brief measures of intelligence have been developed over the years. When deciding to use a brief measure of intelligence, one must recognize and accept a considerable loss of clinical information and much material potentially relevant to diagnosis and treatment. Before turning to a discussion of screening methods, it is useful to review the purpose of screening and to evaluate the use of screening techniques. More detailed discussions of the issues to follow can be found in several sources (Kaufman, 1979a; Kaufman & Kaufman, 1977; Reynolds, 1979, 1981d; Stangler, Huber, & Routh, 1980).

Although nearly all individuals with intellectual disorders will ultimately be identified during their public school careers, it is during the early years that corrective, habilitative efforts have the greatest probability of eventual success. Additionally, parents, teachers, and pediatricians, though good sources of referral, cannot be relied on to identify these children; consequently, numerous brief screening measures of intelligence have been developed. In the course of comprehensive psychological assessments of children or adults, a brief screening measure of intelligence will sometimes be sufficient to meet the clinician's need for information. With young children, brief screening measures are more likely to be used to evaluate large numbers of children in a short time period. In this instance, screening has as its direct goal identifying children who are most likely to develop learning, behavior, or other problems that can interfere with appropriate social, emotional, or academic development.

Screening is conducted on a probability basis and reduces the cost of identifying handicapped children by selecting out (or screening out) those children *most likely* to have problems. A screening test is not a criterion measure. No matter how badly a child performs on a screening test, it does not necessarily mean the child is handicapped. In fact, a good screening test has a built-in pathological bias. Because it is usually considered less tolerable to miss locating a handicapped child than to recommend comprehensive evaluation of a non-handicapped child, whenever a screening test "is in doubt" about a child, it should identify the child as potentially handicapped. This can be accomplished most directly by setting cutting scores to identify the largest number of children that can receive comprehensive evaluations.

Children identified as potentially handicapped through a screening test (or other process) can then be referred for a thorough individual evaluation intended to result in: (1) determining that the child was incorrectly identified and not in need of therapeutic intervention, special assistance, or placement in a special-education program, or (2) confirming and more accurately appraising the child's specific difficulties. The latter appraisal is multifaceted and involves determination of an appropriate classification and delineation of an individual educational program or plan of therapy that capitalizes on children's assets, limits the effects of their liabilities, and makes treatment as palatable and successful as possible. Even in the comprehensive individual assessment, however, one must remember that tests are nothing more than methods for obtaining quantifiable samples of behavior.

Screening tests, as a rule, provide very limited, restrictive samples of behavior and are all but useless with respect to diagnostic decision making and the development of instructional plans. Screening tests are usually less reliable measures of a child's skills, since they are designed to detect areas of deficit or handicap; hence, they do not typically allow for the identification of a child's strengths. From a legal standpoint, the vast majority of screening tests do not meet the requirements of P.L. 94-142 for use in educational placement. The results of a screening test cannot substitute for comprehensive individual assessment information, and screening-test information certainly cannot be allowed to override the results of the individual assessment of the referred pupil. However, when used appropriately, screening tests can enhance, economically, a clinician's or school district's ability to identify and serve the handicapped. Used in an attempt to circumvent, stunt, or substitute for a comprehensive individual evaluation, screening tests can lead to major errors in the identification-programming process and provide a great disservice to the teachers, parents, and other individuals involved. Not all intellectual screening tests are group administered. Some of the best screening tests are individually administered, although individual administration does not elevate the status of a screening measure within the total evaluation process.

Group Screening of Intellectual Function

A number of well-designed group tests are available for use in intellectual screening with youngsters who are at least at the beginning kindergarten stage. One need only review Buros' (1974) *Tests in Print* and the most recent of his yearbook series, *The Eighth Mental Measurements Yearbook* (Buros, 1978), to locate nearly all tests available for the group testing of cognitive skill. In addition to descriptive information on each test, comprehensive reviews of the technical adequacy and general quality of the measures are provided in the *Yearbooks.* There are far too many of these tests to be reviewed here and the reader is thus referred to these sources for information on group tests for intellectual screening and to Ebel (1982) for a more general discussion of the evaluation and selection of group tests.

Group tests are typically not available for use with children below age 5—young children are far less accustomed to formal environments and do not have the necessary attentional, visual-motor, perceptual, and social skills to allow them to sit and concentrate on the test materials for the necessary amount of time without close supervision. Such close supervision and attention is readily available under the circumstances of individual assessment. Individual assessment of children should be the rule below age 5. It is recommended for older persons as well. The use of group tests further removes the clinician from the process and takes away the possibility of obtaining good observational data.

Individual Screening of Intellectual Function

The use of individually administered screening tests need not be an extremely expensive or time-consuming enterprise. Individual screening instruments are available that are valid, reliable, informative, and require only 20–30 minutes for administration. Of these, the most reasonable methods seem to be the use of carefully developed short forms of the major individually administered intelligence tests. These short forms are typically at least as reliable as other brief tests, have more validity information available, are more familiar to educational and psychological personnel, and are traditionally better normed than nearly all other brief tests of intelligence. Short forms of the major scales have an added advantage in that, if an individual is noted to be at risk on the screening measure, the remainder of the scale can be administered without a duplication of effort. The development of short forms of the Wechsler scales has been a popular topic in the psychometric literature for some time and several short forms of the WISC-R have been proposed. Of these, the most useful appears to be the short form proposed by Kaufman (1976d).

Previously, short forms have been developed typically on purely empirical grounds without regard to rational and psychological bases for the inclusion of specific subtests. Although empirical development is necessary, it seems insufficient as the sole method of choosing subtests for a short form. Kaufman's (1976d) four-test short form of the WISC-R was developed on the basis of empirical and rational, psychological characteristics of the various subtests using data gleaned from the large national standardization sample of the test with careful delineation of the short form's psychometric properties.

In choosing subtests for the short form, Kaufman determined that two Verbal and two Performance tests would be included and that each dyad should be truly representative of its respective scale. For the Verbal dyad, the Arithmetic and Vocabulary subtests were chosen. For the 10 possible dyads, the range of correlations with Verbal IQ was but .88 to .93; thus any combination was about equally empirically adequate. The Arithmetic-Vocabulary combination was chosen because: (1) the tests tap diverse mental skills, (2) the verbal-numerical combination is known to be an excellent predictor of school or academic attainment, (3) Vocabulary is the best single measure of g on the WISC-R, and (4) the inclusion of Arithmetic ensures that the Freedom from Distractibility factor (see later discussion of factor analysis of the WISC-R) is represented.

For the 10 possible Performance Scale dyads, the range of correlations was again quite restrictive, though smaller on the average than the verbal dyad-verbal scale correlations. Kaufman (1976d) selected the Picture Arrangement–Block Design dyad to represent the Performance scale. It had the largest correlation with the performance IQ (.89) and has considerable intuitive and rational appeal: Block Design is the best measure of g for the nonverbal scale and is the most reliable of all Performance scale tests. Block Design and Picture Arrangement measure diverse sets of mental skill and Picture Arrangement is more complex than the remaining Performance tasks in addition to being one of the clinically most interesting of all Wechsler tasks. Once chosen from results with the "even" age groups of the standardization sample, both dyads were cross-validated using the "odd" age groups.

Using a method of linear equating described by Tellegen and Briggs (1967), Kaufman generated conversion equations for the estimation of Full Scale IQ from short-form scores at each age level. Since the equations were all so similar, a single equation determined from the intercorrelation matrix of all 11 age groups was used to convert short-form scores to estimate Full Scale IQs. The equation is applicable to the entire age range of the WISC-R and is:

THEOREM 1. Estimated WISC-R Full Scale IQ $= 1.64X_{SF} + 34.1,$

where X_{SF} is the sum of the child's *scaled* scores on the four component subtests. Though easy to use, Kaufman (1976d, Table 3, p. 185) also provides a conversion table for estimating Full Scale IQs based on Theorem 1.

The psychometric characteristics of the Kaufman WISC-R short form are admirable given its brevity. The split-half reliability ranges from .89 to .93 across the age range while short term test-retest reliability estimates range from .83 to .91. At every age, the short form correlates above .90 with the Full Scale IQ. At the appropriate age levels, the WISC-R short-form IQs correlate .80 with the WPPSI and .89 with the WAIS. The short-form estimates of WISC-R Full Scale IQs, on the average, are within 3 points of the Full Scale IQ obtained from administration of the total scale (Kaufman, 1976d). The standard error of estimate of the short-form estimated Full Scale IQs is about 5 points.

Short forms of other individual intelligence tests have also been developed but are not featured here. For adults, Reynolds, Willson, and Clark (1983) have recently developed a short form of the WAIS-R (Wechsler, 1981). For young children, short forms of the WPPSI (Kaufman, 1972) and the McCarthy Scales of Children's Abilities (Kaufman, 1977) are the most important, appropriate individual screening methods (see Reynolds & Clark, 1982, for a discussion of various proposed short forms of these scales). When choosing or developing short forms of existing or new intelligence tests, psychologists would be wise to adhere to the blend of psychological, clinical, and psychometric considerations proposed by Kaufman (1972, 1976d, 1977).

INDIVIDUAL DIAGNOSIS OF INTELLECTUAL DISORDERS

Before proceeding with a formal cognitive assessment, it is essential to understand the legal requirements. As of September 1, 1978, all handicapped children ages 3 to 18 must receive a "free, appropriate public education." Under the provision of P.L. 94-142 (Education for All Handicapped Children Act of 1975), before a child can be identified as handicapped, he or she must be provided with a "full and individual evaluation." This evaluation has to be conducted according to specific requirements: (1) the tests must be presented in the child's native language or mode of communication, (2) the tests must be well normed and used specifically for the purposes for which they were intended (validated), (3) the tests must be administered by an individual trained in their use as they were designed by the producer, (4) no single instrument can be used for appropriate programming, and (5) a multidisciplinary team must conduct the evaluation, consisting of at least one specialist in the area of difficulty. Section 504 of the Vocational Rehabilitation Act of 1973 extends these requirements to the handicapped of all ages.

Obviously, to be consistent with federal law and good psychological sense, evaluation procedures must adhere to strict qualifications. For instance, the stipulation in P.L. 94-142 that "tests and other evaluation materials include those tailored to assess specific areas of educational needs and not merely those which are designed to provide a single intelligence quotient" should be nothing new to competent psychologists who are accustomed to performing comprehensive child studies. Even though this chapter focuses on the use of the major individual intelligence scales, the days should be far behind us when the diagnosis of mental retardation, for example, is made on the basis of a single score from an IQ test. It is imperative that a variety of techniques be employed in the diagnosis of any cognitive disorder at any age, but especially during childhood when the plasticity of the central nervous system is so great and development so rapid. In addition, it is mandated that "tests are selected and administered so as best to ensure that, when a test is administered to a student with impaired sensory, manual, or speaking skill, the test results accurately reflect the student's aptitude or achievement level or whatever other factor the test purports to measure rather than reflecting the student's impaired sensory, manual, or speaking skills (except where those skills are the factors that the test purports to measure)." Most psychological tests are not standardized for use with sensory-impaired populations nor are examiners routinely trained in the skills necessary to communicate effectively with these children. Without specific training in the evaluation and assessment of sensory-impaired children, most psychologists would do well to refer such children to an appropriate specialist. Although one continues to hear horror stories regarding the wrongful diagnosis of hearing-impaired and vision-impaired children based on low levels of performance on standardized intelligence scales, the limitations of tests standardized on normal children for such populations are now better understood and such acts of incompetence are rare. At the preschool level, slight visual or hearing impairments may be less readily apparent, and young children suspected of having cognitive disorders should routinely have hearing and visual examinations.

Many factors influence the outcome of a cognitive assessment and all must be considered when evaluating the performance of an individual. Factors influencing the assessment process are reviewed elsewhere by Kaufman (1979a), Lutey and Copeland (1982), and Matarazzo (1972); readers are cautioned to pay particular attention to external and situational factors when evaluating preschoolers.

It is frequently necessary to arrive at a specific diagnosis when evaluating handicapped individuals. Several systems for the classification of mental and cognitive disorders are available, with which the examiner should be familiar (for example, the diagnostic criteria of P.L. 94-142, the DSM-III, the International Classification of Diseases, and several actuarial systems reviewed in McDermott, 1982). Psychologists and other diagnostic personnel will typically be restricted to the use of a particular system as a function of the location of their employment. In public school settings, the categories and criteria of P.L. 94-142 are almost universally employed, while hospitals and mental health centers most often adopt the DSM-III. Diagnostic personnel in settings where no single system is given exclusionary preference should adopt one system and use it consistently, to foster accurate communication between the different types and levels of personnel who may encounter the individual in question. Accurate diagnostic decision making is difficult and requires hands-on exposure to the many handicapping conditions that can affect children and adults, in addition to thorough academic training regarding the characteristics of these handicaps.

OBSERVING TEST BEHAVIOR

Clinical skills with children are obviously important to the intelligent tester for building rapport and maintaining the proper ambience during the actual testing setting. Although adherence to standardized procedure and obtaining valid scores is quite important, the child must remain the lodestar of the evaluation. Critical to the dynamic understanding of the child's performance is close, insightful observation and recording of behavior during the testing period. Fully half or more of the important information to be gathered during the administration of an intelligence test comes from observing behavior under a set of standard conditions. Behavior at various points in the course of the assessment will often dictate the proper interpretation of test scores, and can offer information on a child's characteristic approach to problem solving, reactions to frustrations or successes, or cognitive style. Many individuals earn IQs of 100, but each in a different manner, with infinite nuances of behavior interacting directly with a person's test performance.

Table 1 provides a sampling of behaviors that will frequently be of interest in the context of an individual assessment in general, but particularly when assessing intelligence and achievement. It will be important, particularly to the generalizability of any inferences made on the basis of the child's behavior during the testing, to observe the child's behavior in other settings such as the waiting room, playground, and at day care or in a formal classroom setting. It is best to make such observations prior to formal testing to lessen the impact of the observation process on the behaviors of interest. Intelligence and achievement tests themselves can be evaluated from an applied behavior-analysis perspective (for example, see Sattler, 1982, Chapter 18, for a brief review) though such is not the featured approach here.

Concomitantly, intelligent testing requires the communication of results in a meaningful manner that is child oriented and not simply a test-by-test recital of results. Though results are often communicated verbally to some staff, the most universal means is through the psychological report. The key to the intelligent tester's report is that it is written about a child, not about a test or series of tests. Further discussions of this can be found in Kaufman and Reynolds (1984) and Shellenberger (1982).

TRADITIONAL NORMATIVE APPROACHES TO TEST INTERPRETATION

The first line of attack in test interpretation is the evaluation of the individual's performance relative to the performance of an appropriate reference group. In the vast majority of cases, this will be the individual's age peers. For the Wechsler scales, the three global IQs would first be examined and compared to the mean level of performance of the standardization samples. Since the Wechsler IQs are standardized within separate age levels and assume an essentially normal dis-

Table 1. Examples of Observations and Behaviors That May Be Useful in the Context of Intellectual and Academic Assessment

1. Appearance. Size, height, and weight; facial and other physical characteristics; grooming and general cleanliness; clothing style (appropriateness for age).
2. Language Development. Articulation, syntax, language patterns, use of standard English, dialects, or slang.
3. Responses to Test Materials and Setting.
    a. *General Activity Level.* Evidence of tension, anxiety, or restlessness, such as nail biting, foot wiggling, fidgeting, excessive talking, blocks in talking, intermittent stutters, voice tremors.
    b. *Attention Span.* Resistance to extraneous stimuli, general distractibility, ability to focus behavior, remaining on task, and sustaining purposive acts.
    c. *Cooperation or Resistance.* Rapport, personal relationship with psychologist, attempts to cooperate, refusal of specific tasks, interest in the various tasks, attempts to perform at a high level of proficiency, motivation.
    d. *Cognitive and Problem-Solving Styles.* Impulsive, quick to respond, contemplates solutions, employs trial and error, develops systematic plan, checks answers, disregards obviously incorrect responses.
    e. *Reactions to Failure, Challenges, and Success.* Continues to work as long as time limits allow, gives up at first hint of difficulty, frequently asks for assistance or special directions, failure on one task reduces interest in following tasks, difficulty heightens interest, seeks challenges, becomes aggressive when meeting failure, withdraws, becomes dependent.
    f. *Attitudes toward Self.* Displays confidence, a superior attitude, frequently says "I can't," seems defeatist, seeks examiner's approval, responds positively to praise and encouragement, sulks, makes disparaging remarks about self or about test materials.

Note. This list is suggestive, not exhaustive, and refers to both behaviors and inferences drawn from those behaviors. Typically both levels of information are important and should be provided.

tribution, the normative evaluation of performance is relatively simple and straightforward. Given the constant mean (100) and standard deviation (15) of the Verbal, Performance, and Full Scale IQs, the relative standing of the individual with regard to age peers is readily revealed from tables in the test manual or a table of the normal curve. However, Wechsler grouped tasks into these three IQ scales on a purely intuitive basis; before making direct interpretations of the scales, evidence for the reality of their existence must be examined. Such evidence comes most directly from factor analysis.

Factor Analysis of the Wechsler Scales

One of the most frequent avenues of research with the Wechsler scales has been factor analysis. A striking consistency of results has occurred across a number of ages and populations that has implications for test interpretation. Some major differences occur across the three Wechsler scales (WPPSI, WISC-R, WAIS-R) that are important to note as well.

Three consistent and pervasive factors emerged for each of the 11 age groups in the WISC-R standardization sample, regardless of whether orthogonal or oblique rotational procedures were employed: Verbal Comprehension, Perceptual Organization, and Freedom from Distractibility (Kaufman, 1975). Each of the 12 WISC-R subtests was found to have a *primary* loading on one and only one of these factors, as shown below:

Verbal Comprehension	Perceptual Organization	Freedom from Distractibility
Information	Picture Completion	Arithmetic
Similarities	Picture Arrangement	Digit Span
Vocabulary	Block Design	Coding
Comprehension	Object Assembly	
	Mazes	

The first two factors bear an obvious relationship to the Verbal and Performance scales, respectively. The third factor was labeled Freedom from Distractibility to follow the historical precedent established by Cohen (1952, 1959) for other Wechsler batteries, and because of research with hyperactive children, showing that drug therapy leads to decreased distractibility and improved memory and arithmetic skills (Wender, 1971).

Tables 2 through 4 show the median varimax loadings obtained for the 11 age groups between 6½ and 16½ years in the normative sample, along with results from a series of replications with various normal and clinical groups. Note that Information had a substantial loading on the third factor for the standardization sample (median = .41). However, this relationship was not obtained for two oblique rotations of the WISC-R factors, so it was concluded that the distractibility factor was composed only of Arithmetic, Digit Span, and Coding. This conclusion has been given additional support from the results of factor analyses of supplementary populations. A distractibility dimension emerged for mentally retarded children and adolescents (Van Hagen & Kaufman, 1975), adolescent psychiatric patients (De Horn & Klinge, 1978), normal groups of Anglos and Chicanos (Reschly, 1978), blacks (Gutkin & Reynolds, 1981), and for children referred to school or clinical psychologists for suspected learning and/or behavioral disorders (Lombard & Reidel, 1978; Stedman, Lawlis, Cortner, & Achterberg, 1978; Swerdlik & Schweitzer, 1978). As indicated in Table 4, the median loadings for these samples on the distractibility factor were above .40 for Arithmetic, Digit Span, and Coding, but only .30 for Information. Thus the existence of the WISC-R Freedom from Distractibility factor, as well as its composition, has been cross-validated for an impressive variety of normal and clinical groups.

Even more striking than the cross-validational evidence for the third factor is the evidence for the first two factors. Verbal Comprehension and Perceptual Organization dimensions have emerged for every sample whose WISC-R subtest scores were subjected to factor analysis, including two groups that did not produce a distractibility factor (the blacks and native-American Papagos investigated by Reschly, 1978). Furthermore, when hierarchical factor solutions have

Table 2. Factor Loadings on the Verbal Comprehension Factor for a Variety of Normal and Clinical Samples

WISC-R Subtest	(1)	(2)	(3)	(4)	(5)	(6)	(7)	(8)	(9)	(10)	(11)	(12)	(13)	(14)	Median
Verbal															
Information	63	63	72	66	70	73	82	59	84	71	76	69	73	70	71
Similarities	64	59	66	67	59	67	75	69	77	69	68	70	66	67	67
Arithmetic	37	43	65	40	42	41	44	43	66	48	39	43	62	24	43
Vocabulary	72	74	76	67	74	57	82	81	82	70	76	82	82	78	76
Comprehension	64	64	74	61	71	53	65	77	82	55	56	72	64	68	64
Digit span	18	35	46	33	31	46	23	28	38	14	—	—	44	19	33
Performance															
Picture completion	35	20	36	32	22	16	30	31	16	24	28	29	37	18	29
Picture arrangement	33	20	39	17	23	46	38	30	48	18	23	25	41	33	30
Block design	27	17	23	20	14	27	37	32	23	22	31	20	33	26	23
Object assembly	21	07	09	14	09	04	20	20	23	28	-10	25	20	19	20
Coding	15	12	35	14	21	26	27	20	07	14	21	11	38	39	20
Mazes	12	18	30	06	16	10	—	08	—	—	—	—	23	—	14

Note. Decimal points are omitted. Loadings of .35 and above are italicized. The groups are as follows:
(1) Standardization sample, ages 6½–16½ (*N* = 2200), 85% white, 15% nonwhite, median varimax loadings for 11 age groups are shown in table. Source: Kaufman (1975).

(2) Anglos, grades 1–9 (*N* = 252). Source: Reschly (1978).

(3) Blacks, grades 1–9 (*N* = 235). Source: Reschly (1978).

(4) Chicanos, grades 1–9 (*N* = 223). Source: Reschly (1978).

(5) Native-American Papagos, grades 1–9 (*N* = 240). Source: Reschly (1978).

(6) Mentally retarded sample, ages 6–16½ (*N* = 80), mean WISC-R IQ = 50.6, 82% white, 18% nonwhite. Source: Van Hagen and Kaufman (1975).

(7) Adolescent psychiatric sample, ages 10½–16 (*N* = 100), 68% white, 32% nonwhite. Source: De Horn and Klinge (1978).

(8) Sample of children referred because of concerns about intellectual ability, ages 7–16 (*N* = 164), mean WISC-R IQ = 85.9, 63% white, 24% black, 13% Latino. Source: Swerdlik and Schweitzer (1978).

(9) Sample of children referred for learning and/or behavior problems, ages 6–13 (*N* = 106), 90% Spanish surname, 8% white, 2% black. Source: Stedman, Lawlis, Cortner, and Achterberg (1978).

(10) Sample of Chicano children referred for school-related problems, mean age = 10½ (*N* = 142). Source: Gutkin and Reynolds (1980).

(11) Sample of Anglo children referred for learning difficulties, mean age = 11 (*N* = 109). Source: Dean (1979).

(12) Sample of learning-disabled children, mean age = 10½ (*N* = 275). Source: Schooler, Beebe, and Koepke (1978).

(13) Sample of low SES children from the WISC-R standardization sample (*N* = 782). Source: Carlson, Reynolds, and Gutkin (in press).

(14) Sample of emotionally disturbed children (*N* = 60). Source: Reynolds and Struer (1982).

Table 3. Factor Loadings on the Perceptual Organization Factor for a Variety of Normal and Clinical Samples

WISC-R Subtest	(1)	(2)	(3)	(4)	(5)	(6)	(7)	(8)	(9)	(10)	(11)	(12)	(13)	(14)	Median
Verbal															
Information	25	32	32	20	26	12	29	33	10	13	09	11	29	25	25
Similarities	34	26	30	15	34	08	45	22	23	33	39	30	34	19	30
Arithmetic	20	26	37	13	37	16	40	39	13	31	-23	37	27	24	27
Vocabulary	24	23	19	26	14	27	31	23	30	27	22	23	26	16	24
Comprehension	30	22	16	20	13	48	38	25	18	33	-12	15	34	19	22
Digit span	12	02	32	14	36	06	10	26	23	22	—	—	19	17	19
Performance															
Picture completion	57	49	44	52	54	83	68	59	83	56	66	47	59	68	57
Picture arrangement	41	53	47	38	43	41	58	52	31	72	59	56	44	49	47
Block design	66	60	66	59	68	62	71	70	75	64	73	70	74	72	68
Object assembly	65	59	57	58	56	70	76	76	68	51	69	80	73	77	68
Coding	20	16	27	16	25	45	30	44	05	37	29	43	19	32	27
Mazes	47	42	47	47	56	67	—	55	—	—	—	—	52	—	50

Note. Decimal points are omitted. Loadings of .35 and above are italicized. The groups are as follows:

(1) Standardization sample, ages 6½–16½ (N = 2200), 85% white, 15% nonwhite. median varimax loadings for 11 age groups are shown in table. Source: Kaufman (1975).

(2) Anglos, grades 1–9 (N = 252). Source: Reschly (1978).

(3) Blacks, grades 1–9 (N = 235). Source: Reschly (1978).

(4) Chicanos, grades 1–9 (N = 223). Source: Reschly (1978).

(5) Native-American Papagos, grades 1–9 (N = 240). Source: Reschly (1978).

(6) Mentally retarded sample, ages 6–16½ (N = 80). mean WISC-R IQ = 50.6, 82% white, 18% nonwhite. Source: Van Hagen and Kaufman (1975).

(7) Adolescent psychiatric sample, ages 10½–16½ (N = 100), 68% white, 32% nonwhite. Source: De Horn and Klinge (1978).

(8) Sample of children referred because of concerns about intellectual ability, ages 7–16 (N = 164), mean WISC-R IQ = 85.9, 63% white, 24% black, 13% Latino. Source: Swerdlik and Schweitzer (1978).

(9) Sample of children referred for learning and/or behavior problems, ages 6–13 (N = 106), 90% Spanish surname, 8% white, 2% black. Source: Stedman. Lawlis, Cortner, and Achterberg (1978).

(10) Sample of Chicano children referred for school-related problems, mean age = 10½ (N = 142). Source: Gutkin and Reynolds (1980).

(11) Sample of Anglo children referred for learning difficulties, mean age = 11 (N = 109). Source: Dean (1979).

(12) Sample of learning-disabled children, mean age = 10½ (N = 275). Source: Schooler, Beebe, and Koepke (1978).

(13) Sample of low SES children from the WISC-R standardization sample (N = 782). Source: Carlson, Reynolds, and Gutkin (in press).

(14) Sample of emotionally disturbed children (N = 60). Source: Reynolds and Struer (1982).

Table 4. Factor Loadings for the Freedom from Distractibility Factor for a Variety of Normal and Clinical Samples

WISC-R Subtest	(1)	(2)	(4)	(6)	(7)	(8)	(9)	(11)	(13)	(14)	Median
Verbal											
Information	*41*	26	33	24	14	*38*	16	-19	*42*	14	26
Similarities	28	26	22	23	22	27	04	-26	28	17	23
Arithmetic	*58*	*45*	*45*	*54*	*49*	*49*	*40*	*52*	*58*	*81*	*49*
Vocabulary	33	12	30	02	17	17	03	20	33	21	17
Comprehension	24	21	06	12	*45*	16	09	21	26	28	21
Digit span	*56*	*40*	31	29	*37*	*65*	*42*	—	*56*	*53*	*41*
Performance											
Picture completion	11	09	12	12	-01	19	01	27	13	*35*	12
Picture arrangement	12	00	*39*	*45*	12	*43*	21	-17	24	*42*	21
Block design	28	22	16	05	23	17	04	*47*	30	22	22
Object assembly	12	18	09	09	13	12	*36*	24	11	07	12
Coding	*42*	*40*	*37*	*43*	*57*	19	*94*	*44*	*38*	28	*42*
Mazes	22	10	20	24	—	22	—	—	23	22	22

Note. Decimal points are omitted. Loadings of .35 and above are italicized. Groups 3 and 5 are omitted from this table because a freedom-from-distractibility factor did not emerge for those two samples. Hence, the loadings shown in Tables 2 and 3 reflect data obtained not from Reschly's (1978) two-factor solutions for blacks and native-American Papagos, but from his three-factor solutions for whites and Chicanos. Groups 10 and 12 are also omitted from this table because Gutkin and Reynolds (1980) only identified two meaningful factors, and Schooler, Beebe, and Koepke (1978) did not even investigate three-factor solutions. The groups are as follows:

(1) Standardization sample, ages 6½–16½ (*N* = 2200), 85% white, 15% nonwhite, median varimax loadings for 11 age groups are shown in table. Source: Kaufman (1975).

(2) Anglos, grades 1–9 (*N* = 252). Source: Reschly (1978).

(4) Chicanos, grades 1–9 (*N* = 223). Source: Reschly (1978).

(6) Mentally retarded sample, ages 6–16½ (*N* = 80). mean WISC-R IQ = 50.6, 82% white, 18% nonwhite. Source: Van Hagen and Kaufman (1975).

(7) Adolescent psychiatric sample, ages 10½–16 (*N* = 100). 68% white, 32% nonwhite. Source: De Horn and Klinge (1978).

(8) Sample of children referred because of concerns about intellectual ability, ages 7–16 (*N* = 164), mean WISC-R IQ = 85.9, 63% white, 24% black, 13% Latino. Source: Swerdlik and Schweitzer (1978).

(9) Sample of children referred for learning and/or behavior problems, ages 6–13 (*N* = 106), 90% Spanish surname, 8% white, 2% black. Source: Stedman, Lawlis, Cortner, and Achterberg (1978).

(11) Sample of Anglo children referred for learning difficulties, mean age = 11 (*N* = 109). Source: Dean (1979).

(13) Sample of low SES children from the WISC-R standardization sample (*N* = 782). Source: Carlson, Reynolds, and Gutkin (in press).

(14) Sample of emotionally disturbed children (*N* = 60). Source: Reynolds and Struer (1982).

been applied to WISC-R data, clear verbal and perceptual dimensions are yielded even after the extraction of a large general intelligence factor (Vance & Wallbrown, 1978; Wallbrown, Blaha, Wallbrown, & Engin, 1975). Tables 2 and 3 present the median varimax loadings for 13 samples on the Verbal Comprehension and Perceptual Organization factors. The median loadings for these cross-validation samples on the nonverbal dimension are quite close to the medians for the standardization sample on the Perceptual Organization factor. The Verbal Comprehension factors for the standardization sample and the supplementary populations are also close in composition. The main difference concerns the Arithmetic and Digit Span subtests: for the standardization sample, these tasks were far more associated with the third than the first factor; for the cross-validation groups, they loaded almost equally on the verbal and distractibility dimensions. Examination of data for the separate supplementary populations revealed that the approximately equal loadings by Arithmetic and Digit Span on the first and third factors characterized the normal as well as the clinical samples.

One important inference to be drawn from the various factor analyses is that the empirical results support the construct validity of the WISC-R. The Verbal Comprehension factor reflects the construct purported by Wechsler to be measured by the Verbal scale. Four Verbal subtests have very high loadings on this factor, and although Arithmetic is a distant fifth, it is clearly associated with the Verbal Comprehension dimension. The fact that Digit Span was the sixth best measure of Verbal Comprehension for the cross-validation samples (but not for the standardization groups) offers tentative support for its placement by Wechsler on the Verbal Scale. Equally good evidence is provided by factor analysis for the construct validity of the Performance Scale. The pattern of loadings on the Perceptual Organization factor suggests that this dimension corresponds to a unitary ability underlying the Performance Scale. Only coding among the six nonverbal subtests is given no empirical support for its inclusion on the Performance Scale.

Review of the WISC-R factor-analytic literature has thus shown that three factors are typically isolated—two relate closely to Wechsler's Verbal-Performance dichotomy, and a third may correspond to a behavioral attribute. These factors are remarkably similar in composition from age to age and across sex (Reynolds & Gutkin, 1980) throughout the entire range serviced by the WISC-R, and also from group to group, whether normal or exceptional populations are tested. The three factors have been isolated for Spanish-speaking as well as English-speaking children (Gutkin & Reynolds, 1980; Reschly, 1978; Stedman, Lawlis, Cortner, & Achterberg, 1978). Furthermore, the factors do not fragment and split into highly specific factors when four or five factors are rotated (Kaufman, 1975).

The robust nature of the various WISC-R factors is important for clinicians to understand because of the implications that these data hold for competent interpretation of the WISC-R. More so than profiles on the old WISC, children's WISC-R profiles should be attacked by featuring the Verbal and Performance scales, and subserving fluctuations in the pattern of subtest scores. The large, omnipresent Verbal Comprehension and Perceptual Organization factors suggest that the Verbal and Performance IQs correspond to real, unitary dimensions of ability in children. As such, profile interpretation should begin by focusing on these global verbal and nonverbal skill areas. This suggestion seems simple enough, but so many methods of interpretation focus on the individuality of the 10 to 12 subtests, as if the WISC-R were a mixed bag of about a dozen separate and diverse skills, each assessing a finite aspect of a child's intellect (see Reynolds, 1980b, for a brief critique). Even a table such as the one appearing in the WISC-R Manual (Wechsler, 1974, Table 12), which presents the differences between *pairs* of scaled scores required for statistical significance, can impel examiners to focus off target. The pairwise comparison technique places a stress on the *subtests* (taken two at a time), rather than on the two major *scales*; furthermore, this procedure offers clinicians a series of statements about a child's strong and weak abilities, but fails to provide a succinct overview or integration of his or her skills.

Later we will present logical and statistical methods for the very necessary look beyond the IQ scales, but intelligent test interpretation begins by first viewing overall performance on *g* (as estimated by the Full Scale IQ) and the Verbal and Performance scales. The third factor will also need to be examined for many children. Gutkin (1979c) provides a formula for estimating a deviation IQ with a mean of 100 and standard deviation of 15 for the Freedom from Distractibility factor.

The third WISC-R factor, which may be a measure of attention/distractibility, anxiety, symbolic ability, sequential processing, or memory, is a particularly intriguing one. Its pervasiveness and robustness on the WISC-R are not matched in factor analyses of other Wechsler batteries. Recent factor-analytic studies of the WAIS-R show a large general factor accompanied by strong Verbal Comprehension and Perceptual Organization factors that correspond to the Full Scale, Verbal, and Performance IQ scales (Gutkin, Reynolds, & Galvin, in press). When WAIS-R distractibility factors do appear for the various adult age groups, they are much smaller in magnitude than their WISC-R counterparts; indeed, for some groups the WAIS-R distractibility dimensions have such small eigenvalues that they are of questionable significance (Naglieri & Kaufman, 1982). Finally, numerous studies of the preschool version of the Wechsler, the WPPSI, have repeatedly located only a large general factor and the two factors corresponding to the *a priori* determined IQ scales (for example, Carlson & Reynolds, 1981; Kaufman & Hollenbeck, 1974).

Normative Evaluation of IQs

Once IQs have been derived, some judgment of the individual's level of intellectual functioning relative to age peers is appropriate. Probably the most readily understandable approach is through the reporting of a percentile rank with a descriptive classification. Wechsler IQs are essentially normally distributed and tables of percentile ranks, expressing the percentage of the population scoring above and below a given score, are available in a variety of sources including Reynolds (1981a), Sattler (1982), and many measurement texts. When reporting the IQ it is helpful to give a descriptive classification in addition to the percentile rank. Wechsler (1974) and others (such as Kaufman & Kaufman, 1977) present various descriptive classification schemes.

The terminology of certain systems can be offensive and care must be given to choosing an appropriate descriptor. The term "mentally defective" for the description of Wechsler or Binet IQs below 70, though perhaps accurate, seems unduly harsh. On the other hand, accuracy is an important concern. For these reasons, a system for descriptive classification of IQ level adapted from Kaufman and Kaufman (1977) is presented in Table 5 (and originally adapted by these authors from Wechsler, 1974).

When reporting IQs, percentile ranks, and descriptive classifications of performance level, it is important to make some statement regarding measurement error. Even though the three Wechsler scales have Full Scale IQs with reliability coefficients in the mid-.90s, considerable error can still be present for individuals. From the reliability estimates, a very practical statistic known as the *standard error of measurement* (S_{em}) can be derived, which allows the establishment of a confidence interval around the reported IQ. Though varying somewhat from scale to scale, the S_{em} of the Wechsler Full Scale IQs is around three IQ points. Since the S_{em} is normally distributed about the true score of the individual, we can band the obtained score to represent any given level of confidence desired, simply by multiplying the S_{em} by the necessary value of z from a table of the normal curve. For example, 1 S_{em} will capture about 68% of a child's scores and 2 S_{em} about 95%. We feel that the 85%–90% level of confidence is appropriate for most clinical purposes; for the Wechsler scales, this requires banding the reported Full Scale IQ with about five points on each side. The primary purpose

Table 5.   Descriptive Classification Corresponding to Various Levels of IQ on the Wechsler Scales

IQ Range	Percentile Ranks	Descriptive Classification
130 and above	98 and above	Very superior
120 to 129	91 to 97	Superior
110 to 119	75 to 90	High average
90 to 109	25 to 73	Average
80 to 89	9 to 23	Low average
70 to 79	3 to 8	Borderline
69 and below	2 and below	Cognitively deficient

Source: Compiled from Kaufman and Kaufman (1977) and Wechsler (1974).

of such reporting is to highlight the concept of error, guarding against overinterpretation and rigidity in the use of cutoff scores.*

Normative evaluation of levels of performance is crucial to intelligent testing. Performance on IQ tests is related to various factors, the most important for children being school attainment. The IQ test makes a good prediction of the child's future level of academic performance, and can help to explain current levels of academic functioning (extensive reviews of predictive studies with IQ tests may be found in Lutey, 1977; and Sattler, 1982). Important information is gleaned for adults as well, including predictions of success in certain jobs, response to various psychotherapies, and the probability of recovery from neurological insult. However crucial, normative interpretation is insufficient for intelligent testing. Much more information lies beyond comparisons of individuals to their peers. Intraindividual differences can be important in altering the predictions made by the IQs, for those predictions assume no major changes occurring in the environment. One must look past the IQs to generate hypotheses for intervention.

IPSATIVE EVALUATION OF TEST PERFORMANCE

Normative assessment of performance on the Wechsler scales proceeds from the assumptions that g is primarily the determinant of the Full Scale IQ, that verbal-comprehension ability is the primary determinant of scores on the Verbal Scale, that perceptual-organization ability is the determinant of scores on the Performance Scale, and, where applicable, that some unitary trait or ability underlies performance on the distractibility factor. A corollary assumption is that fluctuations in a child's or adult's profile are due to chance error. Fortunately, statistics and formulas are available to permit clinicians to test these important assumptions. When the assumptions cannot be refuted by the simple empirical procedures, then examiners should not ordinarily go beyond a normative interpretation of the Wechsler profile. However, when fluctuations between scales and among subtest scores are statistically significant, causing the examiners to reject some or all of the assumptions, then ipsative (intraindividual) evaluation takes over and the clinical "detective work" predominates.

---

*Note that the S_{em} is symmetrical only about the true score, which is obtained by regressing the obtained score to the mean of the distribution via the reliability coefficient where the true score (X_∞) becomes $X_\infty = \overline{X} + r_{xx}(X_i - \overline{X})$. Our recommendation for banding obtained scores is thus technically in error but seems appropriate for several reasons: banding X_i instead of X_∞ avoids considerable confusion when interpreting scores to a psychometrically unsophisticated audience; as long as r_{xx} is above .90, the differences between the two methods are very small within 3 SDs of the mean; the primary purpose of reporting the confidence interval in test interpretation is not to convey detailed technical information regarding the test, but rather to highlight the fact that there is error present in the IQ and help avoid reifying the obtained numbers.

Verbal-Performance IQ Differences

During ipsative assessment of scores, the individual's own mean level of performance becomes the "normative standard" against which scores are held for comparison. The first step in the process is to examine the Verbal and Performance IQs (VIQ and PIQ) to determine whether use of the Full Scale IQ (FSIQ) is justifiable. To do this, the examiner first compares the VIQ with the PIQ to find the difference between these scores. For the WISC-R a difference in these two scores of 12 points is statistically significant at $p \leq .05$ and 15 points at $p \leq .01$; for the WAIS-R the comparable values are 10 and 13, respectively, and for the WPPSI, the corresponding values are closer to 11 and 14. What does it mean if these scores differ significantly? First, it renders the FSIQ inadequate as a summary statistic representing the general level of ability for the individual. It means that the levels of performance on the Verbal and Performance scales are different to the extent that we can be reasonably confident that the differences are real, not due to chance or the error inherent in all less-than-perfectly-reliable tests. It also, by inference, tells us that this individual does not think, reason, or express himself or herself at an equivalent level through the verbal modality of language as when using more concrete, nonverbal methods. The existence of the difference does not, however, tell us why it is there.

Many explanations of V-P IQ differences are possible. Factor analysis is a group data-analysis procedure; as noted earlier, this technique provides strong support for interpretation of distinct Verbal and Performance scales, but it does not explain why an individual child or adult might score substantially higher on one scale than the other. Kaufman (1979a) has offered various potential explanations for VIQ-PIQ differences on the WISC-R, which in most instances are equally applicable to the WPPSI and the WAIS-R. Kaufman suggests that VIQ-PIQ differences for individuals may reflect: (1) sensory deficits, (2) differences in verbal and nonverbal intelligence, (3) differences in fluid versus crystallized intelligence, (4) psycholinguistic deficiencies, (5) bilingualism, (6) effects of black dialect, (7) motor-coordination problems, (8) reactions to time pressures on the Performance Scale, (9) differences in field dependence/independence, (10) differences on Guilford's operation of evaluation, or (11) socioeconomic influences. Proper interpretation of V-P IQ discrepancies requires close observation of children or adults while they perform the various tasks making up the Wechsler scales, in addition to a comprehensive understanding of contemporary theories of intelligence. Once the best explanation of a child's reliable Verbal-Performance difference has been found, this explanation will almost invariably contribute to the development of appropriate teaching methods for the child to reflect strengths in the individual's methods and preferences for learning. For adults, VIQ-PIQ differences can assist in localization of neurological trauma as well as the evaluation of differences in learning. Attempts have been made to link V-P differences to personality characteristics and such factors as obsessive-compulsive tendencies (for example, Blatt & Allison, 1981), but as yet no satisfactory data-based support for these interpretations is available.

Another factor to consider in evaluating the meaning of VIQ-PIQ differences is the frequency of occurrence of a difference score of a given magnitude. For a VIQ-PIQ difference to have *diagnostic* significance, it should be relatively infrequent in the normal population. Large discrepancies between the Verbal and Performance IQs have commonly been associated with a variety of abnormalities, such as neurological impairment (Holroyd & Wright, 1965). However, these clinical assumptions have usually been made in the absence of hard data on *normal* individuals. How can inferences be made relating interscale or intrascale scatter on a Wechsler battery to *abnormalities*, without first considering *normal* VIQ-PIQ discrepancies?

Wechsler (1974) reports the magnitude of VIQ-PIQ differences required for statistical significance at various levels. About 9 points are required for significance at $p < .15$, about 12 points are needed for $p < .05$, and about 15 points between the VIQ and PIQ is necessary for $p < .01$. These values reflect the degree to which the VIQs and PIQs must differ for the discrepancies to be meaningful, as opposed to being due merely to chance error, and are based on the reliability coefficients of the VIQs and PIQs. The probabilities translate into the amount of confidence one should have that the V-P IQ discrepancy stands for a true difference in the individual's verbal and nonverbal intelligence. However, even though statistical significance provides important information for determining whether a child has "real" differences in the abilities underlying the Verbal and Performance scales, the significance or meaningfulness of the discrepancy does not translate to the *frequency of occurrence* of a given V-P difference. Yet it is the frequency of occurrence among a normal population that is most pertinent for understanding abnormal conditions.

In a study of the WISC-R standardization sample, the average child aged 6½–16½ years had a VIQ-PIQ discrepancy, regardless of direction, equal to 9.7 points (SD = 7.6) (Kaufman, 1976c). The mean discrepancy was approximately the same for each of the 11 age groups. Similarly, discrepancies were unrelated to sex and race. In contrast, a trend was noted with regard to socioeconomic status. The mean discrepancy was nearly 11 points for children of professional parents, decreasing steadily down to a mean of about 9 points for children of unskilled workers. For all youngsters in the normative sample, one out of two normal children had a significant VIQ-PIQ difference at the 85% level of confidence (9 or more point discrepancy); one out of three had a significant discrepancy at the 95% level of confidence (12+ points); and one out of four had a significant discrepancy at the 99% level of confidence (15+ points). Thus 25% of normal school-age children have a V-P difference of a magnitude that Wechsler (1974, p. 34) claims "is important and calls for further investigation."

The V-P IQ discrepancies for the WISC-R surprise many clinicians, even though analogous data have been available for years on the 1949 WISC (Seashore, 1951), and the Wechsler Adult Intelligence Scale (WAIS) (Matarazzo, 1972). If earlier studies have been ignored to some extent by clinicians and researchers, it is essential for the WISC-R data to be internalized by test users—particularly in view of current controversy over labeling, and legal definitions of various exceptionalities. Recently, results for the WISC-R and WAIS have been replicated for the WPPSI (Reynolds & Gutkin, 1981c).

Kaufman (1979a) has provided a table summarizing the distribution of VIQ-PIQ differences on the WISC-R that is reproduced here as Table 6. Table 6 shows the magnitude of V-P discrepancies occurring at different frequencies within the normal population. These values provide an index of "unusualness" or "abnormality" of various V-P discrepancies. Entering the rightmost column of Table 6, it is evident that discrepancies of 15 or more points occur less than 25% of the time among normal children; discrepancies of 19 points occur less than 15% of the time; discrepancies of 30 points occur less than 2% of the time; and so on. These values enable examiners to evaluate every significant ($p <$ .01) VIQ-PIQ discrepancy they observe, and determine whether the difference in the child's verbal and nonverbal abilities is unusual or abnormal; they are, therefore, worthy of considerable attention. Separate norms are presented in Table 6 for five different socioeconomic categories, because, as noted above, VIQ-PIQ discrepancies were a function of socioeconomic background, with larger differences associated with the higher occupational groups. Clinicians have the option of using the basal rates for the total group, or for the separate parental occupation categories, based on their personal preferences. Similarly, they may choose any degree of abnormality that makes sense for a given purpose. When merely attempting to describe in a case report whether a child's V-P discrepancy is rare or typical, a criterion such as "less than 15%" seems adequate. However, when examiners are intending to base a diagnosis of an exceptionality partly on the degree of interscale scatter, then a more conservative criterion, such as "less than 5%," or "less than 2%," should be employed.

Whereas tables of these values for the WAIS (Matarazzo, 1972) and the WPPSI (Reynolds & Gutkin, 1981c) are available, Kaufman's (1979a) WISC-R table corresponds almost exactly to the distributions of difference scores for the other scales. Comparable data for the WAIS-R are available elsewhere in this volume, but the WAIS-R distributions resemble closely the WISC-R distributions given the similar correlation between the Verbal and Performance scales and the constant SD. (The distribution of difference scores is a direct function of these variables.)

The focus in this section on the abnormality of profile fluctuations is not intended to minimize the importance of statistically significant differences in a person's abilities. V-P IQ discrepancies that are large enough to be significant are quite valuable, even if they are not large enough to be termed "rare." These significant differences indicate real discrepancies in the individual's abilities, and therefore provide valuable input for making educational and other practical recommendations. The key distinction here is between diagnosis and treatment. When differences are both significant and rare, they may be used as one piece of evidence in formulating diagnostic hypotheses, *and* they are likely to be translatable to remedial action. However, differences that are significant but not unusual in their occurrence have *only* remedial implications; diagnosis of an

Table 6. Percentage of Normal Children Obtaining WISC-R V-P Discrepancies of a Given Magnitude or Greater, by Parental Occupation

Size of V-P Discrepancy (Regardless of Direction)	Parental Occupation					
	Professional and Technical	Managerial, Clerical, Sales	Skilled Workers	Semiskilled Workers	Unskilled Workers	Total Sample
9	52	48	48	46	43	48
10	48	44	43	41	37	43
11	43	40	39	36	34	39
12	40	35	34	31	29	34
13	36	33	31	28	26	31
14	32	29	29	25	24	28
15	29	25	26	21	22	24
16	26	22	22	19	19	22
17	24	19	18	15	16	18
18	20	16	16	14	15	16
19	16	15	13	12	14	14
20	13	13	12	10	13	12
21	11	11	8	9	10	10
22	10	9	7	7	9	8
23	8	8	6	6	8	7
24	7	7	5	5	6	6
25	6	6	4	4	5	5
26	5	5	3	3	4	4
27	4	4	2	2	3	3
28–30	3	3	1	1	2	2
31–33	2	2	< 1	< 1	1	1
34+	1	1	< 1	< 1	< 1	< 1

Source. Kaufman (1979a), reprinted with permission.

abnormality should not be based, even partly, on deviations that occur with reasonable frequency among normal individuals unless forming part of a carefully delineated syndrome.

Fluctuations in Performance on Individual Subtests

The next line of attack for interpreting the Wechsler scales requires the examiner to evaluate the child's performance on each subtest of the Verbal and Performance scales. There must, of course, be statistical and psychometric justification for the interpretation of any individual subtest. First, the subtest must deviate from the mean of all subtests on the same scale by a statistically significant amount, and second, the subtest must have at least adequate "specificity" (reliable unique variance). Both conditions must be met prior to interpretation of a child's performance on any single subtest.

To determine whether a child's performance on any subtest deviates significantly from the mean of all subtests, the Verbal and Performance scales should be considered separately. Using the Verbal scale as an example, the child's mean scaled score on the Verbal scale should be calculated and then subtracted from each subtest scaled score. Exact values are available in Sattler (1982) for determining whether a subtest's deviation is statistically significant; however, the values are all quite close to three–four scaled-score points for the WISC-R and WAIS-R and three for the WPPSI. These are the recommended values for determining whether a difference is real or due to measurement error or other uncontrolled, random factors. Thus any subtest deviating from the mean of all subtests by the designated number of points (or more) on the Verbal Scale should be considered a candidate for individual interpretation that may reflect a significant strength or weakness in the child's ability spectrum. This procedure is then repeated for the Performance Scale.

Once it has been ascertained that a significant discrepancy exists, one must evaluate the amount of specific variance (or subtest specificity) that the subtest possesses and judge whether or not it is adequate to support interpretation of the subtest independent of the general factor. Subtest specificity refers to the amount of variance in a score that is both reliable and unique to that subtest, that is, not shared or held in common with other subtests of the same scale. Subtest specificity is readily calculated as a by-product of factor analysis and is the percent of reliable variance minus either the multiple correlation of all other subtests with the subtest or the communality estimate from the factor analysis. Kaufman (1979a), Carlson and Reynolds (1981), and Gutkin, Reynolds, and Galvin (in press) have calculated the specific variances of the WISC-R, WPPSI, and WAIS-R subtests, respectively, and classified each as possessing ample, adequate, or inadequate specificity. Table 7 summarizes the classifications of each of the sources. From Table 7 it can be seen that adequate specificity exists to allow the interpretation of most of the Wechsler subtests at most ages. However, some significant fluctuations do occur and Table 7 should be a useful guide. The classifications in Table 7 are based on the following criteria: for

Table 7. Classification of Wechsler Scale Subtests According to Relative Proportion of Subtest Specific Variance

Ample	Adequate	Inadequate
WPPSI		
Vocabulary	Arithmetic	Information
Similarities	Geometric design	Comprehension
Sentences	Animal house (age 4)	
Animal house (except at age 4)		
Picture completion		
Mazes		
Block design		
WISC-R		
Information	Vocabulary	Similarities (ages 9½–16½)
Similarities (ages 6½–8½)	Comprehension	Object assembly
Arithmetic	Picture completion (ages 9½–16½)	
Digit span		
Picture completion (ages 6½–8½)		
Picture arrangement		
Block design		
Coding		
Mazes		
WAIS-R		
Digit span	Information	Vocabulary
Arithmetic	Comprehension (ages 25–74)	Comprehension (ages 16–24)
Picture completion	Similarities	Object assembly
Picture arrangement	Block design	
Digit symbol		

Note. Only major age trends noted.

ample specificity, the subtest must display specific variance of at least 25% and specific variance must exceed error variance; for adequate specificity 15% to 24% specific variance and specific variance must be greater than error variance; tests with inadequate specificity fall below 15% and typically show error variance in excess of specific variance.

Once a subtest has been identified as deviating significantly from the mean and as having at least adequate specificity, one still must determine just what interpretation is appropriate for this finding. Behavioral observations taken during the testing may strongly influence this interpretation. It is also necessary to know just what is measured by the subtest(s) in question. This can be determined through a content analysis of the mental operations necessary to perform the tasks called for by the subtest and by reviewing the primary correlates of the subtest in the research literature. Kaufman (1979a), Lutey (1977), and Sattler (1982) are excellent sources of information on the skills tapped by the various subtests, but the examiner must meld this information with his or her own observations of the child's performance. It is also preferable to look for trends in abilities across multiple subtests that appear as strengths or weaknesses not only on each scale, but across scales, rather than becoming too excited about a single subtest that deviates from the child's mean subtest score. It is always appropriate to apply logic, intuition, and good common sense to test interpretation along with one's statistical and psychometric expertise. For individual assessment, neither is totally adequate, especially when attempting to devise appropriate instructional programs for a special-needs learner or gain significant insights into the cognitive structure and function of the individual.

Just as with VIQ-PIQ discrepancies, it is also useful to examine the range of subtest scatter on the Wechsler scales. Both the range of subtest scores obtained by an individual and the number of subtests deviating from the mean of the subtests are of interest. It is frequently quite surprising to clinicians to learn of the results of such investigations with *normal* children, since the notion of scatter has long been associated with a variety of *abnormal* conditions. Kaufman (1976b) has reported on the degree of subtest scatter characterizing the 2200 normal children of the WISC-R standardization sample.

For each normal child aged 6½–16½ years, scaled scores on the 10 regular subtests were rank ordered from high to low. Then, the lowest score was subtracted from the highest score, yielding a scaled-score range for each youngster. Whereas the informally obtained estimates of these ranges from clinicians with years of experience tend to cluster around three–four points, the actual ranges computed for the standardization group averaged an astonishing seven points (SD = 2) (Kaufman, 1976b). This mean range spans more than two standard deviations; furthermore, a mean scaled-score range on the Full Scale of 7 ± 2 characterized each of the 11 age groups, males and females, blacks and whites, and children from each of five parental occupation categories.

In practical terms, a scaled-score range of seven means that the average child's subtest scores ranged from about 6–13 or 7–14. Since normalcy is often defined as ± 1 standard deviation from the mean, even a scaled-score range as large as 9 points (7 + 2) can be considered normal. Thus a range of scaled scores from 3 to 12, from 6 to 15, or from 8 to 17 can legitimately be termed "normal" when empirical guidelines are used. One has to wonder how many times ranges such as these have been interpreted as indicative of marked scatter, and how many times youngsters have been assigned a label such as "learning disabled," at least in part because of the so-called scatter in their WISC-R profiles.

Table 8 provides a summary of the results of Kaufman's (1976b) analysis of scaled-score ranges for this group of children and should serve as a guide to interpreting the range of subtest performance for individual children. To use Table 8, compute the child's ranges on the Verbal, Performance, and Full scales. Subtract the child's lowest scaled score from his or her highest scaled score for each of the three scales. Then enter these values into the pertinent columns in Table 8 to determine whether the child's intrascale scatter is rare or fairly typical. Suppose only the 10 regular subtests are administered, and a girl obtains a Verbal range of 5, a Performance range of 10, and a Full Scale range of 11. Her Verbal scaled-score range of 5 reflects normal variability, because a range of 7 is required to occur less than 15% of the time in the normal population. However, her Performance range of 10 and her Full Scale range of 11 are both reasonably rare, each occurring less than 10% of the time. As with VIQ-PIQ discrepancies, clinicians may select any degree of abnormality that makes sense to them; and they would probably be wise to adapt the specific level to the circumstances surrounding the evaluation and the purposes for which the test scores are intended.

Kaufman (1976b) has also provided results from an analysis of the WISC-R standardization data with regard to the number of subtests deviating significantly from the mean of all subtests on the same scale. More than half the children showed at least one subtest deviating significantly from the scale mean; nearly one-fourth showed at least three significant deviations from the mean of all subtests. These analyses are not restrictive to the WISC-R. Reynolds and Gutkin (1981c) reported values nearly identical to those published by Kaufman (1976b) for scaled-score range and number of deviant subtests for the WPPSI sample of 4–6½ year olds. Comparable data for the WAIS-R are not yet available. However, clinicians would certainly not be far afield if they applied the WISC-R data on scatter, summarized in Table 8, directly to WAIS-R profiles. When doing so, they should eliminate digit span from the computations for the Full Scale score since this subtest is optional on the WISC-R.

The fact that it is normal for children to evidence peaks and valleys in their

Table 8. Degree of Abnormality of an Index of Subtest Scatter (Scaled-Score Range)

Frequency of Occurrence in Normal Population	Size of Scale-Score Range					
	Verbal Scale		Performance Scale		Full Scale	
	5 Subtest	6 Subtest	5 Subtest	6 Subtest	10 Subtest	12 Subtest
< 15%	7	8	9	9	10	11
< 10%	8	9	10	10	11	12
< 5%	9	10	11	11	12	13
< 2%	10	11	12	13	13	14
< 1%	11	12	13	13	14	14

Note. Scaled-score range equals a child's highest scaled score minus his or her lowest scaled score.

ability spectrum has vital implications for assessment. Clinicians and researchers of exceptional populations should routinely consult the baseline data for the standardization sample in order to interpret the profiles of the children they test. No diagnosis of an exceptionality should be based in any way on Wechsler scatter, unless the degree of interscale or intrascale scatter in the child's profile is shown, by empirical comparisons, to be rare within the normal population. Furthermore, no clinical sample should be claimed to exhibit considerable scatter unless there is empirical evidence to show that the indices of scatter, VIQ-PIQ discrepancy, scaled-score ranges, and so on for the clinical group are significantly greater than the indices for normal children.

Results of studies with the WISC-R and WPPSI standardization groups have challenged the stereotype that normal children have "flat" profiles. Now it is time to investigate empirically the stereotypes pertaining to the considerable scatter that supposedly characterizes the Wechsler profiles of individuals with emotional, neurological, and school-related disorders. Fortunately, a number of these studies have been conducted; the interesting results of these investigations are reviewed in the next section.

Subtest scatter and the specific fluctuations occurring for individuals should also be evaluated from the standpoint of theory. Neuropsychological, componential, cognitive, factor, and psychometric models of intelligence all have contributions to make to intelligent test interpretation. Although space limits reviews of such models and their application to intelligence testing, discussions may be found in Kaufman (1979a), Reynolds (1981b), and White (1979). Kaufman (1979a), in particular, provides a thorough discussion of the theoretical underpinnings and meaning of the trait or ability underlying the third WISC-R factor (Freedom from Distractibility).

THE WECHSLER SCALES AND LEARNING-DISABILITIES ASSESSMENT

The Wechsler scales have always held an affinity for researchers and practitioners concerned with learning-disabled (LD) populations or with those variously referred to as having minimal brain damage, minimal brain dysfunction, dyslexia, or other neurologically based learning disorders. The WISC and now the WISC-R have been especially intriguing to these workers as the instruments of choice in evaluating LD children.

The aims of this section are to examine the use of the WISC-R for LD assessment, and to chart some appropriate pathways for future avenues of study. Three main areas will be treated: (1) *factor analysis* of the WISC-R, as related to LD populations; (2) *recategorizations* of the WISC-R subtest scores according to Bannatyne's (1971, 1974) system, an approach that has apparently produced a characteristic group profile for LD samples; and (3) evaluations of *scatter* in WISC-R profiles for LD youngsters since they are frequently stereotyped as having much interscale and intrascale variability.

Learning-Disabilities and Factor Analysis of the WISC-R

A generation ago, it was an impressive psychometric feat to conduct a factor analysis of a multiscore test battery; to accomplish such a task was frequently worth the award of a doctoral degree. Cohen's (1959) landmark factor-analytic investigation was not published until a decade after the 1949 WISC first appeared. Today, the push-button psychometrics of computer technology has resulted in a landslide of factor analyses of the WISC-R.

Pertinent Research Findings. As we have noted, every study conducted to date has supported the construct validity of the Verbal and Performance scales. Robust Verbal Comprehension and Perceptual Organization factors have emerged for children across a host of demographic characteristics, and for a variety of exceptional populations: clinic referrals (Lombard & Riedel, 1978; Swerdlik & Schweitzer, 1978), mentally retarded (Schooler, Beebe, & Koepke, 1978; Van Hagen & Kaufman, 1975), gifted (Karnes & Brown, 1980), learning disabled (Blaha & Vance, 1979; Peterson & Hart, 1979; Schooler, Beebe, & Koepke, 1978), and emotionally or behaviorally disordered (DeHorn & Klinge, 1978; Finch, Kendall, Spirito, Entin, Montgomery, & Schwartz, 1979; Peterson & Hart, 1979; Reynolds & Struer, 1981).

Some investigators did not investigate three-factor solutions (for example, Schooler, Beebe, & Koepke, 1978), but most researchers have explored the third factor and have typically found a dimension labeled Freedom from Distractibility. This factor, not hypothesized by Wechsler in his dichotomous treatment of the WISC-R subtests, usually has significant loadings by at least two of the following three tasks: Arithmetic, Digit Span, and Coding. Occasionally other subtests join in, such as Picture Arrangement (Swerdlik & Schweitzer, 1978; Van Hagen & Kaufman, 1975), Picture Completion (Karnes & Brown, 1980), or Block Design (Dean, 1979; Peterson & Hart, 1979), but the overwhelming consistency from sample to sample is clearly limited to the Arithmetic–Digit Span–Coding triad.

Relevance to LD Assessment. The emergence of solid Verbal Comprehension and Perceptual Organization factors for learning-disabled groups would seem to bode well for the meaningful interpretation of the VIQ and PIQ and the difference between them. For most groups, the latter generalization tends to be true, but there is a mitigating circumstance for learning-disabled children: the consistent findings of the ACID profile—low scores in *A*rithmetic, *C*oding, *I*nformation, and *D*igit Span—for diverse groups of this exceptional population. Rankings of the 10 regularly administered WISC-R subtests are given in Table 9 for seven samples of learning-disabled children. Digit Span, the last member of the ACID profile, is not always administered, though we feel it should be. Relatively low scores on Information and Arithmetic (both directly related to school achievement) will often distort the meaning of the IQ, and a weakness on Coding will likewise render the IQ an inefficient estimate of nonverbal in-

Table 9. Rank Ordering of Subtest Means for a Variety of Learning Disabled Populations

WISC-R Subtest	Anderson, Kaufman, & Kaufman (1976) (N = 41)	Smith, Coleman, Dokecki, & Davis (1977)		Vance, Gaynor, & Coleman (1976) (N = 58)	Zingale & Smith (1978)			Consensus Rankings
		High IQ (N = 132)	Low IQ (N = 76)		High SES (N = 30)	Med. SES (N = 56)	Low SES (N = 36)	
Object assembly	3	1	1	1	1	1	1	1
Picture completion	1	2	2	2	2	2	2	2
Picture arrangement	4	3	4	5.5	3	3	3	3
Block design	5	4	3	7	4	4	4	4
Comprehension	2	5	5	3	5	7	5	5
Similarities	10	6	6.5	5.5	7	5	6	6
Vocabulary	8.5	7	6.5	4	6	6	9	7
Coding	6	8	9	9	8	8	7	8
Arithmetic	7	9	8	10	9	10	8	9
Information	8.5	10	10	8	10	9	10	10
Mean V IQ	82	90	76	91	90	87	82	
Mean P IQ	89	100	80	91	98	96	90	
Mean F-S IQ	84	93	76	91	93	90	84	

Source. Kaufman (1982), reprinted with permission.

Note. The subtests are rank ordered from easiest (highest mean, rank = 1) to hardest (lowest mean, rank = 10) for each learning-disabled population. Subtests are listed from easiest to hardest, based on consensus rankings for the seven samples.

telligence. Despite the factor-analytic construct validity support for Wechsler's VIQ-PIQ dichotomy, there is thus reason to doubt the practical value of the simple VIQ-PIQ discrepancy for learning-disabled or potentially learning-disabled children. Since three-quarters of the ACID profile (ACD) corresponds precisely to the Freedom from Distractibility factor, it is evident that the third factor may hold the key to competent LD assessment.

Avenues for Future Research.   We now understand the factor structure of the WISC-R and do not need to know more about the slight differences in the two or three factors for various ethnic or exceptional groups. Small differences in factorial composition from sample to sample cannot be attributed to ethnic membership or type of exceptionality; they are just as likely to be due to an irrelevant, uncontrolled variable or, most likely of all, to the chance fluctuations that are known to characterize correlation matrices.

Future research in this area should focus on what the factors *mean* in either a theoretical or clinical sense. Does the Verbal Comprehension factor measure so-called general intelligence, or is it more aligned to school achievement or to Guilford's semantic-content dimension? Does Perceptual Organization reflect conventional nonverbal intelligence fluid ability from the Cattell-Horn approach, spatial ability from Bannatyne's regrouping, the cognitive style of field independence, or simultaneous processing? Does Freedom from Distractibility assess what its label claims, or is the third factor more related to successive processing, Guilford's symbolic ability, memory, automatic processing, stimulus trace (Baumeister & Bartlett, 1962), attention concentration, anxiety, or Bannatyne's sequencing ability?

The needed research could be factor-analytic or correlational in nature, for example, by analyzing WISC-R data in conjunction with other instruments that are known to measure constructs such as manifest anxiety, successive versus simultaneous processing, fluid versus crystallized intelligence, and so on. However, better still would be well-designed experimental research where groups known to differ on various constructs could be compared on their WISC-R factor scores. Conducting such construct validation studies for various homogeneously defined populations such as learning-disabled children may show that the factors measure different constructs for different groups and subgroups, or that the factors have to be interpreted differently for individuals under varied circumstances. Regardless of the outcome of such studies, the cumulative results would enhance the interpretation of the WISC-R from a theoretical and clinical base, and may shed much light on the dynamics underlying the ACID profile in groups of learning-disabled children.

Bannatyne Recategorizations

The preceding discussion of WISC-R factor analyses and LD populations leads directly to the topic of recategorizing Wechsler's subtests into Bannatyne's four categories: Conceptual (Similarities, Vocabulary, Comprehension), Spatial (Picture Completion, Block Design, Object Assembly), Sequencing (Arithmetic,

Digit Span, Coding), Acquired Knowledge (Information, Arithmetic, Vocabulary). The relationship to the factor-analytic section is twofold. First, the three WISC-R factors could easily be labeled totally in accordance with the Bannatyne model, namely Conceptual (Verbal Comprehension), Spatial (Perceptual Organization), and Sequencing (Freedom from Distractibility). Second, the characteristic LD profile of low scores on the ACID subtests makes much more sense when interpreted from Bannatyne's four-category approach than from Wechsler's two-scale system.

Pertinent Research Findings. A seemingly characteristic Wechsler profile of Spatial > Conceptual > Sequencing has been found for groups of reading disabled (Rugel, 1974) and learning disabled (Clarizio & Bernard, 1981; Smith, Coleman, Dokecki, & Davis, 1977) children. However, the consistency of this finding, which has almost come to be accepted as fact, has been challenged on several grounds by recent investigations. Some studies have simply not produced the expected relationships among the three Bannatyne categories for LD samples (Thompson, 1981) or failed to find significant differences among the group means (Vance & Singer, 1979). Other investigations have shown different Bannatyne patterns when another variable is introduced in addition to the presence of learning disabilities: Mexican-American LD children showed a Spatial > Sequential > Conceptual pattern (Gutkin, 1979a), and LD youngsters with superior intelligence displayed Conceptual > Spatial > Sequential (Schiff, Kaufman, & Kaufman, 1981).

Furthermore, despite mean differences in Bannatyne categories for *groups*, the proportions of *individuals* in the group displaying the characteristic pattern has generally been quite small. Gutkin's (1979a) Caucasian sample of 53 LD children had substantial differences in the group means of Spatial (25.85), Conceptual (21.47), and Sequential (19.66) abilities; however, only 30% of the individuals in this group displayed the predicted pattern, a value that dropped to a mere 2% when statistical criteria ($p < .05$) were imposed on the comparisons. Similarly, less than half of 60 Israeli LD children displayed the predicted pattern, despite striking differences in the mean scores on the Spatial (27.48), Conceptual (23.33), and Sequential (18.88) categories (Raviv, Margolith, Raviv, & Sade, 1981).

Of equal concern to the negative findings cited above is the emergence of Spatial > Conceptual > Sequential group patterns for exceptionalities other than learning disabilities. Groups such as juvenile delinquents, emotionally handicapped, and even nonimpaired referrals displayed the identical Bannatyne patterning and could not be differentiated significantly from learning-disabled children on the basis of the latter group's so-called "characteristic pattern" (Clarizio & Bernard, 1981; Groff & Hubble, 1981; Henry & Wittman, 1981; Thompson, 1981).

Relevance to LD Assessment. The above findings virtually speak for themselves regarding LD diagnosis. What was once considered an optimistic, exciting approach for diagnosis of learning disabilities has come to a grinding halt. It is reasonable to conclude that differential diagnosis of learning disabilities will not be aided by application of knowledge about the so-called characteristic Bannatyne pattern. One should not conclude, however, that Bannatyne's recategorizations are irrelevant to LD assessment; that would be far from the truth. Although the groupings do not facilitate differential diagnosis, they still provide a convenient framework for understanding the learning-disabled child's assets and deficits. As indicated earlier, the VIQ-PIQ dichotomy is not sufficient for understanding the fluctuations that characterize the profiles of LD samples. The four-category system espoused by Bannatyne still succeeds in making more sense out of many WISC-R profiles, especially of LD children, than does a simple VIQ-PIQ split or even the three-way factor-analytic division. The more that WISC-R profiles can be systematized and understood, the easier it is to translate test results to educational action. Brief discussions and statistics for applying Bannatyne's recategorization to the performance of individual children on the WISC-R can be found in Reynolds (1981c) and Reynolds and Gutkin (1981b).

Another potentially valuable categorization scheme has been proposed by Witkin, Dyk, Faterson, Goodenough, and Karp (1974): Verbal-Comprehension (Information, Vocabulary, Comprehension), Analytic-Field-Approach (Object Assembly, Picture Completion, Block Design), and Attention-Concentration (Arithmetic, Digit Span, Coding). The first category is a variant of the Verbal Comprehension factor and of Bannatyne's Conceptual triad. The latter two categories are identical in composition to Bannatyne's Spatial and Sequencing groups, respectively, but are assigned quite different interpretations by Witkin. Stevenson (1979) applied this approach to a group of 55 learning-disabled children and found a depressed score in attention-concentration, agreeing with the bulk of Bannatyne LD research. The interpretations given the groupings by Witkin are important and worthy of consideration when analyzing the profile of any learning-disabled child. However, Bannatyne's four-category approach is still superior to Witkin's for LD assessment because (1) Information is included in Witkin's Verbal Comprehension grouping, (2) LD children typically score low on this subtest, and (3) Bannatyne offers an Acquired Knowledge grouping, of extreme value for interpreting LD profiles.

Avenues for Future Research. It is surely time to stop looking at Bannatyne scores on the Conceptual, Spatial, and Sequencing categories for heterogeneous groups of learning-disabled children. This approach seems to have no future for differential diagnosis, and no longer will be contributing new knowledge to the field. However, the results of Schiff, Kaufman, and Kaufman (1981) with superior IQ learning-disabled children suggest that it is possible to find a profile that characterizes not only a group, but also substantial proportions of individuals within the group. Perhaps the key variable is to investigate LD populations that are defined rather homogeneously.

A second line of needed research is to explore the utility of Bannatyne's Acquired Knowledge category, frequently forgotten in WISC-R studies. Logically, LD youngsters of average intelligence should perform relatively poorly in the achievement-oriented WISC-R subtests, and this has been born out in the studies which have utilized all four Bannatyne categories (Smith, Coleman, Dokecki, & Davis, 1977; Thompson, 1981; Vance & Singer, 1979). Longitudinal investigations of a potential decline in the Acquired Knowledge scores (and, hence, in the IQs) of learning-disabled children would be of special value; any such decline would imply that VIQ becomes a less valid estimate of verbal intelligence as LD children mature from the primary grades to high school. Indeed, there is certainly a question of whether the VIQ is valid for any learning-disabled child who performs poorly on the Acquired Knowledge subtests, regardless of age. That, too, is an important and researchable issue.

The final avenue of research in this area, and undoubtedly the most important, is the theoretical and clinical meaning of strengths and weaknesses exhibited by LD children in the Bannatyne categories—which brings us full circle to the suggested line of research in the area of factor analysis. Once again, the recommendation is to conduct construct validity investigations of the abilities, traits, processes, or behaviors underlying each Bannatyne category. Whether an LD child's elevated scores in the Picture Completion–Block Design–Object Assembly triad, for example, reflect good Spatial ability, Perceptual Organization, simultaneous processing, or analytic-field-approach is a question that can be answered by well-designed research studies.

Scatter

The stereotypes that learning-disabled children have WISC-R profiles replete with subtest scatter, and are characterized by large VIQ-PIQ differences, still persist in many assessment circles despite the findings presented earlier. For years, these notions were accepted as clinical axioms; now a body of research has accumulated to challenge these stereotypes.

Pertinent Research Findings. As we have noted, normal children have substantial VIQ-PIQ discrepancies, averaging about 10 points (regardless of direction), and it is not unusual for normal youngsters to have differences of 15 or more points. Similarly, considerable subtest scatter characterizes the profiles of normal youngsters.

A number of studies have now been published comparing the VIQ-PIQ discrepancies and subtest scatter of learning disabled and other exceptional groups to the basal levels found in the normal population. Table 10 summarizes these studies. The VIQ-PIQ discrepancies for learning disabled children have tended to be significantly (but not overwhelmingly) larger than normal values, although some studies have shown no difference at all (Stevenson, 1979; Thompson, 1980). A similar finding has emerged for subtest scatter. Of the 436 learning-disabled children listed in Table 10 (spread across seven studies and excluding the group with superior IQ), the mean scaled-score range for the 10 regular WISC-R subtests equals 7.8. This value is not consequentially larger than the 7.0 for normal children. Interestingly, Naglieri's (1979) learning-disabled sample

Table 10. WISC-R VIQ-PIQ Discrepancies and Subtest Scatter Indices for a Variety of Samples

Source	N	Description of Sample	Mean VIQ-PIQ Discrepancy (Regardless of Sign)	Mean Scaled Score Range (High Minus Low Scaled Score—10 Subtests)
Kaufman (1976a, 1976b)	2200	Normal standardization sample	9.7	7.0
Anderson, Kaufman, and Kaufman (1976)	41	Learning disabled	12.5	7.5
Gutkin (1979b)	51	Learning disabled	11.9	7.7
Naglieri (1979)	20	Learning disabled	13.6	8.5
Stevenson (1979)	55	Learning disabled	10.1	7.2
Tabachnick (1979)	105	Learning disabled	—	7.6
Thompson (1980)	64	Learning disabled	10.0	7.6
Ryckman (1981)	100	Learning disabled	—	8.2
Schiff, Kaufman, and Kaufman (1981)	30	Learning disabled (superior IQ)	18.6	9.3
Gutkin (1979b)	23	Minimally brain injured	11.8	7.3
Weiner and Kaufman (1979)	46	Referrals for learning and/or behavior problems	9.2	7.3
Stritchart and Love (1979)	40	Referrals for learning disabilities	9.8	7.3
Moore and Wielan (1981)	434	Referrals for reading problems	11.2	—
Naglieri (1979)	20	Mentally retarded	9.6	6.6
Thompson (1980)	14	Mentally retarded	7.6	5.9
Gutkin (1979b)	10	Mentally retarded	8.5	6.0
Gutkin (1979b)	17	Emotionally disturbed	12.9	7.8
Thompson (1980)	51	Psychological or behavioral disorder	8.4	7.2
Ollendick (1979)	121	Juvenile delinquents	—	7.3
Naglieri (1979)	20	Normal control group	12.6	8.0

had significantly more subtest scatter than the normative population, but *not* more than a local control group. In fact, Naglieri's normal control group had the fourth highest index of subtest scatter among all groups listed in Table 10.

The findings with the conventional WISC-R reported in Table 10 have received some cross-cultural validation. Using a Hebrew translation of the WISC-R, Raviv, Margolith, Raviv, and Sade (1981) compared the scatter for a group of 60 Israeli LD children with a sample of 60 matched controls. The mean VIQ-PIQ discrepancy of 11.6 for the LD sample did not differ significantly from the mean of 10.8 for the normals. Although the mean scatter index of 7.5 for the LDs was significantly greater than the value of 6.8 for the controls, the magnitude of the difference is of little practical consequence.

Only Schiff, Kaufman, and Kaufman's (1981) group of LD children with superior IQs showed an impressively high VIQ-PIQ discrepancy and subtest scatter index, suggesting that certain homogeneously defined exceptional samples may have characteristic amounts of inter- and intrascale variability of potential diagnostic value. Otherwise, conventional learning-disabled, emotionally disturbed, juvenile-delinquent, mentally retarded, and clinic-referral populations tend to be close to "normal" in their profile fluctuations.

Relevance to LD Assessment.   Contrary to existing stereotypes about children with learning disabilities, they do not seem to be characterized by abnormal scatter in their WISC-R profiles. The small difference between LD and normal scatter that has been observed in previous investigations may, in fact, represent a selection bias stemming from the stereotypes; that is, other things being equal, children with apparent WISC-R scatter are more likely to be labeled LD than those with flatter profiles. The data presented in Table 10 strongly imply that the magnitude of VIQ-PIQ discrepancy and the size of scaled-score range are not likely to be very useful in the diagnosis of LD or in its differential diagnosis. Nevertheless, significant strengths or weaknesses in a WISC-R profile are potentially valuable, even when the overall scatter is within normal limits, when planning educational interventions for LD youngsters.

Avenues for Future Research.   Plenty of handicapped samples have been analyzed for WISC-R scatter and the results clearly imply that future research along this line will contribute only minimally to knowledge in this area. Perhaps very homogeneously defined groups such as the LD sample with superior IQs should continue to be examined to determine the diagnostic utility of scatter indexes; heterogeneous or loosely defined samples, however, should be left alone. A more fruitful line of research is to reverse the procedure: identify samples of children with abnormally large VIQ-PIQ discrepancies and/or scaled-score ranges, and examine the characteristics of these empirically defined samples. What porportion of these children with unusual profiles are brain-injured, LD, emotionally disturbed, language disordered, normal, and so forth? By working "backward," we should be able to determine whether much WISC-R profile variability is, indeed, diagnostic of LD, and whether this information contributes significantly to differential diagnosis.

Whenever researchers do evaluate samples of known exceptional children, future studies should meet two additional criteria besides a homogeneous definition: (1) they should be large in size, preferably at least 200, to reduce errors inherent in sampling procedures, and (2) a local control group of normal individuals, similar to the experimental group in background variables but necessarily smaller in size, should be tested to provide an additional pertinent comparison. Naglieri's (1979) study shows the advisability of using a local control in addition to the standardization sample for effective evaluation of abnormal profile variability.

Conclusions

Research since the WISC-R's arrival in 1974, and especially since 1979, has greatly added to our understanding of the role of the WISC-R in LD assessment. We know that the factor structure is rather stable for a variety of normal and exceptional samples, including LD and LD referrals, and that the three-factor solution corresponds reasonably well to the group profiles of children with learning disabilities. Research with Bannatyne's recategorizations has shown that this four-category approach seems to fit LD data even better than the three factors and certainly better than the simple two-scale approach advocated by Wechsler. Unfortunately, the initial optimism of the diagnostic utility of the Bannatyne regroupings has been rebuffed by a stream of studies that mitigate against its use for differential diagnosis.

Finally, we have learned that normal children do not have flat WISC-R profiles, and that virtually all exceptional samples do not possess the stereotypical high VIQ-PIQ discrepancies or large amounts of intersubtest variability. As with the Bannatyne categories, the use of scatter indexes for diagnosis is suspect.

Although the main thrust of the research results seems depressing and pessimistic, there is also reason for hope. The studies have taught us much about learning disabilities and have broken some persistent and long-enduring axioms. If assessment procedures can be improved substantially by the bulk of knowledge gained from the studies reviewed here, then that improvement represents an important advance in the field. Also, the recategorizations have permitted and encouraged the application of psychological theory to WISC-R interpretation. By departing from a simplistic VIQ-PIQ dichotomy, the regroupings have fostered analysis in terms of simultaneous and sequential processing from the neuropsychological and cognitive literature, analytic-field-approach from the cognitive-style literature, and so forth. This application of theory fosters a deeper and more meaningful understanding of the WISC-R profile, leading to a more process-oriented treatment of LD children's strengths and weaknesses. If future researchers succeed in uncovering the constructs underlying each LD child's test profile, then the translation of these processes, traits, or abilities to educational intervention becomes a logical outcome of the investigations.

ESTIMATING PREMORBID LEVELS OF INTELLECTUAL FUNCTIONING

In the neuropsychological assessment of children or adults with head injury or other sudden neurological trauma, premorbid intellectual status may prove to be an important consideration. Frequently, premorbid levels of functioning are estimated clinically from the history, parental background, and teacher reports of academic functioning. Attempts to use "hold" versus "don't hold" marker subtests from the Wechsler scales have been made in an effort to place such estimation on a more empirical, and thereby less subjective, footing. These methods frequently prove to be inaccurate (see Lezak, 1976; Matarazzo, 1972), leaving the clinician with few alternatives other than subjective (clinical) impressions.

Recently, more objective methods have been proposed based on regression modeling from demographic data. Wilson, Rosenbaum, Brown, Rourke, Whitman, and Grisel (1978) have provided formulas for estimating the premorbid IQs of adults on the WAIS given knowledge of their age, race, sex, educational level, and occupational status and their work has been replicated for the WAIS-R (Barona, Reynolds, & Chastain, in press). Using a regression model and the standardization data as a source, Wilson, Rosenbaum, Brown, Rourke, Whitman, and Grisel reported impressive results, obtaining R^2 values ranging from .42 to .54 between those variables and the Wechsler IQs. However, the formulas reported for the WAIS are not accurate for the WAIS-R and the new formulas specific to the WAIS-R must be used (Barona, Reynolds, & Chastain, in press).

Following up on the Wilson, Rosenbaum, Brown, Rourke, Whitman, and Grisel (1978) approach with adults, Reynolds and Gutkin (1979) generated regression equations for predicting the premorbid intellectual status of children using demographic variables, with the WISC-R standardization sample providing the data source. For adults, age and number of years of education were good estimators in the multiple regression; however, for children, the method of standardization eliminates the use of these two variables. The relevant and available demographic variables for children were: socioeconomic status (as determined by parent's occupation), race, sex, geographic region, and urban versus rural residence. All five variables were found to contribute significantly to estimation of the WISC-R Verbal and Full Scale IQs while geographic region dropped out of the equation for the Performance IQ.

The actual regression equations and standard errors of estimate obtained were as follows:

Estimated Verbal IQ = 127.85—3.7 (SES)—8.86 (race)—2.40
   Sex—0.68 (region)—1.16 (residence).
Standard Error of Estimate VIQ = 13.47

Estimated Performance IQ = 121.08—9.18 (race)—2.80 (SES)—
   1.07 (residence)—0.64 (sex).
Standard Error of Estimate PIQ = 13.07

Estimated Full Scale IQ = 126.9—3.65 (SES)—9.72 (race)—
1.79 (sex)—1.20 (residence)—0.41 (region).
Standard Error of Estimate FSIQ = 13.50

For each equation, demographic variables take the following values (descriptions for making these classifications are available in Wechsler, 1974):

Sex: male = 1, female = 2.

Race: white = 1, black = 2, other = 3.

SES (based on father's occupational group): upper = 1, upper middle = 2, middle = 3, lower middle = 4, lower = 5.

Region: Northeast = 1, Northcentral = 2, South = 3, West = 4.

Residence: urban = 1, rural = 2.

These equations essentially provide a shortcut to developing tables to display the mean IQs of groups of children with the same demographic characteristics. Their use in clinical diagnosis and decision making remains to be adequately tested. The multiple Rs obtained for the children were not large, ranging from .37 to .44. However, this method has certain advantages over clinical estimation. The regression equations provide a standardized quantitative procedure for estimating premorbid IQs. Being systematic and quantifiable are major advantages, and the necessary data are typically easily and readily available to the clinician and can quickly be evaluated. Reynolds and Gutkin (1979) provide an example of how this technique might be applied and discuss its limitations and further research needs in more detail. Though much remains to be done, regression modeling to estimate premorbid levels of function appears to be superior to other purely clinically derived estimates.

THE PROBLEM OF CULTURAL BIAS IN INTELLIGENCE TESTING

The issue of potential cultural bias in educational and psychological tests has been with psychology since at least the early 1920s. The past two decades, with their insurgence of support and concern for individual liberties, civil rights, and social justice, have seen the issues of test bias become a substantial focus of concern by psychologists, educators, and the lay public alike. Lawmakers and the courts have continued to evidence increasing concern, as witnessed by the recent passage of the so-called "truth-in-testing" legislation in New York State and similar forthcoming efforts in the federal legislature. Two major federal district-court decisions have recently been handed down deciding, in completely opposite directions, whether intelligence tests are culturally biased against black children (*Larry P.*, 1979, *PASE*, 1980). The issues are many and have been hotly contested, even in the scholarly literature (for example, Reynolds & Brown, 1984). Though treated in depth elsewhere in this volume, a summary of the evidence as it relates particularly to this chapter seems in order.

Much of the furor over bias in testing, as well as the court cases, has centered around the use of intelligence tests to evaluate minority children suspected of mental retardation. Even though definitions and conceptualizations of mental retardation have been modified over the last decade to add emphasis to a child's adaptive behavior (ability to function independently within his or her own culture and within the larger society) and social maturity, level of intellectual functioning remains an important consideration in the diagnosis of mental retardation. Since black children as a group earn a lower mean score on intelligence tests (see Kaufman, 1982; Reynolds & Gutkin, 1981a), a significantly larger portion of black than white children are diagnosed as mildly mentally retarded. In fact, as seen clearly in Table 11, many demographic variables are related to IQ test performance. Although the true cause of the mean difference in performance of blacks and whites on intelligence tests is not known, one (among many) proposed explanations is that the tests are faulty. This explanation has become known as

Table 11. Relationship of Background Variables to the Mean WISC-R IQs Earned by Blacks and Whites, Aged 6½–16½

Variables	Blacks			Whites			Total Group		
	V	P	F-S	V	P	F-S	V	P	F-S
Parental Occupation									
Professional and technical	92	91	91	110	107	109	109	106	108
Managerial, clerical, sales	92	91	90	104	104	104	103	103	103
Skilled	90	87	88	100	101	101	100	100	100
Semiskilled	87	87	86	98	99	98	96	97	96
Unskilled	83	83	82	92	93	92	88	89	87
Geographic Region									
Northeast	95	92	93	104	103	104	103	101	102
North Central	90	89	88	101	102	102	100	101	100
South	85	84	83	101	101	101	97	97	97
West	85	91	87	103	104	104	102	103	103
Residence									
Urban	89	88	87	103	103	103	101	100	101
Rural	84	85	84	100	101	100	98	99	99

Source. Kaufman (1982), reprinted with permission.

Note. Data are from Tables 2, 3, and 4 in an article by Kaufman and Doppelt (1976). Data for nonwhites other than blacks (e.g., Orientals) are excluded from the computations for blacks but are included in the computations for the total group.

the cultural test-bias hypothesis and, briefly, contends that minority children do not earn lower scores on intelligence tests due to less ability but rather due to an inherent cultural bias of the tests that causes the tests to be artifactually more difficult for minority children. These biases are generally felt to stem from the white middle-class orientation of test authors and publishers and the lack of relevant experience of taking such tests among black and other minority children. Although psychologists have been aware of the potential for such problems since the early days of testing (Reynolds & Brown, 1984), most significant research on bias in testing is relatively recent.

The Association of Black Psychologists' early efforts to raise the consciousness of the psychological community were successful in spurring much empirical research on the various issues involved and also resulted in the appointment of an American Psychological Association committee to study the issues (Cleary, Humphreys, Kendrick, & Wesman, 1975). At its 1969 annual meeting, the Association of Black Psychologists adopted the following official policy statement on educational and psychological testing:

> The Association of Black Psychologists fully supports those parents who have chosen to defend their rights by refusing to allow their children and themselves to be subjected to achievement, intelligence, aptitude and performance tests which have been and are being used to: A. Label black people as uneducable. B. Place black children in "special" classes and schools. C. Perpetuate inferior education of blacks. D. Assign black children to educational tracts. E. Deny black children higher educational opportunities. F. Destroy positive growth and development of black people.

Many potentially legitimate objections to the use of educational and psychological tests with minorities have been raised by black and other minority psychologists. Too frequently the objections of these groups are viewed as fact without a review of any empirical evidence (for example, Council for Exceptional Children, 1978; Hilliard, 1979). The problems most often cited in the use of tests with minorities typically fall into the following categories as described by Reynolds (1982):

1. *Inappropriate Content.* Black or other minority children have not been exposed to the material involved in the test questions or other stimulus materials. The tests are geared primarily toward white middle-class homes and values.

2. *Inappropriate Standardization Samples.* Ethnic minorities are underrepresented in the collection of normative reference-group data. Williams (Wright & Isenstein, 1977) has criticized the WISC-R standardization sample for including blacks only in proportion to the United States total population. Out of 2200 children in the WISC-R standardization sample, 330 were minority. Williams contends that such small actual representation has no impact on the test. In earlier years, it was not unusual for standardization samples to be all white (for example, the 1949 WISC).

3. *Examiner and Language Bias.* Since most psychologists are white and primarily speak only standard English, they intimidate black and other ethnic minorities. They are also unable to communicate accurately with minority children. Lower test scores for minorities, then, are said to reflect only this intimidation and difficulty in the communication process, not lowered ability levels.

4. *Inequitable Social Consequences.* As a result of bias in educational and psychological tests, minority group members, who are already at a disadvantage in the educational and vocational markets because of past discrimination, are disproportionately relegated to dead-end educational tracks and thought unable to learn. Labeling effects also fall under this category.

5. *Measurement of Different Constructs.* Related to (1) above, this position asserts that the tests are measuring significantly different attributes when used with children from other than the white middle-class culture. Mercer (1979), for example, contends that when IQ tests are used with minorities, they are measuring only the degree of Anglocentrism of the home.

6. *Differential Predictive Validity.* Although tests may accurately predict a variety of outcomes for white middle-class children, they fail to predict at an acceptable level any relevant criteria for minority-group members. Corollary to this objection is a variety of competing positions regarding the selection of an appropriate, common criterion against which to validate tests across cultural groupings. Scholastic or academic attainment levels are considered by a variety of black psychologists to be biased as criteria.

Contrary to the position of a decade ago, a considerable body of research now exists in each of the above areas of potential bias in assessment. To the extent that the cultural test-bias hypothesis is a scientific question, as it must be to receive rational consideration, it must be evaluated via a thorough consideration of carefully conceived research. As with other scientific questions, one must be guided by the data. Recently the evidence regarding the cultural test-bias hypothesis has been reviewed extensively (Jensen, 1980; Reynolds, 1981e, 1982) and debated (Reynolds & Brown, 1984). Empirical research into the question of bias has failed to substantiate the existence of cultural bias in well-constructed, well-standardized educational and psychological tests when used with native-born American ethnic minorities. The internal psychometric characteristics of intelligence and other aptitude tests behave in essentially the same manner across ethnic groupings, and the tests predict later and concurrent academic performance equivalently for all groups. Although most of this research has focused on adults and school-age children, recent studies have also dealt with preschool tests. Across the age span, with a variety of tests and criteria, the results have been quite consistent. Whatever intelligence tests are measuring for white middle-class children, be it scholastic aptitude, learning potential, or intelligence, they are most likely measuring the same construct when used with native-born ethnic minorities.

The issues regarding cultural bias in psychological and educational assessment are complex and not given to simple resolution. The strong emotions spirited forward from otherwise competent, objective professionals is a further indication of the level of complexity involved in the issues of bias. The controversy over bias will likely remain with psychology and education for at least as long as the nature/nurture controversy, even in the face of a convincing body of evidence failing to support cultural test-bias hypotheses. Bias in intelligence testing will remain in the spotlight for some time to come as well, especially now that the *Larry P.* (1979) and *PASE* (1980) decisions have been appealed, and given their propensity to elicit polemic emotional arguments.

The empirical evidence regarding test bias does not support the contentions of minority spokespersons. Nevertheless, bias is not merely an empirical issue (Flaugher, 1978), and the results of research investigations should not make psychologists any less sensitive to the needs and feelings of minority-group numbers. Instruments should be chosen as supplements to IQ tests that are known to include tasks on which blacks have consistently performed well. An example of a good supplement is the Torrance Tests of Creative Thinking (Torrance, 1974), which measures skills such as figural fluency and flexibility; blacks have been shown to outperform whites on some nonverbal creative skills (Kaltsounis, 1974).

Furthermore, it is incumbent on new test developers to include tasks that call on skills believed to be well developed among minority-group members. That was one goal in the development of the Kaufman Assessment Battery for Children (K-ABC; Kaufman & Kaufman, 1983), an intelligence and achievement test of 2½–12½ year olds derived from neuropsychological theory. This battery includes tasks such as Gestalt Closure and Face Recognition, which resemble tests in the literature that have been shown to be far less culturally dependent (Bogen, DeZure, Tenhouten, & Marsh, 1972; Kagan & Klein, 1973) than most traditional tasks of intelligence tests.

In the meantime, clinicians would be wise to follow these several guidelines in order to ensure nonbiased assessment: (1) assessment should be conducted with the most reliable instrumentation available, and (2) multiple abilities should be assessed. In other words, psychologists need to view multiple sources of accurately derived data prior to making decisions concerning children. Hopefully, this is not too far afield from what has actually been occurring in the practice of psychological assessment, though one continues to hear isolated stories of grossly incompetent placement decisions. This is not to say that psychologists should be blind to a child's environmental background. Information concerning the home, community, and school environment must all be evaluated in the individualized decision-making process. Some would deny services to minority children, claiming that they are not handicapped but only artificially appear so on culturally biased tests. However, the psychologist cannot ignore the data demonstrating that *low IQ ethnic, disadvantaged children are just as likely to fail academically as are white, middle-class low IQ children, provided that their en-*

vironmental circumstances remain constant. Indeed, recall that it is the purpose of the assessment *process* to beat the prediction, to provide insight into hypotheses for environmental interventions that will prevent the predicted failure. Low IQ minority children have the same entitlements to remedial, compensatory, and preventive programs as the white middle-class low IQ child, and ethnic minorities should not be denied services on unfounded assumptions that the test caused the low score and not a deficiency or dysfunction on the part of the child or the child's environment. These issues and the empirical research to date with children are reviewed in detail in Reynolds (1981e, 1982) and Reynolds and Brown (1984). Properly executed, intelligent testing by sensitive well-trained professionals can prevent conflicts over bias since testing is conceptualized entirely as a vehicle to understanding that leads to the betterment of the individual in multiple areas of functioning.

REFERENCES

Ackerman, P. T., Dykman, R. A., & Peters, J. E. (1976). Hierarchical factor patterns on the WISC as related to area of learning deficit. *Perceptual and Motor Skills, 42,* 381–386.

Alcorn, C. L., & Nicholson, C. L. (1975, April). *A technique for programming interpretations and educational recommendations based on the WISC-R.* Paper presented to the annual meeting of the National Association of School Psychologists, Atlanta, GA.

Anastasi, A. (1976). *Psychological testing* (4th ed.). New York: Macmillan.

Anderson, M., Kaufman, A. S., & Kaufman, N. L. (1976). Use of the WISC-R with a learning disabled population: Some diagnostic implications. *Psychology in the Schools, 13,* 381–386.

Arthur, G. (1947). *A Point Scale of Performance, Revised Form II: Manual for administering and scoring the tests.* New York: Psychological Corporation.

Bannatyne, A. (1971). *Language, reading, and learning disabilities.* Springfield, IL: Charles C. Thomas.

Bannatyne, A. (1974). Diagnosis: A note on recategorization of the WISC scaled scores. *Journal of Learning Disabilities, 7,* 272–274.

Barona, A., Reynolds, C. R., & Chastain, R. A. (in press). Premorbid index of intelligence for the WAIS-R. *Journal of Consulting and Clinical Psychology.*

Baumeister, A. A., & Bartlett, C. J. (1962). A comparison of the factor structure of normals and retardates on the WISC. *American Journal of Mental Deficiency, 66,* 641–646.

Berger, M. (1970). The third revision of the Stanford-Binet (Form L-M): Some methodological limitations and their practical implications. *Bulletin of the British Psychological Society, 23,* 17–26.

Binet, A. (1903). *L'étude expérimentale de l'intelligence.* Paris: Schleicher.

Binet, A., & Henri, V. (1896). La psychologie individuelle. *L'Année Psychologique, 2,* 411–465.

Binet, A., & Simon, T. (1905). Méthodes nouvelles pour le diagnostic du niveau intellectuel des anormaux. *L'Année Psychologique, 11,* 191–244.

Blaha, J., & Vance, H. (1979). The hierarchical factor structure of the WISC-R for learning disabled children. *Learning Disabilities Quarterly, 2,* 71–75.

Blatt, S. J., & Allison, J. (1981). The intelligence test in personality assessment. In A. Rabin (Ed.), *Assessment with projective techniques: A concise introduction.* New York: Springer-Verlag.

Bogen, J. E., DeZure, R., Tenhouten, N., & Marsh, J. (1972). The other side of the brain IV: The A/P ratio. *Bulletin of the Los Angeles Neurological Society, 37,* 49–61.

Buros, O. K. (1974). *Tests in print.* Highland Park, NJ: Gryphon Press.

Buros, O. K. (1978). *The eighth mental measurements yearbook.* Highland Park, NJ: Gryphon Press.

Carlson, L. C., & Reynolds, C. R. (1981). Factor structure and specific variance of the WPPSI subtests at six age levels. *Psychology in the Schools, 18,* 48–54.

Carlson, L. C., Reynolds, C. R., & Gutkin, T. B. (in press). Comparative structure of the WISC-R for upper and lower SES groups. *Journal of School Psychology.*

Cattell, J. M. (1890). Mental tests and measurements. *Mind, 15,* 373ff.

Cattell, J. M., & Farrand, L. (1896). Physical and mental measurements of the students of Columbia University. *Psychological Review, 3,* 618–648.

Clarizio, H., & Bernard, R. (1981). Recategorized WISC-R scores of learning disabled children and differential diagnosis. *Psychology in the Schools, 18,* 5–12.

Cleary, T. A., Humphreys, L. G., Kendrick, S. A., & Wesman, A. (1975). Educational uses of tests with disadvantaged students. *American Psychologist, 30,* 15–41.

Cohen, J. (1952). A factor-analytically based rationale for the Wechsler Bellevue. *Journal of Consulting Psychology, 16,* 272–277.

Cohen, J. (1959). The factorial structure of the WISC at ages 7-6, 10-6, and 13-6. *Journal of Consulting Psychology, 23,* 285–299.

Cornell, E. L., & Coxe, W. W. (1934). *A performance ability scale: Examination manual.* New York: World Book.

Council for Exceptional Children (1978). Minorities' position policy statements. *Exceptional Children, 45,* 57–64.

Dean, R. S. (1979, September). *WISC-R factor structure for Anglo and Hispanic children.* Paper presented at the meeting of the American Psychological Association, New York City.

DeHorn, A., & Klinge, V. (1978). Correlations and factor analysis of the WISC-R and the Peabody Picture Vocabulary Test for an adolescent psychiatric sample. *Journal of Consulting and Clinical Psychology, 46,* 1160–1161.

Ebel, R. (1982). Evaluation and selection of group measures. In C. R. Reynolds & T. B. Gutkin (Eds.), *The handbook of school psychology.* New York: Wiley.

Esquirol, J. E. D. (1828). Observations pour servir à l'histoire de l'idiotie. *Les Maladies Mentales.*

Esquirol, J. E. D. (1838). *Des maladies mentales considerées sous les rapports médical, hygiénique, et médico-légal* (2 vols.). Paris: Baillière.

Finch, A. J., Kendall, P. C., Spirito, A., Entin, A., Montgomery, L. E., & Schwartz, D. J. (1979). Short form and factor-analytic studies of the WISC-R with behavior problem children. *Journal of Abnormal Child Psychology, 7,* 337–344.

Flaugher, R. L. (1978). The many definitions of test bias. *American Psychologist, 33,* 671–679.

Friedes, D. (1972). Review of the Stanford-Binet Intelligence Scale. In O. K. Buros (Ed.), *The seventh mental measurements yearbook.* Highland Park, NJ: Gryphon Press.

Galton, F. (1869). *Hereditary genius: An inquiry into its laws and consequences.* London: Macmillan.

Galton, F. (1883). *Inquiries into human faculty and its development.* London: Macmillan.

Goddard, H. H. (1911). A revision of the Binet scale. *Training School, 8,* 56–62.

Goh, D. S., Teslow, C. J., & Fuller, G. B. (1981). The practice of psychological assessment among school psychologists. *Professional Psychology, 12,* 696–706.

Groff, M., & Hubble, L. (1981). Recategorized WISC-R scores of juvenile delinquents. *Journal of Learning Disabilities, 14,* 515–516.

Gutkin, T. B. (1979a). Bannatyne patterns of Caucasian and Mexican-American learning disabled children. *Psychology in the Schools, 16,* 178–183.

Gutkin, T. B. (1979b). WISC-R scatter indices: Useful information for differential diagnosis? *Journal of School Psychology, 17,* 368–371.

Gutkin, T. B. (1979c). The WISC-R Verbal Comprehension, Perceptual Organization, and Freedom from Distractibility deviation quotients: Data for practitioners. *Psychology in the Schools, 16,* 356–360.

Gutkin, T. B., & Reynolds, C. R. (1980). Factorial similarity of the WISC-R for Anglos and Chicanos referred for psychological services. *Journal of School Psychology, 18,* 34–39.

Gutkin, T. B., & Reynolds, C. R. (1981). Factorial similarity of the WISC-R for white and black children from the standardization sample. *Journal of Educational Psychology, 73,* 227–231.

Gutkin, T. B., Reynolds, C. R., & Galvin, G. A. (in press). Factor analysis of the Wechsler Adult Intelligence Scale—Revised (WAIS-R): An examination of the standardization sample. *Journal of School Psychology.*

Henry, S. A., & Wittman, R. D. (1981). Diagnostic implications of Bannatyne's recategorized WISC-R scores for identifying learning disabled children. *Journal of Learning Disabilities, 14,* 517–520.

Herring, J. P. (1922). *Herring Revision of the Binet-Simon Tests: Examination manual—Form A.* London: World Book.

Herrnstein, R. (1973). *IQ in the meritocracy.* Boston: Little, Brown.

Hilliard, A. G. (1979). Standardization and cultural bias as impediments to the scientific study and validation of "intelligence." *Journal of Research and Development in Education, 12,* 47–58.

Hilliard, A. G. (1984). IQ testing as the emperor's new clothes: A critique of Jensen's *Bias in Mental Testing.* In C. R. Reynolds & R. T. Brown (Eds.), *Perspectives on bias in mental testing,* New York: Plenum.

Holroyd, J., & Wright, F. (1965). Neurological implications of WISC Verbal-Performance discrepancies in a psychiatric setting. *Journal of Consulting Psychology, 29,* 206–212.

Hughes, J. (1979). Consistency of administrators' and psychologists' actual and ideal perceptions of school psychologists' activities. *Psychology in the Schools, 16,* 234–239.

Jensen, A. R. (1979). *g*: Outmoded theory or unconquered frontier? *Creative Science and Technology, 2,* 16–29.

Jensen, A. R. (1980). *Bias in mental testing.* New York: The Free Press.

Jensen, A. R., & Reynolds, C. R. (1982). Race, social class, and ability patterns on the WISC-R. *Personality and Individual Differences, 3,* 423–438.

Kagan, J., & Klein, R. E. (1973). Cross-cultural perspectives on early development. *American Psychologist, 28,* 947–961.

Kaltsounis, W. (1974). Race, socioeconomic status, and creativity. *Psychological Reports, 35,* 164–166.

Karnes, F. A., & Brown, K. E. (1980). Factor analysis of the WISC-R for the gifted. *Journal of Educational Psychology, 72,* 197–199.

Kaufman, A. S. (1972). A short form of the Wechsler Preschool and Primary Scale of Intelligence. *Journal of Consulting and Clinical Psychology, 39,* 361–369.

Kaufman, A. S. (1975). Factor analysis of the WISC-R at 11 age levels between 6½ and 16½ years. *Journal of Consulting and Clinical Psychology, 43,* 135–147.

Kaufman, A. S. (1976a). Do normal children have "flat" ability profiles? *Psychology in the Schools, 13,* 284–285.

Kaufman, A. S. (1976b). A new approach to the interpretation of test scatter on the WISC-R. *Journal of Learning Disabilities, 9,* 160–168.

Kaufman, A. S. (1976c). Verbal-Performance IQ discrepancies on the WISC-R. *Journal of Consulting and Clinical Psychology, 9,* 160–168.

Kaufman, A. S. (1976d). A four-test short form of the WISC-R. *Contemporary Educational Psychology, 1,* 180–196.

Kaufman, A. S. (1977). A McCarthy short form for rapid screening of preschool, kindergarten, and first-grade children. *Contemporary Educational Psychology, 2,* 149–157.

Kaufman, A. S. (1979a). *Intelligent testing with the WISC-R.* New York: Wiley-Interscience.

Kaufman, A. S. (1979b). Cerebral specialization and intelligence testing. *Journal of Research and Development in Education, 12,* 96–107.

Kaufman, A. S. (1981). The WISC-R and LD assessment: State of the art. *Journal of Learning Disabilities, 14,* 520–526.

Kaufman, A. S. (1982). The impact of WISC-R research for school psychologists. In C. R. Reynolds & T. B. Gutkin (Eds.), *The handbook of school psychology.* New York: Wiley.

Kaufman, A. S. (1983). Intelligence: Old concepts—new perspectives. In G. Hynd (Ed.), *The school psychologist.* Syracuse: Syracuse University Press.

Kaufman, A. S., & Doppelt, J. E. (1976). Analysis of WISC-R standardization data in terms of the stratification variables. *Child Development, 47,* 165–171.

Kaufman, A. S., & Hollenbeck, G. P. (1974). Comparative structure of the WPPSI for blacks and whites. *Journal of Clinical Psychology, 30,* 316–319.

Kaufman, A. S., & Kaufman, N. L. (1977). *Clinical evaluation of young children with the McCarthy Scales.* New York: Grune & Stratton.

Kaufman, A. S., & Kaufman, N. L. (1983). *Kaufman Assessment Battery for Children.* Circle Pines, MN: American Guidance Services.

Kaufman, A. S., & Reynolds, C. R. (1984). Assessing intelligence and academic achievement. In T. Ollendick & M. Horsan (Eds.), *Child behavioral assessment: Principles and procedures.* New York: Pergamon.

Kohs, S. C. (1923). *Intelligence measurement.* New York: Macmillan.

Korchin, S. J. (1976). *Modern clinical psychology.* New York: Basic Books.

Kuhlman, F. (1912). A revision of the Binet-Simon system for measuring the intelligence of children. *Journal of Psych-Asthenics Monograph Supplement, 1,* 1–41.

Larry P. et al. v. Riles et al. (1979, October). United States District Court for the Northern District of California, C-71-2270RFP, slip opinion.

Lezak, M. (1976). *Neuropsychological assessment.* New York: Oxford University Press.

Lombard, T. J., & Riedel, R. G. (1978). An analysis of the factor structure of the WISC-R and the effect of color on the Coding subtest. *Psychology in the Schools, 15,* 176–179.

Lutey, C. (1977). *Individual intelligence testing: A manual and sourcebook* (2nd & enlarged ed.). Greeley, CO: Carol L. Lutey.

Lutey, C., & Copeland, E. (1982). Cognitive assessments of the school aged child. In C. R. Reynolds & T. B. Gutkin (Eds.), *The handbook of school psychology.* New York: Wiley.

Matarazzo, J. D. (1972). *Wechsler's measurement and appraisal of adult intelligence* (5th ed.). Baltimore: Williams & Wilkins.

McCarthy, D. (1972). *McCarthy Scales of Children's Abilities.* New York: The Psychological Corporation.

McDermott, P. (1982). Actuarial assessment systems for the grouping and classification of school children. In C. R. Reynolds & T. B. Gutkin (Eds.), *The handbook of school psychology.* New York: Wiley.

McDermott, P. (in press). Diagnosis and classification of childhood disorders. In R. T. Brown & C. R. Reynolds (Eds.), *Psychological perspectives on childhood exceptionality.* New York: Wiley-Interscience.

Mercer, J. R. (1979). In defense of racially and culturally nondiscriminatory assessment. *School Psychology Digest, 8,* 89–95.

Moore, D. W., & Wielan, O. P. (1981). WISC-R scatter indices of children referred for reading diagnosis. *Journal of Learning Disabilities, 14,* 416–418.

Naglieri, J. A. (1979). *A comparison of McCarthy GCI and WISC-R IQ scores for educable mentally retarded, learning disabled and normal children.* Unpublished doctoral dissertation, University of Georgia.

Naglieri, J. A., & Kaufman, A. S. (1982, August). *Determining the number of WAIS-R factors using several methods.* Paper presented at the annual meeting of the American Psychological Association, Washington, DC.

Ollendick, T. H. (1979). Discrepancies between verbal and performance IQs and subtest scatter on the WISC-R for juvenile delinquents. *Psychological Reports, 45,* 563–568.

PASE: Parents in Action on Special Education et al. v. *Hannon et al.* (1980, July). United States District Court for the Northern District of Illinois, Eastern Division, C-74-3586RFP, slip opinion.

Peterson, C. R., & Hart, D. H. (1979). Factor structure of the WISC-R for a clinic-referred population and specific subgroups. *Journal of Consulting and Clinical Psychology, 47,* 643–645.

Peterson, J. (1925). *Early conceptions and tests of intelligence.* Chicago: World Book.

Pintner, R., & Paterson, D. G. (1925). *A scale of performance tests.* New York: Appleton.

Raviv, A., Margolith, M., Raviv, A., & Sade, E. (1981). The cognitive pattern of Israeli learning disabled children as reflected in the Hebrew version of the WISC-R. *Journal of Learning Disabilities, 14,* 411–415.

Reschly, D. J. (1978). WISC-R factor structures among Anglos, Blacks, Chicanos, and Native-American Papagos. *Journal of Consulting and Clinical Psychology, 46,* 417–422.

Reynolds, C. R. (1979). Should we screen preschoolers? *Contemporary Educational Psychology, 4,* 175–181.

Reynolds, C. R. (1980a). Two commercial interpretive systems for the WISC-R. *School Psychology Review, 9,* 385–386.

Reynolds, C. R. (1980b). Review of the TARDOR Interpretive Scoring System for the WISC-R. *Measurement and Evaluation in Guidance, 14,* 46–48.

Reynolds, C. R. (1981a). The fallacy of "two years below grade level for age" as a diagnostic criterion for reading disorders. *Journal of School Psychology, 19,* 350–358.

Reynolds, C. R. (1981b). The neuropsychological basis of intelligence. In G. Hynd & J. Obrzut (Eds.), *Neuropsychological assessment and the school-aged child: Issues and procedures.* New York: Grune & Stratton.

Reynolds, C. R. (1981c). A note on determining significant descrepancies among category scores on Bannatyne's regrouping of WISC-R subtests. *Journal of Learning Disabilities, 14,* 468–469.

Reynolds, C. R. (1981d). Screening tests: Problems and promises. In N. Lambert (Ed.), *Special education assessment matrix.* Monterey: CTB/McGraw-Hill.

Reynolds, C. R. (1981e, August). *Test bias: In God we trust, all others must have data.* Invited address to the annual meeting of the American Psychological Association, Los Angeles.

Reynolds, C. R. (1982). The problem of bias in psychological assessment. In C. R. Reynolds & T. B. Gutkin (Eds.), *The handbook of school psychology.* New York: Wiley.

Reynolds, C. R. (in press). Determining statistically reliable strengths and weaknesses in the performance of single individuals on the Luria-Nebraska Neuropsychological Battery. *Journal of Consulting and Clinical Psychology.*

Reynolds, C. R., & Brown, R. T. (Eds.) (1984). *Perspectives on bias in mental testing.* New York: Plenum.

Reynolds, C. R., & Clark, J. H. (1982). Cognitive assessment of the preschool child. In K. Paget & B. Bracken (Eds.), *Psychoeducational assessment of preschool and primary aged children.* New York: Grune & Stratton.

Reynolds, C. R., & Elliott, S. N. (1982, March). *Trends in test development and test publishing.* Paper presented to the annual meeting of the National Council on Measurement in Education, New York.

Reynolds, C. R., & Gutkin, T. B. (1979). Predicting the premorbid intellectual status of children using demographic data. *Clinical Neuropsychology, 1,* 36–38.

Reynolds, C. R., & Gutkin, T. B. (1980). Stability of the WISC-R factor structure across sex at two age levels. *Journal of Clinical Psychology, 36,* 775–777.

Reynolds, C. R., & Gutkin, T. B. (1981a). A multivariate comparison of the intellectual performance of blacks and whites matched on four demographic variables. *Personality and Individual Differences, 2,* 175–180.

Reynolds, C. R., & Gutkin, T. B. (1981b). Statistics for the interpretation of Bannatyne recategorizations of WPPSI subtests. *Journal of Learning Disabilities, 14,* 464–467.

Reynolds, C. R., & Gutkin, T. B. (1981c). Test scatter on the WPPSI: Normative analyses of the standardization sample. *Journal of Learning Disabilities, 14,* 460–464.

Reynolds, C. R., & Struer, J. (1981, April). *Factor structure of the WISC-R for emotionally disturbed children.* Paper presented to the annual meeting of the National Association of School Psychologists, Houston.

Reynolds, C. R., & Struer, J. (1982). Comparative structure of the WISC-R for emotionally disturbed and normal children. *The Southern Psychologist, 1,* 27–35.

Reynolds, C. R., Willson, V. L., & Clark, P. L. (1983). A WAIS-R short form for clinical screening. *Clinical Neuropsychology, 5,* 111–116.

Rugel, R. P. (1979). WISC subtest scores of disabled readers: A review with respect to Bannatyne's recategorization. *Journal of Learning Disabilities, 7,* 48–55.

Sattler, J. M. (1982). *Assessment of children's intelligence and special abilities* (2nd ed.). Boston: Allyn & Bacon.

Sattler, J., Hilliard, A., Lambert, N., Albee, G., & Jensen, A. (1981, August). *Intelligence tests on trial: Larry P. and PASE.* Symposium presented at the annual meeting of the American Psychological Association, Los Angeles.

Schiff, M. M., Kaufman, A. S., & Kaufman, N. L. (1981). Scatter analysis of WISC-R profiles for learning disabled children with superior intelligence. *Journal of Learning Disabilities, 14,* 426–430.

Schooler, D. L., Beebe, M. C., & Koepke, T. (1978). Factor analysis of WISC-R scores for children identified as learning disabled, educable mentally impaired, and emotionally impaired. *Psychology in the Schools, 15,* 478–485.

Seashore, H. G. (1951). Differences between verbal and performance IQs on the WISC. *Journal of Consulting Psychology, 15,* 62–67.

Seguin, E. (1907). *Idiocy: Its treatment by the physiological method* (Reprinted from original edition of 1866). New York: Bureau of Publications, Teachers College, Columbia University.

Sharp, S. E. (1898–1899). Individual psychology: A study in psychological method. *American Journal of Psychology, 10,* 329–391.

Shellenberger, S. (1982). Presentation and interpretation of psychological data in educational settings. In C. R. Reynolds & T. B. Gutkin (Eds.), *The handbook of school psychology.* New York: Wiley.

Smith, M. D., Coleman, J. M., Dokecki, P. R., & Davis, E. E. (1977). Recategorized WISC-R scores of learning disabled children. *Journal of Learning Disabilities, 10,* 437–443.

Stangler, S. R., Huber, C. J., & Routh, D. K. (1980). *Screening growth and development of preschool children.* New York: McGraw-Hill.

Stedman, J. M., Lawlis, G. F., Cortner, R. H., & Achterberg, G. (1978). Relationships between WISC-R factors, wide-range achievement test scores, and visual-motor maturation in children referred for psychological evaluation. *Journal of Consulting and Clinical Psychology, 46,* 869–872.

Stern, W. (1914). *The psychological methods of testing intelligence.* Baltimore: Warwick and York.

Stevenson, L. P. (1979, April). *WISC-R analysis: Implications for diagnosis and educational intervention of LD children.* Paper presented at the meeting of the Council for Exceptional Children, Dallas.

Strichart, S. S., & Love, E. (1979). WISC-R performance of children referred to a university center for learning disabilities. *Psychology in the Schools, 16,* 183–188.

Swerdlik, M. E., & Schweitzer, J. (1978). A comparison of factor structures of the WISC and WISC-R. *Psychology in the Schools, 15,* 166–172.

Tabachnick, B. G. (1979). Test scatter on the WISC-R. *Journal of Learning Disabilities, 12*, 626–628.

Tellegen, A., & Briggs, P. F. (1967). Old wine in new skins: Grouping Wechsler subtests into new scales. *Journal of Consulting Psychology, 31*, 499–506.

Terman, L. M. (1916). *The measurement of intelligence.* Boston: Houghton-Mifflin.

Terman, L. M., & Childs, H. G. (1912). A tentative revision and extension of the Binet-Simon Measuring Scale of Intelligence. *Journal of Educational Psychology, 3*, 61–74; 133–143; 198–208; 277–289.

Terman, L. M., & Merrill, M. A. (1937). *Measuring intelligence.* Boston: Houghton-Mifflin.

Terman, L. M., & Merrill, M. A. (1973). *Stanford-Binet Intelligence Scale: 1972 Norms edition.* Boston: Houghton-Mifflin.

Thompson, R. J. (1980). The diagnostic utility of WISC-R measures with children referred to a developmental evaluation center. *Journal of Consulting and Clinical Psychology, 48*, 440–447.

Thompson, R. J. (1981). The diagnostic utility of Bannatyne's recategorized WISC-R scores with children referred to a developmental evaluation center. *Psychology in the Schools, 18*, 43–47.

Torrance, E. P. (1974). *Torrance tests of creative thinking: Directions manual and scoring guide.* Lexington, MA: Ginn.

Vance, H. B., Gaynor, P., & Coleman, M. (1976). Analysis of cognitive abilities for learning disabled children. *Psychology in the Schools, 13*, 477–483.

Vance, H. B., & Singer, M. G. (1979). Recategorization of the WISC-R subtest scaled scores for learning disabled children. *Journal of Learning Disabilities, 12*, 487–491.

Vance, H. B., & Wallbrown, F. H. (1978). The structure of intelligence for black children: A hierarchical approach. *Psychological Record, 28*, 31–39.

Van Hagen, J., & Kaufman, A. S. (1975). Factor analysis of the WISC-R for a group of mentally retarded children and adolescents. *Journal of Consulting and Clinical Psychology, 43*, 661–667.

Vernon, P. A. (1979). *Intelligence: Heredity and environment.* San Francisco: W. H. Freeman.

Vernon, P. A. (1981). *Speed of information processing and general intelligence.* Unpublished doctoral dissertation, University of California—Berkeley.

Vitelli, R., & Goldblatt, R. (1979). *The TARDOR interpretive scoring system for the WISC-R.* Manchester, CT: TARDOR Publishers.

Wallbrown, F., Blaha, J., Wallbrown, J., & Engin, A. (1975). The hierarchical factor structure of the Wechsler Intelligence Scale for Children—Revised. *Journal of Psychology, 89*, 223–235.

Wechsler, D. (1939). *Measurement of adult intelligence.* Baltimore: Williams and Wilkins.

Wechsler, D. (1958). *Measurement and appraisal of adult intelligence* (4th ed.). Baltimore: Williams and Wilkins.

Wechsler, D. (1967). *Manual for the Wechsler Preschool and Primary Scale of Intelligence (WPPSI).* New York: Psychological Corporation.

Wechsler, D. (1974). *Manual for the Wechsler Intelligence Scale for Children—Revised (WISC-R).* New York: Psychological Corporation.

Wechsler, D. (1981). *Manual for the Wechsler Adult Intelligence Scale—Revised (WAIS-R).* New York: Psychological Corporation.

Weiner, S. G., & Kaufman, A. S. (1979). WISC-R vs. WISC for black children suspected of learning or behavioral disorders. *Journal of Learning Disabilities, 12*, 100–105.

Wender, P. H. (1971). *Minimal brain dysfunction in children.* New York: Wiley-Interscience.

White, W. (Ed.). (1979). Intelligence. Special issue of *Journal of Research and Development in Education, 12*(1).

Wilson, R. S., Rosenbaum, G., Brown, G., Rourke, D., Whitman, D., & Grisell, J. (1978). An index of premorbid intelligence. *Journal of Consulting and Clinical Psychology, 46*, 1554–1555.

Wissler, C. (1901). The correlation of mental and physical tests. *Psychological Review, 3* (Monograph Supplement 16).

Witkin, H. A., Dyk, R. B., Faterson, H. G., Goodenough, D. R., & Karp, S. A. (1974). *Psychological differentiation.* Potomac, MD: Erlbaum.

Wright, B. J., & Isenstein, V. R. (1977). *Psychological tests and minorities.* Rockville, MD. (NIMH, DHEW Publication # (ADM) 78-482)

Yoakum, C. S., & Yerkes, R. M. (1920). *Army Mental Tests.* New York: Henry Holt.

Zingale, S. A., & Smith, M. D. (1978). WISC-R patterns for learning disabled children at three SES levels. *Psychology in the Schools, 15,* 199–204.

FOURTEEN

NEW DIRECTIONS IN INTELLIGENCE TESTING: THE KAUFMAN ASSESSMENT BATTERY FOR CHILDREN (K-ABC)

ALAN S. KAUFMAN

University of Alabama
Tuscaloosa, Alabama

RANDY W. KAMPHAUS

Eastern Kentucky University
Richmond, Kentucky

and

NADEEN L. KAUFMAN

University of Alabama
Tuscaloosa, Alabama

At the time of this writing, the K-ABC has been available for use by psychologists for about eight months. Because of its initial popularity psychologists are struggling to understand the K-ABC: its unique properties, goals, and perhaps most importantly to the practitioner its niche alongside the other more well-known measures of intelligence. Complicating this effort to understand the K-ABC is the fact that the K-ABC is unique from existing intelligence tests in a number of ways. Its administration and scoring rules, which allow an examiner the freedom to reword the oral instructions for some items, or to give credit for responses in foreign languages, are different from existing measures. Its theory of intelligence, of sequential and simultaneous processing abilities, further differentiates the K-ABC from its predecessors. As a result of this "new" theory of intelligence being adopted by the K-ABC authors, the K-ABC requires many practicing psychologists to think differently about using an intelligence test for prediction, about the intellectual performance of many minority-group children, and about the procedures for identifying intellectually gifted children. It is these and other nuances of the K-ABC that psychologists are now beginning to internalize. This chapter will focus on those aspects of the K-ABC that make it distinctive, in the hope that practitioners and academicians alike will be able to better put the K-ABC in perspective. However, before addressing these more substantive issues, an overview of the K-ABC will be presented.

OVERVIEW OF THE K-ABC

The Kaufman Assessment Battery for Children (K-ABC; Kaufman & Kaufman, 1983a) is a new test of the intelligence and achievement of children in the 2½–12½ year age range. Intelligence is defined in terms of mental processing, having its theoretical roots in both neuropsychology and cognitive psychology. The intelligence scales are Sequential Processing, Simultaneous Processing, and Mental Processing Composite (Sequential and Simultaneous), and reflect a processing dichotomy that has been identified and researched independently by cerebral-specialization theorists (Bogen, 1969; Sperry, 1968), by Luria (1966) and his devotees (Das, Kirby, & Jarman, 1975, 1979), and by cognitive psychologists (Neisser, 1967).

Sequential Processing refers to the ability to solve problems in step-wise fashion, where the emphasis is on the temporal or serial relationships among the stimuli; these stimuli, whether verbal or visual, have to be handled sequentially for optimal performance on the items. An example from the K-ABC is Word Order, in which the child has to point to silhouettes of objects in the same order that these objects were named by the examiner. Harder items require the child to name colors for five seconds (an interference task) in between the stimulus and response. In school situations, sequential processing is required to memorize lists of number facts, to sound out words by a phonics approach, to use a step-by-step procedure for mathematical operations such as borrowing, and so forth.

The Simultaneous Processing Scale measures the child's ability to solve problems where many stimuli need to be organized and integrated at the same point in time. These problems frequently are analogic or have spatial overtones; whether they are primarily perceptual or conceptual, they are united by the need for simultaneous synthesis to produce the most appropriate solutions. Illustrations from the K-ABC include identifying a partly completed "inkblot" drawing (Gestalt Completion) and solving visual, mostly abstract, analogies (Matrix Analogies, akin to Raven's Matrices). Simultaneous processing is necessary for grasping configurations of words and letters during beginning reading, for understanding the main ideas of passages at more advanced levels of reading ability, for interpreting diagrams, charts, and maps, and so on.

Both Mental Processing or intelligence scales use stimuli that are generally seen as "fair," that is, as depicting scenes or events that are common or potentially accessible to all children, using actual photographs of people or common objects whenever feasible, and using neutral stimuli such as abstract designs. In essence, the Mental Processing Composite was intended as a measure of the child's fluid intelligence (Horn & Cattell, 1966), the ability to be adaptable, flexible, and "intelligent" when faced with unfamiliar problems. Hence clear attempts were made to eliminate from the K-ABC intelligence scales those traditional tests of verbal or global IQ that are heavily dependent on the acquisition of facts or school-related skills. These crystallized functions are so dependent on nonintellective variables such as subcultural environment, exposure to books, motivation, and adequacy of the child's school and teachers, that their elimination from the K-ABC's measure of intelligence was imperative.

This is not to say, however, that the assessment of school and nonschool-related acquired knowledge is unimportant. These essential aspects of a child's functioning are assessed by the K-ABC Achievement Scale. The Achievement Scale includes tasks that have traditionally been associated with tests of verbal intelligence (verbal-concept formation), school achievement (word reading and reading comprehension) or both (general information, arithmetic). The K-ABC Achievement Scale is interpreted as a measure of the child's applied intelligence, frequently requiring the child to integrate both types of mental processing (for example, Riddles, a test of verbal-concept formation, requires simultaneous integration of sequentially presented stimuli), and assesses Cattell-Horn's construct of crystallized ability.

All K-ABC global scales (Sequential Processing, Simultaneous Processing, Mental Processing Composite, Achievement, and Nonverbal) yield normalized standard scores with a mean set at 100 and SD at 15 to permit direct comparisons of intelligence and achievement for children suspected of learning disabilities, and to foster meaningful interpretation of K-ABC standard scores in relation to IQs yielded by other intelligence measures and standard scores obtained on other major tests of achievement. K-ABC Achievement Scale subtests also yield scores with a mean of 100 and SD of 15 to permit easy comparison of mental processing scores with specific achievement domains. Because of their high reliability coefficients, which will be cited later, the Achievement Scale subtests are quite capable of supporting this metric. Mental Processing Scale subtests, in contrast, yield scaled scores with a mean of 10 and SD of 3 using the familiar Wechsler subtest parameters.

The Nonverbal Scale is a special short form of the K-ABC Mental Processing Scale, for 4–12½ year olds, that includes those subtests that may be administered in pantomime and are responded to motorically. This scale was developed to permit fair assessment of the intellectual functioning of children with hearing impairment and moderate-to-severe speech or language disorders, as well as of youngsters who speak only a foreign language.

TECHNICAL DATA

Standardization

Over 4000 children between the ages of 2½–12½ were administered K-ABCs as part of the standardization, validation, and reliability research programs. A national standardization sample, based primarily on 1980 United States Census data, includes 2000 children, 100 (50 boys and 50 girls) at each 6-month interval from 2–6 (2 years, 6 months) through 2–11 to 12–0 through 12–5.

The sample was stratified based on age, sex, ethnic group (white, black, Hispanic, other), socioeconomic status (parental educational attainment), geographic region, community size, and educational placement. Educational placement was included as a stratification variable to ensure that exceptional children (gifted and talented, emotionally disturbed, learning disabled, and so forth) were systematically and proportionally included in the norming sample rather than arbitrarily excluded. A summary of the representation of the national standardization sample for some of the major stratification variables is given in Table 1. Inspection of this table reveals that the composition of the K-ABC norming sample is quite different from the norming samples of intelligence tests based on 1970 census data, particularly with regard to ethnicity. The proportion of minority-group children in the K-ABC norm group is almost double (27% versus 15%) what was included in the WISC-R norming sample (Wechsler, 1974), reflecting changes within the United States during the decade of the 1970s and emphasizing the need to include Hispanics in normative samples as a separate group.

To develop the K-ABC sociocultural norms, an additional sample of 615 children (119 whites and 496 blacks) was tested, and added to the groups of blacks and whites already tested as part of the national standardization sample. These sociocultural percentile-rank norms are supplementary norms provided for black and white children from different socioeconomic backgrounds (as determined by parental educational attainment), to allow examiners to interpret K-ABC scores according to a child's cultural heritage and opportunities for learning. However, these extra norms are not intended to be used in place of standard scores, which are based on national norms, for decision-making purposes.

Reliability

The mean internal-consistency reliability coefficients (based on subtest split-half coefficients) for the K-ABC global scales for the preschool and school age ranges are shown in Table 2. The reliability coefficients for the four main global scales ranged from .86 to .93 (mean = .90) for children aged 2½ to 4, and they ranged from .89 to .97 (mean = .93) for children aged 5 to 12½ years. The stability of these global scores was assessed by a test-retest study based on 246 children

Table 1. Representation of the K-ABC Standardization Sample by Geographic Region, Race or Ethnic Group, Parental Education, and Community Size (Ages 2-6 through 12-6)

Region	K-ABC Sample N	K-ABC Sample %	U.S. Population %	Race or Ethnic Group	K-ABC Sample N	K-ABC Sample %	U.S. Population %
East	401	20.0	20.3	White	1450	72.5	73.1
North Central	565	28.2	26.5	Total minorities	550	27.5	26.8
South	628	31.4	34.0	Black	311	15.6	14.5
West	406	20.3	19.2	Hispanic	157	7.8	9.1
				Native-American, Asian, or Pacific Islander	82	4.1	3.2
TOTAL		2000					

Parental Education	K-ABC Sample N	K-ABC Sample %	U.S. Population %	Community Size	K-ABC Sample N	K-ABC Sample %	U.S. Population %
Less than high school education	384	19.2	21.1	Central city	579	28.9	27.8
High school education	813	40.6	41.1	Suburb or small town	876	43.8	43.8
Some college	413	20.6	19.8	Rural area	545	27.2	28.3
College degree	390	19.5	18.0				

Table 2. Mean Split-Half Reliability Coefficients for K-ABC Scales and Subtests for the Standardization Sample

Scale or Subtest	Mean for Ages 2-6 Through 4-11	Mean for Ages 5-0 Through 12-6
Global Scales		
Sequential Processing	.90	.89
Simultaneous Processing	.86	.93
Mental Processing Composite	.91	.94
Achievement	.93	.97
Nonverbal	.87	.93
Mental Processing Subtests		
Magic Window	.72	
Face Recognition	.77	
Hand Movements	.78	.76
Gestalt Closure	.72	.71
Number Recall	.88	.81
Triangles	.89	.84
Word Order	.84	.82
Matrix Analogies		.85
Spatial Memory		.80
Photo Series		.82
Achievement Subtests		
Expressive Vocabulary	.85	
Faces and Places	.77	.84
Arithmetic	.87	.87
Riddles	.83	.86
Reading/Decoding		.92
Reading/Understanding		.91

Note. Coefficients were corrected for half-test length using the Spearman-Brown formula. Mean coefficients were obtained using Fisher's *z* transformation.

who were retested after a two- to four-week interval (mean interval = 18 days). The results of this study indicated that the four main global scales were quite stable, but that stability improved considerably with increasing age. Mean coefficients of .83, .88, and .92 were obtained for ages 2½ to 4, 5 to 8, and 9 to 12½, respectively.

The trend toward higher reliability coefficients for older children reflects the known variability that characterizes preschool children's intelligence test performance, and the fact that the K-ABC requires younger children to take fewer subtests. The K-ABC is tailored to the developmental needs of children in numerous ways including the number of subtests administered per age. On the K-ABC, only 7 subtests are administered at age 2½; 9 at age 3, 11 at ages 4 and 5, 12 at age 6, and 13 at ages 7 through 12½. The administration time of the K-ABC shows a corresponding increase with age, ranging from 40 to 45 minutes at age 3 to 75 to 85 minutes at ages 7 through 12½.

The reliability of the K-ABC subtests typically meets or exceeds the levels found on comparable instruments (Kaufman & Kaufman, 1983b). As shown in Table 2 the average internal consistency reliability (split-half) coefficients of the K-ABC subtests ranged from .72 to .89 (mean = .81) for preschool children and from .71 to .92 (mean = .83) for school-age children. Test-retest coefficients for the subtests are presented in the *K-ABC Interpretive Manual* (Kaufman & Kaufman, 1983b). As with the global scales, a distinct developmental trend is evident revealing relatively lower reliabilities for the preschool children and higher reliabilities for the school-age children.

One final reliability property of the K-ABC deserves mention. At ages 4 and 5 on the K-ABC, 11 subtests are administered. However, three subtests at age 5 are "school-age" tasks (two are simultaneous, one achievement) that are not administered to 4 year olds, replacing the three "preschool" tasks (two simultaneous, one achievement) that are intended for ages 2½ to 4. This substitution of subtests raises the question of the continuity of measurement on the K-ABC from the preschool to the school-age levels. As a result, 41 children were administered both the 4 and 5 year levels of the test, in counterbalanced order, to assess the alternate levels reliability of the K-ABC at this age juncture. The resulting coefficients were quite impressive, yielding a mean correlation of .91 for the global scales (Kaufman & Kaufman, 1983b).

Validity

A total of 43 validity studies, conducted by researchers in various parts of the country, are reported in the *K-ABC Interpretive Manual* (Kaufman & Kaufman, 1983b). Many samples of normal and exceptional children are represented in these studies, including: hearing impaired, gifted, educable and trainable mentally retarded, learning and reading disabled, behaviorally disordered, physically impaired, "high-risk" preschoolers, and culturally different American Indians. These validity studies provide the K-ABC user with a wealth of information regarding the construct, concurrent, and predictive validity of the test battery.

Of major validity interest is the relationship of the K-ABC to the WISC-R. This relationship was assessed in 17 investigations, involving 605 children, in the *K-ABC Interpretive Manual* (Kaufman & Kaufman, 1983b). In a study of 182 children from regular classrooms, the Mental Processing Composite correlated .70 with WISC-R Full Scale IQ; this overlap in variance of approximately 50% indicates clearly that the K-ABC intelligence scales share a definite common ground with the popular WISC-R, to many the reigning criterion of intelligence.

On the other hand, an overlap of this magnitude reveals that the K-ABC possesses enough reliable unique variance to be considered a new contribution to the field of intelligence measurement. Similarly, for this large sample of normal children, the mean K-ABC Mental Processing Composite was 113.6, whereas the mean WISC-R Full Scale IQ was 116.7. Therefore, the K-ABC norms, on the average, are predictably about three standard score points tougher than those for the WISC-R. The reader is referred to Chapter 4 of the *K-ABC Interpretive Manual* (Kaufman & Kaufman, 1983b) for additional validity information, and also to the discussions of factor analysis and correlations with measures of achievement that appear later in the present chapter.

ADMINISTRATION AND SCORING

The nuts and bolts of administering and scoring the K-ABC are described in the *K-ABC Administration and Scoring Manual* (Kaufman & Kaufman, 1983a). This manual discusses all aspects of administration and scoring, including establishing rapport, using the easels, subtest starting and stopping rules, and completing the Individual Test Record. Although it is beyond the scope of this chapter to discuss administration and scoring rules in detail, one distinctive aspect of the K-ABC's rules warrant special mention.

Each K-ABC mental-processing subtest allows an examiner to "teach the task," if necessary, on the first three items administered. In "teaching the task," the examiner may use alternate wording, gestures, physical guidance, even a language other than English, to help communicate the task expectations to a child who fails the first trial of *any or all* of the first three items administered (an unscored sample plus the first two actual items given to each child). By building this flexibility into the standardized procedures for administering the K-ABC, examiners always have the opportunity, if not the mandate, to use alternate instructions or procedures to help the child understand the task demands.

This flexibility is particularly important for culturally disadvantaged and preschool-age children who may have difficulty understanding oral instructions that include words or concepts not readily understood by many of these children (Kaufman, 1978). Flexibility in the oral instructions allows examiners to feel more confident that they are assessing a child's mental-processing abilities and not a child's ability to comprehend English oral instructions. Kaufman (1983) gives an expanded discussion of the concept of teaching items and cites data to show that this built-in flexibility does not in any way affect the reliability of the K-ABC.

Having an overview of the K-ABC and its technical data as background, the remainder of this chapter is devoted to discussing four major topics related to the K-ABC: sequential and simultaneous processing, using the K-ABC for predicting school performance, using the K-ABC with minority-group children, and using the K-ABC to identify intellectually gifted children.

SEQUENTIAL AND SIMULTANEOUS PROCESSING

As mentioned earlier, the theory on which the K-ABC is based is a condensation of research in neuropsychology and cognitive psychology. It is precisely because of this diverse support for the theory that the sequential/simultaneous model is used in the K-ABC. Only a theoretical model with a vast and varied research history will suffice for a test that purports to meet the needs of a wide range of preschool and school-age children.

This processing dichotomy provides the foundations for the use of the K-ABC. Therefore, several important questions regarding the dichotomy must be addressed. First, what evidence documents that the K-ABC adequately measures these processes? Second, is there a linear or hierarchical relationship between these two processes? The first question can be answered by studying the results of factor analysis; one way of approaching the second question is to determine whether both processes are equally important for school learning. These questions will be addressed in this section.

Factor Analysis

Das, Kirby, and Jarman (1975, 1979) developed a battery of tasks (such as Raven's Progressive Matrices, serial recall of words) to assess Luria's (1966) constructs of successive and simultaneous processing. Das and his colleagues have presented a great deal of factor-analytic evidence to show that the tasks they used assess these two dimensions (Das, Kirby, & Jarman, 1975, 1979).

In similar fashion, several studies using the K-ABC and some of its earlier, experimental versions have been carried out to assess the factorial validity of the K-ABC intelligence scales (Kaufman & Kamphaus, 1984; Kaufman, Kaufman, Kamphaus, & Naglieri, 1982; Naglieri, Kaufman, Kaufman, & Kamphaus, 1981). Kaufman and Kamphaus (1984) factor analyzed the K-ABC using the national standardization sample of 2000 cases and found considerable support for the sequential/simultaneous processing dichotomy underlying the battery, in agreement with the factor structure identified by Naglieri, Kaufman, Kaufman, and Kamphaus (1981) and by Kaufman, Kaufman, Kamphaus, and Naglieri (1982) for earlier versions of the K-ABC.

Kaufman and Kamphaus (1984) used subtest raw-score intercorrelation matrices for each of 11 age groups between 2½ and 12½ years as the basis for their analyses. The matrix for each age group was submitted to a principal-*components* analysis (1's in the diagonals, no iterations, followed by varimax rotation of all factors with eigenvalues of 1.00 or above) to assist in determining the number of meaningful factors for each age group. Then principal *factor* analysis was performed for each age level, with squared multiple correlations in the diagonals as the initial communality estimates. Iterations were then conducted, and the two-, three-, and four-factor varimax-rotated solutions were examined. Using a variety of statistical and theoretical criteria, two factors consistently emerged as the best explanation of the intercorrelations for each of the eleven age groups.

The varimax-rotated factor loadings for the sequential and simultaneous factors for the mental-processing subtests are given in Table 3. Table 3 also presents mean factor loadings across all age groups and the percent of reliable variance for each factor at each age group.

As shown in Table 3, the subtests that compose the Sequential Processing Scale had the highest mean loadings on the sequential factor (.43–.75) and the Simultaneous Processing Scale subtests loaded highest on the simultaneous factor (.40–.69). Hand Movements was the only subtest to have a substantial loading on the opposite factor (mean simultaneous factor loading = .36).

Other aspects of Table 3 are noteworthy. Word Order and Number Recall are consistently the best measures of sequential processing across the 2½ to 12½ year age range. This is a predictable finding since Word Order is an adaptation of a task used by Luria (1966), and Das, Kirby, and Jarman (1979) used digit-recall tasks as measures of successive processing. Hand Movements is the third best measure of sequential processing on the Mental Processing scales. It is also noteworthy that Hand Movements is the only subtest to show a developmental trend. Hand Movements seems to be a better measure of sequential abilities at the preschool level (mean factor loading = .60) than at ages 5 and above (mean factor loading = .37).

With regard to Simultaneous Processing, Magic Window and Gestalt Closure appear to be the best measures for preschool children and Triangles and Photo Series the best measures for school age children.

The strong simultaneous factor loadings by Gestalt Closure and Triangles are logical, since these tasks share similar properties with Wechsler's Picture Completion and Block Design subtests, both of which have been shown to be good measures of simultaneous processing (Naglieri, Kamphaus, & Kaufman, 1983). The high simultaneous-factor loadings by Magic Window and Photo Series may not be as predictable but they are consistent with Das, Kirby, and Jarman's (1979) notion that it is the mental process required to solve a problem, and not the nature of its stimuli or presentation or response mode, that determines the task's factor loadings. On Magic Window, portions of a pictured object are presented sequentially through a small opening, so the whole object is never in view at one time; for Photo Series, the child is required to organize a large array of photographs of an event (such as a child blowing up a balloon) by placing the photographs in the proper sequence. Apparently, however, as Das and his colleagues contend, it is the mental process that determines the factor loadings on these tasks that have obvious sequential components. For Magic Window, young children need to revisualize the separate parts of an object and mentally integrate them into a whole. With Photo Series, the simultaneous skills necessary to organize a large number of photographs (sometimes as many as 10) without manually rearranging them assumes primacy over the sequential abilities needed to order them chronologically.

Kaufman and Kamphaus (1984) also factor analyzed all of the K-ABC subtests (Mental Processing and Achievement) together. Only two factors emerged at ages 2½ and 3 with a third (achievement) factor emerging for ages 4 through

12½ years. At ages 4–7, achievement subtests not only loaded on the achievement factor but also had substantial and sometimes higher loadings on one or both processing factors. At ages 8 and above the achievement factor was more robust and stable, with achievement subtests consistently having their highest loadings on this factor. It is quite conceivable that the strong achievement factor at ages 8 and above is a result of the homogenizing effects of school instruction.

Perhaps most importantly, the factor analysis of all subtests yields some insights into the relationship of sequential and simultaneous processing to different aspects of achievement. In addition to factor analysis, factor scores for the sequential and simultaneous factors (computed from the principal factor analyses of Mental Processing subtests) were correlated with raw scores on each K-ABC achievement subtest.

The results of these analyses indicate that *both* processes bear important relationships to different areas of achievement. In addition, a few differential relationships can be noted. Both Expressive Vocabulary and Faces and Places are more highly related to simultaneous processing ability than to sequential ability (mean correlations of .51 vs. .30 for Expressive Vocabulary, and means of .46 vs. .32 for Faces and Places). These relationships seem sensible given the visual interpretation and integration required to identify the objects, places, and people pictured on these tasks.

The K-ABC Arithmetic subtest correlated about equally with sequential ($r = .50$) and simultaneous ($r = .48$) processing for ages 3 to 6 years, but simultaneous processing correlated much higher (.62 vs. .42) with arithmetic performance for 7 to 12½ year olds. This finding suggests that when school instruction in mathematics begins, simultaneous processing becomes more important for achievement. The nature of the K-ABC Arithmetic subtest may also provide some clues as to why the task is more related to simultaneous processing for older children. Early items on the Arithmetic subtest require counting, number identification, and naming shapes. Later items, on the other hand, require mathematical problem solving using addition, subtraction, multiplication, and division. This latter type of problem solving requires a child to mentally manipulate several numbers to determine the correct answer; the mental integration of numbers to solve a problem seems logically related to the concept of simultaneous processing.

Kaufman and Kamphaus (1984) further noted that the K-ABC Reading/ Decoding and Reading/Understanding subtests correlated more highly with sequential processing at ages 5 through 7, but for more experienced readers (ages 8 through 12½), both sequential and simultaneous processing correlated equally well with both reading tasks.

Are the Two Processes Hierarchical?

In the previous section, the results of factor analysis offer solid support for the existence of sequential and simultaneous factors at all ages covered by the K-ABC, providing empirical justification for the theoretical foundation on which

Table 3. Varimax-Rotated Factor Loadings of K-ABC Subtests by Age

	Subtest	Factor	2½	3	4	5	6	7	8	9	10	11	12	Mean Factor Loadings
1.	Magic Window	Seq.	17	17	30									21
		Sim.	80	62	47									63
2.	Face Recognition	Seq.	36	23	24									28
		Sim.	34	37	50									40
3.	Hand Movements	Seq.	60	57	62	26	47	39	35	34	37	41	35	43
		Sim.	12	19	25	51	33	32	44	47	43	38	56	36
4.	Gestalt Closure	Seq.	36	20	14	22	12	07	03	07	04	07	04	12
		Sim.	48	50	79	63	55	53	48	57	52	50	44	54
5.	Number Recall	Seq.	59	74	58	62	78	83	77	95	92	74	54	73
		Sim.	38	31	16	24	15	13	12	07	13	09	27	19
6.	Triangles	Seq.			36	21	17	22	13	17	18	25	26	22
		Sim.			47	74	75	71	67	78	69	73	70	69

#	Subtest													
7.	Word Order	Seq.			69	89	79	75	78	53	69	63	96	75
		Sim.			32	34	24	36	25	29	24	26	10	27
8.	Matrix Analogies	Seq.				32	30	25	23	28	23	41	36	30
		Sim.				54	45	42	67	59	62	58	70	57
9.	Spatial Memory	Seq.				30	27	26	22	16	27	36	09	24
		Sim.				68	63	54	52	71	54	56	58	60
10.	Photo Series	Seq.					25	36	26	20	22	17	36	26
		Sim.					76	67	66	67	75	66	63	69
	Percent of reliable variance	Seq.	26	25	27	26	27	28	23	23	26	24	27	
		Sim.	30	23	27	36	34	32	32	39	35	33	37	

Note. Decimal points are omitted from factor loadings. Percent of reliable variance was computed by dividing the rotated eigenvalue by the sum of the split-half reliability coefficients. Seq. = Sequential; Sim. = Simultaneous. Subtest 3 (Hand Movements), 5 (Number Recall), and 7 (Word Order) constitute the Sequential Processing Scale; all other subtests are on the Simultaneous Processing Scale.

675

the K-ABC's definition of intelligence rests. The data also give good support for the construct validity of the Achievement Scale at ages 4 through 12½. Correlations of factor scores on the two processing dimensions with the separate K-ABC achievement subtests reveal that both processes correlate well with performance on these acquired knowledge tasks, and each is particularly related to success on the school-related tasks of reading and arithmetic. These correlational analyses bear on the question of whether sequential and simultaneous processing are hierarchical in nature, but they do not unequivocally answer the question. The paragraphs that follow clarify this issue.

The K-ABC Mental Processing scales include seven tests of simultaneous processing and three tests of sequential processing. This 7:3 ratio, however, does not represent the proportion of subtests actually administered to a given child. The ratio of Simultaneous to Sequential subtests is actually 3:2 at ages 2½ and 3; 4:3 at ages 4 and 5; and 5:3 at ages 6 through 12½.

Some professionals have noted this disproportion in favor of simultaneous subtests and have hypothesized that simultaneous processing is perhaps more important than sequential processing. The stand of the K-ABC authors on this issue is consistent with that of Das, Kirby, and Jarman (1975, 1979), who have maintained that the two processing modes are nonhierarchical and that both processes are important for the successful performance of school tasks.

This disproportion exists for several reasons. First, the nature of the sequential subtests allows them to be administered to practically the entire age range of the K-ABC. In contrast, for the simultaneous scale, developmental changes in the processing demands of some tasks (such as Face Recognition), and the failure of a few skills to emerge until age 5 or 6 years (such as the time concept needed for Photo Series), made it necessary to include some simultaneous tasks only for preschool children and others for ages 5 and above (Kaufman, Kaufman, Kamphaus, & Naglieri, 1982).

Second, the disproportionate number of simultaneous subtests may also be due to the nature of the sequential and simultaneous constructs. Simultaneous processing appears to be more multifaceted. Das, Kirby, and Jarman (1979) used a variety of tasks to measure simultaneous-processing abilities including Wechsler's Block Design, Raven's Coloured Progressive Matrices, and design copying. Similarly, on the K-ABC simultaneous processing is spatial (Triangles), analogic (Matrix Analogies), and perceptual (Gestalt Closure) in nature. Sequential processing appears to be less multidimensional, as a variety of tasks researched in early stages of the development of the K-ABC did not add enough unique measurement to the Sequential Processing Scale.

A better way to assess whether or not the Sequential and Simultaneous Processing scales are hierarchical is to review data. Table 4 summarizes a vast amount of data presented in Chapter 4 of the *K-ABC Interpretive Manual* (Kaufman & Kaufman, 1983b) showing the correlation of the K-ABC intelligence scales with a variety of achievement measures in criterion-related validity studies, using individual and group measures of reading, mathematics, spelling, and other content areas as criteria.

Table 4. Correlations of K-ABC Mental Processing Scales with Various Criteria of Achievement

Criterion	r with Sequential Processing	r with Simultaneous Processing	r with Mental Processing Composite	Source of Data in K-ABC Interpretive Manual
Prediction of Future Achievement				
Woodcock-Johnson (preschool and knowledge clusters; N = 31)	.46	.54	.62	Table 4.22
Various School-Age Achievement Batteries[a]				
Reading (recognition and comprehension; N = 151)	.42	.37	.45	Table 4.22
Mathematics (N = 151)	.37	.46	.50	Table 4.22
Spelling (N = 106)	.40	.26	.36	Table 4.22
General information (N = 88)	.32	.34	.41	Table 4.22
Language (N = 63)	.46	.48	.54	Table 4.22
Composite (N = 151)	.45	.43	.52	Table 4.22
Individual Achievement Batteries (Concurrent)				
Woodcock Passage Comprehension Subtest (N = 592)	.53	.56	.63	Table 4.23

Table 4. (*Continued*)

Criterion	r with Sequential Processing	r with Simultaneous Processing	r with Mental Processing Composite	Source of Data in K-ABC Interpretive Manual
Prediction of Future Achievement				
Key Math written computation items (N = 544)	.34	.44	.47	Table 4.24
Wide-Range Achievement Test (WRAT)				
Reading (N = 114)	.46	.50	.55	Table 4.26
Arithmetic (N = 85)	.43	.54	.56	Table 4.26
Spelling (N = 85)	.35	.43	.44	Table 4.26
Key Math Diagnostic Arithmetic Test (N = 78)	.60	.56	.69	Table 4.26
Stanford Diagnostic Reading Test (N = 63)	.51	.43	.55	Table 4.26
Group Achievement Batteries (Concurrent)[b]				
Reading (N = 369)	.43	.43	.52	Table 4.27

Mathematics (N = 335)	.42	.50	.55	Table 4.27
Spelling (N = 148)	.36	.31	.39	Table 4.27
Language (N = 226)	.46	.44	.54	Table 4.27
Vocabulary (N = 291)	.37	.45	.50	Table 4.27
Work-study skills (N = 257)	.36	.43	.47	Table 4.27
Reference materials (N = 34)	.58	.58	.71	Table 4.27
Social studies (N = 34)	.65	.70	.83	Table 4.27
Science (N = 34)	.51	.55	.66	Table 4.27
Composite (N = 369)	.48	.50	.59	Table 4.27
Mean of All Coefficients in Table	.447	.468	.544	

Source. This table is adapted from a table presented by Kaufman (1983).

[a]Test batteries include Peabody Individual Achievement Test (PIAT), Iowa Tests of Basic Skills (ITBS), and California Achievement Test (CAT).

[b]Test batteries include Gates-MacGinitie Reading Tests, Science Research Associates Achievement Series (SRA), Stanford Achievement Test (SAT), ITBS, and CAT. Correlations with composite for the SRA battery were obtained by averaging the correlations for the separate achievement areas.

Whenever possible data are combined across studies and criterion measures to make the amount of data presented comprehensible and to obtain more stable values based on larger sample sizes. Correlations are not only presented between various achievement criteria and the Sequential and Simultaneous Processing scales, but they are also presented for the Mental Processing Composite to determine if a combination of the two processes bears a stronger relationship to achievement criteria than does either processing scale in isolation.

Overall, the Sequential and Simultaneous Processing scales correlated equally well with various achievement criteria. The average coefficient in Table 4 for the sequential scale is .45 and for the simultaneous scale .47, indicating that both processes are about equally important for achievement. In fact, the slight advantage for the simultaneous scale may merely be a reflection of its higher reliability. The mean coefficient for the Mental Processing Composite with achievement is .54, lending support to the notion that the two processes combined are more important for achievement than either sequential or simultaneous processing alone.

With regard to the various *reading* criteria included throughout Table 4, the average coefficients were .47 and .46 for the sequential and simultaneous scales, respectively. (Mental Processing Composite averaged .54 with criteria of reading decoding and comprehension.) For mathematics, the average coefficients show more of an advantage for the simultaneous scale (mean $r = .50$) than for the sequential scale (mean $r = .43$). In direct contrast, for the spelling measures shown in Table 4, sequential processing (mean $r = .37$) shows a slightly larger correlation with spelling achievement than does simultaneous processing (mean $r = .33$). Mental Processing Composite correlated .54 with arithmetic criteria and .40 with spelling criteria, again reinforcing the notion that both processes afford better prediction of school achievement than is obtainable by either process alone.

The Table 4 data, then, corroborate the data presented by Kaufman and Kamphaus (1984) indicating that sequential and simultaneous processing are both important for school performance. Although there are some trends showing an advantage for a particular process on various school tasks, the advantage seems to be merely a trend, not a distinct or overwhelming advantage. These data are consistent with the notions that school tasks are complex, requiring both processes for effective performance (Kaufman & Kaufman, 1983b), and that sequential and simultaneous processing bear a nonhierarchical relationship to each other (Das, Kirby, & Jarman, 1975, 1979).

Kamphaus and Naglieri (in preparation) assessed the relationship of sequential and simultaneous processing to achievement using an analysis of variance, as opposed to a correlational, approach. They performed several 2×2 analyses of variance (one for each achievement subtest with the exception of Expressive Vocabulary) using data from the K-ABC standardization sample. One grouping variable was the level of processing ability: high sequential and high simultaneous processing, with both scores at or above the 63rd percentile; and low sequential and low simultaneous processing, with both scores at or below the 37th percentile. The other grouping variable was the presence of a significant difference (a standard score difference of 12 points or more, $p < .05$) between the two processing scales (simultaneous > sequential or sequential > simultaneous). In this analysis a significant difference on the second variable (the simultaneous/sequential discrepancy) might be interpreted as indicative of one process being relatively more important for achievement in a particular area.

Kamphaus and Naglieri (in preparation) report that for all dependent variables those who performed well on both processing scales obtained significantly ($p < .05$) higher achievement standard scores than those who performed relatively poorly. This is hardly a surprising finding, but it does demonstrate again that sequential and simultaneous processing are important for school achievement.

With regard to the second variable (sequential > simultaneous or simultaneous > sequential) only two significant ($p < .05$) findings were obtained. Simultaneous processing was relatively more important for achievement on Faces and Places and Riddles. On the Faces and Places subtest the mean standard score for the simultaneous > sequential group was 98.6 and for the sequential > simultaneous group 95.2. On the Riddles subtest the means were 98.8 and 95.3 for the same groups. These findings are consistent with the findings of Kaufman and Kamphaus (1984) showing that these subtests correlated more highly with simultaneous than sequential factor scores for several age groups. Both tests apparently have obvious simultaneous components requiring the mental integration of stimuli to solve the items. The lack of a clear processing advantage for the K-ABC arithmetic or reading tasks is an important finding, as it supports once more the K-ABC authors' contention (Kaufman & Kaufman, 1983b) that achievement in school tasks such as these is complex, requiring both sequential- and simultaneous-processing skills.

The data reported by Kaufman and Kamphaus (1984) and Kamphaus and Naglieri (in preparation), and the data summarized in Table 4, support a nonhierarchical interpretation of sequential and simultaneous processing. Although a considerable amount of data is mounting to support a nonhierarchical relationship between the two processing types, that is not to say that one process may be relatively more important for a particular type of achievement for a certain age group. There are indications, as was cited earlier, of some developmental trends in the relationship of processing styles to achievement. Therefore, developmental research is needed to cross-validate and extend our knowledge of some of these trends.

One final issue regarding the K-ABC sequential/simultaneous processing dichotomy is the possibility that the scales are more appropriately explained by an alternate theoretical model, that is, Jensen's (1973) theory of Level I and Level II (memory-reasoning) abilities. A cursory glance at the K-ABC tasks, noting that all of the Sequential Processing subtests have a memory component, often elicits thoughts of Jensen's model. Evidence from a variety of researchers, however, suggests that using the Level I–Level II processing model as a template for the K-ABC processing scales is untenable.

Recent research results obtained by Jensen (1983) and Reynolds (1983) show that the K-ABC Sequential and Simultaneous Processing scales do not behave in accordance with predictions based on the Level I–Level II model, and they do not accord well with Jensen's "Spearman hypothesis." Research by Kaufman and Kamphaus (1984) also does not support the idea of interpreting the K-ABC scales as constructed from a memory-reasoning model.

Among other reasons why the K-ABC sequential scale is more than a memory scale is the fact that subtests with a clearcut memory component are also included on the Simultaneous Processing Scale: Face Recognition at the preschool ages and Spatial Memory at the school-age level. As evident from Table 3 these subtests have lower loadings on the sequential factor (Face Recognition mean = .28, Spatial Memory mean = .24) than on the simultaneous factor (Face Recognition mean = .40, Spatial Memory mean = .60).

One might ask, then, if the Sequential Processing Scale is nothing more than a sequential short-term recall scale. In this case data also argue against such a contention. Factor analysis of an earlier version of the K-ABC (Kaufman, Kaufman, Kamphaus, & Naglieri, 1982), a battery that included a larger number of tasks than the standardized version, revealed a robust sequential factor for all age groups in the sample and substantial loadings by a task called concept formation. The Concept Formation task is a logical classification task inspired by the work of Jerome Bruner that assesses problem solving and categorization without an obvious short-term memory component. In this same study, Bells, an adaptation of the sequential Knox Cubes memory test, loaded on the simultaneous factor for every age group.

Further evidence that the Sequential Processing Scale is more complex than sequential memory comes from data cited earlier showing that in the factor analyses of all K-ABC subtests, every school-age achievement subtest joined the sequential factor at one age group (Faces and Places) or at several age groups (Arithmetic, Riddles, Reading/Decoding, and Reading/Understanding). In the pattern of correlations between factor scores and achievement subtests, the sequential factor scores correlated as highly as simultaneous factor scores with different achievement subtests (such as Reading/Decoding and Reading/Understanding). Finally, the correlations of the processing scales with different achievement criteria given in Table 4 show that sequential processing is about as important as simultaneous processing for performance in reading, mathematics, and spelling. None of these findings is consistent with an interpretation of the Sequential Processing Scale as simple sequential rote memory.

Hence, although at first inspection one may wonder if the K-ABC Sequential Processing Scale is really just a memory scale, considerable evidence shows that such an interpretation is inappropriate. The Sequential Processing Scale appears to measure complex skills that are related to a number of achievement areas.

THE K-ABC AND PREDICTION

Another distinctive aspect of the K-ABC is the position of the test authors on the use of the K-ABC, or any other intelligence test for that matter, for prediction. For many psychologists, the only value of an intelligence test is its ability to predict future accomplishments. Evidence of this obsession with prediction was most apparent in the landmark *Larry P.* v. *Riles* case, where Judge Peckham decided the fate of intelligence tests primarily on the degree to which they were validated for the purpose for which they were used. The defined "purpose" of intelligence tests according to that testimony was the predictive validity of the WISC, WISC-R, and Stanford-Binet.

The view of the K-ABC authors is that psychologists have been too past or future oriented, with those focused on the past wanting to know the etiology of the child's current dilemmas (hereditary or environmental), and those concerned about the future wanting to know what is in store for the child next year. In fact, children are referred for problems they have *now* and therefore the psychologist should focus on the present problem and what can be done about it in the *present*. The K-ABC intelligence scales were not designed merely to predict the future, but to provide insight into the child's particular problem-solving abilities. It is the goal of the K-ABC user to alter the child's program of instruction to capitalize on problem-solving strengths and deemphasize or circumvent weaknesses. If the intervention is successful, then the consequence is an alteration of the predicted outcome. Children who are predicted to do poorly in school because of relatively low test scores will now perform well because the test results have been used directly to help teach them meaningful skills such as reading or spelling. The ironical outcome of successful intervention is thus to kill the prediction of "inevitable" failure!

Because of this stress on actively using test data, the *K-ABC Interpretive Manual* includes Chapter 7, entitled "Educational Translation." Here, the Kaufmans, in conjunction with coauthor Dr. Judy Gunnison, present a framework for designing educational interventions and give specific examples of how to teach certain reading, mathematics, and spelling skills using a sequential, simultaneous, or sequential *and* simultaneous emphasis. Some pilot-study data are also presented, showing promising results that support the use of the educational remediation strategies suggested in the K-ABC manual.

If one wishes to use a test merely for prediction, it would seem logical to give a test that is most related to a particular achievement area: a test of reading or reading readiness to predict future reading success; an arithmetic test to predict future achievement in mathematics; and so forth. For this reason, the K-ABC Achievement Scale is recommended for use in predicting future school achievement.

Data collected in six separate predictive validity studies support this advice (Kaufman & Kaufman, 1983b). These predictive validity studies, assessing prediction over 6 to 12 month intervals, show the Achievement Scale to correlate .67 to .89 (median = .77) with overall levels of achievement on various group and individually administered standardized achievement batteries (Kaufman & Kaufman, 1983b). The K-ABC Mental Processing Composite was found to be highly predictive of school achievement, but not as high as the Achievement Scale (coefficients of .29 to .65, median = .58). These values for the intelligence scales compare favorably to the results of numerous studies on the WPPSI and WISC-R cited in Sattler (1982). Data from eight predictive validity studies with the WPPSI (Sattler, 1982; White & Jacobs, 1979) reveal that the Full Scale IQ correlated from the middle .30s to the middle .60s (median = .50) with several criteria of achievement. Similarly, several predictive and concurrent validity studies using the WISC-R showed correlations from the middle .50s to the middle .60s (median = .59) between the Full Scale IQ and a variety of measures of achievement (Sattler, 1982). One can conclude from these data that the Mental Processing Composite predicts school achievement about as well as Wechsler's Full Scale IQ, but that both scores are less efficient predictors than the K-ABC Achievement Scale standard score.

In summary, the K-ABC is an efficient predictor of future school performance. It is the job of the K-ABC user, however, to invalidate the frequently pessimistic prediction by altering the instructional program to meet best the processing profiles of children. Rather than train a child's processing weakness, the *K-ABC Interpretive Manual* (Kaufman & Kaufman, 1983b) advises psychologists to pursue curriculum goals, that is, to teach the actual skills via methodologies that take advantage of the child's processing strengths. Using this model, the K-ABC focuses on the present, and on active intervention, rather than on the past or future, or on passivity.

THE K-ABC AND CULTURAL MINORITIES

Any new intelligence test must be more sensitive to the needs of minority-group children. As discussed earlier, the cultural composition of the population has changed dramatically since the 1970 census, with the population of minority-group children nearly doubling. The K-ABC standardization sample, based on 1980 census data, reflects the increase in minority children in the United States; however, proportional representation of blacks and Hispanics is not enough. In addition, several steps were taken during the development of the K-ABC in order to make it maximally useful for minorities.

First, the concept of sample and teaching items, as mentioned in the overview, make the K-ABC more applicable to minority-group children. These items on the Mental Processing Scale give the examiner substantial opportunity to use gestures, rewording of instructions, physical prompts, or a language other than English to ensure that the minority child understands the task demands. If the child understands the task then the examiner is more likely to be assessing intelligence rather than acculturation. The use of a language other than English extends to the point that on all items a correct response given in a non-English language is given credit. Again, the task is to assess mental-processing proficiency (that is, intelligence), not English language fluency.

In addition to the inclusion of sample and teaching items, both rational and statistical techniques were used to remove culturally biased items from the K-ABC. The first procedure was a judgmental review of the items by two black educators and two Hispanic educators. Interestingly, these reviewers identified a very small number of biased items relative to the number identified by statistical procedures. An example of an item identified by these reviewers was the vacuum cleaner on the Gestalt Closure subtest. (The Puerto Rican reviewer said that many inner-city children were not aware of such devices.) The statistical procedures, as indicated, were much more sensitive to bias than the judgmental bias reviews. Many items were eliminated, following analysis of data from a national tryout (prior to standardization), based on a variant of the procedure described by Angoff and Ford (1973). By eliminating items biased against blacks and Hispanics (and against whites, for that matter), the K-ABC addresses the question asked by Judge Peckham in the *Larry P.* v. *Riles* case: why is it that sex-biased items were removed from later editions of the Binet and yet no attempt has been made to remove racially biased items from intelligence tests?

The sample and teaching items, limited oral instructions for the subtests, reduced dependency on elaborate verbalization for responses, acceptance of foreign language responses, and elimination of biased items are probably in part responsible for the finding of smaller standard score differences between white and minority-group children on the K-ABC than have previously been reported for IQ tests. For the total sample of 2½ to 12½ year olds, white children ($N = 1569$) averaged 102 on the Mental Processing Composite as opposed to 95 for black children ($N = 807$). This difference of 7 points is about half the 16-point difference found for the WISC-R Full Scale IQ for the standardization sample (Kaufman & Doppelt, 1976). Global IQs yielded by numerous intelligence tests, not just the WISC-R, have consistently produced a full standard deviation difference between blacks and whites. Similarly, Hispanic children ($N = 160$) earned a mean Mental Processing Composite of 99 on the K-ABC, which is only 3 points below the mean obtained for whites. In contrast, Mercer (1979) found an 11-point white-Hispanic discrepancy using the WISC-R Full Scale IQ.

THE K-ABC AND GIFTEDNESS

Kaufman (1984) discusses in detail the properties of the K-ABC in relation to the identification of intellectually gifted children. The K-ABC has received much attention for the characteristics that render it potentially useful for the diagnosis and placement of the mentally retarded and learning disabled. This use has been a common topic of discussion with the K-ABC, even though the authors (Kaufman & Kaufman, 1983b) feel that the test is focused toward active intervention (see previous section on predictive validity) as opposed to passive placement. Relatively less discussion has been directed toward the use of K-ABC with the gifted, a group for which the K-ABC has some interesting applications.

First, gifted and talented children were systematically included in the K-ABC standardization sample. As noted earlier, exceptional children, including gifted, are not included in the standardization samples for current tests of intelligence. Data from the U.S. Office of Civil Rights indicate that 1.9% of school-age children are enrolled in programs for the gifted and talented. The K-ABC standardization sample approximates this figure by having 1.5% of the standardization sample comprised of children who are enrolled in school programs for the gifted; other exceptional groups such as emotionally disturbed and mentally retarded are also proportionally represented in the sample. Thus the K-ABC sample comes closer than other tests in truly representing children living in the United States, and it specifically includes those youngsters who are most likely to be referred for evaluation on an intelligence test.

Subtests for the Mental Processing scales were generally selected for their ability to assess high-level integrated problem-solving skills, not to serve as "pure" measures of sequential or simultaneous processing. This was done because of the belief that high levels of intellectual functioning are reflected by the ability to solve complex, multifaceted problems. Gestalt Closure is the only simultaneous task and Number Recall the only sequential task that is a relatively "pure" measure of the two problem-solving styles. Excluding these two subtests, all other K-ABC tasks on the mental-processing and achievement portion of the K-ABC require that a child demonstrate the ability to integrate both processes effectively, using auditory and visual modalities, and verbal and nonverbal skills. Simultaneous processing tasks such as Triangles (constructing designs to match a model by using as many as nine triangles) and Matrix Analogies (solving 2×2 abstract visual analogies) require high-level problem-solving/reasoning skills. On the Sequential Scale, Word Order (recalling the correct series of words with the addition of a color interference task on later items) taps a child's ability to change or adapt problem-solving strategies in the middle of the task. On the Achievement Scale, Riddles (combining several attributes to identify a concept) is a complex task assessing verbal fund of information and a child's ability to see relationships between verbal concepts; it also demands *simultaneous* integration of stimuli that are presented sequentially.

K-ABC items were also selected to challenge the gifted child. Clearly items that are very difficult for a particular age group do not contribute a great deal to the assessment of the vast majority of children in that age range. On the K-ABC, however, very hard items (and easy items for retarded children) were retained to challenge the precocious child and gifted preadolescent. Difficult items such as Helen Keller and Robert E. Lee were retained on the Faces and Places subtest, and incomplete drawings of a teapot and mountain climber on the Gestalt Closure subtest challenge adults as well as children.

Generally, it appears that the K-ABC possesses adequate "top" for gifted children. If one considers the upper 2% of children as one criterion for determining intellectual giftedness, then scaled scores of 16 and above and standard scores of 130 and above are needed to identify potentially gifted children. Using these criteria, the mental-processing subtests demonstrate adequate difficulty from ages 2½ through 10½. At age 11½, however, Triangles, Photo Series, and Matrix Analogies only yield maximum scaled scores of 15; at age 12½, these three subtests, which lack adequate difficulty for gifted youngsters, are joined by Spatial Memory. Even though a few subtests lack difficulty at ages 11½ and 12½, the Mental Processing Composite standard score possesses adequate difficulty at all ages. The highest Mental Processing Composite obtainable at most ages is 160, and even at age 12½ it only dips to a maximum standard score of

151. The K-ABC achievement subtests also show adequate difficulty over most of the K-ABC age range. For school-age children as old as 10 years, 9 months, scores of 132 and above are obtainable on four subtests, with only Arithmetic falling below 130 (a maximum of 127 at age 10½). The Achievement Scale standard score shows less ability than the Mental Processing Composite to discriminate among highly gifted youngsters in the 11–12½ year age range, yielding maximum standard scores in the mid 130s.

Another important feature for clinical testing of gifted children is the flexible nature of the K-ABC "stopping points." On the K-ABC a set of items for each subtest is designated for children in each chronological age group. Typically, examiners stop testing after reaching the last item in this set. For the child who passes all items in the last set of items designated for a particular age group, however, the examiner must continue testing beyond the ordinary stopping point until the child misses one item. Because of this rule examiners are able to "test the limits" for highly intelligent children (except those at the upper end of the K-ABC age range).

Another important administration and scoring option for preschoolers and kindergarten youngsters is the out-of-level norms for ages 4 years, 6 months through 5 years, 11 months. Although both 4 and 5 year olds are administered 11 subtests, there are changes in the subtests that comprise the Simultaneous Processing and Achievement Scales. Magic Window, Face Recognition, and Expressive Vocabulary are only administered to 4 year olds; these subtests are replaced by Matrix Analogies, Spatial Memory, and Reading/Decoding for children ages 5 years and above. The out-of-level norms permit the examiner to give the 4-year-old level of the K-ABC to a retarded 5 year old, or to give the 5-year level to a gifted 4½-year old. These norms are particularly applicable for the 4½ year old child being evaluated for a gifted program, because they allow the examiner to challenge this child with subtests that are usually designated only for older children. By administering the subtests intended for 5 year olds, examiners get to evaluate the young child's performance on a novel simultaneous task with a memory component (Spatial Memory), a task of spatial abstract reasoning (Matrix Analogies), and a subtest that measures letter and word reading skills (Reading/Decoding).

In addition to the properties of the K-ABC just mentioned, the theoretical foundation of the test is, according to Kaufman (1984, p. 84), a very important feature of the K-ABC for gifted assessment. As he notes:

> The theoretical foundation of the K-ABC, which is rooted in neuropsychology and cognitive psychology, provides an additional rationale for its use with gifted children. When we attempt to identify a population that excels in a trait, we need to have a secure understanding of the constructs that underlie that trait. For gifted children, it is important to know precisely what an intelligence test measures, and the basis for defining a given set of tasks as a measure of mental ability, before concluding that those who score at the upper extreme are gifted intellectually.

> Neither of the two most popularly used individual IQ tests, the WISC-R or Stanford-Binet, is well founded in theory. Alfred Binet selected tasks for different age

levels of his intelligence test in a fairly arbitrary manner; indeed, one of the main goals in his task selection process was to identify children at the *low* end of the spectrum—those who were likely to have difficulty in school. David Wechsler combined two separate scales to form his intelligence test, one from the Binet tradition (Verbal), the other having its origins in World War I (Performance). To determine which recent immigrants and others with limited proficiency in English were smart enough to serve in the Armed Forces, World War I psychologists developed a series of nonverbal tests. Wechsler adopted the best of these tasks for his Wechsler-Bellevue Performance Scale, and they are retained in the present-day WISC-R and WAIS-R. Whereas research with the Stanford-Binet and WISC-R has shown the practical utility of these instruments for gifted assessment, it is nevertheless true that their component tasks were developed not from systematic theories of intelligence, but from attempts to determine whether children were bright enough to perform adequately within the mainstream of conventional education, or whether adults possessed the minimal skills to serve their country. The K-ABC, derived from theories of children's and adult's intellectual processing of information, would seem to form a more solid and defensible basis of the intelligence of individuals at all ranges of ability than do the existing tests that have conventionally been used for identifying gifted children.

As is reported in the *K-ABC Interpretive Manual* (Kaufman & Kaufman, 1983b), two prepublication studies were conducted with gifted children by independent researchers. Barry, Klanderman, and Stipe administered the K-ABC and Stanford-Binet to a group of children ($N = 50$) referred for possible gifted placement. Mealor, Livesay, and Finn administered the K-ABC to a group of previously identified gifted children ($N = 40$). The gifted referrals achieved a mean Mental Processing Composite of 130.5 and Stanford-Binet IQ of 137.3, demonstrating their superior intelligence on both measures. The higher Binet IQs accord well with research showing the Binet to yield higher scores than are yielded by tests such as the McCarthy Scales and WISC-R. Perhaps most importantly, Barry (1983), in a subsequent analysis of the 50 referrals, compared the overall K-ABC intelligence scores of the 35 children who qualified for gifted placement (a Binet IQ of 130 or above) with the scores earned by the 15 children who did not. The children who qualified for the program earned an average Mental Processing Composite of 135.3, whereas the mean global score for the group that did not qualify was 124. This large discrepancy between the qualifiers and nonqualifiers argues for the use of the K-ABC in making placement decisions for gifted children.

In the Mealor, Livesay, and Finn study, the identified gifted children achieved a mean Mental Processing Composite of 123.1, demonstrating, as did the first group, a high level of intellectual ability. Interestingly, this group scored 5½ points *lower* on the Sequential Scale, whereas the gifted referrals scored 5½ points *higher* on the Sequential Scale. Within the Simultaneous Scale both groups earned almost identical scores on all five subtests, exhibiting particular strengths on reasoning tasks such as Triangles and Matrix Analogies. Both groups also performed well on Riddles, a verbal reasoning task on the Achievement Scale. Apparently, reasoning skills are strong for these children regardless of modality.

These two studies with gifted youngsters suggest stable patterns of performance for highly intelligent children on verbal and spatial-reasoning tasks and less stable performance on sequential-processing tasks. The most startling difference on the Sequential Scale was on the Number Recall task, where the referral group exceeded the performance of the gifted group by *3* scaled score points, a full standard deviation discrepancy. Further studies are certainly needed to delineate the nature of the simultaneous/sequential profile for highly intelligent children.

In summary, the K-ABC has frequently been discussed in terms of its usefulness for making special-education placement decisions when children are referred for a problem. Relatively less discussion has occurred regarding the use of the K-ABC for gifted children, yet there are properties of the K-ABC that make it well suited for use with gifted children.

ILLUSTRATIVE CASE REPORT

Several topics pertaining to the K-ABC have been touched on in this chapter, but these topics just scratch the surface of areas of interest that are covered in the test manuals, that are rapidly appearing in professional journals, and that have been debated at national and state conventions. Rather than try to summarize the topics presented in this chapter, or to reach conclusions prematurely (before clinicians and researchers have had the years of experience with the K-ABC that facilitate the true understanding of a new instrument), we prefer to synthesize information on the K-ABC by ending the chapter with an illustrative case report based on an actual assessment of a child referred for evaluation.

Name: Kevin J.
Date of Birth: 5/17/75
Chronological Age: 7 yrs., 11 mos.

Date of Evaluation: 4/10/83
Grade Level: 2.8

K-ABC Profile

Global Scale Standard Scores

Sequential Processing	89 ± 9	Sequential < Simultaneous ($p < .01$)
Simultaneous Processing	117 ± 7	Sequential < Achievement ($p < .01$)
Mental Processing Composite	106 ± 7	MPC < Achievement ($p < .01$)
Achievement	123 ± 4	

Achievement Standard Scores

Faces and Places	136 ± 11	Strength
Arithmetic	95 ± 11	Weakness
Riddles	129 ± 9	
Reading/Decoding	116 ± 6	
Reading/Understanding	120 ± 6	

Mental Processing Scaled Scores

Sequential Processing

Hand Movements	12	
Number Recall	6	Weakness
Word Order	7	Weakness

Simultaneous Processing

Gestalt Closure	16	Strength
Triangles	10	
Matrix Analogies	8	Weakness
Spatial Memory	15	Strength
Photo Series	13	

Background and Referral Information

Kevin is currently in the second grade at a private school, where his teacher states that he has difficulties maintaining his train of thought. He is described by her as "drifting off" and engaging in self-talk and other fantasy activities. His learning has been inconsistent this year, progressing very well in some areas and very poorly in others. After a very slow start, Kevin has improved dramatically in his reading skills since January of this academic year when a phonics approach was abandoned in favor of a method that focused on letter and word configurations. His speech is frequently fragmented; his teacher has worked with Kevin in an experience-based language development program and reports improvement.

After a Caesarean breech birth, Kevin was treated in the hospital for jaundice. A subsequently healthy child, Kevin's developmental milestones appeared normal, although his language did not progress adequately. He attended a special education preschool program following a psychological evaluation noting this language and other developmental delays; during afternoons he attended a regular nursery school. After Kevin completed regular kindergarten, Mrs. J. rejected the school's recommendation that Kevin be placed in a highly structured special education setting for the purpose of modifying the self-stimulation behavior (e.g., flapping of arms) and short attention span which characterized his classroom behavior. At this point (8-80) a private evaluation at a hospital revealed average intelligence (Stanford-Binet IQ of 101, results that were not considered indicative of Kevin's true potential) along with a diagnosis of "neurophysiological immaturity characterized by some developmental delays." Kevin's great inconsistencies in his ability to use words to convey information were noted, as were his weaknesses in the visual-motor domain and his very poor attention span.

Mrs. J. currently describes Kevin as having "skewed interests and abilities." She states that he has difficulty learning and remembering arithmetic facts, and that he experiences trouble finding the right words to express his thoughts. On the other hand, Kevin can remember visual-spatial facts easily (e.g., where he put something), and has indicated skills in music. Behaviorally, Mrs. J. claims that Kevin daydreams a great deal, and still engages in twitching movements. She states that he interacts appropriately with his 11-year-old sister at home.

Four months ago Kevin was administered the WISC-R and McCarthy Scales of Children's Abilities by a qualified examiner as part of a research study at his school, and these results are discussed in this report.

Appearance and Behavioral Characteristics

Kevin is a handsome, well-built boy of almost 8 who was friendly and cooperative throughout the evaluation session. He offered a steady flow of spontaneous talk, including reading any signs passed in the hallways while confidently walking to the testing room. There were a couple of such reading errors noted, including his reading of a poem he had just written with "eyebrows" substituted for the actual words "brown eyes." This reversal is indicative of other verbal sequencing errors that Kevin made. On a task where he was repeating a series of unrelated numbers spoken by the examiner, Kevin reversed numbers or forgot the entire stimulus set. Other indications of a language difficulty ran throughout the course of the evaluation and were quite consistent. Kevin had trouble retrieving specific words or labels that were necessary for him to communicate adequately the information that he wanted to convey to the examiner. Thus he frequently made these statements: "I can't explain"; "I forgot the word." On a task which required him to solve verbal riddles, Kevin grew frustrated and pounded the sides of his head with his fists in a vain effort to remember the words he needed to solve the problems. Other times he employed rather extensive circumlocution, where he "talked around" the subject, hoping to describe in many different words the specific one he couldn't remember. During the verbal/auditory tasks (especially those involving quantitative concepts or numerical memory) Kevin whispered under his breath the verbal stimuli presented by the examiner in obvious attempts to better store the information, or asked directly for questions to be repeated. On longer verbal items he appeared to have lost the overall meaning and inquired "What do you mean?" or "What did you say again?" This difficulty appeared most acute when Kevin was responding to structured verbal questioning and was only rarely evident when he was talking spontaneously about topics of his own choice. Unstructured tasks (such as the informal interview during rapport making) also produced optimum expressive language skills. It appears, therefore, that Kevin is less impaired verbally when he is "calling the shots" and is free to direct the course and content of communication. A specific example of this behavior was evident when he added a revealing comment after correctly identifying a picture of the Grand Canyon: "It's as deep as a mountain is high."

Kevin was impulsive in his problem solving, spewing forth instant decisions which frequently led to inaccurate responses that he then corrected after he received the visual feedback. His impulsivity was most pronounced when he was faced with an array of stimuli, as when arranging photographs to depict an event or selecting the best response to a visual analogy. Comments indicating great confidence (e.g., "I can do it, I'm doing my best") occurred on several nonverbal tasks. Most of his comments, however, underscored both behavioral immaturity and his vivid fantasy life.

The blend of impulsivity, immaturity, and some loose associative thinking was most dramatic while Kevin was copying a set of abstract designs on blank paper. He talked to his drawings in animated voice, virtually bringing them to life. The abstract geometric forms were turned into concrete objects in Kevin's mind, and he proceeded to call them various objects while "playing" with them as if the two-dimensional drawings were three-dimensional objects. For example, he attempted to "pick up" a drawing he called a "sandwich." He giggled loudly and used sweeping extended arm movements, becoming increasingly excited by the stimuli he was busy producing. The drawings were rapidly made, with two dominant themes: PacMan (the electronic video game) devouring the abstract designs, and ghosts. Kevin uttered many strange slogans while feverishly drawing, such as "kill him in the moustache." He drew a birdlike creature about which he rambled "A chicken—no, it's not a chicken cacciatore either, it's a pledge allegience to the flag." He then spontaneously drew a primitive stick figure ("Here's Harry—he'll show you"), whom he called dumb and ugly (using comic strip technique to indicate Harry saying "I'm Dumm").

Tests Administered

Kaufman Assessment Battery for Children (K-ABC)
Bender-Gestalt Visual-Motor Test
Informal Interview

Test Results and Interpretation

Kevin was given the K-ABC, a test of intelligence and achievement that defines intelligence as the ability to solve unfamiliar problems and that attempts to minimize the roles of language and acquired factual knowledge on the child's intelligence scores. the K-ABC is based on theories of brain functioning, and focuses on whether the child processes information (solves problems) better either *sequentially* (where the child handles stimuli serially, bit by bit, in a stepwise, temporal manner) or *simultaneously* (where the child handles many stimuli at once and integrates them, often spatially, to come up with a solution).

Kevin earned a Mental Processing Composite of 106 ± 7 (90% confidence) on the Kaufman Assessment Battery for Children (K-ABC), classifying his overall intelligence as Average and ranking him at the 66th percentile when compared to other 7 years olds. However, this global score is of little meaning when one examines his separate performance in the two types of problem-solving skills assessed by the K-ABC. Kevin earned a standard score of 117 ± 7 (Above Average, 87th percentile) on the Simultaneous Processing Scale, which is strikingly higher than his Below Average score of 89 ± 9 (23rd percentile) on the Sequential Processing Scale. Thus he is quite adept at processing information holistically, that is, integrating many stimuli at once to solve new problems, but has much less well-developed skills at mentally processing a series of stimuli one stimulus at a time in stepwise or systematic fashion. Kevin's 28-point superiority in favor of Simultaneous Processing is not only highly significant, in a statistical sense, but it is also unusual; differences of 28 points or more occurred less than 10% of the time in the representative normative population of children.

Kevin earned an Achievement standard score of 123 ± 4, indicating Well Above Average success in tasks heavily dependent on acquired factual knowledge and applied, school-related skills. He performed better than 94% of children his age on this scale, and the chances are 9 out of 10 that his true Achievement standard score is in the range 119–127. Kevin scored significantly higher on the Achievement Scale than on either the Mental Processing Composite or Sequential Processing Scale, although his level of achievement was commensurate with his Above Average score on the Simultaneous Processing Scale. Thus Kevin has achieved better than one might predict from his overall intelligence score or from his sequential problem-solving skills, suggesting that he has been able to utilize effectively his excellent simultaneous processing abilities and apply them to the acquisition of facts and skills such as reading. This hypothesis is given support by Kevin's pattern of scores on the separate achievement subtests: He excelled at the tasks most dependent on simultaneous processing for success (99th percentile in identifying famous people and places; 97th percentile in solving verbal riddles, requiring integration of the separate attributes of a concept), but had a noteworthy weakness (37th percentile) on an arithmetic subtest that demands good sequential processing for high quality performance.

Kevin's profile on the Mental Processing subtests was also revealing. He had exceptional strengths on two Simultaneous Processing subtests, one requiring the identification of partially completed inkblot drawings (98th percentile), and the other demanding the recall of the location of objects placed randomly on a page (95th percentile). These assets are offset by a significant weakness (25th percentile) on a Simultaneous Processing test of abstract analogies, and performance below his own average in construction of abstract designs. Evidently, Kevin is most outstanding when solving simultaneous problems that employ concrete, meaningful stimuli (he also did rather well on a Simultaneous Processing subtest requiring him to arrange photographs in the correct order to depict an event), but has difficulty when the problems utilize abstract stimuli.

Not surprisingly, Kevin's most dramatic weaknesses (9th–16th percentile) reflected his global deficiency in Sequential Processing; he performed poorly in repeating digits, and also in pointing to pictures of objects in the same order that they were named by the examiner—sometimes with an intervening "interference" task (naming colors). Kevin performed adequately on the one sequential task that also can be solved in a more simultaneous fashion by school-age children (copying a series of hand movements performed by the examiner), suggesting once again that Kevin is able to spontaneously use his excellent simultaneous skills to good advantage in learning situations. His success on this particular sequential task, as well as his performance on the reading subtests (about 90th percentile in both decoding and comprehension), which require an integration of *both* processes, implies that he may be able to compensate well for his sequential weakness by calling on his better-developed simultaneous strategies.

Kevin's total K-ABC profile, both the intelligence and achievement portions, presents a unified picture of a child with a high simultaneous–low sequential pattern who is also much better able to handle meaningful than abstract stimuli. These results are corroborated by scores on other tests. On the Bender-Gestalt, administered with the K-ABC, Kevin earned a Koppitz error score of 10, which translates to a visual-motor development standard score of only 71. This low level of ability in copying designs reinforces Kevin's difficulties with abstract stimuli.

In addition, WISC-R scores from four months earlier (V-IQ = 111, P-IQ = 104, FS-IQ = 108) reinforce the present K-ABC results. High simultaneous–low sequential is supported by much better performance on the Perceptual Organization factor (75th percentile) than on the Freedom from Distractibility (also known as Sequential) factor (16th percentile). Facility with meaningful versus abstract stimuli was also quite evident from the profile: excellent success on Picture Completion and Picture Arrangement (84th percentile) when compared with Block Design and Coding (25th percentile). Although Kevin's overall performance on the WISC-R and K-ABC is quite comparable, the consistency of his three WISC-R IQs masks the huge Simultaneous-Sequential discrepancy that is immediately evidenced from his global scale profile on the K-ABC, and that can be teased out of the fluctuations in his WISC-R subtest profile.

The McCarthy Scales of Children's Abilities was administered to Kevin at the same time as the WISC-R. His overall General Cognitive Index of 91 clearly underestimates his mental functioning on both the WISC-R and K-ABC, but the pattern of subtest scores on the McCarthy is quite consistent with the hypotheses discussed above. Strengths in Word Knowledge and Opposite Analogies support Kevin's high level of achievement; a strength in Puzzle Solving coupled with a weakness in Draw-A-Design demonstrates his excellent simultaneous processing with meaningful—but not abstract—stimuli; and striking weaknesses in repeating series of words and numbers (5-year level) show his comparatively poor sequential processing. Importantly, Kevin did well on those sequential memory tasks which lend themselves to correct solution by good holistic, visual-spatial (simultaneous) processing: repeating the main ideas of a story, reversing digits, and copying taps on a xylophone. As with the K-ABC results, these findings suggest that Kevin can, and does, employ his simultaneous strengths to facilitate and compensate for his weaker sequential abilities.

Whereas no projective or personality measures were administered to Kevin at this time, the Bender-Gestalt may be evaluated for signs of emotional insta- bility. When Kevin's Bender-Gestalt productions were evaluated for emotional indicators, four were revealed: confused order, increasing size, large size, and expansion. Confused order, or no logical sequence of placement of drawings on the paper, indicates poor planning skills. This finding is not surprising due to the impulsive style of action Kevin demonstrated, as well as his sequential processing weakness. The other three indicators were all aspects of low frustration tolerance and a tendency to act out. All of these aspects of personality or attitude are associated with emotional maladjustment. Reinforcing these measurable signs was the flow of chatter mentioned earlier, as Kevin loudly rambled on about disjointed topics which stimulated and excited him. The overall effect was of observing one deeply engaged in a fantasy world, paying little or no heed to the fact that another human being was present.

Discussion and Recommendations

As indicated by all the many test results, Kevin has a significant problem dealing with abstract symbols, whether they be designs or numbers or concepts. His abstract versus concrete discrepancy is pervasive, and Kevin must be taught with meaningful stimuli in order for him to understand new information and absorb or apply it. Since Kevin's school-related skills, interests, and store of acquired knowledge are unevenly developed, the test results have important implications for any remedial programs that may be planned to facilitate learning. Attempts must be made to stimulate Kevin's interests in some of the *school- related* content that is appropriate curriculum for a child his grade level. This suggestion does *not* mean to discourage his unusually deep current interests; it means rather to work at motivating him to be of prime receptiveness for topics covered in his daily classes. Having him mentally set to explore areas which he can feel are already meaningful to him will increase the likelihood that Kevin will attend well to new and perhaps difficult stimuli. This approach may require careful planning and gradual exposure to the more abstract subjects.

Kevin has simultaneous processing strengths which permit him to excel in visuospatial nonverbal reasoning tasks and those where he can solve problems holistically. However, the visual perceptual difficulties that appeared on the several drawing measures indicate that his real intellectual functioning might even be *superior* to the level that he actually achieved. On the other hand, his weaknesses in sequential processing (dealing with information in a bit-by-bit, successive fashion) may be more severe than measured here because of his ability to compensate for his deficit. Nevertheless, most important to note is the fact that Kevin is learning, and his acquired fund of information is vast.

Any diagnosis at this time is an inferred one at best. Kevin appears to have minor neurological impairment which might account for his language difficulties (a mild dysnomia), the visual-motor perceptual delay when dealing with abstract stimuli, as well as the profile of extreme strengths and weaknesses on the K-ABC and other instruments.

Kevin needs to be taught by methods that call on his simultaneous processing integrities and his excellent ability to deal with meaningful stimuli. These strengths are evident in his behavior at home (his mother's reports of Kevin's interest in music and his good visual-spatial memory) and school (his teacher's indication of improvement in language skills using an experience-based program). Similarly, Kevin's sequential processing weaknesses are evident in his school-work: poor ability to remember arithmetic facts, sudden improvement in reading after departing from a purely phonics approach, reversals in reading, fragmented speech, difficulties maintaining his train of thought.

The success Kevin has had when switched to a more simultaneous approach for learning to read (a method stressing letter and word configurations) suggests that emphasizing Kevin's simultaneous strengths should prove successful in teaching him new material. This likelihood is supported by his spontaneous ability to compensate for his sequential weaknesses by utilizing a simultaneous problem-solving strategy to solve tasks such as copying an examiner's hand movements, copying taps on a xylophone, or repeating a story. Further support is given by his ability to correct many of his errors that are due to impulsive behavior by relying on the visual-spatial feedback that comes from examination of his completed product (as when ordering photographs).

Kevin should be administered a diagnostic arithmetic test to determine the specific content and process areas requiring remediation. Based on the results of this educational testing, Kevin should be taught each skill in a way that deemphasizes his sequential difficulties and focuses instead on his simultaneous problem-solving capacities and his ability to deal with meaningful stimuli. Specific suggestions for teaching mathematics (as well as reading and spelling) are provided in Chapter 7 of the *K-ABC Interpretive Manual* and can be improvised by using available curriculum materials; these suggestions will be communicated to Kevin's teacher after the precise trouble spots are identified. For example, memory for symbols and basic facts can be taught with a simultaneous emphasis by using flashcards that have problems on one side and the answer on the other, and that utilize meaningful stimuli (e.g., pictures of cherries) along with the number.

Since reading comprehension, particularly identifying the meaning of a paragraph or the main topic of a story, is quite dependent on simultaneous processing, several of the remedial suggestions presented in the *K-ABC Interpretive Manual* might be used as enrichment materials for Kevin. At about age 8, Kevin is ready for more advanced reading experiences; his continued growth in reading comprehension may be enhanced by relying on his excellent simultaneous skills. Hence Kevin's teacher might want to encourage him to visualize what he is reading and to draw a picture of what he has read, or to order a series of pictures to match the sequence of ideas presented in a story. One of these procedures, perhaps mental imagery, should be implemented and evaluated a couple of months later to determine if it is an effective enrichment activity. Similarly, the procedures suggested for remediating Kevin's mathematics difficulties need to be monitored to determine their effectiveness. If Kevin's progress is limited, then another set of procedures should be implemented, or modifications made in the existing procedures, until adequate progress in mathematics is made.

Concerning Kevin's self-stimulating fantasy life, one method of consideration might be to make Kevin "aware" of these times with a gentle reminder of what is "appropriate" behavior when in the presence of others or in social situations. Hopefully, he will soon begin to make this distinction for himself, especially if illustrations are used that are meaningful to him. There is the definite possibility that his emotional immaturity is another manifestation of the inferred minor neurological impairment, and perhaps will be outgrown.

REFERENCES

Angoff, W. H., & Ford, S. F. (1973). Item-race interaction on a test of scholastic aptitude. *Journal of Educational Measurement, 10,* 95–106.

Barry, B. J. (1983, April). *Validity study of the Kaufman Assessment Battery for Children compared to the Stanford-Binet, Form L-M, in the identification of gifted nine- and ten-year-olds.* Unpublished Master's Thesis, National College of Education.

Bogen, J. E. (1969). The other side of the brain: Parts I, II and III. *Bulletin of the Los Angeles Neurological Society, 34,* 73–105; 135–162; 191–203.

Das, J. P., Kirby, J., & Jarman, R. F. (1975). Simultaneous and successive syntheses: An alternative model for cognitive abilities. *Psychological Bulletin, 82,* 87–103.

Das, J. P., Kirby, J., & Jarman, R. F. (1979). *Simultaneous and successive cognitive processes.* New York: Academic Press.

Horn, J. L., & Cattell, R. B. (1966). Refinement and test of theory of fluid and crystallized intelligence. *Journal of Educational Psychology, 57,* 253–270.

Jensen, A. R. (1973). Level I and level II abilities in three ethnic groups. *American Educational Research Journal, 10,* 263–276.

Jensen, A. R. (1983, August). *Nature of the black-white differences on various psychometric tests.* Paper presented at the meeting of the American Psychological Association, Anaheim.

Kamphaus, R. W., & Naglieri, J. A. (in preparation). The relationship of simultaneous and successive processing to achievement: A cross-validation of Das.

Kaufman, A. S. (1978). The importance of basic concepts in the individual assessment of preschool children. *Journal of School Psychology, 16,* 207–211.

Kaufman, A. S. (1983). Some questions and answers about the Kaufman Assessment Battery for Children (K-ABC). *Journal of Psychoeducational Assessment, 1,* 205–218.

Kaufman, A. S. (1984). K-ABC and giftedness. *The Roeper Review, 7,* 83–88.

Kaufman, A. S., & Doppelt, J. E. (1976). Analysis of WISC-R standardization data in terms of the stratification variables. *Child Development, 47,* 165–171.

Kaufman, A. S., & Kamphaus, R. W. (1984). Factor analysis of the Kaufman Assessment Battery for Children (K-ABC) for ages 2-½ through 12-½ years. *Journal of Educational Psychology, 76,* 623–637.

Kaufman, A. S., & Kaufman, N. L. (1983a). *K-ABC administration and scoring manual.* Circle Pines, MN: American Guidance Service.

Kaufman, A. S., & Kaufman, N. L. (1983b). *K-ABC interpretive manual.* Circle Pines, MN: American Guidance Service.

Kaufman, A. S., Kaufman, N. L., Kamphaus, R. W., & Naglieri, J. A. (1982). Sequential and simultaneous factors at ages 3–12½: Developmental changes in neuropsychological dimensions. *Clinical Neuropsychology, 4,* 74–81.

Luria, A. R. (1966). *Human brain and psychological processes.* New York: Harper & Row.

Mercer, J. R. (1979). *System of Multicultural Pluralistic Assessment (SOMPA): Technical manual.* New York: The Psychological Corporation.

Naglieri, J. A., Kamphaus, R. W., & Kaufman, A. S. (1983). The Luria-Das successive-simultaneous model applied to WISC-R data. *Journal of Psychoeducational Assessment, 1,* 25–34.

Naglieri, J. A., Kaufman, A. S., Kaufman, N. L., & Kamphaus, R. W. (1981). Cross-validation of Das' simultaneous and successive processes with novel tasks. *Alberta Journal of Educational Research, 27,* 264–271.

Neisser, U. (1967). *Cognitive psychology.* New York: Appleton-Century-Crofts.

Reynolds, C. R. (1983, August). *Changing conceptualizations of race differences in intelligence.* Paper presented at the meeting of the American Psychological Association, Anaheim.

Sattler, J. M. (1982). *Assessment of children's intelligence and special abilities* (2nd ed.). Boston: Allyn & Bacon.

Sperry, R. W. (1968). Hemisphere deconnection and unity in conscious awareness. *American Psychologist, 23,* 723–733.

Wechsler, D. (1974). *Manual for the Wechsler Intelligence Scale for Children—Revised (WISC-R).* New York: The Psychological Corporation.

White, D. R., & Jacobs, E. (1979). The prediction of first-grade reading achievement from WPPSI scores of preschool children. *Psychology in the Schools, 16,* 189–192.

FIFTEEN

MENTAL MEASUREMENT OF MINORITY-GROUP CHILDREN

THOMAS OAKLAND AND RONALD PARMELEE

The University of Texas
Austin, Texas

Few issues have been subject to greater debate in education and psychology than those associated with assessing the mental abilities of minority children. For years, educators and psychologists thought tests offered the most objective and least biased means of assessing children from minority racial-ethnic groups and social classes. Although tests had their flaws, criticisms were directed more justifiably at other techniques that lacked reliability and validity.

However, during the late sixties, criticisms of tests were heard from many quarters. Persons from virtually every academic discipline and political persuasion offered their views about problems associated with testing minority children. These views tended to highlight seven specific concerns (Oakland, 1982):

Tests are discriminatory when pupils are not assessed in their native or dominant language;

Tests are discriminatory when they reflect only Anglo middle-class abilities and attitudes;

Many assessment specialists are poorly trained and insensitive to relevant characteristics of minority children;

Minority children are overrepresented in inferior education programs and underrepresented in superior education programs;

Minority children may remain in ineffective education programs for years;

Parents frequently are not informed or consulted when schools make important decisions regarding their children;

Important decisions often are based on meager information.

The emergence of blacks and other minority groups from second- to first-class citizens during the last 25 years has ushered in a new era. Minorities generally feel a heightened sense of pride in themselves and in their group membership. They increasingly expect their self-pride to be matched by expressions of dignity from others. They resist efforts in which test data are used to denigrate their dignity and pride, to limit their educational and vocational opportunities, and to make behind-the-door decisions that maintain the old ways. Thus they voice strong opposition when tests

Are used to denigrate the dignity and pride of minority groups,

Are used to limit their educational and vocational opportunities, and

Serve to dehumanize decision-making practices.

One must not infer a general dislike for testing. In general, the public's attitudes toward testing are very positive (Learner, 1981). For example in a recent Gallup poll, 81% of U.S. parents described standardized tests as very useful; 85% of minority parents also described tests as very useful. This seemingly contradictory information suggests that, although minorities are concerned about test misuse and abuse, they recognize that tests may be useful. Issues regarding the uses of mental tests with minority children constitute the broad focus for this chapter. More specific attention is given to the role of mental assessment in special education since most of the issues seem to lodge there.

An understanding of certain historical events and trends regarding mental measurement will help to establish a wider context within which to consider our more narrow issues.

HISTORICAL REVIEW OF MENTAL TESTING

Many of the current practices in the field of mental measurement have their origin in the work of Galton (1822–1911). Galton inferred from Darwin's theory of evolution that human beings vary in their genetic mental endowment and that these variations are heritable (Herrnstein & Boring, 1965). Galton's concern for individual differences led to his establishing a laboratory in London where the measurement of physical and mental capacities of individuals was conducted.

Testing for Individual Differences

Individual differences is the most important principle underlying mental measurement. Everyday observation tells us that people differ in their physical and psychological characteristics. Galton recognized the importance of individual differences in understanding people and studied the distribution of ability among them. Galton thought quantitative measurement to be an essential aspect of a fully developed science. He recorded ability measures on many individuals, classified persons according to how they fell along a continuum of abilities, and observed a very large range between those individuals with the greatest and least abilities. His classification system was the first step toward the concept of standardized scores (Wiseman, 1967).

The psychology of individual differences that began to take form in Galton's work was further developed by James Cattell (1860–1944). Cattell also stressed that psychology must rest on a foundation of measurement and experimentation and sought to develop a battery of tests designed to evaluate people. The assessment of human capacity proved to be the central theme of Cattell's work. Establishing the normal range of variation for human mental capacities was his primary goal.

After the work of Galton and Cattell gained greater visibility, interest in mental measurement began to spread rapidly during the last decade of the nineteenth century. In Germany, Oehrn developed tests to measure mental capacities in relation to psychopathology, and Munsterberg used several mental tests with children. In addition to Cattell, in the U.S. Jastrow tested college students at the University of Wisconsin, and Boas, an anthropologist, took various types of anthropological measurements of school children. In 1895, the American Psychological Association appointed a committee to oversee these early ventures into mental measurement.

Binet's Tests

Many features of presently used intelligence tests came from the work of Alfred Binet, who devised the first practical intelligence test in 1905 in France. (Later revisions occurred in 1908 and 1911.)

The French Ministry of Education commissioned Binet and Theophile Simon, a French psychiatrist, to create a practical and objective means for identifying mentally deficient children in order that they might be placed in more appropriate classes. The test that Binet and Simon published in 1905 was the first scale that yielded an overall index of intelligence. The concept of mental age also was developed by Binet, allowing for comparison between children. In developing his test, Binet sought to reveal the differences in the higher cognitive abilities among persons. In 1914, Stern, a German psychologist, suggested that mental age, divided by chronological age, should be regarded as a "mental quotient." Stern's mental quotient has evolved into the intelligence quotient (IQ) and has been used widely in mental tests.

A number of different revisions of Binet's scales were prepared in the U.S., the most famous developed by Terman at Stanford University. This test was the first to use the IQ. The Binet tests were innovative because of their simplicity, the ease and quickness with which they could be individually administered, and their promising psychometric characteristics.

The IQ and Its Meanings

The advent of the Stanford-Binet test and other mental tests that soon followed sparked the continuing debates as to the nature of intelligence. Simply speaking, an IQ expresses an individual's performance on an intelligence test in terms of his or her relative standing among peers in some specified normative population.

The validities of an IQ measure are a function of the quality of the particular intelligence test from which they are derived. The best intelligence tests are standardized on highly representative samples of persons drawn from each age group of the general population.

The more recently developed IQ tests, like the Wechsler tests, utilize standard scores instead of mental ages. Deriving the IQ in this manner allows for a more accurate representation of a child's standing relative to other children of the same age in the norm group.

Since its inception at the turn of the century, the IQs of hundreds of millions of children and adults have been measured and recorded, and the very existence of the concept of IQ has produced increasing controversy. From one author's perspective (Herrnstein, 1971), the measurement of intelligence is psychology's most telling accomplishment to date.

The Development of Group Tests

World War I stimulated a testing movement that was to have considerable impact on psychology. In May, 1917, the American Psychological Association, as part of its contribution to the war effort, formed a committee under the direction of Robert Yerkes to develop examination techniques for recruits. This committee decided that psychological tests offered the most practical solution to their assigned task. Since a large number of individuals had to be processed, the committee decided to develop a group test of intelligence. The efforts of Yerkes' committee produced the Army Alpha Test of Intelligence. A group test for use with illiterates and recruits speaking foreign languages, the Army Beta, was a later product.

The Army Alpha and Beta tests were christened during the first large-scale use of intelligence tests and served as models for most group intelligence tests that followed. These tests introduced the principles of group and self-administering tests and stimulated the development of measures of academic achievement, special aptitudes, interests, and personality characteristics.

A tremendous growth spurt in the testing industry during the 1920s promoted the development of group tests for persons of all ages. Group tests permitted the simultaneous examination of large numbers of persons and also simplified the instructions for administering and scoring. Unfortunately, the application of group intelligence tests was not accompanied by a commensurate degree of technical improvement. The fact that the tests were still crude instruments was often overlooked in the process of gathering scores and drawing practical conclusions from the results. Consequently, hostility and skepticism toward all types of testing came about when the tests failed to meet unwarranted expectations. In retrospect, the indiscriminate uses of tests in the 1920s did much to retard and advance the progress of psychological testing (Anastasi, 1976). Increasing degrees of professionalism in the development of tests and their uses have been observed since the 1930s.

Theories of Intelligence

The early research on intelligence was concerned primarily with its measurement and devoted little attention to theoretical developments (Laosa, 1977). However, the work of five pioneers in the field of mental measurement stands as an exception to this pattern.

Charles Spearman (Spearman, 1927) reported in 1904 an important theory regarding the organization of human abilities. He examined the interrelationships among tests of various abilities and concluded that all intellectual abilities have a general underlying factor (g) in common and a number of specific factors (s) that are unique to each ability. Spearman conceptualized the g factor as general mental energy. It represents the "incentive" rather than the "reproductive" aspect of mental ability. The g factor was thought to be involved in operations of a deductive nature, linked with skill, speed, intensity, and extensity of a person's intellectual output. Spearman hypothesized that g is a function of heredity and that s is a measure of specific learning and experiences acquired by the individual (Fruchter, 1954). This two-factor theory has been a useful conceptual base for measures of general and specific abilities.

E. L. Thorndike (Thorndike, 1927), another pioneer in developing theories of intelligence, thought of intelligence as composed of a multitude of separate elements, each representing different abilities. Thorndike believed certain mental activities may have some common elements that form clusters; he identified three such clusters of mental abilities: social intelligence (dealing with people), concrete intelligence (dealing with things), and abstract intelligence (dealing with verbal and mathematical symbols).

A third pioneer, L. L. Thurstone (Thurstone, 1938), was one of the first to use factor-analytic methods to probe the construct of intelligence. He identified eight primary mental abilities: verbal, perceptual speed, inductive reasoning, word fluency, number facility, memory, spatial relations, and verbal fluency. Thurstone later discovered these primary factors had moderate intercorrelations, leading him to postulate the existence of a second-order factor that permeates the eight primary abilities. This factor resembles Spearman's g.

J. P. Guilford (Guilford, 1967) became the most prominent multifactor theorist in the United States. He developed a three-dimensional structure-of-intellect model that consists of five operations categories (cognition, memory, divergent production, convergent thinking, and evaluation); four content categories (figural, symbolic, semantic, and behavioral); and six product categories (units, classes, relations, systems, transformations, and implications). He believed that intelligence activities could be understood by the kinds of mental operations performed, the type of contents on which the operations performed, and the resulting product.

Perhaps the most significant theoretical impact has been made by Jean Piaget (Ault, 1977; Flavell, 1977) who viewed intelligence as a form of biological adaptation between the individual and the environment. He theorized that biological adaptation is extended by cognition, which allows the individual to move from an immediate action level to a symbolic level through the process of internalization. Piaget saw cognitive processes emerging as a result of a reorganization of one's psychological structures, resulting from interactions between the individual and his environment.

Modern conceptions of intelligence stress the importance of both innate and developmental influences. Intelligence is characterized as a more global concept than was earlier believed with the unique learning histories of individuals determining how intelligence is used. Among the modern theorists, Arthur Jensen (Jensen, 1970, 1980) suggests two major classes of mental abilities: associative (level I) and cognitive (level II). Associative ability involves rote learning and short-term memory. Cognitive ability involves reasoning and problem solving. Little transformation of input takes place within level I, whereas level II processing involves a conscious manipulation of the stimulus input in producing the correct output.

A second modern theorist, Jagannath Das, categorizes cognitive ability by way of an information-processing model. Das' model has two primary modes: simultaneous processing and successive processing. Stimuli are arranged either in a simultaneous or sequential manner in order to make decisions. Equal status is given to both modes as a given task can be solved by more than one mode. Das perceives intelligence as the ability to use information obtained through the simultaneous and successive transformation procedures in order to plan and structure behavior effectively for goal attainment (Das, 1972; Das, Kirby, & Jarman, 1975; Das & Molloy, 1975; Jarman & Das, 1977).

Intelligence has been viewed by some as culturally determined, implying that the qualities that constitute intelligence are a product of time and place. This view of intelligence, known as cultural relativism, is closely related to the idea of intelligence as a set of specific acquired skills or strategies. Jensen (1980) depicts this interpretation as confusing intelligence or g with the instrument measuring it. Instruments that measure intelligence are undoubtedly cultural in the sense that persons must have had some experience with the basic contents of the test. Nevertheless, the trait of intelligence seems to represent a single g factor in all human groups, even though it may not always be valued. The presence of g spans all of human history; it would be difficult to believe that the geniuses of the great civilizations of the past were not well above average in the kinds of behaviors that best characterize g of present intelligence tests.

THE DISTRIBUTION OF MENTAL ABILITY

Common observation tells us that people's similarities outweigh their differences. This same observation holds true with the distribution of mental ability in a given population. Jensen (1980) has explained the individual variation found in human intelligence in terms of polygenic theory. Variations in human intelligence are attributed to a number of small, similar, and independent influences that either enhance or diminish intellectual development. These influences are thought to be primarily genetic, but environmental influences also contribute importantly.

Environmental influences also contribute to the individual variability found in human intelligence. Perinatal influences, such as perinatal anoxia, birth weight, malnutrition, parental nurture, and parental harmony have all been demonstrated to have some influence on intellectual development (Jensen, 1981). The available evidence clearly suggests that intelligence is affected by both genetic and environmental factors. The continuous interaction of heredity and environmental influences creates the cognitive abilities found in every person.

The normal or bell-shaped curve is the common form in which the distribution of mental abilities in humans is represented. Although a perfect normal curve, as defined mathematically, is rarely achieved in the real world, small variations do not significantly change statistical interpretation. Scores on most intelligence tests closely approximate the normal distribution, provided that a representative sample of the population has been tested and that test items have been fairly and evenly graded in difficulty.

For years we thought that test-score distributions that demonstrate mean differences provide evidence of bias. For example, the goal for culture-fair tests was for the various racial-ethnic groups to display similar means and standard deviations. However, cross-cultural studies rarely produced these results. In fact, within the U.S., the means for some racial-ethnic groups are above average (for example, Jews) while the means for others are below average (for example, blacks). Tests were thought to be biased against those groups with lower than average mean scores and biased in favor of those groups with higher than average mean scores (Eells et al., 1951; McGurk, 1967). Using this line of reasoning, one could not contend that tests are biased against *all* minority groups, only those with below-average mean scores.

Some persons (Mercer, 1973; Williams, 1974) contend that racial-ethnic differences on aptitude and achievement tests are largely an artifact of test bias rather than reflecting actual between-group differences. Others (such as, Jensen) contend the tests are equally valid for persons from various racial-ethnic groups and social classes.

The fact that children from *some* minority groups score below average on various measures of mental abilities has been of concern to psychologists and educators for years. The attempt to develop culture-fair measures was only one of many means sought to provide mental ability tests that would be fair and accurate when used with persons from various social classes and racial-ethnic groups. Other approaches to eliminate biases included developing culture-specific tests (Williams, 1972), criterion-referenced measures (Crano, Kenny, & Campbell, 1972), behavioral assessment, translating tests from English to other languages, norming tests to include more minority children, developing separate racial-ethnic norms, developing pluralistic norms, and developing statistical models to use current tests fairly.

Measures of cognitive abilities have been primary targets for scrutiny and even attack for various reasons. Cognitive abilities are highly prized. Thus persons and techniques authorized to assess cognitive abilities hold considerable power and influence over others. Also, the quality of professionalism in assessing intelligence varies greatly within our country—from the scientologists who quackishly hawk IQ testing, to those who hold diplomates from the American Board of Professional Psychology. Furthermore, as we have seen, the psychological literature is inconsistent in its descriptions of the theoretical and conceptual bases of intelligence. Thus the profession is vulnerable to criticisms.

A few psychologists who provided early leadership in developing theories and measures of intelligence (such as Goddard, Yerkes, and Terman) are perceived to be racists by some (Kamin, 1974). They and others infer invidious attempts to develop tests that discredit minority groups. Data that consistently demonstrate group differences and from which erroneous inferences are drawn (for example, blacks are inherently inferior) tend to confirm these concerns.

Critics of testing have asserted often that tests imperfectly predict future behaviors, rigidly shape school curricula, foster a view of people as having innate and fixed abilities, and encourage undesirable biases and expectations (Black, 1963; Gross, 1963). However, many concerns that blacks have about cognitive assessment go far beyond these general problems. Their allegations (such as tests frequently are employed to denigrate their dignity and pride and to limit their educational and vocational opportunities) suggest that testing is seen by many blacks as another means to maintain racially biased social order and institutional practices.

Hispanics also share some of these concerns. However, they emphasize possible biases due to cultural and language differences. Hispanic children from newly arrived or first-generation families have had educational, cultural, and linguistic experiences that are significantly different from other U.S. children and that preclude the use of norm-referenced measures with them—especially those administered in English (Mercer, 1973).

BASIC ASSUMPTIONS UNDERLYING ASSESSMENT

All professions have tools and technology for evaluating qualities and characteristics. Tests constitute potentially useful devices to the behavioral sciences as long as we recognize their strengths and weaknesses. When using tests or other assessment devices, we need to acknowledge certain basic assumptions underlying their use (Newland, 1973).

We assume persons are demonstrating their very best performance when taking tests measuring achievement and aptitudes—considered tests of maximum performance. We endeavor to promote proper attitudes, motivation, test-taking skills, and other qualities that help to ensure persons are performing at the highest level possible.

We assume that the examiners are skilled and knowledgeable in establishing and maintaining rapport, in administering and scoring the tests, in analyzing the results, and in performing other features important to their role. Problems in any one of these areas adversely affect the accuracy and usefulness of the test's results.

Most tests assess but a sample of a domain and rarely assess the complete domain. The sample being observed should be adequate in amount and representative of the domain being assessed. Although we cannot sample every behavior, we can identify those most relevant and observe as many as possible. The accuracy of our judgments is increased by using assessment techniques that permit us to observe a large number of behaviors that are relevant to the domain being assessed. Our confidence is increased when a test has many suitable items rather than a few. Also, observing a child over many days in a variety of settings is better than a single observation. We can have greater confidence that the data are accurate when the results from different assessment techniques and sources yield similar results.

Errors exist in any measure. For some assesment devices, the errors are large, and for others the errors are small. We assume we are able to estimate the magnitude of errors in using a particular instrument by knowing a measure's reliability and validity, and thereby ascertaining our confidence that appropriate statistical interpretations are justifiable. The use of such techniques as the standard errors of measurement and estimate is helpful in this regard. Although their use should be highly encouraged, one must remember that the magnitude of measurement errors is only estimated for any individual—it is never known.

A related issue concerns our confidence in predicting future behaviors. Many of us are responsible for forecasting a person's future behavior: what is the likelihood that David will experience learning problems? What is the likelihood of Chris doing well at MIT? What is the likelihood that Miss Sternberg will be a good supervisor? Although we may have opportunities to assess how previous factors influence present behaviors, rarely can we forecast future events with certainty. The accuracy of our prognostications regarding complex behaviors is directly related to how thoroughly we understand the persons and the important elements of their environments, and to how much control we have over the persons and environmental events affecting them. Also important is the length of time over which our predictions are being made. Predictions regarding a person's future should be made with great caution and reservation, particularly if they involve projections over two or more years.

In working with a multicultural population, we need to be aware of possible social-class and racial-ethnic differences in a test's reliability and validity. A test's psychometric characteristics may be stronger for particular groups of people. For example, relationships between six readiness measures and later reading and math achievement were determined for Anglo, black, and Mexican-American children from middle- and lower-class homes (Oakland, 1978). Important racial-ethnic and social-class differences existed on a number of tests. The correlations between the Metropolitan Readiness Test and the second-grade Metropolitan Achievement Test (MAT) were .43 for the entire sample of 411, but .77 for Anglos, .30 for Mexican-Americans, and .15 for blacks. Correlations between the Slosson Oral Reading and second-grade MAT scores were .71 for middle-class and .14 for lower-class Mexican-American children. Various independent studies, preferably at local levels, should be conducted to help ensure that we can be equally confident in predicting future characteristics of persons from various social classes and racial-ethnic groups.

Another assumption is that persons being tested have been exposed to acculturation patterns that are similar to those of a test's standardized sample. No two acculturation patterns are the same. However, the more similar the person is to those included in the standardization sample, the greater confidence we have that the test was appropriately standardized and validated for our uses.

We often work with persons who have been raised in a highly restricted or different physical or sociocultural setting that provided opportunities for growth and development significantly different from those of most persons. Compared to the acculturation patterns afforded most children within this country, those provided for children who are severely physically or perceptually disabled, emotionally disturbed, severely socially maladjusted, raised in extreme isolation, or raised in foreign countries often are different. The acculturation patterns governing the development of many children from racial-ethnic minority groups or from lower socioeconomic homes also may be sufficiently different to warrant our judgment that the test is inappropriate.

However, we must avoid the notion that all minority or lower socioeconomic children are, by definition, significantly different from children in the mainstream or those in the standardization sample. This position is prejudicial and unwarranted. We must be sensitive to the fact that important differences exist with respect to child-rearing practices, expectations and aspirations, socialization patterns, language experiences, availability of and involvement in informal and formal learning experiences, and values and attitudes; these and other factors may result in acculturation patterns that are not directly comparable to those that are more typical in the United States. The decision as to whether a child's acculturation patterns are similar to those generally reflected in the test's standardization sample can be made for each child individually and only after acquiring a thorough knowledge of the child's background and the characteristics of the test's standardization sample. Also, school systems should consider using local norms as one means of overcoming problems associated with dissimilar acculturation patterns.

HOW IS BIAS DEFINED?

Attempts to resolve questions of test bias are confused by differing definitions of bias. Bias is a complex concept that connotes different interpretations. The number of definitions is large and growing and exceeds the scope of this chapter. Some of the more important definitions are described below. Readers are advised to see Scheuneman (1981), Jensen (1980), Flaugher (1978), Humphreys (1973), Lord (1980), and Berk (1982) for a more extensive review of methods to detect test bias.

Traditional definitions of bias have relied largely on the three conceptions of validity: content, criterion related (including concurrent and predictive), and construct (including internal and external). Most empirically oriented psychologists wisely avoid discussing content validity, per se, as few criteria exist on which to base sound judgments.

Statisticians seemingly favor for detecting test bias those methods which combine judgmental and statistical methods. For example, logical analysis may be employed to establish the relevance of items to the trait being assessed. Statistical techniques then can be used to identify aberrant items—those operating inconsistent with other items presumably measuring that trait. Finally, judgment again may be used to examine possible patterns among the statistically biased items and to further refine one's understanding of the trait (Shepard, 1982). Methods using item bias (as opposed to criterion-related validity) may be preferred because they can be incorporated into the first stages of test construction, thus leading to the early elimination of biases that may eventually compromise the test's validity. Furthermore, regression methods to detect criterion-related bias and factor-analytic methods to detect construct bias may be employed later with greater ease and confidence following the use of item methods.

Psychometrists often define bias through definitions that emphasize the relations between test items to the total test (for example, item-total correlations). However, others prefer definitions that emphasize the entire test and focus on possible bias in selection. Three definitions of bias appear prominently. One holds that a test is more valid for one group than others. This regression approach defines bias in terms of differences in the regression of a criterion measure on an independent variable. Cleary's definition exemplifies this first conception of bias:

> A test is biased for members of a subgroup of the population if, in the prediction of a criterion for which the test was designed, consistent nonzero errors of prediction are made for members of the subgroup. In other words, the test is biased if the criterion score predicted from the common regression line is consistently too high or too low for members of the subgroup. With this definition of bias, there may be a connotation of "unfair," particularly if the use of the test produces a prediction that is too low. [1968, p. 115]

Despite prevailing notions that tests are biased against minority groups, Jensen's conclusions from predictive bias studies indicate that the vast majority of studies indicate:

> The regressions of criterion performance on test scores do not differ for blacks and whites. And almost without exception, when the white and black regressions do differ significantly, the difference is in the intercepts, with the blacks' intercept below the white. This intercept bias results in overprediction of the blacks' criterion performance when predictions for whites and blacks are based on the white or on the common regression line. . . . Thus, contrary to popular belief, the evidence shows that, when predictive test bias is found, it in fact most often favors blacks

in any selection procedure that treats all test scores alike regardless of race. . . . It seems safe to conclude that most standard ability and aptitude tests in current use in education . . . are not biased for blacks or whites with respect to criterion validity. [1980, p. 515]

Though this view is generally held by many statisticians and psychometrists, others challenge the absoluteness of Jensen's generalizations (for example, Scheuneman, 1981, pp. 8–9). Others challenge that traditional views regarding test bias overlook test fairness—an issue that will be considered shortly. Furthermore, these generalizations *may be* applicable principally to one racial-ethnic group (such as blacks); less evidence is available on the other major minority groups that comprise our multicultural society. We must avoid generalizing Jensen's conclusions as being applicable to all minorities within the U.S.

The second model is the frequently used quota system. Using this model, persons are selected in the same proportion as they are found in the population. If a community's population is 80% white and 20% black, one black will be selected for every four whites selected. Two separate cut-off scores are set to allow this selection ratio when between-group differences in mean scores exist.

A third model, the corrected-criterion model (Darlington, 1971), allows us to weigh the social and political implications in using various culture-fair models. A choice of models depends on the relative importance attributed to selecting persons with the highest scores versus giving members of minority groups more opportunities to be selected. A practical effect of this model is to add bonus points to scores of members of certain groups to help ensure a larger selection ratio for them. This method is used in civil-service exams when extra points are awarded to a veteran's score.

SOURCES OF BIAS

Bias exists in many forms. This chapter will examine possible biases from four sources: children, parents, educational personnel, and school-system policies and practices. Basic assumptions underlying assessment also will be examined.

Furthermore, a broad definition for nonbiased assessment is offered at this point. This definition allows other definitions to be subsumed within it.

A nonbiased assessment program provides a quality assessment program that eliminates, minimizes, or at least recognizes the presence of biasing conditions. Bias is apparent from predilections and procedures that prevent or obscure either (1) the full and accurate appraisal of conditions influencing a child's development or (2) the use of information to help maximize a child's development (Oakland, 1981, p. 2).

Sources of Bias in Children

Language.   Children's ability to understand and communicate in English is very important. School success depends in part on being able to understand, speak, read, and write English. Thus knowing children's English proficiency is important in determining whether their language skills are sufficiently developed to enable them to perform adequately on tests and elsewhere in our monolingual educational system.

Many children living in various parts of the United States are exposed to and acquire two languages simultaneously in early childhood. Both are first languages for these children, although one is usually dominant in certain situations or with certain people. Language acquisition and semantic development follow the same developmental pattern in bilingual as in monolingual children. Some researchers have argued that bilingual children initially form a single vocabulary system from the words they know in both languages; only gradually do they learn to differentiate the words of the separate languages and to use them accordingly. Thus bilingual children must learn the restrictions of the labels as they apply to corresponding items in the two languages (Matluck & Mace-Matluck, 1981).

Many concerns about validly testing the mental abilities of minority children relate directly to language and culture. Conventional tests that require a high level of English proficiency cannot be used with children whose English language skills are inadequately developed. Paucity of language may signal a general language deficiency or a language difference owing to exposure to nonstandard dialects, exposure to more than one language during language acquisition, or exclusive knowledge of a language other than English.

The tests used in schools generally are not intended to assess language skills directly but use language as a means of assessing intelligence, achievement, personality, and other characteristics. Students should not be penalized for dialect differences in either the native or second language. Consequently, conventional assessment techniques often must be altered when we work with children with language differences so that we can eliminate biases arising from language and ensure that test results obtained for a particular student are reliable and valid.

Test Wiseness.   The degree to which children are test wise is also a source of test bias in test scores. Tests are administered to children with the presumption that they have acquired requisite abilities and attitudes. Minority children may be deficient in employing test-taking skills, choosing proper problem-solving strategies, and balancing speed and power. We assume that children taking tests understand directions, consider all possible responses before choosing the correct one, concentrate on one item at a time, are not distracted by other items, and are involved and attentive during the entire test. These and similar abilities constitute basic test-taking skills (Oakland, 1972). There is evidence that many children have limited test-taking skills. We do not know how pervasive this limitation is among minority children or to what degree it lowers their performance on tests (Sattler, 1982); however, we do know that a lack of test wiseness contributes to bias. Therefore, we must ensure that children have prerequisite test-taking skills.

Motivation and Anxiety.   Adequate test performance requires that children be properly motivated (Havighurst, 1970). Results from aptitude and achievement tests are valid only when children are performing at their very best. Too often children randomly select answers on a multiple choice test, fail to cooperate, and show their lack of motivation in other ways. Other children may be extremely anxious and unable to concentrate and attend to the test. A nonbiased assessment program must take into account the attitudinal characteristics of children to ensure that they are properly motivated.

Achievement motivation is an area in which cultural groups are believed to differ, possibly accounting for the observed differences in test performance and scholastic achievement (Chapman & Hill, 1971). Achievement motivation helps determine the levels of interest, striving, and effort that persons invest in the development of their intellectual skills, and the levels of attention, concentration, effort, and persistence they apply to the tests.

Minority children may be less motivated to be correct for the sake of correctness alone and are willing to settle for lower levels of achievement success (see Zigler & Butterfield, 1968). Some minority-group children demonstrate motivational deficits that decrease their usual intellectual performance.

Although some children evidence test anxiety, little empirical evidence supports the contention that test anxiety is a salient variable accounting for cultural or racial-group differences in test scores (Jensen, 1980). In general, studies suggest that motivational factors may affect the test performance of some minority children, potentially resulting in low test scores that are a function of factors not related to their cognitive abilities (Gruen, Ottinger, & Zigler, 1970; Terrell, Durkin, & Wiesley, 1959; Zigler & Butterfield, 1968; Zigler & de Labry, 1962).

Cultural Differences.   Children often come from restricted or different physical and cultural settings where the opportunities for growth and development differ significantly from those available to most children (Cole & Bruner, 1971; Newland, 1973). These differences may be seen in child-rearing practices, expectations and aspirations, language experiences, informal and formal learning experiences, and other facets influencing acculturation. The acculturation patterns of minority-group children and children from lower socioeconomic homes may be significantly different from the patterns of children who are included in a test's standardization sample. Confidence in using a test decreases when a child's acculturation patterns differ significantly from the patterns that are normally provided for other children.

Due to the potential differences in the acculturation patterns of minority groups, gaining an understanding of each minority culture is important to one's work. The variation that exists between cultures with regard to cognitive modes of processing information illustrates this point. The standard measures of intelligence (such as the Stanford-Binet and WISC-R) used in U.S. school systems presuppose modes of the neogenetic type. These tests are characteristic of Western linguistic behavior and are typified by test content involving education of relations and correlates. Such constructs may be inappropriate for non-Western cultures that have different cognitive-processing strategies; in addition, it is likely that the constructs measured by any test differ from culture to culture (Biesheuvel, 1972). For this reason, it is important that educators and psychologists be aware of the cultural characteristics of minority children with whom they work. Overlooking cognitive-processing patterns unique to specific ethnic groups represents a potential source of bias in interpreting test data. Knowing the cognitive strategies, values, languages, mores, motivations, and attitudes among different ethnic groups is an important aspect of the assessment process. Understanding how the coping patterns of different ethnic groups facilitate or hinder children's adjustments to their own subculture as well as to the larger culture is also important (Sattler, 1974).

It is frequently alleged that intelligence tests are not relevant to the experiences of ethnic minority children. For example, black children are described as developing unique verbal skills that are neither measured by conventional tests nor accepted by the middle-class-oriented classroom (Williams, 1970). Conversely, Ebel (1975) pointed out that items on intelligence tests represent important aspects of competence in the "common" culture; the items are not reflective of middle-class values alone. He states:

> The bias which accounts for poor test performance by some minority persons is not in the tests so much as it is in the culture, and thus is another problem altogether. So long as the tests under scrutiny truly measure the skills necessary to success in the prevailing culture, minority interests are not well served by blaming "test bias" for poor performance. [1975, p. 87]

Children do not significantly differ from each other solely by the virtue of minority or lower socioeconomic group affiliation. They also vary with regard to intellectual capacity (cognitive functioning), physical characteristics (psychomotor functioning), personality makeup, learning abilities, language functionings (expressive and receptive language skills), and behavioral characteristics. The decision as to whether a child's acculturation patterns are similar to those of children who are included in a test's standardization sample can be made for each child individually only after thorough knowledge is obtained of each child's background and of the test's standardization sample.

Attitudes and Expectations.   The view that a person's behaviors tend to move toward the expectations we have for them (the self-fulfilling prophecy) is widely held. The prevalence of good behavior is assumed to increase when we expect people to be well behaved and we communicate these expectations to them. Children tend to adopt and accept the expectations that their peers, family, and teachers communicate to them. Knowing those expectations for children enables one to appraise their future more accurately and possibly modify interpretations of assessment data. Children who expect to fail on tests often underperform on them. Thus under certain conditions, low expectations can add to testing bias and exacerbate other problems.

Although some persons continue to believe that test results contribute to the development of a self-fulfilling prophecy, the strength of such expectancy effects must be considered carefully. Expectations that some teachers hold of their pupils seem to influence various student characteristics. Some thought the low expectations teachers may hold for most minority pupils might explain, in part, the generally lower mean scores on achievement and intelligence tests for some minority groups. This view is not supported by research (Brophy & Good, 1970).

The self-fulfilling prophecy became a popular explanation for the poor test performance of minority children as a result of the work of Rosenthal and Jacobson (1968). One of their studies supposedly demonstrated that pupils for whom teachers had high expectations obtained significantly higher gains on an IQ test than did a control group of children. However, this study has many methodological problems and has not withstood further investigation (Snow, 1969; Thorndike, 1968). Additional research has indicated that children's cognitive development, for the most part, is not influenced by teachers' knowing children's intelligence test scores.

Parents as a Potential Source of Bias

The characteristics of parents also may bias the assessment process, particularly when one views their role as participatory and active. Most parents are eager to have their children adequately assessed and to receive special services; their presence tends to have a beneficial influence. Unfortunately, others may be unwilling or unable to take an active role or may exert their influence in detrimental ways.

Deficient Parental Support. Parental attention and attitudes shape children's personality traits and ways they apply their abilities. When sufficient parental support is provided, children display more persistence, application, and a desire to excel. The parents' attention and love can convey to children a desire for adult approval and educational success (Gage & Berliner, 1975). The degree to which children perceive their parents as encouraging or discouraging in regard to high educational achievement also has an effect on their aspirations; their aspirations impact their responses to the assessment process. For example, among black children from working-class families in Harlem, high-achieving children in comparison with low achievers came from homes where there was a high level of parental support and interest for children in the family (Greenberg & Davidson, 1972). Parental encouragement seems to be a strong intervening variable between social-class background and intelligence in respect to the child's educational aspirations (Brembeck, 1971). High levels of ambition and educational aspiration may seem to be inappropriate or absurd to parents having relatively low levels of self-esteem, and such parents may fail to encourage their children because they have transferred their own low opinion of themselves to their children (Jackson & Marsden, 1962). The available evidence suggests that a lack of parental support may bias the assessment process by undermining the educational aspirations and motivation of children.

Many minority parents of today were yesterday's children who experienced the inequities and inadequacies of regular and special education programs. As children, some parents were placed in low-ability classrooms or were labeled inferior or deviant because of cultural and language differences. These early experiences may color their current attitudes toward schooling. Toward such parents psychologists and school personnel must exercise skillful and empathic efforts to help them to perceive their children's educational experiences in a different light.

Inadequately Informed Parents.   Some parents may not have the information necessary to help make appropriate decisions for their children. Some may know a Monday night television schedule better than they know their children's school and afterschool schedules. Others are caught up in the "Me generation" and lack a sense of dedication to their children. Some are unable to make objective, intelligent decisions regarding their children's welfare; are uncooperative, apprehensive, and afraid of the school; and may not have time or know how to help. These conditions may prevent or obscure the full and accurate appraisal of a child's needs. The biasing role of parents who are unwilling to become adequately informed about their children's schooling may be difficult to overcome.

Inconsistent Home and School Values.   Children have a right to education, and society correctly expects this right to be exercised. Although the vast majority of parents highly value education, the actions of some are not consistent with allowing the school to be fully effective. For example, working-class parents tend to place less value on formal education and are less likely to be ambitious for their children (Hyman, 1954). Parents may encourage their children to remain at home or to take a part-time job that escalates into full-time. Families may move frequently, disrupting children's educational, social, and emotional development. Schools that experience a 100% student turnover rate yearly are not able to provide quality educational programs nor to use acquired information to help maximize a child's development.

Unproductive Communication Systems.   The communication system between the school and the child's family may be inadequate. Schools often use legalistic and educational terminology when they communicate with parents, perhaps in an attempt to comply with legal requirements. However, many parents often do not understand what is being said or implied and they feel confused and helpless. When asked to affirm school recommendations for their children's education, they may not comprehend the request fully. Such experiences may discourage them from attending other school meetings.

These problems are compounded when a parent's English proficiency is limited. Some parents do not speak English, while others have acquired enough to show survival skills but may not grasp the nuances and complexities of educational terminology. These and other parental influences may impede a nondiscriminatory assessment program.

Tests as Possible Sources of Bias

The use of standardized tests represents an important component of a nondiscriminatory assessment program. However, their use requires us to know their strengths and weaknesses with regard to their psychometric soundness before choosing specific tests to use. In selecting appropriate tests, a thorough evaluation of their reliability, validity, and standardization data is imperative.

Intelligence and other aptitude tests are frequently criticized as exhibiting bias on the basis of their standardization samples, validity, and reliability. Many have argued as follows:

The standardization samples of standardized tests include minorities in insufficient numbers for them significantly to impact item selection;

Standardized tests measure different attributes when used with children outside of the mainstream, white, middle-class culture; and

Standardized tests do not predict any important outcomes or future behaviors for minority children.

As a result of these and other criticisms, psychologists often feel compelled to interpret the results of standardized tests differently depending on the race or ethnic background of the child in question.

In selecting tests for minority children, psychologists and educational diagnosticians must determine whether the child being tested has been exposed to comparable, but not necessarily identical, acculturation patterns relative to the standardization sample. The norms of these tests should provide a meaningful basis on which to interpret a child's test scores. If the purpose of administering a test is to compare a child's performance with other children nationally, then the test's standardization sample should include a large number of children drawn from throughout the United States and stratified on the basis of relevant variables (such as age, gender, socioeconomic status, race-ethnicity, and geography). Judged on these criteria, the norms for some tests (including most group-achievement and aptitude batteries and WISC-R) are fairly adequate, while those for others (such as the Illinois Test of Psycholinguistic Abilities, Peabody Picture Vocabulary Test, and Leiter International Performance Scale) clearly are inadequate (Oakland & Matuszek, 1977). Knowing the precise characteristics of a test's standardization sample is highly important in interpreting a child's test score with confidence.

General national norms may not be the most appropriate standard against which to compare a child's performance. For many decisions localized norms should be used. These can be developed for a region, state, community (school district), or a school campus; culture-specific norms (for example, those only on black children) also may be an appropriate standard. When the characteristics of children within a geographic area are sufficiently different from those in the standardization sample on such characteristics as scholastic aptitude and achievement or educational, social, and cultural experiences, the use of one or more sets of localized norms may be appropriate. Localized norms also are highly desirable when the results will be used for purposes of screening, instructional arrangements, grouping practices, and other programmatic features somewhat indigenous to one institution (for example, a school district).

The availability of both national and localized norms, particularly when reported by various social-class and racial-ethnic groups, provides for greater accuracy and clarity in interpreting test scores. The set or sets of norms to be used should be determined from the nature of the questions being asked of the data.

A considerable body of literature currently exists that does not substantiate a claim of cultural bias against ethnic minority children with regard to the use of well-constructed, adequately standardized intelligence and aptitude tests. The construct validity of a large number of popular intelligence tests has been examined across race and sex with a variety of populations of minority and white children (Gutkin & Reynolds, 1981; Merz, 1970; Oakland & Feigenbaum, 1979; Reschly, 1978; Vance & Wallbrown, 1978). No consistent evidence of bias in construct validity has been found in these studies. For example, in a study comparing the factor structure of the WISC-R across four different racial groups (whites, blacks, Mexican-Americans, and Native American Papagos), Reschly (1978) concluded that the usual interpretation of the WISC-R Full Scale IQ as a measure of overall, general intellectual ability appears to be equally appropriate for all four groups. He also concluded that the Verbal-Performance scale distinction on the WISC-R is equally appropriate across race, and that strong evidence exists for having confidence in the integrity of the construct validity of the WISC-R for a variety of populations.

On the basis of these studies, Reynolds (1981) has concluded that the evidence presently indicates that psychological tests, especially aptitude tests, function in essentially the same manner across race and sex. In addition, these tests seem to be perceived and reacted to in a similar manner and measure the same construct with equivalent accuracy for blacks, whites, Mexican-Americans, and other native-born American ethnic minorities for both genders. Single group and differential validity generally have not been found and appear to be generally absent from well-constructed, standardized psychological and educational tests. The overall results of these studies suggest that test score differences across race are most likely real and not an artifact of test bias.

The empirical evidence regarding bias in the predictive validity of psychological and educational tests suggests conclusions similar to those from studies on construct validity (Reschly & Reschly, 1979; Reschly & Sabers, 1979; Reynolds & Hartlage, 1979; Reynolds & Nigl, 1981). A number of studies have focused on the differential validity of the Scholastic Aptitude Test (SAT) in predicting college performance. The majority of these studies found either no difference in the prediction of criterion performance of blacks and whites or a bias against whites (see Jensen, 1980, and Reynolds, 1982, for reviews). Similar generalizations hold true for the WISC-R.

For example, in a study examining the validity of WISC-R IQs in predicting reading and math performance on the Metropolitan Achievement Test (MAT) for whites, blacks, Mexican-Americans, and Native American Papagos, Reschly and Sabers (1979) report a generally significant underprediction for whites. The greatest amount of overprediction among all nonwhite groups was with the Papagos. In a subsequent study of the predictive validity of WISC-R factor scores with samples of white, black, Mexican-American, and Papago children, Reschly and Reschly (1979) reported a relatively strong relationship of WISC-R scores to achievement for most non-Anglo as well as Anglo groups. Significant relationships were found between the WISC-R factors and measures or achievement for all the tested groups except the Papagos. Concurrent and predictive validities of the WISC-R were examined for 296 middle- and lower-class Anglo, black, and Mexican-American children (Oakland, 1983). Reading and math data on the California Achievement Test were the criteria. The concurrent and predictive IQ-achievement correlations are approximately .70 for the total group for reading and math. No strong SES or racial-ethnic differences appear.

Results of cross-race comparisons of predictive validity in many other individually administered aptitude tests for children have produced similar results (Bossard, Reynolds, & Gutkin, 1980; Reynolds, 1978; Sewell, 1979). Differences that appear tend to favor minority children. There is no strong evidence to support contentions of differential or single-group validity (Reynolds, 1981). The occurrence of racial-ethnic bias in standardized tests is rare and lacks any apparent pattern, with the exception of those tests having poor reliability and high specificity of test content. The bias that does occur seemingly favors low-SES, disadvantaged minority children, or other low-scoring groups. The allegation of cultural bias against ethnic minority children with regard to the use of well-constructed, adequately standardized intelligence and aptitude tests has not been generally supported by empirical research.

Nevertheless, this does not preclude the need to further examine instruments selected for use in a nonbiased assessment program with regard to their psychometric characteristics. Further research on each measure's reliability and validity—based on its uses with particular subgroups for arriving at particular decisions—is needed. Estimates of reliability must be sufficiently high to enable an examiner to ensure that the data are stable and consistent. Validity studies are needed to ascertain the accuracy of the inferences and uses made of the data in different settings and with different subpopulations (Bersoff, 1973). Knowledge of the selected measure's reliability and validity is prerequisite to the development of a nondiscriminatory assessment program. The application of high standards for all assessment techniques will help to ensure a better program in this area.

Professional Personnel as Possible Sources of Bias

Assessment specialists also play a central role in designing and carrying out a nonbiased assessment program. Six general areas are of greatest interest.

Race of Examiner. A popular belief concerning mental testing holds that the lower test scores of blacks and other minority children are due partly to the intelligence tests usually being administered by a white examiner. It is frequently argued that blacks, for example, would perform better with a black examiner. A search of the literature, however, fails to confirm this conclusion (Jensen, 1980). In roughly 83% (25/30) of the studies that have addressed the race-of-examiner issue, no significant relationship was found between the effects of examiner race and mental test scores of whites and blacks. The children in these studies ranged from preschool through grade 12, represented many different geographic locations, and reflected a representative sample of subjects and settings. On the basis of this evidence, one can conclude that the race of the examiner generally is not an important source of variance between whites and blacks on tests of mental ability.

On the other hand, these studies do not lay to rest the issue of the examiner's race. This issue is too complex to be resolved by testing the simple hypothesis that the race of the examiner is a factor contributing to mean-score differences between blacks and whites. The narrow conceptualization of the race-of-examiner issue has resulted in oversimplified research questions and a disjointed body of literature (Graziano, Varca, & Levy, 1982). As an example, race of subject has been viewed as a singular construct. Previous research, however, has pointed out the examiner's age as one factor moderating the race-of-examiner effect (for example, Jensen, 1974). Probably other examiner characteristics such as testing experience also mediate the race-of-examiner effect. Assigning black examiners to test black children is most justifiable when the children have a strong preference to work with black professionals.

Anecdotal evidence suggests that white examiners may contribute to anxiety, fears and suspicion, verbal constriction, strained and unnatural reactions, insecurity, latent prejudice, and other reactions during their interactions with some children as a result of racial differences. Some examiners exhibit paternalism, overidentification, overconcerns, or reactive fears. There is no way of knowing the degree to which these behavioral patterns and perceptions affect the test scores of individual minority children.

Language and Dialect. The nature of the communication process existing between white examiners and minority children represents another source of bias in the testing of minority children. The question arises as to what effect the language of the examiner has on the performance of children from a non-English speaking or bilingual background. It can be assumed, for example, that communication is impeded when verbal and nonverbal clues are misunderstood. Such misunderstanding may result in mistrust, accentuate stereotypic judgments, and contribute to conflict and misinformation. Consequently, it is extremely important that examiners communicate with minority children who use different languages or dialects in a manner that allows for clear understanding.

Some argue that black children do not understand the English commonly used by white examiners, resulting in their scores being lower than when tested by black examiners. However, few studies support this contention. In fact, many black children are bidialectical and have the ability to comprehend black dialects and standard English equally well (Sattler, 1982).

The language of the examiner and of the test does make a difference in testing non-English speaking or bilingual children. Children from these groups frequently obtain higher scores on nonverbal and performance tests than on verbal tests presented in English (Lynn, 1977). It is difficult to conclude that these general findings represent a deficiency in verbal ability relative to nonverbal ability for such a diverse group (Mexican-American, Puerto Rican, American Indian, Chinese, and Japanese). The language used by the examiner has less influence on performance tests and nonlanguage tests than on verbal tests.

In the United States, many Hispanic, Indian, and first-generation Asians speak their native language at home and come into contact with standard English primarily and initially in schools. For children from these backgrounds, examiners should be particularly careful in interpreting verbal test scores and should consider supplementing verbal tests with nonlanguage tests.

Attitudes and Expectations. An adult's attitudes can affect their behaviors toward children. Psychologists and examiners who feel attachment for and are concerned with students are likely to behave quite differently than those who feel rejection or indifference toward them. Moreover, psychologists' attitudes can be affected by children's characteristics. School personnel generally tend to favor bright, achieving, linguistically competent, academically motivated, compliant, conforming students. However, many children who are referred for assessment exhibit quite different characteristics. Furthermore, some persons have strong and fixed opinions of persons of identifiable racial-ethnic and social class groups. These prejudices may prevent people from objectively understanding the individual characteristics of others. Examiners are not immune to these prejudices. They, too, may have biases.

Some believe examiners' expectations about children's test performance may possibly affect minority children differently than white children, placing the minority child in a disadvantaged position. Studies examining whether an examiner's preconceptions of a child's ability level differentially affect the test scores of majority and minority children generally find the examiner's prior expectations have little influence on the intelligence test scores obtained by minority children (Anderson & Rosenthal, 1968; Clairborn, 1969; Dietz & Purkey, 1969; Dusek & O'Connell, 1973; Fielder, Cohen, & Finney, 1971; Fleming & Anttonen, 1971; Ginsburg, 1970; Gozali & Meyen, 1970; Jose & Cody, 1971).

Gender of Examiner. The low performance of children on intelligence tests is sometimes attributed, in part, to the examiner's gender. There has been much conjecture as to whether children perform less well for men than for women. Sattler's (1974) review of the effects of the examiner's gender on intelligence test performance reports that female examiners elicit slightly better performance than male examiners from both male and female subjects. However, because of the unimpressive nature of the empirical evidence, the examiner's gender is likely to be a relatively unimportant factor in evaluating intelligence test performance of minority children.

Deciding Who the Client Is. The American Psychological Association (1972) emphasized the belief in the dignity and worth of the individual, a commitment to freedom of inquiry and communications, and a concern for the best interests of clients, colleagues, and society in general. Psychologists are strongly encouraged to respect the integrity and protect the welfare of the persons with whom they work. When a conflict arises among professional workers, psychologists should be concerned more with the welfare of their clients than with the interests of their professional group.

This principle, however, is not always followed. Some examiners are more concerned with job security, friendships, and serving the institution that employs them. Persons working within this frame of mind will not fully investigate all the factors that may attenuate a child's performance. To find a deficit within the child and to fault the child's home and neighborhood is often easier than to identify important school-related variables that impede the child's development. In a nonbiased assessment program, the examiner has an open mind and investigates school-, child-, and home-related factors that may be hampering a child's development.

Competence. Examiners tend to be highly trained, competent, and dedicated. However, some know assessment superficially and mechanically; are poorly prepared in psychoeducational, child clinical, and behavioral assessment; and generally have not kept up with the advancements made in the field of appraisal and interventions. Some psychologists consider their full-time job to begin after school and devote more effort to developing their private practices than their school-related activities.

Many minority-group and low-income parents depend on the public schools to provide quality educational and psychological services. These parents do not have financial means to purchase such services privately. Thus the standards governing the provision of educational and psychological services in public schools must remain as high as those for the private sector. The competence of examiners working in the public sector represents a very important source of potential bias in the testing of minority children.

School-System Policies and Practices

The degree to which a school system has and willingly uses its financial and professional resources to provide quality diagnostic and intervention services to children may be the single most important factor governing nonbiased assessment programs. Keep in mind that a nonbiased assessment program uses a quality assessment program that attempts to eliminate, minimize, or recognize the presence of biasing conditions. Bias occurs when conditions are present that prevent or obscure either a full and accurate appraisal of a child's characteristics or the use of the information to assist the child's growth and development.

Most responsibilities for delivering a nonbiased assessment program ultimately fall on the school district rather than on private practitioners or state education agencies. Although questions regarding the use of tests with minority pupils in regular education have been raised (Oakland, 1973), the major sources of concerns have been in using tests in special-education programs with minority pupils. Thus the uses of tests in special education with minority pupils is emphasized here.

The Education of All Handicapped Children's Act (Public Law 94-142). The Education of All Handicapped Children's Act (Public Law 94-142) clearly has established the most important standards governing the assessment of handicapped children. Earlier legislation (Public Law 93-380) specified that assessment devices used to classify and place handicapped children will be selected and administered so as to not be racially or culturally discriminatory. P.L. 94-142 and its implementing regulations reaffirmed this mandate concerning nondiscriminatory assessment. Thus an understanding of major provisions of P.L. 94-142 help identify standards useful in the assessment of minority children referred for special education services.

Provisions of 94-142. The law establishes the right to an education for all people between ages 3 to 21 in the least restrictive setting. The *cascade model* (Figure 1) generally has been used as the basis for conceptualizing the least restrictive setting. The model proposes a continuum of special-education services in settings that range from those which are natural and normal for all children (that is, education in the regular classroom) to those which are highly restrictive (that is, state schools or hospitals). The ideal placement is one that provides needed services in the least restrictive setting possible.

P.L. 94-142 also establishes the need for a comprehensive assessment of educational, psychological, medical, social, and linguistic abilities conducted by a multidisciplinary team. Placement decisions are required to draw on information acquired by a multidisciplinary team from various sources. An individual educational plan is written and reviewed annually to focus attention on specific educational needs.

Children with sensory, manual, or linguistic impairment are to be tested in ways that minimize or eliminate the impact of these impairments on the assessment of their cognitive abilities. The tests are to be validated for the specific purposes for which they are used and administered by trained personnel consistent with standardized procedures.

The regulations governing P.L. 94-142 provide for specific due-process procedures that help to establish the parents' rights and allow them to participate when important decisions are made regarding their children. Parents have the right to examine all test results and educational documents pertaining to their children, to receive notices written in their native language when schools are considering making important changes, to object to proposed changes, to be represented by legal counsel and expert witnesses, to have an impartial hearing and judgment, and to appeal decisions made at the hearing to higher courts.

The law seemingly is directed toward improving the diagnostic and intervention services for handicapped pupils, particularly those from racial-ethnic mi-

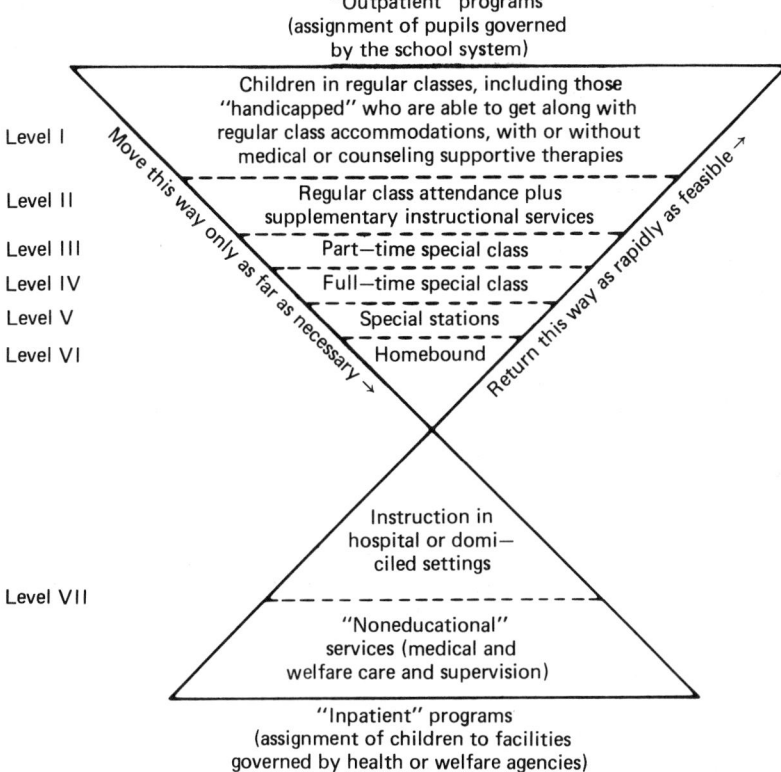

"Outpatient" programs
(assignment of pupils governed
by the school system)

Level I

Children in regular classes, including those
"handicapped" who are able to get along with
regular class accommodations, with or without
medical or counseling supportive therapies

Move this way only as far as necessary →

Return this way as rapidly as feasible →

Level II
Regular class attendance plus
supplementary instructional services

Level III
Part—time special class

Level IV
Full—time special class

Level V
Special stations

Level VI
Homebound

Instruction in
hospital or domi—
ciled settings

Level VII
"Noneducational"
services (medical and
welfare care and supervision)

"Inpatient" programs
(assignment of children to facilities
governed by health or welfare agencies)

Figure 1. Deno's Cascade Model of special education services.

nority groups; to further pupils' educational development in a normal educational setting; to restrict severely the numbers of minorities placed in special educational programs, particularly those programs that are least effective (for example, for the mild mentally retarded children); and to strive to hold the numbers of minority children in special programs and classes proportionate to their representation within the community.

Implementation of P.L. 94-142.

Few school systems with predominantly minority populations are able to comply with the law or to meet its intent. Other school districts with fewer minority children frequently do not have the resources or choose to devote little effort to implementing these regulations.

Note the provision in P.L. 94-142 that tests must be validated for the specific purpose for which they are used. At least three major points follow. First, the law and regulations do not require the use of valid tests, merely those which have been validated. Second, the regulations do not specify conditions for test validation. Third, few attempts have been made by test companies or school districts to establish the validities of tests for minorities for the specific purposes for which they are used.

Information from one large metropolitan district is presented below that shows some of the major problems encountered in delivering nonbiased assessment programs. Difficulties described are not indigenous to this system or even to other large school systems. Major problems exist throughout many of our nation's schools.

Within this district of about one million pupils, teachers refer more than 6000 pupils each month (or about 60,000 yearly) for special education services because special help is needed. Close to 95% of these pupils later qualify for special services. Although the system has more than 300 school psychologists, the number of referrals far exceeds their capacity to conduct psychoeducational appraisals. New referrals are added to the existing list containing 12,000 to 16,000 children waiting to be assessed.

By law, the referred children should be assessed in 60 days. As this is not possible, educational personnel attempt to placate parents' demands and to eliminate lawsuits by communicating their good faith in trying to provide needed services to their children as best they can and as soon as possible.

Many referred children know little English and speak foreign languages. The district is fortunate in being able to assess children in about 30 major languages—the most of any U.S. city. However, it lacks the ability to assess children in more than 200 other languages in which they are legally required to assess. A complete psychoeducational appraisal costs an average of about $900. Annual costs for appraisals of about $48 million places a significant drain on other school resources, and the policy of stealing from Peter to pay Paul is envoked to enable the system to remain solvent. More than 1000 special-education teachers are needed as existing resources clearly do not meet present needs. Many children are placed in private educational facilities whose services frequently cost a minimum of $100 per day. In addition, their programs must be supervised by district personnel, a practice which further increases educational costs.

The effectiveness of the multidisciplinary teams frequently is thwarted by dictatorial practices of the team leader or by district policies that allow the team to recommend only those services that existing school resources provide. Moreover, parental legal rights frequently are annulled when agreements among school personnel are arrived at prior to the multidisciplinary meeting attended by the parents.

Many professional staff, unable to accept the deleterious conditions under which they are forced to work, become discouraged, disheartened, and eventually leave the system. To them, questions about the reliability and validity of the WISC-R when used with black children pale in importance to other large issues.

School-system policies and practices often promote the development of bureaucracies that are insensitive to the individual needs and characteristics of pupils, their families, and educational personnel: the same tests are routinely administered and reported on the approved form using technical jargon to describe analyses rich in statistical patterns and deficient in capturing human qualities. Given the rush to test more pupils, school psychologists and other diagnostic personnel have little time to consult with teachers and parents to help prevent minor problems from increasing in complexity or to carry out primary and secondary prevention programs that may be beneficial for an entire school campus.

Administrators impede the development of good programs for minority children when the school system becomes embroiled in politics, when strikes and attrition contribute to low morale, when rigid boundaries between the home and school are drawn and thus inhibit professionals and parents from forming important and mutually supportive relationships for the benefit of children, and when financial and professional support for regular and special programs is insufficient.

Using Litigation to Improve Assessment

As we have seen, there is no generally accepted definition of bias to which all psychologists can adhere. This unfortunate situation prevails among other behavioral sciences and in the court system too.

Minorities have used litigation as a process to improve assessment and educational services for their children. Various lawsuits have been initiated in an effort to define and clarify appropriate assessment practices or to alter practices alleged to be discriminatory. Litigation clearly has made significant alterations in how minority children are assessed and educated.

During the late 1960s and 1970s, many class-action suits challenged how tests were used in various school systems (Bersoff, 1981; Oakland & Laosa, 1977). Courts in general expressed their reluctance to adjudicate those educational issues and often encouraged the parties to seek out-of-court decisions. No cases involving the cognitive assessment of children have been heard at the Supreme Court level. Thus we must look to lower federal and state courts for direction.

An understanding of the decision in two more recent and well publicized cases may be important in understanding issues central to the topic of this chapter. Both involve class-action suits that allege intelligence tests are biased against black children being considered for placement in classes for the educable mentally retarded (EMR) or educable mentally handicapped (EMH). Many similarities exist regarding the programs and policies in both school systems (San Francisco and Chicago) as well as the evidence and testimony provided to the courts. Judge Robert Peckham issued his opinion in October, 1979 (*Larry P. et al.* v. *Wilson Riles et al.*, No. C-71-277-RFP) regarding the use of the Wechsler Intelligence Scale for Children (WISC) in San Francisco, while Judge John Grady issued his opinion in July, 1980 (*Parents in Action on Special Education et al.* v. *Joseph P. Hannon et al.*, No. 74C 3586) regarding the use of the WISC and Stanford-Binet in Chicago. Both are United States District Judges.

The decisions by the two judges were very different. Peckham ruled in favor of the plaintiffs (the WISC is discriminatory when used in placing black pupils in EMR classes), while Grady ruled in favor of the defendants (the Stanford-Binet and WISC are not discriminatory when used in placing black children in

EMH classes). Sattler (1981) contrasted the written opinions of the two judges on a number of questions. Some of these contrasts appear below.

Q.   What is your understanding of how children are selected for classes for the mentally retarded?

Judge Peckham: . . . The entire placement process revolves around the IQ determination. . . . If the IQ tests are discriminatory, they inevitably must bias the entire process (p. 33).

Judge Grady: . . . An IQ test is not the first level, nor is an IQ score the catalyst for the assessment process. The first level of investigation is the classroom. Unless the child is having difficulty with his studies in the classroom, the question of EMH placement will never arise and there is no occasion for an IQ test (p. 106).

Q.   How much emphasis is given to the IQ in placing children in mentally retarded or educable mentally handicapped classes?

Judge Peckham: The available data suggest very strongly that, even if in some districts the IQ scores were not always determinative, they were pervasive in the placement process. . . . Retardation is defined in terms of the IQ tests, and a low score in effect establishes a *prima facie* case of retardation (p. 33).

Judge Grady: . . . The IQ score is not the sole determinant of whether a child is placed in an EMH class. First, the score itself is evaluated by the psychologist who administers the test. The child's responses are recorded verbatim, and the significance of his numerical score is a matter involving judgment and interpretation. . . . The examiner who knows the milieu of the child can correct for cultural bias by asking the questions in a sensitive and intelligent way. . . . Finally, the IQ test and the psychologist's evaluation of the child in the light of that test is only one component of several which form the basis for an EMH referral (pp. 100–101).

Q.   Was the issue of test validity important in your trial?

Judge Peckham: . . . If defendants could somehow have demonstrated that the intelligence tests had been "validated" for the purpose of EMR placement of black children, those tests could have been utilized despite their disproportionate impact. . . . However, defendants did not make these showings (p. 61).

Judge Grady: We do not address the broader questions of whether these IQ tests are generally valid as measures of intelligence, whether individual items are appropriate for that purpose, or whether the tests could be improved. Those questions are not involved in this case (pp. 91–92).

Q. To what extent do socioeconomic factors account for the findings that black children score lower than white children on intelligence tests?

Judge Peckham: . . . It is clear that socio-economic status by itself cannot explain fully the undisputed disparities in IQ test scores and in EMR placements. . . . The insufficiency of the above explanation leads us to question the cultural bias of IQ tests. The first important inferential evidence is that the tests were never designed to eliminate cultural biases against black children; it was assumed in effect that black children were less "intelligent" than whites (pp. 44–45).

Judge Grady: Defendants' explanation of the IQ difference, that it is caused by socio-economic factors which interfere with the development of intellectual skills, is consistent with other circumstances not accounted for by plaintiffs' theory of cultural bias. It is uncontradicted that most of the children in the EMH classes do in fact come from the poverty pockets of the city. This tends to suggest that what is involved is not simply race but something associated with poverty. It is also significant that many black children who take tests score at levels high enough to preclude EMH placement. Plaintiffs have not explained why the alleged cultural bias of the tests did not result in EMH level scores for these children. Plaintiffs' theory of cultural bias simply ignores the fact that black children perform differently from each other on the tests. It also fails to explain the fact that some black children perform better than most whites. Nationally, 15 to 20 percent of the blacks who take the tests score above the white mean of 100 (p. 105).

Q. To what extent does black children's use of nonstandard English affect their performance on intelligence tests?

Judge Peckham: At the outset, it is undeniable that to the extent black children speak other than standard English, they will be handicapped in at least the verbal component of the tests. . . . Dr. Hilliard and other witnesses pointed out that black children are more likely to be exposed to nonstandard English, and that exposure will be reflected in IQ scores (p. 47).

Judge Grady: The evidence does not establish how the use of nonstandard English would interfere with performance on the Wechsler and Stanford-Binet tests. . . . Dr. Williams testified that a black child might say, "John go to town" instead of "John is going to town," or "John book" instead of "John's book." . . . What is unclear is how the use of such nonstandard English would handicap a child either in understanding the test items or in responding to them. The fact that the child might say "John book" does not indicate that he would not understand the phrase "John's book." Moreover, responding to a test item in nonstandard English should not affect a child's score on the item, since the examiners are specifically instructed by the test manuals to disregard the form of the answer so long as the substance is correct. . . . But there are no vocabulary items on the IQ tests, so far as I can tell, which are peculiar to white culture (pp. 96–97).

Q. Generally, to what extent are intelligence tests racially biased?

Judge Peckham: The answer, as should be clear from the earlier discussion of the history and biases of IQ tests, is that validation has been assumed, not established, for blacks. The tests were developed and standardized in the United States on white, essentially middle-class groups. . . . (p. 67).

Judge Grady: All but a few of the items on their face appear racially neutral. . . . I conclude that the possibility of the few biased items on these tests causing an EMH placement that would not otherwise occur is practically nonexistent (pp. 101–102).

Q. What specific items on intelligence tests do you believe may be racially biased?

Judge Peckham: Cultural differences can also be found in specific test items. Some of these items have in fact become rather notorious, such as the "fight item" on WISC tests. This question asked children what they would do if struck by a smaller child of the same sex. The "correct" answer is that it is wrong to strike the child back. Young black children aged six and seven "missed" this item more than twice as often as their white counterparts. The difference can only be attributed to a cultural variation at that age. Similarly, it may be that such questions as who wrote Romeo and Juliet, who discovered America, and who invented the light bulb, are culturally biased. At a more subtle level, such skills as "picture arrangement" may be tested in a biased fashion if the pictures, which generally are of Caucasian persons, relate to situations more typical of white, middle-class life than the experiences of many black children (p. 48).

Judge Grady: On the WISC and WISC-R, I believe the following items are either racially biased or so subject to suspicion of bias that they should not be used:

1. "What is the color of rubies?"
2. "What does C.O.D. mean?"
3. "Why is it better to pay bills by check than by cash?"
4. "What would you do if you were sent to buy a loaf of bread and the grocer said that he did not have any more?"
5. "What does a stomach do?"
6. "Why is it generally better to give money to an organized charity than to a street beggar?"

7. "What are you supposed to do if you find someone's wallet or pocket book in a store?"
8. "What is the thing to do if a boy (girl) much smaller than yourself starts to fight with you?"

On the Stanford-Binet, I believe the one item which is racially inappropriate is the "aesthetic comparison" on the 4½ year olds' subtest, where the child is asked to tell which of the two persons is "prettier" (p. 68).

Q. Does the use of intelligence tests violate some provisions of Public Law 94-142?

Judge Peckham: . . . Defendants have failed to take the steps necessary to assure the test's validity. They have committed a serious error that Title VII regulations warn against in the employment situation: "Under no circumstances will the general reputation of a test, its author, or its publisher, or casual reports of test utility be accepted in lieu of evidence of validity." Whether or not the tests in fact do what they are supposed to do, the law is that defendants must come forward and show that they have been validated for each minority group with which they are used. This minimal burden has not been met for diagnosing the kind of mental retardation justifying EMR placement (pp. 68–69).

Judge Grady: The requirement that "materials and procedures" used for assessment be nondiscriminatory, and that no single procedure be the sole criterion for assessment, seems to me to contemplate that the process as a whole be nondiscriminatory. It does not require that any single procedure, standing alone, be affirmatively shown to be free of bias. The very requirement of multiple procedures implies recognition that one procedure, standing alone, would well result in bias and that a system of cross-checking is necessary (p. 106).

Q. On the basis of the evidence heard in your court, how did you rule?

Judge Peckham: This court finds in favor of plaintiffs, the class of black children who have been or in the future will be wrongly placed or maintained in special classes for the educable mentally retarded, on plaintiffs' statutory and state and federal constitutional claims. In violation of Title VI of the Civil Rights Act of 1964, the Rehabilitation Act of 1975, defendants have utilized standardized intelligence tests that are racially and culturally biased, have a discriminatory impact against black children, and have not been validated for the purpose of essentially permanent placements of black children into educationally dead-end, isolated, and stigmatizing classes for the so-called educable mentally retarded. Further, these federal laws have been violated by defendants' general use of placement mechanisms that, taken together, have not been validated and result in a large overrepresentation of black children in the special EMR classes (p. 106).

Judge Grady: I have found one item on the Stanford-Binet and a total of eight items on the WISC and WISC-R to be culturally biased against black children, or at least sufficiently suspect that their use is in my view inappropriate. These few items do not render the tests unfair and would not significantly affect the score of an individual taking the test. The evidence fails to show that any additional test items are racially or culturally unfair or suspect. . . . The WISC, WISC-R and Stanford-Binet tests, when used in conjunction with the statutorily mandated other criteria for determining an appropriate educational program for a child, (20 U.S.C. §1412(2) (D) (5)), do not discriminate against black children in the Chicago public schools. Defendants are complying with that statutory mandate.

Intelligent administration of the IQ tests by qualified psychologists, followed by the evaluation procedures defendants use, should rarely result in the misassessment of a child of normal intelligence as one who is mentally retarded. There is no evidence in this record that such misassessments as do occur are the result of racial bias in test items or in any other aspect of the assessment process currently in use in the Chicago public school system (pp. 115–116).

Thus after considering similar and expert testimony, the two judges differed greatly on the major issues regarding the use of these individually administered measures of intelligence. Their decisions add to our uncertainty and further polarize professionals in law, psychology, and education. We are not aware of attempts to have higher courts review these two cases.

Given the air of confusion and conflicting opinions from the social sciences and the courts, yet the need for objective evaluation and direction, the Committee on Child Development Research and Public Policy of the National Research Council established a Panel on Selection and Placement of Students in Programs for the Mentally Retarded (Heller, Holtzman, & Messick, 1982). Their original mission was to determine the factors that account for disproportionate representation of minority students and males in special-education programs and to identify placement criteria or practices that do not affect minority students and males disproportionately. Following their preliminary work, the panel clarified its mission to focus on ways to improve instruction for children. This clarification is noteworthy. Whereas others frequently assume disproportionate numbers of minorities in special programs constitutes *prima facie* evidence of discrimination, the panel questioned under what conditions disproportionate representation is a problem; unequal numbers do not by themselves signify inequality. Disproportion is a problem when children (1) are invalidly assessed for placement in programs for the retarded and (2) receive low-quality instruction.

Instead of recommending procedures that eliminate or reduce disproportions, the panel recommended the following six practices that are intended to redress the inequitable conditions underlying them.

1. It is the responsibility of teachers in the regular classroom to engage in multiple educational interventions and to note the effects of such interventions on a child experiencing academic failure before referring the child for special-education assessment. It is the responsibility of school boards and administrators to ensure that needed alternative instructional resources are available.

2. It is the responsibility of assessment specialists to demonstrate that the measures employed validly assess the functional needs of the individual child for which there are potentially effective interventions.

3. It is the responsibility of the placement team that labels and places a child in a special program to demonstrate that any differential label used is related to a distinctive prescription for educational practices and that these practices are likely to lead to improved outcomes not achievable in the regular classroom.

4. It is the responsibility of the special-education and evaluation staff to demonstrate systematically that high-quality, effective special instruction is being provided and that the goals of the special-education program could not be achieved as effectively within the regular classroom.

5. It is the responsibility of the special-education staff to demonstrate on at least an annual basis that a child should remain in the special-education class. A child should be retained in the special-education class only after it has been demonstrated that he or she cannot meet specified educational objectives and that all efforts have been made to achieve these objectives.

6. It is the responsibility of the administrators at the district, state, and national levels to monitor on a regular basis the pattern of special-education placements, the rates for particular groups of children or particular schools and districts, and the types of instructional services offered to affirm that appropriate procedures are being followed or to redress inequities found in the system.

These recommendations deemphasize the use of global IQ scores and emphasize the assessment of children's functional educational needs and characteristics rather than deficiencies.

Elsewhere we (Oakland, 1982) and others have maintained that improved educational outcomes for minority children should constitute our most important goal and that problems associated with assessing minority children comprise only one component of that goal.

CONCLUSIONS

Issues regarding the cognitive assessment of minority pupils are complex and arise from multiple sources. Through research and writing, the social sciences have devoted much attention to these issues. Psychology seems to be primarily fixated on a set of broad issues involving the psychometric characteristics of tests: how to develop the perfect test or to ascertain a test's psychometric characteristics when used with persons from different racial-ethnic groups and social classes. Although these issues are not unimportant, others deserve priority. To interpret Peckham's decision in *Larry P.* as an indictment of testing misses its major message. We must seek ways to more effectively promote and enhance the cognitive development of significant numbers of minority children. Also, testing should be discontinued when their prevailing effects mislabel people, promote decisions that fail to enhance pupils' psychoeducational development, denigrate the dignity and pride of minorities, and limit their educational and vocational development.

A broader scope is needed, one which reaffirms testing as a technology that should serve members of our society well by identifying their various talents, abilities, and other characteristics. Complementary educational programs involving the pupils, their families, educators, and other segments of the community are needed that foster pupils' cognitive development. School assessments, tied to interventions likely to be beneficial, should be our goal.

REFERENCES

American Psychological Association (1972). *Ethical Standards of Psychologists.* Washington, DC: APA.

Anastasi, A. (1976). *Psychological testing* (4th ed.). New York: Macmillan.

Anderson, D. F., & Rosenthal, R. (1968). Some effects of interpersonal expectancy and social interaction on institutionalized retarded children. *Proceedings of the 76th Annual Convention of the American Psychological Association, 3,* 479–480. (Summary)

Ault, R. L. (1977). *Children's cognitive development: Piaget's theory and the process approach.* New York: Oxford University Press.

Berk, R. A. (Ed.). (1982). *Handbook of methods for detecting test bias.* Baltimore: The Johns Hopkins University Press.

Bersoff, D. (1973). Silk purses into sow's ears. *American Psychologist, 28*(10), 892–899.

Bersoff, D. (1981). Legal principles in the nondiscriminatory assessment of minority children. In T. Oakland (Ed.), *Nonbiased assessment.* Minneapolis: The University of Minnesota.

Biesheuvel, S. (1972). Adaptability: Its measurement and determinants. In L. J. Cronbach and P. J. D. Drenth (Eds.), *Mental tests and cultural adaptation.* The Hague, Netherlands: Mouton Publishers.

Black, H. (1963). *They shall not pass.* New York: Morrow.

Bossard, M. D., Reynolds, C. R., & Gutkin, T. B. (1980). A regression analysis of test bias on the Stanford-Binet Intelligence Scale. *Journal of Clinical Child Psychology, 9,* 52–54.

Brembeck, C. S. (1971). *Social foundations of education.* New York: Wiley.

Brophy, J. E., & Good, T. L. (1970). Teachers' communication of differential expectations for children's classroom performance: Some behavioral data. *Journal of Educational Psychology, 61,* 365–374.

Chapman, M., & Hill, R. A. (Eds.). (1971). *Achievement motivation: An analysis of the literature.* Philadelphia: Research for Better Schools.

Clairborn, W. L. (1969). Expectancy effects in the classroom: A failure to replicate. *Journal of Educational Psychology, 60,* 377–383.

Cleary, T. A. (1968). Test bias: Prediction of grades of Negro and white students in integrated colleges. *Journal of Educational Measurement, 5,* 115–124.

Cole, M., & Bruner, J. (1971). Cultural differences and inferences about psychological processes. *American Psychologist, 26,* 867–876.

Crano, W. D., Kenny, D. A., & Campbell, D. T. (1972). Does intelligence cause achievement? A cross-lagged panel analysis. *Journal of Educational Psychology, 63,* 258–275.

Darlington, R. B. (1971). Another look at "culture fairness." *Journal of Educational Measurement, 8,* 71–72.

Das, J. P. (1972). Patterns of cognitive ability in nonretarded and retarded children. *American Journal of Mental Deficiency, 77,* 6–12.

Das, J. P., Kirby, J., & Jarman, R. F. (1975). Simultaneous and successive synthesis: An alternative model for cognitive abilities. *Psychological Bulletin, 82,* 87–103.

Das, J. P., & Molloy, G. N. (1975). Varieties of simultaneous and successive processing in children. *Journal of Educational Psychology, 67,* 213–220.

Dietz, S. M., & Purkey, W. W. (1969). Teacher expectation of performance based on race of student. *Psychological Reports, 24,* 694.

Dusek, J. B., & O'Connell, E. J. (1973). Teacher expectancy effects on the achievement test performance of elementary school children. *Journal of Educational Psychology, 65,* 371–377.

Ebel, R. L. (1975). Educational tests: Valid? Biased? Useful? *Phi Delta Kappan, 57,* 83–89.

Eells, K. (Ed.). (1951). *Intelligence and cultural differences.* Chicago: University of Chicago Press.

Fielder, W. R., Cohen, R. D., & Finney, S. (1971). An attempt to replicate the teacher expectancy effect. *Psychological Reports, 29,* 1223–1228.

Flaugher, R. L. (1978). The many definitions of test bias. *American Psychologist, 33,* 671–679.

Flavell, J. H. (1977). *Cognitive development.* Englewood Cliffs, NJ: Prentice-Hall.

Fleming, E. S., & Anttonen, R. G. (1971). Teacher expectancy as related to the academic and personal growth of primary-age children. *Monographs of the Society for Research in Child Development, 36,* (5, Serial No. 145).

Fruchter, B. (1954). *Introduction to factor analysis.* Princeton, NJ: Van Nostrand.

Gage, N. L., & Berliner, D. C. (1975). *Educational Psychology.* Chicago: Rand-McNally.

Ginsburg, R. E. (1970). An examination of the relationship between teacher expectancies and students' performance on a test of intellectual functioning. Unpublished doctoral dissertation, University of Utah.

Gozali, J., & Meyen, E. L. (1970). The influence of the teacher expectancy phenomenon on the academic performance of educable mentally retarded pupils in special classes. *Journal of Special Education, 4,* 417–424.

Graziano, W. G., Varca, P. E., & Levy, J. C. (1982). Race of examiner effects and the validity of intelligence tests. *Review of Educational Research, 52*(4), 469–497.

Greenberg, J. W., & Davidson, H. H. (1972). Home background and school achievement of black urban ghetto children. *American Journal of Orthopsychiatry, 42,* 803–810.

Gross, M. (1963). *The brain watchers.* New York: New American Library.

Gruen, G., Ottinger, D., & Zigler, E. (1970). Level of aspiration and the probability learning of middle- and lower-class children. *Developmental Psychology, 3*(1), 133–142.

Guilford, J. P. (1967). *The nature of human intelligence.* New York: McGraw-Hill.

Gutkin, T. B., & Reynolds, C. R. (1981). Factorial similarity of the WISC-R for white and black children from the standardization sample. *Journal of Educational Psychology, 73,* 227–231.

Havighurst, R. (1970). Minority subcultures and the law of effect. *American Psychologist, 25*(4), 313–322.

Heller, K. A., Holtzman, W. H., & Messick, S. (Eds.). (1982). *Placing children in special education: A strategy for equity.* Washington, DC: National Academy Press.

Herrnstein, R. (1971). I.Q. *The Atlantic Monthly, 228*(3), 43–64.

Herrnstein, R. J., & Boring, E. G. (Eds.). (1965). *A sourcebook in the history of psychology*. Cambridge, MA: Howard University Press.

Humphreys, L. G. (1973). Statistical definitions of test validity for minority groups. *Journal of Applied Psychology, 58*(1), 1–4.

Hyman, H. H. (1954). The value-system of different classes. In R. Bendix & S. Lipset (Eds.), *Class status and power*. London: Routledge and Kegan Paul.

Jackson, B., & Marsden, D. (1962). *Education and the working class*. London: Routledge and Kegan Paul.

Jarman, R. G., & Das, J. P. (1977). Simultaneous and successive syntheses and intelligence. *Intelligence, 1*, 151–169.

Jensen, A. R. (1970). A theory of primary and secondary familial mental retardation. In N. R. Ellis (Ed.), *International review of research in mental retardation* (Vol. 4). New York: Academic Press.

Jensen, A. R. (1974). The effects of race of examiner on the mental test scores of white and black pupils. *Journal of Educational Measurement, 11*, 1–14.

Jensen, A. R. (1980). *Bias in mental testing*. New York: The Free Press.

Jensen, A. R. (1981). *Straight talk about mental tests*. New York: The Free Press.

Jose, J., & Cody, J. J. (1971). Teacher-pupil interaction as it relates to attempted changes in teacher expectancy of academic ability and achievement. *American Educational Research Journal, 8*, 39–49.

Kamin, L. (1974). *The science and politics of IQ*. Hillsdale, NJ: Erlbaum.

Laosa, L. M. (1977). Nonbiased assessment of children's abilities: Historical antecedents and current issues. In T. Oakland (Ed.), *Psychological and educational assessment of minority children*. New York: Bruner/Mazel.

Larry P. et al. v. *Wilson Riles et al.* (1972, 1974, 1979). United States District Court, Northern District of California, Case No. C-71-2270 RFP.

Learner, B. (1981). Representative democracy, "men of zeal," and testing legislation. *American Psychologist, 36*, 270–275.

Lord, F. M. (1980). *Application of item response theory to practical testing problems*. Hillsdale, NJ: Erlbaum.

Lynn, R. (1977). The intelligence of the Japanese. *Bulletin of the British Psychological Society, 30*, 69–72.

Matluck, J. H., & Mace-Matluck, B. (1981). Nonbiased assessment: Understanding language characteristics. In T. Oakland (Ed.), *Nonbiased assessment*. Minneapolis: Upper Midwest Regional Resource Center.

McGurk, F. C. J. (1967). The culture hypothesis and psychological tests. In R. E. Kuttner (Ed.), *Race and modern science*. New York: Social Science Press.

Mercer, J. R. (1972). IQ: The lethal label. *Psychology Today, 6*, 44–47, 95–97.

Mercer, J. R. (1973). Implications of current assessment procedures for Mexican-American children. *Journal of the Association of Mexican-American Educators, 1*, 25–33.

Merz, W. R. (1970). *A factor analysis of the Goodenough-Harris Drawing Test across four ethnic groups*. (Doctoral dissertation, University of New Mexico, 1970.) *Dissertation Abstracts International*, 1970. (University Microfilm #70-19, 714)

Newland, T. E. (1973). Assumptions underlying psychological testing. In T. Oakland & B. N. Phillips (Eds.), *Assessing minority group children*. New York: Human Sciences Press.

Oakland, T. D. (1972). Effects of test-wiseness materials on standardized test performance of preschool disadvantaged children. *Journal of School Psychology, 10*, 355–360.

Oakland, T. D. (1973). Assessing minority group children: Challenges for school psychologists. *Journal of School Psychology, 11*, 294–303.

Oakland, T. D. (1978). Predictive validity of readiness tests for middle and lower socio-economic status Anglo, Black, and Mexican American children. *Journal of Educational Psychology, 70,* 574–582.

Oakland, T. D. (Ed.). (1981). *Nonbiased assessment* (a project of the National School Psychology Inservice Training Network). Minneapolis: Upper Midwest Regional Resource Center.

Oakland, T. D. (1982). Nonbiased assessment in counseling: Issues and guidelines. *Measurement and Evaluation in Guidance, 15*(1), 107–116.

Oakland, T. D. (1983). Concurrent and predictive validity estimates for the WISC-R IQs and ELPs by racial-ethnic and SES groups. *School Psychology Review, 12,* 57–61.

Oakland, T. D., & Feigenbaum, D. (1979). Multiple sources of test bias on the WISC-R and the Bender-Gestalt test. *Journal of Consulting and Clinical Psychology, 47,* 968–974.

Oakland, T. D., & Laosa, L. (1977). Professional, legislative, and judicial influences on psycho-educational assessment practices in schools. In T. Oakland (Ed.), *Psychological and educational assessment of minority children.* New York: Bruner/Mazel.

Oakland, T. D., & Matuszek, P. (1977). Using tests in nondiscriminatory assessment. In T. Oakland (Ed.), *Psychological and educational assessment of minority children.* New York: Bruner/Mazel.

PASE: Parents in Action on Special Education et al. v. *Hannon et al.* (1980, July). No. 74 C 3586, United States District of Illinois, Eastern Division, slip opinion.

Reschly, D. J. (1978). WISC-R factor structures among Anglos, Blacks, Chicanos, and Native American Papagos. *Journal of Consulting and Clinical Psychology, 46,* 417–422.

Reschly, D. J., & Reschly, J. E. (1979). Validity of WISC-R factor scores in predicting achievement and attention for four sociocultural groups. *Journal of School Psychology, 17,* 355–361.

Reschly, D. J., & Sabers, D. (1979). Analysis of test bias in four groups with the regression definition. *Journal of Educational Measurement, 16,* 1–9.

Reynolds, C. R. (1978). *Differential validity of several preschool assessment instruments for blacks, whites, males, and females.* Unpublished doctoral dissertation, University of Georgia, Athens.

Reynolds, C. R. (1981, August). *Test bias: In God we trust, all others must have data.* Invited address for the APA Division of Evaluation and Measurement at the annual meeting of the American Psychological Association, Los Angeles.

Reynolds, C. R. (1982). The problem of bias in psychological assessment. In C. R. Reynolds & T. D. Gutkin (Eds.), *The handbook of school psychology.* New York: Wiley.

Reynolds, C. R., & Hartlage, L. C. (1979). Comparison of WISC and WISC-R regression lines for academic prediction with black and with white referred children. *Journal of Consulting and Clinical Psychology, 47,* 589–591.

Reynolds, C. R., & Nigl, A. J. (1981). A regression analysis of differential validity of intelligence tests for black and for white inner city children. *Journal of Clinical Child Psychology, 10*(3), 176–179.

Rosenthal, R., & Jacobson, L. (1968). *Pygmalion in the classroom.* New York: Holt, Rinehart and Winston.

Sattler, J. M. (1974). *Assessment of children's intelligence.* Philadelphia: Saunders.

Sattler, J. M. (1981). Intelligence tests on trial: An "interview" with Judges Robert F. Peckham and John F. Grady. *Journal of School Psychology, 19*(4), 359–369.

Sattler, J. M. (1982). *Assessment of children's intelligence and special abilities* (2nd ed.). Boston, MA: Allyn and Bacon.

Scheuneman, J. D. (1981). A new look at bias in aptitude tests. In P. Merrifield (Ed.), *Measuring human abilities* (*New Directions in Testing and Measurement,* No. 12). San Francisco: Jossey-Bass.

Sewell, T. E. (1979). Intelligence and learning tasks as predictors of scholastic achievement in black and white first-grade children. *Journal of School Psychology, 17,* 325–332.

Shepard, L. A. (1982). Definitions of bias. In R. A. Berk (Ed.), *Handbook of methods for detecting test bias*. Baltimore: Johns Hopkins University Press.

Snow, R. (1969). Unfinished Pygmalion. *Contemporary Psychology, 14,* 197–199.

Spearman, C. E. (1927). *The abilities of man.* New York: Macmillan.

Terrell, G., Jr., Durkin, K., & Wiesley, M. (1959). Social class and the nature of the incentive in discrimination learning. *Journal of Abnormal and Social Psychology, 59,* 270–272.

Thorndike, E. L. (1927). *The Measurement of intelligence.* New York: Bureau of Publications, Teachers College, Columbia University.

Thorndike, R. L. (1968). Review of *Pygmalion in the classroom,* by R. Rosenthal and L. Jacobson. *American Educational Research Journal, 5,* 708–711.

Thurstone, L. L. (1938). Primary mental abilities. *Psychometric Monographs,* No. 1.

Vance, H. B., & Wallbrown, F. H. (1978). The structure of intelligence for black children: A hierarchical approach. *The Psychological Record, 28,* 31–39.

Williams, R. L. (1970). From dehumanization to black intellectual genocide: A reminder. *Clinical Child Psychology Newsletter, 9*(3), 6–7.

Williams, R. L. (1972, September). *The BITCH-100: A culture-specific test.* Paper presented at the annual convention of the American Psychological Association, Honolulu, Hawaii.

Williams, R. L. (1974). Scientific racism and IQ: The silent mugging of the black community. *Psychology Today, 7*(12), 32–41.

Wiseman, S. (Ed.). (1967). *Intelligence and ability.* Baltimore, MD: Penguin Books.

Zigler, E., & Butterfield, E. C. (1968). Motivational aspects of changes in IQ test performance of culturally deprived nursery school children. *Child Development, 39,* 1–14.

Zigler, E., & de Labry, J. (1962). Concept-switching in middle-class, lower-class, and retarded children. *Journal of Abnormal and Social Psychology, 65,* 267–273.

SIXTEEN

TRANSCULTURAL INTELLECTUAL ASSESSMENT

PERFORMANCE BY HISPANICS ON THE WECHSLER SCALES

DAMIAN McSHANE

Utah State University
Logan, Utah

VALERIE J. COOK

George Peabody College of Vanderbilt University
Nashville, Tennessee

The Wechsler Intelligence Scales have been the long-standing "favorites" for North American psychologists attempting to measure a range of cognitive-intellectual skills. Although the Wechslers have held the corner on the market, the market has been changing dramatically in recent years. The Hispanic population of the United States has been increasing—it is currently second only to Blacks as a minority group, is predicted to become the largest minority in coming years, and is currently the largest linguistic minority group. Thus it is mandatory to take close examination of performance by Hispanics* on the Wechsler scales.

Over 70 empirical studies have been identified as directly concerned with performance by Hispanics on the Wechsler scales: Wechsler Preschool and Primary Scale of Intelligence (WPPSI), Wechsler Intelligence Scale for Children (WISC), Wechsler Intelligence Scale for Children—Revised (WISC-R), and the Wechsler Adult Intelligence Scale (WAIS). Studies of Hispanic performance on the Wechsler Adult Intelligence Scale—Revised (WAIS-R) were notably lacking.

---

*From a general perspective, *Hispanic* and *Latino* will be used interchangeably to refer broadly to the varied cultural and geographical settings of Spanish-speaking peoples. Other terms such as *Mexican-American* and *Chicano*, will be used when research literature refers to a specific population cited or when used by the authors to describe particular research experience.

In our critical examination of these studies, we sought to answer such questions as:

Do Hispanics exhibit unique and characteristic performance on the Wechsler scales?

What factors or variables affect Hispanic performance on the Wechslers?

What is the relationship of Hispanic Wechsler performance to other variables and measures of significant interest, especially in predictive terms?

Where does our current research and clinical knowledge base regarding transcultural assessment of Hispanics using the Wechslers seem to lead us?

The following sections individually cover studies concerning Hispanics and the WPPSI, WISC and WAIS, WISC and WISC-R, and WISC-R. Results are summarized for each section and across all studies; a final discussion integrates findings and suggests future needs and directions. Approximately 70 empirical studies concerning Hispanic[1] performance on the WPPSI, WISC, WISC-R, and WAIS are critically reviewed. Hispanics showed significantly different score patterns when compared to other ethnic groups. Verbal IQ was generally lower than performance IQ. However, reliable and consistent internal validity was similar to that for other groups, although small item bias without systematic pattern for Hispanic performance was identified. Evidence in support of external validity was more variable. Dimensions such as age, socioeconomic status (SES), sex, and urban-rural residence significantly affected scores. Sociocultural background accounted for a sizable portion of variance in IQ scores; correlations with sociocultural measures tended to approximate or exceed those with standardized achievement tests (which also were significant). Low significant correlations between IQ and adaptive behavior measures were obtained.

Finally, evidence for and against the effects of language difference (e.g., bilingualism) were reported. A majority of researchers failed to define the nature of language variation in their studies, seriously compromising any possibility of interpreting results. Added to the fact that because ethnicity and/or sociocultural background was not specified sufficiently in most studies, inferences about many aspects of Hispanic performance were probably confounded.

WPPSI

Bergan and Parra (1979) administered Information, Comprehension, Arithmetic, Picture Completion, Geometric Design, and Block Design subtests of the WPPSI to 29 Anglo and 72 bilingual Mexican-American 4 and 5 year olds. The WPPSI was administered in English, Spanish, and in *English* and *Spanish* to equal-sized subgroups of Mexican-Americans. Mexican-American children tested in English scored significantly lower than children tested in English and Spanish and significantly lower than the Anglo group. Mexican-American children tested in both languages differed significantly from Anglo children tested in English. Scores were as follows: Anglo in English, 97.50; Mexican-American in English, 77.00; Mexican-American in Spanish, 86.25; Mexican-American in English and

Spanish, 91.33. Children were also given a letter identification pretest and letter identification instructions under variations in modeling and feedback conditions. There were no significant differences among IQ predictions of letter-testing conditions or instructional variations.

Gerken (1978), giving the WPPSI and the Leiter International Performance Scale to 25 Mexican-American children in the Headstart program and in kindergarten, used 6 examiners (2 bilingual Mexican-American, 2 bilingual Anglo, 2 monolingual Anglo). Significant differences were found for the total group in relation to verbal versus nonverbal tests: WPPSI VIQ, 78.40; PIQ, 98.96; FSIQ, 86.96; LIPS IQ, 102.44. Although there were no examiner effects, significant differences with respect to language dominance groups were obtained:

Spanish	VIQ, 62.33; PIQ, 88.22; FSIQ, 80.30
Bilingual	VIQ, 83.69; PIQ, 104.15; FSIQ, 99.03
English	VIQ, 103.67; PIQ, 108.64; FSIQ, 107.22
Leiter	Spanish, 90.33; Bilingual, 109.23; English, 109.33

Spanish-dominant children scored lower on both VIQ and PIQ, whereas bilingual children only scored lower on VIQ, as compared to English-dominant children. However, both Spanish-dominant and bilingual children evidenced a significant VIQ-PIQ discrepancy (26 points, 21 points), whereas English dominant children did not.

Finally, Henderson and Rankin (1973) administered the WPPSI to 49 Mexican-American 5 year olds and obtained Metropolitan Reading Test scores from school records when they finished third grade ($N = 36$). Split-half procedures resulted in a reliability coefficient of .95, not significantly different from that in the manual. Correlations with the MRT providing a measure of predictive validity were not significant. WPPSI scores for the group were VIQ, 74; PIQ, 91; FSIQ, 80.

WPPSI Summary

If one can summarize *three* studies, the performance of young Mexican-American children on the WPPSI is characterized by very large Verbal-Performance discrepancies, averaging about 20 points; this sort of variation may well be related to language difference and bilingualism. No findings of significant predictive validity for the WPPSI were discovered.

WISC

Language

Of six studies directly concerned with comparing a Spanish version and the English version of the WISC or administration in Spanish versus in English, three found some significant differences favoring Spanish and three found no differences or differences favoring English.

Chandler and Plakos (1969) reported that 47 students of Mexican descent in grades 3–8 who had trouble speaking English and who had enrolled in educable mentally retarded (EMR) classes were given the Escala de Inteligencia Wechsler Para Niños (Spanish version of WISC). Results showed an approximate increase of 12 IQ points over a previous performance (recorded in school records) on the English version. Interestingly, prior WISC (English) records showed an average PIQ-VIQ discrepancy of 7 points (favoring PIQ), and the Spanish version elicited about the same average discrepancy. (Both VIQ and PIQ increased equally.) Ethnicity of examiners was not reported.

Sixty kindergarten and first-grade Chicano children were administered the WISC in English or bilingually by Chicano or Anglo examiners (De Jesus, 1978). A weak but significant effect by language was found for VIQ but not for PIQ. However, there was a strong ethnicity-of-examiner effect, favoring Chicano examiners, for both VIQ and PIQ. Children tested in English by Chicano examiners achieved significantly higher scores than did other treatment groups.

One hundred bilingual Spanish-Americans (grades 3–5, Dallas, Texas) whose primary spoken language was Spanish were each given English and Spanish versions of the WISC (Galvan, 1967). Children scored lower on the English version, with no significant correlation between VIQ on different language versions, no significant correlation for PIQ on the different versions, and no significant correlations between WISC VIQ scores on either version and California Achievement Test scores.

In contrast, Swanson and De Blassie (1971) gave the WISC to 41 first-grade children (6–8 to 7–11 years old) from two rural elementary schools in central New Mexico, who had attended Headstart and went into first grade in 1969 and whose parents (both) were Mexican-American. Half the children were given the WISC with the help of an interpreter; the other half were tested entirely in English. The former group obtained the following mean scores: VIQ, 88.95; PIQ, 101.42; FSIQ, 94.47; and the latter group, these mean scores: VIQ, 91.94; PIQ, 103.4; FSIQ, 96.94. No significant differences were found.

One-half ($N = 150$) of the entire fifth grade of Nogules Elementary School was randomly selected and given the WISC in English (Palmer & Gaffney, 1972). After 1 year, a random sample ($N = 30$) of the original subjects was given a Spanish translation of the WISC developed at the University of Arizona. There were no significant differences between subtests for the two versions. Measured by the Hollingshead (1957) Index of Social Position, the significant correlation between SES and English-version scores did not occur for the Spanish version. Performance in Spanish was remarkably similar to that in English, suggesting to Palmer and Gaffney low skills in both languages. Lack of well-developed language skills coupled with low socioeconomic status suggested impoverished background as an important factor. The authors concluded,

Testing in English of bilingual children does not necessarily handicap them—results achieved reflect an accurate level of performance. Regardless of the language, the subtest scaled scores for the most part fall into the low average range. [p. 63]

Swanson (1975) tested 90 first and second graders in the Hatch, New Mexico, school system whose dominant language was Spanish and whose parents were both Mexican-American. Children were assigned to three groups on the basis of California Test of Mental Maturity IQ (thereby controlling for IQ), undergoing WISC administration in English or in Spanish, or in English with an interpreter. Swanson reported that performance was superior for the English group on all subtests of the Verbal Scale, with the Spanish group consistently inferior. Children who were administered the test in Spanish obtained superior scores in all but two of the subtests in the Performance Scale of the WISC. Thus Swanson concluded that "the use of English in administration of the verbal phase of the WISC and in Spanish administration of the Performance phase are more likely to elicit optimum performance of Mexican-American children."

Finally, 45 bilingual Mexican-American, educable mentally retarded children (8½–11½ years old) were given a variety of tests, including English and Spanish versions of the WISC (Hausman, 1972). The author reported that an analysis of a subject's performance during the Raven Interest Training session proved the most meaningful in terms of assessing learning potential.

Psychometric Properties, SES, Sex, Age, Academic Performance, and Emotional Functioning

Fourteen studies suggest that the psychometric characteristics of WISC performance by Spanish-speaking children varies from those for Anglo children; socioeconomic status (SES), sex, and age affect WISC scores for these ethnic children, but there is little relationship between WISC performance and measures of academic skill or emotional functioning for these three factors.

Spence, Mishra, and Ghozeil (1971) administered the WISC Vocabulary subtest (among other tests) to 99 children whose parents spoke only Spanish (Group 1) and to 47 children whose parents spoke both Spanish and English (Group 2). Mean scores for Group 1 and Group 2 differed significantly (8.25 and 9.69), suggesting to the authors that the Mexican-American children from bilingual home environments had certain intellectual advantages as compared to the children from monolingual homes.

Altus (1953) studied two groups of school children referred for preliminary screening for classes for the mentally retarded, one bilingual and of Mexican descent and the other unilingual and of non-Mexican descent. The children were equated on variables of age, sex, and Performance IQ. Significant differences in IQ on the Verbal Scale averaged 17 points in favor of the unilingual group. Unilingual results were VIQ, 89; PIQ, 86; FSIQ, 87. Bilingual results were VIQ, 72; PIQ, 84; FSIQ, 75. The bilingual group was divided into younger and older groups, and the older group exhibited higher VIQ (by 9.4 points) and PIQ (by 7.1 points). Altus (1953) reported that the higher Verbal IQs of the older group showed some tendency toward narrowing the Verbal-Performance gap and that this may occur with age and increased school attendance, although the relative difficulty of the items showed little change.

Seventy-five subjects, Anglo-American monolinguals, monolingual Spanish-Americans, and Spanish-American bilinguals were selected in relation to language, ethnic group, sex, grade and placed in a $3 \times 2 \times 2$ design (Killian, 1971). WISCs were administered to children who had just finished kindergarten or first grade and then readministered 26 months later (grades 2 and 3). Anglos scored higher on VIQ for both test and pretest. Anglos scored higher on PIQ for the pretest, but Spanish-American performance significantly increased on the retest, and this difference disappeared. Individual subtest variation showed this more general pattern, and Spanish-American children scored significantly higher than Anglos on Object Assembly. Test-retest reliability coefficients over the 26-month period for subtests varied between .29 (Information) and .58 (Block Design). Killian (1971) concluded that Spanish children were deficient in verbal comprehension skills; primary differences among groups seemed to be ethnic rather than in relation to bilingualism. Respective VIQ, PIQ, and FSIQ for bilingual Spanish children were: *1968*, 88, 90, 88; *1970*, 90, 96, 92; for Anglo children: *1968*, 100, 97, 98; *1970*, 97, 97, 97; for monolingual Spanish children: *1968*, 92, 93, 92; *1970*, 91, 99, 94.

A variety of perceptual and language tests, including the WISC, were given to Spanish- ($N = 68$), English- ($N = 57$), and Navajo- ($N = 33$) speaking elementary school children (monolingual upon school entrance) who were referred by teachers for school problems and who had a monolinguistic home environment, no handicapping conditions, no history of severe illness or accidents, and no more than 20 days absenteeism, (Sabatino, Hayden, & Kelling, 1972). Children were matched on age and PIQ. Differences between language groups were significant for Information, Vocabulary, and Similarities subtests. There were no effects due to sex differences. The authors concluded that "the school learning problems experienced by native Spanish-speaking children were the result of their limited linguistic competence in English, the language of instruction in their classroom."

An intensive analysis of the relative value of using the Vocabulary and Block Design subtests of the WISC to predict FSIQ based on six Verbal and five Performance WISC subtests was made (Mercer & Smith, 1972). Tests were administered to 1,310 6- to 11-year-old Anglo, Black, and Mexican-American children attending public elementary schools in Riverside, California. Separate analyses were performed by sex, age, and socioeconomic level for each of the ethnic groups. For Mexican-Americans, no age differences were found. Mexican-American children scored with the following ranges: VIQ, 84.6–90.0; PIQ, 95.7–99.4. They had significantly lower VIQs (approximately 10 points) than PIQs. Lower performance on the WISC of low SES boys was a pervasive tendency, but was most marked among Mexican-American girls. Socioeconomic differences were negligible for boys but significant for girls. Predictions of FSIQ, VIQ, and PIQ from Vocabulary and Block Design subtests were most accurate for FSIQ (.846 with a standard error of 6.74 IQ points). Boys of lower social status had significantly higher VIQs than girls in all ethnic groups. Scores tended to increase with increase in social status, especially for girls. Disappearance of sex differences for middle status Mexican-Americans resulted primarily from greater improvement in the scores of girls with increase in status.

Bechtol (1981), studying internal bias of the WISC for approximately 200 Blacks, 400 Mexican-Americans, and 400 Anglos, reported little evidence for cultural bias against the Blacks and Mexican-Americans. Consistency reliabilities were high across all groups; group by item interactions were often significant, but considered trivial for practical purposes. The groups had highly similar rank orderings of items for difficulty; however, relative differences in item difficulties were dissimilar. Bechtol concluded that because these interactions were substantially reduced when minority children were compared with Anglos two years younger, the results supported a group difference in mental maturity interpretation. Test and item correlations also revealed little bias, and "the small residue of bias present was further attenuated by longer exposure to the Anglo culture (p. 2733)."

Three hundred twenty Mexican-American children attending Riverside, California, public schools, ages 6–11, mostly low SES, were given the WISC (Goldman & Hartig, 1976). Teachers rated each student on a competence scale made up of semantic differential questions (e.g., slow-quick); social grade point averages and academic grade point averages were obtained from cumulative records. Differences between Anglo and Black and Mexican-American scores were all significant, as were variances. IQ was associated with more than twice as much variance in scholastic performance in Anglo children as in Black or Mexican-American children. In fact, IQ accounted for very little variance in scholastic performance in the latter groups. The authors suggested that lower validities for minority children may have been due, in part, to the smaller variance of grade point average for minority children.

Buriel (1978) compared WISC Block Design performances (as well as CEFT and PRFT as measures of field dependence) of 40 second and third generation Mexican-American and 40 Anglo students in first through fourth grades. Anglo children scored significantly higher at the upper grade level (3 and 4). The WISC-BD showed a significant relation to math (not reading) for both groups of children, and the author concluded that the WISC-BD may have the most cross-cultural validity as an index of children's mathematical abilities.

Thirty (15 boys, 15 girls) Mexican-American children enrolled in regular classes in the Laredo (Texas) public schools were selected from a stratified parent population (Milne, 1974) and given the WISC: VIQ, 83; PIQ, 96; FSIQ, 88. Best scores were on Coding, Picture Arrangement, Picture Completion; lowest scores were on Vocabulary, Information, and Digit Span.

Christiansen and Livermore (1970) administered the WISC to 92 Anglo-American and Spanish-American children 13 to 14 years of age who were enrolled in regular public school classes. They divided the sample into four groups of 23 children each on the basis of social class and ethnic origin. Results were as follows for VIQ, PIQ, and FSIQ. Spanish, low SES: 89, 96, 91; Spanish, mid SES: 111, 108, 111; Anglo, low SES: 95, 102, 99; Anglo, mid SES: 120, 109, 116. A 2 × 2 ANOVA found both ethnic origin and social class to affect general intelligence and verbal abilities, whereas only social class related to nonverbal abilities.

Stewart (1976) examined the effects of sex and ethnic variables for 42 mentally retarded students, 42 normal children, and 41 children diagnosed with learning or language problems (Anglos, Blacks, and Mexican-Americans, aged 6–10). Analysis of variance found no significant effects of sex or ethnicity for regular classroom groups. Significant interaction between ethnicity and learning problems, and between sex and retardation, was found. However, regardless of the level of significance, effects did not account for any appreciable amount of the variance.

Burstein (1976) administered the WISC to three separate samples of schizophrenic, emotionally disturbed, and normal children; each sample contained 120 White, Black, or Hispanic children between the ages of 6 and 12 years. Despite statistical significance, the use of signs derived from WISC scores to aid in the diagnosis of emotional disorders was not found to be sufficiently effective to warrant future research. Neither of the discriminant functions was significant for the Hispanic sample, and Burstein felt this reflected the strength of the effects of cultural factors on the WISC scores overriding the influence of psychopathology.

Using Mercer and Smith's (1972) data concerning 1,310 public school children (6–11 years old), including Anglos (505), Blacks (319), and Mexican-Americans (487), Silverstein (1973) factor analyzed WISC scores. (Chicano mean scores on VIQ, PIQ, and FSIQ were 87.2, 97.0, and 91.1, respectively.) Factor I, Verbal Comprehension, was composed of Information (.58), Comprehension (.38), Arithmetic (.39), Similarities (.54), and Vocabulary (.60); and Factor II, Perceptual Organization, was composed of Block Design (.45) and Object Assembly (.45), for Mexican-American children.

Prewitt-Diaz and Munoz (1980) administered the WISC (Spanish version; Moran, 1974) to 100 Puerto Rican students in grades K–9 (10 at each grade level) aged 5–15. Contrary to the findings of Moran (1974), who reported a Puerto Rican mean IQ of 88.01 and a standard deviation of 21.6, these 100 students obtained a mean of 109.9 with a standard deviation of 14.56 (VIQ, 90.20; PIQ, 111.80).

Taleriro and Brown (1963) examined the records of 92 Puerto Rican children, 6–15 years of age, seen in a hospital setting in New York between 1952 and 1961. The children were divided in three age groups: 6 through 8 years, 11 months; 9 through 11 years, 11 months; and 12 through 14 years, 11 months. The respective groups obtained the following scores: VIQ, 78; PIQ, 90; FSIQ, 83; VIQ, 79; PIQ, 87; FSIQ, 81; VIQ, 84; PIQ, 90; FSIQ, 86. Not only did older subjects score higher, but they also showed greater variability in a group. Generally, Information and Vocabulary were consistently poor, although there was a slow but steady improvement with increases in age.

Taleriro and Brown (1963) indicated that the performance of the early adolescent group was similar to that of adult psychiatric Puerto Rican pretests on the Wechsler—VIQ, 84; PIQ, 90; FSIQ, 86—reported by Brown (1960). The adult group showed better verbal comprehension. The authors also compared their results with the performances of 120 children (grades 1–8) tested in Puerto Rico with a Spanish translation and adaptation of the WISC (Wechsler, 1959). These Puerto Rican children obtained a mean FSIQ of 88.

Finally, 110 psychologists estimated "true IQs" from constructed WISC profiles that varied for ethnicity, social class, profile-scatter pattern, and direction of Verbal-Performance Scale discrepancy (Sattler & Kuncik, 1976). Psychologists gave higher IQ estimates to Black and Mexican-American profiles. (Patterns of subtest scores affected estimates.)

WISC Summary

In summary, controlling for the language of WISC administration produced equivocal results. Three studies found Hispanic children to do better in Spanish, whereas three studies found they did as well in English. One of these studies found that English produced better VIQs, whereas Spanish produced better PIQs. PIQ-VIQ differences favoring PIQ by 7–10 points seemed to be obtained regardless of language of administration. Two studies found age or grade effects (one only with PIQ). Another found no age effect but reported sex and sex by SES effects. Although a sex by retardation effect was obtained in the second study, another matched age and PIQ and found no sex effect. No relationship of IQ to emotional disturbance was found for Hispanics. Finally, although high internal consistency (reliabilities, test and item correlations) and similar factor structure were obtained for Hispanic performance compared to performance of Anglos, no consistent relationship to achievement was found. Across these 18 WISC studies PIQ-VIQ discrepancies averaged about 10 points, with significant variation higher and lower. Finally, examiner effects were explored in the following study, with interesting results.

Thomas et al. (1971) involved 72 Puerto Rican families in long-term studies of behavioral and intellectual development. A vast majority of the parents were born in Puerto Rico, came to New York in their late teens, lived in low-income public housing projects, and did not complete high school. Over 95% of the fathers and less than 10% of the mothers were employed. Two Puerto Rican examiners—both female, fluent in Spanish and English, with comparable clinical experience—administered the WISC to 116 children (62 boys and 54 girls) between the ages of 6 years, 0 months and 15 years, 11 months. Examiner B had never met any of the children before, and Examiner A had known the children and their families for years.

The mean Full Scale, Verbal, and Performance IQs reported by Examiner A ($N = 71$) were all at least 10 points higher than those reported by B ($N = 45$). Mean scores for A were: VIQ, 96.5; PIQ, 98.6; FSIQ, 97.2; and for B: VIQ, 79.1; PIQ, 86.1; FSIQ, 80.5. Children tested by A achieved significantly higher scores on all 10 subtests, with greatest absolute differences found for Vocabulary, Comprehension, and Similarities subtests.

In order to intensively study the relation of examiner-child interactions to the level of measured intelligence, 19 subjects were retested by the two examiners. Examining test reports written immediately after each testing session with regard to the examiners' description of the children's behavior produced the following results.

Examiner A made significantly more positive statements about the child's relation to the examiner and the child's approach to test demands. In retrospective interviews focusing on examiner descriptions of the testing session, Examiner A reported spending considerable time with each child before beginning formal testing. She greeted the child in a lively and friendly manner, engaging the child in conversation at once, encouraging the child to ask questions about the examiner, the room, and features of the test, creating the atmosphere of a game and making every effort to draw the child into the test situation as a joint pleasant activity. She encouraged the child to try again if the initial response was "I don't know," and organized breaks and rest periods.

On the other hand, Examiner B described herself as reserved and quiet, approaching the children seriously. She replied willingly to spontaneous questions but in an impersonal way and without pursuing them; followed a set routine; tended to remain silent if the child hesitated or responded "I don't know," and went on to the next item without encouraging the child to try.

Thomas et al. (1971) summarized:

> Examiner A tried to establish a warm, friendly, and mutually cooperative relationship in which the child was encouraged to do well. Examiner B described herself as attempting to establish a friendly but impersonal situation in which formalized rules were followed quite rigidly and in which the child was protected from having to cope with his own inadequacies. [p. 819]

Examiner A obtained significantly larger responses on Verbal subtest items and fewer "I don't know" responses than B. For Examiner B, the correlation between IQ and academic achievement was significant (.01) and accounted for almost 50% of the variance ($N = 26$). For children tested by Examiner A, the correlation between measured intelligence and academic achievement accounted for less than 20% of the variance and did not reach statistical significance (.05).

Thomas et al. (1971) interpreted the above results to suggest that greater verbalization increases the opportunity of saying something right, and that repeated effort after an initial expression of ignorance also increases the possibility of success. They suggested that better performance may occur when "optimizing" rather than "standardized" testing procedures are emphasized. And in attempting to explain higher academic-IQ correlations for Examiner B, the researchers speculated that there is little opportunity for maximizing performance during group-administered achievement tests. Procedures used by most teachers in routine classroom instruction more closely resemble those of Examiner B, suggesting that her test scores may have represented a more accurate reflection of what is actually learned under such instructional conditions.

WISC/WAIS

Murray et al. (1973) administered the WISC and WAIS to 2498 students aged 10–19 years at the Gatesville State School for Delinquent Boys in Texas (Anglo, 1007; Black, 808, Chicano, 663). Scores in terms of VIQ, PIQ, and FSIQ were as follows:

	WISC		WAIS
Anglo:	91.1, 95.5, 92.5	Anglo:	96.3, 98.4, 97.1
Chicano:	75.5, 87.3, 79.3	Chicano:	83.4, 91.1, 85.9
Black:	75.8, 77.2, 74.2	Black:	84.4, 84.4, 83.4

WISC scores were significantly lower than WAIS scores for all ethnic groups. Chicanos evidenced VIQ-PIQ discrepancies for both the WISC (12 points) and the WAIS (7 points).

Overall and Levin (1978) reported the absence of significant difference in effects associated with age, sex, ethnic group, and education in terms of a variety of disturbed diagnostic groupings (776 psychiatric patients), excluding mental deficiency. Highly significant WAIS IQ effects were associated with differences in ethnic group (Mexican-American, $N = 54$), sex, and educational levels independent of diagnostic group.

WISC/WISC-R

Goody (1981) collected data from three samples of 30 children each (Anglo, Chinese, Hispanic) tested on the WISC from 1966–1974 and from similar samples of children given the WISC-R who had been tested from 1974–1979. All 180 subjects were male disabled readers (aged 7½ years to 12 years, 3 months). Monolingual Anglos scored significantly higher on most Verbal subtests, Verbal IQ, and Bannatyne (1968) Conceptual and Acquired Knowledge factors. Chinese scored significantly higher on WISC-R Coding than Hispanics. Chinese scored significantly higher on most Performance subtests and PIQ than Hispanics and Anglos. A majority of the WISC-R profiles exhibited PIQ greater than VIQ, whereas a majority of WISC profiles demonstrated PIQ equaling VIQ (less than 15 point difference) for all subjects. Chinese and Hispanics showed greater PIQ-VIQ differences than Anglos. The main Bannatyne pattern found among Anglos was Conceptual > Spatial > Sequential, and for Chinese and Hispanics Spatial > Sequential > Conceptual. Nearly all of the subtest and IQ scores of the WISC group were consistently higher than those of the WISC-R group.

Maltzman (1981) performed analyses on the same 180 male disabled readers studied by Goody (1982). In addition to Goody's findings, she found that several WISC/WISC-R subtests were predictive of the types of Bender errors made by Anglo and Chinese boys, but no WISC/WISC-R subtest could be found to relate to the number of errors made by the Hispanic-American sample.

Guzman (1976) administered a variety of English and Spanish tests, including the WISC-R and the Escala de Inteligencia Wechsler Para Niños to 52 public and parochial 9-year-old fourth grade students in Corpus Christi, Texas. The group was half boys and half girls; all were of Mexican-American descent, of low socioeconomic background, and bilingual and spoke English as their dominant language (as assessed by Dos Amigos Verbal Language Scales). No sex differences were found, and no differences reported between the WISC and WISC-R.

Munford and Munoz (1980) administered the WISC and WISC-R in a counterbalanced design to 20 Hispanic children (7–12 years old) who spoke fluent English; half were boys and half, girls. As compared to WISC performances, subjects scored significantly lower on WISC-R Similarities, Object Assembly, Coding, Mazes, PIQ, and FSIQ. Girls scored significantly lower on Coding than boys. There was an overall difference of approximately 14 points between Verbal and Performance IQs on both tests. WISC-R scores tended to increase after "practice" on the WISC, but WISC scores tended to decrease after "practice" on the WISC-R. The tests were highly correlated, however. The authors suggested that because the WISC-R was administered first, followed by the WISC, fatigue during the most difficult WISC Verbal section (all Verbal subtests given together) at the end of testing may have accounted for the significant order differences.

Swerdlik (1976) compared WISC and WISC-R scores of 164 Black, White, and Latino children aged 7 years to 15 years, 11 months who had been referred to school psychologists in a midwestern tristate area due to suspected mental deficiency. Seventy-two school psychologists administered the WISC and WISC-R to the children in a counterbalanced order with a specific test-retest interval of not less than a week or more than a month. All subjects obtained significantly higher subtest VIQ, PIQ, and FSIQ scores on the WISC than on the WISC-R. WISC/WISC-R differences increased as the ability of the students decreased. WISC and WISC-R score differences tended to vary significantly for Blacks, Whites, and Latinos. There were no significant subtest differences between ethnic groups.

Swerdlik (1978) again reported the above-mentioned WISC and WISC-R scores administered in a counterbalanced design for 104 White, 39 Black, and 21 Latino students referred for suspected mental deficiency. Latino WISC scores were VIQ, 81; PIQ, 101; FSIQ, 91; WISC-R scores were VIQ, 76; PIQ, 93; FSIQ, 84. Referred Black, White, and Latino children differed less on the WISC and WISC-R than other children in the general population as reported in previous research studies.

Finally, Swerdlik and Schweitzer (1978) compared the factor analytic structure between the WISC and WISC-R for these 164 referred students, but did not separate out different ethnic groups. The WISC exhibited a two-factor solution (Verbal Comprehension and Perceptual Organization), and the WISC-R showed the typical three-factor solution (Verbal Comprehension, Perceptual Organization, Freedom from Distractibility).

WISC and WISC-R performances were compared by Solway (1976) in two samples of juveniles referred to a large metropolitan juvenile probation department ($N = 180$ and 185, respectively). The samples were equated for age, sex, race, and grade level and included Mexican-American subjects. Significant differences for 6 out of 10 subtests and all IQ scores found WISC-R scores lower than WISC scores in every case except for Arithmetic. Actual mean VIQ, PIQ, and FSIQ scores for WISC and WISC-R groups, respectively, were: 83, 89, 84, and 79, 83, 80.

In summary, Hispanic performance on the WISC tended to be significantly higher on the WISC than on the WISC-R in these studies (with one exception). VIQ-PIQ differences for Hispanics averaged about 15 points across studies.

WISC-R

The advent of the WISC-R (Wechsler, 1974) was heralded as "a revision that really is" (Kirchev, 1975). It was concluded, on the basis of inspection of the revisions, that the WISC-R held the potential to be more culturally fair for American minorities than was its predecessor, the WISC. Its psychometric properties and its fairness for minorities seem to have formed the central focus of recent research endeavors. Only one of over 30 articles to be reviewed in this section addressed a topic other than the psychometrics and fairness issue.

It is likely that this focus on WISC-R psychometric properties is, in part, a response to the courts' tendency to target the tests in cases concerning the culturally fair identification of mentally retarded children. Little consensus has been reached among psychologists and educators regarding the nature of "fair" tests or, conversely, test bias. There appears to be agreement, however, that (1) bias is the "other side" of validity and (2) both internal and external validity criteria should be considered in determining appropriate uses for a test. Thus when considering Hispanic children and the validity of the WISC-R, two primary questions emerge: Is the WISC-R performance of Hispanic children similar to that of children from other ethnic groups? (Does the WISC-R have internal validity for use with Hispanic children?) Does the WISC-R predict school success equally well for Hispanic and other children? (Does the WISC-R have external validity for use with Hispanic children?)

Research related to the internal and external validity of the WISC-R will be presented first, followed by a presentation of the relationship of the WISC-R with other variables. Attention will be given to other-than-test factors that influence Hispanic children's performance on the WISC-R. Finally, research regarding the validity of the WISC-R in diagnosing educational difficulties of Hispanic children will be discussed.

Internal Validity of the WISC-R

Is the WISC-R performance of Hispanic children similar to that of children from other ethnic groups? Perhaps the most obvious starting point is the examination of descriptive data. Although researchers have not had the simple description of WISC-R test results as their primary focus, many have reported such descriptive data in the context of their studies. Descriptive WISC-R results reported in the studies reviewed here are summarized in Table 1.

Mercer (1979) and Oakland (1980) reported similar results across the three WISC-R IQs: Anglos obtained higher scores than Blacks and Hispanics on all three measures; Blacks had higher VIQs than Hispanics; whereas Hispanics had higher PIQs and FSIQs than Blacks. These differences were significant, except for the comparison of Blacks and Hispanics on the VIQ. Additionally, Hispanic children obtained higher VIQs than PIQs. The differences between Mercer's and Oakland's results (Oakland's were somewhat higher for all ethnic groups across all IQs) may be related to different sampling procedures. Mercer's data are from the standardization of the System of Multicultural Pluralistic Assessment (SOMPA) and based on a random sampling of children in California public schools, having equal representation of White, Black, and Hispanic children, boys and girls, across an age range from 5–12. Oakland used a stratified random sampling design to select children from grades 1 through 8 (ages 6–14) from the three racial-ethnic groups (Anglo, Black, and Mexican-American), from two social classes (middle and lower), and about equally from both sexes. Oakland did not identify the geographic location of his study.

Oakland (1983) used a similar stratified random sampling procedure to select children from one school district to participate in the second study reported in Table 1. While the same pattern of Anglo, Hispanic, and Black WISC-R IQs were reported for the total sample and across ethnic groups within the middle class, this pattern changed to Anglo, Hispanic, and Black within the lower-class sample. Furthermore, both Hispanic and Black middle-class children scored higher than Anglo lower-class children.

While the WISC-R IQ patterns found in the nonreferred samples are also observed in the referred samples, subtle differences emerge across these referral samples from the Southwest. (Only Swerdlik, 1978, had a non-Southwest sample.)

Hispanic children who were (1) of "verified" Mexican-American ethnicity (Dean, 1979a), (2) known to speak Spanish at home at least part of the time (Dean, 1980), or (3) bilingual Spanish-English speakers who used both languages daily (Lawlis, Stedman, & Cortner, 1980) obtained the highest VIQs and FSIQs of all of the Hispanic children. Dean's 1979 sample met clear criteria for diagnosis of learning disabilities, and his 1980 sample had been referred due to learning difficulties. Both samples were from the Phoenix area; the first was a matched (on sex, age, and SES) sample, the second sample was described as middle to lower-middle class. Lawlis et al. conducted their research with an undefined referral sample from parochial schools.

Gutkin's (1979) groups (diagnosed as learning disabled) obtained FSIQs similar to those of the total public school referral populations (cf. Gutkin & Reynolds, 1980; Reynolds & Gutkin, 1980). Although Anglo children obtained higher IQs than Chicano children, Reynolds and Gutkin (1980) found that the differences favoring PIQ over VIQ were the same for these predominantly lower-class Anglo and Chicano children. Additionally, Gutkin and Reynolds (1980) found no significant differences between Anglos and Chicanos on the three IQs, and the Anglos had a greater Verbal-Performance difference (favoring Performance) than did the Chicanos. It should be noted tha Gutkin and Reynolds did not define *Chicano* in their description of subjects.

Hays and Smith (1980) reported the greatest differences between ethnic groups in their study of juvenile delinquents referred to the probation department for intellectual or psychological evaluations. All of these children were from suspected low income backgrounds.

Swerdlik (1978) reported WISC-R results for children in Illinois, Ohio, and Michigan who had been referred for evaluations due to concerns about their intellectual ability. The mean PIQ obtained by these Latino (term undefined) children suspected of intellectual impairment was higher than the mean PIQs obtained by the Latino children referred for learning disabilities; furthermore, it was within the average range and less than one-half standard deviation below the mean for nonreferred Latino children. Combining this information with the fact that these Latino children had much larger differences between their VIQ and PIQ means than did either their White or Black counterparts in this study, or referred Chicano children in the other studies, leads one to question if the individuals making these referrals might be confusing language differences and intellectual ability.

In summary, mean differences do exist between the ethnic groups. Hispanic children score lower than Anglo children on all three WISC-R IQs, but higher than Black children on the PIQ and FSIQ. While some scholars (e.g., Mercer, 1979; Williams, 1974) would accept these data as evidence of test bias, others (e.g., Clarizio, 1982; Cleary, Humphreys, Kendrick, & Wesman, 1975) argue that such differences may reflect true differences of the ethnic groups and are not simply artifacts of the test. Thus further examination is required to determine the extent to which the WISC-R itself contributes to these differences.

Internal Consistency, Reliability.   A test must be reliable before it can be valid for any group or purpose. The internal reliability coefficient also serves as a measure of test homogeneity, that is, the degree to which all items are measuring a similar construct (Clarizio, 1982).

The first investigator to attend to the internal consistency of the WISC-R for Mexican-American children was Dean (1977), who examined the performance of 53 children referred for learning disabilities. The resulting split-half (odd-even, corrected by the Spearman-Brown formula) reliability coefficients ranged from .75 to .93 for the Verbal subtests and .65 to .79 for the Performance subtests (Coding deleted). The reliability coefficients for the scale IQs were: .95, Verbal; .89, Performance; and .96, Full Scale. These reliability coefficients were comparable to those reported in the WISC-R manual. The standard errors of measurement for the subtests and IQs of these Mexican-American children exceeded those reported for the standardization sample; however, Dean concluded that the WISC-R is reliable for Mexican-American children because the SEMs were less than five IQ points or two scaled score points.

Table 1. WISC-R IQ Means and Standard Deviations in Studies Including Hispanic Children

Researcher(s)	Subjects' Ethnicity	N	WISC-R IQs					
			Verbal		Performance		Full Scale	
			$\overline{X}$	SD	$\overline{X}$	SD	$\overline{X}$	SD
Nonreferred Samples								
Mercer, 1979	Anglo	604	102	15	104	14	103	14
	Black	456	89	14	90	13	88	13
	Hispanic	520	88	15	98	13	92	13
Oakland, 1980	Anglo	106	104	16	106	14	106	15
	Black	117	93	13	95	14	93	13
	Hispanic	92	92	14	98	13	95	14
Oakland, 1983[a]	Anglo total	116					105	16
	Mid-SES	110					111	13
	Low-SES	56					93	14
	Black total	122					92	13
	Mid-SES	67					96	13
	Low-SES	55					87	12
	Hispanic total	108					95	15
	Mid-SES	57					101	15
	Low-SES	51					87	11
Reschly, 1978		223	85	13	93	12	88	12

Referred Samples

Study	Group	N						
Dean, 1979a	Anglo	60	92	11	90	13	90	12
	Hispanic	60	85	12	88	13	87	13
Dean, 1980	Anglo	109	90	20	92	19	90	18
	Hispanic	123	86	14	89	14	86	13
Gutkin, 1979	Anglo	53					82	12
	Hispanic	87					77	9
Gutkin & Reynolds, 1980	Anglo	78	79	14	85	15	80	15
	Hispanic	142	80	13	83	14	80	13
Hays & Smith, 1980	Anglo	41	92	13	99	11	95	11
	Black	46	73	11	787	13	74	12
	Hispanic	30	72	13	86	13	78	12
Lawlis et al., 1980[a]	Hispanic	83					90	12
Reynolds & Gutkin, 1980	Anglo	94	79	16	86	15	81	15
	Hispanic	174	70	12	83	18	75	11
Swerdlik, 1978	Anglo	104	84		93		89	
	Black	39	79		81		80	
	Hispanic	21	76		93		84	

Note: Reported IQs rounded to the nearest whole number.

[a] Author(s) reported "WISC-R IQs" but did not report *which* IQ; assumed to be Full Scale IQ.

Oakland and Feigenbaum (1979) examined the internal consistency of the WISC-R for a stratified sample of 180 Anglo-American, 119 Black, and 137 Mexican-American children from an unnamed school district of 55,000. The Kuder-Richardson alpha levels for the subtests were relatively similar overall and ranged from .70–.90 for Anglos, .64–.87 for Blacks, and .67–.88 for Mexican-Americans. The alphas for the Mexican-American sample were generally lower than those for the Anglo sample, except for Similarities (equal) and Digit Span and Mazes (higher). In contrast, the alphas for the Mexican-American sample were generally higher than those for the Black sample except for Digit Span (equal) and Arithmetic, Picture Arrangement, and Mazes (lower). Oakland and Feigenbaum concluded that there are "no strong indications of test bias from an internal consistency standpoint" (p. 972).

Sandoval (1979) used a more heterogeneous sample that included the 345 Anglo, 330 Black, and 350 Mexican-American children for whom WISC-R data sets were available from the SOMPA standardization sample. The large majority of the alpha reliabilities were within .02. Sandoval concluded that the WISC-R "has high comparable reliability for both majority and minority groups" (p. 922).

Finally, Ross-Reynolds and Reschly (1983) calculated Cronbach alphas for all WISC-R subtests (except Coding and Digit Span) for a stratified random sample of the 252 Anglo, 235 Black, 223 Chicano, and 240 Native-American Papago first to ninth graders included in the Pima County (Arizona) mental retardation prevalence study. The reliabilities ranged from a low of .71 for Black children on Object Assembly to a high of .93 for White children on Vocabulary. The variability across subtests was greater than that across ethnic groups: "variations within the *same* subtest across groups was .05 or less" (p. 145). The reliabilities were greatest for Information and Vocabulary and lowest for Picture Arrangement, Object Assembly, and Mazes for all groups. In general, the Cronbach alphas exceeded the Kuder-Richardson reliabilities reported in the WISC-R manual, though they followed the same pattern.

Thus a pattern has emerged supporting the internal consistency and reliability of the WISC-R in its use with Hispanic children.

Characteristics of Subtests and Items.   Critics of the WISC-R (e.g., Williams, 1970, 1971) have often attributed the mean differences among ethnic groups to the different experiences they bring to the testing situation. They contend that the WISC-R items are biased in that they are not consistent with the concepts and vocabulary associated with cultural minorities. Numerous scholars (e.g., Clarizio, 1982; Cleary et al., 1975) have cautioned against face-level judgments of item bias and directed our attention to the use of statistical procedures to explore such bias.

Sandoval (1979) found that Anglo children's mean raw scores on subtests exceeded those of Black or Mexican-American children by at least one-half of the Anglo standard deviation. The standard deviations of raw scores, however, were comparable across all subtests, except for Object Assembly, where the standard deviation for Blacks exceeded that for Anglos or Mexican-Americans. In contrast, Swerdlik (1978) found no significant differences in subtest scaled scores among the three ethnic groups in his referral sample.

Oakland and Feigenbaum (1979) calculated item difficulty indexes for each child. A series of ANOVAs on the mean scores for each subgroup was done to test between-group differences. Significant differences were found: boys/girls, older/younger, middle SES/lower SES, higher acculturation/lower acculturation, and Anglo/Mexican-American and Black. Unfortunately, they did not explore the effects of combining these independent variables. They concluded, "there is evidence of test bias on the WISC-R" (p. 972).

In a second procedure, Oakland and Feigenbaum calculated the correlation of each test item and the total score for children in each of the 11 groups (see above). These correlations were then correlated to compare the degree of relationship between two sets of correlations from two subgroups; thus a low correlation would indicate bias. Only three of the comparisons were less than .80, two of which were among the ethnic group comparisons (Anglo vs. Black, Black vs. Mexican-American). While Oakland and Feigenbaum may have been too quick in concluding that the test is not biased overall, this position is supported regarding the performance of Mexican-American children.

Dean (1979a) used a stepwise discriminate analysis with WISC-R subtests and IQ composites as predictor variables to identify WISC-R profile patterns in a matched (on sex, age, grade, SES) sample of learning disabled Anglo and "verified" Mexican-American children. The variables that comprised the discriminant function were Similarities, Coding, Picture Completion, and Arithmetic. "With the exception of Coding, the predictive power of subtests taken in unison favored the Anglo-American sample" (p. 793).

Sandoval (1979) completed a comprehensive study of WISC-R item performance patterns among Anglo, Black, and Mexican-American children. He found that the rank order correlations between item difficulties for Anglo and Mexican-American children ranged from .981 on Similarities to a perfect 1.0 correlation on Comprehension, Block Design, and Object Assembly. The rank order correlations of difficulty differences between adjacent items were somewhat lower, but all exceeded .70, "indicating that few items in each subtest are relatively more difficult for one group or another" (p. 922). Item by ethnic group interactions were generally significant; however, significant differences between Anglo and Mexican-American children were *not* found on Arithmetic or the Performance subtests (except Mazes). Following a multivariate ANOVA on the difference in item means across ethnic groups and SES, Sandoval concluded that "the difference in scoring between groups is spread across the items and subtests, although Information and Vocabulary for Blacks and Vocabulary for Mexican Americans do show significant ethnic group effects." A total of 76 items were identified as more difficult for Mexican-American than Anglo children. The nature of the differences in item performance was not readily explained, that is, no pattern was discernible.

The item difficulty patterns of four groups of nonreferred, average children—

Anglos, Blacks, Chicanos, and Bermudians—were compared on each of the Verbal subtests of the WISC-R by Sandoval, Zimmerman, and Woo-Sam (1983). Analyses done separately for 7½ and 10½ year olds identified only a small number of items differentially difficult for one group of children or another and found item difficulty curves for the four groups remarkably parallel, considering the differences in the children's cultures. The authors also cited Cotter and Berk (1981), who studied learning disabled children, and Figueroa (1982), who separated a Chicano population into those whose parents spoke Spanish most of the time and those whose parents did not, as additional empirical support for similar, parallel curves in dissimilar groups of subjects.

Mishra (1983) administered the six Verbal WISC-R subtests to 40 Anglo, 40 Mexican-American, and 40 Navajo subjects matched for grade level (fourth and fifth), sex, and socioeconomic status. With long-linear analytic techniques, results revealed that the performance of subtests was homogeneous across the three cultural groups in Arithmetic, Comprehension, and Digit Span subtest items. Only 10 of the 79 items comprising Information, Similarities, and Vocabulary were found to be biased against Mexican-American subjects (whereas a greater number were biased against the Navajo). Mishra also noted that some of the Vocabulary items identified as biased (failed more often) in the present study were also reported as being culturally sensitive by Martin (1977) using a Cuban-Spanish translation of the WISC-R. Martin found that rank order of item difficulty for some Vocabulary items changed for his Cuban sample or compared to rank order of item difficulty obtained for the normative sample.

Ross-Reynolds and Reschly (1983) focused their item analyses on six of the WISC-R subtests: Information, Similarities, Arithmetic, Vocabulary, Comprehension, and Picture Completion. An outlier analysis was conducted for each subtest, using the White sample as the basis of comparison for the Black, Chicano, and Native American Papago samples. They found that the WISC-R items are virtually unbiased for Blacks (no biased items) and Chicanos (only one biased item on the Vocabulary subtest). In contrast, one-third of the items on the Verbal Scale subtests were interpreted as biased against the Native American Papagos. Their results may be related, in part, to their scoring of some Verbal subtest items as pass-fail when, in fact, they are scores with 0, 1, or 2 points.

In a second analysis, Ross-Reynolds and Reschly calculated point biserial correlations, reflecting the relationship between item responses and subtest scores, for each ethnic group on Information, Arithmetic, and Picture Completion. Whereas the general magnitude and pattern of these correlations were comparable for Anglos, Blacks, and Chicanos (correlations of .4 or greater were found for two-thirds of the items for each group), they were lower and different for the Native American Papagos.

Thus, depending on the method of analysis used, there are mixed results regarding item bias against Hispanic children on the WISC-R. Because test critics have consistently pointed to items they deemed biased, Sandoval and Mille (1980) had 38 Black, 22 Mexican-American, and 40 Anglo-American college students judge the relative difficulty of (1) items that were found to be biased and (2) items that were found to be equally difficult in Sandoval's (1979) study. They found that the judges, regardless of ethnicity, could not discriminate among the biased and fair items.

Even when conceding that some of the WISC-R items may be relatively more difficult for Hispanic children than for Anglo children, the overall pattern of performance across items appears to be comparable across ethnic groups (with the exception of American Indians). Sandoval (1979) concluded:

> The lack of a clear pattern of difficult items and the fact that there exists a large number of items just slightly more difficult for minority group children sprea.. throughout the entire test suggest that general factors rather than specific item content contribute to differences in means.

Because there appeared to be a general factor affecting minority children's performance on the WISC-R items, Reynolds and Willson (1982) attempted to control for a general ability factor through the use of a partial point-biserial correlation between ethnicity and individual subtest performance (where total performance was the controlling variable) in order to evaluate the degree to which ethnic differences might be attributed to differences in or related to specific ability factors. They administered the WISC-R to 252 Whites, 223 Mexican-Americans, and 240 Native American Papagos. White children showed relatively higher levels of performance than Mexican-American children on Information, Similarities, Vocabulary, and Comprehension. Once overall level of performance was equated, no White–Mexican-American differences appeared on any other subtests. This was in sharp contrast to Black–White comparisons that show (according to the authors) once overall level of performance is controlled, no differences on the Verbal factor, Whites exceeding Blacks on the Spatial-Visualization factor, and superior Black performance on such rote tasks as Digit Span.

Cotter and Berk (1981) attacked this issue from a different perspective. WISC-Rs were administered by certified school psychologists to 112 Black, 126 White, and 117 Hispanic learning disabled children between 10.0 and 10.33 years of age who attended school in a large metropolitan county in Florida. Bilingual children were tested by bilingual school psychologists, and it was noted that "the manner in which particular WISC-R items may have been translated from English to Spanish was at the discretion of each bilingual psychologist" (pp. 4–5). The children were then matched on sex and subtest raw score in Black–White or Hispanic–White comparisons. Item-by-group analysis of variance were computed on the delta transformed item means for each of nine subtests (of the 10 regular subtests, Coding was deleted) and two-group comparisons to determine interaction effects. Significant interactions were found on the Information and Comprehension subtests for both the Black–White and Hispanic–White comparisons. In addition, there was a significant interaction on the Vocabulary subtest in the Hispanic–White comparison. Though these interactions were significant, they hold little practical utility in that they accounted for less than 2 percent (.94 to 1.63 percent) of the total subtest variance. Furthermore, the patterns of item bias seemed to offset each other. That is, 11 percent of the items were biased against Blacks as compared to 9 percent biased against Whites, and only 6 percent of the items were biased against Hispanics, whereas 8 percent were biased against Whites. The latter comparison is particularly surprising; however, the reader is asked to remember that the Hispanic children may have been tested in a combination of English and Spanish. This administration procedure confounds the results and adds to difficulty in their interpretation. However, it may be that the biases of items against minority groups is related to a general rather than specific cultural factor.

Factor Analytic Studies. Even the most critical of test critics would agree that there is evidence of "fairness" if a test has similar factor structures for different ethnic groups. Conversely, "If the test measures different factors in the two (or more) groups, we then have evidence that the test does not behave the same, psychometrically speaking, in the advantaged and disadvantaged populations" (Clarizio, 1982, p. 68). We will review Kaufman's analysis of the WISC-R standardization data before reviewing the factor analytic studies of Latino children's performance. A summary of the factor structures reported in the studies to be reviewed is presented in Table 2.

The WISC-R standardization sample of 2200 children included Hispanic children, but they were categorized as "White" or "Nonwhite" based on visible physical characteristics (Wechsler, 1974). Kaufman's (1975) analysis should be used as the primary reference/comparison data in that the norms are used for all children. He did a series of factor analyses, including the principal-components technique, varimax rotations, and oblique solutions. The results of the varimax rotations are of most interest in that the later researchers all used this procedure. When two factors were requested, "the pattern of loadings . . . correspond[ed] perfectly to Wechsler's dichotomous division of the tests for virtually every age group" (p. 137). A third factor emerged at 9 of the 11 age levels, thus Kaufman concluded that the three-factor solution is the best fit. The data from Kaufman's study reported in Table 2 are the median loadings for the 11 age levels. Kaufman's (1975, 1979) organization of the three factors is based on the heaviest loadings of subtests. The first factor, Verbal Comprehension, consists of Information, Similarities, Vocabulary, and Comprehension. The second factor, Perceptual Organization, includes Picture Completion, Picture Arrangement, Block Design, Object Assembly, and Mazes. The third factor, consisting of Arithmetic, Digit Span, and Coding, was labeled Freedom from Distractibility. This organization is even more strongly supported by the oblique factor solutions. Furthermore, one large general factor emerged when using an unrotated principal factor solution. This general factor accounted for 79% to 92% (across age groups, median of 89%) of the common factor variance, thus supporting the concept of the Full Scale IQ. Should the factor pattern for Hispanic children vary substantially from these data, one would question the validity of the WISC-R for use with these children.

Sandoval (1982) conducted a factor analysis for each of the three ethnic groups included in the SOMPA standardization sample. While he found that the three-factor solution worked for Anglos (the third factor explained only 8% of the variance), a two-factor solution was best for Blacks and Mexican-Americans. Though Information loaded more heavily on Factor II than Factor I for Mexican-American children, the two factors overall were quite congruent with those of the Anglo children (see Table 3).

Reschly (1978) conducted factor analyses on the data obtained in the Pima County mental retardation prevalence study. The three-factor solution for Anglos was "virtually identical" (p. 419) to that found by Kaufman (1975). The factor structure was similar for Chicanos, except that Picture Arrangement emerged on Factor III. The first two factors were most comparable for these Chicano and Anglo children (see Table 3). Furthermore, when comparing his results for Chicano children with those of the standardization sample (i.e., Kaufman, 1975), he found that the coefficients of congruence were high for all three factors: .98, .99, and .93 for Factors I, II, and III, respectively. Reschly concluded, however, that either two or three factors may best describe the pattern for Chicano children. Additionally, "regardless of the index used, the proportions of variance attributable to a general factor were approximately the same for all groups and similar to the standardization sample" (p. 421).

The WISC-R factor structure for referred Hispanic and Anglo children is moderately to highly comparable (see Table 3; Dean, 1980; Gutkin & Reynolds, 1980). Again, the utility of Factor III in describing Hispanic children's performance is questionable (see Table 2). Dean (1980) found that Block Design emerged on Factor III for both Mexican-American and Anglo children referred for learning difficulties. Lawlis et al. (1980) found a third factor composed of Coding and Object Assembly for their referred bilingual Mexican-American children. Finally, Gutkin and Reynolds (1980) rejected a three-factor solution for both the Anglo- and Chicano-referred children.

Only Gutkin and Reynolds (1980) found "clean" Verbal Comprehension and Perceptual Organization factors for Hispanic children. Picture Arrangement loaded more heavily on Factor I than Factor II (Dean, 1980; Lawlis et al., 1980), leading one to question the verbal mediation necessary for referred Hispanic children's performance on this subtest. Lawlis et al. (1980) found the most distinctly different pattern, with only three subtests (Picture Completion, Block Design, and Object Assembly) forming Factor II. Finally, Gutkin and Reynolds (1980) reported that the first principal components factor accounted for 86% and 84% of the common factor variance for Anglo and Chicano children, respectively.

In summary, the first two factors are highly similar for Anglo and Hispanic children, although Picture Arrangement had substantial loadings on Factor I in three of the five analyses of Hispanic children's performance. The sensitivity of this subtest to verbal mediation for Hispanic children should be recognized. The validity of Factor III for Hispanic children is highly questionable. The overall factor structure of the WISC-R, however, is highly comparable for Hispanic and Anglo children.

Table 2. WISC-R Factor Structure (Varimax Rotations)

Researcher(s)	Subjects' Ethnicity	N	I	S	A	V	C	DS	PC	PA	BD	OA	Cd	M
							Factor 1							
Kaufman, 1975	WISC-R standardization sample		63	64	37	72	64	18	35	33	27	21	15	12
Sandoval, 1982	Anglo	332	67	61	53	80	62	26	27	38	29	10	18	05
	Black	314	73	61	53	71	71	30	39	34	26	15	25	09
	Latino	307	10	72	54	81	62	48	25	38	19	24	24	20
Reschly, 1978	Anglo	252	63	59	43	74	64	35	20	20	17	07	12	18
	Black	235	66	59	61	75	71	49	25	29	20	10	33	23
	Latino	223	66	67	40	67	61	33	32	17	20	14	14	06
	Papago	240	68	58	42	74	70	30	21	23	14	07	17	14
Dean, 1980	Anglo	109	76	68	39	76	56	NG	28	23	31	-10	21	NG
	Latino	123	80	76	58	89	46	NG	29	48	28	23	17	NG
Gutkin & Reynolds, 1980	Anglo	78	64	83	39	79	76	20	36	25	38	35	01	NG
	Latino	142	71	69	48	70	55	14	24	18	22	28	14	NG
Lawlis et al., 1980	Latino	83	81	73	64	80	76	58	17	47	39	31	12	NG
							Factor 2							
Kaufman, 1975	WISC-R standardization sample		25	34	20	24	30	12	57	41	66	65	20	47
Sandoval, 1982	Anglo	332	18	25	26	17	23	13	48	42	64	77	12	32
	Black	314	23	20	37	24	16	28	41	53	65	65	32	54
	Latino	307	38	20	39	29	28	34	58	41	60	54	32	48
Reschly, 1978	Anglo	252	32	26	26	23	22	02	49	53	60	59	16	42
	Black	235	40	41	34	20	24	08	52	53	33	17	20	44

Nonreferred Samples

Referred Samples

Sample	n	I	S	A	V	C	DS	PC	PA	BD	OA	Cd	M
Latino	223	20	15	13	26	20	14	*52*	*38*	*59*	*58*	16	*47*
Papago	240	22	33	*37*	15	10	*35*	*53*	*44*	*69*	*51*	17	*51*
Referred Samples													
Dean, 1980 — Anglo	109	09	*39*	−23	22	−12	NG	*66*	*59*	*73*	*69*	29	NG
Latino	123	12	24	13	31	−02	NG	*54*	*44*	*62*	*79*	29	NG
Gutkin & Reynolds, 1980 — Anglo	78	*52*	15	*70*	23	34	*59*	*59*	*64*	*51*	*59*	*45*	NG
Latino	142	13	33	31	27	33	22	*56*	*72*	*64*	*51*	*37*	NG
Lawlis et al., 1980 — Latino	83	12	24	31	30	20	15	*93*	25	*45*	*54*	05	NG
Kaufman, 1975 — WISC-R standardization sample		*41*	28	*58*	33	24	*56*	11	12	28	12	*42*	22
Factor 3													
Sandoval, 1982 — Anglo	332	*36*	24	*37*	14	15	*73*	09	11	15	20	30	31
Black	314												
Latino	307												
Reschly, 1978 — Anglo	252	26	26	*45*	12	21	*40*	09	*99*	22	18	*40*	10
Black	235	18	13	27	16	09	*36*	21	24	*58*	*58*	22	30
Latino	223	33	22	*45*	30	06	31	12	*39*	16	09	*37*	20
Papago	240	21	11	09	05	17	09	14	03	05	25	*37*	28
Dean, 1980 — Anglo	109	19	−26	*52*	20	21	NG	27	−17	*47*	24	*44*	NG
Latino	123	24	−20	*63*	29	30	NG	−20	−22	*39*	26	*38*	NG
Gutkin & Reynolds, 1980 — Anglo	78												
Latino	142												
Lawlis et al., 1980 — Latino	83	18	01	33	01	10	27	00	12	04	*36*	*88*	NG

Notes: I = Information, S = Similarities, A = Arithmetic, V = Vocabulary, C = Comprehension, DS = Digit Span, PC = Picture Completion, PA = Picture Arrangement, BD = Block Design, OA = Object Assembly, Cd = Coding, M = Mazes. Decimals have been eliminated; factor loadings of .35 or greater are in italics. NG = subtest not given in administration of WISC-R.

Table 3. Comparability of the Corresponding WISC-R Factors for Hispanic and Anglo Children

Researcher(s)	Factor I	Factor II	Factor III
Nonreferred Samples			
Sandoval, 1982[a]	.94	.94	NA
Reschly, 1978[b]	.99	.98	.86
Referred Samples			
Dean, 1980[b]	.83	.89	.88
Gutkin & Reynolds, 1980	.98	.91	NA

Note: NA = not applicable.
[a]Cosine of the angles formed between the factor vectors.
[b]Coefficients of congruence.

Summary. Is the WISC-R performance of Hispanic children similar to that of children from other ethnic groups? Hispanic children obtain lower Verbal, Performance, and Full Scale IQs than Anglo children, but higher Performance and Full Scale IQs than Black children. Generally speaking, Hispanic children obtain somewhat higher Performance than Verbal IQs, which has led Kaufman (1979, p. 33) to offer caution regarding the interpretation of the VIQ and to suggest omitting the calculation of the FSIQ when using the WISC-R with bilingual children. These patterns are seen with less consistency among samples of referred Hispanic children. Indices of internal consistency are both high and comparable across ethnic groups. There is some evidence of test item bias (against Hispanics) throughout the test. These items cannot be explained by any common characteristic(s) and thus seem to be associated with some general factor rather than specific characteristics of the Hispanic culture. Furthermore, judges could not discriminate between fair and biased items. The underlying factor structure of the WISC-R is comparable across ethnic groups; however, a two-factor solution (Verbal Comprehension and Perceptual Organization) seems to be the best for Hispanic children. These two factors are well aligned with the Verbal and Performance scales of the WISC-R. The results of these studies create a mixed picture of whether the WISC-R has adequate internal validity for use with Hispanic children.

External Validity of the WISC-R

Does the WISC-R predict school success equally well for Hispanic and other children? Traditionally, school success has been operationally defined as performance on standardized achievement tests. The most commonly used index to describe the relationship between the WISC-R and achievement is the correlation coefficient. But Clarizio (1982) noted that for a test to predict equally across groups, the regression slopes, intercepts, and standard errors of estimate should be equivalent. We will review 15 studies examining the external validity of the WISC-R in an attempt to answer our opening question.

Correlational Studies.   The correlation between the WISC-R and achievement tests are more alike for Anglo and Hispanic children from nonreferred samples than they are for referred samples, though there has been but one study of the latter (see Table 4). Oakland and Feigenbaum (Oakland, 1980, 1983; Oakland & Feigenbaum, 1979) explored the relationship between the WISC-R and California Achievement Test (CAT) for three ethnic groups from stratified random samples of boys and girls, lower and middle SES, and grades 1–8. Oakland (1980) found that all of the correlations for Anglo children were significantly higher than those for the minority children. Similarly, Oakland and Feigenbaum (1979) found that the WISC-R predicts reading significantly better for Anglo than for minority children. Contrary to popular belief, the predictive (3 years) correlations were equal to or slightly greater than the concurrent (same Spring) correlations. The magnitude of the differences between the concurrent and predictive correlation coefficients was most remarkable for the Mexican-American children. On further analysis of this group's performance, Oakland found that the predictive and concurrent correlations of the WISC-R and reading were similar for lower-SES children (.60 and .59, respectively), but the predictive correlations were significantly higher than the concurrent correlations for middle-SES children (.77 and .50, respectively). The predictive correlations were significantly higher than the concurrent correlations for mathematics for both the lower-SES children (.58 and .50, respectively) and middle-SES children (.66 and .50, respectively).

Dean (1979b) found that performance on the Iowa Test of Basic Skills (ITBS) could be predicted (over 1½-year span) for WISC-R performance for Mexican-American children (ages 8.3 to 10.5) whose home language was Spanish. The WISC-R best predicted performance on the ITBS Vocabulary test, having correlations of .61, .49, and .59 for the VIQ, PIQ, and FSIQ, respectively. The correlations of the WISC-R subtests with the ITBS subtests ranged from .14 (Coding $\times$ Arithmetic Skills) to .53 (Vocabulary $\times$ Vocabulary). In general, the Verbal subtests were better predictors than the Performance subtests. All correlations of the Verbal subtests with ITBS Vocabulary and Reading were significant. Four of the five regular Verbal subtests correlated significantly with the ITBS Arithmetic Skills; interestingly, Arithmetic was the one subtest that was not a significant predictor. Block Design was the best predictor of the Performance subtests, significantly correlating with Vocabulary (.42), Reading (.31), and Arithmetic Skills (.37). The only other significant correlations among the Performance tests were Picture Completion $\times$ Arithmetic Skills (.31) and Picture Arrangement $\times$ Vocabulary (.33). Furthermore, ITBS Total Scores could be predicted by the VIQ (.63), PIQ (.41), and FSIQ (.55). Thus, although all three WISC-R IQs can predict school achievement, Dean found the Verbal subtests and VIQ to be the best predictor. All of his correlations were lower

Table 4. Correlations of the WISC-R with Achievement Tests

Researcher(s)	WISC-R Score	Subjects' Ethnicity	N	Reading	Math
Nonreferred Samples					
Oakland, 1980	VIQ	Anglo	136	.70	.61[a]
		Black	117	.66	.57
		Hispanic	92	.67	.64
	PIQ	Anglo		.53	.53
		Black		.47	.49
		Hispanic		.47	.44
	FSIQ	Anglo		.71	.65
		Black		.58	.48
		Hispanic		.62	.58
Oakland &	FSIQ	Anglo	180	.72	.65[a]
Feigenbaum, 1979		Black	119	.63	.60
		Hispanic	137	.65	.61
Oakland, 1983	FSIQ[b]	Anglo	166	.73	.67[a]
	(concurrent)	Black	122	.63	.59
		Hispanic	108	.64	.60
	FSIQ[b]	Anglo		.72	.73
	(predictive)	Black		.69	.59
		Hispanic		.75	.71
Dean, 1979b	VIQ	Hispanic	49	.41	.57[c]
	PIQ			.35	.36
	FSIQ			.44	.33
Reschly &	FSIQ	Anglo	212	.56	.55[d]
Reschly, 1979		Black	189	.62	.51
		Hispanic	184	.55	.50
		Papago	202	.41	.43
	VC factor	Anglo		.55	.50
		Black		.65	.46
		Hispanic		.50	.43
		Papago		.35	.38
	PO factor	Anglo		.41	.36
		Black		.41	.38
		Hispanic		.38	.34
		Papago		.27	.31
	FD factor	Anglo		.41	.51
		Black		.53	.50
		Hispanic		.55	.54
		Papago		.37	.42
Referred Sample					
Reynolds &	VIQ	Anglo	94	.56	.41[e]
Gutkin, 1980		Hispanic	174	.42	.41
	PIQ	Anglo		.28	.43
		Hispanic		.03	.25
	FSIQ	Anglo		.48	.47
		Hispanic		.25	.38

[a] California Achievement Test (CAT).
[b] Author reported "WISC-R IQ" but did not report *which* IQ, assumed to be Full Scale IQ.
[c] Iowa Test of Basic Skills (ITBS).
[d] Metropolitan Achievement Test (MAT).
[e] Wide Range Achievement Test (WRAT).

than those reported by Oakland, which Dean attributes to the homogeneity of his sample.

Reschly and Reschly (1979) used a different approach by examining the external validity of the WISC-R factor scores, using data from the Pima County Prevalence Study. The correlations of the FSIQ with scores on the Metropolitan Achievement Test (MAT) were lower than those obtained by Oakland (Oakland, 1980, 1983; Oakland & Feigenbaum, 1979), but all were significant. Reading was best predicted by the FSIQ for both Anglo and Chicano children; and the order of predictors varied for the two groups thereafter. The FSIQ was the best predictor of math for Anglo children, whereas the FD factor score was the best predictor of math for Chicano children. Though the pattern of best predictors varies somewhat for Anglo and Chicano children, the correlations were comparable. Reschly and Sabers (1979) conducted a more detailed analysis of the relationship of the FSIQ with the MAT by examining the correlations for each of the ethnic groups across five grade levels (first, third, fifth, seventh, ninth). In the first grade, the correlations for Chicano children were higher than for Anglo children. By third grade this situation reversed; by seventh grade, prediction of mathematics was fairly comparable for Anglo and Chicano children, although the correlations with reading continued to be slightly higher for Anglo children. The correlations for Chicano children were fairly comparable across grades (within subject areas), whereas marked differences of an uneven pattern across grades were noted for Anglo children.

Reynolds and Gutkin (1980) found low to moderate correlations of the WISC-R with the Wide Range Achievement Test (WRAT) for a sample of referred urban lower-middle-SES 11-year-old (approximately) Anglos and Chicanos. The VIQ was the best predictor of reading and spelling (.44 and .35, respectively) for both Anglo and Chicano children. With regard to mathematics, the VIQ was the best predictor for Chicano children, whereas the FSIQ was the best predictor for Anglo children (though the VIQ and PIQ were comparable). Perhaps the most important finding was that the PIQ had little, if any, relationship to achievement for Chicano children (.03, reading; .25, math; .03, spelling). Reynolds and Gutkin attributed the low correlations overall to the homogeneity of their sample.

Navarro (1978) administered the Portable Rod and Fare Test (PRFT), the Children's Embedded Figures Test (CEFT), the Human Figure Drawing Task (HFDT), and the Block Design Tests (BDT) to 120 fourth grade girls, 60 Chicanos and 60 Anglos. Complete WISC-Rs were also administered to all subjects. Anglos scored higher on the BDT than Chicanos; with a "tuning" treatment, subjects from both ethnic groups improved their performance significantly. The correlations between the field dependence-independence (FDI) measures and the WISC-R subtests were moderate to high among the treatment subjects and low to moderate among the control subjects regardless of ethnicity. Correlation between FDI measures and WISC-R were consistently higher than those among the FDI measures.

In summary, there is a fairly strong and usually significant relationship between performance on the WISC-R and achievement tests for Hispanic children. The degree of similarity in the pattern of this relationship between Hispanic and Anglo children varies across referral status and grade. In general, the Verbal indices are better predictors of achievement test performance for Hispanic children than are Performance indices, which result in substantially lower relationships, especially for referred children. Neither the fact that these correlations are significant for Hispanic children nor the fact that they are comparable between Hispanic and Anglo children is sufficient basis to conclude that the WISC-R is fair in its prediction of achievement test performance for Hispanic children. Thus we will turn our attention to studies that address the comparability of regression equations between the two groups, as suggested by Clarizio (1982).

Regression Studies.   Reschly and Sabers (1979) were the first researchers to attend to the equality of the regression equations (predictor, WISC-R FSIQ; criterion, MAT scores) obtained by different ethnic groups (Anglo, Black, Chicano, and Native American Papago). A total of 10 comparisons was made (5 grade levels for reading and math) across the four ethnic groups on three indices: standard errors of measurement, slopes, and intercepts. The standard errors of estimate were significantly smaller for non-Anglos in four of the 10 comparisons. The slopes significantly differed in three of the 10 comparisons, although the direction of the difference in slopes was inconsistent. When the applicability of a common regression line for these four ethnic groups was tested, three were rejected due to slope differences and an additional six were rejected on the basis of intercept differences; thus a total of nine of the 10 common regression lines were rejected. When eliminating the Papago data, Reschly and Sabers concluded that new common regression equations were appropriate in five of the 10 comparisons. The application of these common regression equations resulted in consistent underprediction of both reading and math for Anglo children, and math for Chicano children. The accuracy in the prediction of reading scores for Chicano children was mixed: underpredicting reading in the first, third, and ninth grades, and overpredicting in the middle grades (fifth and seventh). Although Reschly and Sabers concluded that the WISC-R was a fair predictor of achievement for minority children because it tended to overpredict achievement, their conclusion may have been confounded by the consistent overprediction of achievement for Papagos and the highly mixed picture for Blacks. The application of a common regression line (based on the three ethnic groups) for Chicano children is questionable in that seven times out of 10, the equation resulted in *under*prediction of their achievement.

   Reschly and Sabers did not explore the possibility of a common regression equation based solely on Anglo and Chicano data; however, that was the focus of a study conducted by Reynolds and Gutkin (1980). They calculated separate regression equations (predictors, WISC-R VIQ, PIQ, FSIQ; criterion, WRAT reading, spelling, math) for the Anglo and Chicano children in their referral sample. These regression equations were then compared using a technique developed by Pothoff (1966), which simultaneously considers both the slope and intercept. Of the nine comparisons, only the PIQ × math regression equations were significantly different: the slopes were similar, but the intercepts varied substantially. When they applied a common regression equation, overprediction of achievement resulted for Chicanos, whereas underprediction was the norm for Anglos. They concluded that the relationship between IQ and achievement is consistent across ethnic groups, at least within the referral population.

The lack of regression studies is confounded by the mixed results reviewed here. In the first instance (Reschly & Sabers, 1979), a common regression equation tended to underpredict the achievement of nonreferred Hispanic children. In the second case (Reynolds & Gutkin, 1980), the opposite was true, that is, the common regression equation consistently overpredicted the achievement of referred Hispanic children. Clarizio's (1982) conclusion that the WISC-R is a valid predictor of achievement for Hispanic children is considered premature. His conclusion appeared to be based on his review of the correlational studies, without close attention to his own recommendations regarding consideration of standard errors of estimate, slopes, and intercepts.

Criticisms of the Criterion.   Many critics of the WISC-R (e.g., Mercer, 1979; Williams, 1974) have also criticized the procedures used in establishing external validity. Specifically, they contend that WISC-R IQs should be expected to be highly correlated with standardized achievement test scores in that both the predictor and the criterion are culturally biased. This can be most apparent when considering bilingual, in this case Spanish-English–speaking, children. As noted earlier, the WISC-R Verbal indices appear to be the best predictors of achievement for Latino children, whereas the FSIQ appears to be the best for Anglo children. It makes sense that a measure of English-language skills (i.e., Verbal indices) is highly related to performance on achievement tests requiring facility in reading English. Similarly, the Performance indices, which require only rudimentary understanding of English, might be expected to have lower correlations with English language tests. Some of the researchers (e.g., Reschly & Sabers, 1979; Reynolds & Gutkin, 1980) have recognized the culturally loaded nature of the criterion variable, but none of them have addressed the specific nature of the criteria they used. All three group achievement tests (i.e., CAT, ITBS, and MAT) used in the external validity studies have total reading and math scores based on a composite of subtests. Only Dean (1979b) differentiated between reading vocabulary and reading comprehension; but even he failed to note that the ITBS Arithmetic Skills subtests are composed of written questions of concepts and word problems, that is, no "straight" computation subtest. Both the CAT and MAT have computation subtests, but they also have math subtests that require a great amount of English reading. It is likely that the total reading and total math scores were used, thus the Hispanic children faced achievement tests that required a great amount of English language competency. The lack of definition of both the criterion task and the language preference and proficiency of the Hispanic children only serves to worsen an already cloudy issue.

Grade point averages and teacher ratings have been suggested as potentially "fair" criteria of school success to be considered in the external validation of the WISC-R. To date, only Reschly & Reschly (1979) have used the alternate criterion of teacher ratings. They had teachers rate the children on several scales, although they reported only the correlations of the WISC-R FSIQ and factor scores with teacher ratings of Academics and Attention. The correlations for Anglo and Chicano children were comparable. With the Academics ratings as the criterion, the following correlations for Anglo and Chicano children resulted: FSIQ, .35 and .38; VC factor, .30 and .32; PO factor, .22 and .27; FD factor, .37 and .38. When the criterion was the Attention ratings, the following correlations for Anglo and Chicano children were found: FSIQ, .28 and .30; VC factor, .25 and .23; PO factor, .19 and .21; FD factor, .33 and .31. Although all of these correlations were significant, all were also lower than those reported for the MAT criterion (see Table 4). Interestingly, the Freedom from Distractibility factor emerged as the best predictor for both sets of teacher ratings of both ethnic groups. Furthermore, the pattern from best predictor to worst predictor was identical for both sets of ratings and both ethnic groups (i.e., FD or = FS VC PO), though vastly different from the pattern of predictors for the MAT scores.

The data are too limited to draw any firm conclusions regarding the fairness of the WISC-R in predicting school success using alternative criteria—limited by the number of investigations and limited in that only correlational (and not regression) data have been reported. It does seem, however, that the WISC-R has the potential of being more adequate in these predictions than was its predecessor, the WISC (see earlier discussion of Goldman & Hartig, 1976). Caution is suggested in that teacher ratings of culturally different students have not always been demonstrated to be fair (Cook, Eyler, & Ward, 1981) and we may be looking at another kind of "biased" criterion.

Oakland (1980, 1983) modified the predictor variable rather than the criterion; that is, he examined the relationship between the SOMPA Estimated Learning Potential (ELP) (Mercer & Lewis, 1978) and the traditional school success criterion, achievement test (CAT) scores. The ELP is a WISC-R IQ from which the contributions of sociocultural status have been eliminated via a multiple regression equation. In contrast to the mean WISC-R IQs, the mean ELPs are 100 across ethnic groups. "Lacking clear directions as to its intended uses, many school psychologists and other assessment specialists have considered it [the ELP] as a supplement to or replacement for the IQ" (Oakland, 1983, p. 58). Thus Oakland (1980, 1983) turned his attention to the use of the ELP, in contrast to the IQ, in predicting achievement. (See Table 5 for a summary of his results.)

The concurrent ELP $\times$ CAT correlations for Hispanic children were slightly higher than those for Anglos, and the predictive ELP $\times$ CAT correlations were notably stronger for Hispanic children. However, the WISC-R IQ remains the better predictor of school achievement for both Anglos and Hispanics. The one exception to this conclusion is the slightly higher magnitude of the ELP correlation for middle-SES Hispanic children when predicting achievement over a three-year span.

Table 5. Summary of Oakland's (1980, 1983) Studies Comparing the WISC-R IQ and SOMPA ELP as Predictors of Achievement

Date	Timing	Reading		Math	
		IQ	ELP	IQ	ELP
Anglo					
1980	Concur-rent	.72	.43	.64	.42
1983	Concur-rent	.73	.43	.67	.42
	Predictive	.72	.46	.73	.50
Hispanic (total)					
1980	Concur-rent	.64	.50	.59	.46
1983	Concur-rent	.64	.48	.60	.46
	Predictive	.74	.71	.71	.63
Hispanic (mid-SES)					
1983	Concur-rent	.50	.45	.50	.47
	Predictive	.77	.78	.66	.68
Hispanic (low-SES)					
1983	Concur-rent	.59	.49	.50	.41
	Predictive	.60	.54	.58	.43

Note: Criterion was the California Achievement Test.

Summary. Does the WISC-R predict school success equally well for Hispanic and other children? Performance on the WISC-R is significantly related to performance on standardized achievement tests and to teacher ratings of children, regardless of ethnicity. The magnitude of these relationships is higher for Anglo than for Hispanic children, though there are mixed results regarding the significance of these differences. This confused state is further complicated by the mixed results of the regression studies, with Reynolds and Gutkin (1980) finding overprediction, and Reschly and Sabers (1979) finding underprediction, of achievement for Hispanic children.

Although the use of achievement tests as the criterion has received justifiable criticism, the WISC-R is also significantly related to teacher ratings of children. Additionally, the WISC-R IQ is a better predictor of achievement test scores than is its socioculturally fair modification, the SOMPA ELP.

A great amount of research is needed before a firm conclusion can be drawn regarding the validity of the use of the WISC-R as a predictor of Hispanic children's school success. Specifically, more attention should be given to the development of an alternate (to standardized achievement tests) measure of school success. Furthermore, these researchers need to address the comparability of standard errors of estimate, slopes, and intercepts (i.e., regression lines) as a part of their endeavors. Additional regression studies regarding the prediction of standardized test scores are also needed. Researchers are asked to fully describe their samples and their criterion variables in this process.

WISC-R Correlates with Measures Other than School Success

The assessment of adaptive behavior is required in the identification of the mentally retarded, thus the relationship of the WISC-R with adaptive behavior instruments is of interest. Mercer & Lewis (1978) included such a measure, the Adaptive Behavior Inventory for Children (ABIC), in the SOMPA. Mercer (1979) reported WISC-R $\times$ ABIC correlations for each of the three IQs and each of the three ethnic groups. These correlations were quite similar within the Anglo group: .43 (VIQ), .45 (PIQ), and .48 (FSIQ). There was somewhat greater variability across scales for Blacks: .34 (VIQ), .46 (PIQ), .43 (FSIQ). The greatest variability was found within the Hispanic group: .43 (VIQ), .53 (PIQ), and .48 (FSIQ). Montague (1981) reported correlations of a similar magnitude (median of .46) for his referred Texan sample. In contrast, Oakland (1980) found much lower correlations for his groups of nonreferred Texan children: .31 for Anglos, .21 for Blacks, and .21 for Mexican-Americans. Both Mercer and Oakland concluded that the WISC-R and ABIC measure different constructs, noting that although the correlations were significant, they reflected only low levels of common variance.

One of Mercer's (1979) strongest contentions is that sociocultural background accounts for a substantial amount of the variability in WISC-R scores. Mercer & Lewis (1978) developed a set of Sociocultural Scales, consisting of Family Size, Family Structure, Socioeconomic Status, and Urban Acculturation, as part of the SOMPA. Mercer (1979) reported that the total raw scores of these scales significantly correlated with the three WISC-R IQs for all three ethnic groups: .55 (VIQ), .49 (PIQ), and .58 (FSIQ) for Anglos; .44 (VIQ), .52 (PIQ), and .52 (FSIQ) for Blacks; and .55 (VIQ), .54 (PIQ), and .57 (FSIQ) for Hispanics. While Oakland (1980) found correlations of a similar magnitude between these two measures, the correlations across WISC-R scales were most similar for Blacks and most varied for Anglos. Additionally, all of the correlations were lower than those found by Mercer, that is, .54 (VIQ), .32 (PIQ), .50 (FSIQ) for Anglos; .35 (VIQ), .31 (PIQ), .36 (FSIQ) for Blacks; and .45 (VIQ), .28 (PIQ), and .42 (FSIQ) for Mexican-Americans. Oakland also examined the contributions of each of the Sociocultural Scales to the WISC-R IQs. All correlations with the FSIQ were significant for all ethnic groups. The only correlation within the VIQ that was not significant was that of Family Size within the Black sample. Neither Family Size nor Structure was significantly related to the PIQ for any ethnic group, although Socioeconomic Status and Urban Acculturation was related for all three groups. The WISC-R correlations with the Sociocultural scales often approach and occasionally exceed the correlations with achievement test scores (see Table 4). Additionally, different patterns of WISC-R performance are found across SES levels within ethnic groups. Thus it must be concluded that sociocultural background does make a substantial contribution to the WISC-R scores of children from all ethnic groups.

The Culture Fair Intelligence Test (IPAT, 1973) frequently draws the attention of those who seek an "unbiased" instrument. Smith, Hays, and Solway (1977) compared the WISC-R and Culture Fair performance of 51 adolescents (47% White, 53% Black and Mexican-American) referred to a Houston area juvenile detention ward. In a second study, Hays and Smith (1980) made similar comparisons among 41 White, 46 Black, and 30 Mexican-American adolescents referred to the Harris County (Texas) Probation Department. Both groups were suspected to be from low income families. The correlations between the WISC-R and Culture Fair for each of these two total groups were moderately high and significant: .71 and .58 (VIQ), .70 and .61 (PIQ), and .76 and .64 (FSIQ), for the 1977 and 1980 groups, respectively. The correlations for each ethnic group were somewhat lower, ranging from .27 (Mexican-American, VIQ) to .66 (Black, PIQ). All of the correlations, except that with the VIQ for Mexican-Americans, were significant. The correlations for the Mexican-Americans (ranging from .27 to .43) had little overlap with those for the Blacks (.41 to .66) and were lower than those for the Anglos (.49 to .56). In both studies, the mean FSIQ and Culture Fair IQ were within one point for the Anglos, whereas the mean Culture Fair IQ exceeded the mean WISC-R IQ by 7.5 points for the minorities in the first study and 9 and 8.7 points, respectively, for the Blacks and Mexican-Americans in the second study. Thus those who ascribe to mean differences as bias will conclude that the Culture Fair Intelligence Test is more fair than the WISC-R. The reasonably high common variance of the Culture Fair and WISC-R only underscores this position. The low, nonsignificant correlation of the VIQ and Culture Fair IQ for Hispanic children might be explained by language difference.

While most psychologists would agree that testing linguistic minority children in their dominant language is most fair, few tests have been appropriately translated, adapted, and standardized. The Escala de Inteligencia Wechsler Para Niños, the Spanish WISC, was translated, adapted, and standardized for use in Puerto Rico. Oplesch and Genshaft (1981) compared the performance of 20 Puerto Rican boys and girls living in a small northern Ohio city on the WISC-R and the EIWPN. These children were in the first to third grades and from lower income homes where Spanish was dominant. The children, however, were determined to be bilingual on the basis of the Dailey Language Facility Test. The two tests were administered in a counterbalanced design, with a 4-week interval, by one bilingual examiner. There were no significant differences in the children's performance on the tests, nor were there order or sex effects. Their scores on the WISC-R and EIWPN were, respectively: 93 and 94 (FSIQ), 86 and 93 (VIQ), and 102 and 108 (PIQ). While finding the Verbal-Performance discrepancy typical of research reported earlier in this chapter, the authors attributed the lower VIQ to a combination of lower language skills in both languages, a probable lack of emphasis on language in the home, and the lower SES of the families. Though they concluded that formally determined bilingual children might be tested in either language, they offered cautions regarding the use of either the WISC-R (normed predominately on Anglo children) or the EIWPN, which may have cultural Puerto Rican referents foreign to Puerto Rican children on the mainland (80% of the children were born in the United States). For example, 70% of the children were unfamiliar with the Puerto Rican word for a coin worth 5 cents, whereas only 20% missed the WISC-R equivalent question.

The Testing Situation

The very nature of the standardized testing situation has been considered suspect and a potential source of bias for minority children (Reschly, 1979). When Hispanic children are tested, one of the most suspect elements is that of the examiner, along with the associated language of test administration. Morales (1976) studied these effects by having four examiners, male and female, bilingual (Spanish/English) and monolingual (English), give a battery of tests to 92 young children (grades 1–3) who spoke both English and Spanish. The only significant difference between monolingual and bilingual examiners of the WISC-R was on the Performance Scale (the direction of that difference was not reported). No differences for examiner sex was found. Both the monolingual and bilingual testing conditions tended to predict academic performance (undefined) equally well. The exact nature of the testing situations as compared by Morales is unclear; for example, no definition of monolingual and bilingual testing sessions is offered, no indication of standardized versus nonstandardized test administration is made. Thus it is difficult to draw any conclusions from this brief report of Morales's work. However, Morales and George (1976) presented a more detailed report of this study. Performance IQs for the various conditions were as follows: male, 94.4; female, 89.7; bilingual, 87.4; monolingual, 96.8; male bilingual, 90.0; male monolingual, 98.9; female bilingual, 84.8; and female monolingual, 94.7. The effect of examiners' sex approached significance ($p = .054$). Two stepwise regression analyses investigated predictive ability (classroom performance) of the WISC-R Performance section separately for monolingual and bilingual conditions: for monolingual, $r = BD/.42**$, $OA/.29*$; for bilingual, $r = MAZ/.30*$ ($* = .05$, $** = .01$ level). The authors indicated that the results suggested that examiners' language may override the effects of standardized test administration and some predictive utility may exist for using the WISC-R with Hispanics. The authors speculated about differential arousal rates under cross-ethnic versus same ethnic examiner conditions and possible performance effects.

Rather than focusing on the ethnicity or binguality of the examiner, Piersel, Brody, and Kratochwill (1977) experimentally manipulated the nature of the child's testing experience. They examined the effects of three testing conditions on the performance of 32 minority (64% Black, 35% Mexican-American, 11% mixed ethnicity), low income, inner-city children, ages 8–10. All of these children were in regular education programs, that is, none were receiving bilingual education or special education services.

Six White female school psychologists administered an abbreviated form of the WISC-R under three conditions: (1) immediate feedback and self-charting of the degree of accuracy of item response, (2) a pretesting vicarious modeling experience simulating positive interactions between an examiner and a child, and (3) traditional and standardized administration procedures. As predicted, these minority children achieved the highest WISC-R scores under the vicarious condition ($X = 96.09$, SD $= 11.29$), which was significantly higher than the standardized condition ($X = 88.29$, SD $= 11.42$), which in turn was significantly higher than the feedback condition ($X = 82.71$, SD $= 9.60$). There were no differences between Verbal and Performance trends. When considering the "at risk" level of performance on the WISC-R, it was found that only 14.3% of the children achieved scores one standard deviation below the mean when under the vicarious condition. In contrast, 42.8% in the standardized condition and 52.4% in the feedback condition fell below this point. Piersel et al. emphasized that "some form of desensitization is essential if measures of intellectual assessment are to be used as one of the important sources of information for making decisions about a child's academic future" (p. 1144).

While the data are too sparse to draw firm conclusions regarding the effects of the testing situation on Hispanic children's WISC-R performance, the Piersel et al. study is certainly compelling. Both researchers and practitioners must raise questions to be addressed regarding the transaction of the examiner and Hispanic child in the testing situation (cf. Martinez-Morales & Cook, 1982).

Using the WISC-R in Educational Diagnosis

The most pressing question facing psychologists regarding the use of the WISC-R with Hispanic children is its application to educational decision making. While all of the research discussed thus far can be applied to conclusions regarding the validity of this use of the WISC-R, some investigators have given specific attention to this question.

Bannatyne (1968, 1974) proposed a WISC subtest recategorization system consisting of a Spatial score (Object Assembly + Block Design + Picture Completion), a Conceptual score (Comprehension + Similarities + Vocabulary), and a Sequential score (Digit Span + Coding + Arithmetic). He found that genetic dyslexic children were characterized by a Spatial > Conceptual > Sequential pattern on the WISC. Rugel (1974) reviewed 27 studies regarding reading disabled children, conducting a Bannatyne analysis and finding a pattern consistent with that reported by Bannatyne, Smith, Coleman, Lokecki, and Davis (1977) found Bannatyne's reported WISC pattern on the WISC-R performance of learning disabled children. Thus a "Bannatyne pattern" has often been associated with learning disabilities. Gutkin (1979) examined the WISC-R patterns of 53

Caucasian and 87 Mexican-American school-aged, learning disabled children from a Southwest urban school district. The Caucasian children, as a group, did show the Bannatyne pattern, that is, Spatial (X = 25.85, SD = 6.65), Conceptual (X = 21.47, SD = 6.90), Sequential (X = 19.66, SD = 4.83), though only the Spatial score was significantly higher than the others. A different pattern emerged for the Mexican-American group as a whole: Spatial (X = 24.07, SD = 5.62), Sequential (X = 19.76, SD = 4.12), Conceptual (X = 16.07, SD = 5.52); all differences between scores were significant. This ordering of the recategorized scores for Hispanic children makes sense when one considers the nature of the subtests forming those sources; that is, the Spatial subtests require no language/verbalization; the Sequential subtests require minimal language/verbalization; whereas the Conceptual subtests require extensive language/verbalization.

When applying the Bannatyne pattern as a criterion for individual diagnosis of learning disabilities, Gutkin found that 70% of the Anglo and 80% of the Hispanic children *failed* to demonstrate the Bannatyne pattern. Additionally, only 2% of the Anglos and none of the Hispanics demonstrated statistically significant differences in the predicted direction. Thus Gutkin concluded that the Bannatyne recategorization system "may be of little value when investigating the possible presence of learning disabilities in individual children [regardless of ethnicity]" (p. 181).

Because Hispanic children tend to score lower than Anglo children on the WISC-R, a disproportionate number of Hispanic children may be at risk to be identified as mentally retarded. Reschly and Jipson (1976) examined the prevalence of mental retardation (based on IQ criterion alone) within the four ethnic groups of Pima County, Arizona. Their results are summarized in Table 6.

While either IQ criterion (i.e., -2 SD or $-1^{2}/_{3}$ SD) alone resulted in a disproportionate number of Blacks and Papagos being identified as mentally retarded, the proportion of Anglo children identified under the -2 SD criterion was approximately at the expected level. If the PIQ is used for decision making, as recommended by Kaufman (1979) and Clarizio (1982), the proportion of

Table 6. Expected and Obtained Percentages of Children Under Two IQ Criteria for Identification of Mental Retardation

IQ:		IQ < 70 (<2 SD)			IQ < 75 (<1 2/3 SD)		
Expected	Percentage:		2.3			4.7	
Ethnicity		VIQ	PIQ	FSIQ	VIQ	PIQ	FSIQ
Anglo		2.4	1.2	1.6	4.8	2.0[a]	2.4
Black		10.2[a]	4.7[a]	8.1[a]	22.1[a]	12.3[a]	16.6[a]
Hispanic		10.8[a]	2.2	6.7[a]	24.2[a]	8.9[a]	16.1[a]
Papago		37.5[a]	4.2[a]	14.2[a]	60.8[a]	15.8[a]	37.1[a]

Note: From Reschly & Jipson (1976).
[a]Significantly different from expected.

Chicano identified as mentally retarded under the -2 SD criterion is also at the expected level. Within the Chicano group, however, significant differences were found between the proportions of urban and rural children under this criterion. The percentages of urban Chicano children with IQs below 70 were: 6.8% (VIQ), 0.0% (PIQ), 3.4% (FSIQ). In contrast, the rural Chicano children were distributed as: 15.2% (VIQ), 4.8% (PIQ), 10.5% (FSIQ). These significant differences between urban and rural Chicano children were not found at the 75 IQ criterion. Thus rural Chicano children are more at risk than urban Latino children to be identified as mentally retarded when the IQ is used as the sole criterion.

When additional measures are included in the criterion, however, the percent of minorities identified as mentally retarded is drastically reduced. For example, Reschly (1981) reported the following percentages of Chicano children meeting the criterion of $-1^2/_3$ SD on more than one measure: IQ/ELP, 12.0%; IQ/ABIC, 1.6%; IQ/ELP/ABIC, 0.8%. When the criterion of -2 SD was used, the percent of Chicano children identified as mentally retarded was even smaller: IQ/ELP, 4.0%; IQ/ABIC, 0.8%; IQ/ELP/ABIC, 0.8%. Reschly did not report which WISC-R IQ was used in these calculations, though it is suspected that he used the FSIQ. He did recognize that lower than expected percentages would be found when applying a combined criterion because the measures are not perfectly correlated. Reschly concluded,

> Use of sociocultural and broadly defined adaptive behavior information clearly has the potential to reduce and perhaps eliminate overrepresentation of minorities in programs for mildly retarded persons; however, the "declassification" effect is not restricted to minorities and comes about primarily from the adaptive behavior measure, not the "unbiased" measure of ability, i.e., the Estimated Learning Potential. [p. 18]

The WISC-R in Mexico

Padilla and Roll (1983) indicated that translations of the Wechsler scales have been used in Mexico for decades (cf. Ahumada, Ahumada, & Diaz-Guerrero, 1957) and that recent translations of the WISC-R and other Wechsler tests have been published for use in Mexico and Latin America with the approval of the Psychological Corporation. In order to enable Mexico to avoid relying on U.S. norms for scoring and interpretation, which until recent times has been the case, Padilla and Roll administered the Spanish version of the WISC-R to a standardization sample of 1100 children between the ages of 6 and 16 from randomly selected schools in Mexico City. The tested Mexican children obtained a mean Verbal IQ of 89.2, a mean Performance IQ of 88.0, and a mean Full Scale IQ of 87.3 (SD = 13.7). Using U.S. norms, the mean Full Scale IQ for 6 year olds fell about a half standard deviation below the U.S. mean, and dropped to a level more than a standard deviation below the mean for the older adolescents. The authors state: "It can be reasonably speculated that as Mexican children become older, they have less of an opportunity to learn what is contained in U.S. produced and U.S. culture bases tests, and/or that they have a lower level of motivation to perform on this type of test" (p. 8).

Padilla and Roll (1983) pointed out that a series of thoughtful analyses and cogent arguments, written in the early thirties by George I. Sanchez (1932a, 1932b, 1934a, 1935b), questioning the validity of IQ tests administered to Spanish-speaking children in the southwestern U.S., were virtually ignored. Fifty years later there is a realization that the task of adopting psychological instruments standardized in the U.S. for use across multiple cultural and linguistic groups raises complex conceptual, methodological, and ethical issues. The initial results of the Padilla and Roll Mexican standardization study reinforce their perceptions that such important issues as linguistic equivalence of meaning, examiner variability, cultural variation in response set, and representative sampling have yet to be adequately explored and understood.

WISC-R Summary

Hispanic children tend to score less well than Anglos, but better than Blacks, on the WISC-R. Their Verbal IQ is generally lower than the Performance IQ, and lower than that achieved by Blacks. There is some evidence to suggest that the mean IQ can be raised by providing positive vicarious experience prior to the testing session. There is some evidence to support the conclusion that the WISC-R has internal validity for use with Hispanic children. It is as reliable and internally consistent for Hispanics as it is for other ethnic groups, including Anglos. There is evidence of item bias, but the pattern of differentially difficult items cannot be attributed to any specific factor(s) within the Hispanic culture. The two strong factors that emerge via factor analysis conform with the Verbal Comprehension and Perceptual Organization factors identified in the WISC-R standardization sample. One subtest that varies in its loading between Anglo and Hispanic is Picture Arrangement, which shows up on the Verbal Comprehension factor as well as the Perceptual Organization factor for Hispanic children. The "third" factor, Freedom from Distractibility, is not appropriately used with Hispanic children.

The evidence in support of the external validity of the WISC-R for use with Hispanic children is not so compelling. While the WISC-R is significantly related to standardized achievement scores, the comparability of the correlations for Hispanic and Anglo children is not consistent across studies. Furthermore, one of the two regression studies supports the WISC-R as a predictor of achievement for Hispanic children in that it tends to overpredict achievement. On the other hand the second regression study leads to the opposite conclusion due to the finding of underprediction of Hispanic children's achievement. The WISC-R tends to be a better predictor than the ELP, except for long-term prediction of the achievement of middle-SES Hispanic children. Although the WISC-R correlations with teacher ratings are significant, they are lower than the correlations with standardized achievement tests. Much more research is needed before drawing any firm conclusions regarding the external validity of the WISC-R for use with Hispanic children because the current studies lead to conflicting conclusions.

The sociocultural background of children, regardless of ethnicity, accounts for a sizable portion of the variance in IQ scores. The WISC-R correlations with sociocultural measures tend to approximate or exceed those with standardized achievement tests. Indeed, differences in the patterns of performance, predictions, and results of decision making vary for Hispanic children depending on their socioeconomic status or urban/rural residence (favoring middle-SES and/or urban children).

Not one of the learning disabled Hispanic children had the Bannatyne pattern typically associated with learning disabilities. The inappropriateness of using the Bannatyne pattern as a criterion for identification of a learning disability is further reinforced by the pattern found for learning disabled Hispanic children, that is, Spatial > Sequential > Conceptual—a pattern that coincides with English language proficiency.

Significant but low correlations are found between the WISC-R and adaptive behavior. When a dual IQ and adaptive behavior criterion is applied for the identification of the mentally retarded, a substantially lower proportion of children is so identified. The application of a criterion of two standard deviations below the mean results in a much more proportionate distribution of Hispanic children as mentally retarded than does the criterion of one and two-thirds standard deviation below the mean. In fact, when the Performance IQ is used for decision making on an IQ criterion alone, the number of Hispanic children identified as mentally retarded approximates that expected by application of the normal curve.

SUMMARY

Do Hispanics exhibit characteristic (and unique) performance on the Wechsler Scales? Hispanics consistently obtain lower Full Scale IQs than the standardization sample and intermediate between that for Whites and Blacks. Performance IQ seems to be normally distributed; however, Verbal IQ is typically lower than Performance IQ for Hispanics. For the WPPSI this discrepancy averages about 20 points, for the WISC and WISC-R about 10–15 points, and for the WAIS a slightly smaller difference is typical. Bannatyne factor structure patterns differ from those for learning disabled children and are highly similar to the pattern for American Indians (Spatial > Sequential > Conceptual > Acquired Knowledge). Factor analytic studies suggest a two-factor structure for Hispanics as compared to a three-factor structure for Whites. However, some additional variation from the typical Verbal Comprehension and Perceptual Organization factors is evident; for instance, in various studies Picture Arrangement loads on Verbal Comprehension or on Perceptual Organization or on a third factor. Hispanics consistently performed more poorly on the WISC-R than on WISC. Reliability and internal consistency are usually high for Hispanic performance on the Wechslers, although some item bias is evident. General factors rather than specific item content probably contributed to differences in mean, because there is no clear pattern to significant differences in item difficulty. Adequate test-retest reliability data are not available.

What factors affect the Wechsler performance of Hispanics? The language of test administration, the requested language of response, and the language background of the examinee all affect Wechsler performance, although there are several contradictory findings and a paucity of empirical findings for the WISC-R. A fair number of studies find biodemographic variables, such as age, sex, and SES, to relate significantly to scoring levels. Sociocultural background, experience, and ethnicity seem to account for a significant portion of variation in performance. Examiner characteristics and aspects of the examination process (e.g., ethnicity of examiner, test experience of subject, test format) differentially affect performance. Interestingly, no researchers have explored the potential effects of various handicapping conditions (e.g., poor nutrition, vision) that might adversely affect Hispanic performance. Because Hispanic children show extremely high rates of middle ear disease, very similar to rates for American Indian children, and significant Indian $\times$ Wechsler performance $\times$ middle ear disease/ hearing loss relationships have been empirically documented (see McShane, 1982), this area might be very productive for examination. In a similar fashion, emotional disturbance, family stability, pathology, and other potential mediating factors have not been researched in relation to Hispanic performance on the Wechslers.

What is the relationship of Wechsler performance by Hispanics to other variables and measures, especially in predictive terms? There is little or no data to support predictive validity for Hispanic performance on the WPPSI, WISC, or WAIS. For the WISC-R, measures of internal reliability and consistency are moderately high; correlations between WISC-R performance and achievement measures are significant; but WISC-R regression studies find both overprediction and underprediction of achievement. Clearly the results are mixed, although some might consider these findings as more supportive of predictive validity than not.

DISCUSSION

Clearly, transcultural intellectual assessment of Hispanics using the Wechsler scales has been primarily *etic* in approach, in that it attempts to examine performance from an external, pancultural, or universal perspective, rather than *emic* in approach—trying to understand naturally occurring psychological constructs and phenomena within the context of the particular culture of the studied population (Berry, 1980; Price-Williams, 1975; Sundberg & Gonzales, 1981). In this case, various strategies to establish "equivalence" of a given measurement instrument for use in transcultural applications have not been systematically and adequately explored. *Functional, conceptual,* and *metric* equivalence (Berry,

1980), *linguistic* equivalence (Brislin, 1980), and *scalar* equivalence (Hui & Triandis, 1983; Poortinga, 1983) have not been empirically established for use of the Wechsler scales with Hispanics. Measurement validity (Straus, 1969)—establishing the validity of a given measure within the culture in which it is used—has not been confirmed.

This primary problem of transcultural assessment, test construction, and adequacy still leaves the second major difficulty—that of the *use* of the measure within a particular transcultural context. Researchers have pointed out that the utility of an instrument depends on its susceptibility to a number of culture-specific influences that may affect the interpretability of the obtained data. "[H]ow clearly the instructions are understood, familiarity with the test materials and concepts used, previous experience with working under time pressure, and motivational factors" (Van der Flier, 1982, p. 267) may influence performance. The understandability of test-taking format is important: "In societies not accustomed to the testing ritual, finding the correct answer may be no more of a challenge than finding the spot where it should be marked" (Schwarz, 1963, p. 675). Such factors as social desirability, deviation from accepted norms of ideological and moral beliefs, demand characteristics of the testing situation, and the subjects' approval motive (the degree to which a subject responds as to how he thinks the experimenter wants him to respond) should all be considered (Malpass, 1977: 1074). Other factors, such as socioeconomic status, sex roles, and urban-rural dweller differences, need to be addressed (Furnham & Henry, 1980: 27; Weiss, 1980: 147). Extreme response style, the tendency of certain cultures to endorse extreme items, should be assessed (Chun et al., 1974: 465). The importance of examiner variables—sex, ethnic background, testing style, mono- or bilingual ability of the test administrator—has already been discussed (see Olmedo, 1981: 1983). Hispanic researchers have argued for the use of standardized tests that have been normed for the particular culture group under study (Argulewicz & Sanchez, 1982; Gonzalez & Lanyon, 1982). The sheer amount of overt, covert, controllable, and uncontrollable variables that affect the reliability, validity, and interpretability of a given measure applied in another culture has resulted in "a preponderance of poorly controlled and interpreted studies" (Malpass, 1977, p. 1070). Although the Wechsler Intelligence Scales are probably the most widely used measures of intellectual ability and are the single set of such instruments for which there is the greatest amount of data in relation to Hispanic performance, our understanding of what contributes to unique and similar Hispanic profiles is not very deep. Bilingualism waits to be examined as a mediating variable in more depth; interactive facets of the testing situation itself are just beginning to be explored; and relationships *between* neuropsychological, behavioral, and sociocultural variables have been touched barely at all (see McShane, 1984). It is not surprising that a very similar review of Wechsler performances for American Indians (McShane & Plas, 1984) closely resembles the results of this chapter. Indeed, similarities and differences between Wechsler performances for Hispanics, American Indians, and Asian Americans may provide valuable insights, as McShane completes a metanalysis, now in progress, of the combined published data for these three North American linguistic minorities. Clearly much more work is needed to help us understand and use these measures with Hispanics and other groups.

REFERENCES

Ahumada, I. R. de, Ahumada, R., & Diaz-Guerrero, R. (1957). Consideraciones acero de la estandard: Zacion de pruebas a Latinoamerica, con ilustraciones de la adaptacion del WISC a Mexico. In C. F. Hereford & L. Natialico (Eds.), *Aportaciones de la psicologia a la investigacion transcultural.* Mexico City: Editorial F. Trillas.

Altus, G. T. (1953). WISC patterns of a selective sample of bilingual school children. *Journal of Genetic Psychology, 83,* 241–248.

Anderson, J. G., & Evans, F. (1969). Achievement and the achievement syndrome among Mexican-American youth. In P. Kutsche (Ed.), *Measuring socio-cultural change.* Denver, Colorado Associated University Press.

Argulewicz, E. N., & Sanchez, D. T. (1982). Considerations in the assessment of reading difficulties in bilingual children. *School Psychology Review, 7* (3), 281–289.

Bannatyne, A. (1968). Diagnosing learning disabilities and writing remedial prescriptions. *Journal of Learning Disabilities, 1* (4), 242–249.

Bannatyne, A. (1974). Diagnosis: A note on recategorization of the WISC scaled scores. *Journal of Learning Disabilities, 7,* 272–273.

Bechtol, J. L. (1981). Internal test bias in the WISC. *Dissertation Abstracts International, 41* (07), 2735B.

Bergan, J. R., & Parra, E. B. (1979). Variations in IQ testing and instruction and the letter learning and achievement of Anglo and bilingual Mexican-American children. *Journal of Educational Psychology, 71* (6), 819–826.

Berry, J. W. (1980). Introduction to methodology. In H. C. Triandis & J. W. Berry (Eds.), *Handbook of cross-cultural psychology,* Vol. 2, *Methodology.* Boston: Allyn and Bacon.

Blackman, P. B. (1976). *A comparison between the WISC and WISC-R among White, Black and Chicano children.* Unpublished Ed.'s thesis, University of Iowa, Ames, Iowa.

Brislin, R. W. (1980). Translation and content analysis of oral and written materials. In H. C. Triandis & J. W. Berry (Eds.), *Handbook of cross-cultural psychology,* Vol. 2, *Methodology.* (pp. 389–444) Boston: Allyn and Bacon.

Buriel, R. (1978). Relationship of three field-dependence measures to the reading and math achievement of Anglo American and Mexican children. *Journal of Educational Psychology, 70* (2), 167–174.

Burstein, A. (1976). Schizophrenic patterns on the WISC and their validity for White, Black and Hispanic children. *Dissertation Abstracts International,* 875-A. (University Microfilms No. 76-17, 894).

Chandler, J. T., & Plakos, J. (1969). Spanish-speaking pupils classified as educable mentally retarded. *Integrated Education,* Nov.–Dec. pp. 28–32.

Christiansen, T., & Livermore, G. A. (1970). A comparison of Anglo American and Spanish American children on the WISC. *Journal of Social Psychology, 81,* 9–14.

Chun, K. T., Campbell, J. B., & Yoo, J. H. (1974). Extreme response style in cross-cultural research: A reminder. *Journal of Cross-Cultural Psychology, 5* (4), 465–480.

Clarizio, H. F. (1982). Intellectual assessment of Hispanic children. *Psychology in the Schools, 19,* 61–71.

Cleary, T. A., Humphreys, L. G., Kendrick, S. A., & Wesman, A. (1975). Educational uses of tests with disadvantaged students. *American Psychologist, 30,* 15–41.

Cook, V., Eyler, J., & Ward, L. (1981). *Effective strategies for avoiding within school resegregation.* Nashville, TN: Vanderbilt University Institute for Public Policy Studies.

Cotter, D. E., & Berk, R. A. (1981, April). *Item bias in the WISC-R using black, white, and Hispanic learning disabled children.* Paper presented at the annual meeting of the American Educational Research Association, Los Angeles, CA. (ERIC Document Reproduction Service No. ED 206 631, TM 810 434)

Dean, R. S. (1977). Reliability of the WISC-R with Mexican-American children. *Journal of School Psychology, 15* (3), 267–268.

Dean, R. S. (1979a). Distinguishing patterns for Mexican-American children on the WISC-R. *Journal of Clinical Psychology, 35* (4), 790–794.

Dean, R. S. (1979b). Predictive validity of the WISC-R with Mexican-American children. *Journal of School Psychology, 17* (1), 55–58.

Dean, R. S. (1980). Factor structure of the WISC-R with Anglos and Mexican-Americans. *Journal of School Psychology, 18* (3), 234–239.

De Jesus, N. H. (1978). Effects of ethnicity of examiner and language of test instructions on the test performance of Latino children. *Dissertation Abstracts International,* 2978-B. (University Microfilms No. 7823893)

Figueroa (1982). SOMPA and the psychological testing of Hispanic children. *Metar, 2* (3), 1–16.

Furnham, A., & Henry, J. (1980). Cross-cultural locus of control studies: Experiment and critique. *Psychological Reports, 47,* 23–29.

Galvan, R. R. (1967). Bilingualism as it relates to intelligence test scores and school achievement among culturally deprived Spanish-American children. *Dissertation Abstracts International,* 3021-A3022-A. (University Microfilms No. 68-1131)

Gerken, K. C. (1978). Performance of Mexican-American children on intelligence tests. *Exceptional Children,* March, 438–443.

Goldman, R. D., & Hartig, L. K. (1976). The WISC may not be a valid predictor of school performance for primary-grade minority children. *American Journal of Mental Deficiency, 80* (6), 583–587.

Gonzalez, J. M., & Lanyon, R. I. (1982). A Spanish psychological screening inventory: Norms and validity for Costa Rican adolescents. *Journal of Cross-Cultural Psychology, 13* (1), 71–85.

Goody, M. H. (1982). A comparative study of cross-cultural patterns of intellectual abilities on WISC and WISC-R among Anglo, Chinese and Hispanic educationally handicapped boys with reading disabilities. *Dissertation Abstracts International, 42* (01), 141-A. (University Microfilms No. 8115429)

Gutkin, T. B. (1979). Bannatyne patterns of Caucasian and Mexican-American learning disabled children. *Psychology in the Schools, 16* (2), 178–183.

Gutkin, T. B., & Reynolds, C. R. (1980). Factorial similarity of the WISC-R for Anglos and Chicanos referred for psychological services. *Journal of School Psychology, 18* (1), 34–39.

Guzman, M. D. C. (1976). A comparative study of the WISC revised, the Spanish WISC (Escala de Inteligencia Wechsler Para Niños), PPVT (English version), PPVT (Spanish version), and the CMMS on Mexican-American children. *Dissertation Abstracts International,* 4280-A. (University Microfilms No. 77-742).

Hausman, R. M. (1972). Efficacy of three learning potential assessment procedures with Mexican-American educably mentally retarded children. *Dissertation Abstracts International,* 3438-A. (University Microfilms No. 72-34, 203)

Hays, J. R., & Smith, A. L. (1980). Comparison of WISC-R and Culture Fair Intelligence Test scores for three ethnic groups of juvenile delinquents. *Psychological Reports, 46,* 931–934.

Henderson, R. W., & Rankin, R. J. (1973). WPPSI reliability and predictive validity with disadvantaged Mexican-American children. *Journal of School Psychology, 11* (1), 16–20.

Hollingshead, A. (1957). *The Two-factor Index of Social Position.* New Haven: Author.

Hui, C. H., & Triandis, H. C. (1983). Multistrategy approach to cross-cultural research: The case of locus of control. *Journal of Cross-Cultural Psychology, 14* (1), 65–68.

Jensen, A. (1980). *Bias in mental testing.* New York: Free Press.

Kaufman, A. S. (1975). Factor analysis of the WISC-R at 11 age levels between 6½ and 16½ years. *Journal of Consulting and Clinical Psychology, 43,* 135–147.

Kaufman, A. S. (1979). *Intelligence testing with the WISC-R.* New York: Wiley-Interscience.

Kee, D. M. (1972). Learning characteristics in four ethnic groups. *Integrated Education, 10* (6), 29–32.

Killian, L. R. (1971). Cognitive test performance of Spanish-American primary school children: A longitudinal study, final report. Ohio: *Kent State University.* Sponsoring agency: National Center for Educational Research and Development (DHEW/OE).

Kirchev, A. (1975). A revision that really is—The WISC-R. *Psychology in the Schools, 12* (1), 126–128.

Lawlis, G. F., Stedman, J. J., & Cortner, R. H. (1980). Factor analysis of the WISC-R for a sample of bilingual Mexican-Americans. *Journal of Clinical Child Psychology,* Spring, 57–58.

Malpass, R. S. (1977). Theory and method in cross-cultural psychology. *American Psychologist, 32* (12), 1069–1079.

Maltzman, C. M. (1981). Cross-cultural patterns of response to the WISC/WISC-R and Bender Gestalt Test by Chinese-American, Hispanic-American, and Occidental-American educationally handicapped boys. *Dissertation Abstracts International, 42* (02), 658-A. (University Microfilms No. 8117495)

Marmorale, A. M., & Brown, F. (1979). Psychological testing of nonwhite nonmiddle class child. *International Journal of Group Tensions, 1,* 195–200.

Martin, P. D. (1977). *A Spanish translation, adaption and standardization of the Wechsler Intelligence Scale for Children—Revised.* Unpublished doctoral dissertation, University of Miami.

Martinez-Morales, E., & Cook, V. J. (1982, March). Cultural sensitivity and nondiscriminatory assessment: A transactional model of assessment for Hispanic children. Paper presented at the Multi Ethnic Conference on Assessment: An International Conference, Tampa, FL.

McShane, D. A. (1982). Otitis median and American Indians: Prevalence, etiology, psychoeducational consequences, prevention and intervention. In S. Manson (Ed.), *New directions in prevention among American Indian and Alaskan native communities.* Portland: Oregon Health Sciences University Press.

McShane, D. A. (1984). Alcohol use and cerebral asymmetries. *Journal of Nervous and Mental Disease, 172* (9), 529–532.

McShane, D. A. (1984). Explaining achievement patterns of American Indian children: A transcultural, developmental model. *Peabody Journal on Education, 61* (1), 34–48.

McShane, D. A., & Plas, J. M. (1984). The cognitive functioning of American Indian children: Moving from the WISC to the WISC-R. *School Psychology Review, 13* (1), 61–73.

Mercer, J. R. (1979). *System of Multicultural Pluralistic Assessment (SOMPA) technical manual.* New York: Psychological Corporation.

Mercer, J., & Lewis, J. (1978). *Technical manual: System of multicultural pluralistic assessment.* New York: Psychological Corporation.

Mercer, J. R., & Smith, J. M. (1972). *Subtest estimates of the WISC Full Scale IQs for children.* National Center for Health Statistics (DHEW).

Milne, N. D. M. (1974). Relationships among scores obtained on the Wechsler Intelligence Scale for Children, Columbia Mental Maturity Scale and Leiter International Performance Scale by Mexican-American children. *Dissertation Abstracts International,* 6516-A. (University Microfilms No. 75-9073)

Mishra, S. P. (1983). *Ethnic group bias in WISC-R verbal items.* Paper presented at the annual convention of the American Psychological Association, Anaheim, CA.

Montague, D. J. (1981). Relationships between WISC-R IQ, SOMPA's estimated learning potential, and adaptive behavior in children with academic problems. *Dissertation Abstracts International,* 1615-B. (University Microfilms No. 8121343)

Morales, E. S. (1976). Examiner effects on the testing of Mexican-American bilingual children in the early elementary grades. *Dissertation Abstracts International,* 685-A.

Morales, E. (1977). *Qualitative assessment of the academic performance of bilingual Mexican-American children.* Paper presented at the 85th annual meeting of the American Psychological Association, San Francisco, CA.

Morales, E., & George, C. (1976). *Examiner effects in the testing of bilingual Mexican-American children.* Paper presented at the annual convention of the American Psychological Association, Washington, DC.

Moran, R. B. (1974). *Observations and recommendations on the Puerto Rican version of the Wechsler Intelligence Scale for Children.* Rio Piedras: Puerto Rico University. (ERIC Document Reproduction Service No. ED 088 932)

Munford, P. R., & Munoz, A. (1980). A comparison of the WISC and WISC-R on Hispanic children. *Journal of Clinical Psychology, 36* (2), 452–458.

Murray, M. E., Waites, L., Veldman, D. J., & Heatly, M. D. (1973). Differences between WISC and WAIS scores in delinquent boys. *The Journal of Experimental Education, 42* (2), 68–72.

Navarro, M. S. (1978). *Chicano children's cognitive styles: A review of the literature and effects of a pretest intervention.* (ERIC Document Reproduction Service No. ED 217 075)

Oakland, T. (1980). An evaluation of the ABIC, pluralistic norms and estimated learning potential. *Journal of School Psychology, 18* (1), 3–11.

Oakland, T. (1983). Concurrent and predictive validity estimates for the WISC-R and ELPs by racial-ethnic and SES groups. *School Psychology Review, 12* (1), 57–61.

Oakland, T., & Feigenbaum, D. (1979). Multiple sources of test bias on the WISC-R and Bender-Gestalt Test. *Journal of Consulting and Clinical Psychology, 47* (5), 968–974.

Olmedo, E. L. (1981). Testing linguistic minorities. *American Psychologist, 36* (10), 1078–1082.

Oplesch, M., & Genshaft, J. (1981). Comparison of bilingual children on the WISC-R and the Escala de Inteligencia Wechsler Para Niños. *Psychology in the Schools, 18,* 159–163.

Overall, J. E., & Levin, H. S. (1978). Correcting for cultural factors in evaluating intellectual deficit on WAIS. *Journal of Clinical Psychology, 34* (4), 910–915.

Padilla, E. R., & Roll, S. (1984). *The performance of Mexican children and adolescents on the WISC-R.* Manuscript under editorial review. *Interamerican Journal of Psychology, 16* (2), 122–128.

Palmer, M., & Gaffney, P. D. (1972). Effects of administration of the WISC in Spanish and English and relationship of social class to performance. *Psychology in the Schools, 9* (11), 61–64.

Perez, F. M. (1980). Performance of bilingual children on the Spanish version of the ITPA. *Exceptional Children, 46* (7), 536–541.

Piersel, W. C., Brody, G. H., & Kratochwill, T. R. (1977). A further examination of motivational influences on disadvantaged minority group children's intelligence test performance. *Child Development, 48,* 1142–1145.

Pothoff, R. F. (1966). *Statistical aspects of the problem of biases in psychological tests* [Mimeo Series No. 479]. Chapel Hill, NC: University of North Carolina, Department of Statistics.

Prewitt-Diaz, J. O., & Munoz, G. (1980). *A reliability study of the WISC with Puerto Rican children (grades K–9) in Puerto Rico.* (ERIC Document Service Reproduction N. ED 222 598)

Price-Williams, D. R. (1975). *Explorations in cross-cultural psychology.* San Francisco: Chadler and Sharp Publishers, Inc.

Reschly, D. J. (1978). WISC-R factor structures among Anglos, Blacks, Chicanos, and Native-American Papagos. *Journal of Consulting and Clinical Psychology, 46* (3), 417–422.

Reschly, D. J. (1979). Nonbiased assessment. In G. D. Phye & D. J. Reschly (Eds.), *School psychology: Perspectives and issues.* New York: Academic Press.

Reschly, D. J. (1981). Evaluation of the effects of SOMPA measures on classification of students as mildly mentally retarded. *American Journal of Mental Deficiency, 86* (1), 16–20.

Reschly, D. J., & Jipson, F. J. (1976). Ethnicity, geographic locale, age, sex, and urban-rural residence as variables in the prevalence of mild retardation. *American Journal of Mental Deficiency, 81* (2), 154–161.

Reschly, D. J., & Reschly, J. E. (1979). Validity of WISC-R factor scores in predicting achievement and attention for four sociocultural groups. *Journal of School Psychology, 17* (4), 355–361.

Reschly, D. J., & Sabers, D. L. (1979). Analysis of test bias in four groups with the regression definition. *Journal of Educational Measurement, 16* (1), 1–9.

Reston, J. (1981). *Bilingual education battle just beginning.* Detroit: Detroit Free Press.

Reynolds, C. R., & Gutkin, T. B. (1980). A regression analysis of test bias on the WISC-R for Anglos and Chicanos referred for psychological services. *Journal of Abnormal Child Psychology, 8* (2), 237–243.

Reynolds, C. R., & Willson, V. L. (1982). *Intellectual differences among Mexican-Americans, Papagos, and Whites independent of "g."* Paper presented to the annual meeting of the American Psychological Association, Washington, DC.

Ross-Reynolds, J., & Reschly D. J. (1983). An investigation of item bias on the WISC-R with four sociocultural groups. *Journal of Consulting and Clinical Psychology, 51,* 144–146.

Rugel, R. P. (1974). WISC subtest scores of disabled readers: A review with respect to Bannatyne's recategorization. *Journal of Learning Disabilities, 7,* 48–55.

Sabatino, D. A., Hayden, D. L., & Kelling, K. (1972). Perceptual, language and academic achievement of English, Spanish, and Navajo speaking children referred for special classes. *Journal of School Psychology, 10* (1), 39–46.

Sanchez, G. I. (1932a). Group differences in Spanish-speaking children: A critical review. *Journal of Applied Psychology, 16,* 549–558.

Sanchez, G. I. (1932b). Scores of Spanish-speaking children on repeated tests. *Journal of Genetic Psychology, 40,* 223–231.

Sanchez, G. I. (1934a). Bilingualism and mental measures. *Journal of Applied Psychology, 18,* 765–772.

Sanchez, G. I. (1934b). The implications of a basal vocabulary to the measurement of the abilities of bilingual children. *Journal of Social Psychology, 5,* 395–402.

Sandoval, J. (1979). The WISC-R and internal evidence of test bias with minority groups. *Journal of Consulting and Clinical Psychology, 47* (5), 919–927.

Sandoval, J. (1982). The WISC-R factoral validity for minority groups and Spearman's hypothesis. *Journal of School Psychology, 20* (3), 198–204.

Sandoval, J., & Mille, M. P. W. (1980). Accuracy of judgments of WISC-R item difficulty for minority groups. *Journal of Consulting and Clinical Psychology, 48* (2), 249–253.

Sandoval, J., Zimmerman, & Woo-Sam (1983). Cultural differences on WISC-R verbal items. *Journal of School Psychology, 21,* 49–55.

Sattler, J. M., & Kuncik, T. M. (1976). Ethnicity, socioeconomic status and pattern of WISC scores as variables that affect psychologists' estimates of "effective intelligence." *Journal of Clinical Psychology, 32* (2), 362–366.

Schwarz, P. A. (1983). Adapting tests to the cultural setting. *Educational and Psychological Measurement, 23* (4), 673–686.

Silverstein, A. B. (1973). Factor structure of the Wechsler Intelligence Scale for Children for three ethnic groups. *Journal of Educational Psychology, 65* (3), 408–410.

Smith, A., Hays, J. R., & Solway, K. S. (1977). Comparison of the WISC-R and Culture Fair Intelligence Tests in a juvenile delinquent population. *Journal of Psychology, 97,* 179–182.

Smith, M. D., Coleman, J. M., Dokecki, P. R., & Davis, E. E. (1977). Recategorized WISC-R scores of learning disabled children. *Journal of Learning Disabilities, 10,* 437–443.

Solway, K. (1976). A comparison of the WISC and WISC-R in a juvenile delinquent population. *Journal of Psychology, 94,* 101–106.

Spence, A. G., Mishra, S. P., & Ghozeil, S. (1971). Home language and performance on standardized tests. *Elementary School Journal, 71,* 309–313.

Stewart, D. W. (1976). Effects of sex and ethnic variables on the profiles of the Illinois Test for Psycholinguistics and Wechsler Intelligence Scale for Children. *Psychological Reports, 38,* 53–54.

Straus, M. A. (1969). Phenomenal identity and conceptual equivalence of measurement in cross-national comparative research. *Journal of Marriage and the Family,* 233–239.

Sundberg, N. D., & Gonzales, L. R. (1981). Cross-cultural and cross-ethnic assessment: Overview and issues. In P. McReynolds (Ed.), *Advances in psychological assessment,* Vol. 5. San Francisco: Jossey-Bass Publishers.

Svanum & Bringle, (1982). Race, social class and predictive bias: An evaluation using the WISC, WRAT and teacher ratings. *Intelligence, 6,* 275–286.

Swanson, E. N. (1975). Interpreter and Spanish administration effects on the WISC performance of Mexican-American children. *Dissertation Abstracts International,* 2035-A. (University Microfilms No. 75-21, 319)

Swanson, E., & De Blassie, R. (1971). Interpreter effects on the WISC performance of first grade Mexican-American children. *Measurement and Evaluation in Guidance, 4* (3), 172–175.

Swerdlik, M. E. (1976). A comparison study of the Wechsler Intelligence Scale for Children (WISC) and the Wechsler Intelligence Scale for Children—Revised (WISC-R) for children referred to school psychologists because of concerns about their intellectual ability. *Dissertation Abstracts International,* 5716-A. (University Microfilms No. 77-5899)

Swerdlik, M. E. (1978). Comparison of WISC and WISC-R scores of referred Black, White and Latino children. *Journal of School Psychology, 16* (2), 10–125.

Swerdlik, M. E., & Schweitzer, J. (1978). A comparison of factor structures of the WISC and WISC-R. *Psychology in the Schools, 15 (2), 166–172.*

Thomas, A., Hertzig, M. E., Dryman, I., & Fernandez, P. (1971). Examiner effect in IQ testing of Puerto Rican working-class children. *Journal of American Orthopsychology, 41,* 809–821.

Van de Vijver, F. J. R., & Poortinga, Y. H. Cross-cultural generalization and universality. *Journal of Cross-Cultural Psychology, 13* (4), 387–408.

Van der Flier, H. (1982). Deviant response patterns and comparability of test scores. *Journal of Cross-Cultural Psychology, 13* (3), 267–298.

Wechsler, D. (1974). *Wechsler Intelligence Scale for Children—Revised.* New York: Psychological Corporation.

Weiss, S. C. (1980). Culture Fair Intelligence Test and draw-a-person scores from a rural Peruvian sample. *Journal of Social Psychology, 111,* 147–148.

Williams, R. L. (1970). Black pride, academic relevance and individual achievement. *Counseling Psychologist, 2* (1), 18–22.

Williams, R. L. (1971). Abuses and misuses in testing black children. *Counseling Psychology, 2* (3), 62–73.

Williams, R. L. (1974). The problem of the match and mismatch in testing black children. In L. Miller (Ed.), *The testing of black students.* Englewood Cliffs, NJ: Prentice-Hall.

SEVENTEEN

TOWARD A PSYCHOLOGY OF GIFTEDNESS: A CONCEPT IN SEARCH OF MEASUREMENT

MARY MEEKER

S.O.I. Institute
El Segundo, California

HISTORICAL CONCEPTS OF INTELLECTUAL GENIUS

The earliest descriptive passage of giftedness is found in the apocryphal *New Testament*, called the "Hebrew Gospels":

> And Joseph, seeing that Jesus was vigorous in mind and body, resolved that he should not remain ignorant of the letters, and took him to the Temple where he handed him over to a master teacher. And the teacher said to Joseph. "I will tell you whether he is vigorous in mind. I shall teach him first the Greek letters and then Hebrew." He wrote out the alphabet and began to teach in an imperious tone, saying, "Say, 'Alpha.' " And he gave him his attention for a long time and Jesus made no answer, but was silent. And the teacher said to him, "Say 'Alpha.' " Whereupon Jesus was again silent. "Stupid boy!" the teacher screamed, "Say 'Alpha.' " And Jesus replied, "If thou art really a teacher, tell me the power of the Alpha and I will tell thee the power of the Beta." And the teacher, enraged at this, struck him, saying "Take him from the Temple, he is stupid." [Hollingworth, 1942, p. 193]

The concept of the genius is ancient. Ovid, referring to Caesar and his preparations to complete the conquest of the world, notes the manner in which a genius acts in advance of his years:

> Though he himself is but a boy, he wages a war unsuited to his boyish years. . . . Genius divine outpaces time, and brooks not the tedium of tardy growth. [Hollingworth, 1942, p. 200]

Throughout history people have examined the subject of genius, and it seems that anyone, who wanted to, felt qualified to express an opinion or make that opinion a definition of giftedness. This rampant, unthinking approach to expertise has resulted in interesting contradictions, many of which have led to lingering misconceptions that persist even today as myths that are so well known that laypeople, educators, and psychologists accept them as conventional wisdom, without question. James Gallagher covered them clearly in the "Research Summary on Gifted Child Education" (Meeker, 1966). I compended more of these for the California State Framework for Gifted Minors (Meeker & Magary, 1971).

John Stuart Mill felt that originality characterized genius. That in the interest of the public, freedom should be granted to persons who were so individually creative and original. He further indicated that society, rather than try to fit genius into molds which society approved of, should allow genius to live in an atmosphere of freedom. Other authors amplified the concept that genius constitutes a different species. Hirsch (1962) wrote: "Genius differs in kind from the species of man. . . . It is another psychobiological species, differing as much from man in his mental and temperamental processes as man differs from the ape." Another notion of genius is that of a highly specialized aptitude for specific performance; that is, the genius is thought to lack general ability and to be capable of only certain kinds of intellectual performance. Galton indicated that intellect, zeal and the drive for work was what raised the ordinary person into genius. Some current authors have taken this statement to be definitive of giftedness, rather than, as Galton implied, that hard work and intelligence lead to success. By insisting that giftedness is academic hard work, they led many of their readers to believe that academic success is the only goal of gifted education. Galton formulated the theory that genius (great natural ability) is nothing more nor less than a very extreme degree in the distribution of a combination of traits that is shared by all in various degrees. Galton was the first measurement oriented investigator who attempted to apply a numerical concept to qualities or functions emanating from human thought; thus mathematical concepts of probability and standard deviations within the bell-shaped curve led to the definition of genius.

This notion historically laid the foundation for tests to be expressed as IQ scores. But there was an inherent danger in this approach—a danger that came to haunt the measurement experts. Using population distributions as a basis for measuring a general quality of humanness called intelligence implied that, and rested on, the assumption that intelligence is genetic.

George Bernard Shaw (1952) had a different conception of genius and used Saint Joan as an example. He described her as "seeing farther and probing deeper" than other people. He saw her values as being different from others and credited her with the energy to give meaning to her vision. Shaw was the first to recognize that the peers of "geniuses" wanted to destroy them because their inability to be able to comprehend the depth of the genius' thinking frightened them.

Other writers discuss social conditions under which the exceptional individual contributes to social change and progress, an issue that has impact for educating highly exceptional children. Havelock Ellis (1937), for instance, who studied 975 British men of genius concluded that genius was often subjected to persecution. Of the 975 eminent men studied, 160 had been imprisoned. Shaw describes Saint Joan as always being alone in her venture. Hirsch (1962) describes the genius as being isolated because the act of performing at such an extraordinary level requires solitude as a refuge for their work. Our current knowledge about gifted people today is that many are indeed loners (Meeker, 1971).

HISTORY OF THE GIFTED CHILD MOVEMENT

While the words *intelligence, measurement,* and *gifted* have commonalities, they do at the same time have some contradictions. Measurement means comparison with a fixed amount to ascertain size of proportions using a unit, degree, or standard capacity. The measuring of human intelligence has traditionally consisted of a number or range-between-numbers. When there was a need to define giftedness, the early pioneers studying the phenomenon began with the Binet items to investigate distributions of scores that fell beyond the second standard deviation. Almost as an exercise in finding how children distributed themselves around the mean, Terman and Merrill (1925, 1959, 1960) searched for some standard measurement that would indicate superior to gifted intelligence—at that time called genius.

Using a standard deviation of 15 points and a total of two standard deviations, these researchers also recorded personality descriptions of those children who scored at and above the "genius" level. Until the early sixties, while Terman continued to study gifted childrens' intelligence, measures of intelligence on children were made with the Stanford-Binet. The Binet was the benchmark for measuring intelligence in children until Wechsler developed the WISC scales (conversation with David Wechsler at the American Psychological Association Conference, Philadelphia, Pennsylvania, 1963). Few psychologists questioned whether these tests of intelligence were based on a theory of intelligence; it seems the sophistication of the early psychologists had not progressed beyond the Gaussian curve, the molar score, and the unitary measure. D. Wechsler and L. L. Thurstone were early voices in the wind. Their concern about nondifferentiated measures eventually led Wechsler (1958) to the development of the WAIS with its consequent derivatives, and Thurstone (1938, 1947) to develop the PMA Tests. Thus, when major educational institutions began looking toward identifying the gifted as had been suggested at the Woods Hole Conference, there was a search for psychologists to be employed in the schools to identify gifted students.

In California, pilot studies by the State Department of Education in 1959 led to the conclusion that a combination of measures of achievement and an IQ score of 130 did indeed predict giftedness. In those first years of gifted education there was no attempt to design a program where teachers would teach these gifted students so identified and then retest them on the Binet to see whether they had maintained their gifted scores. This primordial approach to programming for the gifted was "more of the same," that is, more reading or more arithmetic or more spelling. Since the testing for gifted was dictated by the people doing the measuring and these psychologists, who were for the most part clinical psychologists whose expertise centered on tests of intelligence, the practice of testing with the Binet or WISC continued without close examination of how gifted programs affected intelligence. Not to anyone's knowledge, and certainly not reported in the literature, there was a study designed in which there would be pretesting for gifted, as well as selection and post-IQ testing to ascertain what effect a given program had on the gifted score. Partly this was a result of the assumption that intelligence is inherited and thus the measure is correct within the standard error of a given test. Such assumptions and practices continued until 1962, and the inheritance of historical measurement techniques in general centered on statistical distributions of numerical delineations. The larger picture of human giftedness was easily lost because the past techniques were not questioned, and thus until the gifted child movement formally began in California in 1962, few questions arose about human giftedness.

With successful implementation of gifted programs in many other states, the question of the predictive validity of IQ scores arose as many identified as gifted did not achieve commensurately with their indicated score. The first question was: If academic achievement is not the test of giftedness, then what is giftedness? Few recalled that part of test variance is not correlated, but many asked: If gifted is not a number or an IQ score, then what other definitions are there to consider? Educators and psychologists began to realize that the IQ score as a definition did not address the individual differences, creative problem solving, body talent, musical talent, design and art talent, and other unique aspects of intellectual functions, social giftedness, and leadership. A second question was: Are these also functions of intelligence?

The rosters of high schools proliferate with the traditional stereotypes of giftedness. Gifted students are valedictorians, salutatorians, honor rollees, and Merit Scholars; and, among them, most would score more than 130 IQ because of their verbal facility. Few, however, gain fame or recognition for their academic prowess in comparison with other kinds of gifted people. Terman's (1959) follow-up studies confirmed that few made substantial contributions in their fields, yet all had been excellent students and certainly were the pride of their families. Conclusions about their health and happiness as adults indicate that they were no more healthy or happier than their nongifted peers. If the other prong of investigation centering on personality findings had also continued in tandem with the IQ investigations, the understanding of human giftedness in its broadest ranges would have enhanced our knowledge of these special people, but these "soft signs" were dropped from study once the intelligence test became established as the criterion and predictor of giftedness.

CREATIVITY AS AN ASPECT OF GIFTEDNESS

Creativity is a natural human condition, and it is also a life-long process. The assessment of creativity as a form of giftedness is more personality than cognitively oriented. Barron (1959), who researched adults known for their creative productions, found that they were fluent with their words, or their hands, or their ideas. *Motor creative* individuals usually talk with their hands as they express ideas. *Natural creative* individuals also show a gifted level of flexibility in relational thinking (often called inspiration or illumination). Natural creative individuals tend to have unlimited energy and defy time schedules when they work. Typically they also show sensitivity to people's needs or to problems in need of solutions. They easily do the transformational thinking that leads to creative solutions. Creative individuals are known for their unique, original, often surprising ideas. All of these traits could be acquired by the learning process. These characteristics of successful creative adults and children are well documented in *The Creativity Question*, edited by Rothenberg and Housman (1976).

Nevertheless, several points should be clarified:

1. What is the difference between talent and creativity?
2. What is the difference between giftedness and creativity?
3. How do we separate product from process?
4. Can creativity be measured?
5. Can creativity be trained?
6. Are there personal benefits and effects to becoming creative?

We will consider each of the above issues separately.

Differences Between Talent and Creativity

Talent can best be described as a physiological function that is gifted—that is, coordination is of champion quality (such as in athletes, musicians, dancers, artists); whereas creativity may best be defined as the creation of new and excellent music, games, choreography, lyrics, stories, designs, and art forms. We all know technically gifted musicians who have never written and could not create music.

Creativity and Giftedness

The traditional and conventionally accepted definition of giftedness is that of academic achievement. In Guilford's "Structure of Intellect" (1967), these gifted people can be described as excellent producers of information they have studied; they are gifted *convergent producers*, in contrast with the *creative*, who are *divergent producers*. Getzels and Jackson (1962), Torrance (1959, 1963), Robert and Mary Meeker (1978), Gowan and Demos (1964), and Khatena (1977, 1978) were early investigators into the characteristics of the divergent producer or creatively gifted. Estimates range from 20% to 40% as the number of gifted creatives who could be convergently or academically gifted but who rarely work for grades because they are more disposed toward being creative than scholastic. Perhaps we can clarify these concerns when we address issue number three.

Separating Products from the Processes of Being Creative

How do we separate creative products from the processes? Too often, society, specifically buyers, determine whether a product is creative; someone likes it and purchases it—thus the product becomes *creative*. There are many creative products, acknowledged as such, but not popularly accepted as creative. Even people who achieve a reputation for being creative and reach success and acceptance continue to grow and change. The products are a temporal result, but the process continues.

Can Creativity Be Measured?

Guilford's early factor analysis produced a fifth kind of intelligence, divergent thinking, that differed from the other four: *comprehension, memory, evaluation,* and *convergent production.* The tests that accounted for these factors were tests that required thinking along unusual and unknown lines. By 1959, after 15 years of attempts to factor intelligence, the final schematic was developed (Guilford, 1950, 1967). Out of this body of work, the SOI Tests of divergent thinking evolved and by 1974 the three primary tests of divergence centered on figural-spatial, symbolic, and semantic contents. Those tests have been standardized with national norms (Meeker, 1969).

Can Creativity Be Trained?

The answer is yes. There are many studies to substantiate this, based on validated, field-tested materials. Whether society deems these people as creative, however, is another question (Meeker, 1977, 1978).

Benefits from Training in Creativity

Training Intellectual Abilities in Sequential Steps has led to increased self-concept, increased sensitivity, freedom to choose, and consequently better decision-making and analytical skills, feeling of power to solve new problems, ability to roll with disappointments, openness and sensitivity to others, better tolerance for personal differences, and greatly increased sense of humor. The notion that intellectual abilities or thinking skills can be taught needs clarification: procedures to train thinking, reasoning, and creative responses depend on explicit definitions of what they are. That they are "intact" is taken for granted by educators or employers who require the use of them on various tests. The ability, for instance, to work and think at the inferential level is the most abstract level in the Guilford Structure of Intellect. Here are some examples from instructional booklets showing how inferential (Implications) thinking can be developed ranging from rudimentary responses to most complex ones. The most difficult questions on the Wechsler and Binet tests depend on inferential responses.

Symbolic Implications. A critical ability for algebra, mathematics and science problem solving (see Figure 1).

Semantic Implications. A critical thinking and reasoning skill that is necessary for interpretation of verbal information. Figure 2 is one demonstration of how implications thinking can be developed. Again, the exercises begin at a very simple level and are articulated in difficulty. It is important that the inferential aspects are not compounded with difficulty due to use of esoteric vocabulary.

Creativity processes in and of themselves have, when taught, led to specific results; for example, students in creative training have reported that they have become, do, or are as follows:

adventurous	capitalize on mistakes or accidents
change oriented	confident
daring	do not like routine tasks
egocentric	flexible
have a high energy level	independent
interest oriented	intuitive
multiple ideas	multi-interests
are their "own person"	persistent
prefer to work alone	ready sense of humor
risk-takers	self-assured
self-critical	self-sufficient
sensitive	tolerate ambiguity

On SOI Tests of more than 250,000 students, analysis of their test results at the SOI Institute shows only one-third of identified gifted students tested at a gifted level in creative processing skills. Meeker reported similar results in a 1963 study of 69 gifted students who were followed from elementary school through high school (Meeker, 1969, 1984).

MENSA

The major association for gifted adults is MENSA. There are chapters in most of the United States. These are people who have demonstrated high scores (above the 96th percentile) on tests of intelligence, such as the WAIS. A group of 88 Mensa members were recently involved in a complete assessment of medical, psychophysical and SOI abilities. They were part of a much larger group of adults over the age of 50. The study is being carried out at the Veteran's Hospital in Los Angeles under the direction of Karl Syndulko, neuropsychologist, and Wallace Tourtellotte, M.D. (Paper to be presented April, 1985, New York City, International Conference on Geriontrics.)

The intent of this study was to look at body and intellectual functions as

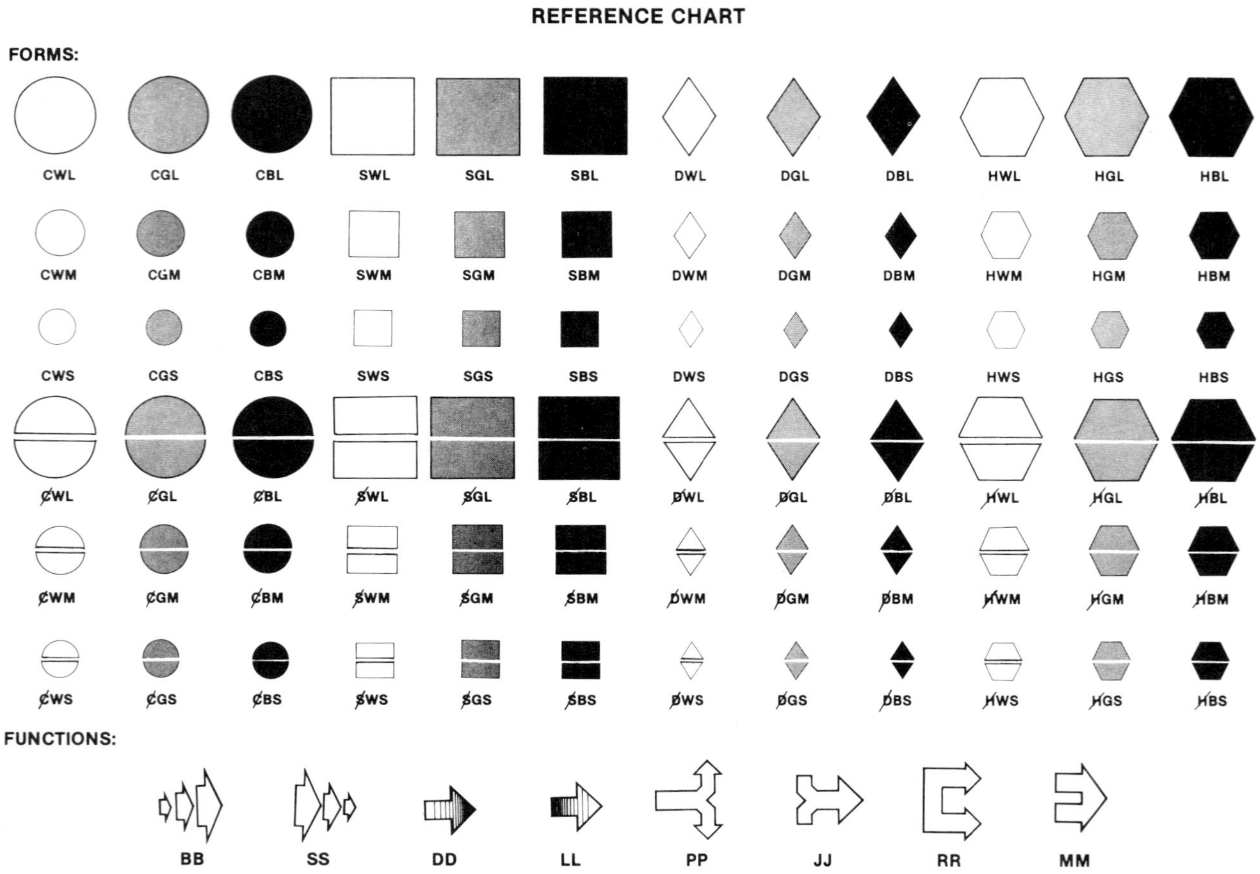

REFERENCE CHART

FORMS:

CWL	CGL	CBL	SWL	SGL	SBL	DWL	DGL	DBL	HWL	HGL	HBL
CWM	CGM	CBM	SWM	SGM	SBM	DWM	DGM	DBM	HWM	HGM	HBM
CWS	CGS	CBS	SWS	SGS	SBS	DWS	DGS	DBS	HWS	HGS	HBS
₵WL	₵GL	₵BL	₰WL	₰GL	₰BL	₱WL	₱GL	₱BL	₦WL	₦GL	₦BL
₵WM	₵GM	₵BM	₰WM	₰GM	₰BM	₱WM	₱GM	₱BM	₦WM	₦GM	₦BM
₵WS	₵GS	₵BS	₰WS	₰GS	₰BS	₱WS	₱GS	₱BS	₦WS	₦GS	₦BS

FUNCTIONS:

BB	SS	DD	LL	PP	JJ	RR	MM

Figure 1. NSI Form and Function Sheet. (*Source:* Reprinted with permission from Robert Meeher. *SOI Module NSI.* SOI Institute, 343 Richmond, El Segundo, CA 90245.)

794

Instructions: On this page f FORM and FUNCTIONS you will fill-in the missing form. Determine what form is needed to complete each of the statements in the boxes; look up the code for that form and enter the code on the line. The first one is already completed so you can see how it is done. You do the remaining lines on this page. The answers are on the back cover.

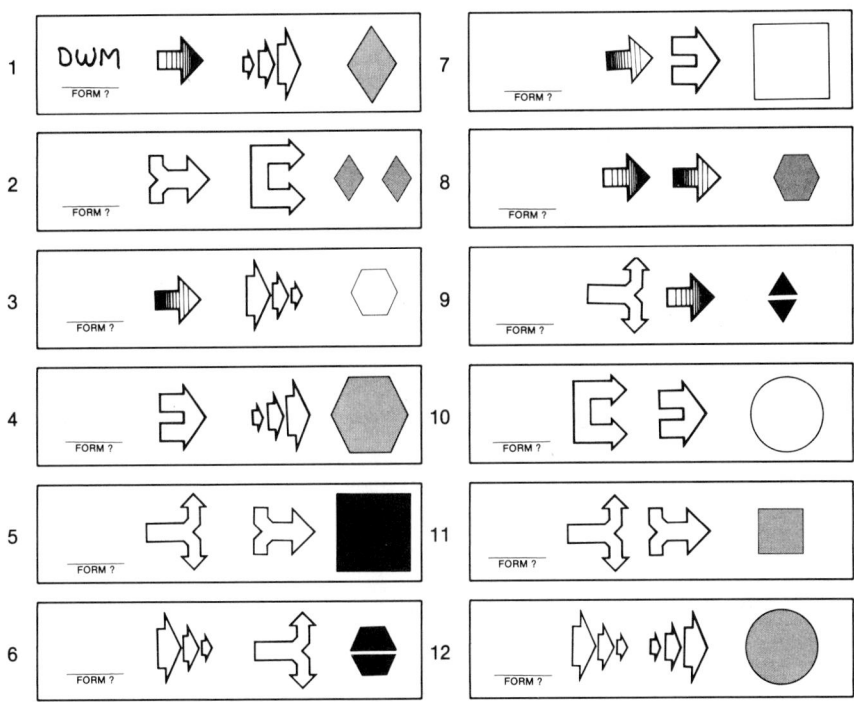

Review: Each box has two functions. That is the only difference between these statements and the ones on page NSI-4 which you have already done. So let's consider these one function at a time so they will be like two NSI-4 problems in each box. Start with the figure(s) on the right and the function next to it. Apply these tests:

IF THIS HAPPENS	THE STARTING FIGURE IS:
Becomes darker...........	Same shape, same size, one shade lighter
Becomes lighter...........	Same shape, same size, one shade darker
Becomes smaller...........	Same shape, same shade, one size larger
Becomes larger...........	Same shape, same shade, one size smaller
Becomes double...........	Same shape, same shade, same size—but one only
Becomes merged...........	Same shape, same shade, same size—but two
Becomes darker...........	Same shade, same size—whole
Becomes joined...........	Same shade, same size—split apart

Now put the code for that figure between the two functions—or if you have difficulty with the codes cut out the figure from the reference chart and put it on the page. Now you have a one function statement, so apply the test once more to find the answer.

Figure 1. (*Continued*)

795

Instructions. Preceding each sentence is a word which can be used as a verb or as a noun. Every sentence has a blank line on which you are to write a word from the box below. The word should fit the meaning of the sentence. These are not easy to do. If you cannot do one, go to the next, doing all you can. Then try to do the ones that were too hard. As you use a word, scratch it out.

1. PATTERN: *as a verb*: I want to pattern _____ after someone I really admire.

    as a noun: I love to design the pattern for a new _____ but I hate to do the hems.

2. CONCERN: *as a verb*: When he continued to be late for work, his supervisor became concerned about the employee's _____.

    as a noun: Your concern may be speed, but mine is _____.

3. PICTURE: *as a verb*: Picture a sunny _____, with the sun _____ on the water.

    as a noun: There was not one picture on the _____ of their rooms.

4. MIND: *as a verb*: When she was asked to mind the _____, she had not learned that the customer expected _____.

    as a noun: The formula for cheap, money making movies includes violence to _____ the mind.

5. INSTITUTE: *as a verb*: When a new manager comes in, _____ procedures are usually instituted.

    as a noun: An Institute is usually a form of business where _____ is carried on.

6. MILK: *as a verb*: Once she got the _____ she wanted, she milked the situation for sympathy.

    as a noun: Cappucino is really hot milk and coffee _____ together.

7. SCREAM: *as a verb*: The parents screamed so frequently at the child that he soon stopped _____.

    as a noun: Some comedians are a scream; some _____ are not; they are just _____.

8. WALK: *as a verb*: We are healthier if we walk up the _____.

    as a noun: When they were fired, they were told to take a walk out of the _____.

9. SMILE: *as a verb*: "Smile and the _____ smiles with you; weep and you weep _____.

    as a noun: The child's smile brings _____ into our hearts.

10. JUICE: *as a verb*: If you juice fresh _____, the liquid is _____.

    as a noun: Fresh frozen orange juice is neither _____ nor often pure.

---

alone, accuracy, assault, attention, building, carrots, clowns, courtesy, day, different, dress, fresh, health, listening, mixed, myself, orange, shining, silly, stairs, store, study, sunshine, walls, world

Figure 2. (*Source:* Reprinted with permission from Mary Meeher, *EMI Module.* SOI Institute, 343 Richmond, El Segundo, CA 90245.)

they change with age. The MENSA subgroup showed significant deviations from the nongifted group, $N = 120$. The largest difference was in Memory. Studies of gifted children have consistently shown the four Memory subtests (Memory for Units, both visual and auditory and Memory for Systems of Digits, both visual and auditory) to be significantly higher than for nongifted. This same finding held up in the Mensa group. They tend to retain gifted Memory through age 81. Age range was 50–81.

Interestingly, the psychophysical measures of reaction times held, too, in that their reaction times were lower than those of nongifted. However, on cognitive abilities related to developmental aspects of vision, the Mensa adults showed normal distributions on visual closure and visual discrimination.

In the area of creativity, there were three tests:

Divergent Production of Figural Units. Drawing ideas in unstructured tests (DFU).

Divergent Production of Semantic Units. Writing a creative story based on a series of previously drawn pictures.

Divergent Production of Symbolic Relations. Solving arithmetic problems creatively.

The writing of creative ideas was a gifted ability for a significant number of the adults.

On the whole, the gifted adults maintained the gifted abilities that were more abstract and cognitive, except for the ones more representative of physiological processes, such as vision closure and discrimination. Within age groups differences between men and women were negligible. A general slowing down was noticed after age 70. This was a trend and not significant.

Dr. Syndulko and Dr. Tourtellotte, who is chief of neurology, will be reporting on the contributions of age to gifted and nongifted adults in 1985 to the International Gerontology Convention in New York City. At the writing of this chapter, the data are analyzed but not formally printed. Further information can be obtained through the Veterans' Hospital, Wadsworth, Los Angeles.

CONCLUSION

There are many kinds of gifted responses among adults: scholastic, leadership, talent, creative. Not all adults are gifted in all aspects. The concept of measurement of giftedness ceases its critical importance once gifted students exit colleges into adult roles. The 1970s and 1980s have seen the greatest funding of gifted programs in the history of education in the United States. Studies of gifted adults who were recognized formally by measurement techniques, whether WISC tests, SOI-LA Tests, or Stanford-Binet tests, are rare. This author has followed 69 gifted students from 1962 until the present when they are functioning as adults. Comparison with nongifted peers finds them, much like the Mensa adults, performing successfully in their jobs. Unlike the preceding generation of Mensa, however, these young adults are marrying much less and are having much fewer children—they were aged 30–36 in 1984. Unquestionably, the multifaceted gifted and talented adults need identification and support for their giftedness as they mature.

REFERENCES

Barron, F. (1959). The creative individual. *CERGA Conference Address.* Los Angeles: California State University at Los Angeles.

Ellis, H. (1937). *On life and sex.* New York: Garden City Publishing Co.

Gallagher J. J. (1960). *What are gifted children like?* American Educational Research Association of the National Education Association.

Gallagher, J. J. (1964). *Teaching the gifted child.* Boston: Allyn & Bacon.

Gallagher, J. J. (1966). *Research summary on gifted child education.* Boston: Allyn & Bacon.

Galton, F. (1982). *Hereditary genius* (2nd ed.). London: Macmillan.

Getzels, J. W., & Jackson, P. W. (1962). *Creativity and intelligence: Explorations with gifted students.* New York: Wiley.

Gowan, J. C., & Demos, G. D. (1964). *The education and guidance of the ablest.* Springfield, IL: Thomas.

Guilford, J. P. (1950, September). Creativity. *American Psychologist,* pp. 444–445.

Guilford, J. P. (1967). *The nature of human intelligence.* New York: McGraw-Hill.

Hirsch, C. (1962). The cognitive functioning of the creative person: A developmental analysis. *Journal of Projective Techniques, 26,* 193–200.

Hollingworth, L. (1942). *Children above 180 IQ: Origin and development.* Yonkers-on-Hudson, NY: World Book Co.

Khatena, J. (1977, Summer). Facilitating the creative functioning of the gifted. *Gifted Child Quarterly, 21*(2), 218–226.

Khatena, J. (1978). *The creatively gifted child: Some suggestions for parents and teachers.* New York: Vantage Press.

Khatena, J., & Torrance, E. P. (1976). *Khatena-Torrance creative perception inventory.* Chicago: Stoetting.

Meeker, M. (1969). *The structure of intellect: Its interpretations and uses.* Columbus, OH: Charles E. Merrill.

Meeker, M. (1970). *California State Framework for Gifted and 32 Subject Matter/Grade Range Frameworks, 1966–70.* Sacramento: California Department of Education.

Meeker, M., & Magary, J. (1971). *California State Frameworks for Curriculum for Gifted Minors.* Sacramento, CA: California State Department of Education.

Meeker, M., & Meeker, R. (1978, July). Measuring creativity from the child's point of view. *Journal of Creative Behavior, 12*(1), 52–62.

Rothenberg, A., & Housman, C. R. (1976). *The creativity question.* Durham, NC: Duke University Press.

Shaw, G. B. (1952). *Saint Joan.* New York: Modern Library.

Terman, L. M. (1925). *Mental and physical traits of a thousand gifted children.* Palo Alto, CA: Stanford University Press.

Terman, L. M. (1959). *The gifted group at mid-life* (Vol. 5). Stanford, CA: Stanford University Press.

Terman, L., & Merrill, M. (1960). *Stanford-Binet Intelligence Scale, Manual for 3rd Revision, Form L-M.* Boston: Houghton Mifflin.

Thurstone, L. L. (1938). The primary mental abilities. *Psychological Monographs,* No. 1.

Thurstone, L. L. (1947). *Multiple factor analysis.* Chicago: University of Chicago Press.

Torrance, E. P. (1959). Current research of the nature of creative talent. *Journal of Counseling Psychology, 6,* 309–316.

Torrance, E. P. (1963). *The measurement of creative behavior in children* (mimeo.). Minneapolis: University of Minnesota, Bureau of Education Research.

Wechsler Intelligence Scale for Children (1949). New York: The Psychological Corp.

Wechsler, D. (1958). *The measurement of adult intelligence* (4th ed.). Baltimore: Williams and Wilkins.

EIGHTEEN

ASSESSMENT OF MENTALLY
RETARDED INDIVIDUALS

KAZUO NIHIRA

University of California
Los Angeles, California

Every society has among its members individuals who, by virtue of impairments in cognitive and neurophysical development, fail to meet societal demands and expectations adequately. These individuals are children and adults whose limited cognitive and neurophysical capacities manifest themselves in a wide spectrum of human abilities ranging from total dependency to near independence. To describe assessment procedures of this highly heterogeneous population, this chapter adopted the most frequently used definition of mental retardation—namely, the definition proposed by the American Association on Mental Deficiency (AAMD). The AAMD's definition incorporates two broad dimensions of human competency—intellectual functioning and adaptive behavior. Accordingly, this chapter describes the state of the art in the psychometric assessment of adaptive behavior, followed by a review of recent trends in the assessment of intelligence in the field of mental retardation.

There are several excellent reviews of well-known scales of intelligence prior to the 1974 revision of the Wechsler intelligence scale for children. Since the Wechsler scale is one of the most frequently used instruments for the diagnosis and classification of mentally retarded individuals, it is important to examine psychometric properties of the revised scale in relation to the old scale as well as to other existing scales of intelligence. The latter half of this chapter focuses primarily on this topic.

DEFINITION AND CLASSIFICATION OF MENTAL RETARDATION

Brief History

In the past, psychological classification of mentally retarded individuals has consisted of three or four categories, such as "moron," "imbecile," and "idiot," or, more recently, "mild," "moderate," "severe," and "profound retardation."

These categories usually represented various ranges on IQ scales. Binet and Simon (1905, 1961) originally developed the Binet scale with an explicit intention of measuring and isolating "scholastic educability" from other aspects of mental subnormality. However, once classification labels were assigned to those who were within a specified IQ range, such labels were regarded as representing not only the individual's level of intellectual functioning, but also his or her socio-behavioral functioning as well—in essence, those characteristics that had been associated with the labels. The idea that intellectual functioning is a single unitary trait that is immutable has reinforced misconceptions concerning the phenom-enon of mental retardation and seriously impeded needed changes in its reme-diation.

Before the advent of the mental test movement at the turn of this century, the definition of mental retardation seemed to have encompassed broader aspects of human capacity with strong emphasis on the individual's ability to manage one's self and one's own affairs adequately (Down, 1876; Goddard, 1914; Howe, 1858). Concerning the problem of mental retardation in the school-age child, Doll (1966) stated: "In all our history, the prime criterion of mental deficiency has been social inadequacy at maturity. In attributing this limitation to intel-ligence alone, we have combined the socially inadequate retarded with the socially adequate retarded" (p. 66). This statement is a precursor to the most widely used definition of mental retardation—in essence, the one proposed by the American Association on Mental Retardation (Grossman, 1983).

The AAMD Definition

In 1959, the concept of social adaptability (now called adaptive behavior) was formally recognized and incorporated in the definition of mental retardation in the AAMD manual of terminology and classification. In the latest edition of the AAMD manual (Grossman, 1983), mental retardation is referred to as "significantly subaverage general intellectual functioning resulting in or asso-ciated with concurrent impairments in adaptive behavior and manifested during the developmental period" (p. 1). As an integral part of the definition, each key term is defined as follows:

1. General Intellectual Functioning is defined as the results obtained by assessment with one or more of the individually administered general intelligence tests developed for the purpose of assessing intellectual func-tioning.
2. Significantly Subaverage Intellectual Functioning is defined as approxi-mately IQ 70 or below. This upper limit is intended as a guideline; it could be extended upward through IQ 75 or more, depending on the reliability of the intelligence test used.
3. Adaptive Behavior is defined as the effectiveness or degree with which

individuals meet the standards of personal independence and social responsibility expected for their age and cultural group.

4. Developmental Period is defined as the period of time between birth and the 18th birthday.

The AAMD definition indicates that two criteria—level of intelligence and level of adaptive behavior—must be considered in making the diagnosis. A diagnosis of mental retardation is appropriate only when an individual falls into the retarded category in both intellectual functioning and adaptive behavior functioning.

For reporting and descriptive purposes, the AAMD classification manual recommends a four-level classification system—mild, moderate, severe, and profound—based on IQ ranges (see Table 1). The narrow band or zone of uncertainty between levels indicates that clinical judgment about all information, including the IQs, from more than one test if available, and the information about intellectual functioning from other sources is necessary to determine the individual's level.

The classification manual further recommends the procedure for diagnosing and determining level of retardation as follows (Grossman, 1983, p. 13):

1. Recognize that a problem exists (for example, delay in developmental milestones).
2. Determine that an adaptive behavior deficit exists.
3. Determine measured, general-intellectual functioning.
4. Determine whether there is retardation of intellectual functioning.
5. Determine the level of retardation as indicated by level of measured intellectual functioning.

Thus a low IQ by itself neither defines mental retardation nor specifies the level of retardation. The individual must also show a corresponding deficit in adaptive behavior. This second criterion is somewhat more difficult to specify. Because there are different environmental expectations at different ages, the deficit in adaptive behavior will vary for different age groups.

Table 1. Level of Retardation Indicated by IQ Range

Term	IQ Range for Level
Mild mental retardation	50–55 to approx. 70
Moderate mental retardation	34–40 to 50–55
Severe mental retardation	20–25 to 35–40
Profound mental retardation	Below 20 or 25

ADAPTIVE BEHAVIOR APPRAISAL IN DIAGNOSIS AND CLASSIFICATION

The AAMD classification manual provides some guidelines for the appraisal of adaptive behavior in diagnosis and classification (Grossman, 1983, p. 25). During the infancy and early childhood period, adaptive behavior may be reflected in sensory-motor skills, communication skills (including speech and language), self-help skills, and socialization (development of ability to interact with others). Delays in the development of these behavior skills may represent potential deficiencies in adaptive behavior. During the childhood and early adolescent period, adaptive behavior deficits may be manifested in difficulties in application of basic academic skills in daily life activities, application of appropriate reasoning and judgment in coping with the environment, and inadequate social skills (inability to handle participation in group activities and interpersonal relationships). During the late adolescent and adult period, vocational and social responsibility and performance become important; thus adaptive behavior appraisal may involve the extent to which the individual maintains himself independently in community living.

Implicit in this appraisal is the concept that mental retardation is not a permanent condition; an individual may meet the criteria of mental retardation at one time in life but not at another time. It is possible for him or her to change the status or level of mental retardation as a result of change in adaptive behavior or environmental expectations in regard to age-related social norms or specific environmental settings.

PSYCHOMETRIC ASSESSMENT OF ADAPTIVE BEHAVIOR

Existing Scales of Adaptive Behavior

The Vineland Social Maturity Scale (Doll, 1947) had been the most well-known standardized instrument of Social Competence (now called Adaptive Behavior) prior to 1960. Since then, there has been an upsurge of interest in measuring adaptive behavior and today there are numerous scales of adaptive behavior. One review lists 110 instruments (Individualized Data Base Project, 1977), and another lists 132 (Walls, Werner, Bacon, & Zane, 1977). These measures vary greatly, not only in quality and norming, but also in intended purpose. Some scales are designed to assess primarily severe and profoundly retarded individuals, while others are designed to measure the vocational readiness of mildly retarded people. Some scales are designed to obtain a detailed appraisal of a person's competency in order to set training objectives rather than to assist in diagnosis and classification. Users must, therefore, be careful to choose the instruments most suited for their specific populations and needs. The AAMD classification manual provides the following list of scales that have adequate norms (Grossman, 1983, p. 43):

Broad-ranged scales or scales for multifunctioning levels:

AAMD Adaptive Behavior Scales (*R, M*)
AAMD Adaptive Behavior Scales—school version (*R, M*)
Adaptive Functioning Index (*R*)
Behavior Modification Technology Assessment Instrument (*R, O*)
Camelot Behavior System Checklist (*R*)
Client Centered Evaluation Model (*R, M*)
Minnesota Developmental Programming System (*R*)
Progress Assessment Chart (*R*)
Vineland Social Maturity Scale (*R*)

Scales with limited functioning level or specialized contents:

Adaptive Behavior Inventory for Children (*R*)
Balthazar Scales of Adaptive Behavior (*R, T, O*)
Cain-Levine Social Competency Scale (*R*)
California Preschool Social Competency Scale (*O*)
Competitive Employment Screening Test (*R*)
Fairview Developmental Scale (*R*)
Fairview Social Skills Scale for Mildly and Moderately Retarded (*R*)
San Francisco Vocational Competency Scale (*R*)
Social and Prevocational Information Battery (*T*)

In the parentheses, "*R*" indicates behavior rating scales; "*M*" indicates scales, including subscales measuring maladaptive behavior; "*T*" indicates a test battery; and "*O*" indicates the scales requiring direct observation and testing. Some of the scales designated as "*R*–behavior rating" recommend that the rater observe the actual behavior of the ratee if the rater is not sure about his or her judgments regarding specific scale items.

Components of Adaptive Behavior Scales

In a comprehensive review of the literature, Meyers, Nihira, and Zetlin (1979) described the characteristics of 23 frequently used instruments of adaptive behavior. The review noted the diversity of contents: Some are designed to tap a broad spectrum of behavior subsumed under the traditional notion of social competency, while others emphasize in-depth measures of selected areas of social competency, such as vocational readiness or independent living skills in the community.

Most scales of adaptive behavior are composed of several subscales or behavior domains (in essence, coherent groups of related activities, with items organized in developmental sequence within each behavior domain). Although each scale has its unique internal organization and item expression, it is possible to identify the frequently used behavior domains in most scales.

The common domains of adaptive skills and competence are *self-help skills* (feeding, dressing and undressing, toilet training, grooming, and so on); *physical development* (fine and gross motor coordination, ambulation, vision and hearing, and so on); *communication skills* (articulation, expression, comprehension, the use of language in social situations, and so on); *cognitive functioning* (money handling and budgeting, number and time concepts, reading cooking instructions, writing own address, and so on); *domestic and occupational activities* (cleaning, cooking, washing, assembly work, machine operation, job search skills, and so on); *self-direction and responsibility* (initiative, care of personal belongings, carrying out assigned activities, and so on); and *socialization* (social interaction, cooperation with others, participation in group activities, and so on).

The recent emphasis on the rehabilitation in the least restrictive environment has increased concern about problem behavior of some mentally retarded persons in community settings. This trend is reflected in the inclusion of maladaptive behavior domains in some scales of adaptive behavior. The common domains of maladaptive behavior are verbal and nonverbal stereotyped behavior, inappropriate self-stimulation, verbal and physical aggression, antisocial or rebellious behavior, and so forth. Since an individual's adaptation in any environment is a function of both behavioral competency and behavioral control, the domains of maladaptive behavior should not be neglected in the assessment of adaptive behavior.

AB-IQ Distinction

Statistical correlations between adaptive behavior and IQ seem to vary considerably in relation to the nature of adaptive behavior measures and the type of populations sampled (see the review by Meyers, Nihira, & Zetlin, 1979). Across different AB scales, IQ has been found to correlate moderately or highly with domains of communication skills, as well as cognitive and language development, regardless of the type of population sampled. On the other hand, somewhat lower correlations with IQ have been reported for domains of self-help skills, self-direction, and socialization.

Somewhat higher AB-IQ correlations have been found among heterogeneous groups of individuals, such as the residents in state institutions, than among more homogeneous groups of children in special education programs. The AB-IQ correlations tend to be higher among profoundly retarded individuals. This is understandable since, for this range of development, the measures of IQ and AB both share similar clusters of items (for example, sensory development, fine and gross motor coordination, and so on). These items are radically different from the type of test items designed to assess the ability to handle abstract thought and symbolic processes at the higher level of the IQ continuum. At the lower end of the continuum, the operational definition of IQ tends to blend in with the adaptive behavior construct. In general, the two measures indicate moderate to high degree of statistical correlations.

However, the two measures differ significantly in their expressions and purposes:

1. Most measures of adaptive behavior attempt to assess the typical or average performance of an individual, where IQ tests seek to assess the individual's highest potential for performance.

2. Adaptive behavior information is a description of an individual's everyday behavior in his or her natural environment, while intelligence is a trait inferred from an individual's response to standard stimuli in a controlled clinical interview.

3. The IQ concept has originated from the need to provide objective assessment of the individual's potential for academic achievement, while the AB construct emphasizes an individual's current ability to cope with his or her environmental demands, most of which are nonacademic in nature.

4. Because of its predictive purposes, the IQ test items, by selection, emphasize relatively stable qualities of an individual, while there is no such emphasis in the characteristics of the AB items.

5. In terms of their expression and purposes, the AB-IQ distinction can be best illustrated by an analogy that the AB is to IQ as the quality of life of an individual is to his socioeconomic status. The SES is typically inferred from education, occupation, and income level. The quality of life in this context is a description of an individual and his or her environment in terms of nutrition and diet, level of safety and comfort in his physical environment, economic security, variety of cultural and intellectual stimulations, and opportunities for social and interpersonal relationships. There is no question that the SES and the quality of life are correlated in the general population, but the two constructs differ significantly in their style of expressions and type of information they provide.

PSYCHOMETRIC ASSESSMENT OF INTELLIGENCE

The Stanford-Binet and the Wechsler tests have been by far the most widely used tests for the evaluation of mentally retarded individuals (Silverstein, 1963; Stevens & Heber, 1968). Consequently, a great deal of effort has been expended in research with the Binet, the WISC, and the WAIS. A comprehensive review of the literature prior to 1970 was published by Silverstein (1970). Zimmerman and Woo-Sam (1972) also published their review of literature on research with the WISC, which included studies with mentally retarded children.

Since the WISC was revised and renormed in 1974, a large number of studies concerning the nature of this new test have been published. Most of the studies have been concerned with the comparability of results between the WISC-R and its predecessor, the WISC. This has been a legitimate concern of the school psychologist since periodic reevaluations of children in special education programs have been mandated. Other studies were concerned with the issue of whether there have been any changes in concurrent or factorial validity, or the diagnostic use of the WISC subtests pattern. Only those studies with a primary interest in the assessment of mentally retarded subjects have been reviewed in this section.

Comparison of the WISC-R with Other Scales

WISC-R versus WISC. Since the publication of the Wechsler Intelligence Scale for Children—Revised (WISC-R) in 1974, a large number of studies have examined the comparability between the WISC-R and WISC. These studies have indicated a consistent tendency for the WISC-R to yield lower IQ scores than did the WISC. Zimmerman and Woo-Sam (1979) reviewed the extensive literature on WISC versus WISC-R comparisons for a wide variety of children. In 33 studies that employed the counterbalanced design, WISC-R IQ scores averaged 5.4 points lower than WISC IQ scores. In six studies with a matched sample design, WISC-R IQ scores averaged 5.1 points lower than WISC IQ scores. Eleven studies compared 13 samples where the WISC was administered initially, followed by the WISC-R after a period ranging from one day to 48 months. WISC IQ scores averaged 2.1 points higher than WISC-R IQ scores. Careful review of these studies led Zimmerman and Woo-Sam to conclude that these differences could not be attributed to ability, age, referral status, or race.

The significant difference between WISC and WISC-R scores found in the general population also applies to mentally retarded children. Table 2 summarizes the results of studies of WISC-R versus WISC score comparisons from mentally retarded children and adolescents. The studies with the counterbalanced design tested approximately half of the subjects with the WISC first and then the WISC-R within a relatively short time period; the order of the test administrations was reversed for the second half of the subjects in order to control practice effects. The average difference in the Full Scale IQs varied between the studies, ranging from 3.4 points to 10.8 points in favor of the WISC. The variation was mostly larger than the standard error of measurement of 5.5 points. Thus decisions concerning special class placement should take into account the marked differences in scores obtained from these two tests. Many children who are at the borderline or just above the cut-off score will be classified for EMR placement, not because the children's intellectual capacities are declining, but because the test norms are different.

On the other hand, the naturalistic studies in which the WISC-R has been administered several years after the administration of the WISC usually have found much smaller differences in the Full Scale IQs, averaging from 0 points to 3.6 points, in favor of the WISC (see Table 3). The small differences between the WISC and WISC-R under these conditions may possibly indicate practice

Table 2. Studies Comparing the WISC-R and WISC (Counterbalanced Design)

Investigator	N	Age in Years	Average Interval	WISC FSIQ	WISC-R FSIQ	Correlation	Discrepancies		
							VIQ	PIQ	FSIQ
Berry & Sherrets (1976)	28	8–15	14 dy.	78.4	75.0	—	4.4	3.2	3.4
Hamm et al. (1976)	48	10&13	39 dy.	70.0	63.4	.89	5.8	7.9	6.5
Catron & Catron (1977)	62	12–14	20 dy.	65.3	59.7	—	5.1	6.2	5.6
Rowe (1977)	44	12–16	17 dy.	66.5	61.7	—	4.0	4.8	4.9
Solly (1977)	12	8–12	3 dy.	76.2	65.4	—	—	—	10.8

809

Table 3. Studies Comparing the WISC-R and WISC (WISC Followed by WISC-R)

Investigator	N	Age in Years	Average Interval	WISC FSIQ	WISC-R FSIQ	Correlation	Discrepancies		
							VIQ	PIQ	FSIQ
Thomas (1980)	93	6–14	3 yr.	78.2	75.9	—	3.2	.96	2.3
Udziela & Barclay (1983)	45	12–17	7 yr.	66.8	64.8	—	1.8	2.8	2.0
Martin (1979)	81	9–19	4 yr.	66.9	68.8	.83	3.9	.20	1.9
Gironda (1977)	20	12–16	3 yr.	63.9	64.0	.54	2.0	−0.4	−0.1
Reschly & Davis (1977)	48	8–16	1½ yr.	76.7	73.0	.87	7.0	.04	3.6

effects, but are more likely the effects of educational programs and interventions. Since, in many school districts, the WISC has been replaced by the WISC-R for the mandated periodic evaluations of children in special education programs, any discrepancies between the two evaluations require careful interpretation.

Catron and Catron (1977) observed that administration of the WISC-R requires significantly longer time than the WISC—the average difference being more than 15 minutes—and the subtests that yielded the greatest difference in scores were as follows: Information, Arithmetic, Similarity, Block Design, and Coding. In the previously mentioned review of literature, Zimmerman and Woo-Sam (1979) concluded that the newly normed WISC-R is a more current measure of intellectual abilities of today's children than is the WISC, with norms based on the children in the 1940s. The apparent "drop" in scores from the WISC-R merely reflects the fact that the average WISC-R IQ of 100 for children in the 1970s is significantly higher than the average WISC IQ of 100 for children in the 1940s. Expanded educational opportunities and widespread exposure to television and other media may have contributed to the elevation of norms during the past 25 years. Reschly and Davis (1977), finding significantly greater differences in the Verbal scale IQ and in several Verbal subtests, speculated that the effect of environmental influences may have been greater on Verbal items as opposed to Performance items. However, most of the studies reviewed documented approximately equal discrepancies in both Verbal and Performance IQ scores between the WISC and WISC-R.

WISC-R versus WAIS.

Comparability of scores between the WISC-R and the WAIS is a serious question since, at the age of 16, children may be tested with either of the two tests. In the earlier review by Silverstein (1970), two studies that compared the WISC and WAIS with EMR children noted Full Scale IQ difference of 11 points in favor of the WAIS. The two recent studies in Table 4 compared results of the WISC-R and WAIS with EMR students and reported a correlation of .81, but mean differences of 11.6 and 12.7 points with WAIS scores higher than WISC-R scores. These findings are also in agreement with a recent review by Zimmerman and Woo-Sam (1982). For five studies of EMR students reviewed, the mean correlation was .85, but the difference between the Full Scale IQs was consistently large (12.5), with the WAIS higher in all cases. These results appear conclusive that the WISC-R and the WAIS cannot be considered interchangeable in determining the level of mental retardation of an individual.

WISC-R versus PPVT.

The Peabody Picture Vocabulary Test (Dunn, 1959) is a popular instrument because it is easily administered, reasonably short, and requires little or no vocalization from the individual being tested. The test has been widely used for initial screening of children who are experiencing academic difficulty. Consequently, numerous studies have been conducted to investigate the relationship between the PPVT and other tests of general intelligence. Sattler (1974), in a review of 25 studies that compared the PPVT and WISC, concluded

Table 4. Studies Comparing WISC-R and WAIS (Counterbalanced)

Investigator	N	Age in Years	Average Interval	WISC-R FSIQ	WAIS FSIQ	Correlation	Discrepancies		
							VIQ	PIQ	FSIQ
Craft & Kronenberger (1979)	30	M = 16	37 dy.	63.6	75.2	—	12.6	8.6	11.6
Nagle & Lazarus (1979)	30	M = 16	10 dy.	63.3	76.0	.81	13.8	9.3	12.7

that the PPVT consistently overestimated the WISC IQ scores of mentally retarded children.

After the WISC-R was published, it became necessary to investigate whether the PPVT has the same relationship with the WISC-R as with the original WISC. Four such studies have been reviewed and summarized in Table 5. They indicate the same general patterns of findings for the WISC-R and PPVT as those obtained for the WISC and PPVT previously. Zimmerman and Woo-Sam (1982), in a review of 19 studies that compared the PPVT and WISC-R with mentally retarded or referred children, found a mean correlation of .55, ranging from −.11 to .86, between WISC-R IQs and PPVT IQs, with PPVT IQs averaging 6 points higher than WISC-R IQs. These studies supported Sattler's (1974) contention that scores from the WISC and PPVT should not be considered interchangeable, especially when applied to a mentally retarded population.

WISC-R versus PPVT-R. The PPVT, which was revised recently (Dunn, 1981), will probably replace the original as a screening or evaluation instrument for mentally retarded individuals. However, only a few studies have examined the relationship between the PPVT-R and other tests of general intelligence (see Table 5).

Prasse and Bracken (1981) reported that the PPVT-R had insignificant correlations (.14, .11, and .16) with the WISC-R's Verbal, Performance, and Full Scale IQ scores, and had a significantly lower mean score than the WISC-R for a sample of EMR children. This is a surprising result since the PPVT has shown moderate correlations with WISC-R IQs in numerous studies and yielded consistently higher mean IQ scores than the WISC-R.

However, Naglieri (1982) reported a correlation of .58 between the WISC-R and PPVT-R, with both tests yielding similar means. Naglieri noted that the nonsignificant correlations in Prasse and Bracken's study are due to a restricted range of abilities. Further studies are necessary before a conclusion can be made.

Binet versus WISC-R. Since 1972, two of the most widely used intelligence tests for mentally retarded children have been either revised or restandardized: the WISC in 1974 and the Stanford-Binet in 1972. However, only a few published studies have examined the effect of these recent changes on the previously established relationship between these two well-known tests (see Table 6). Kaufman and Van Hagen (1977) compared the WISC-R and the restandardized Stanford-Binet (Terman & Merrill, 1973) in 45 educable mentally retarded children and adolescents. The correlations of WISC-R Verbal, Performance, and Full Scale IQs with S-B IQ were .73, .65, and .82, respectively. Two other studies of children referred for suspected mental retardation or learning disability also reported similar correlations (Bloom, Raskin, & Reese, 1976; Raskin, Bloom, Klee, & Reese, 1978). These recent figures are of the same order of magnitude as the corresponding correlations between the 1949 WISC and the 1960 Stanford-Binet for mentally retarded children (Silverstein, 1970; Zimmerman & Woo-Sam, 1972).

While the level of correlations remained stable, an ominous gap in the mean

Table 5. Studies Comparing WISC-R, PPVT, and PPVT-R

WISC-R versus PPVT

Investigator	N	Age in Years	WISC-R FSIQ	PPVT	Correlation Between PPVT and WISC-R Scales		
					VIQ	PIQ	FSIQ
Richmond & Long (1977)	16(B)	8–14	71.8(B)	69.9	.75	.36	.71
	23(W)	8–14	79.2(W)	86.8	.77	.32	.65
Covin (1977)	—	—	72.1	75.2(A)	.59	.19	.45
	50	M = 8.5	72.1	75.5(B)	.50	.06	.29
Hodapp & Hodapp (1980)	47	6–16	74.8	86.9	.53	.25	.50
Vance, Prichard, & Wallbrown (1979)	65	M = 12.8	67.3	73.5	.66	.50	.63

WISC versus PPVT-R

Investigator	N	Age in Years	WISC-R FSIQ	PPVT-R	Correlation Between PPVT-R and WISC-R Scales		
					VIQ	PIQ	FSIQ
Prasse & Bracken (1981)	67	11.3	59.8	55.0	.14	.11	.16
Naglieri (1982)	38	9.6	57.7	59.9	.58	.48	.59

Note. (B) = Black, (W) = White; (A) = Form A, (B) = Form B.

Table 6. Studies Comparing WISC-R and Binet (1972)

Investigator	N	Age in Years	WISC-R FSIQ	Binet IQ	Correlation Between Binet and WISC-R Scales		
					VIQ	PIQ	FSIQ
Raskin et al. (1978)	50	6–11	79.9	82.5	.84	.70	.83
Kaufman & Van Hagen (1977)	45	M = 11.5	46.8	53.8	.73	.65	.82
Bloom et al. (1976)	50	6–16	78.9	81.7	—	—	.81

IQs for the same group of subjects has appeared between the two tests. In the study by Kaufman and Van Hagen (1977), the mean 1972 S-B IQ of 53.8 was about 7 points higher than the mean WISC-R Full Scale IQ of 46.8 ($t = 7.77$, $p < .001$). The higher IQ scores from the Binet than from the WISC-R, though in lesser magnitude, is also shown in three other studies (Bloom, Raskin, & Reese, 1976; Bloom, Reese, Altshuler, Meckler, & Raskin, 1983; Raskin, Bloom, Klee, & Reese, 1978). These findings sharply differ from the previous studies that compared the WISC and the Binet, in which the mean IQs were virtually identical between the two tests in all studies with mentally retarded subjects reviewed by Silverstein (1970) and Zimmerman and Woo-Sam (1972).

It has been well established that the WISC-R tends to yield lower IQ scores than the WISC. The current findings that WISC-R IQs are lower than Binet IQs for the same group of subjects may merely reflect the different norms for the 1974 edition of the Wechsler scale. At this point, it seems appropriate to ask a question: Are the WISC-R IQ and Binet IQ, the two most popular measures of intelligence, equivalent or interchangeable?

To examine this question, Bloom, Raskin, and Reese (1976) compared the WISC-R IQs and the Binet IQs for individual cases in the intelligence classifications based on the AAMD terminology (Grossman, 1983). Despite an obtained high correlation of .81 for the Binet IQs and WISC-R IQs, and the proximity of the two means (WISC-R Full Scale IQ $= 78.9$, and Binet IQ $= 81.7$), 27 out of 50 referred children did not fall in the same classification category (for example, mild retardation, moderate retardation, and so on). True score ranges were then computed for each child using the standard error of measurement. In 12 out of 50 cases, the true score ranges still failed to overlap within the same classification category. These results are quite unsatisfactory, given the fact that educational placement decisions are frequently based on the scores from these tests. It appears that the WISC-R IQ and Binet IQ are not interchangeable for the purpose of the AAMD intelligence classification. One must exercise extreme caution, therefore, in making judgments or decisions about a child's performance based on his or her test score alone.

Constancy of WISC-R IQ

In a previous review, Silverstein (1970) concluded that the S-B test, as administered to mentally retarded children and adolescents, appears to have satisfactory test-retest reliability, but the evidence for long-term constancy of IQ is equivocal. Recently Vance, Blixt, Ellis, and Debell (1981) compared the WISC-R scores after a two-year time interval for a sample of 75 LD and EMR children and adolescents. The stability coefficients were .80 for the Verbal IQs, .91 for Performance IQs, and .88 for the Full Scale IQs. During the two years, the mean Verbal IQ decreased 1.87 points ($t = 2.11, p < .05$), while the mean Performance IQ increased 2.04 points ($t = 2.57, p < .05$), resulting in no appreciable change in the mean Full Scale IQ. It was speculated that the special classes for these children may have stressed teaching areas of nonverbal skills, such as motor coordination, perceptual training, and thinking using concrete objects.

Other studies examined the stability of WISC-R IQs for an ethnically diverse sample of 382 LD, EMR, or behaviorally impaired students over a three-year period (Elliott, Piersel, & Gavin, 1983; Elliott, Piersel, Witt, & Argulewicz, 1982). The stability coefficients for the total sample for Verbal IQ (.81), Performance IQ (.78), and Full Scale IQ (.85) were similar to those in the previous studies. However, analysis by each racial-ethnic group revealed that white subjects' IQs were significantly more stable than blacks' on all three scales, and more stable than Mexican-Americans' on Performance and Full Scale IQ. On the basis of these results, Elliott et al. (1982) recommended the periodic reevaluation of white handicapped children with a short form version of the WISC-R.

Elliott et al. (1983) also examined changed scores for each student and found that the changes for 80% of the students were not more than ±10 points. These recent studies provide some additional evidence for the stability of WISC-R IQ scores in mentally retarded school children and adolescents. The differential stability of IQ scores for three racial-ethnic groups is worthy of further consideration. Elliott et al. (1983) offered a plausible explanation that, after three years of schooling, students in the minority groups have had to make more adjustments to the majority culture and its educational system than did students in the majority group.

In younger children suspected of developmental delay, the IQ measures appear to be more stable than for their normal peers. Goodman and Cameron (1978) administered the Bayley or Binet to a clinic population of 289 children mostly under 5 years old and reevaluated them in the subsequent two-year period. The test-retest correlations computed for separate age groups ranged from .76 to .95. This is in sharp contrast to the range of stability coefficients in IQs (.40 to .50) between 1 to 3 years of age in normal children. The study also indicates that within the retarded range, the lower the IQ, the higher the stability coefficient. For children with IQs under 48, the stability coefficients for boys and girls first tested after age 2 were .86 and .87, respectively. These figures compare with the lower stability coefficients of .70 and .67 for boys and girls with IQs in the 48–79 range, and are significantly higher than the stability coefficients among their normal peers. Analysis of change scores for each child indicates that 71% to 94% of the children, depending on initial IQ level and sex, changed less than one standard deviation during the two-year period. The maximum fluctuation occurred in the 51–80 IQ range, rather than in the IQ-over-80 group. This result partly contradicts the frequently encountered clinical assumption that the younger or brighter a mentally retarded child, the more likely he or she is to improve.

Extension to MR Population

The Wechsler tests do not have as low a floor as the Stanford-Binet and were not designed for the assessment of severely retarded children. Ogdon (1975) extrapolated WISC-R IQs that were both below and above the value published in the WISC-R manual (Wechsler, 1974). For retarded children, WISC-R IQs are extrapolated to IQs in the 30–39 range. The regression equation on which the extrapolation is based and the cautions regarding the clinical use of these IQs are also presented. With the low IQs, the reliability may be attenuated due to the smaller number of items successfully completed to establish the scaled score.

Diagnostic Uses of WISC-R Subtest Pattern

Bannatyne's Recategorization. Since the publication of the WISC-R, there has been an upsurge of research on its subscale patterns for the differential diagnosis of the learning disabled children, most frequently in accordance with Bannatyne's (1971, 1974) scheme for recategorization of the WISC-R subscales. Bannatyne proposed a three factor grouping of the WISC subscales—Spatial, Sequential, and Conceptual categories—to provide the clinician with a practical tool to facilitate the identification and diagnosis of various subgroups of learning handicapped students. The Spatial category consists of Block Design, Object Assembly, and Picture Completion subscales. These subscales are supposed to measure the ability to recognize spatial relationships and manipulation of objects in three-dimensional space. The Sequential category consists of Picture Arrangement, Digit Span, and Coding subtests, and is thought to measure the ability to retain and reproduce sequences of visually and auditorily presented stimuli. The Conceptual category consists of Comprehension, Similarities, and Vocabulary subtests, and is thought to measure the ability to use concepts and abstract reasoning. Bannatyne later added a fourth category called "Acquired Knowledge," which consists of Information, Arithmetic, and Vocabulary subtests.

Rugel (1974) reviewed previous studies and found that, as a group, the learning disabled children manifested a score pattern with the following rank order (from least difficult to most difficult): Spatial, Conceptual, Sequential, and Acquired Knowledge. The pattern of performance for educably mentally retarded students was shown to be: Spatial, Sequential, Conceptual, and Acquired Knowledge. Most of these previous studies have either examined within-group patterns of performance or compared the performance of a handicapped group with a group of normal subjects.

Several recent studies attempted to determine not only if a learning disabled (LD) population exhibited the profile as proposed by Bannatyne, but whether it would discriminate them from other clinically meaningful groups, such as educable mentally retarded (EMR), emotionally handicapped (EH), or otherwise impaired individuals.

Clarizio and Bernard (1981) compared LD, EMR, EH, other impaired, and nonimpaired children and found that the Bannatyne profile was characteristic of all groups except the EMR group, in which the Verbal score was the lowest in relation to their other abilities. Henry and Wittman (1981) concluded that the LD students did not significantly differ from EMR or EH students in the proportion of students conforming to Bannatyne's pattern. In a study by Webster and Lafayette (1980), a discriminant function analysis correctly classified 99% of the LD students. However, the same analysis also classified 100% of the EMR and EH students in the LD category. Thompson (1981) reported that the Bannatyne pattern of Spatial, Conceptual, and Sequential not only failed to characterize the LD group, but was actually characteristic of the behavioral disorder group. Furthermore, the percentage of individual children demonstrating the pattern was low, and there was no significant difference among the groups in the frequency with which the Bannatyne pattern was demonstrated. Bannatyne's recategorization may have some validity in differentiating a normal population from a handicapped population, but appears to have no value for differentiating subgroups of handicapped or atypical children.

Verbal-Performance IQ Discrepancy.   Verbal-Performance IQ discrepancies have been explored based on the notion that mentally retarded persons tend to do better on Performance than on Verbal items (Seashore, 1951). Contradictory evidence has been reported in the literature (Silverstein, 1970; Zimmerman & Woo-Sam, 1972). Many studies have reported significant Verbal-Performance IQ discrepancies in mentally retarded persons, but some have reported nonsignificant discrepancies or even discrepancies in the "wrong" direction. Using the WISC-R, a few recent studies investigated the validity of Verbal-Performance IQ discrepancies for the purpose of differential diagnosis. Petersen and Hart (1979) reported no differences in the Verbal-Performance IQ discrepancy scores when comparing six subcategories of high-risk children. In comparing six clinically meaningful subcategories of a handicapped population, Thompson (1980) found as follows: (1) the mentally retarded group had significantly lower Verbal IQ, Performance IQ, Full Scale IQ, Verbal Comprehension Deviation Quotient (VCDQ), and Perceptual Organization Deviation Quotient (PODQ) scores, and (2) there were no significant differences between the groups on any of the difference scores. Law, Box, and Moracco (1980) also reported nonsignificant differences between EMR, LD, and normal groups of children.

Factor Score Profile.   Groff and Linden (1982) compared the WISC-R factor score profiles between two groups of mentally retarded subjects (8–11 years and 13–16 years) and a nonretarded group (the factor analytic studies will be reviewed in the next section). The younger retarded group was matched on CA with the nonretarded group, and the older retarded group was matched on MA with the nonretarded group. The comparison on the three factor scores—Verbal Comprehension, Perceptual Organization, and Freedom from Distractibility—did not show a significant difference between the retarded and nonretarded groups in their pattern of intellectual strength and weakness. The results were interpreted to be consistent with an expectation of the developmental theory of retardation but contrary to a prediction of the difference theory of mental retardation.

Factor Analysis of WISC-R

Factor analytic studies of the WISC subtests' intercorrelations have shown at least two meaningful factors that approximately correspond to the Verbal and Performance subscales of the tests. Traditionally, the two factors have been referred to as the Verbal Comprehension factor and the Perceptual Organization factor. A third factor, Freedom from Distractibility, has frequently emerged in studies with mentally retarded populations, but not (or not as prominently) for normal subjects (see reviews by Silverstein, 1970; Zimmerman & Woo-Sam, 1972). Thus, the Freedom from Distractibility factor has been assumed to represent a dimension of individual difference unique to the mentally retarded population.

Since publication of the WISC-R, there has been an upsurge of factor analytic studies to compare the factor structure between the WISC-R and its predecessor. Kaufman (1975) factor analyzed the standardization population data for the WISC-R and found the three WISC factors—Verbal Comprehension, Perceptual Organization, and Freedom from Distractibility—at each age level from 6½ to 16½ years. The WISC-R factor structure, particularly the first two factors, was found to be more stable and in closer agreement with the Wechsler Verbal-Performance dichotomy than was the structure of its predecessor. The study also provided strong evidence for the presence of the Freedom from Distractibility factor in the general population.

The three-factor structure of the WISC-R has been demonstrated repeatedly in studies with mentally retarded children and adolescents (Van Hagen & Kaufman, 1975), and with educable mentally retarded students (Cummins & Das, 1980; Groff & Hubble, 1982). In these studies, the WISC-R factor structure was found to be equivalent to the factor structure of the WISC for mentally retarded as well as for normal subjects.

Vance, Wallbrown, and Fremont (1978) applied the Wherry-Wherry hierarchical factor method and delineated the *g*-factor in addition to the three factors found in other factor analytic studies. The result was interpreted in terms of Vernon's hierarchical structure of intelligence paradigm. This study also indicated the robustness of the three-factor structure of the WISC-R tests.

A few studies, however, failed to identify the third factor, Freedom from Distractibility (Petersen & Hart, 1979; Schooler, Beebe, & Koepke, 1978). Schooler et al. (1978) speculated that the absence of Digit Span and Maze subtests from their factor analysis may have been the reason for their failure to identify the third factor. Petersen and Hart (1979) reported the homogeneity of their samples with respect to the Freedom from Distractibility, and attributed to it the disappearance of the third factor in their study.

PREVIEW OF THE FUTURE

Among a number of recent developments in the measurement of intelligence, one study that deserves special mention is the Kaufman Assessment Battery for Children (K-ABC) (Kaufman & Kaufman, 1983). The development of the K-ABC is guided by the simultaneous and successive processing model proposed by Das and his colleagues (Das, Kirby, & Jarman, 1975). Factor analytic evidence of the two mental processes for mentally retarded, as well as for general populations, has been presented in several studies (Cummins & Das, 1980; Das, Kirby, & Jarman, 1979; Jarman, 1978). These two process factors appear to be meaningfully related to WRAT achievement scores in EMR children (Cummins & Das, 1980; Das & Cummins, 1978).

The simultaneous-successive dichotomy is reminiscent of Bannatyne's spatial and sequential categories, and two of the WISC-R factors—Perceptual Organization and Freedom from Distractibility. While the WISC-R subscales tend to provide factorially complex measures involving the two mental processes and academic achievement, the K-ABC subscales have been developed to measure each of the two separate mental processes. Another promising feature of the K-ABC is that the test is designed to provide separate measures of achievement. Thus the Kaufman approach may lead to naturalistic studies, as opposed to laboratory studies, of adaptive intelligence (or achievement) as separate from the neuropsychologically based mental processes.

On a slightly different topic, there have been many indications that professionals in the field of mental retardation are dissatisfied with the current practice of "clinical judgment" supplemented by adaptive behavior rating scales for diagnosis and classification on the adaptive behavior dimension. Roszkowski and Spreat (1981) proposed development of a statistical method for incorporating adaptive behavior information into the determination of mental retardation level. An aternative approach would be to provide well-defined standards for making the clinical judgment. Either approach will likely yield a more reliable and more standardized system of classification. The potential benefit of a statistical or actuarial approach, if carefully developed, would probably outweigh the potential danger of oversimplification of complex adaptive behavior information. Any attempt to use adaptive behavior information, whether clinical or actuarial, in the classification procedure should take into consideration the effect of environmental demands and expectations.

REFERENCES

Bannatyne, A. (1971). *Language, reading, and learning disabilities.* Springfield, IL: Thomas.

Bannatyne, A. (1974). Diagnosis: A note on recategorization of the WISC scaled scores. *Journal of Learning Disabilities, 7,* 272–274.

Berry, K. K., & Sherrets, S. A. (1976). A comparison of the WISC and WISC-R scores of special education students. *Journal of Pediatric Psychology, 3,* 14.

Binet, A., & Simon, T. (1961). New methods for diagnosis of the intellectual level of subnormals. *L'Anée Psychologique, II, 1905.* In J. J. Jenkins & D. G. Paterson (Eds.), *Studies in individual differences.* New York: Appleton-Century-Crofts. (Original work published 1905)

Bloom, A. S., Raskin, L. M., & Reese, A. H. (1976). A comparison of WISC-R and Stanford-Binet Intelligence Scale classifications of developmentally disabled children. *Psychology in the Schools, 13,* 288–290.

Bloom, A. S., Reese, A., Altshuler, L., Meckler, C. L., & Raskin, L. M. (1983). IQ discrepancies between the Binet and WISC-R in children with developmental problems. *Journal of Clinical Psychology, 38,* 600–603.

Catron, D. W., & Catron, S. J. (1977). WISC-R vs. WISC: A comparison with EMR children. *Journal of School Psychology, 15*, 264–266.

Clarizio, H., & Bernard, R. (1981). Recategorized WISC-R scores of learning disabled children and differential diagnosis. *Psychology in the Schools, 18*, 5–12.

Covin, T. M. (1977). Relationship of Peabody and WISC-R IQs of candidates for special education. *Psychological Reports, 40*, 189–190d.

Craft, N. P., & Kronenberger, E. J. (1979). Comparability of WISC-R and WAIS IQ scores in mentally educable handicapped adolescents. *Psychology in the Schools, 16*, 502–504.

Cummins, J. P., & Das, J. P. (1980). Cognitive processing academic achievement, and WISC-R performance in EMR children. *Journal of Consulting and Clinical Psychology, 48*, 777–779.

Das, J. P., & Cummins, J. (1978). Academic performance and cognitive processes in EMR children. *American Journal of Mental Deficiency, 83*(2), 197–199.

Das, J. P., Kirby, J., & Jarman, R. F. (1975). Simultaneous and successive synthesis: An alternative model for cognitive abilities. *Psychological Bulletin, 82*, 87–103.

Das, J. P., Kirby, J., & Jarman, R. F. (1979). *Simultaneous and successive cognitive processes.* New York: Academic Press.

Doll, E. A. (1947, 1965). *Social maturity scale.* Circle Pines, MN: American Guidance Service.

Doll, E. A. (1966). Recognition of mental retardation in the school-age child. In Phillips, I. (Ed.), *Prevention and treatment of mental retardation.* New York: Basic Books.

Down, L. (1876). *The education and training of the feeble-in-mind.* London: Lewis.

Dunn, L. M. (1959). *Peabody picture vocabulary test: Manual of direction and norms.* Nashville, TN: American Guidance Center.

Dunn, L. M. (1981). *Peabody picture vocabulary test—Revised.* Circle Press, MN: American Guidance Service.

Elliott, S. N., Piersel, W. C., & Galvin, C. A. (1983). *Stability of WISC-R IQs for handicapped children.* Paper presented at the APA convention, Anaheim, CA.

Elliott, S. N., Piersel, W. C., Witt, J. C., & Argulewicz, E. (1982). *WISC-R test stability and the practice of psychological re-evaluations.* Paper presented at the Annual Convention of the American Psychological Association, Washington, DC.

Gironda, R. J. (1977). A comparison of WISC and WISC-R results of urban educable mentally retarded students. *Psychology in the Schools, 14*, 271–275.

Goddard, H. H. (1914). *Feeble-mindedness: Its causes and consequences.* New York: Macmillan.

Goodman, J. F., & Cameron, J. (1978). The meaning of IQ constancy in young retarded children. *The Journal of Genetic Psychology, 132*, 109–119.

Groff, M., & Hubble, L. (1982). WISC-R factor structure of younger and older youth with low IQs. *Journal of Consulting and Clinical Psychology, 50*, 148–149.

Groff, M. G., & Linden, K. W. (1982). The WISC-R factor score profiles of cultural-familial mentally retarded and nonretarded youth. *American Journal on Mental Deficiency, 87*(2), 147–152.

Grossman, H. J. (1983). *Classification in mental retardation.* Washington, DC: American Association on Mental Deficiency.

Hamm, H. A., Wheeler, J., McCallum, S., Herrin, M., Hunter, D., & Catoe, C. (1976). A comparison between the WISC and WISC-R among educable mentally retarded students. *Psychology in the Schools, 13*, 4–8.

Henry, S. A., & Wittman, R. D. (1981). Diagnostic implications of Bannatyne's recategorized WISC-R scores of identifying learning disabled children. *Journal of Learning Disabilities, 14*(9), 517–520.

Hodapp, A. F., & Hodapp, J. B. (1980). Correlation of the PPVT and WISC-R: A function of diagnostic category. *Psychology in the Schools, 17*, 33–36.

Howe, S. G. (1858). *On the cause of idiocy.* Edinburgh: McLachlan & Stewart.

Individualized Data Base Project (1977). *Performance measures of skill and adaptive competencies in the developmentally disabled.* Report of the Individualized Data Base Project. Pomona, CA: University of California, Los Angeles, The Neuropsychiatric Institute Research Group at Pacific State Hospital.

Jarman, R. (1978). Pattern of cognitive ability in retarded children: A reexamination. *American Journal of Mental Deficiency, 82,* 344–348.

Kaufman, A. S. (1975). Factor analysis of the WISC-R at 11 age levels between 6½ and 16½ years. *Journal of Consulting and Clinical Psychology, 43,* 135–147.

Kaufman, A. S., & Kaufman, N. L. (1983). *Kaufman Assessment Battery for Children: Interpretive manual.* Circle Pines, MN: American Guidance Service.

Kaufman, A. S., & Van Hagen, J. (1977). Investigation of the WISC-R for use with retarded children: Correlation with the 1972 Stanford-Binet and comparison of WISC and WISC-R profiles. *Psychology in the Schools, 14,* 10–14.

Law, J. G., Jr., Box, D., & Moracco, J. C. (1980). A validation study of recategorized WISC-R scores of learning disabled children. *Education, 101,* 195–199.

Martin, F. (1979). Is it necessary to retest children in special education classes? *Journal of Learning Disabilities, 12,* 388–392.

Meyers, C. E., Nihira, K., & Zetlin, A. (1979). The measurement of adaptive behavior. In N. R. Ellis (Ed.), *Handbook of mental deficiency, psychological theory and research* (2nd ed.). Hillsdale, NJ: Lawrence Erlbaum.

Nagle, R. J., & Lazarus, S. C. (1979). The comparability of the WISC-R and WAIS among 16-year-old EMR children. *Journal of School Psychology, 17,* 362–367.

Naglieri, J. A. (1982). Use of the WISC-R and PPVT-R with mentally retarded children. *Journal of Clinical Psychology, 38,* 635–637.

Ogdon, D. P. (1975). Extrapolated WISC-R IQs for gifted and mentally retarded children. *Journal of Consulting and Clinical Psychology, 43,* 216.

Petersen, C. R., & Hart, H. D. (1979). Factor structure of the WISC-R for a clinic referred population and specific sub-group. *Journal of Consulting and Clinical Psychology, 47,* 643–645.

Prasse, D. P., & Bracken, B. A. (1981). Comparison of the PPVT-R and WISC-R with urban educable mentally retarded students. *Psychology in the Schools, 18,* 174–177.

Raskin, L. M., Bloom, A. S., Klee, S. H., & Reese, A. (1978). The assessment of developmentally disabled children with the WISC-R, Binet and other tests. *Journal of Clinical Psychology, 34*(1), 111–114.

Reschly, D. J., & Davis, R. A. (1977). Comparability of WISC and WISC-R scores along borderline and mildly retarded children. *Journal of Clinical Psychology, 33,* 1045–1048.

Richmond, B. O., & Long, M. (1977). Brief report on the WISC-R: III. WISC-R and PPVT scores for black and white mentally retarded children. *Journal of School Psychology, 15,* 261–263.

Roszkowski, M., & Spreat, S. (1981). A comparison of the psychometric and clinical methods of determining level of mental retardation. *Applied Research in Mental Retardation, 2,* 359–366.

Rowe, H. A. H. (1977). "Borderline" versus "mentally deficient." *Australian Journal of Mental Retardation, 4,* 11–14.

Rugel, R. P. (1974). WISC subtest scores of disabled readers: A review with respect to Bannatyne's recategorization. *Journal of Learning Disabilities, 7,* 48–55.

Sattler, J. (1974). *Assessment of children's intelligence.* Philadelphia: Saunders.

Schooler, D. L., Beebe, M. C., & Koepke, T. (1978). Factor analysis of WISC-R scores for children identified as learning disabled, educationally mentally impaired, and emotionally impaired. *Psychology in the Schools, 15,* 478–485.

Seashore, H. G. (1951). Differences between verbal and performance IQs on the Wechsler intelligence scale for children. *Journal of Consulting Psychology, 15,* 62–67.

Silverstein, A. B. (1963). Psychological testing practices in state institutions for the mentally retarded. *American Journal of Mental Deficiency, 68,* 440–445.

Silverstein, A. B. (1970). The measurement of intelligence. In N. R. Ellis (Ed.), *International Review of Research in Mental Retardation* (Vol. 4). New York: Academic Press.

Silverstein, A. B. (1982). Note on the constancy of the IQ. *American Journal on Mental Deficiency, 87,* 227–228.

Solly, D. C. (1977). Comparison of WISC and WISC-R scores of mentally retarded and gifted children. *Journal of School Psychology, 15,* 255–258.

Stevens, H. A., & Heber, R. (1968). An international review of developments in mental retardation. *Mental Retardation, 6*(2), 4–23.

Terman, L. W., & Merrill, M. A. (1973). *Stanford-Binet Intelligence Scale, Form L-M. Manual for the third revision.* Boston: Houghton Mifflin.

Thomas, P. J. (1980). A longitudinal comparison of the WISC and WISC-R with special education students. *Psychology in the Schools, 17,* 437–441.

Thompson, R. J. (1980). The diagnostic utility of WISC-R measures with children referred to a developmental evaluation center. *Journal of Consulting and Clinical Psychology, 48,* 440–447.

Thompson, R. J. (1981). The diagnostic utility of Bannatyne's recategorized WISC-R scores with children referred to a developmental evaluation center. *Psychology in the Schools, 18,* 43–47.

Udziela, A. D., & Barclay, A. G. (1983). A note on WISC-WISC-R differences with mentally retarded and borderline functioning adolescents. *Psychology in the Schools, 20,* 27–28.

Vance, H. B., Blixt, S., Ellis, R., & Debell, S. (1981). Stability of the WISC-R for a sample of exceptional children. *Journal of Clinical Psychology, 37,* 397–399.

Vance, H. B., Hawkins, N., Wallbrown, F., & Engin, A. (1978). Analysis of cognitive abilities for mentally retarded children on the WISC-R. *Psychological Record, 28,* 391–397.

Vance, H. B., Prichard, K., & Wallbrown, F. H. (1978). Comparison of the WISC-R and PPVT for a group of mentally retarded students. *Psychology in the Schools, 15,* 349–351.

Vance, H. B., Wallbrown, F. H., & Fremont, T. S. (1978). The abilities of retarded students: further evidence concerning the stimulus trace factor. *The Journal of Psychology, 100,* 77–82.

Van Hagen, N. M., & Kaufman, A. S. (1975). Factor analysis of the WISC-R for a group of mentally retarded children and adolescents. *Journal of Consulting and Clinical Psychology, 43,* 661–667.

Walls, R. T., Werner, T. J., Bacon, A., & Zane, T. (1977). Behavior checklist. In J. D. Cone & R. P. Hawkins (Eds.), *Behavioral assessment: New directions in clinical psychology.* New York: Bruner / Mazel.

Webster, R. E., & Lafayette, D. (1980). Distinguishing among 3 subgroups of handicapped students using Bannatyne's recategorization. *Journal of Educational Research, 73,* 237–240.

Wechsler, D. (1974). *Manual for the Wechsler Intelligence Scale for Children—Revised.* New York: Psychological Corporation.

Zimmerman, I. L., & Woo-Sam, J. W. (1972). Research with the Wechsler Intelligence Scale for Children: 1960–1970. *Journal of Clinical Psychology,* Monograph Supplement, No. 33.

Zimmerman, I. L., & Woo-Sam, J. W. (1979, August). *Exploring WISC versus WISC-R differences.* Paper presented at the American Psychological Association meeting, New York, NY.

Zimmerman, I. L., & Woo-Sam, J. J. (1982, April 9). *Concurrent validity of the Wechsler Intelligence Scale for Children—Revised.* Paper presented at the Western Psychological Association, Sacramento, CA.

NINETEEN

GROUP TESTS OF INTELLIGENCE

ROGER T. LENNON

(Retired President and Chairman, The Psychological Corporation)

This chapter discusses group tests of intelligence, or mental ability, or cognitive functioning under various other labels. A *group test* means simply one that is designed for administration to a number of subjects at the same time. This chapter will consider the origins of group intelligence tests, relative merits of group and individual tests, the rapid post-World War I diffusion of group tests, changing concepts and rationales for group tests, problems and issues in the use of group tests, descriptions of several of the most widely used group tests, and speculation regarding the future of group testing.

ORIGINS OF GROUP TESTS

Efforts to devise group-administrable forms of intelligence tests date back almost to the beginning of the intelligence-testing movement itself. The advantages of being able to test simultaneously a large number of subjects, preferably without the necessity for highly trained examiners to conduct the testing, were so apparent as to prompt numerous workers in the field to prepare group forms of the early individual scales. Indeed, it was possible even in 1910 for Whipple to report in his *Manual of Mental and Physical Tests* that "Most mental tests may be administered either to individuals or to groups" (1910, p. 7). Group versions of tests of verbal analogies, opposites, vocabulary, arithmetic, information, and sentence completion, among others, were reported in the literature prior to 1914. Despite these early efforts, however, the group intelligence test in more or less its current form, characterized by completely objective scoring, is commonly attributed to the work of Arthur S. Otis and the prominence that his work attained as part of the Army Alpha and Beta tests administered to more than 1,700,000 U.S. Army recruits in World War I. Otis' (1959) own recollection, in a television interview with Walter Durost, is enlightening:

Otis: Well, it came about something like this. Although I majored in engi-
        neering for my first two years, I changed over into psychology and eventually
        I found myself in one of Dr. Terman's classes. He was telling us about the
        Binet scale and how he had translated it and introduced it in this country
        and he was impressing on our minds the need for testing every child so
        that they could be properly understood. Well, it seemed to me that he was
        not going to be able to train enough psychologists or teachers to test all
        the children, at least since the Binet took an hour for one child. If a teacher
        had a roomful of children, say, 30, well she'd have to spend 30 hours to
        get them all tested. Well, that would be an hour a day for five days a week
        for six weeks. So I told Dr. Terman that I thought that we were very much
        in need of a group test by which a whole roomful of pupils could be tested
        at one time. I said, why don't I make that a subject for my doctor's
        dissertation and he said, well, if you can do that, why it certainly would
        be wonderful, so go to it—more power to you. So I said, well that's what
        I'll do. Then I had to cast about for, well, how to make a group test. Well,
        first thing I realized was that we couldn't do it orally so we'd have to have
        the children have some kind of a paper before them to write their answers
        on. And I realized also that it would not do to have them write out long
        answers, partly because it would take too long for the teachers to read
        them and score them and partly because it would be hard for them to
        decide without a great deal of training as to whether they should give credit
        for this answer or not. So I decided, well, the best way to solve that problem
        is to have a question with five alternative answers. So, I looked through
        the Binet scale and I saw that one type of question that they asked was,
        "What is the opposite of so and so?" And, "What word is similar to this?"
        And they had analogies, and arithmetic problems. So I thought, well, I'll
        see if I can adapt those to this alternative answer proposition, you see. Well,
        I found that you could say, "What is the opposite of brave?" And then
        you could give ugly, and so and so and so and so, and then the right
        answer, of course, would be, say, cowardly—opposite of brave, cowardly.
        And then I give these other alternative answers. And then the child is simply
        to underline and that would save all the writing. They could go right ahead
        and as soon as they had an answer in their mind, they could indicate it
        and then go right on to the next one. So I thought up a great many questions,
        items as we call them, and I administered them to a large number of children
        down in San Jose. Then, of course, there is the job of standardizing, or
        validating, as we call it, in order to make sure that a test is going to test
        what we want. It's a test, we have to validate it. Well, validating it means
        to take each individual item and determine as best we can whether it
        measures something significant—whether it helps to measure intelligence.
        Now the best way that I thought of to do that was to have the teachers
        divide their classes into two groups which we would call a good group and
        a poor group, meaning a bright group and a dull group. Then we would

have them answer all of these questions—the whole class—then we would tabulate the results and, in the case of each question, we would see how many of the dull group passed it and how many of the good group passed it, and if we found that the tendency was for the good group to pass it a large percent and the poor group to fail it to a large extent, we would call it a good diagnostic item. Whereas if there were just as many of the poor group who got it as the good group, well then, we threw that out and we said that's no good, that's not diagnostic. So I drew up the items that way and selected out of about 120, perhaps 80 that were diagnostic and that formed my original test.

Durost: Now in that original test, you had many different subtests. You've mentioned some of them and you maintained these as separate entities with separate time limits and everything else. Now I think you have developed by implication something that is very, very important. Your original attempt in developing an intelligence test was to make one that would do in a group situation what the Binet did in an individual situation. But this does not imply, does it, that an individual test is necessarily better than a group test?

Otis: No, I think that it is quite possible that a group test is better because in an individual test the teacher has to use judgment as to whether the answer should be scored plus or minus, whereas in the standard test that we use now in groups no judgment is needed. But I think that the ultimate criterion is how reliable is the test after you've made it. And, if we find that the group test is more reliable, that is, if it gives more nearly the same result each time that you give it, that is the final criterion. If the group test turns out to be just as reliable as the Binet and can be given in half an hour instead of an hour with a whole group of pupils instead of just one at a time, so much the better.

Durost: Would you care to comment on the group test as compared to the individual test from the point of view of this predictive efficiency?

Otis: Well, I should think that the mere fact that the tests are validated on the basis of the comparison of how well the child actually does in school, whether he succeeds in understanding the teacher promptly and is able to make rapid progress over against having to be told two or three times and not making rapid progress, and if we use items that were chosen distinctly to distinguish and discriminate between those two groups, then we are testing just what we want to test. We are finding out with the test just what we want to find out.

Durost: Would you tell us how your involvement with the Army Alpha Test came about?

Otis: Yes. Well, when World War I began, Major Yerkes, a psychologist at
Yale University, conceived the idea that it would be very desirable to test
the intelligence of the draftees as soon as they came into the Army so that
the superior officers could pick out officer material and could place the men
in the various functions of the Army to the best advantage. So he invited
some other psychologists, Dr. Whipple, Terman, Yerkes, and Haggerty, to
form with him a committee to consider the possibility of doing this testing.
It was Major Yerkes' idea at the time that they would have to train a lot
of psychologists to give the Binet. He didn't know anything about any
group tests. . . . So, fortunately perhaps, Dr. Terman presumably had a
copy of my test in his pocket with him at the time. You see this incident
occurred, this incident of World War I, occurred just at the time that I
was finishing my doctor's degree, and I had this manuscript of the test and
it was pretty well standardized. Dr. Terman had been convinced that it
was fairly sound and workable, and so he probably told him that they
needn't bother with giving the Binet to everybody because there's a young
fellow out at the University in my class who has made up a group test. He
presumably convinced them that they should send for me and make up
some group tests which, of course, was done. They enlisted the help of
perhaps 100 or so psychologists from all over the country and we got
together and made up as many items as we could. They just followed my
group test. They said, "Well, he made up opposites, we'll do that, and he
made up analogies, we'll do that," and they made up groups of tests just
like what I had in my test practically, and we tried those out on a number
of personnel of the Army. Very much to the surprise of everyone, including
our psychologists, we found that the privates did the most poorly, and the
corporals did better, and the sergeants did better, and the second lieutenants
did better, and the first lieutenants did better, and the captains did better,
and the majors did better, and the lieutenant colonels did better, and the
colonels did better, and the majors, and the generals did the best of all.
Well, that sold intelligence testing to the Army completely, of
course . . . .

The development and administration of group intelligence tests to World War
I inductees was a dramatic and powerful demonstration of psychology's potential
contribution to national interests and utilization of human resources. As Otis'
memoir indicates, much of the credit for this accomplishment is attributable to
Robert Yerkes, who was president of the American Psychological Association
at the outbreak of World War I. Yerkes moved energetically to enlist psychology
in the national war effort and one of his initiatives was the organization of a
Committee on the Psychological Examination of Recruits. It was this committee
that was responsible for the development of Army Alpha and Beta tests and
that provided the support for the training of examiners, the collection of test
data, and their application to the classification of inductees. The criteria that
the committee adopted to guide its development of group tests are noteworthy;

most of them would still be regarded as appropriate today. They included characteristics such as substantial correlations of results with measures of intelligence known to be valid, measurement of a wide range of abilities, objectivity and rapidity of scoring, multiple forms, resistance to malingering and cheating, independence of school training, minimum of writing needed, intrinsically interesting material, and economy of time.

The success of the Army testing program was not lost on school people. Beginning in 1918 group tests of intelligence designed for use with school pupils began to be published. By 1925 at least 50 such group scales had been published, and many more were to follow in the succeeding decade. Otis published the first school version of his scale in 1918 and many of the psychologists who had been involved in the development of the Army tests prepared similar scales for school use in the early 1920s, including indeed some identified as revisions of Army Alpha or Beta. The readiness of school systems to incorporate group intelligence testing was astonishing. Within a year after its initial publication, the publisher of the first Otis test reported that it had had to print about a million copies to keep up with the demand. Terman in 1923 estimated that about two million American elementary and secondary pupils would take an intelligence test that year and that within a few years that number would rise to five million. In the mid-1930's one publisher—World Book Company—was offering 11 group intelligence tests, and at least a half-dozen other publishers were represented by one or more tests of this kind. The use of group intelligence or mental ability tests has by now become well-nigh universal in American elementary and secondary schools, despite prohibitions against their use in a few school jurisdictions predicated chiefly on the belief that these tests are culturally biased and hence potentially harmful to certain categories of pupils. It would be a rare graduate of an American school in recent years who has not had the experience of taking a group ability measure once or more in the course of his or her school career.

Over the years that group intelligence tests have been achieving this level of use in American schools, they have also been increasingly adopted in commercial and industrial organizations as aids in personnel selection. Special editions of group intelligence tests originally developed for school use or tests developed specifically for this adult industrial market have enjoyed wide popularity, although precise information on the magnitude of such use is not available. Litigation attacking the "fairness" of some of these tests for certain minority groups, while not always successful, has had the effect of making some employers hesitant about inclusion of these measures in their selection and placement procedures.

RELATIVE MERITS OF GROUP AND INDIVIDUAL TESTS

As previously noted, efforts to develop group as well as individual forms of mental tests characterized the work of scholars in the field from the beginning. It was inevitable that the relative merits and demerits of the two types of examination should have become a subject of inquiry from the beginning, and the literature records the elements of the debate—if indeed it could be called a debate. It is instructive to note what Whipple, in the 1914 edition of his *Manual,* had to say on the matter.

> Most mental tests may be administered either to individuals or to groups. Both methods have advantages and disadvantages. The *group method* has, of course, the particular merit of economy of time; a class of 50 or 100 children may take a test in less than a fiftieth or a hundredth of the time needed to administer the same test individually. Again, in certain comparative studies, *e.g.,* of the effects of a week's vacation upon the mental efficiency of school children, it becomes imperative that all S's should take the tests at the same time.

> But, on the whole, and especially when careful analytic work is contemplated, the group method, save for the preliminary trial of a method, is out of place. There are almost sure to be some S's in every group that, for one reason or another, fail to follow instructions or to execute the test to the best of their ability. The individual method allows E to detect these cases, and in general, by the exercise of personal supervision, to gain, as has been noted above, valuable information concerning S's attitude toward the test. Moreover, with the group method E must be content with bare quantitative performance: he has no opportunity for the skillful adaptation and variation of the attunement that we have mentioned; he can only surmise what has lain in S's mind between instruction and performance, between stimulus and response, nor can he tell what effect the compulsion to work with other S's may have had upon any given S. [1914, pp. 7–8]

This citation is important not only as a reflection of the understanding of the merits of the two types of administration prevailing in the early days of intelligence measurement, but also because of the enduring pertinence of the identification of the strengths and weaknesses of the two modes of testing. Whipple undoubtedly was speaking for the majority of psychologists in voicing the preference that he did for individual testing. The advantages of group testing, however, and repeated demonstrations of its effectiveness, even as measured by correlations with results of individual tests, proved irresistible. One does not often hear now of situations in which a practitioner wishes or needs to decide whether to administer a group or an individual test; the relative uses of the two types of instruments and the situations in which it is necessary or desirable to resort to one or the other are clearly perceived. It is recognized that group tests ordinarily make greater demands on understanding written and spoken language than do individual tests, and thus may place at a disadvantage subjects either of foreign language background or of seriously deficient reading skills. It is also true that group tests are almost always time limited and may thus have an element of speededness harmful to a few examinees; it needs to be observed, however, that almost all the group tests now in wide use have been designed to minimize the effect of speed on performance. Obviously the group test does not generate a protocol rich in clinical detail as the individual test is likely to, though with respect to the great majority of subjects and of uses made of test results, this limitation is not serious. The reliance on multiple-choice items, now almost universal in group tests, has given rise to the criticism that results of group tests are unduly influenced by guesswork or chance, and to the further criticism that they place too great a premium on the recognition process rather than the supposedly more creative processes tapped by the individual tests; empirical evidence on the reliability and predictive validity of the two types of tests suggests that these differences are not of major significance.

However lively the discussion about the relative merits of individual versus group modes of testing intelligence was in the early years, it lost much of its urgency as the character of group measures changed in the mid-1930s and subsequently, as outlined in the following section. Originally, group intelligence measures were justified on the ground that they accomplished more efficiently the same mission as the individual test. We have seen that Otis explicitly sought to devise items that would measure precisely the same functions as were measured by Binet items; and the most common type of validity evidence proffered for early group tests was their respective correlations with the individual tests for which they were designed as surrogates. With the passage of time, however, the group tests took on a life and character of their own, transcending their original role as alternatives to well-regarded individual tests. Current group tests embody their own definitions of intelligence, mental ability, or cognitive functioning; their validity is not regarded as best evidenced by their correlations with individual test results but rather by their demonstrated predictive validity in the types of situations for which they are commonly used.

CHANGING CHARACTER OF GROUP TESTS

The concept of intelligence or mental ability underlying almost all the group tests that enjoyed wide popularity in the 1920s was of a "general" ability that manifested itself in an individual's performance across a wide variety of, or perhaps most, tasks of a cognitive nature. If any theory as to the nature of intelligence could be said to characterize these tests, it would be that of Spearman's g, though there was little explicit attention to theoretical underpinnings of the tests. Psychologists, to be sure, entertained varying notions about the nature of intelligence as a famous 1920s article in the *Journal of Educational Psychology* made clear; but whatever the differences on particulars, there was large agreement on the unitary character of the trait.

This view of intelligence influenced the selection of content and the scoring and interpretation of results of the early group tests. Although the test makers embodied a variety of tasks in their tests, and often organized their tests into separate sections such as vocabulary, analogies, arithmetical reasoning, and so on, these varieties of content were chosen because of their supposed suffusion with g, with little regard for their mutual independence or possible diagnostic utility. The use of varieties of tasks was intended, as one author expressed it, to facilitate "sinking different shafts" to permit a comprehensive sampling of the hypothesized general ability. Scores on the several parts were summed to yield an overall measure of mental ability, most commonly expressed as a mental age and an IQ defined as the traditional (though now largely abandoned) ratio of mental age to chronological age. Even those tests that offered verbal and nonverbal, or language and nonlanguage, features treated these as different modes of assessing the same presumed general ability, as evidenced by the usual practice of combining the two measures into a single IQ.

However, as research into the nature, organization, and development of mental ability proceeded, giving rise to new theories and concepts, group tests began to reflect these emerging points of view, most notably with respect to selection of content and proposed interpretations of scores.

Typical of group tests that sought to respond in one way or another to changes in theories or concepts of mental organization were publications such as the following:

1. *California Test of Mental Maturity.* First published in 1936, CTMM sought to go beyond the provision of a single measure of intelligence, and even of a language and nonlanguage measure, to yield scores on several more specific components. It purported to make a "diagnostic evaluation of various mental abilities," seeking to capitalize on the interest in factor-analytic investigations of intelligence, though its development was not, strictly speaking, based on a factor-analytic approach. The diagnostic potential of CTMM attracted great interest, though early reviewers voiced reservations about whether the diagnoses would prove to be sufficiently reliable or useful to warrant the added testing time required. Indeed it was not long before users were calling for a shortened form, which was forthcoming. In the shortened form, the subtests became so abbreviated as to render diagnostic profiling even more suspect. CTMM, in its original and subsequent editions, has proved to be one of the most popular of group intelligence tests, though it seems fair to say its lasting success did not derive from the provision of "factor" scores. Most users seemed satisfied with a language, nonlanguage, and total IQ.

2. *Chicago Tests of Primary Mental Abilities.* The PMA tests appeared in their first commercially published edition in 1941. They represent the first major series of group tests explicitly based on a factor-analytically derived theory of mental organization. Leon Thurstone, author of PMA, and his colleagues, had, through a series of factor-analytic studies, identified seven group factors that he termed "primary mental abilities." These factors, which appeared with greatest consistency in the research, included verbal comprehension, word fluency, number, space, associative memory, perceptual speed, and reasoning. (In the ultimately published battery no tests of perceptual speed or associative memory are included.) Tests to measure these factors were chosen which, in factor-analysis language, loaded heavily on the factor in question and had relatively small loadings on any of the other factors. In seeming contradiction to the emphasis on relative independence among the factor scores, PMA

did provide for the calculation of a single IQ-like score. PMA did not enjoy the sustained widespread acceptance of some of the competing group tests, perhaps because it was perceived as requiring too much time for administration or because users were not persuaded of the practical utility of the diagnostic information provided by the several factor scores.

3. *Holzinger-Crowder Unifactor Tests.* This battery of tests, published in 1953, was, like PMA, a clear reflection of a multifactor concept of intelligence. Limited in application to the high school grades, it provided separate measures of verbal, numerical, spatial, and reasoning factors. It also yielded a single IQ-like index, though the spatial score did not enter into this total. HCUFT was supported by a large body of information on the predictive validity of the separate factor scores against a wide variety of high school achievement measures together with information on the reliability of differences among the separate scores. The battery, though published for more than a decade, enjoyed only modest success.

4. *Davis-Eells Games.* This test, published in 1953, was the work of Allison Davis, Kenneth Eells, and colleagues at the University of Chicago, who had become persuaded that the typical group intelligence tests available in the 1940s were seriously unfair to inner-city black children because of differences between the culture in which such children grew up and the mainstream, predominantly white culture. They sought to produce a set of tests that would overcome or minimize this presumed prejudice and that might bring to light other facets of mental functioning than the conventional tests. They labeled the ability being measured as "problem-solving ability" and refused to label the score on their test an IQ. The content of the test was largely pictorial and the administration required much more verbal direction-giving by the examiner than was true for most tests. The content was also designed to be familiar and interesting to inner-city minority children. Although the tests initially attracted great attention in the climate of concern for cultural differences, they failed to establish a significant lasting presence in American schools. School users found the tests cumbersome to administer and time consuming and were disappointed when the results failed to prove as predictive of school success as those of conventional tests.

5. *Army General Classification Test.* During World War II, the Army, as well as the Navy and the Air Force, undertook to develop its own classification test for use with all inductees. The resulting test, the *Army General Classification Test,* clearly reflected the influence of the factor-analytic movement. The test consisted of equal numbers of items measuring verbal, numerical, and spatial abilities, though the scores on all three types of material were finally summed into a single measure. Not long after the end of World War II, a civilian edition of GCT was published but, unlike the civilian versions of Army Alpha after World War I, it enjoyed little popular acceptance.

Other examples could be cited of group tests that sought to reflect research findings on the nature and organization of mental ability or different perceptions of measurement needs. (One such publication, *Differential Aptitude Tests*, is discussed at length later in this chapter.) It is notable that the group intelligence tests that continue to enjoy the most widespread use, particulary in schools, are by and large revised current editions of the older, more traditional types of tests. As the author has written elsewhere,

> Someone familiar with the intelligence tests of the early '20's would feel at home with today's versions. If we have departed from dedication to *g*, we have not traveled very far. . . . The factor approach, which for a time seemed likely to give rise to quite different types of ability measures, simply did not live up to its early promise, at least with respect to widely-useful instrumentation. [Lennon, 1984, p. 11]

Whether this persistence of traditional types attests to the fundamental validity of that approach, or whether it signifies a divorce of psychometric practice from psychological theory, or unresponsiveness to it, or whether we are still in need of useful new formulations of the concept of intelligence, is not clear.

But if the content of group intelligence tests and the constructs that they purport to measure have remained relatively stable over the years, today's group tests are conspicuously superior to their early antecedents in several ways. Items are more carefully written and edited and subjected to far more intensive and extensive experimental tryout than was true in the early years. Accommodation of the tests to the requiments of mechanical or electronic scoring has resulted in almost total reliance on objective item types, particularly multiple-choice items. The normative data provided for current group tests greatly exceed in extent and quality the data provided for the early tests. Applications of item-response theory have resulted in development of more coherent scales and contributed to comparability of results over various levels and forms of a given group of tests. More important, perhaps, than these technological advances is the increasing sophistication brought by the test authors to issues of test validity and to the explication in the respective test manuals of the rationales that support the test design and use.

Illustrative of this heightened sophistication or sensitivity is the circumstance that most of the group tests in most common use today no longer describe themselves as tests of "intelligence," "mental ability," or "general ability." Rather, these tests now are labeled tests of "academic aptitude," "scholastic aptitude," "school ability," "cognitive skills," or similarly unpretentious designations. This change is not merely cosmetic, though it may be assumed that it was prompted in part by widespread criticism of the group of tests known as "intelligence" tests. The new test names seek to indicate more precisely the intended functions of the tests and thus the bases for the selection of test content. Manuals for the better current group tests are attentive to the technical standards developed jointly by the American Psychological Association, the American Educational Research Association, and the National Council on Measurement in Education, and provide more explicit discussion of construct, content, and criterion-related validity.

ISSUES AND PROBLEMS IN THE USE OF GROUP TESTS

The past two decades have been marked by persistent, widespread, and vigorous criticism of testing of all kinds, both from professional groups and from the general public. Of all categories of tests, group intelligence tests have probably been the most common target. Some of the criticisms directed against tests in general, or intelligence tests in particular, have been addressed elsewhere in this volume and there is an extensive literature dealing with the merits of the criticisms. Nevertheless, it will be useful here to treat briefly a few of the complaints most commonly raised against group tests.

Cultural Bias

Certain subgroups in the population, notably blacks and Hispanics, consistently do less well on the average than subjects in general. Critics argue that these systematic differences are attributable to "unfairness" in the tests. According to this view, the typical content of these group tests is unfair to minority groups because it is saturated with white, middle- or upper-class values and beyond the experience of the minority groups. Further, the norm groups for the tests are perceived as not adequately representing minority subjects, making it impossible to evaluate the performance of a minority examinee in relation to an appropriate reference group. The result of the inappropriateness of the content and norms is a systematic underestimating of the ability of minority examinees, which in turn leads to diminution of educational and other opportunities.

Defenders of the tests argue on the other hand that "fairness" can only be evaluated in terms of the ability of the tests to predict performance on relevant criteria for all groups. If cultural differences in the experiences of minority and mainstream groups have in fact affected the learnings of minority subjects in ways that are hurtful to their performance in school or in other realms of interest, then tests that seek to predict success in these realms should properly reflect that fact. Regarding representation of minorities in norm groups, most widely used tests developed during the past decade have had proper representation of such groups in their standardization.

Complaints about cultural unfairness of the tests have prompted a few school districts to discontinue their use, as noted earlier. Most users apparently have concluded that whatever the merits of the bias criticisms, the tests serve sufficiently useful purposes for minority and other subjects to warrant their continued use. The criticism has had beneficial consequences; it has stimulated test authors and publishers to greater sensitivity to minority concerns in the development of test content, often involving the use of panels of minority reviewers of drafts of test items and special attention to the inclusion of samples of minority subjects in the test-development process.

Limited Sampling of Abilities

A long-standing criticism of group intelligence tests has been that the tests sample an unduly restricted set of intellectual skills. The emphasis on verbal abilities, on abstract thinking, and in some instances on reading comprehension, characteristic of many group tests, is seen as productive of a surely incomplete and possibly distorted picture of an examinee's intellectual functioning. We are all familiar with the complaint that these tests do not measure creativity, originality, artistic ability, or other rightly prized human attributes. Critics contend that the tests conduce to an overvaluing of the abilities represented to the disadvantage of other equally worthy talents.

The typical group test undoubtedly relies on a fairly limited array of tasks: vocabulary, analogies, series completion, spatial abilities, quantitative skills, general information, classification, syllogistical reasoning. There certainly is no representation that an examinee's performance on this or a similar set of tasks provides a comprehensive description of his or her intellectual functioning, even though the composite measure derived is presumed to have considerable generality. Obviously there are practical limits to the numbers and kinds of tasks that can be set in any test and decisions as to which types should be included are based on the contributions the types can make to the most common uses to which the test will be put. In principle, test makers would generally subscribe to expanding the types of abilities sampled in their tests; but they would maintain that the types of content most commonly included in present tests are by and large among the ones best suited for the purposes for which the tests are most often used.

Limited Utility of Test Results

A recurrent criticism of group intelligence test results is that they are poor predictors of the criteria most commonly of interest: school success, occupational success, general adjustment to life, and so on. It is further argued that the information provided by group intelligence tests toward the prediction of such criteria is duplicative of other readily available information, such as school grades, or that the information is too diffuse and general to serve helpfully in planning instruction or proffering career guidance. Thus according to these critics, it is not worth the time and expense required to give these tests.

Fortunately, these are issues that lend themselves to empirical approaches. The contributions of group intelligence-test scores in the prediction of various criteria, alone or in combination with other information, can be measured, as it has been in countless studies. There is little room for doubt about the substantial predictive validity of group intelligence tests against a wide variety of academic attainment criteria. Success in the prediction of vocational and occupational criteria has been less good but still sufficient to persuade many people of the usefulness of tests for these purposes.

The criticism that the results of most current group intelligence tests are of limited value in planning instructional interventions is a cogent one. The information provided by these tests can help teachers make judgments about setting appropriate instructional goals, about the probable learning pace of pupils, about the levels of abstraction with which pupils can deal, and even about courses in which the pupils are likely to experience success or failure. The test results do not, nor are they intended to, provide explicit guidance with respect to day-to-day instructional tactics or curricular planning. Tests that would serve these purposes better are clearly desirable and the next generation of ability tests may well move in this direction. It is to be noted, however, that research to date on the so-called "aptitude-treatment-interaction problem" has had but limited success in setting a theoretical framework for the development of such instruments.

Expectancy Issues: The Pygmalion Effect

One of the most severe charges leveled against results of intelligence tests, both individual and group, is that their results create in the minds of teachers expectations about pupil achievement that in turn affect the way the teachers treat these pupils. It is said that teachers tend to regard pupils who do poorly on these tests as "slow learners," "academic risks," or, even in the absence of such labeling, to anticipate that these pupils will do poorly at academic tasks. These expectations lead the teachers to assign such pupils to slow groups, to set more limited academic goals for them, to reduce the pace of instruction—in short, to behave precisely in ways that will fulfill the prophecy. Few would deny that this type of teacher behavior does, in fact, occur. The proper response, however, would appear to be not to deny the teacher of information about the pupil's mental ability or any other relevant characteristic, but rather to provide for better understanding of the limitations of any information about learners, the necessity for systematic reconsideration of this information at frequent intervals, and an appreciation of the fact that some pupils with poor intelligence test scores achieve relatively well, so that no pupil's prospects for achievement should be written off solely on the basis of an intelligence test score. Teachers must entertain expectations of the attainments of individual pupils if they are to try in any significant sense to individualize instruction. Such expectations are likely to be more realistic if they are based in part on the results of good intelligence tests. Teachers in general have a sufficiently clear understanding of the meaning of intelligence test results so that their behavior toward pupils is not so rigidly determined by these results as this criticism would imply.

Reliability and Long-Term Consistency

In the early days of group testing it was commonly assumed that the results of group tests were likely to be on the average less reliable than results of individual tests. Such a belief stemmed from the circumstances that the group tests tended to be shorter and to sample a smaller variety of functions than the individual tests; further, individual test scores were generated under the direction of a trained examiner who could eliminate some of the sources of error that would lower the reliability of results. In fact, this presumed lessened reliability was sometimes advanced as a reason for preferring an individual to a group test in clinical practice. It is now clear from the published reliability data for individual and group tests that these differences do not in fact exist. Published reliability coefficients for the best of the group tests compare favorably with those for Stanford-Binet or the Wechsler scales; even at the primary grades group tests manifest quite adequate reliabilities.

There has also been over the years a tendency to question the long-term stability of group intelligence test results. Long-term studies of the results of these tests, however, demonstrate a quite remarkable stability over periods ranging from three to nine years. Results of tests administered three years apart correlated .83 with each other, and between tests administered six years apart .82. Thus it is fair to conclude that whatever these group tests are measuring is an attribute of impressive constancy, at least under ordinary school conditions.

TYPICAL GROUP INTELLIGENCE TESTS

This section presents descriptions of six group "intelligence" tests, although, as noted earlier, none is identified in its title as an intelligence test. The tests described are among the most widely used tests in this category and they may be considered typical. All have been judged by professional reviewers and competent users to have satisfactory psychometric properties and to serve well the purposes for which they are most commonly used.

Otis-Lennon School Ability Test

The Otis-Lennon School Ability Test series is the current edition of the Otis tests. Predecessor editions included Otis Group Intelligence Scale, Otis Self-Administering Tests of Mental Ability, Otis Quick-Scoring Mental Ability Tests, and Otis-Lennon Mental Ability Test. The present edition is available in two forms: *R*, published in 1979, and *S*, published in 1983. The series is organized in five levels: Primary I, for grade 1, Primary II, for grades 2 and 3, Elementary, for grades 4 and 5, Intermediate, for grades 6 through 8, and Advanced, for grades 9 and above. Primary I and Primary II levels require about 80 minutes for administration while the upper levels require about 40–45 minutes; speed of response is reported not to have an important influence on test scores.

The Otis-Lennon series, according to its *Manual for Administering and Interpreting*, was

> Designed to provide an accurate and efficient measure of the abilities needed to acquire the desired cognitive outcomes of formal education. . . . The concept of ability that underlies the test is that of a general intellective ability—Spearman's *g* as modified by Vernon. . . . The Otis-Lennon tests concentrate on assessing the verbal-educational factor. [p. 4]

According to the authors, the designation of the test as a school ability test rather than a mental ability test, as in previous editions, does not signify a departure from the rationale underlying the previous editions or any major difference in the nature of the abilities measured. For most examinees, performance on the test is considered indicative of learning abilities in some nonschool as well as school situations.

The content of the two Primary levels of the series is pictorial in nature, requiring no reading. Item types include analogies, classification, following directions, quantitative reasoning, and verbal comprehension. At the three upper levels the content comprises several types of verbal and nonverbal items, sampling a variety of mental processes: verbal, figural, and quantitative reasoning, and verbal comprehension.

Norms for age and grade groups are provided based on a carefully selected sample of about 130,000 pupils in 70 school systems. These norms permit the expression of an examinee's score in terms of its percentile or stanine standing in an age or grade group; they also permit the derivation of what is termed a "School Ability Index," having the same constants as the familiar IQ (mean of 100, and standard deviation of 16).

Data are provided on reliability of Otis-Lennon results, including both Kuder-Richardson coefficients and test-retest coefficients, both indicating a high degree of dependability in the results. Evidence is presented for the predictive validity of Otis-Lennon scores against a variety of achievement test criteria and teacher grades.

For uses other than in school situations, there is little empirical validity information. Thus for employment or other out-of-school selection purposes, other instruments may seem more appropriate, particularly in view of the explicit designation of the Otis-Lennon tests as "school ability" tests. For use in school situations where a global measure of mental ability is desired, the Otis-Lennon tests offer ease of administration, scoring convenience (all levels may be machine-scored), and straightforward interpretation.

Test of Cognitive Skills

The Test of Cognitive Skills, published in 1981, is a major revision of, and intended as the successor to, the California Short-Form Test of Academic Aptitude. It is designed to serve the same purposes as previous editions, including particularly the prediction of academic achievement. The content seeks to tap abilities important to learning, such as reasoning, problem solving, evaluating, discovering relationships, and remembering—in other words, abilities of a relatively abstract nature that are vital to success in an educational program. The materials are organized in five levels, 1–5, covering respectively grades 2–3, grades 3–5, grades 5–7, grades 7–9, and grades 9–12. The test at all levels may be administered in less than an hour.

The Test of Cognitive Skills, at all levels, comprises four subtests, designated Sequences, Analogies, Memory, and Verbal Reasoning. Separate scores are provided for all four parts as well as a total score designated a Cognitive Skills Index. Scores are interpreted through reference to age and grade percentile rank and stanine norms. Special interpretive aids are provided to facilitate use of the Test of Cognitive Skills in conjunction with the California Test of Basic Skills or the California Achievement Tests. The test at all levels may be scored by hand or by machine.

School and College Ability Tests, Series III

The School and College Ability Tests, Series III, is the current edition, published in 1979, of a series developed by Educational Testing Service but now distributed by CTB/McGraw-Hill. While the developers have explicitly disavowed that School and College Ability Tests are "intelligence" tests, their content and declared purposes clearly warrant their consideration within this category of tests. The professed aim of School and College Ability Tests is to measure what are termed "developed abilities." The abilities the tests seek to measure are those known to be predictive of success in school. Unlike some other group ability measures, School and College Ability Tests do not claim to emphasize abilities not specifically taught in school; the most important criterion in selection of content is its relation to school learning.

The tests are organized in three levels, designated Elementary, Intermediate, and Advanced, covering respectively grades 3–6, grades 6–9, and grades 9–12. All tests may be administered in a single 40-minute class period.

The tests measure verbal and quantitative abilities. Separate verbal and quantitative scores are derived as well as a total score; all scores are interpreted through reference to national percentile ranks and stanines. Users are encouraged to compare verbal and quantitative performance and appropriate information is provided for the interpretation of such differences. Acceptably high reliability coefficients are reported, and validity coefficients against grade point averages are in the range commonly found.

Tests in the School and College Ability Tests series may be scored either by hand or by machine.

Cognitive Abilities Test, Form 3

This is the current (1978–1982) edition of a test series that has been widely used over a long period of years. It undertakes to assess verbal, quantitative, and nonverbal abilities. The authors state in the test's manual that the tests "have attempted to emphasize relational thinking—the perceiving of relationships among abstract elements in a variety of media and settings." The primary purpose of the test is to enable schools to understand individual pupils' learning needs and cognitive styles so that they may better match instruction to them.

The test is organized in two levels—a Primary Battery for Kindergarten through grade 3, and a Multi-Level edition for grades 3 through 12; students at various grade levels are exposed to appropriate sections of the content. The

Primary Battery comprises four tests: relational concepts, multimental concepts, quantitative concepts, and oral vocabulary, and may be administered in about an hour. It requires no reading and administration is paced to reduce the influence of speed of response. The Multi-Level edition comprises three batteries: verbal, nonverbal, and quantitative. The verbal battery includes vocabulary, sentence completion, verbal classification, and verbal-analogies items. The quantitative battery includes items on quantitative relations, number series, and equation building. The nonverbal battery includes items on figure classification, figure analogies, and figure synthesis. Time required for administration of all three batteries is approximately 100 minutes.

Separate scores are derived for the verbal, nonverbal, and quantitative batteries, and users are discouraged from attempting to combine the separate scores into any single index. Nevertheless, the intercorrelations of the battery scores are substantial—high .60s and .70s, and it is probable that Cognitive Abilities Test measures a general factor to about the same extent as other tests in this category.

Scores on all three batteries may be interpreted by reference to carefully developed norms that permit translation of the scores to normalized standard scores within age groups, having IQ-like constants (mean of 100 and standard deviation of 16). Scores may also be expressed as percentile ranks or stanines within age or grade groups. Reliability of the battery scores is satisfactory, and validity coefficients against achievement test scores are of approximately the same order as reported for other tests of this kind. The authors report particular care in the test-development process to achieve cultural, social, and gender balance.

All tests in both the Primary Battery and the Multi-Level edition may be scored by hand or by machine.

Differential Aptitude Tests, Forms *V* and *W*

Forms *V* and *W* of the Differential Aptitude Tests series are the current edition of a series first published in 1947. The premise underlying the tests is that persons do not have "intelligence" in the sense of a single unitary ability, but rather several abilities—"intelligences"—that may vary in amount within each individual. The battery thus undertakes to measure several presumed abilities, including some very similar to those tapped in the usual group intelligence test but also some not commonly found in such tests. The battery does not attempt to justify itself, therefore, as a measure of a unitary intelligence but rather as a multifaceted assessment of important abilities, which, considered singly or in various combinations, are predictive of numerous educational and vocational criteria. The tests are provided in a single level, covering grades 8 through 12; they have also enjoyed some use with out-of-school groups as vocational guidance instruments.

Differential Aptitude Tests comprise eight subtests: verbal reasoning, numerical ability, abstract reasoning, clerical speed and accuracy, mechanical reasoning, space relations, spelling, and language usage. Not all subtests need be administered to every examinee, though this is the recommended procedure. The individual tests require from 6 to 30 minutes; administration of the complete battery calls for a little more than three hours of testing time.

Norms are provided based on a representative national sample of students in grades 8 through 12. Separate norms are provided for male and female subjects because substantial sex differences were found to occur for some of the abilities. Scores on each test may be expressed as percentile ranks or stanines within grade groups.

Despite the disclaimer that Differential Aptitude Tests are intelligence tests, provision is made for calculation of an Index of Scholastic Ability based on the verbal reasoning and numerical ability tests, which is said to serve the same purposes as scores derived from other mental ability tests.

Differential Aptitude Tests are supported by an unusual wealth of validity information, indicating correlations of scores on all the tests with a wide variety of achievement test results and teacher grades. Accessory material, including individual profile charts and a handbook on use of the charts in counseling, contribute to the usefulness of the battery. Differential Aptitude Tests also offer a Career Planning Program through which the test results and examinee responses to a Career Planning Questionnaire covering educational and vocational plans and achievement data are analyzed through a computer program to provide a Career Planning Report.

Obviously, Differential Aptitude Tests provide more information than the typical instrument in this category. The utility of this additional information, calling as it does for increased testing time, must be evaluated in terms of the desired purposes of any given testing.

Wonderlic Personnel Test

Illustrative of a short test of mental ability intended for use in industrial and commercial organizations is Wonderlic Personnel Test (1945). The original forms of Wonderlic were abbreviated editions of Otis Self-Administering Tests designed for administration in 12 minutes. Additional forms equivalent to the original forms have been issued over the years. The Wonderlic test is organized in spiral-omnibus form and is essentially self-administering. Content includes vocabulary, arithmetic, and information items. A single score is derived that may be interpreted through reference to norms based on job applicants in a large number of occupations.

The Wonderlic, and tests like it, have proved vulnerable to legal challenges on grounds of unfairness to minority job applicants. On the average minority applicants characteristically do less well on Wonderlic than majority examinees, and in the absence of persuasive validity evidence courts have ruled that use of these tests for employment purposes discriminates illegally against minority applicants. As a partial response to such rulings, the author and publisher of Wonderlic have accumulated and made available a large body of normative data for black examinees, suggesting that if these normative data are used in interpreting scores of black examinees, less adverse impact in hiring decisions will result.

As an initial screening device for a wide variety of occupations where some measure of general ability is desired, Wonderlic has enjoyed long-continued wide acceptance. Despite its widespread use, validity data are limited, partly owing to the great practical difficulty of obtaining adequate criterion data for suitable samples of employees.

THE OUTLOOK FOR GROUP INTELLIGENCE TESTING

The use of tests of the type herein considered "group intelligence tests" shows no signs of diminishing significantly despite the severe criticisms to which they have been subjected over the past twenty years from both within and without the profession. No dependable statistics exist on the total number of these tests administered each year in the United States, but the results of scattered surveys taken from time to time in school districts, or states, or regions, and the opinions of informed groups, such as members of the National Council on Measurement in Education, indicate that present levels of use will continue for the foreseeable future, at least in schools, which constitute by far the largest user group. Minority groups will probably continue to object about the now-familiar issues of unfairness and cultural bias, but authors and publishers have been responsive to these concerns and future editions, or new tests in this category, will presumably offer fewer grounds for this type of criticism. The use in the future of this type of test in industry is less certain, given the legal challenges and the declared preference of courts for tests that are manifestly job related. The matter of appropriate strategies for validating tests in industrial situations is at this time in a state of agitation, and the confidence with which employers may use tests of this type will depend somewhat on the outcomes of professional considerations of these validity issues.

Tests in this category will, it seems clear, less and less be identified as intelligence or mental ability tests; indeed, these labels persist in only a few of the widely used tests. Even such terms as academic aptitude, or scholastic aptitude, which are less controversial, may give way to designations thought to be more descriptive and more specific. These differing test names will reflect changing concepts and theories of the nature and organization of cognitive functioning. Schools would welcome tests that measure processes, or functions, or abilities, more demonstrably indicative of appropriate instructional intervention than are the present tests. The emphasis on "cognitive skills" or "cognitive abilities" is probably a harbinger of changes to come in this category of tests.

The term IQ itself may be a casualty of these shifts in the conceptualization of what the tests measure. The term is so deeply embedded in the profession, not to say the culture, and its continuing use so reinforced by individual tests, that its elimination will be slow in coming if indeed it happens at all. The term

IQ has emotional connotations for many, hindering rational discussions; is subject to numerous misconceptions in the minds of both professionals and lay persons; and, in its traditional ratio form, suffered from serious statistical defects. Although it is not clear that terms proposed as alternatives will not suffer from the same problems, the manuals for most of the current tests can surely be read as encouraging the use of such alternatives.

More and more, tests in this category will be adapted for administration, scoring, and interpretation by computer. Ironically, some of the very features that facilitated the development of group tests—objective scoring, self-administration, and controlled timing, for example—are precisely features that permit easy adaptation to computer administration, which again makes the tests in a sense "individual." Finally, the possibility of storing test content in the computer with instant access to any part of it, and of creating an interactive situation between examinee and test, is likely to hasten the development of so-called "adaptive" testing. A substantial technology already exists for this type of testing, which permits the administration to a given examinee of those test items that are most appropriate in difficulty. The items presented to the examinee depend on his or her response to previous items; as the examinee passes an item, he or she is given a more difficult item, and as he or she fails an item, he or she is given an easier item. Adaptive testing permits more reliable testing per unit of testing time. As computers become more prevalent in schools and workplaces, adaptive testing is likely to become more popular because of the increased efficiency that it permits.

REFERENCES

Anastasi, A. (1976). *Psychological testing* (4th ed.). New York: Macmillan.

Bennett, G., Seashore, H., & Wesman, A. (1972–1981). *Differential Aptitude Tests.* Cleveland, OH: The Psychological Corporation.

Buros, O. K. (1936). *Educational, psychological and personality tests of 1933, 1934, and 1935.* New Brunswick, NJ: Rutgers University.

Davis, A., & Eells, K. (1953). *Davis-Eells Games.* Yonkers, NY: World Book.

DuBois, P. H. (1970). *A history of psychological testing.* Boston: Allyn and Bacon.

Holzinger, K., & Crowder, N. (1953). *Holzinger-Crowder Uni-Factor Tests.* Yonkers, NY: World Book.

Lennon, R. T. (1978). Perspective on intelligence testing. *Measurement in Education 9*(2). Washington, DC: National Council on Measurement in Education.

Lennon, R. T. (1980). The anatomy of a Scholastic Aptitude Test. *Measurement in Education, 11*(2). Washington, DC: National Council on Measurement in Education.

Lennon, R. T. (1984). *Trends in testing: 1983.* Georgia Educational Researcher, 3 Athens, GA. Georgia Educational Research Association.

Otis, A. S. (1959). *The origins of group intelligence testing.* Televised interview with Dr. Walter N. Durost.

Otis, A. S., & Lennon, R. T. (1979, 1983). *Otis-Lennon School Ability Tests.* Cleveland, OH: The Psychological Corporation.

School and College Ability Tests, Series III (1979). Monterey, CA: CTB/McGraw-Hill.

Sullivan, E. T., Clark, W. W., & Tiegs, E. W. (1937). *California Test of Mental Maturity.* Monterey, CA: CTB/McGraw-Hill.

Test of Cognitive Skills (1981). Monterey, CA: CTB/McGraw-Hill.

Thorndike, R., & Hagen, E. (1982). *Cognitive Abilities Test, Form 3.* Chicago, IL: The Riverside Publishing Co.

Thurstone, L. L., & Thurstone, T. (1941). *The Chicago Tests of Primary Mental Abilities.* Chicago, IL: Science Research Associates.

Whipple, G. M. (1910, 1914). *Manual of mental and physical tests: Simpler processes.* Baltimore: Warwick and York.

Wonderlic, E. F. (1945). *Wonderlic Personnel Test.* Northfield, IL: E. F. Wonderlic.

PART THREE

APPLICATIONS

TWENTY

INTELLIGENCE AND MENTAL HEALTH

BENJAMIN B. WOLMAN

International Encyclopedia
of Psychiatry, Psychology,
Psychoanalysis, and Neurology
New York, New York

The relationship between intelligence and mental health can be explored in two ways: (1) the extent to which the level of intelligence affects mental health, and (2) the extent to which the level of mental health affects intelligence. Let us start with exploring the impact of intelligence on mental health. There are several possibilities, such as the following: (1) low levels of intelligence are associated with and/or represent poor mental health; (2) high levels of intelligence and especially the highest ones are indicative of poor mental health; and (3) there is no correlation between intelligence and mental health. The examination of these complex relationships must start with clearly stated definitions of both intelligence and mental health.

DEFINING INTELLIGENCE

Spearman (1904) proposed the *two-factor theory of intelligence*. The two factors consist of g plus s, with g standing for the *general intelligence factor*, which accounts for the positive intercorrelations among the tests, and s representing the *specific factors* for specific abilities, such as number concepts, arithmetic reasoning, word knowledge, verbal reasoning, memory, and so on. These specific factors contribute in varying amounts to the global g factor. Those functions, such as vocabulary, that correlate highly with overall intelligence scores are regarded as being more saturated with g than the functions that have low correlations with general intelligence, such as sensory discrimination. R. B. Cattell claims to have been influenced by Spearman's two-factor theory in the development of his *Culture-Fair Intelligence Test;* in fact, Cattell (1971) in his factor-analytic research has isolated two gs rather than one. These are identified as g_c and g_f. The g_c factor is labeled *crystallized general ability.* While g_c is primarily verbal (in essence, vocabulary tests) and acquired by cultural experience, it also involves numerical skills, memory, and mechanical knowledge. Each of these represents a skill that has been acquired by educational and cultural experiences. The g_f factor represents *fluid ability,* which is more culture-free. It is involved in perceptual and performance tests dealing with spatial judgment and inductive reasoning, including matrices, analogies, and classifications. High fluid ability is frequently seen in the poorly educated, the so-called street people, who are nevertheless bright. Their ability to write well or express themselves other than colloquially may be poor, but they may be superior in reasoning and problem solving. Hebb (1942) has developed a theory of intelligence along similar lines by structuring intelligence in terms of two levels or concepts—Intelligences A and B. *Intelligence A* is the innate biological potential, and *Intelligence B* is the later development of that intelligence by the environment, mostly to the stage or level where it can be observed and measured. In *Vectors of Mind,* Thurstone (1935) first isolated and identified three primary group factors based on the correlations among 15 intelligence tests. By 1947 he had identified seven independent abilities from a correlational matrix involving 60 group intelligence tests. He identified these seven independent primary mental abilities as V (verbal meaning found in vocabulary and disarranged sentences), W (word fluency found in anagrams and word naming), N (number of ability in computations), M (memory in rote learning), S (spatial relations from forms and designs), P (perceptual speed from visual similarities and differences), and R (reasoning ability found in induction exercises and syllogisms) (see Morrow & Morrow, 1977, pp. 103–104).

NATURE OR NURTURE

There is an abundant evidence concerning the genetic determinant of intelligence (Bouchard & McGue, 1981; Dixon & Johnson, 1980; Fuller & Simmel, 1980; Taylor, 1980). The IQ correlations between blood relatives are quite convincing, although contemporary research yields more moderate correlation coefficients, compared to those obtained a few decades ago. However, the genetic factor is still considered a highly relevant and clearly established determinant of one's level of intelligence (Taylor, 1980).

Some authors go even further. Burt (1972), Jensen (1969, 1980), and Shockley (1972) maintain that intelligence, at least 80% of it, is inherited, and blacks score significantly (at least 15 IQ points or one standard deviation) lower than whites. In a way, they follow in the footsteps of Terman (1916) who wrote that Indians, Mexicans, and Negroes are genetically inferior.

However, Klineberg (1931) found no racially related differences in intelligence between French, German, and Italian children, but the IQ scores were higher in urban versus rural groups, obviously related to environmental stimulation. Wolman (1951) critically examined the literature concerning intelligence of Jewish adolescents in the United States and in Israel. Wolman found no evidence of Jewish genetic superiority and abundant proof of environmental influences, especially through parental encouragement and guidance.

Apparently the child's experience in early years of life exercises great influence on his later intellectual functioning. The preschool years are of considerable importance for future development of curiosity, learning sets, and other intellectual functions. The early environmental stimulation contributes to higher scores on mental tests, whereas inadequate stimulation may be responsible for mild mental retardation (Ramey & Baker-Ward, 1983).

Wechsler Adult Intelligence Scale (1944) has created the opportunity for relating the cognitive functions of perceiving, remembering, judging, and conceptualization to emotional elements of personality organization. The WAIS, in addition to being an intelligence test, offers significant clues for clinical diagnosis. In fact, one may doubt the existence of a pure and impersonal intelligence test. Clinicians have discovered "that high-level efficiency could be primarily defensive while leading to elevated IQ scores, whereas clinical improvement sometimes meant the lowering of IQ scores. The previously hyperalert person whose concentration was now more relaxed and less anxiously vigilant failed to reach as great heights of success on items which rewarded vigilance" (Allison, 1978, p. 357).

Evidently intellectual competence as measured by intelligence tests is not a purely intellectual matter. A child's cognitive development is greatly influenced by motivation and attention span as well as by stimulation and encouragement. Mental development is a product of several factors, especially of innate abilities and learning, and the latter is provided by the child's environment. Even the best seed will not develop into a tree if it is placed in arid soil, and the child's intellectual competence is definitely influenced by social adjustment (Scarr, 1981; Wolman, 1982).

DEFINING MENTAL HEALTH

A group of psychiatrists and sociologists led by Dr. Srole (1962) conducted a study of mental health in New York. The sample included 1,660 adults in midtown Manhattan. The researchers found that only 18.5% of the population could be considered to be in good mental health, and 36.3% had marked mental symptoms. About 7.5% of the people suffered from severe mental symptoms, while 2.7% were totally incapacitated by their disorder, with 10.2% severely disturbed. In summary, 23.4% of the population, including the previously mentioned 10.2%, were impaired in their functioning to a significant degree.

Since success gives pleasure and failure displeasure, the issue of mental health has been often related to economic factors. The socioeconomic success rates high in our society, and nothing is simpler than to deduce that the lower socioeconomic classes are "unhappy" and those who "can afford" are "happy." Subsequently, poor mental health was ascribed to the economically poor.

Several research workers have linked the *severity* of mental problems to socioeconomic factors (Dohrenwend, 1977). The sociologist Hollingshead and psychiatrist Redlich studied mental health in New Haven, Connecticut (1958). They implied that the higher socioeconomic classes suffer from mild emotional problems, while the lower socioeconomic classes had a much higher ratio of severe cases. In addition, Srole and associates (1962) found in New York City that 30% of the affluent class were mentally well, compared to 4.6% of the poor class.

I would like to suggest five criteria of mental health, as follows:

1. Achievement

The inability to actualize one's mental and physical potential is one of the signs of mental disorder, and the greater the discrepancy between promise and fulfillment, the more severe is the disorder.

There are several cases of gifted individuals who function well in their professions as scholars, scientists, and creative artists, but who are unable to act in a balanced and rational manner in their personal lives. Apparently poorly integrated personality permits adequate functioning in the conflict-free ego spheres, but it fails in conflict-laden areas.

2. Emotional Balance

The second criterion of mental health is *emotional balance*. The reactions of healthy individuals correspond to the quality and quantity of stimuli. Normally, people react with pleasure to situations that enhance their well-being. Happiness is generally attained when one's wishes come true, whereas grief is the reaction to failure or loss. Normal reactions are *appropriate* to the stimuli.

Normal emotional reactions are also *proportionate* to the stimuli. An emotionally well-balanced individual reacts to a loss in a manner *proportionate* to the magnitude of the loss and to the ensuing hardships. Moreover, a well-balanced individual will do whatever is possible to regain the loss and to prevent its recurrence. In short, normal emotional behavior is appropriate, proportionate, and *adjustive*.

In addition, emotional balance implies also the ability to *control* one's emotions. Emotionally disturbed individuals may react instantly to an annoying stimulus without considering potential dangers and may perpetuate their moods because they are unable to control them. Rational emotional reaction is appropriate, proportionate and adjustive; it is also distinguished by *self-discipline and ability to control overt expression of one's emotions.*

3. Cognitive Functions

The third criterion of mental health is related to *cognitive functions.* An erroneous perception, an oversight of danger, and the inability to distinguish fantasy from reality may jeopardize one's existence. A realistic perception of what is going on in the outer world and in one's own life increases one's chances for survival and helps in adjustment.

In most mental disorders the perception of the outer world is disturbed, but not as a result of malfunction of the sensory organs as is the case in sight or hearing impairments. An individual who misconstrues or misinterprets what he perceives is said to be *delusional*. Delusions are distorted perceptions; hallucinations are perceptions without external stimulation, such as seeing ghosts and hearing voices.

4. Social Adjustment

The fourth criterion is *social adjustment*. Human beings interact with one another in cooperation and competition, love and hate, peace and war. The term *social life* denotes both the friendly or cooperative and the hostile or competitive aspects of human interaction.

There are no ideal societies. Every social group has its share of the constructive life-preserving and cooperative factors, as well as the disruptive, destructive, and antisocial forces. No society can afford a free display of destructive forces.

I have suggested four types of interaction, namely one hostile (*H*) and three friendly (*I, M,* and *V*). When hostility is acted upon in self-defense and conducted in a rational manner, it is normal and justifiable. However, when hostility is irrational and acted out indiscriminately, it is pathological.

The first phase of friendliness is called *instrumental* (*I*), that is, using others toward the satisfaction of one's own needs. Newborn infants and little children must be instrumental because they must be on the receiving end. Instrumentalism is perfectly normal at this stage of development, and some degree of instrumentalism must be preserved into adult years, for whoever endeavors to earn a living, his or her intentions are instrumental. An instrumental attitude is a relationship to other people in which one tries to use others or their services in order to satisfy one's own needs. It is a *taking* attitude. The infant versus mother is the prototype of instrumentalism.

However, hardly anyone can live all his or her life in an instrumental way, because other people would not tolerate it. As soon as the child enters social relationships with other children, he or she becomes aware of the fact that life cannot be a one-way street. If the child asks for favors, he or she must return favors. Through the dual process of development and learning, the child gradually enters the next phase, which is called *mutual* (*M*), that is, a *give and take* relationship. Genuine friendship and mature sexual relations are mutual, since each partner tries to satisfy his or her own needs and, at the same time, is willing to satisfy the needs of the partner.

People who have developed the ability to satisfy each others' needs, may enter into a relationship in which they are the *givers*. Genuine charity, helping poor and underprivileged people, and idealistic self-sacrifice for one's religion, country, or political convictions are examples of *vectorialism*. A vectorial attitude implies giving without expecting anything in return.

Parenthood is the prototype of vectorialism. Mature parents are willing to do whatever they can for their children without expecting anything in return. Immature parents involve their children in their own emotional problems and exploit their children emotionally. These parents are instrumental; normal parental attitude is vectorial.

A socially adjusted individual acts in a rational way in all three directions. He is instrumental in the bread-winning functions, mutual in friendship and marriage, and vectorial in regard to his or her children and to those who need help. An exaggeration in instrumentalism, mutualism, or vectorialism breeds disorder.

5. Self-Esteem

The last, but certainly not the least, criterion of mental health is *self-esteem*. An individual who perceives oneself to be physically healthy or attractive, intelligent, influential, or outstanding has the feeling of power. Power can be defined as the ability to satisfy needs.

People whose self-confidence was developed in childhood by their parents have more courage and depend less on others. Gradually one's own abilities, efforts, and achievements begin to count more than other people's opinion. Well-adjusted people are aware of the fact that not everyone will like them, and they act in accordance with what *they themselves* think is right. *The dependence on one's own judgment is an important factor in personality integration and mental health, provided it is based on a realistic estimate of one's own potentialities and environmental opportunities.*

Mental Retardation

Does mental retardation cause or is it associated with mental disorders? Suppose an individual obtains a low score on a mental test. This person might have considerable difficulties in mastering school subjects and probably fail on most of them. This person may be unable to attend an academic high school. Low scores on mental tests are indicative of a poor level of comprehension and reasoning abilities.

However, this person may perform adequately on a simple job, such as shipping clerk, messenger person, elevator operator, or bellhop. The person may relate pleasantly to his or her parents and siblings and be very friendly to the neighbors. In teens and early adult years he or she may act adequately in courtship and sex, and eventually marry. As an elevator operator in a department store or as a shipping clerk, he may support his family the best he can. During the evening, he and his wife may watch television, and on weekdays go shopping, visit relatives, and go to movies.

Is there any pathology there? Is a below average IQ indicative of psychopathology?

The American Association on Mental Deficieny's (AAMD) definition of mental retardation refers to subaverage general intellectual functioning existing concurrently with deficits in adaptive behavior and manifested during the developmental period. AAMD introduced two systems of classification. The first system was based on etiology in which mental retardation was regarded as a manifestation of some underlying disease process or mental condition, such as, for example, hydrocephalus or chromosomal abnormality in Down syndrome. The second classification system was related to subaverage intelligence scores and behavioral maladjustment (Heber, 1961).

Several researchers noted a relationship between IQ and adaptive behavior (Meier, 1977). The AAMD revised definition emphasized the importance of adaptive behavior as follows: "Mental retardation refers to significant sub-average general intellectual functioning existing concurrently in adaptive behavior and manifested during the developmental period" (Grossman, 1977). According to Leland (1983), the three following behavioral patterns represent adaptation:

1. **Independent Functioning:** Independent functioning is defined as the ability to accomplish successfully those tasks or activities demanded by the community in terms of survival demands for that community and in terms of expectations for specific age groups.

2. **Personal Responsibility:** Personal responsibility is defined as both the willingness of individuals to accomplish those critical tasks they are able to accomplish (usually under some type of supervision) and their ability to assume individual responsibility for personal behavior. This ability is reflected in decision making and choice of behavior.

3. **Social Responsibility:** Social responsibility is defined as the ability of the individual to accept responsibility as a member of a community group and to carry out appropriate behaviors in terms of group expectations. This is reflected in levels of conformity, social adjustment, and emotional maturity. It is further analyzed in terms of the acceptance of some level of civic responsibility leading to complete or partial economic independence.

Independent functioning is closely tied to age expectations and is the most carefully examined aspect of adaptive behavior (Leland et al., 1967). There is a time when children are expected to feed themselves, to be toilet trained, to walk, to dress themselves, and so on.

Personal responsibility asks the question: Does the individual do the types of things that he or she can do? This includes such activities as brushing one's teeth, making beds, housekeeping, and so on. Apparently, when individuals do what they are able to do with a minimum of supervision or demand, they demonstrate personal responsibility. This is primarily a matter of motivation. To be willing to assume responsibility for one's own behavior, and to be willing to recognize that the consequences of this behavior are closely related to decisions and choice of behaviors, is a demonstration of "good" personal responsibility.

Social responsibility relates to coping with critical demands of the community. If individuals are not aware of these demands or cannot judge appropriate interactions, their presence in the community may become undesirable (Leland, 1973).

The relationship between mental retardation and behavioral maladjustment is a controversial issue. Some authors maintain the following:

> Trying to differentiate the mentally retarded is like trying to catch and hold the wind. Behaviors, whether erratic, unpredictable or hypoactive, seen among some may be due to brain injury, to extreme infantilism, or to serious emotional disturbance and/or psychosis. . . . Mentally retarded individuals, whether young or old, are as different and as individual as any of their nondeficient peers. [Karp, Morgenstern, & Michal-Smith, 1978, p. 750]

Apparently, the frequency of mental disorders in mentally retarded is a highly controversial issue. According to Webster (1963), mental retardation is a clinical development syndrome that usually includes an impairment in emotional as well intellectual development. LaVietes (1978), after carefully analyzing research data, concluded that the "high risk for development of psychiatric disorders can be ascribed to factors inherent in intellectual limitations, to the life experiences of such a child, and to the interaction between the two" (p. 202). Moreover, according to LaVietes,

> Low self-esteem is almost ubiquitous in mildly to moderately retarded children. They perceive their disappointment to others in some undefined way. Because he has failed the parent, the child feels in danger of losing parental love and support. He develops an increased need for praise and approval but has a decreased ability to elicit it. His low self-appraisal is aggravated by experiences within the family inasmuch as siblings, even younger ones, advance more rapidly and may resent the retardate's presence. Outside the family there are fewer environmental supports. He is excluded from social and community life. There is the stigma of attending a special school, and possibly of having a peculiar appearance. Other children may tease, avoid, ignore, or depreciate him. There are limits in social opportunities with peers, real difficulties in negotiating with the environment, and in mastering the ordinary tasks of childhood at appropriate developmental points. Encounters with the environment leave him feeling incompetent and ineffective. Yet he is overly dependent upon others for survival. In reaction to these chronic traumas, the retarded child reacts variously with distrust, withdrawal, inhibition, anxiety, fear of challenge, anger, and regressive or aggressive sources of satisfaction. Retarded children in institutions that are overly restrictive, controlled, and lacking in individualization and social structure of families, receive minimal stimulation for the development of appropriate interactive behaviors. Children become prone to excessive dependence, fears of the unfamiliar, rigidity, excess fantasy, and other maladaptive devices for coping with stress. [p. 203]

Sociocultural Factors

Children who are labeled as "borderline or retarded may be found to be unmotivated or poorly adjusted," and "children who are called 'disadvantaged' usually come from homes that we would characterize as having low levels of intellectual stimulation" (Scarr, 1981, p. 1165); for instance, parents who enjoy reading, will probably buy books for their children, foster their intellectual curiosity, and encourage mental development. It is still a question whether the lower test scores obtained by children of a low socioeconomic status (SES) are more related to inadequate cultural nourishment (*Cultural Index*) or poverty, or to some genetic factor (Horn, Loehlin, & Willerman, 1980; Scarr & Weinberg, 1978).

A study by Rice, Cloninger, and Reich (1982) admitted that one's IQ and socioeconomic status (SES) are somehow related, but they rejected the idea that the SES is identical with the Cultural Index. It is quite possible that disturbed behavior of some or of many mentally retarded individuals is a product of their feeling inferior, rejected, ostracized, or discriminated against, rather than a direct outcome of their low level of intelligence that, unquestionably, contributes to the biased social attitude in our achievement-oriented public opinion.

The widespread prejudice against intellectually inferior people is inherent in mental tests. Most intelligence tests probably make correct predictions concerning academic and possibly occupational success, but they can't say much in regard to behavioral competence, which is of utmost importance, especially in regard to mentally retarded individuals. It may be that a simple IQ assessment is rather irrelevant as far as prediction of the individual's future behavioral competence (Leland, 1981, 1983).

Minority Group Children

As previously mentioned, Burt, Jensen, and Shockley link the level of intelligence to hereditary and racial factors. Several authors critically examined this issue and challenged the use of mental tests with minority group children (Hobbs, 1975; Oakland, 1977, 1980). It seems that there are no culture-free tests, and attitudinal, perceptual, and behavioral differences between white and black children are ignored by most tests. Small wonder that the content of mental tests derived from experiences of white children is unwillingly and unwittingly unfair to children with a different sociocultural background and different environmental experiences (Barclay, 1983).

At the 1983 Annual Convention of the American Psychological Association held at Annaheim, California, A. R. Jensen further elaborated on his theory and claimed that "the black-white difference of one standard deviation on mental tests cannot be explained by idiosyncratic cultural or linguistic factors" (Cordes, 1983, p. 3). Moreover, according to Jensen, "It was found, that the average white-black difference on a test of items judged least culturally loaded was almost twice as large as the difference on a test of items judged most culturally loaded" (Cordes, 1983, p. 3). Furthermore, the black-white difference "is predominantly a difference in *g*," and the *g*-factor [Spearman's *g*] reflects abstract reasoning, stimulus encoding, discrimination, comparison, short-term memory, retrieval from long-term memory, and perhaps, above all, the speed of mental processing. Jensen maintained that problem-solving strategies and predicting and monitoring one's own behavior are readily trainable, whereas the speed of encoding, short-term memory, retrieval of long-term memory, and other mental functions related to the *g*-factor have a neural base and could be of genetic origin.

Jensen's theories have been widely criticized. At the present time, they are hypothetical statements that lack empirical evidence. The fact that minority group children often, but not always, obtain lower scores than white children can be traced to a variety of factors. Many researchers pointed to the lower socioeconomic status of minority groups, and thus to their limited exposure to cultural influences. It seems imperative that psychologists who test minority group and underprivileged children should not overlook the impact of these factors on test performance and the resulting test scores. It is also often a matter of language comprehension, familiarity with testing materials, experience, and so on (Van der Flier, 1982).

It is interesting to note that even when the language barrier is removed by translation, the test scores might reflect other cultural differences. For example, Padilla and Ross (1983) administered the Spanish translation of WISC-R to 1100 children in Mexico City. The age of children was from 6 to 16. The full IQ score for 6-year-old Mexican children was one-half standard deviation below the U.S. score. The Mexican score was slightly more than one standard deviation for 14 to 16 year olds. Apparently, as Mexican children grow older, they have less learning opportunities and the gulf between them and U.S. children grows.

Several years ago, as a young psychologist, I was assigned to measure the intelligence of children in an underdeveloped country. I used the Simon-Binet tests. One of the questions was: "What will you do if you miss the train?" Bright children in Paris and other metropolitan areas should have answered: "I will wait for the next train," but all children that I tested, answered: "I will go home." When an exceedingly bright boy repeated the same answer, I lost my composure and asked: "Why couldn't you wait for the next train?" The boy gave me a contemptuous look and said: "Do you expect me to stay overnight at the railroad station?" I did not know that there was only one train a day.

There is no question that Tay-Sachs disease, Krabbe's disease, Down syndrome, Hurler syndrome, Sanfilippo syndrome, Gaucher's disease, hydrocephalus, and cretinism, as well as several other organic syndromes, are associated with low IQ and represent serious cases of mental disorder. They certainly do not meet any of the previously mentioned criteria of mental health, and they are cases of both mental disorder and defective intelligence (Boll, 1978).

However, not every case of a low IQ represents mental disorder. Not all oak trees are the same size and not all people must have the same IQ, and the behavior of individuals with an IQ below the average is not always and not necessarily maladaptive (Balthazar & Stevens, 1975).

Genius

Decades of longitudinal research by Terman and associates related genius to an exceedingly high level of inherited intelligence. In 1921 Terman embarked on a comprehensive study of 1528 California children from 2 to 19 years of age. The IQ's of the children ranged from 135 to 200. Terman labeled the children as geniuses or near geniuses, depending on the levels of their IQ scores. Over the years, Terman (1925–1947) published four volumes describing the mental and physical traits of the gifted children. He found these children to be superior to the control group in practically every aspect: they were in better physical and mental health, they excelled in scholastic achievements, and they conducted an active life. They had a considerable number of outstanding ancestors, and the incidence of mental disorders in their parent was 0.4%, far below the national averages.

Years later, in 1959, Terman published a follow-up study in the fifth volume of his work, and called it "The Gifted Group in Mid-Life." The gifted children did not live up to what was expected of them. Most of them have become able and well-adjusted adults, but certainly not geniuses (Albert, 1975).

Apparently IQ is not the only and probably not the most significant aspect of a genius. Mozart, Beethoven, Rembrandt, and Picasso, as well as several other geniuses, did not display in their behavior signs of unusually high, superb levels of intelligence. IQ represents a certain level of intellectual abilities, but genius is a person whose contribution enriched humanity in one or more areas of cultural endeavors. Genius is an unusually *creative* individual, be it a composer, sculptor, painter, dancer, inventor, poet, or scientist, but not necessarily a person with an exceedingly high IQ (Anderson, 1959; Bloom, 1977).

Several authors linked genius and creativity to some type of mental disorder. Lombroso (1907) described several instances of unusually creative behavior associated with psychotic behavior. Lombroso maintained that geniuses are afflicted by epileptoid psychosis and their moments of inspiration and creativity resemble epileptic fits. However, Lombroso admitted that these insane-geniuses have made major contribution to the progress of mankind.

In *General Introduction to Psychoanalysis,* Freud maintained that genius is a person who "longs to attain honor, power, riches, and the love of women, but he lacks the means of achieving these gratifications. So, . . . he turns away from reality and transfers all his interest and his libido to the creation of wishes in the life of fantasy, from which the way might readily lead to neurosis" (1935, p. 327).

Some psychoanalysts followed in Freud's footsteps, while others expressed certain doubts. Kris (1952) did not subscribe 100% to the idea that geniuses turn away from reality.

I have (Wolman, 1967, 1982) strongly opposed this idea. I quoted several instances of creative abilities free of pathology and, on the other hand, an unlimited number of cases of mental disorder not associated with any creative ability whatsoever. The fact that some artists might be afflicted with mental disorder does not prove that art is a product of insanity and every artist must be a mentally disturbed person. The so-called "schizophrenic art" is not art at all. Creative work is a combination of great abilities combined with superb self-discipline, and mental disorder reduces and may destroy any creative effort.

Maslow (1970) studied the lives of several prominent people, such as Einstein, Beethoven, Lincoln, and others. On the basis of this study, he prepared a list of 15 traits of individuals who obtained a high level of self-actualization:

1. The individuals who found self-actualization live very close to reality, and they judge life in a realistic and accurate manner.
2. Self-actualized individuals accept themselves for whatever they are and, at the same time, they are ready to accept others.
3. Self-actualized individuals display a great deal of spontaneous behavior; although they avoid antisocial or unusual actions, they show a great deal of originality and spontaneity in their thinking and overt behavior.
4. These people are usually devoted to solving a general problem. Their life is perceived as a mission rather than a satisfaction of their own personal needs.
5. Once in a while they have to move away from people in order to contemplate in solitude the problems they are coping with and to develop a more detached viewpoint.
6. They are not conformists. They develop their own ideas, rather independent of the *Zeitgeist* and cultural influences of their times.
7. The people who found self-actualization appreciate life; although they are not naive optimists, they love life and they admire its beauty.
8. Some of them can reach beyond observable facts and have a deep feeling of ecstasy going beyond usual human experiences.
9. All of them are very much involved with social problems and display sympathy and compassion for humanity.
10. They develop close personal relations with a small number of friends.
11. Their approach to other people is thoroughly democratic, and they show respect for all other individuals regardless of race, creed, age, and so on.
12. They would never choose inappropriate means to reach their goals. They enjoy just as much the road to achievement as they do their final goal.
13. Most of them have a good sense of humor.
14. They are creative and have esthetic inclinations; they are interested in poetry, science, music, and inventions.
15. Throughout their lives they retain intellectual independence and an independent outlook on life.

People who enjoy good mental health are usually capable of achieving whatever could have been achieved in their lives. Therefore, if one's achievement falls short of his potentialities, which include the totality of heredity and environmental factors, one must conclude or at least suspect the existence of mental blocks that thwart success. As previously mentioned, achievement proportionate to one's potentialities is a highly relevant indicator of mental health. Some gifted individuals could not put their talents to use because they were afflicted by mental disorder, but mental disorder was never a source or a catalyst for creative work.

Intelligence and Psychopathic Personality

Antisocial behavior is not related to a particular level of intelligence, and moral convictions are not necessarily related to moral behavior. Consider the great moralist Tolstoy and the inspiring writer Balzac. Whereas their writings conveyed a high level of moral convictions, their personal lives were far from exemplary. Religious and political fanatics who commit horrible acts against humanity often believe that it is their moral responsibility to punish the disbelievers and murder the opponents. Many members of terrorist movements who practice indiscriminate violence against innocent people believe in the moral aspects of their behavior and whitewash their crimes committed "in the name" of this or another ideal.

There is a distinct clinical category of antisocial behavior related to a distinct personality pathology. In 1837, J. C. Prichard called it *moral insanity*; today it is called psychopathy or sociopathy. I described sociopaths as "narcissistic hyperinstrumentals," void of guilt feelings, lacking compassion for anyone except themselves:

> A sociopath is narcissistic in that the primary object of his affection is himself. He is hyperinstrumental in that the primary mode of expressing that affection is through gaining benefits from others to satisfy his own needs. [Krauss & Krauss, 1977, p. 362]

Some sociopaths are rather dull, some very bright. Embezzlers, racketeers, extortionists, swindlers, and a garden variety of violent and nonviolent criminals are usually shrewd and calculating individuals. A catatonic schizophrenic or a psychomotor epileptic or a "stoned" drug addict may attack whoever is in their way. Violent sociopaths avoid confrontation with overwhelming forces and prefer to mug, hold up, or murder weak victims. Powerful crime syndicates are run by highly sophisticated individuals, and no one can doubt the strategic talents of Hitler and his generals.

Differential Diagnosis

As early as 1905, Binet and Simon pointed to the possibility of differential diagnostic assessment of alcoholism and psychosis. Binet assumed that mentally retarded individuals' correct and erroneous answers are given for a limited number of years, while psychotics and alcoholics tend to "scatter" their right and wrong replies over a large number of years. Binet's hypothesis was refuted by Matarazzo (1972). According to Matarazzo, there is a partial evidence that even normal individuals may score lower on a test if they are in a state of temporary and transient anxiety.

Matarazzo (1972), after twenty years of research, concluded that patients who suffered injury or lesion in the left cerebral hemisphere obtain lower scores on verbal IQ (VIQ) than on their performance IQ (PIQ) reverse with the right hemisphere. Matarazzo's conclusions were confirmed ten years later by Bornstein and Matarazzo (1982) with a *caveat* that the difference between VIQ and PIQ cannot serve as a sole diagnostic clue.

Furthermore, Bornstein and Matarazzo's (1982) survey of recent literature noted gender differences, namely test scores of males are more affected by hemisphere brain lesions than are the scores obtained by females. Apparently, the laterality of brain dysfunctions is more pronounced in males than in females. However, lesions to the frontal lobes do not affect seriously intelligence test scores (Black, 1976).

The Hammer and the Anvil

It seems that the nature-nurture controversy concerning mental disorders can be solved by comparing it to the hammer-anvil issue. Eighty years ago the science of behavioral genetics was practically nonexistent, and Freud could have maintained that parents have a shorter way to affect their children's mental health than through the genes. At the present time there is still little, if any, evidence that neuroses and psychoses are genetically determined, but one need not overlook the possible role of genetic factors within the framework of the socio-psycho-genic theory of mental disorders (Wolman, 1973).

Several years ago two parents brought to my office their oldest, 16½-year-old daughter. The girl was clearly schizophrenic; she told me that she came to my office before and that we knew each other for a long time. She asked why did I change my name. Her 15-year-old sister was a reasonably balanced and well-adjusted girl. On subsequent visits the parents asked: "Where did we go wrong?"

They maintained that they treated both girls equally, which is practically impossible. However, assuming that the difference in parental attitudes did play a certain role in their oldest daughter's disorder, one need not overlook the possible and significant role of genetics. I see no point hypothesizing an alleged "schizophrenic predisposition" (Wolman, 1970), but one may accept a more probable hammer-and-anvil hypothesis. When the same hammer (parental behavior) hit a genetically weak surface (the older girl), it caused grave damage. However, a similar hammer blow on a genetically stronger surface (the younger daughter) could have caused a negligible damage.

Schizophrenia and Intellectual Processes

I believe that schizophrenia is a product of inappropriate parent-child relationship. As mentioned above, there are three types of positive social relationship, depending on the objectives of the participants. Whenever an individual enters a relationship with the objective of receiving, it is an *instrumental* type, for the partner or partners are used for the satisfaction of the individual's needs. The infant-mother relationship is the prototype of instrumentalism. The infant is weak, the mother is strong; the infant must receive, yet cannot give. Whenever an individual enters a relationship with the objective of satisfying his or her own needs and also the needs of others, it is a *mutual* relationship. Friendship and marriage represent mutualism and sexual intercourse is probably the prototype of mutualism. Whenever an individual's objective is to satisfy the needs of others, it is a *vectorial* relationship. Parenthood is the prototype of vectorialism; parents are strong, infants are weak; parents give love and support and protect their children.

In normal families, parents are perceived by their children as strong and friendly adults who relate to each other in a *mutual,* give and get manner and have a *vectorial* attitude toward the child, regardless of what the child may be or do. Parental love is unconditional; the smaller and weaker the child, the more vectorial the parental attitude.

The intrafamilial relationship that produces schizophrenia does not fall into the usual descriptive categories of rejection, overprotection, overindulgence, and so on. The schizogenic family relationship represents a *reversal* of *social positions* and, as a result, causes in the mind of the child who will become schizophrenic a confusion in social roles of age, sex, family position, and so on.

Mother confuses the child by presenting herself as a martyr. She appears to be strong, for she controls the entire family and imposes her will on everyone in the household. She does it in a protective-hostile manner with the child: she tells the child that he is weak, sick, stupid, or ugly, and that she must protect him and do things for him. Yet she presents herself as a self-sacrificing, suffering, almost dying person.

She cannot tolerate any independence, any growth of the child, any success not brought about by mother. The mother is possessive, controls her children's lives, and demands from the child an unlimited love, gratitude, and self-sacrifice for the self-sacrificing tyrant-martyr mother.

The future schizophrenic starts his life in the same way as does any other child. He is helpless and depends on aid from outside. His attitude is instrumental, as he depends upon "narcissistic supplies." Soon he cannot fail to realize that there is something wrong with his parents. The child lives under the threat of loss of his martyr-type mother and nonparticipant baby-father. All schizophrenics, as Sullivan amply observed (1953), are panic-stricken. The child begins to worry about his parents and takes on a premature and much too costly protective hypervectorial attitude toward them. In order to survive, he must protect his protectors. *Vectoriasis praecox* (my name for schizophrenia) sometimes begins very early and depletes the child's mental resources (Wolman, 1966, 1970).

Certainly no woman could destroy her child without the active or tacit approval of her husband, and the fathers of schizophrenics participate in the development of schizophrenia in offspring. The father-mother relationship causes the woman to demand from the child what she failed to get from her husband.

When the "mutual" interparental relationship fails, chances are that mother will develop an instrumental, exploitative attitude toward the child.

The fathers trigger the tragic involvement. They expect the child to give them what they failed to receive from their wives. Most of these fathers are seductive to children of both sexes, spreading confusion with regard to age and sex identification. Some of them fight against their own wives and children and some schizophrenic families live under the father's tyranny in terror.

Schizophrenia has been thus interpreted as an *escape for survival.* It is a process of downward adjustment in an irrational struggle to stay alive. The schizophrenic withdraws from social contacts, avoids emotional involvement, and regresses into a lower level of intellectual functioning, as if acting on an unconscious belief that this is the only way to survive.

I distinguished five levels and several syndromes of hypervectorial (schizotype) disorders. In the hypervectorial disorders the *neurotic* stage includes phobic, neurasthenic, and obsessive-compulsive patterns. The schizoid *character neurosis* corresponds to what is usually called the schizoid personality. The next level in schizophrenic deterioration is *latent schizophrenia,* which represents the individual who is still in control but who is on the verge of breakdown. Next comes manifest schizophrenia, called *vectoriasis praecox.* The last *dementive level* represents the end of decline and a complete collapse of personality structure. All five levels represent an ever-growing dysbalance of cathexis of sexual and hostile impulses.

The decline of the controlling force of the ego is the most significant determinant of each level. As long as the ego exercises control, it is neurosis. When the ego comes to terms with the symptoms, it is character neurosis. When the ego is on the verge of collapse, it is latent psychosis. When the ego fails, it is manifest psychosis, or full-blown schizophrenia in one of its four syndromes. Finally, a complete dilapidation of the ego and behavior on the *id* level is typical of the severely deteriorated, dementive stage.

Schizophrenia and Intellectual Functions

It is typical for the hypervectorial (that is, schizophrenic) type thought process to confuse and to merge and combine several nonrelated issues. On milder neurotic, character neurotic, and latent psychotic levels the judgment of the hypervectorials is usually *contaminated.* As their mental health deteriorates, their judgment ability deteriorates, and there is a growing tendency to confuse wish with reality. The *intellectual abilities* of manifest schizophrenia fluctuate, and the same person may obtain different scores on mental tests. Their attention span on prepsychotic levels is quite high, and they may perceive minute details, but they have a limited ability to establish hierarchic order of what was perceived. The schizophrenic mind works as a camera and unselectively registers everything in its field of vision, but it is unable to distinguish between relevant and irrelevant issues. On prepsychotic—that is, on neurotic and character neurotic and latent psychotic levels—there is a progressing tendency for inconsistent communication and descriptions in a most detailed manner. Paranoid schizophrenics are unable to distinguish between real events and their imagination. Catatonic schizophrenics live in fear of letting their emotions go loose, and therefore refrain from any action. However, when they make good progress in psychotherapy, as I saw on several occasions, paranoid and catatonic schizophrenics have adequately restored their intellectual functions.

I cannot say the same about hebephrenics who regress to primary and irrational ways of thinking. The disturbance in reality testing and in cognitive functions and reasoning is quite pronounced; the recovery of hebephrenics and of simple-deteriorated schizophrenics is exceedingly difficult and not always possible.

There is little, if any, hope for schizophrenics who end up in the fifth, lowest level of dementia. In terms of personality dynamics, *dementia* represents decay and destruction of a human personality structure. Apparently, in the fifth or dementive level of schizophrenia, there is just *id*. Ego and superego do not interfere and perhaps are nonexistent. Imagine a neonate, and imagine that he grows physically and lives on the pleasure principle (in essence, the principle of immediate gratification of needs). Repetitive movements, aimless activity, mannerisms, and no control of bowels and bladder remind one of severe mental defectives.

One may therefore conclude that milder levels of mental disorder have little, if anything, to do with one's intelligence. It may be true, however, that even mildly disturbed individuals, called neurotic, often act in an irrational manner and fail in their endeavors. They may act in a rational manner in nonemotional, conflict-free areas, and fail to use their intelligence in emotionally laden fields. Thus, though their level of intelligence is not impaired by neurosis, their ability to *apply* their intelligence might be substantially reduced. Similar observations have been derived in therapy with depressed patients: on prepsychotic levels, depressed patients' intelligence is not impaired, but it might become affected by manifest manic-depressive psychosis.

Severe mental disorders definitely affect intellectual functioning, especially when they hurt a not-yet developed personality structure. Returning to the hammer-anvil pictorial presentation, one must be aware of the fact that in early childhood the anvil is quite fragile, and the earlier the blows, the more severe is the damage.

Early Deprivation

In one area, intelligence and mental health are closely related—namely, in early childhood deprivation. Several researchers adduced convincing evidence regarding the impact of early deprivation on both mental health and intelligence.

Horney described two maternity wards. In one ward the nurses were instructed to take care of the newborn infants in a matter-of-fact manner. In the second ward they were instructed to take care of the infants in an affectionate and cheerful manner; whenever they had a free minute, the nurses picked up the infants, smiled, cuddled, and talked to them. The researchers found a clear difference in the growth and development of the infants: the infants in the smiling ward grew faster, better, and were more healthy (Horney, 1939).

Several years ago, reports arrived that a well-established institution for foundlings in a Latin American country had a high mortality rate for infants. A committee of physicians was sent to discover the causes of mortality. The investigators discovered that the staff was efficient, the hygiene immaculate, and the care perfect. However, something strange attracted the attention of the visitors—namely, the mechanization of child care. Every nurse took care of eight babies; she had no time to show attention or to display affection for the infants. The nurses worked like robots, feeding the babies, changing diapers, taking physical care of them, but leaving them alone. The infants grew in a sterile atmosphere: there was neither cuddling nor affection. Most of the infants lay prostrate in their cribs, wailing and whimpering, and many of them developed all types of diseases. The infants had no resistance to the diseases, and some of them behaved as if they wished to die. The inability to laugh and play, the lack of language development, and mental marasm, was described by Dr. Spitz (1945) as "hospitalism." *Hospitalism* indicates a set of symptoms caused by lack of attention, affection, and approval.

Karen Horney (1939) maintained that the fundamental need of human beings is *to be accepted,* to receive love, and to obtain approval of parents or parental substitutes. Certainly it is important to gain satisfaction in the form of food, shelter, and so on, but the feeling of *being accepted,* called by Horney *safety,* seems to be far more important than the immediate receiving of gratification. H. S. Sullivan (1953) followed a similar line of reasoning. Sullivan felt that children who receive milk without affection develop tensions and anxiety. Anxiety, caused by conflict between the desire to receive gratification of primary needs and the inability to accept them because of parental disapproval, may not enable some children to develop into normal adults.

Apparently, human beings cannot live alone. Normal social development is predetermined by the degree of parental acceptance. Children brought up by rejecting or overdemanding parents enter kindergarten or school already harmed, and they may not be able to develop wholesome social relations with peers. These children don't trust themselves, or they don't trust other people, or they are afraid to show affection. Many people are unable to develop good social relations with their friends, acquaintances, and relatives just because they are afraid to be hurt, and thus they withdraw or develop hostile attitudes toward people.

A newborn child is narcissistic, Freud wrote, which means that his entire libido is invested in or directed toward himself. This *primary narcissism* is normal for a little child who cannot survive unless he is a selfish, narcissistic creature. However, if he receives a sufficient amount of attention from loving parents, part of his libido becomes invested (or, as Freud called it, *cathected*) in the people who have given him this love. In normal individuals the libido is balanced, partly cathected in themselves and partly in others. This balance is necessary for survival. An individual who has no libido invested in himself would not care about himself, would not do anything to protect his own life, and may become a menace to himself. Inadequate self-cathexis of libido or inadequate self-love may be dangerous to one's survival.

INFANTILE AUTISM AND SCHIZOPHRENIA

It is my contention that an extremely inadequate supply of love or a total lack of love given to the child during the earliest days of life can adversely affect the child's mental growth. I believe that the so-called autism is precisely such a case. It seems to me that *infantile autism* is merely a syndrome of childhood schizophrenia (Mahler, 1952; Rimland, 1964; Wolman, 1970).

A schizophrenic child is a child, and growth and maturational processes complicate the clinical picture. As a result, there are several schizo-type-behavioral patterns in childhood, depending on the age of the child, sex, severity of damage, level of development, specific family influences, and so on.

One important distinction should be made when attempting to relate childhood schizophrenia to adult schizophrenia. Schizophrenia in adulthood is a failure of the impoverished ego. The ego has lost most of its resources in object cathexis, has been hard pressed ("overdemanded") by the superego to control its id, failed in that, and finally is unable to control the id and ceases to be the steering wheel of the organism. In childhood schizophrenic disorders, the ego has never had the chance to assume that role. Schizophrenia in infancy or *vectoriasis praecocissima is a mental catastrophy that takes place even before the ego has the opportunity to grow and to assert control over the id.* It is not easy, therefore, to divide this earliest point of schizophrenia into the clinical syndromes, such as catatonic, paranoid, and so on.

The symptomatology of schizophrenia in adults has been presented in order of increasing severity ending in the dementive level (Wolman, 1966). Analysis of the symptomatology of infantile schizophrenia is made in reverse order, starting with the most severe syndromes. The logic of such an order is obvious. In regard to adults, the assumption is that personality structure is regressed; in childhood schizophrenia, the growth has been prevented.

As a rule, the earlier the damage is caused, the more it affects the personality. Accordingly, the following types or degrees of severity of childhood schizophrenia are closely related to the age of onset of the damage.

The first and most severe level, *pseudo-amentive schizophrenia,* roughly corresponds to dementive schizophrenia in adults, the last and most severe level of regression. The second and slightly less severe level is *autistic schizophrenia,* which corresponds to simple deterioration and hebephrenia in adults. The third level, in order of decreasing severity, is *symbiotic schizophrenia,* more or less corresponding to catatonia. The fourth level, *aretic schizophrenia,* corresponds to some extent to the adult paranoid schizophrenia.

The proposed four types of infantile schizophrenia correspond to the stages and manners in which the hypervectorial disorder was produced. Pseudo-amentive childhood schizophrenia is formed on a preverbal, pre-ego formation level.

The three other types are formed slightly later, but all of them originate in the first two years of life.

Childhood schizophrenia follows the general schizophrenic principle of downward adjustment or regression for survival. All stages and phases of the hypervectorial disorders follow the same main principles of giving up of one's libidinal resources and, as a result, impoverishment of one's ego.

Schizophrenia in childhood is even more variated than in adult years. When a storm breaks young trees and saplings, no one can predict how each tree will look afterward. Some may be cut in two; some, fortunately, may lose only a few branches; some may survive the damage, while others may be completely destroyed, uprooted, or blown away.

All schizophrenic children are children whose childhood has been taken away—they are *children without childhood,* their *vectoriasis* (schizophrenia) is *praecocissima.*

I use the terms autism, infantile autism, and autistic schizophrenia as synonymous to describe a severe syndrome of infantile schizophrenia. Thus the following discussion will be limited to certain interpretations of this particular syndrome.

I believe that autism is a withdrawal mechanism. The archaic ego, barely formed in the first year of life, withdraws from contact with the outer world, which does not supply supportive libido cathexes. Autism is morbid, but it is a *morbid adjustment* for survival. The child blocks out emotions and withdraws from social contact. He fears people, because any contacts he has had have been painful and horrifying. Whenever mother gave milk, she scolded; whenever the infant called for help, mother became furious; whenever he cried at night, mother and father became mad (see Rimland, 1964).

No child is born autistic. Autism is a part of the schizophrenic downward adjustment; it is a withdrawal in order to avoid more damage. The child is overwhelmed by hostile attitudes and has no alternative but to surrender; there is no use to fight against mother. The autistic child is a child who has given up growth, desire, initiative, emotions, and social contacts in order to survive. When it is impossible to obtain approval for one's actions, inactivity is the only possible avenue of existence.

Apparently, intelligence and other mental functions are not totally separate entities independent from environmental influences. As previously mentioned, even the best seed will not turn into a plant if it was placed in arid soil. Innate abilities, big and small, may never come to fruition in a destructive environment. The earlier in life the hammer hits, the greater the damage. In some instances the blow can be devastating and the destruction irreversible to both intelligence and mental health.

REFERENCES

Albert, R. S. (1975). Toward a behavioral definition of genius. *American Psychologist, 30,* 140–151.

Allison, J. (1978). Clinical contributions of the Wechsler Adult Intelligence Scale. In B. B. Wolman (Ed.), *Clinical diagnosis of mental disorders.* New York: Plenum.

Anderson, H. H. (1959). *Creativity and its cultivation.* New York: Harper & Row.

Balthazar, E. E., & Stevens, H. A. (1975). *The emotionally disturbed, mentally retarded: A historical and contemporary perspective.* Englewood-Cliffs, NJ: Prentice-Hall.

Barclay, A. (1983). Testing the mentally retarded. In B. B. Wolman (Ed.), *International encyclopedia of psychiatry, psychology, psychoanalysis, & neurology* (Progress Volume). New York: Aesculapius.

Binet, A., & Simon, T. (1905). Méthodes nouvelles pour le diagnostic du niveau intellectuel des anormaux. *Année Psychologique, 11,* 191–244.

Black, F. W. (1976). Cognitive deficits in patients with unilateral war-related frontal lobe lesions. *Journal of Clinical Psychology, 32,* 366–372.

Bloom, A. R. (1977). Genius. In B. B. Wolman (Ed.), *International encyclopedia of psychiatry, psychology, psychoanalysis, & neurology* (Vol. 5). New York: Aesculapius.

Boll, T. J. (1978). Diagnosing brain impairment. In B. B. Wolman (Ed.), *Clinical diagnosis of mental disorders: A handbook.* New York: Plenum.

Bornstein, R. A., & Matarazzo, J. D. (1982). Wechsler VIQ differences in cerebral dysfunction: A literature review with emphasis on sex differences. *Journal of Clinical Neuropsychology, 4,* 319–334.

Bouchard, J. J., & McGue, M. (1981). Familial studies of intelligence: A review. *Science, 212,* 1055–1059.

Burt, C. (1972). Inheritance of general intelligence. *American Psychologist, 27,* 175–190.

Cattell, R. B. (1971). *Abilities: Their structure, growth and function.* Boston: Houghton Mifflin.

Cordes, C. (1983). Jensen refines theory linking g-factor to processing speed. *APA Monitor, 14,* 3–20.

Dixon, L. K., & Johnson, R. C. (1980). *The roots of individuality.* Monterey, CA: Brooks-Cole.

Dohrenwend, B. P. (1977). Socioeconomic states and mental disorders. In B. B. Wolman (Ed.), *International encyclopedia of psychiatry, psychology, psychoanalysis, & neurology* (Vol. 10). New York: Aesculapius.

Freud, S. (1935). *Introductory lectures to psychoanalysis.* New York: Perma Giants. (Original work published 1916.)

Freud, S. (1939). *An outline of psychoanalysis.* New York: Norton. (Originial work published 1938.)

Fuller, J. L., & Simmel, E. C. (1980). *Behavior genetics: Principles and applications.* Hillsdale, NJ: Erlbaum.

Grossman, H. J. (Ed.) (1977). *Manual on terminology and classification in mental retardation.* Washington, DC: American Association on Mental Deficiency.

Heber, R. (Ed.) (1961). *A manual on terminology and classification in mental retardation* (2nd ed.). Washington, DC: American Association on Mental Deficiency.

Hebb, D. O. (1942). The effect of early and late brain injury upon test scores and the nature of normal adult intelligence. *Proceedings of the American Philosophical Society, 85,* 275–292.

Hobbs, N. (Ed.). (1975). *Issues in the classification of children.* San Francisco: Jossey-Bass.

Hollingshead, A. B., & Redlich, F. C. (1958). *Social class and mental illness.* New York: Wiley.

Horn, J. M., Loehlin, J. C., & Willerman, L. (1980). Aspects of the inheritance of intellectual abilities. *Behavior Genetics, 12,* 479–516.

Horney, K. (1939). *New ways in psychoanalysis.* New York: Norton.

Jensen, A. R. (1969). How much can we boost IQ and scholastic achievement? *Harvard Educational Review, 39,* 1–123.

Jensen, A. R. (1980). *Bias in mental testing.* New York: Macmillan.

Karp, E., Morgenstern, M., & Michal-Smith, H. (1978). Diagnosing mental deficiency. In B. B. Wolman (Ed.), *Clinical diagnosis of mental disorders.* New York: Plenum.

Klineberg, O. (1931). A study of psychological differences between "racial" and national groups in Europe. *Archives of Psychology, 20,* 1–58.

Kris, E. (1952). *Psychoanalytic interpretation of art.* New York: International Universities Press.

La Vietes, R. (1978). Mental retardation: Psychological treatment. In B. B. Wolman (Ed.), *Handbook of treatment of mental disorders in childhood and adolescence.* Englewood Cliffs, NJ: Prentice-Hall.

Leland, H. (1973). Adaptive behavior and mentally retarded behavior. In G. Tarjan, R. K. Eyman, & C. E. Meyers (Eds.), *Sociobehavioral studies in mental retardation.* Washington, DC: American Association for Mental Retardation.

Leland, H. (1981). Assessment of adaptive behavior. In B. Bracken & K. Paget (Eds.), *Psychoeducational assessment of preschool and primary age children.* New York: Grune & Stratton.

Leland, H. (1983). Adaptive behavior measurement. In B. B. Wolman (Ed.), *International encyclopedia of psychiatry, psychology, psychoanalysis and neurology* (Progress Volume). New York: Aesculapius.

Leland, H. et al. (1967). Adaptive behavior: A new dimension in the classification of mentally retarded. *Mental Retardation Abstracts, 4,* 359–387.

Lombroso, C. (1907). *Genio degenarozione.* Milan: Sandron.

Mahler, M. S. (1952). On child psychosis and schizophrenia: Autistic and symbiotic infantile psychoses. *The Psychoanalytic Study of the Child, 7,* 286–305.

Maslow, A. (1970). *Motivation and personality* (rev. ed.). New York: Harper & Row.

Matarazzo, J. D. (1972). *Wechsler's measurement and appraisal of adult intelligence* (5th ed.). New York: Oxford University Press.

Meier, J. H. (1977). Mental retardation. In B. B. Wolman (Ed.), *International encyclopedia of psychiatry, psychology, psychoanalysis, & neurology* (Vol. 7). New York: Aesculapius.

Morrow, J. P., & Morrow, R. S. (1977). Intelligence theories. In B. B. Wolman (Ed.), *International encyclopedia of psychiatry, psychology, psychoanalysis, & neurology* (Vol. 6). New York: Aesculapius.

Oakland, T. (Ed.). (1977). *Educational and psychological assessment of minority children.* New York: Bruner-Mazel.

Oakland, T. (Ed.). (1980). *Non-biased assessment.* Minneapolis: University of Minnesota Test.

Padilla, E. R., & Ross, S. *The performance of Mexican children and adolescents on the WISC-R.*

Ramey, C. T., & Baker-Ward, L. (1983). Early experience and mild mental retardation In B. B. Wolman (Ed.), *International encyclopedia of psychiatry, psychology, psychoanalysis, & neurology:* (Progress Volume). New York: Aesculapius.

Rice, J., Cloninger, C. R., & Reich, T. (1980). Analysis of behavioral traits in the presence of cultural transmission and assortative mating: Applications to IQ and SES. *Behavior Genetics, 10,* 73–92.

Rimland, B. (1964). *Infantile autism.* New York: Appleton-Century-Crofts.

Scarr, S. (1981). Testing for children. *American Psychologist, 36,* 1159–1166.

Scarr, S. & Weinberg, R. A. (1978). The influence of "family background" on intellectual attainment. *American Sociological Review, 43,* 674–692.

Shockley, W. (1972). Dysgenics, geneticity, raceology: A challenge to the intellectual responsibility of educators. *Phi Beta Kappa, 53,* 297–307.

Spearman, C. (1904). *The abilities of man.* London: Macmillan.

Spitz, R. (1945). Hospitalism—An inquiry into the genesis of psychiatric conditions in early childhood. *The Psychoanalytic Study of the Child, 1,* 53–74.

Srole, L., et al. (1962). *Mental health in metropolis.* New York: McGraw-Hill.

Sullivan, H. S. (1953). *The interpersonal theory of psychiatry.* New York: Norton.

Taylor, H. F. (1980). *The IQ game: A methodological inquiry into the heredity-environment controversy.* New Brunswick, NJ: Rutgers University Press.

Terman, L. M. (1916). *The measurement of intelligence.* Boston: Houghton Mifflin.

Terman, L. M. (Ed.). (1925–1947). *Genetic studies of genius* (4 vols). Palo Alto, CA: Stanford University Press.

Terman, L. M. & Oden, M. H. (1959). *Genetic studies of genius* (Vol. 5). The gifted group at midlife. Palo Alto, CA: Stanford University Press.

Thurstone, L. L. (1935). *The vector mind: Multiple factor analysis for the isolation of primary traits.* Chicago: University of Chicago Press.

Van der Flier, H. (1982). Deviant response patterns and comparability of test scores. *Journal of Cross-Cultural Psychology, 13,* 267–298.

Webster, T. G. (1963). Problems of the emotional development of young and retarded children. *American Journal of Psychiatry, 110,* 37–43.

Wechsler, D. (1944). *The measurement of adult intelligence.* Baltimore, MD: Williams & Wilkins.

Wolman, B. B. (1951). The Jewish adolescent: A bibliographical review of the current psychological and educational literature in USA and Israel. *Jewish Social Studies, 13,* 333–344.

Wolman, B. B. (1966). *Vectoriasis praecox or the group of schizophrenias.* Springfield, IL: Thomas.

Wolman, B. B. (1967). Creative art and psychopathology. *American Imago, 24,* 140–150.

Wolman, B. B. (1970). *Children without childhood.* New York: Grune & Stratton.

Wolman, B. B. (1973). *Call no man normal.* New York: International Universities Press.

Wolman, B. B. (Ed.). (1978). *Clinical diagnosis of mental disorders.* New York: Plenum.

Wolman, B. B. (Ed.). (1982). *Handbook of developmental psychology.* Englewood Cliffs, NJ: Prentice-Hall.

Wolman, B. B. (1982). Die kreative Kraft des Unbewussten. In G. Ammon (Ed.), *Handbuch der dynamischen Psychiatrie* (Vol. 2). München: Reinhardt.

TWENTY-ONE

CLINICAL APPLICATIONS

IRLA LEE ZIMMERMAN

University of California Neuropsychiatric Institute
Los Angeles, California

JAMES M. WOO-SAM

Orange County Mental Health Clinic
Anaheim, California

In the *Dictionary of Psychological and Psychoanalytic Terms, clinical* is defined as:

> Characterizing the method of studying the individual as a unique whole. Specific behaviors are observed and specific traits may be inferred, but the goal is that of understanding (and helping) the particular individual. [English & English, 1958, p. 90]

As far as the process itself, *clinical* implies:

> Relying upon the *intuitive* judgment of the clinician rather than upon measurement; the intuitive integration of measurement findings with direct observations. [English & English, 1958, p. 90]

Does the administration of an intelligence test permit a clinician to observe specific behaviors, and can these observed behaviors lead to the inferring of specific traits that characterize an individual as unique? Clearly, the very process of testing an individual adult or child provides the clinician an opportunity to observe behavioral reactions. However, two questions must be asked. (1) Does the evaluation process provide a situation for the observation of a broad sampling of behavior? (2) Do these observed behaviors have relevance that allow for description of the individual as unique?

In clinical practice, these are not taken as assumptions, but as givens. Consider, for example, a not uncommon situation: the WISC-R is given to two 15-year-old boys. One obtains a full-scale score of 98, the other a full-scale score of 100. Can the clinician make inferences on the basis of the test performances that distinguish between the two boys? The clinician who does not or cannot should not be testing.

The following sampling of quotes provides a historical perspective of the way various authors have sought to conceptualize intelligence tests as providing more than IQ scores.

Although no theoretical framework was provided, Downey (1917) discussed the extension of the Binet Scales for use with adults:

> In conclusion, I would emphasize the value of the . . . tests as a direct aid in analysis of an individual's make-up. . . . This value would outweigh that of expression of the results in terms of an intelligence quotient. [1917, p. 155]

At the other end of the age scale, Stutsman, in writing of her observations in administering the Merrill Palmer noted:

> Many responses threw light on the child's environmental adjustment and many reactions give an insight into temperamental make-up, revealing what a mine of possibilities were ignored by one who utilized the test situation to get differences in mental development alone. [1931, p. 243]

Following the introduction of the scale that was to bear his name, Wechsler (1944) drew on his extensive clinical experience to arrive at the following hypotheses:

> Although the primary purpose of an intelligence examination is to give a valid and reliable measure of the subject's global capacity, it is reasonable to expect that any well conceived intelligence scale will furnish its user with something more than an IQ or MA. In point of fact, most intelligence examinations, when administered individually, make available certain amount of data regarding the testee's mode of reaction, his special abilities and not infrequently, some indicators of his personality traits. [1944, p. 146]

Cronbach, acknowledged as an elder statesman in the field of measurement, concluded (of the Wechsler):

> The test is, however, a distillation of clinical experiences, and this contributes both to its strengths and to its weaknesses. It is a useful sample of complex behavior in which emotional and intellectual factors are intertwined. [1960, p. 202]

In his review of the measurement of personality from the Wechsler scales, Frank noted:

> Although the tests Wechsler developed are entitled tests of "intelligence," it is apparent that in most clinical situations, certainly as regards the evaluation of adolescents and adults, the psychologist is equally (if not more) interested in deriving some hypotheses regarding the personality of the individual he is testing as he is his level of intelligence, per se. [1970, p. 185]

Sattler pointed out such features in the testing of children:

> The examiner has numerous opportunities to observe children's behavior in the course of administering the Stanford-Binet. Because there are varied test materials, children have the opportunity to react in many different ways, and in the process may reveal some facets of their personality. [1982, p. 131]

In essence, the above authors have voiced the conviction that intelligence tests do provide the medium for the observation of personality traits. The clinician's role is to use these observations to distinguish one individual from another.

Attempts to provide a theoretical basis for the systematic observation and interpretation of tests of intelligence can be traced to the pioneering work of Rapaport and his colleagues (1945, 1946). Their approach was embedded in psychoanalytic theory stressing ego psychology, which conceptualizes the individual as a whole, whose behavior is adaptive as well as pathological, with an organized, enduring ego structure. Since cognitive functioning is a prominent aspect of ego structure, intelligence is an essential element of personality functioning. Schafer summarized these issues:

> Patterns of past intellectual achievement, of current problem-solving methods, and of verbalizations, as these are elicited by a standardized intelligence test, almost always illuminate important dimensions of personality, especially if they are approached with relevant concepts from psychoanalytic ego psychology. Beyond establishing general intellectual level, these cognitive patterns reflect established defense and adaptive policies, characteristic rigidity, flexibility or looseness of ego integration, and the degree to which controls and defense are undermined and the ordinary impersonal, detached intellectual functions are neurotically or psychotically invaded by primitive representations, conflicts, and narcissistic preoccupations. [1954, p. 426]

Discussing children, Fromm pointed out:

> Intelligence is a *function* of the total personality, mutually interdependent with education, life experiences, emotions, conscious and unconscious wishes and yearnings, attitudes, and conflicts. [1960, p. 225]

Fromm used this concept as a basis for developing a system of test interpretation for the Cattell and Binet scales.

Waite attempted to delineate the specific contribution of the intelligence test (as compared to projective measures) in understanding personality. Unlike the Rorschach, a test such as the Wechsler,

> by the nature of the types of response processes it demands of the patient, discourages regression. It requires the application of purely reality-oriented thought processes which are addressed to the external problem at hand and which are uncontaminated by trends in unconscious fantasy life. [1961, p. 92]

By 1978, Allison could summarize as follows:

> The intelligence test, rather than being viewed as a catalogue of relatively inde-
> pendent, specific traits or abilities, now could be seen as reflecting meaningful
> clusters or configurations of personality organizations. [1978, p. 356]

The dynamic theorizing just presented is by no means limited to those with
psychoanalytic leanings. Even Piaget, writing from a developmental framework,
could point out:

> Affective life and cognitive life . . . are inseparable although distinct. They are
> inseparable because all interaction with the environment involves both a structuring
> and a valuation, but they are none the less distinct, since these two aspects of
> behavior cannot be reduced to one another. . . . An act of intelligence . . . involves
> . . . an internal regulation (the value of the solutions taught and of the objects
> concerned in the search), but these two controls are of an affective nature and
> remain comparable with all other regulations of this type. Similarly, the perceptual
> or intellectual elements which we find in all manifestations of emotion involve
> cognition in the same way as any other perceptual or intelligent reactions. [1950,
> p. 48]

The basic assumption that personality and other behavior characteristics are
revealed in the act of responding to a test of intelligence will be explored in the
next section.

HISTORICAL SURVEY OF RESEARCH

In this section, the research literature bearing on the interaction between intelligence and personality is reviewed.

As early as 1914, Hart and Spearman (1914) began to study the selective
effects of psychosis and apparently degenerative mental diseases on different
mental functions. Binet himself had observed that psychotics and chronic alcoholics "scattered" their successes and failures over a larger number of age
levels than did the mentally retarded (Wells, 1927). Pressey and Cole (1918)
attempted to quantify the indices of variation seen in the scatter of scores on a
Binet by giving added weights to passes and failures according to their distance
from the individual's mean. Wells (1927) confirmed the likelihood of extreme
scatter in psychotic adult records, but at the same time warned that scatter need
not mean pathology. Hunt (1936) reviewed more than 20 articles concerned with
scatter, confirming selective deficit in function. However, Harris and Shakow
(1937, 1938) were able to point out in their review that scatter could not
distinguish between the test results of retarded, neurotic, and normal children.
By using an adequate control group of normal adults, they found that only
mental age related to the amount of scatter. Whatever hope remained for the
diagnostic value of using scatter on the Binet suffered a setback by the study

of Kendig and Richmond (1940), again using a control group of normals. The selective effects of mental disorder on the Binet could not be confirmed for dementia praecox, although extreme variation seemed more characteristic of the patient group. An even more detailed examination of mental disorders, by Roe and Shakow (1942), introduced the concept of grouping Binet items according to content, such as conceptual thinking, associative thinking, and learned material. Correcting for age, they were unable to find specific profiles, but presented a theory of mental deterioration in a sequence from the most vulnerable, conceptual thinking, to the least, vocabulary and old learning. The suggestion that vocabulary was less vulnerable in mental disorder was actually antidated by the work of Babcock (1930) and others. Using the Binet vocabulary as an estimate of the mental age of the patient, she compared this with a variety of other tests considered most vulnerable to mental disorder or brain damage. Results over the years were equivocal.

Despite negative and equivocal results, the hypothesis of selective deficit was not questioned. Instead, clinicians faulted the measuring devices. The Binet, then the most widely used test, was criticized on the basis of its omnibus format, random placement of items, verbal focus, child-oriented content, and inadequate norms for adults. As Hunt (1936) cogently remarked, the Binet was an "exceedingly blunt instrument."

With the introduction of the Wechsler Bellevue (Wechsler, 1939), much of the criticism surrounding the measuring instruments abated. Created by a clinical psychologist who had spent years in the study of psychiatric patients, the Wechsler Bellevue was considered both a measure of intelligence and a clinicodiagnostic device. It provided separate norms for adults and children on a variety of both verbal and performance tasks, thereby answering the major objections to the Binet. The selective deficit hypothesis was presented in the form of a ratio of subtests that would differentiate between abilities less vulnerable to deterioration and those that did not "hold up." Scatter was now defined as a two-point difference between subtests, and various diagnostic groups were considered to demonstrate different scatter patterns. Furthermore, Wechsler recommended analyzing the actual responses given (qualitative or content analysis) for their diagnostic import. By 1958, Wechsler devoted an entire section of his book (Wechsler, 1958) to the clinical interpretation of the latest form of the Wechsler.

Over the ensuing years the Wechsler Bellevue and its revisions (Wechsler Adult Intelligence Scale, or WAIS, 1955; Wechsler Adult Intelligence Scale—Revised, or WAIS-R, 1982), and the children's versions (Wechsler Intelligence Scale for Children, or WISC, 1949; Wechsler Preschool and Primary Scale of Intelligence, or WPPSI, 1967; Wechsler Intelligence Scale for Children—Revised, or WISC-R, 1974), have been subjected to countless studies, a number of which focus on personality variables. Summaries of these studies include reviews covering the adult versions by Rabin and his coworkers (for example, Guertin, Ladd, Frank, Rabin, & Hiester, 1966; Guertin, Ladd, Frank, Rabin, & Hiester, 1971; Rabin, 1945), while Littell (1960), Zimmerman and Woo-Sam (1972), and Woo-Sam and Zimmerman (1973) covered studies focusing on children. The research that deals with aspects of personality ranges from studies of personality traits and attributes (such as anxiety, impulsivity, and cognitive styles) to comparisons of the characteristics of diagnostic groups (such as schizophrenic, juvenile delinquent, organic, neurotic, and learning disabled).

The introduction of the Wechsler scales reinforced the old belief that clinical groups would have greater scatter than normals, a difference presumed to have diagnostic significance. Results with the WISC-R are representative of outcome for all Wechsler forms. To begin, the meaning of test scatter on the WISC-R was clarified as Kaufman (1976b) presented results for "normal" children, that is, those of the standardization sample. His findings revealed that the presumably normal, flat profile, in which subtest scores deviated by less than three points from the child's own mean, occurred in only 19% of the normal population. Interestingly, the same percentage of flat profiles has been reported by Vance, Wallbrown, and Blaha (1978) in their classification of profiles of children with reading disabilities.

Any lingering hope that the large amount of scatter seen in the test results of normal children would at least be surpassed by that of clinical samples was demolished in a review of two thousand cases by Zimmerman and Woo-Sam (1978), as well as by further studies by Gutkin (1979) and Hale and Landino (1981), among others. All three studies found that emotionally disturbed, delinquent, learning-disabled, retarded, and brain-damaged children showed no more or less scatter than did the standardization sample. In other words, extensive scatter proved to be both typical and "normal," and thus of limited use as a diagnostic feature.

As scatter proved to be of little diagnostic value, researchers turned to schemes that combined the subtests into categories such as those suggested by Bannatyne (1974). The spatial > conceptual > sequencing > acquired knowledge profile was assumed characteristic of learning-disabled children. However, recent studies found the pattern unable to identify individual learning-disabled children and to be equally characteristic of emotionally handicapped children (Groff & Hubble, 1981; Thompson, 1981). Kaufman and Reynolds (1982) concluded almost morosely that Bannatyne scores had no future either for differential diagnosis or to contribute new knowledge to the field.

Finally, Kavale and Forness (1984) explored the differential diagnosis of learning disability on the Wechsler scales, using the technique of meta-analysis to provide a quantitative system of the findings from 94 studies. They concluded that "no recategorization, profile, factor cluster, or pattern showed a significant difference between learning disabled and normal samples" (1984, p. 136).

Attempts to generate personality and behavioral descriptions from the Wechsler scales similar to those used with the Minnesota Multiphasic Personality Inventory are relatively rare. The Personality Assessment System (PAS) developed by Gittinger (1967) represents one such approach. Henrichs, Krauskopf, and Amolsch (1982) attempted to develop an atheoretical actuarial method to obtain personality descriptions, which were then compared to the PAS. The two sets of personality descriptions were found to have a distinct resemblance.

Studies exploring the relationship of certain personality characteristics to specific Wechsler subtest performance produced mixed results. Bassett and Gayton (1979) attempted to replicate the search for a relationship between bodily concern (as inferred from sick-bay calls of prisoners) and Object Assembly scores, with negative results. However, Brannigan and Ash (1977) found that impulsive children showed the predicted evidence of poor social judgment as based on their low Comprehension scores. Chavez, Trautt, Brandon, and Steyaert (1983) found no effects from "test anxiety" on WAIS Digit Span and Digit Symbol performance. Yet the premorbid social competence of process schizophrenics was significantly related to their Picture Arrangement scores, in a study by Edinger (1976).

The clinical evaluation of the Wechsler proved discriminating in these studies: Zimmerman and Lambert (1961) were able to distinguish between well-adjusted and disturbed school children on the basis of behavior observed during the administration of the WISC. In a much later study, Zimmerman, Bernstein, and Eiduson (1983) found that behavior ratings made during the administration of the WISC-R to normal (unreferred) 6 year olds were better predictors of both school adjustment and achievement at age 7 than was the IQ alone.

Whether schizophrenic thinking could be reliably determined from responses to WAIS verbal subtests was explored by Bilett, Jones, and Whitaker (1982). Although the sample was small ($n = 12$), ten experienced clinicians were considered "surprisingly accurate" in discriminating schizophrenic from other hospitalized or normal adolescents.

A clinical versus an actuarian approach may favor the latter, particularly with an increase in statistical sophistication. Leli and Felshow (1981) compared clinical judgment to clinical actuarian prediction. Results suggested that an actuarian index should be incorporated into the clinical judgment strategy of psychologists attempting to identify brain impairment. In another study, Leli and Scott (1982) used a discriminate function created from two WAIS indexes of intellectual deterioration, which correctly classified 16 of 17 Alzheimer's disease subjects. Whether brain damage leads to specific WAIS patterns was explored by Milberg, Graffenstein, Lewis, and Rourke (1980), using a discriminant function analysis of the Information, Vocabulary, and Similarities subtests. Temporal lobe versus generalized seizure patterns could be differentiated (hit rate 77%, cross-validation 79%). A language-related memory deficit in temporal lobe epilepsy was hypothesized.

The previous section has provided a survey of current research approaches to inferring personality from tests of intelligence. However, most clinicians use these tests to derive hypotheses, typically qualitative in nature, regarding the subject's personality. The following section describes such a clinical approach.

In the following pages, a potpourri of clinical clues are presented for the Wechsler Intelligence Scale for Children—Revised (WISC-R), focusing particularly on the 12 subtests. The decision to report on the WISC-R is a practical one. Clinical clues are developed from a long period of experience with an instrument. The Wechsler Adult Intelligence Scale, newly revised (WAIS-R) will require time before such material will become available. Meanwhile, these examples, although representing only a small sampling of the rich mine of behavior elicited by the Wechsler, may represent a prototype from which examiners may develop their own contributions.

The WISC-R, like all other Wechsler scales, represents a standardized set of stimuli, typically presented in a specified sequence. Verbal and performance subtests interlace in a predefined order. To the experienced examiner, each subtest has its own contribution. As each subtest is administered, specific behaviors are elicited and may be observed. In the following section, the contribution of the WISC-R subtests are considered in detail as they represent a clinical approach to children's functioning. Each subtest is considered in terms of its position in the scale, its factorial contribution, specificity, and clinical implications.

Needless to say, the primary role of a test of intelligence is just what the name implies, an opportunity to measure intellectual ability, allowing for a comparison of an individual with his or her peers. Proper interpretation of test results must be based on a detailed understanding of the statistical properties of the test, what Kaufman and Reynolds (1983) point out as the "psychometric groundwork for intelligent testing." A naive search for subtest differences (as indicating specific "traits" or skills), even if these are large enough to be statistically rare, not only contribute little to diagnosis, but often result in overlooking the real contribution of the test in understanding the child. In other words, the essence of clinical interpretation is the use of an intelligence scale to obtain information above and beyond that based on an IQ alone. Clearly, obtaining an IQ, far from being the end of the clinician's task, must be considered only the beginning.

Accepting that variation between and among the subtests is a normal feature, and in and of itself of little diagnostic value, it is still essential for the examiner to understand the makeup of the WISC-R before any attempt at interpretation is to begin. A basic understanding is grounded in the factor-analytic studies of Wallbrown, Blaha, Wallbrown, and Engin (1975), Kaufman (1976a), and Silverstein (1977), all of whom used the standardization data to describe the composition of the test. These findings, which will be described for each subtest in turn in the following section, first indicate that the WISC-R is indeed a good measure of intelligence, as determined by the contribution of the subtests to the construct, general intelligence (g) noted in the Wallbrown, Blaha, Wallbrown, and Engin (1975) hierarchical factor-analytic approach. Furthermore, the WISC-R is also measuring the verbal and performance abilities inherent in the dichotomous test format, and paralleled by the first two WISC-R factors, verbal comprehension and perceptual organization. An additional factor described in test results of normal children in the standardization sample as well as a number of samples of minority children and those referred for various reasons, has been labeled Freedom from Distractibility. This factor includes the subtests Arithmetic, Digit Span, and Coding. All the above factors have been confirmed in such widely varied groups as Mexican-American, black, and American Indian (Reschly, 1978; Sandoval, 1982) and referred and clinical groups including the mentally retarded (Van Hagen & Kaufman, 1975), gifted (Karnes & Brown, 1980), learning handicapped (Swerdlik & Schweitzer, 1978; Vance & Wallbrown, 1977), delinquent (Hubble & Groff, 1981), psychiatric (De Horn & Klinge, 1978), and epileptic subjects (Richards, Fowler, Berent, & Boll, 1980).

Another aspect of the WISC-R that is critical in interpreting test findings involves the specificity of the subtests. Specificity describes the ability of each subtest to measure something unique in itself, apart from its general contribution to the measure of general intelligence or the factors just cited. From the findings of Silverstein (1977) and Kaufman (1979), examiners can feel fairly confident in interpreting differences between and among most of the subtests at all age levels. In the following section, the specificity of each subtest in turn will be described. In other words, the analysis of a test protocol must be based on the examiner's awareness of such aspects as the generality of scatter and the specificity of the particular subtest in question. As an aside, it is not surprising that four of the most interpretable subtests, that is, those with the highest subtest specificity, are found in one of the most frequently cited profiles of learning disability, ACID (Arithmetic, Coding, Information, Digit Span) (Ackerman, Dykman, & Peters, 1976).

The above results were cited in some detail because they represent the bedrock of any interpretation of the WISC-R. Scatter and ensuing profile variations represent aspects of individual differences reflected in a child's response to the WISC-R. Children, whether "normal" or subsumed under such diagnostic categories as learning disabled, mentally retarded, brain damaged, or emotionally disturbed, respond differently to a complex measure such as the WISC-R. Such differences, whether we refer to scatter or an interpretation of specific responses, reflect the uniqueness of an individual child, and tell of his or her uniformity and diversity of functioning. Far from idealizing the so-called "flat profile" as normal, the clinician must appreciate the sudden flickers of talent, the strengths and lags represented by the typical uneven profile, whether given by a "normal" child or by one assumed to have problems.

WISC-R ADMINISTRATION: VERBAL VERSUS PERFORMANCE ASPECTS

Before considering the contribution made by each subtest in the WISC-R, a number of aspects specific to the verbal and performance section will be considered.

The verbal subtests require the child to express his or her answers verbally. Part of the focus on interpreting verbal subtests, then, is on what might be considered the continuum of responses. One extreme consists of answers that are "popular" in the sense used in the Rorschach, that is, so commonplace that they seem to be elicited by the question, or are "overlearned" automatically by most children. The other extreme covers responses that are original, neither taught nor expected, sometimes creative, amusing, often "odd." Projection may be involved: a more stereotyped answer has been replaced by an answer drawn from strong feeling or emotion in the child's own life. Unique responses are of clinical value, and should be studied carefully. Often specific questioning about the meaning of a response can develop important information about a child's preoccupations or concerns. The continuum of popular-original answers may relate to Guilford's (1967) concept of "convergent" versus "divergent" thinking. Typically, tests of intelligence measure convergent thinking, so that when a child gives a divergent answer he or she is departing from expected or typical behavior. Because of the format of intelligence tests, then, divergent answers tend to be unusual and even undesirable, as can be seen on such subtests as Arithmetic or Information. However, they may also be witty or amusing, with their own engaging philosophy. For example, responding to Comprehension "Why are criminals locked up?" one child responded wisely, "That's easy. If they weren't locked up they'd just walk right out of jail!" (Flumen & Flumen, 1979, p. 82).

Many other aspects can be observed during the administration of the verbal subtests. For example, how readily does the subject respond to the verbal items? Is he or she sufficiently cooperative to provide a valid test performance? Must questions be repeated? Could this indicate a hearing problem, limited understanding of English, wandering attention, or a low level of comprehension? Or is this a device used to allow the subject more time to think about the question? Does this suggest a suspicious orientation, a search for the "trick" involved because the question is seen as "too easy"? Asking the child to repeat the question can serve as a check both on hearing and on attention and memory.

How much probing is necessary? Must the child be urged to respond? Is he or she apt to fall into an immediate "don't know" before even trying to respond? Can the examiner's insistence on a response reduce a perfectionistic orientation, an unwillingness to guess or to be wrong? Does the subject tend to block on responses ("I know, I just can't think . . .")? Do such approaches characterize initial responses, or are they seen only at the upper limits of the child's ability, where they would, of course, have more adaptive connotations of realistic appraisal of one's abilities?

How does the child express answers? Are there problems in articulation? Difficulties with syntax? A loss of words, a possible aphasia? Do speech patterns suggest a specific background?

How fluent are verbal responses? Are answers expressed in one or two words, or with many? Are responses to the point, or is extraneous information added? Is such information given in a compulsive need to cover all possibilities, or is it completely irrelevant? In either case, do responses suggest any preoccupations of (diagnostic) importance?

If a child must be urged to respond, how close to the mark are his or her guesses? Do they indicate that the unwillingness to respond initially is paired with considerably more knowledge than the child is willing to exhibit without coaxing? How aware is the subject of the adequacy of his or her answers? Is he or she "humiliated" by failing items? Does this lead to expressions of impotence and perplexity that indicate a loss of ability? Are responses perseverated, so that the same answer is given to ensuing questions? How does the child concentrate on questions? Does he or she use special aides, such as closing the eyes, or "writing" on the table with one finger? Can he or she be reassured as to performance, or does he or she brood over failures?

What kinds of verbalizations are seen in the child's responses? Do the questions elicit personal references? Are these indications of immaturity? Does the child seem self-centered, applying everything to him or herself? Or is he or she describing a current, transient crisis? Are responses bizarre, unrealistic, naive, or dependent?

The above are just a sampling of impressions to be obtained during the administration of the verbal subtests. An equally rich pool of observations can be obtained from the performance subtests. For example, comparing responses to verbal and performance tasks can be noted. Are there marked differences in approach to the two kinds of tasks? Does the child seem more at ease with one than the other? Does he or she tend to verbalize while working, naming objects, describing his or her own moves, or merely chattering on about other topics during assembly tasks? Does verbalizing direct his or her moves, or merely describe them?

How quickly does the child understand the various performance tasks? Does he or she need to have instructions repeated for each item? It he or she aware that certain items are timed? Does this upset performance, or enhance it?

Does the child use a trial-and-error approach to assembly tasks, or begin by visualizing the problem before making a move? Does he or she work systematically with swift, sure moves? Does the child recognize the object or picture he or she is working on? Are there specific items or pictures that are misperceived, and can these give a clue as to some preoccupation? Which hand is used? Is there any confusion in handedness?

With the interspersing of verbal and performance subtests, similarities and differences between approaches to the two kinds of tasks tend to be highlighted. For example, some children all but sigh with relief at the change of pace. The profile on the front page of the WISC-R answer blank allows for a picture of verbal versus performance progress. This can be augmented by the construction of a profile in which the subtests are listed in order of administration. Does the curve of scores on the alternating verbal and performance subtests show a relatively flat, a sawtooth, ascending, or decending slope? Such a curve may clarify variations in motivation and attention, or the effects of fatigue on performance.

Information

On the WISC-R, this subtest consists of 30 items, arranged in order of increasing difficulty, which involve the recall of facts sampling a broad range of knowledge. It contributes substantially to the construct of general intelligence (g) and is also an excellent measure of verbal comprehension. Its ample specificity allows the clinician to stand on firm footing in generating hypotheses concerning meanings of high and low scores.

This subtest serves as the introduction to all Wechsler scales, and for good reason. It is probably among the least threatening of all the subtests. The child has little need to expand on responses; a simple one-word answer is usually adequate. Therefore the child who finds it difficult to express himself or herself, or is hesitant to talk, or is shy has a benign introduction to the scale. Initial items call for simple, overlearned responses, guaranteeing early successes and an opportunity for the child to be reassured as to the adequacy of his or her response, and praised or reinforced for successes. At the same time, enough items at the upper level ensure that the child will need to cope with the stress of serially more difficult items. In other words, the child moves from the presumably encouraging effects of initial successes and the examiner's praise and encouragement through items gradually increasing in difficulty. How does the child respond to the combination of pressure and support? Phlegmatically? Calmly? Anxiously? One child rapidly concluded "Getting hard, I can't!" and "You're making them too hard, I won't do any more!" She could not be calmed by the examiner's reassurance that these were items she had not yet learned. Such extreme behavior in the face of frustration accurately indicated future problems in establishing a remedial program.

On the other hand, some children respond initially to information items with brash, self-confident comments ("Easy! . . . cinchy!"), only to find themselves embarrassed when succeeding items prove beyond their ability. Will this provide a learning experience that prepares the child to be more cautious or apprehensive on succeeding subtests? Or does the child find it necessary, after failing questions at the upper limits of information, to "brag" once again of his or her ability on the new easy items of Picture Completion, only to stumble again on items as he or she continues?

Information is also characterized by simple, nonthreatening items, often with school-like implications. Therefore failures can be rationalized as "not taught" yet. The child usually can accept the serial nature of the subtest in which initial overlearned items are eventually followed by items far beyond his or her age level. The parallel to a classroom situation is particularly germane.

The content of items on Information rarely threaten the child, or elicit phobic thoughts. Therefore the examiner would be alert to emotional reactions seen on this subtest. Equally, unusual or bizarre responses are particularly unexpected. These would give evidence of the extent of disturbance and the pervasiveness of emotional problems, in that they might intrude in what is usually a benign setting.

On the other hand, a child may reveal the ability to cope with pressure by his or her response to questions beyond his or her ability. One bright 6 year old, asked why oil floats on water, responded roguishly, "Because it has water wings?"

Other contributions can be gained from this subtest. For example, deviant answers are unusual and might indicate emotional disturbance, or, in contrast, suggest the child's failure to hear the question. (By asking the child to repeat what was just asked, the need for a hearing test might be determined.)

Extremes of attention are also clarified on this subtest. An example is the *boundary* item, where two countries are to be named. Does the child seem satisfied with naming only one, forgetting the second? There are no time limits on this subtest, and questions may be repeated, which may indicate why attention problems need not necessarily lower Information scores.

School attitudes are often clearly indicated on Information, where geography, measurements, history, and science items are administered. Spontaneous comments can reveal the child's feeling about his or her own achievement, or the general demands of the classroom, such as problems in remembering names and dates.

In all, Information represents a simple, nonthreatening introduction to the WISC-R and a chance for the examiner to gather initial impressions leading to clinical hypotheses. Succeeding subtests will provide further clues and perhaps confirm the initial impressions.

Picture Completion

This subtest, the second in the scale, and the first performance measure to be presented, consists of 26 incomplete pictures. These pictures are of common objects with increasingly more subtle omissions, which must be identified by the child. Picture Completion contributes substantially to the construct of general intelligence (g) and is also a measure of perceptual organization. It has ample specificity for younger children (6 to 8) and adequate specificity for older children (8 to 17), so that deviant scores can be interpreted individually across all age levels.

Like Information, one-word answers (and occasionally, pointing) are usually adequate, and initial items are simple enough for most children to assure success. Again, a shy, hesitant, or nonverbal child has a benign introduction to the performance section.

Picture Completion offers a number of clinical speculations. This is the first subtest in the scale where the child faces time limits. Here the pace of responses can be noted: for instance, are they immediate, variable, or slow? Does awareness of timing influence the rate of performance? Some children "race the clock" as a way of life, while others feel threatened at the idea of time limits. Carrubba (1976), however, found no specific deficits on this or other subtests attributable to the obvious use of a stopwatch, and concluded that in general, anxiety did not seem aroused by timing, and if present, was apt to lower all scores rather than those on timed tests alone.

Like Information, the prosaic content of this subtest rarely elicits emotional reactions or bizarre responses. Therefore such behavior is particularly important when observed in this neutral setting. High scores suggest a perceptive, visually alert child. Clinically, scores that are higher than expected have been related to an attitude of "overalertness" seen in, for example, a troubled child who may be aware of family disruptions long before these are acknowledged, or divorce is imminent. Extremely low scores are not particularly common. Specific failures might be explored to see if they suggest cultural impoverishment, in that the child cannot recognize the object presented, and thereby fails to discriminate the missing object.

Stylistic aspects to be observed on Picture Completion include naming versus pointing to identify missing objects. The verbal component on this subtest may relate to the level of terminology available to the child. Types of errors can be informative: for instance, irrelevant or multiple responses may point to preoccupations or perseverative ideas. Severe emotional problems may be suggested by responses verging on the bizarre, while impulsivity may lead to responses made without properly surveying the picture.

In sum, this simple nonthreatening task introduces the child to performance measures and allows for observations of his or her response to a perceptual task.

Similarities

This subtest consists of a list of 17 paired concepts of increasing difficulty, which the child has to identify as being alike or the same in some way. Contributing substantially to the construct of general intelligence (g), Similarities is an excellent measure of verbal comprehension. This subtest has ample specificity only for younger children (6 to 8); for older children (8 to 17) its contribution is principally to the verbal-comprehension factor.

In contrast to Information, this subtest is apt to be difficult, and for younger children even the initial items can be insurmountable. Bishop and Butterworth (1979) noted an unexpected tendency for otherwise normal children to fail to master the "set" required (how things are the same or alike). However, the advantages of Similarities tend to surpass its disadvantages, such as a limited number of initial simple, overlearned items. Respones offer the examiner an opportunity to develop various hypotheses concerning a child's functioning, regardless of age level.

Similarities is an excellent measure of concept formation for younger children, allowing for evaluation of the development from concrete to more abstract levels of reasoning. For some children, Similarities proves to be the first real challenge on the WISC-R, and they fail to establish the "set" of sameness on the first item. Coaching can be given on the first two items, and the child's responsiveness gauged (frequently, to break the tendency to name "differences"). After the first four items, the more abstract items are introduced, and again, coaching is allowed on the first two of these items to help the child raise the level of abstraction. Some children continue the same concrete responses, while others make the transition automatically. The child who can use the suggestions of the examiner to establish the proper set shows an encouraging flexibility and adaptability.

Failures on this subtest may represent a lag in achieving the concept of "sameness," usually not well established before the age of six. Younger children may also suffer the effects of excessive "coaching" by well-meaning teachers or parents who attempt to establish the concept of sameness before the child is able to understand what is involved. Such children are likely to perseverate the concept of shape, appropriate for the first item, to successive pairs of concepts. For older children, failures are characteristic of those who are less able, or who tend to be more concrete in their thinking. High scores are usually clear evidence of intelligence or ability, although out-of-line successes merit a question as to the possibility of coaching at home or school. Emotional reactions are rarely elicited, as noted for previous subtests, thereby suggesting the extent of disturbance.

Similarities can also reveal certain aspects of rigidity. As an example, a brain-injured child who had correctly identified the number of pounds in a ton in Information failed to respond to the *pound-yard* item, which in terms of placement is actually a bit easier. Here his interpretation of "yard" as *place* was so entrenched that he could not utilize his understanding of the other term to think of another interpretation. The hypothesis developed on this subtest was confirmed by other signs of rigidity detected throughout the scale. Other evidences of rigidity may be seen in the child who denies the possibility of similarity, revealing a negativistic response to difficult questions. In sum, Similarities is a challenging task that allows the examiner to observe and measure the way the child approaches verbal-conceptual tasks.

Picture Arrangement

This subtest consists of 13 sets of cartoons of increasing difficulty, which tell a coherent story when they are arranged in proper sequence. Picture Arrangement is a measure of the contruct general intelligence (g). It is an excellent measure of perceptual organization and has ample specificity, so that deviant scores can be interpreted with a degree of confidence.

The playful, game-like aspects of this "picture puzzle" task can be counterpointed by its level of difficulty for younger or less able children, who may be unable to grasp the idea of sequential pictures. Picture Arrangement presents both a sample construction and help as needed on the first four items, so that the child's ability to respond to coaching can be viewed. Does he grasp the point of the story, once presented, or merely remember and imitate the sequence? Do the coached items raise the child's awareness as to the meaning of the task? How much learning takes place, and at what point? What are errors like? Is the first card moved to the last position in a ritualistic way, or does the child reproduce the moves made on the previous items? Are visual clues indicating sequence overlooked?

Other clinical clues may relate to the child's style of responding and to his or her understanding of the "story" in each item. This subtest taps a number of emotional themes: fire setting, theft, disobedience, to mention but a few. Some children may respond to specific sequences as deliberately selected to refer to their own problem (such as fire setting). Errors are worth exploring. A simple question about the story may clarify its meaning to the child.

How aware is the child of the social implications of each sequence? Are certain themes more difficult than others? One bright 11 year old could pass every item but *gardener* and *rain*, where parental authority was involved. Her ambivalence over her stepmother's role in her life proved to be paramount.

How does the child feel about this subtest? Is he or she so apprehensive or challenged that he or she "jumps the gun" and tries to peek while the items are being set up? Is this behavior crude and obvious, or does it show a bit more subtlety? Both behaviors may suggest a highly competitive youngster who plays by his or her own rules, but the level of maturity differs.

The pace of response can be measured on Picture Arrangement. Does the child take about the same time for each of the easier items, suggesting a smooth, even functioning, or does he or she dash through some constructions only to bog down on others? Do errors reflect a failure to check details, even though he or she understands the sequence? As items become more difficult, how does the child use his or her time? Is there a mature slowing down, as alternatives are considered, or must pictures actually be positioned before the child can reject a placement? Are failures due to excessive time taken to understand the theme?

In sum, Picture Arrangement allows for the observation of the child's understanding of the subtleties of social interaction, in a problem-solving format.

Arithmetic

This subtest has 18 items consisting of common arithmetic problems of increasing difficulty. Items are presented orally, and must be solved without use of paper or pencil. This subtest contributes to the construct of general intelligence (g), and contributes to the freedom-from-distractibility factor. It has ample specificity, so that deviant scores can be interpreted with confidence.

As the fifth subset of the WISC-R, Arithmetic returns the child to school-like questions. Clinically, this subtest may prove to be a good entry at which to begin exploring the child's attitude toward testing and toward school. By this point, the child is usually at ease in the test situation, and can discuss his or her understanding of the examination. (Ideally, this has been covered before testing begins, but occasionally a child rejects entering into any such discussion until more at ease or aware of what he or she faces.) Why is he or she being seen? Does he or she feel there will be profit from responding, or does the child interpret the whole situation as attempting to prove he or she is "retarded" or "crazy"? An obligation to the child is to clarify the process, and to assure that the examination does prove to be meaningful and positive. As an example, a child who is sure he or she doesn't "know" arithmetic (and thereby need not try to master the subject in the classroom) can gain confidence from the initial easy items. As successes build, he or she may be reassured about ability. The effect of positive feedback has many times proved to be a turning point in a child's school achievement.

Bizarre or unusual responses are rare on this subtest, and should be explored for the information they may give about the child's functioning. In all, this subtest allows for an estimate of academic skills with emphasis on attention and concentration.

Block Design

This subtest consists of eleven two-color designs of increasing complexity printed on cards. The subject is required to reproduce the designs from red and white blocks by analyzing the pattern into its components and then reproducing it.

Block Design contributes substantially to the construct of general intelligence (g) and is an excellent measure of perceptual organization. Its ample specificity ensures that deviant scores can be interpreted with some confidence. Observation of the child's approach to the task also offers the opportunity to draw a variety of clinical inferences.*

The child's approach to the designs should be noted. With only two colors to use, the likelihood of the proper diagonal or solid color block turning up by chance may be a factor in success. Does the child notice such chance associations? Can he or she utilize these combinations? Or are blocks handled randomly? If the child uses such an approach, how successful is it? Do trial-and-error productions on one design allow the child a head start on the next? How systematic is the child? Does he or she show an anxious twirling of blocks, a block-by-block assembly, or are the correctly colored sides exposed conscientiously before construction even begins?

How realistic is the child in his or her approach? Does the child resist being shown how to copy design number three, trying to take the blocks away from the examiner? Is this show of brashness confirmed by subsequent success, or is the child unable to understand the critical role of diagonal blocks in further designs?

Block Design provides an indication of the child's ability to work under the pressure of time limits and the frustration of increasingly difficult items. For instance, does the child continue to work until a design is completed, even if this means going beyond the time limit? How does the child approach the problem? Can he or she analyze the design into its components and then duplicate its segments? Does he or she recognize the symmetry of the designs or is each section done separately without awareness of the duplication?

In sum, Block Design allows for observation of the way a child conceptualizes the interrelationships between shapes and patterns.

Vocabulary

This subtest involves 32 words of increasing difficulty that are to be defined by the subject. This subtest contributes substantially to the construct of general intelligence (g) and is an excellent measure of verbal comprehension. It has adequate specificity so that deviant scores can be interpreted individually. However, its role as a measure of verbal fluency may eclipse its value as a measure of word knowledge alone. The reason for this can be seen when responses are

---

*Scores on Block Design may be contaminated by games, such as "Track Four," which use the Kohs blocks.

evaluated clinically. Although pathological answers are readily elicited (for example, *knife*—"you can kill cats by stabbing them!"; *nail*—"hurt myself with a hammer"; *thief*—"steals, he could murder me when I sleep"), a survey of the Massey, Sattler, and Andres (1977) scoring guide reveals that answers indicating a preoccupation with emotionally upsetting themes can still meet the criteria for a 1- or 2-point score. Therefore the contribution of this subtest is more often based on content than on a high or low score alone.

In essence, an examination of Vocabulary can reveal a great deal about a child's preoccupation with such themes as fears, guilt, aggression, or the like. At the same time, scoring categories are broad enough so that such preoccupations need not lower or raise the score, or be reflected on the profile. When disturbed content prevails, so that vocabulary status might be questioned, the examiner can explore this issue further by administering the Peabody Picture Vocabulary Test—Revised (PPVT-R), where expressive verbal fluency is not required, and emotional associations minimized, to establish specific strengths or weaknesses in word knowledge.

In sum, this subtest is considered one of the best measures of general intelligence, and provides a reliable measure of verbal fluency, along with a variety of clinical clues.

Object Assembly

This subtest consists of four cutup objects, each consisting of six to eight pieces, to be assembled within a time limit. A poor measure of the construct general intelligence (g), it is nevertheless an excellent measure of perceptual organization. However, with only four items, this subtest is one of the least reliable in the WISC-R, and subtest specificity is so low that interpretation of deviant scores taken alone is questionable. Nevertheless, Object Assembly can provide a source of clinical clues as to the child's work habits when facing performance rather than verbal materials. Visual-motor coordination and the ability to visualize the whole from its parts are skills that can be readily observed during administration of this subtest.

As in other performance subtests, there is a sample item to orient the child to the task, and provide a degree of reassurance and familiarity. The difference between the child's approach to labeled items (both *girl* and *horse* are named as presented) to those where the child is required to figure out the object may be worth noting. A dependent child may demand to know what he or she is constructing. Insisting that pieces are missing or that the object doesn't make sense may characterize responses of suspicious, hostile youngsters. Some children can put various parts together without recognizing or completing the whole. Others fit one or two pieces together without awareness, and take their preliminary constructions apart in a futile further try. Bizarre responses, such as piling pieces on top of each other, are rare and indicate marked immaturity or regression.

Orientation toward authority can be estimated during administration of this subtest through such simple tasks as reboxing the puzzle pieces. Does the child help the examiner? Is this done spontaneously, in the spirit of cooperatively "cleaning up"? If not, does the child respond to the suggestion to help? Does behavior once requested continue on the further items, or must the child be asked each time, with no carryover? All such observations can be telling indications of the child's level of maturity and cooperation.

In sum, Object Assembly taps the child's understanding of the way objects could be assembled from their component parts, and as such, fleshes out the picture of overall functioning.

Comprehension

This subtest consists of 17 items of increasing difficulty in which the child is asked to explain why certain procedures are followed, or what should be done in a given situation. More than any other subtest, it elicits personal, individualistic, revealing content, rich in clinical clues.

Comprehension contributes substantially to the construct general intelligence (g), and is also an excellent measure of verbal comprehension. Specificity on this subtest is adequate for the interpretation of deviant scores. However, it is in the opportunity to observe the child coping with pertinent questions concerning practical situations that proves to be the greatest contribution of this subtest to the scale.

Only this initial item can be explained to the child who has difficulty understanding the task, but this is an unlikely situation, particularly in view of the position of the subtest toward the end of the scale. The use of questioning to elicit the required number of answers on many items ensures that the child will not be penalized for a failure to supply different answers spontaneously. However, while scores will not reflect the need for questioning, a child who requires such prodding differs from one who spontaneously generates a variety of responses. Some children search for the most abstract answer possible, and rest on their laurels. Others need constant structuring and encouragement to do what is expected. In contrast, a child who is something of a self-starter, and/ or spontaneously verbal, or one who attends carefully to instructions, may produce a variety of answers without prompting.

In a more subtle manner, items alternate between those in which the multiple answer is specifically requested, and those where no such suggestion is implied. Does the child note the difference between the two kinds of questions (that is, "give some reasons why")? Does the child begin to supply multiple answers to all questions, before being asked for a second idea? A more passive or concrete child may respond only as questioned, while an active or "field-independent" one will spontaneously pick up on the demands of the items. A child with obsessive trends may flood the examiner with responses, in a no-stone-unturned approach. The degree of relevance maintained in such a response set should be evaluated in order to assess the child's coping skills.

Particularly valuable for eliciting clinical clues are the items that tap such practical but potentially traumatic situations as *loss* or *fire*, as well as explore relationships to authorities such as *firemen, policemen*, and *inspectors*.

Clinically meaningful responses are frequently elicited on Comprehension. An item such as *finding a wallet*, for example, can elicit such themes as the following: guilt ("Give it back, say you didn't take it"); passivity ("Give it to your mother," that is, avoid independent action); sociopathic responses ("Take the money"); difficulty in coping ("Don't do nothin"); denial ("I never stole anything!"); or experience ("I never been to a store"). Such clinically meaningful responses rarely merit at 1- or 2-point score. However, besides the obvious intellectual aspects, a variety of clinical implications can be drawn from such responses.

Another example that assumed some notoriety is the *fight* item, once assumed to be unfair to minority children, whose failures were said to reflect the mores of the subculture. On the contrary, recent item analyses of the WISC-R responses of Mexican-American, black, and Anglo children, as well as referred youngsters and even children from another culture (Burmuda) revealed the item to be, if anything, proportionally easier for minority children (Astwood, 1976; Sandoval, Zimmerman, & Woo-Sam, 1983; Vance, Gaynor, & Coleman, 1977). Apparently children with siblings, no matter what their culture, "overlearn" to pick on someone their own size ("Don't hit your little brother!"). On the other hand, while this item is often answered correctly, unscored addenda ("Walk away— but me, I'd hit 'em!"; "Leave 'em alone, 'cause my mother would get me good!") tell more about the child than does the score alone, and explain why high and low scores might not contribute nearly as much as such comments to the clinical aspects of interpretation.

Still another interpretation of Comprehension is based on the research of Brannigan and Ash (1977). They found that children judged to be impulsive rather than reflective (on the basis of their scores on the Matching Familiar-Figures Test) were more apt to have their Comprehension scores surpassed by Information by 2 or more weighted score points. The authors concluded that such impulsive children did not use their knowledge as effectively as reflective children in dealing with problem situations involving social judgment.

In general, the verbal-comprehension loading of this subtest means that highly verbal children are apt to have an advantage on this subtest. On the other hand, such a diversity of ideas can be expressed in the responses, that the very richness of Comprehension in terms of clinical clues may be the element that masks its specificity in profile analysis.

In sum, since Comprehension presents practical, everyday situations and allows the child to come up with his or her own solutions, whether conventional or unique, it must be considered the richest clinical measure in the WISC-R.

Coding

This subtest consists of a simple (*A*) and advanced (*B*) form, given to younger (ages 6 and 7) and older (8 to 17) children, respectively. The child is presented with a key consisting of symbols matched to marks or numbers, and must copy the symbols into the blank spaces that conform to the proper mark or number.

Coding contributes relatively little to the construct general intelligence (g), instead measuring the freedom-from-distractibility factor, at least for many subjects. Its ample specificity allows for the interpretation of deviant scores with some confidence.

Coding can be a valuable source of clinical clues, particularly when school problems are being explored. Requiring fine motor skills and pencil use, this task can reveal the child's level of development involving such abilities. Also Coding frequently throws light on a child's approach to a new learning task. How well does he or she accept this subtest? Are instructions grasped immediately, or are errors made on the sample items? Does the child understand the value of memorizing symbols as he or she goes along? Does the child work faster as experience accumulates? (Recording the number of items completed in each of four 30'' intervals making up the 2-minute total can give an estimate of this.)

How accurate are the symbols? Can the child insert them in the small squares? Does he or she make any errors? Is he or she concerned or even aware of the absence of an eraser? Does the child tend to agonize over errors, slowing performance, or can he or she go on? Immediate memory can enhance performance on this subtest, and may be revealed by whether the child needs to check constantly with the key to proceed. The more efficient child may glance back at earlier entries to recall the proper symbol. (A useful check on memory is to ask the child to write down all the symbols he or she recalls after completing the subtest.)

Motivational aspects are often reflected in a successful performance on Coding. How persistent is the child? Must he or she be urged to continue? Some children note the length of the total subtest and immediately begin to evade such "hard work." Others stop dead at the end of the first line, and must be urged to go on. Refusing to work past a certain point may be characteristic. What is the child's approach? Is the child fast and accurate, fast and careless, slow and accurate, or slow and error prone? Is there a change in response from the beginning to the end of the subtest? Does the child overcome initial apprehension, and improve, or does he or she become discouraged and show a decline in performance? Are there evidences of fatigue? Do these tend to show in terms of errors or in a slowing of performance?

Visual as well as motor aspects may be involved in the coding performance. Are glasses needed? Does the child put his or her nose into the paper? Do specific errors reflect visual problems, motor problems, or a lack of understanding? Which hand is used? Is this the child's usual hand, or has there been a change perhaps due to injury? Is the child ambidextrous? Or is handedness not yet established? What is the role of the other hand? Even if impaired, can it be used as a "helper," holding down the answer sheet? If left handed, does the child write in the "crooked" position? (This can result in the hand covering the key, so that a second answer sheet must be supplied and correctly positioned.)

In sum, Coding allows for observation of the child's fine motor skills as well as such behaviors as persistence and flexibility.

Digit Span

This subtest, which is a supplementary verbal measure, consists of two sets of digits presented orally to the child. For the first list, the subject is to repeat numbers, ranging from three to nine digits, in the order that they were read. For the second list, the subject must repeat the digits (increasing from two to eight digits) backward. As an alternate subtest, Digit Span is not administered to all subjects and is typically given to only half of those children otherwise completing a standard WISC-R. However, this subtest has a great deal to contribute to clinical interpretation.

Digit Span contributes relatively little to the construct general intelligence (g). It does contribute to the freedom-from-distractibility factor, and has ample specificity to allow for interpretation of deviant scores with some degree of assurance.

The child's approach to Digit Span can reveal attention problems. Various approaches to memory tasks can be observed. Some children close their eyes during digit presentation, or repeat numbers subvocally as they are given. Others repeat the digits forward several times before attempting to reverse them. Such reactions suggest the child's awareness of memory problems and the efforts used to overcome these deficits.

Occasionally, successes on digits backward may surpass those on the easier digits forward. In that the initial task may have failed to challenge the child, and full attention was not engaged, only for him or her to find the more difficult task sufficiently intriguing, a possible oppositional trend can be hypothesized.

In sum, Digit Span allows for the rapid evaluation of attention and memory along with other clinical clues.

Mazes

This subtest, which is a supplementary performance measure, consists of seven paper-and-pencil mazes of increasing length and complexity, which are to be completed within a time limit. Although rarely administered routinely, because of the length of the scale, Mazes merits administration when time permits. Mazes contributes relatively little to the construct general intelligence (g), but proves a good measure of the perceptual organization factor. Its ample specificity and its clinical implications justify its addition to the scale.

With both a sample to illustrate the task to the child, and help as needed on the first two items, this subtest offers another evaluation of a child's learning style and coping skills. Is the idea of drawing the path grasped immediately, or is coaching required before the task is understood? The child who delays starting while he plans ahead, and then completes the maze in one continuous move, can be compared to one who begins, perhaps rashly, but can then stop and look ahead, realizing at that point the need to plan moves.

The kinds of errors the child makes should always be evaluated. For example, when the performance is characterized by overshooting alleys and exits, impulsivity might be hypothesized. Cutting through the walls may indicate a loss of control or incoordination. Failure to meet the time limits in an otherwise perfect performance may reflect excessive caution or perfectionism.

In all, this subtest allows an evaluation of planning and foresight, justifying its inclusion as a regular addition to the WISC-R.

SUMMARY

The present chapter has attempted to indicate some of the rich clinical features to be obtained from administration of a test such as the WISC-R. An individual's responses often reveal unique qualities of his or her personality structure, and give clues about both motivations and behavior. Needless to say, the above ideas are based on empirical evidence, clinical experience, and theory, not necessarily on research. Also they are by no means exhaustive. Examiners need to look not only for these but for the many other clues to be found in the protocols they administer, and to integrate measurement findings with direct observation. If the rich interaction that occurs when a child or adult is administered an intelligence test is ignored, and the clinician reports only a few sterile scores, both the testee and those concerned with his or her welfare have been shortchanged.

REFERENCES

Ackerman, P. T., Dykman, R. A., & Peters, J. E. (1976). Hierarchical factor patterns of the WISC as related to areas of learning deficit. *Perceptual and Motor Skills, 42,* 381–386.

Allison, J. (1978). Clinical contributions of the WAIS. In B. Wolman (Ed.), *Clinical diagnosis of mental disorders.* New York: Plenum.

Astwood, N. C. (1976). A comparison of American and Bermudian children on the WISC-R. *Dissertation Abstracts International, 36,* 6368B.

Babcock, H. (1930). An experiment in the measurement of mental deterioration. *Archives of Psychology, New York,* No. 117.

Bannatyne, A. (1974). Diagnosis: A note on recategorization of the WISC scaled scores. *Journal of Learning Disabilities, 7,* 272–273.

Bassett, J. E., & Gayton, W. F. (1979). Object Assembly and bodily concern, a behavioral extension to prisoners. *Journal of Consulting and Clinical Psychology, 47,* 984–985.

Bilett, J. L., Jones, N. F., & Whitaker, L. C. (1982). Exploring schizophrenic thinking in older adolescents with the WAIS, Rorschach, and WISC. *Journal of Clinical Psychology, 38,* 232–243.

Bishop, D., & Butterworth, G. E. (1979). A longitudinal study using the WPPSI and WISC-R with an English sample. *British Journal of Educational Psychology, 49,* 156–168.

Brannigan, G. C., & Ash, T. (1977). Social judgment in conceptually impulsive and reflective children. *Psychological Reports, 41,* 466.

Carrubba, M. J. (1976). The effects of two timing procedures, level of trait anxiety, and their interaction on performance on the WISC-R. *Dissertation Abstracts International, 37,* 2070A.

Chavez, E. L., Trautt, G. M., Brandon, A., & Steyaert, J. (1983). Effects of test anxiety and sex of subject on neuropsychological test performance. *Perceptual and Motor Skills, 56,* 923–929.

Cronbach, L. J. (1960). *Essentials of psychological testing* (2nd ed.). New York: Harpers.

DeHorn, A., & Klinge, V. (1978). Correlations and factor analysis of the WISC-R and PPVT for an adolescent psychiatric sample. *Journal of Consulting and Clinical Psychology, 46*, 1160–1161.

Downey, J. E. (1917). The Stanford Adult Intelligence Tests. *Journal of Delinquency, 2*, 144–155.

Edinger, J. D. (1976). Wechsler Picture Arrangement and premorbid social competence among process schizophrenics. *Journal of Personality Assessment, 40*, 52–53.

English, H. B., & English, A. C. (1958). *Dictionary of psychology and psychoanalytic terms.* New York: McKay.

Flumen, A. L., & Flumen, L. B. (1979). WISCOs and WPPSICLEs. *Journal of School Psychology, 17*, 82–85.

Frank, G. H. (1970). The measurement of personality from the Wechsler tests. In B. Maher (Ed.), *Progress in experimental personality research.* New York: Academic Press.

Fromm, E. (1960). Projective aspects of intelligence testing. In A. I. Rabin & M. R. Haworth (Eds.), *Projective techniques with children.* New York: Grune & Stratton.

Gittinger, J. W. (1967). *Introduction to the personality assessment system.* A paper presented in symposium on clients: A new approach based on abilities, to the American College Personnel Association.

Groff, M., & Hubble, L. (1981). Recategorized WISC-R scores of juvenile delinquents. *Journal of Learning Disabilities, 14*, 515–516.

Guertin, W. H., Ladd, C. E., Frank, G. H., Rabin, A. I., & Hiester, D. E. (1966). Research with the Wechsler Intelligence Scale for Adults: 1960–1965. *Psychological Bulletin, 66*, 385–409.

Guertin, W. H., Ladd, C. E., Frank, G. H., Rabin, A. I., & Hiester, D. E. (1971). Research with the Wechsler Intelligence Scales for Adults: 1965–1970. *The Psychological Record, 21*, 286–339.

Guilford, J. P. (1967). *The nature of human intelligence.* New York: McGraw-Hill.

Gutkin, T. B. (1979). WISC-R scatter indices: Useful information for differential diagnosis? *Journal of School Psychology, 17*, 368–371.

Hale, R. L., & Landino, S. A. (1981). Utility of WISC-R subtest analysis in discriminating among groups of conduct problem, withdrawn, mixed, and non-problem boys. *Journal of Consulting and Clinical Psychology, 49*, 91–95.

Harris, A. J., & Shakow, D. (1937). The clinical significance of numerical measures of scatter on the Stanford Binet. *Psychological Bulletin, 34*, 134–150.

Harris, A. J., & Shakow, D. (1938). Scatter on the Stanford Binet in schizophrenic, normal, and delinquent adults. *Journal of Abnormal and Social Psychology, 33*, 100–111.

Hart, B., & Spearman, C. (1914). Mental tests of dementia. *Journal of Abnormal Psychology, 9*, 217–264.

Henrichs, T. F., Krauskopf, C. J., & Amolsch, T. J. (1982). Personality descriptions from the WAIS: A comparison of systems. *Journal of Personality Assessment, 46*, 544–549.

Hubble, L. M., & Groff, M. (1981). Factor analysis of WISC-R scores of male delinquents referred for evaluation. *Journal of Consulting and Clinical Psychology, 49*, 738–739.

Hunt, J. McV. (1936). Psychological experiments with disordered persons. *Psychological Bulletin, 33*, 1–58.

Karnes, F. A., & Brown, K. E. (1980). Factor analysis of the WISC-R for the gifted. *Journal of Educational Psychology, 72*, 197–199.

Kaufman, A. S. (1976a). Factor analysis of the WISC-R at 11 age levels between 6½ and 16½. *Journal of Consulting and Clinical Psychology, 43*, 135–147.

Kaufman, A. S. (1976b). Do normal children have "flat" ability profiles? *Psychology in the Schools, 13*, 284–285.

Kaufman, A. S. (1979). *Intelligent testing with the WISC-R*. New York: Wiley Interscience.

Kaufman, A. S., & Reynolds, C. R. (1983). Clinical evaluation of intellectual function. In I. B. Weiner (Ed.), *Clinical methods in psychology*. New York: Wiley Interscience.

Kavale, K. A., & Forness, S. R. (1984). A meta-analysis assessing the validity of Wechsler Scale profiles and recategorizations: Patterns or parodies? *Learning Disabilities Quarterly, 7,* 136–156.

Kendig, I., & Richmond, W. V. (1940). *Psychological studies in dementia praecox*. Ann Arbor, MI: Edwards.

Leli, D. A., & Filshov, S. B. (1981). Actuarial detection and description of brain impairment with the Wechsler Bellevue Form 1. *Journal of Clinical Psychology, 37,* 615–622.

Leli, D. A., & Scott, L. H. (1982). Cross-validation of two indexes of intellectual deterioration on patients with Alzheimer's disease. *Journal of Consulting and Clinical Psychology, 50,* 468.

Littell, W. M. (1960). The WISC—A review of a decade of research. *Psychological Bulletin, 57,* 132–162.

Massey, J. O., Sattler, J., & Andres, J. (1977). *WISC-R scoring criteria*. Palo Alto, CA: Consulting Psychology Press.

Milberg, W., Graffenstein, M., Lewis, R., & Rourke, D. (1980). Differentiation of temporal lobe and generalized seizure patterns with the WAIS. *Journal of Consulting and Clinical Psychology, 48,* 39–42.

Piaget, J. (1950). *The psychology of intelligence*. New York: Harcourt Brace.

Pressey, S. I., & Cole, I. W. (1918). Irregularity in a psychological examination as a measure of mental deterioration. *Journal of Abnormal Psychology, 13,* 285–294.

Rabin, A. I. (1945). The use of the Wechsler Bellevue Scales with normal and abnormal persons. *Psychological Bulletin, 42,* 410–422.

Rapaport, D. (1945, 1946). *Diagnostic psychological testing* (Vols. I and II). Chicago: Year Book Medical Publishers.

Reschly, D. J. (1978). WISC-R factor structures among Anglos, Blacks, Chicanos, and Native American Papagos. *Journal of Consulting and Clinical Psychology, 46,* 417–422.

Richards, H. C., Fowler, P. C., Berent, S., & Boll, T. J. (1980). Comparison of the WISC-R factor patterns for younger and older epileptics. *Journal of Clinical Neuropsychology, 2,* 333–341.

Roe, A., & Shakow, D. (1942). Intelligence in mental disorder. *Annals of the New York Academy of Science, 42,* 361–490.

Sandoval, J. (1982). The WISC-R, factorial validity for minority groups and Spearman's hypothesis. *Journal of School Psychology, 20,* 198–204.

Sandoval, J., Zimmerman, I. L., & Woo-Sam, J. M. (1983). Cultural differences on WISC-R verbal items. *Journal of School Psychology, 21,* 49–55.

Sattler, J. M. (1982). *Assessment of children's intelligence and special abilities*. Boston: Allyn & Bacon.

Schafer, R. (1954). *Psychoanalytic interpretation in Rorschach testing*. New York: Grune & Stratton.

Silverstein, A. B. (1977). Alternative factor analytic solutions for the WISC-R. *Educational and Psychological Measurement, 37,* 121–124.

Stutsman, R. (1931). *Mental measurement of preschool children*. Yonkers, NY: World Book.

Swerdlik, M. E., & Schweitzer, J. (1978). A comparison of the factor structure of the WISC and WISC-R. *Psychology in the Schools, 15,* 166–172.

Thompson, R. J. (1981). The diagnostic utility of Bannatyne's recategorized WISC-R scores with children referred to a developmental evaluation center. *Psychology in the Schools, 18,* 43–47.

Van Hagen, J., & Kaufman, A. S. (1975). Factor analysis of the WISC-R for a group of mentally retarded children and adolescents. *Journal of Consulting and Clinical Psychology, 43,* 661–667.

Vance, H. B., Gaynor, P., & Coleman, M. (1977). Item analysis of the WISC-R. *Psychology in the Schools, 14,* 132–139.

Vance, H. B., & Wallbrown, F. H. (1977). The hierarchical factor structure of the WISC-R for referred children and adolescents. *Psychological Reports, 41,* 699–702.

Vance, H. B., Wallbrown, F. H., & Blaha, J. (1978). Determining WISC-R profiles for reading disabled children. *Journal of Learning Disabilities, 11,* 657–661.

Waite, R. R. (1961). The intelligence test as a psychodiagnostic instrument. *Journal of Projective Techniques, 25,* 90–102.

Wallbrown, F. H., Blaha, T., Wallbrown, J. D., & Engin, A. W. (1975). The hierarchical factor structure of the WISC-R. *Journal of Psychology, 89,* 223–235.

Wechsler, D. (1939). *Measurement of adult intelligence.* Baltimore: Williams & Wilkins.

Wechsler, D. (1944). *Measurement of adult intelligence.* Baltimore: Williams & Wilkins.

Wechsler, D. (1949). *Manual for the Wechsler Intelligence Scale for Children.* New York: Psychological Corporation.

Wechsler, D. (1955). *Manual for the Wechsler Adult Intelligence Scale.* New York: Psychological Corporation.

Wechsler, D. (1958). *The measurement and appraisal of adult intelligence.* Baltimore: Williams & Wilkins.

Wechsler, D. (1967). *Manual for the Wechsler Preschool and Primary Scale of Intelligence.* New York: Psychological Corporation.

Wechsler, D. (1974). *Manual for the Wechsler Intelligence Scale for Children—Revised.* New York: Psychological Corporation.

Wechsler, D. (1982). *Manual for the Wechsler Adult Intelligence Scale—Revised.* New York: Psychological Corporation.

Wells, F. L. (1927). *Mental tests in clinical practice.* Tarrytown-on-Hudson, NY: World.

Woo-Sam, J. M., & Zimmerman, I. L. (1973). Research with the Wechsler Preschool and Primary Scale of Intelligence: The first five years. *School Psychology Monograph, 1,* 25–50.

Zimmerman, I. L., Bernstein, M., & Eiduson, B. T. (1983, April 30). *Early precursors of school success.* Paper presented at the Western Psychological Association Convention, San Francisco, CA.

Zimmerman, I. L., & Lambert, N. M. (1961, September 1). *The relationship between individual psychological tests and school screening procedures for the identification of emotionally disturbed children.* Paper presented at the American Psychological Association Convention, New York.

Zimmerman, I. L., & Woo-Sam, J. M. (1972). Research with the Wechsler Intelligence Scale for Children: 1960–1970. *Journal of Clinical Psychology Monograph, 33,* 1–44.

Zimmerman, I. L., & Woo-Sam, J. M. (1978, April 22). *The meaning of scatter on the WISC-R: Clinical findings versus normative data.* Paper presented at Western Psychological Association Convention, San Francisco, CA.

TWENTY-TWO

CLINICAL USES OF THE WAIS-R: BASE RATES OF DIFFERENCES BETWEEN VIQ AND PIQ IN THE WAIS-R STANDARDIZATION SAMPLE

JOSEPH D. MATARAZZO

Oregon Health Sciences University
Portland, Oregon

DAVID O. HERMAN

The Psychological Corporation
New York, New York

TWO USES OF INTELLIGENCE TEST RESULTS

Individually administered tests of intelligence are one of the important tools of psychological assessment used by professional psychologists in a variety of settings. Examples of such settings include private offices, public and private schools, public and private mental health clinics and institutions, university hospitals, the personnel offices of industrial companies, and the counseling centers of colleges or universities, among others. As would be expected, the purposes to which the results yielded by such tests of intelligence are put varies considerably from one setting to another and, often, from one client to another even within a single setting. Such variety notwithstanding, the use made of such information in all these settings may be categorized under two main headings.

The first category involves the use of these tests as a standardized yardstick by which to ascertain an individual's standing relative to his or her peers on the *intellective* dimension, namely general (measured) intelligence. Specifically, each of the several Wechsler or Stanford-Binet scales, as well as a variety of other such tests, yields one or more summary IQ values that enable the practitioner to ascertain whether the particular individual just examined scores below average, average, above average, or at any other point relative to age peers along a scale from the first to the 100th percentile of such measured ability. The practical need for such an objective index of relative standing led Binet and Simon to develop the first such test and that need has guided the development of each new test developed between 1905 and the present.

A second category in which the results of such a test are used was discovered serendipitously by Binet. This second use goes beyond classification on the intellective dimension and involves an examination of the *intratest* performance of the individual in the hope that such information also will be an aid in classifying this individual on a nonintellective dimension of *psychopathology*. Binet was the first to suggest that his scale could provide more than merely a cognitive index when he observed that psychotic or alcoholic individuals appeared to "scatter" their "passes" and their "failures" on individual items of the Binet scale over a larger number of year levels than did mentally retarded patients. Unfortunately, three decades of subsequent research failed to provide verification of Binet's observation that psychopathology is associated with "unevenness" of functioning in subparts of the Stanford-Binet scale (Matarazzo, 1972, p. 428).

Nevertheless, Wechsler (1939) agreed with Binet and devoted many pages of the first edition of his textbook to the belief that his newly introduced Wechsler-Bellevue scale could provide rich diagnostic information above and beyond a simple IQ score. However, as reviewed in detail elsewhere (Matarazzo, 1972, Chapters 13, 14, and 15), despite a voluminous literature that accumulated over the next 45 years devoted to testing Wechsler's belief, no robust evidence exists today that any of the numerous neurotic, psychotic, or personality-disorder forms of psychopathology are associated with reproducible evidence of intersubtest scatter (pathognomonic differential patterns of *profiles*) on any of the Stanford-Binet or Wechsler scales. There is, however, modest evidence that an increase in situational, momentary, or state anxiety, even when induced in normal individuals, may lead to a differentially lower score on one or more subtests of the Wechsler scales. Modest evidence also exists that parental child-rearing practices also may produce differential lowering of one or another Wechsler scale subtest as the child grows older (Matarazzo, 1972). However, adequate cross-validation of these two promising leads is not as yet available.

VIQ-PIQ DISCREPANCIES AND DIFFERENTIAL DIAGNOSIS

The picture regarding unevenness of performance is not totally bleak, however. In fact, the most persuasive evidence supporting the notion of scatter published to date is on the relationship between the presence or absence of a *well-documented* neurologic diagnosis of *brain dysfunction* and a corollary discrepancy shown by that individual in Verbal IQ *versus* Performance IQ. Andersen (1951) first suggested, on the basis of a statistical analysis of the Wechsler-Bellevue (W-B) subtests, that there might be a relation between the brain hemisphere (left versus right) with cerebral dysfunction and a deficit on certain W-B subtests. Specifically, he reported that patients with left-hemisphere damage performed less adequately on the *verbal* subtests and better on the *performance* subtests than patients with right-hemisphere damage. Subsequently, Reitan (1955) reported a pattern of results that has been confirmed many times. Unlike earlier researchers who unsuccessfully attempted to verify Wechsler's hypothesis that some of his subtests "hold up" in "brain damaged" patients and other subtests "don't hold up," Reitan employed well-selected cases with *verified* lesions in the right or left cerebral hemisphere. Using this improved methodology, Reitan found that patients with left-hemisphere lesions scored poorer on the Wechsler Verbal Scale subtests than on the Performance Scale subtests. Conversely, he demonstrated that patients with right-hemisphere lesions obtained poorer scores on the Performance Scale subtests than the Verbal Scale subtests. In addition, patients with damage diffused throughout both hemispheres obtained a pattern of results on the W-B subtests similar to that of patients with right-hemisphere lesions. Subsequent investigators confirmed these earlier findings of Andersen and Reitan following the replacement of the W-B in 1955 by the Wechsler Adult Intelligence Scale (WAIS). A detailed review of this emerging early literature (Matarazzo, 1972, Chapter 13) provided moderately strong supporting evidence that *groups* of patients with *verified* lesions or injury in the *left* cerebral hemisphere earned a significantly lower mean *Verbal* IQ relative to their own Performance IQ. And, of equal diagnostic importance, patient groups with damage in the *right* cerebral hemisphere earned a differentially lower mean *Performance* IQ. Two subsequent updatings of this growing literature (Bornstein & Matarazzo, 1982; Matarazzo, 1980) added additional support to the validity of these patterns.

The results of this latest Bornstein and Matarazzo (1982) literature review of studies that utilized only the W-B are summarized in Table 1; those that used only the WAIS are summarized in Table 2. As may be seen in both tables, and with only several exceptions that will be discussed shortly, the findings from over two dozen independent samples of patients affirmed the validity of the hypothesis that the mean Verbal IQ (VIQ) is lower than the mean Performance IQ (PIQ) in patients with left-hemisphere dysfunction and that the reverse is true in patients with right-hemisphere involvement.

Although it is evident in Tables 1 and 2 that these group findings were duplicated, almost without exception, in study after study, the caution was added in the earliest of these literature reviews that such research findings as shown in our Tables 1 and 2 were based on *group means* and should be interpreted with that limitation in mind. In particular, it was cautioned that although such differences in group means are very useful for suggesting leads for further research toward a better understanding of brain-behavior relationships, the practicing clinician should remember that the differential diagnosis of such lateralized cerebral dysfunction in the *individual patient* always should be supported by corroborating or disaffirming evidence derived from physical findings and, where none are present, at the very least from the clinical history of that patient plus other neuropsychological test findings. The basis for this caution stems from the fact that for any individual any number of organismic and demographic variables may potentially influence the magnitude of the Verbal IQ, the Perfor-

Table 1. Wechsler-Bellevue 1 Verbal and Performance IQ for Subgroups of Adult Patients with Lesions in Different Hemispheres of the Brain

	Left	Right	Diffuse	Control	Sex Male	Female	Etiology	Author
VIQ	93.7[b]	102.3			16	15	Epileptics	Meyer & Jones (1957)
PIQ	98.8	99.9						
VIQ	79.7	91.1	80.7		47	11	Mixed	Klove & Reitan (1958)
PIQ	90.3	80.1	78.2					
VIQ	88.4	99.7	93.4	100.7	66	13	Mixed	Klove (1959)
PIQ	98.4	87.8	93.1	102.6				
VIQ	88.0	101.0	95.0	114.0	76[a]		Mixed	Doehring, Reitan, & Klove (1961)
PIQ	97.0	84.0	93.0	117.0				
VIQ	81.7	93.8	91.6		60	8	Mixed (Recent)	Fitzhugh, Fitzhugh, & Reitan (1962)
PIQ	90.8	78.8	89.4					
VIQ	68.0	75.5	72.9		31	44	Mixed (Chronic)	Fitzhugh, Fitzhugh, & Reitan (1962)
PIQ	71.9	73.4	78.1					

	Group	Source	n	n				
VIQ	Temporal Lobe Epileptics	Dennerll (1964)	33	27	86.2			106.0
PIQ					96.5			93.5
VIQ	Temporal Lobectomy (Sample I)	Meier & French (1966)	18	12	92.1			102.1
PIQ					100.8			99.4
VIQ	Temporal Lobectomy (Sample II)	Meier & French (1966)	22	18	90.2			99.8
PIQ					93.9			91.4
VIQ	Mixed	Leli & Filskov (1981)	57	43	103.8	105.0	123.1	95.5
PIQ					108.2	92.9	124.7	97.5

Note. The practicing psychologist should study the many qualifications cited in this chapter, which must be considered when attempting to apply the findings in this table to the *individual*. The research psychologist also should adhere to the requirements outlined by Reitan for classifying groups of patients and cited earlier in this chapter.

[a] Proportion of males and females not reported.

[b] In this table, each patient subgroup is compared *with itself* on **VIQ** versus **PIQ** (for example, 93.7 versus 98.9 and 102.3 versus 99.9, respectively, for the two Meyer & Jones, 1957, subgroups).

Table 2. Wechsler Adult Intelligence Scale Verbal and Performance IQ for Subgroups of Adult Patients with Lesions in Different Hemispheres of the Brain

	Left	Right	Diffuse	Control	Sex Male	Sex Female	Etiology	Author
VIQ	68.9[b]	72.8	70.4		47	51	Mixed Chronic Seizures	Fitzhugh & Fitzhugh (1964)
PIQ	73.7	68.3	72.2					
VIQ	94.9	107.2	90.2	100.0		44[a]	Mixed	Satz (1966)
PIQ	105.1	99.7	87.0	97.0				
VIQ	92.3	106.6	98.6	104.2		70[a]	Mixed	Satz, Richard, & Daniels (1967)
PIQ	104.9	96.1	94.7	99.3				
VIQ	75.8	89.1				49[a]	Mixed	Parsons, Vega, & Burn (1969)
PIQ	83.3	78.7						
VIQ	85.4	86.1				51[a]	Mixed (Minimal Deficit)	Vega & Parsons (1969)
PIQ	89.5	75.2						
VIQ	65.8	91.8					Mixed (Maximal Deficit)	
PIQ	76.7	77.7						
VIQ	90.3	98.8	92.0		92		Mixed	Zimmerman, Whitmyre, & Fields (1970)
PIQ	91.3	93.4	81.5					
VIQ	79.8	91.5	83.2	99.8		88[a]	Mixed	Simpson & Vega (1971)
PIQ	83.4	78.7	79.5	98.8				
VIQ	94.6	99.1		98.9	40		Missile Wound	Black (1973)
PIQ	96.4	95.6		97.8				

Measure					n	n	Type	Reference
VIQ	88.7	96.6		102.2	90		Missile Wound	Black (1974a)
PIQ	94.7	89.2		99.7				
VIQ	95.1	98.1	94.6	99.8	150		Missile Wound	Black (1974b)
PIQ	98.5	93.6	89.3	101.2				
VIQ			93.7	106.0	10		Head Injury	Becker (1975)
PIQ			80.3	107.1				
VIQ	99.2	99.0			44		Missile Wound	Black (1976)
PIQ	102.5	100.1						
VIQ	96.6	102.6	95.9	102.0	152	109	Mixed	Todd, Coolidge, & Satz (1977)
PIQ	90.6	95.9	88.3	97.5				
VIQ	87.1	110.3			55		Mixed	McGlone (1977)
PIQ	98.0	94.5						
VIQ	98.9	99.1				37	Mixed	
PIQ	97.4	94.0						
VIQ	83.1	106.8			40		Mixed	McGlone (1978)
PIQ	94.3	93.3						
VIQ	99.1	98.9				37	Mixed	
PIQ	99.2	94.7						
VIQ	72.1	96.4	87.0		24	2	Head Injury	Uzzell, Zimmerman, Dolinskas, & Obrist (1979)
PIQ	80.8	78.9	77.4					

[a] Proportion of males and females not reported.

[b] In this table, each patient subgroup is compared *with itself* on VIQ versus PIQ (for example, 68.9 versus 73.7, and 72.8 versus 68.3, and 70.4 versus 72.2, respectively, for the Fitzhugh & Fitzhugh, 1964 subgroups).

mance IQ, and, therefore, any resulting difference between their magnitudes. As reviewed in separate chapters in detail elsewhere (Matarazzo, 1972), such potentially influential variables include illiteracy, rural versus urban background, years of education, and professional versus blue-collar occupational history, among others. Additionally, even in patients with corroborated physical findings and a clearcut diagnosis of injury to the brain, the Wechsler scale laterality findings apparent in our Tables 1 and 2 will not necessarily be present. One such example is the possible "overrepresentation" of the left-hemisphere effect in the mean scores of "grab bag" samples of left-hemisphere patients that has been discussed in detail by Smith (1966, 1981) for cases of patients with *aphasia* who have lost their capacity for speech. Smith (1981) also provides a lucid discussion of numerous other pathological conditions that may profoundly influence brain-behavior functions and thus the interpretation of a VIQ-PIQ discrepancy (or its lack) in any given individual case. All this means, of course, is that the clinical significance of a difference between a person's Verbal and Performance functioning on the Wechsler scales cannot be interpreted *carte blanche*, but only after due weight is given to the myriad factors that may have contributed to it in this particular individual. We will now turn to what recent research suggests *may* be one such seemingly important variable.

SEX AND VIQ-PIQ DISCREPANCIES IN THE DIAGNOSIS OF ORGANICITY

Research by Landsdell (1962) and McGlone (1977, 1978), reviewed by Inglis and Lawson (1981), appears to constitute moderately strong evidence, again only from group means, that the *sex* of the individual may moderate the expression of a Verbal IQ versus Performance IQ discrepancy in documented cases of patients with right- versus left-hemisphere involvement. Building on this suggestion by Inglis and Lawson, Bornstein and Matarazzo (1982) added to the earlier Matarazzo (1972, 1980) literature reviews the most recent VIQ-PIQ studies and re-reviewed the earlier published literature with the sex of the patient as the focus and produced the findings broken down by sex summarized here in Tables 1 and 2. Table 1 includes 10 different samples of patients that were reported in eight different studies in which the W-B I was used; Table 2 includes the 18 patient samples reported in 16 studies that employed the WAIS.

As is clear from the group means shown in Table 1, despite the use of both female and male patients in the 10 patient samples included in that table, there were *no* exceptions to the pattern of a lower mean VIQ in left-hemisphere patients and, conversely, a lower mean PIQ in patients with a right-hemisphere lesion discussed above. That same pattern holds in Table 1 across a variety of patient populations and with groups that included relatively large as well as relatively small numbers of females.

The brain laterality and VIQ versus PIQ results with the WAIS shown in Table 2, for the most part, also are consistent with the observation that left-hemisphere involvement is associated with a lower mean VIQ and right-hemi-sphere involvement with a lower PIQ. As also is seen, however, there are four exceptions to these two VIQ versus PIQ patterns in the 18 published samples in Table 2. These four exceptions are found in the right-hemisphere group in the study by Black (1976), in the left-hemisphere group reported by Todd, Coolidge, and Satz (1977), in the left-hemisphere group of sample two reported by McGlone (1977), and in the negligible-mean difference in the left-hemisphere group in sample two in McGlone (1978). An analysis of possible explanations for these four exceptions was offered by Bornstein and Matarazzo (1982) in their literature review. Specifically, they dealt with the first exception by suggesting that the results of the Black (1976) study might have been due to the fact that Black's patients were male soldiers with wounds restricted to the *frontal* lobes, and that previous research suggests that such frontal lesions typically have a minimal impact on intelligence test results.

The second exception is apparent in the results of the Todd, Coolidge, and Satz (1977) study. As seen in Table 2, these authors' findings *confirmed* a lower PIQ in right-lesioned subjects but their additional search *failed* to reveal a lower VIQ in their left-hemisphere group of patients. Finding no explanation for this latter finding, Bornstein and Matarazzo concluded that unless other explanations are forthcoming, this Todd, Coolidge, and Satz study should be considered an example of a bona fide exception to the VIQ versus PIQ laterality hypothesis relating to means of groups so clearly supported in the data reviewed in Tables 1 and 2.

The third and fourth seeming exceptions in Table 2 are from samples reported by McGlone (1977, 1978). However, as evident in Table 2, *both* these "deviant" McGlone samples consisted *exclusively* of *female* patients. In contrast, as also is clear in that table, the counterpart male samples published in each of these same two McGlone studies did, in fact, show very clearly the left and right WAIS scale VIQ versus PIQ laterality effects reported by other investigators. Although such research is being pursued, to date no firm evidence has been published to explain why males appear to show a VIQ versus PIQ brain laterality effect whereas females show less of this effect.

It also is of some interest to note in Tables 1 and 2 that the three samples of patients with *diffuse* dysfunction that did *not* show the previously suggested pattern of VIQ *larger* than PIQ (sample 2 in Fitzhugh, Fitzhugh, & Reitan, 1962; Fitzhugh & Fitzhugh, 1964; Leli & Filskov, 1981) also were each reported from studies that had a high proportion of females.

Despite the single Todd, Coolidge, and Satz exception, and viewed collectively, the results from the 28 patient samples summarized in Tables 1 and 2 permit two conclusions that add important *actuarial* information, to be used judiciously with other information, to the armamentarium of the clinician who is called in consultation to render an opinion on a particular patient. The first is that, *on the average*, patients with a lesion or injury in the left hemisphere will tend to show a lower VIQ relative to PIQ, whereas patients with a lesion in the right hemisphere will show a lower PIQ relative to VIQ. The second conclusion one also may draw from this emerging but as yet not persuasively robust research literature is that this Verbal IQ deficit in left-hemisphere patients and Performance IQ deficit in right-hemisphere patients may, on the average, be found more often in male patients than in female patients. However, this second conclusion is still in its embryonic phase and considerable more research is needed before it will have been demonstrated more securely that the sex of a patient influences the laterality findings so clearly evident in our Tables 1 and 2. Thus for example, in the first studies designed to investigate these two conclusions using the WAIS-R, Bornstein (1983, 1984) *confirmed* the findings of a lower VIQ in left and a lower PIQ in right-hemisphere patients using this newest of the Wechsler scales. However, he *failed* to find that sex masked this laterality effect. Instead he found that *both* his male and female left-hemisphere patients had a lower mean VIQ, and that the reverse pattern (lower PIQ) also was true of both female and male right-hemisphere patients. Obviously much more research is needed before the sex of the patient will be as important a variable for the practitioner to evaluate as the results to date suggest clearly is the case for cerebral laterality and VIQ versus PIQ differences. Nevertheless, in their latest review of this literature, one which added still other studies to those presented here in Tables 1 and 2, Bornstein and Matarazzo (1984) still find evidence that the sex of the patient *may* play a role in the laterality effect.

VIQ VERSUS PIQ DIFFERENCES IN CLINICAL PRACTICE

Even though the first of these conclusions appears more robust than the second, conditions that may provide exceptions to each of these two emerging conclusions always are considered by the psychologist-practitioner offering an opinion in any given case. Thus, as given emphasis above, the data in Tables 1 and 2 represent group means and thus clearly will not be observed in the assessment results of each and every *individual* patient. In an earlier publication (Matarazzo, 1972), a review is provided of a number of other patient variables (such as age, acute versus chronic lesion, aphasia, Turner's Syndrome, and so on), which must be considered in an individual case in order to evaluate appropriately the clinical significance of an observed discrepancy between a person's Verbal IQ and Performance IQ. However, one overriding issue involving a VIQ versus PIQ difference is critically important and must be taken into consideration in the evaluation of every single patient. Unfortunately, despite its importance, to date too little attention appears to have been accorded it. That issue is that the use of Verbal versus Performance IQ difference scores will be handicapping, if not totally misleading unless, as suggested elsewhere (Matarazzo, 1972, pp. 389–391), the practitioner takes into account the *base rates* of such VIQ versus PIQ differences among the *normal* subjects that Wechsler found in his original standardization samples. To begin with, one must recall that for the W-B I the correlation between VIQ and PIQ was .71 and that, for the WAIS, this same *r* ranged between .77 and .81 for different age samples, and that for the WAIS-

R it averaged .74 across the 9 age groups (Wechsler, 1981) with a range between .67 and .80. It follows from these r values of *less* than 1.00 that in appraising the meaning of VIQ versus PIQ discrepancy one must thus expect a certain amount of variability in VIQ versus PIQ even among normal individuals. As reported by Wechsler, the mean difference in the WAIS standardization sample between VIQ and PIQ was approximately zero ($-.02$ points), although with a standard deviation of 10.02. (The *mean* of approximately zero should not surprise the reader inasmuch as Wechsler arbitrarily normed each of the VIQ scores to a VIQ mean as close to 100 as possible and he likewise normed the PIQ scores to a mean of 100). This mean of zero means, of course that, for the 1700 subjects who participated in the standardization of the WAIS, the positive and negative VIQ versus PIQ differences were equal and on the whole symmetrically distributed. Nevertheless, the 10.02 point standard deviation of this seemingly neglible mean difference of $-.02$ makes clear to a reader with a knowledge of basic statistics that, independent of sign, a WAIS VIQ-PIQ difference greater than 10 points will be encountered among *normal* individuals in about 32 cases in 100, a difference of 15 points in 13 cases in 100, and a difference of 20 points 5 times in 100, and so on. Given the standard deviation of a difference score, experts in psychometrics and test construction understand such base rates and their implications but, unfortunately, such experts rarely are the same individuals who provide actual clinical services to patients presenting real-life challenges. Conversely, many psychologists who are engaged in such professional clinical work are sufficiently far removed from their graduate training related to such statistical-psychometric issues that the tendency is increased to forget the influence in the case of a given patient of such base rates. However, a number of writers have addressed this issue and their contributions are cited elsewhere (Matarazzo, 1972, p. 389; Matarazzo, Carmody, & Jacobs, 1980, pp. 13–15) as well as here in the next section.

Nevertheless, many users of the Wechsler scales have failed to distinguish between two distinct aspects of VIQ-PIQ differences. The *first* of these concerns the *base rates* of the IQ differences as they occur in a meaningful population, usually the normative sample. Information of this kind answers the question of how often one may expect to find a difference score of a given magnitude in the population. This first base-rate question may be approached in either of two ways. One is purely *statistical,* and involves computing the standard deviation of the VIQ-PIQ difference scores in the population; then, by referring to a table of normal-curve statistics one may determine the proportion of the population with difference scores of any given magnitude. (This technique was referred to above in the discussion of how often various Verbal-Performance differences on the WAIS would be encountered in a normal population.) The other way to approach base rates of the VIQ-PIQ differences involves preparing a frequency distribution of the VIQ-PIQ difference scores *actually obtained* in a normative sample, and computing the percentage of individuals with such difference scores at each of a variety of different magnitudes. (Data of this kind for the WAIS-R will be presented later in this chapter.)

The second major aspect of verbal-performance differences concerns not how often they actually occur in the population, but rather their *reliability and statistical significance*. This aspect of the discrepancy between a Verbal and a Performance IQ relates to the error of measurement (degree of unreliability) inherent in test scores obtained on a single examination. It deals not with how frequently a VIQ-PIQ difference actually occurs in a population but, rather, addresses the question of whether or not the individual's obtained VIQ-PIQ difference is "real" in the sense of being statistically significantly different from zero. Stated differently, this approach permits one to assess the probability that the VIQ-PIQ difference score earned by this individual could have been obtained if his or her "true" difference score were zero. Clearly there may be times when *psychometric* information of this type, which deals with the unreliability of a difference score, will be important to the examining psychologist, but experience suggests that such times will be fewer than many have believed in the past.

For our present purposes we will refer to the question of how frequently VIQ-PIQ differences of a particular magnitude in the population actually occur as a question of *base rate*. The second aspect of these VIQ-PIQ differences, which concerns whether a particular difference is psychometrically large enough to be considered "real," we will refer to as a question of *statistical significance*. As will be shown later in this chapter, these two types of questions that one may ask about a given VIQ-PIQ difference have quite different answers and, unless the questions are kept distinct, their answers may confuse and mislead the practitioner.

Parenthetically, it should not be inferred that these distinctions are new, for psychometricians have long been aware of the statistical issues involved. Readers may be interested in an excellent article written for clinicians over 25 years ago (Payne & Jones, 1957), which clearly states the questions and presents the proper statistical formulas for answering them. What that article did not do was to compare *base-rate* data obtained by statistical formula with *base-rate* data obtained by actually tallying the frequency of each difference score occurring in a normative sample. (The two procedures should and do yield nearly identical results as demonstrated in a companion paper to this chapter by Grossman, Herman, & Matarazzo, in press.) Data based on the distributions of actual difference scores will be discussed in depth later in this chapter.

Information about the base rates of various difference scores is often more important to the psychologist-practitioner than the information yielded by the standard error of measurement that lies at the heart of the statistical significance of a VIQ-PIQ difference. For example, even if the VIQ versus PIQ discrepancy obtained is significantly different from zero in the statistical or psychometric sense, is it also of a magnitude that in community-living adults occurs in one person out of five, or in one out of 30, or one out of 100? As will be discussed in the remainder of this chapter, this base-rate approach offers a unique perspective for evaluating the clinical importance of VIQ-PIQ difference, and contrasts with evaluating the purely statistical-psychometric significance of such differences.

STATISTICAL VERSUS EMPIRICAL INDICES OF ABNORMALITY

A bit of historical perspective may help explain the clinician's need for base-rate information on the VIQ versus PIQ discrepancy score. Before the time the very first studies reviewed here in our Tables 1 and 2 were being conducted, individual psychologist-practitioners had amassed years of *practical clinical experience* with the W-B and WAIS, and from that experience, although not recorded in a form for empirical analysis, they had accumulated an intuitive knowledge of the range of VIQ versus PIQ difference one could expect to find in normal as well as abnormal conditions. A published example of the use of such individually acquired clinical base rates involved a 21-year-old woman seen in 1957 by one of the present writers and his colleagues (see Matarazzo, 1972, pp. 414–417, for details). She was referred to the medical psychology consultants by the chief of neurosurgery with a request for any leads that might help the latter establish a differential diagnosis between what could be a clinically difficult to verify brain tumor and catatonic schizophrenia, each of which condition he felt was compatible with her history and clinical findings. The psychologist's findings on the W-B I included a Verbal IQ of 98 and Performance IQ of 70. Based only on clinical experience with the Wechsler scales, the opinion could be proffered as early as 1957 that, whereas such a 28-point VIQ-PIQ differential in a high school graduate of average ability had never been observed even in the most disabling forms of acute schizophrenia or other major psychiatric disorders, such a large VIQ-PIQ discrepancy was not infrequently observed in patients with traumatic and other head injuries in which the clinical history was specific for brain injury. Surgery was immediately performed and a large tumor was removed from the patient's right hemisphere. Subsequent reexamination with the WAIS three months later produced a Verbal IQ of 104 and a Performance IQ of 104, validating the clinical opinion that the right-hemisphere tumor was associated with the initial 28-point VIQ-PIQ differential. Unfortunately, too few examples were published that were based on such accumulated actual *empirical* clinical experience, and thus the earliest published discussions of what practitioners should view as an abnormal VIQ versus PIQ difference were based exclusively on inferences from considerations of statistical significance (that is, is the obtained difference statistically significant from zero?). As an aid to the clinician-practitioners for whom the distinction between the two types of VIQ versus PIQ questions has not been clear, we turn now to a fuller treatment of this issue of statistical significance.

Statistical Significance of VIQ-PIQ Differences

Wechsler was a practicing clinical psychologist who, before assuming his clinical and university responsibilities at the Bellevue Hospital in 1932, had studied in London with the statistician Karl Pearson. Not surprisingly, then, in the publication of his first test (the W-B I) Wechsler (1939, pp. 118–144) included not only the VIQ-PIQ mean difference at each age but also the necessary statistical information from which a reader could compute the *standard error of measurement* of such a difference. Wechsler also published similar statistical information about VIQ-PIQ difference obtained on each of his subsequent scales, namely, his 1949 WISC, 1955 WAIS, 1967 WPPSI, 1974 WISC-R, and 1981 WAIS-R scales. Thus from 1939 on Wechsler provided information on a statistical "band of error" not only for any given individual's VIQ and PIQ viewed separately but, also, the error band for the *difference* between these scores.

Subsequent writers amplified on the potential use of such statistically derived information about VIQ versus PIQ differences. The article by Payne and Jones (1957), cited earlier, offers a concise but comprehensive discussion of various questions about the interpretation of VIQ-PIQ differences. A number of writers have followed in the statistical tradition by providing solutions for interpreting whether any obtained VIQ-PIQ difference differs significantly from zero by use of the published standard errors of measurement of that particular Wechsler scale (Field, 1960; Fisher, 1960; McNemar, 1957; Naglieri, 1982; Reynolds, 1979; Silverstein, 1981a, 1982). Each of these writers, following Wechsler's initial suggestions, provides the information from which a practitioner can compute the statistical band of error associated with the VIQ-PIQ discrepancy of any magnitude obtained on any client or patient. In a further contribution to this important issue, Kaufman (1979) devotes a whole chapter, as well as other sections of his textbook on the WISC-R, to a lucid discussion of serious errors that a school psychologist or other practitioner can make if VIQ versus PIQ differences are interpreted without considering a host of other nonstatistical variables that potentially influence such differences.

Empirically Obtained Abnormal VIQ-PIQ Differences

During the 1960s and 1970s research of the type summarized here in Tables 1 and 2 was helping give birth to a new specialty in psychology which in time was called *clinical neuropsychology*. With the accumulation of more and more of the findings shown in our two tables, this new type of psychologist began to be called in as an expert witness in complex courtroom litigation involving alleged injury to the brain of individuals involved in automobile, industrial, and other serious accidents. Such real-life courtroom experiences added a new element on top of the base of the earlier hospital experiences of most of these clinicians. Specifically, a major change occurred in the *setting* in which the validity of a clinical diagnosis was determined and, as necessary, debated. Shortly after Binet and Simon developed their first intelligence scale and Rorschach developed his inkblot projective test, hospital- or community-based American and British psychologists increasingly were called in to consult on the differential diagnosis of a patient. Typically in these cases the psychologist, a referring colleague, and the patient were the only individuals that were involved. Such a hospital-based practice and setting permitted the attending clinician and the consultants involved to exercise their clinical skill to the best of their ability, including using changes in the patient's clinical status with the passage of time as a powerful aid for validating or amending the initial clinical diagnosis. That the practice of neurology and neurosurgery and clinical psychology each was based on a great deal of art was acknowledged by all knowledgeable hospital personnel. The electroencephalogram and psychological tests were useful tools as aids to the clinical judgments involved, but not one of these clinicians claimed that such diagnostic tools were completely valid measures of the presence or absence of a "brain injury" in any given patient. Nevertheless, the clinical psychologist who practiced in such a hospital built up his or her own "norms" by which one might recognize the expression of "organic" or "functional" psychopathology and, based on such accumulating individual "actuarial" norms, was able to provide rich clinical input into the diagnostic decision that would eventually evolve over time. However, developments in the insurance industry as well as a marked increase in the use of clinical psychologists in personal-injury cases changed the venue of these earlier hospital practices from exclusively the hospital to the hospital *plus* the courtroom. The more recent personal-injury cases now involved the patient, numerous physicians and other psychologists, insurance carriers, and plaintiffs' and defendants' attorneys. Furthermore, there was the added dimension that on the verity of this clinical diagnosis rode very large potential sums of monies. Issues of the reliability and validity of psychological assessment instruments, plus the adequacy and representativeness of the samples on which such tools were standardized, no longer were important primarily to the practitioners of psychology and few others. For example, the experience of psychologists in the courtroom quickly revealed that neither juries, attorneys, nor judges appeared to comprehend how statistical abstractions based on the performance of a standardization sample of subjects hundreds or thousands of miles away could lead the psychologist–expert witness "to conclude within reasonable medical or psychological probability" that the particular patient whose case was being heard did or did not show evidence of a brain injury.

Empirical studies specifically designed to provide "normative" and other comparison data for use as yardsticks by which to remedy this situation were therefore undertaken (for example, Matarazzo, Carmody, & Jacobs, 1980; Matarazzo, Matarazzo, Gallo, & Wiens, 1979; Matarazzo, Matarazzo, Wiens, & Gallo, 1976; Matarazzo, Wiens, Matarazzo, & Goldstein, 1974; Matarazzo, Wiens, Matarazzo, & Manaugh, 1973). One contribution of such empirical base-rate studies was the publication of the actual Wechsler scale and other test scores of *each* subject in several small samples and an accompanying analysis of the *empirical frequencies* with which each such score, or a difference between pairs of scores, *actually occurred* in samples of patient and normal groups.

Information of this kind was important for two reasons. First, it bypassed questions of the statistical significance of VIQ-PIQ differences, which juries found confusing, and which were at best tangentially relevant to the diagnosis of brain injury. Second, these empirical data on base rates clarified the meaning of such abstractions as the standard errors of difference scores by making objective the actual deviance of a particular VIQ-PIQ difference. Subsequent experience confirmed that attorneys, judges, and juries who bear the responsibility for assessing the quality of the diagnostic conclusions that are offered in sworn expert testimony find opinions backed by empirical base-rate data relatively easy to comprehend and accept.

In an important contribution to this accumulating literature, Kaufman (1976, 1979) published a wealth of comparable empirically obtained base-rate information showing the frequency with which VIQ-PIQ differences of varying magnitudes actually occurred among the 2200 children who served as the standardization sample for the WISC-R published in 1974. Specifically, using the actual empirical IQ score data from the sample of 2200 youngsters on whom Wechsler, Kaufman, and the latter's colleagues at The Psychological Corporation standardized the WISC-R, Kaufman began by computing the VIQ versus PIQ discrepancy obtained by each of the youngsters. He next counted and published the actual numbers (and percentages) of these youngsters whose empirical VIQ versus PIQ discrepancy was 0, 1, 2, 3 . . . and up to 35 and more points. He not only published such frequencies of actual occurrence for the whole sample of 2200 children but, equally importantly, he also regrouped and published subsets of these VIQ-PIQ differences by sex, age, race, parental occupation, and, finally, by five different full-scale IQ groups (that is, 120 and above, 110–119, 90–109, 80–89, and 79 and below). With these tables in hand a school or clinical psychologist can readily discern how frequently the VIQ-PIQ difference shown by a particular client or patient actually also occurred among the 2200 normal children who constituted Wechsler's WISC-R standardization group.

The utility of such empirical data becomes clear from Kaufman's example that the use of the *standard error statistical-psychometric approach* to these 2200 cases would reveal that a VIQ-PIQ difference of 12 points is statistically *significantly different from zero* at the .05 level of probability. He added, however, that if, instead, one consults his empirical tables derived from the same 2200 cases, such tables reveal that such a 12-point VIQ-PIQ difference *actually was shown* by 30% of these 2200 normal youngsters. Clearly an administrative action labeling such a school child exceptional or emotionally disturbed only on the basis of this .05 level of statistical significance would be a professionally unsupportable act despite its basis on a scientific foundation as significantly different from zero (namely, a *p* of .05). It is because assessment data gathered by school, by clinical, and by neuropsychologists are playing increasingly important roles in markedly influencing human lives in our schools, clinics, hospitals, employment settings, and courts of law that test constructors, as well as other psychologists, must be encouraged to collect their data and present it in a manner that will be useful to those who must base practical actions on them. As an early step in that process Matarazzo (1972, p. 390) collated and published the empirically derived VIQ and PIQ *mean* values obtained in seven studies of samples of patients with left and right cerebral-hemisphere dysfunction. As cited by Kaufman (1976, p. 744) that table (updated as Tables 1 and 2 here), as well as the VIQ-PIQ difference scores subsequently published by Matarazzo and his colleagues (Matarazzo, Carmody, & Jacobs, 1980; Matarazzo, Matarazzo, Gallo, & Wiens, 1979) for small samples of normal and patient groups and described earlier in this present section, served an interim role but could not substitute for the actual normative table and its subsets published by Kaufman (1976) from the 2200 youngsters on whom the WISC-R was standardized. Accordingly, as a further contribution to the accumulating pool of such needed base-rate reference norms, we next present here comparable empirical data from the WAIS-R standardization sample.

ACTUAL WAIS-R VIQ-PIQ DIFFERENCES BY AGE AND FSIQ

There are, of course, many ways by which the raw data from the VIQ versus PIQ difference shown by each of the 1880 normal individuals on whom the WAIS-R was standardized could be analyzed and presented. As suggested above the state of the art based on research on the Wechsler scales (see our Tables 1 and 2 as examples) suggests that at the present time the use of such a WAIS-R VIQ versus PIQ discrepancy occurs more frequently in clinical neuropsychology (brain-behavior relationships) than in clinical psychology and related specialties that more often deal with forms of psychopathology other than neuropathology. As also suggested, experience indicates that information relative to such VIQ-PIQ differences that neuropsychologists would find useful in their work with adult patients are normative data that help provide answers to two questions. First, do such actuarially observed VIQ-PIQ differences occur as frequently in one *age group* as they do another? And, second, do they occur as frequently in one *IQ group* as they do in another?

Age and VIQ-PIQ Differences

The data in Table 3 and Figure 1 are relevant to the first of these two questions. The reader should note that the numerical data in Figure 1 and in Tables 3 and 4, which we tabulated from the WAIS-R standardization data, are "rounded off" and thus do not always add up precisely to the indicated totals. Several features of Table 3 are noteworthy. First, WAIS-R VIQ-PIQ differences are approximately *normally distributed* for each of the three age groups (16–24, 25–44, and 45–74) represented in the table as well as for the total sample of 1880. This is evident in the *numerical* data for each age group, which are shown in Table 3, as well as visually in the graphical plots of these three distributions (plus their total) that we constructed (but have not included here) using the data shown in Table 3. To highlight this normal distribution in visual form we did, however, construct Figure 1 for all 1880 subjects from the percentage data for each magnitude of VIQ-PIQ difference shown in the last column of Table 3.

Although Wechsler (1981) did not present the mean of the 1880 VIQ versus PIQ differences that actually occurred in the WAIS-R standardization sample,

Table 3. Frequencies and Percentages of Differences Between Verbal and Performance IQs in WAIS-R Standardization Sample (Different Age Groups)

Magnitude of VIQ-PIQ Difference in Points	16–24 (N = 600)			25–44 (N = 550)			45–74 (N = 730)			All Ages (N = 1880)			
	N	(%)	(CUM %)	N	(%)	(CUM %)	N	(%)	(CUM %)	N	(CUM N)	(%)	(CUM %)
30+	4	0.7	0.7	1	0.2	0.2	5	0.7	0.7	10	10	0.5	0.5
26–29	3	0.5	1.2	2	0.4	0.5	5	0.7	1.4	10	20	0.5	1.1
23–25	9	1.5	2.7	5	0.9	1.5	11	1.5	2.9	25	45	1.3	2.4
22	6	1.0	3.7	4	0.7	2.2	4	0.5	3.4	14	59	0.7	3.1
21	4	0.7	4.3	5	0.9	3.1	4	0.5	4.0	13	72	0.7	3.8
20	5	0.8	5.2	8	1.5	4.5	4	0.5	4.5	17	89	0.9	4.7
19	5	0.8	6.0	1	0.2	4.7	6	0.8	5.3	12	101	0.6	5.4
18	6	1.0	7.0	4	0.7	5.5	7	1.0	6.3	17	118	0.9	6.3
17	3	0.5	7.5	2	0.4	5.8	4	0.5	6.8	9	127	0.5	6.8
16	8	1.3	8.8	4	0.7	6.5	7	1.0	7.8	19	146	1.0	7.8
15	7	1.2	10.0	5	0.9	7.5	5	0.7	8.5	17	163	0.9	8.7
14	10	1.7	11.7	8	1.5	8.9	13	1.8	10.3	31	194	1.6	10.3
13	5	0.8	12.5	10	1.8	10.7	15	2.1	12.3	30	224	1.6	11.9
12	12	2.0	14.5	11	2.0	12.7	15	2.1	14.4	38	262	2.0	13.9
11	16	2.7	17.2	13	2.4	15.1	16	2.2	16.6	45	307	2.4	16.3
10	17	2.8	20.0	14	2.5	17.6	13	1.8	18.4	44	351	2.3	18.7
9	13	2.2	22.2	10	1.8	19.5	12	1.6	20.0	35	386	1.9	20.5
8	15	2.5	24.7	21	3.8	23.3	17	2.3	22.3	53	439	2.8	23.4
7	18	3.0	27.7	12	2.2	25.5	27	3.7	26.0	57	496	3.0	26.4
6	15	2.5	30.2	13	2.4	27.8	25	3.4	29.5	53	549	2.8	29.2
5	22	3.7	33.8	16	2.9	30.7	27	3.7	33.2	65	614	3.5	32.7
4	22	3.7	37.5	20	3.6	34.4	23	3.2	36.3	65	679	3.5	36.1

	n	%	cum %	n	%	cum %	n	%	cum %	n	%	cum f	cum %
3	20	3.3	40.8	11	2.0	36.4	32	4.4	40.7	63	3.4	742	39.5
2	27	4.5	45.3	30	5.5	41.8	22	3.0	43.7	79	4.2	821	43.7
1	16	2.7	48.0	24	4.4	46.2	29	4.0	47.7	69	3.7	890	47.3
0	21	3.5	51.5	25	4.5	50.7	33	4.5	52.2	79	4.2	969	51.5
−1	23	3.8	55.3	17	3.1	53.8	27	3.7	55.9	67	3.6	1036	55.1
−2	17	2.8	58.2	16	2.9	56.7	34	4.7	60.5	67	3.6	1103	58.7
−3	19	3.2	61.3	20	3.6	60.4	30	4.1	64.7	69	3.7	1172	62.3
−4	24	4.0	65.3	23	4.2	64.5	29	4.0	68.6	76	4.0	1248	66.4
−5	20	3.3	68.7	19	3.5	68.0	26	3.6	72.2	65	3.5	1313	69.8
−6	14	2.3	71.0	23	4.2	72.2	24	3.3	75.5	61	3.2	1374	73.1
−7	15	2.5	73.5	19	3.5	75.6	20	2.7	78.2	54	2.9	1428	76.0
−8	11	1.8	75.3	15	2.7	78.4	15	2.1	80.3	41	2.1	1469	78.1
−9	17	2.8	78.2	11	2.0	80.4	23	3.2	83.4	51	2.7	1520	80.9
−10	18	3.0	81.2	9	1.6	82.0	13	1.8	85.2	40	2.1	1560	83.0
−11	13	2.2	83.3	14	2.5	84.5	18	2.5	87.7	45	2.4	1605	85.4
−12	16	2.7	86.0	13	2.4	86.9	14	1.9	89.6	43	2.3	1648	87.7
−13	15	2.5	88.5	9	1.6	88.5	8	1.1	90.7	32	1.7	1680	89.4
−14	12	2.0	90.5	10	1.8	90.4	9	1.2	91.9	31	1.6	1711	91.0
−15	11	1.8	92.3	5	0.9	91.3	8	1.1	93.0	24	1.3	1735	92.3
−16	3	0.5	92.8	9	1.6	92.9	9	1.2	94.2	21	1.1	1756	93.4
−17	5	0.8	93.7	6	1.1	94.0	6	0.8	95.1	17	0.9	1773	94.3
−18	2	0.3	94.0	5	0.9	94.9	4	0.5	95.6	11	0.6	1784	94.9
−19	9	1.5	95.5	1	0.2	95.1	9	1.2	96.8	19	1.0	1803	95.9
−20	5	0.8	96.3	2	0.4	95.5	3	0.4	97.3	10	0.5	1813	96.4
−21	4	0.7	97.0	5	0.9	96.4	8	1.1	98.4	17	0.9	1830	97.3
−22	5	0.8	97.8	3	0.5	96.9	1	0.1	98.5	9	0.5	1839	97.8
−23–25	7	1.2	99.0	7	1.3	98.2	4	0.5	99.0	18	1.0	1857	98.8
−26–29	2	0.3	99.3	8	1.5	99.6	3	0.4	99.5	13	0.7	1870	99.5
−30+	4	0.7	100.0	2	0.4	100.0	4	0.5	100.0	10	0.5	1880	100.0

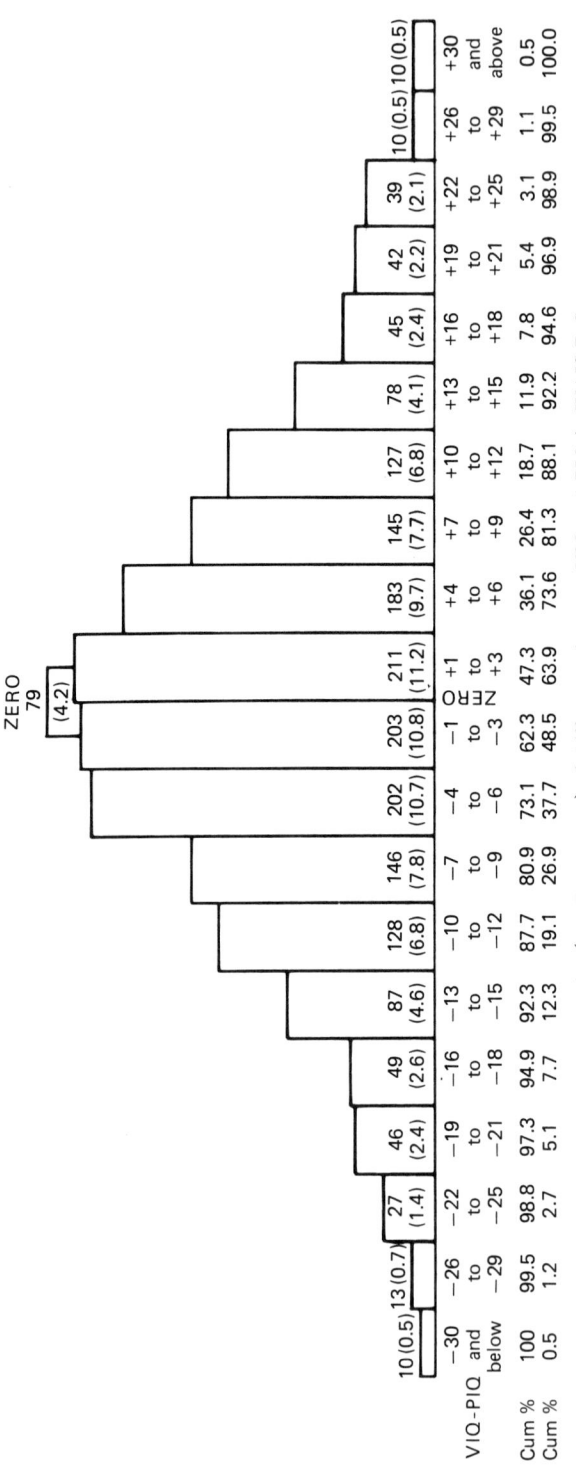

Figure 1. Frequencies (and Percentages) of Differences between VIQ and PIQ in WAIS-R Standarization Sample.

the data in the last column of our Table 3 and their graphic presentation in our Figure 1 permit a reader to infer that such VIQ-PIQ discrepancies distribute themselves around a mean difference of zero. In point of fact, when we went back and computed the actual VIQ-PIQ difference for *each* of the 1880 individuals, the mean of these 1880 VIQ-PIQ differences was almost exactly zero (namely −.10) with a standard deviation of 11.12. Additionally, as published in the WAIS-R Manual (1981, p. 46) the average correlation between VIQ and PIQ across the nine age groups constituting the 1880 individuals was .74. As discussed in an earlier section of this chapter, being able to *infer* this symmetrical (normal) distribution of VIQ-PIQ differences around a mean of zero from the standard deviations and coefficients of correlation published in the WAIS-R Manual may be helpful in some applied uses of these VIQ versus PIQ differences. However, the *actual* empirical data on frequency and percentage of occurrence of VIQ-PIQ differences of varying magnitudes that we here show in our Table 3 and Figure 1 will often be of more direct use to the practitioner, especially the clinical neuropsychologist.

The second noteworthy feature of the data in Table 3 is the very large *range* of VIQ-PIQ differences actually manifested by the 1880 *normal* individuals in the standardization sample. Thus entering the extreme right column of Table 3, one discerns that 10 of these 1880 normal individuals showed a VIQ-PIQ difference of +30 or more points and 10 others of them a difference of −30 or more points. The full range was from +49 to −43 points. We shall return shortly (in relation to Table 5) to the implications for the practitioner of this high number of "deviants" from "normality," which occurred in what was a carefully selected, representative cross section of community-living American adults.

The third point to note in Table 3 follows from this last point pertaining to the group as a whole. Perusal of the frequencies of the various VIQ-PIQ differences for the three separate age groups reveals that extremely high positive and extremely high negative differences occurred approximately equally in each of the three age groups. For example, reading across, a difference of +20 points or more occurred in the three different age groups in 5.2, 4.5, and 4.5% of the cases, and of −20 points or more occurred in 4.5 (100 − 95.5), 4.9, and 3.2% of the cases, respectively.

The conclusion that the data in Table 3 permit is that *age* per se appears to exert no effect on VIQ-PIQ discrepancies on the WAIS-R. Rather, VIQ-PIQ differences of small and large magnitudes occur in each age group and are normally and symmetrically distributed around a mean of zero in each age group.

Full Scale IQ and VIQ-PIQ Differences

Leaving age and turning next to the breakdown in Table 4 of the same 1880 V-P differences into subsets classified by *Full Scale IQ,* one sees that the third feature discussed above of the age data in Table 3 is *not* present in the FSIQ data in Table 4. Rather, the ranges resulting from the percentages of cases of

Table 4. Frequencies and Percentages of Differences Between Verbal and Performance IQs in WAIS-R Standardization Sample (Different FSIQ Groups)

Magnitude of VIQ-PIQ Difference in Points	79 & below (N = 165)			80–89 (N = 302)			90–109 (N = 924)			110–119 (N = 312)			120+ (N = 177)			All Ages (N = 1880)			
	N	(%)	(CUM %)	N	(%)	(CUM %)	N	(%)	(CUM %)	N	(%)	(CUM %)	N	(%)	(CUM %)	N	(CUM N)	(%)	(CUM %)
30+	0	0.0	0.0	0	0.0	0.0	5	0.5	0.5	1	0.3	0.3	4	2.3	2.3	10	10	0.5	0.5
26–29	0	0.0	0.0	0	0.0	0.0	1	0.1	0.6	6	1.9	2.2	3	1.7	4.0	10	20	0.5	1.1
23–25	0	0.0	0.0	0	0.0	0.0	19	2.1	2.7	3	1.0	3.2	3	1.7	5.6	25	45	1.3	2.4
22	0	0.0	0.0	2	0.7	0.7	8	0.9	3.6	3	1.0	4.2	1	0.6	6.2	14	59	0.7	3.1
21	0	0.0	0.0	2	0.7	1.3	5	0.5	4.1	3	1.0	5.1	3	1.7	7.9	13	72	0.7	3.8
20	0	0.0	0.0	1	0.3	1.7	6	0.6	4.8	8	2.6	7.7	2	1.1	9.0	17	89	0.9	4.7
19	1	0.6	0.6	2	0.7	2.3	5	0.5	5.3	3	1.0	8.7	1	0.6	9.6	12	101	0.6	5.4
18	0	0.0	0.6	2	0.7	3.0	6	0.6	6.0	4	1.3	10.0	5	2.8	12.4	17	118	0.9	6.3
17	0	0.0	0.6	1	0.3	3.3	3	0.3	6.3	5	1.6	11.5	0	0.0	12.4	9	127	0.5	6.8
16	0	0.0	0.6	2	0.7	4.0	10	1.1	7.4	3	1.0	12.5	4	2.3	14.7	19	146	1.0	7.8
15	0	0.0	0.6	1	0.3	4.3	9	1.0	8.3	5	1.6	14.1	2	1.1	15.8	17	163	0.9	8.7
14	1	0.6	1.2	6	2.0	6.3	12	1.3	9.6	8	2.6	16.7	4	2.3	18.1	31	194	1.6	10.3
13	2	1.2	2.4	4	1.3	7.6	16	1.7	11.4	4	1.3	17.9	4	2.3	20.3	30	224	1.6	11.9
12	1	0.6	3.0	4	1.3	8.9	23	2.5	13.9	8	2.6	20.5	2	1.1	21.5	38	262	2.0	13.9
11	3	1.8	4.8	4	1.3	10.3	31	3.4	17.2	2	0.6	21.1	5	2.8	24.3	45	307	2.4	16.3
10	6	3.6	8.5	4	1.3	11.6	21	2.3	19.5	10	3.2	24.4	3	1.7	26.0	44	351	2.3	18.7
9	4	2.4	10.9	10	3.3	14.9	12	1.3	20.8	6	1.9	26.3	3	1.7	27.7	35	386	1.9	20.5
8	8	4.8	15.8	9	3.0	17.9	21	2.3	23.1	12	3.8	30.1	3	1.7	29.4	53	439	2.8	23.4
7	5	3.0	18.8	10	3.3	21.2	23	2.5	25.5	11	3.5	33.7	8	4.5	33.9	57	496	3.0	26.4
6	4	2.4	21.2	10	3.3	24.5	25	2.7	28.2	10	3.2	36.9	4	2.3	36.2	53	549	2.8	29.2
5	7	4.2	25.5	12	4.0	28.5	32	3.5	31.7	9	2.9	39.7	5	2.8	39.0	65	614	3.5	32.7
4	7	4.2	29.7	15	5.0	33.4	25	2.7	34.4	12	3.8	43.6	6	3.4	42.4	65	679	3.5	36.1
3	7	4.2	33.9	6	2.0	35.4	41	4.4	38.9	6	1.9	45.5	3	1.7	44.1	63	742	3.4	39.5

	n	%	cum %	n	%	cum %	n	%	cum %	n	%	cum %	n	%	cum %	n	cum n	%	cum %
2	11	6.7	40.6	14	4.6	40.1	35	3.8	42.6	15	4.8	50.3	4	2.3	46.3	79	821	4.2	43.7
1	6	3.6	44.2	20	6.6	46.7	31	3.4	46.0	4	1.3	51.6	8	4.5	50.8	69	890	3.7	47.3
0	13	7.9	52.1	15	5.0	51.7	37	4.0	50.0	9	2.9	54.5	5	2.8	53.7	79	969	4.2	51.5
−1	7	4.2	56.4	13	4.3	56.0	35	3.8	53.8	8	2.6	57.1	4	2.3	55.9	67	1036	3.6	55.1
−2	11	6.7	63.0	7	2.3	58.3	30	3.2	57.0	12	3.8	60.9	7	4.0	59.9	67	1103	3.6	58.7
−3	10	6.1	69.1	15	5.0	63.2	32	3.5	60.5	9	2.9	63.8	3	1.7	61.6	69	1172	3.7	62.3
−4	10	6.1	75.2	20	6.6	69.9	31	3.4	63.9	7	2.2	66.0	8	4.5	66.1	76	1248	4.0	66.4
−5	8	4.8	80.0	5	1.7	71.5	34	3.7	67.5	13	4.2	70.2	5	2.8	69.0	65	1313	3.5	69.8
−6	5	3.0	83.0	12	4.0	75.5	29	3.1	70.7	13	4.2	74.4	2	1.1	70.1	61	1374	3.2	73.1
−7	10	6.1	89.1	9	3.0	78.5	27	2.9	73.6	2	0.6	75.0	6	3.4	73.4	54	1428	2.9	76.0
−8	2	1.2	90.3	10	3.3	81.8	16	1.7	75.3	7	2.2	77.2	6	3.4	76.8	41	1469	2.1	78.1
−9	4	2.4	92.7	6	2.0	83.8	30	3.2	78.6	8	2.6	79.8	3	1.7	78.5	51	1520	2.7	80.9
−10	2	1.2	93.9	7	2.3	86.1	21	2.3	80.8	6	1.9	81.7	4	2.3	80.8	40	1560	2.1	83.0
−11	0	0.0	93.9	8	2.6	88.7	23	2.5	83.3	9	2.9	84.6	5	2.8	83.6	45	1605	2.4	85.4
−12	3	1.8	95.8	6	2.0	90.7	24	2.6	85.9	6	1.9	86.5	4	2.3	85.9	43	1648	2.3	87.7
−13	3	1.8	97.6	5	1.7	92.4	16	1.7	87.7	4	1.3	87.8	4	2.3	88.1	32	1680	1.7	89.4
−14	1	0.6	98.2	7	2.3	94.7	14	1.5	89.2	5	1.6	89.4	4	2.3	90.4	31	1711	1.6	91.0
−15	2	1.2	99.4	3	1.0	95.7	11	1.2	90.4	5	1.6	91.0	3	1.7	92.1	24	1735	1.3	92.3
−16	0	0.0	99.4	3	1.0	96.7	12	1.3	91.7	3	1.0	92.0	3	1.7	93.7	21	1756	1.1	93.4
−17	0	0.0	99.4	1	0.3	97.0	11	1.2	92.9	4	1.3	93.3	1	0.6	94.3	17	1773	0.9	94.3
−18	0	0.0	99.4	1	0.3	97.4	7	0.8	93.6	2	0.6	93.9	1	0.6	94.9	11	1784	0.6	94.9
−19	0	0.0	99.4	2	0.7	98.0	12	1.3	94.9	3	1.0	94.9	2	1.1	96.0	19	1803	1.0	95.9
−20	1	0.6	100.0	2	0.7	98.6	6	0.6	95.6	1	0.3	95.2	0	0.0	96.0	10	1813	0.5	96.4
−21	0	0.0	100.0	2	0.7	99.3	7	0.8	96.3	7	2.2	97.4	1	0.6	96.6	17	1830	0.9	97.3
−22	0	0.0	100.0	0	0.0	99.3	6	0.6	97.0	1	0.3	97.8	2	1.1	97.7	9	1839	0.5	97.8
−23–25	0	0.0	100.0	1	0.3	99.7	14	1.5	98.5	2	0.6	98.4	1	0.6	98.3	18	1857	1.0	98.8
−26–29	0	0.0	100.0	1	0.3	100.0	7	0.8	99.2	3	1.0	99.4	2	1.1	99.4	13	1870	0.7	99.5
−30+	0	0.0	100.0	0	0.0	100.0	7	0.8	100.0	2	0.6	100.0	1	0.6	100.0	10	1880	0.5	100.0

very high plus or very high minus VIQ-PIQ differences become progressively *smaller* as one proceeds in Table 4 from right to left (from the highest to the lowest, FSIQ groups). Specifically, as perusal of Table 4 reveals, to encompass 95% of the VIQ versus PIQ discrepancies that actually were present in the group of 177 individuals with a FSIQ of 120 and higher required a range of these VIQ versus PIQ differences that extended approximately from +25 to −25. However, to encompass a comparable 95% of these VIQ-PIQ differences in the other four FSIQ groups (reading from right to left in Table 4) required the progressively smaller ranges of approximately +22 to −22 (FSIQ 110–119); +22 to −22 (90–109); +18 to −18 (80–89); and only +13 to −13 (79 and below). This same finding is revealed in a different format in Table 5, which we constructed by selecting from Table 4 the percentages shown there for each of the magnitudes of interest to us, namely, 10 (or more), 13, 15, and 22 points, respectively. Thus entering Table 4 for FSIQ 120 and above shows that a cumulative percentage of 6.2 of those 177 individuals had a V > P of 22 or more points and, entering the bottom of that same column, another 3.4% (100 − 96.6%) had a P > V of 22 or more points. These two figures (6.2 and 3.4) are reproduced in the first row of the *last* column of Table 5. The remaining numbers in Table 5 were derived in the same manner and present the percentage of individuals whose difference scores fell outside the ranges of +22 to −22, +15 to −15, +13 to −13, and +10 to −10 points in each of the five different FSIQ subgroups, as well as the full sample of 1880 individuals. The numbers shown in the last row of Table 5 for the *total* of each column were obtained by computations based on each of the *actual* subsets of 1880 individuals and, due to rounding off, are not exactly equal to the sum of the two part columns (V > P and P > V) presented in that Table (that is, the value of 24.3 as the sum of 11.9 plus 12.3 in the last row under the 13+ points column).

Two conclusions follow from these empirical data in Tables 4 and 5. First, contrary to what one may have anticipated, normal, community-living adults in the lowest FSIQ group (IQ of 79 and below) show relatively fewer (including extreme) plus or minus VIQ versus PIQ differences than do individuals with higher FSIQs. Thus, in Table 4 one finds that only a single individual (.60%) in this lowest IQ group showed a VIQ-PIQ difference of +15 points and more and only three individuals (1.8%) of −15 and more (100 − 98.2), with progressively larger *percentages* (4.3 and 5.3, 8.3 and 10.8, and 14.1 and 10.6, and 15.8 and 9.6%) of such individuals as one proceeds (from left to right) up the FSIQ groups in that table. Second, the proportion of individuals with large differences between the Verbal and Performance IQs increases progressively with each increase in FSIQ, becoming most frequent in individuals with the highest FSIQ. This may be seen most readily by reading up from bottom to top in each of the "total" columns in Table 5; namely, from FSIQ of 79 and below up through each successively higher FSIQ group. Study of the WISC-R table in Kaufman (1976, p. 743), which is most comparable to our WAIS-R Table 4 (and its summary in Table 5) reveals a similar finding; namely, that the children

Table 5. Percentage of Cases in the WAIS-R Standardization Sample with Differences Between Verbal (V) and Performance (P) IQs of Different Magnitudes

WAIS-R Full Scale IQ	N	10+ Points			13+ Points			15+ Points			22+ Points		
		V > P	P > V	Total	V > P	P > V	Total	V > P	P > V	Total	V > P	P > V	Total
120 and above	177	26.0	21.5	47.5	20.3	14.1	34.5	15.8	9.6	25.4	6.2	3.4	9.6
110–119	312	24.4	20.2	44.6	17.9	13.5	31.4	14.1	10.6	24.7	4.2	2.6	6.7
90–109	924	19.5	21.4	40.9	11.4	14.1	25.4	8.3	10.8	19.2	3.6	3.7	7.3
80–89	302	11.6	16.2	27.8	7.6	9.3	16.9	4.3	5.3	9.6	0.7	0.7	1.3
79 and below	165	8.5	7.3	15.8	2.4	4.2	6.7	0.6	1.8	2.4	0.0	0.0	0.0
Total Group	1880	18.7	19.1	37.8	11.9	12.3	24.3	8.7	9.0	17.7	3.1	2.7	5.8

with FSIQs of 79 and below had relatively fewer plus or minus VIQ versus PIQ differences of 15 or more points. As shown in our Table 5, only 2.4% of the adults with a WAIS-R FSIQ of 79 and below had a V-P or P-V difference as large as 15 points or more. Furthermore, as with the WISC-R standardization sample, the percent of the WAIS-R sample with a VIQ versus PIQ difference of 15 points (plus or minus) or more increased progressively (reading up in Table 5) in each of the succeeding IQ subgroups (9.6, 19.2, 24.7, and 25.4%, respectively).

Nevertheless, it is important to cast into practical perspective the percentages shown in our Tables 4 and 5 of Verbal versus Performance differences that occurred in the different FSIQ groups in the WAIS-R standardization sample. Particularly noteworthy in Tables 4 and 5 is the degree of *symmetry* revealed by the frequency of plus and minus differences around each mean in most of the FSIQ groups. Thus reading across in the second *row* from the bottom of Table 5 (FSIQ of 79 and below) reveals that the percentages that occur in Table 4 of V > P and P > V of 10 points or more were 8.5 versus 7.3; of 13 or more points were 2.4 versus 4.2; of 15 or more points were 0.6 versus 1.8, and of 22 points or more were .00 versus .00. Thus these pairs of percentages are approximately equal at each magnitude of V-P difference. Perusal in Table 5 of the comparable data in the *rows* containing the individuals in FSIQ group 80–89 and also 90–109 reveals a comparable symmetry in the VIQ-PIQ differences with a positive (V > P) as against a negative (P > V) sign. However, this symmetry breaks down in the WAIS-R standardization subgroups with the two highest FSIQs shown in Table 5. As evident in that table (but less clearly so in Table 4 and not at all in the data from all 1880 subjects shown in Figure 1), high FSIQ individuals (FSIQ of 110–119 and of 120 and above) showed somewhat *more* occurrences of a larger Verbal over Performance IQ than they did the reverse. Interestingly, Wechsler (1939, Table 25, p. 128) found this also was the case in the standardization sample for the W-B. The comparable WAIS standardization data (Wechsler, 1958, Table 25, p. 104) were reported in a form that precludes a comparable interpretation for that scale. It also is noteworthy that in the 1939 W-B standardization data just cited, very high percentages of the adults aged 20 to 49 (74.3%) in the lowest FSIQ group earned a larger PIQ relative to their own VIQ than earned a larger VIQ relative to their own PIQ (23%). The remaining 2.7% showed a difference of zero in VIQ versus PIQ. Why the individuals in the WAIS-R standardization group with an FSIQ of 79 and below (see our Tables 4 and 5) did *not* show a similarly greater frequency of higher Performance than Verbal IQ, whereas the opposite pattern (Verbal higher than Performance) *was found* in the two highest FSIQ groups (110–119 and 120 and above) is not clear.

We return next to an issue that we earlier discussed in general terms but that we now may consider for its relevance to the WAIS-R data. Specifically, how does the statistical significance of VIQ versus PIQ differences on the WAIS-R compare to these *empirically observed* base rates shown in our Figure 1 and Tables 3, 4, and 5?

Contrast of Approaches: Statistical Significance versus Empirical Base Rates

As suggested earlier and elaborated by the writers cited, data regarding the *statistical significance* (relative to a "true" difference from zero) of an obtained VIQ versus PIQ difference have at times been misunderstood to reflect the actuarial *abnormality* of the difference. Too often the result has been conclusions about an examinee that are clinically unsound. The example of a 12-point V-P difference on the WISC-R given by Kaufman (1976, p. 744) and discussed by us earlier is a case in point. Silverstein (1981a, Table 1) elaborates on this WISC-R example.

Our Table 6 on the WAIS-R data to which we turn next was constructed to make that same point by contrasting the statistical probability that an individual's VIQ-PIQ difference could have been obtained by chance if his or her "true" difference score were zero, with the frequency with which the obtained difference score actually occurred in the WAIS-R standardization sample. The VIQ-PIQ differences of the magnitude required to be statistically significantly different from zero at four probability levels already have been published for the WAIS-R and are reproduced here in the middle column of our Table 6. Specifically, the WAIS-R Manual (Wechsler, 1981, Table 14, p. 35) indicates that for the 1880 individuals constituting the nine different age groups shown in that table, an average VIQ versus PIQ difference of 7.15 (rounded off to 7) is significantly different from zero at the .15 level of probability and a difference of 9.73 (rounded off here to 10) is significantly different from zero at the .05 level of probability. Naglieri (1982, Table 2, p. 320) carried out the further computations and reported that across all 1880 subjects, VIQ-PIQ differences of 8 points and 13 points, respectively, are required to reach the .10 and .01 levels of statistical significance. These four values, based on the standard error of measurement, are the differences required for statistical significance in our Table 6.

Returning to the *last* column of either our Table 3 or Table 4 for the comparable *empirically* observed data on the same 1880 individuals yields the magnitudes of VIQ versus PIQ differences that actually occurred in the standard-

Table 6. Statistically Reliably Different and Actually Empirically Different Magnitudes of VIQ and PIQ Discrepancies (Regardless of Sign) Across All Ages in the WAIS-R Standardization Sample

p Value	Magnitude of VIQ versus PIQ Difference Required to be Statistically Reliably Different from Zero	Magnitude of VIQ versus PIQ Difference Actually Empirically Observed at Each Level of Probability
.15	7	16
.10	8	19
.05	10	23
.01	13	30

ization sample. The empirically observed data shown in the last column of Table 6 were derived as follows. Entering Table 3 one sees that .50% of the 1880 adults obtained a V-P difference of +30 or more points and another .50% earned a difference of −30 or more points. Adding .50 to .50 yields 1.00%. The last column of Table 6 records this 30-point difference opposite the p level of .01. The magnitudes of VIQ-PIQ differences that actually occurred in 5, 10, and 15% of the cases are 23, 19, and 16 points respectively, and were derived from Table 3 in a similar manner. For example, entering the cumulative percentage sub-column of the last column of either Table 3 or 4 reveals that 7.8% of the 1880 individuals had a VIQ-PIQ discrepancy of +16 or more points and another 7.7% (100 − 92.3) had a VIQ-PIQ difference of −16 or more points. Adding these percentages reveals that 15.5% (7.8 plus 7.7) of the 1880 actually showed a VIQ versus PIQ difference of 16 or more points regardless of sign. Rounding these two values off reveals that, as shown in the right-hand column of our Table 6, about 15 out of 100 (p of .15) of these 1880 individuals actually (*empirically*) showed a VIQ versus PIQ difference of 16 or more points. That same last column in Table 3 (or Table 4) reveals that a difference of 19 points was earned by 5.4 plus 5.1% (100 − 94.9) or, summing the two (5.4 + 5.1) and rounding off, 10% (p of .10) of the 1880 individuals. The .05 and .01 percentiles are derived in the same manner. This procedure reveals that, regardless of sign, VIQ versus PIQ differences of 30, 23, 19, and 16 points actually occurred in the WAIS-R stand-ardization sample in proportions of .01, .05, .10, and .15, respectively. Each of these four magnitudes of discrepancy and their respective p values are shown in the last column of Table 6.

The contrast in the two columns shown in Table 6 is striking and reinforces the point made earlier that psychometrically based probabilities, while valid for their intended purposes (that is, determining whether such a discrepancy is statistically significant from a true value of zero), cannot *ipso facto* be used for other purposes. Thus the data in our Table 6 reveal that a VIQ versus PIQ difference (regardless of sign) of 10 points is sufficiently deviant that it differs significantly from zero at the 5% level of confidence. Such statistical reasoning notwithstanding, perusal of the last column of either Table 3 or Table 4 (and graphically in Figure 1) reveals that, in the WAIS-R standardization sample, 18.7% of these normal adults showed a V-P difference of +10 points or more and another 19.1% (100 − 80.9) showed a comparable difference of −10 points or more, for a total of 37.8%. Thus whereas as shown in the middle column of Table 6 a VIQ versus PIQ difference of 10 points is psychometrically "deviant" at a p level of .05, such a 10-point difference actually was found in the scores of 37.8% of these community-living (and therefore inferentially clinically normal) adults.

The summary data in Table 7 were developed in a similar manner from the last column of Table 3 (or Table 4) and present the percentages of the 1880 individuals who showed each magnitude of plus or minus VIQ versus PIQ difference, as well as the cumulative percentage for each of these magnitudes regardless of sign. Thus the data in the second from the *last* column of Table

Table 7. Cumulative Percentage Distributions Across All Ages of the Differences (Regardless of Sign) Between WAIS-R VIQ and PIQ

Size of Difference Between VIQ and PIQ	% V > P (+ Difference)	% P > V (− Difference)	Sum of + and − Differences	WAIS-R Cumulative Percentage[b]
30 and above	.5	.5	1.1[a]	100.0
26–29	.5	.7	1.2	98.9
22–25	2.1	1.4	3.5	97.7
19–21	2.2	2.4	4.7	94.2
16–18	2.4	2.6	5.0	89.5
13–15	4.1	4.6	8.8	84.5
10–12	6.8	6.8	13.6	75.7
7–9	7.7	7.8	15.5	62.2
4–6	9.7	10.7	20.5	46.7
1–3	11.2	10.8	22.0	26.2
0	—	—	—	4.2

[a]The percentages in this table do not sum exactly due to "rounding off" errors.
[b]Percent at or below the larger of the two numbers in column 1.

7 reveal that a VIQ versus PIQ difference of 30 or more points occurred in .50 plus .50% (for a total, due to rounding errors, of 1.1) of the 1880 individuals. As described earlier this 1.1% is represented in the last column of Table 6 as a 30-point difference for a p level of .01. The remaining data in Table 7 were derived in a similar manner. Thus it may be computed in Table 7 that an *actual* VIQ versus PIQ difference of 22 or more points occurred with a p value of 5.8% (100 − 94.2 for discrepancies over 19–21 points in the last column of Table 7). Rounding off this 5.8%, one concludes that 5% of the 1880 individuals had a VIQ versus PIQ difference at the lower end of the range of 22–25 points, namely about 23 points. This is consistent with the data in the last column of Table 6, derived from Table 3, which reveal that a VIQ-PIQ difference of 23 points occurred with an actual probability of 5 times in 100 (p of .05). Data for the .01, .10, and .15 levels of probability comparable to those shown in Table 6 also are derivable from the last column in Table 7 or, as *actually* was done above, from the last column of either Table 3 or Table 4.

Returning to Table 6, it is apparent that the differences between the conclusions a clinician would draw from using the actual, empirically obtained data in this third column versus the statistically derived data in the middle column would impact the life of an examinee quite differently. Specifically, whereas a VIQ versus PIQ difference of 13 points is shown in the middle column of Table 6 to be a statistically significant difference with a probability value of .01, the data in the last column of Table 3 reveal that such a 13-point (or greater) difference actually occurred in 11.9% of the cases in the plus direction and in 12.3% (100 − 87.7) of the cases in the minus direction for a total of 24.3% of the time in the 1880 individuals in the standardization sample. As discussed above, the VIQ versus PIQ difference of 10 points, which is statistically significant at the .05 level, actually occurred in 37.8% of the standardization sample. One must ask how pathological is a *statistically* significant difference of 13 points (*p* of .01) if it *actually occurs* in 24.3% of normal, community-living American adults? In fact, it was a data pool of "intuitive" statistics similar to this one (namely a *p* of .243) that accumulated from examining many hundreds of patients that led one of the present authors to suggest that a VIQ versus PIQ difference of 15 points is merely the *initial* datum that should stimulate the clinician to search for corroborating, extratest evidence from the *clinical or social history* that such a difference of 15 points is associated with a potentially significant diagnostic finding (Matarazzo, 1972, pp. 389–390). Furthermore, it is well known to the practicing clinician that differences (fluctuations) in VIQ as well as PIQ also occur in *each* of these two IQ part scores (and thus their difference) when one reexamines the same individual on a second occasion. In fact, subsequent research on test-retest changes in a small sample of normals administered the WAIS twice revealed that *increases* from first to second administration of 10–15 points in either VIQ, PIQ, or FSIQ, while rare, were not so infrequent as one earlier might have believed without benefit of such actuarially determined (observed) base rates (Matarazzo, Carmody, & Jacobs, 1980, Table 6, p. 101). Because of the clinician's need for such actuarial base-rate information, a companion study to the one reported in the present chapter was undertaken by us, of the magnitudes of increases and decreases that *actually occurred* in VIQ, PIQ, and FSIQ in the 119 *S*s in the WAIS-R standardization sample who were administered the WAIS-R and then retested with it two to seven weeks later (Matarazzo & Herman, 1984b).

IMPLICATIONS FOR CLINICAL PRACTICE

A wide body of research, some cited earlier in this chapter, suggests that, above and beyond the random errors associated with chance, a number of variables may produce a discrepancy between any given person's VIQ and PIQ. As discussed in relation to Tables 1 and 2 of the present chapter, an accumulating literature strongly suggests that dysfunction in the left hemisphere of the brain is, on the average, differentially associated with a lower Verbal IQ whereas a dysfunction in the right hemisphere is, on the average, associated with a relatively lower Performance IQ. Furthermore, early (but less robust) research suggests that this "laterality" effect *may* be more pronounced in males than in females (Bornstein & Matarazzo, in press). A number of other conditions appear able to produce a discrepancy in the VIQ versus PIQ of any given patient. Examples include aphasia, Turner's Syndrome, acute versus chronic lesions in a brain hemisphere, as well as occupation, magnitude of Full Scale IQ, and so on.

With the actual WAIS-R frequencies of occurrence of the different magnitudes of VIQ versus PIQ discrepancies shown here in our Figure 1 or Tables 3 through 7, a practitioner now has *empirical norms* against which to begin the professionally challenging search for extratest correlates of a potentially clinically meaningful difference between an individual's Verbal IQ and Performance IQ. Thus, depending on the specifics of the individual being examined, there may be times when a *difference of a few points is clinically meaningful* (that is, as revealed in other clinical or test findings), and other times when further search of the clinical history and physical and other neuropsychological test findings reveals no clinical corroboration of a VIQ-PIQ difference of 20 or more points. This is not surprising, inasmuch as at this stage in the development of the science on which the practice of psychology is based there still is no substitute for wide clinical experience and good judgment. Until other research is available, the normative WAIS-R data included in Figure 1 and Table 3 would suggest, as also suggested for the WAIS (Matarazzo, 1972, pp. 389–390), that a VIQ versus PIQ difference of plus or minus 15 points is worthy of further clinical study even though, as shown in the last column of Table 3, a difference of this magnitude or greater occurred in 17.7% (8.7 plus 9.0) of the standardization sample.

However, the caution offered earlier may need repetition here. Namely, many times an extensive clinical inquiry will yield no corroborating evidence that a 15 or 20 point or more Verbal versus Performance difference is meaningful. As but one example, the WAIS-R data presented in our Table 5 reveals that 9.6% of these community-living, normal individuals with an FSIQ of 120 and above actually showed such a difference of 22 or more points. This is fully consistent with the experience of psychologists who examine graduate students, law students, medical students, business executives, and other individuals who score at the top of the scale of measured intelligence. On the other hand, neuropsychologists of any experience can readily recall a patient with demonstrable brain injury who showed little or *no* difference in Verbal versus Performance IQ but who did show profound deficit as assessed by a number of other types of neurological and cognitive-neuropsychological measures. Furthermore, as stated above, the results discussed in relation to the mean values shown in our Tables 1 and 2 *suggest* also that, for the W-B and WAIS, a VIQ-PIQ discrepancy may be masked in the female patient relative to a male patient. Thus if further comparable research with the WAIS-R bears out this potential influence of the sex of the patient, for individuals 16 years and older sex as a variable (but, as shown here in our Table 3, apparently not age) will have to be taken into consideration in giving clinical meaning to any obtained Verbal-Performance IQ discrepancy.

A Further Caution in Interpreting WAIS-R Base Rates

Furthermore, to return to our Tables 5, 6, and 7, and to underscore the complexity of the challenge for the practitioner using these tables, it is possible that a not insignificant number of the 1880 adults in the WAIS-R standardization sample *did* at one time in their lives suffer a brain injury, and thus the large VIQ-PIQ differences shown in these community-living, "normal" individuals are reflecting a number of "real" cases of brain injury rather than its absence as the latter might be inferred by a reader superficially perusing only the tables in the present chapter. New information on the damaging *prenatal* effects on the brain of the fetus due to maternal smoking, ingestion of alcohol, or prescription and nonprescription drugs, is appearing in scientific journals at an alarming rate. Unconsciousness due to head trauma experienced in household accidents, diving during swimming, falls from bicycles, automobile accidents, falls backward off a chair, and so on are not uncommon childhood and adult experiences. Only future research will help us unravel what proportions of the adults in a "normal" population such as the WAIS-R standardization sample were, in fact, showing in their VIQ versus PIQ discrepancy score the residuals of such not uncommon head traumas.

What this means is that the rule of thumb that a 15-point or more discrepancy in VIQ versus PIQ ordinarily should be further examined and clarified is only that; namely, a rule of thumb that should be used wisely by a professional psychologist—pursued vigorously in some contexts and put aside in others. In clinical neuropsychology, as in other specialties, there still is no substitute for wide clinical experience and good professional judgment. The WAIS-R base rates included in this chapter and the companion articles by Matarazzo & Herman (1984a, 1984b) are intended to serve as only another example of *aids* to such judgment and not as substitutes.

REFERENCES

Andersen, A. L. (1951). The effect of laterality localization of focal brain lesions on the Wechsler-Bellevue subtests. *Journal of Clinical Psychology, 7,* 149–153.

Becker, B. (1975). Intellectual changes after closed head injury. *Journal of Clinical Psychology, 31,* 307–309.

Black, F. W. (1973). Memory and paired-associate learning of patients with unilateral brain lesions. *Psychological Reports, 33,* 919–922.

Black, F. W. (1974a). Cognitive effects of unilateral brain lesions secondary to penetrating missile wounds. *Perceptual and Motor Skills, 38,* 387–391.

Black, F. W. (1974b). The cognitive sequelae of penetrating missile wounds of the brain. *Military Medicine, 139,* 815–817.

Black, F. W. (1976). Cognitive deficits in patients with unilateral war-related frontal lobe lesions. *Journal of Clinical Psychology, 32,* 366–372.

Bornstein, R. A. (1983). VIQ-PIQ discrepancies on the WAIS-R in patients with unilateral or bilateral cerebral dysfunction. *Journal of Consulting and Clinical Psychology, 51,* 779–780.

Bornstein, R. A. (1984). Unilateral lesions and the Revised Wechsler Adult Intelligence Scale: No sex differences. *Journal of Consulting and Clinical Psychology, 52,* 604–608.

Bornstein, R. A., & Matarazzo, J. D. (1982). Wechsler VIQ versus PIQ differences in cerebral dysfunction: A literature review with emphasis on sex differences. *Journal of Clinical Neuropsychology, 4,* 319–334.

Bornstein, R. A., & Matarazzo, J. D. (1984). Relationship of sex and the effects of unilateral lesions on the Wechsler Intelligence Scales: Further considerations. *Journal of Nervous and Mental Disease, 172,* 707–710.

Dennerll, R. D. (1964). Prediction of unilateral brain dysfunction using Wechsler test scores. *Journal of Consulting Psychology, 28,* 278–284.

Doehring, D. G., Reitan, R. M., & Klove, H. (1961). Changes in patterns of intelligence test performance associated with homonymous visual field defects. *Journal of Nervous and Mental Disease, 132,* 227–233.

Field, J. G. (1960). Two types of tables for use with Wechsler's intelligence scales. *Journal of Clinical Psychology, 16,* 3–7.

Fisher, G. M. (1960). A corrected table for determining the significance of the difference between verbal and performance IQ's on the WAIS and the Wechsler-Bellevue. *Journal of Clinical Psychology, 16,* 7–9.

Fitzhugh, K. B., & Fitzhugh, L. C. (1964). WAIS results for Ss with longstanding, chronic, lateralized and diffuse cerebral dysfunction. *Perceptual and Motor Skills, 19,* 735–739.

Fitzhugh, K. B., Fitzhugh, L. C., & Reitan, R. M. (1962). Wechsler-Bellevue comparisons in groups with "chronic" and "current" lateralized and diffuse brain lesions. *Journal of Consulting Psychology, 26,* 306–310.

Grossman, F. M., Herman, D. O., & Matarazzo, J. D. (in press). Statistically inferred versus empirically observed VIQ-PIQ differences in the WAIS-R. *Journal of Clinical Psychology.*

Inglis, J., & Lawson, J. S. (1981). Sex differences in the effects of unilateral brain damage on intelligence. *Science, 212,* 693–695.

Kaufman, A. S. (1976). Verbal-Performance IQ discrepancies on the WISC-R. *Journal of Consulting and Clinical Psychology, 44,* 739–744.

Kaufman, A. S. (1979). *Intelligent testing with the WISC-R.* New York: Wiley-Interscience.

Klove, H. (1959). Relationship of differential electroencephalographic patterns to distribution of Wechsler-Bellevue scores. *Neurology, 9,* 871–876.

Klove, H., & Reitan, R. M. (1958). Effect of dysphasia and spatial distortion on Wechsler-Bellevue results. *AMA Archives of Neurology and Psychiatry, 80,* 708–713.

Lansdell, H. (1962). A sex difference in the effect of temporal-lobe neurosurgery on design preference. *Nature, 194,* 852–854.

Leli, D. A., & Filskov, S. B. (1981). Actuarial detection and description of brain impairment with the Wechsler-Bellevue Form I. *Journal of Clinical Psychology, 37,* 615–622.

Matarazzo, J. D. (1972). *Wechsler's measurement and appraisal of adult intelligence* (5th and enlarged ed.). New York: Oxford Press.

Matarazzo, J. D. (1980). Psychological assessment of intelligence. In H. I. Kaplan, A. M. Freedman, & B. J. Sadock (Eds.), *Comprehensive textbook of psychiatry III* (3rd ed.). Baltimore: Williams & Wilkins.

Matarazzo, J. D., Carmody, T. P., & Jacobs, L. D. (1980). Test-retest reliability and stability of the WAIS: A literature review with implications for clinical practice. *Journal of Clinical Neuropsychology, 2,* 89–105.

Matarazzo, J. D., & Herman, D. O. (1984a). Relationship of education and IQ in the WAIS-R standardization sample. *Journal of Consulting and Clinical Psychology, 52,* 631–634.

Matarazzo, J. D., & Herman, D. O. (1984b). Base rate data for the WAIS-R: Test-retest stability and VIQ-PIQ differences. *Journal of Clinical Neuropsychology, 6,* 351–366.

Matarazzo, J. D., Matarazzo, R. G., Wiens, A. N., Gallo, A. E., Jr., & Klonoff, H. (1976). Retest reliability of the Halstead Impairment Index in a normal, a schizophrenic, and two samples of organic patients. *Journal of Clinical Psychology, 32,* 338–349.

Matarazzo, J. D., Wiens, A. N., Matarazzo, R. G., & Goldstein, S. G. (1974). Psychometric and clinical test-retest reliability of the Halstead Impairment Index in a sample of healthy, young, normal men. *Journal of Nervous and Mental Disease, 158,* 37–49.

Matarazzo, R. G., Matarazzo, J. D., Gallo, A. E., Jr., & Wiens, A. N. (1979). IQ and neuropsychology following carotid endarterectomy. *Journal of Clinical Neuropsychology, 1,* 97–116.

Matarazzo, R. G., Wiens, A. N., Matarazzo, J. D., & Manaugh, T. S. (1973). Test-retest reliability of the WAIS in a normal population. *Journal of Clinical Psychology, 29,* 194–197.

McGlone, J. (1977). Sex differences in the cerebral organization of verbal functions in patients with unilateral brain lesions. *Brain, 100,* 775–793.

McGlone, J. (1978). Sex differences in functional brain asymmetry. *Cortex, 14*, 122–128.

McNemar, Q. (1957). On WAIS difference scores. *Journal of Consulting Psychology, 21*, 239–240.

Meier, M. J., & French, L. A. (1966). Longitudinal assessment of intellectual functioning following unilateral temporal lobectomy. *Journal of Clinical Psychology, 22*, 22–27.

Meyer, V., & Jones, H. G. (1957). Patterns of cognitive test performance as functions of the lateral localization of cerebral abnormalities in temporal lobe. *Journal of Mental Science, 103*, 758–772.

Naglieri, J. A. (1982). Two types of tables for use with the WAIS-R. *Journal of Consulting and Clinical Psychology, 50*, 319–321.

Parsons, O. A., Vega, A., & Burn, J. (1969). Different psychological effects of lateralized brain damage. *Journal of Consulting and Clinical Psychology, 33*, 551–557.

Payne, R. W., & Jones, H. G. (1957). Statistics for the investigation of individual cases. *Journal of Clinical Psychology, 13*, 115–121.

Reitan, R. M. (1955). Certain differential effects of left and right cerebral lesions in human adults. *Journal of Comparative and Physiological Psychology, 48*, 474–477.

Reynolds, C. R. (1979). Interpreting the index of abnormality when the distribution of score differences is known: Comment on Piotrowski. *Journal of Consulting and Clinical Psychology, 47*, 401–402.

Satz, P. (1966). Specific and non-specific effects of brain lesions in man. *Journal of Abnormal Psychology, 71*, 65–70.

Satz, P., Richard, W., & Daniels, A. (1967). The alterations of intellectual performance after lateralized brain injury in man. *Psychonomic Science, 7*, 369–370.

Simpson, C. A., & Vega, A. (1971). Unilateral brain damage and patterns of age-corrected WAIS subtest scores. *Journal of Clinical Psychology, 27*, 204–208.

Silverstein, A. B. (1981a). Reliability and abnormality of test score differences. *Journal of Clinical Psychology, 37*, 392–394.

Silverstein, A. B. (1981b). Verbal-Performance IQ discrepancies on the WISC-R: One more time. *Journal of Consulting and Clinical Psychology, 49*, 465–466.

Silverstein, A. B. (1982). Pattern analysis as simultaneous statistical inference. *Journal of Consulting and Clinical Psychology, 50*, 234–240.

Smith, A. (1966). Certain hypothesized hemispheric differences in language and visual functions in human adults. *Cortex, 2*, 109–126.

Smith, A. (1981). Principles underlying brain functions in neuropsychological sequelae of different neuropathological processes. In S. B. Filskov & T. J. Boll (Eds.), *Handbook of clinical neuropsychology.* New York: Wiley.

Todd, J., Coolidge, F., & Satz, P. (1977). The Wechsler Adult Intelligence Scale discrepancy index: A neuropsychological evaluation. *Journal of Consulting and Clinical Psychology, 45*, 450–454.

Uzzell, B. P., Zimmerman, R. A., Dolinskas, C. A., & Obrist, W. D. (1979). Lateralized psychological impairment associated with CT lesions in head injured patients. *Cortex, 15*, 391–401.

Vega, A., & Parsons, O. A. (1969). Relationships between sensory-motor deficits and WAIS verbal and performance scores in unilateral brain damage. *Cortex, 5*, 229–241.

Wechsler, D. (1939). *The measurement of adult intelligence.* Baltimore: Williams & Wilkins.

Wechsler, D. (1958). *The measurement and appraisal of adult intelligence* (4th ed.). Baltimore: Williams & Wilkins.

Wechsler, D. (1981). *Manual for the Wechsler Adult Intelligence Scale—Revised.* New York: The Psychological Corporation.

Zimmerman, S. F., Whitmyre, J. W., & Fields, F. R. J. (1970). Factor analytic structure of the Wechsler Adult Intelligence Scale in patients with diffuse and lateralized cerebral dysfunction. *Journal of Clinical Psychology, 26*, 462–465.

TWENTY-THREE

EDUCATIONAL APPLICATIONS OF INTELLIGENCE TESTING

ANN E. BOEHM

Teachers College, Columbia University
New York, New York

Intelligence tests play a significant role in assessing both groups and individuals in educational settings. In an extensive review, Carroll (1978) concluded that, despite the controversy surrounding intelligence tests, their use has been and continues to be influential in shaping educational policy and practice. In the past, scores from intelligence tests have led to widespread ability grouping. More recently, massive federal funds allocated to the early intervention program Head Start were largely retracted when the effectiveness of this program was questioned, based partly on the fact that IQ gains were not maintained after a few years in school.

This chapter focuses on educational applications of intelligence tests with school-age children. The results of these intelligence measures have at least three major areas of educational application:

1. **Selection and Placement.** Applications related to selection or placement in classes or programs based on assessed learning rate (intelligence).

2. **Screening, Diagnosis, and Remedial Planning.** In addition to affecting decisions related to selection or placement, screening is used to rule out questions of general intelligence in understanding other learning problems. In the diagnostic process intelligence measures are used not only to determine the general level of cognitive functioning, but also to formulate hypotheses regarding relative strengths and weaknesses that might lead to planning effective learning strategies and remedial programs. In addition, an intellectual evaluation helps in determining appropriate levels of expectation for school achievement.

3. **Accountability, Research, and Evaluation.** IQ measures are often included among outcome measures related to program effectiveness. In addition, they are among the measures used in research to account for pupil characteristics.

Each of these three areas of application will be reviewed in this chapter. The applications to be discussed are based both on group and individual intelligence measures, although major emphasis will be placed on individual tests. Many documented misuses and abuses of these measures (Bersoff, 1979, 1981, 1982; Kaufman, 1979; Lutey & Copeland, 1982; Oakland, 1977; Sattler, 1982) will not be detailed in this chapter. The perspective taken here is consonant with that summarized by Oliver (1976) when speaking about the American College Testing Program:

> Anyone who thinks that a test score reflects all of the needed educational infor-
> mation or reflects all aspects of human talent or is an indication of human worth
> or value, does not understand the nature of testing. Tests simply provide some
> information that, when properly used, is extremely valuable in making better
> educational decisions.

Undoubtedly the authors of the most widely used individual tests of intelligence, the *Stanford-Binet* (Terman & Merrill, 1973) and the *Wechsler Scales* (Wechsler, 1967, 1974) would have agreed with Oliver's statement. Binet and Simon and Wechsler were careful to point out the limitations of their instruments in assessing the construct of intelligence. Binet and Simon (1916) believed in careful obser-vation and study of individuals over an extended time period and regarded the results of their scale as only tentative and not as a total indicator of functioning. Wechsler (1975) viewed intelligence as a multifaceted entity consisting of nu-merous components that could be only imperfectly and incompletely tapped by an intelligence test.

It is also clear that, other than for purposes of placement, the results of intelligence tests can not be translated directly into educational practice. The cognitive processes underlying performance on intelligence tests are not assessed directly (Resnick, 1979; Sattler, 1982; Sternberg & Wagner, 1982). Information processing approaches to the assessment of intelligence provide a promising direction for the future. Assessment of cognitive competence is needed relative both to success in academic areas and in everyday life situations (Brown & French, 1979). The advantages of the information-processing approach to cog-nitive functioning are inherent in the careful breakdown of cognitive tasks into their component levels and applications so that, in a given area, processes used to solve problems are identified. Specific strengths or limitations in problem-solving strategies can then be translated into educational objectives and practice. The present research direction, along with the cognitive processes identified, addresses the concerns raised by Carroll (1978) who concluded his review by stating, "Despite a few promising signs in recent research efforts, the present scene in intelligence testing is essentially one of stagnation, with much talk but little progress" (p. 93). Carroll, however, was hopeful that with continued study, research relevant to information processing will "permit more rigorous state-ments about the nature of the cognitive abilities measured by standardized mental tasks" (p. 59), and that cognitive measures will have increased relevance to schooling and to educational practice.

SELECTION AND PLACEMENT APPLICATIONS

From its beginning, the systematic assessment of intelligence has had as its purpose an education application. When Alfred Binet, along with Henry Simon, developed the first individual test of intelligence in 1905 (Binet & Simon, 1916), it was developed as a means of "insuring the benefits of instruction to defective children" (p. 9). In 1904, a commission named by the French Minister of Public Instruction was charged with the task of developing procedures of systematic diagnosis so that decisions were neither haphazard nor based on subjective impressions. Based on extensive preliminary work with normal and subnormal children in the Paris elementary schools, Binet and Simon developed their "Psychological Method" to assess general intelligence in order to differentiate between children of normal and subnormal ability. Carroll (1978) cited earlier work by Galton (1869) who had focused on sensory discriminations and reaction times in the assessment of ability, and by Cattell (1885) who suggested that such tests might predict scholastic success for college students. But it was Binet and Simon who focused on generating tasks with which normal, as compared to subnormal, children of increasing age could meet success. Binet and Simon recognized that one could not strictly measure "intelligence" through use of a scale, but could only understand the process of development and at what point different levels of retardation corresponded. Intelligence was viewed as involving a fundamental faculty of utmost importance to practical life — namely, judgment: "To judge well, to comprehend well, to reason well, these are the essential activities of intelligence" (Binet & Simon, 1916, p. 43). The extent to which children could judge, comprehend, and reason well in relationship to their normal age-mates was, and continues to be, the major basis for placement in special classes or programs.

Class placement is the major application of intelligence test results in educational settings. Resnick (1979) summarized three broad applications of tests in schools: the management of instruction, public accountability, and legitimization of schooling. The management of instruction according to Resnick involves three applications of tests: sorting, grading, and monitoring. Intelligence tests are the major measure by which children are "sorted" or placed into programs or classes. When used for purposes of placement, the individual's performance (in essence, score) on an intelligence test in addition often serves to establish expectations regarding achievement. Resnick (1979) suggested that in the future intelligence tests may be used as well to set limits on expectations the public has and demands from schools regarding their responsibility for pupil achievement.

Selection for Classes for the Mentally Retarded

The "sorting" function specified by Resnick is broadly, but not uniformly, employed to determine who will be admitted to or assigned to particular programs. With few exceptions, current federal and state practices mandate the use of intelligence tests for assignment to classes for the retarded. These intelligence measures, however, are usually supplemented by other achievement tests, teacher and parent observations, and measures of adaptive behavior. Depending on the state, a measured IQ score below 70, 75, or 80 is a major basis for placement in classes for the educable mentally retarded. One exception, however, is California, which, following the case of *Larry P. v. Riles* (1979), which examined the disproportionate number of black children placed in classes for the educable mentally retarded, based largely on IQ scores, banned the use of intelligence tests as the major basis for placement into classes for the educable mentally retarded. However, this ruling does not restrict the use of intelligence tests as a major basis for replacement into classes for the gifted, a topic to be discussed in a later section. Resnick (1979) suggested that the controversy regarding the use of intelligence tests for purposes of placement results not only from possible errors in placement, but also from the belief held by many, including herself, that given appropriate program modifications, children can be maintained within the educational mainstream.

Placement decisions have far-reaching implications for the child's future. Therefore, serious attention must be paid to the possibility of error, be it based on measurement error inherent in any test or inaccurate interpretation based on inadequate supportive evidence. Salvia and Ysseldyke (1981) suggest three types of testing errors that can occur in the placement process, including use of the wrong test, the wrong interpretation, and examiner mistakes that can range from clerical errors in scoring to failure to recognize the child with a hearing loss or the child who does not have a command of English.

While placement decisions should never be based on an IQ score alone, assessment reports are usually passed through the administrative hierarchies of school systems, and the IQ score often serves as the ultimate basis for placement, and supportive evidence, pro or con, is not necessarily reviewed. Recommended follow-up testing has not always been carried out. This was the case when the New York Supreme Court upheld the State's first educational malpractice award (*New York Times*, 1978). A young boy with a severe speech defect was assigned to a class for the educable mentally retarded based on an IQ score of 74. Despite the assessor's recommendation for reevaluation, he remained in EMR classes for 13 years without retesting. Later retesting indicated functioning within the normal range.

Experts in the field urge that rigid cut-off points not be used (Kaufman, 1979; Sattler, 1982; Wigdor & Garner, 1982). "Precise cut-off points, formulas, or minimum IQ requirements distort the meaning of what is measured and prevent intelligent test interpretation" (Kaufman, 1979, p. 13). Reporting the score as falling within a band of scores reflective of the standard error of measurement, recommended by Salvia and Ysseldyke (1981) and Sattler (1982), among others, may help alleviate this pitfall. This practice would be particularly important for children with borderline scores. A further recommendation might be the administration of two individual intelligence tests to individuals for whom there is a question regarding appropriate placement. The extra time and cost would be worth the extended sample of functioning on which to base a placement decision.

These extra steps are important as well for the child who is borderline at the trainable level of retardation. Placement in classes for the retarded, either EMR or TMR, will result in children having been so labeled and consequently instructed with a different set of expectations. Shepherd (1984) cautions, for example, that expectations for the trainable mentally retarded might prevent the child who comes from a highly involved home environment who might benefit from some training in basic academic skills from receiving training in these skills. In many TMR classes the teaching program and teacher expectations are focused only on self-help and other adaptive behaviors.

While the ramifications of labeling for the retarded are more serious than for other groups, such as the "gifted," inappropriate expectations, be they too high or too low, can be harmful to any child. Furthermore, being labeled as a slow learner, whatever the degree of retardation, tends to stick (Sattler, 1982; Wigdor & Garner, 1982).

Specific Learning Disabilities

A significant discrepancy between ability and achievement is the primary basis for identifying children with specific learning disabilities according to the Education for All Handicapped Children Act of 1975 (PL 94-142). According to PL 94-142 (*Federal Register*, 1977), children with handicapping conditions must be educated at public expense in the least restrictive environment; this usually results in special services, often in the form of special classes. Diagnosis, the development of individualized education programs (IEPs), and placement are based on input from a team of people, including the teacher, parent, school psychologist, and other appropriate specialists. Davis and Shepard (1983) questioned, however, whether professionals engaged in the identification of learning disabled students (including teachers of the learning disabled, school psychologists, and speech/language specialists) were (1) knowledgeable of and employed tests for identification that are psychometrically adequate, and (2) appropriately interpreted ability-achievement discrepancies. They sent a detailed questionnaire to 542 learning disability (LD) teachers, 130 school psychologists, and 179 speech/language specialists in the State of Colorado. The results, based on a 74% return rate, indicated that the group as a whole both frequently used and often preferred to use tests that reviewers had indicated were technically inadequate. Although the WISC-R was the preferred instrument among the school psychologists sampled, the *Peabody Picture Vocabulary Test* (PPVT) (Dunn & Dunn, 1981) was rated by learning disabilities teachers as having more value and relevance. The authors concluded that, if the limitations of inadequate instruments are taken into account, these instruments can provide information useful to the diagnostic process. However, users were not necessarily aware of inadequacies related to standardization, reliability, and validity. Furthermore, many of the respondents overestimated (in essence, inaccurately interpreted) the extent of discrepancy between scores on intelligence and achievement tests. If such misinterpretation is as widespread an error as indicated by Davis and

Shepard (1983) and as suggested by Kaufman (1979), many children are misplaced in special education classes.

The Committee on Ability Testing (Wigdor & Garner, 1982) pointed out that a common misuse of test scores occurs when children are assigned to LD classrooms based on significant differences between school performance (interpreted as performance on achievement tests) and "ability to learn" (interpreted as performance on intelligence tests). According to the Committee, "It has been demonstrated over and over that the differences between the two kinds of tests cannot be directly interpreted in this fashion. Both categories of tests measure developed abilities and, therefore, they both give indications of 'ability to learn' " (p. 163). The Committee further cautioned that since the correlation between the two types of test is high, measurement error might account for a large portion of the observed differences and the findings might be reversed on retesting.

The Committee on Ability Test (Wigdor & Garner, 1982) noted as well that while PL 94-142 has brought public education to previously unserviced children, it also has had the effect of removing children from regular classrooms and of increasing the amount of tracking in schools. In addition, the fundamental challenge of such tracking, according to the Committee, lies in the extent to which instruction is more effective than that offered in the regular classroom.

Davis and Shepard (1983) also direct attention to the widespread reliance of professionals on "clinical" or "professional" judgment in arriving at decisions regarding learning disabilities, often placing tests secondary to these judgments. They reported that many of the professionals that they surveyed were not aware of the steps essential to ensure the reliability and validity of their clinical judgments. Davis and Shepard concluded that little confidence can be placed on these "professional judgments" at present because these professionals do not necessarily understand the process of hypothesis testing and do not verify their judgments.

Classes for the Gifted

Increased attention to the "gifted" has resulted in special classes or programs being established across the country for this group of learners. These programs vary from separate class placement to enrichment experiences that can occur either within or outside the mainstream classroom. At present, few statewide programs are mandated for the "gifted," with the majority of programs mandated only at local or district levels. The nature of these programs will be determined by the definition of "giftedness" held by the particular school or district. A major issue arises here since there is no one accepted definition of "giftedness." Experts in the field point to the diverse groups of children designated as "gifted" by educators (Borland & Jacobs, in press: Marland, 1972, Renzulli, 1977; Tannenbaum, 1983). Giftedness is not, however, a uniform trait, and children labeled as "gifted" differ in their talents. Most schools employ a multi-trait approach when identifying the gifted, which can encompass not only academic ability and achievement, but also creative abilities or special talents. Each of these characteristics involves problems of definition and reliable measurement.

Where programs for the gifted exist, the IQ score is often the major criterion for initial screening, if not final placement. Under parental pressure to provide enriched learning opportunities for the gifted, schools are faced with the challenge of determining who the "gifted" are and must engage in screening large numbers of children for possible placement. While some systems engage in individualized screening procedures using brief measures, such as the *Slosson Intelligence Test* (SIT) (Slosson, 1983), others administer group tests of intelligence. In some systems the testing stops at this point, with selection decisions based on a brief sample of behavior obtained from a screening instrument or on group-administered intelligence test scores. Although brief tests, such as the Slosson, have value in the screening process, their use alone is inappropriate to placement decisions. Lutey and Copeland (1982) cite research in which the Slosson, for example, overestimates intelligence in the upper ranges and underestimates intelligence at the lower ranges of functioning when compared to other measures of intelligence. They recommend that the Slosson not be used at the extreme levels of intellectual functioning unless modifications are made that take into account the large standard deviations in these ranges.

Sattler (1982) indicated that "Group intelligence tests are about as successful as teacher nomination in identifying gifted children; they tend to provide lower IQs than individually administered intelligence tests" (p. 437). Sattler recommended the individual intelligence test as the method of choice for identifying gifted children. Carroll (1978) reviewed a number of characteristics that differentiate group from individual tests of ability. These characteristics include the following: (1) the need to answer as many questions as possible within a given time limit: (2) recognition rather than production answers; and (3) tasks that often require the examinee to read.

Many "gifted" children who encounter difficulty with reading or who have problems with verbal expression might thus be excluded from classes for the gifted at the screening level. Borland and Jacobs (in press) urge that final placement decisions *never* be based on group test scores and note that missing one or a few items, for whatever reason, can result in significantly lower scores.

Those systems that require administration of a more comprehensive intelligence test often turn to the *Stanford Binet* as the preferred measure (despite the absence of adequate reliability and validity data in the manual for the 1972 Edition), viewing it as providing more ceiling and floor than do either the Wechsler scales or the *McCarthy Scales of Children's Abilities* (MSCA) (McCarthy, 1972). However, at increasing chronological age levels, the *Binet* tasks become largely verbal in nature. This characteristic of the *Binet* is likely to change with the forthcoming revision. At present, however, the possibility exists of enhanced placement opportunities for children from highly verbal, enriched environments when selection decisions are based on the *Binet*. Thus, as children are placed in classes for the gifted, the question of which test is used is of great importance and possible ethical concern. Martin (1983) pointed out that instruments used with young children ages 5 through 8 (Binet, MSCA, WPPSI, WISC-R) are problemmatic since they do not produce comparable scores. Both the MSCA and WPPSI produce scores lower than the Binet. For example, the

Stanford-Binet yielded higher IQ scores than the WPPSI (Zimmerman & Woo-Sam, 1970), with the largest discrepancies occuring in the "superior" range. Gerken, Hancock, and Wade (1978) reported that preschoolers obtained higher scores on the *Stanford-Binet* than on the *McCarthy scales*. Where districts set arbitrary cut-off scores of, for example, an IQ of 130 or 140, for placement in a class for the gifted, but do not specify the test to be used, an issue arises regarding the professional's responsibility in test selection (Martin, 1983). The variability in the young child's day-to-day performance is another issue of concern.

Borland and Jacobs (in press) urge that broad-based identification procedures be used in identification of the gifted. Multiple sources of information must also be considered, including tests, observations, past records, and recommendations by teachers, parents, and the children themselves. Such a procedure, according to Borland and Jacobs, will ensure that well-informed individuals will be in control of the decisions made, not test scores.

Many independent schools require scores from an individual intelligence test as part of the admission process. The role that these results play varies with the school. But, for many schools, level of intellectual functioning is a prominent criterion for admission. For example, in New York City, Administration of the WPPSI through the *Educational Records Bureau* (ERB) is a standard part of the admission process at the early grade levels.

Group Measures and Grouping

In addition to placement in special classes or programs, intelligence tests, particularly group intelligence tests, have been used in schools since the 1920s to track children into homogeneous groups for purposes of instruction. Although the benefits of homogeneous grouping have been seriously challenged, the practice continues to exist. In a comprehensive review, Carroll (1978), traced the development, use, and limitations of group tests of intelligence. Group measures will not be detailed here except to point to the significant impact their use has had on educational practice. When the prevailing view in our history prior to World War II considered intelligence as an inherited capacity that was not highly responsive to environmental experience, the IQ scores were widely perceived as unchanging (Block & Dworkin, 1976; Carroll, 1978; Jensen, 1980; Skodak-Crissey, 1975). Group measures were widely administered and served as the basis for placing learners into homogeneous classes, for labeling them as slow, average, or fast learners, and had the end result of establishing expectations in parents and teachers. Teachers, in particular, were led to believe that there was little they could do to alter the child's inherited capabilities as reflected by test scores (Carroll, 1978). The format of many of the group measures that developed in the 1930s and 1940s is largely the same today. Some yield single scores, such as the *Henmon-Nelson Tests of Mental Ability* (Lamke, Nelson, & French, 1973), and the *Otis-Lennon School Ability Test* (Otis & Lennon, 1979); others yield verbal and nonverbal scores (*Cognitive Abilities Test*, Thorndike & Hagen 1978) or multiple scores (*California Tests of Mental Maturity,* Sullivan, Clark, & Tiegs, 1964), which allow evaluation of the learner's relative strengths and weaknesses. Areas represented by tasks on both group and individual tests have been summarized by Salvia and Ysseldyke (1981) and include areas such as verbal comprehension, number knowledge, classification, analogies, completion items, and spatial relationships.

By placing students into homogeneous groups, educators hoped to be effective in matching instruction to pupil needs. Carroll (1978) summarized the general goals and outcomes of this sorting process:

> Bright pupils would presumably be given instruction that allowed them to progress faster through the assigned curriculum units, with appropriate "enrichment" through the introduction of additional material. At the high school level, such pupils would be more likely to be assigned to college-preparatory courses in mathematics, science, social studies, language, and the humanities. The less able students were given instruction with simpler content and at a slower pace; at the high school level they were encouraged to take courses in business, shop, and other vocational subjects. [p. 71]

Findings regarding the effectiveness of the tracking process have been inconclusive (Carroll, 1978; Resnick, 1979; Salvia & Ysseldyke, 1981). It may be that the class groupings that resulted did not result as well in instruction matched to learner needs. According to Glaser and Nitko (1971), "The fundamental task of testing and measurement (in education) is to provide information for making basic, essential decisions with respect to education's instructional design and operation" (p. 625).

Public controversy regarding the consequences of intelligence testing began as its use became widespread (Cronbach, 1975). The prevailing belief in the innate, fixed nature of intelligence was repeatedly challenged. Basic assumptions underlying intelligence tests that "learning of any given skill is a function of *motivation, opportunity,* and an *innate ability to learn* and that individual differences in the mastery of skills for which motivation and opportunity are equal therefore reflect differences in the ability factor alone" were viewed as unwarrented. (Schwarz, 1971, p. 310). It has been well documented that individuals do not have equal opportunity and motivation to acquire skills through their day-to-day experiences. (Anastasi, 1958; Hunt, 1961; Sattler, 1982; Scarr, 1981; Schwarz, 1971; Wigdor & Garner, 1982). Kaufman, 1979. Scarr (1981) clearly documented that even given the same heredity (identical twins), environmental factors impinge on cognitive functioning. Measured intelligence is related to opportunity to learn reflected by socioeconomic factors, geographic location in which the child is reared, and the cultural and language background of the child.

Since the 1950s, the "fairness" of tests to the economically disadvantaged and minority groups has been increasingly challenged (Kaufman, 1979, 1982; Sattler, 1982; Thorndike, 1971). Litigation and federal and state legislation have focused on the civil rights of all individuals, with particular attention to disadvantaged and minority groups, as well as to children with handicapping conditions (Bersoff, 1975, 1981, 1982; Oakland, 1977; Oakland & Matuszek, 1977; Reynolds, 1982; Thorndike, 1971).

The report of the Committee on Ability Testing (Wigdor & Garner, 1982) indicated an overall decline in the use of group intelligence tests in the past ten years. Some localities, such as New York City, ban their use altogether. While tracking into fast or slow classes is viewed less favorably at the present time than in the past (Carroll, 1978; Resnick, 1979; Sylvia & Ysseldyke, 1981; Wigdor & Garner, 1982), the Committee on Ability Testing underscored the fact that grouping for purpose of instruction continues to be a widespread practice. At the elementary school level children are grouped within classrooms for instruction in different subject areas. They are selected under Title I for compensatory education, usually in reading or mathematics, and they are selected for enrichment opportunities. According to the Committee on Ability Testing an increased amount of tracking occurs at the junior high school level and "some form of tracking within comprehensive high schools is virtually universal where students can choose from a variety of programs" (p. 156). However, while grouping learners for purposes of instruction continues, current practice involves the use of multiple measures in arriving at decisions that include achievement test scores, teacher judgment, and other information about the child. According to the Committee on Ability Testing, tests play a supplementary role in the majority of schools, where they may be used to confirm judgments already made based on past performance and observation, or to supplement these judgments. Achievement tests play the predominant role in selection for classes for compensatory education and intelligence or other aptitude tests in selection for enrichment or special classes for the gifted.

Issues Related to Labeling and Placement

Labeling of students, along with separation from peers that can result from placement decisions, has a number of drawbacks. A major problem is that labels assume a concrete reality. Scores add to the problem, for the public tends to view scores, particularly IQ scores, as fixed and unchanging even though psychologists and educators in general recognize that these scores can change and reflect measurement error (Wigdor & Garner, 1982). The Committee on Ability Testing reported that the general populace often believe retardation to be an unchanging state as well. The outcome of their review underscored the fact that assignments to special classes *tend to be stable.* The Committee's concern centered as well on whether actual educational benefits result to children placed in special classes. They pointed out that effective instruction does not necessarily take place and concluded that "The amount of concern might be different . . . if there were widespread confidence that such placement were to the educational benefit of the children" (p. 162). Similar concerns were voiced by Carroll (1978), Kaufman (1982), Resnick (1979), and Sternberg and Wagner (1982).

Parents are likely to be concerned and anxious when their child is considered for placement in a class for the educable mentally retarded or for the learning disabled. Possible guilt and doubt are evoked as to their own role and to the future meaning of these decisions. In contrast, when placement is recommended into a class for the gifted or into enrichment programs, parents are usually pleased and proud. High expectations tend to be formed by both parents and teachers. Unrealistic demands may be placed on the child, who, like any other child, will demonstrate areas of relative weakness as well as relative strength. Borland and Jacobs (in press) caution that gifted education should be a humane reaction to the fact of individual differences in learning, not a tracking system that invites fierce competition and undue pressure on children.

Like the child labeled as "educable mentally retarded" or "learning disabled," the child labeled as "gifted" may encounter difficulty with peers based on that label. Being singled out or ridiculed as the "brain" or "egghead" is no more attractive than being singled out as the "retard." Moreover, many children do not like to be separated from their peers. When special classes are formed, this separation is most extreme. In many school systems children receive enrichment experiences and at the same time remain a member of the regular class group. On the other hand, the learning disabled child who goes to the "resource room" for extra help may experience this extra help as a stigma if only children with learning problems are afforded this opportunity. The location of different special learning services in the same resource room might help confront this issue, as well as provide a model of peer-appropriate behavior for all children.

Other Issues Related to Test Use in the Educational Setting

Intelligence, as reflected by test scores, is a well-documented predictor of school achievement. However, intelligence tests are biased towards abilities required by the school; they do not tap the range of human ability. This is not surprising, since it was to predict the likelihood of success with regular instruction that Binet and Simon developed the first intelligence scale. Until the present time, the content of most intelligence tests consisted of tasks and operations largely taught in schools. As Anastasi (1982) explains:

> Typical intelligence tests designed for use with school-age children or adults measure largely verbal abilities; to a lesser degree, they also cover abilities to deal with numerical and other abstract symbols. These are the abilities that predominate in school learning. Most intelligence tests can therefore be regarded as measures of scholastic aptitude or academic intelligence. [p. 348]

Increased attention, however, currently is being directed toward investigating cognitive processes involved in problem solving (Glaser, 1984; Resnick, 1976, 1979; Sternberg, 1982, 1983). Researchers, such as Brown and Campione (1982), Glaser and Pellegrino (1982), and Sternberg (1983), are investigating mental operations used by very able students and slow learners, as they solve problems. Tasks are developed to tap the means by which learners respond to the input of external information, organize that information, and retrieve information from memory. Brown and French (1979) stressed the need to investigate learning processes required to cope with everyday life situations as well as those processes needed to be successful with school learning.

When funds become available for programs to help children with special learning needs or talents, identification of appropriate individuals is initiated. In the past, the need to make rapid placement decisions has sometimes resulted in employing assessors who are minimally trained. As a result, these assessors might not make necessary observations of essential factors, such as different but appropriate response patterns according to the child's background, primary language spoken other than English, and visual, auditory, or motor problems that might be related to low IQ scores. The misidentification of individuals as educable mentally retarded led to placement of a disproportionate number of minority group children being placed in EMR classes in California, with class action suits initiated by parents resulting in the IQ test being put "on trial" (*Larry P. v. Riles*, 1979). As a result there are severe restrictions on the use of intelligence tests with minority children in California. The problem here is not necessarily with the test, a point later made by Judge Grady (*Pace v. Hannon*, 1980) in a similar case brought to court in Chicago. The problem lies with the misuse of these tests out of the context of other data or with using tests with inappropriate technical data. Sternberg (1983) stated as follows: "I would hasten to add that the problem is not intrinsic to the tests, but to their use (or misuse). Such tests can be valuable if they are used cautiously, in conjunction with multiple other sources of information, and if *their validity for individual cases is seen as always doubtful*" (p. 12). Currently, these cautions are not necessarily practiced. All too frequently decisions are made, as in selection for classes for the gifted or the learning disabled, on brief or inadequate measures. Davis and Shepard (1983) and Salvia and Ysseldyke (1981) lend support to the fact that evaluators frequently use tests with inadequate psychometric characteristics. Furthermore, the bureaucracy that exists within educational systems sugggests that even given appropriate test selection, administration, and interpretation, recommendations can be passed by so that attention is again focused on the score, this time, however, by persons without adequate psychodiagnostic training, but with responsibility for implementing placement decisions.

Finally, Resnick (1979) questioned whether IQ testing for special education placement will be as common in the future as it is today. Based on the evidence, Resnick argued that structured instructional programs for the educable mentally retarded, learning disabled, and normal but economically disadvantaged groups are not that different. Fully aware that placement in special education brings state and federal funds to schools, which in turn permits greater pupil service and a more favorable pupil-teacher ratio, Resnick suggested that "If cost were not an issue, it would be possible to by-pass the entire IQ-based selection process for special education by simply offering all children who fell below certain standards of academic performance instruction in such favorable settings" (p. 207). If money and personnel were available, testing could then be focused directly on the learner in relationship to instructional goals, which, according to Resnick, would allow ongoing monitoring of instruction and the interaction between learning and the learning processes used. The same concerns apply to classes for the gifted.

In summary, the educational application of intelligence tests for purposes of selection and placement must be governed by the following:

1. Tests are imperfect measures of current functioning. The scores yielded are not unchanging but can go either up or down.

2. Functioning on tests is related to the child's culture and experiences. The scores obtained reflect as well the repertoire of responses available to the child at the time of testing (Cleary et al., 1975).

3. Multiple sources of information should be used in making placement decisions. Tests with adequate psychometric characteristics should be used.

4. Testing should be viewed as a process of hypothesis generation and testing.

5. Current intelligence tests used for selection and placement do not assess directly the processes by which problems are solved.

SCREENING, DIAGNOSTIC, AND REMEDIAL APPLICATIONS

The use of intelligence tests for placement decisions primarily focuses on total scores. Educational diagnosticians have long found it useful as well to review a child's performance by subtests and items on individual measures of intelligence in order to raise hypotheses about cognitive strengths and weaknesses that can lead to instructional planning. The time and expertise required to administer major individual tests of intelligence or cognitive functioning, such as the Binet, Wechsler scales, McCarthy Scales, or *Kaufman Assessment Battery for Children* (K-ABC) (Kaufman & Kaufman, 1983) would not be well used if these tests only yielded a total score or scores from subtests and indices. The competent examiner who has administered the intelligence test, usually along with other tests, has had the special opportunity to observe closely a large sample of behavior. Behavioral observations are made of how the child approaches tasks, responds to items of increasing complexity in the different areas assessed, and reacts when difficulty is encountered. In addition, observations should be made of the child's receptive and expressive abilities, facility with language, and physical, sensory, and motor characteristics. When placed in the context of developmental expectations, and taking into account the child's cultural background, these observations lend important input to the use of test results beyond the scores yielded. If the examiner is a member of an assessment team, observations will be shared. If the psychologist is carrying out the evaluation independently, the observation will be integrated with other findings into recommendations and actions.

The focus of this section will be on screening, as well as diagnostic and remedial applications of intelligence tests for instructional planning matched to the child's needs. It will be assumed that these tests will be used in the context of other information gained from parents, teachers, past records, ongoing observation, and other testing. The considerations detailed in this section may take place in conjunction with placement decisions previously detailed, or the teacher or parent concerned about a child's progress, general academic performance, or behavior may refer a child for evaluation. An intelligence test is often a part of that evaluation. The parent or teacher again expects more than a score and seeks information concerning the child's learning rate and offers suggestions regarding how best to help that child learn.

Interpretation that leads to appropriate results is a complex processes of hypothesis testing. The goals are to make sense of an individual's test performance in light of research on that test and its limitations for minority groups, the disadvantaged, and other groups. Kaufman (1979) indicated that proper test interpretation requires the grouping and regrouping of tasks in order to uncover strengths and weaknesses. Subtests should be scrutinized in terms of their stated purpose, the abilities that appear to be tapped, and their relationship to school performance. Sattler (1982) reviewed the pros and cons of intelligence testing from the research literature and cautions that "Our intelligence tests, which measure success in school quite effectively, are value-laden. They represent primarily such societal values as schooling, verbal abilities, and abstraction and concept formation skills" (p. 63). The meaning of these societal values for each child must be determined.

Detailed analysis of subtests into their component abilities is not uniformly successful across the major individual intelligence tests. For example, Sattler (1982) reviewed the outcomes of Binet content analyses (Lutey, 1977; Sattler, 1965) to profile successes and areas of difficulty for purposes of interpretation. He urged caution in using systems, such as the Binetgram (Sattler, 1965), which classifies the items across subtests into seven arbitrary categories based on their face value. Difficulties that ensue according to Sattler include the fact that items might have been placed in other categories, that categories are not represented at all age levels, and that the nature of task demands change at different age levels. Sattler notes that the grouping of tasks into arbitrary categories can facilitate hypothesis generation but cannot lead to diagnostic statements regarding such areas as memory, language, or numerical reasoning. Tasks on the Binet, as well as on other individual intelligence tests, tap more than one cognitive ability. The examiner is unable to identify *why errors were made* based on the sample of behavior tested.

As with the Binet, the task demands on the Wechsler verbal and performance subtests also change with age. While the majority of tasks on the Binet require mostly nonverbal responses with very young children, after age 4, the task demands become increasingly verbal. Although on the Wechsler tests school-age children are administered subtests organized into a *Verbal Scale* and a *Performance Scale,* the starting and stopping points, and therefore the content of these subtests, changes with increasing age. Early items on the WISC-R "information" subtest, for example, tap basic information, such as the number of days in the week, while later items involve knowledge influenced by schooling, such as identifying who Charles Darwin was or what he did.

Analyzing and Interpreting Performance across Subtests

Sattler (1982) recommended a successive level approach to test interpretation. He detailed this approach for the WISC-R, but the approach is useful with other tests that yield verbal and nonverbal, or subtest scores. With existing measures of intelligence, translation of findings into diagnostic statements and instructional programs is not straightforward or direct. Interpretation involves a process of hypothesis generation and testing, a stance taken by most experts in the field (for instance, Kaufman 1979, 1982; Mercer 1979; Palmer, 1983; Salvia & Ysseldyke, 1981). Some experts (Bryant, 1983; Roswell & Natchez, 1977) include trial remediation in the diagnostic process.

Five levels of test interpretation are suggested by Sattler (1982) that include in descending order the following: (1) full-scale IQ; (2) verbal and performance IQs; (3) intersubtest scatter; (4) intrasubtest scatter; and (5) qualitative analysis (p. 193). A number of studies summarized by Kaufman (1979, 1982) suggest another level of analysis—factor analysis. Consideration of subtest performance by factor areas might occur following level-2 interpretations. These successive levels of interpretation will be considered in the present chapter as their meaning relates to possible educational applications.

The Full Scale Score

The Full Scale score provides educators with information about an individual's performance as it compares to the standardization population. The Full-Scale IQ score provides the most reliable and valid estimate of intelligence (Thorndike, 1975). The examiner has the responsibility of determining whether the child tested was represented in the standardization population, an issue of paramount importance given the pluralistic nature of our population.

Many children across the U.S. may not be represented in the standardization sample. Even in well-standardized tests minority groups are underrepresented (Oakland & Matuszek, 1977; Reynolds, 1982). Federal legislation (1977) specified in The Education for All Handicapped Children Act of 1975 (PL 94-142) that tests must be administered in the child's native language. Most major tests have been translated to fulfill this requirement. A number of problems continue to persist (Kaufman, 1979, 1982; Oakland & Matuszek, 1977; Reynolds, 1982; Sattler, 1982).

Most translated tests have not been standardized on a representative sample.

Test administrators may not be sufficiently fluent in the respective language to pick up subtleties of meaning conveyed by the child.

The form of translated materials may not represent the form by which ideas are represented in another language or culture.

Children from different cultural backgrounds approach problems differently and have different cognitive styles.

A translation to another language, Spanish for example, does not necessarily represent dialect differences.

The Committee on Ability Testing (1982) urges utmost caution when using tests to evaluate bilingual children. Bilingual children have a differential command of both languages that can interfere both with complying with procedural direction and task demands (Kaufman, 1979; Wigdor & Garner, 1982). Many of these same issues pertain to black children who come from backgrounds where nonstandard English dialects are spoken (Kaufman, 1979, 1982; Oakland & Matuszek, 1977).

The individual's performance on verbal tasks, as opposed to nonverbal tasks on intelligence measures, have been of considerable interest in the assessment process. One approach to formulating educational interventions based on intelligence tests results has been to review discrepancies that occur between the Verbal Scale and the Performance Scale on the Wechsler tests. Considerable attention has been focused in the research literature on these differences. The results are far from clear. Wechsler (1974) suggested a 15-point difference, a difference that can be expected by chance to occur 1 in 100 times on future testings, as meaningful for interpreting the differences between the Verbal and Performance Scales. (Both Sattler and Kaufman recommend the consideration of 12-point differences, the .05 level, meaningful to generate hypotheses.) Kaufman (1976a) provided important baseline data regarding the extent of verbal-performance discrepancies among the WISC-R standardization population. Discrepancies between the verbal and performance scores obtained by the standardization occurred frequently: 9 or more points in 50% of the sample, 12 or more points in about 33% of the sample, and 15 or more points in 25% of the sample. Thus there is considerable variability in normal children. A discrepancy of 15 points, the difference viewed by Wechsler as noteworthy, occurs in one out of every four children. Furthermore, verbal scores were higher than performance scores as often as performance scores were higher than verbal scores for each age group, sex, race, and IQ level. Socioeconomic background was the only variable where there were differences, and then only at the two extremes of the distribution (Kaufman, 1976a). As might be expected, verbal scores were higher than performance score for children of professionals, while performance scores were higher than verbal scores for children of semi-skilled and skilled workers.

Thus, while discrepancies of 12 or 15 points might be noteworthy to the examiner, they must be interpreted with great caution for purposes of instructional planning. By reporting the error band around these subscale scores, users can highlight the extent of probable overlap. Some users look for larger verbal-performance differences (Shepherd, 1984) because difference of the magnitude of 25 points or more are truly unusual. These differences can guide the thinking of the examiner regarding what should be done next in terms of diagnosis or trial remediation. For example, the child from an advantaged home environment with a verbal IQ score of 138 and a performance IQ score of 118 is scoring extremely well on both portions of the test. Yet, while the difference may be "noteworthy," it may not be meaningful. On the other hand, the child from a disadvantage background who attains a performance IQ score of 108 and a verbal IQ score of 92 may be exhibiting an important outcome of his or her environment. Verbal abilities are fostered in environments where verbal exchange takes place between parents or primary caregivers and children (Caldwell & Bradley, 1979). It is likely as well that children learn how to respond to the types of items assessed by tests. The advantages afforded by middle class upbringing may help the child develop test-taking skills as well as helping them become familiar with the content areas tapped by tests. Where verbal abilities have been poorly developed, tests that minimize these abilities should be used to obtain a yardstick regarding a child's reasoning abilities (Salvia & Ysseldyke, 1981). Finally, large discrepancies between verbal and performance scores do not necessarily indicate a problem. Both Sattler and Kaufman suggest multiple bases for verbal-performance discrepancies that can range from psychopathology to environmental deprivation to sensory deficits.

As the assessor evaluates performance on intelligence tests, including verbal performance discrepancies, attention should be directed to the culture and experiences of the child being assessed. Salvia and Ysseldyke (1981) urge that assessors go beyond scores and look as well at task requirements and demands in light of the child's background experiences and opportunities: "Simply knowing the kind of behavior sampled by a test is not enough, for the same test item may create different psychological demands for different children" (pp. 246–247). Kaufman (1979, 1982), Reschly (1982), and Reynolds (1982), Sattler (1982), also underscore the importance of cultural factors, past experience, training, and the child's personal style on test responses. Responses offered might be correct in terms of the child's experience, language background, and culture, but be scored as incorrect according to the test criteria or not recognized as correct by the examiner due to a culturally different response style. Thus, in making educational applications from intelligence test results, the assessor must take into account many factors and consider alternative hypothesis.

Kaufman (1979, 1982) reviewed research related to a series of possible explanations of verbal-performance discrepancies. The results, while not conclusive, reveal a number of factors quite consistently. The accuracy of verbal responses, for example, will be affected by expressive difficulties, whatever the cause. Children from bilingual backgrounds receive lower verbal IQ scores (Oakland & Matuszek, 1977) than do children from monolingual backgrounds. Even when tests are translated into the child's native language, it cannot be assumed that the language bias has been removed: "Translating a test from English to Spanish may not remove biases; it may serve to increase them" (Oakland & Matuszek, 1977 p. 61). Kaufman (1979) cautioned, for example, that if a psycholinguistic deficiency is present or a fine-motor problem is observed, then the full-scale IQ score may become meaningless. Kaufman suggested that evaluators use factor groupings where tasks high on verbal comprehensions or perceptual-motor characteristics can be separated out of the analysis.

The literature regarding verbal-performance discrepancies on the Wechsler profiles is both conflicting and inconclusive for populations described as delinquent, neurologically impaired, and learning disabled (Kaufman, 1979, 1982). Kaufman (1979) concluded: "Poorly defined samples or samples that fail to control for essential variables are probably responsible for the discrepancies. However, another likely source of the problem is the fact that a V-P discrepancy may signify quite different things for different individuals" (p. 25). The latter point underscores the diversity of factors—hearing, vision, expressive language difficulty, and so forth—that may account for discrepancy.

Kaufman (1979) and Sattler (1982) cited possible abilities tapped by each Wechsler subtest, as well as those shared with other subtests, which might be useful as examiners formulate hypothese and engage in follow-up assessment. As examiners review specific responses, hunches relevant to school learning can be raised with regard to how items are passed. For example, does the child offer clear direct responses? Or does he/she talk around a response? The child who has clear access to vocabulary or to past learning is more likely to be successful with school tasks than the child who must search for responses and has difficulty expressing them. Kaufman (1982) concluded: "Significant V-P discrepancies and strengths and weaknesses in the subtest profile have *educational* significance, but they do not have *diagnostic* significance as well unless the fluctuations occur infrequently in the normal population" (p. 166).

The Relevance of Factor Analytic Studies for Educational Practice

Factor analytic studies have been employed to understand possible reasons for functioning on individual intelligence tests. The outcome of these studies, reviewed by Kaufman (1979, 1982) and Sattler (1982), will be regarded here only with respect to a number of possible alternatives the assessor can raise that might influence educational practice.

Kaufman (1975) conducted a series of factor analytic studies on the WISC-R standardization sample at each of 11 age levels. He identified three factors, consistent with those identified by Cohen (1959) on the WISC-R: "verbal comprehension," "perceptual organization," and "freedom from distractibility." While the "verbal comprehension" and "perceptual organization" factors closely corresponded to the subtest composition of the Verbal and Performance scales (supporting their construct validity), the "freedom from distractibility" factor included subtests from both scales (Arithmetic, Digit Span, and Coding), tasks that appear to require attention, concentration, and memory abilities. These factor groupings provide the assessor with another means of reviewing a child's test performance. Kaufman (1979) indicated, for example, that if a child has a motor problem, cognitive abilities assessed by subtests in the "perceptual organization" grouping may not yield an accurate estimate of ability in that area. Kaufman provided examples of alternative interpretations possible for children with the same IQ score, but with different patterns of subtest scores within factors. A major implication for educational practice arises here. Hypotheses regarding possible educational meanings of scores in terms of strengths and weaknesses must be reviewed from many perspectives.

Other groupings of subtests might lead to other hypotheses. For example, Meeker used Guilford's SOI model to classify WISC tasks in terms of operations, products, and content levels of operations tapped (Meeker, 1969, 1975). The same model was used by Meeker to classify tasks on the Stanford-Binet (Meeker, 1965, 1969). Kaufman (1979) reviewed Bannatyne's (1974) work. He spelled out four categories of subtests, "verbal conceptualization," "spatial," "sequencing," and "acquired knowledge" (the latter having subtests in common with the other categories). Both Kaufman (1979) and Sattler (1982) cautioned that low functioning on subtests in a factor area may not be directly interpreted as a deficiency in that area. Instead, hypotheses can be generated that need to be tested. Reynolds (1981) suggested that the child's own mean level of performance in each category serves as the point of reference when interpreting task performance in each category other than "acquired knowledge" (due to overlap of tests) in much the same way that Sattler (1982) recommended procedures for reviewing functioning on the Verbal and Performance scales.

A number of studies have identified a LD profile in which performance was better in spatial than in conceptual tasks, which, in turn, was better than in sequencing tasks (Cordoni, O'Donnell, Ramaniah, Kurtz & Rosenshein 1981; Kaufman 1979; 1982).

Kaufman (1981), reviewing the "state-of-the-art" of the WISC-R in the assessment of learning disabilities, concluded that both the V-P discrepancies and degree of scatter demonstrated by children labeled as LD was not that different from children in the normative population. He concluded that "The magnitude of V-P discrepancy and the size of scaled-score range are not likely to be very useful in the diagnosis of LD or in its differential diagnosis" (p. 523). While there are characteristic factor patterns for children demonstrating different learning needs, there are no characteristic patterns of scatter. Patterns serve a descriptive, rather than a diagnostic, function (Kaufman, 1981). Factor performance by minority group membership has been summarized by Reschly (1978). Factor analytic studies of the WPPSI have been summarized by Sattler (1982); and studies related to scatter were analyzed by Reynolds (1982) and Reynolds and Gutkin (1981).

Analysis of Scatter Between Subtests

When a child's functioning on the subtests included on the Wechsler Verbal and Performance scales is reviewed, additional information for formulating hypotheses regarding strengths and weaknesses relevant to educational planning is possible. However, it is important to note that the SEMs of subtest scores are greater than those of the Verbal, Performance, or Full scale IQ scores. Furthermore, Sattler (1982) stressed that profile analysis is dependent on significant differences between subtest scores, as well as on the Verbal and Performance IQ scores.

Thorndike (1975) reported correlations of stability on the WISC-R subtests over time to range from −.08 to .39, with a median of .15. These findings compared with the stability coefficient for the total score of .79 for the same children. Educational decisions, therefore, cannot be based on interest scatter, even if the differences are statistically significant. Their use is warranted to review current functioning only, to identify areas of relative strength and weakness, and to raise hypotheses that require further assessment. Wechsler (1974) recommended ±3 scaled points between subtests as the minimal level for interpretation, but recommended differences of ±5 scaled points for more secure interpretation. Both Kaufman (1979) and Sattler (1982) further recommend that the child's subtest scores be interpreted in relation to his or her mean performance on the Verbal and Performance scales. On each scale, then, the child's mean performance serves as the yardstick for interpreting subtest performance. Only those subtests that differ significantly from the mean can be viewed as being a peak or a valley.

When Kaufman (1976b) reviewed scatter among the standardization sample, the outcome of this study revealed considerable scatter. Thus children as a whole are likely to demonstrate considerable scatter. Lutey and Copeland (1982) recommended that it is in general inappropriate to interpret performance on individual subtests. Therefore extreme caution must be exercised in carrying out scatter analysis and in considering its meaning for the child's schooling. Whatever the pattern of scores, the test administrator has the often difficult responsibility of getting at their root and of following through on hunches through further testing or observation and of providing necessary supportive evidence. The subtests included provide behavior samples of diverse abilities. They were not intended by Wechsler to provide diagnostic measures of comprehension, arithmetic, or abstract reasoning.

The Meaning of Subtests for Schooling

Sattler (1982) further recommended that evaluators look at scatter as it occurs *within* subtests since items increase in difficulty and sometimes form. The examiner should be attuned to unique or unusual verbal and nonverbal responses offered by the child to specific items. A test question can set off concerns about home events; unusual thought process can be observed; unusual solutions to problems can be pinpointed. Each of these observations can serve to generate further hypotheses. Children can pass or fail items for different reasons. They can pass them, for example, because they are good at making logical connections or because they have had lots of practice with parquetry blocks; they can fail them because they have never experienced a vocabulary term before, or because they have difficulty retrieving from memory the word meaning.

Numerous studies have investigated various patterns of subtest functioning (Kaufman 1982; Reynolds, 1982; Sattler, 1982). Baseline data are needed regarding the occurrence of various patterns within the normal population. No single pattern or profile indicative of neurological impairment, schizophrenia, or learning disabilities has been identified. While poorer performance on some subtests is associated with different clinical problems, not all individuals demonstrating a particular subtest deficiency have the associate clinical problem. Numerous studies with individuals diagnosed as LD has led Kaufman (1981) to conclude that there is no single Wechsler LD pattern.

Translation of Results into Remediation

As an outcome of profile analysis, hypotheses may have been raised regarding areas of relative strength and weakness with the goal of developing appropriate instruction. However, test scores and patterns of abilities revealed across subtests cannot be translated directly into educational prescriptions. The hypotheses raised must first be confirmed or disconfirmed by further testing and observation. However, the direct connection to educational prescriptions and remedial strategies is suggested by a number of current publications that prescribe educational interventions based on subtest scores or patterns on the WISC-R (Nicholson & Alcorn, 1983; Searls, 1975; Whitworth & Sutton, 1978) or the Stanford-Binet (Whitworth & Sutton, 1982). It is unlikely that the activities recommended will impede the child's development. The issue raised is that the child may not have a problem in the area as targeted so that training efforts may be misdirected or may result in minimal improvement. Programs designed to provide practice in behaviors related to areas of relative weakness or strength do not necessarily get at process. With practice children may become better puzzle builders or become familiar with facts related to their environment. But the degree to which these practiced skills transfer or are reflected in improved overall cognitive functioning is questionable. The problems encountered in formulating meaningful recommendations are reflected in the frustration school personnel often experience in understanding and translating the meaning of IQ scores to why a child is having difficulty with a particular school subject and instructional intervention that needs to take place.

Proponents of information-processing approaches to intelligence believe more direct and meaningful translation of test performance in the cognitive area is possible (Glaser & Pellegrino, 1982; Resnick, 1976; Sternberg, Ketron, & Powell, 1982; Sternberg & Powell, 1983; Sternberg & Wagner, 1982). Brown and French (1979), referring to implications for future directions in intelligence testing, use as a model Soviet testing philosophy, which focuses on potential development, as opposed to current or completed development. Information yielded from current intelligence measures was also seen as necessary, along with information related to competencies that can be revealed through diagnoses and developed for purposes of remediation. But "completed development" as measured by current IQ tests does not provide information relevant to what Brown and French call the "width of an individual's potential zones," which can be assessed by accounting for the amount of additional information or additional cues required to solve problems and the amount of transfer that occurs with new but parallel items. This approach, based on detailed task analysis and observation of transfer through test-teach-test formats, is implicit to the approach advocated by Brown and French. It is also reflected in Feuerstein's (1979, 1980) approach to assessment of learning potential and to instructional enrichment. Detailed task analysis permits progressive cycles of pretest-teach-monitor, teach, and so forth, which can translate directly into educational objectives and curricular activities. The impact of this approach is currently in the early stages of development as it relates to intelligence testing, although significant gains have been made. Brown and French (1979) and others (Glaser, 1984; Sternberg & Powell, 1983) have advanced work in the area of information processing, so that tests of the future may be based on validated task analyses and the determination of the degree of transfer to other related tasks. The time and efficiency with which an individual engages in such tasks, according to Brown and French, would lead to indices of learning-to-learn.

The large gap between what current IQ tests measure and what schools teach also impedes the translation of results into educational practice (Sternberg and Wagner, 1982). Major problems, according to Sternberg and Wagner, include the following:

1. Tests do not tap processes that might be built into school learning.
2. Tests do not measure directly the skills required in school tasks such as reading.
3. Motivational factors that interact with both tests and school tasks are not accounted for.
4. Limitations exist in research methodology that probes the interface between theory and practice.

Theoretical models increasingly are serving as a basis for reviewing the results of existing psychometric tests (Lutey & Copeland, 1982) and for the development of new measures, such as the K-ABC (Kaufman & Kaufman, 1983). Kaufman and Kaufman draw upon neuropsychology as a major basis for organizing the K-ABC into scales representative of successive and simultaneous processing. An achievement scale is also included to differentiate between tasks of cognitive functioning as opposed to acquired learning, represented by achievement.

On the Wechsler scales, McCarthy, and the Binet, however, most tasks assess acquired learning based on past experience, versus new learning. If an incorrect response is made (for example, puzzle pieces, are reversed, or concrete or imprecise word definitions offered, one can observe what was wrong and can raise hypotheses as to why, but it is not possible to determine from that test performance processes the individual used to solve the problem. This limitation makes direct translation into educational objectives or programs problematic. Sattler (1982) noted the limitation of existing intelligence tests for measuring processes underlying the child's responses, but did not elaborate on the issue. As Sternberg and Wagner (1982) explain, ". . . it is not clear just what one is to train. Second, the decision regarding what to train is made on the basis of factors derived from individual-differences data" (p. 52). The test examiner must then engage in follow-up testing in those areas of concern that are task analyzed into their subcomponents from which educational objectives can be determined.

Instructional recommendations based on patterns of functioning on IQ tests may exceed the purpose for which these tests were developed—that is, to measure either general intelligence or the ability to succeed in mainstream school environments. Brown and French (1979) stated the problem succinctly when they referred to problems that arise in the use of intelligence test results: "Controversy concerning the efficacy of IQ tests arises when they are either overinterpreted or called upon to fulfill functions they were never designed to meet" (p. 218), including an essentially diagnostic function.

While translation of intelligence test subtest performance into programs of intervention is not a direct process, areas of relative weakness or strength can lead to intensive investigation, the outcome of which is intervention. An increasing body of literature suggests positive benefits from training of at least some of the intellectual skills tapped by the Wechsler tests. For example, Brown and Campione (1982) reported considerable success at improving comprehension skills of seventh-grade problem learners with adequate decoding skills when appropriate questioning strategies were modeled. Comprehension strategies are detailed by Collins and Smith (1982) and involve a careful task analysis of the processing skills involved. Possible remedial strategies are also detailed for each level at which comprehension errors occur. Processing skills are detailed for comprehension monitoring and for hypotheses' generation and testing.

The meaning of the improved performance that results is also questioned by Brown and Campione. For example, if intelligence tests are used as outcome measures, does improved functioning imply improved "intelligence", or have participants been trained to the test? The authors suggest that this issue can be partly confronted by reviewing efficiency of learning, or "the extent of training needed to bring a student to mastery" (p. 227). A related question is addressed by Gettinger (1978) and Gettinger and White (1979) who studied time-to-learn by fourth- through sixth-grade students in a series of six types of school learning tasks. Units in each of the six subject areas were repeated eight times with criterion tests presented following each trial. Time-to-learn measures correlated with standardized achievement tests higher than the results of IQ tests correlated with these achievement measures.

The issue of transfer is of paramount importance to the position taken by Brown and Campione when instruction is geared to modifying cognitive skills. "Intelligence is the efficiency of new learning and the breadth of transfer. Improved intelligence, therefore, must involve learning-to-learn skills" (Brown & Campione, 1982, pp. 227–228). They concluded that cognitive skills can be modified and that such training can be relevant to schooling. Sternberg (1983) and Sternberg and Wagner (1982) provided criteria for training intellectual skills based on information-processing theory and research.

Motivational Factors

That intelligent behavior involves motivational factors was underscored by Wechsler (1975) who pointed out that intelligence is goal-directed and concluded that "What intelligence tests measure, what we hope they measure, is something much more important: the capacity of an individual to understand the world about him and his resourcefulness to cope with its challenges." (p. 139). Motivational factors are implied here rather than directly manipulated by the testing situation. But, for behavior to be goal-directed or for the individual to be resourceful in coping with life's challenges, motivation is entailed. Critics of intelligence tests question whether individuals from other than achievement-oriented environments are motivated to complete items on intelligence tests that can result in lowered measured intelligence rather than cognitive deficits (Kaufman 1982; Salvia & Ysseldyke, 1981).

Sternberg (1983) and Sternberg and Wagner (1982) also include motivational factors among the eight prerequisites to be accounted for by intellectual skills training programs. But, Sternberg (1983) concluded that inadequate intellectual performance cannot be accounted for only in terms of motivational deficits and stressed that *both* intellectual and motivation stimuli must be included in a training program.

CONSIDERATIONS OF BIAS AND OTHER CRITICISMS IN FORMULATING EDUCATIONAL APPLICATIONS

Intelligence testing in the educational arena has been the target of repeated waves of criticism and attack (Lennon, 1978; Reynolds, 1982.) Lennon (1978) critically reviewed the dimensions of this attack. A primary criticism of intelligence tests is that they are culturally biased, particularly toward minority groups. This criticism is based on differential test performance on the part of individuals from different backgrounds, the recognition of different experiential opportunities and cultural expectations, and possible language handicaps, among other factors (Kaufman, 1979; Oakland & Matuszek, 1977; Reynolds, 1982; Sattler 1982). But Lennon (1978), who reviewed test use in terms of here-and-now performance, also stated, "If background factors have, in fact, contributed to the creation of handicaps to learning, surely it is better to know this than not to know it in the planning of instructional programs" (p. 3).

Potential sources of bias in intelligence testing and the outcomes of this testing that have become of increasing concern to psychologists and educators have been reviewed by Jensen (1980) and Reynolds (1983). Bias, according to Reynolds (1983), involves a series of complex issues and must be considered from many perspectives. Reynolds recommends consideration of the possibility of the following:

1. Inappropriate content.
2. Inappropriate standardization procedures.

3. Examiner and language bias.

4. Inequities in social consequences.

5. Measurement of constructs having different meanings for different groups.

6. Differential validity.

Zinoman (1983) also summarized potential biasing conditions that should be minimized, if not eliminated in the educational use of testing. In addition to many of the factors raised by Reynolds, Zinoman also alerted assessors to consider bias either introduced by parents or existing in the referral process and in the policies and practices of the school district.

The educator should be aware of a number of other factors when interpreting the results of intelligence tests to educational practice. For example, Wechsler (1974) reported significant changes in IQ scores upon retesting, with the greatest effects demonstrated on the Performance Scale scores. The Performance IQ improved upon retesting after an interval of six to nine months, roughly equivalent to an academic year, 9½ points compared to an increase of 3½ points on the Verbal Scale and 7 points on the full-scale score. If intelligence tests are used as pre- and post-measures of a program's effectiveness, the issue of practice should be taken into account.

The emerging appearance of computer-based scoring and interpretive systems and their future use in educational settings must be considered with great caution. The score profiles are usually presented as falling within confidence bands. Interpretative statements may be more problematic, particularly if important examiner observations are not incorporated and if all possible hypothesis are not reviewed along with recommendations for follow-up assessment. However, the increasing use of computer-based testing may lead to the development of new measures of intelligence based on adaptive testing procedures. The possibility of programs devised to adjust content to the individual responses, to route testees to higher or lower levels of the task or to items of increasing cognitive complexity, provides an exciting avenue for the future. As summarized by Anastasi (1976), "Adaptive testing also provides greater precision of measurement for individuals at the upper and lower extremes of the ability range covered by the test" (p. 304).

ACCOUNTABILITY, EVALUATION, AND RESEARCH

The overall effectiveness of ongoing instruction as well as of innovative or experimental education programs is a primary concern of school administrators and funding agencies. Improvement in cognitive functioning among specified target groups has been a major goal of many of these innovative programs. IQ tests have been used as outcome measures in programs such as Headstart. Furthermore, IQ measures are likely to be among the pre- and post-test measures used to assess intellectual growth effected through programs focused specifically on training cognitive skills. Lennon (1978), speaking of issues related to intelligence testing in the educational enterprise, succinctly summarized their essential role in the description of groups for a broad range of educational research issues, including "program evaluation, accountability studies, research enterprises where matching of groups on mental ability or some other construct is called for" (p. 8).

In addition to such outcome measures, Resnick (1979) suggested that intelligence tests may play a major role in the future if schools become legally responsible for ensuring that students learn basic skills. Under such circumstances, as schools seek to set limits to their responsibility, the IQ test, according to Resnick (1979) could again enter the picture to determine expectations, "now in the guise of insurance against malpractice" (p. 210). However, Resnick believes that yet-to-be developed measures that sample key learning processes related to school tasks may better serve this purpose. At present, Resnick views mastery testing as the most effective means available to monitor learning.

The Committee on Ability Testing (1982) reported that a result of increased national and state involvement and financing has been the proliferation of mandated testing for numerous purposes, including "tests for selection, placement, diagnosis and remediation, guidance, program evaluation, and certification of competence" (p. 152). Schools are the foremost users of standardized tests (Wigdor & Garner, 1982), and intelligence and ability tests are among these tests.

The program Headstart is a primary example of how continued funding was in part contingent on the results of intelligence tests. During the 1960s, great hope was fostered with the Great Society's programs for the poor. Project Headstart was launched with early education interventions at the preschool level and increased availability of health and nutrition programs seen as a major force in reducing the inequities of those coming from disadvantaged backgrounds. The availability of educational opportunity for all provided hope for blacks and other minorities of a more equal role in society. With extensive federal funding, Headstart programs were launched, often in haste, across the country. Programs ranging in duration from eight weeks to a year long were established with goals as diverse as providing parents with needed health information and facilities for their children to providing children with structured exposure to cognitively based curriculum. Decisions regarding the necessity to evaluate program effectiveness were initiated in many instances well after the programs themselves were started. Thus there was no true control group. Where programs were established, the most needy children were enrolled. When programs were required to account for their effectiveness, assessment was based largely on IQ scores, achievement scores, and readiness tests, regardless of the program's goals. The tests measured the effectiveness of programs with diverse goals and different durations in the same way. The initial gains of the experimental group were not maintained. The results of the Westinghouse-Ohio Study (Cicirelli, Evans, & Schiller, 1970) were later placed on Congressional Record. Genetic influences were again viewed as exerting a more important influence than environment on intellectual functioning (Jensen, 1969). Detailed documentation and review of Headstart programs has been presented by Zigler and Valentine (1980). The long-term effects with children who participated in programs with emphasis on cognitive goals have been repeatedly demonstrated (*Carnegie Quarterly*, 1978); Schweinhart & Weikart, 1980). These long-term benefits include fewer retentions, fewer referrals, fewer school dropouts, as well as more favorable emotional and social ratings and better history of employment. The possibility of such unpredicted long-term effects must be considered in cognitive skills training programs as well.

The history of intelligence testing and the use of the resulting IQ scores indicate that the results of intelligence tests are closely related to public policy (Bersoff, 1982; Kamin 1975; Skodak-Crissey, 1975). Zigler and Trickett (1978) noted the impact evaluation results have had in constructing social policy. According to these authors, improvement in the IQ score has been used as the major outcome measure in many programs for the following reasons: (1) IQ tests have been well developed and standardized; (2) they are often easy to administer; (3) the results relate to many other school behaviors; and (4) the prevailing desire of those involved is to demonstrate that programs are beneficial. Zigler and Trickett (1978) suggest that social competence (of which IQ is one indicator) should also be a primary outcome measure of program effectiveness.

If a major goal of the school continues to be on cognitive functioning, intelligence tests in their present and future forms are likely to be used to evaluate program or strategy effectiveness. Subject characteristics, including cognitive ability, must be accounted for in research directed to understanding cognitive processes learners employ as they learn basic skill areas, solve problems of increasing complexity and access, or organize and store information in a world where electronic forms are increasing in importance.

SUMMARY

Intelligence tests were initially developed by Binet and Simon to provide systematic, reliable, and objective means of assessing children's abilities. The purpose of this early testing in the Paris schools was to foster more adequate educational planning than had been practiced. The scale that resulted was devised to replace judgments, often based on subjective observations, with unbiased judgments based on objective tasks.

This chapter has focused on three major applications of intelligence testing in educational settings: (1) selection and placement of children for purposes of instruction; (2) the use of test performance for instructional planning; and (3) accountability, evaluation, and research. Although the major individual intelligence tests currently available serve a useful function in determining overall learning rate as it relates to school tasks, outcomes must be evaluated in relation to possible sources of bias and other assessment procedures. Issues of labeling and variability in scores should be reviewed on an ongoing basis.

The analysis of results across and within subtests is essential to formulating and testing hypotheses related to instructional planning. Intelligence tests, however, were neither designed nor intended to provide prescriptive instructional information (Lennon, 1978). Current intelligence tests must be used in the context of other assessment information and viewed as selected samples of behavior. The evaluator has the important responsibility for understanding the technical characteristics and the possible effects of diverse background experiences, as well as the learner's physical characteristics and language skills when interpreting results. While the results from intelligence tests cannot be directly translated into the design of instructional programs, they can suggest differences in abilities and thus be useful when selecting among curricular alternatives and when developing remedial programs. Users should remember the importance of working with learner strengths. Reynolds (1981) reported disappointing results when programs focused on remediating weakness, whereas focusing on developing strengths proved more successful. Information-processing approaches provide a promising direction for the development of future tests, the results of which can be translated directly into educational practice. New test formats that involve the careful analysis of cognitive tasks into their component parts and that provide learning opportunities can allow more direct instructional intervention. Such procedures are likely as well to make the process and outcomes of testing more accessible to teachers and parents.

The use of intelligence tests for purposes of accountability in educational settings is likely to continue and, according to Resnick, perhaps increase. Individual pupil characteristics must be determined and understood as researchers evaluate the interaction of cognitive functioning with learning.

REFERENCES

Anastasi, A. (1958). *Differential psychology: Individual and group differences in behavior* (3rd ed.). New York: Macmillan.

Anastasi, A. (1982). *Psychological testing* (5th ed.). New York: Macmillan. (4th ed., 1976).

Bannatyne, A. (1974). Diagnosis: A note on recategorization of WISC scaled scores. *Journal of Learning Disabilities, 7,* 272–274.

Bersoff, D. N. (1975). Professional ethics and legal responsibilities: On the horns of a dilemma. *Journal of School Psychology, 13,* 359–376.

Bersoff, D. N. (1981). Testing and the law. *American Psychologist, 36,* 1047–1056.

Bersoff, D. N. (1982). The legal regulation of school psychology. In C. R. Reynolds & T. B. Gutkin (Eds.), *The handbook of school psychology.* New York: Wiley.

Binet, A., & Simon, T. (1916). *The development of intelligence in children* (E. S. Kite, trans.). Baltimore: Williams & Wilkins.

Block, N. J., & Dworkin, G. (1976). *The IQ controversy.* New York: Pantheon Books.

Borland, J., & Jacobs, H. (in press). (*The gifted child in the school.*) New York: Teachers College Press.

Brown, A. L., & Campione, J. C. (1982). Modifying intelligence or modifying cognitive skills: More than a semantic quibble? In D. K. Detterman & R. J. Sternberg (Eds.), *How and how much can intelligence be increased.* Norwood, NJ: Ablex.

Brown, A. L., & French, L. A. (1979). The zone of potential development: Implications for intelligence testing in the year 2000. In R. J. Sternberg & D. K. Detterman (Eds.), *Human intelligence.* Norwood, NJ: Ablex.

Bryant, N. D. (1983). *Preventing and remediating the effects of LD: Remedial principles vs. folklore, fads, and failure* (Monograph #1). New York: Research Institute for the Study of Learning Disabilities, Teachers College, Columbia University.

Caldwell, B. M., & Bradley, R. H. (1979). *Home Observation for Measurement of the Environment.* Little Rock, Arkansas: Center for Child Development and Education, University of Arkansas of Little Rock.

Carnegie Quarterly. (1978). *New optimism about preschool education: Three reports from Ypsilanti, Michigan. Carnegie Quarterly, 26,* 5–8.

Carroll, J. B. (1978). On the theory-practice interface in the measurement of intellectual abilities. In P. Suppes (Ed.), *Impact of research on education: Some case studies.* Washington, DC: National Academy of Education.

Cattell, J.M. (1885). Über die Zeit der Erkennung und Benennung von Schriftzeicheh, Bildern un Farben. *Philosophische Studien, 2,* 635–650.

Cicirelli, V. G., Evans, J. W., & Schiller, J. S. (1970). The impact of Head Start: A reply to the report analysis. *Harvard Educational Review, 40,* 105–129.

Cleary, T. A., Humphreys, L. G., Kendrick, S. A., & Wesman, A. (1975). Educational uses of tests with disadvantaged students. *American Psychologist, 30,* 15–41.

Cohen J. (1959). The factorial structure of the WISC at ages 7-6, 10-6, and 13-6. *Journal of Consulting Psychology, 23,* 285–299.

Collins, A., & Smith, E. E. (1982). Teaching the process of reading comprehension. In D. K. Detterman & R. J. Sternberg (Eds.), *How and how much can intelligence be increased.* Norwood, NJ: Ablex.

Cordoni, B.K., O'Donnell, J.P., Ramaniah, N.V., Kurtz, J. & Rosenshein, K. Committee on Ability Testing (see Wigdor & Garner, 1982).

Cordoni, B. K., et al. (1981). Wechsler Adult Intelligence Score patterns for learning disabled young adults. *Journal of Learning Disabilities, 14,* 404–407.

Cronbach, L. J. (1975). Five decades of public controversy over mental testing. *American Psychologist, 30,* 1–14.

Davis, W. A., & Shepard, L. A. (1983). Specialists' use of tests and clinical judgment in the diagnosis of learning disabilities. *Learning Disability Quarterly, 6,* 128–138.

Dunn, L. M., & Dunn, L. M. (1981). *Peabody Picture Vocabulary Test—Revised (PPVT).* Circle Pines, MN: American Guidance Service.

Feuerstein, R. (1979). *The dynamic assessment of retarded performers: The learning potential assessment device, theory, instruments, and techniques.* Baltimore, MD: University Park Press.

Feuerstein, R. (1980). *Instructional enrichment: An intervention program for cognitive modifiability.* Baltimore, MD: University Park Press.

Galton, F. (1869). *Hereditary genius: An inquiry into its law and consequences.* New York: Appleton.

Gerken, K. C., Hancock, K. A., & Wade, T. H. (1978). A comparison of the Stanford-Binet Intelligence Scale and the McCarthy Scales of Children's Abilities with preschool children. *Psychology in the Schools, 15,* 468–472.

Gettinger, M. (1978). *Is time-to-learn or intelligence a stronger correlate of school learning?* Unpublished doctoral dissertation. New York: Columbia University.

Gettinger, M., & White, M. A. (1979). Which is the stronger correlate of school learning? Time to learn or measured intelligence? *Journal of Educational Psychology, 71*(4), 405–412.

Glaser, R. (1984). Education and thinking: The role of knowledge. *American Psychologist, 39*(2), 93–104.

Glaser, R., & Nitko, A. J. (1971). Measurement in learning and instruction. In R. L. Thorndike (Ed.), *Educational Measurement* (2nd ed.). Washington, DC: American Council on Education.

Glaser, R., & Pellegrino, J. (1982). Improving the skills of learning. In D. K. Detterman & R. J. Sternberg (Eds.), *How and how much can intelligence be increased.* Norwood, NJ: Ablex.

Hunt, J. M. (1961). *Intelligence and experience.* New York: Ronald Press.

Jensen, A. R. (1969). How much can we boost IQ and scholastic achievement? *Harvard Educational Review, 39,* 1–123.

Jensen, A. R. (1980). *Bias in mental testing.* New York: The Free Press.

Kamin, L. J. (1974). *The science and politics of IQ* Potomac, MD: Erlbaum.

Kamin, L. J. (1975). Social and legal consequences of IQ tests as classification instruments: Some warnings from our past. *Journal of School Psychology,* Special Issue, *13,* 317–323.

Kaufman, A. S. (1975). Factor analysis of the WISC-R at 11 age levels between 6-½ and 16-½ years. *Journal of Consulting and Clinical Psychology, 43,* 135–147.

Kaufman, A. S. (1976a). Verbal-performance IQ discrepancies on the WISC-R. *Journal of Consulting and Clinical Psychology, 44,* 739–744.

Kaufman, A. S. (1976b). A new approach to the interpretation of test scatter on the WISC-R. *Journal of Learning Disabilities, 9,* 160–168.

Kaufman, A. S. (1979). *Intelligent testing with the WISC-R.* New York: Wiley.

Kaufman, A. S. (1981). The WISC-R and learning disabilities assessment: State of the art. *Journal of Learning Disabilities, 14,* 520–526.

Kaufman, A. S. (1982). The impact of WISC-R research for school psychologists. In C. R. Reynolds & T. B. Gutkin (Eds.), *The handbook of school psychology.* New York: Wiley.

Kaufman, A. S., & Kaufman, N. L. (1983). *Kaufman Assessment Battery for Children* (K-ABC). Circle Pines, MN: American Guidance Service.

Lamke, T., Nelson, M., & French, J. (1973). *Henmon-Nelson Tests of Mental Ability* (rev. ed.). Boston: Houghton Mifflin.

Larry P. v. Riles. 495 F. Supp. 926 (N. D. Cal, 1979).

Lennon, R. T. (1978). Perspective on intelligence testing. *NCME Measurement in Education, 2*(9), 1–8.

Lutey, C. L. (1977). *Individual intelligence testing: A manual and source book* (2nd ed.). Greeley, CO: Carol L. Lotey.

Lutey, C. L., & Copeland, E. P. (1982). Cognitive assessment of the school-age child. In C. R. Reynolds & T. B. Gutkin (Eds.), *The handbook of school psychology.* New York: Wiley.

Marland, S. P., Jr. (1972). *Education of the gifted and talented: Report to the Congress of the United States by the Commissioner of Education.* Washington, DC: U.S. Government Printing Office.

Martin, R. P. (1983). Ethics column. *The School Psychologist (Division 16 Newsletter), 38*(2), 6, 10.

McCarthy, D. (1972). *McCarthy Scales of Children's Abilities.* New York: Psychological Corporation.

McLoughlin, J. A., & Lewis, R. B. (1981). *Assessing special students: Strategies and procedures.* Columbus, OH: Charles E. Merrill.

Meeker, M. (1965). A procedure for relating Stanford-Binet behavior samplings to Guilford's structure of intellect. *Journal of School Psychology, 3,* 26–36.

Meeker, M. (1969). *The structure of intellect: Its interpretation and uses.* Columbus, OH: Charles E. Merrill.

Meeker, M. (1975). *WISC-R Template for SOI Analysis.* El Segundo, CA: SOI Institute.

Mercer, C. D., (1979). *Children and adolescents with learning disabilities.* Columbus, Ohio: Charles E. Merrill. *New York Times,* November 7, 1978. "$500,000 Award for Wrong Diagnosis as Retardate" by Max H. Seigel.

Nicholls, J. G. (1979). Quality and equality in intellectual development: The role of motivation in education. *American Psychologist, 34,* 1071–1084.

Nicholson, C. L., & Alcorn, C. L. (1983). *Educational applications of the WISC-R: A handbook of interpretive strategies and remedial recommendations.* Los Angeles, CA: Western Psychological Services.

Oakland, T. (Ed.). (1977). *Psychological and educational assessment of minority children.* New York: Brunner/Mazel.

Oakland, T., & Matuszek, P. (1977). Using tests in nondiscriminatory assessment. In T. Oakland (Ed.), *Psychological and educational assessment of minority children.* New York: Brunner/Mazel.

Oliver, T. (1976, Spring). *NCME Newsletter.*

Otis, A. S., & Lennon, R. T. (1979). *Otis-Lennon School Ability Test.* New York: Harcourt Brace Jovanovich.

Pace v. Hannon. 506 F. Supp. 931 (N.D. Ill. 1980).

Palmer, J. O. (1983). *The psychological assessment of children* (2nd ed.). New York: Wiley.

Renzulli, J. S. (1977). *The enrichment triad model: A guide for developing defensible programs for the gifted and talented.* Mansfield, CT: Creative Learning Press.

Reschly, D. (1978). WISC-R factor structures among anglos, blacks, Chicanos and Native American Papogos. *Journal of Consulting and Clinical Psychology, 46,* 417–422.

Resnick, L. B. (Ed.). (1976). *The nature of intelligence.* Hillsdale, NJ: Erlbaum.

Resnick, L. B. (1979). The future of IQ testing in education. In R. J. Steinberg and D. K. Detterman (Eds.), *Human Intelligence.* Norwood, NJ: Ablex.

Reynolds, C. R. (1981). Neuropsychological assessment and the individualization of instruction: Considerations in the search for the aptitude and treatment interaction. *School Psychology Review, 10,* 343–349.

Reynolds, C. R., & Gutkin, T. B. (1981). Test scatter on the WPPSI: Normative analyses of the standardization sample. *Journal of Learning Disabilities, 14,* 460–464.

Reynolds, C. R. (1982). The problem of bias in psychological assessment. In C. R. Reynolds & T. B. Gutkin (Eds.), *The handbook of school psychology.* New York: Wiley.

Reynolds, C. R., & Clark, J. H. (1983). Assessment of cognitive abilities. In K. D. Paget & B. A. Bracken (Eds.), *The psychoeducational assessment of preschool children.* New York: Grune & Stratton.

Rosewell, F. G., & Natchez, G. (1977). *Reading disability* (3rd ed.). New York: Basic Books.

Salvia, J., & Ysseldyke, J. E. (1981). *Assessment in special and remedial education* (2nd ed.). Boston: Houghton Mifflin.

Sattler, J. M. (1965). Analysis of functions on the 1960 Stanford-Binet Intelligence Scale, Form L-M. *Journal of Clinical Psychology, 21,* 173–179.

Sattler, J. M. (1982). *Assessment of children's intelligence and special abilities* (2nd ed.). Boston: Allyn & Bacon.

Scarr, S. (1981). *Race, social class, and individual differences in IQ.* Hillsdale, NJ: Erlbaum.

Schwarz, P. A. (1971). Prediction instruments for educational outcomes. In R. L. Thorndike (Ed.), *Educational measurement* (2nd ed.). Washington, DC: American Council on Education.

Schweinhart, L. J., & Weikart, D. P. (1980). *Young children grow up: The effects of the Perry Preschool Project on youths through age 15.* Ypsilanti, MI: High/Score Press.

Searls, E. I. (1975). *How to use WISC scores in reading diagnosis.* Newark, DE: International Reading Association.

Shepherd, M. J. (1984). (Personal communication.) Teachers College, Columbia University.

Skodak-Crissey, M. (1975). Mental retardation: Past, present and future. *American Psychologist, 30,* 800–808.

Slosson, R. L. (1983). *Slosson Intelligence Test* (SIT). East Aurora, NY: Slosson Educational Publications.

Smith, M. S., & Bissell, J. S. (1970). The impact of Headstart: The Westinghouse-Ohio Headstart evaluation. *Harvard Educational Review, 40,* 51–104.

Sternberg, R. (1983). Criteria for intellectual skills training. *Educational Researcher, 12*(2), 6–12, 26.

Sternberg, R. J., Ketron, J. L., & Powell, J. S. (1982). Componential approaches to the training of intelligent performance. In D. K. Detterman & R. J. Sternberg (Eds.). *How and how much can intelligence be increased.* Norwood, NJ: Ablex.

Sternberg, R. J., & Wagner, R. K. (1982). *Understanding intelligence: What's in it for educators?* (ERIC Report 227-110 (ED)) Washington, DC: National Commission on Excellence in Education (ED).

Sternberg, R. J., & Powell, J. S. (1983). The development of intelligence. In P. Mussen (Ed.), *Carmichael's handbook of child psychology, Vol. III, Cognitive development.* (J. H. Falvell & E. M. Markman, Vol. Eds.). New York: Wiley.

Sullivan, E. T., Clark, W. W., & Tiegs, E. W. (1964). *California Test of Mental Maturity, 1963 Revision.* Monterey, CA: California Test Bureau.

Tannenbaum, A. J. (1983). *Gifted children: Psychological and educational perspectives.* New York: Macmillan Company.

Terman, L. M., & Merrill, M. A. (1973). *Stanford-Binet Intelligence Scale, Form L-M: 1972 Norms Edition.* Boston: Houghton Mifflin.

Thorndike, R. L. (1971). Educational measurement for the seventies. In R. L. Thorndike (Ed.), *Educational measurement* (2nd ed.). Washington, DC: American Council on Education.

Thorndike, R. L. (1975). Mr. Binet's Test 70 years later. *Educational Researcher, 5,* 3–7.

Thorndike, R.L., & Hagen, E. (1978). *Cognitive Abilities Test (CAT).* Atlanta: Houghton Mifflin Co.

U.S.O.E., (1977, December 29). *Federal Register.* Education for All Children Act of 1975.

Wechsler, D. (1967). *Manual for the Wechsler Preschool and Primary Scale of Intelligence.* New York: Psychological Corporation.

Wechsler, D. (1974). *Wechsler Intelligence Scale for Children—Revised, Manual.* New York: Psychological Corporation.

Wechsler, D. (1975). Intelligence defined and undefined, a relativistic appraisal. *American Psychologist, 30,* 135–139.

Whitworth, J. R., & Sutton, D. (1978). *WISC-R Compilation.* Wilmington, DE: Jastak Associates.

Whitworth, J. R., & Sutton, D. L. (1982). *Stanford Binet, Form L-M, Compilation.* Wilmington, DE: Jastak Associates.

Wigdor, A. K., & Garner, W. R. (Eds.). (1982). *Ability testing: Uses, consequences and controversies. Part I: Report of the Committee.* Washington, DC: National Academy Press.

Zigler, E., & Trickett, P. K. (1978). IQ, social competence and evaluation in early childhood intervention programs. *American Psychologist, 33,* 789–798.

Zigler E., & Valentine, J. (Eds.). (1980). *Project Head Start: A legacy of the war on poverty.* New York: Free Press.

Zimmerman, I. L., & Woo-Sam, J. (1970). The utility of the Wechsler Preschool and Primary Scale of Intelligence in the public schools. *Journal of Clinical Psychology, 26,* 472.

Zinoman, E. A. (1983). *Non-biased psycho-educational assessment: 1983.* Draft, the University of the State of New York, the State Education Department, the Bureau of Pupil Services.

NAME INDEX

SUBJECT INDEX